THE
HISTORY OF YONKERS

THE
HISTORY OF YONKERS

WESTCHESTER COUNTY, NEW YORK

By

The Rev. Charles Elmer Allison

Reprinted from the 1896 Edition
with Addition of a Bibliography

HARBOR HILL BOOKS
Harrison, New York
1984

Library of Congress Cataloging in Publication Data

Allison, Charles Elmer, 1847-1908.
　The history of Yonkers.

　Reprint. Originally published: New York: W.B. Ketcham,
1896.
　"Limited to 500 numbered copies" -- T.p. verso.
　Bibliography: p.
　Includes index.
　1. Yonkers (N.Y.)--History.　2. Yonkers (N.Y.)--
Biography.　I. Title.
F129.Y5A4　　1984　　　　　974.7'277　　　　　84-12826
ISBN 0-916346-51-X

THIS EDITION IS LIMITED TO

500 NUMBERED COPIES

OF WHICH THIS IS NO. *357*

HARBOR HILL BOOKS,　P.O. BOX 407, HARRISON, N.Y. 10528

Charles E. Allison

...THE...
HISTORY OF YONKERS

FROM THE EARLIEST TIMES TO THE PRESENT, INCLUDING AN ELABORATE DESCRIPTION OF ITS ABORIGINES; A NARRATIVE OF ITS DISCOVERY, AND EARLY SETTLEMENT BY THE DUTCH AND OTHER EUROPEANS; A RECORD OF EVENTS WITHIN ITS BORDERS DURING THE PHILIPSE PERIOD OF MORE THAN ONE HUNDRED YEARS; ITS STIRRING SCENES AS A PART OF THE FAMOUS "NEUTRAL GROUND OF THE REVOLUTION"; ITS FARMS AND FARMERS; ITS HAMLETS; ITS GROWING VILLAGE ON THE NEPPERHAN, AND ITS DEVELOPMENT TO THE BUSY CITY OF TO-DAY; TOGETHER WITH AN HISTORICAL ACCOUNT OF ITS SCHOOLS, CHURCHES, SOCIETIES, INDUSTRIES, BANKS, NEWS- PAPERS, ETC., ETC.; FINELY ILLUSTRATED WITH VIEWS OF ITS PUBLIC BUILDINGS, PRIVATE RESIDENCES, MANUFACTORIES, AND WITH PORTRAITS OF MANY OF ITS CITIZENS.

BY THE

REV. CHARLES ELMER ALLISON

Pastor of the Dayspring Presbyterian Church; President of the Yonkers Historical and Library Association

ISSUED UNDER THE AUSPICES OF THE YONKERS BOARD OF TRADE

NEW YORK:
WILBUR B. KETCHAM
2 COOPER UNION

Copyright, 1896,
BY
Wilbur B. Ketcham.

PREFACE.

"THE YONKERS," from about 1646 until 1788, when the township was erected, was the name of a tract lying between the Amackassin and the Spuyten Duyvil, the Bronx and the Hudson. During that period, "The Yonkers," or "The Yonkers Plantation," was also the name of a precinct, which comprised the greater part of what was subsequently known as the town of Kingsbridge. During the Philipse period the southern part of "The Yonkers" was called "Lower Yonkers," while the northern part, that is, Yonkers of the present day, was generally known as Philipsburg. When the town was erected in 1788, it received its present name from the Legislature. In 1855, the incorporated village within the town, was also called Yonkers. In 1872, the city of Yonkers was incorporated. The southern part of the town was not included within the boundaries of the new city. In 1872, the southern portion of the town was set off by the Legislature, as the town of Kingsbridge. The Supervisors in 1873, confirmed the act of the Legislature. In 1874, the town of Kingsbridge became a part of the Twenty-fourth Ward, of New York City. Wherever the name "The Yonkers," or "Yonkers" occurs in this history, the context designates whether reference is made to the whole area or only to a part.

Occasionally brief duplicate records of interesting facts have been made, first that the description of a period under review may be more graphic, and second that chapters devoted to special subjects, schools and churches, for instance, may be more complete.

In the preparation of this history, the author has turned over the pages of Van Der Donck, De Vries, De Leat, Juet, O'Callagan, Schoolcraft, Bancroft, Redpath, Lossing, Devens, Lamb, Wilson, Bolton, Scharf and others. Indebtedness to them for important historical data is here acknowledged.

Bolton had the great advantage of acquaintanceship with those whose early lives touched the period of the Revolution. He conversed with men who had conversed with the patriot fathers. He also transcribed for his "History of Westchester County" and for his "History of the Church in Westchester County" interesting historical documents. Yonkers and other portions of the county should cherish the memory of the Rev. Robert Bolton. He held back from oblivion numerous facts, the record of which nourishes both patriotic and devout sentiment.

Scharf's "History of Westchester County" is a vast storehouse of information. Probably no county in the United States, except those within the borders of which are large cities like New York and Chicago, has such a voluminous history. Some of the ablest and most scholarly clergymen, lawyers, physicians, scientific and business men the county ever enrolled among its citizens contributed to its pages. How much patient research Scharf's history represents, none realize except those who have critically read it. Multiplying years will multiply its value. The chapter on Yonkers, by the Rev. David Cole, D.D., is, as to arrangement and method, admirable; and as to language, crystal clear. Every page evidences painstaking effort to attain accuracy. Rev. Dr. Cole, Thomas Edsall, Esq. (the able historian of Kingsbridge), the Hon. James Wood, Mr. Henry B. Dawson, and other contributors to Scharf's history, have furnished, by their historical records, a fund of information, of which the author has availed himself. Miss Agnes Emily Kirkwood's history, entitled "Church and Sunday-school Work in Yonkers" is another volume which has been consulted. Very few, if any, towns have a more carefully written record of the work of their Sunday-schools.

Mr. Thomas C. Cornell, for a long time a resident of Yonkers, and for some time the City Engineer, years ago made valuable records and maps, without which a part of the history of the Village of Yonkers could not have been written. Honor to his memory. Judge T. Astley Atkins, during his long residence in Yonkers, has from time to time contributed papers on local history. The author of this history, in its preparation, turned over many files of the Village of Yonkers newspapers, and of the papers published in the City of Yonkers. *The Yonkers Statesman* (weekly) and *The Yonkers Gazette* (weekly) contain very interesting articles from the careful pen of Judge Atkins. They embody the discoveries of his original research, and are especially valuable. Among them are papers entitled: "Nappeckamack," "Philipse Manor during the Revolution," "Philipse Mills, 1776," "Philipse Bridge, 1778," "The Nineteenth Century Dawns on Yonkers," "At the Old Church Door, or Glimpses of Yonkers in 1823," "Nodine Hill," and "Yonkers, Half a Century Ago." Judge Atkins has also contributed to the *Statesman* several legends of Manor Hall. Reference is made to them in Chapter VI. of this history. His papers will increase in value as the years increase. Much that is recorded in Chapter XI. was derived from the volume, "Yonkers in the Rebellion," of which T. Astley Atkins and John W. Oliver were the editors.

The author gratefully acknowledges the courtesy of clergymen, lawyers, physicians, and other professional men; also the kindness of business men, including secretaries of organizations, city officials, and others, who have furnished valuable historical data.

History honors the fathers and teaches the youth. Its motto is *"Et Patribus et Posteritati."* "It has a great office, to make the past intelligent to the present, for the guidance of the future." With the earnest wish that this History of Yonkers, despite its defects, may be a worthy memorial of the fathers and brothers, many of whom wrought faithfully for Church and State, and now belong to the buried generations, and that it may promote the welfare of present and future citizens, it is submitted to the perusal and lenient judgment of its readers by the author.

CHARLES ELMER ALLISON.

YONKERS-ON-THE-HUDSON,
   November 1, 1896.

INTRODUCTION.

"History is Philosophy, teaching by examples."

YONKERS, on the banks of the American Rhine, and on the rim of the American Metropolis, is a city quaint as to name, and thrice favored as to situation. Its name was evolved from the Holland "Jonkheer"—Eng., "Young Nobleman." Its site is beautiful, advantageous, historic. From the brows of commanding hills, charming landscapes outspread their rival glories. Northward are the famed highlands, the wide, quiet and hazy Tappan Zee, rimmed with romance, song and story; the tranquil vale of the winding Nepperhan—"rapid-flowing water;" and the valleys of the Sprain and Grassy Sprain, into which the reservoirs in the skies pour their waters to be stored in the reservoirs among the hills, for the city's use.

Eastward are the blue hills of Long Island, against which glide the glistening sails of ships oceanward or homeward bound. Nearer, the valley of the Bronx, replete with Revolutionary lore. Nearer still, the historic hills, where a patriot army left its footprints, uplift their sombre forests, and smiling fields. Tippett's brook, seaward bound, softly sings through the meadows between these and the opposite heights.

Westward, the superb valley of the Hudson unfolds its purple glories. Sloops and yachts and stately steamers emerge from the obscuring shadows of the hills, and miles of massive Palisades, Nature's masonry, stand out against the horizon. In the south, Bartholdi's Statue of Liberty holds aloft its symbolic torch above the waters of the commodious harbor, where ride the navies of the world. At night the southern sky reflects the gleam of a thousand city lamps, while the many-colored lights of the river craft and the bright beams in the windows of happy Yonkers' homes, sparkle like stars. River, mountains, hills and dales are a perpetual inspiration. How this superb scenery refreshes the spirit, and enriches life, is indicated by lines from the musical pen of a graceful writer.

"AT HER WINDOW IN YONKERS.

"Let me watch the sunset splendor
   Set the river all aglow,
While the creeping, weird-like shadows
   Darker in the mountains grow.
Oh, superb and classic river,
   From the mountains to the sea,
History, and song, and story,
   Have enshrined and circled thee!
All the white sails that float onward
   To the highlands and the bay,
Seem to waft a benediction
   To my burdened heart to-day;
Words from lips that now are voiceless;
   Words from pens that move no more;
Loves from hearts of the beloved,
   That lie sleeping on thy shore.

"Let me watch the distant headland,
   Crowned with sapphire and with gold,
Evening's purple robe is draping
   To the river, fold on fold.
Kingly in the shade or sunlight,
   Restful to the heart's unrest,
Quiet to the life unquiet,
   Blessing to the soul unblest!
Lit by bastions of the sunset,
   Crowned with stars in midnight hours,
Wearing kingly Winter's ermine,
   Clothed in queenly Summer's flowers,
Still forever growing dearer,
   As the changing seasons roll,
Like a dream that has no ending,
   Satisfying all the soul.

"Headland, stretching to the river!
   River, stretching to the sea!
Rest, and strength, and light, and beauty,
   More than human love to me!
River, headland, everlasting!
   Stronger far than human creeds,
Do you draw me to the Father,
   And support me in my needs!"

The cultured citizen gathers inspiration from another source. While beholding the present glories of city, scenery and environments, he also surveys with far-sighted ken the historic past. The nineteenth century is swiftly drawing to its close. This is a fitting time to contemplate the three hundred years lying between the Indian village Nappeckamack, which Henry Hudson saw on the east bank of "The Great River of the Mountains," just after the dawn of the seventeenth century, and this modern city, as seen just before the dawn of the twentieth century—some of its buildings erected upon the very ground in which the savages fastened the poles of their wigwams. It is a far call from that "rapid-water settlement," where the tawny wild man, clad in furs and feathers, spoke his Algonquin tongue, to this populous American city, in whose busy marts, and in whose homes, thirty or more languages are spoken to-day.

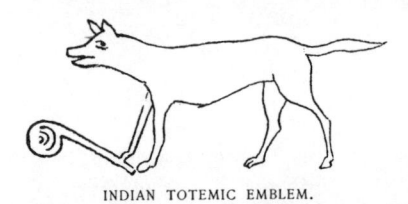

INDIAN TOTEMIC EMBLEM.

Nappeckamack and Yonkers! What numerous and momentous events are crowded between them! What food for profitable reflection they furnish men of thoughtful habit! What contrasts they suggest! Savagism and civilization; rude, bark-covered huts of bent hickory saplings, and "quarries blossoming into the air"; forest paths and city avenues; canoes and river steamboats; crude decorations and modern fine arts; unlettered ignorance and ripe scholarship; hieroglyphics of the woods and classics of the libraries; scant and unsystematized knowledge and synthetized facts of keen-eyed Science, the wonder worker; blind, stumbling, frightened superstition and clear-eyed, radiant, Christian faith.

It is proposed to conduct the reader by instructive narrative through the seventeenth, eighteenth and nineteenth centuries, from Indian occupation, and its totemic emblem, to Dutch possession under the orange, white and blue flag of the Netherlands, which floated from the tapering mast of the Half Moon, thence to English control under the red flag of Britain, and then to the self-government of the great Republic, beneath the protecting folds of whose three-colored banner of liberty forty thousand or more citizens to-day have their homes on the sloping hills and in the beautiful valleys of the stately Hudson, the sinuous Nepperhan, and the gliding Bronx.

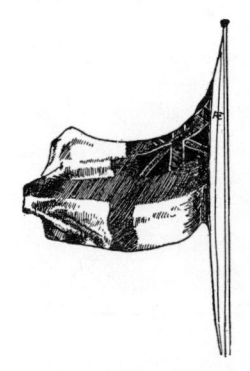

FLAG OF HOLLAND.

It is hoped that those who shall peruse these pages will derive much profit, as, looking backward, they shall see, while past decades multiply into centuries, the forests, full of feathered songsters and wild animals, the Indian lodges and trails, the coming of strange ships up the river, the swinging axe of the frontiersman clad in quaint Dutch dress, the disappearing woods and wigwams, the smoke curling above the settler's log cabin, the slow moving sail-boats, the primitive road through the woods and stony fields, the rising walls of the Manor House (standing to this day), dark-skinned slaves at work in field and hall, the burning stumps in the clearings, the mills with their creaking and dripping wheels, their floors strewn with sawdust, or their beams and rafters coated with cobwebs and grain dust, fenced fields, pasturing herds and flocks, waving harvests, the foot-post, the mounted mail-carrier with his saddle-bags, cavalcades of gay guests winding northward under the forest trees toward Manor Hall, the roadside tavern with its horse shed, the rumbling stage coach, and its passengers in their old-time costumes, old St. John's Church and the devout worshippers rendering their tribute of praise, then shrill fifes, throbbing war-drums, unfurled battle-flags, marching Continentals in blue and buff, or in ragged regimentals, courtly French cavaliers in their elegant uniform, England's redcoated troops and hired Hessians conversing in strange language, cowboys and skinners, lawless marauders, then the peaceful hamlets, farm-houses, barns, roadside school-houses, ripening harvests, the first steamboat churning on its northward way, multiplying dwellings, the Sabbath-going bell, "sprinkling the air with holy sounds," the screaming locomotive awakening the drowsy village into an activity which quickly developed it into a busy town, whose streets, in the dark days of the Republic's peril, resounded with the tread of marching feet— a town which has now attained the proportions of a populous city, whose near future glows with bright promise of swift and continued growth.

FLAG OF GREAT BRITAIN.

FLAG OF THE UNITED STATES OF AMERICA.

As the well-informed observer looks backward into, and through these historic centuries, the populous city fades from sight, as a dissolving view, and lo! an Indian village, with surrounding forests, and here and there a maize-field. The blue sky overarches hills and valleys, rivers and mountains, and the same stars "march forth in their battalions at midnight." All else is changed. It is the dawn of the seventeenth century, and the wigwam village in the woods, at the mouth of the Neperah, is Nappeckamack.

"The steepled town no more
Stretches along the sail-thronged shore;
Like palace-domes in sunset's cloud,
Fade sun-gilt spire and mansion proud;
Spectrally rising where they stood,
I see the old primeval wood;
Dark, shadow-like, on either hand
I see its solemn waste expand:
It climbs the green and cultured hill,
It arches o'er the valley's rill,
And leans from cliff and crag, to throw
Its wild arms on the stream below,
Unchanged alone, the same bright river
Flows on as it will flow forever!
I listen, and I hear the low
Soft ripple, where its waters go;
I hear behind the panther's cry,
The wild bird's scream goes thrilling by,
And shyly on the river's brink
The deer is stooping down to drink."

But again, Clio, muse of history, waves her magic wand, and lo! another scene. Wigwams, red men, familiar mountains, hills and valleys, fade from sight, and a great sheet of ice appears. It is the glacial epoch, the ice-age, and we are looking backward, not through hundreds of years only, but through thousands of years. We are contemplating "terrestrial map-making." The divine Builder is laying the foundations.

CONTENTS.

			PAGE.
CHAPTER	I.	Laying the Foundations,	9
CHAPTER	II.	Nappeckamack and the Tawny Villagers,	14
CHAPTER	III.	Henry Hudson Ascends "The Great River of the Mountains," 1609,	33
CHAPTER	IV.	Traders and Settlers Arrive, 1609–1646,	39
CHAPTER	V.	Dr. Adriaen Van Der Donck and Colen-Donck, or De Jonkheers Landt, 1646–1672,	47
CHAPTER	VI.	The Philipses and Philipsburgh, 1672–1775,	55
CHAPTER	VII.	"The Yonkers" During the Revolution, 1775–1783,	85
CHAPTER	VIII.	The Dawn of Peace, 1783–1788,	119
CHAPTER	IX.	The Town of Yonkers, 1788–1855,	130
CHAPTER	X.	Town and Incorporated Village, 1855–1872,	169
CHAPTER	XI.	Yonkers During the Rebellion, 1861–1865,	199
CHAPTER	XII.	The City of Yonkers, 1872–1896,	226
CHAPTER	XIII.	Yonkers Schools,	269
CHAPTER	XIV.	Yonkers Churches,	275
CHAPTER	XV.	Yonkers Societies,	301
CHAPTER	XVI.	Yonkers Industries,	338
CHAPTER	XVII.	Yonkers Banks,	371
CHAPTER	XVIII.	Yonkers Board of Trade,	379
CHAPTER	XIX.	Yonkers Newspapers,	385
CHAPTER	XX.	Land and River Transportation,	390
CHAPTER	XXI.	Yonkers Citizens,	396
CHAPTER	XXII.	Yonkers Cemeteries,	452
		Bibliography,	455

INDEX TO PORTRAITS, ILLUSTRATIONS, ETC.

Allison, Charles E.,	Frontispiece	Cobb, Raffaelle,	300	Gaul, Henry,	248
Allison, William, Commission of,	94	Cobb, Lyman, Jr.,	372	Getty, Robert P.,	163
Alison, John,	281	Cobbling-stone, The, in Somers,	10	Getty, Samuel E.,	332
Anderson, Henry M.,	300	Cochran, William F.,	357	Gibson, James T.,	335
Aqueduct, Croton, 1842,	155	Cochran, William F., Residence of,	411	Gibson, Wm. Augustus,	227
Arbuckle, John W.,	310	Coe, Frederick A.,	168	Glacier, An Alpine,	10
Archibald, William,	168	Cole, David,	282	Goodale, J. Warren,	409
Archibald, Andrew,	381	Colton, Ellsworth E.,	309, 335	Gorton, Charles E.,	403
Archer, Henry B.,	238	Condon, Richard L.,	268	Grenadier, An English,	91
Arlington Chemical Company's Factory,	364	Conklin, S. William,	303	Halley, William,	310
		Constable, William P.,	250	Harrigan, John C.,	230
Armory of the Fourth Separate Company,	308	Coons, William S.,	332	Harrington, Edwin I.,	335
		Cooper, Samuel L.,	245	Hatfield, John G.,	300
Artillery, American,	115	Copcutt, John,	345	Havey, Peter H.,	409
Back, Frederick A.,	225	Copcutt, John B.,	381	Hepenstal, Charles,	300
Badge, American Revolution, Sons of the,	313	Corley, Charles R.,	281	Hermance, Edgar M.,	335
		Corinthian Yacht Club,	316	Hessian,	91
Baird, Henry M.,	400	Cornell, Thomas C.,	236	Hessian Trooper's Boot,	91
Baldwin, Wm. Delavan,	350	Courter, James C.,	227, 228	Hicks, Henry R.,	252
Ball, Nelson A.,	233	Culver, Charles R.,	255	High School and Public Library,	270
Banker, Garret N.,	335	Curran, Patrick,	249	Hobart, Alvah S.,	281
Banks:		Curran, Thomas F.,	230	Hobbs, Bailey,	225
Yonkers Savings Bank,	373	Currency, Continental,	98	Hobbs, John,	153
First National Bank of Yonkers,	374	Cutting, George R.,	281	Holden, Edwin R.,	386
People's Savings Bank,	375	Daly, Joseph F.,	230	Holden, John G. P.,	386
Citizens' National Bank,	377	Davenport, Frederick M.,	281	Holder, Frank T.,	360
Baptist Church, Nepperhan Avenue,	292	Devitt, John J.,	415	Hollywood Inn,	327
		Deyo's Elevator and Mill,	369	Holthusen, A. H.,	281
Baptist Church, Warburton Avenue,	284	Doctor of Colonial Days,	70	Horton, David,	147
		Donohue, F. X.,	230	Housel, Harold C.,	243
Baragwanath, Thomas H.,	281	Doran, Daniel A.,	403	Houston, E. Alex.,	248
Bashford, Johanna C., Miss,	373	Doty, William H.,	240	Hubbell, John H.,	268
Beaudrias, Isidore J. B.,	404	Downing, Isaac G.,	300	Hudson River Day Line:	
Belknap, Ethelbert,	268	Dutch Patroon,	51	Steamer Albany,	392
Bell, J. Harvey,	227	Early Settlers,	42	Steamer New York,	393
Bell, W. A., Residence of,	193	East, William Palmer,	256, 409	Hudson, The,	190
Bell, Stephen T.,	300	Edgar, William B.,	268	Hulbert, Charles F.,	249
Bellows, John,	381	Eickemeyer, Rudolf, Sr.,	185	Hunt, James M.,	230
Benedict, Albert C.,	335	Eickemeyer, Rudolf, Jr.,	268	Immanuel Chapel, Presbyterian,	298
Bixby, James T.,	281	Ellis, Matt. H.,	202	Indian, A North American,	15
Bloomingdale, J. B., Residence of,	195	Embree, John,	409	Indian Head, Looking North,	35
Bloomingdale, L. G., Residence of,	194	Ewing, Gen. Thomas,	381	Indian Specimens, 16, 17, 23, 27, 30, 31, 32, 40	
Bosworth, Enos J.,	281	Eylers, John,	240		
Bowen, William B.,	281	Fancher, Charles H.,	268	Infantryman, 1812–1834,	149
Brandt, E. N.,	332	Feeser, Albert M.,	281	Jenkins, J. Foster,	252
Brennan, John F.,	230, 268	Fiedler, Justus H.,	268	John, David,	332
Brennan, John F., Residence of,	173	Fisher, William H.,	403	Kaler, George H.,	248
Brevoort, Henry F.,	405	Fitch, James S.,	268	Kearns, James, Jr.,	247
Brevoort, James Renwick,	398	Fitzgerald, Michael,	248	Kellock, Robert,	247
Bright, William J.,	409	Flag, Canoe Club,	316	Kellogg, Wm. C.,	230
Broderick, John J.,	248	Flag, Confederate, 1861,	205	Ketcham, William E.,	400
Brown, Charles F.,	251	Flag, Confederate Battle,	205	Ketcham, Wilbur B.,	409
Brown, Harold,	360	Flag, Corinthian Yacht Club,	317	Kings Bridge, View of,	86
Brown, H. Beattie,	332	Flag of France,	117	Kipp, Augustus,	204
Browne, Valentine,	251, 335	Flag, Palisade Boat Club,	315	Kirkwood, Alexander O.,	233
Brownell, Andrew S.,	268	Flag of the Thirteen United Colonies,	88	Kitching, J. Howard,	206
Bruce, William P.,	281			Knapper, Frank,	233
Bruce, James M.,	400	Flag, United States, 1777,	99	Krebs, George P.,	281
Burns, Arthur J.,	230	Flag, Yacht Club,	316	Lake, William H.,	233
Burns, Jeremiah,	197	Flannery, P. J.,	381	Land, Arthur,	310
Burns, J. Irving,	231	Flying Machine, The,	71	Lawrence, Arnett O.,	233
Butler's Business College,	274	Foerst, John,	247	Lawrence, James V.,	268, 354
Cabin of Round Logs,	71	Forsyth, Edward Albro,	418	Lawrence, J. Joseph,	388
Callan, Peter A.,	335	Fowler, Peter U.,	381	Lawrence, William F.,	426
Canoes,	317	Fox, Alfred,	389	Lawrence, William H.,	168
Canoe Club,	316	Frazier, Charles H.,	403	Leliva, C. E. V.,	381
Canoe Club Emblem,	317	Frazier, Thomas M.,	310	Life Saving Corps, Badge of,	317
Carver, Alexander B.,	281	Freeman, James E.,	281	Light, Robert B.,	303
Catholic Slavonian-Hungarian Church,	294	French Soldier,	114	Lings, Albert A.,	281
		Fulton's First Steamboat,	139	Locher, P. Albert,	281
Chadeayne, Charles L.,	409	Fulton, James C.,	310	Lockwood, Jos. A.,	240
Clark, Eugene C.,	360	Garrison, Hyatt,	249	Lyceum League of America, Badge of,	319
Clark, John,	367	Garthwaite, Albert N.,	310		

McIntyre, James D.,	303
McLaughlin, James,	239
McVicar, Thomas,	233
McVicar, W. H.,	309
Mackay, George D., Residence of,	179
Mahony & Flood Building,	261
Mallinson, Charles E.,	310
Mallinson, George S.,	310
Mallinson, Horton W.,	310
Mangin, John,	175, 239
Manor Hall (1682),	58
Manor Hall (1842),	156
Manor Hall Crest,	66
Manor Hall and the Soldiers' Monument,	174
Map of Yonkers, 1847,	161
Map of the Village of Yonkers, 1868–1872,	170
Marine, 1776,	93
Martin, Edwin K.,	380
Martin, Edwin K., Residence of,	177
Martin, John,	310
Mason, John M.,	168
Masten, Joseph,	227
Matchlock Gun,	41
Methodist Episcopal Church, Central,	290
Miles, Charles A.,	235, 335
Miller, Joseph,	243
Millward, James,	227
Mitchell, Edward J.,	203
Moffat, Henry,	335
Moller, William,	252
Molloy, Anthony,	281
Monastery, The, of The Sacred Heart,	297
Mooney, Michael,	248
Morrell, E. M.,	332
Morris, Wm. Hopkins,	206
Mott, Abraham C.,	300
Moultrie, Frank J.,	430
Mulcahey, Thomas F.,	247
Municipal Building,	419
Murray, Felix,	233
Nappeckamack House,	162
Newman, Chester W.,	381
Nisbet, William F.,	268
Nodine, Isaac C.,	303
Nugent, Arthur W.,	249, 310
Nugent, Charles F.,	310
Odell, James B.,	212
Old Dock, The,	154
Oliver, Edwin A.,	388
Oliver, John W.,	387
O'Neill, Francis,	433
O'Neil, John,	310
Oriental Apartment House,	448
Osborn, George W.,	239
Osterheld, Henry,	352
Otis Brothers & Co.'s Elevator Works,	349
Otis Electric Company,	349
Otis, Elisha G.,	346
Otis, Charles R.,	268, 347
Otis, Norton P.,	227, 348
Otis, Norton P., Residence of,	435
Paddock, Prince William,	168
Paddock, Walter H.,	381
Pagan, John, Jr.,	248
Palisade Boat Club,	315
Palisaded Village of Indians, A,	16
Palisades, The,	18, 24
Park Hill Country Club House,	311
Park Hill Station, The Elevator at,	391
Peake, Cyrus A.,	230
Pearsall, Clarence H.,	233
Peck, Sidney S.,	225
Peene, George,	403
Peene, John G.,	227, 246, 248
Peene, Joseph,	403
Peene, Joseph, Sr.,	225
Phillips, R. Oliver,	268
Philipse, Mary,	93
Philipse, Sir Frederick,	56
Philipse (The) Coat of Arms,	57
Police Officials,	239
Porteous, J. Lindsay,	335
Post, William H.,	168
Potter, Adrian M.,	230
Presbyterian, First, Church and Manse,	287
Presbyterian Church, Westminster,	288
Presbyterian Church, Dayspring,	291
Prime, Ralph E.,	225
Prote, John B.,	225
Prote Storage Warehouse, Mill Street,	257
Pruyn, John I.,	309
Pruyn Furniture and Carpet Co.,	260
Pyne, P. H.,	335
Quick, Edwin A.,	439
Quick, S. Francis,	365
Quinn, Henry J.,	239
Radcliff, Peter E.,	440
Radcliff, Abram S.,	440
Radcliff, P. Edward,	440
Rand, William W.,	400
Rayner, George,	382
Read, Jacob,	151, 240
Reevs, Gabriel P.,	225
Reevs, Gabriel,	230, 243
Reformed Church, First,	283
Reformed Church, Park Hill,	293
Revolutionary Powder Horn and Canteen,	85
Reynolds, Edgar U.,	248
Richardson, Wm. H.,	381
Riley, Wm. H.,	230
Rowland, John,	247
Sahagian, Aslan,	442
Sanders, James P.,	225, 303
Sawyer, Benjamin F., Jr.,	219
Schlesinger, Leopold J.,	300
Schlobohm, John H.,	248
Schopen, Emil,	332
Scrugham, William Warburton, Sr.,	168
Scrugham, William Warburton, Jr.,	230
Seals:	
Board of Education,	269
Columbia Lodge,	306
Grand Army of the Republic,	307
Police Department,	239
Yonkers Bicycle Club,	312
Yonkers Historical and Library Association,	322
For the Prevention of Cruelty to Children,	336
Sherman, William H.,	332
Shipman, Albert K.,	310
Shonnard, Frederic,	268
Shotts, John C.,	200
Shrive, William G.,	443
Silkman, Theodore H.,	232, 252
Skinner, Charles E.,	249
Skinner, Halcyon,	182
Slade, James,	225
Smith, Alexander,	355
Smith, Warren B.,	356
Smith Brothers & Co.'s Mills:	
Tapestry Weaving Mills,	358
Moquette Mills,	358
Print Mills,	359
Worsted Mills,	359
Soldier, A, with Matchlock Gun and Lighted Fuse,	41
Soldiers' Monument, 213, 214, 215, 218, 220, 221	
Southwick, John,	249
Stahl, Charles,	247
Stahlnecker, Wm. G.,	227
Stamps,	83
Statesman Building,	389
Stewart, James,	381
Stewart, Robert,	247
St. Andrew's Memorial Protestant Episcopal Church,	296
St. John's Church (1792),	79
St. John's Rectory and Glebe,	143
St. John's Protestant Episcopal Church, Chapel, Parish House and Rectory,	279
St. John's Riverside Hospital,	333
St. Joseph's Seminary,	286
St. Joseph's Hospital,	334
St. Mary's Catholic Church,	285
Sugar Refinery, National,	353
Sutherland, Leslie,	248
Swift, Samuel,	227, 335
Taylor, Allen,	225
Thayer, Stephen H.,	230
Thomas, Edwin L.,	253
Thompson, Wm. B.,	309
Tierney, John J.,	240
Tillotson, George H.,	310
Tompkins, F. J.,	259
Tompkins, Abraham H.,	248
Tompkins, Alden C.,	409
Tompkins, Joseph M.,	243
Tompkins, R. B.,	225
Trevor Memorial Parsonage,	286
Underhill, Caleb F.,	234
Union Soldier,	201
Unitarian Congregational Church,	289
Valentine House, The,	95
Van Cortlandt Mills,	60
Van Cortlandt Manor House,	61
Van Pelt, Reuben W.,	168
Veitch, William H.,	447
Verplanck, Philip,	381
Von Storch, Henry F.,	219
Walsh, Michael,	249
Walsh's, Thomas A., Pharmacy,	368
Ward, Charles P.,	409
Waring, Charles E.,	376
Waring, Jarvis A.,	188
Waring, John T.,	343
Waring, William C.,	341
Waring, The, Hat Manufacturing Company,	342
Warneck, John,	243
Warren, Nathan A.,	335
Washburn, Benjamin S.,	403
Washington, George,	105
Washington's Camp Chest,	106
Washington's Uniform,	107
Washington's Camp Utensils,	108
Washington's Portfolio,	109
Washington's Pistol Holsters,	110
Washington Market,	258
Water Tower, Elm Street,	241
Water Tower, Lake Avenue,	242
Weller, James H.,	227, 237
Weller & Welsh Building,	254
Wells, Lemuel, Estate of (1813, 1843),	141, 158
White, Frederick,	310
Wheeler, John,	450
Widdemer, Ephraim S.,	281
Wiggins, Lewis H.,	225
Woodruff, Frederick H.,	239
Yachts,	316
Yerks, Elijah M.,	300
Yonkers College of Music,	273
Yonkers, To the North,	178
Young Men's Christian Association Badge,	324

GENERAL INDEX.

Airey, Frank, 398.
Aldermen, 254, 255.
Alexander, John W., 398, 399.
Alison, Rev. Dr. Alexander, 398.
Alison, Rev. John, 298.
Allison, General William, 93, 94.
Allison, Rev. Charles E., 252, 291, 312, 321, 323, 401.
Allison, William, 258.
Alpine Landing, 100.
Amackassin, 20.
American Flag, 90, 98, 99, 117, 121.
Anderson, Henry M., 377, 402.
Andrus, H. J., 365.
Andrus, J. E., 284, 365.
Andre, Major, 114, 117.
Aqueducts, 154, 155, 242, 250.
Arcers or Archers, 52.
Archer, Anthony, 31, 74.
Archer, Henry B., 257, 402.
Archer, John, 30, 74.
Archibald, Andrew, 402.
Archibald, William, 168, 402.
Armitage, Rev. Dr. Thomas, 398.
Arnold, Benedict, 117.
Arnold, Dr. E. S. F., 162, 165.
Artists, 398.
Asbury, Bishop Francis, 77.
Assessments, 193, 264.
Atkins, T. Astley, 144, 170, 322, 398, 400.
Authors, 399.
Avenues (See Streets and Roads).
Babcock, Rev. Luke, 84, 278, 279.
Back, Frederick A., 402.
Baird, Rev. Dr. Robert, 155, 399.
Baird, Rev. Dr. Henry M., 324, 399.
Baird, Rev. Dr. Charles W., 399.
Baird, Edward P., 170.
Baird, H. M., Jr., 398.
Baker, F. A., 398.
Balch, Dr. G. B., 235, 308, 397, 400.
Baldwin, Anson, 157, 224.
Baldwin, Ebenezer, 137.
Baldwin, Edward, 398.
Baldwin, E. K., 170.
Baldwin, Wm. Delavan, 402.
Ball, Nelson A., 404.
Bangs, F. N., 192, 398.
Bangs, John K., 400, 401.
Bank, The Yonkers, 160, 373.
Banker, Dr. Garret N., 236, 397, 404.
Banks, 180, 371.
Baragwanath, Rev. T. H., 289.
Barbecue, 148.
Bartlett, F. E., 398.
Bartlett, W. H. C., 399.
Bashford, H. W., 160.
Bashford, John, 160.
Bates, H. A., 324.
Beaudrias, Isidore J. B., 398, 404.
Behrends, Rev. Dr. A. J. F., 401.
Belknap, Ethelbert, 344, 405.
Belknap, W. H., 344.
Bell, Alonzo, 193.
Bell, E. Y., 398.
Bell, J. Harvey, 255.
Bell, Stephen F., 301, 404.
Bell, William A., 193, 397, 404.
Bellows, John, 404.
Benedict, Dr. A. C., 237, 397.
Bennett, Dr. J. C., 397.

Bible, 54, 79, 118.
Bible Society, 196, 321.
Bills, O. A., 195.
Bixby, Rev. Dr. J. T., 289, 400.
Blackburn, Walter, 398.
Bliven, W. W., 398.
Blizzard, 251.
Bloomingdale, Joseph B., 405.
Bloomingdale, Lyman G., 405.
Board of Trade, 379-384.
Bogart, Ernest L., 401.
Bogart, R. W., 196.
Bosworth, Rev. E. J., 292.
Bowden, Dr. G. W., 398.
Bowers, Henry, 321.
Brennan, John F., 398, 405.
Brevoort, Henry F., 405.
Brevoort, James Renwick, 398, 406.
Bridge, Free, 65.
Bridges, 69, 99.
Broderick, John, 406.
Bronck, Heer Jonas, 44.
Bronx River, 44, 126.
Brooks of Yonkers, 126, 128.
Brown, Dr. Elizabeth S., 398.
Brown, George R., 336.
Brown, Harold, 362.
Brown, Charles Franklin, 406.
Brown, Dr. H. Beattie, 324, 397, 406.
Browne, Dr. Valentine, 236, 407.
Brownell, Andrew Simmons, 406.
Bruce, Rev. W P., 293.
Buchanan, E. G., 398.
Buckmaster, Dr. C. W., 398.
Buel, O. P., 398.
Buildings, Old, 71, 74.
Bunker, Albert, 354.
Bunker, Geo. R., 354.
Burial Ground, 64, 452.
Burial, Indian, 30, 31.
Burns, Arthur J., 262, 407.
Burns, Jeremiah, 407.
Burns, James Irving, 398, 407.
Business Men of Village, 191, 192.
Butler, William Allen, 197, 330, 399.
Butler, William Allen, Jr., 398.
Cadman, Rev. S. Parkes, 252, 289, 401.
Camp Meetings, 148.
Campbell, John C., 100.
Carver, Rev. Dr. Alexander, 252, 280, 312.
Carver, Dr. J. H., 398.
Carpet Factories, 165, 181, 196, 355, 363, 365, 366.
Cemeteries, 169, 247, 452.
Census, 130, 222, 265.
Centenarians, 401.
Chadeayne, Charles L., 408.
Chedsey, F. B., 398.
Chevaux-de-frise, 87.
Church Bells, 143, 144, 146, 250.
Church (R. C.), 134.
Churches, 44, 54, 76, 77, 79, 125, 133, 143, 162, 179, 229, 275, 278, 279.
  African Methodist, 289.
  Armour Villa Park (Chapel), 298.
  Bethel (Mosholu), 143, 155, 162, 179.
  Central Methodist, 179, 180, 289.
  Christ Episcopal (Riverdale), 179.
  Congregational (Oost Dorp), 54, 275, 276.
  Dayspring Presbyterian, 180, 196, 291.
  Dutch Reformed (New Amsterdam), 275.

Churches (Continued.)
  Dutch Reformed (Sleepy Hollow), 59, 79.
  Edge Hill Chapel (Spuyten Duyvil), 179.
  First Methodist (North Broadway), 153, 154, 162, 179, 284.
  First Methodist (Tuckahoe), 133, 143, 153, 162, 179, 283.
  First Presbyterian, 163, 179, 180, 287.
  First Reformed, 155, 156, 157, 162, 180, 195, 285.
  French Protestant (New Amsterdam), 275, 277.
  French Protestant (New Rochelle), 275, 277.
  German Methodist, 292.
  Grace (Gospel Mission), 299.
  Hebrew Synagogue, 298.
  Immanuel (Chapel), 297, 298.
  Mediator (Kingsbridge), 179.
  Mile Square (S. S.), 179.
  Nepperhan Avenue Baptist, 292.
  Park Hill Reformed, 292.
  Presbyterian (Riverdale), 179.
  Protestant Episcopal (New Amsterdam), 275.
  Sacred Heart (R. C.), 297.
  Salvation Army, 299.
  Slavonian-Hungarian (R. C.), 295.
  St. Andrew's Memorial, 295, 296.
  St. John's Evangelical Lutheran, 291.
  St. John's (Tuckahoe), 133, 143, 160, 162, 180, 283.
  St. John's, 77, 112, 117, 123, 133, 134, 143, 144, 154, 159, 162, 179, 180, 278.
  St. Joseph's (R. C.), 290.
  St. Nicholas' United Greek (R. C.), 293.
  St. Mary's (R. C.), 160, 162, 180, 285.
  St. Paul's, 180, 288.
  St. Peter's (R. C.), 295.
  Unitarian Congregational, 180, 289.
  Warburton Avenue Baptist, 162, 163, 179, 196, 197, 286.
  Westminster Presbyterian, 180, 196, 288.
Church, Need of, 76.
Church Prejudices, 133.
Circuit Riders, 77, 125, 133, 143, 155, 180.
Citizens of Yonkers, 396.
City Clerks, 254.
City Officials, 253.
Civil Service Examiners, 250.
Civil War, 192, 194, 199, 224.
Clapp, Everett, 170, 189.
Clark, Dr. E. F., 397.
Clark, Eugene C., 363.
Clark, John, 370, 408.
Clark, Salter S., 398, 401.
Clergymen, 77, 398, 400, 125, 133, 143, 162, 179, 275.
Closter, 100, 153, 154.
Cobb, F. Eugene, 371.
Cobb, George W., 170, 376.
Cobb, Lyman, Sr., 399.
Cobb, Lyman, Jr., 162, 169, 324, 331, 371, 410.
Cobb, Raffaelle, 309, 371, 410.
Cochran, Mrs. Eva S., 280, 296, 330, 331.

Cochran, William Francis, 280, 326, 331, 410.
Coe, Frederick Augustus, 412.
Cole, Rev. Dr. David, 180, 195, 285, 313, 323, 399.
Colgate, James B., 197, 291, 328.
Colton, Dr. Ellsworth E., 412.
Condon, Richard L., 412.
Confiscated Property, 122.
Conklin, S. William, 412.
Connett, E. V., 344, 345.
Constable, William, 134.
Constable, William P., 258, 412.
Cook, Captain Joel, 159.
Coons, Dr. William S., 397, 413.
Cooper, Samuel Lispenard, 413.
Cooper, Rev. Elias, 133, 143.
Cooper, James Fenimore, 86, 104.
Copcutt, John, 155, 157, 181, 345, 413.
Copcutt, John Boddington, 413.
Corley, Rev. Charles R., 272, 286.
Cornell, Thomas Clapp, 155, 160, 336, 414.
Count de Rochambeau, 113.
Courter, James C., 227, 415.
Couzens, M. K., 126, 241.
Cowboys and Skinners, 86, 103, 108, 112, 116.
Cozzens, Frederick A., 162, 197, 219, 399.
Crops, 76, 150.
Crosby, Enoch (the Spy), 101, 104.
Crosby, Miss Mary, 401.
Culver, Charles R., 376, 415.
Currency:
    Indian, 25, 76.
    Dutch, 42, 76.
    English, 150.
    Continental, 98.
    U. S., 150.
    U. S. (Civil War), 193, 195, 223.
Curtice, Ebenezer, 162, 176, 196.
Curran, Patrick J., 415.
Curran, Thomas F., 415.
Cutting, Rev. Geo. R., 288, 312.
Daly, Joseph F., 255, 398, 415.
Davenport, Rev. F. M., 284.
Dawn of Peace, 119.
Dawson, H. B., 189, 399.
Dayboats, 391, 392.
Debating Society, 166.
Debt (Bonded), 265.
Declaration of Independence, 90.
De Cordova, R. J., 401.
Deey, Dr., 397.
De Marmon, Dr. Paluel, 397.
Demund, The Rev. Isaac S., 285.
Denniston, Dr. R. J., 398.
Devitt, John, J., 415.
Deyo, Andrew, 368.
Dispatches, Military, 93, 140.
Donohue, J. C., 398.
Donohue, J. C, Jr., 398.
Donoghue, Francis X, 256, 398, 416.
Doran, Daniel A., 416.
Doty, Oliver W., 164.
Doty, William H., 254, 373, 416.
Downing, Isaac G., 416.
Draft, The, 194.
Drawbridges, 228.
Dress, Dutch, 42, 73.
Dress, Indian, 15, 17.
Drummond, W. P., 155, 195.
Dunwoodie, Major, 86.
Dunwoodie Station, 229.
Dutch Land Purchases, 42.
Dutch Settlers, 42, 49.
Dutton, Rufus, 376.
Early Settlers, 42.
Earthquakes, Slight, 251.
East India Company, 33.
Easton, C. P., 323, 398.

Edgar, William Bell, 162, 416.
Education, 54, 79, 80.
Education, Board of, 249, 262, 263, 269.
Eickemeyer, Rudolf, 162, 166, 184.
Elections, 81, 135.
Elevator Works, 166, 346.
Ellis, Matt. H., 256, 416.
Ellsworth, W. W., 324.
Elting, E. J., 192, 377.
Elting, Peter J., 377.
Eschmann, F. W. R., 321, 365.
Essick, S. V., 398.
Ewing, General Thomas, 252, 313, 398, 417.
Ewing, Thomas, Jr., 398.
Ewing, Hampton D., 398.
Excise Board, 170.
Excise Commission, 170, 232.
Eylers, John, 418.
Fair, An Old-time, 81.
Fancher, Charles H., 418.
Farrington, Thomas O., 192.
Fay, Dr. R. P., 336, 398.
Feeder, J. W., 398.
Feeser, Rev. A. M., 295.
Ferguson, James, 398.
Ferguson, J. H., 398.
Ferry at Spuyten Duyvil, 53.
Ferry at Yonkers, 391.
Fire Arms, 181.
Fire Bell, 232.
Fire Commissioners, 261.
Fiedler, Justus H., 418.
Fire Department, 165, 166, 172, 197, 232, 240, 258, 261.
Fire of 1791, 137.
Firemen, Salaried, 258.
Fire-Ships, 92.
Fire-Whistle (1896).
First Inhabitants, 12.
Fisher, William H., 252, 257, 418.
Fishermen, 154.
Fitch, Hedding S., 398.
Fitch, James Seely, 337, 398; 418.
Fitch, Theodore, 254, 398.
Fitzgerald, Michael, 418.
Flag, American, 90, 98, 99.
Flag, English, 81, 90.
Flag, Holland, 81.
Flagg, Dr. L. W., 155, 397.
Flagg, Dr. R. N., 336, 397.
Flagg, Ethan, 155, 227, 371.
Flagg, Howard W., 344.
Flagg, Wilbur W., 344.
Flandreau, J. M., 173.
Flannery, Patrick J., 419.
Flood, Edward J., 419.
Flour Mill, 164, 338.
Flowers, Imported, 42.
Francis, George W., 155, 178.
Frazier, Charles H., 419.
Freeman, Rev. J. E., 296, 326.
Freemasons, 153, 195, 301, 302.
French Soldiers, 112, 115, 117.
French War, 81.
Foerst, John H., 419.
Foote, Rev. W. C., 155, 178.
Forbes, Dr., 397.
Forrest, Edwin, 165, 401.
Forsyth, Edward Albro, 419.
Fowler, Peter U., 105, 377, 419.
Fox, Alfred, 388.
Fox, Joseph, 388.
G. A. R., 252, 307, 308.
Garrison, Hyatt L., 391, 419.
Garrison, John, 391.
Gas Lights, 193.
Gas Light Company, 166.
Gates, Dr. A. W., 163, 397.
Gates, Dr. H. S., 163, 397.
Gaul, Henry, 420.
Geary, John F., 398

Getty, E. V. V., 398.
Getty, Robert P., Jr., 398.
Getty, Robert Parkhill, 155, 164, 166, 170, 224, 227, 371, 420.
Getty, Dr. Samuel E., 397, 421.
Getty Square (1813), 142.
Getty Square (1843), 156, 157.
Gibson, Dr. J. T., 397.
Gilman, Theodore, 313, 321, 324.
Glacial Man, 12.
Goodale, James Warren, 421.
Gorton, Charles Eugene, 251, 271, 376, 398, 401, 421.
Grant, General U. S., 247.
Greshon, John P., 155.
Half Moon, 33, 38.
Halliday, Alexander, 398.
Halls, Public, 159, 195, 250.
Hamilton, Charles H., 377.
Hamlets, 123, 169.
Harkness, Dr. James, 397.
Harrigan, John C., 398, 421.
Harrington, Dr. E. I., 325, 397.
Harris, E. D., 322.
Hartley, Edward, 398.
Hasbrouck, Dr. Stephen, 397.
Hasbrouck, Washington, 179.
Hatfield, John G., 422.
Hat Manufacturing, 341.
Havemeyer, J. C., 284, 324, 401.
Hawley, David, 398.
Hawley, Samuel, 398.
Health Board, 175, 235, 257.
Heathcote, Colonel, 76.
Heermance, W. L., 323.
Henderson, Dr. ———, 398.
Henry, Dr. ———, 397.
Henry Clay (Steamer), 187.
Hepenstal, Charles, 302, 422.
Hermance, Edgar M., 422.
Hermit of Yonkers, 197.
Hessians, 81, 91.
Hibbard, Dr. T. R., 397.
Hicks, Henry R., 422.
Hillhouse, Thomas, 398.
Hobart, Rev. Dr. A. S., 287, 312.
Hobbs, Bailey, 155, 156, 422.
Hobbs, John, 153.
Holden, Edwin, 386.
Holden, John G. P., 397, 422.
Holder, Frank T., 362.
Holls, F. M., 398.
Hollywood Inn, 326.
Holthusen, Rev. A. H., 291.
Home Guards, 217.
Hooper, Dr. P., 397.
Hooper, M. R., 274.
Horse Racing, 81.
Horan, J. F., 398.
Horton, David, 138, 146, 147.
Hospital, St. John's, 331.
Hospital, St. Joseph's, 334.
Hospital Association, 196.
Hotels, 131, 132, 137, 141, 142, 158, 160, 162, 164, 165, 251.
House Furniture, 72.
Houses (1800–1825), 136.
Houses, Dutch, 54, 71.
Houses, Indian, 14.
Houses, Log, 54, 71.
Houses, Old, 71, 72, 74, 142.
Housel, Harold C., 423.
Houston, E. Alex., 423.
Hover, Joseph, 398.
Howland, Egbert, 170, 371.
Howland, Joseph, 137.
Hoyt, A. B., 204.
Hubbard, J. H., 398.
Hubbard, S. F., Jr., 315.
Hubbell, John Henry, 423.
Hudson, Henry, 33.
Hudson, Park, 165.

Hudson River Day Line, 392.
Hudson River, 11, 35, 114, 126.
Hudson River Obstructions, 87.
Huguenots, 70.
Hulbert, Charles F., 423.
Hunt, James M., 256, 398, 423.
Ice Manufacturing, 339.
Indians, 14.
Indian Bones, 148.
Indian Names, 20.
Indians, Stockbridge, 109.
Indian Queen Tavern, 131, 132, 162.
Industries, 181, 338, 339.
Ingersoll, Dr. John, 138.
I. O. of G. T., 196.
Irwin, Benoni, 398.
Jackson, A. V. W., 401.
Jenkins, J. Foster, Dr., 162, 237, 397, 401, 424.
Jenkins Medical Association, 401.
John, David, 424.
Jones, Alfred, 398.
Kaler, George H., 424.
Kearns, Jr., James J., 424.
Keeler, John H., 377.
Keith, Dr. H., 336.
Kellock, Robert, 424.
Kellogg, William Channing, 256, 337, 424.
Kennedy, Dr. Miriam, 398.
Keskeskick, 20, 44, 47.
Ketcham, Rev. Dr. W. E., 284, 322, 400.
Keyes, E. R., 284, 398.
Keyes, M. S., 398.
King, Dr. ———, 397.
King, Dr. N. S., 398.
King, Rufus, 322, 401.
King Philip's War, 81.
Kingsbridge, 53, 86, 160, 226.
Kipp, Augustus, 204, 425.
Kirkwood Family, 400.
Kirkwood, Alexander Ogilvie, 140, 313, 400, 425.
Kitching, General J. Howard, 205, 206.
Knapper, Frank, 425.
Kniffen's, 138.
Knox, Isaac H., 170, 196, 269.
Krebs, Rev. Geo. P., 292.
Kroeber, Dr. C. H., 398.
Lafayette, General, 114.
Lake, William Henry, 425.
Land and River Transportation, 390.
Language, 17, 18, 20, 22, 39, 42, 49, 54, 67, 69, 70, 136.
Latin or Teutonic Control, 41.
Law, W. W., 365.
Lawrence, J. Joseph, 387.
Lawrence, Justus, 170, 189, 196.
Lawrence, Samuel, 112.
Lawrence, Arnett Odell, 425.
Lawrence, James V., 425.
Lawrence, William H., 425.
Lawrence, William Frederick, 426.
Lawyers, 124, 189, 330, 398.
Lectures, 190, 196.
Legends of Manor Hall, 58.
Leliva, Carl, Edward, Wilhelm, Philip, Von, 426.
Leo, Dr. Stephen, 398.
Lewis, Dr. Dio, 400.
Libraries, 166, 269.
Light, Robert B., 426.
Lincoln, President, 192, 194, 195, 205, 207.
Lings, Rev. Albert A., 290.
Liquor Traffic, 23.
Littlewood, Dr. F. B., 397.
Lockwood, Charles, 180, 263, 292, 337.
Lockwood, Jos. A., 426.
Logan, Edgar, 398.
Logan, Edgar, Jr., 397.
Loomis, Dr. C. L., 397.
Lowerre, Geo. B., 162.

Ludlow, Thomas F., 170.
Lyall, Mrs. Jennie L., 252.
Mackay, George Devereux, 324, 426.
Macomb, General Alex., 134.
Macomb, Mrs. Mary P., 160.
Macomb, Robert, 137, 142.
Mahony, Daniel J., 427.
Mails, 75, 145.
Mangin, John, 427.
Mangin, Captain John, 173, 175, 240.
Manhattan Island, 9, 19, 34, 35, 39, 40, 41, 42, 51.
Manor Hall, 57, 59, 62, 66, 67, 68, 134, 137, 139, 141, 159.
Manor Hall, Legends of, 55, 64, 68.
Manor of Philipsburgh, 56, 58.
Manor, Significance of Word, 56, 58.
Map of Yonkers (1785), 122, 126.
Map of Yonkers (1813), 141.
Map of Yonkers (1843), 157, 158.
Map of Yonkers (1868–1872), 170.
Marmon, Dr. ———, 397.
Marsh, Dr. C. D., 397.
Martin, Edwin Köenigmacher, 379, 380, 382, 427.
Mason, Benjamin, 179.
Mason, John Mitchell, 162, 269, 428.
Masten, E., 398.
Mather, Warham, 76.
McAdoo, W. E., 398.
McAdoo, William Gibb, Jr., 430.
McCready, W. J., 398.
McLaughlin, James, 430.
McLaury, Dr. J. S., 397.
McVicar, Thomas, 431.
McVicar, William H., 430.
Medical Association, 196, 324.
Miller, Joseph, 428.
Miller, Rev. D. Henry, 163.
Miles, James, 156.
Miles, Charles Adna, 397, 428.
Mile Square, 53, 55, 108.
Mill Dams, 158.
Mills, 59, 75, 76.
Missionaries, Foreign, 196.
Mitchell, Edward J., 428.
Moffat, Henry, 429.
Molloy, Rev. Anthony, 295.
Monastery, 297.
Monroe, Rev. Henry, 78, 278.
Monument, 251.
Mooney, Dr. ———, 398.
Mooney, Michael, 429.
Morrell, Dr. E. M., 332, 398.
Morris, Clara, 401.
Morris General W. H., 205, 206, 212.
Morris, Lieut. E. Y., 202.
Morris, Thomas F., 169, 376.
Morse, Edward L., 398.
Morse, G. Livingston, 324.
Morse, W. G. M., 398.
Mosholu, 61, 111, 133, 193.
Mott, Abraham C., 430.
Mott, E. C., 398.
Mott, W. R., 344.
Moultrie, Francis J., 430.
Mount St. Vincent, 165.
Mount Vernon, 164, 165.
Mulcahey, Thomas F., 430.
Mulligan, Dr. Berrian, 398.
Murray, Felix, 430.
Nappeckamack, 14, 15.
Nepperhan Avenue, 140.
Nepperhan River, 14, 15, 49, 52, 99, 128, 390.
"Neutral Ground," 86, 98, 116.
"Neutral Ground," Spy of, 104, 116.
New Amsterdam, 39, 40, 41, 42, 45, 51.
Newman, Chester W., 431.
Newspapers, 80, 81, 117, 125, 135, 148, 166, 189, 191, 192, 197, 198, 250, 385, 389.

New York, 83.
Nichols, Hezekiah, 153.
Nichols, John A., 271.
Nisbet, William Fulton, 431.
Nodine Family, 138.
Nodine Hill, 138.
Nodine Hill, Sunday Services, 196.
Nodine Hill Tower, 99, 112.
Nodine, Isaac Cooley, 432.
Nugent, Arthur W., 432.
Nursery Rhymes, 71.
Odd Fellows, 159, 303, 304.
Odell, Abraham, 103.
Odell, General Jacob, 140.
Odell, James B., 212, 432.
Officers of the City, 253.
Olaff Park, 169.
Oliver, Edwin A., 387, 388.
Oliver, John W., 195, 197, 321, 386.
Olmstead, John, 162, 373.
O'Neill, Francis, 432.
Osborn, George W., 434.
Osterheld, George, 162.
Osterheld, Henry, 166, 433.
Otis, Elisha G., 162.
Otis Elevator Works, 166, 186.
Otis, Charles Rollin, 162, 434.
Otis, Norton Prentiss, 162, 192, 271, 337, 435.
Paddock, Walter Halsey, 436.
Paddock, Prince William, 154, 436.
Paddock, Obed, 154.
Pagan, John, Jr., 436.
Palisades, 20, 98, 99, 100.
Palmer, Rev. Dr. A. J., 252, 284.
Palmer, Joseph H., 399.
Park Hill, 229.
Parks, 229, 383.
Parton, Arthur, 398.
Patriots of the Revolution, 87, 397.
Patroonship, 43.
Peake, Cyrus Augustus, 398, 436.
Pearsall, Clarence A., 436.
Peck, Sidney Starr, 436.
Peek, Cornelius W., 164.
Peek, Peter F., 164.
Peene, George, 391, 437.
Peene, John G., 391, 437.
Peene, Joseph, 152, 153, 391.
Peene, Joseph, Jr., 391, 437.
Pentz, George B., 187, 256, 376.
Phillips, Richard Oliver, 336, 397, 437.
Philipse Brand, 69.
Philipse and Philipseburg, 55, 84.
Philipse Family, 56.
Philipse, Frederick (1), 53, 55, 56, 57, 59.
Philipse, Frederick (2), 62, 63.
Philipse, Frederick (3), 64, 65, 84, 90, 91.
Philipse, Mary, 63, 121.
Philipse, Susanna, 64.
Physicians, 70, 124, 138, 162, 163, 175, 397.
Pierson, Alphæus, 144.
Pike, Dr. Horace B., 235.
Plank Walks, 163, 171.
Police Commissioners, 252.
Police Department, 173, 236.
Police Headquarters, 419.
Pooley, Dr. J. H., 195, 397.
Population, 49, 69, 130, 135, 149, 150, 166, 169, 181, 197, 227, 268.
Porteous, James Lindsay, 397, 438.
Post, William H., 438.
Postage Rules, 132.
Postmasters, 263.
Post-Offices, 75, 133, 145, 147, 264.
Potter, A. M., 398.
Potter, Adrian M., 438.
Poucher, George W., 398.
Prime, A. J., 316, 398.
Prime, Dr. Wendell, 401.
Prime, Ralph E., 205, 211, 226, 270, 322.

Prime, Ralph E., Jr., 398.
Prime, W. C., 398.
Prote John B., 438.
Pruyn, John Isaac, 260, 438.
Public Works, Department of, 247.
Pyne P. H., 397, 438.
Quakers, 77, 78.
Quick. S. Francis, 370, 438.
Quick, Edwin A., 439.
Quinn, Henry Joseph, 440.
Radcliff, Peter E., 440.
Radcliff Abram S., 440.
Radcliff, P. Edward 440.
Radford, Hon. William, 169, 195, 197, 206, 376.
Railroads, 149, 156, 160, 169, 194, 392.
Railroad Fare, 162.
Railroad Station, 197.
Rayner, George, 190, 258, 352, 440.
Rayner, George, Jr., 337.
Read, Jacob, 150, 441.
Real Estate, 162.
Receipt for Rent, 62.
Reed, Charles, 376.
Reid, John, 314.
Reid, Rev. Dr. John, 287.
Reevs, Dr. Gabriel P., 321, 441.
Reevs, Gabriel 262, 441.
Reevs, George 398.
Reformed Church. The First, 156, 157, 180.
Reinfelder, Dr. M. J., 397.
Reservoirs 242, 243.
Reynolds, Edgar Underhill, 441.
Richardson, William H., 441.
Rickoff Andrew J., 271.
Riley, William H., 398, 441.
Ritter, J. G., 398.
Riverdale, 165.
Rivers and Brooks, 126.
Roads, 51, 53, 70, 71, 171, 228, 229.
Robinson, Henry A., 398.
Rockwell, Samuel D., 132, 159, 190, 371.
Roman Catholics, 60, 78.
Romer, William, 398.
Rowe, Captain, 101.
Rowland, John, 442.
Russell, William C., 401.
Ruton, Isaac B., 145.
Ryan, Father, 160.
Sahagian, Aslan, 442.
Sanders James P., 206, 442.
Sanders, Rev. Dr. H. M., 287.
Saunders, David, 162, 181.
Saw Mill, 49.
Saw Mill River, 49.
Sawyer, Rev. Dr. R. A., 180.
Sawyer, Jr., Benjamin Franklin, 442.
Schell, Rev. Dr. E. A., 252, 443.
Schlesinger, Leopold J., 442.
Schlobohm, John H., 443.
Schopen, Dr. Emil, 322, 397, 443.
Scribner, Hon. G. Hilton, 101, 162, 189, 197, 313, 400.
Schools, 79, 80, 134, 147, 153, 155, 159, 162, 169, 176, 178, 187, 249, 269, 274.
Scrugham, W. W., Sr., 155, 156, 166, 171, 188.
Scrugham, William Warburton, 263, 443.
Seabury, Dr. J. H., 397.
Settlers, Early, 40, 46.
Seward, Rev. Dr. D. M., 180, 287.
Seymour, Charles W., 398.
Seymour, W. H., 321.
Sherman William H., 398, 443.
Shonnard, Frederic 143, 154.
Shonnard, Major Frederick, 107, 401.
Shotts John C., 307, 444.
Shrive, William Glenn, 444.
Silkman, J. B., 398.
Silkman, Theodore Hannibal, 444.
Skinner, Albert L., 184.

Skinner, Charles E., 184, 445.
Skinner, George B., 162, 181.
Skinner, Halcyon, 181.
Skinner, John W., 32.
Slade, James, 445.
Slavery, 41, 69, 125, 129, 131, 149.
Sloops, 54, 139, 148, 152, 390.
Small, Dr., 398.
Small, J. C., 398.
Smith, Alexander, 355.
Smith & Sons' Carpet Mills, 355.
Smith, David H., 363.
Smith Duncan, 398.
Smith, Rev. Dr. T. Ralston, 338.
Smith, Thomas, 162, 385.
Smith, Wallis, 374.
Smith, Warren B., 188 329.
Societies 301, 337.
Southwick, John H., 445.
Southworth, Dr. R. J., 397.
Southworth, Mrs. E. D. E. N., 401.
Sproull, John F., 324.
Spuyten Duyvil, 165, 169.
Spy of the Neutral Ground, 101, 104.
Stages, 71, 136, 147, 159, 160, 228.
Stahl, Charles, 445.
Stahlnecker, Oliver, 132.
St. Aloysius' Academy, 178.
Stamp Act, 83.
Standard, Rev. Thomas (M.D.), 77, 277.
Steamboats, 128, 149, 192, 251, 391, 392, 393.
Steamboat Accidents 187, 188.
Steamboat Pier, 153.
Stengle, George 398.
Stewart, David, 155.
Stewart, George, 155, 285.
Stewart, James, 155, 445.
Stewart, James, 344.
Stewart, Robert L., 445.
Stilwell, 170, 398.
Stout, Jacob, 137.
Streets (See Roads).
Streets, Lighted, 111, 193.
Strong, Dr. F. L., 398.
Sugar Refinery, 354, 363.
Sunday-school Teachers, 196.
Sutherland, Leslie, 445.
Swasey, Dr. I. N., 397.
Sweny, W. H., 398.
Swift, Samuel, 337, 375, 445.
Tavern Indian Queen, 131, 132.
Taxes, 264.
Taylor, Allen, 326, 398, 446.
Thayer, Stephen H., 256, 446.
Thayer, Stephen Howard, Sr., 446.
Thomas, Walter, 321.
Thomas, Edwin L., 446.
Thompson, William Bryan, 446.
Tibbetts Brook, 52, 61, 128.
Tierney, John J., 446.
Tilden, Hon. Samuel J., 400.
Tippett, George, 52.
Tojetti, Virgil, 398
Toll Gates, 136, 147.
Tomlinson, David, 398.
Tomlinson, Theodore, 398.
Tompkins, Abraham H., 251, 446.
Tompkins, Frederick J., 447.
Tompkins, Joseph M., 447.
Tompkins, Robert B., 447.
Tories, 88, 89, 91, 93, 103, 121.
Towndrow, Thomas, 162.
Trade, Board of, 379, 384.
Traders and Settlers, 40, 46.
Train, F. S., 398.
Train, F. C., 398.
Travel and Transportation, 136, 137, 138, 149, 152, 153, 156, 159, 160, 163, 169, 171.
Treaty, Dutch and Indian, 40, 41.
Trevor, J. B., 196, 197.

Trotter, Dr. R. R., 336.
Tuckahoe, 105, 106, 123.
Tymeson, Eugene 184.
Underhill, Edward, Sr., 181.
Underhill, Caleb Fowler, 447.
Upham, Dr. Geo. B., 162.
Upham, Dr. W. R., 397.
Valentines, 148.
Valentine, Elizabeth, 107.
Valentine, Thomas, 97, 106, 108.
Valentine, Nathaniel B., 96, 106.
Van Cortlandt, 47, 48, 60, 61.
Van Pelt, Reuben Whalen 447.
Vark Aaron, 141, 145, 157.
Vault Hill, 89.
Veitch, William H., 447.
Veneer Mill, 181.
Verplanck, Philip, 448.
Village Business Men, 191.
Village News Items, 191.
Village Newspapers 189.
Village Officers, 169.
Von Storch, Henry Ferdinand, 448.
Voting, 134.
Wading Place, 53.
Wages, 44, 69.
Walloons, 42.
Walsh, Michael, 449.
War :
  Indian 28, 29, 38, 40, 45, 82.
  French and Indian, 81, 82.
  Dutch and English, 51, 81.
  Revolution, 85, 159.
  (1812), 140, 148.
  Civil, 199.
War Prices, 124.
Waring, Charles E., 155, 376, 377, 449.
Waring Factory, 159, 341.
Waring, John T., 153, 162, 170, 200.
Waring, Jarvis A., 449.
Waring, William C., 341, 449.
Warneck, John, 449.
Warren, Dr. N. A., 335.
War Ships (British), 91, 148.
Washburn, Benjamin Secor, 449.
Washington, General, 81, 121.
Washington's Headquarters, 74.
Washington, Inauguration of, 351.
Washington, Prayer of, 107, 135.
Water Board, 241.
Water Power, 157.
Water Commissioners, 240.
Weaving, 76.
Weller, James H., 237, 449.
Wells Estate, 156, 157, 158, 159, 160.
Wells Estate, Map of, 158.
Wells, Horace D., 157.
Wells, Lemuel 139, 154, 156.
Wells, Lemuel W., 253, 156, 157.
Welsh, William, 450.
West India Company, 41, 50.
Wetmore, Rev. James, 77.
Wheeler, John, 450.
Whigs and Tories, 81.
Whitney, S. R., 401.
Whitney, Frank, 398.
Wide Awakes, 192, 200.
Wiggins, Lewis H., 451.
Wigwams, Indian, 14.
Wilde, Dr. Norman, 401.
Wilson, W. W., 241.
Winslow, F. S., 398.
Winters, Old-Time, 107.
Wisewell, M. N., 179.
Woodlawn Cemetery, 169, 229, 247.
Woodruff, Frederick H., 451.
Woodworth, W. W., 169.
Wynkoop, Richard, 321.
Xavier, Rev Henry F., 290, 398.
Xavier, Frank E., 388.
Yerks, Elijah M., 451.
Y. M. C. A., 197, 324.

Yonkers:
- Advantageous Site of, 11.
- After the Revolution, 119.
- Altitude of, 11.
- An Indian Trading Port, 50.
- At Close of Eighteenth Century, 131.
- Banks, 371.
- Board of Trade. 379.
- Boundaries of, 226.
- Cemeteries, 452.
- Census of, 130, 265, 267.
- Church Attendants, 54, 60.
- Churches, 275, 299.
- Citizens of, 191, 231, 396.
- City of, 226.
- Commuters, 159.
- Dock, 139, 148, 153, 154.
- Drives, 247.
- During Rebellion, 192, 199.
- During Revolution, 85.
- Early Customs of, 71, 73.
- Elections, 134, 227.
- Farm Life of, 131, 150.
- First Houses of, 53, 73.
- First Saw Mill of, 49.
- First Settlers, 12, 14, 42, 48, 49, 53.
- Flora of, 11.

Yonkers (Continued):
- Foreign Born Population of, 226.
- Geological Structure of, 10.
- Growth of, 181, 227.
- Hamlets, 123, 149, 169.
- Hermit, 197.
- Historical Relics in, 100.
- Historical Places in, 99.
- Improvements of, 228.
- Industries, 338.
- In Middle of Seventeenth Century, 49.
- Land and River Transportation of, 390.
- Land Purchases in, 122.
- Languages Spoken in, 12, 19, 22, 49, 54, 59, 136.
- Letters from, 95.
- Militiamen, 137.
- Names of, 14, 47, 49, 51, 53, 80, 131, 401.
- Newspapers. 385.
- Number of Buildings in, 164.
- Number of Dwellings in, 164.
- Number of Families, 267.
- Owners of, 12, 14, 42, 44, 47, 51, 53, 92, 121, 122, 123, 130, 157.
- Part of Neutral Ground, 116.

Yonkers (Continued):
- Political Meetings, 156.
- Population 135, 136, 149, 166, 169.
- Proposed Annexation. 231.
- Real Estate, Value of, 70, [149, 152, 154, 157, 162, 163, 165.
- The Name of a Boat, 70.
- Town of, 130.
- Trustees of, 169.
- Under Dutch. 47, 81.
- Under English. 51, 58.
- Under Glacial Man, 12.
- Under Indians, 14.
- Under N. Y. State, 130.
- Under U. S. A., 135.
- Village Items, 192.
- Volunteers, 200.
- (1609), 14, 39.
- (1609–1646), 39, 47.
- (1646–1672), 47, 54.
- (1672–1775), 54, 85.
- (1775–1783), 85, 119.
- (1783–1788), 119, 131.
- (1788–1855), 131, 169.
- (1855–1872), 169, 227.
- (1872–1896), 227, 267.

THE HISTORY OF YONKERS.

CHAPTER I.

LAYING THE FOUNDATIONS.

"We have come in search of truth,
    Trying with uncertain key
    Door by door of mystery;
We are reaching through His laws,
To the garment hem of Cause.

"As with fingers of the blind,
    We are groping here to find
    What the hieroglyphics mean
Of the Unseen in the seen."

ROCK readers inform us that, ages ago, the highlands of America were covered with a great ice sheet, which overlaid the region where now the cities, near the mouth of the Hudson, uplift their spires and domes. Then the only walls visible were vast and rugged walls of ice which skyward reared their pinnacles and bergs and glittering towers. Those ice walls constituted a part of the mighty glacier with which the Divine Builder was at work, laying the foundation for future cities in which millions should dwell. Nothing in those chill precincts was then visible, but ice to the north, east and west. It was the edge of the great North American glacier, which terminated along the latitude of the New York City of to-day, losing its vast bergs into the Atlantic Ocean, and piling its detritus along its foot. A glacier, it will be remembered, has its origin in the hollows of mountains, where perpetual snow accumulates. The ice makes its way down towards the lower valleys, where it gradually melts until it terminates exactly where the melting, due to the contact of the warmer air, earth, and rain of the valley, compensates for the bodily descent of the ice from the snow reservoirs of the higher mountains. The North American glacier was a continent of ice moving with resistless progress. Mountains were paved away and some of them levelled by the gigantic ice plow, or plain masses of gravel and rock were moved from the north, and deposited where, in subsequent ages, men were to build populous towns. Manhattan Island and Long Island are merely a part of the dump of this monstrous mass of ice—simply square miles of ice-ground rock, covered with the gravelly deposits of the glaciers. When the gigantic work was completed, and the Almighty Builder had no more use for the glacier, He melted it. Then the ice period was ended. It was followed by the era of more or less equable temperature now enjoyed.

The glacier disappeared, but the register of its work abides. The Divine Architect left records of the way He shaped the coast, and laid the foundations for human habitations. Savants, who read and translate the hieroglyphics on the rocks, inform us that those inscriptions record the history of the formation of the hills and valleys now covered by the long avenues and numerous buildings of the peopled town.

The surface of Westchester County is one of the pages of this history. "The geological formations are very ancient. They consist mainly of micaceous gneiss, or granite. The former largely predominates. The exposed surfaces indicate subjection to immense heat and pressure, with so great displacement that the strata, in some districts, are nearly vertical, outcropping in numerous parallel ledges, not continuous, but *en echelon*, and giving inclinations to hillsides." A number of minerals are found. A coarse crystallized limestone (marble) appears here and there. The granite affords building stone of fine quality. Over the primary rocks trap boulders are strewn. The effects of glacial action and drift deposit are visible in *moraines*. Glaciers become laden with stones and earth falling from the heights above, or coming down in crushing avalanches of snow and stones. The stones and earth make a band along either border of a glacier, and such a band is called a *moraine*. At Croton Point, on the Hudson, and elsewhere in the county, are evidences of glacial *moraines*. Deep striæ and lighter scratches still remain upon exposed rock surfaces, and others are smoothly polished. Immense numbers of boulders are scattered throughout the county. The most of them are granite, and these are thought to have been brought from Massachusetts and New Hampshire. Some are of conglomerate from across the Hudson River, and others have great numbers of shells and fossils.

AN ALPINE GLACIER.

A boulder at Somers is remarkable. It is an immense mass of red granite, mentioned in the old deeds as the "Cobbling Stone," and "was doubtless brought there by a glacier or dropped from an iceberg." Similar records of the work of the gigantic ice-plow and ice-sledge are also found in the regions around Westchester County.

The terminal *moraine* of the great North American glacier can be traced from Montauk Point, Long Island, for hundreds of miles westward, with such occasional interruptions as are made by rivers and hills. Glaciers have a slow movement, varying from a few inches to three or four feet a day, according to the slant of their beds and their volume. Nothing could resist the southward progress of the mighty ice continent. Mt. Washington was buried to its top, and the Catskills carry the scars of this great plow to the present day. The débris thus worn from the heights was borne along in and under the glacier for hundreds of miles. Some of it, ground to sand and gravel, was strewn along the coast, forming part of the continental shelf, or slightly submerged coast, that adapts itself to the contour of the land. Other large masses were dropped at the ice foot, where they are seen to-day in the form of worn and mossy boulders. For this reason the country near New York harbor is a mineralogical compendium of the whole country to the north. It is a part of the locality where the monstrous ice-sledge dumped its gravel and boulders.

A boulder of labradorite, for instance, which was found on Long Island, must have been brought down from the Adirondacks, because no labradorite exists south of these mountains. The green mica, mixed with field spar, that is characteristic of the bluffs at the upper end of Manhattan Island, the jasper that extends under the Hudson at Weehawken, the serpentine of Castle Point, are found across the East River, and glacial scratches have been discovered on the top of the Palisades, which point to Prospect Park, Brooklyn, where boulders of trap, such as the Palisades are made of, are not uncommon. Over two hundred varieties have been found on Long Island, and preserved in cabinets in the great cities south of Yonkers. A number of fossils, probably from Helderbergs, have also been found across the East River. The gneiss,

THE "COBBLING-STONE" IN SOMERS.

that so well illustrates glacial action in Central Park by its smoothed and rounded "sheep backs," extends under East River at Hell Gate, and crops up in ridges on the land beyond. It is this rock that was blasted away at vast expense to clear the channel in East River.

These sentences, descriptive of celestial map-making, and transcribed in large part from other pages, will interest those who desire to know the rock-written history of Yonkers and neighboring sections, as translated by scientists. The cautious reader will not unhesitatingly accept, as the truth of history, the conclusions of all geologists, for some of them are disciples of a science falsely so called; but he will listen with grateful interest to those of more solid judgment and devout spirit. Able teachers of a true science find on the rocks a story of the successive ages of creation, which corresponds to the series of graphic visions and pictures unveiled to the eyes of the author of the first book of the inspired volume. What these reverent scholars have to say about nebula, cosmogonic days, the various past ages—Azoic, Silurian, Devonian, Carboniferous, Mesozoic, Tertiary, and the Quaternary, or present age, is of profound interest, but the scope of this history does not afford space for more than has already been recorded, and by this brief record different readers will be differently impressed.

The devout student, who finds "sermons in stones," will read with a conviction that by whatever method the foundations were laid, a Divine Builder laid them. The lover of the beautiful will render a tribute of praise because a throne so beautiful was fashioned for a city so queenly—a throne* commanding a view of mountains grand and river glorious.

"I thank God," says Washington Irving, "that I was born on the banks of the Hudson! I think it an invaluable advantage to be born and brought up in the neighborhood of some grand and noble object in nature—a river, a lake, or a mountain. We make a friendship with it; we in a manner ally ourselves to it for life. It remains an object of our pride and affections, a rallying point, to call us home again after all our wanderings. 'The things which we have learned in our childhood,' says an old writer, 'grow up with our soul, and unite themselves to it.' So it is with the scenes among which we have passed our early days; they influence the whole course of our thoughts and feelings; and I fancy I can trace much of what is good and pleasant in my own heterogeneous compound to my early companionship with this glorious river. In the warmth of my youthful enthusiasm I used to clothe it with moral attributes, and almost to give it a soul. I admired its frank, bold, honest character—its noble sincerity and perfect truth. Here was no specious, smiling surface, covering the dangerous sand-bar or perfidious rock; but a stream deep as it was broad, and bearing with honorable faith the bark trusted to its waves. I gloried in its simple, majestic, epic flow; ever straight forward. Once, indeed, it turns aside for a moment, forced from its course by opposing mountains, but it struggles bravely through them, and immediately resumes its straightforward march. Behold, thought I, an emblem of a good man's course through life, ever simple, open and direct; or if, overpowered by adverse circumstances, he deviate into error, it is but momentary; he soon recovers his onward and honorable career, and continues it to the end of his pilgrimage. . . . . The Hudson is, in a manner, my first and last love; and after all my wanderings, and seeming infidelities, I return to it with a heartfelt preference over all the other rivers of the world."

Multitudes, contemplating the valley of the Hudson, will consider the rich and fertile soil, the favorable climate, and the wonderful vegetation. They will cite, for example, the flora of the county, in the beauty of which Yonkers shares. The great State of New York has a remarkably large flora. One botanist, years ago, reported fourteen hundred and fifty flowering plants and sixty ferns and lycopodiaceæ, in the State; and in Westchester County, the number of plants growing some years ago, without cultivation, was more than eleven hundred and forty-six ferns and their allies. At the time of that writing, eighty-eight plants had been introduced into the county from Europe. Of the flowering plants, fifty were first-class trees, reaching a height of thirty feet and upwards; thirty-four were second-class trees, which attain a height of fifteen to thirty feet, and sixty-nine were shrubs. Since the botanist above quoted wrote, doubtless many other plants have been introduced. Those in some of the conservatories of the city are very beautiful. Among the plants in the Greystone greenhouse, for instance, is a sago palm, claimed to be "two hundred years old, in fine condition, with seventy-five fronds (in 1895) three feet long." It is said that this palm was formerly in the possession of George Washington.

Other readers of the rock-written records of the region about the mouth of the Hudson will reflect upon the vast commercial advantages bestowed upon those who dwell on the banks of the royal river:

---

* The highest point in the town has been determined by the United States Coast Survey to be 516 feet above the level of the sea.

"Of all points from the St. Lawrence to Florida, New York Bay presents the most commanding facilities for entering North America, and penetrating to its heart. For extent of navigable water, the Hudson River has no peer among the rivers discharging from our coast. And the country it drains lies on a line intermediate between extreme climates, and for all conditions essential to agriculture, manufactures and commerce, is unsurpassed between the oceans. But its supreme importance lies in this—that it is the main artery of, and key to, the continent. When the thoughtful citizen looks at New York Harbor, as related through the Hudson River to our vast Northern lake chain, or traces from it inland the immense water connections time has developed, and especially when he thinks of the tremendous commerce now going in and out through these connections, he must feel profoundly the importance of the valley and harbor of the Hudson."

Who was the first inhabitant of this region, after the glacier had melted, and the foundations for human habitations were laid? Ethnologists assure us that the Indians were not the first people on the banks of the Hudson. "The traditions of the Indians referred in a very vague way to long journeys from the Northwest, and great suffering from cold on their way hither, and of contests with a people who occupied the country before them. Of their own history they were lamentably ignorant. Their computation of time, by moons and revolving cycles, led all investigation into inextricable confusion. Any event beyond an individual's recollections floated vaguely in the boundless past." "A curious tradition of the present Iroquois records that when the *Lenni Lenapi*, the common ancestors of the Iroquois and other tribes, whose language is still widely spread among the Indians, advanced from the Northwest to the Mississippi, they found on its eastern side a great nation more civilized than themselves, who lived in fortified towns and cultivated the ground. At first they granted the new-comers permission to pass through their territories, to seek an eastward settlement, but treacherously attacked them while crossing the river. This conduct gave rise to inveterate hostilities, that terminated in the extermination or subjugation of their opponents, and the establishment of the red men in these regions."

Some archæologists and ethnologists inform us that the Skraelling, called the "Glacial Man," was the first to appear on this coast. What they consider evidences of the so-called "Glacial Man" are found, at the present time, in the gravels of the Trenton River, New Jersey, consisting of stone implements, that seem to have been lost while engaged in hunting and fishing. "With the disappearance of the ice, and the moderation of the climate, the men of the ice period spread along the Atlantic coast from Labrador to Florida, their descendants being the modern Eskimo and Greenlander, whose ancestors were driven northward by the red man when he conquered the country." Stone implements abound at Trenton, but none of that class have as yet been found in the region of the Hudson. The conclusion of some ethnologists is, that the glacial man, "ruder than the rudest red savage, and in appearance resembling the present Eskimo," was the first inhabitant of the banks of the Hudson, and that his language was very primitive. The reader who remembers that reliable scientists insist upon being assured of facts, and also upon grouping or classifying a sufficient number of facts to justify their inferences, will be inclined to consider the opinions of many students of antiquities as interesting and working hypotheses, rather than demonstrated truth. One record is reliable. It abides forever. Whether the first inhabitant was a "Glacial Man" or not, he was a descendant of the first parents of the whole race, for all nations of the earth were made of one blood. As to the Indians, universal texture and black color of the hair, and polysynthetic speech, point directly to primordial unity of origin—one racial stock. One historian says: "When we look at the conditions on either side of the continent, we cannot suppose that it was at all impossible for men at any indefinitely remote period to have found their way hither. The climatic changes of past periods may have made the route by Behring's Strait (now thirty-six miles wide at its narrowest point between Asia and North America) entirely practicable. The route by the Aleutian Islands is not difficult now to canoe navigators. The Pacific currents frequently cast the wrecks of Japanese vessels upon the northwestern shores. The islands of the South Pacific afforded a probable way of communication, and it is believed that many have disappeared, comparatively recently, beneath the surface. On the Atlantic side the difficulties were by no means insurmountable, even if we ignore 'the lost Atlantis.' The trade winds and equatorial currents carried Cabral and his Portuguese fleet, bound around the Cape of Good Hope, to the American shores, and led to the discovery of Brazil. On his second voyage Columbus found, in a house on the island of Guadaloupe, the stern part of a European vessel. In various periods of the past the same forces may have brought men to these shores. It is probable that America was peopled from various sources, and at widely separated periods."

In the dense forests of Mexico remains of an ancient city have been discovered in which were found walls of hewn stone, admirably put together with mortar, and enriched by sculptures in bold relief, and hieroglyphical inscriptions exactly resembling the Aztec MSS. in the museums of Europe, and in the publications of Humboldt; well-executed, *vaulted* roofs, and obelisks, covered with mythical figures, and pictorial hieroglyphical inscriptions. Not only are the western Indians very like their nearest neighbors, the northeastern Asiatics, but in language and tradition it is confidently affirmed there is a blending of the people. The Eskimo on the American, and the Tchnktchis on the Asiatic side, understand each other perfectly.

Whoever were the first inhabitants of these shores, and by whatever route they came, the period arrived when the red men, "the painted brothers of our common race," dwelt on the banks of the Hudson, the Nepperhan, the Sprain, Tippett's Brook, and the Bronx. One of their villages was at the mouth of the Neperah. They called it Nappeckamack.

CHAPTER II.

NAPPECKAMACK AND THE TAWNY VILLAGERS.

"And still the lofty hills abide,
   Where sped their moccasined feet,
Still floods and ebbs the river's tide,
   Where skimmed their birch bark fleet.

" But from the hills, and river's shore,
   Their dusky race has fled;
The pale-face thoughtlessly treads o'er
   The places of their dead."

WHAT music dwells in the Indian language! How graphic are its sonorous sentences! Poor in words expressing abstract thought, but how replete with word-pictures, which convert the listener's ears into eyes, enabling him to see what he hears!

Nappeckamack is one of those expressive Indian words. The beautiful Neperah or Nippirau (written Nippiorha in the Royal Charter), impetuously rushing toward the stately Shatemuc (Hudson), flashed upon the receptive mind of the red man at once a picture and a picture-word, descriptive of the glancing stream and the village on its banks—Nappeckamack, "the rapid-water settlement!"

It was a fortified or palisaded village, probably the largest in the territory now known as Westchester County, and was situated near the confluence of the Neperah and Shatemuc. History describes an Indian village as a collection of hickory sapling huts, bark-covered. Most of the houses presented the same appearance, but differed as to dimensions. Their size varied with the number of families in the tribe. Two or more rows of long, bark-stripped, slender hickory saplings, cut with rude stone implements by the wigwam builders, were set in the ground in straight lines. The rows were as far apart as the proposed width and as long as the proposed length of the house. The width was seldom greater than twenty feet; the length of some of the houses as great as one hundred and forty feet. The tops of the poles were bent together in the form of an arch and made fast. The appearance of an Indian village house has been likened to that of a garden arbor. Split poles, which served for laths, were fastened to the sides and roof. They were covered with bark secured to the lathing by withes. A hole was left in the crown of the roof that smoke might escape. Floors were unknown. There was only one door, and that was in the end of the house. Totemic emblems were rudely painted on the wigwam. It was occupied by as many as sixteen or eighteen families. They kindled and kept their fires in the middle of their house and from one end to the other. Each family repaired at night to its own part and its own mats.

A collection of such houses constituted a village, which was built in a sheltered spot. A central place were used for the transaction of public business and for amusements and ceremonies. The side of a steep and high hill, or a level plain near a stream of water, or a plateau on a hill-top, was the site the Indians usually selected for their village. The foundations of the strong stockade enclosing their fortified villages were constructed of logs laid on the ground. On both sides of such logs palisades were set in the ground. The upper ends were crossed and bound together. These stockaded villages were the Indians' castles. Families of the same sub-tribe, or chieftaincy, repaired to them in winter. But the red men were migratory, and in cold weather, as well as in warm, they ranged their forests and hunting-grounds for game, and at convenient places set up temporary wigwams, which they covered with the bark of trees, filling the crevices with twigs and mud. They also covered their lodges with the skins of wild animals. Spring and summer found them on the sea coast, or at river side or lake side in search of fish.

Nappeckamack commanded the approaches on the north of the territory of the tribe living in Nepperhaem. Another "Mohegan Castle," or fortified village called Nipinichsan, on the north shore of Papirinimen (Spuyten Duyvil Creek), commanded the southern approaches. The portion of land known to the whites as "Berrian's Neck" was the site of the ancient Nipinichsan of the red men. It forms the northern bank at the mouth of the *Spyt den Dyvel Kil*, or channel. The village overlooked the Shatemuc and Papirinimen. It was both a dwelling-place and a place of defence against the warlike Sank-hi-can-ni (fire-workers), dwelling on the west shore of Shatemuc. Nappeckamack and Nipinichsan were not the only Indian villages within the forest-covered territory afterwards known as "the Yonkers." Tradition reports that there was one on the eastern edge of Boar Hill and another on the site of the present Riverdale. The last remembered Indian village in the town was on the rising banks of the Neperah, where years ago stood the residence of Abraham Fowler (east side of the Saw Mill River road and a few rods south of the Tuckahoe road).

The furniture of a wigwam was simple. It consisted of mats and rushes and beds of evergreen boughs. Over the boughs were spread skins and furs, which were easily obtained, because the woods and streams of the tract now known as Yonkers then abounded in fur-bearing animals. Nappeckamack, the Indian village of the distant past, appears so near, when observed through the lenses of history, that the moccasined villagers can be seen coming and going as of yore. They were an agile race, broad-shouldered, slender-waisted, nimble-footed, some of them portly. Their complexion was brownish-yellow, or cinnamon-hued, their sunken brown or black eyes dull and sleepy, except when their passions were excited, noses broad but prominent, cheek-bones high, hair very coarse, long, and jet black (except that of the aged), beard scant, and the little that Nature gave them often carefully plucked out, jaws powerful, teeth snow white, hands and feet small, and bodies lithe; some of the girls and young women comely and graceful.

Their dress, usually simple, was sometimes elaborate. The men usually went bareheaded. The Weckquaeskeck Indians, who had a village on the site of the present Dobb's Ferry, wore their hair shorn to a cock's-comb on top, with a long lock depending on one side. In the summer the Indians of Nepperhaem and other portions of the country wore nothing but a short garment of dressed skin, called "Indian breeches" by the settlers. The women robed themselves in two garments, an under robe of dressed deer skin and an outer robe of similar material. The outer robe was girt at the waist with a belt, and extended below the knees. The lower border of this skirt was ornamented with great art and nestled with strips, tastefully decorated with wampum. The skirt of an Indian woman's outer robe was sometimes ornamented with wampum worth from one hundred to three hundred guilders. Moccasins of deer and buffalo skins were worn by both men and women; some of them were ornamented with their favorite wampum. The women bound their hair behind in a club of about a hand long, in the form of a beaver's tail. Over this they drew a square cap. "Some of the caps were ornamented with wampum. Sometimes an ornamented headband was worn around the forehead. This confined the hair smooth. Around their necks were various ornaments, decorated with wampum. They valued them as the lady of to-day values her pearl necklace." The Indian women also wore bracelets, costly ornaments and beautiful girdles. Sometimes the young women painted a few black stripes on their faces.

When an Indian brave especially desired to favorably impress a favorite maiden he wore on his head a band manufactured and braided of scarlet deer hair, interwoven with soft, shiny red hair. The men painted themselves uniformly, particularly their faces. They selected various colors, and sometimes were so disguised by paint as hardly to be recognized by acquaintances. In the winter the women and children did not go abroad much, but when they had occasion to leave their villages they robed themselves in winter garb. The men, as a defence against the inclemency of the weather, greased themselves with bear and raccoon fat. They also were clothed in winter in bear skins and those of buffaloes, deer and weasels. The most elegant garments of American Indians were mantles made of feathers overlapping each other.

In his "History of the New Netherlands" Wassenares thus describes Indian dress: "The tribes are in the habit of clothing themselves with otter skins, the

A NORTH AMERICAN INDIAN.

fur inside, the smooth side without, which, however, they paint so beautifully that at a distance it resembles lace. When they bring their commodities to the traders, and find they are desirous to buy them, they make so little matter of it that they rip up the skins with which they are clothed and sell them also, returning naked to their homes. They use the beaver skins mostly for the sleeves and the otter for the rest of the clothes." Bancroft, in his "History of the United States," devotes several chapters to the red men. He does not specify the Indians of Manhattan Island and neighboring regions as those whose dress he describes. What he writes of Indian garb, however, gives a clearer idea of that which was probably the more elaborate dress of the Indians in the Hudson River valley. He says: "The clothing of the natives was in summer but a piece of skin, like an apron, round the waist; in winter a bear skin, or more commonly made of the skins of the fox and beaver. Their feet were protected by soft moccasins, and to these were bound the broad snow-shoes on which, though cumbersome to the novice, the practised hunter could leap like a roe. Of the women, head, arms and legs were uncovered; a mat or a skin neatly prepared, tied over the shoulders and fastened to the waist by a girdle, extended from the neck to the knees. They glittered with tufts of elk-hair dyed in scarlet, and strings of shells were their pearls and diamonds. The summer garments, of the skins of the moose and deer, were painted in many colors, and the fairest feathers of the turkey, fastened by threads made from wild hemp and nettle, were curiously wrought into mantles. The claws of the grizzly bear formed a proud collar for a war chief; a piece of an enemy's scalp, with a tuft of long hair painted red, glittered on the stem of his war-pipe; the wing of a red bird or the beak and plumage of a raven decorated his locks; the skin of a rattlesnake was worn round the arm of their chiefs; the skin of the polecat, bound round the leg, was their order of the garter—emblem of noble daring. A warrior's dress was often a history of his deeds. His skin was tattooed with figures of animals, of flowers, of leaves, and painted with shining colors. Some had the nose tip-ped with blue, the eyebrows, eyes and cheeks tinged with black and the rest of the face red; others had black, red and blue stripes drawn from the ears to the mouth; others had a broad black band, like a ribbon, extending from ear to ear across the eyes, with smaller bands on the cheeks. When they made visits, and when they assembled in council, they painted themselves brilliantly, delighting especially in vermilion."

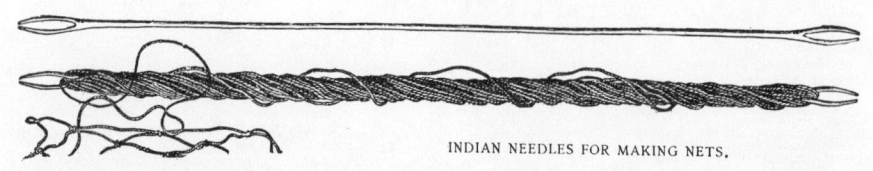

Verrazano, who sailed along the coast of North America in 1524, probably reached the entrance of New York Harbor, but it is doubtful whether he entered the harbor, as the weather was threatening, and he did not know the locality. He speaks of the natives whom he met as being "dressed out with the feathers of birds of various colors—the finest-looking tribe and the handsomest in their costumes" of any that he had found on his voyage. Among those who came on board his vessel were "two kings, more beautiful in form and stature than can possibly be described"; one was perhaps forty years old and the other about twenty-four. "They were dressed," he continues, "in the following manner: the oldest had a deer skin around his body, artificially wrought in damask figures, his head without covering, his hair was tied back in various knots; around his neck he wore a large chain ornamented with many stones of different colors. The young man was similar in his general appearance." "In size," he says, "they exceed us, their complexion tawny, inclining to white, their faces sharp, their expression mild and pleasant, greatly resembling the antique." "The women," he says, "were of the same form and beauty, very graceful, of fine countenances and pleasing appearance in manners and modesty. They wore no clothing except a deer skin, ornamented like those of the men." Some had "very rich lynx skins upon their arms and various ornaments upon their heads, composed of braids of hair, which hung down upon their breasts upon each side." The older, and the married people, both men and women, "wore many ornaments in their ears, hanging down in the Oriental manner." In disposition they were generous, giving away whatever they had; of their wives they were careful, always leaving them in their boats when they came on shipboard, and their general deportment was such that with them, he says, "we formed a great friendship."

These Indians, whom Verrazano met in 1524, "the finest-looking tribe and the handsomest in their costumes," were probably the Matonwacks (Montauks) of Long Island. Those whom Hudson met in Newark Bay, "clothed in mantles of feathers and robes of fur," were probably Raritans. As their wigwams were not far away from "the rapid-water settlement," we may presume that the villagers of Nappeckamack knew their dress well; and unless human nature in that day differed very much from the human nature of to-day, we may be assured that if the Montauk or the Raritan belle had a costume unusually fine the Nappeckamack belle would soon hear all about it, and either possess one like it or with skilful fingers fashion a robe fairer and finer.

SQUAW AND PAPOOSE.

Though fond of baubles and finery, the Indians were a slovenly and dirty race. While the European studies to keep his skin clean, the Indian's aim was to make his shine by means of accumulated oil, grease and paint. Soot scraped from the bottoms of kettles, the juices of herbs of various tints, rendered adhesive by combination with unctuous substances, were lavishly used to make his appearance particularly hideous and terrific. It is evident that the red man's taste was singular. When the sailors who had first come out in the "Half Moon" saw their Indian friends for the second time their persons were adorned with axe-heads and shovel-blades, given in exchange for furs. Stockings were in use for tobacco pouches. Afterward they learned a better use for axe-heads, shovel-blades and stockings. The early French writers relate an amusing instance, which shows the confusion of Indian ideas in matters of dress. A Huron girl was presented by the Ursuline nuns, who had educated her, with a complete and handsome suit of clothes in the Parisian style. It was her marriage present. A few days after the marriage the nuns saw the Indian bridegroom arrayed in the whole of his bride's attire and parading backward and forward in front of the convent. His pleasure increased when he observed the nuns crowding to the windows to see him.

SENECA-IROQUOIS LONG HOUSE.

History not only describes the huts of Nappeckamack, and the forms and features and dress of the copper-colored villagers roaming the forests of Nepperhaem like wild animals, but also has something to say about their lineage, nation or tribe and family. One method by which ethnologists grouped the red men was that of classification by language. All the northern part of the United States was occupied by two great peoples, "the Iroquois" and "the Algonquin." In the northern and central and western parts of New York, and on both sides of Lake Erie and Lake Ontario were the Iroquois and their affiliated tribes. They are known in history as the "Five Nations." By occupying the summit lands and the sources of the great navigable rivers of the continent east and northeast of the Alleghanies, they placed themselves on vantage ground, and held in subjection a vast extent of country. They were savages, fierce, wild and cruel; but they were also brave and skilful warriors, wise legislators, keen diplomatists and eloquent orators. They were the "Romans of America." The French sobriquet, "The Iroquois," is a term founded on an exclamation which these warlike people employed in their responses to public speakers.

A second great division of the red men was composed of those who spoke what the French called "Algonquin." That is a French contraction of *Algomequin,* a word of the Algonquin language, signifying "those on the other side of the river," i.e., the St. Lawrence River. The Algonquin was a most widely diffused language, and most fertile in dialects. It extended from

INDIAN PIPES.

the icy regions of the north to the southern boundary of South Carolina, and from the Atlantic to the Mississippi. "It was the mother tongue of those who greeted the colonists of Raleigh at Roanoke, and of those who welcomed the pilgrims at Plymouth. It was heard from the bay of Gaspé to the valley of Des Moines; and from Cape Fear, and it may be from Savannah to the lands of the Esquimaux; from the Cumberland River of Kentucky to the southern bounds of the Mississippi."

The Hudson River Indians spoke the Algonquin. This was the language of the red villagers in "the rapid-water settlement."

The red men were divided into tribes, and sub-tribes, each having its token painted on person or on cabin. The Indians on the banks of the Neperah were confederated with the Mohicans (Mohegans was the Connecticut spelling of the word), and with them constituted one tribe or nation. The Mohegans occupied the country along the east bank of the Shatemuc (Hudson) River, and eastward to the Connecticut River; and from Long Island Sound northward to the mouth of the Mohawk River, and perhaps to Lake Champlain. Long Island was also occupied by Mohegan tribes. Mohegan was a phrase which denoted "enchanted wolf." This was the badge or arms of the tribe, rather than the tribe itself. Some Mohegans called themselves Muhhekaniew. On the west bank of the Shatemuc were the Minci, another tribe of Algonquin lineage.

It is difficult to ascertain the name of the family, or

THE PALISADES, OPPOSITE YONKERS.

chieftaincy, which occupied the territory now included within the Yonkers boundaries. Authorities differ. By some they are called Weckquaskecks, and by others Reckgawawances, or chieftaincy of the Wappingers, or Wapanachki—"Men of the East," and as "the oldest sons of their grandfather," the *Lenni Lenapes* or the "Original People," their territory extending to about the middle of what came to be known as Beekman's patent (Dutchess County).

One of the writers who holds the first of these opinions, that is, that the Indians of the Yonkers territory were, as to their family, Weckquaskecks, says: "The Weckquaskeck family occupied the territory between the Hudson and the Bronx, and from Sing Sing to the Spuyten Duyvil, and on Manhattan Island were the Manhattans." The historian who maintains the latter opinion says: "The Hollanders, at first, called the Indians on Manhattan Island, Manhattans, but later still it came to be known that there were no Manhattans. The word Manhattan is a compound Algonquin descriptive term, not referring to a tribe but to a beautiful landscape. The Indians on Manhattan Island bore the name Reckwawances. They were a sub-tribe of the Wappingers, and were subsequently known as Reckgawawances. Their territorial jurisdiction extended on the east to the Bronx and East Rivers, and on the south included Manhattan Island, which, however, was only temporarily occupied during the seasons of planting and fishing, their huts there constituting their summer seaside resorts, and remaining unoccupied during the winter. Their tract on the mainland was called Kekesick—literally 'stony country.' Tuckaren was their sachem in 1839. There is very great certainty that it was the Reckgawawances who sold Manhattan Island to Director Winnit in 1626, and that they were the 'Manhattae' or Manatthanes, so called by De Laet in 1633-40. Nipinichan was their castle, or palisaded village on the north shore of Papirinimen or Spuyten Duyvil Creek, and Nappeckamack was their similarly fortified village at the mouth of the Neperah.

"From the district occupied by the Reckgawawances, the chieftaincies of the Wappingers extended north and east. On the north came in succession the Weckquaesgecks, who were especially conspicuous in the wars with the Dutch, the Sint-Sinks, the Tankitekes and the Kitchawongs, as far as Anthony's Nose." The author quoted above agrees with Schoolcraft as to the significance of the term Monatum, but objects to his extending the term to the Indians whom the Dutch found on New York Island. He says: "It was the Dutch, and not the Indians, who first called the island Manhattan. The Indians gave the name Manna-hata to the region on the west of the Hudson, and near the Elysian Fields at Hoboken. The term was taken to Holland and was at once adopted as defining the bay and harbor, also as the name of the native inhabitants. From this the island came to be called Manhattan."

The red men who lived in the "rapid-water settlement," at the mouth of the Neperah, had their totemic emblem. The Wappingers bore the totem of the wolf, and the Mohicans proper that of the bear, by virtue of which they were entitled to the office of the chief sachem, or king of the nation. De Lancey, the historian, says that the Indians of Westchester County were Mohicans of the Turkey tribe, a clan of the *Lenni Lenape*, a Delaware stock of North American aborigines, while the historian Wilson says, "A snake-skin tied around the head, from the centre of which projected the tail of a bear or a wolf, or a feather, indicated the totem or tribe to which they belonged."

Each local tribe had its sachem, whose extent of power depended on his personal capacity. Bravery, prudence, eloquence and cunning swayed these rude men. The sachem represented his tribe in national council, which assembled when concerted action was required. Local tribes declared war for themselves, but they could not declare a general war. Death was the penalty for treason. The decisions of the general council were honored.

In the foregoing reference to the lineage, tribe and family to which the dwellers in Nappeckamack belonged (Algonquin lineage, Mohegan tribe* and either Weckquaskeck or Reckgawawance family), the term Algonquin has been used for denominating their language. The words which the red men on the banks of the Neperah spoke, as they convened about hunting and fishing, love and war, would sound in our ears as jargon. Scholarly interpreters enable us to form some idea of the language which was spoken, but not written, by the aborigines.

Very many ways of spelling their words are in vogue, all evidently aiming to express the Indian sounds. All their names and other words which we have are based upon the reproducing of their spoken

---

*Dawson, the historian, was of the opinion that the Indians occupying the tract subsequently known as "the Yonkers" were not Mohegans but Manhattans, a branch of the Munseys. He held that the east side of the Hudson, south of Albany and down to Tappan Sea, were occupied by the Mohicans (Mohegans), and that the fierce Manhattae occupied Staten and Manhattan Islands as far north perhaps as the east shore of Tappan Bay.

sounds in our own letters. If a Dutchman, Frenchman or an Englishman undertook to write the same word from an Indian's mouth very different appearing and sounding words would be recorded. And as very many of our New York Indian terms and names represent an English spelling of a Dutch or French translation of an Indian sound, we should never be surprised at a variety of spelling.

The Algonquin language, which was that of the Nappeckamack Indians, was agglutinative. Those wild men in "the-rapid-water-settlement" strung words together in an extended compound. "They concentrated in a single expression a complex idea or several ideas, among which there was a natural connection. The universal tendency was to express in the same word, not only all that modified or related to the same object or action, but both the action and the object." A learned writer says that, as a rule, Indian geographical terms are of two classes—general or generic, and specific or local. In specific names the combination may be simple, as Coxackie—*co*, object, and *acke*, land; in others, intricate, as Maghaghkemeck, in which *acke*, land, is buried in consonants and qualifying terms. Wa-wa-na-quas-sick is a somewhat lengthy combination—*wa-wa* is plural or many; *na* signifies good; *quas* is stone or stones; and *ick* "a place of stones." It all means a pile of memorial stones thrown together to mark a place or event. Wa-wa-yaun-da—*wa-wa*, plural, more than one, or we; *yaun*, home, or by the prefixed plural, homes; *da*, town or village; complete, "our homes or places of dwelling."

The Indian names of streams, places and persons in the territory within and near what is now known as Yonkers illustrate the significance of pictorial Algonquin words, and afford some idea of the language spoken on the banks of the Hudson, Nepperhan, and other Yonkers streams, before the Europeans came. Among the names of streams are *Shatemuc* (the Hudson); *Mamaroneck*, "the place where fresh water falls into the salt"; *Pocantico*, from the Indian Pockhantes, "a river between the hills," descriptive of "a weird stream which pours its swift current through the foldings of a hundred hills"; *Bisightick*, the Indian name of Sunnyside Brook, which flows past the late residence of Washington Irving; *Kitchawan*, "a large and swift flowing current"—the original name of the Croton River—the present name is evidently from the name of the illustrious sachem *Kenotin; Armonperahin*, name of the Sprain River; *Armeperahin*, supposed to be the west branch of the Sprain River; *Aquehung*, name of the Bronx; *Cisqua*, a stream tributary to the Croton; *Mosholu*, name of Tippett's Brook; *Weckquasqueck*, name of a rivulet flowing into the Hudson at Dobb's Ferry; *Shoraskappock*, the confluence of the Spuyten Duyvil and the Hudson; *Amackassin*, the rivulet flowing into the Hudson at the north boundary of Yonkers; *Muscoota*, the Harlem River, possibly meaning "the river of the grass lands"; *Muscoot* is the Indian name of a stream in the town of Somers; *Armonck*, name of Byram River; *Mehanas*, name of a stream in North Castle; *Pockeotessen*, a stream in Rye; *Wisquaqua* (called by the English Wicker's Creek), a stream flowing into the Hudson at the upper landing, Dobb's Ferry; *Niperhan*, called by the Christians Yoncker's Creek; *Papirinamen*, name of Spuyten Duyvil Creek.

Among the Indian names of places are *Ossin-ing*, "stone upon stone," the Indian name of Sing Sing; *Weec-quaes-guck* or *Weckquaskeck*, "the place of the bark kettle," Indian name of the settlement on the site of Dobb's Ferry; *Alpiconck*, "place of elms," or "leaves," or "rich foliage," a village on the site of the present Tarrytown; *Sackhoes*, a village on the site of the present Peekskill; *Senasqua* (one of the softest of Indian words), the Croton Point meadow; *Castoniuck*, an Indian village on the east bank of the Hudson. The name survives in the town of Niuck or Nyack, on the west shore opposite the site of the old Indian village; *Meahagh*, name of Verplank's Point; *Amawalk*, probably a corruption of *Appamaghpogh*, *Amaghpogh* or *Amanogh; Tuckahoe*, literally *Tuckah*, "the bread," a root which the Indians gathered for food (Bolton gives another possible origin of the word); *Keskeskeck*, "stony country," which lies over against the flats of the Island of Manhates, mostly east and west; *Paperinimen*, an island on what was afterward known as the Westchester side of King's Bridge; *Sigghes*, an Indian rock west of the Albany post road and a landmark constituting a point in the northern boundary of Yonkers; *Amackassin*, name of an Indian rock on the Hudson Rriver shore, and near the mouth of the rivulet *Amackassin*. This was the "great stone," the copper-colored stone, which the Indians believed to be an enchanted rock. *Kapsee* (or as it should have been written, *Kapsic*, if its alleged signification, "safe place of landing," is correct), an extreme point of land on Manhattan Island, still known as Copsie Point, between the Hudson and East Rivers. The Indian name for the Palisades is supposed to have been *Wehawken*, the term *awk* indicating a structure of rocks resembling trees. The whole county of Westchester was denominated *Laaphawachking*, "place of stringing beads."

Among the names of persons were *Tackaren*, an Indian sachem who sold Nepperhaem to Van Der Donck; *Sepham*, an Indian sachem, whom tradition says lived on one of the Tuckahoe hills and exercised all authority among the tribes of the neighboring valleys; *Claase Dewilt, Karocapacomont,* and her son *Neameran,* native Indians, and former proprietors of Lower Yonkers; *Katonah* and *Orowapum,* Indian sachems, the former an Indian chief who held sway in what is now the town of Bedford, and the latter a sachem who owned lands in what is now White Plains. It is said that *seaump* (samp), for pounded corn, *hickora* (hickory), *opossum, raccoon, canoe, moccasin* and *tobacco* are Indian words.

This brief reference to the structure and words of the Algonquin language, spoken by the Indians of Yonkers, suffices to explain why scholars have denominated it polysynthesis, literally "a much putting together."

A few additional sentences will help to an understanding of the spirit of the people as unbosomed in their songs. "Let me write the songs of a nation and I care not who makes its laws" said a philosopher. Songs explain feelings and interpret character. "Words are the language of thought, tones are the language of emotion, going to the very fount of tears." Emotion is world-wide, and music is the universal language. It is "the color of the invisible, the language of the unspeakable." Do not our own songs and hymns reveal our longings and aspirations? "The *Miserere* is the prayer of a mourning heart; the *Te Deum* is an ocean of gratitude, whose bursting tides throw their spray over every sail; while the *Jubilate* is the chime of a thousand bells." The Indians "stood around and sang," when some of Hudson's crew went ashore, before sailing up the bay, but none of the Indian songs of that day have been preserved. We have, however, Algonquin songs of a nearer period, and while the dialect may differ from that spoken by the Indians on the Nepperhan, the spirit they breathe assists to an understanding of the life of the red men, who sang in the ancient forests of what is now called Yonkers. The following brief extracts are from songs of Western Indians who speak the Algonquin tongue. A stanza or two from a cradle song, a war song and a death song will suffice to reveal the feelings of the Indian in wigwam, in battle, and of the warrior in the death hour.

Schoolcraft sought the assistance of a gifted lady, Mrs. Elizabeth Oakes Smith, when he wished the cradle song put into English verse. He says, "This lodge and forest chaunt is almost too frail a structure to be trusted without a gentle hand amid my rougher material." In order to realize how soothing its monotonous tones were, it is to be remembered that the *e-we-yea* of the Indian woman's song is entirely analogous to the lullaby of our language. More verses of these songs can be found in Schoolcraft's volume. These will help us to a better understanding of the red man and his language:

INDIAN CRADLE SONG.

Wa wa-wa wa-wa wa yea,	(Swinging twice, lullaby,)
Nebaun-nebaun-nebaun,	(Sleep thou thrice,)
Nedaunis-ais, e we yea,	(Little daughter, lullaby,)
Wa wa-wa wa-wa wa.	(Swinging, thrice.)
Nedaunis-ais, e we yea.	(Little daughter, lullaby.)

Swinging, swinging, lul la by,
   Sleep, little daughter, sleep;
'Tis your mother watching by,
   Swinging, swinging, she will keep,
Little daughter, lul la by.

The original words of the Western warrior's war song were taken down from a young Chippewa warrior of Lake Superior. They are from the Algonquin of Schoolcraft, and were put into English verse by Mr. C. F. Hoffman:

INDIAN WAR SONG.

a. In the beginning of this song the warrior has turned his eyes to the clouds:

O sha' wau oug,	(From the place of the south,)
Un dos' e wug,	(They come,) *repeat.*
Pe nä' se wug,	(The birds, *i.e.,* the warlike birds.)
Ka baim wai wa' dung-ig.	(Hear the sound of their passing screams on the air.)

b. The idea of ravenous birds in the sky still prevails:

Tod ot' to be	(I wish to change myself to be)
Pe nä' se,	(A bird.)
Ka dow we a' we yun,	(His swift body—to be like him.)

c. The warrior now rises above all thoughts of fear:

Ne wā be na,	(I cast it away,)
Ne' ow a.	(My body.)
Ne wa' be na,	(*Repeats.*) This is a high symbolical boast of personal bravery.
Ne' ow a.	

I.

Hear not ye their shrill piping screams on the air?
Up, braves! for the conflict prepare ye—prepare!
Aroused from the canebrake, far south, by your drum,
With beaks whet from carnage the Battle Birds come.

II.

O God of my fathers, as swiftly as they,
I ask but to sweep from the hills on my prey;
Give this frame to the winds on the prairie below,
But my soul—like the bolt—I would hurl on the foe!

The death song is also from the Algonquin of Schoolcraft and was put into English verse by Hoffman.

INDIAN DEATH SONG.
("A' BE TUH GE' ZHIG.")

a. In opening this song the warrior is to be contemplated as lying wounded on the field of battle:

| A' be tuh ge' zhig | (Under the centre of the sky) |
| Ne ba' baim wä' wä. | (I mutter my baimwäwä.*) |

b. His thoughts revert to the star of his destiny:

| Ain dah' so gezhig | (Every day, thou star,†) |
| Ke ga' gun o wa' bom in. | (I gaze at you.) |

c. He sees the birds of carnage hovering over the field:

A' be tuh geézh-ig,	(The half of the day)
Ai be yaun,	(I abide—gazing,)
Pe nä se wug.	(Ye warlike birds.)

I.

Under the hollow sky,
  Stretched on the prairie low,
Centre of glory, I,
  Bleeding, disdain to groan;
But like a battle-cry
  Peal forth my thunder moan—
    Baim-wa-wa!

II.

Star, morning-star, whose ray
  Still with the dawn I see;
Quenchless through half the day,
  Gazing, thou seest me.
Yon birds of carnage, they
  Fright not my gaze from thee—
    Baim-wa-wa!

---

* Baimwäwä is the sound of passing thunders, which will convey a just idea of the violence of the figure.

† It is the morning star that is here alluded to.

[The reader who desires to know something about Indian tunes is referred to the *Century Magazine* of January, 1894, in which may be seen the musical notes of a love song, dance song and funeral song, recorded by a gifted writer, who, a few years since, made a personal study of Indian life, and transcribed several hundreds of Omaka, Ponka, Otoe and Dakota melodies].

How did the Indians occupy their time? In imagination we draw near to Nappeckamack and observe the villagers. Yonder is a troop of laughing Indian girls. They are not carrying school books, for they know nothing about books. They have baskets of bark and are going to gather wild strawberries or other wild fruit. They know where to find the most luscious. The Indian women are at work, doing much that the fair Christian women of to-day think, and rightly think, should be done only by men. How do they prepare their food? Here is one cooking. She has kindled a fire on the ground by rubbing two dry sticks rapidly together. She is boiling food in a stealite bowl or vessel of rude pottery. She handles it with wooden spoons. Indians of some localities boiled water by throwing heated stones into it. If it is the season for young corn we note that the squaws are roasting or boiling it, or they are preparing "succotash" by boiling sieva beans with green corn. If the corn is dry we may see the tawny cooks grinding it with stone pestles, in stone mortars or in bowl-like depressions in the rocks, in or near the village. Yonder is one preparing "Noohik" by moistening corn meal and breaking it upon heated stones. The pale face calls this "nocake" or "hoecake." Their food, known as porridge or pap, was called by some "sapsis," by others "dundare" (literally, boiled bread), in which they mixed beans of different colors.

CORN DIGGER.

They ate beavers' tails, the brains of fish, which, with their "sapsis," ornamented with beans, were their state dishes and highest luxuries. They knew how to preserve meat and fish by smoking, and when hunting, or while on a journey, carried with them corn roasted whole. They had venison and other meats, also fish and oysters. Dogs' flesh was one of their greatest delicacies. They knew nothing about intoxicants, but had a popular drink, prepared by pounding together, into a fine pulp, hickory nuts and walnuts, and mixing it with water. It was the pale face who brought them alcoholic liquor, "fire-water." This proved to thousands of them "liquid damnation." It is "Satan in solution," and was more fatally deceptive to them than the many poisons with which they were acquainted. It bit them like the deadly serpents in their forests, and stung them like the adders from which they knew enough to spring away, but with which they were, despite their caution, sometimes poisoned.

The Indians feasted when they could, but they knew what a compulsory fast was. The records of the stoical manner in which they conducted themselves in times of famine are pathetic. Think of them, driven by the intense cold, compelled to sit indolently in the smoke, round the fire in their cabins, and fast for days together.

BIRD AND TORTOISE PIPE, FOUND IN NEW CASTLE.

DUCK'S HEAD PIPE, FOUND IN BEDFORD.

CALUMET, OR PEACE PIPE.

They knew little about raising crops. They never broke in a single animal to labor. They had no iron or any other metal except specimens of native copper from the shores of Lake Superior. They prized these as ornaments and spear heads. They had no flocks, nor herds nor poultry. They had patches of tobacco and corn. Pumpkins were cultivated in a rude, primitive way. They used the shoulder blade of a deer, or clam shells, or rude stone implements to dig up the soil. Necessarily they tilled light soil, because it was more easily stirred, and, as it was soon exhausted, they selected places near the shore for their corn planting ground, for fish was their fertilizer. A salt water fish (Mendahen) was spread on the field to restore fertility. Maize was the Indian's winter food. In order to keep it in good condition through the winter, they selected the dryest places, and having buried it, they covered it with boughs and coarse grass.

The red man's manufacturing was as primitive as his agriculture. Among their manufactured articles were boats, pipes, war clubs and shields, bows and arrows, axes, mortars and pestles, gouges, sinkers, fish lines and nets, hammer stones, ornamental and other stones, rude pottery, skinning tools, adzes, hatchets, spear heads, scrapers and mauls. Their light boats could be carried from stream to stream. They were constructed of light wooden frames and covered with white elm or birch bark stretched on slender wooden ribs, and sewed together with thongs made from the dry sinews of the deer, or with roots and fibres. Sometimes gums were used to make them water-tight. At the seams they were fashioned skilfully, and with taste. Their heavy canoes were made of logs hollowed. Whitewood tree trunks

THE PALISADES, OPPOSITE YONKERS—LOOKING DOWN.

were charred and the burnt portion was scraped away with stone gouges. When some of the Long Island Indians sold their lands to the white man, they reserved "the whitewood trees suitable for making canoes of." These canoes varied in length. Some were thirty feet or more. One of their large canoes was capable of holding from twelve to fourteen men, or one hundred and fifty bushels of corn. It is thought that the Indians manufactured pottery at the place on the Hudson now known as Croton Point. A trench discovered there contained charcoal and fragments of earthen vessels. Perhaps there was a crude kiln there. The baskets of the Indians were ingeniously made of birch bark, and were watertight. They also manufactured baskets of splints, rushes or grass. Bows, for their wars, or their hunting, were skilfully fashioned from ash or hickory and were strung with deer sinews. Arrows were made of jasper, quartz, flint, hornstone, and other varieties of stone. They heated the stone and dropped water upon it, or with blows they fashioned it arrow shape. The sharp stones with which they pointed their arrows were sometimes fastened with hard resin. Occasionally, to-day, flint chips are found where the Indian arrow maker wrought. Some of their arrows were of elegant construction and tipped with copper, and when shot with power would pass through the body of a deer as certainly as the bullet from a rifle. Sometimes American Indians tipped their arrows with eagles' claws.

Their fish lines and nets were made of twisted fibres of dogbane and the sinews of the deer. Hooks were fashioned of the sharpened bones of fishes and birds. Sinkers were made by notching opposite edges of flat stones. The Indians made pipes of stone, also of clay; some resembling birds and other animals. Many represented the beaver. Varieties of granite, greenstone, syemite, sandstone and porphyry were selected as material to shape into axes. Some were heavy and some light. The heavy axes weighed six or eight pounds; the light, half a pound. The handle was made fast by binding pieces of rawhide around the wood and the groove in the stone. Sometimes a young growing tree was cleft, and the axe head inserted and left until the wood grew around it. Flint or jasper leaf-shaped cutting tools were the saws and knives of the Indians. They were chipped to an edge. Some spear heads were about two inches long, others eight or ten inches. Large numbers of grooved stone hammers and mauls have been found along the Hudson. The Indians used pierced tablets to twist bow strings. The tablets also served as ornaments. Several spear heads of hammered copper have been found in Westchester County. These spear heads and the flint and jasper arrow heads indicate that the red men of this section trafficked with those of other tribes. The copper evidently came from Lake Superior. The Indians wrought their ceremonial stones with great care. Rank was indicated by them, and they inspired reverence and strangely influenced the people, who were superstitious. Flint drills, or those of reed, were turned by a bow string. With these holes were drilled in stones.

Indian money, called "seewan" by the Dutch and "wampum" by the English, was made of shells cast on shore by the sea. According to one writer, wampum signifies "white." Another says that, in the language of the Iroquois, it means "muscle." It was made from the inside of conch shells. This was their silver. From the inside purple face of the shell of the quahong they made "sucki." This signifies "black." It was their gold. They chipped out small pieces, and ground them down into beads about the size of a straw and one-third of an inch long. These they bored longitudinally with sharp stones and strung them on hempen threads or on the dried sinews of animals, and wove them into strips as broad as one's hand and about two feet long, which they called belts of wampum. They were divided into pieces of different values. The black, or purple, was twice the value of the white. Three purple beads were equal in value to an English penny.

Wampum served also as an ornament. Ten thousand or more beads were sometimes wrought into the belt of some great chieftain. It distinguished the rich from the poor. It was a tribute from the conquered to the conqueror. Treaties were ratified with it, alliances confirmed, friendships sealed. It cemented peace and atoned for murders committed. The wampum belt was sent with all public messages, and sometimes—marked with curious hieroglyphics—was preserved as a record of important transactions between rival tribes. Long Island was called "Seewan-Hacky," the island of shells. Immense quantities of wampum were manufactured there. The district about Byram Lake was called "Cohemong," which meant "the place where wampum is made." The Indians who lived where these shells were found might be called "the bankers of the savage world." The ruling tribe on Long Island was the Montauks, who possessed the eastern extremity of the Island. They owed their supremacy to the abundance of clams in their waters, from which they made Indian money. They were able to supply the Indians of all tribes westward almost to the Great Lakes with money. Thus Montauk became the seat of financial power. The remains of "Indian shell beds" were visible some years ago in the rear of the fort on Berrian's Neck, the ancient Niperichsen of the Mohegans. This neck forms the northern bank at the mouth of the noted *Spyt den Dyvel Kil*, or channel.

The Indians had a knowledge of dye stuffs which surprised the Europeans. Van Der Donck, who lived among them, wrote: "They know how to prepare a coloring wherein they dye their hair a beautiful scarlet, which excites our astonishment and curiosity. The color is so well fixed that rain, sun and wind will not change it. Although they do not appear to possess any particular art in this matter, still such beautiful red was never dyed in the Netherlands with any material known to us. The colored articles have been examined by many of our best dyers, who admire the color and admit that they cannot imitate the same; and remark that a proper knowledge of the art would be of great importance in their profession." The same writer says that their red, blue, green, brown, white, black, yellow, etc., were mostly made of stone, which they prepared by pounding, rubbing and grinding; and he adds: "To describe perfectly and truly how they prepare all these paints and colors is out of my power."

American Indians had a limited knowledge of medicine. They knew the medicinal value of hemp, thoroughwort, spurge, the inner bark of the horse-chestnut and butternut, mayweed, water pepper, spicewood, sassafras, slippery elm, pine, spruce, bearberry, gooseberry root, blackberry, cranesbill, white oak bark, wormwood, puff-balls, yellow dock, onions and other products of the fields and trees. They knew how to prepare emetics, cathartics, rubefacients, infusions, decoctions, astringents, and, if necessary, poisons. Incised wounds they sewed together with strings from the inner bark of the basswood or fibres from the tendons of deer.

Their principal medical treatment was sweating baths. These were earthen ovens around which heated stones were placed to raise the temperature. Sometimes a vapor bath was prepared in a tent covered with skins and warmed by means of hot stones. One author says that the patient crept into the heated earthen oven and after he remained there and perspired for a certain time, "he was taken out and immersed suddenly in cold water—a process which served to cure, or certainly to cause death."

They used beaver's oil in many forms and as a remedy for many ailments. "It was the calomel of Indian allopathic practice, and the Dutch took to it and greatly valued it." The open-air life, the exercise and the general habits of the red men contributed to their health. They were strong. Their medicine man was both doctor and magician. He worked upon their imaginations and excited their superstitious susceptibilities. With great solemnity he used the ceremonial stones, which were the most finely wrought of Indian stone work, made of fine and beautifully striped slate, and drilled so that they could be carried upon a rod or handle. It would seem that the magician's arts were relied upon to work a cure when medicine failed. Those who lingered with hopeless illness or were helpless from age were sometimes neglected and sometimes put to death.

While we are studying the red villagers and their customs, we observe the nimble-footed Indian girls and boys at play around the wigwams on the banks of the Neperah and in the woods. Our curiosity is aroused as to the training of these tawny children; and Bancroft, with charming grace, tells us what we wish to know. He begins with infancy and describes the cradle and the babe, and then the education of the child, older grown. Hear him: "How helpless the Indian infant, born without shelter amid storms and ice! But fear nothing for him; the sentiment of maternity is at his side, and so long as his mother breathes he is safe. The squaw loves her child with instinctive passion, and if she does not manifest it by lively caresses, her tenderness is real, wakeful and constant. No savage mother ever trusted her babe to a hireling nurse; no savage mother ever put away her child to suckle that of another. To the cradle, consisting of thin pieces of light wood, and gaily ornamented with quills and beads and rattles, the infant is firmly attached and carefully wrapped in furs, and then swathed, its back to the mother's back, is borne as the topmost burden, its dark eyes now cheerfully flashing light, now accompanying with tears the wailings which the plaintive melodies of the carrier cannot hush. Or while the squaw toils in the field, she hangs her child, as spring does its blossom, on the boughs of a tree, that it may be rocked by breezes from the land of souls, and soothed to sleep by the lullaby of the birds. Does the mother die, the nursling—such is Indian compassion—shares her grave.

"On quitting the cradle, the children are left nearly naked in the cabin to grow hardy and learn the use of their limbs. Juvenile sports are the same everywhere; children invent them for themselves; and the traveller, who finds through the wide world the same games, may rightly infer that an innate power instructs childhood in its amusements. There is no domestic government; the young do as they will. They are never earnestly reproved, injured or beaten; a dash of cold water in the face is their heaviest punishment. If they assist in the labors of the household, it is as a pastime, not as a charge. Yet they show respect to the chiefs, and defer with docility to those of their cabin. The attachment of savages to their offspring is extreme, and they cannot bear separation from them. . . . From their insufficient and irregular supplies of clothing and food, they learn to endure hunger and rigorous seasons; of themselves they become fleet of foot and skilful in swimming; their courage is fed by tales respecting their ancestors, till they burn with a love of glory to be acquired by valor and address. So soon as the child can grasp the bow and arrow, they are in his hand; and as there is joy in the wigwam at his birth and his first cutting of a tooth, so a festival is kept for his earliest success in the chase. The Indian young man is educated in the school of nature. The influences by which he is surrounded kindle within him the passion for war; as he grows up he in his turn begins the war song, of which the echoes never die away on the boundless plains of the West; he travels the war path in search of an encounter with an enemy, that he, too, at the great war dance and feast of his band may boast of his exploits, may enumerate his gallant deeds by the envied feathers of the war-eagle that decorate his hair, and keep the record of his wounds by shining marks of vermilion on his skin." The laborious manner of the life of the pale face the red men esteem slavish and base as compared with theirs, and the learning on which we pride ourselves they regard as frivolous and useless.

The Indians loved oratory. Some of them were natural orators. They were extremely fond of method, and were displeased with any irregular harangue, because it is difficult to be remembered. A speaker would hold in one hand a small bundle of sticks. Having finished speaking upon one point he would put down one little stick, the second point finished he would lay down another stick, and thus continue until all the points were covered. Indians delighted to assemble together and hear what messengers from abroad had to say. They arranged themselves in a semi-circle in two or three rows.

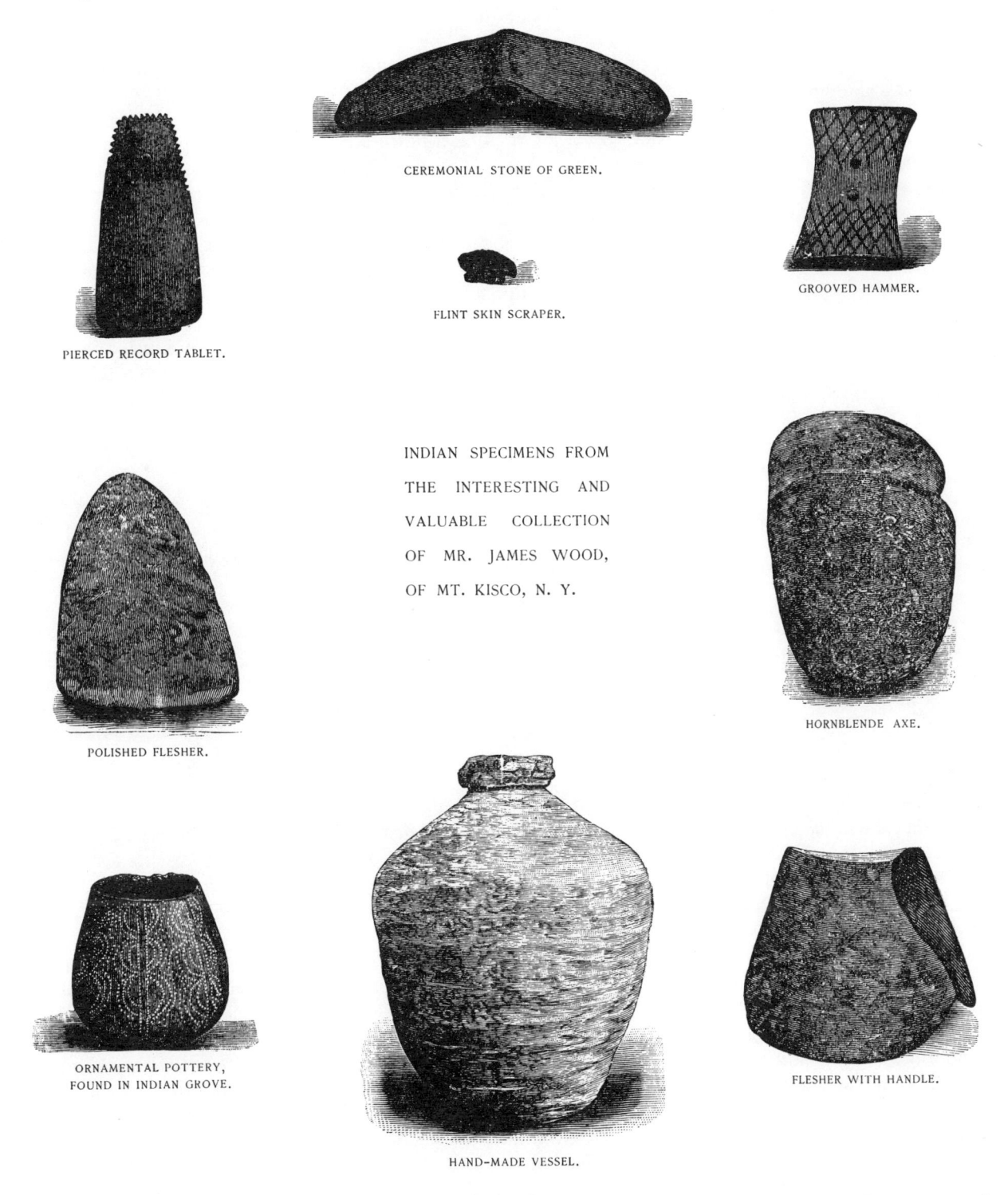

CEREMONIAL STONE OF GREEN.

FLINT SKIN SCRAPER.

GROOVED HAMMER.

PIERCED RECORD TABLET.

INDIAN SPECIMENS FROM THE INTERESTING AND VALUABLE COLLECTION OF MR. JAMES WOOD, OF MT. KISCO, N. Y.

POLISHED FLESHER.

HORNBLENDE AXE.

ORNAMENTAL POTTERY, FOUND IN INDIAN GROVE.

HAND-MADE VESSEL.

FLESHER WITH HANDLE.

One writer about American Indians says: "The old men sit in the foremost ranks, the warriors next, and the women and children hindmost. The business of the women is to take exact notice of what passes, imprint it on their memories—for they have no writing—and communicate it to the children." The painted and tattooed chiefs were adorned with skins and plumes, the beaks of the red bird or the claws of the bear. Sometimes they had pipes in their mouths as they listened. They preserved profound silence. Seated with their knees almost meeting their faces, they gave solemn attention to the speaker, who spoke energetically and dramatically. Decorum was never broken. Speakers did not endeavor to get and hold the floor by undignified methods, nor did angry debate disturb the assembly. Questions of order were unknown. When a general council was called a tribe sent orators of personal merit and of ability as representatives.

The amusements of the dusky men of the forests consisted of running races, leaping, games with small stones, shooting at a mark and racing in canoes along swift river or placid lake. They also engaged in dances, either ceremonial, or war, or religious. They delighted in fishing and hunting. They caught fish with hooks or nets or spears. *Wigwaws* was a process of fishing after dark, similar to that termed *bobbing* at the present day.

Game abounded in the section now known as Yonkers and in neighboring territory. Among the animals were wildcats, wolves, bears, beavers, otters and minks. The low ground east of the "Bronx Dale" is called "Bear Swamp." Savage bears inhabited that wide domain of forest and morass. Deer were numerous in some parts of Westchester County as late as 1780. In 1638 a dense forest, in which deer herded plentifully, covered the middle and upper parts of Manhattan Island, where a few of the islanders lived in almost primitive barbarism. Wolves roamed at large through this wilderness and committed occasional ravages. Buffaloes also roamed through parts of what is now known as Westchester County. Van Der Donck, writing in 1656, says: "Buffaloes are also tolerably plenty. These animals mostly keep toward the southwest, where few people go. Half of the buffaloes have disappeared and left the country." The vast gorges of the highlands and the vales about North Salem abounded with buffalo. At Poundridge was an extensive trap. The English settlers found it well preserved, and called it a pound. It was a dozen feet or more in height. The logs of which it was constructed were kept in place by saddle-stones. It enclosed about one acre of ground. The entrance was narrow. Rows of stakes extended in each direction from the entrance, crossing the valleys and reaching up the hillsides. The ridges between the south and southwest valleys descend at this point. Early in the morning the Indian hunters, sufficient in number to cover, as guards, considerable territory, would begin to "beat the bush" many miles distant from the trap. They yelled so frightfully that animals of every kind ran before them. If the pursued game attempted to escape on either side, the hunters bounded along the ridges and drove them back. Thus, hard pressed, the fleeing animals came to the rows of posts or palisades, and rushed between them into the acre or more inclosed by the logs held together by the stones. When the narrow entrance was closed great numbers of deer and other animals were at the mercy of their captors.

Van Der Donck wrote that when the Indians went a-hunting bears they dressed themselves, "as Esau did, in clothes which have the flavor of the woods," that they might not be discovered by the sharp-smelling animals.

The wars of the red men were terrible, not by reason of the great numbers engaged, because it was rarely that more than two score set out on the war path. A party of half-a-dozen was especially to be feared by their foes, or by those they determined to attack. "When the resolution was once taken to attack a distant tribe, the chief, to whom the command of the expedition was assigned, entered on a course of the most rigid training and preparation. He examined the condition of the arms at the disposal of his followers, and commenced a series of incantations to learn the will of the Great Spirit, who was considered to preside over war. Orations of the most inflammatory description were delivered; the wampum belt was thrown on the ground, and was lifted by him only who was judged worthy to fill the post of second in command. The leader then began his series of mystic observances. He was painted black all over, and fasted most rigidly, never eating, nor even sitting down, until after the sun had set. From time to time, however, he drank a strong decoction of some consecrated herbs, with a view to give vivacity to his dreams or hallucinations, which were carefully noted down and scrutinized by the sages and old men. He was next subjected to the powerful action of the vapor bath; afterwards carefully washed, and painted anew in bright and varied colors, in which red was the most predominant. The great war chaldron was next brought out and placed over a huge fire. Into that chaldron every one present, as well as those allies who had consented to take part in the expedition, threw some offering. A grand feast was now prepared. The chief sang his war song. Other noted warriors, with faces painted in a most frightful manner, followed his example, each rising in turn from his seat and describing the great actions which he and his ancestors had performed, all being accompanied by the war dance to the sound of a tom-tom, a kettle-drum, the only instrument of music they had.

"Having now worked their passions up to the fiercest pitch, and converted themselves from men into demons by the force of song, revelry and rivalry, they proceeded to arm, having passed the night in exciting orgies, and marched forth with their manitous, or little gods, placed in a common box, as guardian spirits, occasionally yelling their terrific war whoop as they went along."

With passions uncontrolled, absolute freedom of action, excessive thirst for excitement and display, long-continued peace was not to be expected, and a state of war became the common lot and condition of the whole people. The whole tendency of their education and habits led to that point, and to be a great warrior was every Indian's highest aim. The party on the war path skilfully followed a trail and were eager to meet the foe.

It was their custom to cautiously steal upon an enemy while he was asleep. They concealed themselves in the neighborhood of a village, where unsuspecting men and women and children dwelt. Out from their ambush they would rush on a single foeman, or perhaps upon a squaw and her children. The scalp was swiftly severed from the head with three strokes, and then the exulting brave returned to his companions to hang the bloody trophy in his wigwam, or to go in triumphant procession from village to village to hear orators recount his deeds to the elders and chief people, and to gain high titles of honor by the number of scalps taken with his own hand. Sometimes a war party of two or three would set out, and, after entering their foemen's territory, would hang on the skirts of an enemy until the moment arrived for striking a blow.

They declared war by sending a belt, painted red, or a bundle of bloody sticks. Peace was declared by burying the tomahawk. The great calumet of peace, "like our modern flag of truce," had a sacred character, and ensured security to ambassadors.

Sometimes captives were adopted, but often tortured, and then killed. On the way to the village of his victors the most cruel sufferings were stoically borne by the captive. His hands were crushed between two stones, his fingers torn off or mutilated, the joints of his arm scorched and gashed, "while he himself preserved tranquility and sang the songs of his nation." Terrible tortures and death awaited him at the end of his journey through the forests, unless he could escape. How stoical they were is indicated by the manner in which they conducted themselves when they were attacked at Greenwich, Conn., by the Dutch. The Indian village there consisted of three rows of houses or huts ranged in streets, each eighty paces long, and backed by a mountain which sheltered it from the northwest wind. The Dutch surrounded it, and, after a desperate conflict of an hour, one hundred and eighty Indians lay dead on the snow outside their dwellings. Their huts were then burned by the Dutch, and the Indians either were consumed in the flames or, if they rushed forth, were shot. It was afterwards reported that five hundred Indians, or perhaps seven hundred (for they had assembled to celebrate some festival), were killed. "Throughout the entire carnage not one of the sufferers—man, woman or child—was heard to utter a shriek or moan."

A trader with the Southern Indians, who was in their country forty years, says: "The men are expert in shooting with the bow and throwing the feathered dart and tomahawk into the flying enemy. They resemble the lynx with their sharp, penetrating, black eyes, and are exceedingly swift of foot, especially in a long chase. They will stretch away through the rough woods by the bare track for two or three hundred miles in pursuit of a flying enemy with the continued speed and eagerness of bloodhounds, till they shed blood. When they have allayed this, their burning thirst, they return home at their leisure, unless they chance to be pursued, as is sometimes the case, whence, the traders say that an Indian is never in a hurry but when Satan is at his heels." When a murder was committed the next of kin was the avenger. How the nephew of a Weckquaskeck Indian avenged the blood of his uncle is rehearsed in a later chapter of this volume.

The war cry of the Indians on Manhattan Island was "Woach, Woach, Ha, Ha, Hach, Woach!" and if the Indians of the "rapid-water settlement" were the tribe which occupied Manhattan Island in the summer, that war cry was heard under the forest trees in the valleys and on the hills of Yonkers, over which now brood the doves of peace.

"Indian notions of a Supreme and Almighty Creator were crude and thoroughly carnal. To all religious systems they were entire strangers. They acknowledged the existence of a God in heaven from all eternity. Their principal aim was to escape the ire of the Evil One. They offered him sacrifices when they were sick or unsuccessful in war or in the chase. They believed in a multitude of minor spirits, or tutelary guardians, and supposed that all animated creatures, whether human beings or wild animals, the elements, and even the planets, had their good spirits to watch over them. The spirit was the Indian manitou, which protected him from infancy to his death. It was represented by the head of a man, carved in miniature, on a stick. Every Indian had one or more of these, which he carried around his neck in a bag, or suspended on a string. To these they addressed themselves on all important occasions, on a voyage, on the approach of a storm, intrusting to them even the guardianship of their camp during the night preparatory to engaging in an attack on an enemy's quarters.

"They acknowledged the distinction between body and soul, believing the latter to be immortal, and to go, if good in this life, when the body ceased to live, to a place toward the south, where the climate was so fine that it had no need of covering there; where abundance of every good thing would be had without the labor of production; while, on the other hand, the souls of the wicked would be driven to another place, where they never should enjoy rest, contentment or peace. With these impressions, a belief in ghosts easily followed, and was so general that the moanings of the winds at night through the trees of the surrounding forest, or the howlings of the wild animals in the wilderness were believed to be the lamentations of the spirits of the wicked, condemned to wander thus about without shelter or repose. Superstition—twin sister of Ignorance—held them also in strongest bondage, and one of their most common practices was to hunt or drive the devil from among them, which they did by jumping, bellowing and grinning, as if possessed. Large fires were kindled, around and over which they danced, rolling, tumbling, bending, and making the most violent contortions, until the perspiration burst from every pore. Medicine men throve upon the ignorance and simplicity of their dupes. Their influence was almost unbounded. If, as a physician, he could not cure, he became a magician, and danced and sang around his patient, invoking his god with loud cries."

It is not surprising that, being without a knowledge of the true God, the Indians were spiritually debased. They did not realize the sacredness of marriage, nor the wickedness of murder. Infanticide passed uncensured. They were cruel, vain, boastful, unforgiving. They were thieves, and gloried in it. Though moved by generous instincts, they were suspicious, resentful, and harbored enmity. If the whites had treated them with uniform kindness, and had not given them "fire-water," much bloodshed would have been avoided. Peaceful at the advent of the Dutch, then hostile, they became more wild and savage, the fierceness being aggravated by drawing lines.

"An Indian about to die would calmly chant his last song, or for the last time address his hearers, with pride speaking of his deeds. When he ceased to breathe his body was kept in the wigwam in a sitting posture. When it was buried, a stone was put under the head, and in the sitting posture the body was left in the grave. Beside it remained a kettle, pot, platter, spoon, money, maize, venison, pipe, manitou, tomahawk, quiver and strung bow. The dead sat in the narrow house arrayed in his most splendid apparel, and furnished with what they thought his spirit would need on the long journey to the country of his ancestors. Festivals in honor of the dead were frequent, when food was given to the flames, that so it might serve to nourish the departed. The traveller would find in the forests a dead body, placed upon piles, shrouded in bark and attired in warmest furs. If a mother lost her babe, she would in like manner cover it with bark and wrap it in beaver skins; at the burial place she would put by its side its cradle, its beads and its rattles; and, as a last service of maternal love, would draw milk from her breast and burn it in the fire, that her infant might still find nourishment on its solitary journey to the land of shades. The southwest was the gentle region round which tradition gathered. There was the paradise where maize and beans grow spontaneously; there dwelt the shades of the forefathers of the red men.

"In mourning, the women beat their breasts, tore their faces and called the name of the departed, day and night. They painted their faces black and shaved their heads in token of sorrow, and burned their dark tresses on the grave of the dead, especially if he had been a relative or had been slain in battle."

They called their burial grounds Tawasenthas, "places of many dead." In Nepperhaem were at least two or three burial grounds. "The principal one," says Bolton, "is two miles northeast of Manor Hall, on what was once known as Blackwell's Hill." Years ago the graves were distinctly marked by rude mounds of earth. An Indian burial ground, about one-eighth of a mile northeast of the site of the present monastery, was pointed out to the writer, in 1895, by Mr. John Archer, who was then in his seventy-ninth year

His grandfather, Mr. Anthony Archer, lived, during the Revolution, at the southeast corner of the road to Eastchester (Ashburton Avenue) and Archer's Lane (Nepperhan Avenue). The location of the Indian cemetery was shown Mr. John Archer by his father. As to whether it is the burial ground to which Bolton refers, the writer is uninformed. Its site is the eastern slope of Wild Boar Hill. The ground is a part of the property once known as the Blackwell estate. As there are now no near and permanent landmarks it is difficult to so describe the spot that it may be located in future years. It is about one hundred and fifty feet north of the Shonnard line and about the same distance south of the little brook, which, flowing eastward, empties into the Nepperhan. The rivulet is known as Weston's Brook, but every year it flows with lessening volume, and will doubtless soon disappear altogether. Mrs. Ann E. Odell, the widow of Jacob Delancy Odell (General Jacob Odell's son) whose home was once in the Odell house on the east side of the Saw Mill River road, about one half a mile north of the Tuckahoe road, said, in 1896, "that the men of their family, years ago, had plowed up Indian bones when at work in the field." In 1895, there was a growth of locusts and of bushes on the site of the Indian burial ground. A fine white oak tree was near the wall just west of the little locust grove. The spot is about one thousand feet west of the crematory. About the year 1828, the top of the mound covering the graves was two feet, more or less, above the surface, and there was then "a sort of trench around the mound." The mound has now (1896) almost disappeared. It is overgrown with blackberry and other vines. Plowmen, years ago, plowed up bones in this vicinity.

AN INDIAN TRAP.

"Another Indian burial ground was nearly covered some years ago," so writes Bolton, "by the barn and other buildings of Benjamin Fowler, Esq.," who lived about eight hundred feet southwest of the entrance to the present St. Mary's Roman Catholic Cemetery. The site of this burial ground of the Indians is on the west of the Sprain road, and at the entrance to the Sprain Valley.

The descendants of the chief, Tackarew, continued to live in "the Yonkers" for more than half a century after the sale of the lands to Van Der Donck. General Jacob Odell (an officer in the war of 1812) used to narrate an incident associated with the Indians. He said "that in his boyhood, he was accustomed to go with other boys up on the Odell Hill, east of their Saw Mill River farm house, which stood just north of where the present railroad bridge spans the highway, to see the Indians, some of whom had their rude dwellings at that place. One beautiful moonlight night he saw an old Indian, whom they called Waco, lying flat on his back, looking up into the heavens. The old red man said, 'Boys, there will be snow to-morrow,' and he was right." The next day there was one of the heaviest snow falls Mr. Odell ever saw.

After the Revolution there were two or three Indian huts about where the present Mulford Street is. The last hut stood near the southeast corner of the present St. Joseph's Avenue and Mulford Street. Two or three, and sometimes four of the Indians used to go to Mr. Anthony Archer's house on cold winter evenings, and lie down before the fire which was burning in the large fire-place. Mr. Archer would shake with laughter as he told how, when the hour came for him to retire, he would ask the Indians whether it was not time for them to go home, and the only response the comfortable guests gave their host was their simple but expressive "Ugh!" The self-invited guests remained all night, and when Mr. Archer came into the room in the morning, his tawny visitors were gone. They had risen early, and, without pilfering anything, had withdrawn.

CAUGHT IN AN INDIAN TRAP.

The last Indian in that neighborhood died in the hut which stood near the site of the present St. Joseph's Church, and was buried in the Indian burial ground above described, in what were known as Weston's Woods.

Evidently long before the Revolution the Indians were fast disappearing from the county. The Rev. Mr. Muirson, in a letter to the Gospel Propagation Society, in 1708, says of the Indians of Rye: "They are a decaying people. We have not now in all this parish twenty families, whereas not many years ago there were several hundred. . . . I have taken some pains to teach some of them, but to no purpose. for they seem regardless of instruction." Some Indians at Rye became slaves.

The Indians evidently preferred the forests to civilized life. They withdrew from the settlements, but a few remained. Indian Hill in Yorktown became memorable as the last spot in Westchester County inhabited by a band of aborigines. Individual families lingered longer, and a strain of Indian blood still courses in the veins of some families now living in the county. A resident of Yonkers in 1896, whose jet black hair, dark complexion, dark eyes and wiry form are characteristically striking, traces his descent from an Indian squaw who lived in Westchester County at an early period. According to the Eleventh United States Census, there were fifteen civilized Indians in Westchester County in 1880, and in 1890 there were four. Bolton says that up to a late date "great numbers of Indians occupied Wild Boar Hill." He adds, "From here they are all said to have taken their departure in a single night." Old residents used to speak of an Indian and his wife who lived within the southeastern part of the limits of the present town. They made baskets and sold them to the people. When times were hard the farmers assisted them, giving them pork and potatoes.

"One of the last remnants of the tribe of the red men, if not the last in Yonkers, was a noble Indian by the name of Shuctamen, who occasionally visited the village, but was oftener to be seen in his canoe cruising along the various fishing grounds of the Hudson." "The passing away of a race is sad. The wail of the red man, as he looked for the last time upon the graves of his kindred and set his face toward the sunset, touches a responsive chord in all sympathetic breasts":

> "I will go to my tent and lie down in despair,
> I will paint me with black and sever my hair;
> I will sit on the shore where the hurricane blows,
> And reveal to the God of the tempest my woes;
> I will weep for a season, on bitterness fed,
> For my kindred are gone to the mounds of the dead."

BIRCH BARK CANOE.

CHAPTER III.

HENRY HUDSON ASCENDS "THE GREAT RIVER OF THE MOUNTAINS." 1609.

"I have seen it in a vision,
Seen the great canoe with pinions,
Seen the people with white faces,
Seen the coming of this bearded
People of the wooden vessel
From the region of the morning."

AT FIVE o'clock Wednesday afternoon, September 2, 1609, a clumsy kind of brig, with square sails upon two masts, cast her anchor in a "great lake of water as we could judge it to be." High hills, like friendly sentinels, saluted commander and crew, "a very good land to fall in with, and a pleasant land to see." Captain Henry Hudson was looking from the deck of his Dutch galliot at the hills now known as the Naversinks. The "great lake of water, as we could judge it to be," was the Lower Bay, and the Half Moon or Halve Maen (Crescent) was at the portals of one of the finest harbors in the world.

A mixed crew of twenty men, Netherlanders and Englishmen, among them the captain's son, manned the ship—a vessel of about eighty tons burden. The flag she floated was the orange, white and blue flag of the United Provinces. The prudent commander sent out boats to take soundings. He wished to ascertain where the channel was. If he ran aground and wrecked his vessel her owners would suffer loss, his great project would come to naught, and he would be at the mercy of the savages, whose canoes skimmed over the waters around him. Before making record of his vessel weighing anchor, cautiously sailing through the Narrows and furrowing the waters of the Hudson, we will inquire as to where this ship sailed from, and what her captain was seeking on this strange coast.

In 1607, a company of London merchants contributed to fit out an expedition to discover, if possible, a northern strait, that voyages to Asia might be shortened and less expensive. The immense profits of voyages to the east influenced the merchants to invest money in this enterprise. They chose Henry Hudson, an Englishman by birth, to be captain of their ship. His son accompanied him. He coasted the shores of Greenland, sailed northward, but encountered such vast fields of ice that he was compelled to turn back. He returned to England. The next year he sailed again, still hoping to find a new water-way to China. In this voyage he ascertained that the seas which divide Spitzbergen and Zova Zembla afford no water-way to the spicy Orient. He now had failed twice to discover the shorter route, but he was not discouraged. Van Meteren, the historian, who was then the Dutch minister at the Court of St. James, transmitted messages from the Hollanders to Hudson, for the tidings of his voyages had reached Amsterdam, where there were enterprising merchants with a genius for business—men who knew how to "coin thought into gold."

In 1609—memorable year—Hudson, the Englishman, arrived at Hague, a city of the Netherlands, thirty-one miles from Amsterdam. The officers of the Dutch East India Company met and carefully discussed former discoveries in the northern seas. Some said that it would be a waste of time and money to again attempt the navigation of the vast oceans in the frozen north. Hudson, the explorer, stood before them, full of enthusiasm. He believed that Asia might be reached through Polar seas. While the Directors were hesitating, inclined to postpone the voyage a whole year, an astute diplomat, ambassador to Holland from France, and watchful of the interests of his sovereign, Henry IV., began to negotiate with Hudson. This stimulated the East India Directors, and they promptly entered into an agreement with the English captain. The Amsterdam Chamber defrayed the expenses. They contracted to pay Hudson "as well as for his outfit, as for the support of his wife and children," eight hundred florins ($320) and "in case he do not come back (which God prevent) the Directors shall further pay to his wife, two hundred florins, ($80) in cash." If he found the water-way to India the Directors promised to reward him "in their discretion."

It is April 4, 1609. The Half Moon was ready to set sail for China by a new route, which her commander hoped to discover. A number were assembled probably at that point in the Amsterdam harbor where there is a tower called "Schreyers Toren," or "Weepers' Tower," because here relatives and friends bade those outward bound for long sea voyages, good-by, often amid tears, as the ship cast her moorings and proceeded on her way into the Zuyder Zee. The farewells were spoken, the conference of Hudson with friends on shore was ended, the final order was given, the eventful voyage was begun.

On the fifth of May the Half Moon reached the north cape of Norway. Hudson found fogs and fields of ice. Then he turned west. On the tenth of May he took in water at the Faroe Isles. Early in July the Half Moon needed repairs. A gale had rent her canvas and carried away her foremast. In this crippled condition the ship sailed past the vessels of fishermen, who had come to the Newfoundland Banks from France.

When Hudson reached the coast of New France (now the coast of Maine) he anchored in a very good harbor, and sent his men on shore to find a forest tree, suitable for a new mast. When the mast had been shaped and fitted, and the sails mended, the voyage was resumed. From this harbor Hudson sailed southward, until he reached Cape Cod (discovered in 1602). Then he stood out to sea, to the south and east, and did not land again until he neared Chesapeake Bay. While the Half Moon was riding at sea off this bay, Hudson gave orders to turn her prow northward. He entered a great bay, now known as Delaware Bay, on August 28th, and spent a day acquiring knowledge of the currents and soundings of the Delaware. Resuming his voyage he sailed along a low sandy coast, and on Wednesday, September 2d, at five o'clock in the afternoon, he anchored in a "great lake of water as we could judge it to be." The next day he approached the "bold" land, and saw what appeared to be three separate rivers. He stood towards the northermost, which was probably Rockaway Inlet, but his progress in this direction was soon arrested by shoals. When he had sounded, and found only ten feet of water on the bar of this stream, he ordered the prow of the Half Moon to be turned about to the southward, and sounded his way to an anchorage within Sandy Hook.

On the morning of September 4th he sent out a small boat to explore, and to ascertain the depth of the water. A good harbor was found, where the sea "was four and five fathoms two cables length from the shore." A great many fine fish were discovered. Indians were seen along the coast, and towards evening they came out in their canoes, and paddled around the strange boat. They brought with them green tobacco and offered it as a peace offering. On the 5th a landing was made from the Half Moon. The natives stood around and sang in their fashion. The historian wishes that he could record that song, and the opinions the savages expressed in their wigwams that night, as, with suppressed excitement, they conversed in their Algonquin tongue about the big canoe with white wings, and the strangely dressed men on board. Had Europeans ever been there before? Gomez is said to have sailed along the coast to the latitude of New York in 1525. Records seem to indicate that Verrazano had passed the bar the year before (1524) and had anchored at the entrance of the Narrows, but it is doubtful whether he crossed New York Bay for there was "a violent contrary wind which blew in from the sea, and forced a return to the ship and a regretful leaving a region so commodious and delightful." The records seem to conflict as to this. The Indians had a tradition, said a Moravian missionary, that before they knew that there were any people with a *"white skin"* some of them, who had been out a-fishing, espied at a great distance that which some thought was an uncommon large fish or other animal, while others were of opinion that it was a house. They sent runners and watermen off to carry the news to the scattered chiefs, who assembled on what is now known as Manhattan Island, and prepared to make a sacrifice, thinking that it might be the Manitto (the Supreme Being) coming to visit them, The tradition, which is too lengthy to be transcribed in full for these pages, reports that when the strangers landed from the big canoe, they gave the red men fire-water, which intoxicated them. The journal of Hudson's mate makes no record of such landing, and Van Der Donck asserts that he had often heard the old Indians, who recollected the arrival of Henry Hudson's ship, say, that previous to that date (1609) they were entirely ignorant of the existence of any other nation besides their own, and that they looked at the ship as a huge fish or sea monster. Certain it is, that history has no record of what the red men said on the day when some of Hudson's crew landed. It is recorded that their food was Indian corn, which when roasted the sailors found excellent. Some of them had pipes of red copper, with earthen bowls. Each of their boats was a hollowed tree. They slept on bulrushes, or on the leaves of trees. They were friendly, but had to be watched, otherwise they would slyly steal, and carry away what they fancied. It was specially noticed that the woods abounded in "goodly oakes," and the newcomers never ceased to admire the great girth of the trees.

On the 6th, John Coleman, an Englishman, who had been with Hudson on his previous voyages, was sent, with four seamen, to sound the Narrows. They passed through Kill von Kull to Newark Bay. "The sweetness of the inner land and the crisp saltness of the distant sea were mixed in one delicious breeze," and they reported the country as pleasant with grass and flowers as any they had ever seen. While returning to the Half Moon late in the afternoon, Indians in two canoes came out, and John Coleman, either by accident or design, was shot through the throat with an arrow. Night came on. They had so great a stream that their grapnel would not hold them. The frightened sailors, their light out and their way lost, were tossed about on the troubled sea until ten o'clock the next morning, when, with the corpse of their officer, they were received on board the Half Moon. Coleman was buried on a point of land near by, which was called "Coleman's Point." About two days afterward, when large canoes, one of which was filled with armed men, came off to the vessel, Hudson suspected their intentions and allowed only two of the savages to come on board. These he determined to detain. He dressed them in red coats, whereupon the remainder returned to shore. Presently another canoe, with two men, came to the vessel, and one of these was also detained, probably as a hostage, but he contrived to jump overboard soon after, and swam ashore. Whereupon Hudson weighed anchor, stood up through the Narrows, and finally anchored

LOOKING NORTH TO INDIAN HEAD. OPPOSITE YONKERS.

in full view of the forests of Manhattan Island. On the morning of the 12th, the natives in eight and twenty canoes crowded about him, bringing beans and very good oysters. He was now probably opposite the present "Battery," and in the beautiful bay, which is about fifteen miles in circumference. Under the bright autumnal sun of that day, fair and warm, the captain of the Half Moon stood, and from his vessel's deck gazed around. Behind him were the Narrows through which, as through a gate, he had sailed in from the great ocean. Before him, forest-crowned Palisades and the gently swelling banks of Manhattan, "as fair a land as can be trodden by the foot of man." Before him also a noble stream, flowing from the north, with a broad, deep channel. Now he hoped he had found the long sought for strait, so gigantic were the proportions of this river. How insignificant the streamlets of European lands as compared with it.

The wind was adverse, and he could only move with the flood tide. His English mate, Robert Juet, kept the log book "which has the charm of quaintness and the advantage of being written by an eye-witness on the very spot where the first impressions of the noble river were received." This journal of the vessel's progress from day to day enables the historian to record a brief description of Henry Hudson's ascent of the river which bears his name, and of his return voyage. Drifting with the flood tide and anchoring when it ebbed, eleven and one-half miles were gained on the 13th, and they anchored at a place from which a "high point of land" was seen, "which shewed out to us bearing north by east, five leagues off us." If we knew the point to which the log book record referred, we could determine where the Half Moon was anchored. Some writers are of the opinion that the "high point of land" was the north end of the Palisades, opposite the present Dobb's Ferry. They claim that if any one will take an observation of the direction of the river line, northward from off Eighty-fifth Street, New York, he will discover that although the Palisades are on the west side of the river, yet "they bear strangely upward to the northeast from that point of observation."

Others think that Hook Mountain, just north of Nyack was the "high point of land." From the fact that it could be seen from such a great distance down the river (five leagues or fifteen miles, as Juet writes) the Dutch sailors used to call it "Verdrietig Hook," or "Tedious Point," because when the winds were light or unfavorable they had it in view for a long and tedious time. It has been thought that Hudson saw this point from an anchorage in the river near Spuyten Duyvil Creek. The Half Moon, according to some authorities, passed Nappeckamack, the Indian village at the mouth of the Neperah, on the 14th of September, for on that day a favorable wind was obtained, and the ship was carried from either off Eighty-second street, or from near Spuyten Duyvil Creek, thirty-six miles up stream. Bancroft says that the anchorage on the night of the 12th was just above Manhattanville, and that the flood tide of the morning and the evening of the 13th brought the Half Moon near the present Yonkers, from which point it was wafted rapidly northward on the 14th.

Whether the dusky dwellers on the banks of the Neperah saw the Half Moon—the white-winged sea bird, as it must have seemed to them—near Nappeckamack on the evening of the 13th of September, 1609, or sailing northward, past their village and up the Shatemuc (Hudson) on September 14th, there was evidently great commotion among them. What running to and fro! What comparisons of views among the braves, the squaws and the children! What conjectures and speculations among the superstitious villagers! With what swift feet they must have hastened to the high banks, from which they could watch with wondering eyes the strange canoe with wings outspread. In all probability Indians were gazing at it from the top of the Palisades also. "What must have been the wonder of the Nap-pe-cha-mak settlement," says one writer, "when they beheld the apparition . . . off the mouth of the Nepperhan—especially when we conjure up old Master Hendrick Hudson, standing upon the poop of his round built yacht, and Master Robert Juet and brother officers, in their tall shovel brim hats and doublets." Little did any of the red men realize what the coming of the pale face meant to their race. How soon they were to disappear, and another people possess their lands, drive their plowshares through their "places of many dead," and build their homes on the shores of their stately Shatemuc, their winding Neperah, and their placid Aquehung. Well it was for them that all this was hidden from view, as they watched the Half Moon until it sailed out of their sight.

On the 14th the ship reached the very portals of the Highlands, "the land grew very high and mountainous"—so runs the record of the log book. On that day, the 14th, the two savages who had been held as hostages, made their escape through the port-holes of the vessel and swam ashore. The moment the ship was under way they hailed the crew and expressed their indignation at the treatment to which they had been subjected, by uttering loud cries of scorn and anger. On the 15th twenty leagues more were made. Pages have been written about the "Highlands." The entry in the log book is simply "passing by high mountains." Indian corn and pompions were procured from the friendly natives. On the night of the 15th six miles more were sailed, then their progress, for a time, was impeded. They grounded on sand banks, or mud flats. Then they came to a place where there were "shoals in the middle of the river and small islands, but seven fathoms of water on both sides." Possibly they were about opposite the site of the present city of Hudson. On the 18th they did not advance, but were all day "riding still." On the afternoon of that day either the captain himself, "or our master's mate" went ashore in one of the boats of the natives with an aged chief of a small tribe of the river Indians. He was taken to a circular, arched-roof house, covered with bark, the granary of the beans and maize of the last year's harvest, while outside enough lay drying to load three ships. The country impressed him "as the finest land for cultivation that he ever in his life trod upon." Two mats were spread out as seats for the stranger, food was immediately served in neat wooden bowls, men were sent at once with bows and arrows for game, and soon returned with pigeons, a fat dog was killed and skinned with sharp shells, and haste made to prepare a feast. How curiously the red men must have observed their guest, and how intently they must have gazed at the Half Moon riding at anchor in the river. What attempts must have been made to ascertain whence the stranger, clad in strange costume, came and whither he was bound. He refused to tarry long, and they, supposing him to be afraid of their weapons, took their arrows, broke them in pieces, and threw them into the fire. For more than a century the river Indians preserved the memory of this visit.

On the 19th Indians brought on board beaver and other skins and sold them for a trifle. On the 20th the precaution was taken to send a boat up ahead of the Half Moon in order to take soundings. On two occasions the Europeans entertained Indian guests on board the Half Moon while in the northern waters of the Hudson. At one time, probably on the return of the Half Moon, the captain persuaded two old Indians and their squaws, and two maidens of sixteen and seventeen years, to dine with him in the cabin of his vessel, and he said that "they deported themselves with circumspection." At another time he treated the sachems to wine until they were merry, and one of them was so drunk that he could not leave the Half Moon until the next day. This was on the 21st of September, and at this very moment the eminent French navigator, Champlain, was upon the waters of the lake which bears his name, and within one hundred miles of Hudson. It is passing strange that one from a Christian country should have corrupted the red men by offering them intoxicants. The first glimpse we get of the famous explorer is in the church at St. Ethelburge, Bishopsgate Street, London, in the summer of 1607, whither he had gone with his crew to partake of the Sacrament before sailing in search of a passage to "Asia and the North Pole." We have greater esteem for him, as we see him worshipping in the London church, than we have as we see him on the American river, making red strangers drunk—strangers who never heard of the coming of the Son of God to give Himself for men, both when He was living and when He was dying. Would that some faithful missionaries had been brought on the Half Moon.

> " 'Tis theirs to free, exalt, and not debase
> The painted brothers of our common race."

Hudson's flimsy reason for his course is recorded in the log book: "Our master and his mate determined to try some of the chief men of the country whether they had any treachery in them." After drinking the wine and aqua-vitæ, "one of them was drunk, and that was strange to them, for they could not tell how to take it." Hudson lived in a period less enlightened than the present and therefore was less culpable than those who to-day debauch their fellowmen with poisonous drink for the sake of "the yellow dust which men call gold."

There are conflicting opinions as to the point reached by the explorers. It is generally supposed that the Half Moon attained the latitude of Castle Island, just below Albany, about one hundred and fifty miles from the mouth of the river. An exploring small boat ascended a little above to where the water was more shallow. "Seven foot and unconstant soundings" convinced the disappointed explorer that he had not found a strait, but had reached the head of a river, and "found it to be at an end for shipping to go on in." He commenced his return on September 23d, leaving the friendly tribes persuaded that he would revisit them the next year. In two days the Half Moon had sailed southward about thirty miles. On the 24th "we went on land," says the mate, "and gathered good store of chestnuts." The monotony of the progress by water was diversified on the 25th by a brisk walk along the west shore. The next day the wind was contrary, though the weather was fine. The opportunity was seized to bring to the ship a quantity of logs as specimens of the richness of the country in timber for shipping purposes.

A stiff wind, which was blowing out of the north on September 27th, filled their sails, and would have sent them many miles southward had they not struck upon a bank of mud. They did make a few leagues progress, however, and on or about that day they were within a few miles of the site of Newburgh. Think of Hudson contemplating the wooded hills and mountains of that region!

> "One still
> And solemn desert, in primeval garb,
> Hung round his lonely bark."

When in Newburgh Bay, "the people of that country came aboard us, and brought some small skins with them, which we bought for knives and trifles. At three o'clock they departed." It was on the 28th that the explorers were at the northern entrance to the Highlands. where they anchored about two days. On one side they saw "Storm King," and on the other side "Breakneck." The channel is narrow, the wind was strong, and the cautious pilot felt safer at anchor than between those threatening mountains, "because the high land hath many points, and a narrow channel, and hath many eddy winds." The Half Moon rode at anchor in Newburgh Bay on the 29th and 30th. Observing the sloping hills of the shore, they concluded that it was "a very pleasant place to build a town on." The wind changed, and on October 1st they sailed southward one and twenty miles. Juet recorded in his log book that an Indian "got up by our rudder to the cabin window, and stole out my pillow." It would seem that the Half Moon anchored probably in the vicinity of Stony Point. It was no sooner perceived from the shore to be stationary than a party of the mountain Indians came off in their canoes to visit it, apparently filled with wonder at everything it contained. While the attention of the crew was occupied with their visitors on deck, one of the savages managed to run his canoe under the stern of the Half Moon and to climb up the rudder, and through a window, into the cabin, from which he abstracted one of the pillows, and a few articles of wearing apparel, "two shirts and two bandoleers," but he was detected. "Our master's mate shot at him, and struck him on the breast and killed him." Hereupon all the other savages departed with the utmost precipitation, some taking to their canoes and others to the water. Evidently the lightning-flashing and thunder-bearing weapon terribly frightened them. Then the ship's boat was manned and sent to recover the stolen pillow and apparel; but as the boat was returning one of the Indians in the water seized hold of it with the intent, as was supposed, of upsetting it. "The cook took a sword and cut off one of his hands, and he was drowned." Now the savages were thirsting for revenge. The next day afforded them an opportunity to make an attack, because after the Half Moon had made another seven leagues southward, the strong flood tide and the light wind compelled them to come to anchor, probable not far from Shorackappock: that is, the junction of Papirinamen and Shatemuc (Spuyten Duyvil Creek and Hudson River). Here they were visited by a canoe, on board of which was one of the savages they had kidnapped, and who had escaped. The red warriors were armed with bows and arrows. Juet, the mate of Hudson's vessel, says: "We perceived their intent, and suffered none of them to enter our ship, whereupon two canoes full of men with bows and arrows shot at us after our stern, in recompense whereof we discharged six muskets and killed two or three of them; then above one hundred of them came to a point of land to shoot at us; then I shot a falcon (a small cannon) at them and killed two of them, whereupon the rest fled into the woods. Yet they manned off another canoe with nine or ten men, which came to meet us; so I shot at it also a falcon, and shot it through and killed one of them; then our men with muskets killed three or four more of them, so they went their way." The Half Moon now descended several miles and dropped anchor off "a cliff that looks the color of white green." Evidently they were near the site of Hoboken. The storm of October 3d gave them much trouble with their anchorage; but, sheltered in the Upper Bay, they rode safe. The next day the weather was fair, and with a favorable wind the Half Moon sailed out between the headlands which sentinel the Narrows. "Seeking the far East in the service of the East India Company, Hudson had sailed into the heart of the new empire of the West, and had discovered better than he knew."

The underskipper advised spending the winter at Terra Nova (Newfoundland) and continuing their exploration the next season; but the captain "discerned the temper of his motley crew," and feared a mutiny unless a move were made homewards. Juet records: "We continued our course toward England without seeing any land by the way all the rest of the month of October. On November 7th the Half Moon arrived at Dartmouth." There the vessel was arbitrarily delayed, for the English authorities no sooner ascertained whence the Half Moon, a Dutch ship with an English captain, had come than they detained both ship and captain. Hudson could only forward his reports to his employers. Probably he never saw Holland again. The Half Moon with her cargo reached Amsterdam, July, 1610. The next year another expedition was fitted out by the Muscovy Company, the expenses being defrayed by private gentlemen. Hudson sailed toward the northeast again until the ice obstructed his progress, then he proceeded westward, and, after many trials and hardships, discovered the bay and strait known to the world as Hudson's Bay and Hudson's Strait; but his superstitious crew greatly magnified the dangers by which they were surrounded, and at last arose in mutiny. They placed Henry Hudson, their commander, in a shallop, to drift helplessly over "the dreary waste of frozen waters, which are, alas! his tomb and his monument."

CHAPTER IV.

TRADERS AND SETTLERS ARRIVE.—1609-1646.

"I hear the tread of pioneers
 Of nations yet to be ;
The first low wash of waves, where soon
 Shall roll a human sea.

The rudiments of empire here
 Are plastic yet and warm ;
The chaos of a mighty world
 Is rounding into form."

WHEN the cargo of the Half Moon was unloaded on her return to Holland, fur merchants began to realize that a trade with the red men on the banks of "The Great River of the Mountains" would yield rich profits, for they were informed that fur bearing animals abounded in the new country, and that the "wild men" would willingly exchange beaver, otter, mink and wildcat skins for inexpensive trinkets. Furs as an article of dress were highly esteemed in Holland, where the winters are severe. Russia supplied the trade. The field of the East India Company's operations was not America, but the Orient, and, in 1611, they dispatched two more vessels to the North, still hoping that their captains, cruising among the icebergs, might discover a water-way to Asia. Although their Company did not enter into the new country to trade, nothing prevented the Directors or other merchants beginning a business there as private individuals. Private enterprise did become active. About the year 1610 a number of associated merchants contracted with Hudson's Dutch mate to take command of the ship they prepared to send to "The Great River of the Mountains." Some who had sailed in the Half Moon constituted a part of the crew. The traders were supplied with a quantity of bright baubles, cheap gewgaws and other articles which the "wild men" valued more than the white and yellow metals the pale face called silver and gold.

This was the beginning of an enlarging and profitable trade, and doubtless the tawny dwellers on the Neperah were soon adorned with some of these gewgaws. Among the voyagers who subsequently came to the New Netherlands were Hendrick Christiaensen and Adrian Block. They "chartered a ship with the skipper Ryser," and made a voyage, taking back with them to Holland two Indians, sons of sachems. When the Hollanders saw these cinnamon-hued men from the forests of America their interest in the new country increased. Christiaensen afterward came over in command of the Fortune, and in order to traffic more advantageously, established a trading post on Manhattan Island. He built rude houses of boards and roofed them with bark from the Manhattan forests. He sailed in the Fortune up the river and if he passed Nappeckamack in the day time the natives were furnished with a new theme of exciting conversation. Had a record of the conversations of those wild villagers, about the pale face and his boats, been preserved, how eagerly would it be perused by multitudes of readers.[a]

Christiaensen built a fort on an island near the confluence of the Mohawk and the Hudson and named it "Nassau." He mounted eleven swivel guns and two cannons on Fort Nassau and garrisoned it with ten or twelve men. This early trader was killed by one of the wild men who had accompanied him to Holland. The savage was immediately dispatched. The command of the ship devolved upon Cornelius Hendricksen.

While the Fortune was up the river the Tiger, commanded by Adrian Block, accidentally caught fire. Block and his crew with difficulty escaped to the shore. The vessel burned to the water's edge. At about the present site of No. 39 Broadway, New York, Block built four small habitations and began to make plans for the future. He had been bred to the law, but had renounced his profession to study the science of navigation, and now circumstances made him, for a time, a ship builder. Although poorly provided with tools, he set to work to construct a new ship on the charred remains of the Tiger. In the Spring of 1614 he launched the Onrust, or Restless. It is reasonable to believe that during the progress of the work, wild villagers from the "rapid-water settlement" on the Neperah sometimes hastened over their turnpike, the forest path, to Manhattan Island to see the pale face make his big canoe. This was the first vessel built in that port. It was thirty-eight feet over the keel, forty-four and one-half feet over all, eleven and one-half feet beam, and of sixteen tons burden.

With this yacht Block ventured through the dangerous channel now known as Hell Gate, and sailed through Long Island Sound, thus ascertaining that what was previously supposed to be a part of the main land is an island many miles long. A small three-cornered island which Block saw he called after his own name, and to this day it is known as "Block Island." He reached Salem Harbor and then sailed back to Manhattan Harbor. The Fortune was returning from "Fort Nassau" and Block was informed that a "wild man" had killed her former master, thereupon the captain of the Fortune was transferred to the Restless, and Block returned to Holland in the Fortune.

He appeared before the States General, and when they had heard his description of the country and its products, a charter was granted to the merchants he represented. It was issued October 11, 1614, and was "a distinct act of sovereignty over the country between New France and Virginia." It was the first document to officially give this portion of the western continent the name of "New Netherland." The charter provided for the erection of a second fort, and a fortress (but not a regular fort) was built on Manhattan Island in 1615. The Battery, as it now exists, is chiefly made land. Fort Nassau, near the confluence of the Mohawk and Hudson, had been occupied about three years and had fallen into decay. In 1617, when the ice was melting, a freshet swept away fortifications and warehouse, completing the partial destruction of former years. A redoubt was built four miles further up the river than Castle Island, and at that place, in 1618, a memorable council was held. Its influence upon the future of Manhattan Island, of the territory afterwards known as Yonkers, and upon the whole country claimed by the Dutch and English is one of the most important facts recorded in the history of that period. The Spaniards were in Mexico and South America, the Dutch and English were occupying territory now a part of the United States, and the French were in Canada, but the encroachments of the French from the north threatened the pioneer settlers of Teutonic race and faith. The council held a few miles below what is now Albany raised a perpetual barrier against the French. It was a council of the Dutch and the chiefs of the Indians. The Five Nations wanted arms and ammunition. Their warriors, who were unused to defeat, had been compelled to flee from the banks of Lake Champlain and Lake George before the Canadian Algonquin Indians, assisted by the French, whose strange weapons "scattered swift and mysterious death." The Iroquois warriors at first thought a gun was "the devil" and would not touch it, but smarting under defeat they realized the necessity of getting possession of the white man's weapon. For a musket they would willingly give twenty beaver skins, and for a pound of powder they were glad to barter the value of several dollars. At the council* which was called they agreed to bring furs to the Dutch, in exchange for guns and ammunition. Representatives from such tribes of the Algonquin family as the Lenni-Lenapes, Mohicans, and Minquas were present. The treaty made on that memorable occasion was faithfully kept. Thereafter, the Dutch were allied with these Indians, against the French, and subsequently the English profited by the compact.

* Politically the Indian was free. Each tribe had a chief, but the chief had little real power. All important matters were settled by councils. The records of these councils were kept in a peculiar manner. The Indian could not write, but he could make pictures that would often serve the purpose of writing. The treaty made by the Indians with William Penn was commemorated by a belt made of "wampum," or strings of beads. It represented an Indian and a white man clasping each other by the hand in token of friendship. That was the record of the peace established between them. But quite independent of any picture, the arrangement of the beads and their colors had a meaning. When a council was held, a belt was made to show what had been done. Every tribe had its "wampum" interpreters. By examination of a belt they could tell what action had been taken at any public meeting in the past.

TREATY BELT, GIVEN BY THE INDIANS TO PENN.

A thoughtful writer says, "the question of the domination and development of the continent of North America by a Latin or a Teutonic race and faith—the most momentous and far reaching question ever brought to an issue on this continent—depended almost entirely upon this other question which side should win and hold the friendship of that powerful confederation of red men who overawed or held in tribute the Indians from the Mississippi to the Atlantic, and from Lake Champlain to the Chesapeake." The Dutch succeeded, and Manhattan Island, the Yonkers, and other sections were saved from French influences. At that council the Dutch upheld one end of the long wampum belt, and the Iroquois upheld the other end. The middle portion was made to rest upon the shoulders of the representatives of the Algonquin tribes. "The pipe of peace was smoked, and a tomahawk was trampled under foot until it had disappeared under the loose soil, while the Dutch, on their side, promised to build a church on the spot consecrated by this burial of the implement of war."

A SOLDIER, WITH MATCH-LOCK GUN AND LIGHTED FUSE.

England and Holland both claimed the Hudson River Valley and other territory in the New Netherlands on the ground of earliest discovery. The English had taken cognizance of the Dutch traffic on the Hudson River and warned the Holland government of the impropriety of visiting, for purposes of traffic, the coasts to which England laid claim. The States General were foresighted. They realized that if they would hold the New Netherland they must absolutely possess it, and now they began to encourage the West India Company. This they had previously failed to do. The company bound itself to people the disputed territory. Having been chartered in 1621, in 1623 it was ready for complete organization. Modeled after the East India Company, it was invested with enormous powers. Its five boards, or chambers were located in five cities. New Netherland affairs were entrusted to the Amsterdam Chamber, among whose eight directors were De Laet, Van Rensselaer and Paauw. This company continued to control the New Netherland until 1664, although its monopoly was abolished in 1638. Traders had been coming to the "Great River of the Mountains" ever since the Half Moon returned to Holland (1610). In 1622 pioneers began to plan for emigrating and settling in the new country. At that time Manhattan Island was a rough, rocky ridge. The southern portion, and the shores in some places were alluvial sand beds, while marshes and ponds also appeared. One of the largest bodies of water was the "Collect Pond," nearly two miles in circumference and fifty feet deep. It covered the site of the Tombs and the adjacent territory, and was connected with marshes on the Hudson by a rivulet on the line of Canal Street, which takes its name from this fact. The lower part of the island has been considerably widened by filling in the rivers on either side. The appearance of Manhattan Island at that period has been thus described: "Nature wore a hardy countenance, as wild and untamed as the savage land holders. Manhattan's twenty-two thousand acres of rock, lake, and rolling table-land, rising in places to an altitude of one hundred and thirty-eight feet, were covered with sombre forests, grassy knolls and dismal swamps. The trees were lofty; and old, decayed and withered limbs contrasted with the younger growth of branches, and wild flowers wasted their sweetness among the dead leaves and uncut herbage at their roots. The wanton grape-vine swung carelessly from the topmost boughs of the oak and the sycamore, and blackberry and raspberry bushes, like a picket-guard, presented a bold front in all the possible avenues of approach. Strawberries struggled for a feeble existence in various places, sometimes under foliage, through which no sunshine could penetrate, and wild rose bushes and wild currant bushes hobnobbed, and were often found clinging to frail footholds among the ledges and cliffs, while apple trees pitifully beckoned with their dwarfed fruit, as if to be relieved from too intimate an association with the giant progeny of the crowded groves. The entire surface of the island was bold and granitic, and in profile resembled the cartilaginous back of a sturgeon. Where the Tombs prison now casts its grim shadow in Center Street was a fresh water lake, supplied

MATCH-LOCK.

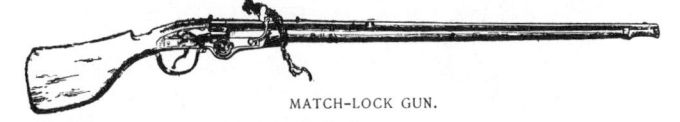

MATCH-LOCK GUN.

[In the records of 1619 are these significant words, relating to emigration to Virginia: "About the last of August came in a Dutch man-of-war that sold us 20 Negars." This was the beginning of African slavery in the English Colonies of America. At that time every leading nation of Western Europe traded in negroes. The system gradually spread over the country and a little more than one hundred and fifty years later (*i.e.* about 1776) every one of the thirteen American Colonies held slaves. There was, however, this marked difference. At the north, negroes were usually kept as house servants, and in the south they were also employed as field hands.]

by springs from the high ground about it, so deep that the largest ships might have floated upon its surface, and pure as the Croton which now flows through the reservoirs of the city. It had two outlets —small streams, one emptying into the North, the other into the East River." In New Amsterdam, in 1622, were a number of families who desired transportation to New Netherlands. They were Walloons, fugitives from Belgian provinces for conscience sake. They spoke the French language. The West India Company sent thirty of these families to the New Netherlands. Some of these settlers came to Manhattan Island. Soon after more Walloons came. The ship which brought them reached Manhattan Harbor in 1623. Adriaen Van Der Donck, who purchased the site of Yonkers, did not arrive from Holland until 1641, when Kieft was governor, but during the years intervening between 1623 and 1641 many events occurred without the record of which the history of Yonkers would be incomplete.

While the New Netherlands were under the jurisdiction of Holland six directors administered its affairs. They were May, Verhulst, Minuit, Van Twiller, Kieft and Stuyvesant. The four last mentioned were called Director Generals. Lands in what was afterwards called "the Yonkers" were bought during the administration of Kieft, the fifth director. The first director, Cornelius Jacobsen May commanded the ship which brought the thirty Walloon families. He came in 1623. The seat of his jurisdiction was mainly the Delaware River. Cape May was named after him. The second director was William Verhulst, who succeeded May in 1625. It is thought that he also lived on the banks of the Delaware. It was during the year 1625 that settlers on Manhattan Island were gladdened by the arrival of two large ships freighted with cattle, horses, swine and sheep. The Indians must have been surprised when they saw these four-footed animals removed from the ships. They had no flocks and herds. The dog was their only domestic animal—"a worthless creature resembling a cross between the fox and the wolf, the lazy sharer of his cabin and playmate of his children." The red men must also have been surprised when they saw the fruit, and vegetables, and plants, and flowers which the pale face began to raise when he had imported the seed. The cotton plant, for instance, was unknown in this country until 1621, when the seeds were planted in Virginia. Van Der Donck wrote, "The flowers in general which the Netherlanders have introduced in the New Netherlands are the white and red roses of different kinds, the cornelian roses and stock roses, and those of which there were none before in the country, such as eglantine, several kinds of gilly flowers, jenoffelins, different varieties of fine tulips, crown imperials, white lilies, the lily frutularia, anemones, baredames, violets, marigolds, summer sots, etc. The clove tree has also been introduced, and there are various indigenous trees that bear handsome flowers, which are unknown to the Netherlands. We also find there some flowers of native growth, as for instance, sunflowers, red and yellow lilies, mountain lilies, morning stars, red, white and yellow maritoffles (a very sweet flower), several species of bell flowers, etc., to which I have not given particular attention, but amateurs would hold them in high estimation, and make them widely known."

SEVERAL PICTURES OF EARLY SETTLERS.

DUTCH COUNTRY PEOPLE OF OLD TIMES.

DUTCH WOMEN OF OLD TIMES.

DUTCH WOMAN OF THE TIME SKATING.

Peter Minuit, the third director, arrived May 4, 1626. He was invested with the title, "Director General." It was he, who as Governor of the Colony, purchased the island of Manhattan (22,000 acres) for beads, buttons, brightly colored clothes and other dazzling trinkets valued at sixty guilders—twenty-four dollars. This was his first official act. It had been the policy and practice of Spain, regardless of honesty to arbitrarily and by force seize the Indians' lands, but the Holland Government dealt honorably. When granting land it was always on the inflexible condition that after receiving a land grant from the Chartered Company the Indian title must be extinguished by payment of a satisfactory price. This gained the Hollanders the confidence of the red men, "and established a claim to the enduring respect of the world . . . the annals that illustrate it throw a glory on the Holland name." Doubtless some of the trinkets and brightly colored clothes were soon adorning the red men and the red women on the banks of the Neperah. Little did they realize what Manhattan Island would be worth in future years. Its present estimated value is more than two thousand millions ($2,000,000,000).

After the island of Manhattan had been purchased, Director General Minuit bought, for the company, Long Island, Staten Island, Governor's Island, the shores of New Jersey opposite Manhattan Island, all the county of Westchester and other large tracts along the Hudson, the Connecticut and the Delaware Rivers. The deeds of the earliest sales of Westchester tracts are not extant.

In 1626, the work of constructing a regular fort on Manhattan Island was begun. Fort Amsterdam was located at the southern point of the island in order to guard the entrance to both rivers. That point was also the site of the little village of rude huts. The population was about two hundred. Outside the walls of the fort a brick or stone warehouse was erected. Here the company stored their goods which awaited shipment. In one corner of this building was the village store. It came to be a place much frequented by the Indians. Here they sold furs and drank the pale face's "fire-water," and soon the families in Nappeckamack must have felt the blight of this traffic, which for three centuries has cursed the homes on the banks of the Neperah.

In addition to the fort and warehouse a grist mill was erected. It was operated by horse power. Subsequently wind mills were erected for sawing logs and for other purposes. The Indians were afraid of the wind mills. The loft of the horse mill was furnished with a few seats and used for religious service. While the settlement of the province had been undertaken with no higher aim than commercial speculation, the moral and spiritual necessities of the people were not entirely overlooked. Two "comforters of the sick" had been sent over with the governor, and their specified duties were to read the Bible and lead in devotional exercises on every Sabbath morning.

In 1626, a Weckquaesgeck Indian, whose home was in what is now called Westchester County, went to Manhattan Island to sell beaver skins. Perhaps he went from Weckquaesgeck, which was the principal village of the tribe, and was situated on the site of the present Dobb's Ferry. His young nephew, a boy of about twelve, was with him. Three of the governor's negro servants met him by the Fresh Water Pond, seized and robbed him, and then murdered him. The boy escaped, and influenced by his Indian training, meditated revenge. Sixteen years afterward he killed a white man and an Indian war broke out.

During the administration of Director General Minuit, he and Governor Bradford, of New Plymouth, conducted a correspondence about the vexed question of the boundary. Each gave the other assurances of esteem, but Bradford did not fail to remind Minuit that the New Netherlands were English territory. Friendly Indians were the bearers of the letters. Contrast these tawny letter carriers running through the forests, along the old Westchester path, from New Amsterdam bound for New England, with the New York and Boston express mail train of to-day.

The institution of Patroonship began during Minuit's administration. By this institution the Hollanders hoped to induce emigrants to settle in the New Netherlands. Less than three hundred colonists were on Manhattan Island, while the population of Boston was rapidly increasing, and as many as four thousand people were on the banks of the James River in Virginia, although the colony there was planted only two years before Hudson ascended "the Great River of the Mountains." The settlement on Manhattan Island was more for trading than agriculture, and thereby was weakened, for the trader, looking for quick profits, is apt to be a rover. Besides that, the West India Company had at first a monopoly of trade, and, "except as to the one matter of business integrity, the company laid very little restraint upon its directors, who became stern autocrats. This also retarded the growth of the Dutch settlements. It was unknown among the colonists of New England. They were absorbed with religious ideas, did not make money-getting the first object, had upon them no jealous European eyes, and threw open their area for free appropriation, not even imposing settlers' respect for Indian titles. Under this easy sway New England grew with wonderful rapidity." The Dutch system did not encourage single farms; it looked to manors. The Hollanders had feudalistic ideas.

On June 7, 1629, a "Charter of Privileges and Exemptions" was granted the West India Company. It comprised thirty-one important articles. Having received this, the company issued proposals for the settlement of the province. The colonies to be granted were to resemble the lordships in the Netherlands, where the country-people were subordinate to their landlords. Every one who, within four years, would plant a colony of fifty persons over fifteen years of age would become owner of any manor he colonized, and would receive the title of Patroon. If the memorial tract were on a river he would receive title to a water front of sixteen miles. If the tract were on both sides of a river the extent would be eight miles along each bank. As to the distance inland, the specifications were that the lord of the manor should have ownership indefinitely far into the interior. Indian title must be extinguished by payment of a satisfactory price. Each Patroon was to provide immediately for the support of a minister and schoolmaster.

The oldest grants of memorial patents of which deeds are extant are those of Staten Island and Hoboken and of the present counties of Albany, Columbia and Rensselaer, the former to Michael Paauw in 1630, and the latter to Kiliaen Van Rensselaer, pearl and diamond merchant, in 1631. Paauw also owned the site of Jersey City. He named his patent Pavonia. The name Paauw is the Dutch for peacock, which translated into Latin is Pavonia. The estate of Van Rensselaer was called Rensselaerwyck. One historian cites more than thirty score land grants bestowed before the close of the Dutch administration (1664). Many of them were memorial patents.

In 1632 Minuit's administration came to an end. Van Twiller, his successor, arrived in 1633 in a warship. One hundred soldiers came with him. A clergyman, the Rev. Evardus Bogardus, also came with the new Director General, and before the end of 1633 a separate church building (a plain wooden structure) was erected. It refreshes one's spirit to find in the annals of these years the record of the lay readers and of the minister of the Gospel who gave wholesome instruction. Perhaps some of the Indians from Nepperhaem on the Neperah learned from these men about the Great Spirit who had walked among men, and about the beautiful life He lived. But the work of evangelizing the "wild men" was discouraging, and it was made more difficult by the dissipated whites who set such an unchristian example. The red men were adepts at theft, which was deemed by them honorable than otherwise, but much more degraded peoples than they have been Christianized. Soon after Van Twiller's arrival an English ship sailed into the New Amsterdam harbor. It had been sent out by London merchants to trade in furs on "Hudson's River." Van Twiller refused permission. It was not "Hudson's River" but the "Mauritius," and the colony belonged to the Dutch Republic. He unfurled from the Fort Amsterdam flag-staff the colors of the West India Company and fired a salute. The English ensign was run up the mast of the English ship, and defiantly she ascended the river. Several days afterward the Dutch followed and brought back to New Amsterdam the English vessel and the cargo of furs which the officers had begun to collect. The cargo was confiscated and the empty vessel sent back to England.

In 1636 the day's wages of a laborer were eighty cents during harvest. A good cow brought thirty pounds, a pair of oxen forty pounds, a horse fifty pounds, and a negro slave averaged, as to money value, sixteen dollars. That was about the time Herr Jonas Bronck (from whom Bronx River derives its name) came into Westchester County. He was the first settler. He erected a mill and laid out a plantation directly opposite what is now the village of West Farms. About the time of the arrival of this European in what is now Westchester County, the first college of the country was established in the colony of Massachusetts—Harvard dates from 1636.

Director General Kieft arrived in 1638. One regulation of his is curious. He ordered that the town bell on Manhattan Island should be rung every evening to announce the hour of retiring. A ferry had been established before Kieft's arrival. It was from the vicinity of what is now Peck Slip to a point a little below the present Fulton Ferry. Cornelius Dickson, who had a farm in the vicinity, came out at the sound of a horn, which was kept hanging against a tree near the water's edge, and he ferried the waiting passengers across the river in a skiff for the moderate charge of three stivers in wampum. There was on Manhattan Island a road which had been formed by travel from the fort towards the northern part of the Island, crooking about to avoid hills and ravines. It might have been more truthfully called a path. Upon either side of it, although at considerable distances apart, farms were laid out; and some English colonists, who removed to this hitherto uncultivated district from Virginia, brought with them cherry and peach trees, and there planted them. Kieft thought it well to secure more land for the West India Company, and he purchased from the Indian chiefs all the territory now comprising Queens County. He also secured in Westchester County a tract called by the Indians *Kekeshick*, "stony country," which is a part of the territory subsequently called "the Yonkers."

"Appeared before me Cornelius Van Thenhoven, Secretary of the New Netherlands, Frequemeck, Rechgawac, Packanniens, owners of *Kekeshick*, which they did freely convey, cede, etc., etc., to the behoof of the General Incorporated West India Company, which lies over against the flats of the Island of Manhates, mostly east and west, beginning at the source of said kill, till over against the high hill of the flat lands—to wit, by the great kill, together with all the rights, estate and title to them, the grantees, etc., etc. In testimony of the truth of which this is subscribed by witnesses.

"Done 3d of August, 1639, at Fort Amsterdam, in New Netherland.

"Cornelius Van der Hoyken,
"Davidy Piettersen de Vries, } As Witnesses.

"In presence of me,
    "Cornelius van Thenhoven, Secretary."

Up to this time the relations between the Dutch and the Indians had been on the whole friendly. The Indian nature had generous instincts; but as a savage he was suspicious and revengeful. White men intent upon trade gave the "wild men" fire-water, and it made them wilder. The pale face also supplied them with fire-arms, despite the West India Company, which forbade that traffic under penalty of death. Kieft dealt unjustly with the Indians. In 1641 an old wheelwright was killed by the nephew of the Indian whom the negroes murdered. Kieft sent at once to the chief of the Weckquaesgeck tribe (Westchester County Indians) to demand satisfaction. The latter refused to give up the criminal on the ground that he was but an avenger after the manner of his race. A party of eighty soldiers was dispatched against the Weckquaesgecks with orders to exterminate them by fire and sword. The guide professed to know the way to the Indian village, but he lost the track just at nightfall. "The night was clouded and dark, and when the expedition reached Armeperahin (west branch of the Sprain River, which flows in the rear of Dobb's Ferry), Van Dyck, the ensign, called a halt, notwithstanding the entreaties of his men to push on ere the savages should have warning of their approach. An hour and a half was thus lost. The guide then missed his way, whereupon Van Dyck lost temper and made a retrograde movement to Fort Amsterdam, whither he returned without having accomplished the object for which he had been detailed." The expedition, however, was not without its effect. The Indians observed, by the trail of the white men, how narrowly they had escaped destruction, and immediately sued for peace, which Cornelius Van Thenhoven concluded with them in 1642, at the house of Jonas Bronck. It is not to be supposed that the Weckquaesgeck Indians were cowardly because they sued for peace. They were valiant warriors. "Yea," says De Vries, "they say they are manetto—the devil himself." About the time of these events the European male population on Manhattan Island was estimated to be four hundred, consisting of Dutch, English, French, Walloons, Danes and others. Eighteen languages were spoken on the Island.

In 1643 Captain De Vries, while rambling through the woods near his plantation at Vriesendale, met a drunken and enraged Indian who complained to "the good chief" that the whites had sold him brandy and stolen his beaver coat at Hackinsack, and he vowed revenge. Before night he shot a white man. The chiefs deplored the murder, but pleaded for the murderer. They told the Governor that the criminal was the son of a chief, and that the brandy had crazed him. "Even your own men," they said, "get drunk and fight with knives. If you will sell no more drink to the Indians you will have no more murders." They offered two hundred fathoms of wampum—a blood atonement of money—as a purchase of peace. Kieft refused to accept any expiation less than the head of the fugitive. Rum had kindled another holocaust. Indians were shockingly massacred at Pavonia. They were Weckquaesgecks from what is now Westchester County and Tappaens, who had fled there from the Mohawks (eighty in number) who had made a descent from the north to levy tribute. In obedience to Kieft's cruel orders they were attacked. The Dutch slaughtered them. Neither woman nor child was spared. Forty Indians were also killed at Corlearss Hook. Soon eleven tribes of savages proclaimed open war against the Dutch. Every settler on whom they laid hands was murdered. Women and children were dragged into captivity, and though the settlements around Fort Amsterdam extended at that period thirty English miles to the east and twenty-one to the north and south, the enemy burned the dwellings, desolated the farms and farm-houses, killed the cattle, destroyed the grain, hay and tobacco and laid waste the country all around and drove the settlers panic-stricken into Fort Amsterdam. From the shores of the Housatonic to the valley of the Raritan, death, fire and captivity threatened unspeakable horrors. In one week the smiling country was transformed into a frightful and desolate wilderness. Rich and poor, the strong and helpless, the old and the young shared the same fate. Blood flowed in rivers, and, what was often worse, children were carried into helpless captivity. The Weckquaesgecks attacked the house of Anne Hutchinson, who had been driven out of New England by the Puritans, and had settled within the bounds of the Pelham of to-day. They killed her, her daughter and her son-in-law and carried her young granddaughter into captivity. She remained with the Indians four years, and was then sent to her friends. She had forgotten her native tongue, and was unwilling to leave the Indians.

In October, 1643, the whole available fighting force of the Dutch was not over two hundred men, besides fifty or sixty Englishmen. The seven allied tribes numbered about fifteen hundred warriors, and were likely to descend on them at any moment. The only tolerable place of safety was Fort Amsterdam, and into it women and children were huddled promiscuously, while husbands and fathers mounted guard on the crumbling walls. Kieft sent an expedition to Connecticut, and six hundred Indians (men, women and children) were killed in one night. Finally a treaty of peace was made. The war had been in continuance (in 1645) five years, with an interval of only a few months of peace. During the last two years it was estimated that over sixteen hundred Indians had been killed, and not many more than one hundred men remained on Manhattan Island. Some had gone to Fort Orange (Albany) and others had returned to Holland. The treaty of peace was made in 1645.

Kieft then went to Fort Orange in order to secure the friendship of the Mohawks and other tribes in that vicinity who had just made peace with the French. So slender at this time were the Governor's resources that he was obliged to borrow money of Van Der Donck in order to make the customary presents to the savages. Van Der Donck was one of the pioneer settlers near Fort Orange. It was he who subsequently purchased the site of Yonkers, and from him the city derives its quaint name.

CHAPTER V.

DR. ADRIAEN VAN DER DONCK AND COLEN-DONCK, OR DE JONKHEERS LANDT. 1646–1672.

> A primal glory far and near
> Salutes the thoughtful pioneer,
>   Viewing the scene.
> A greater glory not revealed,
> Is by the vail of time concealed
>   From vision keen.
>
> Not forest trees, but tapering spires,
> Not solitude, but hearthstone fires,
>   Hid by the years.
> And all unknown, the future fame
> Of Yonkers, with its quaint old name,
>   From De Jonkheers.

THE title to the territory first known as Kekeshick and Nepperhaem, and subsequently known as "the Yonkers," passed from the Indians to the Dutch Republic, which claimed the New Netherlands by reason of priority of discovery, but admitted that the title claimed was not perfect until the Indian title had been extinguished by purchase. Afterward the title vested in the West India Company. From that company it passed to Adriaen Van Der Donck, who was one of the most prominent pioneer settlers, first near Fort Orange (Albany), and then in New Amsterdam (New York).

It was about 1646 that the Indian sachem Tacharew granted lands in Nepperhaem (the name of the country bordering the Nepperhan and frequently applied to the village on its banks) to Adriaen Van Der Donck. The Indians had previously sold the same lands to the West India Company, but they did not regard a sale as final if the purchaser failed to hold possession. If the land was not occupied they sold it to others. They understood the right of occupation and use and nothing more; therefore sometimes the purchaser was compelled to repurchase in order to obtain a quit claim. Probably Van Der Donck never lived on the shores of the Nepperhan, but previous to 1649 he had built a saw-mill on that stream, and laid out a farm and plantation. It seems to have been his intention to live on his *bowerie* or farm, which included a "planting field" on the plain or flat, a part of the tract afterward known as the Van Cortlandt estate. The beautiful flat surrounding the old Van Cortlandt House (now made more beautiful by grading) was the ancient corn ground of the Indians. Probably the house Van Der Donck had begun to build before going to Holland in 1649 was on that plain, and perhaps located a little distance north of the site of the mills afterward built by Van Cortlandt, and yet standing. The old house of Jacobus Van Cortlandt still stood there early in the nineteenth century. It was taken down about 1825. Perhaps Van Der Donck's house was farther south and near Spuyten Duyvil. One writer says: "That indispensable requisite of a Dutch farm, salt meadow, was lacking. In search of this Van Der Donck found about a mile above the *wading place* (near Kingsbridge) 'a flat with some convenient meadows about it,' which he promptly secured by purchase from the Indians and a further grant from Kieft." His new acquisition, together with the former, gave him an estate which extended from the Shatemuc (Hudson) to the Aquehung (Bronx) and from Papirinamen (Spuyten Duyvil Creek) to Amackassin, the rivulet which flows into the Hudson near the north boundary of the present city of Yonkers. The southern boundary of the tract was an irregular line. Its course was from the Hudson (Mauritius, the Hollanders called it) to "Bronck's river," and it included some at least of what was afterward called Fordham Manor. The boundary lines of Colen-Donck were almost the same as those of the town of Yonkers, as described by the Legislature in 1788. Van Der Donck's lands extended sixteen miles along the Hudson, and their proprietor, invested with all the rights and privileges contained in the Charter of 1629, became a member of the order of Patroons.

The history of Yonkers would be incomplete without at least a brief biography of the pioneer from whom the city received its name. The Hollanders called him "De Jonkheer." It signifies "young gentleman" or "young nobleman," and was a title of courtesy which he held in common with other prominent colonists of New Netherland. His estate was called "Colen-Donck" by the Hollanders, that is, the "Colony of Donck." Another name they gave it was "De Jonkheer's landt." The English called it "Ye Youncker's land," and so was evolved "The Yonkers," and finally Yonkers. Colen-Donck, in whole or in part, was in possession of Van Der Donck or his relatives about twenty-six years (1646–1672).

The name Van Der Donck signifies "from the Donck." Donck is a village in South Holland. Adriaen Van Der Donck was born in Breda, Holland. He graduated at the famous University of Leyden, "the Athens of the West." After graduating he studied law and was admitted to the bar. Patroon Kiliaen Van Rensselaer, an Amsterdam pearl and diamond merchant, knew him as a man of attainments and promise, and desired him to emigrate to New Netherland and become the sheriff of his colony, the successor of Sheriff Planck. The colony was known as Rensselaerswick, and was a great feudal estate, including the entire territory comprised in the present counties of Albany, Columbia and Rensselaer. Van Der Donck came to New Netherland in 1541, when William Kieft was Governor. He erected a house on the first island below Fort Orange (Albany) and there dwelt. The island, which is on the west side of the Hudson, was named Castle Island. As early as 1646 he was styled "the Yoncker." He was sheriff of Patroon Van Rensselaer's colony about five years. Being a man of judgment, he realized that the most potent and powerful restraints are not those of force, but of an educated conscience, and he soon perceived how sorely the pioneer settlers needed religious instruction. He also deplored the debased condition of the untutored savages. He informed Van Rensselaer of the condition of the colony, and urged him to send the Christian scholar, Rev. Dr. Johannes Megapolensis, to Rensselaerswick, "for the edifying improvement of the inhabitants and the Indians thereabouts." The good Doctor reached Fort Orange on August 11, 1642. Through Van Der Donck's influence a church was built, and the future owner of "the Yonkers" doubtless was in the little congregation which worshipped in that quaint old church, with its canopied pulpit, pews for the magistrates and deacons, and nine benches for the people. While the devout Dutch dominie was preaching he would sometimes see ten or more Indians in the congregation, each with a long pipe in his mouth. They could not understand what an all-important and loving message he was bringing to their pale face brothers from Him whose ambassador he was and whom he served. They would stare at him, and when service was dismissed would enquire why he stood there alone and made so many words while all the rest were silent. The Christian scholar slowly acquired their language, and by degrees, as he could make them understand his message, he told them the old story which is ever new—the story of the Bethlehem manger and the Middle Cross, the world's altar where the Christ hung on the nails for them and theirs. Multitudes think of Van Der Donck as the pioneer settler whose chief honor was the acquiring of a large estate, now the site of the beautiful city of Yonkers, and of his perpetuating his name by that acquisition. There are others, however, who believe with Addison that "the best perquisites of a place are the advantages it gives a man of doing good." They honor Van Der Donck's memory because he was instrumental in bringing to New Netherland a missionary of the cross who learned the language of the aborigines and told them the story of Immanuel, "God with us." If any of the red men became Christians under the preaching of the devoted minister, their title to the sweet fields beyond the swelling flood meant so unspeakably much to them then, and means so much to them now, that in gratefully meditating upon their happiness we cease to think of a to any earthly estate however vast and valuable.

In 1643 a controversy arose between Van Der Donck and one of the agents of Van Rensselaer. It appears that Van Der Donck undertook to plant for himself a colony at Katskill, which Van Rensselaer held was a violation of articles in the Charter of Freedom, which provided that no person against his will should approach near his colony, which he had power to enlarge.

In the year 1645 Van Der Donck married Mary Doughty, the daughter of the Rev. Francis Doughty, a New England clergyman, who in 1642 had been driven with many of his friends by the persecuting Puritans from Massachusetts on account of religious views, and had settled on Long Island.

Van Der Donck had another sharp controversy with Van Rensselaer's agent, who insisted that he should rebuild a cottage which had been destroyed by an accidental fire, or that he should compensate the Patroon for its loss. Both men were angered, and Van Der Donck went to Fort Orange (Albany) to live. Van Rensselaer died in Holland in 1646. With his death Van Der Donck's connection with that Patroonship terminated. He still desired to become a Patroon himself, and upon removing in 1646 to Manhattan Island looked for a desirable estate. He finally selected the territory which became known first as the fief or colony of Nepperhaem, or, as he called it after his own name, Colen-Donck, and then as De Jonkheers landt, Ye Younckers land, De Jonkheers, The Yonkers, Yonkers. Previous to 1664 Colen-Donck or De Jonkheers was a part of the province of New Netherland. After 1664, when the Dutch surrendered New Netherland, and the first English Governor renamed the whole, and the parts of the surrendered territory, "the Yonkers" came to be popularly known as a portion of the "North Riding," on the maine—a part of Yorkshire. In 1683 it came to be known as "the Yonkers" in Westchester County. During the Philipse period the southern part of "the Yonkers" was "Lower Yonkers," and the territory within the boundaries of the present city of Yonkers was generally called Philipsburgh.

The Director General was kindly disposed toward Van Der Donck, because in 1645 he had assisted at Fort Orange (Albany) in negotiating a treaty of peace with the Mohawks. He made the Governor loans, which enabled him to purchase the customary presents for the Indians. Van Der Donck, having acquired the desired estate, was invested with all the rights and privileges contained in the Charter of 1629. (For text of the Charter, see Scharf's Westchester County.) He obtained his grant in 1646. His lands extended sixteen miles along the Hudson, north of Manhattan Island, and eastward to the Bronx River. The Indian chiefs Tackarew, Claes and other red men received from Van Der Donck a satisfactory price for the lands. His estate was erected as a manor in 1652, six years after the date of the grant. The Jonge Heer, being now a member of the privileged order of Patroons, enjoyed all the feudal appendages attached thereto, such as power to erect a church or churches, to administer jurisdiction, to decide civil suits, to impose fines, to pronounce the first sentence and to exercise all other rights belonging to the jurisdiction.

Van Der Donck was out of the country during a part of the six years after the date (1646) of his grant. Before 1649—the year he went to Holland—he had built, as previously recorded, a saw mill on the Neperah (probably south of the present Manor Hall), and had begun to build a house at what was afterward called Van Cortlandt, or perhaps south of that.

The records of those early days are so brief and few that only an outline picture of Colen-Donck, as it appeared about the middle of the seventeenth century, can be drawn. A few white men were at work building a saw mill on the banks of the Nepperhan, which the Dutch soon began to call De Zaag Kill (English, the saw creek). A few white men were also at work building a dwelling-house in the woods several miles south of the site of the saw mill. Some, if not all of them, were probably dressed in the quaint Dutch costume of that day, and they doubtless conversed in the Dutch language. Around them were Indians conversing in their Algonquin tongue, now and then addressing the pale face workers in broken Dutch. Since only about half-a-dozen years before there were eighteen languages spoken in New Amsterdam, we may believe that among the laborers conversing in Dutch and the red men conversing in Algonquin, there were also workmen from Manhattan Island who spoke English or other languages.

As these woodchoppers swung their axes, the trees came "rustling, crackling, crashing, thundering down." The white chips flew in every direction as the beams were hewn. Painted savages stood by and watched with curiosity the pale face woodmen. Probably Indian boys and girls also looked on with interest, for children love to play around the place where men are at work. At noontime the woodmen laid down their tools and ate their food under the trees. Game and fish were plentiful. If it was in the warm season of the year, the forest was melodious with the singing of birds—more melodious than forests are near populated towns. Mingled with the warbling of birds was the rippling of the sparkling Nepperhan (swiftly flowing over its rocks and sands), "the music of whose liquid lip was to them companionship." The merry laughter of the swift-footed Indian children at play and their unconscious grace of form and motion must have recalled to the European woodmen their own former homes in the dear and far-away fatherland. Probably Van Der Donck himself occasionally came up from Manhattan Island to observe the progress of the work on his saw mill and dwelling-house in the woods; and he may have anticipated the pleasure he would enjoy in making the improvements which suggested themselves to his trained and observing mind. "Man proposes but God disposes." It does not appear that the Hollander's hopes were realized. He was a public-spirited citizen, and was sent to Holland, after opposing the Governor of New Netherland, to champion the interests of his constituents. That was in this wise:

In 1647, William Kieft's administration came to an end, and in May of that year, Peter Stuyvesant, the last of the Dutch governors, arrived at Manhattan Island. Very soon he was at variance with Van Der Donck and other leading citizens, who were determined to have a more representative government. Finally Stuyvesant reluctantly yielded, and a Board of Nine Men were chosen. At the second election Van Der Donck and Oloff S. Van Cortlandt, a thriving merchant and one of the richest men in New Amsterdam, were chosen members of the Board. Influenced by Van Der Donck, the Board determined to send a delegation to Holland to demand certain reforms. The controversy became so heated that Van Der Donck was thrown into prison. This high handed measure was followed by an indignation meeting. Van Der Donck's friends considered him a political martyr. He and others were chosen delegates to Holland to represent the Nine Men. They carried with them the celebrated "Vertoogh van Niew Nederlandt" (Remonstrance of New Netherland). The Vertoogh, probably, was the composition of Van Der Donck, and although written for political purposes, is a most important work, because it begins with the discovery of the country, and tells of the aboriginal inhabitants, of the wild animals, of the origin of the West India Company, and the conditions of New Netherland up to date. Stuyvesant dispatched his attorney to Holland and both parties appeared before the States General.

The scope of this history does not permit a more extended biography of Van Der Donck. He remained in Holland to guard the interests of the people of New Amsterdam. He so well accomplished his mission in behalf of the oppressed commonalty as to procure from the States General their mandate recalling Stuyvesant to Holland, of which he was made the bearer. But the States, being on the eve of a war with England, and needing the assistance of the rich and successful West India Company, the latter was enabled, not only to procure the revocation of Stuyvesant's recall, but to detain its bearer in Holland.

In 1650, a contract was made by the West India Company with Van Der Donck and others for the transportation of two hundred persons to New Netherlands. One historian says that "the Yonkers" soon became a place of considerable trade with the Indians, and that vessels were loaded in the place for Amsterdam, Holland. There is no good reason for doubting that sloops began to land at Colen-Donck two and a half centuries ago, for Van Der Donck's saw mill was built on the Neperah, about the middle of the seventeenth century, and it may be that in 1650, or soon after, vessels were laden in Colen-Donck for a foreign port. Probably furs constituted the most valuable part of the cargoes.

In 1652, Van Der Donck received from the University of Leyden the honorary degree, *Juris utrinsque Doctor,* or "Doctor of both laws" (civil and canon). His titled name was written Adriaen Van Der Donck, J.U.D. About the year 1652, he secured the erection of his estate on the Hudson into a manor. Unable to obtain permission to return to Manhattan Island, his family were obliged to sail without him, and he employed his forced leisure in writing a history of New Netherland. The book is extant. The "Remonstrance," and the "Description of New Netherland" are the sources to which all writers, ever since, have gone for information as to the early history of what is now New York. In the summer of 1653 Van Der Donck arrived from Holland. His life was overruled as all lives are. "There is a divinity that shapes our ends, rough hew them how we will." He wished to settle on his new estate. Circumstances, over which he had no control, prevented his living on it any length of time, if, indeed, at all. He was sorely disappointed, but if he had had his own way, probably his book would not have been written. His apparent loss was a great gain to all succeeding generations. Unwittingly he gave a name to a city. He died on Manhattan Island in 1655, leaving his manor to his wife, who with some small children survived him. "Of Van Der Donck's relatives or descendants we have nothing trustworthy. His mother, Agatha, and his brother, Daniel, are said to have come to America in 1652, and we read of an Anna and a Guisbert Van Der Donck, who may have been Daniel's wife and son. One Cornelius Van Der Donck received land from Stuyvesant in 1655. This may have been a brother." One historian says that the Van Der Doncks are now known by the name Vanduck, or Vandunck, and that they live principally on Long Island.

Before 1666 his widow married Hugh O'Neal of Patuxent, Maryland, and in 1671 she went to Maryland to live. Colen-Donck remained in her possession till 1667; but whether she carried out Van Der Donck's building project, or whetheer shever derived any income from the manor is unknown.

In Van Der Donck's time New Amsterdam was a town with a fort, church within the fort; and peaked-roof cottages clustering near. The houses were chiefly of wood, with thatched roofs, some of them covered with sods, the chimneys mostly of wood. Some of the houses, however, especially those on the plantations, were partially constructed of brick and stone. The *boweries* were nearly all located on the two rivers or on the great kill or on the bays and lagoons of the East River. A rough palisade near the present Wall Street was a defence against Indians and wild beasts. The outlying plantations were also generally protected against Indians and wild animals by wooden palings. Deer herded plentifully in the dense forests which covered the middle and the upper parts of the Island. Wolves and bears roamed at large. As late as 1680 a bear hunt took place in an orchard between what are now Cedar Street and Maiden Lane, New York City. In 1650 hogs rooted in the highways of New Amsterdam and damaged orchards and plantations. In 1652 an ordinance was passed forbidding the shooting with fire-arms at partridges and other game within the limits of the town. Broadway was an Indian path which ran over the highland from what is now the Battery to the site of the present Central Park. The present Bowery was also then an Indian track. Broad Street was a marshy piece of ground, through the middle of which a drain was made, partially then developed into a canal. The Mauritius (Hudson) came up to a hill on which Trinity Church stands. The East River flowed along Pearl or Great Dock Street almost to Broadway. The narrow point of highland extending from the present Battery to the present Wall Street was the site of the infant city. What is now the Battery was a reef of rocks often covered by the tide. The island was covered with woods, meadows, fens, lakes, swamps, rivulets, pasture-grounds, wagon roads, some lofty hills, forests with herds of deer and roaming wolves and bears. An inlet offered a safe harbor to Broad Street, and a canal and brook opened a way into the heart of the settlement. In the interior of the island were farms and *boweries*. Venison was so plenty that sheep were scarcely raised. The West India Company owned *boweries* or plantations on the island, which were stocked with cattle and leased at a fixed rent. Clearings were made by the trees being cut and burned in the fields. Corn was ground and boards sawn by horse and wind-mills. The Indians were afraid of the wind-mills. Wampum passed as currency.

DUTCH PATROON, OR LANDED PROPRIETOR.

"Along shore might have been seen perhaps an Indian lazily paddling his canoe laden with tobacco and maize toward the mouth of the gracht (at foot of Broad Street). Possibly out in the bay lay the Hope drying her sails. She has just arrived from Curacoa with her cargo of salt and cattle and slaves; and further out the Blue Cock is about hoisting sail for Fatherland, and the jovial rhythm of her crew weighing anchor sounds cheerily over the sun-lit waters."

The Dutch capitulated September 7, 1664. This was the date of "the downfall of the Dutch dynasty," as Irving terms it. The English under Richard Nicolls took possession of New Amsterdam, which at that time had a population of fifteen hundred. The fleet which Nicolls commanded had been sent to Manhattan harbor by Charles II. of England, who patented the whole province to his brother James, Duke of York and Albany (subsequently King James II.). One of the first acts of Nicolls, the first English Governor, was to rename New Netherland and its parts in the English language and in the English manner. This he did by using mainly the name and titles of the Duke of York, who was the Lord Proprietor of the Province, and by whom he was appointed chief of the commission to capture it, and then command it as its Governor. It was a very natural thing for him to do, but its result has been to fasten forever on what is now the chief city of the western hemisphere the most inadequate name—New York. New Amsterdam became New York, Fort Amsterdam became Fort James, Fort Orange became Albany. The Dutch language was proscribed, the English was to be used in future in all civic matters.

As the entire region surrounding old York in England, from which the Duke took his title, forms the county there called Yorkshire, and as it is one of the largest in England it was early, for convenience sake, divided into three districts, termed in the peculiar dialect of that region Ridings, which, from their position, were termed East, West and North Ridings of Yorkshire. This example Governor Nicolls faithfully followed. He called Long Island, Staten Island and Westchester, as the region nearest to "New

York," "Yorkshire," and divided it into three "Ridings," the "East," "West" and "North" "Ridings." The region now Suffolk County formed the "East Riding," Staten Island, Kings County and the town of Newton in Queens County formed the "West Riding." The remainder of what is now Queens County, together with what is now Westchester County—being all the territory on the main north of the Harlem River and south of the Highlands, between the Sound and the Hudson—he called the "North Riding." As the portion of the "North Riding" on the main, Westchester County was legally and popularly known till the year 1683, when it received its present name, Westchester County, being one of the twelve original counties into which the State was then divided by act of the first Legislature of New York, which sat in the Hall of Fort James.

The Governor also seized all the property of the Dutch West India Company, and obliged the Dutch to renew their title to lands in the name of the Duke of York.

About ten or eleven years after the death of Van Der Donck, Mr. and Mrs. O'Neal appeared before Governor Nicolls and his council. The wife applied for a new patent, confirming her in possession of Colen-Donck, which she had received from her first husband. The Indians, who had formerly owned the land, acknowledged that they had sold it to the late Patroon Van Der Donck. The Patent of Nepperhaem was given at Fort James (formerly Fort Amsterdam), on the Island of Manhattan, by Richard Nicolls, the Governor. The record of the acknowledgment of the Indians is as follows:

"This day came Hugh O'Neale and Mary, his wife (who in right of her former husband laid claime to a cert^n parcele of land upon the Maine not farre from Westchester, commonly called Younckers land) who bro't severall Indyans before the gov^r to acknowledge the purchase of said lands by van der Donck, commonly called ye Youncker. The said Indyans declared ye bounds of the sd. lands to be from a place called by them Macackassin at ye north so to run to Neperan and to ye Kill Soro-quappock, then to Muskota and Papperinemain to the south and crosse the country to ye eastward by Bronckx his Ryver and Land. The Indyan Propryetors name who was chief of them is Tackareeck living at the Nevisans, who acknowledge the purchase as before described, and that he had received satisfac^n for it—Claes ye Indyan hav^g interest in a part acknowledged to have sould it and received satisfac^n of van der Donck. All the rest of the Indyans present, being seven or eight acknowledged to have rec^d full satisfaction."

The date of this instrument, 1668, is evidently a clerical error. It was probably 1666. The word Nevisans in the document refers to the Naversink Highlands in New Jersey.

This acknowledgement having been made, Hugh O'Neal and his wife received a grant of the whole estate. Not many days after, Mr. and Mrs. O'Neal assigned their patent to Mrs. O'Neal's brother, Elias Doughty, of Flushing, Long Island. Doughty disposed of it in several sales. He sold about one hundred and fifty acres to John Arcer, or Archer (as this Dutch name was Anglicized) of Oost Dorp (now Eastchester). Archer was the founder of the village of Fordham, and the extreme lower portion of "the Yonkers," which he bought subsequently, a part of the manor of Fordham.*

The next sale by Doughty was on June 7, 1668, to John Heddy (perhaps Hadden). It was a tract of three hundred and twenty acres in the Yonkers, a part of the present Van Cortlandt Park, New York City. The next sale by Doughty was made to William Betts and George Tippett. Their lands were north and northeast of Spuyten Duyvil Creek. The deed is dated July 6, 1668. The tract included about two thousand acres, extending across from the Hudson to the Bronx, south of an east and west line, which lay along the north side of " Van Der Donck's planting field," about five hundred feet south of the present Yonkers city line. The purchase included all south of that line except Papirinamen, for which Tippett received a separate deed of gift from Doughty. (Edsall's monograph, in the rooms of the New York Historical Society, contains a map of this purchase with an appendix of deeds.) Betts was an Englishman, and by trade a turner. Tippett was at Flushing before he bought lands in "the Yonkers." "While he lived in 'the Yonkers' the swine of the New Harlem people used to run at large at the upper end of Manhattan Island, and sometimes straying across the *wading place* (there was no bridge there at that early date) at low tide, failed to return. Tippett would be charged with their detention, and the whole community hauled into court as witnesses. Tippett's 'ear mark' for his own swine was said to be 'the cutting of their ears so close that any other marks might be cut off by it.'" Tippett's Brook (now called Tibbitt's Brook) derives its name from George Tippett, this early settler. During the Revolution the Tippetts adhered to the side of the Crown. In consequence, their property was confiscated by the State, the Tippetts having removed to Nova Scotia. The property was sold to Samuel

---

*Probably some of the Archers living in Yonkers at the present time are of the family to which John Arcer (who purchased lands of Elias Doughty, Van Der Donck's brother-in-law) belonged.

Berrian, the son-in-law of George Tippett. (The Rev. William Berrian, some time rector of Trinity Church, was of this family.) The value of land in "the Yonkers" in 1668, may be estimated by the record of "Heddy's" purchase. His three hundred and twenty acres, which now constitute a portion of Van Cortlandt Park, cost him a horse for two hundred acres, and five pounds for one hundred and twenty acres.

One square mile on the Bronx River (still known as "Mile Square") came into the possession of Francis French, Ebenezer Jones and John Wescott. Doughty sold that tract to them in 1670. All the rest of Colen-Donck was sold on November 29, 1672, to Thomas Delaval, Thomas Lewis and Frederick Philipse, each purchasing one-third. This sale is of special interest because it marks the end of the period during which "the Yonkers" was owned, in whole or in part, by Van Der Donck, or some relative of his. It also marks the beginning of the period of over one hundred years in which the title to a part at least, and much of the time to a very large part, of "the Yonkers" was in some member of the Philipse family. Colen-Donck was granted to Van Der Donck in 1646. Doughty, his brother-in-law, held title to some part of it until 1672. The title to all, or to a part, of "the Yonkers," therefore, was in that family over a quarter of a century. Frederick Philipse bought a part of "the Yonkers" in 1672. During the Revolutionary War (1779) the State of New York confiscated the Philipse estate. The title, therefore, to a part, and most of the time, to a large part of "the Yonkers," was in the Philipse family over a century.

Colen-Donck, or "the Yonkers," as it came to be called (a part of the "North Riding" on the maine, one of the three districts of Yorkshire), could not be reached from Manhattan Island by bridge until 1693, when the "King's Bridge" was built by Mr. Flypsen (Frederick Philipse). Previous to that travel was by the *wading place* east of the site of Kingsbridge. Soon after the village of Fordham was settled, the people of New Harlem established a new ferry between New Harlem and Bronx-land. They attempted to divert eastern travel to it from the *wading place* by obstructing the banks at Spuyten Duyvil ("spouting devil"). But travellers removed the obstructions and still crossed the ancient ford without paying toll. Spuyten Duyvil, "a nearer and more convenient passage to and from the island and the Maine," was selected, and in 1669 the ferry was removed and located there. Johannes Verveelen was made ferryman. There was allotted to his use the "island or neck of land Papirinamen," where he was required to provide a dwelling-house, furnished with three or four good beds, for the accommodation of travellers; also provisions at all seasons for them, their horses and cattle, with stabling and stalling; also a sufficient and able boat to transport passengers, horses and cattle on all occasions." The rates of "ye ferryman" were "for lodging any person 8 pence per night, in case they have a bed with sheets; and without sheets 2 pence in silver." The rates for transporting travellers, their horses and cattle are also on record. "A causeway was also required to be built across the meadow from Papirinamen to Fordham, of which Verveelen was to bear one-third of the expense and Fordham the remainder. Archer called on Betts, Tippett and Hadden to help him build his share of the '*causey*.' They demurred, being more interested in having a bridge made over the Bronx to Eastchester. The dispute came before the Governor, who decided that Betts, Tippett and Hadden should first aid with the causeway, and then the Fordham people should help them build the bridge. For so doing the ferry was made free to Betts, Tippett and Hadden. Verveelen kept the ferry many years, and was succeeded by his son Daniel, who was ferryman until the erection of King's Bridge in 1693."

That portion of Yorkshire called "the Yonkers"—a part of the "North Riding" on the maine—was, during this period, a forest-covered country. Indians and wild animals still made it their abode. Doubtless there were some clearings, for the Indians had had their maize fields, and the Dutch settlers living in log cabins must have begun to chop down the forest trees here and there.* As early as 1641 De Vries was opposed to making war on the Weckquaesgeck Indians, who owned and inhabited what is now Dobb's Ferry, because the Dutch settlers were all scattered among them, and their cattle were running wild in the woods. The bloody war which lasted about five years drove the panic-stricken pioneers into Fort Amsterdam; but as the treaty of peace was made in 1645, and as Frederick Philipse did not purchase until 1672, a period of over twenty-five years had afforded old settlers time to reoccupy and rebuild and others to locate. What the population of "the Yonkers" was is not known. "Many probably made their first dwellings along the river in caves, by digging in the bank, but they soon learned from the Indians the construction of bark wigwams, which afforded a much more comfortable abode and

---

* Brodhead says in his history that permanent agricultural colonization was begun along the Hudson River as early as 1623. Washington Irving gave as the date of the erection of "Wolfert's Roost," 1656.

which when improved by the devices which suggested themselves to the European mind became the log cabins renowned in song and story. The house of logs from which the bark had been peeled was a mark of gentility, and a second story was a luxury, although the occupant might have to reach his chamber under the roof-poles by ascending steps on the outside or by climbing up a perpendicular ladder within the house. A dwelling of logs hewn and squared with the broad axe was the highest of the kind. But about 1635 a class of emigrants began to arrive in New Netherland who gave a new character to the Hudson region. They were Hollanders and Huguenots who came with large amounts of ready money to occupy vast grants of land, most of which had manorial rights attached to them."

The Albany road was opened to the Neperah River, or "De Zaag Kill" (the Saw Creek), about 1669, and the Boston road on the line of the old Westchester path was opened to Eastchester about 1671. Governor Nicolls was very successful in his treatment of the savages, and preserved constant peace with them by mildness and generosity. Six or seven sloops sailed up and down the Hudson between the towns and carried the peltry and Indian goods. "It was a far longer and more dangerous voyage in those days than a voyage to Europe is now." Indian goods were blankets, woollens, guns, powder and lead. In return payment was made in beavers' and other furs.

The scattered settlers in "the Yonkers" during this period (1646–1672) probably, occasionally at least, attended public religious service in the fort in New York. Those who understood English may have gone over to Oost Dorp, or Westchester, where the Puritans or Independents held service. The only printing press in the colonies in 1668 was at Cambridge, Mass., but Puritan literature did not circulate in New York. One of the earliest efforts of Governor Lovelace, who arrived in 1668, was to procure a printing press for the purpose of having published a catechism and some chapters of the Bible, which the Rev. Thomas James, the first minister at Easthampton, Long Island, had prepared in their own tongue for use among the Indians. There is no record of any Yonkers Indian learning to read the Bible or any other book, but Christian settlers must have told them of the Saviour. It is not to be supposed that the pioneer settlers were unacquainted with learning. Lovelace wrote to the King about New York: "I find some of these people have the breeding of courts, and I cannot conceive how such is acquired," In 1670 the three daughters of Anthony De Milt were known as the best Latin scholars in New York— not even excepting the Dutch minister, who had been educated in Holland. Mrs. Stuyvesant (Judith Bayard) spoke French naturally as the granddaughter of a French Huguenot minister, and also Dutch and English, was a rare musician, in dress a French woman of fashion, while Mrs. Bayard herself was, for her day, highly educated. Several of the New York citizens had superior homes. That of Cornelius Steenwyck, who moved to Harlem in 1652, had handsome carpets, marble tables, velvet chairs, fine paintings and silver. If there was this luxury a few miles south of the Neperah, surely some of the homes in "the Yonkers" must have indicated refinement, although the people did live in plain dwellings in the woods and among the Indians. Among some, superstition prevailed in those days. In 1665 Ralph and Mary Hull were tried in New York for witchcraft, but acquitted. Several years later than 1668 Katherine Harrison, a widow from Wethersfield, Conn., was charged by the people of Westchester with witchcraft, but, proving her innocence, was allowed "to remaine in the towne of Westchester." It will be remembered that "the Yonkers" during this period, after the English captured New Amsterdam, was a part of the kingdom of Charles I., of the protectorship of Oliver Cromwell and of the kingdom of Charles II. The principal events in Europe during the years in which these rulers held their places of power, especially the public questions of interest in England and Holland, were discussed in the log cabins and other primitive dwellings in "the Yonkers" in the Van Der Donck period (1642–1672) of Yonkers history. The disputes about colonial boundaries especially interested those sturdy pioneers in Colen-Donck, for the Dutch settlements, spreading to the east and to the west, came in collision with the English upon the Connecticut and with the Swedes upon the Delaware. The border contests with the English continued as long as the Dutch held possession of the country. Among the prominent Dutch of the colony were Van Der Donck's successors, the Philipses of Philipsburgh.

CHAPTER VI.

THE PHILIPSES AND PHILIPSBURGH. 1672-1775.

>Well nigh a hundred circling years
>Dwelt princely lords in affluence great,
>In Manor Hall, and proudly rode
>The forests of their vast estate.
>At nuptial feast, where pleasure cheered,
>And guests their merry-making had,
>An Indian, tall and grave, appeared,
>In scarlet blanket closely clad.
>From door of banquet hall he spoke
>With measured words, and strange, and few,
>Which in the nearing days of war,
>To wondering bride proved sadly true,
>"From you shall these possessions pass,"
>(For thus the portent message came),
>"What time the eagle shall despoil
>The tawny lion of his mane."
>
>——*Manor Hall Legend.*

DURING more than one-third of the three centuries which the recorded history of Yonkers covers, most of the territory within the bounds of the present city was owned by three members of the Philipse family, each of whom was named Frederick, and each of whom was known as the lord of the manor. It is to be remembered, however, that the term lord of the manor is a technical one, and means simply, the owner, the possessor of the manor, nothing more. The lords of the manors in the colony of New York were never invested with the powers, privileges, rights and burdens of the old feudal manors of England with their military tenures. The grant of a manor did not carry with it a title. Under English law the Sovereign alone is the "source of honor," and the sole power that can, or ever could, grant a title or confer nobility. It is, therefore, incorrect to write "Lord Philipse." "The word *Manor* is an English corruption of the French word *Manoir*, a habitation, or mansion, in which the owner of land dwelt permanently, and that is derived from the Latin verb *Maneo*, to remain, to abide in a place, to dwell there." Another derivation of the word has been given, but it is very doubtful.

Frederick Philipse, the first lord of the manor, purchased a portion of the tract included in the present Yonkers in 1672, and owned nearly all* of it about thirty years. The manor was confirmed to Frederick Philipse in 1693, with the customary privileges of the lordship, of holding court-leet, court-baron, exercising advowson, etc. He died in 1702. His grandson, Frederick Philipse, the second lord of the manor, owned the territory included within the boundaries of the present Yonkers about forty-nine years. He died in 1751. Frederick Philipse, the third lord, and the son of the second, owned the manor about twenty-eight years. It passed out of his possession in 1779, when it was confiscated by the State. The three Philipses, therefore, were owners of the territory embraced within the boundaries of the Yonkers of to-day, about one hundred and seven years.

---

*Mile Square was not included in the patent of 1693. In 1685, John Doughty, of Flushing, sold sixty-four acres near the Bronx, in *one square mile* to Francis French, Ebenezer Jones and John Wescott.

The Philipses were a noble family of Bohemia. "The Honorable Frederick Philipse, of Friesland in Holland" came to Nieuw Amsterdam in the time of Stuyvesant, as early, at least, as 1653, perhaps with Stuyvesant in 1647. The orthography of the name varies. On a banneret-shaped vane, which surmounts the east end of the old Dutch church at Sleepy Hollow is the monogram V̄. Probably the vane was designed by Philipse himself. It appears that the original spelling of the name was "F-e-l-y-p-s-e," Felypse (in full, Felypsen). The English is Philipse. Philipsen means son of Philip. Upon one of the two silver cups of the Communion Service given to the Sleepy Hollow church by Frederick Philipse and his wife, is graven the name *Fredryck Flypse*, and upon the other the name of his wife, *Catharina Van Cortlandt*. His name alone with the same orthography is graven upon the baptismal bowl.

The Philipse family left Bohemia for Friesland, one of the Holland provinces. At what date is not known. There is a tradition that they migrated by reason of religious persecution. It is said that the earliest generation of the family embraced the doctrines of Huss, and that the Honorable Viscount Felyps (the grandfather of Frederick Philipse, the first lord of the Manor of Philipsburgh), being dead, his widow was constrained to quit Bohemia with her children. She fled to Holland with what little property she could save from the wreck of their estate. Unable to provide better for her son Frederick, she bound him to a carpenter, and he became an excellent workman. Another account is that the Prince of Germany permitted the Philipses to migrate with their servants, furniture and property. "Besides their high rank as nobles, they appear also to have held the office of Grand Veneurs, or keepers of the deer forests in Bohemia, as there is still preserved in the family the collar and badge of office, consisting of a gold chain set with amethysts, diamonds, rubies and emeralds, to which is suspended a deer beautifully chased in gold." Frederick Philipse and his wife Margaret Dacre (said to have been of the Parish of Dacre in England) emigrated to New Amsterdam. Their son, Frederick Philipse, subsequently the first lord of the manor, was with them. One writer says that he, the son, was a carpenter by trade and came under an engagement with the West India Company for five years, during which time he worked in the forts at Nieuw Amsterdam and Esopus. Subsequently he abandoned his trade, became a merchant and was very successful. In 1662 he married Margaret Hardenbroek. Peter Rudolphus De Vries, her first husband, had left her a fortune. Her daughter was adopted by her second husband, and is known in history as Eva Philipse. His first wife died in 1690 or 1691. She was an energetic lady who bought and traded in her own name, and often went to Holland in her own ships as supercargo. She took her children to Europe and gave them a thorough education.

SIR FREDERICK PHILIPSE, THIRD LORD OF THE MANOR.

In 1692 he married Catharina Van Cortlandt, the widow of John Dervall, a merchant of wealth. She brought her husband two fortunes—one from her first husband and the other from her father. By the Manor Grant, dated 1693, he procured the erection of the tracts he had purchased into a manor, which he called the Manor of Philipseborough, but which was subsequently called the Manor of Philipsburgh. The island of Papirinamen was included in it.

He had conducted a large trade with the Five Nations. His shipping trade with the East and West Indies had also proven profitable. Governor Stuyvesant granted him lots in New Amsterdam. He was known as the "Dutch millionaire." For more than a score of years he was a member of the New York Common Council under all the colonial Governors from Sir Edmund Andros (1674) to the

Earl of Bellomont (1698). "He was intimate with all the leading men of the colony in church and state, and was historically connected with every important New York event of his time. He entertained the Governors and their satellites at stated intervals with cold ceremony. In summer his invited guests, equestrian parties in gay attire, might often have been seen on Manhattan Island crossing King's Bridge and passing through the woods beyond. He dressed with care and precision, wearing the full embroidery, lace cuffs, etc., of the period, and his head was crowned with the absurd and detestable monstrosity—a periwig, with flowing ringlets."

After he became lord of the manor his power was baronial, and though he ruled with consideration he was still imperious in his will, and made himself felt as a lord. During his mercantile life his extensive and complicated relations gave him wonderful opportunities and exposed him to extraordinary temptations. Complicity with piracy, smuggling and the slave trade were persistently charged upon him, and strong efforts were made to throw him out of the Common Council and bring about the confiscation of his great estate. It was said that he was engaged in an unlawful trade with the buccaneers of Madagascar, but the accusation was not proved. All the owners of merchant vessels were more or less under suspicion, for immediately following their return from prolonged voyages there was a marvellous flush of cheap India goods and Arabian gold pieces in New York. These matters are rehearsed in our colonial history. Through real personal merit, however, together with high family association and the power of his wealth, he became a man of almost unlimited influence, and continued to exert it to the end of his life. He was not a man of letters, but apt and shrewd almost to craftiness. Although an official adviser to the king's commander-in-chief, he never advised. In the political controversies, which were more deadly bitter in his time than they have ever been since, he laid his hand upon his purse and waited to see which party was likely to win. During the revolution of 1689 he so balanced himself upon the fence as to protect his own property interests, and came down upon the right side in the end. From 1693 to his death, November 6, 1702, he lived in Castle Philipse at Tarrytown. He built a dwelling-house and a mill at the mouth of the Nepperhan and a dwelling-house, mill and church near the mouth of the Pocantico. It may be that Castle Philipse was used primarily as a trading port. It is best seen from the bridge below, which is connected with Irving's laughable legend of the headless horseman. The mill at Sleepy Hollow, through all the palmy days of the Manor (says the historian, Mrs. Lamb), was where the tenants brought their grain to be ground and from where the lord shipped his flour to the metropolis; but it should not be forgotten that he built a grist mill at Philipsburgh probably before 1700.

THE PHILIPSE COAT OF ARMS.

The dwelling-house he erected on the north bank of the Nepperhan, near the mouth of the Hudson, is the southern part of Manor Hall. At the time it was erected (probably 1682) it terminated in the rear by a huge slanting roof-shed. The northern part of the Hall was not built until over forty years after the death of the first lord and about sixty-three years later than the probable date of the building of the southern part. The oldest part faces the Nepperhan, and extends from the south front to the south side of the present east and west hall. Probably when the oldest part was completed the present east and west hall space was covered with an outside portico of dimensions coinciding with the hall. The foundation walls of the house are two feet wide, those of the superstructure are one foot and eight inches in width. The chimney breasts and hearthstone are seven feet in width. The southern part of the house is built of brick imported from Holland. The brick trimmings of all the openings of doors and windows are also said to have been brought from Holland. The south wall is of gneiss stone rubble work. Foundation, outer walls, beams, rafters, doors and staircase are very substantial. The floor beams are of hewn oak, nine inches by eight, and are laid three feet apart. The floor planks were evidently sawn by hand in a sawpit. The stone (not blue stone) with which the old kitchen under the west room is laid is one foot six inches square. In front of the south entrance door are Nyack red stone platform and steps. The old-style front and rear doors are constructed so as to permit opening the upper half, while the lower half remained closed. The great massive door which swings in the centre of the southern front was manufactured in Holland in 1681, and imported by the first Lady Philipse in one of her own vessels. It is as dark as ebony, and shows where the upper and lower halves, which formerly opened separately, have been cemented together. The eastern front door was constructed in the same style. A door which admits to one of the upper rooms in the oldest part of the building swings on wooden hinges. The first-story windows are provided with outer shutters, those in the second story with inside shutters. The bolts and hinges were evidently made by a blacksmith. On each side of each chimney is a deep closet. The Dutch fire-place of the second story (southwest room) is of a style much oftener found at the present day in books than in buildings. Within it is an iron fire-back dated 1760. It is a rude casting, upon which is a representation of the ravens bringing food to Elijah. It is a mere caricature truly, but possibly the work of some local smith, and thus valuable. The fire-place jambs are about three feet deep and are faced in old Delft blue and white tiles, each five inches square, and all bearing Scriptural illustrations and appropriate references, chapters and verses being designated. There are in this fire-place one hundred and six tiles. The flooring of the fire-places is of Holland brick.

As the building was erected in an exposed place it seems to have been necessary to provide for the escape of those within it in time of danger. The house has what have been thought, by some, to be secret passage ways, and "it is believed from evidence gained in near excavations that there is from the cellar of the house an underground passage to a well now covered by Woodworth Avenue—a passage for escape in case of a raid." Mr. William H. Doty, long time city clerk, is of the opinion that the passage way to Woodworth Avenue was to afford access to what may have been a storage vault, but the coachman of Judge Woodworth (some time proprietor of the Manor House) used to say that he had gone through an underground passage all the way down to the Hudson River. Mr. John C. Campbell, (who was born in 1821,) said in 1896, that when he was about ten years old his father took him to Manor Hall and showed him a dry cistern in front of the south door on the east front (several feet southwest of the site of the monument). The cistern was about twelve feet deep. From the bottom of the cistern, which was reached by wooden steps or a ladder, led an arched passage way toward the Hudson. The passage way was large enough for a man six feet tall to walk through. It led all the way to the Hudson, but the river at that time came nearer the Hall than now. Mr. Campbell also said that he did not go down through the passage way. Judge Atkins wrote the author in 1896: "The old well was in front of Manor Hall, opposite the kitchen door, i. e., the *north* door, now out of Court room on east front. It supplied spring water and was very deep and quite over the usual diameter of country wells. I have looked into its mouth and sought to pierce its darkness. I know of no such cistern as Mr. Campbell describes. The legend of my boyhood days ran thus—that from the well a secret passage led under Manor Hall. There was on the west circumference of the well—say ten feet below the curb—a chamber in which butter, etc., were kept—hence, probably the legend. I have utilized it in my heretofore published 'Legend of Manor Hall.' Adjoining the fire place in the city clerk's room is the secret closet. It did not connect with any passage way. If that way existed it has not been found in our day."

Mr. Robert P. Getty in 1896 pointed out for the writer a spot in the northwest corner of the Manor Hall cellar, which he said he believed was the opening at one time to the subterranean passage way leading west. From the ice-house in front of the north door, (east front) another subterranean arched passage way led as far north as the present Wells Avenue, and no farther. The ice-house was formerly,

MANOR HALL, 1682.   DRAWN BY MR. JAMES ROSS.

it is said, a powder magazine. Mr. James Sheridan, the superintendent of the Manor House in 1896, said that once there was a well west of and near the kitchen or dining-room. More extended reference to the old Hall is made on subsequent pages of this chapter.

Frederick Philipse built a grist mill before 1700, probably on the north bank of the Nepperhan, south of Manor Hall. It may have been erected on the site of the original mill of Van Der Donck. It seems probable that about 1683 he built a mill and a dwelling house in Sleepy Hollow, near the mouth of the Pocantico, and that Castle Philipse and its "armament" were a later development (perhaps by 1693 or soon after) from the simple house of that date. It is said that the Philipse dwelling house on the Pocantico was originally built of logs, also, that it is still in part of that material, and that the provision in the cellar walls of "Castle Philipse" at Sleepy Hollow may be seen to this day. According to Bolton, the historian, Frederick Philipse erected his first manorial residence (subsequent to 1680) on the west bank of the Pocantico, and this building, "on account of its great strength and armament was styled 'Castle Philipse.' There the first lord of the manor lived in rugged feudal style until the lower manor house was built at Yonkers."

The Rev. Dr. Cole, another Yonkers historian, differs from Bolton. His opinion is that Frederick Philipse lived at Yonkers first, and as to the date of the building of Manor Hall he adds: "If Mrs. Lamb's statement that the first Mrs. Philipse (Margaret Hardenbroek) had the south front door of the house made in Holland, and brought over in one of her own ships in 1681 is correct, it gives strong probability to the claim that the southern part of Manor Hall was built in 1682. At any rate this identifies it with the first Mrs. Philipse, showing that it was built before 1691, when, at latest, she died. And it shows that she was taking pride in the building, as if she meant it for her own residence, and not for a mere tenement house. Probably nothing can be proved, but let us suggest a theory: It is claimed, both, that the south part of this building was erected in 1682, and that part of Castle Philipse, at Tarrytown, was erected in 1683. If it be asked why two manor houses were erected, we answer, neither of these two houses were built for a manor house. Mr. Philipse owned one-third of upper Yonkers (his one-third no doubt included the site of our City Hall and the adjacent mill started by Van Der Donck) from 1672, ten years before the date claimed for the Yonkers building, and he owned the Pocantico site from 1680, three years before the date claimed for the Tarrytown building. Now Mr. Philipse was not a 'lord' in 1682 or 1683, nor for many years later, but simply a plain merchant, intent on business. He bought this site in 1672, as the site of Van Der Donck's mill, long established, and he secured the Pocantico site in 1680 as a site for a new mill. And he built the two houses, here and at Tarrytown, not for manor houses, but for plain country residences with the mills. He often wrote of the two sites as 'the upper mills,' and 'the lower mills,' and our theory is that the house here, near the old Van Der Donck mill site, was built by him, in 1682, for his own personal residence, and that he and his first wife lived in it till the death of the latter in 1690 or 1691. One reason for this belief is that this already cleared spot offered the strongest immediate attractions for residence. Another is, that for years before 1682, Philipse had an actual business going on here, and it would be natural for him to settle in the vicinity of it, and a third is, that for several years after 1682, Philipse's business must have called him almost daily to the city. Ten miles less of drive (his quickest mode of traveling) would be a great consideration. And still a fourth is, that more money and care were evidently put upon this building, at Yonkers, than on the one at Tarrytown, as if this were intended to be the better and more serviceable house.

Frederick Philipse also built a church at Sleepy Hollow, but the date is uncertain. It is thought to be the oldest church edifice in New York State. Washington Irving who believed that the Reformed Dutch congregation of the Manor of Philipsburgh worshipped in a log house prior to the erection of the old stone church, said that some casual reference to worship in a log house exists in one or more letters connected with the Van Cortlandts and not long since extant. On the tablet in the west wall of the church is the inscription, "Erected and Built by Frederick Philipse and Catharina Van Cortlandt, his wife, in 1699," but that tablet is known to have been placed there probably not earlier than 1837, when the building was renovated and the entrance changed from the south side to the west end toward the road. No one remembers to have seen it over or near the old door on the south side. It has long been thought to be erroneous. The inscription is in plain modern English, but the old Dutch settlers were very tenacious of the Dutch language. They conversed and wrote and read and sang in Dutch. The minister preached in Dutch and the church records down at least to April 28, 1777, were all kept in Dutch, and as far down as Sept. 25, 1785, the ordinances were administered in Dutch. On that day the Rev. Stephen Van Voorhees, (pastor from 1785 to 1788) baptized the little girl Lovine Hauws in *English* and it raised a small tempest in the congregation. The people were deeply offended, and they hardly considered the child baptized at all . . . with such a tenacious spirit among the people it is morally certain that they would never have tolerated such a thing as an inscription in English. Everything else was Dutch, and that would have been Dutch also." The bell was cast to order in Holland in 1685, and presented by Frederick Philipse. It bears the inscription, "Amsterdam, 1685, '*Si Deus pro nobis quis contra nos.*'" It is not probable that the bell was ordered fourteen years before the church was built. It is true that the inscription on the tablet in the west wall records that Catharina Van Cortlandt, the wife of Frederick Philipse was associated with her husband in building the church. She became his wife in 1692, but as several circumstances indicate an earlier date for the building of the church, it is probable that Catharina Van Cortlandt did not aid in erecting the edifice. In her will she refers to the church erected by her late husband. The interments in the old Dutch church yard began to be made probably between 1645 and 1650, and a coffin under the church is said to bear a date (in brass-headed nails) somewhere among the fifties, that is, between 1650 and 1660. Both 1694 and 1697 are given as the date of the organization of the church. The first pastor served from 1697 to 1724. It is very evident that there is great uncertainty as to when Frederick Philipse erected the old Dutch church at Sleepy Hollow. As the Dutch speaking people of Philipsburgh probably attended there before a church was erected in their own place (1752-'53) the venerable old house of worship on the Pocantico will always have an especial interest for Yonkers people. A very interesting account of the old church and the old burial ground may be found in the Rev. Dr. John A. Todd's history of Mount Pleasant (Chapter III., Vol. II., Scharf's Westchester County.)

Frederick Philipse's business talent and foresight were shown by his building a toll-bridge over the Spuyten Duyvil and securing to himself and family the revenue therefrom. As early as 1680 the Council of Governor Andros had ordered "Spouting Devil" to be viewed with reference to building a bridge there to accommodate the travel between Manhattan Island and "the Maine." The municipal officials again considered the project in later years, but the "great expense" deterred their undertaking the work. In 1693 Frederick Philipse offered to build a bridge at his own expense, if he could have certain "easy and reasonable toles, to wit, 1 penny for each head of neat cattell, 2 pens for each mann and horse, and 12 pens for each score of hoggs and sheep that shall pass the said brige; and 9 pens for every boat, vessell or canoo that shall pass the said brige, and cause the same to be drawne up." In June, 1693, the franchise was granted Mr. Fredryck Flypsen for ninety-nine years (the royal charter granted somewhat more liberal tolls than he at first asked). After sunset the toll was higher than throughout the day. The bridge was to be twenty-four feet wide, and to be free for all the king's forces and was to be named the King's Bridge. It was built during that year, a few rods east of the site of the present bridge, which was built probably in 1713 or soon after. The first bridge had a draw for the passage of such craft as navigated the Harlem, and a gate, set up at the end, where the keeper collected the tolls. A public house was kept open at the north side for the "entertainment of strangers." The bridge was owned by Mr. Flypsen's grandson and great grandson until it was forfeited by the latter, Colonel Frederick Philipse, because of his adhesion to the crown in the War of Independence. When Madam Knight crossed the bridge, December, 1704, *en route* to Boston, she was charged threepence "for passing over with a horse."

A few years after the bridge was built slaves were brought to the country for Frederick Philipse. It

VAN CORTLANDT MILLS.

will be remembered that the West India Company's Charter of Privileges and Exemptions made provision for furnishing slaves to the Patroons for the purpose of encouraging agriculture. The Company agreed to furnish the colonists with "as many blacks as they conveniently could." These they brought from the West Indies, and negro slavery existed in Westchester County almost from its first settlement. The English settlers were not adverse to availing themselves of the supposed advantages of negro labor. The Quakers brought slaves with them from Long Island. While slavery thus existed throughout the county the number of slaves was never large. About the year 1698 a cargo of negroes brought from the coast of Guinea was landed at Rye, and there delivered to the son of Mr. Frederick Philipse of Philipsburgh. It was charged that the parties concerned in this transaction had dealings with pirates, and this intimation may have caused some alarm to the inhabitants of some parts of the shore of the Sound. Captain Kidd was then in the height of his career and the shore of Long Island had been frequently visited by him and other free-booters. It is recorded that native Indians were also enslaved in Westchester County (See Bolton, Vol. I., page 529, revised edition).

The death of Mr. Philipse occurred just after the dawn of the eighteenth century. He died in the communion of the Dutch Church. The record of his death, made in the family Bible by his widow, is as follows: "Anno 1702, the 6th of November, Sunday night at ten o'clock, my husband, Frederick Philipse died, and lies buried in the church yard in the manor named Philipseborough." Catharina Van Cortlandt, second wife of Frederick Philipse had no children. The sons and daughters of Frederick Philipse and his first wife Margaret Hardenbroek, (including Eva, the adopted daughter,) were Eva, Philip, Adolphus, Annetje and Rombout. The first lord of the manor left all his real estate in New York City (including his city residence on Stone Street, between White Hall and Broad), and Bergen County to his two daughters, Eva and Anna. The Philipsburgh Manor he left in two sections—one from Dobb's Ferry (so called from a Swedish family of early settlers, who kept a ferry there) northward to his son Adolphus, and the other from Dobb's Ferry southward, including Philipsburgh. "the Yonkers" of to-day, to his son Frederick.

THE VAN CORTLANDT MANOR HOUSE. BUILT 1748.

Eva Philipse's husband was Jacobus Van Cortlandt, an eminent New York merchant, second son of the Right Honorable Oloff Stevenson Van Cortlandt, a native of Cortlandt in Holland, who came out to this country in the military service of the West India Company. Jacobus Van Cortlandt was also a large landed proprietor in the town of Bedford. It was he who in 1699 purchased from his father-in-law, Frederick Philipse, fifty acres, known as "George's Point," it being part of the Betts and Tippett tract. He added to his purchase until his estate came to include the greater part of the old Betts and Tippett purchase, and it was kept in the family intact until acquired by the city of New York for the present New York City Van Cortlandt Park in the old Lower Yonkers. He made a mill pond *circum* 1700. It is now called Van Cortlandt Lake. The pond was made by damming Tippett's Brook, a stream called by the Indians Mosholu, and subsequently known as Mill Creek, Yonkers River and Tibbett's Brook. He set up a saw mill and grist mill there. The place during the eighteenth century was known as Van Cortlandt's Mills. It may be that the old Betts and Tippett's house stood on the fifty acres Jacobus Van Cortlandt bought, perhaps on the site of the old Van Der Donck house, and it is not improbable that Van Cortlandt occupied it. The dwelling house which he or his vendor built stood a little north of the mill and on the banks of the mill pond. It was taken down in 1825. The date (1748) of the Van Cortlandt mansion which stands "in solitary state" in Van Cortlandt Park (Van Der Donck's ancient planting field) is seen in figures upon the southern wall. That mansion was erected by Frederick Van Cortlandt the son of Jacobus Van Cortlandt and Eva Philipse his wife. North of the lake and west of the present railroad track is an ancient burial place, probably that of the Betts and Tippett family, within the seventeenth century.

Philipse Philipse went to Barbadoes before the death of his father, who owned an estate there. Philip married Maria Sparkes, the daughter of the governor of the island. Philip and Maria both died in 1700. Their son Frederick, an only child, might have lived on the island had not his grandfather, Frederick (first lord of the manor), in order to prevent his remaining, sold the estate there. The grandson was sent by his mother's relatives to England, where he was educated and remained until grown up. Had he come to his grandfather's home in his childhood probably he would have adhered to the Dutch Reformed Church. But his English training made him loyal to the Church of England. It was he who was the benefactor of the first church built in Philipsburgh, now known as St. John's Church, Yonkers.

Adolphus Philipse died after he had enlarged his estate, which extended northward from Dobb's Ferry. He was unmarried and his nephew, Frederick, owner of the estate south of Dobb's Ferry, heired the northern section, including the added Putnam County tract, designated "the Highland Estate." Thus the manor, after being divided forty-seven years (till 1749) was reunited and became one.

Frederick Philipse, the second lord of the manor, married Joanna, the daughter of Governor Anthony Brockholst. In his home in Philipsburgh on the banks of the Nepperhan, and elsewhere, he was interested in the public welfare. He studied the interest of both church and state. It was he who enlarged the manor house on the Nepperhan in 1745, by extending it to the north, changing its front to the east, and giving it its imposing array of windows, its two porticoes as now seen, and its surrounding balustrade, from which views of the river and Palisades are commanded. Close under the gable roof were sleeping places for some, perhaps all, of the thirty family servants and twenty-one negro slaves. The marble mantels were imported from England. "The carved (supposed) Indian's head and centre piece, over the mantel in what was the drawing room, is so finely modeled that it were not unworthy of Grinling Gibbon's handiwork."

The second lord of the manor laid out garden and grounds, in which flourished valuable trees and choice shrubs and flowers, and through which, in all directions stretched graveled walks, bordered with box. "To the west the greensward sloped gradually toward the river, dotted with fine specimens of ornamental trees, and emparked and stocked with deer. There was also a summer house of ample proportions embowered in honeysuckle, sweet briar and jasmine, the herbary redolent of rue and rosemary, sweet marjorie and thyme. These all were to be found there after the Revolution." The addition to the house copied in good degree the features of the older part. It was built for ages of wear. The evidences of this appear, as one examines and inspects the whole as it remains, until this day.

The second lord of the manor presided over his tenants and serfs like a right royal old feudal sovereign. There were two great rent days for the manor when he feasted the tenantry, one in January at Philipsburgh (Yonkers) and the other a few days subsequent at Sleepy Hollow. In lieu of rent, a couple of fat hens, or a day's work was often received. The farmers near the river paid higher rates for being granted greater privileges. Among the interesting relics of colonial times which the Valentine family preserved are numerous receipts given for rent.

Op. Nippera, Des 20 Mars, No. 1727.
den 20 Mars heft Theis Valentin en syn Moeder hier gebracht 13½ boschel
tarwe von de heur von land vor ye Tahr Ao 1726.

Yonkers, January ye 28 day, 1734-'5.
Then received of Mr. Matthiase Vallentine 7½ bushels of Rent wheat on
behalf of Mr. Philipse.   I said received by me,
William Peck.

The courts leet and baron were held yearly at the house of John Cockles, the site of the tavern subsequently built and known as the Nap-pec-ka-mak House. That stood where the Getty House now stands. The court took cognizance of all criminal matters, and sometimes inflicted capital punishments. In the administration of justice the baronial lord presided either in his own person or that of his steward.

The second lord of the manor gave substantial proof of his interest in the church by devising in 1751 a farm east of the Nepperhan as a glebe and as a residence for the rectors. He directed his executors to expend towards "erecting, building and finishing a Church of England, £400, out of the rents that are due or shall be due from the Manor of Philipsburgh." He also directed that the church should be built on the aforesaid farm (part of which is the land of the present St. John's and Oakland cemeteries), but his son wisely decided to build nearer the Hudson and just south of the Nepperhan.

Occasionally the old dorp of Philipsburgh and the landing appear to have been "enlivened by the march and embarkation of troops." The following is an extract from the journal of Lewis Morris, Judge of the Admiralty:

"June 4, 1746, returned home, dined in Westchester, when the detachments from Queens County and Westchester marched to Colonel Philipse's, in order to embark for Albany on board of Captain Conradts Derrike's sloop, who lay there for that purpose."

The second lord of the manor died in 1751, and was buried in the family vault in the Dutch church at Sleepy Hollow. The New York *Gazette* for July 29, 1751, thus notices his death: "Last Friday Evening departed this Life, in the 56th year of his age, the Honorable Frederick Philipse, Esq., one of his Majesties Justices of the Supreme Court of this Province, and a representative in our General Assembly for the County of Westchester. He was a Gentleman conspicuous for an abundant Fortune; but it was not his wealth that constituted his Merit. His Indulgence and Tenderness to his Tenants, his more than parental affection for his Children, and his incessant liberality to the Indigent surpassed the splendor of his Estate and procured him a more unfeigned regard than can be purchased with opulence or gained by Interest. There were perhaps few Men that ever equalled him in these obliging and benevolent Manners, which, at the same time that they attracted the Love of his Inferiors, created him all the Respect and Veneration due to his rank and station. That he was a Lover of his Country is gloriously attested by his being repeatedly elected into the Assembly for the last 27 years of his life. He had a disposition extremely social, and was what few ever attain to be, *a good Companion*. But what I have said of his Character is far from being a finished Portrait; it is only a sketch of some few of his Excellent Qualities. Many features, I am sure, have escaped me; but I dare say that those I have attempted are not set off with false colors, but drawn faithfully from the Life."

He had ten children, five of whom (Susanna, Maria, Anthony, Joanna and Adolph) died young. Frederick became the third lord of the Manor. Philip married Margaret Marston, Susanna married an intimate personal friend of Washington, Captain (afterwards Colonel) Beverly Robinson, whose estate was confiscated in 1779 by reason of his adherence to the Crown. Mary, who was born in 1730, is said to have been a beautiful and accomplished lady. She passed her girlhood and young womanhood in Manor Hall. Colonel (afterwards General) George Washington met her in 1756 at the New York City residence of her brother-in-law, Beverly Robinson. The charm of her beauty, her personality and her culture greatly impressed him. That he proposed marriage to her is a story strongly discredited. She was married in 1758. The bridegroom was Col. Roger Morris, who was born in England. The fashion, the rank, the beauty and the scholarship of the metropolis were assembled at the Manor Hall in Philipsburgh (Yonkers) to celebrate the bridal of Mary Philipse. The wedding took place in the drawing room, that is in the southeast room, the ceiling of which is highly ornamented with arabesque work, showing heads in low relief, and figures of festive character, representing music and dance. Bolton says: "The wedding, we are assured, was a pleasant romance of the Hudson. The leading families of the province and the British forces in America had representatives there. . . . As early as two o'clock in the afternoon the guests began to arrive. The Rev. Henry Barclay, rector of Trinity Church in New York, with his assistant Mr. Auctmuty, was there at three o'clock. Half an hour later the marriage was solemnized under a crimson canopy, emblazoned with the golden crest of the family (a crowned demi-lion, rampant, rising from a coronet) in the presence of a brilliant assembly. The bridesmaids were Miss Barclay, Miss Van Cortlandt and Miss De Lancey.

"The groomsmen were Mr. Heathcote, Captain Kennedy and Mr. Watts. Acting Governor De Lancey (son-in-law to Colonel Heathcote, lord of the Manor of Scarsdale) assisted at the ceremony. The brother of the bride, the last lord of the Manor —decorated with the gold chain and jeweled badge of office of his family as keeper of the deer forests of Bohemia—gave away the bride, for her father had been dead seven years. Her dowry in her own right was a large domain, plate, jewelry and money.

MARY PHILIPSE.

"A grand feast followed the nuptial ceremony, and late on that brilliant moon-lit night most of the guests departed. While they were feasting, a tall Indian, closely wrapped in a scarlet blanket, appeared at the door of the banquet hall, and with measured words said, 'Your possessions shall pass from you when the eagle shall despoil the lion of his mane.' He as suddenly disappeared. This message was as mysterious as the writing on the wall at Belshazzar's feast. The bride pondered the ominous words for years, and when, because they were royalists in action, the magnificent domain of the Philipses was confiscated by the Americans, during the Revolution, the significance of the prophecy, and its fulfillment were manifested. Such is the story of the wedding as told by Angevine (son of the favorite colored valet of Philipse) who was sexton of St. John's Church at Yonkers for forty-five years."

Colonel Morris, Robert Orme and George Washington were General Braddock's aids in the battle in which Braddock was killed. Colonel Morris died in England in 1794, and Mary, his widow, died in 1825 at the age of ninety-six. They were buried near Saviour-gate Church, at York, England. Their son was Captain Henry Gage Morris, R.N. They had another son (who was also a captain of the royal navy) and two daughters. There is a portrait of Mary Philipse as she appeared in her beautiful youth. It is preserved at Philipstown in the Highlands.

Frederick Philipse, the third and last lord of the Manor, who was born in 1720, and died in Chester, England, in 1785, was the oldest of the second lord's children. He received a liberal education. In Rivington's *Royal Gazette* occurs a notice of the Commencement at King's (now Columbia) College. It reports that the audience assembled at Trinity Church. "After prayer, and a Latin speech by the President, an elegant salutatory oration was delivered with great propriety of pronunciation and gracefulness of action by Mr. Frederick Philipse. The audience was then entertained with a discourse on the happiness of connubial life by Mr. Beverly Robinson, whose just observations on the subject did him much honor. Degrees were after this conferred on the following gentlemen: Beverly Robinson, Frederick Philipse, Nathaniel Philipse, A.B., Philip Pell and the Rev. Henry Munroe, M.A." The *Royal Gazette* reporter, in private conversation with his friends may have remarked that the discourse on the happiness of connubial life by the young Virginian, Beverly Robinson of New York City, was characterized by a significant tenderness, because among his auditors at the Commencement in Trinity Church, was Miss Susanna Philipse from Philipsburgh, on the Hudson, the fair sister of his college classmate, Frederick Philipse, who was present to see him and her brother graduate, but as history does not report that they were engaged at that time, nor that she was at the Commencement, and as the trusted historian is not permitted to depend on his imagination for his facts, it is sufficient to remark that evidently the salutatory Latin oration of her brother was not so pleasing to the gentle maiden as some of the sentences which her brother's college mate and her lover must have spoken to her in choice English with "great propriety of pronunciation and gracefulness of action," as, leaning on his arm, she strolled with him under the ancient and shapely shade trees near Manor Hall.

Frederick Philipse became a colonel in the militia, and was in his time and is in written annals frequently called "Colonel Philipse." He married Elizabeth Rutgers, a widow, the daughter of Charles Williams. Their family was large, but their children have a place in British rather than American history. Colonel Philipse was an ardent Episcopalian. The two acres on which St. John's Church and adjoining buildings stand were his gift. He expended the money necessary for the building of the church in accordance with his father's will. The church (subsequently called St. John's) was erected 1752-53. He was a member of the Colonial Assembly, but being of a retiring disposition he did not seek public life. "On assuming his estate in 1751 he thoroughly refurnished the manor house, and afterwards maintained a very showy style of living, of which, however, his wife is said to have been the inspiration. She was very fond of display. An aged lady of Yonkers, remembered by several aged citizens of the city, knew Mrs. Philipse well. She stated that it was her pride to appear on a road skilfully reining four jet-black steeds with her own hands. Anthony Archer (who was born in 1746 and died about 1837, aged nearly ninety-two years) when he was about eighteen years old worked for Colonel Philipse nearly a year making terraces west of the manor-house and its garden. Eight or ten carmen from New York were employed. It was a very stony place. There was an old burying-ground under the new sections, which was covered up. "The ground between the garden and the river (now about between Dock Street and Wells Avenue) was occupied as a deer paddock. Several deer were kept in it. There was a high picket-fence around it; but sometimes the deer broke out and made for the tobacco plantations of the farmers (almost every farmer then raised tobacco). The deer were as fond of tobacco as of cabbage, and in their raids upon it sometimes did much damage. One day a fine buck was observed to be studying the paling, apparently with a view to escape. He was looking toward the Palisades. At length, drawing back, he made a spring, and, clearing the fence, soon took to the river. He was not overtaken until half-way across, and then he made a bold resistance to the attempt to capture him. . . . It is supposed that the deer disappeared at the time of the Revolution."

A controversy which arose about the construction of the "Free Bridge" furnishes a record of one event in Colonel Philipse's life. The King's Bridge was unpopular by reason of its tolls, also its barrier gate, which made the belated traveller furious as he shouted to awaken the drowsy gate-keeper several rods away. A popular subscription was started in 1756 for building a free bridge. Benjamin Palmer (he who attempted to found a city, as a rival to New York, on an island in the Sound, since called City Island) headed the movement, and when enough was subscribed he attempted to build it where the first bridge had stood, a few rods from the present one. Colonel Philipse, who owned the shore on Papirinamen, naturally objected. Palmer had to go further down the Harlem. He interested with him Jacob Dyckman on the island and Thomas Vermilye on the Westchester side, and they began to work from the land of the former. Colonel Philipse knew that if that bridge were built no more tolls would be paid at his bridge, and he tried to prevent its construction. Twice in one year he caused Palmer's impressment "as a soldier to go to Canada," which compelled him to employ and pay for a substitute. But despite opposition the structure was completed at the close of 1758. It was opened with a grand barbecue on New Year's Day, 1759, and hundreds of people attended from New York City and Westchester County and "rejoiced greatly." A new road was built to connect with the Boston and Albany roads, and for a time all travel ceased across King's Bridge. Colonel Philipse's bridge-keeper, finding his occupation gone, threw up his lease, and the proprietor had to advertise for a new tenant. It is probable that attempts to collect tolls were abandoned soon afterward.

In 1674 Frederick Philipse was elected a member of the Venerable Society for the Propagation of the Gospel, and his name appears in the list of vestrymen of Trinity Church, New York, from 1779 to 1782.

The record of Colonel Philipse's sympathy with the Crown during the Revolution, of his imprisonment, and of the confiscation of his estate is in the latter part of this chapter. He died in Chester, England, in 1785, and was buried in the Cathedral Church of that city where there is a tablet to his memory on which is the following inscription, a fac-simile of which was made by the late Ethan Flagg, Esq., of Yonkers, during a visit to Chester in 1882, and brought to Manor Hall, Yonkers, where it is now suspended on the east wall of the southwestern second floor room, which was several years ago designated as the room of the Common Council, "Committee on History and Historical Relics:"

"Sacred to the Memory
of
Frederick Philipse, Efquire, Late of the
Province of New York; A Gentleman in Whom
the Various focial domeftic and Religious,
Virtues were eminently United. The Uniform
Rectitude of His conduct commanded the
Efteem of others; Whilft the Benevolence of His
Heart and Gentleness of His Manners secured
their Love, firmly attached to His Sovereign
and the British Constitution, He opposed, at
the Hazard of His life, the late Rebellion in
North America; and for this Faithful discharge
of His Duty to His King and Country He was
Proscribed, and His Estate, one of the Largest in
New York, confifcated, by the usurped Legislature
of that Province. When the British Troops were
withdrawn from New York in 1783 He quitted
A Province to which He had always been an
Ornament and Benefactor, and came to
England, leaving all His Property behind Him;
which reverse of Fortune He bore with
that calmness, Fortitude and Dignity
which had distinguished Him through
every former stage of Life.
He was born at New York the 12th day of September
in the year 1720; and Died in this Place the 30th
day of April, in the Year 1785 Aged 65 Years."

Manor Hall, in Yonkers, to which reference is made on the first pages of this chapter is said to be one of three remaining Manor houses, and is a venerable relic of colonial times. It is an old patrician house and "one of the last links which bind us to the remote period of tomahawks and scalping knives." The New York *Tribune* of November 27, 1895, published the statement that when the Manor Hall was erected at Yonkers in 1682, there was a block house near by for defense against the Indians, but the authority for the paragraph was not given by the *Tribune* writer. The Hall is the only American building of feudal times that has public ownership,* and when, in 1895, it was proposed to erect on its grounds new municipal buildings, which in the opinion of many would overshadow it and possibly eventually result in its being demolished, many citizens vigorously protested, their views being voiced by public speakers, one of whom (the Rev. S. Parkes Cadman) said in substance: "The owner of a valuable painting by one of the old masters has a legal right to destroy it, but not the moral right. In a wide and broad sense you have no right to encroach upon Manor Hall or its surroundings." This was said at a public meeting in Music Hall, November 27, 1895, called by the Mayor of Yonkers to hear discussed the question of erecting a municipal building on Manor Hall grounds. A bulletin of the Yonkers Historical and Library Association, published January, 1896, records the proceedings of the meeting. Remarks were made by Colonel W. L. Heermance, and addresses delivered by Judge T. Astley Atkins, John C. Havemeyer, Esq., the Hon. James Wood and the Hon. G. Hilton Scribner.

Manor Hall is the keystone of the arch of Yonkers history, connecting ye ancient "De Jonkheers" and the modern Yonkers. It has stood within the Indian, Dutch, British and American periods of our country's history. With what interest the Yonkers Indians, clad in their mantles of furs and feathers, or in garments purchased from the Europeans, must have watched the unloading of the brick brought from Holland for the construction of the building. Perhaps they assisted in carrying the old south door and other parts designed for the house, from the ship to the shore, and to the site of the building. How strange their language as they conversed about the way the pale face workman laid the stone and fashioned the timber for his big wigwam. It will be remembered that when the southern part of the old Hall was building, wild animals were roaming the ancient forests of "the Yonkers." In 1691, about nine years after the probable date of the building of Manor Hall, the Assembly passed an act offering twenty shillings for each grown wolf killed in Westchester County by a Christian, and for such a wolf killed by an Indian, one-half the sum.

MANOR HALL CREST.

Said an orator, who realized the value of the educational influences of bronzes and buildings over books: "Let me put up the statues, and I care not who write the biographies. Most biographies are even more short-lived than the men they commemorate. Books for the most part come and go with the generations which produce them. Eagerly read at first, and potent for a time, they retire at last into the dusky alcoves, while bronze and marble stand out under the stars defying the storms and the seasons, and speak on to millions of people from generation to generation." The Manor Hall grounds were ornamented in 1891 by a graceful monument erected near the east entrance to the Hall, in honor of the Yonkers soldiers and sailors who fought to save the Union. Thus were brought into significant juxtaposition memorial stones of the sturdy pioneers of the country, the patriot fathers of the Republic and the brave men who imperiled their lives that "a government of the people, for the people, and by the people might not perish from the earth."

The old Hall is a splendid specimen of colonial architecture, being a curious mixture of Dutch and English, and belonging, properly speaking, to two eras, the southern part having been erected in 1682, and the remainder in 1745. The monument whose polished stones are appropriately inscribed, is exceptionally beautiful. It is "frozen music." The granite standard bearer, who keeps his station at the top of the carved capital (in his left hand the Nation's ensign, and in his good right hand the hilt of his sword) is guarded by four heroes in bronze, the infantryman, the cavalryman, the artilleryman and the marine, reminding the thoughtful citizen that to-day the flag is guarded by the Home, the Bible, the Sabbath and the Church, whose spire, like a jewelled finger, points toward Heaven whence all blessings descend from our fathers' God. The granite lips of the color-bearer are mute, yet they speak to the

*The Van Cortlandt Manor is still occupied as a residence. The Van Rensselaer House, the great house (still standing) above Albany along the river, never was the Manor House properly.

spirit's finer ear of dark days when "all the avenues of our great cities ran with rivers of burnished steel," and "the land shook under the tread of armed men as a floor beaten with flails."

The venerable Hall is vocal with the voices of the elder and buried generations. In the light of broad day when city officials and other citizens, intent on business are congregated in the offices, the sounds of the active Present drown the lighter voices of the Past. But one who enters the deserted old edifice in the twilight, or when the moonbeams silver its walls, can almost, among the shadows, touch hands which long ago vanished and hear voices long hushed, and fragments of songs that nobody now sings. He seems to hear the stately lords issuing orders, as aforetime, to their slaves and servants, the soft and low voices of mothers and maidens singing lullabys in the nursery to little children, the patter of whose feet and the prattle of whose lips are sweet music. A confusion of tongues salutes the ear— Algonquin and Dutch, and the language of the slaves ("God's image in ebony") the strange sentences of uniformed Hessian yagers, and chasseurs, and of courtly French cavaliers, the familiar words of Continental officers in their buff and blue, it may be the measured words of Washington himself in grave converse, speaking in kindly but serious tones, and withal, as an officer accustomed to authority, for it is said that the old southwestern chamber, on the second floor of the Hall, was the scene of several important councils of war.

Indeed, the metaphysical law of the association of ideas finds abundant illustration and demonstration in the multitude of thoughts which throng the mind of the well-informed citizen as he looks out through the small, heavy sashed window panes of the old Hall toward the broad river shimmering in the moonlight, and upon western mountain walls and encircling steeple-crowned hills. More than these are seen from the venerable "coigne of vantage." Shadowy forms moving through the long corridors of the patient and achieving years pass in review. Behold painted Indians in their mantles of furs and feathers, Dutch sailors and pioneer settlers in their tall shovel brim hats and doublets, industrious tenants of the Manor, negro slaves, colonial soldiers with their long flint-lock muskets and their powder-horns, on their way to Canada to fight the French and Indians, British and Hessian; Continental and French battalion with their shrill fifes and rattling drums, farmers with their droves of cattle and sheep moving down the dusty country road, ye old time dwellers in drowsy hamlet and village on their way to the sloop landing, the soldiers of the Union marching with measured steps through the village streets to boat or train, bound for southern battlefields, whence many never returned, and the citizens of the busy city, professional and business men, and horny handed laborers, many of whom weary with the march of life long since fell out of the ranks of the never-halting procession.

What a contrast between the scenes in the Manor House of to-day and those of ye ancient times. A gifted writer (E. Eldon Deane) says, "The banquet hall must have looked cheerful indeed with its blazing hearth, and many a time have the sounds of merriment and good cheer rung out into the silent night without. It is a pleasant exercise of the imagination to people this house with its gay company— the gentlemen in their long-skirted coats and ruffles, knee-breeches, silk hose and silver buckles, the ladies with their long trains over richly brocaded petticoats, beribboned caps and coiffures—and withal to observe their courtliness of manner and address, even to the most trivial affairs or speech."

The Hall represents the period in which the American feudal system (differing from that of England) existed—a system which cost the State of New York dear. It was in 1845, that the Anti-Rent agitation put an end to the last vestige of the system in America.

It seems almost incredible that there could have been such feudal power, but a little more than a century ago. "This Manor, down to 1776, was the domain of potentates who had more personal prerogatives and power within their limit than Queen Victoria has to-day within her realm." Vast is the difference between the feudalism of those days and the wide-spread freedom we enjoy to-day. It is not surprising that the venerable Manor House has deeply interested thoughtful men both at home and abroad. In the standard hand-book of travel, published by Carl Boettiger, there is mention of Yonkers, "not of its magnificent Hudson River or the classic Palisades, not of its excellent churches and schools, not of its extensive factories and business places. Not a word about these, but simply that in Yonkers is the Philipse Manor Hall." Washington and some of his generals are said to have passed several days and nights within it about the time of the battle of White Plains, in October, 1776. It is also said that the southwest room in the second story was Washington's bed-chamber. The ancient structure is the center around which naturally the events of Yonkers' history group themselves. A charming paper on the Hall, written by Mrs. Mary J. Lamb, the historian, may be found in *Appleton's Journal* of March 22, 1874.

In subsequent chapters of this volume are recorded the names of the successive private owners of Manor Hall before it came into the possession of the village of Yonkers. It is said that it was "Farmer Wells" who had the building painted brown. Its original color was that of St. John's Church. The house and grounds were purchased in May, 1868, by the village authorities for their headquarters, with a view also to preserve the historical structure. The north side of the dining room was entirely covered by the mass of colonial wood-work which may now be seen behind the Judge's desk in the court room. It faced south and had one fire-place. The chimney shelf and fire-place may be seen behind the Judge's chair. It was swung round to its present position by order of the village authorities. "The south side," says Judge Atkins, who directed the improvements, "is substantially as I found it, save for the north and south partition."

It became necessary to remove the beams and garret floor of the north end of the building in order to construct what is now known as the Common Council Chamber. The work was done with great skill and taste. On the tablet in the east and west hall is the following inscription:

Philipse Manor House,
Erected in 1682 by Frederick Philipse, Esq.,
Manor of Philipsburgh, Created 1693.
Confiscated by Act of Legislature of New York, 1779.
Sold by Commissioners of Forfeiture, 1785.
Occupied as a Private Residence until 1868.
Purchased by the Village of Yonkers in that year.

Around a building so old and so historical as Manor Hall must cluster many legends. Those who desire to read the Manor Hall legends are referred to *The Yonkers Statesman* papers by Judge Atkins: I. "The Legend of the Manor Well."—*Statesman*, May 24, 1890. II. "Mile Square Legends."—*Statesman*, September 24, 1890. III. "A Legend of the Manor—The Secret Closet."—*Statesman*, May 29, 1891. IV. "A Legend of the Nepperhan."—*Statesman*, October 9, 1881.

The preceding pages of this chapter have been devoted to a record of the Philipses and their two Manor Houses and two churches. Philipsburgh (called Philipseborough by the first lord of the manor) also has a history, but it is closely interwoven with that of the three lords of the manor. Their influence, and that of other manorial lords in Westchester County, may be inferred from the record that in 1769 one-third of the population of the county lived in the two manors of Cortlandt and Philipseborough, and probably five-eighths of the people of the county were at that time inhabitants of the manors of Cortlandt, Scarsdale, Pelham, Morrisania, Fordham and Philipseborough. The population of the county in 1771 was 21,745. Of these six manors, Cortlandt was the largest and Philipsburgh the most valuable.

Cortlandt Manor, which was granted in 1697, comprised a tract ten miles in width, extending easterly across the northern part of the county twenty miles. The manor of Philipsburgh extended twenty-four miles along the Hudson—from Croton River to Spuyten Duyvil Creek and from the Hudson to the Bronx. The land of Betts, Archer, Tippett and Heddy in Lower Yonkers and the tract called "Mile Square" were never included in the Manor, but instead constituted from about 1666 until after the Revolutionary War what was known as the "Precinct of Yonkers." The territory of the present city, except Mile Square, was not a part of that precinct. Papirinamen was, however, a part of the manor. The territory within the boundaries of the present city (except Mile Square) was called Philipsburgh. The Tappan salt meadows, lying on the west of the Hudson, opposite Irvington and Dobb's Ferry, were also a part of the Philipse estate. The larger and more valuable portion of Westchester County was embraced in the manors, and fourteen of the twenty-one townships into which the county was divided by the act of 1788 were formed from them. The annual rental of the Philipseborough Manor was four pounds, twelve shillings, which the owner was to pay "on the first day of the Annunciation of the Blessed Virgin Mary, at our fort in New York."

Concerning the manorial grants it has been said: "They had a peculiar and interesting relation to the settlement of the county and its early progress. To a degree they aided and facilitated the locating of settlers upon the lands, making less means available for the establishment of homes, and affording strong protection at a time when settlements were weak and needed such supports, for the lords of the manor were bound to look after and care for the welfare of their tenants. They built mills and churches, and threw around those infant communities the strength of the state. The rental required was not exorbitant, and the long term of the leases gave security to the lessees. In that transition state of development the arrangement was not without its benefits to occupants and tenants, as well as to the manorial proprietors, who had some special perquisites and prerogatives. But at the best the relation was necessarily tentative and could not long stand the test of a free government. "It was a mediæval and feudal tenure which could not long endure. It was a patriarchal period in which men gained strength to stand for individual independence. Though, as seen, the grants were mostly made under the English *regime*, they had mainly to do with Dutch settlers and inhabitants. The New England pioneer was generally too sturdy and aggressive an individuality to take kindly to such Patroon supervision. But the manorial state was only temporary, and such extraordinary rights and privileges as were thus conferred gave way before the stress of times that tried the souls of men and ushered in a new era in which manhood as against lordhood became the unit of measure for the state. And yet the manorial condition was an education in such higher direction, for it taught respect for the forms of law and order without which self-government itself is impossible." No man has a right to do what he pleases unless he pleases to do what is right. License is not synonymous with liberty, albeit many think it is.

"Happy is that people who have no history." "Blessed is that nation whose annals are dull" are two proverbs, which, if true, would incline to the opinion that the people of Philipsburgh, as Yonkers was called, despite the one man power of the lord of the manor, were comparatively contented during the Philipse period. Theirs was a quiet and for the most part an uneventful life, its monotony broken by happenings in New York City, tidings from the fatherlands, by the excitements of the old French and Indian war and toward the close of the period by the controversy with England. Some of the people doubtless occasionally visited the old country, and brought back news from the old home. Nothing was more common than notices in the journals of "gentlemen intending for Great Britain by the next packet." As the population increased the ascendancy of civilization over barbarism was established. The Indians decreased and most of them disappeared. The harsh life of the pioneer gradually moderated into the well-directed life of the sturdy yeoman. Wolves, wild cats, foxes and other wild animals were destroyed. The vocation of the people was that of an agricultural and pastoral district, and while the soil was rich, labor was hard. During the first part of the period the white settlers were cutting down trees, burning underbrush and stumps, building log houses in the clearings, making roads and building bridges. Before fences were built ear marks and brand marks were necessary to identify stock roaming through the woods. The brand mark of Frederick Philipse was V. F.

The pioneers and their successors must have worked hard, enjoyed hearty appetites and sound sleep. We infer that labor was well paid from the fact that it was in near localities at least a part of the time, perhaps all the time. In 1680 a day laborer in Connecticut received two shillings, and some times two shillings and sixpence per day. The harvesting of crops in old times and previous to the invention of labor-saving machines and improved farm implements, was a very arduous operation. The conditions of life in a farming country may be more equal than those in a city, but it is (or was before the introduction of machinery, the equality of sordid, continuous, excessive, manual labor. "A community of farmers must be a community of hard workers, where in the seasons of harvest the day of toil must be from sun to sun. There is undoubtedly something very charming and poetic about the scent of new mown hay and the lowing of cattle, but to swing the scythe under a burning sun, or to drive an ox-cart in midwinter is not the work of a holiday. Agriculture is not the royal path to wealth and leisure. If the farmer is the most independent of all men he is the hardest driven by his work. He must grub and plow and hoe until every joint in his body is stiff; he must fight the weeds in the ground, and the weavil, cankerworm and potato-bug above ground, the frost that kills his apple blossoms, the crows that dig up the newly planted corn, the hail that cuts the ripening grain. Nature is the hardest of masters; you must wring out of her hands all she gives you."

The population[*] was small during the Philipse period. A missionary writing to England in 1708, reported that he occasionally preached in Yonkers where the population was two hundred and fifty souls. He may have referred to "Lower Yonkers" or "Little Yonkers," as that section was sometimes called, for after Frederick Philipse purchased the territory the present Yonkers came to be called Philipsburgh, or The Lower Mills of Philipsburgh, and sometimes Philipse.

Probably conversation in Philipsburgh during the first years of the Philipse possession was for the most part in Dutch. A missionary in Yonkers (from England) wrote, in 1704, that at Yonkers (he may have referred to Lower Yonkers) "there is a small congregation of Dutch, who have only a reader, and

---

[*] The population of the whole county in 1698, was 1,063; in 1703, 1,946; in 1712, 2,818; in 1723, 4,409; in 1731, 6,033; in 1737, 6,745; in 1746, 9,235; in 1749, 10,703; in 1756, 13,257, and in 1771, 21,745. In 1755 there were only seventy-three slaves held in the county.

therefore some of them who understand English repair to the church at Westchester." Another missionary, the Rev. Henry Munroe, in a letter dated Philipsburgh, February 1, 1766, wrote, "The Manor of Philipsburgh extends about twenty miles in length on the east side of Hudson's River, containing about three hundred families; the people are for the most part of Dutch extraction, together with some settlers from New England." A distinctive colony of a people whose character and history are very interesting, the French Huguenots, many of them from La Rochelle, France, made a home for themselves in New Rochelle. Their language was, of course, French. The Dutch, the English, the French, the negro slaves from the coast of Guinea (landed at Rye in 1698 in the interests of Frederick Philipse), and probably others, were among the inhabitants of the then sparsely populated territory now known as Yonkers. When land was purchased by Frederick Philipse, it was of comparatively small* value; perhaps all that lay within old Colen-Donck was not worth in 1682, fifty cents an acre, and probably that part of the manor house which was built in or about that year did not cost over twenty-five hundred dollars. The price paid in 1670 by Philipse and Lewis for "the south half of the Nepperhan" (at and near its mouth) "with its mill privileges and also about three hundred acres of land adjoining it," was £150.

It is alleged that a portion of the county records were consumed in Bedford when the village was burned on July 2, 1779, by a party of British Light Horse under Lieutenant Colonel Bonastre Tarleton. If that is true some papers with which a more complete history could be written must have been consumed. But the records extant enable us to partly reproduce the picture those early times presented.

Before roads were opened, the Hudson and tributary streams (nature's highways) enabled the pioneer settlers to visit Manhattan Island for trading and supplies. The periauger was in constant use for water transportation. Charlevoix calls it pirogue, a canoe formed of the trunk of a tree, while Cooper in his "Water Witch" says, "It partook of a European and of an American character; it possessed the narrowness and the clear bow of the canoe, from which its name was derived, and the flat bottom and lee boards of a boat constructed for the shallow waters of the low countries." By his last will (dated 1702) Frederick Philipse devised among other property, "the boat Yoncker," with her furniture, apparel and appurtenances, etc., to his grandson, born in Barbadoes. The time came when market-sloops made their periodical trips between the many landing places on the Hudson, and on the Sound, and the neighboring city. They were generally owned wholly or in part by well-to-do farmers living in the vicinity of the landing places, and were not infrequently navigated by younger members of the family, who discharged the double duty of captains and marketmen. Sloops carried both passengers and freight.

A YONKERS DOCTOR OF COLONIAL DAYS.

The Indian path was the first highway through the woods. The next roads were the tortuous paths which led from one settlement to another, and over these nearly all their transportation was done by oxen yoked to rude and cumbersome carts. The cart wheels were constructed from roughly-hewn oak with strong felloes, upon which pieces of iron were spiked to protect them from wear. They had no continuous tires. Wagons were very rare. Oxen performed nearly all the animal labor of the farm. The road known subsequently as the Albany Post road had been opened to the Saw Kill about 1669, and the Boston Post road had been opened (on the line of the Indian trail known as "The old Westchester Path") to Eastchester about 1671. This Indian trail led from Manhattan Island to a wading place not far from the mouth of the Byram river and thence through the present town of Greenwich, perhaps to Stamford and beyond. It was used by the Dutch and English from the very first occupation of the country, and long before any towns or plantations appeared along its course it formed a line of travel between New York and New England. The rude ox-cart seems to have been the first vehicle. Wagons were rare. There were but few horses. These were chiefly used under the saddle, the women often riding upon pillions behind the men. The time came when box wagons, without springs, were used

* Old documents record what the Indians received for their lands. For example, the purchase price of Pekantico (mainly in the present township of Greenburgh) was a quantity of wampum, and other goods enumerated in the deed of conveyance to Frederick Philipse as follows: " 10 fathoms of duffils, 10 blankets, 8 guns, 7 shirts, 1 anker of rum, 25 pounds of powder, 10 bars of lead, 21 iron pots, 5 earthen cans, 12 steels to strike fire, 2 coopers' addz, 2 half vats of beere, 70 fathoms of wampum, 7 pairs of stockings, 6 howes, 12 axes, 9 kettles, 40 knives, 6 brass tobacco boxes, 6 coates, 2 drawing knives." The lands lying south of these along the Pocantico and also in the present town of Greenburgh were purchased with similar articles including " yearthen jugges."

by some farmers. "The chaise was a kind of two-wheeled gig, having a top, and sometimes drawn by one and sometimes by two horses; the chair had two wheels, but no top. The sulky which was much used differed from the chair, chiefly in having room but for one person. Ladies took delight driving about alone in open chairs to the amazement of European travellers who deemed that a paradise in which women could travel without protection. Physicians needed and bestrode stout nags, always carrying saddle-bags and the few simple surgical instruments then known. The infallible lancet was stored in the big pocket-book, as at least once a year, usually in the spring, a good bleeding was deemed a necessity. The very rich for state occasions had their coach drawn by four horses of Flemish blood with coachman and outriders in appropriate liveries.

THE "FLYING MACHINE."

Such equipages, however, were few in number and attracted great attention when upon the road. Blooded horses were not scarce as the county developed, for many of the gentry kept racing stables. In winter the people rode about in huge sleighs, some of which were of great length and had covers, half extending. The horses were decked with a profusion of brass bells, strung upon leather straps. When the youths and maidens went for long drives they carried foot-stoves, (tin-boxes pierced with holes, and set in wooden frames and enclosing iron cups filled with hot embers.)"

The stage coach began running to Boston in 1772. A stage road to Philadelphia had been established in 1732, and stages had also run to Boston once a month, taking a fortnight on the road. The first stage coach, so-called, seems to have run in 1756 between Philadelphia and New York. In 1766 the "Flying Machine" was put on and probably was an improvement on the former "stage coach" and "covered Jersey wagon." The fare was twenty shillings from New York to Philadelphia. It was not until after the Revolutionary War that the stage route was established between New York and Albany. The date was 1785. In 1787 stage communication was had with Boston three times a week in summer and twice a week in winter, and the towns in Westchester County had a stage from New York City every other day.

The people at first lived in some temporary structures until they could build their log cabins or rude stone cabins. After the period of log-houses came that of the Dutch farmhouses, built chiefly of wood or rough stone, though some were probably of brick with a stone foundation. A brick-yard was established in New Amsterdam in 1660. The Dutch pattern, familiar to the settlers in their old country home, was a house of one story with a long incurve, overshot roof, extending beyond the house walls, making a piazza in front, and in some instances another in the rear. The ceilings were timbered, and were built low for the purpose of getting sufficient heat from the wide open-tiled fire-places, which were the only protection they had against a vigorous climate. The author of the "History of Brooklyn," writing about the Dutch period, says of the large fire-places in the old-time Dutch houses:

"They often extended across half the end of the room, and as the only artificial light came from small dipped candles, the open fire-place, heaped high with blazing wood, with its warmth and added light, was the family gathering-place, around which, on the long winter evenings, the household and visitors met to gossip, to tell of what was going on in the colony and to talk about old times in the fatherland. Here the children learned both the hopes and fears of the fathers in their new home and the history and legends of the Dutch home across the seas. And at bed-time came the nursery rhymes, some of which have been handed down to the present time, and have been preserved and translated by Mrs. Gertrude Lefferts Vanderbilt. One of them runs:

'Trip a trop a tronjes,
De varkens in de boonjes,
De koejes in de klaver,
De paarden in de haver,
De eenjes in de waterplass,
So groot myn kleine —— was.'

CABIN OF ROUND LOGS.

"Which is freely translated thus: that the father's and mother's knee was for the child a little throne upon which he might be as happy as were the little pigs among the beans, the cows among the clover, the horses among the oats, and the ducks splashing in the water; at the last line, the child being tossed up high, his name falling into the verse, 'So great my little —— was!' This was part of the Mother Goose of that day."

While Washington Irving's entertaining "History of New York" is so largely a mixture of fact and fancy that one finds it difficult to know where the record of fact ends and that of fancy begins, yet it gives an insight into the spirit of the period under review. He says of the old Dutch house: "As to the family, they always entered in at the gate and most generally lived in the kitchen. To have seen a numerous household assembled around the fire, one would have imagined that he was transported back to those happy days of primeval simplicity, which float before our imaginations like golden visions. The fire-places were of a truly patriarchal magnitude, where the whole family, old and young, master and servant, black and white, nay, even the cat and dog, enjoyed a community of privilege, and had each a right to a corner. Here the old burgher would sit in perfect silence, puffing his pipe, looking in the fire with half-shut eyes, and thinking of nothing for hours together; the goede vrouw on the opposite side would employ herself diligently in spinning yarn or knitting stockings. The younger folks would crowd around the hearth, listening with breathless attention to some old crone of a negro, who was the oracle of the family, and who, perched like a raven in a corner of the chimney, would croak forth for a long winter afternoon a string of incredible stories about New England witches, grisly ghosts, horses without heads, and hairbreadth escapes and bloody encounters among the Indians." Irving also describes the customs and costumes, the parties, the furniture and the amusements of the Dutch period.

Another interesting writer about this period is Mrs. Catharine Van Cortlandt. She says that "the houses of the middle class and farmers were of rough stone or of brick and that the windows were filled in with small panes of glass; the heavy wooden outside shutters swung upon massive iron hinges. They usually had a crescent cut near the top to admit the early light, and were held back by an iron in the shape of an S inserted in the stone wall. As ground was cheap, these houses were large in extent and commonly a story and a half in height, the roof sloping steeply from the ridge pole, and dormer windows broke its uniformity. Double-pitched houses were of later date, as were those in the interior of Westchester County, shingled on the sides as well as on the roof. The front door was invariably divided into halves; in the upper half were two bull's-eyes of glass to light the hall, and it was graced with a heavy brass knocker. The lower half had a heavy latch. A wide piazza surrounded the house. In the villages a front stoop was common, with benches on each side. Here the families took their evening rest, and neighbors discussed the questions of the day. The houses mostly had a southern exposure. Attached to them was usually an extension generally built of brick for the kitchen and the servants. Many bricks were brought from Holland, but these extensions were most frequently built of rough brick from the kilns on the Hudson River of which early mention is made. The fire-places occupied a very large space, and in some very old houses, were built cornerwise. Tiles, usually of Scripture scenes, adorned the fire-places. Some were of quite fine ware, entirely white, as in the Van Cortlandt Manor House where one or two were spared by the soldiers when removing the rest to use as plates. The fire-irons, fenders and andirons were of solid brass, and always as brilliant as hands could make them, forming with the fire, a perfect picture; but alas for those who could not get close to that fire. The furniture of the humble homes was very plain as compared with that of the manor houses. In some of the pioneer houses of the colony, food was served in one dish in the centre, from which each helped himself. The pallet on the floor—'the Kermis bed,' as the Dutch called it—was an occasional resort, even in good houses. The Labadist travellers in 1688 sojourned in a tavern near the Hudson that put its guests to sleep on a horse bedding of hay before the fire; and a hundred years later, Chateaubriand found an inn on the New York frontier where everybody slept about a central post that upheld the roof, heads outward and feet toward the centre. This was the manner common in England in King Alfred's day, thirteen centuries ago.

"Such poor people in the colonies as possessed tastes too luxurious to enjoy a deer-skin on the hearth, were accustomed to fill their bed-sacks and pillows with fibrous mistletoe, the down of the cat-tail flag, or with feathers of pigeons slaughtered from the innumerable migrating flocks. Cotton from the milkweed, then called 'silk-grass,' was used for pillows and cushions."

The reader who desires to know more about the houses, furniture, habits, entertainments, dress, etc., of the people of the period under review, will find a detailed account in Scharf's History of Westchester County, which contains descriptions of tall eight-day clocks, four-post bedsteads (the posts handsomely carved and supporting a canopy or tester hung with dimity or fringed chintz curtains and fringed valance to match), great feather beds, and the skill the drowsy man required to compose himself in them for comfortable sleep, bright brass warming pans, wood dishes, pewter platters and dishes, which were often valued as heirlooms, majestic Delft teapots, old time silver tea-service, tinder boxes (matches were unknown), floors sprinkled with white sand and curiously stroked into angles and curves with a broom, wooden bowls, fashioned from knots of maple trees by the Indians, and sold to the housekeepers, tin-plate stoves for the parlor and sitting-room, the spear-like spits in the kitchen on which revolved the turkey, or saddle of mutton, or roast of beef (the spit was turned by one of the little darkies who peopled the kitchen of every great household), the crane swinging from the chimney-piece and bearing innumerable pots and other paraphernalia of the *cuisine*, "killing-time," Christmas and other holidays, dipping tallow candles, soap making, knitting (the knitting sheath was of silver or homely goose-quill) samplers upon which little maidens worked their alphabet or numerals, or Scriptural text, spinning, shoemaking by the travelling shoemaker, and dressmaking by the tailoress, the first carrying of umbrellas, a practice which the people deemed effeminate, riding, skating, hunting,* fishing, erection of May poles, weddings, descriptions of bridal and other costumes, controversies among denominations, drinking customs, smuggling, the stocks, the pillory and the whipping-post, capital punishment and the cruel manner in which it was inflicted, old-time inns—these and other subjects receive attention in Scharf's history.

The dress of the people in this period varied with their fortunes, and the change from the log cabin epoch to that of the wealthy and courtly inhabitants of the broad manors. The men who first ventured into the woods learned from the Indians to wear dressed skins. Deer skin and buckskin, raccoon and fox skins, wolf and bear skins were used for wearing apparel. "Indian stockings" or moccasins, were worn to some extent instead of shoes.

The men of the towns and farmsteads were ambitious, as well as their women-folks to dress in the manner of the best fashion at home. Nearly everything used in the pioneer's family was raised and manufactured on the premises. Flax was an important crop, and its preparation consumed much time and labor. It was dressed, spun and woven at home. During the greater portion of the year the people wore only linen garments, and their beds were also furnished with linen coverings. The fleeces of their sheep were scoured, carded, spun and woven by the hands of those who wore the woolen clothes in winter and slept under the blankets they had themselves made. The loom occupied a room in every home. The skins of their animals were tanned and dressed at home, the tan-vat being a necessary adjunct to every well-regulated establishment. The people made their own shoes or were supplied from leather of their own making by the itinerant shoemaker, who sojourned in the family till his work was completed.

Long hair was universal in the days before periwigs. Cutting the hair short was the brand of disgrace, and the mark of identification affixed to a servant who ran away before his term of indenture had expired. Puritanism was somewhat successful in its fight against long hair, but when the periwig re-appeared in the reign of Charles II. it proved too enticing for human nature to resist. . . . After 1750 the decline of the wig began, but the natural hair was curled, frizzled, powdered, queued and clubbed. . . . Homespun linsey became the ordinary wear in the farmers' houses.

Eating and drinking at funerals were carried to such an excess that the Legislature interfered. Funerals sometimes became the occasion of drunken brawls and riot. They were very expensive by reason of the expense of providing viands and liquors, and for other reasons. The "underbearers," who carried the coffin, walking with their heads and shoulders covered with the pall-cloth, wore plain gloves, but the pall-bearers, the minister and many of the friends were presented with costly gloves of silk and leather. So many gloves were received by persons of wide social connections that a considerable revenue was derived from the sale of them. If the means of the family permitted, fine linen scarfs caught on one shoulder with a bow of white or black ribbon and fastened under the opposite arm with ribbon were furnished the clergy, physicians and pall-bearers. Mourning rings were large and elaborate. . . . If the distance to the burying ground was short, the deceased was carried on a bier. The slaves followed with spotless napkins pinned over the left arm, a little above the elbow.

The foregoing brief description of the customs and costumes of the people of the period preceding that of the Revolution, and of the homes in which they lived would be more interesting if some of those old dwelling houses were still standing that they might be visited and seen and photographed, but

---

* At the close of the colonial period there were deer on Long Island, hares and rabbits in abundance, and the air was thick with wild fowl in the seasons of flight.

very few if any remain. The southern part of Manor Hall, built probably in 1682, the northern part built in 1745, the Van Cortlandt mansion built in 1748, in what was known as Lower Yonkers, are well preserved. The old south wall of St. John's Church, erected in 1752 or 1753, still stands as a monument, serving to keep in grateful memory the fathers who planned and gave for God's glory and the good of their brother men. "Others have labored and ye are entered into their labor."

One by one the old-time Yonkers houses in which men lived before or during the Revolution have been demolished. Several stood near the mouth of the Nepperhan, several at Tuckahoe, and several at Mile Square. Others were scattered along the old highways and private roads. A picture of the Revolutionary house, in which the Valentines lived and which Washington made his headquarters, is extant. It shows the slave quarters which formed a part of the dwelling. The Rich house, near the cemetery in Mile Square, and the Valentine house, north of and near the present Leake and Watts Orphan House, were probably built before the Revolution. Only a few years since an old dwelling which stood north of the present Fern Brook Street (in the rear of the site of the gas works) was demolished. It is said to have been a counterpart of "The Century House," yet standing on the Dyckman meadows, below Kingsbridge. Mr. John Archer, a life resident of Yonkers (in 1896 in his eightieth year) describes a Yonkers farmhouse which stood at the southeast corner of the road to Eastchester (Ashburton Avenue) and Archer's Lane (Nepperhan Avenue, north of the Arch). It was the dwelling of Anthony Archer (familiarly called "Tony" Archer) who died in Yonkers, in 1832, aged ninety-two years. He occupied it during the Revolution. It was a one story farmhouse with an attic. One end of the old building was built of stone. Its old fashioned fire-place was over fourteen feet wide. The jambs were about five feet. Mr. John Archer said that when he was a boy, eight or ten years old, he "got many a nap on the end of the great back log which lay in that huge fire place." The log was "as large as a barrel" and "about fourteen feet long. It was dragged into the house by a horse and with crowbars rolled into the fire-place. The horse was driven into one door and out of the other."

Down as late as about the middle of the nineteenth century a log cabin stood on what is now Vineyard Avenue, near the site of the present Hook and Ladder and Hose Carriage House. The old cabin was reached from the Eastchester road (Ashburton Avenue) by a path through the field. The chimney was on the outside of the south wall. A more modern dwelling had been added, and with the log house constituted one dwelling.

Another old building which probably belonged to the Philipse period was a house of rough stone which stood on the west side of Guion Lane (Nepperhan Avenue) near the present School Street. The Frederick Post house, still standing, was probably built before the Revolution. Its site is a few rods north of the stone bridge which arches the New York and Putnam Railroad near the Lincoln Station. The Dyckman farmhouse on the west side of the Albany Post road, and a few rods north of the north boundary of Yonkers, is also a very old dwelling. It has large fire-places, low ceilings and windows with small sash. Within this dwelling is an old fashioned stove, probably a "Franklin." It probably was built before the Revolution. An old time stone farmhouse is still standing in what was known as Lower Yonkers. It is situated on the west side of the present South Broadway (the old turnpike) and north of the present Van Cortlandt Park. It is said to have sheltered, in turn, officers of both the Continental and British armies. Another Yonkers dwelling, now known as the Pulver House, dates back to colonial times. It stands on the west side of the Saw Mill river road, and almost opposite the Woodhill M. E. Church. Two old-time farmhouses standing on Jerome Avenue, are antique relics. One of them is at the corner of Yonkers and Jerome Avenues. The Oakleys owned it during the Revolution. A short distance south of the northern boundary of Yonkers is a lane, the corner of which is from the Grassy Sprain road to Central Avenue. The Isaac Lent house stands on the north side of that lane. Its shingled sides, board shutters, old fashioned doors and large fire-place indicate that it is a very old dwelling. A burial ground for slaves was near it. A house on the north side of the Tuckahoe road, east of Central Avenue, and another on the west side of the street leading from Yonkers Park to the Tuckahoe railroad station also bear marks of great age.

On the east side of the Saw Mill river road, and just north of the railroad bridge over the highway is the Abraham Odell house. It is a Dutch farmhouse and originally was a long building, with eaves so low, that one standing on the ground could touch them with his hands. The low-ceiled rooms were all on one floor. That part of the old structure which was nearest the road has been demolished. The part still standing was repaired years ago and enlarged by the addition of a second story. The improvements were made under the direction of John Delancy Odell, the son of Jacob Odell, a general during the war of 1812. The house occupied in 1896 by the St. Andrew Golf Club stands about seventy-five or one hundred feet south of the enlarged Revolutionary house. That Club has recently purchased another house which is also an interesting historical building.*

One of the inconveniences of the pioneer settlers of Philipsburgh was their deprivation of regular mails, but they were not thereby as much inconvenienced as settlers more remote from New York. Letters were first carried by private conveyance. In 1672 Governor Lovelace established a post to "sett forth from this citty of New Yorke monthly and thence travail to Boston, from whence within that Month hee shall return againe to this citty, . . . all persons paying the Post before the Bag be sealed up." The postman was directed to allow passengers to accompany him; he was "to advise where the most commodious place will be to leave the Letters out of your road, which, when having it once well fixt, you are not only to leave the Letters there, but at your return you are to call for answers." Governor Dongan, in 1684, ordered that for a better correspondence between the colonies of America, a post-office be established, and that the rate for riding post be per week, for every single letter not above hundred miles, threepence; if more, proportionately. At the very time the Government arrangement commenced this, transferring of letters was "practiced in some places by foot and horse messengers." In 1692 a royal patent constituted Thomas Neale postmaster general of Virginia and other posts of North America. This is the first mention of the office of postmaster general in America, and the beginning of a new era. A post-office scheme for British America was devised in 1700 by Colonel Hamilton of New Jersey, the son of Governor Andrew Hamilton. He obtained a patent, and the profits accruing, and afterwards sold it to the crown. In 1704 Lord Cornbury wrote to the Lords of Trade: "The post that goes through this place goes Eastward as far as Boston, and Westward he goes no further than Philadelphia, and there is no other post upon all this continent." In 1708 from Boston there was a post, by which the New York citizen could hear once a week in summer and once a fortnight in winter. Parliament established a post-office in the colonies in 1710. The chief post-office in North America was in New York. In 1730 the postmaster in New York published a notice inviting application for the office of *foot post to Albany this winter*. December 6, 1747, it was announced that "Cornelius van Denbergh, as Albany post, designs to set out for the first time this winter on Thursday next. All letters to go by him are desired to be sent to the post-office or to his home, near the Spring Garden." When Benjamin Franklin was made postmaster general of the colonies, he soon established a weekly mail through the winter months. Previous to that there had been a weekly mail in summer. Letters which left Philadelphia Monday morning reached Boston Saturday night. Franklin himself set out on a tour of inspection, and, travelling patiently over the routes, erected mile-stones, some of which are probably still standing.

Letters to distant places were generally carried by messengers on horseback. At first a satchel or a pair of saddle-bags sufficed, then a light vehicle was required, finally the stage coaches, which were first started for the benefit of passengers, became the proper means of transportation for the ever-increasing mail matter. An independent post-office was established in New York in 1775, at the suggestion of William Goddard, the publisher of the Maryland *Journal*, and John Holt, the New York printer, was appointed postmaster. There is no doubt that the "Sons of Liberty," a popular association of Americans, were connected with the movement, for one of the first acts of its members was to send through this office threatening letters to the leading members of the Tory party.

In the development of the county, proximity to New York City was from the first an important element to its advantage. Here was a ready market for the products of the soil. Until mills for grinding grain were built, the flour was made by hand-grinding in a mortar; and afterward, the mills in the county being few in number, much of the grain was carried long distances upon the backs of horses. "The early settler entered upon his work of raising the supply for his family and neighbors with the knowledge of a sure and easy disposal of the surplus of his crop. The soil was remarkably productive. There is no doubt that in a coasting trade much was sent both north and south, to Rhode Island and

---

* *The New York Times* of Nov. 24, 1895, has a description of it. It is at Mount Hope, on the Lawrence farm, about three-quarters of a mile north of the northern boundary of Yonkers. The first house there was a rude log cabin, near the site of the present old house. The house still standing was erected in 1729 and bears every indication of age. It is small, and the ceilings of the small rooms are so low, that one standing on tiptoe can touch them. The large wide ash-boards forming the floors are nailed down with curious hand-made nails, some of which by actual measurement are over an inch wide across the heads. The primitive latches are still on the doors, and the huge fire-place can be plainly seen in the kitchen. The entire half of a tree could easily be put in old time fire-places, and indeed they used to draw big logs from the woods right up to the fire. Joseph Lawrence buried his money during the troublous times, near where the kitchen now stands. While digging for a cellar a few years ago, a gold guinea dated 1753 was found. It was given as a souvenir to Mr. Wallace Smith, cashier of the First National Bank, Yonkers One or two more of these gold coins have also been recently found; the finder of one had it made into an engagement ring. An old revolutionary spur was picked up there one day by a ploughman.

Boston and the Carolinas, direct for the villages of the county; but the vast bulk of what it had to sell went through New York City, the port of entry to the mother country and various other lands of greater or less distances. At first wheat, barley, rye, peas and Indian corn were exported, but afterward live stock, hemp, flax, apples, onions, tobacco, cheese, pickled oysters, prepared, and then other articles, as tar, bacon, butter, candles, linseed oil, inferior cloths, and for a short time hats." Among those who performed farm-labor were negro and Indian slaves. The first mills were saw-mills and grist-mills. There were also tanneries in the county. Every farmer kept sheep and had wool spun in his own house. The weaving was done by men who kept and worked small hand-looms in their houses. Blankets and sheetings and coarse cloths were produced in very considerable quantities. Much flax was raised and was also spun at the firesides of the people, where the hum of the large and small wheels sounded through the day and evening. The linen was of remarkable excellence.

With the exception of the frequently seen grist-mills, saw-mills and an occasional fulling-mill the aggregate amount of whose manufactured products did not generally exceed the demands of the several neighborhoods in which they were respectively situated, there were no manufactories of any kind within the county. Blacksmiths, wheelwrights, masons, carpenters, tailors, shoemakers and storekeepers on the roadside, and the tavernkeepers on the corners were very often farmers on a small scale.

Continental currency was first wampum * or sewant, which was commonly measured by spans, and the Indians in their traffic with the Dutch always chose as traders those men who could cover the greatest length between finger and thumb. The wampum was counterfeited in time, imitations being made in Europe of porcelain, but this base article could not impose on the Indians. Beaver skins were the next fiat money of the day. It was divided into "whole beavers," and "half beavers," the former being rated at about three dollars. The little Dutch money that was in circulation was known as Hollands. The relative value of sewant, beavers and silver money was a matter of legislation.

Smugglers in New York harbor, and for a long distance up the Hudson would bring their cargoes to the numerous secure nooks on the river shore in Westchester County, and when the contraband goods were once unloaded and run into the back country, they might defy detection. The smugglers by their illicit trade stocked the bars of tapsters, and the cellars of the manorial lords with wines, etc., and furnished the Indians and slaves with cheap liquor, the drinking of which resulted in "calamities." The fine fixed in 1656 was for the first offence, five hundred guilders, and for the second the forfeiture of the "barque, yacht, boat, or canoe," whose owner attempted to evade the customs officers.

How and where the people of Philipsburgh and Lower Yonkers (the Yonkers Plantation or Precinct) worshipped during the Philipse period (1672–1775) is rehearsed in this volume in the chapter on the Yonkers churches. It will suffice to record here that no church was built in Philipsburgh until 1752–53. The voice of public praise and prayer was heard at first in the dwelling house of the pioneer or in a barn. Governor Nicolls took cognizance of the neglect of worship in the colony, and in 1665 summoned delegates to a general meeting at Hempstead, Long Island. "The Duke's Laws" were promulgated. They ordered among other things that a church capable of accommodating two hundred persons should be built in the most convenient place in each parish, and that only ordained Protestant ministers be permitted to officiate. These laws were in operation until the first Provincial Assembly in 1683. In 1684 Mr. Warham Mather, a religious teacher, was chosen at a town meeting to be minister for a year, Westchester, Eastchester and Yonkers uniting in his support. The Assembly of 1691 passed for the County "An Act for settling a ministry and raising a maintenance for them in Westchester County." This and other acts were sent to Parliament for approval. Colonel Heathcote wrote: "When I first arrived in the Province, (1692) I found it (Westchester County) the most heathenish country I ever saw in my whole life which called themselves Christians." He ordered the captains to assemble all the companies and acquaint them that in case they would not in every town agree among themselves to appoint readers and pass the Sabbath in the best manner they could till such times as they could be better provided, that they should every Sunday call the companies under arms and spend the day in exercise. In 1693 the County Court of Sessions, on account of great disorders and debaucheries committed on the Lord's day ordered that in every town "for want of an able minister," the inhabitants should employ a reader "to read out of good books two sermons every Lord's day," and that "noe person shall sitt tippling in a public ordenary on the Lord's day." In 1701 the Society for the Propagation of the Gospel in Foreign Parts was incorporated in England by royal charter of King William III. The Church of England missionaries in

---

* It is a fact of interest that as late as the summer of 1831 several bushels of wampum were sent from Babylon, Long Island, to be used by the Indians of the Western Territories for the purpose of conventions and treaties.

Westchester County were men who loved God and their brother men. How faithfully they labored amid discouragements and how much good they accomplished is a part of the history of Philipsburgh and other portions of the county. Bolton's "History of the Church in Westchester County" contains a more complete record than space in this volume provides. One of those faithful missionaries, the Rev. John Bartow, wrote from Westchester, in 1706, to the Secretary of the Missionary Society: " Sir—My great business is to plant the Church of England among prejudiced, poor, and irreligious people, who are more apt to receive than to give, who think it a hardship to pay their dues; and we dare not use the law for fear of bringing odium on the Church, and on all occasions expect to be civilly treated by the minister. My task is greater than I can bear. I will hold out as long as I can with submission to the divine will, who feedeth the fowls of the air, trusting He will still feed me, by your means, when you come to be sensible of our wants." In 1711 the Rev. John Bartow wrote from Westchester, which was then the county seat and principal village: "The inhabitants of our Parish live scattered and dispersed up and down the woods, so that many cannot repair constantly to the church, by reason of their great distance from it." The "Parish" referred to included then the more recent towns of Westchester, West Farms, Morrisania, Kingsbridge, Yonkers, Eastchester, Pelham and New Rochelle.

An historian writes, "Certain it is that no class of persons contributed more to influence the people of this county (Westchester) during its colonial existence than the clergy of the various religious societies. The Connecticut Congregationalists, the Huguenot, the Reformed Dutch and the Church of England ministers, served in their presence and labor not merely to supply the religious wants, but to counteract the lowering tendency of the situation and circumstances of the new settler. Whenever any demoralization appeared for the time, we can easily trace it to the absence of this exalted power for the common good."

It was during the rectorship of one of the Church of England missionaries, the Rev. Thomas Standard, M. A., M. D., that the first Yonkers church was built (1752-53). The first Methodist society of the Wesleyan Methodists formed in this country was in New York City, the second in Ashgrove, Washington County, and the third in New Rochelle. In 1740, George Whitfield visited and preached in Rye, N. Y. It would seem that there was an organized Methodist society in White Plains as early as 1741–43. In 1771 the Rev. Joseph Pilmoor, one of John Wesley's missionaries, then stationed in New York, advocated Methodism as he spoke to the people of New Rochelle, and at the beginning of the next century "the powerful appeals made to the hearts and consciences of the people by the itinerant preachers of Methodism dealt the infidelity of the Thomas Paine type a blow from which it has never recovered."

Francis Asbury, afterwards bishop, preached in 1771 at Rye and neighboring points. One of the places in which he preached was Tuckahoe, Yonkers, and a Methodist society was formed there in 1771. (That was ten years before Sabbath Schools were established in England.) The New Rochelle circuit was not formed until 1787, and in 1797 the First Methodist Church of Yonkers was organized at Tuckahoe (incorporated 1855), and is there to-day. It will be noted that the formation of the New Rochelle circuit and the organization of the Methodist Church at Tuckahoe occurred a few years after the close of the Philipse period (1672–1775).

The Rev. James Wetmore, a Church of England missionary, writing from Rye in 1727 or 1728, speaks about there being nearly one hundred negroes in the parish, some of whose masters would not allow them to be instructed and others of whom would not allow them to be baptized, so that there was only one negro in the parish baptized. He adds, "I had two negroes of my own which I baptized, but I have lately sold them out of the parish, and I have another which I have instructed, and design to baptize."

As to the Quakers, numbers of them were east and north of Yonkers. The persecutions of Quakers in New England had caused them to look to the Dutch for protection. They had settled on Long Island. Flushing, L. I., was their headquarters. John Harrison, of Flushing, had purchased from the Indians in what is now Westchester County, a tract about nine miles long and nearly three broad. A strong Quaker element came from the older settlements on Long Island up through Harrison's purchase, and gave character to the early settlements in some parts of the county—a character which still remains. "The Dutch who had settled along the Hudson River and the English who occupied the towns along the Connecticut border, entertained no very friendly feelings for each other. Their enmity and jealousies kept them apart, and on this account, a district of considerable width running north and south between them had remained comparatively unoccupied. Into this the Quakers rapidly pushed, purchasing the lands from those who had obtained titles therefor. The line of settlement ran through the present towns of Harrison, North Castle, New Castle, Yorktown, Lewisburgh and North Salem, and through Putnam, Dutchess and Columbia Counties. For a time the Quakers in the town of Harrison and several other towns constituted the majority of inhabitants. Being so near to Philipsburgh and Lower Yonkers, their influence must have been felt, and some of them doubtless became residents.

As to the Roman Catholics, it is said that the first mass in Westchester County was said at the house of Dominick Lynch, on Throgg's Point, in the town of Westchester. He was a prominent man during the Revolution. This mass was probably said after the Revolutionary War, and therefore little is to be recorded of Roman Catholic influence in "the Yonkers" during the period under review. The "Duke's Laws," promulgated in 1665, reveal the fact that the Government during the Philipse period was not in sympathy with the Romanists. One clause in those laws is that "no minister shall be admitted to officiate within the Government but such as shall produce testimonials to the Governor that he received ordination from some Protestant bishop."

During the Philipse period the feeling between differing Protestant sects was by no means fraternal. The Rev. James Wetmore wrote in 1741, that some of his members were "corrupted with the wild enthusiasm of this new sect." He referred to "this new Methodism, or rather downright distraction in the shape it now appears among the itinerant sectaries." In 1743 he complains that the people are unsettled in their principles, and go after all sorts of teachers that come in their way, and "many of them are much confused by the straggling Methodist teachers that are continually among us." The Rev. John Walton, a graduate of Yale, went to Rye in 1723, and to White Plains in 1726. He was a Presbyterian, "highly gifted as a preacher, although self-willed and erratic, eloquent and persistent." The Rev. Mr. Wetmore wrote of Walton as "a bold, noisy fellow, with a voluble tongue, drawing the greatest part of the town after him." Mr. Wetmore also wrote: "I find my cares and labors much increased by having two" (probably one at White Plains and the other at Rye) "Independent Methodist teachers settled by that party in my parish, besides exhorters and itinerants, that frequently call people together and instill wild and enthusiastic notions into them. They have made much confusion in the remote parts of my parish, but chiefly among those who were always Dissenters." Two years elapsed and this "wild set" had become organized and had two Independent Methodist "teachers" settled in his parish.

The Presbyterians were also prejudiced against the Methodists in this period. The Rev. Henry Munroe, another Church of England missionary wrote a letter dated, "Philipsburgh, Feb. 1, 1766," in which he says: "The people" (in the manor of Philipsburgh) "are for the most part of Dutch extraction, together with some settlers from New England. Their religion savors much of that of their mother country. Some adhere to the Church of Holland, and have a very good house of worship on Colonel Philipse's estate within twelve miles of my church, others of them are Independents according to the New England plan—indeed to speak more plainly, according to no plan at all—seduced by every kind of doctrine, every wandering and enthusiastic spirit; these have another house of worship about four miles distant from the former. There are likewise some Quakers and several Anabaptists, who give me a good deal of trouble and uneasiness in opposing their erroneous principles with which even some of the members of my congregation are deeply *tinctured*. Besides these there are many of them who profess no religion and have no concern about it. Those that attend divine service constantly and regularly at my church are about twenty families, and though I cannot depend on all these as true and professed members of the Church of England, some of them halting, as if it were between two opinions, yet I must do them the justice to say that they are a good sort of people, and desirous to learn. Many of the other denominations are already so far reconciled to our church as to come frequently to hear me preach, so that my church is often crowded with Dissenters; and I have so far got the better of their prejudices as to prevail with some of them to buy common prayer books and bring their children to be baptized by me, which you know, sir, is not very common among Dissenters."

The Rev. Mr. Wetmore, rector of Rye, in 1730, writes concerning the Quakers: "Where any of them settle, they spare no pains to infect their neighborhood. Where they meet with any encouragement, they hold meetings day after day. Celebrated preachers are procured from a distance, and a 'great fame' is spread before them 'to invite many curiosities. Our people of credit," says he, "will often go to their meetings, especially their great and general meetings," which he thinks are very pernicious and ought to be suppressed. "Swarms of them make frequent visits hither" (Harrison). They "hold their yearly meetings, monthly, quarterly and weekly meetings, *yea, and sometimes daily*." They scatter books all over the parish; and Mr. Wetmore, who is a ready writer, feels constrained to write and print two letters and three dialogues in refutation of their arguments. These he hopes will be of great service to "stop the growth of Quakerism in these parts."

A writer describing the Dutch in New York says: "They were faithful church-goers, who loved their 'kerck' and respected their 'dominie.' An hour-glass which stood on the clerk's desk was to indicate when the sermon, which was expected to be sixty minutes long, should close. When the time came to receive the offering, the deacon went around carrying a long black pole to which was attached a bag. A bell fastened at the end of the pole awakened sleepers. The sexton notified the people of the hour of service by rapping at their doors with his ivory-headed cane and calling out, 'Church-time!'" Each family compensated him for this service by paying two shillings a year. It was he who carried to the clerk all written requests for the prayers of the congregation. "The clerk had a long rod, slit at the end, into which he inserted the note and handed it up to the minister, who occupied a very high pulpit, in the shape of a half globe, raised on the top of a demi-column, and canopied with a sounding-board. The minister wore a black silk mantle, a cocked hat and a neck-band, with linen cambric 'beffy' on his breast, for cravats were then uncanonical." *

The old church at Sleepy Hollow is the one to which the Rev. Henry Munroe referred when writing from Philipsburgh in 1766. He speaks of it as a "good house of worship on Colonel Philipse's estate, within twelve miles of my church." The Dutch-speaking people of Philipsburgh attended the old church at Sleepy Hollow for many years. This fact, and the fact that the first lord of the manor built the church, and that in recent times Washington Irving's polished pen has so charmingly described it, insures the deep interest of the Yonkers citizens in the venerable building, probably the oldest church building in the State of New York. The reader will find in the Rev. Dr. Allen's lecture, descriptions of the small, thin and yellow bricks brought from Holland to construct it; the thick walls, the small windows, seven feet from the floor, and guarded by heavy iron cross-bars, as a protection from Indians or other enemies; the old vane (bearing the monogram V̄⁻) on the eastern end of the church, the bell, the belfry, the Communion service and baptismal bowl, the hard oak benches on which the sturdy Dutchmen sat one or two hours, and listened to sound sermons in Dutch, the elevated seats (called thrones) on either side of the pulpit for the Philipses, the church gallery where the legendary character, Ichabod Crane, led the band of rustic singers, the phebe birds, and one of them perching on the sounding-board and looking down at the dominie, etc., etc. All these, and many more interesting sentences, may be found in Dr. Allen's lecture.

ST. JOHN'S CHURCH, CONSECRATED, 1792.
BUILT, 1752-52; WOOD WORK BURNED, 1791; RESTORED IN ORIGINAL FORM (EXCEPT STEEPLE), 1792; STEEPLE REBUILT, 1804.

Educational facilities were slender while the county was sparsely settled. "The mother was the teacher and the Bible the text-book." The catechism was taught in Dutch. The Venerable Society for the Propagation of the Gospel in Foreign Parts founded a school in 1713. Their abstracts say: "To a schoolmaster at Yonkers, in the province of New York, where there is a large congregation of Dutch and English, for instructing the younger sort of both nations in the Catechism and Liturgy, £5 per annum upon producing a certificate of his teaching thirty children that summer." In 1719 Mr. Jones was allowed fifty shillings "for teaching children to read at Mile Square."

In 1766 the Rev. Henry Munroe wrote from Philipsburgh to the Secretary of the Missionary Society requesting him to send the usual number of books for the mission library, the number already received being inconsiderable. Books were few in the early days, and there was little to develop literary taste;

---

* The reader who desires to know about other church customs in the colony during the Philipse period is referred to the Chapter on Manners and Customs in Scharf's "Westchester County." The Rev. Dr. John K. Allen, the pastor of the Reformed Church at Tarrytown, delivered, in 1884, a lecture on "The Legendary History of the Old Dutch Church of Sleepy Hollow." An extract from this very instructive and entertaining lecture may be found on pages 298, 299 and 300 of Vol. II., Scharf's "Westchester County."

but the Dutch were not illiterate. Westchester County had several very good schools, principally under the direction of some of the Huguenot immigrants, who were gentlemen of culture and not accustomed to agricultural pursuits. In 1763 the Rev. John P. Tetard purchased a farm of sixty acres in Lower Yonkers, near King's Bridge, lying on the old Boston road, to which he removed about three years later. In 1772 he opened there a French boarding school, probably the first in New York, where, besides French, he taught "the most useful sciences, such as geography, the doctrine of the spheres, ancient and modern history, etc." (Tetard's Hill was fortified during the Revolutionary War.)

Evidently some of the people of the colonies loved learning during the Philipse period of Yonkers history. Previous to the Revolution among the colleges founded were Harvard (1636), William and Mary (1692), Yale (1700), Princeton (1746), Pennsylvania University (1749), Kings, Columbia (1754), Brown (1764), Queens, Rutgers (1770), Dartmouth (1769), Hampden and Sidney (1775). In 1764 the first medical college was founded at Philadelphia. In the times preceding the Revolution there was not to be found in all New England, an adult born in the country who could not read and write, so complete and universal were the means of instruction.

In 1683, the New York Province, the Governor, Council and representatives (the first legislature of New York which sat in the Hall of Fort James, formerly Fort Amsterdam) enacted that the Province of New York "bee divided into twelve Countyes," one of which was Westchester. Eight of the original counties were east of the Hudson and four west. The acts of the Assembly of 1683 were transmitted for the approbation of the Duke of York, but he did not return the approving papers. He ascended the throne as James II., and merged the provinces north of the Delaware into one province. The act relating to the counties was passed again in 1691. Westchester was represented in the first legislative assembly of the colony which met in 1691. From 1683 to 1759 the town of Westchester was the shire town of the County. The New York *Post Boy* of February 13, 1758, reports the burning of the Court House there. The last court there was held November 6, 1759.

It will be perceived from the foregoing history of the acts of the Assembly that the territory first called Kekeshick and Nepperhaem, then "Colen-Donck" or "De Jonkheers" ("the Yonkers") and then Philipsburgh in Yorkshire, a part of "the North Riding on the Maine" came to be Philipsburgh, Westchester County. It so continued to be known until after the Revolution. It may be that Lower Yonkers and Philipsburgh (or the Lower Mills of Philipsburgh) were regarded as parts of "the Yonkers." The fact that there was a Lower Yonkers, may perhaps justify the conclusion that Philipsburgh was regarded as Upper Yonkers, and that both Lower Yonkers and Philipsburgh were included in "the Yonkers." A rare map engraved and published according to Act of Parliament, October 10, 1776, and published in America for the first time in 1892 designates "Younkers" as located at the mouth of the Nepperhan where, at that time, there was a fort.

At the beginning of the Philipse period any newspaper which the inhabitants of Philipsburgh or the Yonkers precinct may have received, came from England or other foreign country. The first American newspaper was not published until 1690, when a sheet was issued in Boston. It was proposed to publish it monthly, but it was immediately suppressed by the authorities. The Boston *News Letter* was published in 1704. *The New York Gazette*, the first paper issued in New York City was published in 1725 by William Bradford (father of Andrew Bradford, who in 1719 had begun to publish *The American Weekly Mercurie* in Philadelphia). *The New York Gazette* was a weekly printed on a half sheet of foolscap with large and worn type. *The New York Journal and Register* (the first New York daily) was not published until after the Revolution. Its first number appeared in 1788.

In 1754 four newspapers were published in Boston, two in New York, two in Philadelphia, and one, the *Virginia Gazette*, at Williamsburgh, Va. It was first issued by William Parks who had previously published for nine years the *Maryland Gazette*, at Annapolis, Holt's *New York Gazette*, Gaine's *New York Gazette and Mercury*, the *New York Post Boy*, and Rivington's *New York Gazetteer* were the newspapers which during the latter part of this period were read in the houses in Philipsburgh. Westchester County advertisements are found in the New York papers of those times. The *New York Post Boy*, March 14, 1765, announces that "last week was killed at Morrisania at the farm of Lewis Morris, Esq., in the county of Westchester, where it was reared, an ox of six years old, that weighed nineteen hundred and forty-seven pounds." The following is an advertisement of an earlier date (March 23, 1747): "Stolen, on Sunday night, the 8th of March, out of the estate of John Ryder, at Philipseborough, in the county of Westchester, a large brown horse, about fifteen hands high, has a small star on his forehead and goes narrow with his hams behind. He is branded in several places, but not very plain, on his foreshoulder with I. H., and on his left thigh with J. R. Whosoever takes up the said horse and brings him to his said owner shall have five pounds reward and all reasonable charges paid by John Ryder."

In the New York papers of the period are also found advertisements appertaining to the country farms to be disposed of, runaway slaves to be recovered, stage lines started, wrecked vessels that would be restored, prices of merchandise, etc.

The papers from abroad brought tidings of events in the reign of the monarchs of whom the citizens of Philipsburgh and Lower Yonkers were subjects, for it will be remembered that when the flag of Holland was lowered from the Fort Amsterdam flag-staff, and the banner of Great Britain unfurled, Colen-Donck or De Jonkheers, came under the sway of the latter government. Its rulers were Charles II., James II., William III. and Mary, William III., Anne, George I., George II. and George III. The British flag floated over Colen-Donck, and over Lower Yonkers and Philipsburgh, as the tracts were called in the Philipse period. In 1673, just after Frederick Philipse became owner of the territory within the boundaries of the present Yonkers, the Dutch retook New York, but in the next year a treaty between England and Holland gave it over to England. The British government was represented in the colony by Nicolls, Lovelace, Andros, and a number of other men of influence. The last in the line was Governor Tyron, who was in New York City at the beginning of the Revolutionary War.

One of the Acts which interested the Philipsburgh people was that of 1694, which directed that two fairs should be held in the county, the first to be "kept" at Westchester in May, and the second to be "kept" at Rye in October, each yearly, and to be "held for four days inclusive, and no longer." Courts were held on each of the days of the fairs. The fairs were not exhibitions for prizes like modern fairs, but places for trade. Cattle, horses, grains, provisions, etc., were exposed for sale or barter. Great numbers attended, "including the county politicians, who, of course, were present as their successors are now, solely for the good of their country." Such fairs had been held from time immemorial in England. Horse racing on Rye flats was a favorite pastime for many years during this period.

A letter dated Westchester, October 29, 1733, and published in the New York *Weekly Journal*, at that time, describes an election of a representative from the county of Westchester. It records that the electors came on horseback. Those constituting one company came in the following order, "First rode two trumpeters and three violins; next four of the principal freeholders, one of which carried a banner on one side of which was affixed in gold capitals: 'King George,' and on the other in golden capitals, 'Liberty and Law;' next followed the candidate, Lewis Morris, Esq., late chief justice of this province, then two colors; and at sunrising they entered upon the green of Eastchester, the place of election, followed by above three hundred horse of the principal freeholders of the county." They had started from New Rochelle, where they had spent the night. Those who were unable to find shelter under roof sat till daylight by a large fire in the street.

"About eleven o'clock appeared the candidate for the other side, William Forster, Esq., schoolmaster, appointed by the Society for the Propagation of the Gospel. . . . Next him came two ensigns, borne by two of the freeholders, then followed the Hon. James De Lancey, Esq., chief justice of the province of New York, and the Hon. Frederick Philipse, Esq., second judge of the said province and baron of the exchequer, attended by about three hundred and seventy horse of the freeholders and friends of the said Forster and the two judges. They entered the green on the east side, and riding twice round it their word was 'No land tax.' . . . About an hour after, the high sheriff came to town finely mounted, the housings and holstercups being scarlet, richly laced with silver. Upon his approach the electors on both sides went into the green, where they, after having read his majesty's writ, bid the electors proceed to the choice, which they did." Lewis Morris, Esq., was elected.

During this period the people of "the Yonkers" were interested not only in local politics, but in Indian wars, French wars, and political struggles against the English government. They heard, with sympathy for the New Englanders, of the King Philip war (1675) which threatened the extermination of the European population in New England. It was during this war that there were fears in "the North Riding on the Maine, Yorkshire," of an Indian outbreak, and men were summoned to aid in the fortifications and defense of Fordham. The people of Philipsburgh heard also with great interest reports of the war between southern Indians and the whites. Toward the close of the seventeenth century, they were greatly interested in the northern campaign, for the hostile Indians on the northern and western frontiers began to receive powerful aid and encouragement from the French in Canada, who, when the mother country was at war with England, carried on hostilities with the English colonies and frequently accompanied by their savage allies made destructive inroads into New England and New York. For instance, in 1690, a party from Montreal burned Schenectady, New York. After the event an expedition was sent against the French and the Indians, and doubtless Westchester County men, and perhaps citizens of Philipsburgh were among the troops. In 1754 the long conflict, known as the French and Indian war began, and the sense of common danger led the colonists to make a united effort. The French who had colonized Canada and the interior of the continent were determined to divide the continent and take the larger portion for France and for Catholicism. Doubtless the Jesuit missionaries counseled this. It was the French and Indian war which brought George Washington, a young Virginia surveyor, into prominence. Braddock's defeat and the rescue of his army shook the confidence of the people in the prowess of the British soldiery and gave Washington a hold on popular esteem which was never afterward shaken. How the English officers at first under-estimated those of the colonies may be inferred from the record that when Washington ventured to suggest that the troops be moved with caution, Braddock flew into a passion, stode up and down his tent, and said that it was high times when Colonel Buckskin could teach a British general how to fight. It will be remembered that one of Braddock's aids was Col. Roger Morris, who married Mary Philipse, and whose wedding was in Manor Hall. With what sorrow the people of Philipsburgh must have read of the defeat and death of the English general. They were furnished with new themes for conversation when tidings came of the ruin of Acadia (the event upon which Longfellow based his poem Evangeline), and of battles in Canada and on Lake George. Upon their tongues were such names as Abercrombie, Montcalm, Amherst, Howe, Wolfe, Montgomery, Prideaux, Pontiac, Arnold and Washington. The seven years of war made it necessary to send soldiers from Westchester County, as well as from more northern counties. The rolls of Westchester County indicate how largely the county contributed to swell the armies sent forth to the several campaigns. A well-organized militia force existed. As the fortunes of the several battles, sieges and marches varied, the firesides of the country homes were illumined or darkened. When, for example, the capitulation of Fort William Henry at Lake George in August, 1757, was reported (seven officers and fifty men of the garrison, all New Yorkers, thereby becoming prisoners of war) a deep thrill of indignation stirred every breast, but the feeling was more intense when the word came that the French General Montcalm, under his own eyes and in the face of about three thousand of his regular troops, suffered his Indian allies to rob and strip officers as well as men of all they had, and left most of them naked." These wars were the prelude to the American Revolution. They were a training school for both officers and men. With what joy must the people of Philipsburgh have heard in 1759 that the French had surrendered Niagara. What must have been their pleasure when Montreal was surrendered in 1760, and Canada in 1763. By the treaty of peace made at Paris in 1763, all the French possessions in North America eastward to the Mississippi from its source, to the river Iberville, and thence through Lakes Maurepas and Pontchartrain to the Gulf of Mexico, were surrendered to Great Britain. The French were far-sighted. When the treaty was signed a French statesman said, "There now, we have arranged matters for an American rebellion in which England will lose her empire of the west." They anticipated that the colonies would become strong and would renounce their allegiance to the crown. England feared such a result. More than once it was proposed in Parliament to re-cede Canada to France in order to check the growth of the American states.

If England had legislated for the interests of the colonies, the people might have continued loyal, for they had a warm attachment to the crown; but they were exasperated by the course pursued by the home government.

Before the Revolutionary War began, one event caused great excitement in Philipsburgh. Lawlessness, possibly the outcome of the wars, was displayed in Westchester County. In May, 1765, five hundred men—country levelers they were called—at first reported to be two thousand strong, marched down to Kingsbridge (Lower Yonkers) and sent into town the threat to Mr. Van Cortlandt that unless he would give them a grant forever of his lands they would enter the city and pull down his house and also one belonging to Mr. Lambert Moore. The ringleaders were arrested and condemned.

The trade and manufactures of the colonies were systematically restricted for the selfish benefit of England; but though these oppressive enactments were heavily felt by the colonists, they made no resistance so long as the imperial authority confined itself to measures which, however harsh or injurious, were not clearly unconstitutional. But in 1761 parliament authorized sheriffs and officers of the customs to use writs of assistance, or general search warrants, which empowered them to enter stores and private dwellings and search for merchandise which it was suspected had not paid duty. It was this which caused James Otis in Massachusetts to vigorously protest. Two years later Patrick Henry in Virginia defended that colony. The spirit of freedom continually manifested itself. Early in 1776 a serious affray occurred in New York. The soldiers wantonly cut down the liberty pole which had stood for several years in the park. A conflict ensued in which the people came out best. Another pole was erected in the northern part of the city.

It was at length decided to tax the colonies against all their protests. The French and Indian wars had left a heavy burden upon Great Britain, which parliament attempted to shift to the shoulders of the colonies. The Stamp Act passed the House of Commons in 1765. The hated stamps reached New York later than the other colonies. They were brought over in the ship Edward, which arrived on October 23, 1765, but the people openly resisted their distribution by violence. In 1766 the act was repealed, and there were outbursts of popular rejoicing. Parliament, however, maintained the principle that it had a right to tax the colonies, and in 1767 passed an act imposing duties on tea, glass and paper. Indignation was again aroused, and yet we read of the people in New York City firing guns and crackers on June 4, 1768, and illuminating the town on the king's birthday. After 1774 the people ignored the "imperial parliament." They acknowledged the king, but insisted that if he wanted money from his American dominions, he had to get it, as he always had got it, by applying to the Assembly of the colony, through the Governor, for a grant. In the new seats of the race, as in the old, an Englishman was to be taxed only by his own representatives.

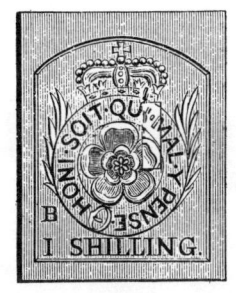

A STAMP.

New York was the first to recommend a non-importation of English merchandise as a measure of retaliation against Great Britain. The people were now self-dependent. If they wished more cloth, they could raise more sheep and sow more flax-seed. They used sassafras, balm and sage in the place of tea and patriotically declared that it was more wholesome. They made women's shoes cheaper and better than in England. Cards appeared recommending that no true friend of his country should buy or import English goods. New York was the first to invite a general conference of all the colonies. There must have been excitement in Philipsburgh when the tea-laden, storm-shattered Nancy was turned back to Europe by the Committee which took possession of her at Sandy Hook, without permitting her to enter the harbor, and when the cargo of the London had been overhauled in Whitehall slip, and eighteen chests of tea which had been concealed in her hold were emptied into the East River. Dawson, the painstaking historian (once editor of the Yonkers *Gazette*) claims that this act was more significant than the Boston "tea-party," because it was done in open day by undisguised citizens. Space will not permit the record of many more of the interesting incidents of the period. The patriot rejoices to read "Freeman's" masterly papers in Holt's *New York Gazette*, of the distribution by post-riders of the *Constitutional Courant* secretly printed in New Jersey and bearing as a headpiece the picture of a severed snake, of the songs written for the Sons of Liberty, of the mob in New York City, of the arrival of the hated stamps, and the vessels at New York and Philadelphia lowering their colors to half-mast, and the bells of Philadelphia tolling, of the "Stamp Act Congress in New York," of gentlemen wearing homespun clothes, for the merchants refused to buy goods in England until the Stamp Act was repealed, of the distribution of manuscript placards, of the commander of the fort in New York being reported to have said that he would "cram the stamps down their throats with the end of his sword," and the Sons of Liberty threatening to storm the fort and burn the stamps, of the mob hanging Governor Colden in effigy, of the celebration of Guy Fawkes day in New York, "a dangerous anniversary for a revolutionary assemblage," of the discovery of packages of stamps in a vessel at the dock in New York, and burning them in tar barrels, of the soldiers cutting down the "Tree of Liberty" in New York, and the citizens throwing brickbats at them and then erecting another liberty pole on the same day, of a collision between soldiers and citizens in New York City, January, 1770, when one citizen was killed, three wounded and a large number injured. This is claimed to have been the first conflict of the war of the American Revolution. All these events must have been the themes of excited conversation in Philipsburgh and Lower Yonkers. New York at the time had about 25,000 inhabitants and what interested its citizens was also of interest to the country. Nor were denunciations of oppression confined to the city. An ardent patriot, for example, addressed "the Knaves and Fools in the town of Rye," asking the "Fools" what in the world could have put it into their heads that it were better for them to have their "faces blackened and be negroes and beasts of burden for the people of England," than to live and die like their forefathers in a state of freedom. "I really could not have believed," he adds, "that there

A STAMP.

A STAMP.

had been so many *asses* in all America as there appears to be in your little paltry town. Instead of *Rye Town*, let it hereafter be called *Simple Town*. It seems you are such *geese* as not to know when you are *oppressed* and when you are not."

In March, 1775, the Committee of Inspection in New York ordered that circular letters be written to all the counties* in the colony . . . requesting them to elect deputies to meet in provincial convention at the city of New York on April 20th of that year, for the *sole* purpose of appointing delegates to represent the colony in the next congress, to be held at Philadelphia on May 10th. Thereupon several Westchester County citizens, among whom Philipsburgh and Lower Yonkers are not reported to have been represented, met at White Plains to devise means "of taking the sense of the county upon the subject."

These citizens made arrangements to notify the principal Freeholders of the different towns and districts of the county that a meeting would be held on April 11, 1775, in the court house at White Plains at 10 o'clock to consider the most proper method of taking the sense of the Freeholders of the county upon the expediency of choosing deputies. The Conservatives or Tories also sent out a circular. They were willing to abide by what they considered were the loyal and judicious measures already taken by their worthy representatives in the General Assembly of the Province for a redress of American grievances.

White Plains was a little village scattered along the wide-spread Post-road. The county court house was formerly located in the town of Westchester. At this time the court house was in White Plains, on the west side of the stage road to New York. Captain Hatfield kept a tavern in White Plains. The Tories met there. The tavern in which the Whigs met was probably kept by Isaac Oakley. The Whigs at noon quietly crossed the old Post-road and reassembled at the court house. They organized a meeting and appointed Colonel Lewis Morris, chairman.

Having obtained information that the Whigs were assembled at the court house, the Tories walked down from their tavern. It is said that the two men who walked at the head of the Tories on their way to the court house were Isaac Wilkins of the borough of Westchester and Frederick Philipse of the Manor of Philipsburgh. Both of these men were members of the General Assembly of the colony. It was Isaac Wilkins who wrote for the press the papers which were published over the *nom de plume*, A. W. Farmer (A Westchester Farmer). He was the spokesman for the Tories and said that the meeting was unlawfully called and for unlawful purposes. He declared that they (the Tories) did not intend to contest the matter by a poll, for that would tacitly acknowledge the authority which had summoned them thither, but that they were present to protest against such disorderly proceedings and show their detestation of all unlawful committees and congresses. They also declared their determined resolution to "continue steadfast in their allegiance to their gracious and merciful sovereign, King George the Third, to submit to lawful authority, and to abide by and support the only true representatives of the People of this colony, the General Assembly." They then gave three cheers, and returned to Captain Hatfield's tavern, singing as they went, with a loyal enthusiasm, the grand and animating song of

"God save great George, our King,
Long live our noble King!" etc.

The Whigs who remained at the court house unanimously voted to send deputies. When their business was transacted "they gave three huzzas for our gracious sovereign," and quietly dispersed. The records indicate that the two taverns that day did a great business in selling liquor.

Colonel Lewis Morris, the chairman, prepared an official narrative of the origin of the meeting, and of its proceedings, which was published. Those who protested against the meeting having returned to Hatfield's tavern, drew up and signed a declaration and protest in which they expressed their "honest abhorrence of all unlawful congresses and committees," and announced their determination, at the hazard of their lives and properties, to support the King and the Constitution. They also expressed their confidence in the General Assembly, which they believed would guard their rights. That declaration was signed by Frederick Philipse, Isaac Wilkins, the Rev. Luke Babcock, and over three hundred more. Colonel Morris alleged that many of the Tories who signed the declaration were tenants, and that many were under age, and not entitled to vote. The declaration, with names of the signers, was published in *Rivington's New York Gazetteer*, and is dated April 13, 1775. That was six days before the shots fired at Lexington and Concord set the whole country ablaze. Soon an army of twenty thousand patriots gathered around Boston, threatening "to drive Gage and the British into the sea."

* At the time of the Revolution there were fourteen counties in New York, the most westerly of which lay on the sides of the Mohawk, about forty miles from Albany. The inhabitants at this time were Dutch, French, English, Scotch and Irish.

CHAPTER VII.

"THE YONKERS" DURING THE REVOLUTION. 1775–1783.

" What constitutes a state ?
. . . .
Men who their duties know,
But know their rights, and knowing, dare maintain."

"Lay down the axe, fling by the spade,
  Leave in its track the toiling plough.
The rifle and the bayonet blade
  For arms like yours were fitter now;
And let the hands that ply the pen
  Quit the light task and learn to wield
The horseman's crooked brand, and rein
  The charger on the battlefield."

FIERCE flames leaped with vindictive swiftness from the mouths of Continental muskets at Lexington, Mass., April 19, 1775. There "the embattled farmers fired the shot which was heard round the world." It was a volley like the lightning flash and the startling thunder clap in the heavens, where lurid clouds have long been gathering with angry mutterings. The herald who spurred his horse along the Old Boston Road to New York, carried the news of the fray at Lexington and Concord. Dusty and travel-stained, he arrived in New York at noon, April 23, 1775. The tidings, shouted at the threshold along the historic highway, kindled a flame of patriotic zeal. In the farmhouses, country stores, blacksmith shops and taverns of Lower Yonkers and Philipsburgh, the excited people conversed about the fight and its probable consequences. Comments were made by the Philipses in their manor hall on the banks of the Nepperhan, by the Van Cortlandts in their mansion at Van Cortlandt Mills, and by all the Whigs and Tories living in humbler dwellings. A few days later the people within "the Yonkers" were conversing about large numbers of New York citizens aiding to unload at King's Bridge and the near hills upward of five-score cannon, which for security had been carted out of the city. Tidings of the capture of Ticonderoga increased excitement. It was a fortress which had cost Great Britain eight million pounds sterling, and was "the key of the gateway of Canada." The report of the battle of Bunker Hill added new fuel to the fame of patriotic zeal. Then came tidings from Philadelphia where the Continental congress had appointed George Washington, of Virginia, commander-in-chief of the army. The patriot fathers who lived in Philipsburgh and Lower Yonkers, and whose sacred dust now consecrates the soil, mourned the death of their countrymen at Lexington, and Concord and Bunker Hill, and determined to battle, if necessary, for the freedom in the defense of which those heroes gave their lives. But many in Westchester County were not in sympathy with the methods the patriots were adopting to obtain redress of wrongs. For example, it is recorded that in the town of Scarsdale only three families were in favor of the patriot cause, and although this may not be strictly true, it suffices to indicate the drift of feeling in that township.

REVOLUTIONARY POWDER-HORN AND CANTEEN.

Most of the people in the county were plain farmers, living quiet lives. The next seven years gave their territory historical prominence, and made its history an important part of the history of the struggle of Americans to erect, among nations, a government of the people, and for the people and by the people. Lower Westchester became the famous "Neutral Ground" and the scene of bitter strife and frightful desolation. "The Yonkers," previous to the Revolution, was comparatively unknown, but to-day, millions of school children and older students of history are reading about Washington's retreat from New York to White Plains, and other movements of the patriot army in Westchester County. "The Yonkers" was one of the first places the enemy occupied when he left Boston for Halifax and returned to the colonial coast. Lower Yonkers, New York City, Long Island and Staten Island were the last places from which the royal army withdrew at the close of the war. The history of unnumbered sections in the United States is of local interest only. The history of "the Yonkers" during the Revolution is of world-wide interest.

Romance has also woven a spell around the region. Sunnyside is only about six miles north of the northern boundary of the town and Sleepy Hollow only a short distance further. Washington Irving makes mention in "Wolfert's Roost," of "the ancient dorp of Yonkers" and of the valley of the Nepperhan "dotted by Dutch farmhouses." He refers to the hills and valleys, . . . "locked in by the mazy windings of the Neperah and the Pocantico." Of skinners and cowboys he writes as those "famous in the heroic annals of Westchester County, the former fought or rather marauded, under the American, and the latter under the British banner, but both in the hurry of their military ardor were apt to err on the safe side and rob friend as well as foe. Neither of them stopped to ask the politics of the horse or cow which they drove into captivity; nor when they wrung the neck of a rooster did they trouble their heads to ascertain whether he were crowing for Congress or King George." James Fenimore Cooper, in his book "The Spy: A Tale of the Neutral Ground," describes "the house of entertainment for man and beast." It was known by its old sign, written in red chalk on a rough board suspended from its gallows-looking posts, as "Elizabeth Flanagan, her hotel." Cooper locates it at the "Four Corners," which are only about six miles north of the northern boundary of Yonkers.

VIEW OF KING'S BRIDGE. FROM AN OLD CUT.

The "Four Corners" are where the road to Unionville crosses the east and west road to Tarrytown. The house was a rendezvous for the American soldiers and particularly, according to Cooper, for the Virginia dragoons under "Major Dunwoodie" and "Captain Lawton." It was at one of their convivial meetings in the "Hotel Flanagan" that Captain Lawton is represented to have sung his song "to a well-known bacchanalian air, several of his comrades helping him through the chorus with a feu or that shook the crazy edifice they were in." It was at the "Four Corners" that Thaddeus Kosciusko fixed his headquarters, when the American army lay encamped in the vicinity.

Yonkers, to which attaches such deep interest by reason of its history, romance and song, is especially inviting to the patriot and student. Bolton, Dawson, Edsall, Morris, Todd, Irving and other writers who have recorded the stirring events of the Revolutionary period, have rendered the city and other portions of the county and the country large service. Their volumes have furnished most of the historical facts recorded on the pages of this chapter.

In May, 1775, the Continental Congress resolved that a Post should be immediately taken and fortified near King's Bridge to prevent communication between New York City and the country being interrupted by land. The maintenance of land communication was all the more important because it was doubtful whether they could prevent the British closing water communication. Only two bridges and those not far apart, connected Manhattan Island with the main land. One of them (King's Bridge), spanning the Spuyten Duyvil Creek, afforded access from Manhattan Island on the south to Lower Yonkers on the north. The other (the Free Bridge), over the Harlem River, afforded access from Manhattan Island on the west to the main land (then a part of Westchester County) on the east. The Albany and Boston roads part at King's Bridge.

The Continental Congress on May 25th also resolved that experienced men shall be immediately sent to examine the Hudson River in order to discover where "it will be most advisable and proper to obstruct navigation." They hoped by obstructing the river, and by fortifying the Highlands on both sides of the Hudson, to prevent the enemy controlling* the river. Subsequently a *chevaux-de-frise* was constructed. It extended from a point on the east shore, near Fort Washington (just south of Yonkers), to a point on the west shore a little north of Fort Constitution (Fort Lee). A short distance north of Fort Constitution there was a redoubt at the western terminus of the obstruction.

The Continental Congress also resolved that the militia of New York colony (not to exceed three thousand) should be armed and trained, and in constant readiness to act at a moment's warning. They were to serve until the end of the year 1775. One of the regiments of this force was the Fourth of Duchess. The colonel was James Holmes of Bedford, an experienced soldier of the former war. Philip Van Courtland was the lieutenant-colonel. Three of the ten companies of this regiment were largely from Westchester County. A number of these militiamen were subsequently in service at Ticonderoga, and some are said to have served in Canada.

Another resolution of the Continental Congress was that the Provincial Congress of New York should determine the number of men sufficient to occupy several designated Posts in Lower Yonkers. When these resolutions were received on May 29th by the Provincial Congress, that portion of them which directed the fortification of King's Bridge was referred to a committee of which Colonel James Van Cortlandt was a member. He had been elected a deputy to the Provincial Congress by a Westchester County committee in which Lower Yonkers was represented by Frederick Van Cortlandt. The committee appointed to view the ground near the bridge reported on June 3rd, favoring a Post for three hundred men on the hill adjoining Hyatt's tavern, which stood on Manhattan Island, west of the Free Bridge and near the King's Bridge road. Commanding points on Tippett's and Tetard's Hills in Lower Yonkers were suggested for additional works. At the places indicated forts were afterwards erected by the Americans, and when captured by the British were strengthened and garrisoned by them for many years.

The Provincial Congress of New York, complying with the resolution of the Continental Congress, requiring a complete reorganization of the militia of the colony, adopted a "Military Bill." It provided that every portion of the colony should be divided into districts or beats, each district to include as nearly as possible eighty-three men and boys capable of bearing arms. The ages of those liable to military duty ranged from sixteen to sixty. One-quarter of the entire force was to be organized as minute-men. The companies were to be formed into regiments and the regiments into brigades. All were to be commanded by a major-general, who should be appointed and commissioned by the Provincial Congress. Every man between the ages of sixteen and fifty was to provide himself with a musket and bayonet, a sword, a tomahawk, a cartridge-box to contain twenty-three rounds of cartridges, a knapsack, one pound of gunpowder and three pounds of balls. Drills were to take place monthly. Upon those who refused to respect these enactments heavy penalties were to be imposed. The county of Westchester furnished guides as well as militiamen. There are, however, records of only four companies of Westchester County minute-men—one at Poundridge and Lower Salem, two at Bedford, and one (nineteen men) at White Plains. It is not surprising that the trying circumstances in which the quiet farmers found themselves during the breaking down of the old and strong government, and the upbuilding of a new and experimental government should have resulted in division of sentiment as to the wisdom of the proceedings of the Continental and Provincial Congresses and their various committees, which were empowered to act when congress was not in session.

The Manor of Philipsburgh included six "Districts" or "Beats." The officers chosen by the company in Lower Philipsburgh—the Yonkers of to-day—were Isaac Vermilyea, captain; Israel Honeywell, first-lieutenant; Dennis Lent, second-lieutenant, and Hendrik Odell, ensign. The company at Lower Yonkers held two elections. At the second they elected John Warner, captain; Jacob Post, first-lieutenant; Samuel Lawrence, second-lieutenant, and Isaac Post, ensign. The second election was held because at the first the company had chosen for their captain John Cock, who kept the old tavern

---

*How important the control of the Hudson was considered is shown by the attempt of the enemy to gain it. Before the war closed the British Government planned a great campaign to obtain possession of the river and other waters to the north, in order to sever New England from the other colonies. Burgoyne was to come down from the north, Clinton to move up from New York, and St. Leger, with his Tories and Indians, was to march from Lake Ontario, through the interior of the State to Albany, where the three British generals hoped to eat Christmas dinner together, and rejoice over the fatal blow "Mr. Washington" and other "rebels" would have received, had the plan been successfully carried out. During the Civil War a similar plan was adopted by the Union Army commanders. They sought by army and navy to get possession of the Mississippi River, and thus divide the Confederacy into two parts

on the north side of King's Bridge. He understood military tactics, but the county committee, doubting his loyalty, objected to his holding the captaincy. It was necessary to be watchful.

In August, 1875, the Provincial Congress provided for the punishment of any person found guilty before any city or county committee of attempting to furnish the enemy with provisions, or holding with them a correspondence in order to give them helpful information. It was also enacted that, although "this congress have a tender regard to the freedom of speech, the rights of conscience and personal Liberty, as far as indulgence in these particulars may be consistent with our general security, yet for public security be it

"*Resolved*, That if any person or persons shall hereafter oppose or deny the authority of the Continental, or this Congress, or the Committee of Safety or the Committees of the respective Counties, Cities, Manors, Precincts or Districts of this Colony, or dissuade any person or persons from obeying the recommendations of the Continental, or this Congress, or the Committee of Safety, or the Committees aforesaid, and be thereof convicted, . . . that the committee (which tries the accused) shall cause such offenders to be disarmed, and for the second offence . . . to be committed to close confinement at their respective expense."

If any person was discovered to be enlisted or in arms "against the Liberties of America," he was to be confined in custody. For the second offence the punishment was close confinement and confiscation of estate. This act caused great excitement and aroused intense bitterness. Men armed and organized themselves and established strong patrols for security.

In September, 1775, the Committee of Safety resolved, in order to secure needed weapons for the troops, that all arms fit for use, which were in possession of those who had not signed the General Association in the colony, should be impressed, the owner to be paid the value of the weapon taken from him. Then excitement increased. Some citizens of the county said "that if any came to their houses to take away their arms they would fire upon them." Subsequently the Provincial Congress abrogated this resolution of the Committee.

On the first day of 1776 the distinctive flag of the thirteen united colonies was raised at Washington's headquarters near Boston. It had thirteen stripes of red and white, as now, but had upon its corner the red and white cross which then marked the British flag. When the Declaration of Independence had eliminated the royal element, the crosses in the standard were replaced (1777) by stars as at present.

The second in command of the Continental army was Charles Lee. He came from Boston to put New York City in condition to be defended, if the enemy should attempt to capture it. His line of march through Westchester County was along the well-known Boston Post-road between Byram River and King's Bridge. In January, 1776, the Committee of Safety issued *Instructions for Recruiting Officers*. The pay of the privates was to be five dollars per month. Each was to receive as a bounty, a felt hat, a pair of yarn stockings, and, if they could be procured, a hunting shirt and a blanket, and the men were to provide their own arms. The Committee of Safety directed the Westchester County Committee to prevent barrels of beef and pork being sold and removed from the county. They were of the opinion that the provisions might be needed by the Continental army.

It is evident that while the Whigs were actively making preparations for defense against Howe, should he come from Halifax to New York, the Tories were not idle. At the close of the year 1775, scores of cannon were accumulated near the northern point of Manhattan Island. About fifty were at John Williams'—the Williamsbridge of the present day. Another collection was at King's Bridge, and the third within two hundred and fifty yards of Isaac Valentine's house. They were entirely unguarded, and on the night of January 17, 1776, were spiked or "loaded with stones and other rubbish." The local committee of Westchester County seized a large number of residents of Westchester, Eastchester and Mamaroneck and some residents of Yonkers (probably Lower Yonkers), and subjected them to examination. Among those who were apprehended was a Yonkers schoolmaster. Many were discharged. It was discovered that the rat tail files used for spiking the guns had been purchased by a Mamaroneck man. He and another suspect were imprisoned. In January, 1776, the Committee of Safety agreed to give Jeremiah Allen twenty shillings apiece for clearing and unspiking the whole of the guns, and for removing those at Williams' to Valentine's. He raised them on fires of several cords of wood,

FLAG OF THE THIRTEEN UNITED COLONIES.

kindled day and night to soften the spikes. The guns thus unloaded and unspiked were subsequently mounted on the works erected by the Americans on the hills about King's Bridge. In February, 1776, the skeleton regiment of Westchester County minute-men, Colonel Drake commanding, was ordered to New York, leaving a sufficient guard at the cannon near King's Bridge. In the same month, Augustus Van Cortlandt, clerk of the City of New York, gathered together the public records of that city and, removing them to Lower Yonkers, concealed them in Colonel Van Cortlandt's family vault, which is northeast of the Van Cortlandt mansion, on the hill known as Vault Hill, east of the present New York and Putnam railroad branch, to Getty Square.

General Washington suspected that the Royal army, which was then encamped in Boston, would soon be transferred to New York. He wrote to the commanding officer of the American forces in New York informing him of his suspicions. The letter was received March 13, 1776. He also appealed to the Provincial Congress to do all they could to prevent the British taking possession of New York, and promising to "come or send to their assistance." A resolution was passed which authorized the establishment of a military magazine in Westchester County. Colonel Drake was to repair immediately to the county and purchase twelve hundred barrels of the best pork, and have the same safely stored, and to purchase flour for the use of five thousand men for a month. When General Howe, the stepbrother of the King, was compelled by the Americans to leave Boston there was an informal agreement between him and Washington that he should be permitted to retire unmolested, on condition that the city should not be burned. When the fleet sailed it carried with the army nearly fifteen hundred loyalists who feared to remain. It was not known to what part of the coast Howe would direct his course when he returned from Canada, whither he had sailed. Washington anticipated his coming to New York.

General Lee was ordered from Manhattan Island to the south and General Lord Stirling took command of the Continental troops in New York City. Colonel Drake and Colonel Thomas received orders to draft two hundred men out of their regiments and with as many more volunteers to proceed to New York and assist in throwing up fortifications. The members of the several local committees chosen in May, 1776, to serve one year were Israel Honeywell, Jr., Abraham Storm, Peter Van Tassel, Glode Requean, Abraham Ledew, James Hammond, Joseph Younge, Gershon Sherwood, James Requean and Thomas Champenois. These ten were citizens of Philipsburgh (the Yonkers of to-day). The Lower Yonkers members, five in number, were William Hadley, William Betts, Thomas Emmons, John Crawford, Frederick Van Cortlandt. These and other Westchester County men whose names are recorded as deputies to Congress and members of the State Convention, by accepting these prominent positions became conspicuous in the estimation of the British government as "rebels," but their grateful countrymen, who appreciate their unrecorded sacrifices and sufferings, call them "patriot fathers," and they do well thus to honor them. A monument to the memory of these and other heroes of 1776 should be erected on the site of Washington's headquarters—Valentine Hill—and Washington's prayer there might appropriately form a part of the inscription.

Congress, taught by experience, had directed that enlistments should be made for three years instead of six months. Tidings came to Philipsburgh that the colonies had formally been declared to be in rebellion, that mercenaries had been employed to assist in reducing them to subjection, that Indians were to be employed by the Home Government for the purpose of harassing the frontier and threatening the inland settlements and villages, and that the slaves were to be withdrawn from their masters and armed in the service of the king. Great Britain was making vast preparations. By a treaty with some of the petty German states, seventeen thousand Hessian mercenaries were hired to fight against America. Twenty-five thousand troops were levied, an immense squadron was fitted out to aid in the reduction of the colonies and a million dollars were voted for the extraordinary expenses of the war department.

The Commander-in-chief came to New York, and while the patriots were entrenching Long Island, other points were not overlooked. In June the citizens of Lower Yonkers heard that Washington had visited their territory and had inspected the grounds near the Spuyten Duyvil Creek, "esteeming it a pass of the utmost importance in order to keep open communication with the country." King's Bridge and Fordham Heights were important places from a military standpoint.

Soon two regiments from Pennsylvania were fortifying the grounds above King's Bridge. Bodies of militia were assisting them. Washington designated seven points as well calculated for defence. In the order which he issued on July 2, 1776, directing Mifflin to repair King's Bridge, and to make haste in forwarding the works near, is the memorable sentence, "The time is now at hand which must probably determine whether Americans are to be freemen or slaves."

General Howe, who had embarked his forces at Halifax in the middle of June, reached New York harbor a short time before the Declaration of Independence was made. When he was in the lower bay it was not known whether he would embark his troops on Long Island, or Staten Island or somewhere along the North and East Rivers. At the beginning of July he landed a force of seven or eight thousand on Staten Island. A part, or all of them, were probably there July 2, 1776. It was on that date that Frederick Philipse wrote as follows to a "Committee to Detect Conspiracies":

"Philipseborough, July 2, 1776.

"Gentlemen—I was served on Saturday evening last with a paper signed by you, in which you suggest that you are authorized by the Congress to summon certain persons to appear before you whose conduct had been represented as inimical to the rights of America, of which number you say I am one.

"Who it is that has made such a representation, or upon what particular facts it is founded, as you have not stated them, it is impossible for me to imagine; but, considering my situation and the near and intimate ties and connexions which I have in this country, which can be secured and rendered happy to me only by the real and permanent prosperity of America, I should have hoped that suspicions of this harsh nature would not be easily harbored. However, as they have been thought of weight sufficient to attract the notice of the Congress, I can only observe that, conscious of the uprightness of my intentions and the integrity of my conduct, I would most readily comply with your summons, but the situation of my health is such as would render it very undesirable for me to take a journey to New York at this time. I have had the misfortune, Gentlemen, of being deprived totally of the sight of my left eye, and the other is so much affected and inflamed as to make me very cautious how I expose it for fear of a total loss of sight. This being my real situation, I must request the favor of you to excuse my attendance to-morrow; but you may rest assured, Gentlemen, that I shall punctually attend as soon as I can, consistent with my health, flattering myself in the meantime that upon further consideration you will think my being a friend to the rights and interests of my native country is a fact so strongly implied as to require no evidence on my part to prove it, untill something more substantial than mere suspicion or vague surmises are proved to the contrary.

"I am, Gentlemen,
"Your most obedient, humble servant,
"Frederick Philipse.

"To Leonard Gansevoort, Philip Livingston, Thomas Treadwell, Lewis Graham, Gouverneur Morris, Thomas Randall, Esquires."

Throughout the land were echoing the notes of the old Liberty Bell at Philadelphia, upon whose ample curve is the prophetic inscription, "Proclaim liberty throughout the land unto all the inhabitants thereof." The British flag had waved over "the Yonkers" more than one hundred years. By authority of the Continental Congress in session at Philadelphia, July 4th, and of the State government in session at White Plains, July 9th, another flag was thereafter to float on land and sea. The standard of the new government was the crosses and the stripes. The next year (June 14, 1777) the stars and stripes, now one of the oldest prominent banners in the world, were flung to the loyal winds that love them well.

The Declaration of Independence was read in City Hall Park, New York, on July 9th. The populace pulled down the leaden statue of George III., and cast it into bullets. The head of the statue was sent to Fort Washington to be placed on the flag-staff. It was left temporarily at Moore's tavern. By the aid of John Cock, the tavern-keeper, whom the committee would not permit to serve as captain of the Lower Yonkers company, the head was stolen, and buried, probably at his tavern. Subsequently it was dug up and sent to England, "to convince them at home of the infamous disposition of the ungrateful people of this distracted country."

The murky and muttering war cloud was drawing nearer "the Yonkers." General Clinton came to New York from his unsuccessful siege of Charleston, and Admiral Howe, the brother of General Howe, came from England. The whole British force now in the vicinity of Manhattan Island amounted to almost, if not quite, thirty thousand men. Nearly half of them were the hated Hessians, whom the King of Great Britain had hired at thirty-six dollars a head. Washington's army was inferior in numbers, poorly equipped and imperfectly disciplined. Many of the troops were sick, and many dispirited. Their numbers were also decreasing.

Before the Declaration of Independence was made the General Assembly of New York was styled "The Provincial Congress of the Colony." The State government which the patriots organized was styled "The Convention of the Representatives of the State of New York." After approving the Declaration of Independence on July 9th (at White Plains), the convention ordered five hundred copies printed and sent to all the county committees. As the British army advanced the "Convention" migrated from place to place, holding brief sessions at Harlem and at Fishkill in Dutchess County. From Fishkill it retired to Kingston, where it adopted the State Constitution framed by a committee of which John Jay was chairman. The "Convention," or some of its committees, remained in session during the operations of the army in New York State, and was constantly in communication with General Washington. As the Provincial Congress, and its committee to detect conspiracies, had hurriedly left New York, before the day appointed for the hearing of Frederick Philipse, evidently proceedings against him were at this time suspended.

On the afternoon of July 12, 1776, two of the British warships, the Phœnix and the Rose (one of forty and the other of twenty guns), and three tenders "taking advantage of the tide and fresh breeze," left Staten Island and stood northward. Their purpose was "to obstruct supplies coming down the river," and probably to encourage the conservative farmers of Westchester County to follow the example of those on Staten Island in declaring for the King. Much to the "surprise and mortification," and regret of the patriots, the frigates safely passed the American batteries and unfinished *chevaux-de-frise* above Fort Washington. They came to anchor near the mouth of the Spuyten Duyvil Creek. A dozen guns from the batteries on Tippett's and Cock's hills, in Lower Yonkers, were fired at them and "did great execution." The vessels weighed anchor, and sailed past Philipsburgh and as far as Tarrytown. Subsequently they moved north as far as the Highlands, and inflicted damage. At Fort Montgomery a thirty pound shot was fired at one of the tenders which was sounding the river. The shot caused her to put about, and run down to the place where the frigates were anchored.

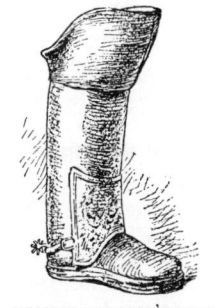

HESSIAN.

HESSIAN TROOPER'S BOOT.

While lying off Tarrytown they were attacked by a fleet of American galleys, which had been built in Connecticut and Rhode Island. The English ships were much superior, yet the Americans gallantly fought them two hours. In order to attack the British fleet in New York waters the Americans were preparing fourteen fire-ships in New York. A movement against the English war vessels on the Hudson was made by two of the fire-ships. While they were waiting for an opportune time to make the attack, an event occurred which forms part of the history of Yonkers.

Frederick Philipse had given his *parole*. Nevertheless he seems to have been feared as a British sympathizer. He was taken into custody by an order from Washington on the ninth of August, and removed from his Manor Hall on the Nepperhan to New Rochelle, where he was closely confined, under guard, for eleven days, when he was removed to Connecticut, and gave his *parole* that he would not go beyond the limits of Middletown.* He was accompanied by Angevine, his faithful colored valet, who afterward went with Mr. Philipse to England, and survived him but one year. They are interred in the same churchyard. Charley Philips, son of Angevine, lived for many years on the banks of the Hudson, and was sexton of St. John's Church forty-five years. After the Philipse family had left Philipsburgh (1777), John Williams, Steward of the

---

* It was the custom of the patriots to remove suspected and dangerous Tories to Kingston, or Morristown, N. J., or Hartford, Conn., or Litchfield, Conn., or Philadelphia, Pa., or elsewhere. Mr. Philipse was given permission to visit New York City, subject to recall. He was summoned to return. Dawson, the historian, says that the order for his recall was not delivered in time for him to go back to Connecticut, and that his failure to return was assigned as the reason for confiscating his estate in Westchester County and elsewhere. Mr. Dawson reflects upon the two Jays and Morris. A judicial mind reserves decision until all the facts are known. The recorded facts of the history of Frederick Philipse's disloyalty are evidently very meagre. Mr. Dawson also reflects upon Frederick Van Cortlandt for using his influence to have the tavern-keeper, who was elected captain by the Lower Yonkers Company, rejected by the County Committee. It is, however, recorded that through the aid of the rejected captain the leaden head of the statue of King George, which the patriots intended to place on the flag-staff at Fort Washington, was stolen and concealed and sent to England to increase the bitterness there. Evidently the county committee had good reason, although they might not have put it on record, for doubting the loyalty of the Lower Yonkers tavern-keeper. And evidently the patriots also had unrecorded reasons for arresting Frederick Philipse; and despite the fact that "he continued to be a member of the colonial party of the Opposition in New York until seized by the military power and sent into exile," they feared him. The inscription on the tablet to his memory recites "that he opposed, at the hazard of his life, the late rebellion in North America, and for the faithful discharge of his duty to his king and country he was proscribed." The patriots were engaged in an unequal struggle with British and Hessians. The issue was doubtful. About the time of Philipse's arrest, they were in such straits that, when calling out the Westchester County militia to guard the exposed shores of the River and the Sound, they ordered each man who had no arms "to bring with him a shovel, spade or pick-axe, or a scythe straightened and fixed on a pole." They sorely needed sincere sympathy and financial aid. If Frederick Philipse, with his large influence and wealth, had manifested sincere interest in their struggle, no harm would have come to him from them.

AN ENGLISH GRENADIER.

Manor, had possession of the Manor until its confiscation in 1779. Mr. J. Henry Williams, an officer of the Yonkers Savings Bank, is a descendant of John Williams, the Steward of the Manor.

It was about the middle of August when the American fire-ships attacked the British fleet. The tide being favorable and the night quite dark, the sloops were allowed to drift. Noiselessly they drew near the enemy. It would appear that the tender of the Rose was anchored in front of the war ships as a lookout. The Americans steered one of their ships toward this vessel and succeeded in laying it alongside of it. As soon as they grappled the tender, they lighted their combustibles. In the light of the flames the other fire-ship was skilfully steered to the side of the Phœnix. The trained seamen on board the frigate endeavored to keep the fire-ship off, but the Americans grappled their enemy and for nearly fifteen minutes the sloop, which was burning fiercely, lay by the side of the Phœnix. Within that time the British frigate was set on fire in four places. It seemed that the vessel would be entirely consumed, but "almost miraculously" it was rescued by a naked sailor, who sprang on board the fire-ship, and, by speedy use of an axe, "disengaged the chain of the grappling which had linked the two vessels together." Then the frigate sunk the sloop. Having escaped the conflagration, "the Phœnix either cut or slipped her cable, let fall her foresail, wore around and stood up the river, being immediately veiled from the spectators by the darkness of the night. . . . The Rose and the other two tenders remained at their moorings, although it was said that one of the tenders was deserted by her crew for a time. The tender which was first grappled was burned to the water's edge." It was towed to the shore by the Americans, who secured cannon, cutlasses, grappling chains, etc., from the wreck. Of the captain of one of the fire sloops nothing was afterward heard, and "it is probable that he perished in his attempt to fasten his sloop to the tender, or when attempting to make his escape by swimming." Washington wrote, "His bravery entitled him to a better fate." Whether this attack took place off Tarrytown or off "the Yonkers," seems to be uncertain. One historian, who holds that it was off "the Yonkers," says that the British frigates and tenders were anchored off the shore afterward known as Mount St. Vincent, and that a number of American officers and soldiers watched it from Tippett's hill, Lower Yonkers. At sunrise the frigates and remaining tender fled down stream, ran through the *chevaux-de-frise* and joined the main body of the fleet off Staten Island.

The battle of Long Island took place on August 27th. Every boat and craft at or near King's Bridge was impressed by General Heath on the 29th, and hurried down to Washington for use in his masterly retreat from Long Island to Manhattan Island. "These preparatory arrangements to retreat from Long Island were made with great alertness, yet profound secrecy. Verbal orders were sent to Colonel Hughes, who acted as quartermaster-general, to impress all water craft, large and small, from Spuyten Duyvil on the Hudson round to Hell Gate on the Sound, and have them on the east side of the city by evening. The order was issued at noon, and so promptly executed that, although some of the vessels had to be brought a distance of fifteen miles, they were all at Brooklyn at eight o'clock in the evening." Let citizens remember with gratitude that the God of the Republic, their fathers' God, concealed the movements of the imperilled patriot army, on that critical night, with a dense fog, and saved the retreating troops. Had Washington and his generals been captured they probably would have been hung. General Green advised the burning of New York, but Congress voted that it should not be damaged. They expected to regain the town, should it be lost.

On the 31st the inhabitants of Yonkers began to drive their horses, cattle, hogs and sheep into the interior. The State treasure-chest was brought up to King's Bridge, and thence immediately removed up into Mr. Odell's house in the valley of the Nepperhan. Two days after the battle of Long Island, the convention adjourned from Harlem to Fishkill, and its committee followed, holding sessions, while on its way, at King's Bridge, at the house of Mr. Odell on Philipse Manor, at the public house of Blagge at Croton River, and possibly elsewhere. The committee transacted necessary business, a part of which was the removal of military stores endangered by the movements of the enemy, and the ordering of all the bells to be taken from the churches, and all brass knockers from the doors of houses, that they might have metal to melt up for cannon. It was during this gloomy period that the British sent their vessels to the Sound in order to cut off water communication with New York on the east. One of the islands they occupied was Montresor's, now Randall's, and an American detachment attacked them there.

On Sunday, September 15th, in order to draw the attention of the Americans from the preparations he was making on Long Island to occupy New York, Howe sent two warships and two tenders up the

Hudson as far as Bloomingdale. The same day the Royal army took possession of New York. Washington's headquarters,* about this time, were on Harlem Heights.

While Washington was in Harlem there was an almost daily correspondence between his headquarters and the State government at Fishkill. The letters from headquarters were those of Colonel Tilghman, of Washington's staff. They were addressed to the Committee of Correspondence, consisting of William Allison, R. R. Livingston, Henry Wisner and William Duer. "The 'express,' by means of which the letters were carried to and fro between Harlem and Fishkill, was, after the fashion of the day, a chain of horsemen, stationed at intervals of thirty miles along the old Albany Post-road, which at that time was, and still is, the main highway along the east bank of the Hudson. At this period the road was not exposed to the enemy. It is interesting as showing the speed of the 'express' to note that the writers at either end of the line acknowledged the receipt of letters written on the previous day." It was during the months of September and October, 1776, that almost daily a horseman carrying a communication from Washington's Aide to the State government at Fishkill and a horseman bringing a letter sent from Peekskill and directed to headquarters, rode through "the Yonkers." The letter of Duer, written on October 21st, was directed to Tilghman at headquarters, Valentine Hill. These letters, thirty-seven in number, were published in 1895 in the New York *Times* by Major Frederic Shonnard of Yonkers. They are of great interest as revealing the devotion of the patriots and the spirit of their period. One of the letters suggests that "if it became necessary to abandon the country below the Highlands, the chain of mountains might be rendered impregnable." In one of his letters Duer says: "The complexion of our Affairs is, as I confess, not pleasing, and did you know the Political Character of too many of the Inhabitants of this state as well as I, you would think it on that Account still more Gloomy. . . . We are not to expect to purchase our Liberties at a cheaper Rate than other nations have done. . . . Experience will make us both brave and wise."

AMERICAN MARINE, 1776.

How serious the secret movements of the Tories were may be inferred from the attempts that were made to capture or kill General Washington. A servant was bribed to poison the food furnished for his table. She, however, became alarmed and conscience-stricken, and revealed the plot. Surely, Providence was the protector of the chosen leader.

The Whigs were compelled to make many arrests. One company of Tories (not Yonkers men), who had enlisted to serve the British, having been apprehended, were marched off to Philadelphia. They must have been dumbfounded when they ascertained that their names and conspiracy were known. One Tory pathetically wrote to a friend: "I have been cruelly rode on rails, a practice most painful and dangerous."

When it became evident that it would not be advisable to attempt to hold New York, Washington determined to take post at King's Bridge, and along the Westchester shore. Part of the army had no tents. He planned to supply them with boards for barracks. Five thousand men were to be left on Manhattan Island, and nine thousand were to occupy King's Bridge and its dependencies. On the 8th of October Heath was instructed to fell trees across some of the roads leading toward the bridge, and to dig holes in the highways. The next day sixteen thousand boards were ordered for the barracks at King's Bridge, also brick and stone for ovens. The farmers in Lower Yonkers felt the curse of war in those days. Barns, cornfields and orchards were pillaged and fences were pulled down for firewood.

A commissary was appointed to purchase all the cattle in the county suitable for table meat, and to drive them down to King's Bridge, as fast as the army needed them, leaving enough to supply the families. Farm animals were driven into the interior, out of the enemy's reach. Grain was threshed out in order that the soldiers might be supplied with straw. Colonel Drake, of New Rochelle, was commanded to call out a part of the Westchester County militia to watch the enemy's ships, and to prevent all communication with the Tories.

In order that the Americans might not successfully attack them, the Royal army was intrenching the Manhattan Island high grounds overlooking Harlem plains from the south. The Americans, for defence against British attack, were throwing up intrenchments on the high grounds overlooking Harlem plains from the north. Those were gloomy days for the patriots. By the evacuation of New York, they had lost quantities of flour and had also lost heavy guns, which they greatly needed.

* The building is still standing. Its site is on the present 159th Street, northwest of the 155th Street bridge. Before the Revolution it was the mansion of Colonel Morris, the husband of Mary Philipse. It was subsequently owned by Madame Jumel, the widow of Aaron Burr.

General Howe planned to attack Washington from the east. To withdraw the attention of the Americans from that direction, he sent, on the ninth of October, the Phœnix, the Roebuck and the Tartar up the Hudson. They passed Fort Washington and Fort Constitution, subsequently called Fort Lee, but received considerable damage in their masts and rigging, and some on board were killed or wounded. To the surprise and mortification of Washington, they passed the obstructions in the Hudson. The work of obstructing the river had not yet been completed. Some deep waters near the east shore were yet navigable. The vessels moved up as far as Dobb's Ferry and anchored. On their way they captured two or three small craft and sank a sloop which had on board a machine for blowing up the British fleet. Two new ships, which had been purchased to add to the obstructions in the channel, but which had not yet reached their destination, were driven ashore near Yonkers. "One express after another brought Washington word of these occurrences. First he sent off a party of rifle and artillery men with two twelve pounders to secure the new ships, which, retreating from the enemy, had run aground at Yonkers. To prevent, if possible, the men-of-war, already up the river, from coming down and others from below joining them, Washington gave orders to complete the obstructions. Two hulks which lay in Spuyten Duyvil creek, were hastily ballasted by men from General Heath's division, and men were sent up to get off the ships which had run aground at Philip's Mills that they might be brought down and sunk immediately." One of them was afterward recovered by a party of men sent by General Clinton from King's Bridge. The British vessels drove two galleys ashore at Dobb's Ferry, and captured them. In the evening the squadron moved up to Tarrytown and, anchoring off that place, remained there while the British were attacking the Americans on the Westchester shore of Long Island Sound, and subsequently at White Plains.

General Howe embarked on the East River in flat-boats, batteaux, etc. The naval portion of the movement was under the personal supervision of Admiral Lord Howe. No less than forty-two sails passed the mouth of the Harlem River, going eastward. It was evident that this movement was no feint. The Royal army was landed at nine o'clock in the morning of October 12th, at Throgg's Neck, a peninsula which stretches about two miles into the Sound. The landing was covered by a British frigate. The watchful Americans had stationed there twenty picked riflemen to defend the pass. They were ordered to take up the flooring of the bridge if the enemy should land on Throgg's Neck. A guard also kept watch of the fording place at the head of the creek.

The movements of Howe at Throgg's Neck turned the left flank of the American army. Information was sent to Washington by express to his headquarters on Harlem Heights. In order to strengthen the guard at the bridge, he sent Colonel Prescott, the hero of Bunker Hill, with his regiment. Other troops, consisting of both artillery and infantry detachments, were also sent as reinforcements. Among the armed Americans on duty there was the Westchester militia, under Colonel Drake. The advance of the entire British army was checked at that old Westchester bridge. The fight there has been called the "Lexington of Westchester." Washington had many heavy cares

COMMISSION OF COLONEL (SUBSEQUENTLY GENERAL) WILLIAM ALLISON, AN OFFICER OF THE AMERICAN REVOLUTION.

during those dark days. While stationing his troops to protect Westchester County he was compelled to order a regiment of New Hampshire militia, then at White Plains, to march to Fishkill, "with all possible dispatch," for the assistance of the Committee of Safety in holding the dissatisfied in check. He called a meeting of the general officers at King's Bridge. By earnest appeals to the troops, he endeavored to inspire them with his own patriotic fervor and faith, and lofty sense of duty. General Lee, having returned from the south, was given command of the troops then in Westchester County. They constituted the greater part of the army.

THE VALENTINE HOUSE, KNOWN AS "THE REVOLUTIONARY HOUSE."

Accompanied by his generals, who were at headquarters, the Commander-in-chief rode beyond King's Bridge on the 14th, and by personal reconnoissance acquainted himself with the roads and ground. His sympathy must have gone out for the people of the stripped country. Not only had farm animals, grain, hay and straw disappeared, but many of the citizens had fled from their homes, the Tories, doubtless, to New York City, Canada and elsewhere, and the Whigs into the interior. Among other precautions which the patriots took during those dark days were such as would insure the safety of public documents. The records of New York City and of the Borough of Westchester had been hidden safely in private houses and elsewhere until a committee was appointed to remove them to Kingston, Ulster County. The committee were empowered to call a military guard to attend said records in their removal.

On October 16th a council of war was held at the headquarters of General Lee. Washington, the Commander-in-Chief, Major-Generals Lee, Putnam, Heath, Spencer and Sullivan, Brigadier-Generals Lord Stirling, Mifflin, McDougal, Parsons, Nixon, Wadsworth, Scott, Fellows, Clinton and Lincoln were present. Green was on Harlem Heights at the headquarters of the army. It was decided to abandon all of Manhattan Island except Fort Washington. The attempt to hold that was against Washington's judgment, yet, in deference to the expressed will of the Continental Congress, preparations were made to defend it.

About this time the Albany road needed repairing. Colonel Drake's regiment of Westchester militia received orders to put it in repair. It was feared that the warships Phœnix, Roebuck and Tartar, then lying off Tarrytown, might inflict damage. In order to watch those ships, two regiments of Massachusetts militia, detailed from the command of Major-General Lincoln, were sent up the river. They were to oppose any landing of the enemy's force. The headquarters of that small division, and probably of the two remaining regiments, were on Valentine Hill.

Strong pickets were established, and frequent night patrols were made through all the region about King's Bridge. Washington moved his headquarters to King's Bridge. At noon, October 20th, the entire military force of the Americans, except four regiments detailed to garrison Fort Washington, were withdrawn from Manhattan Island. Every important height and pass, and all the advantageous ground between New Rochelle and the Hudson River, were occupied by detachments of the American army. Detachments were also watching the Westchester shore of the Sound.

Four letters written at this period from Yonkers by the devoted patriot, G. Selleck Silliman, to his wife are extant. One is dated "In the Woods at Yonkers" (probably Lower Yonkers). In one he says: "This day we have been obliged to carry our chaplain out to our alarm post in the woods in order to have Publick Worshipp there, which was performed there, as the enemy did not come to disturb us."

General Howe at one o'clock Friday morning, October 18th, sent a detachment on flat-boats from Throgg's Neck across the mouth of a river or bay at Pell Point. Colonel Glover, with his American guard, did not discover this movement until daylight. The spectacle must have been imposing when the main body of the Royal army—well uniformed as they were—following the advance detachment, moved in two hundred boats, formed into four grand divisions, and convoyed by small armed vessels. An express was dispatched to General Lee with information of Howe's movements.

Colonel Glover ambuscaded the advance guard of the royalists, and from behind stone walls his well-posted troops arose and poured an effective fire into their ranks. That occurred at Pelham. Lee sent his entire brigade to hold the enemy in check. Glover fell back three miles and bivouaced. Writing from Mile Square he says, "After fighting all day without victuals or drink, lay as a picquet, all night, the heavens over us and the earth under us, which was all we had, having left our baggage at the old encampment we left in the morning."

Washington's headquarters were moved to Thomas Valentine's house, Valentine Hill. A line of entrenched encampments was formed along the high grounds west of the Bronx from Valentine Hill to Chatterton Hill, opposite White Plains. On October 20th the royalists began their march toward White Plains. Some of their war ships were on the Hudson, off Tarrytown, and others were on the Sound, at first off Throgg's Neck and then off Myers' Point (southeast of New Rochelle).

Washington hurried his troops along Valentine Hill* to White Plains, where his unprotected stores were. One brigade was ordered to move from King's Bridge up the Albany road to Dobb's Ferry, and to join the division at White Plains, after receiving baggage, to be brought by boat.

Napoleon said that God is with the army which has the heaviest cannon; but he learned that He who holds the winds in His fists could gather together the snows of the north and blow them over his thousands of troops. Washington believed, with Franklin, that "if a sparrow cannot fall to the ground without God's notice, a nation cannot rise without His aid." While the great Commander-in-chief had his headquarters in the house of Thomas Valentine he publicly invoked the aid of the God of battles. The record of his prayer there is in another part of this chapter.

The royalists moved toward New Rochelle and bivouaced. Washington, planning for the future, determined to establish a magazine of provisions "to the north of the Highlands, and remote from the North River," for the enemy controlled navigation, and the question as to how the American army should be supplied with provisions became serious.

It is probable that on the second day after the enemy occupied Pell's Neck, Colonel Rufus Putnam made a personal reconnoissance of his strength and position. It is said that he disguised himself and set out for White Plains. When within three or four miles of that place, he saw a house with men about it. "He surveyed them through his field-glass, and having ascertained that the house was a tavern (Ward's tavern—see map) and that the men were not British soldiers, he rode up and called for oats for his horse. Sitting down quietly, he listened to the conversation. The men were Whigs. Colonel Putnam learned that a large body of the Royal army was lying near New Rochelle, about eleven miles from White Plains, where there was a great quantity of American stores guarded by only about three hundred militia. He also ascertained that a detachment of the enemy was posted at Mamaroneck, only about seven miles from White Plains. He waited no longer at the tavern, but hastened, by way of Philipsburgh, back to headquarters to report to Washington."

On Tuesday, the 20th, the royalists took possession of Mamaroneck. It was about four o'clock on Wednesday morning, the 21st, that Major-General Heath's troops, who, in light marching order, had moved up from near King's Bridge, passed Washington's headquarters on Valentine Hill. After a weary, all-night forced march they reached Chatterton Hill, opposite White Plains, at four o'clock on Thursday morning. While Heath's column was hurrying toward White Plains, another detachment of the patriot army made a brilliant dash on the enemy at Mamaroneck, handling them "very roughly," wounding and killing a number, capturing thirty-six prisoners, a pair of colors, sixty stand of arms and other property.

During the night of October 22d a division of the American army, under General Sullivan, reached White Plains. On October 23d Washington's headquarters were established at White Plains. During this trying period he had been "almost the whole time on horseback."

---

*Mr. Nathaniel B. Valentine, who has lived on Valentine Hill all his life and who is a descendant of Thomas Valentine, said in 1896: "The troops, moving along what is now Jerome Avenue, passed the site of the present Roman Catholic Seminary, and continued northward along the Mile Square road to the Tuckahoe road, striking that highway about half a mile west of the site of the present pumping station, thence along the Tuckahoe road to what is now Central Avenue (then a winding country road). Following the old highway, they reached White Plains. In some places Central Avenue follows the course of the old road. To-day Jerome Avenue, east of the seminary on Valentine Hill, is a wide and graded street. In Revolutionary times it was a winding road, and so narrow that it was known as 'the lane.'" It was only recently made a modern avenue.

When General Lee commenced his laborious march toward White Plains, "it was attended with much difficulty, for want of wagons and artillery horses. The baggage and artillery were carried or drawn off by hand. When a part was forwarded, the other was fetched on. Sometimes the toiling column was in open view of the enemy." Had they attacked the Americans it is thought they could have captured the greater number of their cannon, wagons and horses. Among the relics of the northward march along Valentine's hill is the following receipt:

"Valentine Hill, January 27, 1777.
"These may certify that on or about the 25th of October last I ordered Thomas Valentine's one yoke of oxen and cart to be taken for the public service.
"They carried a load to ye White Plains. There I discharged them. I am informed they were further taken on their return, and that Mr. Valentine hath not received them.
"B. Lincoln."

General Lee while on this retreat made a dash upon the enemy. He threw a party of his command over the Bronx on Wednesday night, October 23d. Two hundred and fifty Hessians, who constituted an outpost of the enemy, were near Ward's tavern, between Tuckahoe and Scarsdale. On Thursday morning the American party killed ten of them and captured two. It is said that the enemy also made a dash and captured the baggage of General Lee and Captain Alexander Hamilton. The movement, under such circumstances, of eight thousand men with a train of one hundred and fifty wagons, which filled the wood for four miles, and with artillery—often within half a mile, and within open sight of an active, powerful and well-equipped enemy, and with very little loss, demonstrates the sagacity and perseverance of the patriot fathers.

The whole American army, except about fourteen hundred left on Mount Washington, and a few near King's Bridge, was concentrating at White Plains. The small detachment left at Fort Independence (near King's Bridge), in Lower Yonkers, had orders to burn the barracks, which had been erected at much expense, quit the post, and (by way of the Hudson River) join the army at White Plains.

It was on October 25th that the heads of the columns of the main body of the royalists, moving with great caution, arrived at Scarsdale, northeast of and near the present Yonkers boundary. The Royal army encamped there, in a line parallel with the Bronx River, and north of the opposite side of the little stream, on which General Lee, with his heavily laden column, was transporting the baggage and stores of the American army toward White Plains. In many places the royalists and the Americans were not more than a mile apart. In one place, if not in others, the "toiling Americans" were in sight of their powerful foe. The records seem to indicate that Howe planned an attack on Lee's column, but that the Americans by a forced march along a more westerly road got beyond his reach.

Early in the morning of October 20th, the Royal army struck its tents in the encampment at Scarsdale, and in two columns, right in front, moved toward White Plains. The right column was composed mostly of British, and the left mostly of German troops. The records of the skirmish at Hart's Corners with New England troops sent to delay their advance, and the description of the battle of White Plains,* in which the patriots acquitted themselves nobly, belong to the general history of the county and the country. It is said that the firing at that battle could be heard on Valentine Hill. Washington's army at White Plains probably numbered somewhat more than thirteen thousand, ill armed and in rags. Many, if not most, of the officers were inexperienced, having but a few months before left the desk or the plough.

Why General Howe retreated from White Plains is partially explained by the record of the treason of one Dumont, the adjutant of Colonel Morgan, the commander at Fort Washington. On November 2d, he passed undiscovered out of the fort and into the camp of Lord Percy at Harlem, carrying with him the plans of Fort Washington, and full information as to the garrison. Percy sent the information to Lord Howe, who prepared to march to Fort Washington. He had been outgeneralled by the American commander, and evidently concluded that it was useless to try to successfully attack him in his stronger position on the hills of North Castle.

Detachments of the royalists had occupied Lower Yonkers October 27, 1776, the day before the battle of White Plains. The enemy did not withdraw from "the Yonkers" until the bitterly cold winter of 1782-'83, that is, about six years after they took possession. The German troops, which Howe had left

---

* Mr. J. C. L. Hamilton, who lives a short distance north of Yonkers, informs the writer that he has the muster roll of the artillery company which was commanded in the Revolution by his great-grandfather, Alexander Hamilton. That company fought at White Plains.

at New Rochelle, to keep open the communication between his fleet and his army, were ordered to march to King's Bridge. The fourth brigade of the British troops marched to Mile Square and Valentine Hill. Other detachments of the Royal army were moved to different parts of Lower Westchester. Howe pushed toward Dobb's Ferry and encamped there on the 6th. The next day he moved his park of artillery under strong escort down to King's Bridge. "The Yonkers" was in the hands of the foe. Washington called a council of general officers. The conclusion to which they came was shown by the troops of New Jersey, Pennsylvania and the more southern States being ordered to file off the lines in order to march to Verplanck's Point, whence they were transported by the King's Ferry across the Hudson. General Heath's division of patriot soldiers marched to Peekskill to defend the Highlands. Washington left White Plains to take command of the army across the Hudson, for he apprehended that the British would now proceed against Philadelphia. He first took post with General Green at Fort Lee. General Lee, with about four thousand men, was left at White Plains and North Castle to watch the enemy, secure the stores and to subsequently join Washington and the main army. The main body of Howe's army broke up their encampment at Dobb's Ferry and marched down to King's Bridge. They inflicted terrible outrages upon the inhabitants of Lower Westchester. "The distinction of Whig and Tory was lost in one general scene of ravage and desolation." Hessian and British troops were equally notorious, and what the soldiery spared was frequently carried away by their wives and mistresses, who formed a part of the retinue of the army. Fort Washington was attacked by a force greatly outnumbering the gallant defenders. After a stubborn defence it was surrendered. More than five hundred of the assailants were killed or wounded. It is recorded that Washington sent a message from Fort Lee, on the opposite shore, that if the defenders could hold the fort until evening he would send them assistance. Even after the Americans had thrown down their arms they were butchered, and Washington wept as he saw the enemy thrust their bayonets into the brave patriots. The garrison, numbering over two thousand, were made prisoners of war and crowded into the foul jails of New York. The captured fort was named Fort Knyphausen.

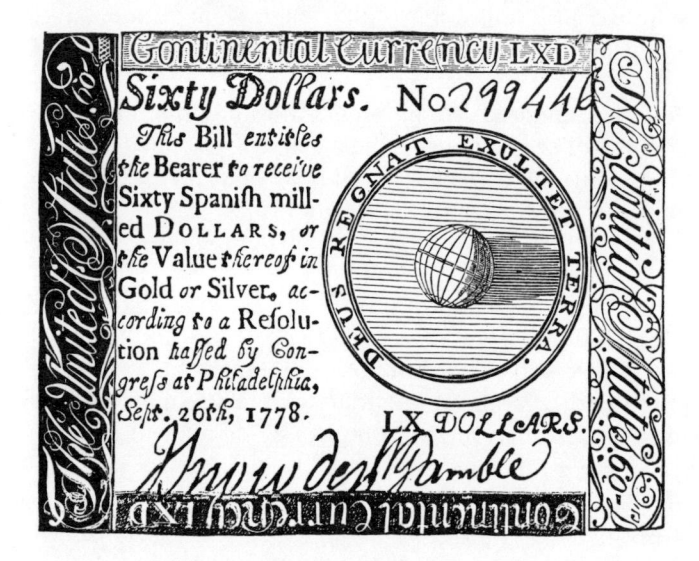

CONTINENTAL CURRENCY.

Two days after the surrender, Cornwallis crossed the Hudson with a body of six thousand men, and, ascending the Palisades opposite "the Yonkers," marched southward against Fort Lee. The thrilling story of Washington's retreat through New Jersey and the pursuit of the royalists, so close that the music of their bands was frequently heard by the rear guard of the American army, is well known to readers of history.

The year 1777 came and went, but before it had gone Congress voted "that the flag of the United States be thirteen stripes, alternate red and white, and the Union be thirteen white stars in the blue field." *

* For full record of how the first American flag—the stars and stripes—was made, see *New York Daily Tribune*, April 28, 1893. General Washington and the committee of Congress called upon a young lady, Mrs. John Ross, whose husband, the son of a clergyman, while assisting at night, with other young men, in guarding powder upon one of the city wharves of the Delaware, had received an injury from which he died. Mrs. Ross was noted for her exquisite skill in needlework and embroidery. After the death of her husband, who had been an upholsterer, the young widow was heroically conducting the business alone. In 1893, her grandson, Mr. George Canby, a Philadelphian, wrote an account of the making of the first flag. It is as follows :

General Washington, with her uncle, Colonel Ross, and the committee of Congress, called upon the talented and sprightly young widow—who not only was a great favorite of her uncle, but enlisted his earnest sympathy—and asked her if she thought she could make a flag from a design, a rough drawing of which General Washington exhibited. She replied with diffidence and becoming modesty that "she did not know, but would try." With quick appreciation, however, she noticed that the stars as drawn showed six points, and then told General Washington and the other gentlemen present that the correct star should have but five points. To the answer given that they understood that, but that a great number would be required, and the more regular form with six could be more easily made than one with five points, she promptly responded in a most practical way by deftly folding a scrap of paper in a way readily remembered as one of the little arts of her trade, and then, with a single clip of her scissors, which in the quaint old way were hanging ready at her side, she displayed to the astonished eyes of the august committee a true, symmetrical five-pointed star.

This at once decided not only that point in her favor, but other suggestions of hers were agreed to, and after the design was partially redrawn on the table in her little back parlor she was left to make her sample flag according to her own ideas of the arrangement of the stars, the proportions of the stripes and the general form of the whole. Upon its completion it was presented to Congress, and the committee soon thereafter had the pleasure of reporting to Betsy Ross that her flag was accepted as the National standard, and

In the spring of 1778 General Howe was superseded by Sir Henry Clinton. In the summer of 1778 Washington was again for several weeks at White Plains. The British, after the battle of Monmouth, had retreated to New York, and the Americans, from their former post on the hills of Westchester, awaited further movements on the enemy's part. Washington also attempted to co-operate with the French fleet, which had just arrived, in an attempt to capture New York. The plan, for various reasons, failed, but the army remained at White Plains and Rye, from July 20, 1778, to September 15, 1778.

Before describing Washington's movement of troops in Lower Westchester in 1781, after the French under Rochambeau had marched across the country from Newport, and joined him on the hills north of Yonkers, attention will be called to the skirmishes and dashes of detachments along the highways, over the hills and through the valleys of Philipsburgh and Lower Yonkers, under subordinate officers stationed in the county between 1776 and 1781, and to the ravages of cowboys and skinners.

UNITED STATES FLAG, ADOPTED 1777. THIRTEEN STARS.

A bare recital of the names of some of the hills, valleys, streams and bridges, and of a few of the private and public houses in "the Yonkers," with which are associated events of the Revolution, is sufficient to indicate how rich in history and romance the locality is. The "Neutral Ground," of which it forms a part, will always be famous in the annals of the nation. Among historic hills are Locust, Wild Boar, Odell, Fort Field, Tuckahoe Heights, Valentine, Woodlawn Heights, Tetard, Tippett's and Vault. The bridges of historic interest are King's Bridge, Free Bridge, Philipse Bridge, the "Tony" Archer Bridge, Tuckahoe Bridge, Valentine's Bridge, Hunt's Bridge, the bridge across Tippett's Brook, near Van Cortlandt ridge, and Williams' Bridge. Streams which have a place in the annals of the War for Independence are the Hudson, the Bronx, Spuyten Duyvil Creek, the Harlem, the Nepperhan, Tippett's Brook and the Sprain. Among historic roads are Broadway, Ashburton Avenue, the Boston road, the Mile Square road, the Bronx road, the Saw Mill River road, the Tuckahoe road, the Sprain road, and the private road in the valley of Tippett's Brook. Tuckahoe, Mile Square, Mosholu, Fieldston, Riverdale and Van Cortlandt also have their thrilling chapters of history. St. John's Church, Manor Hall, the Van Cortlandt Manor, the Hadley house, the Frederick Post house, the Valentine house, Guerno's tavern, Hunt's tavern, the Ryche house, the old parsonage, the Archer house and the Odell house are among buildings of interest. Some of them are still standing, others were long since demolished.

Let one who desires to behold the scenes of thrilling events take his station at some commanding view-point in historic Yonkers. The lofty and shapely high service brick water-tower on Nodine Hill affords magnificent views of many square miles of surrounding country. One who mounts the two hundred and sixteen steps of its winding iron stairway, and looks out from the arched windows of the observatory, is amply repaid.

To the west the Palisades uplift their beetling crags. On the 18th of November, 1776, two days after the capture of Fort Washington, several thousand troops, consisting of two battalions of light infantry, two companies of chasseurs, two battalions of British, and two of Hessian grenadiers, two of Guards,

she was authorized to proceed at once to the manufacture of a large number for disposal by the Continental Congress. As soon as the committee had left her, such sudden and unexpected good fortune in her modest business undertaking for the moment seemed almost too much for the brave little woman's courage. As she was silently and thoughtfully considering her ability to meet the requirements of this seemingly too great responsibility, her uncle, Colonel Ross, who, as soon as possible, had parted from the other members of the committee, quickly returned alone, and, laying down a note of large denomination on her table, cheerily told her how useful he knew money would be to her, and advised her to purchase immediately all the bunting she could get hold of in Philadelphia. The unusual sight of such a large amount of money and her uncle's good words of encouragement dispelled her momentary trepidation, and from that time on her busy hands and those she called to assist her found no idle moments. A record has been discovered and published that in May, 1777, Congress made an order on the Treasury "to pay Betsy Ross £14 12s 2d for flags for the fleet in the Delaware River," which shows that the resolution of June 14, 1777, was not the birth of the flag by any means.

At this day, to the descendants of Betsy Ross, it does, indeed, seem most unfortunate that absolutely nothing is known of what was done or what became of the original or first made flag. According to a tradition in the family, it was first run up and floated to the breeze, as an experiment, from the masthead of a merchant ship lying at or near Race Street wharf. But of the circumstances attending it we have nothing authentic. When it is remembered what a disordered condition public affairs were in at that time, the great diversity of feeling which existed in the minds of even serious-minded folks in regard to the important events transpiring, it is not to be wondered that little note was made of many interesting events, the actors in which did not realize their historical importance. It is, however, an important fact to chronicle that the business of flag making, as established at that time by Betsy Ross, was continued by her and her immediate family for some sixty odd years. Her eldest daughter by her last husband, John Claypoole, my aunt, Mrs. C. S. Wilson, did not entirely relinquish the business, which had never been interrupted, until the year 1857; so that there is no difficulty whatever in our family tracing the American flag back to its original starting point.

All published pictures of my grandmother are fictitious, as she left no portrait whatever. She was born (Elizabeth Griscom) January 1, 1752; married first Ross, second Ashburn, third Claypoole, and died in my father's house in this city, February 11, 1836, aged eighty-four years, when I was a little boy six years old; so that I am one of the very few living who have pleasant recollections of the maker of the first Star Spangled Banner.

and the thirty-third and forty-second regiments under Lord Cornwallis, made a landing opposite Yonkers and climbed the Palisades, in order to march southward and attack Fort Lee. On October 18, 1778 (two years after the date of Cornwallis' landing), Lord Grey, after coming up the Hudson in barges, disembarked his troops at Closter landing to cut off Baylor's light dragoons, stationed at Tappan. The situation of Baylor had been betrayed by some Tories. His detachment consisted of one hundred and four horsemen. The barn in which they had sought shelter for the night was surrounded by the enemy's troops, and Baylor's men were all bayoneted.

As to whether the troops of Cornwallis in 1776, and those of Grey in 1778, climbed the Palisades at the same place, the author is uninformed. Near the present winding carriage road at Alpine (formerly Upper Closter) landing, are pointed out to-day the outlines of an old road, said to have been abandoned as early as during the first quarter of the nineteenth century, perhaps earlier. It may be that the troops of one of the British generals reached the top of the mountain by that road. In 1895 Mr. John C. Campbell * (then aged about seventy-four) said that his father, David Campbell (3d), used to speak about the British climbing the Palisades up a ravine, nearly opposite the present Public Dock of Yonkers, about half a mile south of the Upper Closter (now Alpine) landing.

On the Yonkers side of the river, in plain sight from the commanding observatory of the Nodine Hill tower, is the Philips Manor Hall, on the north bank of the Nepperhan River. Beginning at that point, and, from the observatory, sweeping a circle to the north, the east, the south and back to the west at a point (St. John's Church) on the south bank of the Nepperhan, many of the events † of the Revolution will be recalled.

On May 28, 1779, the left column of the British forces was at "Philipse," and the right column of the new encampment was placed in Eastchester, in all likelihood along the Mile Square road, but extending down to the creek.

A letter, which came into the possession of Miss Eliza M. Storms, when her father, Brigadier-General Henry Storms, died in 1874, at his residence in North Tarrytown, refers to British troops at Philips' or Mile Square, in 1779:

"WEST POINT, July 25, 1779.

"SIR—All the white Ink I now have—indeed all that there is any prospect of getting soon—is sent in phial Nº. 1, by Colº. Webb. The liquid in Nº. 2 is the counterpart, and brings to light what is wrote by the first, by wetting [the Paper] with a fine hair brush. These you will send to C—Junr as soon as possible, & I beg that no mention may *ever* be made of your having received such liquids from me, or any one else. In all cases & at all times, this prudence & circumspection is necessary; but it is indispensably so now, as I am informed that Governor Tryon has a preparation of the same kind, or something similar to it, which may lead to a detection if it is ever known that a matter of the sort has passed through my hands.

"I beg that you will use every possible exertion through C—and other channels, to ascertain with a degree of precision the enemy's Corps, and how they are disposed of. I wish to know where every Regiment lyes, in order [that I may] regulate my own movements with more propriety. To learn with certainty what Corps are on Staten Island—Long Island, and on what part of it. The City of York. Between the City & the bridge—at Philips's or Mile square, &c., would be extremely useful to me at all times, but more so at this.

---

* Mr. John C. Campbell of Yonkers was born on the Palisades, and lived there most of his life. He informed the author in 1895 that the first name of his great-grandfather, of his grandfather and of his father was David. During the Revolutionary War David Campbell (1st) lived about half a mile from the site of the present Closter (N. J.) railroad station. He had a farm of one hundred acres, more or less. The British came and took his cattle and horses and the corn from the corn-crib. He ran to a swamp for safety, but was chased by a soldier who cut his head with a sword. The old man had an oval silver plate set in his skull where he had received the wound. He was ninety-four years old when he died. David Campbell (2d) was a United States soldier soon after the Revolution, but never returned home from the army. It is thought that he was killed or died of wound or disease while serving his country. David Campbell (3d) lived on the Palisades all his life, and died there a few years ago at the age of ninety-seven.

† The record of many others could be preserved for future generations if the old families of Yonkers should pen the stories which have come down from the elder generations and still linger as household tales. Many a fireside narrative will never appear on the printed page, and in time will have been lost in oblivion. Stories of Indians, Dutch, English, Highlanders, Hessians, French, Negro slaves, cowboys and skinners have been among the themes of folk-talk in Yonkers. This family is said to trace its descent from a Hessian; that family is related to Van Wart, one of the captors of Andre; the ancestor of that family was hung by the cowboys and was cut down in time to save his life; and the family which lives in yonder house has such and such a Revolutionary relic. While looking with interest at relics of the Revolution and of the War of 1812 in a dwelling which stands where the Willow Hill road branches off from the Albany road (just north of Yonkers), Mr. Charles Allen Embree, who was present, said to the writer: "I have at Nepera Park a sword of finer workmanship than the General Odell sword of 1812 which you have in your hand. It was carried by Mr. Nicholas Fursman, who was a soldier of the Revolution. He lived in the Sprain Valley at the corner of the Sprain road and the present Jackson Avenue. The sword he carried is finely wrought. It was borrowed by George Jackson of Yonkers, who carried it in the War of 1812." Mr. Embree, in whose possession the sword is at the present time, is a descendant of Mr. Fursman. On a map, engraved and published according to Act of Parliament, October 10, 1776 (a rare map, reproduced in this country for the first time in 1892), a fort is designated as located on the north bank of the mouth of the Nepperhan at "Younker."

"I am informed that in the afternoon of the 21st, 40 Sail of Vessels passed Eastward by Norwalk. I have also received advice that a number of Troops imbarked at Dobb's Ferry, & fell down the River on the 22nd. In short, that General Clinton & Sir George Collier were with this Fleet. But these things not being delivered with certainty, rather perplexes than informs the judgment. I have heard nothing further of either of these Fleets—nor do I know whether the one in the Sound had Troops on board or not. Let me hear from you soon on the subject of this letter.

"I am, Sir,
"Ye most obedt Serv.,
"Go. WASHINGTON.

"Majr Talmadge, 2nd Regt. L. Dragoons."

The passages in brackets are interlined in the original letter.

Who was C. referred to as a "channel" of information? Could it have been Enoch Crosby, the Westchester spy, of whom Cooper has written under the name of Harvey Birch? The initial would answer for him certainly.

Northeast of the Manor Hall, and just outside of the Hudson River Railroad tracks at the foot of ——————— Street, south of the site of the present Palisade Club boat-house, is a point of land on which Washington is said to have landed. The Hon. G. Hilton Scribner, of Yonkers, was taken to the place years ago by Dr. Alfred Robinson, who narrated the incident, but did not give his authority for it.

Northeast of, and near Manor Hall, is Locust Hill. In Revolutionary days American troops were encamped there. North of that hill is Wild Boar Hill. A spy, who had made the woods then there his hiding place, was captured and taken to Poughkeepsie and hung. It is said that after a skirmish an American soldier, a member of a Rhode Island regiment, was found on the ground about one hundred and fifty feet north of the road to Eastchester (Ashburton Avenue), near the northwest corner of the present St. John's Hospital. In after years, when workmen were making an excavation there for the foundation of a barn, they found a skeleton, but could not account for it being on that spot. Mr. Richard Archer heard of it and went over to inform them that it was there his father, Anthony Archer, helped to bury the body of a soldier of the Revolution.

Anthony Archer (3d) related that his father had told him that a skirmish took place on the crown of the present Ashburton Avenue, and after it was over he went to the place and found two dead soldiers —one, who had been shot in the face, was leaning against a tree, and the other was lying on a stone. He then went down and brought up to the spot John Williams, who at that time was the superintendent of the Manor property, and they two buried the men near the site of the present Hudson River Railroad station, or near the foot of the present Locust Street. At another time there was a High Dutchman (or Hessian) shot in Yonkers, and they buried him there also. Drowned people seem to have been buried near the foot of the present Locust Street. There used to be a cove there, and sometimes bodies of those who had been drowned floated into it and were buried near the river.

It was on Wild Boar hill that the American water guard were wont to watch in order to intercept traders on their way down the Hudson to the British lines. One day three of the guard conceal themselves in the cedars then standing east of the site of the present St. Joseph's Church. They hear the clatter of horses' hoofs. A company of light dragoons is approaching. Among them rides a happy officer. It is Captain Rowe of the Yagers. It has been his daily duty to make a reconnoitering tour from King's Bridge round to Mile Square. This is his last tour. He is engaged to an accomplished Harlem lady, Miss Elizabeth Fowler, and has resigned his military commission that he may marry her; but alas for him and the lady he loves! Suddenly there is a sharp report, and the captain, reeling in his saddle, falls. With disciplined celerity the Yagers make captives of the water guard; but the captain has received a mortal wound. The Yagers hastily send to the parsonage, within the grounds of the present Oakland cemetery, and procure the horse and gig of Mrs. Babcock, the widow of the Rev. Luke Babcock. But who is to drive? Yonder at the corner of the Eastchester road and Archer's lane—the present-day Ashburton Avenue and Nepperhan Avenue—is an old-fashioned farmhouse, the home of Anthony Archer, the grandfather of John Archer, who to-day lives a few rods distant from the site of the old dwelling, which years ago was demolished. The British troop press Mr. Anthony Archer into their service as driver. They dispatch a messenger to bear to the affianced lady the sad tidings of her lover's severe wound. Tenderly the pale captain is conveyed down to the private road * in Tippett's Valley. They halt to obtain a drink

---

* The entrance to that road in those days was east of the present railroad track, but west of the brook. When the first Croton Aqueduct was built the entrance was changed to a point a short distance west of the present railroad station. The road once extended all the way to Van Cortlandt Mills.

of water at the farmhouse of Frederick Post, a few rods northwest of the present stone bridge which arches the railroad near the Lincoln station. Then they resume their sad southward way. When they arrive at the Van Cortlandt Mansion the dying officer faintly speaks a few words to his broken-hearted bride-elect, is exhausted by the effort, and lies in her arms a bleeding corpse.

> "O that some sweet bird of the south
> Might build her nest in every cannon's mouth,
> Till the only sound from its rusty throat
> Would be a wren's or a blue bird's note."

At or near the bridge spanning the Nepperhan, a short distance from the parsonage, which stood near the beautiful cluster of large trees in the present Oakland cemetery, opposite the present carpet factory, Eden Hunt, a brother of Major David Hunt, was mortally wounded. He and his comrades were endeavoring to escape from Colonel De Lancey, who was pursuing them. Mr. Hunt rode a better horse than those of his companions, and was some distance ahead of them. When he reached the road to Eastchester (Ashburton Avenue), he turned into it instead of going forward on the Post-road. It was a fatal mistake for him. Two soldiers, who were members of the British Refugee Corps, waylaid and attacked him. The rest of the party retreated by the Albany road.

The parsonage, near which Eden Hunt was wounded, was known, in 1778, as the Babcock house. The widow of the Rev. Luke Babcock and Miss Sarah Williams, who was the sister of Mrs. Frederick Philipse, occupied it. Lord Howe fixed his headquarters there. Colonel Gist, an American officer, was said to have been a devoted admirer of Mrs. Babcock. Perhaps this accounts for his stationing his troops, when opportunity offered, at the foot of Wild Boar hill, directly opposite the manse. In the year 1778, the colonel's corps was attacked at its post near the parsonage. While he was calling on the accomplished widow, her house was quietly surrounded by armed men. An interesting account of the attempt to surprise the American colonel and his command is recorded in *The Weekly Statesman* of April 15, 1880. The article is entitled "Philipse Bridge," and is from the pen of Judge Atkins. The British commander, Lieutenant-Colonel Simcoe, wrote the following account:

"Colonel Gist, who commanded a light corps of the rebels, was posted near Babcock's house, from whence he made frequent patrols. Lieutenant-Colonel Simcoe had determined to attack him, when a deserter, coming in at night, gave an account of his position. The following morning was fixed upon for the attempt. General Kniphausen, who commanded at King's Bridge, approved the enterprise and ordered a detachment of the Yagers to co-operate in it. Lieutenant-Colonel Emmerick undertook to lead the march, having in his corps people who were well acquainted with the country.

The following disposition was made. Emmerick's infantry, followed by the Queen's Rangers (who were royalists), were to march through the meadows on the side of Valentine's hill, opposite Cortlandt's ridge, and pass between the rebel sentries to Babcock's house, where they would be in the rear of Gist's encampment, which they were immediately to attack. Lieutenant-Colonel Tarleton, with the whole of the cavalry, was to proceed to cover the right and arrive at Valentine's hill by daylight; a detachment of Yagers, under Captain Wreden, were to march on Cortlandt's ridge and to halt opposite the Gist encampment; and a larger detachment of Yagers, under Major Pruschank, were at the same time to be ready to force Philips' bridge, then to proceed to the bridge opposite Babcock's house, and to cut off the enemy's retreat by that road. The signal for these divisions moving on was to be the noise of storming Gist's encampment.

Lieutenant-Colonel Emmerick conducted the march in so able a manner, and the whole corps followed with so much silence, that the enemy's sentinels were passed without alarm, and this division gained the heights in the rear and could see the whole chain of sentinels walking below them. Major Ross was detached, to possess himself of Post's house to preserve a communication with Lieutenant-Colonel Tarleton on Valentine's hill; the remainder of the Rangers inclined to the right toward Gist's camp, and Lieutenant-Colonel Emmerick was directed to secure the Saw Mill River road.

Firing soon began; and, it was apparent, from Lieutenant-Colonel Emmerick's quarter, whom the enemy had discovered. Lieutenant-Colonel Simcoe immediately moved rapidly into the road and directly up the steeps to the enemy's camp, as a nearer way than through the thickets: he attained it and, to his great surprise, found that Major Pruschank had not forced Philips' bridge, as had been intended, but had crossed and joined Captain Wreden on Cortlandt's ridge; and that Colonel Gist had escaped through the passage which had been so unaccountably left open. Lieutenant-Colonel Tarleton fell in with a patrol of cavalry and dispersed it; and the Queen's Rangers, as soon as they got possession of Gist's camp, having ambuscaded themselves, took a patrol, which came forward on hearing the firing. The troops set fire to Gist's huts and also to their camp. The Americans reported that the royalists had left unguarded one pass—a bridge known as Warner's. When the enemy was discovered, John Odell, an American captain, led his troops through the woods west of the Nepperhan River, where they were joined by Colonel Gist. It is recorded that Mrs. Babcock, who was looking out of one of the dormer-windows of the Manse, by waving her handkerchief, aided the escape of the retreating soldiers.

The parsonage was the scene of a raid made by a gang of cowboys in the winter of 1780. Having broken into the house, they proceeded to take everything of value. The ladies had no one to defend their household valuables. The robbers' faces were blackened and they were otherwise disguised. When they withdrew from the Manse, their leader bowed low to the helpless widow, and repeated the doggerel:

"Fare you well and fare you better,
And when I die I'll send you a letter."

Colonel James Van Cortlandt successfully used his influence in behalf of the ladies, and their stolen property was returned. Many years ago, when the trees which grew near the site of the Gist encampment were cut down, balls buried six inches in the wood were found.

Mr. John Archer said, in 1895, that at one time during the Revolution his grandfather, Anthony Archer, had the care of the parsonage. When some American officers were taking an evening meal there, Mr. Archer, their host, served tea, a great luxury in those days. A lieutenant said: "Where did you get this?" "None of your business," exclaimed his captain; "if you like it, drink it, and ask no questions!" It seems that Mr. Archer, who was in politics a neutral, had a small perianger, with which he was accustomed to go down to New York, for he had a pass from the British. He brought back provisions. It was necessary to purchase them in New York, for what the people raised in Philipsburgh was stolen.

The old Saw Mill River road is of great historical interest. A short distance north of the railroad bridge which spans it, about half a mile north of the road to Tuckahoe, is the Odell house. The name Odell was at first spelled Wayhull, then Woodhill (or Wardell and then Wodell). William Odell, of Connecticut, was the emigrant ancestor of the family. His son William was one of the proprietors of Rye in 1661–62. Members of the family* settled in Rye, Greenburgh and Yonkers. Abraham Odell, of Revolutionary times, married Miss Rebecca Dyckman, who emigrated from Holland. Mr. and Mrs. Abraham Odell lived in an old Dutch farmhouse in the Saw Mill Valley, about seventy-five or one hundred feet north of the house occupied in 1895 by the St. Andrew Golf Club. The house was originally a long, old-fashioned building, the eaves so low that one standing on the ground could touch them with his hands. All the rooms were low-ceiled and on one floor. The part of the house nearest the road has been demolished. The part still standing, in 1895, was repaired and raised by the addition of a second story. That was done by Jacob Delancy Odell, the grandson of Abraham Odell.

Abraham Odell, who lived in the old house during the Revolution, was an American soldier. His holsters are now a valued relic in the possession of Mr. Charles H. Odell, who lives north of, and near the Yonkers boundary, where the Willow hill road to Hastings branches off from North Broadway. The old holsters are of heavy leather, brass-mounted, and are large enough to carry two horse-pistols, each fourteen or more inches long.

One night a party of Tories, with blackened faces, came to the Odell house on the Saw Mill River road, and demanded of Mr. Odell his money. He refused to reveal where it was hidden. They took him across the road, and hung him to a pear tree, a few rods north of the cider mill which then stood there. They then went into the house to compel Mrs. Odell to inform them where the money was. While they were in the house, one of the family, perhaps Jonathan, the oldest son, cut Mr. Odell down, and he then hid in a field of buckwheat. The Tories probably did not live far away, for Mrs. Odell thought she recognized the voices of some of them. She refused to reveal where the money had been hidden. They knocked her down and broke three of her ribs. Then they took the feather-beds out into the road and ripped them up, hoping to find the concealed coin. The next morning, the daughters

---

*See pedigree of Odell family in Bolton's "Westchester County," Vol. II., page 653, revised edition.

gathered together the feathers which remained heaped in the highway. Jacob Odell, the son of Abraham, was a young man during the Revolution and took up arms in defence of his country. In the War of 1812 he was a general of militia. In a subsequent chapter will be found reference to him.

It was up the Saw Mill River road that a large force of British and Hessians moved in February, 1780, to attack the Continental troops, near Young's, at the "Four Corners," about four miles east of Tarrytown, and within the American lines. The Tories informed the enemy that the rebels were stationed at Young's. An expedition was dispatched from Fort Knyphausen (formerly Fort Washington). It was nearly midnight, on that cold night in February, 1780, when between four and five hundred infantry, and one hundred horsemen set out from the fort to move northward through Lower Yonkers and Philipsburgh, and thence up the Saw Mill Valley road to Young's. The snow was deep, and they sent back the sleighs which they had secretly collected, and the two field pieces with which they had set out. Bolton says that a Yonkers man, Mr. Robert Reed (or Rheade), who lived on the Saw Mill River road, having obtained certain information that the attack on the Americans at Young's was to be made, and that the enemy's troops were about to march, instantly mounted his horse, and rode up to the American quarters—a distance of thirteen or fourteen miles—in order to warn Lieutenant-Colonel Thompson, and that the horse upon which he rode died a few minutes after his arrival.

The Americans attempted to hold their ground, but they were greatly outnumbered and several score of them were captured. An American named Mahen, who was from Massachusetts, "was pursued by two of the enemy's horse, the snow being almost up to his hips; they gained fast on him; he inquired if they would give him quarter; they replied: 'Yes, you dog, we will quarter you,' and this was repeated. Mahen, in despair, resolving to give them a shot before he submitted to his fate, turned and fired at the first horseman, who cried out, 'The rascal has broken my leg!' when both of them wheeled round and rode off, leaving Mahen to rejoice at his fortunate escape." *

---

* It was at the "Four Corners" the Spy of the Neutral Ground, of whom Cooper writes, was, according to the novelist, held a prisoner in the hotel kept by Elizabeth Flanagan. It has long been known that Harvey Birch, the hero of Cooper's novel, was a real personage, and that his true name was Enoch Crosby. He was a strapping fellow, six feet tall, and twenty-seven years old. A most accurate description of the spy and his exploits was made in an address delivered before the Westchester County Historical Society by Mr. Joseph Barrett. Mr. Barrett says that Crosby's operations did not take him to New York City; on the contrary, they were confined entirely to the country districts along the Hudson. The facts were mainly derived from ex-Chief-Justice John Jay, to whom Cooper was also indebted for the sketch which he developed into the romantic figure of "The Spy."

Following Mr. Barrett, however, we find that Judge Jay erred in his notion that Crosby's operations ever took him into New York City; on the contrary, they were confined entirely to the country districts along the Hudson.

Crosby was born in Harwich, Barnstable County, Mass., January 4, 1750, and at the breaking out of the Revolution was a shoemaker at Danbury, Conn. He had previously been a tanner and currier. He was an ardent patriot, and enlisted before the battle of Lexington in Benedict's company, of Waterbury's regiment, which was attached to that branch of the Canada expedition of August, 1775, commanded first by Schuyler and then by Montgomery. His term of enlistment expiring, he returned to Danbury after the occupation of Montreal, and then travelled over Dutchess and Westchester Counties as a peripatetic shoemaker. Thus he not only acquired that intimate knowledge of the country that was to prove so valuable to the American cause, but also was brought into contact with the Whigs and Tories, the bummers, raiders, cowboys and skinners who infested the neutral ground between the lines of the opposing armies.

His first work as a spy was accidental. Determining to re-enlist, he tramped southward toward the American forces, through Westchester County, in September, 1776, and on the way met a Tory, who fell into the belief that Crosby was one of his own stamp. Crosby did not undeceive him, and, as the stranger had a loose tongue, the young American was soon put in information of all the Tory secrets in that part of the country. Having learned so much, it occurred to him that he might as well prosecute the adventure which fortune had placed in his hands, and he asked to be taken to a meeting of Tories, which his companion had told him was to be held near by, to raise a company for the King's service. He must have played his part admirably, for he gained audience with all the important royal sympathizers of the neighborhood, including the secret enemies of the patriots, and laid a most admirable plot for their discomfiture.

Learning that a meeting of the Tory band was to be held on a certain night, he slipped away on the previous morning, and by a forced march across the country reached at midnight the house of a Mr. Young, eight miles from White Plains, whom he knew to be a true American. Prevailing on this man to accompany him, they aroused Messrs. Jay, Duer, Sackett and Platt, the Committee of Safety at White Plains, and Crosby gave them the news which he had gathered with so much daring and adroitness. They ordered out Captain Townsend's company of mounted rangers, who swept across the country under Crosby's lead, surprised the assembled Tories, and ere daylight dawned had every man of them prisoners and on their way to White Plains.

The fame of this exploit went everywhere through the American lines. Crosby, then a strapping fellow of twenty-seven years, nearly six feet tall, broad and muscular, talked to Mr. Jay about re-enlisting, but that sagacious gentleman represented to him that in no way could he do so much for his country as by continuing in that line of duty for which this one achievement seemed to mark him as specially fitted. "Our greatest danger," said Mr. Jay to him, "is our secret foes. We know how to guard against our enemies in the field, but we have no defence against secret enemies, who profess to be friendly to us and plot their treason in midnight cabals. One who can counteract these influences is entitled to more credit than he who fights in the ranks." Crosby demurred at first, but finally accepted the employment of a spy on the condition that if he should die in their service, the committee would see that his name was vindicated. With much feeling Mr. Jay and his associates gave him this solemn assurance, and Crosby consecrated himself to his dangerous and arduous task.

Carrying a pass from the committee, which was to be used only in cases of extreme necessity, and disguised as a travelling cobbler, he set out on his secret mission to discover and entrap the bands of Tories forming under cover. This was in the late fall of 1776. Very shortly he applied for a shoemaker's job at a farmhouse, and discovering that a Royalist company was being enlisted in the vicinage, professed a desire to enlist, but declined to give his name because the roll might fall into the hands of the rebels. He gained the confidence of the Tory leaders so completely that he was allowed to examine the roll, and was shown an immense haystack in a meadow near the captain's house, which proved to be a framework covered with hay and capable of concealing forty or fifty men. A meeting of the company having been arranged for the next evening, he left his bed in the captain's house during the night previous,

Just east of the Saw Mill River Road, and on the heights, where to-day the waters of the Fort Field reservoir lie sparkling in the sunlight, in plain view from the Nodine Hill water-tower observatory, is the Fort Field of Revolutionary fame. It adjoins the site of the reservoir, and extends to the northeast. Its area is about twenty-five or thirty acres. In 1895, Mr. Peter N. Fowler, of Yonkers, said that it is called a fort because the Hessians who were encamped there during the Revolution constructed earthworks on those heights. He also said that when plowing there he had turned up pieces of earthenware, evidently parts of broken jugs, and he had concluded that those Hessians were heavy drinkers.

Northeast of the water-tower observatory are Tuckahoe Heights, where the advance corps of the American army was stationed, just before the battle of White Plains. Near the Eastchester road was Mr. Valentine Odell's property, where a company of the horsemen of De Lancey, the leader of the Westchester Tory light horse corps, killed or mortally wounded nine patriots. A touching incident in connection with the occurrence is on record: "A dog belonging to one of the Americans who fell took up his quarters at Mr. Caleb Smith's, who lived a mile below. The ladies of Mr. Smith's family were in the habit of frequently visiting their neighbor, Mr. Odell. The dog would go with them half way and then return. It appears that nothing could ever tempt him to pass the fatal spot." In 1778 a detachment of De Lancey's corps, commanded by Captain Barnes, went to Hart's Corners on a plundering expedition. Major Leavenworth, of the Massachusetts line, planned an ambuscade. He concealed a detachment west of the hill, on the farm of the late Isaac Lent. Some of the patriots were purposely stationed in plain

reported to the committee at White Plains, and was back in his bed before the family were stirring. The band was duly surrounded and captured, Crosby among them, by Townsend's rangers, and marched to confinement in the old Dutch Church at Fishkill, where they were examined by the committee. By collusion, Crosby escaped from the church, but was compelled to rush past the sentinels in the dark. They fired at him, but he escaped unhurt.

By agreement with the committee he was known as John Smith. Twelve miles northwest of Marlborough he wormed out of a Tory farmer the information that an English captain was hiding in a cave near by, and trying to recruit a company. Repeating his ruse of a desire to enlist, the spy discovered that a meeting was to be held on Tuesday, November 5, 1776, at a barn on Butter Hill. Suggesting to the captain that they had best leave the cave separately, he departed, and sent word to the committee. Crosby arrived at the barn in due time with the Tories and lay down with them in the hay. Presently he heard a cough outside, the signal agreed upon, which he answered, and the barn was quickly filled with the rangers. Colonel Duer, of the Committee of Safety, had come with them for the express purpose of protecting Crosby, and, indeed, had given the signal. The English captain was ordered to call his roll, but Crosby did not respond to his name. Townsend, who was not in the secret, prodded him out with a bayonet from the hay, and, recognizing the man who had escaped him at Fishkill, promised to load him with irons. He shackled the spy, took him to his own quarters and confined him in an upper room. But when Townsend had drunk after dinner plentifully of wine, which the maid, instructed by the Committee of Safety, had enriched with a gentle opiate, and was sleeping soundly, she unlocked the door with the key which she took from Townsend's pocket and led Crosby forth to freedom.

By such methods Crosby was instrumental in the capture of many Tory bands. He spent several weeks in the family of a Dutchman, near Fishkill, where he was known as Jacob Brown. He had numerous fictitious names, of which Harvey Birch was one. In December, 1776, he was sent to Bennington, Vt., by orders of the committee. The object of his journey was accomplished, for, besides apprehending a number of secret enemies of the country in that region, he obtained such information as enabled him to surprise a company of them much nearer home. This was at Pawling, Dutchess County, and, fearing to trust himself again to the vengeance of Captain Townsend, he arranged with Colonel Morehouse, a Whig of the neighborhood, to raise a body of volunteers and capture them. When their rendezvous was surrounded, Crosby, he having again made a false enlistment, was dragged out from under a bed, where he had taken refuge, and complained that his leg was so much injured that he could not walk. The accommodating colonel took him on his horse, and, of course, he soon got away.

For three years Crosby continued in the employ of the Committee of Safety, but at last the Tories, marvelling much at the detection of their covert undertakings, fixed suspicion upon him. A band traced him to the house of his brother-in-law in the Highlands, and beat him until they left him for dead. They were followed by a company of Whigs, who pursued them to the Croton River, where some were killed and others driven into the stream. It was months before Crosby recovered, and it was then plain that his days of usefulness as a spy were past. He joined Captain Philip Van Cortlandt's company, and was appointed a subordinate officer. While on duty at Teller's Point, in the spring of 1780, he decoyed a boat's crew from a British ship in the stream to the shore by parading on the beach a soldier dressed in Lafayette's uniform. He had his ambuscade set for them, and captured them all. In the following fall his enlistment expired and he retired to private life. His whole pay from the government was but two hundred and fifty dollars, so that any remuneration he received from the Committee of Safety must have been very little. In October, 1781, in partnership with his brother Benjamin, he bought three hundred and seventy-nine acres of the forfeited Roger Morris estate, near Brewster's. A part of this tract is now covered by the Croton Reservoir. He erected a frame house on the east branch of the Croton River, a short distance east of the Upper Iron Bridge at Croton Falls, where he lived a quiet life many years. The property is now owned by Joel B. Purdy. Later, Crosby built the house now owned by his grand-daughter, Mrs. S. E. Mead, of Golden's Bridge. It stands north of the old house. In this house Crosby passed the later years of his life, and died June 25, 1835. He was interred in the old Gilead burying-ground, near Carmel, Putnam County. He married the widow of Colonel Benjamin Green. Colonel Green was also a soldier of the Revolution, and after the close of the war settled near the present Somers Centre depot. After the colonel's death his widow remained in the house until her marriage with Crosby, which was brought about by Dr. Ebenezer White. In the course of conversation on one occasion, Crosby asked the doctor if he would not find a wife for him. The doctor promised to try and do so. He finally bethought him of the Widow Green in her lonely state. The widow was apparently pleased with the recommendation of his friend Crosby, as set forth by the doctor, and an introduction took place, followed shortly afterwards by marriage.

He was a justice of the peace nearly thirty years. His exploits became known to the public through the Astor trials and the publication and dramatization of Cooper's novel. When it was produced at the Lafayette Theatre, Laurens Street, N. Y., he was induced to sit in a stage box. The crowd rose and cheered him with great enthusiasm, to which he responded with a bow. He was so modest that the world would never have known from him of his services to his country.—*Scharf's "Westchester County."*

sight on the hill a little below the church. Returning from Hart's Corners Captain Barnes saw the Americans on the heights and ordered his men to move off by the opposite side. The concealed patriots fired, and the Royalists surrendered. Sixty-four men—the whole company—were thus captured.

Captain Honeywell, on his way back from Morrisania with a few patriots, stopped for refreshments at the house occupied by Jacob Vermilyea. The enemy, under command of Captain Totten, surrounded the house and fired upon it. One of the Americans was killed. The nine who were captured rose upon their guard and escaped.

Benjamin Hunt, a Continental officer, succeeded on one dark night, with about fifteen men, in making prisoners of thirty Royalists. It was near the site of the school-house that he gave orders as if to a detachment of many men: "Lieutenant ——— to the right!" "Captain ——— to the left!" When the enemy had laid down their weapons and had ascertained that they had been deceived by the stratagem of the American officer, great must have been their mortification.

The British horsemen were accustomed to come down to the foot of the Tuckahoe Bridge over the Bronx to water their horses. The river had been bridged there as far back at least as 1728. Some patriots who were in the encampment of the American army on the hills to the west determined to ambuscade the Royalists. They concealed themselves on the shore of the river, but instead of the usual small number of horsemen coming down that day nearly the whole force came. The hidden Americans prudently remained in concealment, otherwise they would have been overpowered.

WASHINGTON'S CAMP CHEST, USED DURING THE REVOLUTION.

Eastward from the Nodine Hill tower observatory and just across the valley of Tippett's Brook is the famous Valentine Hill. It was rented at the commencement of the Revolutionary War, and was occupied all through the struggle by Thomas and Gilbert Valentine, grandsons of the pioneer settler who came to the hill when deer and other animals were roaming through the ancient forests, and wild turkey were coming in flocks to feed on the acorns and beech-nuts. Benjamin Valentine, the ancestor of this family, was a dragoon in the French military service, Canada. He removed to New York about 1680. He had three sons, one of whom—Mathias—was the pioneer settler on Valentine Hill. Mr. Nathaniel B. Valentine said, in 1895:

"Mathias Valentine built what is known as 'the Revolutionary house,' that is, the oldest house. It was torn down in 1840. The north end of the dwelling was stone, and was built in the century before the Revolution. It stood about four hundred or five hundred feet northeast of a later dwelling which we call 'the Valentine house.' The old well, still in use, from which water is drawn by a sweep, is about fifty feet south of the site of the Revolutionary house. The well is on the south side of Valentine Street, the course of which is from Yonkers Avenue to the present Jerome Avenue. Its distance southwest of the front porch of the present Roman Catholic Seminary is about six hundred feet. The distance of the site of the old Revolutionary house southwest from the seminary porch is about five hundred and fifty feet.

"Thomas Valentine, my great-grandfather, lived in that house during the Revolution, and Washington made it his headquarters for a brief time in 1776.

"Nathaniel, the son of Thomas Valentine, was a youth during the Revolutionary War. One night, his father, his brothers and himself being at home, the skinners came to the house and succeeded in getting the door open. His brother Thomas seized an old-fashioned shovel, thrust it into the fire in the fire-place, and threw the burning coals out among the marauders, who stood in the dark. They continued to wrangle, and finally got the old gentleman outside his house. In the darkness one of the skinners drew a pistol and fired. The powder blackened the breast of Nathaniel, the youth, and he carried the marks to his grave. It was Nathaniel who said that on many a still night he could hear the singing of the Hessians, who were encamped north of Fort Washington.

"I have given away many bullets and buckles and other relics of the Revolution. Several relics were found recently. When the Stewart Brothers contracted to build the present seminary Mr. Thomas Coyle was one of the sub-contractors. While at work on the grounds, he or his men found two silver coins, one of which he gave as a souvenir to Mr. James Stewart, and the other to Mr. Robert Stewart.

"I have preserved the old chest in which the family buried linen sheets and other household property. It was necessary for those then living here to resort to such measures, otherwise the marauders would have stolen everything valuable. I have the iron knocker taken from the door of the kitchen, which was the oldest part of the Revolutionary house. The part of the dwelling which Washington occupied was a later addition and was built near the road. I also have the step stone on which Washington must have stood, for it was in front of the front door of the headquarters. It should form a part of the monument, which the Westchester County Historical Society has promised to erect on the site of the Revolutionary house.

"I also have in my possession a picture of the headquarters. My great-grandfather is represented in the picture as standing by the side of Washington, who was conversing with him the day he (the General) rode off toward White Plains. Some of the British were then on the hill where West Mount Vernon has been built. Looking through their field-glasses they saw Washington at that time. The American army went up the back road, and came out at the Tuckahoe Road, near the Sprain Road. A physician was killed in this neighborhood. It is my impression that his home was near. We have been accustomed to speak of him as 'the little doctor.' He attempted to escape from the enemy, who perhaps thought he was a spy. They pursued and killed him. He was buried about seventy feet west of the Revolutionary house, under a cherry tree, which remained there many years. On modern maps of Yonkers a place on the hill is designated as Glen Washington. That is only a fancy name given since 1850 by land speculators.

"Elizabeth Valentine, who died in the Valentine house in 1854, at the age of eighty-eight years, was a little girl about ten years old when she saw Washington at the headquarters on Valentine Hill. The General took her up on his lap, and the paternal kindness he showed her in her childhood she never forgot. She used to speak of the days of 1776 as hard times, and said that when the American army marched away from Valentine Hill toward White Plains many of the soldiers were barefooted. Some had the flint locks of their muskets tied on with strings of tow, that is, of the coarse part of flax. Probably frequent firing had loosened the locks."

It was Elizabeth Valentine who narrated the story of Washington offering prayer one morning in front of his headquarters, and it was her custom, when she was an old lady, after reading a portion of Scripture, to turn to the text she had heard Washington quote in his prayer. When the writer first heard from Mr. Nathaniel B. Valentine the story of the prayer of the first Commander-in-chief of the American armies, he caused it to be published in the Yonkers *Statesman* of October 10, 1884, and suggested that it should form a part of one of the inscriptions on the proposed monument. It would then be recorded in school histories and exert a shaping and salutary influence upon millions of the future citizens of the Republic. French boys may honor Napoleon as their hero, but American youth have a nobler ideal, and it is doubtful whether even the most discerning and observing teacher realizes how great an influence Washington exerts upon young Americans. Being dead, he yet speaketh. In one of the Yonkers public schools, several years ago, probably just after the death of President Garfield, some of the boys were requested to write the name of their hero, and some of the girls the name of their heroine.

Of the boys fifty selected Washington, sixteen their fathers, thirteen Garfield and five Lincoln. Of the girls twenty-three selected Mrs. Garfield, fifteen their mothers, three Florence Nightingale and two Martha Washington. In 1895 Major Frederick Sherman caused the story of Washington's prayer on Valentine Hill to be published in one of the New York dailies. The following is in substance his report:

"A short time before the battle of Chatterton Hill, in White Plains, Washington occupied the old Valentine homestead as a temporary headquarters. At this time Elizabeth Valentine, an aunt of Nathaniel B. Valentine, was living there with her parents. She, although then a child, was profoundly impressed by the visit to her home of such a notable personage, and retained a vivid recollection of the incidents of the occasion to the end of her long life.

"She was always glad to tell of them—recalling nothing more clearly than the fact that the General made a prayer in the presence of herself and others, at about the time of his departure for what proved to be the battlefield of Chatterton Hill, in the course of which he quoted the 22d verse of the 22d chapter of Joshua, which reads as follows: 'The Lord God of gods, the Lord God of gods, he knoweth, and Israel he shall

WASHINGTON'S UNIFORM.

know; if it be in rebellion, or if in transgression against the Lord (save us not this day).'

"When it is considered that the words were uttered by the Commander-in-chief of the Revolutionary forces, at such a supreme crisis in the long struggle for independence, when the chances of success seemed more than doubtful, all that read them will regard this utterance as being eloquent and impressive to a degree hardly equalled by any other human expression of which history contains a record.

"Oh! who shall know the might
Of the words he utter'd there?"

Bolton narrates several incidents associated with Valentine's hill. He says that, "on one occasion a party of cowboys forced their entrance into Mr. Valentine's house; seizing the proprietor, Thomas Valentine, they demanded his life or his money, whereupon, disbelieving or affecting to disbelieve him, they threatened, on his again refusing, to hang him instantly. Obtaining no satisfactory answer, they carried him to the foot of a cherry tree, near the corner of the old garden, and had placed the cord around his neck, when he suddenly threw it off, exclaiming, 'Don't be such . . . fools as to hang a man when he hasn't any money.' The coolness and apparent sincerity of his language served effectually to disarm the robbers; for they not only desisted from their purpose, but released him."

"Two instances of heroic courage in a female of the family (Susan Valentine, afterwards Mrs. Vredenburgh) deserve record. These marauders, like all other villains, frequently proved themselves great cowards. Miss Susan Valentine, when a young woman, prevented a large party from entering the house by threatening them single-handed with a large oven shovel, solemnly protesting she would split the head of the first man that dared to cross the threshold. Her courage and determination alone served to protect the house from plunder. On another occasion an intimate friend, Mr. Sneden, had entrusted her with the care of £30 in gold and silver, not daring to carry this amount about his person, as he was going a long journey into the interior.

WASHINGTON'S CAMP UTENSILS.

"On receiving her charge, Miss Valentine, for greater security, concealed it in her dress, designing to keep it there until the owner's safe return.

"The same evening of Mr. Sneden's departure a party of skinners forced their way into her bedroom, dragged her from the bed and demanded her money. This she either denied possessing, or refused to hand it over; whereupon, becoming violent, she called to her brother. During the scuffle that followed her brother's entrance, she contrived to crawl out at the foot of the bed, hoping in this way to escape unobserved. In this she was disappointed; the villains observed and again seized her. In the violent attempt made to extricate herself the second time, the money fell on the floor, or, as she herself described it, 'was fairly shook out of her.' The freebooters greedily seized it and marched off, delighted with the success of their enterprise."

On the sixth of June, 1778, Sir William Erskine fell back toward Valentine's hill. Soon after, the Queen's rangers, whose encampment was on Odell's hill, marched to White Plains, as part of the escort of the English Commander-in-chief. At the time the attempt was made to surprise Gist, the American officer, in the Manse which stood within the grounds of the present St. John's cemetery, Colonel Tarleton, with the whole of the English cavalry, received orders to proceed to this hill to cover the right. In 1778, Odell's hill was again occupied by the Continentals after Lieutenant-Colonel Simcoe had withdrawn.

Eastward from the Nodine Hill water-tower observatory is Mile Square, where detachments of both armies found good camping ground, for it was sheltered and near the water. A day or two before the battle of White Plains a strong force, composed of British mounted troops, were reconnoitering in this section, and for this purpose were riding along the road which extends through the place. The American Rifle Corps were there in 1776. They moved over the Bronx River to fall upon the British flank as the Royalists were marching toward White Plains. After the battle of White Plains, a detachment of the enemy marched down to Mile Square and occupied the intrenchments on the hill. They rebuilt Hunt's bridge. Colonel Emmerick's British light horse were quartered at Mile Square and for several summers the British hussars were billeted there. Their headquarters was the Ryché house. Often the cavalry horses could be seen tied to the long cords which stretched from the trees in the apple orchard. The guards patrolled the roads, and lines of videttes stretched along the near hills.

In 1778, a large body of patriots was on the opposite side of the Bronx. An ambuscade was formed by the enemy in an orchard at the place where the roads fork to Hunt's bridge and Valentine's hill. It was thought if the yagers and cavalry should engage with the patrol, which might come to Valentine's hill, that the Americans in large force would hasten to the assistance of their patrol. Then the infantry and Highlanders might rush out of the woods, where they were concealed, and, "occupying the fences, do severe and cool execution upon them, as they were on the bridge and in the deep hollow." Some of the officers, who got upon a fence out of curiosity, were discovered by the Americans, and thus the enemy's plans failed.

In September, 1778, Sir Archibald Campbell advanced with the seventy-first regiment of Scotch Highlanders to Mile Square. Another body of Highlanders, commanded by General Grant, soon after occupied the territory from the Hudson to Hunt's bridge, which spanned the Bronx River. Colonel James De Lancey, who regarded Mile Square as within the British lines, kept a recruiting officer at Jones' house during the whole course of the war. Gainos, a Frenchman, kept an old hotel on the road from Mile Square to Philipsburgh (now Yonkers). The Americans, when on Valentine Hill, procured strong drink and food of him. When they withdrew from that section, Gainos removed to White Plains. The tenants whom he left in charge of the place were attacked at midnight by the cowboys. One of the marauders was killed. His comrades, when retreating, threw the headless body into the adjoining well. Bolton, writing some years ago of the place, said: "This tragical event has given rise to strange stories, and has thrown over this spot a veil of horror, which is heightened by the loneliness of the situation. Some benighted countryman has construed the gnarled and fantastic cedars, which surround this spot, into the headless form of the cowboy, seated on the well, and the sweeping blast or gurgling brook into his doleful groans. The common people still regard this place with superstitious dread, no one daring to approach it after dusk."

South of the Nodine Hill water-tower observatory are the present Woodlawn Heights, in what was formerly known as Lower Yonkers. Tarleton and Simcoe, the two British officers, with a few hussars, were patrolling and making an observation of the country. About sixty Stockbridge Indians, who were skilful with the musket, had just joined the American army. The Indians were concealed around Devaux's farm. Simcoe was describing a private road to Tarleton. The dragoon, who was his

WASHINGTON'S PORTFOLIO, ON WHICH HE WROTE HIS DISPATCHES DURING THE REVOLUTION.

orderly, alighted and took down a fence of Devaux's farmyard for the officers to pass through, but for some reason they decided not to proceed, and putting spurs into their horses were soon out of sight. Well it was for them. Had they rode out upon that farm, the Indians would probably have either captured or killed them.

What is known as "The Massacre of the Stockbridge Indians" took place in the vicinity of Woodlawn Heights, Lower Yonkers. The details of the fight, and of the massacre are given in Simcoe's *Military Journal*. They may also be found in Edsall's "History of King's Bridge," Scharf's "Westchester County." Lieutenant-Colonel Emmerick was patrolling out the old "Mile Square Road" on August 20, 1778, but was compelled to return to his camp at King's Bridge. The Indians were delighted, thinking that the whole British force had been put to flight. Spies informed the British officers of their impression, and measures were taken to ambuscade and capture them. The yelling red men, outnumbered and outflanked, were driven from the fences into the open fields. They fought with bravery, but the English mounted men got among them. The braves pulled several of the cavalrymen from their horses, but eventually were compelled to flee. They were swiftly pursued over the fields, across the lane, down through Van Cortlandt's woods, over Tippett's Brook, into the woods on the ridge beyond, where a few survivors found concealment among the rocks and bushes; here the cavalry pursued them, but, being unable to scale the rocks, called upon the fugitives to surrender, promising them, as a condition for so doing, life and protection. Upon this three ventured to throw themselves upon the mercy of the British soldiers, and were immediately drawn out to the bridge (afterward called Indian Bridge) crossing Tippett's Brook, and cut to pieces. Notwithstanding the strictest search that could be made for the remainder, four managed to escape to the American lines beyond Croton. One of the survivors, by the name of

Job, lived to a good old age, gaining his livelihood by fishing on the banks of the Hudson; but whenever he could be tempted to relate the horrors of that day, the big tears would start in his eyes, and he would sob like a child. Nimham, the old Indian chief, called out to his people to fly, "that he was old, and would die there." He wounded Simcoe, and was killed by Wright, his orderly hussar. The son of the chief was also a victim of that fight. Tarleton had a narrow escape in the pursuit down the ridge. In striking at an Indian he lost his balance, and fell from his horse, but, luckily for him, his red foe had no bayonet and had discharged his musket. French, an active youth, bugle-horn to the hussars, struck at an Indian, but missed his blow. The red man dragged him from his horse, and was searching for his knife to stab him, when, French's hand being loosened, he drew out a pocket pistol and shot the Indian through the head. One man of the Legion cavalry was killed, and one of them, and two of the hussars were wounded. During the pursuit Simcoe joined the battalion of rangers, seized Husted's Heights, and captured a captain and several men of the American light troops, but the main body escaped. The bodies of many of the Indians were buried in a small clearing in Van Cortlandt's woods, since known as the "Indian Field." Nearly forty Indians were killed or desperately wounded.

South of the Nodine Hill water-tower observatory are King's Bridge and Fordham Heights. In January, 1777, a large force of Americans, under the command of General Heath, moved down to the enemy's posts near King's Bridge, to make an attack upon them. The victory had just been gained at Princeton by Washington, and he wrote to Heath to "move down toward New York with considerable force as if you had a design upon the city." Washington aimed to compel the British to withdraw from New Jersey. The force moved at night and in three columns, General Heath being with the centre column. The calculation was that the three divisions should reach King's Bridge about the same time.

The right column, under General Lincoln, was to march from Tarrytown along the Albany Post-road to the heights above Colonel Van Cortlandt's, and halt there. The centre column, under General Scott, was to move from below White Plains along the centre road and halt on Valentine Hill, near the present Dunwoodie railroad station. The left column, under Generals Wooster and Parsons, was to move from New Rochelle and Eastchester to the top of Williams' Bridge Hill and halt.

The right column, under Lincoln, surprised the guard above Van Cortlandt's, capturing arms, equipage, etc. The centre had orders from Heath to cannonade Valentine's house (east of and near King's Bridge) if the guard quartered there resisted. Two hundred and fifty men, the advance detachment of the centre column, moved with double quick into the hollow between the house and Fort Independence to cut off the guard. Just then the left column, under Wooster, struck the enemy's pickets near the top of Williams' Bridge Hill. Two British light horse who were reconnoitering out on the Boston Road, came unexpectedly on the head of Wooster's column where the road descends to Williams' Bridge. Before they could turn, a field-piece dismounted one, who was taken prisoner, while the other galloped back, crying, "The rebels! the rebels!" which set all the outguards and pickets running to the fort, leaving arms, blankets, provisions, tools, etc., behind. The American left and centre were then moved into the hollow, between Valentine's and Fort Independence, and the surrender of the fort demanded and refused. The garrison consisted of a body of Hessians and Colonel Rogers' rangers.

In the histories of the towns of King's Bridge and Westchester may be found details of the various attacks and counter-attacks at this time, of some of the Americans being quartered in huts in the woods, back of Colonel Van Cortlandt's; of their plan to pass a thousand men on the ice over Spuyten Duyvil Creek, which the moderating weather prevented; of the freshet in the Bronx, of the sending to New Castle for a twenty-four brass-pounder and a howitzer to cause the enemy to believe that Fort Independence was to be besieged, of the cannon at the third discharge being dismounted by its own recoil, of there being no live shells for the howitzer, and of the alarmed British garrison on Montressor's (Randall's) Island, seeing the numerous fires kindled by a detachment of patriots, sent to Morrisania, burning their buildings and fleeing to New York, under the impression that the Americans were about to cross to New York and attack the city.

WASHINGTON'S PISTOL HOLSTERS, OF HEAVY PATENT LEATHER.

On the 29th a severe snow-storm threatened and the American generals concluded that, as they had no artillery with which to take the fort, it would be advisable to immediately move the troops back before the storm came on to places where they could be sheltered. The movement began at dusk. Lincoln's division marched to Dobb's Ferry and Tarrytown, Scott's to White Plains and Wooster's to

New Rochelle. They were not safe in their quarters before the snow fell heavily. Indeed it fell heavily while they were marching back. "The boldness of these operations by raw militia, and for so long a period, in face of the strong force of British and German veterans in New York, speaks volumes for the spirit of our grandsires in their determined contest for independence."

A redoubt, semicircular in form, was yet standing several years ago (and may be to-day) on the old Bussing farm, just north of the old King's Bridge town line, and distant about one thousand feet northeasterly from the Williams' Bridge station on the Harlem Railroad. It commanded the road and bridge across the Bronx, and was one of the series of works thrown up by Washington along the heights of the Bronx, and extending northerly to White Plains, at the approach of Howe.

A camp of light troops and cavalry was established at the foot of Tetard's Hill, between King's Bridge and the Free Bridge. It was long occupied by Emmerick's chasseurs, formed in 1777, Simcoe's rangers and other Royalist troops. The King's Bridge was made the *barrier* and the old tavern on the north side became the *watch-house*. A detailed description of the forts about King's Bridge may be found in Edsall's "History of King's Bridge." The map which illustrates that history was drawn by Mr. M. K. Couzens, of Yonkers. The forts were erected by the Americans before they withdrew from New York, and were occupied by the British after the patriots had retreated to White Plains. They were strengthened and garrisoned by the enemy for many years. The "Neutral Ground" extended from King's Bridge, or Van Cortlandt, as far north as Croton.

An outpost of light troops was established by the Royalists near Mosholu, and maintained throughout each year. The force was usually composed of German mounted and foot yagers, and a company of chasseurs, formed of detachments from the different Hessian regiments in New York. In 1778 there were five companies of foot and one of mounted yagers under Lieutenant-Colonel Von Wurmb; in 1779 the yagers and Lord Rawdon's corps. Their camp was on Frederick Van Cortlandt's farm, near his house, which was burned about 1826, and the residence occupied at one time by Waldo Hutchins was erected on its site. The members of this outpost made frequent patrols out Mile Square Road, over Valentine's Hill and Boar Hill to Philipse's Mills and back by the Albany Post-road. Two three-pound Amusettes were sometimes taken on these rounds. The rangers of Simcoe and De Lancey, the yagers of Von Wurmb and the chasseurs of Emmerick were often met and engaged by troops of American light horse and the fiery Colonel Armand and other dashing leaders on the high-roads and by-ways. Johnson, a spy, was hung near Spuyten Duyvil and the North River during the Revolution.

In order to obtain intelligence of the first movement of the enemy, the American officer, Major Hull, selected a certain number of families on whose fidelity he could rely, and formed a line of them, extending from King's Bridge to his most advanced guards. "He requested these persons to come to him at night, that he might communicate to them his plan of securing information, which he said would depend on their good faith, alertness and secrecy. He told the man who lived nearest King's Bridge that whenever he perceived any extraordinary movement, or whenever the enemy passed the bridge, to take a mug or pitcher in his hand, and in a careless manner go to his neighbor, who composed one of the line, for some cider, beer or milk, and give him notice, and then immediately return home. His neighbor was to do the same, and so on until the information reached the station of Major Hull. Every individual thus employed was faithful to the trust reposed in him. The enemy could make no movement without the detachment being informed, and prepared to meet or avoid them. Major Hull rewarded, as he was authorized, these good people, who could not, in their situation, perform a duty of this nature without personal risk. Yet they ceased not to exhibit the virtues of patriotism and constancy, by a faithful devotion to their country's interests, while exposed to imminent danger, and surrounded by hardships and privations." They constituted the "pitcher contingent."

In 1830 many remaining traces of the period of the Revolution were pointed out between Spuyten Duyvil and the present Riverdale. Caltrops lay on the bank which slopes to the river. It is recorded that they had been thrown there to impede the charge of mounted men. One of the relics was an old chariot covered with gilt, and said to have been taken from some British officer. There were also old English muskets, and a grindstone upon which was the regal R. It had been remounted on a frame, and for a time was utilized. A number of cannon balls have been dug out of the bank of the Hudson in "the Yonkers." An old stone farmhouse yet standing, west of South Broadway, was then regarded as one of the best buildings in the vicinity. It can be seen from the west windows of the New York and Putnam cars. During the Revolutionary War, officers of both armies occupied it in turn, and it has been said that on more than one occasion Washington was within it.

Yonder on the Hudson shore, southwest of the Nodine Hill water-tower observatory, is the old Lawrence house,* and Valentine Lane, north of the Leake and Watts Orphan House grounds. During the Revolution Washington and several of his officers were seen grouped in council under the large chestnut tree east of the house. This incident was narrated many years ago by Mrs. Rebecca Valentine, the widow of Elijah Valentine. Vischer's rock or Fisher's Point lies southwest of the Nodine Hill water-tower. The Groshan place was one of the Yonkers houses which suffered from the raids of marauders. More than once they made their attacks. It is recorded that the cowboys took money and farm stock, and that they compelled those dwelling there "to find other shelter out of doors while they filled the rooms with straw and quartered themselves therein for the night." It is also recorded that "a cow and horse belonging to the family were concealed for some time in one of the bedrooms; while the family silver was stowed away between the wainscoat."

Two or three hundred yards north of the present Park Hill railroad station is the place where, according to Bolton, General Washington, pursued by the enemy's patrol, escaped up the eastern slope of what is now known as Park Hill. Doubtless the historian recorded the story as it was narrated to him, but it is hardly credible.

In plain sight from the Nodine Hill water-tower observatory is St. John's Church. It was not known by that name in the Revolutionary period. In those times it was a small structure. The south wall and old door of the original building are still standing. A bronze tablet is affixed to the door. Both armies used the church as a hospital. An American soldier of the Revolution, who was killed in the neighborhood, is known to have been interred beneath the floor of the sacred edifice, but no reason has been assigned by history or tradition for the selection of the church as the soldier's sepulchre.

We have now, from the Nodine Hill water-tower observatory, swept a circle of the historic ground, from Manor Hall on the north bank of the Nepperhan, to the church on the south bank. Some of the events which have occurred within this circle of vision have been briefly narrated. These events belong to a period of about six years (1776–81). Washington was back on the east side of the Hudson in 1778. The British, after the battle of Monmouth, had retreated to New York, and the Americans, from their former post on the hills of Westchester, awaited further movements on the enemy's part. Washington also attempted to co-operate with a French fleet which had just arrived, in an attempt to capture New York. The plan, for various reasons, failed, but the army remained at White Plains and Rye from July 20th until September 15th. One reason why the American commander came back to the east side of the Hudson in 1778 was because it was rumored that the English purposed to attack Boston, and he desired to place his army where it could march quickly to the aid of that city, if necessary.

The closing events remain to be recorded. Yonder, to the northwest of the Nodine Hill water-tower observatory, is the valley of the Sprain. On the Greenburgh hills, by the side of a little brook which flows into the Sprain, are the remains of the French ovens used by Count De Rochambeau. He marched across the country from Newport in 1781 and made a junction with Washington on the banks of the Hudson. A fascinating description of the French army encamped along those hills was read several years ago by its author, Josiah S. Mitchell, Esq., of White Plains, before a social club of that village. The American army was encamped in two lines to the west, with the right resting on the Hudson River, and the French in one line on the hills to the east, extending as far as the Bronx River. The valley of the Nepperhan lay between them. The French encampments made a gallant display along the Greenburgh hills. Some of the officers took a pride in decorating their tents and forming little gardens in the vicinity. Mr. Mitchell says:

"Five long years of exhausting struggle had passed since the two signal lanterns in the steeple of the 'Old North Church' in Boston warned the people that the British army had set out on its first march to subjugate the turbulent colonists of Massachusetts, and with ceaseless persistence the war then begun at Lexington and Concord was continued, until the misfortunes of 1780, occasioned by the treason of Arnold, the loss of Charleston and the annihilation of the army by Cornwallis at Camden, filled the people with sad forebodings. . . . At this critical moment the splendidly appointed French army arrived, and thereafter every step was a step forward, and through this aid the war was brought to a successful close in two years.

"It is about this French army—the admiration of Europe, perfect in equipment and discipline, and

---

*The house of Samuel Lawrence is still standing. It is on the north side of Valentine Lane, opposite the grounds of the Orphan House. The house and the farm, which included the grounds of the Orphan House, were given to Mr. Lawrence for his services as a guide to Washington. Mr. Abram Dyckman, another guide, was killed at the corner of the road to White Plains, and what is now Eleventh Avenue, Mount Vernon.

unsurpassed in magnificence, as it lay encamped in the summer of 1781 on the hills from White Plains to the Nepperhan—that I propose to speak, and briefly and imperfectly to describe the dress and appearance of the regiments, and the distinguished officers in command, leaving you, at your leisure, to follow them through their subsequent career—for they made history in Europe.

"The officers of this army, from Rochambeau to the youngest lieutenants, were of high birth, and most of them of great experience, for some of whom destiny had in store a brilliant future, for others a tragic end.

"The Count de Rochambeau, the chief in command, was a hero who had won varied commissions on hard-fought battle-fields; he had distinguished himself at Weisbourg, at Fribourg, and as aide-de-camp to the Duke of Orleans at the siege of Namur; at Langfeldt, under the eyes of his King, he received wounds and glory. His skill and bravery in many battles marked the steps in his promotions until he reached the highest rank. At the close of our war he returned to France and became an active partisan in the French Revolution and a prisoner in the Bastile. When his name was called for execution it was found that the cart which transported the prisoners to the place of execution was already filled, and the officer in charge pushed him back, saying, 'Stand back, old fellow; your turn will come later!' but the head of the bloody Robespierre fell before his turn came.

"Next to Rochambeau came the old Baron Viomeuil, who had been in service since 1740, and now commanded the ancient brigade of Bourbonnais, which lay on Nelson's hill—the ridge east of the Nepperhan—the oldest regiment of France, whose morning reveille had greeted every rising sun for centuries.

"Next in command was the Chevalier de Chastelleux, a man of culture who rendered great service to Rochambeau in his interviews with Washington.

"On the same ridge east of Nelson's were the Royal Deux Ponts, and the old Soisonnais, commanded by Count de Viomeuil, a brother of the baron; and farther east lay the regiment of Saintonge, commanded by Count de Custine, who had served in Prussia under Frederick the Great. On his return to France he took an active part in the Revolution and perished under the guillotine.

"The French left wing covered Chatterton's hill and White Plains, and was composed of Lauzun's legion, its commander distinguished for the elegance of his person, and his courtly and fascinating manners. He was favored by fortune, courted by the nobility, the delight of the gay city of Paris, a special favorite of Washington and one of the bravest men in the army. He afterwards became engaged in the turmoils of the French Revolution, and, with de Custine, perished under the guillotine.

"The old Odell mansion, still standing, was the headquarters of General Rochambeau, and with him, as aide-de-camp, was young Berthier, who rose to distinction and high command under the great Napoleon. When he became Field Marshal of France and Prince of Wagram, some of the Greenburgh girls exultingly boasted that they had danced with him at Colonel Odell's. You all know his sad death.

"There at the headquarters was that chivalrous young Swede, the Count de Fersen, first aide-de-camp of Rochambeau. He was one of the heroes of Yorktown, and you will find his portrait in a group of officers in Trumbell's picture of the surrender of Cornwallis, in the rotunda of the capitol at Washington. On his return to France he became devoted to the Bourbons and commanded the famous Swiss body guard of Louis XVI. He was an especial favorite of Marie Antoinette, and, in the memorable flight to Varennes, de Fersen was the disguised coachman of the Royal fugitives. He afterwards became the favorite of Charles XIII., of Sweden, and was finally tortured to death by a mob in Stockholm.

"Now, let us look a moment at the beautiful dress and elegant equipments of the French regiments. The old Bourbonnais and all the infantry wore long waistcoats and coats of white cloth with crimson lapels, white buttons and pink collars. The Soisonnais wore sky-blue collars, yellow buttons and red lapels. The Royal Deux Ponts had a blue uniform with yellow collars and lapels. Upon the buttons of each soldier was the number of his regiment. The uniform of the artillery was gray, with lapels of red velvet. The non-commissioned officers wore a cluster of white plumes. The chasseurs wore white and green, and the grenadiers red.

"These officers and regiments were intimately connected with three great eras of France—the old Monarchy, the Revolutionary period, and the Empire. The object of their present junction with the American army in Westchester County was to capture New York; but General Clinton had, by addition to his forces, made it advisable to change the plans to a southern campaign.

"Immediately after the arrival of the French the days were spent in exchanging visits between the officers of the two armies—our army, under Washington, occupying the high grounds between the Nepperhan and the Hudson. The Americans were charmed with the beautiful equipment of the French allies, and the French surprised at the fine discipline of the Americans; and each had something to learn of the other. No jar or collision occurred between the officers of the two armies, although composed of men so different in race, habits, and religion.

"It is amusing to find, in the diaries and letters of the officers of both armies, mention of incidents in the exchange of courtesies between them. Dr. Thatcher speaks of a dinner given by some French officers to the officers of the regiment to which he was attached. They were received, he says, in an elegant marquee; the dinner, served in French style, consisted of soups, roast beef, etc. The officers, he tells us, were accomplished gentlemen, free and affable in their manner. What else could be expected of the highest nobility of the most polite court in Europe?

"On the other hand, M. Blanchard, the French commissary, did not express so much pleasure with a dinner he took with Washington. 'The table,' he says, 'was served in the American style—vegetables, beef, potatoes, lamb, chickens, salad, pudding and pies, all being put on at the same time. They gave us, on the same plate, beef, potatoes, lamb, etc.'

"There can be nothing more pleasing to an American than the admiration with which Washington was regarded by the French; and I cannot close this branch of my sketch without giving you the impressions of the Marquis de Chastelleux in regard to Washington, as expressed in his account of his travels in America, written at this time.

"The marquis had been invited by Lafayette to come and be presented to the Commander-in-chief. As he approached, he found the headquarters in a large farmhouse, with a spacious tent before it for the General, and smaller tents in the adjoining fields for his guards, and everything in perfect order. He writes: 'As I rode up, I observed Lafayette in front of the house conversing with an officer, tall of stature, with a mild and noble countenance. It was Washington himself. I alighted, and was presented by Lafayette, and was invited into the house, where I met many prominent officers, and, although dinner was over, a fresh dinner was prepared for me. . . . I soon found myself at ease near the greatest and best of men. The goodness and benevolence that characterize him are evident from everything about him, but the confidence he gives birth to never occasions improper familiarity, for the sentiment he inspires is a profound esteem for his virtues and a high opinion of his talent. The continent of North America, from Boston to Charleston, is a great volume, every page of which presents his eulogium."

UNIFORMS OF FRENCH SOLDIERS IN AMERICA.

The object of Washington in concentrating the forces in Westchester County having failed, by reason of the great accessions to the army of Sir Henry Clinton in New York,* plans were formed for a southern expedition to crush Cornwallis, and the scene of gayety at and around the old Odell homestead terminated on the 19th of August, when the encampment was broken up and "Westchester County from White Plains to Peekskill was alive with the tramp of troops, the gleam of arms in the summer sun, and the lumbering of artillery and baggage-wagons along its roads. And the brilliant French army left the green hills of Westchester County, which had witnessed its brief and joyous sojourn."

"On the 8th General Washington," says a French writer, "reviewed both armies. The American army, which he inspected first, was composed of four thousand five hundred men, at the utmost, among whom were some very young men and many negroes. They had no uniforms, and appeared poorly equipped. . . . The Rhode Island regiment alone appeared to the French officers to be well dressed." When the French and Americans made an exploration toward New York the recorded testimony of the French writer is: "I cannot repeat too often how greatly I have been surprised at the American army. It is inconceivable that troops, almost naked, poorly paid, and composed of old men, negroes and children, should march equally well on the road and under fire. I have shared this astonishment with M. de Rochambeau himself, who continued to speak of it to us on the return march. I hardly need to speak of the coolness of General Washington; it is known; but this great man is a thousand times greater and more noble at the head of his army than at any other time."

One day a company of mounted men passed through Yonkers, moving southward. Colonel Armand, the celebrated French cavalry officer, was making a daring and successful attempt to surprise a large piquet of green yagers, stationed at Warner's store (Mosholu), under the command of De Wurmb. Bolton, who describes the movement, says: "For this purpose Armand left his quarters above the Croton and proceeded down the main Post-road to Yonkers. After passing that place, and when in the neighborhood of the enemy's encampment, he started his whole corps on a full gallop. The yagers had taken the precaution to post a sentinel at Hadley's spring, but the poor fellow became so perfectly alarmed and powerless on seeing the furious onset of Armand's horse, that he could give no alarm, and was instantly dispatched. The consequence was, the whole corps were killed or made prisoners. Colonel Armand then made good his retreat, passing in front of the Van Cortlandt residence and returning by way of Tippett's valley. In the meantime, the British bugle sounded to horse, and his enemies were in full pursuit. On arriving at the Van Cortlandt house a vigorous search was made for Armand, who was by this time far advanced on his retreat to the Croton."

* During the Revolution the enemy's war vessels were from time to time in Yonkers waters. In 1780 the Vulture floated past with Andre on board to consummate the treachery of Arnold, and the Vulture went down with the tide, but Andre never trod her deck again. While the French were on the hills north of Yonkers (1781) two sloops of war, two tenders and one galley—all British—went up the Hudson, probably to destroy stores, provisions, etc., then moving from West Point to Tarrytown. The account of the fight off Tarrytown, where two American sloops put in, may be found in Scharf's "Westchester County" (Vol. II., page 229). When the British boats were returning, they were fired at from the fortifications at Dobb's Ferry. One of the shells burst on board the largest ship; thereupon eighteen or twenty men jumped overboard. Three or four swam ashore, and the rest were supposed to have drowned.

A military movement was made southward while the allied armies were on the Greenburgh hills. The expedition was planned by Washington in order to cut off Colonel James De Lancey, stationed south of Vault Hill, and Major Pruschanck, another British officer. He occupied Cortlandt Ridge, in command of the yager horse. Washington's plan was to take post himself on Valentine's hill, the Duke of Lauzun was to move to Williams' Bridge, and remain there until daylight the following morning. General Lincoln was to be piloted down from Tappan to Yonkers.

Lauzun's command of mounted men reached Williams' Bridge and halted. General Lincoln's command, in the meantime, had landed about half a mile below Philipse's mills, on land afterward owned by Thomas W. Ludlow. It was then occupied by Isaac Post. Major Lawrence, the guide, conducted the force along the shore southward, missing Colonel Emmerick, who, with his corps, was moving north to Boar Hill. Lincoln's command, after moving southward along the shore of the Hudson, turned eastward. They crossed the hills and reached Tippett's Brook in order to avoid Pruschanck's corps stationed below, on Cortlandt Ridge. General Lincoln passed the Van Cortlandt residence and kept close to the edge of Gun and Locust Hills. He had arrived in the vicinity of General Montgomery's house (then occupied by his widow), and had not been observed by the sentinels on the opposite side, when the enemy's patrol fired. De Lancey, instantly on the alert, commenced his retreat in face of General Lincoln's advancing columns. Totten, De Lancey's lieutenant, seemed determined to make a stand, but soon received positive orders from De Lancey to retire, which he did, just in time to avoid the surprise. As this attempt to surprise the British outposts was unsuccessful, it is unnecessary to detail the movements in connection with it of the troops with Washington and those with the Duke of Lauzun.

The last important movement was on the part of Washington and de Rochambeau with about five thousand troops. It was a part of the plan for wresting New York City from the British, or else forcing them to draw upon their troops in the south for the protection of the city. The American commander understood that the fleet of De Grasse would co-operate. The project miscarried, because the British were more strongly re-enforced than had been anticipated.

Washington determined that he would reconnoiter their works at all events. On July 21, 1781, Lincoln and Chastelleux made a reconnoissance of the works to the north of New York Island. Some advanced by the old Albany Road, some down the Saw Mill Valley, and the third column by the Eastchester Road. Scammel's light infantry was in advance to prevent the intelligence of the general movement spreading. Sheldon's cavalry and the Connecticut troops were to go to the eastward of Westchester township and scour Throgg's Neck; his infantry and the Count de Lauzun's lancers were to scour Morrisania. The main body arrived at Fort Independence at daybreak. The British on New York Island did not seem to know what was going on. While the troops kept the enemy in check, Washington and Rochambeau, accompanied by the engineers of their staffs and with an escort of dragoons, reconnoitered the British position. A map prepared by Washington's engineer, now at the Historica Society Library in New York, with its pencil-marks and memoranda, brings the whole movement down almost to an eye-witness standpoint. They rode across country from the Hudson to the Sound. The British shelled them from several points, but the cortege proceeded leisurely on their business.

AMERICAN ARTILLERY, DRAWN BY OXEN.

Before withdrawing from Westchester County and hastening with the allied armies to capture Cornwallis at Yorktown, Va., Washington endeavored to leave upon the enemy's officers in New York City the impression that his plan was to capture the city. Letters were written and sent in such a way that they would be intercepted. He stationed some of his troops on Vault Hill, north of the Van Cortlandt mansion, and lighted camp-fires there. All the time he was making arrangements to secretly withdraw and join Lafayette before Yorktown in Virginia. Some years ago, there were the remains of a considerable fort on the north end of Vault Hill or ridge.

Mr. Jasper Stymets, an aged resident of Dobb's Ferry, who died about 1850, at the age of ninety years, or thereabouts, said that the Americans and French, when leaving Greenburgh for Yorktown, Va., marched up the Nepperhan Valley, thence along the first cross-road (now the north line of Greenburgh) to the Albany Post-road and thence northward to King's Ferry at Verplanck's Point.

In September, 1781, or 1782, a British force of five thousand men moved out across King's Bridge to Valentine's hill, as an escort to young Prince William Henry (afterwards King William the Fourth). Sir Guy Carleton was with the Prince. They made an incursion as far as Valentine's hill.

The spectator, who to-day looks out upon Yonkers, with all its beauty and wealth, can hardly realize what a ravaged country it was during the Revolution. The Rev. Timothy Dwight, D.D., sometime president of Yale College, was a chaplain in the United States army before presiding over the college. He and Dr. Thatcher, who kept a military journal, described the *Neutral Ground* in Westchester County. The distinguished clergyman's description is graphic. He says:

"In the autumn of 1777, I resided for some time in this county. The lines of the British were then in the neighborhood of King's Bridge, and those of the Americans at Byram River. The unhappy inhabitants were, therefore, exposed to the depredations of both. Often they were actually plundered, and always were liable to this calamity. They feared everybody whom they saw, and loved nobody. It was a curious fact to a philosopher, and a melancholy one, to hear their conversation. To every question they gave such an answer as would please the inquirer; or, if they despaired of pleasing, such a one as would not provoke him. Fear apparently was the only passion by which they were animated. The power of volition seemed to have deserted them. They were not civil, but obsequious; not obliging, but subservient. They yielded with a kind of apathy, and very quietly, what you asked, and what they supposed it impossible for them to retain. If you treated them kindly, they received it coldly, not as a kindness, but as a compensation for injuries done them by others. When you spoke to them, they answered you without either good or ill nature, and without any appearance of reluctance or hesitation; but they subjoined neither questions nor remarks of their own; proving to your full conviction that they felt no interest either in the conversation or yourself. Both their countenances and motions had lost every trace of animation and feeling. The features were smoothed, not in serenity, but apathy; and, instead of being settled in the attitude of quiet thinking, strongly indicated that all thought, beyond what was merely instinctive, had fled their minds forever.

"Their houses, in the meantime, were in a great measure scenes of desolation. Their furniture was extensively plundered or broken to pieces. The walls, floors and windows were injured, both by violence and decay, and were not repaired because they had not the means to repair them, and because they were exposed to the repetition of the same injuries. Their cattle were gone. Their enclosures were burnt when they were capable of becoming fuel, and in many cases thrown down when they were not. Their fields were covered with a rank growth of weeds and wild grass.

"Amid all this appearance of desolation, nothing struck my eye more forcibly than the sight of the high road. Where I had heretofore seen a continual succession of horses and carriages, life and bustle—lending a sprightliness to all the environing objects—not a single, solitary traveller was seen, from week to week, or from month to month. The world was motionless and silent, except when one of these unhappy people ventured upon a rare and lonely excursion to the house of a neighbor no less unhappy; or a scouting party, traversing the country in quest of enemies, alarmed the inhabitants with expectation of new injuries and sufferings. The very tracks of the carriages were grown over and obliterated, and, where they were discernible, resembled the faint impressions of chariot wheels said to be left on the pavements of Herculaneum. The grass was of full height for the scythe, and strongly realized to my own mind, for the first time, the proper import of that picturesque declaration in the song of Deborah: 'In the days of Shamgar, the son of Anath, in the days of Jael, the highways were unoccupied, and the travellers walked through by-paths. The inhabitants of the villages ceased; they ceased in Israel.'"

Dr. Thatcher thus writes of the county as it appeared in 1780:

"The country which we lately traversed, about fifty miles in extent, is called *Neutral Ground*, but the miserable inhabitants who remain are not much favored with privileges which their neutrality ought to secure to them. They are continually exposed to the ravages and insults of an infamous banditti, composed of Royal refugees and Tories. The country is rich and fertile, and the farms appear to have been advantageously cultivated, but it now has the marks of a country in ruins. A large proportion of the proprietors have abandoned their farms; the few that remain find it impossible to harvest the produce. The meadows and pastures are covered with grass of a summer's growth, and thousands of bushels of apples and other fruit are rotting in the orchards. We brought off about two hundred loads of hay and grain, and ten times the amount might have been procured had teams enough been provided. Those of the inhabitants of the neutral ground who were Tories have joined their friends in New York, and the Whigs have retired into the interior of the country. Some of each side have taken up arms, and become the most cruel and deadly foes. There are within the British lines banditti, consisting of lawless villains, who devote themselves to the most cruel pillage and robbery among the defenceless inhabitants between the lines; many of them they carry off to New York, after plundering their houses and farms. These shameless marauders have received the names of cowboys and skinners. By their atrocious deeds, they have become a scourge and terror to the people. Numerous instances have been related of these miscreants subjecting defenceless persons to cruel tortures, to compel them to deliver up their money, or to disclose the places where it had been secreted. It is not uncommon for them to hang a man by the neck till apparently dead, then restore him, and repeat the experiment, and leave him for dead. One of these unhappy persons informed me that when suffering this cruel treatment, the last sensation which he recollects, when suspended by the neck, was a flashing heat over him like that which would be occasioned by boiling water poured over his body; he was, however, cut down, and how long he remained on the ground insensible he knows not. A peaceable, unresisting Quaker, of considerable respectability, by the name of Quincy, was visited by several of these vile ruffians; they first demanded his money, and after it was delivered they suspected he had more concealed, and inflicted on him the most savage cruelties in order to extort it from him. They began with what they call scorching, covering his naked body with hot ashes, and repeating the application till the skin was covered with blisters; after this they resorted to the halter, and hung the poor man on a tree by his neck, then took him down and repeated it a second, and even a third time, and finally left him almost lifeless."

Mr. Lancaster Underhill, of the town of Eastchester, who lived to the great age of ninety-eight, during many a severe winter night during the war lay concealed beneath the body of an ox cart, which he had covered with hay, and as each morning came was grateful that his house had not been burned.

Evidently many of these sufferers were secretly aiding the Americans. Even their enemy was compelled to praise them. General Howe wrote, in 1777, of the Dutch along the Hudson: "I can do nothing with this Dutch population. I can neither buy them with money nor conquer them with force." Surely that is an eloquent eulogium to their patriotism. They could exclaim in their dire distress: "Behold my desire is . . . that mine adversary had written a book. Surely I would take it upon my shoulders and bind it as a crown to me." It must be remembered that they revealed this "stubborn virtue," when, at times, the outlook was very dark, and ridicule was heaped upon the patriot generals and their cause. It may be that occasionally a newspaper from New York fell into their hands. In, for instance, a copy of *Rivington's Royal Gazette* they read sentences ridiculing Washington and his army. That paper, on August 7, 1780, contains the following paragraph:

ROYAL FLAG OF FRANCE.

"A POLYPHEMUS.—Our old acquaintance, Mr. Washington, we learn is approaching us, *Polyphemus-like*, with hasty and ample strides. His dire intents (supported by myriads of heroes and in his train a thirteen-inch mortar drawn by eight *charming, lively oxen*) are given out to be another coup upon Powles Hook. His last halt was at Paramus, some thirty miles off.—*Rivington's Royal Gazette*, August 7, 1780.—EDITOR."

But the New York City papers were not the only newspapers in the colonies. Doubtless the American troops, in their encampments near Yonkers, received papers from towns not in British possession; and the people of Philipsburgh and Lower Yonkers soon heard of the coming of La Fayette, De Kalb, Steuben, Pulaski, Kosciusko, and other liberty-loving foreigners. They heard with grateful joy of victories at Trenton, Princeton, Bennington and elsewhere. They were thrilled when tidings came of the capture of Burgoyne's splendid army, with its train of brass artillery, five thousand muskets and an immense quantity of ammunition and stores. The gloom into which Arnold's treason* plunged them disappeared when the perfumed breezes which blew across their valleys bore the martial airs of France, and the lilies of France floated over their hills by the side of their own beautiful new banner, the stars and stripes. Public service at the church (now St. John's) was discontinued, for a time at least, by act of the vestry. The communion plate of the church was carried off to New York for safe keeping. When the Rev. George Panton, A.M., was appointed missionary to Philipsburgh he endeavored to counteract the demoralizing influence of the armies and of the lawless gangs which infested the neutral ground. After he withdrew, in 1782, ministers of different denominations were permitted to occupy the pulpit. The Methodist circuit riders, who, before the Revolution, preached at Tuckahoe, probably endeavored to hold in that place occasional services; but, on account of the advice of neutrality given by Wesley, Methodist itinerants were unpopular in the county during the Revolution.

Although schools were broken up and regular church services discontinued, and even needed

* Andre was captured about twelve miles north of Yonkers.

food sometimes plundered, the devout among the people knew where to obtain comfort. They had the Word* of God.

In that inspired volume they read the sure promises of Him who stands

"Behind the dark unknown,
Keeping watch above His own."

In great distress, the patriots kneeled in their humble homes, in the valleys and on the hills of "the Yonkers." From their environment of desolation their cry went up to their fathers' God, to whom Washington, from military headquarters on Valentine Hill, appealed, when he prayed. Their answered prayer is the American Republic.

---

*The Varians at Scarsdale hid their favorite cow and their family Bible in the cellar. When the British, on their way in 1776 from New Rochelle to White Plains, came up, those in search of plunder effected an entrance into the house by hacking at the door with their sabres, and afterward in the same way got into the cow-stable, only to find the cow gone. The sabre-marks of the British were to be seen in the eighties of this century, and perhaps are yet visible, in the woodwork of both the front door and the door to the stable.

At the time of the Revolution the cheapest Bibles were valued at not less than two dollars a volume. The Varian Bible is an ancient English Bible, bearing date 1715. Mr. Charles H. Odell, who lives on the Post-road, a few rods north of the Yonkers northern boundary, has the Bible which Miss Rebecca Dyckman (wife of Abraham Odell) brought from Holland. Mr. and Mrs. Abraham Odell lived on the east side of the Saw Mill River Road.

CHAPTER VIII.

THE DAWN OF PEACE. 1783–1788.

"Blessings from God's liberal hand
Flow around this happy land.
Kept by Him, no foes annoy;
Peace and freedom we enjoy."

THE Treaty of Peace by which the United States were formally acknowledged by Great Britain to be free, sovereign and independent, was signed September 3, 1783. As early as the autumn of 1781 the war clouds began to break away. On October 23d of that year a swift courier rode into Philadelphia, bearing to Congress news of the surrender of Cornwallis. Great was the happiness of the Philadelphians when they heard the night watchmen, on their rounds, crying: "Ten o'clock, and Cornwallis is taken!" On the next day, when Congress assembled and Washington's dispatch was read to that august body, the members, exulting and weeping, went in concourse with the citizens to the Dutch Lutheran Church and turned the afternoon into thanksgiving. The note of rejoicing sounded throughout the length and breadth of the land, for it was evident that the dominion of the Briton in America was broken. The war virtually terminated with the surrender of Cornwallis. New York City and neighboring territory remained in the hands of the enemy longer than any other part of the country. In May, 1782, the command of the British forces in the United States was transferred from Sir Henry Clinton to Sir Guy Carleton, who was friendly to American interests. Washington made no effort to dislodge the foe.

After the winter of 1782-83, which was bitterly cold, British troops were withdrawn from "the Yonkers" and King's Bridge. In April, 1783, gladness was poured into the hearts of the residents of Lower Yonkers and of Philipsburgh by those who brought tidings of an up-river celebration. The Proclamation of Congress that the war was at an end was published to the army at Newburgh at noon, April 19, 1783, exactly eight years from the day the embattled farmers had fired the famous shot at Lexington. The mountains around Newburgh Bay were ablaze with bonfires, kindled by the happy soldiers who were celebrating the great event. The independence of their country was achieved.

The next month a man-of-war, sailing southward, passed "the Yonkers." Sir Guy Carleton, the British commander, was on board. He was returning from his interview with Washington. On that occasion the first grand salute was given by the British authorities to the American flag, and to General Washington, Commander-in-chief of the American forces. An interesting account of this will be found in the *Magazine of American History* for November, 1885. Mr. Jasper Stymets, an aged resident of Dobb's Ferry, who died about 1850, at the age of ninety years, heard the firing. The inscription on the monument recently erected at Dobb's Ferry is misleading,* in that it records that the interview took place there. Perhaps the fact that both sides of the river were known as Dobb's Ferry accounts for the error. Carleton met Washington at Tappan Sloat and Orange Town on the opposite shore of the river. The principal purpose of the interview was not to arrange for the evacuation of American soil by the British, but to arrive at the correct interpretation of Article VII. of the Treaty of Peace, which prohibited the British authorities from destroying records, official documents, wills, etc., or carrying away any slaves. "The silver lining now fast obscuring the dark clouds of strife brought new life and hope to the patriot fathers,

* See J. C. L. Hamilton's papers in *The Sing Sing Republican*, 1895.

but to the dusky descendants of Ham it quenched hope. Liberty for the Americans was continued slavery for them." Washington and Carleton met to interpret the true meaning of the article referring to carrying away slaves.

Probably there was in no part of the thirteen colonies more rejoicing than in the Yonkers, for no section had suffered more, and few, if any, had suffered nearly as much. Because the war-storm, with its iron hail, had been so severe and had continued so long, the smiling fields were all the more beautiful when again robed with the woven sunbeams of peace. Grateful indeed were the Yonkers patriots when foreign invaders withdrew, and war-worn Continentals began to enjoy their well-earned rest. By heroic sacrifices and struggles they had won independence for themselves and their children. They had caused thrones of oppressors to tremble. Now their war drums had ceased to throb and their battle flags were furled. No longer were their homes threatened with attacks of soldiers or lawless marauders. The martial airs of shrill fifes and of bugles had died away among the hills. The people trembled no more at the sharp report of muskets, the roar of cannon, the hoarse shouts of powder-blackened men, and the groans of the wounded. The music which greeted "the Yonkers" in those pleasant summer days of peace was that of "warbling bands" of singing birds, of whispering breezes, and of low-voiced brooklets—

" Sending numerous crystal calls
From thousand tiny waterfalls;
Dusk bumble-bees about the grass
(Anacreons of field and hill)
Drowned with their droning double-bass
The dragon-flies' soprano shrill;
And south winds touched melodious stops
In whispering wood and murmuring copse."

The old flint-lock musket standing unused in the corner of the farmhouse and the battle sword resting undisturbed in its scabbard on the wall aroused the curiosity of questioning children, who, during the long nights of winter, listened to stories of red-coats, Highlanders, Hessians, the French, Continentals, cowboys, skinners and Indians, while their rapt faces were lighted up by the blaze of the crackling hickory logs, burning in the roaring fire-place.

In November, 1783, an historical body of men moved southward along the old Albany Post-road. General Washington and George Clinton, Governor of New York State, were on their way to take possession of New York City. The renowned General and noble Governor were escorted by a body of Westchester light horse, commanded by Captain Delavan. Washington's face was not now care-worn as it had been on Valentine's hill in the anxious days of 1776. Would that art had fastened forever on canvas a picture of those patriots as they appeared on that winter day when moving across the bridge over the Nepperhan and past the old church (now known as St. John's). With what eager eyes would the citizens of the great Republic, especially those residing in historic Yonkers, study that picture! Washington on this southward march halted at the Van Cortlandt mansion and spent the night there. The next day he passed out of "the Yonkers," and, amid the acclamations of the people, rode victorious across King's Bridge, over which he had retreated northward seven years before. The remnant of the British army had crossed to Staten Island and Long Island for embarkation, when, on the 25th of November, Washington and the Governor and other officers of the State and City of New York were met at the Bowery by Knox and citizens, and in orderly procession made their glad progress into the heart of the town.

An American lady, who was at that time very young and had resided in the city during the latter part of the war, has given us an account of the striking contrast between the American and British troops. "We had been accustomed for a long time," said she, "to military display in all the finish and finery of garrison life; the troops just leaving us were as if equipped for show, and with their scarlet uniforms and burnished arms made a brilliant display; the troops that marched in, on the contrary, were ill-clad and weather-beaten and made a forlorn appearance, but then, they were our troops! And as I looked upon them and thought upon all they had done and suffered for us, my heart and my eyes were full, and I admired and gloried in them the more because they were weather-beaten and forlorn."

Doubtless mingling with the throng of exulting citizens who saw the Americans take possession of the City of New York were residents of "the Yonkers," and, when they returned to their homes between the Hudson and the Bronx, with what profound interest must their friends have listened to their description of the thrilling scene, as the Continentals, in their blue and buff or in their ragged regimentals, marched between cheering throngs of citizens. The low rafters of the plain, old-fashioned houses in the valleys and on the hills of "the Yonkers" must have rung with laughter, and there must have been mingled indignation and hilarity* in the tavern at Philipsburgh, Tuckahoe and Mile Square when those who had been down to "York" told how the British, before withdrawing, had unreefed the halyards of the tall flag-pole on the Battery and greased the pole to prevent the hoisting of the American flag, and how, after some time had elapsed, Sergeant Van Arsdale climbed the staff, tore down the British standard and rove the new halyards by which the three-colored banner of freedom was run up by Lieutenant Anthony Glean, while the multitude heartily cheered, and the artillery boomed forth a national salute of thirteen guns. When in "the Yonkers" family circles the story was told of the night of Evacuation Day and the display of fireworks, introduced by the representation of a dove descending with the olive emblem, the more thoughtful and devout listeners must have rendered a tribute of praise to Him who had sent to the war-scourged land the dove of peace, with "wings of silver and feathers of yellow gold." The period in which peace dawned witnessed changes among the people of "the Yonkers." During the war many Whigs in the lower part of the county—the neutral ground—had retired into the interior of the country for safety, and Tories had joined their friends in New York, or had fled elsewhere. Colonists who had rendered themselves obnoxious to the new powers sought homes in Newfoundland, St. Johns, Halifax, Montreal, Quebec, and in the wilds of Nova Scotia. Doubtless their descendants are living in those countries to-day. Some Tories went to the West Indies or Bermuda. Many more fled to the mother country. The exodus entailed ruin of fortunes, loss of occupation, separation of families, and seven years of distress. Many were reduced from affluence to the most abject poverty, others died in obscurity. The Britons having withdrawn from "the Yonkers," nothing prevented any Whigs who may have fled from returning to their homes. Probably some Tories also came back. The bitterness of Tory and Whig in those days was intense. The war having closed, the impoverished but sturdy yeomen of "the Yonkers" began to rebuild their homes and fortunes and their civil and religious institutions. To acquire title to the lands they occupied was a matter of great importance to them. The State owned the ground they were tilling, having confiscated all of the Philipse Manor in 1779. Provision had been made by the Legislature to sell the land in plots, not to exceed five hundred acres or one farm. This would enable tenants to become owners of the farms they occupied. Provision had also been made for the appointment of Commissioners of Forfeiture in the four districts (eastern, western, middle and southern) into which the State was divided. "The Yonkers" belonged to the southern district. The Commissioners were to sell all forfeited lands in their several districts respectively, and their deeds were to operate as a warranty of the State against all claims. Subsequently John Jacob Astor, evidently influenced by the opinion which the Attorney-General of England gave, bought the interest of Captain Morris and his two sisters (children of Colonel Roger Morris and his wife Mary Philipse) for £20,000 sterling. Mr. Astor made a compromise with the State of New York, for which he received $500,000. As the time for purchasing the farms approached, interest increased. The sales, which were private, were made in 1785; some in 1786. Edward Couenhoven's tavern at Tarrytown, where the Commissioners sat to transact their important business, and where probably most of the sales were made, was a place to which many journeyed in those days. It may be that the Commissioners also sat at White Plains and in the tavern at Philipsburgh.

Agreeable to the instruction of Isaac Stoutenburgh and Philip Van Cortlandt, Commissioners of Forfeiture, unto John Hills, surveyor, a map had been made from surveys. It is dated 1785.

All who constituted the groups in and around the old tavern at Tarrytown have long since descended to their graves, but our imagination depicts their appearance. We see their old-time dress, and hear their conversation about the weather, the health of "the folks at home," the roads, bridges, crops, farms, stock, and market prices of produce. Some talk about the war recently closed, and it may be bitter words about the Tories are spoken. Others are interested in politics. Federalists and Anti-Federalists have their arguments for and against the proposed Constitution of the United States. The former quote the arguments of their party leaders, Washington, Jay, Madison and Hamilton. The latter quote their own trusted statesmen, among whom are Jefferson—then absent, as Minister Plenipotentiary

---

* An American flag was flying in New York before the Royalists withdrew. An English officer ordered it down, saying, "This is a British garrison until 12 o'clock." His order was not obeyed, and he attempted to haul it down; thereupon the patriotic housewife belabored him over the head with her broomstick until the powder flew from his wig. He retreated and left the flag floating.

to France—Madison, Monroe, Burr, George Clinton and Galletin (Jefferson subsequently formed a more favorable opinion of the Constitution). Some are grouped near the tavern, others are in the bar-room, which was a popular place, for in those days the blessed Temperance reformation had not yet widely exerted its beneficent influence, and every one, including clergymen and other church officers, drank intoxicants.

The subject uppermost in the minds of the farmers was the purchase of lands. The Commissioners recorded on their books and on the map the names of purchasers. When those (Philipsburgh) (Yonkers) yeomen rode homeward, the word home had a new meaning to them. The one-man power of Frederick Philipse was forever at an end. They were no longer tenants only, but proprietors. They were citizens of a nation in which there is no king but God, who created all men free and equal. By the Commissioners' sales, the seventeen and one-half square miles of Yonkers, as now bounded, came into the possession of about three-score owners. Mile Square had not belonged to Frederick Philipse, but evidently a part of it had been confiscated, for a portion of it was sold by the Commissioners. Several names on the map, which do not appear in the subjoined list, are names of occupants and not of grantees. Several Yonkers buyers purchased more land than is here designated, but part of their tracts were outside present Yonkers boundaries. The subjoined figures approximate accuracy. The survey could not have been perfect, as the time was brief between the date of the appointment of the surveyor and the date of the sales. For that matter it is a question whether, with modern excellent instruments, we have knowledge of the exact number of acres in the city. The irregular lines of the Hudson River shore on the west, and the banks of the Bronx on the east, render it difficult to ascertain the area to a rood or a rod.

Names of those who purchased lands in "the Yonkers" from the Commissioners of Forfeiture and the number of acres each bought:

#	Name	Acres	#	Name	Acres
1	John Lawrence,	488	32	Eleazer Hart,	154
2	Ward Hunt,	343	33	Isaac Odell,	144
3	Abraham Odell,	324	34	Robert Reid,	141
4	Jacob Post,	323	35	Elisha Barton,	135
5	Cornelius P. Low,	320½	36	Dennis Post,	135
6	Isaac Lawrence, Jr.,	308	37	Nicholas Underhill,	134
7	Benjamin Fowler,	305	38	Caleb Smith,	130
8	Samuel Lawrence (estimated),	300	39	Dennis Lent,	128
9	Isaac Post,	293	40	John Devoe,	126
10	Thomas Sherwood,	290	41	Abigail Sherwood,	125
11	Isaac Vermilye,	273¾	42	Frederick Underhill,	125
12	Evert Brown (estimated),	267	43	Hon. Richard Morris (estimated),	117
13	Henry Odell,	259	44	Henry Brown,	113
14	Mary Vincent,	240	45	Parsonage Lot,	107
15	Thomas Valentine,	238	46	Elnathan Taylor,	99
16	Jacob Vermilye,	221	47	Frederick Van Cortlandt (about),	98
17	William Crawford,	202	48	Margery Rich,	92
18	John Lamb,	202	49	John Guerino,	89
19	Robert Johnston, }	190	50	William Hyatt,	89
20	Lewis Ogden, }		51	Mary Valentine,	76
21	Thomas Barker,	189	52	Abijah Hammond,	69
22	Isaac Smith, }	185	53	Jacobus Dyckman,	45
23	Thomas Smith, }		54	David Hunt,	41
24	Shadrach Taylor,	184	55	Abraham Lent,	41
25	John Williams,	177	56	Philip Livingston,	31
26	Patience Burnett,	173	57	Stephen Oakley,	29½
27	Peter Forshee,	170	58	Charles Duryea,	29
28	Jacob Smith,	165	59	Stephen Sherwood,	24½
29	Joseph Oakley,	164	60	Sarah Archer,	18½
30	John Bowne,	156	61	Mary Merrill,	14¾
31	Andrew Bostwick,	155½			

[The names Jesse Husted and James Cortright are on the map, but Husted was probably a tenant of Frederick Philipse and Cortright's land was eventually a part of Hammond's sixty-nine acres.]

By the Acts respectively of 1786 and 1792 the Legislature first conveyed, and then confirmed, the property described as the Glebe to St. John's Church forever. Two acres where the church stands, two where Thomas Sherwood, the gardener, lived, and about two acres of meadow adjoining the Saw Mill River and the road, being a part of the Glebe land, were reserved and excepted from C. P. Low's purchase. Mr. John Williams, one of the purchasers, had been the steward of the Philipsburgh Manor under Colonel Frederick Philipse. John Guerino was a Frenchman, who kept a tavern near Hunt's Bridge. The property purchased of the Commissioners by C. P. Low, whose name appears in the foregoing list, was the Manor Hall property. Low was a New York merchant. He bought the Manor Hall property and three hundred and twenty acres of land for £14,520. He never occupied it, but on May 12, 1786, sold it to William Constable, also a New York merchant.

From the foregoing record it appears that, in 1785, "the Yonkers," as now bounded, was owned by between sixty and seventy persons, and a study of the old map leads to the conclusion that the number of houses within the limits of the present city were in 1785 between three score and four score.

There were then in Yonkers, as now bounded, eight highways, and at least two, probably a number more, private roads. Two of the highways were the cross-roads to the town of Eastchester, lying east of the Bronx. One of these, the southern or Mile Square Cross-road, led from the Albany Post-road, beginning at the site of the present first Methodist Church, to Hunt's Bridge, a little north of the present Yonkers Avenue Bridge, over the Bronx. The northern, or Tuckahoe Cross-road, led from the Saw Mill Valley to the Bronx at Tuckahoe.

The other highways were the Albany Post-road; the road leading from the present southern boundary of Yonkers to Mile Square; the Saw Mill River Road, leading northward and out of "the Yonkers," from the southern cross-road; the Mile Square Road, leading from Hunt's Bridge, northward to the Sprain Valley, thence north, and out of "the Yonkers"; the Bronx Road, leading from Hunt's Bridge, northward to the northern, or Tuckahoe Cross-road, and the Bronx Road leading from the Tuckahoe Bridge northward and out of "the Yonkers." A road, probably private, led from the northern, or Tuckahoe Cross-road, northward to the lands of Patience Burnett, but not quite up to the northern boundary line of "the Yonkers."

There was a private road beginning at the southern cross-road to Eastchester (at a point near the present Dunwoodie Railroad station), and extending southward through the valley of Tippett's Brook. In all probability there was another private road by which the traveller could journey eastward from the Albany Post-road (beginning at a point north of Van Cortlandt's) to the private road in Tippett's Brook Valley, and across the brook to the highway leading northeast to Mile Square. That private cross-road was perhaps part of the highway subsequently known as Highland Avenue, and to-day as McLean Avenue, which crosses the stone bridge arching the New York and Putnam Railroad. (The present Lincoln Railroad station is near that bridge.) The present highway leading along the west shore of the Bronx from the southern boundary line of Yonkers to Mile Square is a modern road. There were three bridges over the Bronx. One was known as Hunt's Bridge. Some distance north of that was the Lower Valentine Bridge. The Upper Valentine Bridge spanned the Bronx at Tuckahoe.

At Philipsburgh, Tuckahoe and Mile Square were little clusters of houses. The six houses at Philipsburgh were the old Manor House, the church, two mills, a tavern and a fish-house. The tavern, which was known as Hunt's tavern, stood on the site of the present Getty House. The flour-mill was on the north bank of the Saw Mill River, and southwest of Manor Hall. The saw-mill was on the south bank, and near the Post-road Bridge which spanned the stream just north of the present Getty Square. A little school-house, about one mile and a half south of Manor Hall, stood near the Albany Post-road, and not far from the present southern boundary of Yonkers. The south shores of the Saw Mill River (north of what is now Getty Square) were several feet lower than now.

Sixteen of the nineteen houses at Tuckahoe were small dwellings. One was a public house known as Underhill's tavern. A blacksmith-shop and school-house were there, the latter about three hundred yards from Troublesome Brook. About half a mile northwest of the blacksmith-shop was a race ground. At Mile Square were thirteen small houses, among them Reynolds' and Guerino's taverns.

Several other places, well known to the Yonkers people of that date (1785), are designated on the old map made for the Commissioners of Forfeiture. A little less than half a mile south of the northern boundary was "Forshee's Landing" on the Hudson. At that point a little rivulet flowed into the Hudson. Bostwick's Public Landing was about two miles north of Manor Hall. A little north of Bostwick's was "Great Bass Cove," and a little south of it was "Little Bass Cove." A point of land constituting a part of the south bank of the mouth of the Nepperhan projected into the Hudson, and was called "Philip's Point." The rock Sigghes, an ancient landmark, well-known to surveyors, and located about one-half of a mile northeast of the mouth of the Amackassin, is designated on the map. About five hundred yards northeast of the confluence of the Grassy Sprain and the Sprain is a rock known as "Cat Rock," so called, because numbers of wild-cats once frequented the hill. Beavers' dams were in the Bronx, about a thousand feet south of the northern boundary of "the Yonkers." Wild Boar Hill is designated on the map as "Boar Hill." It is said to have received its name "from the animal that once frequented the solitudes of its ancient forests. So troublesome and numerous had this animal become at one period, that the Provincial Government was compelled to pass laws for its destruction." Down to about 1846 white oak trees abounded on Hog Hill. The swine ate the acorns. Wild pigeons flocked there to eat the acorns, and many were shot. "Strawberry Hill" is north of the present High Street. "Blackwell's Hill" is east by north of what was known a few years ago as the "Morsemere Shooting Range." The top of "Blackwell's Hill" is about half a mile northeast of Greystone—a little more to the east than to the north.

No reliable record has been found of any lawyer residing in Philipsburgh during this period (1783–1788). Israel Honeywell, of Westchester, was Judge of the Court of Common Pleas from 1734 to 1737, and again from 1740 to 1743, but it is not probable that he was the Israel Honeywell who at this time resided in Yonkers. The Yonkers Honeywell (one of the first delegates to the Convention to represent the Episcopal Church of Yonkers) was probably he who, in 1775, was the First Lieutenant of the Philipsburgh Company. In other parts of the county were the homes of well-known members of the bar, some of them absent from home, rendering their country important public service. Among those absent was John Jay, the first Chief-Justice of the United States, and subsequently Minister to Great Britain. Another prominent Westchester County lawyer of this period was Gouverneur Morris, of Morrisania, who went to France in 1787, and remained in Paris until 1795, as the American Minister. Daniel D. Tompkins, who was one of the Governors of New York State, and one of the Vice-Presidents of the United States, was born at Scarsdale, and during this period was a student. He graduated from Columbia College in 1795. Aaron Burr had cases in the Westchester County courts between 1785 and 1794, and Alexander Hamilton also tried cases in the court of the county about this time, but they were few in number.

As to physicians, Mr. Nathaniel B. Valentine said, in 1895, that there was a Dr. Forbes practising medicine in "the Yonkers" in early years, probably at the time of the Revolution, but whether he lived in the place is not known. Dr. Samuel Adams, a Scotchman by birth, and a surgeon in the British army, who went upon the medical staff of the American forces during the Revolution, settled near Mount Pleasant and practised his profession for many years. His surgical skill caused him to be employed in difficult cases in all parts of the county. Records are extant of Dr. John G. Wright, who lived in the town of Eastchester. He was a college-mate of Alexander Hamilton. Dr. Jacob Shaw also practised medicine in the town of Eastchester. Dr. Benjamin Hunt, a son of Moses Hunt, of Long Reach, Eastchester, resided in Eastchester on the road to Bedford and Vermont, at the corner of the road to Mile Square, where Abraham Valentine lived in 1797. The records lead to the inference that he may have lived there during the period under review. Dr. Benjamin Hunt was in Eastchester previous to 1810, but how long before is unknown to the writer. Dr. Matson Smith settled at New Rochelle in 1787, and lived there for years. Notwithstanding his youth at the time of his settlement, he quickly established a remarkably large practice, which covered most of the southern towns of the county. Dr. Brewster was in White Plains. Dr. Francis Fowler was practising there about the beginning of the nineteenth century.

Dr. John Ingersoll probably came later than this period (1783–1788). He migrated to Yonkers from the vicinity of Horseneck (West Greenwich), Conn., prior to 1804. His home was where Alderman Hicks now (1896) lives—on the Tuckahoe Road, several hundred feet southeast of the present pumping-station of the Yonkers water-works.

These old-time physicians needed strong horses, for they had rough riding on some occasions. They carried saddle-bags, and the few simple surgical instruments then known. The infallible lancet was stored in the big pocket-book, as at least once a year, usually in the spring, "a good bleeding was deemed a necessity."

While citizens were giving needed attention to their private business, they did not neglect public affairs. By the Act of 1779, provision had been made for the temporary government of the southern part of the State "until the enemy should abandon it, or be disposed." A record is preserved of an election held at David Hunt's tavern in Philipsburgh in the winter of 1783, when a supervisor, clerk, constable, assessors, collector, commissioners and overseers of roads, and "damage viewers" were chosen.

Devout citizens endeavored to sustain public worship even during the period when the people were scourged by war. When peace dawned, their efforts were renewed. The Rev. George Paton, the Episcopal missionary at Philipsburgh, had resigned in 1782, and for about seven years the people of that hamlet were without a settled clergyman. The war had rendered the holding of regular services difficult while it lasted; the influences of the armies depraved and loosened morals. An opportunity to acquire even a common school education was not afforded the youth. In 1784, Mr. Andrew Fowler, then a lay-reader, who subsequently became a clergyman, sometimes read prayers and sermons in the church. As he was engaged as a lay-reader and school-teacher at New Rochelle, he could only occasionally officiate at Philipsburgh. He made record of the earnest efforts of the widow and children of the Rev. Luke Babcock, a former missionary, to persuade the people to attend divine service. The church was first incorporated in 1787, and during that year was first represented in the Convention. Augustus Van Cortlandt and Israel Honeywell were the first delegates. "The Yonkers" then had no other church edifice. A record is extant of the incorporation of "the Reformed Dutch Church at the Lower Mills in the Manor of Philipsburgh" in 1784. The trustees were Isaac Vermilye, William Hadley, William Warner and "Cobus" Dyckman. No further information about that church has been obtained. Perhaps those interested in the incorporation of it did not complete the organization.

Talbot, Moriarty, Van Nostrand, Garrettson, Ware, and other Methodist circuit riders preached in various places in Westchester County. Earnest exhorters supplemented their labors, which resulted in the organization of churches in later years. Doubtless at Tuckahoe, where a Methodist Society had been formed in 1771, and at other places in "the Yonkers," their coming was welcomed by a faithful few. Their names are written on the pages of Conference, but the shining records of their abundant labors and sacrifices, are they not written in the book of the chronicles of the King, whose they are, and whom they serve?

It was much more difficult for lawyers, physicians, clergymen and business men to reach distant places in those early days, than it is to-day. Public travel was in its infancy; the hardy traveller bestrode his own good horse, and started on a distant journey, however, with little more concern than the traveller of to-day boards a railway train. A stage line was begun in 1785, between New York and Albany. In 1787 stage communication with Boston was had three times a week in summer and twice a week in winter, and the towns in Westchester County had a stage from New York City every other day. What would the people of that day have thought of express trains, river and ocean steamers, telegraph, cables, telephones, phonographs, cylinder presses, and modern bicycles, and road carriages moving without horses? And what will the people of the twentieth century have to say about "the slow people of the nineteenth century"?

Newspapers were published in New York City twice or three times a week. The first daily paper published in New York was *The Daily Advertiser*. It made its appearance in 1785. These papers were insignificant in size as compared with the "blanket sheet" of to-day. The country was small as to population. "The Yonkers" in 1790 had only 1,125 inhabitants, including 170 slaves. There were 27 more males than females. Westchester County had 24,003, including 1,419 slaves. There were 390 more males in the county than females. In 1786 New York City had only 23,614, a little more than half the population of Yonkers in 1896. The population of the whole State of New York in 1790 was only 340,120. The whole country had in 1780 only 2,945,000, and in 1790 only 3,929,214.

Among the domestic events recorded in the newspapers of that period were the evacuation of Charleston, Savannah and New York by the British, Washington's resignation of his commission, the adoption of decimal currency, the appointment of the first Minister to England, Shay's rebellion, and the reports of the adoption of the proposed Constitution of the United States in order to secure a more perfect government, for the Republic was imperilled by reason of the absence of central authority. The confederation was a rope of sand—a loose union of independent commonwealths—a confederacy of sovereign states. There was no chief magistrate, and no judiciary. Congress had but a shadow of authority, and that shadow, instead of proceeding from the people, emanated from the States, which were declared to be sovereign and independent. The debt was $38,000,000, and could not be paid. The princely fortune of Robert Morris was exhausted, and himself brought to poverty in vain effort to sustain the credit of the government. For three years after the Treaty of Peace public affairs were in a condition bordering on chaos. The imperilled state of the Republic was viewed with alarm by the sagacious patriots, who had carried the Revolution to a successful issue. It was seen that unless the Articles of Confederation could be replaced with a better system the nation would go to ruin. In 1787 the Constitution of the United States was finished by the Convention in Philadelphia, and it was sent to the several Legislatures for ratification or rejection. Then followed the famous series of papers entitled "The Federalist" in support of the Constitution. This great political agitation was the first of a long series recorded in the annals of the country. Those who favored the new form of government were called Federalists, and those who opposed were called Anti-Federalists or Republicans. The Yonkers farmers and other citizens were discussing with great interest the question of the adoption or rejection of the new Constitution. The delegates from Westchester County to the Convention, convened in Philadelphia in 1788 to consider the Federal Constitution, were Thaddeus Crane, Richard Hatfield, Philip Livingston, Lewis Morris, Lott W. Sarls and Philip Van Cortlandt. They all voted to ratify, and their support was needed, as the vote was close—thirty to twenty-seven. "The Yonkers" was now a part of a nation, "strong enough for safety, liberal enough for freedom."

Among the foreign events which the newspapers reported and the people of "the Yonkers" discussed were these which occurred during the reign of George III. in England and of Louis XVI. in France, which was just on the eve of the bloody Revolution.

The first part of this chapter makes reference to the old map drawn in 1785 by order of the Commissioners of Forfeiture. This map, supplemented by other historical documents, furnishes interesting records of the streams, hills, valleys, farms, dwellings, roads, school-houses, etc., of "the Yonkers" near the close of the eighteenth century. The map was brought to light about fifteen or sixteen years ago by Judge Atkins, a painstaking historian of Yonkers, who discovered it at the residence of Mrs. Van Wyck, a grand-daughter of General Van Cortlandt, one of the Commissioners of Forfeiture. It is a large map on stout paper. The portion relating to the town of Mount Pleasant is missing.

After Judge Atkins discovered the map, another Yonkers lawyer, having heard that such a map was extant, also found it. Mr. Matthew K. Couzens, some time Civil Engineer and Surveyor of Yonkers, had been searching for the map about thirty years in the Albany and Westchester County archives and elsewhere, for he had frequently found references to it. Having heard of its whereabouts, Mr. Couzens supplemented its missing parts by his own surveys. Reducing the scale, he made a complete map. This, at much expense, he published, together with an accompanying "Index to Grantees and Occupants of the former Manor of Philipsburgh." The index contains brief descriptions, dates of deeds, certificates of sale, and places of record, and is highly valued by searchers of titles. It was published in 1880, and shows the grants in the territory of the Yonkers of to-day and also of Greenburgh. The old map, as supplemented by Mr. Couzens, not only designates the boundary streams (Amackassin, Bronx and Hudson) of Yonkers, but also other streams, large and small. There are a score of these, more or less. In the following list of the names of rivers and rivulets, many of the names are more modern than the date of the old map, on which are designated the Hudson, the "Bruncks," the "Amackassin," the Nepperhan, the Sprain, the Grassy Sprain, Tippett's Brook, Troublesome Brook, "Turkey Hoe" Rivulet, Fern Brook, Sunny Brook, Jack's Brook, Nodine Hill Brooks and a number of other streams, many of the smaller of which have almost, if not altogether, disappeared.

The three prominent Indian names of the Hudson were Shatemuck, *Co-ho-ha-ta-te-a* and Mohegan, or Mohegan-ittuck, or Mahicannituck ("River of the Mohegans" or of the "Mahicans"). The Minces, who occupied the west bank of the Hudson, called the river Mohegan-ittuck. The Mohegans themselves, who occupied the east shore, called it Shatemuck. The Mingoes (Iroquois) called it *Co-ho-ha-ta-te-a*. On the map of Alonzo Chaves, reconstructed from the description of Oviedo, about 1537, the Hudson is designated Rio de Sanct Antonio, River of Saint Antony. Henry Hudson called it "The Great River of the Mountains." The Dutch named it Mauritius, in honor of Maurice, Count of Nassau. By some Europeans and settlers it was called Nassau. Montagne was also one of its names. About 1682 it became generally known as the North River, to distinguish it from the Delaware or South River. The name Hudson's River had been applied to it by the English not long after its discovery by Hudson in 1609. The noble stream in the German's fatherland is honored by those who call the Hudson "The American Rhine." It is indeed a beautiful and a classic stream. "The Yonkers" frontage on the Hudson ("The Great River of the Mountains") is about four and one-third miles.

The Bronx rises in Westchester County, north of Yonkers, and flowing southward empties into the East River. It is almost twenty-five miles long. The Yonkers frontage on the Bronx is about six and one-half miles. The river flows between Yonkers and Eastchester. Its Indian name was Aquehung. Its present name is derived from Jonas Brunck or Bronx, who, about 1639-40, arrived from Hoorn, Holland. He was of Swedish extraction. His last European residence was Amsterdam. With his family, farmers, female servants and his cattle, he arrived in the ship "Fine of Troy," in New Amsterdam in 1639. He purchased in 1641 from the Indians, five hundred acres lying between the Muscoota (Harlem River) and the Aquehung (Bronx). Part of the tract is the present Morrisania. Herr Brunck (or Bronx) was probably the first European settler in Westchester County. He erected a stone house covered with tiles, a barn, tobacco house and two barracks. From the old map of Bronxland on file in the office of the Secretary of State at Albany, it appears that Bronx's house was not far from the present station of the Port Chester Branch Railroad, and "from the inventory of his estate, it is quite certain that he was a gentleman of learning and refinement, for he had in his library books written in several languages, used silver on his table, and had napkins and table-cloths, and as many as six linen shirts. The books were many of them religious." The river is referred to as "Brunck's, his river." Vast quantities of trout and other fresh-water fish once abounded in its waters. Though unnavigable it was formerly a stream of some magnitude. Beaver were once very common on the Bronx and neighboring streams. About two and a half miles north of Hunt's Bridge was Beaver Pond. On the map of 1785 "beaver dams" are designated (at the northeastern corner of "the Yonkers") in the Bronx River, about one thousand feet south of the present northern boundary of the city. "The beavers afforded an excellent example, not only sociable by dwelling near each other, but by joining in a work which was for the benefit of the community. Water was as needful for the beaver as for the miller, and it is a very curious fact that long before millers ever invented dams, or before men ever learned to grind corn, the beaver knew how to make a dam, and to insure itself a constant supply of water. The dam was by no means placed at random in the stream, just where a few logs may have happened to lodge—but it was set exactly where it was wanted, and it was made so as to suit the force of the current: in those places where the stream runs slowly the dam was carried straight across the river, but in those where the water had much power the barrier was made in a convex shape, so as to resist the force of the rushing water. The power of the stream could, therefore, always be inferred from the shape of the dam which the beavers had built across it. Some of these structures were of great size, measuring two or three hundred yards in length and ten or twelve feet in thickness, and their form exactly corresponded with the force of the stream. They made their houses close to the water and communicated with them by means of subterranean passages, one entrance of which passed into the house or lodge—as it was technically named—and the other into the water, so far below the surface that it could not be closed by ice. The 'lodges' were nearly circular in form, and closely resembled the well-known snow houses of the Esquimaux, being domed, and about half as high as they were wide, the average height being three feet and the diameter six or seven feet. They were so thick and well lined that during severe frosts they were nearly as hard as solid stone." A beaver was seen in the Bronx as late as 1790.

One of the legends of the Bronx is that during the Revolution a British general, presumably Sir William Howe, hearing of the existence of the river, and imagining it to be navigable, ordered the commander of the fleet, then lying in New York, to sail up the river. As the river is only a few feet deep, "the humor of the legend may be appreciated."

Joseph Rodman Drake, M.D., author of "The Culprit" and of the popular poem, "The American Flag," resided many years on the Bronx in the town of West Farms. He often wandered along its banks. In his poem on the Bronx are the following lines:

> "I sat me down upon a green bank side,
>   Skirting the smooth edge of a gentle river,
> Whose waters seemed unwillingly to glide,
>   Like parting friends, who linger while they sever.
> Enforced to go, yet seeming still unready,
>   Backward they wind their way in many a wistful eddy."

* * * * * *

> "And I did leave thy loveliness to stand
> Again in the dull world of earthly blindness,"

* * * * * *

"Yet I will look upon thy face again,
My own romantic Bronx, and it will be
A face more pleasant than the face of men.
Thy waves are old companions. I shall see
A well-remembered form in each old tree,
And hear a voice long loved in thy wild minstrelsy."

The Nepperhan ("rapid flowing water") of the Indians became the prosaic Dutch De Zaag Kill ("the Saw Creek") and the English Saw Mill River. Irving, in his charming history of "Wolfert's Roost," on the site of his own residence, "Sunnyside," writes of "the region of hills and valleys, bright fountains and limpid brooks, locked in by the mazy windings of the Nepperhan and Pocantico." Coming down from the north, and flowing several miles through Yonkers, this stream, having a heavy fall between the Saw Mill River Bridge (near the cemetery) and its mouth, empties into the Hudson. The Revolutionary events associated with it are recorded in the former chapter of this volume.

The Indian Mosholu became Tippett's Brook. It was also called Mill Creek and Yonkers River. The artificial pond which Jacobus Van Cortlandt formed by throwing a dam across it at Van Cortlandt about 1700 A.D. is now known as Van Cortlandt's lake, where New York and Yonkers young men and maidens glide in rowboats in summer, gathering white water lilies in their hands, and on skates in winter, gathering red roses on their cheeks. The Van Cortland Mills still standing there were probably built about 1700 A.D. Tippett's Brook (the name has been corrupted into Tibbitt's Brook) empties into Spuyten Duyvil Creek. It is a tidal stream. The tide backs up as far as the old Van Cortlandt Mills, and the lads, who know where to take fish and and other food from the water, report that "there is good crabbing there." Many years ago sloops came up nearly to Van Cortlandt's.

The Harlem, called by the Indians Muscoota, was once a favorite resort for the angler. The Indian Papirinamen was called by the Dutch Spuyten Duyvil. This name is found in the early colonial records. It means "Spouting Devil," and "may have arisen from some peculiar *upburst* of water as the tide rushed over the reef which obstructs the channel at that point." One or two other theories as to the origin of the name are recorded. Irving's quaint and humorous legend of Anthony the Trumpeter will ever meet with popular acceptance.

The rivulet Amackassin, which is near the northern boundary of Yonkers, flows west by south and empties into the Hudson. The Armonperahin of the Indians became the Sprain or Trout Brook of the whites. It rises north of Yonkers and, flowing several miles through the town, empties into the Bronx. During the Revolutionary War the French allies encamped in Greenburgh built their ovens on the shores of a rivulet tributary to the Sprain. The remains of the ovens are yet visible. Along the banks strolled the handsomely uniformed officers and privates of the famous French regiments. Their beautiful uniform is described in the former chapter of this history. The Indian Armonperahin is supposed to be the west branch of the Sprain River. The author has not succeeded in ascertaining satisfactory information as to the origin of the name Sprain. Can it be a corruption of the last syllables of the Indian name?

Troublesome Brook, once known as Smith's Brook, near its confluence with the Bronx, rises in Greenburgh and flowing south and southwest (about two miles and a quarter, more or less, through Yonkers) empties into the Bronx. "Turkey Hoe" rivulet, as it is designated on the map R, of 1785, rises near the Greenburgh line, and flowing south about two miles empties into the Sprain, about one mile west of the Bronx. Sunny Brook rises on Valentine Hill and flowing southeast and northeast through "Glen Washington" (so named since 1850 by land speculators) empties into the Sprain. A brook in Mile Square, having two branches, rose near the Bronx Road. One branch flowed east and north, the other east and south. From the point of junction the stream flowed about a mile easterly and emptied into the Bronx. A rivulet emptied into the Bronx at Reynold's tavern.

Nodine Brook (east of Nodine Hill) flows down through the little vale east of the Oakland cemetery rocky cliffs, and bending southeast hastens sparkling and rippling past the present "Valley Farm" house, and joins Tippett's Brook. When the Croton Aqueduct and later the present New York and Putnam Railroad were constructed, culverts were built to permit the waters of this rivulet to flow unobstructed to its confluence with Tippett's Brook.

On the east side of Nodine Hill was another brook. One branch rose east or northeast of the present Dayspring Presbyterian Church, and the other branch rose among the rocks east of Van Cortlandt Park Avenue (formerly Garnet Street). These branches poured their waters into a swamp south of the present Elm Street. Only a few years ago rabbits were taken by hunters in that swamp, which is now filled in, and is almost covered with dwelling houses and streets. The brook flowed from the swamp westward and into the Nepperhan at the present Elm Street Bridge. The walled sluice-way, through which the stream ran, may yet be seen south of and near the bridge.

Jack's Brook rose on the hill north of what is now known as Park Hill Railroad station, and gliding toward what is now Brook Street, and along the line of the present Morgan Street, flowed into the Nepperhan, near the corner of the present Main Street and Nepperhan Avenue. Then the country road or lane known as "Guion Lane" descended on the north side to the bridge over the brook, and ascended on the south side to a country road, now known as Main Street. New Main Street was not then opened south of Guion Lane. A short distance west of the corner, the bank was ten feet (more or less) higher than it is now. Where the Jack's Brook Bridge was, has been filled in a number of feet to the present Nepperhan Avenue grade. In the rear of the present building at the northwest corner of Main Street and Nepperhan Avenue was a small pond.

Many years ago, near the confluence of Jack's Brook and the Nepperhan River, there was a small house in which lived a colored man whose name was Adam. Once he was a slave of Lemuel Wells. Jacob Read, long time Supervisor of Yonkers, said in 1895 that, in his boyhood, he used to go with other Yonkers lads, and sit on a big rock there to listen to Adam, who had seen Washington, and who entertained his young auditors with stories of the Revolution.

Fern Brook rose east of the present South Broadway, on lands once owned by Isaac Post. It flowed westward and emptied into the Hudson, about one mile south of the mouth of the Nepperhan. Years ago Thomas W. Ludlow had a saw-mill,* near the pond which was formed by damming up Fern Brook. The mill burned down. It stood at the southwest corner of Fern Brook Street and Hawthorn Avenue. Fernbrook Carpet Mills received their name from this stream.

The old map of 1785, as supplemented by Mr. Couzens, shows a number of small and unnamed brooks. About a dozen, more or less, flowed into the Hudson, a dozen or more into the Nepperhan, and several into the Bronx. The music of the liquid lips of many of them is heard no more. They now are silent, as are those who once strolled along their banks, whose throbbing and loving hearts long since ceased to beat, whose hands have vanished, and the sounds of whose voices are still.

> " Like the dew on the mountain,
> Like the foam on the river,
> Like the bubble on the fountain,
> . . . . gone, and forever."

* There was a grist-mill years ago on the Palisades. Its water-wheel was turned by a stream which came over the mountain.

CHAPTER IX.

THE TOWN OF YONKERS. 1788–1855.

"And sweet homes nestle in these dales,
And perch along these wooded swells,
And blest beyond Arcadian vales
They hear the sound of Sabbath bells."

SECTION I.

THE TWILIGHT OF THE EIGHTEENTH CENTURY. 1788–1800.

FROM July, 1776, when the Provincial Congress, then sitting at White Plains, ratified the Declaration of Independence, "lamenting the necessity which rendered that measure unavoidable," until 1789, when the Government of the United States, framed by the Convention of 1787, went into operation, New York was an independent sovereign state, mistress of herself, and as such was one of the thirteen independent sovereignties, so acknowledged by the British Treaty of Peace in 1783. While in this condition her Legislature divided her territory into counties and townships, and made some changes in the counties from what they had been under the Province of New York. The state was divided into sixteen counties, one of which was Westchester. On the same date (March 7, 1788), Westchester County was divided into twenty-one towns, one of which was called Yonkers. The Act took effect April, 1789. The name of the township was suggested by that of "a tract of land called 'the Yonkers.'" Yonkers is bounded on the north by the town of Greenburgh, on the east by the middle of the Bronx, on the south by the town of Westchester and the Spuyten Duyvil Creek, and on the west by the Hudson. Its northerly boundary is coincident with the northern bounds of the tract called "the Yonkers." The first part of the period of sixty-seven years (which begins with the erection of the township in 1788 and closes with the date of the incorporation of the village of Yonkers in 1855) is uneventful. The tract was sparsely settled. At the beginning (1788) the population was probably not much, if any, over one thousand, including slaves, and it remained small during all the years previous to 1849, when the Hudson River Railroad began operations.

CENSUS OF YONKERS. 1790.

Number of Heads of Families,	152
Free White Males of 16 Years and Upwards,	265
Free White Males under 16 Years,	220
Free White Males, including Heads of Families,	458
All other Free Persons,	12
Slaves,	170
Aggregate Total,	1125
More Males than Females,	27

During the twilight of the eighteenth century the people of Yonkers were living quiet lives. They were cultivating their farms and improving their homes. A few were employed on the sloops and in the grist-mills, saw-mills, blacksmith shops, taverns and country stores. Theirs was the monotony of the country, varied by an occasional visit to New York, then a small city of a little more than thirty-three thousand population. It was just reaching to the present City Hall Park. To the plain yeomen of

Yonkers each returning season of the circling year brought its own pursuits and pleasures. Spring unlocked the brooks, adorned the woods with wild flowers, carpeted the fields, and "rocked her infant blossoms on the trees." Seeds of future harvests were scattered in the brown furrows which polished plowshares turned. Summer came with ripening sun and showers. As mowers, with their whetstones sharpened dulling scythes, the clink-clank rang across the fields. New-mown hay perfumed the air. When the sky was lurid with the approaching thunder storm the hastily loaded hay wagon was hurried from the field and through the wide doorway of the weather-beaten barn, near which the lusty cock "led his speckled harem," and the house dog lay half asleep. With appetites made keen by hard labor in the pure open air, the slaves and other farm hands heartily enjoyed their nooning. When "twilight let her curtain down and pinned it with a star," the weary workmen welcomed the hours of rest. They watered and fed the stock, and, after milking the cows, and attending to the chores, they washed their sunburnt hands and faces at the well in the farm-yard, had their supper, and early with their lighted tallow candles sought their low-ceiled bed-rooms to sleep sound and to wake and work in the fresh morning before sunrise while the dew was yet on the grass.

When the brown and mellow days of autumn came, and the woods were "dyed with new glory," the golden corn was sheafed to await husking, and the treasures of laden orchards and nut trees were stored. Then came winter, when blinding zigzag snowflakes piled their white drifts, and familiar sights

> "Took marvellous shapes; strange domes and towers
> Rose up where stye or corn-crib stood,
> Or garden wall or belt of wood.
> A smooth white mound the brushpile showed;
> A fenceless drift where once was road."

Across the quiet valleys echoed the sound of the woodman's axe, or the regular blows of the flail falling on the distant barn floor. Sometimes, when leisure permitted, the farmer drove over the snow-drifted roads to Lawrence's* tavern at Hunt's Bridge, or to Van Cortlandt or Mosholu, or Mile Square, or Tuckahoe. If he drove to Philipsburgh at the mouth of the Nepperhan, after tying his horse under the tavern shed he probably went over to the bar-room, or to the store to talk with some neighbor about the health of "the folks at home," and about farm and stock, the market price of crops, the news from "York," or elsewhere, and of course, as an American citizen, about politics. At the Indian Queen tavern the landlord or others could give him the latest information about the affairs of the town. That old time inn is an institution of the past, but it continued to be seen in Yonkers in all its simplicity till the steamboats interfered with the stage business, or until the railroad period. That style of tavern has thus been described: "The word 'hotels' was not applied to houses of entertainment hereabout till within the nineteenth century. Such places were previously called 'inns' or 'taverns.' Through Yonkers lay a prominent stage-route—that between New York and Albany. At short intervals along this route places of halting for the many passing stages and of refreshment for the travellers and the horses were established. One who will follow the old route from the metropolis to the State Capitol will find very many of these old houses still standing, but fallen, of course, into disuse. They were substantially all of one type—long, low buildings two stories in height, with an open stoop and portico extending along the entire front. A sign post stood before each one with an arm from which swung a large sign, adorned with a coarse daub, under which the name of the proprietor of the tavern and within or over which the name of the tavern was painted. In front of each was a water trough, and adjoining each was a very long horse shed, of sufficient dimensions to receive and cover many teams and wagons, and provided with an ample number of feed-boxes, from which horses, during a brief tarry, might partake of their oats or other food, as the case might be.

"Within the tavern was sure to be, first of all, a bar-room, to which the halting guest seldom failed to pay his first respects. The next essential feature was the dining-room, where the food was always of the substantial kind. The vegetables, eggs and milk almost always came from the proprietor's own garden and farm close at hand. And the waiters were, in nearly every case, the wife and children of the proprietor, assisted by the negroes, who, in the early days, were almost always slaves. In the second story of the house were the bed-rooms, the furniture of which was of the simple primitive style. The

---

* Probably located there about the close of the eighteenth century. See quaint, but unsatisfactory map of Yonkers, filed at Albany in 1796.

bedsteads were high, corded, and surmounted with the old-fashioned frame and tester, whose object seemed to be to keep all air from the sleeper below. The beds were of straw beneath, and feathers overlying, and the straw, feathers, linen quilts and counter-panes all came as raw material, and as to weaving, from the neighborhood of the homes they adorned. These houses have now been largely superseded by the modern 'hotels.' On off-roads, or in remote districts, their type still prevails. When one would think of 'the Yonkers' of earlier days, he must go back to one of these taverns.

"Down to 1852, there stood upon the site of our present and imposing Getty House (southeast corner of Getty Square) a tavern of the old type. It had been built by Jacob Stout, between 1796 and 1802, in place of the old David Hunt's tavern of previous days. The earlier tavern had been associated with all the public acts of the lords of the manor. In it they had held their courts, and administered the laws of which they were alike the makers and appliers. After their days, from the erection of the town of Yonkers (1788 and 1789), the town meetings were held at this tavern. And, of course, all the public stir of the little hamlet always centred around it, or its successor, built by Mr. Stout. Never did a stage drive up without encountering all the idlers of the place. And at times it found waiting for it many, too, who were not idlers, but who depended on its arrival to bring them the news which formed the great relief to the community's quiet routine. The low politicians and the local wise-heads, real and pretentious, were always sure to be at the tavern in the evenings. Such was the picture. Its like can still be seen in sparsely settled localities along the great routes of travel. It continued to be seen in Yonkers, in all its simplicity, till the steamboats began to interfere with the business of the stages, and to a considerable extent till 1849, when the Hudson River Railroad came and entirely broke it up. The old tavern was finally removed in 1852, to make room for a house of quite another type. What the name of the earliest tavern, or the name of its proprietor had been before 1756, we cannot find. In 1756, the proprietor was Edward Stevenson, and in 1783 it was conducted by David Hunt. In 1813, the house was called 'The Indian Queen Inn.' It was subsequently called 'The Eagle Hotel,' and 'The Nappeckamack House,' which possibly was 'a fancy name given to it by some of its frequenters.' Its most common name among the people was 'The Stage House.' It was removed in 1851 to make room for the present Getty House. It now stands, much altered and enlarged, at the northwest corner of New Main Street and Nepperhan Avenue."

Yonkers citizens, who at any time within this period (1788–1800) waited at the old "Indian Queen Inn" for the stage, were accustomed to see the letters and papers taken from the mail-bags and kept in the little country post-office until called for.*

When the Sabbath ("seventh golden link in the iron chain of toil") came, and weary labor had space to wipe his brow and rest, and opportunity was given to meditate on the rest reserved for the faithful when life's work is done, those who reverenced the sanctuary could attend divine service either

---

*The modern style of envelope was unknown. The letters were folded and sealed with sealing wax. Postage stamps were unknown. The amount of postage was written upon the back of the folded sheet. The amount of postage depended on the size of the letter and the distance it was carried. (For names of Yonkers postmasters see Chapter XII.)

During the colonial period various rates of postage were fixed by legislation. For example, in 1702, letters from New York to Philadelphia were carried for 4 pence half penny. In 1765, all letters, etc., from New York to any place within 60 English miles thereof and thence back to New York, single 4 pence, double 8 pence, treble 1 shilling, ounce 1 shilling, 4 pence.

During the period of Confederation various acts were passed, some greatly increasing the rates of postage and some reducing them. In 1782, by Act of Congress, postage rates were as follows: Any distance not exceeding 60 miles, 1 pennyweight, 8 grains; upwards of 60 miles and not exceeding 100, 2 pennyweights, 16 grains; and so on, 16 grains advance for every 100 miles and for single letters to and from Europe, 4 pennyweights, double, treble, etc., for increased sizes.

The Act of February 20, 1792, was the first Act, subsequent to the adoption of the Constitution, fixing rates of postage on domestic letters. It established the following rates, to take effect June 1, 1792:

For every single letter not exceeding 30 miles, 6 cents.
For every single letter over 30 miles, and not exceeding 60 miles, 8 cents.
For every single letter over 60 miles, and not exceeding 100 miles, 10 cents.
For every single letter over 100 miles, and not exceeding 150 miles, 12½ cents.
For every single letter over 150 miles, and not exceeding 200 miles, 15 cents.
For every single letter over 200 miles, and not exceeding 250 miles, 17 cents.
For every single letter over 250 miles, and not exceeding 350 miles, 20 cents.
For every single letter over 350 miles, and not exceeding 450 miles, 22 cents.
For every single letter over 450 miles, 25 cents.
For every double letter, double the said rates.
For every triple letter, triple the said rates.
For every packet weighing 1 ounce avoirdupois to pay at the rate of four single letters for each ounce, and in that proportion for any greater weight.

Subsequently from time to time the rates of postage were changed. *The Act of March 3, 1847, authorized the Postmaster-General to prepare postage stamps, which when attached to any letter or packet, shall be evidence of payment of postage chargeable therefor.—Extracts from U. S. Government Reports.*

The first stamps issued were the denominations of five and ten cents. These stamps are now obsolete, and they would not be recognized by the post-offices. The five-cent stamp contained the portrait of Franklin, made after a painting by John B. Longacre, in

at the old Episcopal Church, near the mouth of the Nepperhan (first called St. John's Church in 1795), or at the Methodist Church in Tuckahoe (erected in 1797), or at the Episcopal Chapel in Tuckahoe (erected in 1798). These were the only church edifices until 1828. "The Reformed Dutch Church at the Lower Mills in the Manor of Philipsburgh," which was incorporated in 1784, does not seem to have done much, if any more than incorporate, for nothing more seems to be recorded.

The Rev. Elias Cooper, A.M., was the rector of St. John's and also of the branch chapel at Tuckahoe. He was a good man, "a friend to the poor, an ornament to the Church and exemplary in the discharge of every relation and professional duty." He served the Church twenty-seven years (1790–1816). During his pastorate he organized and taught a school. The people to whom he preached were for the most part plain country people who walked to the house of prayer from the few near-by dwellings or rode on horseback or in plain old-time vehicles from their distant farm-houses. They entered the little church at Yonkers through the circular-headed doorway in the south wall--the doorway which can be seen to this day, but now with fastened doors, upon which is affixed a bronze tablet with appropriate inscription. When the good rector arose to read from the book of the great King and the great king of books, whose pages are fragrant with the odor of sanctity and luminous with the smile of God, and when he preached he spoke as the ambassador of One who looks not upon the outward appearance but upon the heart. We hear again the responses of the worshippers and their old-fashioned singing. Their tongues have long been silent in the grave, but in a temple not made with hands they continue to praise their King, "chanting in richer melody than when on earth." At Tuckahoe earnest circuit riders preached first in private houses and then in the church which was dedicated on Christmas Day, 1797. Those devout itinerants were in journeyings often, in perils of flooded roads, in perils of heat and of heavy snow-drifts, in weariness and painfulness, scoffed at and ridiculed; but none of these things moved them if only they could win men to Him, whose they were and whom they served. The record of a circuit rider, the Rev. David Hunt, an Irish divine, furnishes proof of their willingness to preach the Gospel anywhere they could find hearers. About 1792 he preached in the village of Sing Sing in a cider mill. Afterward he held services there in a barn, where, in 1793, a box served for his pulpit, boards for seats, and the hay-mows for galleries. Many readers of history peruse with more interest the records of presidents, senators, governors and generals; but those who value the influences which contribute most to the stability of Church and State, because they ennoble the character of individuals and families, will appreciate the services of these men, who left the world's honors for others to win, and went forth in the spirit of him who said:

> "The vows
> Of God are on me, and I may not stop
> To play with shadows or pluck earthly flowers,
> Till I my work have done and rendered up account."

In those days there was not the fraternal feeling between religious denominations which is prevailing more and more as the years unroll. Now Christians "do not build their denominational fences so high that they cannot shake hands over the pickets." They did then. The travelling Methodist preachers were regarded as setters forth of strange doctrines. We read of one, the Rev. Thomas Ware, who "came along through Shrub Oak, Yorktown, probably in 1786, inquiring for a place to preach in." Peter Badeau said: "My grandfather opened his house for that purpose, and my father invited him, after preaching, home with him. He was one of the first Methodists I ever saw. He left an appointment for

---

which the first Postmaster-General is represented wearing a white neckerchief and a coat with a fur collar. The color of the stamp is a light brown, and there is a border of fine straight lines around the entire stamp.

The ten-cent stamp contained a portrait of Washington, made from Stuart's painting. Its color was black and it had in the upper corners the letters "U. S." These two stamps were all that were used until 1851, when letter postage was reduced to three cents, and a new series of stamps came in.—*Newspaper Clipping.*

Yonkers was a post-office hamlet as early as 1797. From an article by Judge Atkins, one of the historians of the city, the following is taken:

"'I have delved,' says the friendly searcher, 'among the Catacombs, and have extracted the following from one of the worthy and ancient mummies of the Department. The earliest official records indicate that the post-office at Yonkers, N. Y., was in operation January 1, 1797. Alpheus Pierson enacted the rôle of postmaster. Eight years prior to this there were just seven post-offices in the state of New York—Fishkill on the north and New York City on the south being the nearest and handiest to the thousand and more dwellers in Yonkers. Of the twenty extant in the year 1793 in New York State, one was at King's Bridge. Imagine the hilarity of our good people when, in the year 1797, Yonkers was added to the list, and the little village of Philipsburgh, where the Saw Mill Creek enters into the Hudson,' no longer depended upon King's Bridge or Fishkill for its postal facilities.

"The district covered by Philipsburgh and Lower Yonkers had been incorporated as the town of Yonkers only as lately as 1788, and the United States authorities had named the new post-office as such in consequence, although that portion about the 'Saw Mill' continued to be known by the former name." There was once a post-office at Mosholu, also.

preaching there again in two weeks, which was filled by Rev. Cornelius Cook, who passed on to the north, and left an appointment for another preacher two weeks later. Two or three preachers followed him in succession, but I do not remember their names. Then the deacons of the Church got alarmed, declaring that the Methodists were preaching false doctrines, and advised my grandfather to shut his doors against them, which he did; but my uncle, Jacob Badeau, believed the doctrines they taught, and got them another place at Mr. Thomas Kirkham's, about a mile off, where they preached many years, till the old man died, and a society was raised up and a meeting-house built at Shrub Oak Plains. Some years later they built another at the head of Lake Mahopac." The names of those devout men who rode the New Rochelle circuit from 1787 to 1831 are recorded in another place in this volume. They kept the faith of old. Being dead, they yet speak.

The first mass said in Westchester County was said at the house of Dominick Lynch on Throgg's Point in the town of Westchester, where the Academy of the Sacred Heart is now located. Lynch was a prominent man during the Revolution. He was of New York, and in 1795 purchased the farm of Lewis Graham on Throgg's Point, and it was in his house on this farm that the first mass was said. That Article in the Constitution which declares that Congress shall make no law respecting the establishment of religion or the free exercise thereof had been enacted. It is now incorporated in the fundamental law.

In May, 1791, a conflagration in Yonkers greatly excited and saddened the people. The Episcopal Church, which had stood about thirty-eight or thirty-nine years, accidentally took fire, but fortunately it was only partially destroyed. The stone walls remained intact. When the ruins were examined the skeleton of a full-sized man was discovered behind what remained of the pulpit. The next year (1792) the building was restored in its precise original form as to the exterior, but the interior was slightly modified at the rebuilding. The steeple was not rebuilt until 1804.

About ten years after the Revolution New York State took steps for the establishment of a system of popular education in the state at large. In 1795 the Legislature, for the encouragement of schools, promised to give annually for nine years for school purposes in the County of Westchester £1,192, upon condition that the voters of each town should appropriate a sum equal to one-half of what was received. The first year Yonkers received £25 7s. This was reduced the following years.

From such small beginnings have arisen the splendid system of public schools which are to-day the city's glory and pride, and with the churches, in which sound doctrine is taught, are her defence. The best fortresses are such churches, and the best standing army is public schools.

In 1789, the supervisors appropriated to Yonkers for the support of the poor £57 5s and 6d. This amount is insignificant as compared with the funds distributed at this time by the Commissioner of Charities, not to speak of the large amount distributed by the churches, and other benevolent institutions, and by private charity.

Voting previous to 1787 was *viva voce*. That method was abolished by the Legislature in February, 1787, and therefore, previous to the dawn of the nineteenth century the citizens of Yonkers began to use the ballot—*

> "A weapon that comes down as still
> As snowflakes fall upon the sod,
> But executes a freeman's will
> As lightning does the will of God."

In the southern part of the town of Yonkers, Alexander Macomb, a wealthy merchant of New York (from whose son Robert the Harlem River Dam received its name, in 1791), purchased more than 3,500,000 acres of land in northern New York at 8d per acre. Adirondack Mountains were long known as Macomb's Mountains. Daniel Halsey, an innkeeper, kept the old tavern at King's Bridge between 1789 and 1793. In 1797–99 Alexander Macomb (he was General-in-chief of the United States army from 1828 until his decease, June, 1846) also purchased the tract of land—at King's Bridge—which was the "ancient island or hummock" of Paparinamin. In 1796, William Constable sold the Manor Hall property, Yonkers, to Jacob Stout, of New York, for £13,500.

During this period (1788–1800) the farmers and other citizens of Yonkers depended chiefly on New

---

* The record of those who during this period served Yonkers and other towns as supervisors, county clerks, sheriffs, district attorneys (two of them are designated assistant attorney generals) surrogates, county judges, associate judges of the Supreme Court, chief justice of the Supreme Court, assemblymen, residents of Westchester County in the Continental Congress in 1788, may be found in Scharf's "History of Westchester County". The chapter of that volume entitled "The Civil History," by the Rev. William J. Cumming, pastor of the Presbyterian Church at Yorktown, records the names of those officers.

York City papers for the news from the county, state, nation, and from foreign countries. The papers published in New York City in 1789 were the *New York Journal*, a weekly (two dollars), the *Gazette of the United States*, a bi-weekly (three dollars), the *New York Packet*, a tri-weekly (two dollars), *The Daily Gazette* and *The Daily Advertiser* (six dollars), and *The Commercial Advertiser*, established in 1797 (now the oldest New York newspaper). These sheets were very small as to size in comparison with the "blanket sheet" of to-day. The States of the Union were few, the cities in the country were small towns, and the villages of the county were hamlets. For instance, the village of Peekskill, Westchester county, which had during the Revolution only about twenty houses, could not have had in 1788, the beginning of the period under review, many more buildings. The population of the whole county of Westchester in 1790 was only 24,003. Towns, now flourishing cities, were then only villages. Albany, which became the State Capitol in 1797, had in 1790 a population of only 3,506. In 1790, New Haven had 4,500, and Hartford 4,090. New York, in 1790, had about as large a population as Yonkers in 1890. That of New York was 33,131, and of Yonkers, a century later, 32,033. Philadelphia and Boston, in 1780, were smaller than Yonkers in 1790. Philadelphia had 28,522 and Boston 18,038. In 1790, sites of some present large cities of world-wide fame were a howling wilderness and forests through which wild animals roamed. The city of Buffalo, for example, was then unknown. In the latter part of this period (1788–1800) the population of Westchester County, including slaves, was only 27,347. Albany had in 1800 a population of 5,349, New Haven 5,127, Hartford 5,347. New York, which had 60,487 in 1800, was just reaching the lower corner of the present City Hall Park, and beginning to extend along the Boston Road (Bowery), and along Broadway. Philadelphia, in 1800, had 41,220, and Boston 24,037.

As the newspapers of the period (1788-1800) were brought up to Yonkers by sloop or stage coach, the people read about what was transpiring during the years of the administration of two presidents, Washington and Adams, and of two governors, George Clinton and John Jay. History, now a century old, they were perusing as the news of the day. From different states came reports of the ratification of the Constitution. From the village of Poughkeepsie, where the second State Convention was convened (1788) to consider the Federal Constitution, came tidings that after an able debate the famous document had been ratified by a close vote—thirty to twenty-seven. When the Yonkers Federalists heard it they rejoiced, and were proud of the Westchester County delegates—Crane, Morris, Hatfield, Sarls, Livingston, and Van Cortlandt—all of whom had voted in favor of the Constitution, for they realized that the country needed a more perfect government than the old Confederation, and that "no government can give us happiness at home which has not the strength to make us respected abroad." The papers brought to Yonkers tidings of events transpiring in New York City. They reported the mobbing of the doctors. They commented on the celebration of the adoption of the Constitution, and described the splendid parade, one of the features of which was a ship bearing the name of Hamilton, and drawn through the streets by ten milk-white horses.

In 1789 was the first presidential election, but New York did not appoint electors. The papers brought news of the election of George Washington as President, and John Adams as Vice-President. Doubtless many Yonkers people went down to Wall Street, New York, to witness the inauguration. So many visitors from various parts had reached the little city the day before that the taverns and boarding houses were full, and many are said to have slept in tents on "the Common." The Hudson was studded with boats bearing visitors and long caravans of carts began to arrive before daybreak from Westchester, Long Island and the Jerseys. We may believe that this was an occasion of special interest to the veteran soldiers of the Revolution who lived in Yonkers, for it afforded them another opportunity of seeing their beloved commander. Chancellor Livingston administered the oath of office in front of Federal Hall, where at this day stands Washington in bronze. In 1789 he stood, clad in a homespun American suit, white silk long stockings, silver shoe buckes upon his polished shoes, a steel hilted dress sword, and his hair dressed and powdered according to the style then in vogue, and gathered up in a bag. He took the Bible, kissed it, and reverently and with much emotion said, as he stood with closed eyes: "I swear, so help me God." "It is done," declared the Chancellor; "long live George Washington, President of the United States!" Then the huzzas of the populace rent the air, and doubtless, Yonkers people united in that cheer and through eyes moist with gratitude they saw the President proceed, first to the Senate Chamber, and then to St. Paul's Church, where the Chaplain of the Senate read prayers.

In 1790, the Yonkers people were reading of the French Revolution, of the establishment of the National Capitol at Washington; in 1791, of the scourge (yellow fever) in New York, and of the Indian war in the Northwest; in 1792, of the second election of Washington; in 1793, of the progress of education, as shown by the incorporation of Hamilton Oneida Academy at Clinton, N. Y. (chartered in 1812 as Hamilton College), and about two years later (1795), by the incorporation of Union College, Schenectady. In 1793, they were reading of the cotton-gin invention, which gave amazing impetus to the culture and use of cotton, revolutionizing the industrial prospects and political power of the South by making cotton "King." In 1794, came tidings of the "Whiskey Insurrection"; in 1797, of the election of John Adams as President, and Thomas Jefferson as Vice-President of the United States. In 1798, the Yonkers people were reading of the war with France, of the French Revolution, the partition of Poland, the execution of Louis XVI., the Reign of Terror, the fall of Robespierre, the overthrow of the Directory, of the administration of the First Consul (Napoleon), of the reign of George III., and the great political disturbances in England.

Section II.

YONKERS IN THE MORNING OF THE NINETEENTH CENTURY. 1800–1825.

When the nineteenth century dawned upon Yonkers, agriculture was yet the principal industry. The manufacturing period was in the hidden future. It is recorded that "the style of the agriculture" was "in the first order." The lower part of Westchester County had "considerable ornamental farming and gardening." Where "the seats of opulence" were, was "cultivated with much taste." Evidently the old-time "seats of opulence" differed much from those of the present day. Architecture was then "a compound combining New England lightness and elegance with Dutch heaviness and durability." In the early years of the century, the town of Yonkers shared in the prosperity of other parts of the country. A strong impulse to improvement was given by the demand in foreign markets for the products of American soil during the distracting and devastating war on the European continent. Farmers obtained fabulous prices. The number of vessels which weekly sailed from New York, freighted for foreign markets, seems incredible. The prosperous people improved their dwellings, barns, farms and roads. The population* in 1800 was only 1,176, and growth was slow. In 1800 there were 175 taxable persons between the Greenburgh line and the Spuyten Duyvil Creek. In 1810 there were 204, and at that date there were 93 persons entitled to vote, while the taxable property of the town was valued at somewhat over $400,000. The number of taxable persons in 1825 was 249.

It is recorded that at the dawn of the century English was the chief language, but "Dutch and German were both considerably spoken by many people. In a few instances, public worship in the county was in Dutch. "In dress and clothing, a wide range is allowed to fashion, and probably something to folly, while an almost infinite variety prevails. In large and populous places, British fabrics are principally worn, and villages conform as far as convenience will permit. In the country, clothing is home-made."

Early in the nineteenth century, the old Albany Road, which had been opened to the Saw Mill River about 1669, and afterward up to Albany, received a new name. By Act of the Legislature, it became "The Highland Turnpike." The "Turnpike" was required by the Legislature to be, as to its *road-bed*, north of the Highlands, twenty-two feet wide, and south of the Highlands, beginning at Peekskill, twenty-eight feet wide, and the extreme width of the road was to be four rods, but the old fences were never disturbed by the Company. When they constructed a new section, they made the width according to law. There were two toll-gates in Yonkers. One of them was away down the Post-road or Turnpike at the old well. A historian who graphically describes Yonkers as it appeared about 1823, says: "The authorities located the toll-gate a full mile to the south of the desperate bad quagmire which dominated the road between the Rich and the Post boundary line. It is said that every once in a while the stage-coach, on its way from and to the city, would sink so deep in the mire that the neighboring farmers would come with their teams to pull it out, and set it on all fours again on the road beyond." The author above quoted, writing of Yonkers in the dawn of the nineteenth century, refers to the discomforts

---

*In 1811 the Rev. Timothy Dwight, President of Yale College, passed through Westchester County, and wrote of the town of Eastchester as follows: Except "a small scattered village, the rest of the township is covered with plantations." Of the town of Mamaroneck he wrote: "It is wholly a collection of plantations and can scarcely be said to contain even a hamlet. It is set, however, with a number of good houses and excellent farms." Of the whole county, he wrote: "It is universally settled so far as the nature of the ground will admit, and it is almost merely a collection of farms."

of the people in severe winters, by reason of poor roads. "With very few and poor roads it made a vast difference at that time whether the winter was good or bad, or how long navigation was closed and the cove at the mouth of the Saw Mill River inaccessible to the sloop from Partition Street, New York. Certain it is that, from 1796 until the new century came smilingly in, the winters were Arctic in their severity. Three long and dreary ice-bound winters! In '96 not a skiff put out from our inlet until after the 28th of November. Christmas that year was, says an old record, 'intensely cold.' '97 was no better, and '98 but little. The lowest the mercury marked that dreary winter was two above zero, and navigation was suspended during what is called a 'very early, long and severe winter.' The new century did not open with such severe weather. The year 1800 was six days old before the river was frozen, and navigation hindered, and the weather remained mild for fully five years, until 1806, when it was a 'remarkably cold and variable winter, deep snows, heavy rains and high winds and much distress among the poor.'"

During this period (1800-1825) among transfers of property were several of special interest. Alexander Macomb purchased from 1799 to 1804 at Lower Yonkers, adjoining parcels, mostly salt meadow, aggregating nearly one hundred acres, bounded by Van Cortlandt, the Albany Road, the Harlem and Spuyten Duyvil, and by Tippett's Brook. In December, 1800, he obtained from New York authorities a water grant, extending across the creek, just east of King's Bridge (which reserved, however, a passage way fifteen feet wide for small boats and craft). He erected a four-story frame grist-mill, extending out over the creek. Its power was supplied by the alternate ebb and flow of the tide against the undershot wheel. Macomb's extensive real estate venture proving disastrous, the Paparinamin and the mill were sold in 1810 and purchased by his son Robert. Between 1796 and 1802, Jacob Stout built a tavern in place of the old Hunt's tavern of previous days. It came to be known as "The Nappeckamack House" or "The Indian Queen Inn." It stood where the Getty House now stands. The Manor Hall property, consisting of the Manor House, stables, mills and three hundred and twenty acres of land, was conveyed on April 1, 1802, by Jacob Stout, of New York, to Joseph Howland. Mr. Howland, who lived in Norwich, Conn., transacted business in New London, Conn., which at that time was an important port. Subsequently he established a branch of his business in New York. After buying the Yonkers property, for which he paid $60,000, he made the Manor House his residence. As a citizen and a vestryman of St. John's Church, he studied the interests of the people and of the town. The steeple of St. John's Church had not been rebuilt in 1792, when the church was repaired, after the fire in 1791, which destroyed tower, roof and other woodwork. Twelve years had now elapsed, and the good rector, the Rev. Elias Cooper, together with Mr. Howland and others, interested themselves in securing funds to rebuild the steeple. Trinity Church, New York, gave $300. Yonkers parishioners also contributed. Through Mr. Howland's influence, Mr. Ebenezer Baldwin, an esteemed acquaintance of his, residing at Norwich, Conn., was at this time (1804) brought to Yonkers. Mr. Baldwin used to relate an interesting incident of those times. He said that, during the time his carpenters were rebuilding the steeple of the church, one day (July 12th), on their return from their nooning, they were informed that Alexander Hamilton [*] had been shot the day before at Weehawken by Aaron Burr, and that a special messenger had just gone by to inform Hamilton's friends up the river.

Mr. Baldwin resided in Yonkers about forty-one years, exerting a salutary influence. He realized the importance of educating the children and youth, and was much interested in schools. In his own youthful days he had been offered a college education, but his filial and fraternal love was very tender, and because he believed that his father and brother and sisters needed him at home he thrust aside the honors a professional life offered him. As a business man he achieved success, and left an honored name. He was instrumental in establishing a school in Yonkers, in which his younger brother, Erastus, was the first teacher, In the War of 1812 he raised a company of thirty volunteers, and, taking them to Brooklyn, maintained them at his own expense. After the war, the Yonkers company, together with one recruited at New Rochelle and another at New Castle, were organized as a battalion, and Mr. Baldwin was commissioned as Major and placed in command. Thereafter he was addressed as Major Baldwin. His own worth and the social standing and influence of his descendants are a part of the history of Yonkers. He left four children—Judge Anson Baldwin, Ebenezer Baldwin, Jr., Mrs. William

---

[*] All of Hamilton that could die lies in Trinity Churchyard, New York, close by the middle of the south wall:
"Let the sound of those he wrought for,
And the feet of those he fought for,
Echo round his bones forevermore."
A quaint and time-worn construction of stone, with its obscuring inscription, but poorly marks his sepulture.

C. Waring and Mrs. Alexander Smith. Among the names of the third generation of this well-known family registered in the Yonkers directory are Mr. Hall F. Baldwin, Mrs. Ethan Flagg, Mrs. John T. Waring, Mrs. Professor Henry M. Baird, Mr. Warren B. Smith and Mrs. William F. Cochran.

A professional man, well-known in the town during this period, was Dr. John Ingersoll. He was born about 1745; the place of his nativity is unknown. He came to New York State, near the vicinity of Horseneck, now West Greenwich, Conn., prior to 1804, and his home in Yonkers was on the Tuckahoe Road, near the present pumping station of the Yonkers water-works. "His practice obliged him to ride from King's Bridge to the outskirts of White Plains, and he would encounter the darkest night and most pitiless storm rather than neglect his duty at the bedside of a patient. Until inebriety conquered him, he was fairly successful as a physician." He was especially favored in some cases, but his surgery is recorded to have been unskilful—probably by reason of lack of training in that department. He died in 1827 of delirum tremens. Two other physicians, well-known in Yonkers, were the brothers, Amos W. and Horatio S. Gates, who came probably in the twenties.

During this period a prominent hill in Yonkers received the name which it bears to this day. Henry Brown, who had bought one hundred and thirteen acres on the hill in 1785, from the Commissioners of Forfeiture, sold lands west of the present Walnut Street to George Oakley, who sold his seventy acres to John Guion. (In early days we find frequent record of Guion's mills at the east end of the glen.) Farmer Brown sold the top of the hill, east of the present Walnut Street, to Peter Nodine, who, previous to buying this farm, lived near Tuckahoe. He was evidently a descendant of the Huguenot Naudin. That name is on the New Rochelle town records, among those of the early settlers, between 1695 and 1710. Access to the farm on "Nodine Hill," was by a narrow lane, beginning at Guion's lane near Guion's mills. Peter Nodine died in 1816, leaving a large family. His children were Frederick, Clark, Thomas, Elizabeth and George. The present generation of this family, like those of other old Westchester County families, narrate interesting incidents which have come down from the generations which lived in this historic region during Indian and Revolutionary days. Elizabeth, the daughter of Peter Nodine, who lived in a small house west of the present Nodine Hill water-tower, was accustomed, when advanced in years, to speak of a lad, a member of their family circle in early days, who when sent on errands would at times hide behind a cherry tree because he was afraid of some of the Indians. During the Revolutionary War, and before Peter Nodine removed to the hill, the British soldiers drove away his cattle. They "strung him up" to compel him to reveal the place where his money was hidden. He had concealed it in the crevice of a rock. In Revolutionary times housewives used to bake corncake in an oven outside the house. On one occasion the British soldiers came to the house of Peter Nodine.* He was not at home. They insisted upon his wife giving them the corncakes, and when she refused they attempted to take them from the oven. Thereupon she seized the long-handled shovel which was used to withdraw the cakes from the oven and, beating the soldiers over their heads, drove them away. Frederick Nodine, the son of Peter, served in the War of 1812.

A well-known Yonkers man of the century was David Horton. For many years he was honorably prominent in the town. He descended from the Hortons of White Plains. Stephen Horton, his father, removed to Yonkers at the beginning of the century (1801). His son David was then a babe, one year old. Probably he is the only living person in 1896 who saw Yonkers at the dawn of the nineteenth century. His reminiscences of the town are recorded on a subsequent page of this chapter.

In 1807 the Yonkers people heard that an odd appearing craft was on the stocks in New York. The New York papers published the announcement that the boat would start from Cortlandt Street at half past six o'clock Friday morning, August 4th, and make a trip to Albany. Broad smiles were worn by many who heard this report. One man in New York was heard to accost another with: "John, will thee risk thy life on such a concern? I tell thee she is the most fearful wildfowl living, and thy father ought to restrain thee!" The boat was provided with twelve berths, and every one was taken through to Albany. The round trip fare was fourteen dollars. Robert Fulton, a New York artist, was superintending the construction and completion of the boat, which he proposed to propel by steam. He had named it Clermont, the title of the country-seat of Chancellor Livingston, who, by influence and money, was furthering the enterprise. Surmise the conversation of the Yonkers people on that summer forenoon

---

* Of the later descendants of Peter Nodine, Clark served in the war for the Union, as a member of the Sixth Artillery, and Robert S., his son, as a member of the Twenty-second Massachusetts, and Edgar C. as a member of the Sixth New York Artillery. Benjamin Clark Nodine was an officer in the regular army and served in the war for the Union. Edgar Nodine, a cousin of Edgar C., was also a Union soldier. Another Union soldier was a nephew of Clark Nodine. Other relatives of the Nodines who were in the Union army were Uriah Wilson, of the Twelfth Wisconsin Light Artillery, and several Kriffens, one of whom commanded a battery.

of 1807, as they looked down the river and saw the black smoke rolling from the stack of the approaching craft which was to revolutionize navigation. She was coming up the Hudson at the rate of almost five miles an hour, her exposed paddle-wheels (fifteen feet in diameter) churning the water, and leaving a long white wake of foam. The steersman sat at the stern of the boat working a tiller, as in an ordinary sail boat. This first steamboat on the Hudson was provided with masts and sails.

By the end of the first decade new life seems to have appeared all along the river, " waking up the Dutch-speaking and Dutch-worshipping people, as evidenced by packet boats regularly advertised to run from New York for such out-of-the-way and distant places as Tappan and Tarrytown, and Yonkers people could gather on the bluff in the rear of the church every Thursday evening—and probably did so gather in great numbers—to feast their wondering eyes upon the steamboat." . . . But as Yonkers had no pier the steamboats did not make a landing along her shores. At the bulk-head, where the Nepperhan Street of to-day merges into Dock Street, was the sloop landing and a scene of activity. "It was the old Philipse landing of Revolutionary days, and of days long before, too, for that matter. This landing place was at the bottom of a cove into which the Nepperhan flowed at this point, and a hard place it was, too, for a sailing vessel to get into in those days unless wind and tide were propitious in the extreme. Away out in the river, and now covered by the Main Street Bridge over the railway, there arose a large black rock. To this the ancient mariners had affixed a large ring. Now when the wind and tide were unpropitious a cable was passed from boat to ring, the boat swinging into the cove where they could kedge up to the wharf. When the wind was fair they made a straight line for the wharf from the channel, but this was rarely done. . . . At this time (1823) a sloop left Yonkers' dock Monday and Wednesday of each week for freight or passengers. For passengers twenty-five and fifty cents each; for freight, rates unknown. It is said that at this date the sloops carried but few passengers. Those 'sloop days' were great business days for the town. Farmers brought produce from every quarter to the boats; the store in the Square did a rushing business. In fact the chief sales were made on those days when the farmers, having delivered their loads to the sloop captain, returned to the Square, tied their horses to the trees and posts or put them under the Indian Queen sheds, and proceeded to make a day of it. Twelve or fifteen years later a dock was built far out into the river. . . . Up to this time (1823) no steamboat had ever yet slowed up to take Yonkers passengers aboard as they did . . . three years later, when John Bashford rowed out any intended passenger to put him on board any steamer upon payment of eighteen pence. The time we write of was those good old days when trading sloops took passengers from Albany to New York for five dollars, and when the authorities gave out that no 'ferriage shall be paid for a sucking child,' and that 'servants who use a *birth* shall pay two-thirds fare.' . . . It was before the day of the new pier, or even before John Bashford made his adventurous trip to the 'Paragon Car of Neptune,' as it sped up or down the river."

FULTON'S FIRST STEAMBOAT.

About 1813 Mr. Lemuel Wells became a resident of Yonkers, and was honorably identified with the place until his death in 1842. It will be remembered that the Manor Hall with its buildings and three hundred and twenty acres of land had been sold by the Commissioners of Forfeiture to C. P. Low, a New York merchant, for £14,520; that he never occupied it, but in 1786 conveyed it to William Constable, also a New York merchant. In 1796 Mr. Constable sold it for £13,500. Jacob Stout, of New York, was the purchaser. He sold it in 1802 to Joseph Howland, of Norwich, Conn. In 1813 it was for sale at auction. "A courtly gentleman with a gold-headed cane and a slight limp in his gait appeared on the scene—a perfect stranger to every one—and bid up the property to $56,000. This was none other than Mr. Lemuel Wells." He was in stature about six feet; his shoulders were broad, his complexion light; his weight, in his prime, about one hundred and eighty pounds. His native state was Connecticut. When he was a young man he had learned the art of manufacturing jewelry. Subsequently, as a goldsmith with a store in Wall Street, New York, he became well known. His only child, a son, died in Manor Hall, Yonkers, just before he was twenty-one years old. Mr. Wells was "a genial, whole-souled country gentleman, beloved and looked up to with reverence by the simple-hearted country folk among whom he came." . . . When he purchased the Manor House with about four hundred acres of adjoining land he was about fifty-two years of age. His property extended along the Hudson from near the present Point Street to a point on the river just below the present St. Mary Street. It appears that he did not buy with the intention of selling his tract either in large or small plots. He was seldom induced to sell or even to lease any of it, but he was not particularly averse to settlers, and would offer now and then to build a house on his property for them as tenants.

Just after Mr. Wells came an incident occurred which added another page to the interesting history of the old Albany Post-road. It was at the close of the War of 1812. A Treaty of Peace had been signed at Ghent in December, 1814. A Yonkers citizen of the present (1896), Mr. A. O. Kirkwood, thus describes the incident: "As soon as tidings of the signing of the Treaty of Peace reached this side of the water couriers were dispatched to various points with the intelligence, in order to save the further shedding of blood. It may be remembered that the bloody battle of New Orleans was fought eight days after peace was declared. Three messengers with dispatches were sent from New York to the Legislature, assembled at Albany. Two of these were John Pulver (of Holland descent), a lieutenant in the Light Dragoons (whose cavalry sword and trappings were subsequently in the possession of his two daughters, residing on Riverdale Avenue, Yonkers), and a certain Marvin Garrison. Major Pulver, as he was called, was subsequently a Yonkers farmer. The stage coach, with relays of horses at different points, was the only means of travelling. The couriers started at the same time, but there was a rivalry as to which should reach the Capitol first. They kept abreast until Poughkeepsie was reached. Then Garrison hired a private conveyance. But Pulver would not be outdone. He had been a stage-driver before the war, and knew all about horses. So he gave the regular driver two dollars for the privilege of driving the last few miles this side of Hudson. And he *did* drive. A spectator remarked, on seeing the stage dash past, that either Satan or one of his imps must have the reins. Arrived at Hudson, Pulver immediately sought Major Plumb, an old acquaintance, who kept a livery stable, and asked for a team of horses. The Major had a horse which had run away so often that no one cared to drive it, and said to Pulver that he might take it and another of his horses. So a fresh start was taken with a sleigh, as there was deep snow. The runaway soon found that he had a master. The team was kept at the top of its speed; the twenty-eight miles between Hudson and Albany were covered in as short a time as was possible for a fast team and a furious driver, and Pulver drove into Albany to a stable near the Capitol two hours ahead of his competitor, the runaway horse dropping dead soon after.

"Lieutenant Pulver received, on his return to New York, the reward for the victory in the 150-mile race. And so, though not ranking with Paul Revere's ride of the Revolution or Sheridan's ride of the Rebellion, Pulver's ride of 1814 is cherished in the memory of his descendants."

General Jacob Odell was a prominent citizen of Yonkers in the first part of the nineteenth century. He lived on the east side of the Saw Mill River Road, just a little distance north of the site of the present New York and Putnam Railroad Bridge which spans the highway. Reference to him is made in a previous chapter of this volume. He was a general of State militia in the War of 1812, and in later years a number of the members of his old command were accustomed to ride up in a body from New York City every year to pay their respects to him and enjoy his hospitality.

Yonkers, as it appeared in 1804 when Mr. Ebenezer Baldwin came, in 1813 when Mr. Lemuel Wells came, and in 1823 when the Rev. John West came as rector of St. John's Church, has been described by those who put on record the descriptions of older people, and who made a study of old maps. In 1804 it was a hamlet of about a dozen houses. Its row of splendid horse-chestnut trees skirting the Post-road (the only road in the hamlet) was much admired by every traveller. What is now Guion Street is a part of what was then known as Guion's lane. The western terminus of the lane was at the Post-road, opposite the site of the present St. Joseph's Hospital. Its general course was northeast through the fields. It was identical with the present Guion Street, and followed nearly the present New Main Street to the present Nepperhan Avenue. It also followed the course of the present Nepperhan Avenue (once called Guion Street), with slight deflections to the north side of the present Elm Street. Thence it curved westward, and its course was nearer the Saw Mill River than the present avenue until near the front of the present stone house west of what is now Chestnut Street. Thence its course was along the present avenue until it reached what is now known as "Copcutt's Lane" (south of the mill at the Glen). That lane is a part of the old Guion lane. Its course was thence west and north, across a wooden bridge spanning the Saw Mill River, and thence east by south along the high bank (course of present Garden Street), out to the present Nepperhan Avenue, thence along what was once known as "Archer's lane" to the Eastchester Road (Ashburton Avenue). The Guion Lane proper really terminated at Guion's mills. At the corner of "Archer's lane" and the road to Eastchester (east side of "Archer's lane") the farmhouse of Anthony Archer stood during the Revolution. The mill at the east end of the "Glen" was under the direction of John Guion. The cross-road, now known as Ashburton Avenue, led to the Saw Mill River, but this was quite out of the little settlement. There was also a lane leading to the sloop landing upon the present Nepperhan Street. There were the old Manor House, the old mill (southwest of the Manor House), and north of the mill the miller's house, standing in what is now the middle of Dock Street. Just above the dam was the cooper shop occupied by Thaddeus Rockwell.

A new tavern, then recently built by Jacob Stout, occupied part of the site of the Getty House. The old tavern, then used as a carriage shop, stood northeast of it, and to the west of the carriage shop, in front of the site of the present building (Hawley Block), on the west corner of the present Palisade Avenue and Getty Square, was a country store, kept by Multus Cooper and Aaron Vark. There were also a small saw and grist-mill, just north of the present *Yonkers' Statesman* Publishing House (13 Main Street); a house belonging to St. John's Church, standing partly between the church and the road, and occupied by Gilbert Guion; Mr. Howland's farmhouse, then newly built; the old house on Guion Street, near the present School Street, and, perhaps, three or four other buildings of less importance. All of these buildings, with one or two exceptions, were situated on Mr. Howland's property, and constituted the whole hamlet of Yonkers of that day.

Nine years later (1813), when Mr. Lemuel Wells purchased the Manor House and adjacent land, the

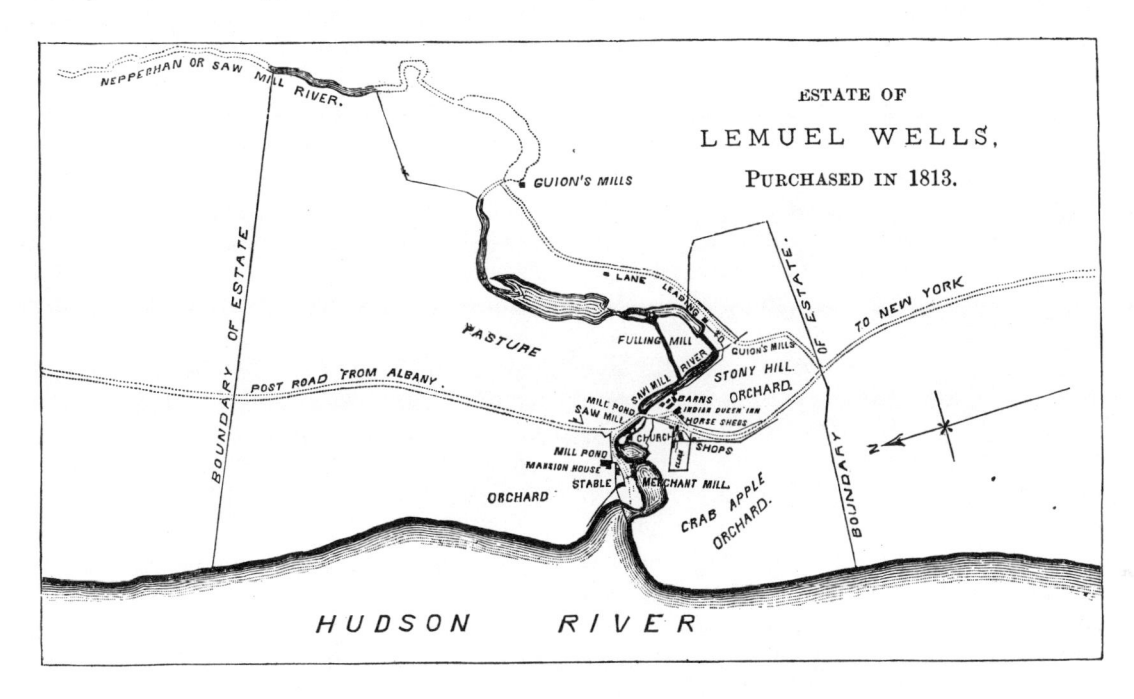

place had somewhat changed. At the south end of the town were many farms, most of them small, but well cultivated. There was already a cluster of houses near the Albany and Boston Roads, which parted at King's Bridge. At the north end of the town and along the line of the Bronx and Saw Mill Rivers, the farms were larger and the population sparse. Much of the land along the Hudson and north of the Manor House was heavily timbered. In front of the Manor House was a lawn, and on the north a flower and vegetable garden with its box-lined beds. Behind the mansion a sloping lawn and an orchard reaching on the north to about the present Wells Avenue, and to the river's edge on the west. North of the garden was the farm-yard, barn and stables, and a lane leading to the Post-road at the turn by the little tenement-house which stood on the west side of the road, just as one rises the hill at the present gas office (northwest corner of Wells Avenue and North Broadway). A small farmhouse also stood on the west side of the road further up. This has also given place to a more modern building. No other building stood on the Post-road—now known as North Broadway—until the Simpson farm was reached. Pastures, orchards and meadows only, and uninhabited. To the south that vast plot east of the Post-road and west of New Main Street was known as the "Stony Hill Orchard." At the corners where New Main Street and Palisade Avenue meet were the post-office, a wheelwright's shop, a store and a stable nearest the Nepperhan. South of what is now New Main Street stood the Indian Queen

Inn (subsequently called the Nappeckamack House), and its sheds along what is now the south side of Getty Square. The old inn (Hunt's tavern) in which the lords of the Manor of Philipsburgh in the previous century had held court's-leet and court's-baron, had been removed. South of the church was a homely building used as a blacksmith shop, and below that, nearly at the top of the hill on the west side of the Post-road, was a small tenement house. The old church stood on the open square, nearly opposite the inn. On the Saw Mill River, at the west side of the road, were a small saw-mill, a country grist-mill, cooperage and timber yard. On the lane leading along the south side of the Manor House at the waterside stood a flour-mill. North of the Nepperhan there was a lovely cove at the mouth of the little river. It has since been filled in. The Nepperhan fell into the Hudson in native purity, confined but an instant, as it were, on its way down to feed the race of the saw and other mills. It is difficult at the present day to picture this vast tract, save as above stated, entirely uninhabited and but slightly improved. Probably, however, a lovelier spot did not exist on the face of the earth.

Of the twenty-six buildings of all kinds, including barns, sheds and little shops, then on the three hundred and twenty acres of land, about twelve could have been utilized as dwellings, five were mill buildings for grinding grain and plaster and for sawing and fulling, seven were barns and sheds, and one is represented as containing "shops." One, an old stone building, in "the lane leading to Guion's mills," was perhaps as old as the Manor House itself. The site of the building now standing at the north of Getty Square was, in 1813, a "nest of bushes and briars." It has since been raised several feet by filling. The slope from the Post-road to the river and the hills to the east were in part laid out in pasture grounds and orchards, and in part covered with a waste of trees. It is said that "the succession of boulders was so continuous that one might have stepped from what is now Getty Square to the present Glenwood, without setting his foot upon the ground." In later years, when the Hudson River Railroad was building, the laborers scoured the hillside as far up as the Post-road, and even further, removing rocks to the river for filling.

The Yonkers citizen of that day who stood on the Post-road wooden bridge, which spanned the river just north of the present Getty Square, could see the sparkling Nepperhan curving down the valley, gliding under the bridge, its waters near the Hudson spreading over a broad area now covered by streets and buildings. The Post-road coming down from the north under a high and closely-wooded bluff on the east side, since set back to make room for business places, met at the bridge a row of beautiful horse-chestnut trees that fell off to the west along the north side of the stream, skirting it all the way round to the site of the old mill near Manor Hall. Mr. Wells, in 1822, told Silas Cornell and Dr. Bloodgood, of Flushing, L. I., who visited Yonkers, to procure horse-chestnuts from those trees, that he had counted the rings on one of them which he had recently removed, and that they indicated that the tree was sixty years old. He said he supposed it to have been imported from Europe by Colonel Philipse. This agreed with a statement made by Anthony Archer, who had been one of Mr. Philipse's employees, and who died in 1837 at ninety-two years of age. Within the spacious lawn in front of the Manor House (the lawn extended to the Post-road) were grand old trees, domestic and foreign, some of them English yews, also supposed to have been imported by Colonel Philipse as early as 1762. There was also a profusion of the richest plants and flowers. Along the south of the lawn was a row of locust trees.

Yonkers in those days was rural indeed. There was little to change the daily routine. "The New York and Albany stages passed up and down every day, and stopped for resting and dining at the old inn on the Post-road, and, in later years, at John Bashford's hotel, at the sloop landing. At that old inn, too, the town-meetings were held for many years. The inn was, of course, the headquarters of the gossipers and politicians, the centre of rally for those eager for the latest news, and for those eager to retail it. And with the tavern and Judge Vark's country store, as prominent centres of evening and holiday diversion, the country folk were able to interchange opinions and partly escape monotony."

In the lower part of Yonkers (subsequently known as the town of Kingsbridge) Robert Macomb was an extensive land owner. By act of the Legislature he was authorized to construct a dam across the Harlem from Bussing's to Devoe's Point, and to use the waters for milling purposes. He erected at much expense the causeway and bridge known as "Macomb's Dam." Its gates admitted the flood tide from the East River but obstructed the ebb, thus converting the Upper Harlem into a mill-pond, having its outlets underneath the old mill and through a race-way made on the Westchester side into Spuyten Duyvil Creek. The race supplied power to a marble sawing mill, which stood on the quay between it and the creek, and of which Perkins Nicolls was proprietor. Robert Macomb became involved, and the property was sold in 1818. . . . Plans were made for mill seats and a manufacturing village, but proved abortive. The old grist-mill stood idle during many years and at length was made useless by the removal of Macomb's Dam.

In 1820 Frederic Shonnard, son of a French officer who belonged to the famous body guard of Frederick the Great, purchased an estate in Yonkers about two miles north of Manor Hall. It consisted of two hundred and twenty acres, for which he paid less than one hundred dollars an acre. During the first quarter of the nineteenth century Yonkers people on Sundays assembled for divine service in the three houses of public worship to which reference was made on a previous page of this chapter, that is, at St. John's on the hill near the Nepperhan, at the Methodist Church at Tuckahoe and at the Episcopal Chapel in Tuckahoe. Some also, it may be, worshipped in an old school-house which stood near Warner's store. Mosholu, which is an old hamlet and post-office skirting the Albany Post-road, known early in the century as "Warner's," where many years ago there were a school-house, store, blacksmith and wagon shop and a cluster of dwellings. A Methodist charge existed there as early as 1826, having thirty-six members, and it is probable the Methodists were worshipping there before 1826 and within the period now under review. There was no church building there until 1835.

The Rev. Elias Cooper, A.M., who was for about twenty-seven years rector of St. John's, died in 1816, aged nearly fifty-nine years, and was buried in St. John's cemetery. A tablet to his memory was erected in the wall of St. John's Church by his beloved people and is there to this day. The Rev. Mr. Cooper's successor was the Rev. William Powell, A.M., who resigned in 1819. The Rev. John Grigg, A.M., became rector in 1820 and resigned in 1823. His successor was the Rev. John West, A.M., who came in 1823, and remained until 1828. The Tuckahoe Episcopal Chapel still remained under the care of the St. John's rector. At the Tuckahoe Methodist Church and probably also in the school-house at "Warner's," Mosholu, the circuit riders who belonged to the New Rochelle Circuit officiated. The names of the preachers who rode on that circuit from 1800 to 1825 are the Rev. Brown (Davis), Wilson, Chicchester, Campbell, Pickett, Thacker, Dougherty, Hunt, Coleman, Sawyer, Crawford, Redstone, Hibbard, Bull, Caulfield, Lyon (Zalmar), Andrus, Peck, Thomas, Ames, Smith (Eben), Swayze, Ames, Lyon (Jonathan), Phoebus, Thacker, Sykes, Smith (Arnold), Bushnell, Emery, Carpenter, Ostrander, Richardson, Woolsey, Jewett, Seney, Thomas, Bangs, Seaman, Martindale and Rice. In 1804, the Rev. James Coleman was alone on the circuit. In subsequent years there were from two to four on the circuit each year.

ST. JOHN'S RECTORY AND GLEBE, ON SAW MILL RIVER ROAD IN 1809.

The congregations worshipping in those days in the little hamlets of the town were composed for the most part of plain people, clad in plain garb. In 1823 there were only nine gold watches reported in Yonkers, and only five four-wheel carriages. In 1804, St. John's Church had only forty communicants. In 1818, a church bell was heard for the first time in the town. It was presented to St. John's Church by Mr. Joseph Howland. Thereafter the soft music of the village church bell "fell at intervals upon the ear in cadence sweet." Many long-time citizens, now in life's twilight, recall hallowed hours and vanished forms, as that old bell salutes them. They listen, on Sabbath mornings and evenings, for its familiar tones, as for the voice of a friend, and, hearing them, their eyes glow underneath their white hair, as fire burns on the hearth when there is snow on the roof. With the bells which swing in other church spires of the town are also associated hallowed memories. As their notes fall on the ears of the devout, they sound as sweet as those of which the poet wrote:

> "Bells,
> Whose sounds so wild would
> In the days of my childhood
> Fling round my cradle
> Their magic spells."

Most of those who heard the oldest church bells in Yonkers, when they first from their spires called to prayer and praise, now belong to the generations which are sleeping "the iron sleep." One reflecting upon these rapid changes among the people of the town is reminded of Tom Hood's lines:

> "And many a heart that then was gay
> Within the tomb now darkly dwells,
> And hears no more those evening bells.
> And so 'twill be when I am gone,
> That tuneful peal will still ring on,
> While other bards shall walk these dells,
> And sing your praise, sweet evening bells."

A Yonkers historian of the present day (Judge T. Astley Atkins) in a paper entitled, "At the Old Church Door; a Glimpse of Yonkers in 1823," presents a well-drawn picture of the congregation in St. John's Church and of Yonkers at that time. He says:

"Alpheus Pierson, postmaster, churchman and capitalist, had been dead some years. He was postmaster, so the records tell us, in 1797, and died in office. . . . He bequeathed to St. John's Church one hundred Spanish milled dollars—a permanent fund, the interest of which is to be appropriated for supporting the rector. Aaron Vark had succeeded Pierson as executor, postmaster and village store-keeper, but the great change had not yet come; for as Yonkers was at the close of the Revolution so it was at the end of the first score of years of the nineteenth century. Only in people had it materially changed.

"The old church remained watchful on the hill by the side of the Nepperhan. The old side door on the green was open on all proper occasions. It stands yet with its quaint brick arch and its old-fashioned doors, but its importance is gone, for through it may no man find entrance to the sanctuary. And when in those days the old bell called what a notable assembly answered the call. There came Lemuel and Eliza Wells, from the Manor, who, entering the old door, passed between the high-backed pews on either side and turned up the single aisle of the church eastward toward the chancel where at the left the large square pew was occupied by the owner of the Manor. In those primitive days no rent was paid. It was later and in more degenerate times that the 'rent' and 'no rent' battle was fought in the church; in those days when Nathaniel Valentine left the church because the 'renters' gained the day, and fixed Mr. Wells' rent at twenty dollars, and the other pews at eight dollars per annum. It is notable that Squire Vark, the successor of the lamented churchman, opposed this terrible scandal of the church, but the Squire would not be driven to such an extremity as secession. Then directly across the chancel, in another high-backed square box, sat the Van Cortlandts, of Spuyten Duyvil or King's Bridge. From Tuckahoe came Benjamin Taylor, John Browne, Benjamin Lent and their families, the aforementioned Valentine from his 'hill' at Mile Square, Abram Valentine (senior warden) from Spuyten Duyvil and the Bibbys from the same place, while the Browns and Devoes of the Heights (now Woodlawn), the Howlands from their mill away up the Saw Mill River and the younger Posts from near by helped materially to fill up the little church in the year '23. The great sounding board still overshadowed the pulpit. Charley Phillips, ex-slave, served as sexton. In the little gallery at the west end, entrance to which was gained by the belfry, presided the village favorite, Vreedenburg, commonly and most irreverently called 'Gus.' No organ marred the sacred loft. Only Gus' tuning fork, and his magnificent voice in those happy days to start the common voice of praise. It was natural that many fair eyes rested often but furtively upon the little gallery, and it was but natural, too, that Gus was 'consequential.' At least the other boys said so, and it must have been true. Moreover, when the rector paused for responses, was it not Gus who led all the church, and was not his 'Amen' loud and impressive?

"It was during the hey-dey of this popularity that sweet Hannah Brown, of Lower Yonkers, flirted with and soon led Gus captive—not quite to the altar, but very near it, for alas! one day the handsome leader offended her and she cut him, and all the boys and girls from Spuyten Duyvil to Greenburgh said Hannah was right. . . . It was about this time that the Rev. John West was rector of St. John's and doubtless enjoyed the income of the Spanish milled dollars, but he did not stay many years. Even a shorter time stayed his predecessor, John Grigg, the former five and the latter three years. As with pastors, so with wardens, vestrymen, sexton and chorister and responder—all are gone. Even the old church was too good for this earth, and they pulled down its sacred walls, leaving a scant window or two, and the dear old doorway and its weather-beaten doors to link us to the past. May this prevent the sacred memories which still linger around the spot being dissipated and lost in the mists of time. . . . By far the most important man in the Yonkers of that day was the aforementioned Aaron Vark. The country store which stood where Factory Street cut through at the Square was his, his also the little addition thereto called the post-office. Afterwards it was a shanty in James Street. The judge, as he was familiarly called, was not only store-keeper and postmaster, but dealt out law to the villagers, drew wills with his quill and teeth with his 'turn-key,' prescribed for the sick and dispensed the drugs, besides taking acknowledgment of legal papers as well as drawing them. At Vark's store affairs political were discussed, and as about all the prominent men of the town were Democrats, the barrel-heads and counters, during the canvass, were usually occupied. Vark and Brevoort, Simeon and Caleb Smith (so many years supervisor) and others of like persuasion, while the little band in the opposition ranks, Federalist or Whig as the case and time might call, could be summed up in the names of Barnabas Fowler and an Oakley or two. It was many years after that before the opposition waxed strong enough to have a ticket of its own in the town. About the time Mr. Wells bought the Manor, Vark bought the little nine-acre farm of Elijah Rich—the little strip between the Post-road and the river below the present Vark Street. Quite near the Rhinelander (now Shonnard) south line lived Ruleff Stephens. Still further north lived the Roberts of Pomona Hall, a house somewhat notorious in those days as the temporary refuge of Burr, immediately after his duel with Hamilton. Over the Saw Mill River were the prosperous farmers, Oliver and Aaron Rhead. They lived next to the parsonage over beyond the burying ground. Down along the Saw Mill lived another Anthony Archer, son of the Revolutionary Archer. Along down the Post-road below Vark was the little farmhouse of Margery Rich, and the old Post farmhouse by the river and brook—afterwards the doubtful Fern Brook. Then on Valentine's lane was Samuel Lawrence's house. Up in the woods towards 'Tibbett's' Brook another Post's house stood, a testimony to the good old times.

"At this time Guion's mills had become Dingee's, and Hiram Searl, mahogany sawyer, owned Pierson's house. Away down the Post-road Scott Rockwell lived at the toll-gate and gathered toll. . . . How can the village of that day (1823) be described? There was the open space now called the 'Square.' On a slight rise of ground where the hotel now stands stood the two-story tavern called the Indian Queen, the veritable inn occupied by David Hunt at the outbreak of the Revolution. Here the Albany stages stopped while the postmaster went through the process of sifting the mail in search of Yonkers letters. Captain Isaac B. Ruton kept the inn creditably, and was withal a popular man. It was truly an exciting hour when the Albany stage, which had left that place the day before, dashed over the bridge in the hollow and up the little hill to the door of the inn, the driver throwing off the mail bag to Vark and the reins to the waiting hostler. The coaches were the same old-fashioned thoroughtrace, leather lined, green-baize curtained affairs used in the last century, and which have in some instances been preserved in our times. Ordinarily the fare to and from New York was one dollar, but in times of vigorous opposition the fare dropped to fifty cents. The stage from the city was always in before dinner time. It bore the mail, the 'Northern Mail' which, as an ancient authority tells us, 'is dispatched on the east side of the Hudson *via* Poughkeepsie to Albany every Monday, Wednesday and Friday at half-past seven A.M., and on the west side alternate days *via* Goshen and Kingston.' In those days a single letter within thirty miles cost eight cents, and the roads were so bad and the conveyance so limited that a post-office order was issued stating that postmasters are not to forward pamphlets in the mail when it is very large, or when it is carried with great expedition or on horseback. Verily, those were yet primitive days. A concession was about this time made, in that 'an extra land mail' was sent out on the east side of the river on Tuesdays and Thursdays. Need one wonder that there was unwonted excitement when the mail stages arrived in front of the Indian Queen?

"The church, hotel, store, post-office, a tumbled-down building or so, together with a patch of underbrush by the bridge, fully occupied the Square. Out of the Square on the west ran a narrow lane, now broadened into Main Street, and which led to the saw-mill. Near this mill in a little house south of the river lived Thaddeus Rockwell, late Justice of the Peace, and Obed S. Paddock. Here the lane ended, and the south bank of the Saw Mill River, then densely wooded, afforded no path to the Hudson. Little use would a path have been, for there was nothing to go to there after the mill was passed. The Nepperhan flowed unbridged and untamed to the river around Philip's Point, a steep and hardly accessible bluff, now much cut away and levelled.

"As one left the Square, passing north just before crossing the bridge, a little tavern stood on the left or south bank of the Nepperhan. Across the bridge a lovely and strictly rural sight met the eye. To the right of the bridge as one crossed was a little dam, from which water was carried in a race to the saw-mill. From this dam the water flowed under the bridge and through a shaded ravine at the left of the road, where afterward was a mill-pond foul and horrible. Along the edge of the ravine at the left of the road, after crossing the bridge, was a row of horse-chestnut trees, magnificent in proportion, inviting in their shade, their trunks and a little hand-rail guarding against an upset into the ravine. At the right of the road was a steep, inaccessible cliff, uncovered in part and partly covered by soil and grass; great masses of rock project here and there, threatening the passer-by. At the end of the chestnut trees and at the turn of the cliff were the projecting gardens of Manor Hall, which here pushed the already narrow road well up under the cliff. The hall itself formed the central portion of the picture at this end of the village. From the front porch the eye ranged up the hill on north and east and south, down to the bridge and across to the church, distant but a few hundred feet. From the west porch the view of the river, distant about three hundred feet, was unobstructed. The wooded point on the southwest cut off the view down the river, but west and northwest nothing interfered with the view. South of the hall itself the lane led from the village centre to the bulkhead where Nepperhan Street now merges into Dock. Beyond this front all was water. . . . Above this wharf at the lower dam was a flour-mill run by Mr. Penny. Three houses, occupied by the workmen, stood near by. These, with the out-buildings pertaining to the Manor, were all the buildings down this lane, excepting the little store at the wharf, which latter was of no consequence."

The foregoing descriptions of Yonkers in 1804, in 1813, and in 1823, transcribed, for the most part, from the pages of local historians, are pen-pictures of the hamlet in the first quarter of the nineteenth century. A description by an eye-witness has a peculiar interest. The Venerable David Horton, in February, 1896, ninety-six years old, was a long-time resident. He is the remaining link between the former times and the present—the last leaf upon the tree.

> " The mossy marbles rest
> On the lips he used to press
> In his bloom.
> And the names he loved to hear
> Have been carved for many a year
> On the tomb."

He heard the old church bell ring when it summoned the elder generation. He is passing the twilight of his long life in White Plains, surrounded by loving children and grandchildren. "Looking out of life's western windows," he is calmly waiting the time when he shall hear the bells of the celestial city. In February, 1896, he celebrated his ninety-sixth birthday. The following sentences are from the published report of the celebration of his ninety-fifth birthday:

"Saturday, February 9, 1895, was the ninety-fifth birthday of Mr. David Horton, of this town, and the day was fittingly celebrated by a dinner-party at his residence, on Mamaroneck Avenue, south of the village, which was attended by about fifty friends of Mr. Horton and family, from far and near.

"A jolly party it was that assembled. The venerable host was in his usual good spirits, and the members of his family spared nothing that would contribute to the enjoyment of the guests.

"Among the decorative features of the dinner table was a large cake, surmounted by ninety-five small lighted candles, the gift of Mrs. Chapman; also a basket of ninety-five varieties of flowers, from Ex-Supervisor Jacob Read, of Yonkers. Many other handsome gifts were received.

"Among those present were Dr. and Mrs. Van Kleeck, Supervisor Secor, and Ex-Supervisor Jacob Read. Rev. Charles Douglas, of New Jersey, and Miss Amanda M. Douglas, the authoress, who are nephew and niece of Mr. Horton, were prevented attending by the weather, as was also Mr. Horton's venerable neighbor, Mr. Bartholomew Gedney, who is in his ninety-third year.

"Mr. Horton was born in White Plains on February 9, 1800, in a house on Broadway on the site now occupied by the convent. From the time he was a year old he resided in Yonkers, until 1865, when he removed to White Plains. His farm in Yonkers is now what is known as Dunwoodie. Mr. Horton was a member of the Benton Grays, a State militia company in Yonkers, over sixty years ago. He served as Road Commissioner of Yonkers for many terms.

"Mr. Horton is full of interesting reminiscence and anecdotes of his early days. From the hills of Yonkers, in 1807, he saw the first steamboat built, Robert Fulton's Clermont, as it sailed up the Hudson on its trial trip. He has distinct recollections of the War of 1812.

"During his thirty-one years' residence in White Plains, Mr. Horton has been engaged in farming, which has been his lifelong occupation. Up to a few years ago he gave his personal attention to the farm, but since that time, on account of failing sight, the management has devolved upon his sons, Louis and William. Mr. Horton's general health continues first-rate, and he maintains a remarkable degree of strength. In appearance, he is little if any older than twenty years ago.

"Mr. Horton has seven children living and nine grandchildren.

In 1895 he said in substance: "I was born in 1800. My grandfather, Daniel Horton, lived at White Plains during the Revolution. General Lafayette called at grandfather's house. My grandmother, Mrs. Ann Horton, saw him at the time. He patted her son Stephen, who was then a lad, and told him he would take him to France with him. When the British were coming toward White Plains grandmother took the children and some valuable articles and rode off on horseback to Bedford, to be out of harm's way. A part of the battle of White Plains was fought on grandfather's farm. The British burned his house and barn.

"The lad, Stephen Horton, grew to manhood and married. When I, his son, was about one year old, that was in 1801, he removed to Yonkers and lived in the Sprain Brook Valley, on a farm which included within its boundaries the site of the present Roman Catholic cemetery (St. Joseph's). When I was a child of about seven years of age I attended school in a school-house* located on the Turnpike (North Broadway), between the dwellings of Mr. Samuel Lyons, and Mr. William A. Dyckman. Mr. Dyckman's home was in the town of Greenburgh and Mr. Lyons' home was in Yonkers. One lived about one-quarter of a mile north of the school-house and the other about one-quarter of a mile south. I recall my teacher there and an incident associated. I remember that he permitted the scholars one day to go out of school and stand in the road to see a steamboat on the river. A school-house stood on the Saw Mill River Road, near the house of Mr. Vincent Fowler, the father of Abram Fowler. Mr. Vincent Fowler's house was on the east side of the Saw Mill River Road, about three or four hundred feet south of the Tuckahoe Road. The school-house was at the corner of the Tuckahoe Road and Saw Mill River Road. One of the school-books in use in the schools was Dabol's Arithmetic, another was the American Preceptor, a third was the Juvenile Expositor. That had grammar and two or three other kinds of reading. I remember several Yonkers teachers. The name of one was O'Neal, another was Josh Hatfield. During my boyhood, there was a hotel where the Getty House now stands. It was kept by Mr. Reynolds. Colonel Williams afterwards kept it. Another who kept the tavern was Isaac B. Ruton. He was captain of a sloop. When I was a small boy Alpheus Pierson kept the store in Yonkers. Afterwards it was kept by Judge Vark. He was a boy when he first went into the store. I think he was a German. For a time he was engaged in wagon

DAVID HORTON.

making. Pierson took a liking to him and employed him in the store as a clerk. When Vark was proprietor of the store he was also a magistrate and used to go to Bedford and White Plains to hold court. He was postmaster also. He kept the store until he was quite an old man.

"Before the stage coach carried the mail it was carried by mounted carriers. A mail carrier would ride up to Judge Vark's store and the judge would unlock the mail-bag, take out the mail, select the Yonkers mail, replace the rest, relock the bag and give it back to the carrier. The bag was large enough to carry a bushel and a half, more or less. Envelopes were not used. The letters were folded and sealed with wax. Each mail carrier had a certain distance to ride. Probably eight or ten persons could ride in the mail coaches which came into use. The coach was drawn by four horses.

"In the early part of the century the road from New York got to be a turnpike and they had two toll-

---

*Early in the century there was a school-house near Warner's store, Mosholu, and another on the road to Mile Square, near Devoe's.

gates. One gate was above Kingsbridge. Afterward they moved it about two miles further north. The people built a bridge about a mile from Kingsbridge. After that they could shun Kingsbridge.

"The sloops in early days were brought up into the Saw Mill River. No pier had yet been built out into the Hudson. In the Nepperhan were two beams across which a plank was laid. Passengers walked out on that plank to the sloop. When the tide began to fall the boatmen would float their sloop out into the Hudson and take the freight out to it in a boat. They made the sloop fast to a ring in a big rock. The dock extending out into the Hudson was built after Mr. Wells came to Yonkers.

"The first sloop I can remember was called the 'Belvedere.' I was a small boy when the Belvedere ran. Another sloop was called the Eveline. I remember that when they got the Belvedere a few farmers joined together and took stock in a sloop. I used to see my mother when about to go to the boat put a tub of butter in one end of a bag and a stone in the other; when the bag was placed on the horse's back the weight of the stone balanced that of the tub of butter.

"When James Madison was re-elected to the Presidency, the successful party in Yonkers celebrated the victory by a barbecue at the "big rock" (on Hudson Street, near present Lutheran Church). The men came on horseback, the ladies riding on pillions behind their escorts. The day was fine overhead, but the mud was deep. It had rained the night before and the ox was not well roasted—not more than half done. Jacob Odell, the son of General Odell, was then a boy. He and I, and other boys, dined off the head of the roasted ox. That was very good.

I knew the Valentines when they kept slaves. My father had a slave named Harry Evison. Harry was left to mother and myself by my father, when he died. We told Evison that if he would remain with us five years, we would give him his freedom; but before the five years had expired the slaves were emancipated.

"The Rev. Elias Cooper preached in Yonkers during my boyhood days. I do not remember any Methodist service in Yonkers previous to 1809, when a camp-meeting was held in Bishop Sherwood's, about a quarter of a mile northeast of where the Tuckahoe Methodist church now stands. I was then nine years old. Not long after the camp-meeting a service led by Harry Cronk, a lay reader, was held in the woods where the present St. Joseph's Catholic cemetery is. I think that was about 1810, but am not certain. Afterwards the Methodists came and held meetings in private houses and then built a church.

"When I was fourteen years old the family moved to the 'Valley farm' (Dunwoodie, Yonkers). Peter Nodine was a neighbor of ours. He owned forty acres of land on Nodine Hill and about nine acres, more or less, down on the road from Yonkers to Eastchester (the present Yonkers Avenue). Benjamin B. Post, Jacob Post, both farmers, and Isaac Post, a brother of Jacob, were also our neighbors. When I was fourteen years old John Nodine, our hired man and I went down to the dock at Manhattanville to drive horses and draw fascine. They were building breastworks east of the Hudson. My father and our neighbors were assisting. The breastworks in some places were built of stone, and in other places of fascines which were unloaded from sloops and drawn by teams from the Manhattanville dock to the breastworks. There were gates in the breastworks. During the War of 1812 the English vessels were lying off Portchester.

"When I was a young man I used to drive to New York, taking down potatoes, apples, pork, pickles, wood, etc. Once when plowing, not far from Manor Hall, I plowed up human bones. The physician who examined them said that they were the bones of an Indian.

"I do not remember the first New York paper we took. We received one paper which was published up the river, but I cannot recall where, perhaps at Sing Sing." *

Mr. Horton was born before any newspaper was published in Westchester County. The first Westchester County paper was the *Somers Museum and Westchester Advertiser*. It appeared in 1809. A Peekskill newspaper in size 19x12 appeared in 1816, and another Peekskill paper in 1830. The *Westchester Herald and Farmers' Register* was the first Sing Sing paper. It was published in 1818. During this period (1800–1825) the New York papers were the *Commercial Advertiser* (1797), *Evening Post* (1801), William Coleman, William Cullen Bryant, William Leggett and Park Goodwin had been its editors. In 1800 there were only two hundred newspapers in the United States.† In 1824 New York

* Mr. Horton died May 11, 1896.

† One of the country papers of that date was the *Ulster County Gazette*, not much over one foot in length. A copy of it, dated 1800 A.D., is now in the possession of Isaac Nodine, of Yonkers. It is printed in heavy black lines in mourning for Washington, and contains an account of his funeral. It also contains quaint advertisements, among which is the announcement that a slave woman will be sold on a given date.

City had twelve daily newspapers, with a circulation varying from one thousand to four thousand copies.

The city and county papers brought to the Yonkers people news of what was transpiring during the administration of three presidents, Jefferson, Madison and Monroe, and of four governors, Clinton (George), Lewis, Tompkins (a Westchester County man, afterwards vice-president of the United States), Clinton (Dewitt), Yates, and the first part of Dewitt Clinton's second term. As the Westchester County villages were yet small hamlets, and as the largest cities in the country were yet small towns, life was comparatively quiet and uneventful. As late as the year 1810, the mail between Canandaigua and Genesee River was carried on horseback—part of the time by a *woman*.

Telegraphs were unknown, and the first railroad for carrying passengers was not opened until September, 1825, and that was in England. No locomotive was in use in this country until 1829. The population of Westchester County in 1800 was less than 28,000, including slaves. Buffalo was a hamlet. At Albany, in 1800, were only 5,349 people, and in the whole State of New York only 589,051, including 10,417 free colored citizens, and 20,903 slaves. New York State then ranked third in population. New York City in 1800 had a population of less than 61,000, Boston less than 26,000 and Philadelphia less than 42,000. The site of Chicago was a wilderness. A fort was built there in 1804. The population of the whole country was only 5,308,483, including 893,602 slaves.

In 1820, toward the end of the period of Yonkers' history under review, Westchester County had 33,131 inhabitants, Albany 12,541, New York State, which had risen to the first rank as to population, had 1,332,706. New York City had 123,706, Boston 43,298, Philadelphia 63,802. The population of Chicago in 1820 is unknown. Its first census was not taken until 1837, when it was a village with 4,170 inhabitants. The population of the United States in 1820 was 9,633,822, of whom 1,538,022 were slaves.

The Yonkers people of that period were reading about the duel between Hamilton and Burr, Oliver Evans' steam carriage and steamboat (on the Delaware), Rumsey's steamboat (on the Potomac), Fitch's steamboat (on the Delaware), Stevens' steamboat (on the Hudson), Fulton's steamboat trip to Albany, Stevenson's steam locomotive in England, the War of 1812, the defeat of the English warships by the Americans, the new song (the Star Spangled Banner), the burning of Washington City by the British, General Jackson's victory at New Orleans, the visit of Lafayette to America, the passage of the law of 1817 by the New York Legislature (it enacted that every negro, mulatto or mustee within the state, born before the Fourth of July, 1799, should from after the Fourth of July, 1827, be free), the admission of new states to the Union, the purchase of Louisiana, the Indian War on the banks of the Tippecanoe River and the opening of the Erie canal, in derision called by some "Clinton's Ditch" (begun in 1817, finished in 1825). From abroad came reports of the punishment of the Barbary States by the United States, and news about Napoleon and his Waterloo defeat, George IV. in England, and other personages and events, long since passed into history.

INFANTRYMAN, 1812-1834.

SECTION III.

FROM PERIOD OF HAMLETS TO THAT OF INCORPORATED VILLAGE. 1825–1855.

In 1825 there were hamlets in Yonkers, but no large village. In 1855 the village of Yonkers had become large enough to convince public-spirited citizens that it should be incorporated. During the years intervening between these dates, life in the town began to be more active. Several causes of the change are evident. Steamboats were plowing the Hudson River and making landings (first in 1831) at Yonkers. Trains began to run in the forties: first those of the New York and Harlem Railroad along the eastern boundary, passing through a small part of the town; and then those of the Hudson River Railroad, passing through the whole length of the western part of the town. Real estate in Yonkers came into market, being released from the hand which had held it. The New York business man appeared as a resident; New York City was growing. In 1850 its population was much more than half a million, and the whole country was increasing in population. Manufacturers began to avail themselves of the

Saw Mill River water-power. In 1844 the electric telegraph came into use in the country, a wire having been stretched during that year from Washington to Baltimore, over which sped the historic message, "What hath God wrought?"

But previous to the forties, before the steam-cars began to run, the population was small. In 1825 it was only 1,621, with 249 taxable persons. In 1845 there were only 2,517 people living in the town and the number of taxable persons was less than 300. In 1855 the population had increased to 7,554 and of taxable persons to 1,629.

In order to reproduce a picture of the township as it appeared before emerging from its rural quiet, it will be necessary to record details which at first may seem beneath the dignity of history, but it is no less an authority than Macaulay who, when writing a history of his country, said that he would cheerfully bear the reproach of having descended below the dignity of history, if he could succeed in placing before his countrymen of the nineteenth century a true picture of their ancestors.

And it was an Oxford University professor who, when he proposed to write a history, said he would not make it a record merely of kings and conquests, "a drum and trumpet history," but a history of the people.

Mr. Jacob Read, a representative of the Yonkers people who were engaged in farming during 1825 and 1855 and intervening years, is still (1896) a resident of the town, which for fifteen years he served as Supervisor. In 1895 he said, in substance:

"I came to Yonkers in February, 1829, when a boy in my eleventh year. I recall distinctly the prominent farmers of Yonkers from 1829 to 1855, and their mode of life. I also recall the kind of crops they raised, and how they marketed their produce. Through the twenties and thirties and up to the forties, the principal crops were oats, rye, wheat, corn, hay, potatoes and pickles. The potatoes were of the 'blue nose' and 'kidney' variety. Afterward came the 'Early Rose.' We did not have, as farmers do now, a number of varieties, all dug out of the same hill! The fruits were apples, peaches, pears and cherries. The apples were 'pound sweets,' 'catheads,' and 'fall pippins.' The peaches of Yonkers in the latter part of the thirties and the first of the forties were very fine. The cherries were of the Dyckman variety, a sour cherry and excellent. We used to call tomatoes 'love-apples,' but nobody ate them. I never ate tomatoes until 1847. We had good walnuts and chestnuts. The garden truck the farmers raised was for their own use only. None was sent to market until about 1835. All the cabbage for market, for example, was raised at Bergen Point and Long Island. Nor did the Yonkers farmers send any milk to New York. It was kept in milk-rooms, for there were no ice-houses. The milk-rooms had stone bottoms, and were cool. Tables in those days were supplied with plenty of fresh meat. I remember that Mr. David Horton, with whom I lived, would kill a sheep in summer, or a lamb or a pig in the fall, so as to have fresh meat, and would send a quarter over to Mr. Vermilye Fowler's, or Mr. Nattie Valentine's, or Mr. David Oakley's; and when they killed, they returned the favor. The poultry in the farmyards also supplied the tables. Barrels of salted meats and hogsheads of cider, as also butter, lard, turnips and potatoes stocked the cellar. Blacksmiths, wheelwrights and carpenters made many agricultural instruments which they are not expected to make to-day.

"Beef and ham were smoked in the farmers' smoke-houses. Up to 1845 sheep were kept. The lambs were sold in New York. A man came up from Manhattan Island during a period of years and bought lambs of the farmers. Pork and poultry were also sent to New York. Large droves of cattle and sheep from the north passed through Yonkers down the Albany Post-road. Perhaps as many as two hundred or two hundred and fifty cows and from three hundred to five hundred sheep would be in a single drove. Two or three men or two men and a boy could manage a drove, as the line fences were all up and the gates were closed. The drovers 'put up' at old Uncle Post Dyckman's on the other side of Kingsbridge.

"Hay was sold in New York. Marketing was done by land as well as by river. A team would be sent to New York with a load on Sunday night in order to be there for the Monday morning market. The team was returned the next day and again sent down on Wednesday, back Thursday, and down again on Friday. Butter sold at from ten cents to a shilling a pound. Loose sugar, that is, brown sugar for every-day use, was purchased in quantities of seven pounds. White sugar was purchased by the 'loaf.' A 'loaf' of white sugar weighed about ten or twelve pounds. It was more expensive than brown sugar. We didn't see any of that white sugar around except when there was company. Then it was cut off the loaf and placed on the table. We used to count money by pounds, shillings and pence up to about 1841. One and thripence was fifteen cents; one and ninepence, twenty-two cents; two and tupence, twenty-seven cents. In these early days we used 'dips,' that is tallow candles. The candles were made by hanging wicks over alder rods (from which the bark had been peeled) and dipping them into the mixed mutton and beef tallow; the beef tallow hardened the candles. The alder rods were selected because they were light and easily handled. After the candles were made the rods were carefully stored away for the next year's use. In later years sperm oil and kerosene oil were used. Coal was not in use in Yonkers until about 1839 or 1840. Then Mr. Ebenezer Baldwin, who kept a lumber yard, brought in twenty tons, but its sale was slow. Nobody at first had a coal-stove. Everybody used open fire-places or 'Franklin' stoves. The 'Franklin' was used in parlors. It was open in front like a fire-place. On one side stood the tongs and on the other the shovel, their brass tops polished bright.

"I recall distinctly the routine work of each year on the Yonkers farms. January and February were the months in which wood was cut for summer use. Enough wood was cut in the winter to last all summer. Fire-wood was drawn from the woods by ox teams. When the snow was deep we would put a chain around the tree we had chopped down, and, with our oxen, would drag the tree to the wood-shed, breaking a road through the snow, which in those winters fell plentifully. I have seen it three feet deep, and of course there were often heavy drifts. We used to pile the woodshed full of fire-wood and then pile it up outside. Loads of chips were brought to the yard from the woods. Chips made a quick fire for boiling the tea-kettle. Besides the wood we cut for home use we cut a good deal of cordwood to be taken to New York by our teams. We had no buck saws, but used axes and sometimes cross-cut saws. Besides getting in our wood, we threshed oats, rye and wheat in January and Febru- ary, calculating always to get through before the first of March, which was the month for repairing stone walls and rail fences, and for cut- ting brushes and briars and heaping them up in piles to burn. In April the farmers were generally dig- ging out stone and building stone walls. They were also at that time getting ready to plow their corn ground and also to plow for oats, which were sown in April. In May we planted our corn ground and also planted potatoes and plowed our pickle ground. Every farmer had his pickle patch, some re- serving four acres and some five or six for that crop. In June the pickles were planted. That was a very important crop. Not one-quarter of the pickles were taken to the Yonkers pickle factories. The fact of the business is that Yonkers, Ford- ham, West- Farms, East- chester and Greenburgh were the prin- cipal pickle pro- ducers for the New York mar- ket. It was a former Yonkers man who estab- lished the pickle industry in one of the western states. In June we also put our cheese peppers in beds to be afterward trans- planted. A good many of them were raised.

JACOB READ.

June was also the month for plowing and hoeing corn and potatoes. In the latter part of the month we plowed for buckwheat and turned over our turnip ground. Turnips were raised to feed the cattle, not for market. June was the month in which the sheep were sheared and in which cherries were picked and taken to market. I have taken down to the city as many as sixteen hundredweight of cherries. In July we were plowing and hilling corn, which we tried to finish before the beginning of haying and harvesting, which was our July and August work. In July we also plowed and hoed our pickle crop. Apples were taken to market in August and pickles were picked in the last part of the month. That was the principal work. We also at that time dug potatoes and took them and our apples to market. This work extended into September. Forty-five bushels of apples were a load for a team. September might have been called our marketing month, for then we were gathering our crops and taking them to market. We also were topping our corn at that time, but we did not husk it until October, which was also the month for picking some varieties of apples, digging some kinds of potatoes and for making cider. In November we were yet busy husking corn and digging potatoes. We were also, during this and other winter months, threshing grain, killing hogs and poultry, cutting wood, etc.

"The crops in Yonkers were fine. In the forties over here in the valley (Tibbett's Brook), at the Horton farmhouse, near the present Dunwoodie Railroad station, and a little south of the road to Eastchester (Yonkers Avenue), we would get up the oxen and take the cart, which held forty-five bushels, out to the potato patch in November and there dig potatoes and fill the cart and have them in the wagon-house or cellar by noon. We would get another cart-load in the afternoon. We calculated that six hills of the variety, which was very large, would fill a bushel basket. They did fill it. Some of those potatoes were from six to eight inches long, and they were good, too! I remember that sometimes after supper we went to the barn to sort apples and potatoes. We made two candlesticks by cutting holes in two large turnips. We put a dip in each. One dip would be burning at one end of the heap of potatoes or apples, and the other at the other end of the heap. We sat there in the barn and worked. Just before stopping work, one of the men would go into the house and put some of those potatoes in the hot ashes of the open fire-place. When we all came in from the barn the potatoes were nicely baked, and there we sat, before going to bed, and enjoyed those mealy and white baked potatoes.

"As to the price of farm land. The Horton farm of two hundred acres, at what is now called Dunwoodie, was bought in 1833, or 1834, for $6,000. A little more than a score of years afterward, when the village was incorporated (1855), the average price of a lot on Warburton Avenue was about $150 or $200. Opposite Manor Hall the price was $200. Judge Woodruff owned the property at that time. As to the upper end of what is now Warburton Avenue—they would almost give you a lot in that locality if you would go up there. In 1872, when the city was incorporated, those lots opposite Manor Hall were worth $500 and $600 each. When Dr. Gates bought of Levi P. Rose two or three acres on the hill, opposite the present First Reformed Church, he paid for it $3,900. In 1893, a part of that property was offered the city, for a City Hall property, for $130,000.

"I recall one event which created great excitement in Yonkers in 1842 or 1843. A dam above Ashford (a place subsequently called Ardsley by Mr. Cyrus W. Field), about five miles north of Yonkers, gave way, by reason of a sudden and heavy fall of rain, owing to a cloud-burst. Oliver Rhead, whose farm was in the Saw Mill River Valley, a little north of St. John's cemetery, saw the river rising rapidly, and, mounting his horse, rode swiftly down to Yonkers to alarm the village. The Wells and Paddock dam, north of the present Elm Street Bridge, was then comparatively new, but for some time it resisted the pressure of the flood. In those days there were no factories or other buildings near the dam to be damaged. At last the water broke through, and with irresistible force rushed through the little village. It gullied out Mechanic (now New Main) Street, about seven feet. It also gullied out Mill (now Main) Street, west of Getty Square. At that time the 'Tony Archer Bridge,' a wooden structure, near the present cemetery (Oakland), spanned the Saw Mill River. It had upright side posts surmounted with railing. The water overflowed that bridge and the bridge over the Saw Mill River, just north of the present Getty Square. The Saw Mill River Road was covered. The water ran up over the stone wall, and as far as the old parsonage, in what are now Oakland Cemetery grounds. It also overflowed 'Gilly Guion's lane.' I was on my way to a political meeting to be held at Bashford's tavern, which stood on the north bank of the Nepperhan, west of Manor Hall. When I reached the 'Tony Archer Bridge,' near the parsonage lot, I attempted to ford the water which was running over the bridge. The current swept me and my horse down stream, and, after regaining solid ground, I rode down to the Post-road Bridge and forded it without accident. I recall the deep gully in Mechanic Street, near the site of the present Getty House. A few days after the flood, a young horse belonging to Anson Baldwin was taken to be shod at Archibald's (afterward Peter Nodine's) blacksmith shop. The horse was restless and succeeded in breaking away from the tie-post. He ran around into Mechanic Street, fell into the deep gully and was killed. The gully was full of boulders."

From 1839 to 1849 Captain Joseph Peene ran the sloop Ben Franklin three times a week from the bulkhead at Yonkers to the foot of Murray Street in New York. His cargo consisted principally of country produce and largely of pickles. Westchester County has long been known as a section producing fine pickles, and Yonkers was one of the chief pickle and shipping ports. The farmers would come aboard with their produce, often as many as fifteen or twenty in a single trip, bringing their lunch baskets with them. No charge was made for the trip, and they provided their own food. All hands usually returned to Yonkers in the Ben Franklin the next day.* An eye-witness said he had often seen the line of pickles and produce wagons extending from the bulkhead to the side of Manor Hall, awaiting their turn to unload upon the deck of Captain Peene's boat. From 1825 to 1855 men were coming to live in Yonkers whose lifework is a part of the history of the town. Among well-known citizens in the twenties were Vark, Horton, Fowler, Wells, Dyckman, Bashford, Gates, Ackerman, Odell, Denslow,

---

* There were only two or three horses in the hamlet in the early forties. Farmers with their oxen or teams of horses came to the boat-landing, the tavern or the country stores, but the villagers, save two or three, had no horses. The proprietor of "Fairy Grove" was King Griffen, a colored man of large proportions, and great weight (avoirdupois). He kept a team of kicking mules. One day, when the boat arrived at the pier, who should step off but the Hon. Martin Van Buren, then President, or ex-President, of the United States. He had come to be a guest of Mr. Thomas W. Ludlow, but as his arrival on that boat was unexpected, Mr. Ludlow had not driven up to meet him. Mr. Griffen was the villager to whom fell the honor of escorting the distinguished visitor to the home of his host. The streets of Yonkers, that day, witnessed a demonstration of Republican simplicity which would have filled the imposing courts of Europe with awe. Behold the President (or ex-President) of the United States, and the "King" of Yonkers, in the same

Paddock, Grigg, West, Crosby, Ruton, Valentine, Taylor, Browne, Lent, Ingersoll, Baldwin, Nodine, Devoe, Smith (Caleb), Stephens, Roberts, Rhead, Pulver, Dingee, Searl, Garrison, Shonnard, Waring, Nichols and others. The rectors of St. John's Church were the Rev. Messrs. John Grigg, John West and Alexander H. Crosby. The preachers at the First Methodist Church (on the Albany Post-road), and probably at the Tuckahoe Methodist Church, were the Rev. Messrs. Hibbard (1828) and Seaman (1829). Previous to 1825 the Tuckahoe Church was in the New Rochelle Circuit, and the ministers in the twenties were Bushnell, Richardson, Woolsey, Jewett, Seney, Thomas, Bangs, Seaman, Martindale, Andrus and Rice. As to who preached in the Tuckahoe Methodist Church from 1825 to 1828 the author is uninformed. The New Rochelle Circuit ministers were: Martindale, Rice, Sandford, Smith (J. M.), Bowen, Woolsey and Cochran. The names of those who preached in the Methodist Church at Mosholu are recorded in Edsall's "History of King's Bridge."

In the following brief annals of 1825 and 1855, and the intervening years, which record the steady improvement of the town, are references to some of the citizens who came in the thirties, forties and fifties, and were prominently identified with the growth of the place.

In 1825, at Van Cortlandt, an ancient structure, the residence of the earliest generation of Van Cortlandts, was taken down to make way for improvements. It stood on the bank of the mill-pond (now Van Cortlandt Lake) a little north of the old mill. It was even more ancient than the old Van Cortlandt mansion. which still stands, "in solitary state," in the present Van Cortlandt Park, then in Yonkers, but now a little south of its southern boundary line. The mansion now standing there was erected in 1748.

In the summer of 1828 a Methodist Church was dedicated in Yonkers. It stood on a site gratuitously deeded by Mr. Lemuel Wells. At first it fronted south on the Eastchester Road (present Ashburton Avenue), the course of which was across the site of the present fire-engine house plot (west of the present St. John's Hospital). The road came out on the Post-road (North Broadway) south of the church. Steps led from the Eastchester Road up into the church. The building was a frame structure, originally small and painted white. Its blinds were green. It had a gallery and a plain pulpit. In 1854 the building was turned to face the Albany Post-road. It was then lengthened and widened at the pulpit end by the addition of wings, and it was otherwise improved.

In 1826 the Rising Star Lodge, No. 250, Free and Accepted Masons, was organized. It was reorganized in 1851. As early as 1828 the hat industry was established in Yonkers by Messrs. William C. Waring and Hezekiah Nichols, who began the business of making hat bodies for silk hats. Their factory was in the "Glen." In 1829 Major Joseph Delafield, a gentleman of liberal culture, purchased, in the lower part of what was then Yonkers, a farm of two hundred and fifty acres on the Hudson River, between Spuyten Duyvil and the site of the present village of Riverdale. He named his place Fieldston from a family seat in Great Britain, and the name was in general use until villages having each its own name sprang up. After the southern part of Yonkers had been set off as a separate township, the people decided by ballot as to what should be the name of the new town. Kingsbridge received only a few more votes than Fieldston.

In the thirties, more citizens were enrolled, among them John Hobbs, the honored school-teacher, Joseph Peene and John T. Waring, who became residents of prominence. Lemuel W. Wells, called "Farmer Wells," came in 1836. Either in the twenties or soon after, Jarvis Waring came. The rector of St. John's Church was the Rev. Smith Pine. The preachers at the First Methodist Church on the Albany Post-road, and probably at the Methodist Church in Tuckahoe, were the Rev. Messrs. Seaman, Hibbard, Smith, Evans, Oldron, Bangs, Davis and Hatfield.

In 1831 Lemuel Wells constructed a steamboat wharf, one-eighth of a mile long. Previous to that steamboats made their landings on the other side of the river at Closter (now Alpine) landing, and at

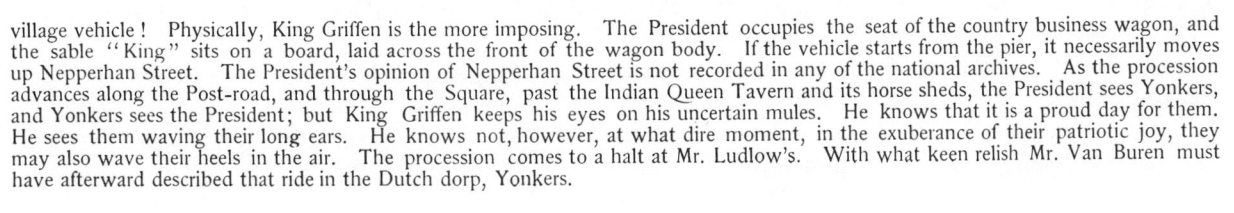

---

village vehicle! Physically, King Griffen is the more imposing. The President occupies the seat of the country business wagon, and the sable "King" sits on a board, laid across the front of the wagon body. If the vehicle starts from the pier, it necessarily moves up Nepperhan Street. The President's opinion of Nepperhan Street is not recorded in any of the national archives. As the procession advances along the Post-road, and through the Square, past the Indian Queen Tavern and its horse sheds, the President sees Yonkers, and Yonkers sees the President; but King Griffen keeps his eyes on his uncertain mules. He knows that it is a proud day for them. He sees them waving their long ears. He knows not, however, at what dire moment, in the exuberance of their patriotic joy, they may also wave their heels in the air. The procession comes to a halt at Mr. Ludlow's. With what keen relish Mr. Van Buren must have afterward described that ride in the Dutch dorp, Yonkers.

Lower Closter, about half a mile south of the Upper Closter landing. The boats had considerable patronage on the west side. Yonkers passengers were taken to and fro in row-boats. Mr. John C. Campbell (in 1896 about seventy-six years of age), an old resident, said in 1895 that he lived on the west shore in his childhood and youth, and that in those days there were no houses on the Palisades. At the foot of the mountain opposite Yonkers, and near the site of the present mill-dock, was a small public house. A rough wagon-road led down the Palisades. The New Jersey farmers brought their farm produce down to the dock, and there they bought shad of the fishermen. Two steamboats, the Orange and the Rockland, were running from Nyack. They made landings at Upper Closter, at Yonkers (after the dock was built), and at Lower Closter.

It was in 1831 that the whole interior of St. John's Church was remodelled. Transepts and chancel were added, the gallery put in, and the organ built in 1849. In 1833 a new school-house (30 x 40) was built by Lemuel Wells, north of the old school-building, which stood near the corner of the road to Eastchester and the Albany Post-road. In 1836 a country road was opened from the old Highland Turnpike (Albany Post-road) to the Saw Mill River Road (once known as Guion's lane, between Guion's mills and the Post-road). Subsequently this country road was called Mechanic Street, and now is known as New Main Street. In 1835 the Methodists built a small frame church at Mosholu, on the west side of the Post-road. The ministers in the Kingsbridge circuit preached there.

In 1837 a dam the Saw Mill River, the present Elm Lemuel Wells and Obed Paddock. lands on the west Messrs. Paddock fall came to be water power," Island "the at the east end of sixth." The was begun in 1837, 1842. John B. engineer. The the old distributing Avenue and For- York, is forty and Between five and Aqueduct are now bounded. pense, including tributing pipes, was built across north of and near Street Bridge by Prince W. and Mr. Wells owned of the dam and the on the east. That called the "fifth that on Chicken fourth," and that the Glen "the Croton Aqueduct and completed in Jervis was chief entire length from reservoir on Fiftieth Street, New a half miles. six miles of the within Yonkers as The whole expense, $1,800,000 for dis- and amount paid for right of way and other incidental charges, was $10,375,000. Including commissions and interest, the whole cost was $12,500,000. New York had at that time a population of about 300,000. While the workmen were constructing this aqueduct Yonkers farmers had new themes for thought and conversation. They began to realize that a growing city was reaching out into the suburbs. In 1840 the population of New York was 312,710.

THE OLD DOCK, YONKERS.

In 1837 the country suffered from business disasters. In 1838 a Yonkers citizen, riding along the Post-road through Yonkers, was asked by his fellow-traveller: "Upon what terms would you accept ten acres of land here, if offered as a gift?" Evidently they were just then riding through a stony or otherwise unattractive part. About the end of the thirties a parsonage was gratuitously deeded to Christ Methodist Episcopal Church (the original corporate name of the First Methodist Church on North Broadway) by Mr. Frederick Shonnard and his wife.

In the forties more men of influence came into the town as residents. Among them were the Rev. Henry L. Storrs, rector of St. John's; the Rev. Victor M. Hulbert, pastor of the Greenville Church and Yonkers Reformed Church Mission, and then pastor of the Yonkers Reformed Church. The Methodist ministers of the Yonkers circuit, who preached in the Methodist Churches on the Albany Post-road (corner of road to Eastchester), the Mosholu Methodist Church and the Tuckahoe Methodist Church were the Rev. Messrs. Burch, Wright, Selleck, Green and Keys. Among other men well-known in Yonkers as recent comers were Ethan Flagg, William Warburton Scrugham, Reuben W. Van Pelt, Charles Waring, Samuel D. Rockwell, John Copcutt, John P. Groshon; Messrs. Francis and Foote, the teachers; Thomas C. Connell, the young engineer; Levi P. Flagg, the young physician; the Bairds, and Robert P. Getty, ex-New York Alderman, ex-member of the New York Board of Education, and in subsequent years U. S. Government Inspector and one of the projectors of the New York Elevated Railway system; Mr. Bailey Hobbs came in 1840 and Mr. Wm. P. Drummond in 1849. About 1841 Mr. David Stewart, who came from Scotland to America in 1835, settled at Mosholu, and about two years afterward he leased a farm within the boundaries of the present town of Yonkers. He and his wife were "model Christians." He served the First Reformed Church as elder for fourteen years. Three of his sons learned the mason's trade, and for many years the firm of Stewart Brothers (first James and David, Jr., and then James and George) was a well-known firm. Some of the largest buildings in Yonkers, among them the Roman Catholic Seminary on Valentine Hill, were constructed by them. Mr. George Stewart, an elder in the First Reformed Church, was one of the principal founders of the Ludlow Street Chapel, which is now the Second Reformed Church of Yonkers. A memorial window to Mr. George Stewart was placed in 1896 in the east window of the New First Reformed Church by the members of his Bible-class. Mr. James

CROTON AQUEDUCT, 1842—NEPPERHAN AVENUE, YONKERS, N. Y.

Stewart, in 1863, went out as first lieutenant with Company H, Seventeenth Regiment. His company was sent to Fort McHenry, and did duty thirty days, but returned without having participated in any engagement. Mr. Stewart, as president of the National Curling Club, is well known among American and Canadian lovers of the game of curling.

Mr. William Warburton Scrugham was the first resident lawyer in Yonkers of whom there is certain record. Coming from White Plains, where he studied law, he built his law office himself on the Post-road in Yonkers (see map of 1847). It then stood a long distance from any other building. As Supervisor of the town for many years, as Lieutenant-Colonel, Colonel, and finally Brigadier-General of state militia, and by election in 1859 as Judge of the Supreme Court of the State of New York, he was widely and favorably known. A more extended sketch of his life will be found in a subsequent chapter. In 1840 a school-house was erected at Mosholu. In the same year Mr. Wells built two school buildings and founded two schools; one for boys and the other for girls. Both schools became well known in subsequent years. The seminary for boys was on Locust Hill Avenue (No. 72). Its first principal was a Mr. Burrill, but it came into prominence under Mr. George W. Francis, A.M. The girls school-building stood between North Broadway and Palisade Avenue, some distance north of the present St. John's Hospital. Mr. George W. Bleecker was the first manager of this seminary. He was succeeded by Mr. William C. Foote, A.M. Mr. Francis and Mr. Foote are remembered with gratitude and love by many Yonkers people who, in their youthful days, were instructed by them.

In 1841 a Whig meeting was held at the "Indian Queen Inn." Prior to the early forties the Whigs in Yonkers were few as to numbers. Mr. John Bashford, who kept the hotel on the dock, was the Democratic leader and Mr. Edward F. Shonnard was the Whig leader. Judge Vark and Colonel Oliver Denslow were prominent Democrats, and the elder Wells was a Whig. At the Whig meeting in 1841 the speakers were Lemuel Wells and "Old Joe Hoxie," a well-known stump speaker, and Judge Suffern from Rockland County. A joint meeting, addressed by Horace Greely, was at another time held in Kellinger's barn. A great Fourth of July meeting, which was held in front of the old carriage shop of James Bashford, about where the present Hudson Street enters South Broadway, was addressed by the young lawyer, William W. Scrugham. It was his first public speech. Mr. Bailey Hobbs, an honored citizen of Yonkers, informed the writer in 1895 that he heard that speech and was delighted with it. Although now (1896) an aged man, Mr. Hobbs can repeat some of the Independence Day address of the gifted Scrugham.

About 1841 a mission movement was started in Yonkers by Mr. Eben S. Hammond (then a senior in the Theological Seminary at New Brunswick) and others, which resulted in the organization of the First Reformed Church in 1843. Previous to that there were only two churches (St. John's and First Methodist on North Broadway) on the Hudson River side of the town as now bounded; but there was a Methodist Church at Mosholu, south of the present Yonkers boundary. About 1841 there were no three-story buildings around the Square, which subsequently came to be known as Getty Square.

In 1841 the New York and Harlem Railroad trains began to run to Fordham. They ran to Williams' Bridge in 1842, to Tuckahoe (Yonkers) and White Plains in 1844, and to Croton Falls in 1847. This road along the eastern boundary, and traversing a small section of the town, was the first railroad in Yonkers. A long-time employee of the road said that the first running of the trains through the county excited the curiosity of the people. Crowds surveyed it from the adjoining hills. Stages from the important villages were immediately put on for the nearest station, as the work advanced. From the present Getty Square, Yonkers, to Williams' Bridge is about six miles. James Nodine and James Miles (who in his youth came from England to New York in a sailing vessel, and who died in Yonkers in 1895, "the oldest hackman of the city"), drove stages from Yonkers to Williams' Bridge. The stage-fare was twenty-five cents. It is stated as a matter of fact that the railroad company suffered severely at first from the dishonesty of conductors, who collected the fare on board the trains.*

MANOR HOUSE AND SURROUNDINGS IN 1842.

Lemuel Wells died February 11, 1842, aged eighty-two years. "He left a widow, but neither child nor will. He had four brothers—Elisha, Levi, Horace and Jared—all of whom had died before him, and three of whom had left children, to the number of sixteen in all. These children, at the time of Mr. Wells' death, were all living, except one, Jared, Jr., who was represented by a single living child. By operation of the law the title to Mr. Wells' estate passed to his widow, with these fifteen children and one grandchild of his brother." The heirs all bore the name Wells except six, viz.: Mrs. Augustus Flagg, *nee* Lydia Wells; Mrs. Chester Hart, *nee* Elvey Wells; Mrs. Ralph Shipman, *nee* Marilla Wells; Mrs. Bildad Rowley, *nee* Nancy Wells; and Mrs. John W. Paterson, *nee* Ann E. Wells.

Among these heirs a partition suit was maintained and finally, by order of the Court of Chancery in that suit, the title became vested by master's deed in one of the heirs—Mr. Lemuel W. Wells, known as

---

*In 1826 a charter was granted to the Mohawk and Hudson Railroad Company for a railroad to run from Albany to Schenectady, sixteen miles. In 1830 work was commenced on the road, which went through populous towns along the open streets, without restriction or fear of the consequences, and travelled across fields, uphill and down. The road was finished in 1831. Both locomotive engines and horses were used on the road and the tickets were sold at stores or shops or by the conductor, and the trains proceeded at a very slow rate. Stationary engines were at the top of the hills, and the train was hauled up hill or let down hill by a strong rope. The brakemen used hand levers. The first steam railroad passenger train was run on this road in 1831. The engine was named "John Bull," and was imported from England. It weighed four tons. There were fifteen passengers on the two coaches, among whom were Thurlow Weed and Ex-Governor Joseph C. Yates.

"Farmer Wells," who came to Yonkers in 1836, and died in 1861. An elaborate abstract of title to the property at the date of the settlement of the partition suit referred to, tracing its history from the grant of Van Der Donck in 1846, was made out, and even published for general use. This abstract has ever since been the final appeal upon questions of title to lots within the boundaries of the Wells estate. Of course, to property lying outside these acres, but within the old Philipse Manor, all questions of title can be determined beyond dispute by going back to the deeds given by the Commissioners of Forfeiture in 1785. About the time Mr. Wells died, Yonkers was a hamlet of one hundred people—more or less—and a little more than a score of houses. That was about the population of the place in 1844, two years after Mr. Wells' death.

When "Farmer Wells" was placing the Wells estate in market, he sold to John Copcutt, for $17,500, "the first water power," west of the present Warburton Avenue, near Main Street. The old flour-mill there had burned about 1839. The fire was seen in New York, and before the city firemen ascertained how far north it was, they had started to run to it. Upon discovering that it was so far away, they turned back. Mr. Copcutt converted the mill into a mahogany saw-mill. About the same period, the second water power, including land on both sides of Main Street, was sold to Messrs. Mitchell and Hutchinson for $6,500, and the mill property (owned and occupied in 1861 by John T. Waring and Anson Baldwin) for $4,750.

A map of the Wells estate, which was divided in 1843, assists to a clearer knowledge of the village, as it appeared at that time, that is, about six years before the Hudson River Railroad began to run trains to Yonkers. In 1843 there was in the village no road to the Hudson River from the Albany Post-road, except that which led to the long wharf which Mr. Wells had built in 1831. The Post-road was much narrower than it is now. As late as 1865, the present South Broadway was only forty feet wide (sidewalks eight feet in width and roadway twenty-four feet). Its total width now is seventy-five feet, the sidewalks being fifteen feet each. A passenger coming north in the Albany stage from New York (then a city of about 360,000) would have seen, as he entered the Wells estate, about half a dozen houses south of St. John's Church. Thomas O. Farrington's, Widow Kniffen's, William Van Wagenen's and Judge Aaron Vark's dwellings were below the present St. Mary's Street. Judge Vark lived near the site of the present St. Joseph's Hospital. The level ground now known as "the flats," south of the present Hudson Street, was a farm where corn and grass grew, and where cows pastured. Our stage passenger, on nearing St. John's Church (then a small edifice as compared with the present building), would have seen, had he looked through the west window of the stage, James Bashford's carriage shop, which stood on a plot, now a part of Hudson Street, opposite the site of the present Railroad station. Just north of Mr. Bashford's shop was his dwelling house, within the St. John's Church grounds of to-day. North of the church, and on what is now the corner of South Broadway and Main Street, was an unoccupied dwelling house belonging to the Wells estate. On its ground floor were two apartments, which, being opened into one, constituted "The Long Room." It was there the small congregation of the present First Reformed Church worshipped in 1841, first as a mission and then as a church, before 1845—the year their first edifice was built. North of the dwelling house, and on a plot now a part of the present Main Street, was the country store and post-office kept by Judge Vark, at the corner of the Post-road, and a short lane which led to the grist-mill and saw-mill on the south bank of the mill-pond. Across the street was the tavern, "The Nappeckamack House," with its horse shed. South of that, and on the site of the present Yonkers Savings Bank, was the dwelling of Lemuel W. Wells ("Farmer Wells"), the nephew of Lemuel Wells. Horace D. Wells lived on the site of the present High School building. At the west end of the Post-road wooden bridge was an old stone building, previously used as a mill. A portion of the water-wheel still remained. The water which supplied the power to that mill came down in an underground wooden sluice-way (about four feet by two feet in size). It flowed from the third water power, east of the present Palisade Avenue.

The brushes and briers which once grew on the low south bank of the Nepperhan River, north of what is now Getty Square, were all covered up before 1843. The ground at that point is now six or seven feet higher than the original bank of the river. A few shops and other places of business stood there in 1843. Along Mechanic, now Main Street, were a few dwellings. On the west side of Guion Street, now Nepperhan Avenue, and nearly opposite the present School Street, was the old stone house possibly built before the Revolution. Dr. Amos W. Gates, Hiram Searls, and a few others lived on or near that street. Dr. Gates' house is still standing. Its site is on the east side of the present Nepperhan Avenue, a few rods south of Elm Street.

One standing on the Post-road Bridge in 1843 could see the clear, sparkling Saw Mill River curving down the valley, rushing under the bridge and out into the Hudson, its waters near the Hudson overflowing a large tract now filled in and covered with railroad tracks, docks and buildings. The south bank of the Nepperhan was a high bluff—a level plateau—forty feet above the river. (It was dug out, and the gravel and stones used to fill in the ground on the south side of the Nepperhan River when Main Street was graded.) North of the Nepperhan River were the Manor House with its farmhouse and outbuildings, the flour-mill, the Methodist Church and old parsonage, the school-house and a dwelling house (still standing) nearly opposite the church.

There were in 1843 the two seminaries, that for boys on the crown of Locust Hill, and that for girls east of the Albany Post-road, and north of the present St. John's Hospital. The girls' seminary was subsequently enlarged and in use as a hotel known as the Peabody House.

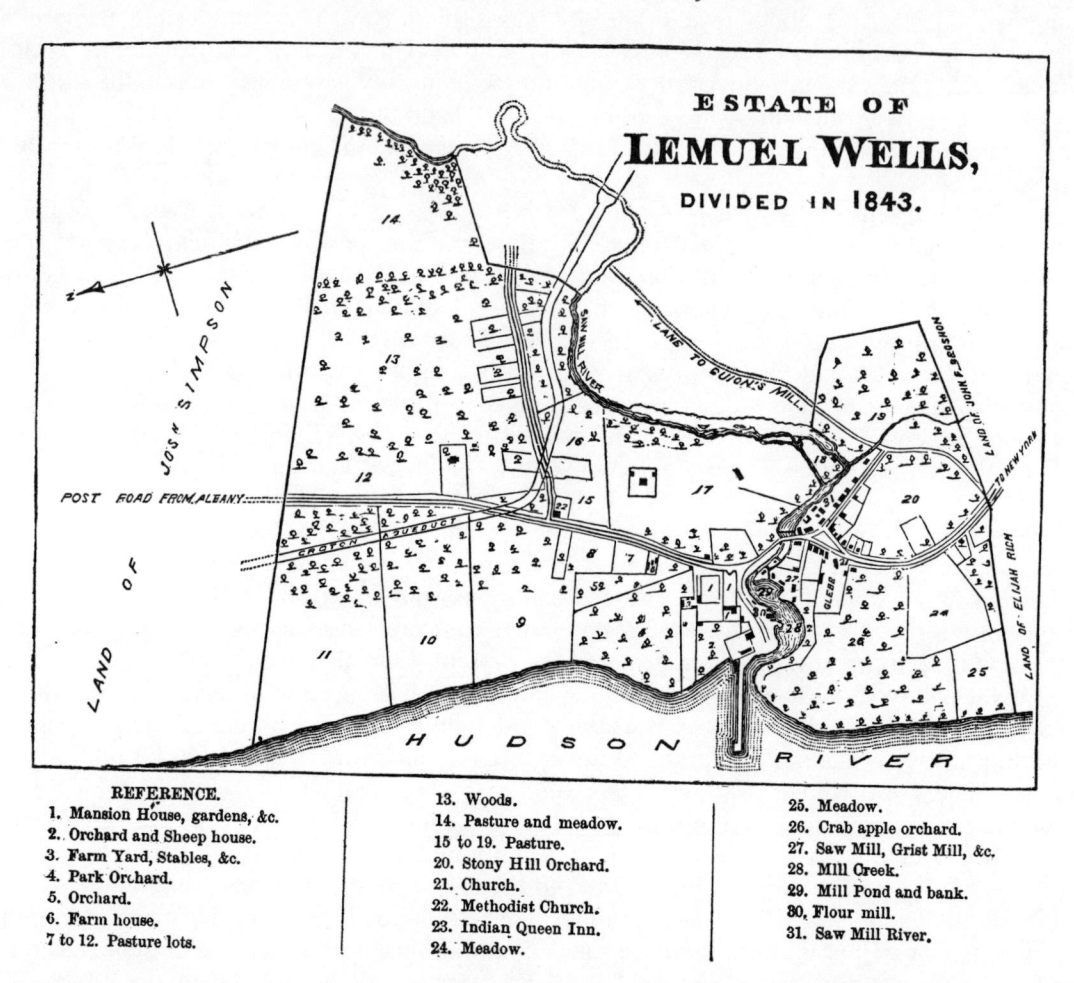

ESTATE OF LEMUEL WELLS, DIVIDED IN 1843.

REFERENCE.
1. Mansion House, gardens, &c.
2. Orchard and Sheep house.
3. Farm Yard, Stables, &c.
4. Park Orchard.
5. Orchard.
6. Farm house.
7 to 12. Pasture lots.
13. Woods.
14. Pasture and meadow.
15 to 19. Pasture.
20. Stony Hill Orchard.
21. Church.
22. Methodist Church.
23. Indian Queen Inn.
24. Meadow.
25. Meadow.
26. Crab apple orchard.
27. Saw Mill, Grist Mill, &c.
28. Mill Creek.
29. Mill Pond and bank.
30. Flour mill.
31. Saw Mill River.

All the buildings shown on the map of 1813 remained in 1843, except the old mill, which had stood on the north bank of the Nepperhan, southwest of Manor Hall. It had burned, but was replaced with a new one. The mill which burned may have been the original mill of Van Der Donck, but very probably was a larger mill, built before 1700, by Frederick Philipse.

The row of chestnut trees still skirted the west bank of the Saw Mill River from near the Post-road Bridge to a point in what is now Warburton Avenue, near the southwest corner of the present Dock Street. The trees stood about fifty feet apart and were very large, some of them sixty feet high. Between the Post-road Bridge and the first horse-chestnut were several tall poplars along the mill-pond west of the Post-road. Before Hutchinson and Mitchell built a mill dam (forming the second water power) across the Nepperhan, a little south of Dock Street, the cattle used to walk down the Post-road from a barn which stood on the site of the present office of the Gas Company (north corner of Wells Avenue and North Broadway). They passed under the overhanging branches of the horse-chestnut tree nearest the Post-road Bridge and dam into the stream to drink. The Rev. Dr. Cole, writing of Yonkers in this period, says: "The spacious front lawn of the Manor House extended to the Post-road, and was at this time (1843) a sweep of beauty. The broad entrance-way to it was at the head of the present Dock Street; . . . the Post-road coming down from the north under a high and closely wooded bluff on its east side, since set back to make room for business places, met at the bridge a row of beautiful horse-chestnut trees, that fell off to the west, along the north side of the stream, skirting it all the way round to the site of the old mill. One of those old horse-chestnut trees was still standing (1886) at the crossing of Dock Street and Warburton Avenue. It was a cherished object to the city, and special care was taken to guard it from injury by keeping it boxed." The tree stood until Warburton Avenue was laid with asphalt, when it was cut down. While outside of Manor Hall grounds there were pastures and orchards and tilled fields, yet it remains true that when Mr. Wells died (1842) "the condition of nature over by far the largest part of the land had been but little disturbed by cultivation. The region was rough beyond description, and it continued so for a few years later." In 1843 there were but six roads traversing Mr. Wells' three hundred and twenty or more acres, all of which, except the Albany Post-road, have since been more or less changed. They were Ashburton Avenue, Nepperhan Avenue, Guion Street, Nepperhan Street and New Main Street.

After the sale of portions of the Wells estate to the amount of about $70,000, it was determined to divide the remainder among the heirs, and it was accordingly divided into six portions, as nearly equal as circumstances permitted.* In 1844 Waring's factory in the "Glen" burned, and in the same year a new building was erected for the industry on what is now known as Elm Street. Afterward this building became a part of the carpet factory property. In 1844 or 1845 Mr. Samuel B. Rockwell, subsequently one of the founders of the Yonkers Savings Bank, removed from New York and made Yonkers his home. He continued to do business in New York, and was one of the first of the city business men to go down daily from Yonkers. He travelled by way of the Harlem Railroad and was soon followed by others who preferred Yonkers to New York as a place of residence. Yonkers (including Kingsbridge) was at that time a country town of about 2,500 inhabitants, and New York was a city of about 371,000. The Yonkers passengers took the Harlem Railroad train at Williams' Bridge.

In 1845 the old Episcopal parsonage and glebe, excepting the land included within the boundaries of the present St. John's cemetery, were sold for $6,500, and a new parsonage was built near the church. In the same year Mr. John Copcutt's veneer mill was built on the foundation of a grist-mill which had been burned. In the year 1845 the patriotic citizens of Yonkers honored Captain Joel Cook, a hero of 1776, who was living in Yonkers. He had belonged to Colonel Meig's regiment. During the war he escorted 1,500 men from Teller's point to the neighborhood of King's Bridge. In compliment to the services of the old veteran his fellow townsmen presented him a gold medal, bearing the following inscription:

Presented to
CAPT. JOEL COOK,
by the citizens of Yonkers
in honor of his patriotic services in defence of
Liberty,
July 4th, 1845,
at the battles of
Lexington, Danbury, White Plains, Trenton and Stony Point,
Springfield and Tippecanoe.

It was in 1845 that Nepperhan Lodge, No. 181, Independent Order of Odd Fellows, was chartered. The petition for it was made by Samuel W. Chambers, James Borlane, Horatio S. Gates, M.D., Ezra B. Keeler, Alfred H. Hyatt, William Mann, James Hughes, Peter Garrison, William Henry Garrison, William P. Reviser, and Matthias Warner. (In 1855 the charter was surrendered. Subsequently other lodges of Odd Fellows were established). In 1845 a public hall was built by Mr. Ethan Flagg, the first hall provided for the citizens. It is still standing at the corner of what were then called Factory and Mechanic Streets, now Palisade Avenue and New Main Street. The hall occupies the second floor, and is known as Flagg's Hall. It had a seating capacity for two hundred and fifty persons. For a long time it was used for all kinds of public meetings.

In 1846 the nucleus of the present No. 2 school-building was erected. Those who built it are said to have expressed the hope that it was "large enough for all time," but since 1846 it has so often

* For description of this division, see *Yonkers Examiner*, September 26, 1861. Judge Wm. W. Woodworth purchased Manor Hall, and resided there. He sold it to Mr. Jas. C. Bell, who sold it to the Village of Yonkers.

been remodelled and enlarged that those who knew the original building could hardly tell where it is in the present large edifice. Pupils were received from the school-house on North Broadway.

In 1847 the Episcopal Chapel at Tuckahoe was consecrated, but the parish did not become independent until 1853.

Mr. Thomas C. Cornell, a young engineer, who, in 1847, was employed in the construction of the Hudson River Railroad from Spuyten Duyvil to Dobb's Ferry, and who, when his section of the road was finished, decided to make his home in Yonkers, did almost all the surveying in the place for many years. In 1847 he made a map of the part of Yonkers about the mouth of the Nepperhan, showing Manor Hall and the lower part of the Saw Mill River with all buildings and other improvements, as they stood in the summer of that year, that is, immediately before the construction of the Hudson River Railroad. A study of this map will help the reader to realize how Yonkers appeared about eight years before the village was incorporated.

Among the buildings which are designated on the map of 1847 is John Bashford's hotel. Mr. Bashford also had a store and a coal yard. He was the postmaster at that time and his place down at the sloop wharf west of Manor Hall was a popular centre of Yonkers life. The political influence of Mr. Bashford and his personal magnetism made him a prominent villager. He was captain of the Yonkers Militia, and his son Henry was his color-bearer "from the time he was old enough to carry a flag." At the time of his death (1848) Mr. Bashford was only forty-seven years old. One of his daughters is Mrs. Thomas C. Cornell, another became the wife of William Hindlaugh. Her portrait was on the bills of the Yonkers Bank until 1865, when the bank became National. Mr. Henry W. Bashford, the son of John Bashford, came to be a well-known citizen of Yonkers. A familiar scene in 1847 was the stage-coach turning from the Albany Post-road and passing down the present Nepperhan Street to the stage-house. The present Dock Street south of Manor Hall is more a modern street. Mr. John Bashford's hotel was well kept. The passengers upon nearing it saw "a long, two-story house of reddish-brown color, but with no accompanying sign-post or proprietor's name in sight, and with no external indications that it was an inn. It stood near the Hudson at the mouth of the Nepperhan, whose water then ran clear as the water of a mountain brook. Broad verandas, also two stories high, covered its whole front. The building was handsomely shaded by several large willows, and the high wooded bluff, towards which the house almost faced, looked down on it from the opposite side of the creek, while the gardens and the open ground, and the fields behind the house all combined to give the place the air of an ample, quiet, rural home by the water side."

In 1847 Father Ryan said his first mass in Yonkers in the principal room of a dwelling house near where Nepperhan Avenue now crosses the Nepperhan River, and subsequently continued his work in a vacant store-room in the adjacent dye factory of Samuel Morgan. The dwelling house and the dye factory were long ago burned. In the summer of 1848 Father Ryan hired, at three dollars a week, the upper story of the first three-story brick building in Yonkers, then just erected by Mr. Flagg, corner of Factory and Mechanic Streets (the present Palisade Avenue and New Main Street). In 1848 Father Ryan began the erection of a brick church on what is now known as St. Mary's Street. The first mass was said in it on Christmas, 1848. In 1847 Mrs. Mary C. P. Macomb, owner of the tract of land known as Paparinamin (then in the town of Yonkers), laid out her estate into streets and plots. Stores and shops were built. A frame church was erected, and thus the village of Kingsbridge had its origin. Mrs. Macomb, as early as 1830, lived near Spuyten Duyvil, and with gracious hospitality entertained well-known guests, among whom was the poet Edgar Allen Poe.

In 1847 the Hudson River Railroad was in process of construction. When it was proposed to build the road its projectors encountered many hindrances. Among them was the attitude of the owners of the land along the river front. They were very generally hostile to the improvement, and claimed excessive damages. They insisted that the scheme would not only impair the beauty and value of the river front, but would seriously interfere with the quiet and comfort of the residents. About 1849 ox-teams were more frequently seen on the roads of Yonkers than horses. Horses were comparatively few in number.

In 1849 the Hudson River Railroad began its operations. It was a single track road, with "turn-outs" where needed. This at once caused the New York and Albany stages to be withdrawn and it also competed with the steamboats. In that year the following announcement was published in *The New York Herald:* "Passenger trains will commence to run between New York and Peekskill on Saturday, the 29th instant (September, 1849), stopping at the following places and at the rate of fare

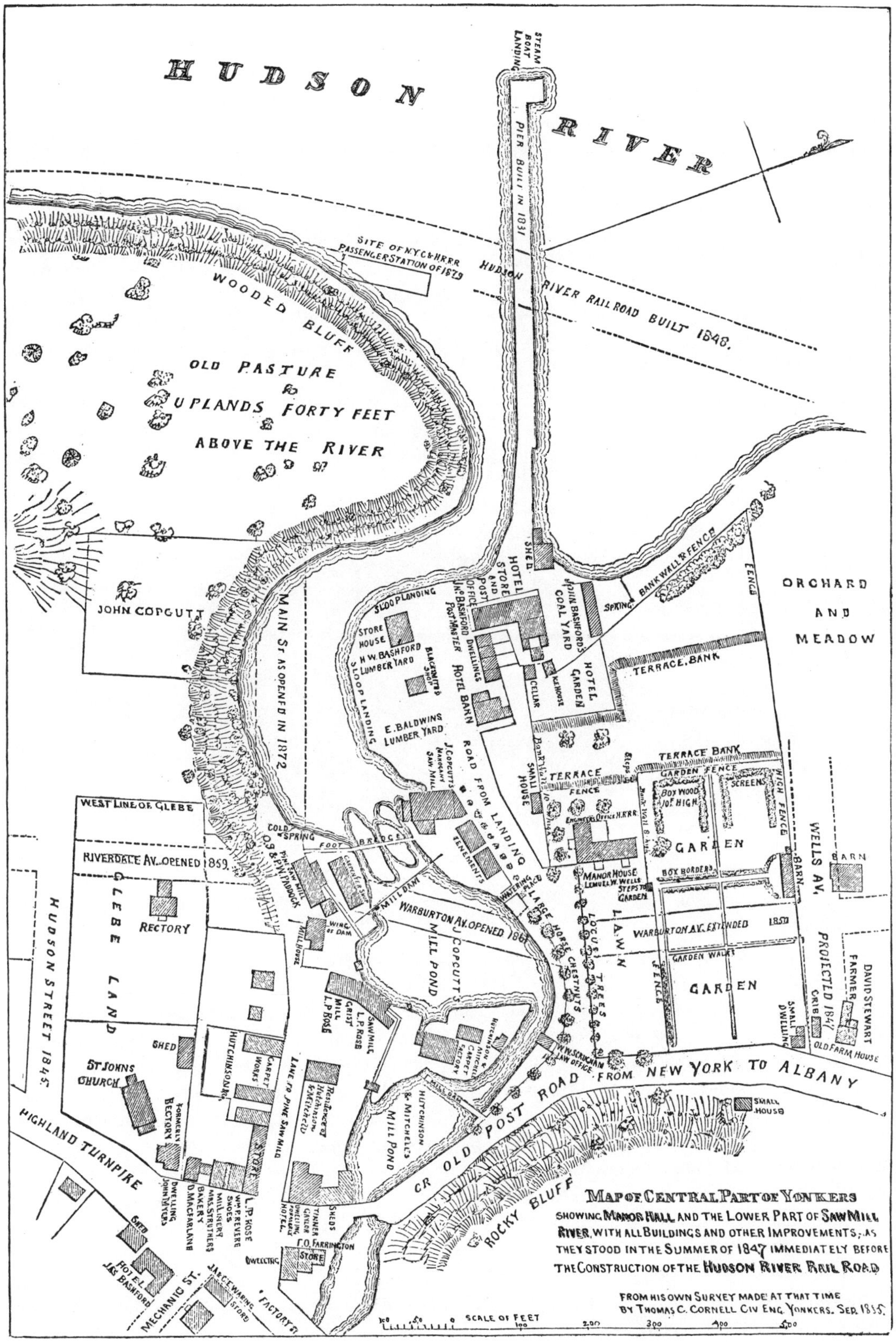
MAP OF CENTRAL PART OF YONKERS
SHOWING MANOR HALL AND THE LOWER PART OF SAW MILL RIVER, WITH ALL BUILDINGS AND OTHER IMPROVEMENTS, AS THEY STOOD IN THE SUMMER OF 1847 IMMEDIATELY BEFORE THE CONSTRUCTION OF THE HUDSON RIVER RAIL ROAD
FROM HIS OWN SURVEY MADE AT THAT TIME BY THOMAS C. CORNELL CIV ENG. YONKERS. SEP. 1885.
SCALE OF FEET
HUDSON RIVER
STEAM BOAT LANDING
PIER BUILT IN 1831
SITE OF N.Y.C. & H.R.R.R. PASSENGER STATION OF 1879
HUDSON RIVER RAIL ROAD BUILT 1848.
WOODED BLUFF
OLD PASTURE & UPLANDS FORTY FEET ABOVE THE RIVER
JOHN COPCUTT
MAIN ST AS OPENED IN 1872
WEST LINE OF GLEBE
RIVERDALE AV. OPENED 1859.
GLEBE LAND
RECTORY
HUDSON STREET 1845
ST JOHNS CHURCH
SHED
HIGHLAND TURNPIKE
MECHANIC ST.
FACTORY ST.
HOTEL JAS BASHFORD
ORCHARD AND MEADOW
TERRACE BANK
GARDEN
LAWN
LOCUST TREES
LARGE HORSE CHESTNUTS
MANOR HOUSE LEMUEL W. WELLS
WARBURTON AV. OPENED 1861
WARBURTON AV. EXTENDED 1850
WELLS AV. PROJECTED 1847
BARN
DAVID STEWART FARMER
OLD FARM HOUSE
MILL POND
J. COPCUTTS MILL POND
ROAD FROM LANDING
OLD POST ROAD FROM NEW YORK TO ALBANY
ROCKY BLUFF
HOTEL STORE AND POST OFFICE
JOHN BASHFORDS COAL YARD
HOTEL GARDEN
HOTEL BARN
H. W. BASHFORD LUMBER YARD
E. BALDWINS LUMBER YARD
SLOOP LANDING
STORE HOUSE
FOOT BRIDGE
COLD SPRING
MILL DAM
TENEMENTS
GRIST MILL L. P. ROSE
SAW MILL L. P. ROSE
CARPET WORKS
HUTCHINSON & MITCHELLS MILL POND
LANE TO PINE SAW MILL
F. O. FARRINGTON STORE
SMALL HOUSE

respectively stated, viz., Manhattanville, twelve and one-half cents; Yonkers, twenty-five cents, etc. Omnibuses will be provided at the junction of Chambers Street and Hudson Street to convey passengers who furnish themselves with tickets at the engine-house, at Thirty-first Street, until the rails are laid to that point. Trains will start at eight A.M., twelve noon, and four P.M. N.B.—Stockholders during the present week free of charge."

Property was now in demand, and the faces of new residents began to be seen on the streets of the village. One evidence of growth during this period was the increase in the number of churches. In 1842 before the railroad was built there were five churches, viz., St. John's, the First Methodist Episcopal of Tuckahoe, St. John's Protestant Episcopal Chapel at Tuckahoe, Methodist Episcopal, corner of North Broadway and the present Ashburton Avenue, and the Methodist Church at Mosholu. Only two of these churches were near the Manor Hall, Yonkers. It will be remembered that the Reformed Dutch Church was organized in 1843 and St. Mary's in 1848. Therefore, the year before trains began to run on the Hudson River Railroad, there were seven churches in Yonkers, including the Mosholu Church, four of which were near Manor Hall. The Mount Olivet Baptist Church (now Warburton Avenue Baptist), which was located on the site of the present Temperance Hall, was organized in 1849, and the First Presbyterian in 1852.

In 1849 Mr. John T. Waring established himself in the hat manufacturing business further down the Saw Mill River than the site of the former factory. Still later he oc- cupied the building on the north side of Elm Street. In the fifties more prominent citizens came, among them Doc- tors Upham, Arnold, Reinfelder, Jenkins, Messrs. Olmsted, Lyman Cobb, Jr., George Osterheld, Rudolph Eickemeyer, Elisha G. Otis, Thomas Town- drow (founder of the first Yonkers newspaper), and Thomas Smith, his associate; David Saun- ders, John M. Mason, F. S. Cozzens, Seaman Lowerre, William B. Edgar, George B. Skinner, G. Hilton Scribner and others. With the senior Otis came his sons, Charles R., then a youth about eighteen years of age, and Norton P., who was enrolled as a school-boy in No. 2. He became Mayor of Yonkers in 1880. It was in 1852 that Mr. Ebenezer Curtice came and took charge of the public school. About 1850 Robert Grant's morocco factory was established at the corner of Nepper- han Avenue and New Main Street. It was during the fifties that the Rev. Dr. A. B. Carter became rector of St. John's, the Rev. Messrs. Perry, Brown (Paul R.), Hoyt, Sanford, Brown (George), Hagany and Ward served the First Methodist Church on North Broadway, as pastors. Five of these seven Methodist ministers, viz.: Perry, Brown (Paul R.), Hoyt, Sanford, Brown (George), and Hagany were probably the preachers at Tuckahoe also, because between 1836 and 1852 Kingsbridge (or Mosholu), Yonkers (on Broadway), and Tuckahoe belonged to the Yonkers Circuit. The Rev. Nathaniel Mead was at Tuckahoe in 1858–59, and the Rev. W. H. Evans in 1859–60. The Rev. Dwight M. Seward (subsequently the Rev. Dr. Seward) became pastor of the Reformed Dutch Church. The Rev. Charles Jones, during 1853–58, was rector of St. John's Episcopal Church at Tuckahoe, which became an independent parish in 1853. The Rev. Augustus St. Clair was the supply at that church from 1859 to 1860, and subsequently the incumbent. The Rev. John Ryan, S. J., had charge of the Roman Catholic Mission in Yonkers. He was assisted from time to time by his colleagues at St. John's College, Fordham. He was succeeded by the Rev. Hippolyte Bienvenue, S. J. These were in Yonkers before the fifties. In 1851 the Rev. Thomas Preston, later the Right Rev. Monsignor Preston— a prelate of the Papal household—was made the first resident pastor of Yonkers. He was temporarily succeeded in 1853 by the Rev. John McMahon. In 1854 the Rev. Eugene Maguire was put in charge. It was during his time that St. Mary's cemetery was opened in the Sprain Valley on land given by Mr. John Murtha. In 1855 the State Census reported the usual attendance of the Roman

"THE NAPPECKAMACK HOUSE," OR "THE INDIAN QUEEN INN," AS IT APPEARED IN 1851.

Catholic Church in Yonkers as eight hundred, "which would indicate a Roman Catholic population of from twelve to sixteen hundred." It was in 1847 that the first prayer-meeting of Baptists in Yonkers was held in the house of Mr. Peter F. Peek. The first sermon preached in Yonkers by a Baptist clergyman to a Baptist audience was delivered by the celebrated Rev. John Dowling, D.D., of New York, in Mr. Peek's parlors in 1847. In 1849, at the residence of Mr. B. F. Crane, the Rev. D. Henry Miller (afterward Rev. Dr. Miller) offered a resolution that a Baptist Church be organized. It was adopted, and seven persons enrolled themselves that evening as members. Rev. Mr. Miller became the first pastor and preached his first sermon in Flagg's Hall. The meetings were held there until a church was built. It was occupied in 1852. The First Presbyterian Church was organized in 1852, by forty-six former members of the Reformed Dutch Church, who had desired to transfer that to the Presbyterian connection, but were outvoted by other members. The Rev. Dr. Seward, pastor of the Reformed Church, became pastor of the Presbyterian. The Rev. Mr. Hulbert succeeded him as pastor of the Reformed Church (this was the second time he was pastor of that Church). The Presbyterians worshipped in Getty's Hall before their church was built and dedicated (1854). The brothers Amos W. and Horatio S. Gates were well-known physicians in Yonkers. Horatio S., after a few years, abandoned practice and removed to California, where he died wealthy. The elder Dr. Gates remained. He was skilful and his practice was lucrative. He lived in Yonkers more than fifty years. He built for himself a dwelling house on the east side of Nepperhan Avenue, northeast of the present Nepperhan Church. Subsequently he bought of Levi P. Rose the hill (south of the present Getty House) for which he paid $3,800. (The old Gates property, four acres [south of the Getty House], was offered to the city in 1893 for City Hall grounds for $130,000.) Dr. Gates used to drive down to King's Bridge and up into the town of Greenburgh and White Plains and over to Westchester. His term for ordinary professional visits were fifty cents if near by, and one dollar if at a distance. His second residence was built on his property south of the present Getty House and Getty Square Railroad station. It is known in 1896 as the Nisbet residence.

ROBERT P. GETTY.

It will be remembered that previous to 1844 the walks were not planked. The first plank walk was laid to Mr. Scrugham's office, which stood some distance from other buildings. Afterward a plank walk was laid on the west side of Warburton Avenue. In 1850 Dock Street was laid out by Judge Woodworth. Previous to the incorporation of the village there was no Prospect Street. Riverdale Avenue from No. 30 Main Street to King's Bridge was constructed at different dates. It was continued from St. Mary's Street to Riverdale in 1853 by the town authorities. Warburton Avenue was laid out from No. 29

Main Street, north of the village line, in 1854. The stone house on the west side of the avenue, north of the brown stone front row, was on the grade of the road. The avenue at that point was filled in to the present grade, when it was graded.

Previous to the incorporation of the village there was a country road from Factory Street (Palisade Avenue) to the summit of Nodine Hill. It was subsequently straightened and graded, and is now known as Elm Street.

In 1851 Mr. Robert P. Getty bought the Nappeckamack House, and, removing it to the northwest corner of New Main Street and Nepperhan Avenue, converted it into a tenement house (still standing in 1896). The Getty House, a structure of light-colored brick, was built on the site of the Nappeckamack House in 1851.* It fronts 108 feet on Broadway and 160 on New Main Street, is in the form of an **L** and four stories high. It cost between $40,000 and $50,000. When the hotel was finished (1852) one hundred and sixteen ladies, in admiration of Mr. Getty's enterprise in projecting and erecting such a splendid hotel, and including within it a hall for public lectures and concerts, presented him with a flag to wave over the building. The presentation was in the hall, and the eloquent address which was made by Colonel (afterwards Judge) Scrugham and the response by Mr. Getty were reported in full in the *Hudson River Chronicle* (June 8, 1852).

On this occasion a salute of five guns was fired. Mr. Getty had expected to name the hotel "The Havemeyer," in honor of his friend, ex-Mayor William F. Havemeyer, of New York, "but a number of his friends during the night took the liberty to express their own feeling and the general sense of Yonkers people by placing upon the front of the building the letters which are seen upon it to-day (1896): 'The Getty House.'" The hall in the hotel was used for public gatherings until about 1866 or 1867, when it was no longer opened as an assembly hall, because it had come to interfere with the quiet of the guests. The managing proprietors of the hotel before 1860 were: Messrs Henry Durell, Edward Dusenberry and Robert L. Buckland. In May, 1860, Mr. Oliver W. Doty, an experienced inn-keeper of Poughkeepsie, assumed its management, but, dying in a few months, was succeeded in the same year by his son William H. Doty, who was its proprietor more than twenty-five years.

The Yonkers flour-mill, standing on the site of the former Hutchinson and Mitchell factory, was built in 1851 or 1852, not long after the factory had been burned. It was devoted to grist-work and the general grinding of grain, and was successively operated by Messrs. F. S. Miles, Miles & Peek, Peek & Wolf, Peter F. Peek, and Cornelius W. Peek, its proprietor in the eighties.

In 1852 a property on St. Mary's Street was purchased by the Rev. Thomas S. Preston, pastor of St. Mary's Church. A small school-house (15 x 25) was at once erected on it. The parish school, which had been opened with less than a dozen scholars (boys and girls) in a basement of a dwelling house in the early spring of that year, was transferred from the dwelling house (northwest corner of St. Mary and Clinton Streets) to the new school-house.

It is recorded that in 1852 there were 537 buildings in the town. The buildings within the territory subsequently set off as Kingsbridge township are probably enumerated in this record. The number of buildings in the city of Yonkers in 1884 is recorded in Chapter XII.

In 1851 the sister city of Yonkers—Mount Vernon—appeared on the map as a small settlement. It originated in the enterprise of some New York citizens who desired to escape the exorbitant rents asked at that time in the city. Five farms in the town of Eastchester, belonging severally to Colonel John R. Hayward, Sylvanus Purdy, Andrew Purdy, and his two sons, John and Andrew O., and containing 369½ acres, were deemed suitable for a new village, because they were between two railroads. The Home Industrial Association bought these farms, and gave orders for surveys and grading avenues and streets. The first name given was Monticello, but for post-office reasons that of Mount Vernon was afterwards chosen. Contemporary with the settlement just described was that of West Mount Vernon, under the direction of the Teutonic Home Association, composed mainly of Germans, five hundred in number, who purchased about 131 acres and rapidly established themselves in the town.

West Mount Vernon and Central, and several adjoining places, were incorporated as one village in

---

*Until about this time (1850) the dwellings near Bowling Green, New York City, and those facing the beautiful harbor were the residences of New York's first families. The Battery was the fashionable resort of New York citizens.

1869, and as a city in 1895. The seal of the city of Mount Vernon bears the motto, "*Urbs Jucundarum Domium*" ("A City of Happy Homes").*

In 1852 there were in Yonkers 537 buildings, not including those in the southern portion subsequently set off. The land that year at the southern end of the town of Yonkers (Spuyten Duyvil) was in three farms, which were purchased (1852) by Elias Johnson, David B. Fox, and Joseph M. Fuller, of Troy, N. Y. They had surveys and plans made for a village to be called Fort Independence, but it was called Spuyten Duyvil. Streets were opened and several houses erected on the hill, and a foundry was established at its base.

In 1850–1855, Edwin Forrest resided in Yonkers. He built and occupied the Castle (now known as Mount St. Vincent) under the name of Fort Hill. The Forrest property was part of the large farm which Captain John Warner, of the Revolutionary army, bought of the Commissioners of Forfeiture in 1785. In 1856 Mount St. Vincent, the mother-home of the Sisters in the archdiocese of New York, was founded on the former Forrest property. The property of Forrest was bought by the Sisters of St. Vincent de Paul. The old edifice of stone, built by Forrest, presents a fine specimen of the English castellated style. The convent has a large number of paintings and fine works of art. It also has a fine collection of minerals presented by Dr. E. S. F. Arnold. Sister Maria (Mary C. Dodge) wrote an interesting history of the institution.

When Messrs. Hutchinson and Mitchell removed from West Farms in the forties, they built several small dwelling houses in Yonkers, on the south side of the lane leading from the Post-road to Paddock's mills. Some who lived in those dwellings wove carpet with hand-looms in their own houses. In 1851 or 1852, the carpet factory of Hutchinson & Mitchell was burned. They had used hand-looms in the factory, and conducted the business of carpet-weaving on a small scale. In 1852, lots (25 x 100) on the west side of Nepperhan Avenue, now worth more than a thousand dollars, could be bought for fifty dollars, ten dollars paid down.

In 1853 the village of Riverdale, and in 1856 "The Park, Riverdale," were laid out. Riverdale Park is now a place of beautiful country homes. In 1853 Hudson Park (a part of a tract on which a cluster of houses called "Cooperstown" was subsequently built) was laid out.

Previous to 1852 there was no provision in the village of Yonkers for extinguishing fires. The fire

---

* If the residents are loyal to the principles of the early settlers of their town (Eastchester) it is indeed a city of happy homes, for when in 1664 ten families, under the auspices of Thomas Pell, who some years before had purchased the lands of the Indians, emigrated from Fairfield County, Conn., they signed articles of agreement which contained among other paragraphs the following:

Imprimus, that we by the grace of God, sitt down on the track of land lieng betwext Huthesson's broock, whear the house was, untell it com unto the river, that runneth in at the head of the meados.

2. That we indeavor to keepe and maintayn Christian love and sivell honisty.
3. That we faith-fully conssall what may be of infirmyti in any one of us.
4. Plainlie to dealle one with another in Christian love.
5. If any trespas be don, the trespaed and the trespaser shall chuse tow of this company, and they a thirde man if need be requiered, to end the mater, without any futher trubell.
6. That all and every one of us, or all that shall be of us, do paye unto the minister, according to his meade.
7. That none exceed the quantity of fifteen acres, until all have that quantity.
8. That every man hath that meadow that is most convenient for him.
9. That every man build and inhabit on his home lot before the next winter.
10. That no man make sale of his lot before he hath built and inhabited one year, and then to render it to the company or to a man whom they approve.
11. That any man may sell part of his alotment to his neighbor.
12. That no man shall engrosse to himself by buying his neighbor's lot for his particular interest, but with respect to sell it, if an approved man come, and that without much advantage, to be judged by the company.
13. That all public affairs, all bridges, highways, or mill, be carried on jointly, according to meadow and estates.
14. That provision be endeavoured for education of children, and then encouragement be given unto any that shall take pains according to our former way of rating.
15. That no man shall give entertainment to a foreigner who shall carry himself obnoxious to the company except amendment be after warning given.
16. That all shall join in guarding of cattle when the company see it convenient.
17. That every man make and maintain a good fence about all his arable land, and in due time a man chosen to view if the company's be good.
18. That every man sow his land when most of the company sow or plant in their fields.
19. That we give needed encouragement to Mr. Brewster, each other week to give us word of exhortation, and that when we are settled we meet together every other weeke, one hour, to talk of the best things.
20. That one man, either of himself, or by consent, may give entertainment to strangers, for money.
21. That one day, every spring, be improved for the destroying of rattlesnakes.
22. That some, every Lord's day, stay at home, for safety of our wives and children.
23. That every man get and keep a good lock to his door as soon as he can.
24. That a convenient place be appointed for oxen if need require.
25. If any man's meadow or upland be worse in quality, that be considered in quantity.
26. That every man that hath taken up lottes shall pay to all publick charges equal with those that got none. That all that hath or shall take up lots within this tract of land mentioned in the premises shall subscribe to these articles.

In 1666, the inhabitants of Eastchester obtained a farther grant from the native Indians, Ann-hooke and others.

which destroyed the mill on what is known as Mill Street awakened some of the people to the need of fire apparatus. Mr. Robert P. Getty procured at his own expense, and brought to the town, a small "goose-neck engine." The first fire company was organized under the name of "Protection Engine Company No. 1," with George L. Condit as foreman. Not long after the organization of the engine company, Mr. Getty also purchased a second-hand hook and ladder truck, and in 1853 Hope Hook and Ladder Company No. 1 was organized, with David Chambers, foreman. Mr. A. M. Grant next bought an engine and housed it near his factory, and a company was formed under the name of Lady Washington Engine Company No. 2. A. G. Van Orden was the first foreman. Before 1874 water for use at fires was had only from the Hudson, or the Nepperhan, or from cisterns.

In 1854 the Yonkers Gas Light Company was organized, chiefly through the public spirit of Colonel Scrugham. The gross sales of gas for the first year (1855) were about 1,000,000 feet at $4 per 1,000 feet, and the gas was about the strength of two candles. (Street gas-lamps were erected in 1861, about six years after the incorporation of the village.)

In 1854 the business of manufacturing hat machinery was established in Yonkers by Mr. George Osterheld, a brother of Mr. Henry Osterheld, who was subsequently a member of the firm of Osterheld & Eickemeyer. In 1854 Mr. Rudolph Eickemeyer, who became the widely known inventor, removed to Yonkers and was associated with Mr. Osterheld. About 1854 the Otis Elevator Works were established in Yonkers. More extended reference to this large industry is made on another page of this volume. In 1855 Mr. George B. Skinner began the manufacture of sewing-machine silk in Yonkers on the east side of the Nepperhan in a stone building which had been erected a year or two before for a cotton factory.

Previous to 1854 a pile of old books lay in the tower of St. John's Church. They were labelled the property of a Young Men's Library Association. There is a tradition that that Association, finding itself in a decline, had turned its books over to St. John's Church. As far as is known, no other movement toward a public library was made till 1854. Early in that year a few residents established a library and reading-room, chiefly for the benefit of the young men of the place. At a public meeting held in the Getty House, Mr. Thomas O. Farrington was appointed chairman and Mr. Henry W. Bashford, secretary, Mr. Josiah Rich made an address. A constitution was adopted, officers elected, and rooms hired in the building, afterward No. 21 South Broadway (Wheeler's Block), and fitted up for the use of the Library Association. Eleven life members and one hundred annual members were enrolled the first year and several hundred books were donated. St. John's gave one hundred and twenty volumes (said to have been the books which had been stored in the tower). Among those who donated books were Mr. George P. Putnam (the publisher, then a resident of Yonkers), the Rev. Robert Baird, D.D., and Mr. Russell Smith. The first officers of the Society were Josiah Rich, president; Thomas O. Farrington, vice-president; Henry W. Bashford, secretary; William N. Seymour, treasurer, and Henry M. Coffin, librarian.

The Yonkers Debating Society, a part of the same movement, held its first meetings in 1854. Its public debates were in Flagg's Hall. The Lecture Committee was also an outgrowth of the Library Association, and the files of the village papers published after the incorporation of the village (1855) contain reports of lectures by men whose names are well known to the whole country.

The population (including Kingsbridge) was 7,554 in 1855, and the number of taxable persons was 1,629. The property valuation was $4,290,672, as against $1,275,809 in 1850. It was evident to the thoughtful people that a stronger government was needed, and they were talking about incorporating their growing village.

The city papers which were coming to Yonkers during this period (1825–1855) were the *Commercial Advertiser* (established 1797), the *Evening Post* (founded 1801 by Coleman, and edited by Bryant, Leggett and Godwin), the *New York Sun* (established as a penny paper in 1833 by Day, and soon passed into the hands of Beech. At first the sheet was about ten inches square), the *New York Herald* (established 1835, first as a penny paper by Bennett), the *New York Times* (established 1850 by Raymond). *The New York World* was not in existence during the period under review. It was first issued in 1860, and as a religious paper. The Yonkers people were also, during a part of this period, reading their local paper, *The Yonkers Herald* (established 1852 by Mr. Thomas Towndrow and Mr. Thomas Smith). (Mr. Towndrow, a collector of Westchester County news for New York papers, had been caused to think of establishing a newspaper in Yonkers by the suggestion of Mr. Thomas C. Cornell.)

These papers were bringing to the Yonkers people reports of the events which occurred during the administrations of nine United States Presidents, and twelve New York State Governors. The Presidents were Adams, Jackson, Van Buren, Harrison, Tyler, Polk, Taylor, Filmore and Pierce. The Governors were Clinton, Pitcher, Van Buren, Throop, Marcy, Seward, Bouch, Wright, Young, Fish, Hunt and Seymour. Among the events about which the Yonkers people were reading and talking during the *twenties* were the Black Hawk War, the United States Bank bill, the tariff, the declaration of nullification by South Carolina, the duel between Clay and Randolph, and the foreign events in the region of George IV., of England; Charles X. and Louis Philippe, of France, and of Frederick William III., of Germany.

In the *thirties* they were interested in the running of the first steam passenger train in America (Albany to Schenectady), the Seminole War, the Clay Compromise, the admission of new states, the affairs of Texas, of which Lamar was President; of Mexico with her Presidents, Santa Anna and Bustamente; the young Queen of England, Victoria; Louis Philippe, of France; Frederick William III., of Germany; the Mormons, the capture and execution of the pirate Gibbs, the nullification outbreak in South Carolina under Calhoun and others; the meteoric shower of 1833, the attempted assassination of President Jackson, the invention of the telegraph, the taking of daguerreotypes, and the tremendous conflagration in the City of New York (1835).

In the *forties* they were reading about the great temperance reformation under the leadership of the Washingtonians and Father Mathew, Fremont's explorations, the comet of 1843, the Second Advent excitement of 1843, the discovery of ether, the invention of the sewing-machine, the Spiritualists, the sending of food to starving Ireland, the conquest of Mexico, the discovery of gold in California, the Astor Place riots in New York, the yellow fever and cholera epidemics, the veto of the U. S. Bank bill, and the resignation of the President's Cabinet; the affairs of Texas, of which Houston was President; the Revolution in France and the proclamation of a Republic with Bonaparte as President; William IV., of Germany; the outbreak of the Hungarian Revolution, and the events in Great Britain under Victoria.

In the *fifties*, the visit of Jenny Lind, "the Swedish Nightingale"; the victory of the yacht America, the reception of Kossuth, Perry's expedition to Japan, the Crystal Palace in New York, the sinking of the Arctic, the passage of the Fugitive Slave Law, the Emperor Napoleon, the repealing of the Missouri Compromise, and the troubles in Kansas arising from the slavery agitation.

DECEASED CITIZENS.

1. PRINCE WILLIAM PADDOCK.
2. WILLIAM H. POST.
3. WILLIAM WARBURTON SCRUGHAM.
4. FREDERICK A. COE.
5. JOHN M. MASON.
6. REUBEN W. VAN PELT.
7. WILLIAM ARCHIBALD.
8. WILLIAM H. LAWRENCE.

CHAPTER X.

TOWN AND INCORPORATED VILLAGE. 1855–1872.

> "New life the quiet valley fills:
>   Behold a transformation scene.
> The humming of the busy mills
>   Blends with the murmuring of the stream;
> And loud among the circling hills
>   Echoes the puffing engine's scream."

THE village of Yonkers was incorporated April 12, 1855. It extended one mile and seven-tenths along the Hudson River. Its average breadth was eight-tenths of a mile. Edward P. Shonnard's farm was on the north and Thomas F. Ludlow's on the south. The area of the incorporated village was about nine hundred acres. About seventeen years elapsed before Yonkers was incorporated as a city. During these years the population increased almost threefold. At the time of the incorporation of the village the number of inhabitants in the whole town, including Kingsbridge, was 7,554. About five years later the village alone had 7,500, and the town 12,000. Before the city was incorporated the population of the town had increased to 20,000.

New centres of interest began to attract attention. Tuckahoe, Mile Square, Mosholu, Van Cortlandt, Kingsbridge, and Spuyten Duyvil were old-time and familiar names. Hudson Park in Lower Yonkers was laid out in 1853, and several years afterward the cluster of dwellings known as Cooperstown appeared. In 1853 four gentlemen purchased a tract in Lower Yonkers, which was laid out as the village of Riverdale. "The Park, Riverdale," was laid out in 1856. During the same year Mount St. Vincent was founded. The Woodlawn Cemetery Company began to improve the grounds at Woodlawn in 1864. The first interment was made January 14, 1865. Now scores of thousands sleep "the iron sleep" in that "city of the dead." Olaff Park (southerly portion of the Van Cortlandt estate) was laid out in 1869. Augustus Van Cortlandt, who came to reside upon his estate at Lower Yonkers in 1853, was Supervisor of Yonkers in 1859, and in the same year Member of Assembly. His residing there gave additional importance to that locality. In 1867 the Spuyten Duyvil Rolling Mill Company was organized. The population of Spuyten Duyvil considerably increased, and in 1859 a school-house was built in the hamlet. A school-house was erected at Kingsbridge in 1872. In 1871 the Spuyten Duyvil and Port Morris Railroad was opened. The stations were Spuyten Duyvil and Kingsbridge. From 1855 to 1872 the following-named citizens were officers of the village of Yonkers:

1855–56, L. W. Wells, R. W. Van Pelt, W. C. Waring, F. S. Gant, Thomas O. Farrington, Jacob Read, Trustees; William Radford, President; William H. Post, Clerk. 1856–57, L. W. Wells, Bailey Hobbs, T. O. Farrington, Peter F. Peek, R. W. Van Pelt, Charles C. Merchant, Trustees; William Radford, President; William H. Post, Clerk. 1857–58, Charles C. Merchant, H. F. De Voe, R. W. Van Pelt, R. P. Getty, Ethan Flagg, Bailey Hobbs, Trustees; William W. Woodworth, President; William H. Post, Clerk. 1858–59, Ethan Flagg, Edward Underhill, L. M. Clark, John Copcutt, R. P. Getty, Bailey Hobbs, Trustees; William W. Woodworth, President; William H. Post, Clerk. 1859–60, Ethan Flagg, John Copcutt, Amos W. Gates, James C. Bell, L. M. Clark, Bailey Hobbs, Trustees; Robert P. Getty, President; William H. Post, Clerk. 1860–61, L. M. Clark, Amos W. Gates, James C. Bell, John Copcutt, Ethan Flagg, John Wheeler, Trustees; Thomas F. Morris, President; Lyman Cobb, Jr., Clerk. 1861–62, Joseph P. Disbrow, L. M. Clark, John Copcutt, Edward Underhill, John Wheeler, Justus Lawrence,

Trustees; John T. Waring, President; Lyman Cobb, Jr., Clerk. 1862–63, William Radford, Joseph P. Disbrow, James W. Mitchell, Edward Underhill, Justus Lawrence, James Stewart, Trustees; John T. Waring, President; Lyman Cobb, Jr., Clerk. 1863–64, William Radford, Thomas O. Farrington, James W. Mitchell, Hall F. Baldwin, G. Hilton Scribner, James Stewart, Trustees; Everett Clapp, President; Lyman Cobb, Jr., Clerk. 1864–65, Thomas O. Farrington, L. P. Rose, James W. Mitchell, Hall F. Baldwin, Robert J. Douglass, G. Hilton Scribner, Trustees; Everett Clapp, President; Lyman Cobb, Jr., Clerk. 1865–66, Levi P. Rose, Patrick White, James W. Mitchell, Thomas Smith, Robert J. Douglass, Heman L. White, Trustees; James C. Bell, President; Lyman Cobb, Jr., Clerk. 1866–67, Patrick White, Charles Byrnes, James W. Mitchell, Thomas Smith, Stephen H. Thayer, Heman L. White, Trustees; James C. Bell, President; Lyman Cobb, Jr., Clerk. 1867–68, Robert P. Getty, Charles Byrnes, George B. Skinner, C. W. Malliband, Stephen H. Thayer, Ethan Flagg, Trustees; Justus Lawrence, President; Lyman Cobb, Jr., Clerk. 1868–69, Robert P. Getty, Hugh McElroen, Frederick A. Back, George B. Skinner, Ethan Flagg, Stephen H. Thayer, Trustees; Justus Lawrence, President; William H. Post, Clerk. 1869–70, Hugh McElroen, Ralph E. Prime, Frederick A. Back, Thomas Smith, Stephen H. Thayer, John W. Oliver, Trustees; Isaac H. Knox, President; J. G. P. Holden, Clerk. 1870–71, Ralph E. Prime, Hugh McElroen, Albert Keeler, Ebenezer Baldwin, John W. Oliver, William August Gibson, Trustees; Isaac H. Knox, President; William H. Doty, Clerk. 1871–72, Hugh McElroen, Anthony Imhoff, Albert

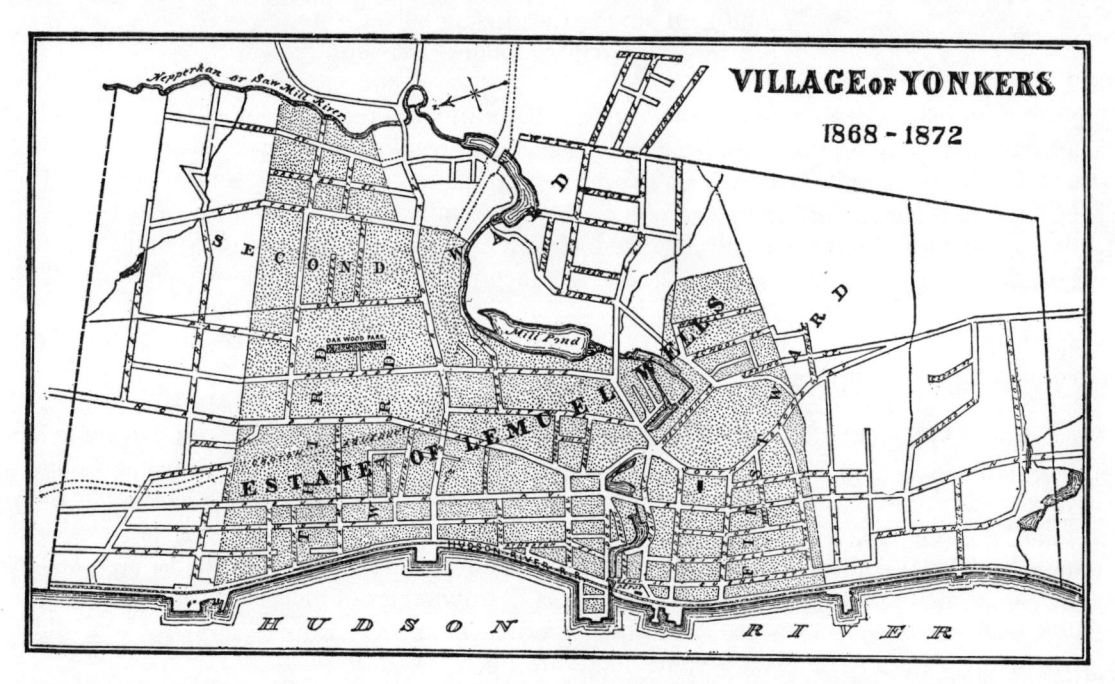

VILLAGE OF YONKERS 1868–1872

Keeler, Ebenezer Baldwin, William August Gibson, Joseph Peene, Trustees; Robert P. Getty, President; William H. Doty, Clerk. To June 25, 1872, Anthony Imhoff, William Macfarlane, Albert Keeler, John Wheeler, Joseph Peene, H. L. Garrison, Trustees; Robert P. Getty, President; William H. Doty, Clerk.

The first treasurer was Mr. John Stilwell. His successors were Messrs. Egbert Howland, Evert K. Baldwin, Samuel D. Rockwell, Bailey Hobbs and George W. Cobb. The town justices presided in the village court until 1866, when a police justice was elected to serve about four years. T. Astley Atkins, Esq., was elected. Judge Atkins held his court in the village hall over the engine-house on Palisade Avenue, until Manor Hall was purchased (May, 1868), for the Village Hall, and the great dining-room and kitchen connected with it were converted into a court-room. In 1870 Edward P. Baird was elected, to serve four years. Before his term of office expired, the city was incorporated, and the city court of Yonkers thereby created.

In 1857 the granting of licenses to sell intoxicating liquor was by the County Board of Commissioners of Excise. In 1870, by an Act of the Legislature, local Boards of Excise were appointed throughout the state. The town of Yonkers had its Board, and the incorporated village of Yonkers had its Board also. It consisted of the Village Board of Trustees. In 1872, when the town government was abolished and the city government succeeded, commissioners were appointed by the Mayor. The village government began to improve the place. Forty or more streets* were officially opened during these seventeen years. Some of them had been previously opened by property-holders, and were adopted by the village. Many sidewalks were improved. About a dozen years before the city was incorporated there were few, if any, plank walks. When pedestrians passed along what is now Warburton Avenue, if the weather was rainy, they had to leap from one stone to another to keep out of the mud. When Mr. William W. Scrugham built his law office on the west side of the Post-road, near the road leading to the Manor House, the small one-story frame building stood at quite a distance from any other house. A plank walk, which was laid, probably in 1844, from the wooden bridge to the law office, was the first walk now known to have been put down in the village. The next was laid on the present Warburton Avenue from Ashburton Avenue, north to about the present Wood place, where a dwelling house had been erected. It was put down early in the fifties. Other sections of it were subsequently laid. As the villagers walked along that walk in wet weather, the water splashed up between the planks. Street lamps were yet unknown.

The first house built on the road now known as Warburton Avenue was the stone house which is yet standing (west side of the street and north of the present brown stone front row, a short distance south of Ashburton Avenue). The avenue was officially opened and confirmed from 29 Main Street, north to the village line in 1854. When the grading was completed the stone house was left below the grade, as it remains to-day. About a quarter of a mile north of the present Ashburton Avenue (opened to the river in 1858) there stood, in the early days, on the land through which Warburton Avenue was opened, a cluster of large oak trees. Great numbers of pigeons flocked there. They also

---

* 1. *The Present Broadway.*—This was the old Post-road from the south end of Manhattan Island ("the Battery") to Albany. We have no date for its beginning, but it is undoubtedly as old as the days of Forts Amsterdam and Orange. In the infancy of the province it had been formed with the least possible labor, following the driest ground, over or on the edges of the hills. But early in this century, about 1806, the "Highland Turnpike Company" was chartered for the purpose of improving this road. This company straightened it in many places, improved it generally and collected toll upon it for many years. These circumstances gave to the road, in addition to the old, familiar and still-preserved name of "The Post-road," the name of "The Highland Turnpike," by which it is designated in many documents. Of course, the present width and beauty of this most prominent avenue of Yonkers, and the excellent quality of its roadway and sidewalks, are improvements, most of which have come upon it since the date of the village organization of 1855. They were effected in part by the village and in part by special legislation.

2. *The present Ashburton Avenue, only from North Broadway eastward.*—This, on the map of 1843, was nothing but a country road "to Mile Square." At its Broadway end it came out on the south side of the Methodist Church, instead of the north, as Ashburton Avenue does now.

3. *The present Nepperhan Avenue, extending from South Broadway, nearly opposite Washington Street, to Robert Avenue.*—That part of this avenue which lies between South Broadway and New Main Street is a new opening made within the city period. That part of it which lies between New Main Street and Ashburton Avenue was formerly very crooked. It is especially interesting to know that it ran round by the edge of "The Glen," below the dam and west of Mr. Copcutt's silk-factory. In later days, however, it has been much straightened all the way from New Main Street to the Aqueduct Arch. The "lane leading to Guion's mills" on the map of 1813 was, as far out as these mills, nearly coincident with Nepperhan Avenue. But it is further important to know that the whole of the old Guion's lane was once known as part of the "Saw-Mill River Road." The openings or confirmations of the new parts of the present Nepperhan Avenue were as follows: From Chestnut Street to Ashburton Avenue, September 21, 1868, and from Ashburton Avenue to Robert Avenue, December 6, 1869. The history of Nepperhan Avenue is very interesting as a study, and must be understood for the satisfaction of any one who undertakes to read the annals of Yonkers since the purchase of Mr. Wells.

4. *The present Guion Street, extending only from the Mansion House on South Broadway to New Main Street.*—This is part of the original "lane leading to Guion's mills." The name Guion Street had been attached to the whole of that lane for some years before 1868 and 1869, but we have just shown that in these two years "Nepperhan Avenue" was substituted as a designation for most of it. See No. 3.

5. *The present Nepperhan Street* (wholly different from *Nepperhan Avenue*), *extending from Buena Vista Avenue, opposite the Hudson River Railroad Station, to the junction of Dock Street and Warburton Avenue.*—This is part of what the map of 1813 represented as a road leaving the Post-road, and running round the edge of the Saw-Mill River to the sloop wharf, just below the old grist-mill. On the map of 1843 it still appears without change. But it has since been extended westward to Buena Vista Avenue. To make clear this street and some others near at hand, but subsequently opened, we have already given an enlarged map of the spot and its vicinity as seen in 1847, just before the opening of the Hudson River Railroad. This map has before been of use to us in illustrating many matters referred to in the early part of our work.

6. *The present New Main Street, extending from Getty Square southward to a junction with South Broadway.*—This street, from Getty Square to Nepperhan Avenue, was from its opening long known as Mechanic Street. From Nepperhan Avenue to South Broadway it was laid out under the village charter, and was known as Spring Street. The part once called Mechanic Street dates as a country road from August 25, 1836, but it was widened and graded by the village, and confirmed as a village street September 5, 1870. As illustrating some designations already given of the present Broadway and the present Nepperhan Avenue, it may be added that when this road was opened, in 1836, it was described as extending from the "Old Highland Turnpike" to the "Saw-Mill River Road."

Such were the only public roads, traversing the three hundred and twenty acres of Mr. Wells down to 1843. From 1843 to 1872, however, and especially during the village period—seventeen years in length—many streets were first laid out by private enterprise, and the following important ones were, at the dates we give with them, officially opened or confirmed. Compare them with our map of 1847, as far as they are indicated on that map:

Atherton Street, from Wells Avenue to Locust Street, June 5, 1865.

Ashburton Avenue, from Broadway west to the river, March 23, 1858, and from Broadway east to the village line, November 26, 1866. This is the old road to Mile Square, and had been known as Ashburton Avenue before the incorporation of the village, in 1855.

Bashford Street, from Dock Street to Wells Avenue, July 6, 1868.

Buena Vista Avenue, from Hudson Street to St. Mary Street, June 13, 1859.

Clinton Street, from Hudson Street to St. Mary Street, November 5, 1866.

Cottage Place, from 29 Irving Place to end of Willow Place, October 3, 1859.

flocked in large numbers on Nodine Hill. North of the present Oliver Avenue, and west of the present No. 7 public school, is a rocky and wooded hill, which was then called "Pigeon Hill." Where the First Dayspring Presbyterian Church stands (southwest corner of Oliver Avenue and Walnut Street) were large cedar trees. The pigeons flocked into those, and also into the grove on "Pigeon Hill." Traps were set on the hill for them, and decoy pigeons were placed near. When a flock flying overhead, attracted by the decoys, settled down to eat the grain strewn on the ground, the fowlers, from their concealment within booths of foliage, would spring the traps, and catch under the nets great numbers of the fluttering game. They shot those which escaped from the nets.

In October, 1855, there was no fire apparatus under the jurisdiction of the village authorities. The engines and hook and ladder belonged to private citizens. At a special meeting, a small majority voted in favor of appropriating three thousand dollars to purchase the apparatus owned by private residents. The vote in favor of the measure was forty-six. Thirty voted against it. The engine of Mr. A. M. Grant was purchased, and in 1856 fire limits were designated. None except citizens within the fire limits were taxed to support the fire department. In 1859, an engine formerly owned by Chanfrau, in his play "Mose," was purchased at a cost of five hundred dollars by Mr. Cornelius B. Lawrence and twelve others. Subsequently they sold it for six hundred dollars, and bought of the New York Fire Department the engine known as "Howard 34." At first the village trustees, with the exception of Leonard M. Clark, did not consider that it would be wise to recognize these gentlemen as a part of the Fire Department, but in January, 1860, they decided that the company should be so recognized, provided it paid all

Dock Street from North Broadway to the Hudson River, laid out by Judge Woodworth in 1850, but subsequently adopted by the village.
Elm Street, from Palisade Avenue (once at this point called Factory Street) to the summit of Nodine Hill, March 12, 1860. This was a road, and known as Elm Street before the incorporation of the village in 1855.
Glenwood Avenue, from Ravine Avenue to Warburton Avenue, July 2, 1860, and from Warburton Avenue to Park Avenue, November 8, 1860.
Gold Street, from Warburton Avenue to the Hudson River, July 1, 1867.
Hawthorne Avenue, (first called Grinnell Street), from Main Street to Ludlow Street, confirmed from Main Street to St. Mary Street, September 3, 1860, and from St. Mary Street to Ludlow Street, October 24, 1870.
High Street, from Broadway to Oak Hill Avenue, September 3, 1860.
Hudson Street, from Broadway to Buena Vista Avenue, June 13, 1859.
Irving Place, from Warburton Avenue to North Broadway, June 6, 1859.
Jefferson Street, from Prospect Street to Vark Street, March 23, 1868.
Kellinger Street, from the Mansion House to Park Hill Avenue, October 24, 1859.
Lamartine Avenue, from North Broadway to the Hudson River Railroad, August 3, 1868.
Locust Street, from 103 Warburton Avenue to the Hudson River, November 3, 1862.
Locust Hill Avenue, from 13 Palisade Avenue to Ashburton Avenue.
Main Street, from Getty Square west to the Hudson River, July 7, 1856. The route of this street has now been much changed by straightening and widening.
Morgan Street, from 120 Nepperhan Avenue to Brook Street, June 1, 1868.
Mulford Street, from 42 Oak Hill Avenue to Vineyard Avenue, September 5, 1870.
Oak Hill Avenue, from 139 Ashburton Avenue to High Street, September 3, 1860.
Orchard Street, from 211 Ashburton Avenue north to village line, April 11, 1870.
Palisade Avenue, from Getty Square to Lake Avenue south of Ashburton Avenue (the lower part formerly known as Factory Street), July 30, 1855; north of Ashburton Avenue, August 17, 1857.
Point Street, from 321 Warburton Avenue to Glenwood Station, October 5, 1868.
Prospect Street, from 57 South Broadway to Buena Vista Avenue, July 6, 1868. This had been a street and known by this name even before the incorporation of the village in 1855.
Ravine Avenue, from Lamartine Avenue north nearly to village line, October 24, 1870.
Riverdale Avenue, from 30 Main Street to Kingsbridge, made up at different dates, and finally opened as one street. Confirmed from St. Mary Street to Riverdale, September 26, 1853, by the town authorities, and from St. Mary Street to Main Street by the village, August 1, 1859.
School Street, from 140 Nepperhan Avenue to Kellinger Street, October 24, 1859.
St. Mary Street, from 105 South Broadway to 146 Buena Vista Avenue, July 2, 1860.
Union Place, from 255 Warburton Avenue to Hudson River Railroad, November 7, 1864.
Vineyard Avenue, from 191 Ashburton Avenue to Lake Avenue, January 16, 1865.
Washington Street, from 81 South Broadway to 44 Clinton Street, March 23, 1858.
Warburton Avenue, from 29 Main Street north to village line, July 27, 1854 (since extended to city line).
Wells Avenue, from 65 North Broadway to the Hudson River Railroad, August 16, 1855. This had been a road known as Wells Avenue before the incorporation of the village.
Willow Place (first called Smith Street) from 118 Warburton Avenue to Cottage Place, October 3, 1859.
Wood Place, from 180 Warburton Avenue to Cottage Place, October 3, 1859.
Woodworth Avenue, from 27 Wells Avenue to Glenwood Avenue, March 12, 1860.
These were the best-known streets in 1872, and the dates of opening or confirmation are the prominent dates.—Scharf's "History of Westchester County."

When Main Street was opened (1856) from Getty Square to the Hudson River, the gravel and stones dug out of the south side were thrown upon the low ground on the north side to fill up to grade. The bank east of the present Hudson River Railroad station was forty or more feet high. Passengers going to the station passed through Hudson Street, then northward. On the top of the high bank, east of the station, was formerly a burial ground. The Philipses are said to have buried their negroes there. At what is now the corner of Main and Warburton was a spring called the "coldspring." Its waters were pure and refreshing. A narrow foot-bridge spanned the Nepperhan at that point. The wagon bridge was of timber, with rails on each side. At one time, a citizen who lived at the northeast corner of the present Main and Warburton, had rowboats to let to those who wished to row on the mill-pond, east of the present Warburton Avenue.

its expenses, and should be of no expense to the village. After nine years of creditable service, the company disbanded. In 1863, the Mazeppa Hose was organized by a company of young men. Their organization was, however, short-lived. They had a fire carriage, which, before disbanding, they sold to Hudson Hose Company No. 1. That company was organized January 8, 1868. The hose carriage cost the Hudson Hose Company two hundred dollars. At considerable expense they decorated it. Subsequently the City of Yonkers bought it for three hundred and fifty dollars. The first foreman of Hudson Hose Company was Ralph L. Bush. William R. Wilkinson, who was foreman eight years, did much to promote the interests of the company. Tenders were provided for carrying hose. Usually runners drew them. These runners were called "jumper boys," "a sort of fireman's primary school." The presence of the boys around the company's house was not desirable, but they were sometimes useful.

Daniel Blauvelt was the first Chief of the Fire Department. F. Bennett was the first assistant engineer. The successor of Mr. Bennett was Robert F. Rich. Mr. Blauvelt resigned his position in 1863. His successor was Eli L. Segar, whose assistant was John S. Waterman. The third chief was Anthony B. Archer. His assistant was John S. Brown. The fourth chief was Samuel L. Smith.

In 1867 the Board of Representatives decided to have two assistant engineers. In that year Samuel L. Smith was chief and John Crowley first engineer. The second engineer was David Chambers. The department's numerical strength is indicated by the number of votes. One hundred and sixty-one were polled. In 1869 Samuel L. Smith was again elected chief. The first engineer was L. F. Searles; H. S. Myers was the second. L. F. Page was elected chief in November, 1869, when Mr. Smith resigned. John H. Mathews was elected chief November 4, 1870. L. F. Page, on September 18, 1871, was again elected chief. His first assistant was John Coon. R. Tansy was the second assistant. That was the last election of the village Fire Department. During all these years under review, water to extinguish fires was drawn from the Hudson or the Nepperhan, or from cisterns. It was not until after the city was incorporated that a reservoir was constructed. The conflagration of 1869 aroused public-spirited citizens to the necessity of providing a better water supply. The village trustees at that time decided to submit to the people the question of providing such supply, and the trustees also consulted engineers. At the election in 1869 the majority

RESIDENCE OF JOHN F. BRENNAN, 198 PALISADE AVENUE.

of votes in favor of storing water to extinguish fires was large. The trustees then called another popular meeting "to vote upon the question of bonding the village to the extent of $225,000 for the expense of introducing water." At an election held January 9, 1872, to vote upon this question, the majority was against the proposition. Nothing more was done while Yonkers remained a village.

Prior to August 10, 1866, the police service was not satisfactory. It is said to have been largely used for political ends, and rowdies and roughs were free to come and go. On July 14, 1866, a special town meeting was held at Flagg's Hotel. Lyman Cobb, Jr., Justice of the Peace, presided, and J. G. P. Holden, Town Clerk, acted as secretary. Supervisor Isaac H. Knox offered a resolution that $20,000 be raised by tax for the metropolitan police fund to pay for the services of fourteen New York City policemen, of whom four at least should be mounted. It was adopted, after an exciting debate, by a vote of seventy-six ayes to forty-seven nays.

On August 10, 1866, a detail from the metropolitan police force arrived in the village of Yonkers, which became the thirty-second sub-precinct of the metropolitan police force. Captain Alanson S. Wilson was in command. James M. Flandreau and John Mangin were sergeants. There were twelve patrolmen. Captain Wilson took possession of the building known as Melah's, on Dock Street, near Warburton Avenue. The lock-up was at that time on James Street. On August 16th Patrolman George W. Osborn was detailed to the force in place of Joseph H. Wilson, who returned to New York.

The police had hardly taken possession of their new quarters when information was received by telegram that a prize-fight was supposed to be about to take place either on the Jersey shore or within the town limits; and Sergeants Flandreau and Mangin left the station, accompanied by a posse of patrolmen, to do whatever they could to prevent the fight. At half-past twelve they arrested upward of thirty men, who had arrived from New York on the train which reached Yonkers ten minutes before midnight, and took them to headquarters on a charge of being suspicious characters. The next morning the

MANOR HALL AND THE SOLDIERS' MONUMENT.

prisoners were marched to Judge Atkins' court, where they were discharged, upon condition of their leaving the place.

The first roundsman in Yonkers was Cornelius Weston. He was appointed July 22, 1867. The next day Patrolman Charles W. Austin was given like honor. Previous to the coming of the police the whole neighborhood had been infested and overrun with harness thieves. "More than $3,000 worth had been carried off from various carriage houses and stables." This was broken up. The record of various arrests, of the suppression of a riot at Dudley's Grove, of the capture of horse thieves and burglars, of "the battle in the Glen," may be found in *The Yonkers Gazette* of January 6, 1877, which also records the names of all the police officers who served from August 10, 1866, down to January 6, 1877.

On March 30, 1871, the Act providing for the formation of a local police force was signed by the Governor of the State and the men from the old metropolitan force were given a specified time in which to elect whether they would remain on the Yonkers force or return to New York. The Yonkers police force was organized April 10, 1871, and consisted of John Mangin, captain; James M. King and Charles W. Austin, sergeants; George W. Osborn and James McLaughlin, roundsmen, and eighteen patrolmen. There were also one doorman and one hostler. The names of the patrolmen are recorded in *The Yonkers Gazette* of January 6, 1877. In the same paper of that date is the record of various arrests and other interesting information about the force.

Telegraph connection between headquarters and New York was effected June 20, 1867. Other telegraphic and telephone connections also were made after the city was incorporated. On the organization of the Yonkers police the law directed that the police commissioners should be the president of the village, supervisor of the town, senior justice of the peace, treasurer, and receiver of taxes. The first board of police was consequently composed as follows: Ethan Flagg, Supervisor; Robert P. Getty, President of the village; Augustus Van Cortlandt, Justice of the Peace; George W. Cobb, Treasurer and W. W. Woodworth, Receiver of Taxes. Mr. Flagg, by virtue of his office, was president of the board, and George W. Cobb was chosen secretary and treasurer. This board was subsequently changed when, on being elected James C. Courter, supervisor, took Ethan Flagg's place and Thos. Smith that of Mr. Van Cortlandt. When Mr. Smith retired Lyman Cobb, Jr., filled the vacancy. Kellog Francis, being the successor of W. W. Woodworth as receiver of taxes also took his place on the board of police. The board was reorganized when Yonkers became a city in June, 1872. James H. Mealing was one of the members of the Yonkers police force when it was organized, April 10, 1871. *The Yonkers Gazette* of January 6, 1877, gives an interesting sketch of the sagacious dog "Leo," belonging to Patrolman Mealing. How Leo helped capture a sneak thief in New York, and how he accompanied the officer on his nightly rounds in Yonkers, scaling fences, and dashing around houses, and rendering various other services, may be found recorded in the *Gazette* of that date.

As early as 1855, a Board of Health was organized in the town, but no effective sanitary work seems to have been done. A new board was organized in 1858. Edward S. F. Arnold, M.D., became health officer that year. His successor was James H. Pooley, M.D. Both of these physicians were efficient officers, and their reports reveal their advanced views of the sanitary needs of the growing town. In 1866 a "Metropolitan Sanitary District and Board of Health" were created by law. The town of Yonkers was a part of the "District." Dr. Pooley was its sanitary inspector. Westchester County did

JOHN MANGIN.

not remain under the jurisdiction of the Board of Health of New York City when the local government of the city was reorganized by the laws of 1870. The village was without a Health Board until 1871, when the appearance of small-pox admonished the authorities. Thereupon the village trustees effected an organization. That was in August, 1871. Horace B. Pike, M.D., was appointed village health officer. In April, 1872, a code of rules or regulations for the suppression of small-pox, for abolishing nuisances, and for reporting deaths and granting burial permits, was adopted by the village trustees.

Just before the city was incorporated, the Yonkers public schools were Numbers 1, 2, 3, 4, 5 and 6. There probably was also a school at Spuyten Duyvil, in a school-house erected in 1859; and probably a school at Kingsbridge, in a school-house erected in 1872. The one-story frame school-house on North Broadway, near Wells Avenue was yet standing in the sixties. Each of these schools within the present boundaries of Yonkers was independent of the other, prior to the incorporation of the city, and for some time after.

No. 1 was located at the northeast corner of the Saw Mill River and Tuckahoe Roads. It was built probably as early as the first quarter of the nineteenth century, perhaps earlier. Mrs. Jacob DeLancey Odell, a lady advanced in years, informed the writer in 1896 that when she was a little girl the young people used to assemble in a school-house at the corner of the Saw Mill River and Tuckahoe Roads to attend singing-school. It is probable that Mr. David Horton attended school in that school-house when he was a boy. The window-frames of the small building were old-style, and the panes of glass small. This old district school-house was torn down recently, but many now living remember its appearance. The desks were against the walls on three sides of the room. When the scholars faced the centre of the room they leaned back against the desks. When slates were to be used or any writing done the pupils turned around and sat facing the wall. A row of boys extended from the end of the room where the teacher's desk stood (near the entrance door), along the side of the building and half-way along the end, opposite the entrance end of the building. Beginning at that point, a row of girls extended along to the opposite side, thence back to the entrance end of the school-house. The row of benches on which the small scholars were seated was in front of the benches on which the larger scholars sat. When a little lad in this district school was weary writing with his slate resting on his lap, he turned and sat astride his small bench, and lying flat, with his face near the bench, wrote and ciphered. The back of each small bench was a horizontal slab about two inches thick. Sometimes the urchins would turn their backs toward the centre of the room, face the older scholars, and lean their little slates on the horizontal slab which formed the back of the seat, their feet dangling underneath the slab. The teachers in the earlier times boarded around, but later, more modern customs prevailed.

Mr. Ebenezer Curtice, who had studied in the Albany Normal School came to Yonkers in 1852. He taught in No. 1 as early as about 1859, and for nearly, or quite, fifteen years, but not continuously. In 1896 he said that when he taught there the average attendance was about twenty-five. There was no uniform series of school-books. Some children would bring one kind and some another. Among the books were Daboll's Arithmetic, Webster's Elementary Spelling Book, McGuffie's Readers, Olney's Geographies, Pinneo's Grammar and Webster's Dictionary.

In the previous chapter of this volume is a brief record of the early history of the school known as No. 2. Before the erection of the building which was the nucleus of the present No. 2, Lewis H. Hobby, and subsequently John Hobbs, were teachers in Yonkers. Joseph Denslow succeeded Mr. Hobbs, and was the teacher until 1846, when the school was removed to the present location from the school-house which Mr. Wells had erected, in 1833, at or near the northeast corner of the Albany Post-road, and the road to Eastchester (Ashburton Avenue). The successors of Mr. Denslow were Mr. Lockwood, Mr. Howe, and Mr. Ebenezer Curtice. Mr. Curtice was the principal of No. 2, five years. He had five assistants and the average attendance was probably about five hundred scholars. The school was erected into a free school in 1858. The principal at that time was M. B. Patterson. He was succeeded by Thomas O'Reilly, in 1862. Andrew J. Hannas was elected in 1865, and John A. Nichols (subsequently Master of Arts) in 1867. Mr. Nichols was the principal of No. 2, when the city was incorporated.

No. 3 was at Mosholu, but when the lower part of Yonkers was set off in December, 1872, as the town of King's Bridge, that No. 3 ceased to be a Yonkers school. After the city was incorporated a new school-building was erected (about 1884 ?) on Hamilton Avenue, and was named No. 3.

No. 4 was located at Mile Square just off the present Trenchard Avenue. The building is larger now than it was originally. The annals of that school are not known to the writer. Mr. Thomas C. O'Reilly became its principal September 1, 1862. No. 5 is at the corner of Central and Underhill

Avenues, near Tuckahoe. It is an old, barnlike structure. The author has no data for its history. It is now abandoned. No. 8 was built recently at Bronxville, and receives the scholars whose homes are near the former school-building (No. 5).

Early in the fifties a school meeting was held in No. 2 and, although only about seven were required for a quorum, there was not a sufficient number to transact business. A citizen was sent for in order to complete the quorum, and then $4,000 were voted to build two school-houses, at $1,000 each, and to pay other estimated expenses of the schools under the jurisdiction of the meeting. When the other citizens heard of that action they deemed it frightfully extravagant. The two school-houses were built, one on "the flats" and the other in a lot on the east side of Warburton Avenue. Miss Agnes Bell taught there. Afterward, when No. 6 was erected (1862), Mr. John Ackerman bought the small school-

"OVERCLIFF." RESIDENCE OF EDWIN K. MARTIN, PARK HILL.

house and the lot. He sold it to Mr. John W. Oliver, who moved it from its former site (about one hundred feet south of where it now stands) to its present position on Wood Place.

No. 6 was established in 1861. On June 16, 1862, the school-house on Ashburton Avenue, east of Warburton Avenue, was occupied. The principal was James Weir Mason. Thomas Moore became principal in 1863 and was in that position when the city was incorporated.

During the period under review (1855–1872), among parish schools was St. Mary's, held in a small school-house (15 x 25) on what is now St. Mary Street. The school building was erected in 1852. In February, 1856, there were twenty-two girls in the school and about the same number of boys, but the number soon increased. In 1860 Father Lynch completed a new school-house. The new building (50 x 55, two stories high, with basement and attic) cost about $10,000. Sisters Chrysostom and Winnefred taught the girls and Brother Clementian (subsequently vice-President of Manhattan College) was director of the boys' school. He had three assistants. The school roll carried three hundred names of girls and boys in 1860, when the new building was occupied. The death of Father Lynch occurred in 1865. In that year the Rev. Charles T. Slevin became pastor. When he came the teachers of the girls' school were Sisters Ann Cecilia and M. Maurice. Few, if any, changes were made in the school until after the city was incorporated.

In 1868 property on South Broadway, opposite Guion Lane, was purchased at a cost of $42,000. The grounds comprise four and one-half acres. St. Aloysius' Boarding Academy for boys was located there. The pupils were young boys. The house was also the headquarters of a community of the Sisters of Charity, of which the first Superior was Sister Ann Cecilia. In 1871, Sister Mary Pius took charge as Superior. In 1887, St. Aloysius' Academy was removed to Mount St. Vincent.

In 1871, St. Joseph's parish having been set off from St. Mary's, the Rev. A. A. Lings, the pastor (formerly assistant at St. Mary's), bought a building plot at the corner of Ashburton Avenue and Oak Hill (now St. Joseph Avenue). A building was completed in 1872, and St. Joseph's Parish School was opened with about three hundred scholars.

During this period (1855–1872) there were several private schools in Yonkers. Two were founded by Mr. Wells in 1840. It was he who built two school-buildings: one of them was on Locust Hill

YONKERS, TO THE NORTH. AS SEEN FROM THE NATIONAL SUGAR REFINERY.

Avenue; the other between the Albany Post-road and the present Palisade Avenue. The latter stood some distance north of the road to Mile Square (Ashburton Avenue). The building was subsequently enlarged and used as a hotel (known as "The Peabody House") after its use as a school-building. The private school for boys, on Locust Hill, was in charge of George W. Francis, A.M., an alumnus of Williams College and bred to the law. He did not practise law, but became a teacher. Mr. Francis came to Yonkers in 1845, and took charge of the boys' school. He bought the Locust Hill Avenue school-building in 1847. His school was a boarding and day school. He retired from teaching in 1860, and sold the school-building in 1862. The private boarding and day school for girls was in charge of the Rev. William C. Foote, A.M., a Yale alumnus, whose uncertain health prevented his becoming a pastor. He came to Yonkers in 1845 and became Principal of the Seminary for Girls and Young Ladies. His pupils ranged in age from ten to twenty. Many ladies, now residing in Yonkers, were educated in that well-known seminary. Mr. Foote had many assistant teachers. About 1855, a New York teacher took charge of the girls' school, but it was soon discontinued. A boys' school was opened there by Professor Nathaniel W. Starr. It closed in 1847, and the building was no longer used for a school. The Rev. Mr. Foote, having discontinued teaching two years, resumed his work as a teacher, in a building on North

Broadway (west of his residence). He conducted a prosperous school there for about fifteen years, and then retired.

A school for boys was founded in 1854, and conducted in a building on the west side of South Broadway, south of, and near, St. John's Church. The first principal was Washington Hasbrouck, the second, Moses N. Wisewell, and the third, Benjamin Mason. Mr. Mason was an alumnus of the University of New York. His school was called the "Yonkers Collegiate and Military Institute." It was a boarding and day school of wide reputation, and was discontinued in 1880. The village papers have references to several other private schools. One was Prescott Seminary, for young ladies. It was located on Buena Vista Avenue. Eliza S. Shaw was the principal. A French and English school for young ladies was opened at the former residence of Dr. H. L. Gates (No. 28 South Broadway). One of the principals was Miss Foster, another Miss Shippey. Madame Migy, a French lady, had a boarding and day school for boys. The Rev. William H. Gilder, A.M., was principal of the Yonkers Literary Institute, which held its sessions in the hall over Hoyt Brothers' (now Weller & Welsh) store. Mr. and Mrs. J. Freeman Silke had a select school in Hudson Street. Peter Keiper was principal of a German-American

RESIDENCE OF GEORGE D. MACKAY, NORTH BROADWAY.

school. Miss Emily A. Rice was principal of a boarding and day school on Locust Hill Avenue, but the writer is not informed as to whether it was established before Yonkers became a city.

The churches and chapels in the town of Yonkers, during this period (1855–1872), were St. John's Protestant Episcopal, First Methodist (at Tuckahoe), St. John's (at Tuckahoe), First Methodist (corner of North Broadway and Ashburton Avenue), Reformed, St. Mary's Roman Catholic, Warburton Avenue Baptist, Nepperhan Avenue Baptist (then a chapel), First Presbyterian, Westminster Presbyterian (on west side of Warburton Avenue, a short distance southwest of the site of the present church), Dayspring Presbyterian (then a chapel), St. Paul's Protestant Episcopal, Hope Unitarian (church built in 1858), Central Methodist (no church edifice then erected), St. Joseph's Roman Catholic, Woodhill Methodist (then a union chapel), Methodist Episcopal Church, Bethel (Mosholu), Church of the Mediator (King's Bridge), Presbyterian Church (Riverdale), Christ Protestant Episcopal Church (Riverdale), Edge Hill Chapel (Spuyten Duyvil). A Sunday-school was established in 1868 at Mile Square, and in 1870 preaching services were conducted by the Rev. Dr. Cole in the house of Mrs. Isaac S. Valentine, at Mile Square. The rectors of St. John's Church were the Rev. A. B. Carter, the Rev. Dr. T. A. Jagger and the Rev. Dr.

William S. Langford. Between 1853 and 1858, Yonkers was dropped from the Yonkers Methodist Circuit, and Mosholu and Tuckahoe left. In 1858 Tuckahoe was made a separate station. The Methodist preachers of the Yonkers Circuit, who ministered at Yonkers and Tuckahoe in 1855–56, were the Rev. J. B. Hagany, and in 1857–58, the Rev. P. Ward. Methodist ministers at Mosholu from 1855 to 1872 were the Rev. Messrs. Lovett, Bainbridge, Brown, Shrive, Smith, Ostrander, Gallahue, Henry, Plested and Tarleton. (After 1875 the Mosholu congregation at Kingsbridge.) From 1858 to 1872 (when Yonkers became a city), the Methodist ministers at Tuckahoe were the Rev. Messrs. Mead, Evans, Hough, Sanford, Prentice, Draper (Doctor of Divinity), Vernon, Ackerly and Haviland. The pastors of the First Methodist Church (North Broadway) were the Rev. Messrs. Hagany, Ward, King (Doctor of Divinity), Keyes, Wakeley, King (second appointment), Crawford (Doctor of Divinity), Bottome and Stratton, Doctor of Divinity.

The rectors of the St. John's Protestant Episcopal Church at Tuckahoe (parish erected in 1853), were the Rev. Messrs. Jones, St. Clair, Doremus and Ives. The last two were supplies only. The Rev. Victor M. Hulbert, D.D., was pastor of the Reformed Church (second term), from 1852 to 1865. The Rev. David Cole, D.D., was called December 8, 1865, and is the pastor to this date (1896). The pastors of St. Mary's (R. C.) Church were the Rev. Eugene Maguire, the Rev. Edward Lynch (with the Rev. Messrs. Mullady, Biretta, Brady, Byrne and Oram as successive assistants), the Rev. Charles T. Slevin (with the Rev. Messrs. Lings, Goodwin and Byron as successive assistants). The pastors of the Warburton Avenue Baptist Church were the Rev. Dr. D. Henry Miller, the Rev. J. R. Scott, the Rev. J. C. C. Clark and the Rev. Dr. A. J. F. Behrends. The Rev. Dr. Dwight M. Seward and the Rev. Dr. T. Ralston Smith were pastors of the First Presbyterian Church. Mr. Rollin A. Sawyer (now the Rev. Dr. Sawyer), a student in the Union Theological Seminary, New York City, was, in 1856, a missionary in the village, under the auspices of the Mission School, which held its sessions in No. 2 public school-building. Mr. Ebenezer Curtice was for some time superintendent of that mission. In 1858 the Westminster Presbyterian Church was organized, and the Rev. Mr. Sawyer became the pastor. The services were held in Getty Lyceum, and then in a hall at the corner of North Broadway and Wells Avenue, known as "The Lecture Room." The other Westminster pastors during the period under review (1855–1872), were the Rev. Samuel T. Carter, son of the well-known New York publisher, and the Rev. Lewis W. Mudge (now Dr. Mudge), formerly a tutor in Princeton College. The rectors of St. Paul's Protestant Episcopal Mission (a mission in 1858, organized as a new parish December, 1858), were the Rev. Messrs. Darius R. Brewer, D.D., Uriah T. Tracy, S. J. Fuller and D. F. Bangs.

The Rev. Dr. A. A. Livermore, editor of the *New York Christian Inquirer*, a resident of Yonkers, preached for the Unitarians, whose church (Hope Unitarian) was established in Yonkers in 1856. He resigned his pastorate in 1863. The pastors who succeeded him were the Rev. Messrs. Williams, May and Burr. The pastors of the Central Methodist Church were the Rev. Messrs. George W. Lord and Frederick S. Barnum. The Rev. Isaac Jenkins was pastor of the African M. E. Zion Church. The Rev. Albert A. Lings was pastor of St. Joseph's (R. C.). Mr. John McCoy and Mr. A. V. Wittmeyer (afterward a New York City pastor) were in Yonkers as missionaries, under the auspices of the Home Missionary Society of the village. On April 28, 1872, two days before Yonkers became a city, Dayspring Chapel was dedicated. Mr. Charles Lockwood, a New York merchant residing in Yonkers, and other Yonkers citizens, were deeply interested in the building of this Nodine Hill house of worship. The name was suggested by Mr. William Allen Butler, the poet-lawyer. Mr. Lockwood and he were members of the First Presbyterian Church. The Dayspring Presbyterian Church was not organized until about seven years after the city was incorporated. The rectors of the Church of the Mediator, at Kingsbridge, were the Rev. T. James Brown, C. W. Bolton, S. J. Richmond and W. T. Wilson. The pastors of the Riverdale Presbyterian Church were the Rev. Messrs. G. M. Boonton and H. H. Stebbins. The rectors of Christ Church, Riverdale, were the Rev. Messrs. E. M. Peck and George D. Wildes, D.D. The services at Edge Hill Chapel, Spuyten Duyvil (erected 1869), were conducted by the pastors of the Riverdale Presbyterian Church.

Previous to the establishment of a bank in the village, banking was done by Yonkers citizens in New York City. Judge Vark, Messrs. Baldwin, Waring and others, did business with the old Irving Bank, Greenwich Street, New York. "The Yonkers Savings Bank," the oldest Yonkers bank, was incorporated April 13, 1854, and began business June 13th of that year. "The Bank of Yonkers," now known as the First National Bank of Yonkers, N. Y., began business on August 10, 1834. The People's Savings Bank of the town of Yonkers was incorporated April 5, 1866. It was opened for business April

27, 1867. The Citizens' National Bank of the city of Yonkers was incorporated December 5, 1872, and began business February 1, 1873. All the banks therefore, except the last named, were established before the city was incorporated. The detailed history of these banks, including the names of their original trustees will be found in a subsequent chapter. A glance at those names will acquaint the reader with those who were among the substantial business men of the town just before the incorporated village merged into the city.

It will be remembered that previous to the incorporation of the village, the saw-mill, grist-mill, glue factory and other industries were established. The hat industry was established in 1828; Copcutt's Veneer Mill in 1845; Hutchinson & Mitchell's Carpet Factory in which hand looms were used, about 1846; Grant's Morocco Factory, 1850; Otis Elevator Works, 1854; Osterheld & Eickemeyer, 1854, and the manufacture of illuminating gas in 1854.

In 1855, Mr. George B. Skinner established in Yonkers the business of manufacturing sewing silk and twist. He located on the east side of the Nepperhan river, in the stone building which had been erected a year or two before for a cotton factory. In 1868 Mr. William Iles, who had been superintendent, became a partner and the firm was George B. Skinner & Co. Messrs. William Macfarlane and William Wertney began the manufacture of machine twist in the basement of George B. Skinner's factory, in 1859. In 1862, or 1863, he moved to a frame building on Chicken Island, and in 1865 to a building which Ethan Flagg had just erected on James Street, in which the Fair of the Sanitary Commission at the time of the civil war had been held. Mr. David Saunders started, in 1857, his business of jobbing and of manufacturing machinery in a room in Peek's flour mill, and then moved below the dam into Copcutt's building, subsequently known as the Pencil Factory. He was burned out in 1868, and after the fire built his factory on Alberton Street, occupying it in 1870. The manufacturing establishment of Messrs. D. Saunders' Sons is to-day one of the prominent industries of Yonkers.

Edward Underhill, Sr., established a brewery in Yonkers in 1858. It is located on Chicken Island. The first barrel of ale was brewed on March 1, 1858. The present building was erected in 1861. A sugar refinery was established by Edward Underhill, Sr., in 1862. It was located on the river, south of the railroad station. Brown sugar was extracted from molasses, and sent to New York to be purified and converted into white sugar. Mr. William C. Waring was for a time associated with Mr. Underhill in this business. In 1863, the firm was Underhill & Waring. In 1864, it was Waring & Cole, in 1865, Cole, Doren & Read, in 1866, Doren & Read, and in 1870, Howell & Co. In 1866, D. H. Smith began the manufacture of soda water in Yonkers, and his business has developed to goodly proportions.

During the war, the manufacture of fire-arms was established on Vark Street by "The Starr Arms Company," and it was a thriving industry. In 1867 the Clipper Mowing Machine Company occupied the building on Vark Street for the manufacture of mowing machines. This was the building which was erected in 1862 or 1863, for the manufacture of fire-arms. The Mowing Machine Company was in business until 1874 or 1875, when it dissolved.

The population of the town of Yonkers (including Kingsbridge) was 12,756, the year (1865) the Smith Carpet Factory,* was established in Yonkers. Most of the residents were within the boundaries of the incorporated village. Proprietors of hat, morocco, machine, elevator, gas, silk, sugar and other industries, and their employees, together with merchants, grocers, teamsters, boatmen, New York business men, farmers and professional men, passed and repassed on the streets and avenues, and met in the village churches and halls. New faces were frequently seen. It may be that some perfumed fops, with light brains, made up their estimates of the men they met in the village, in those days, as such persons are apt to do, by their outward appearance. But among those plainly dressed citizens were some whose fruitful minds were devising that which would bring to the town great wealth.

Yonkers resembles other cities in that some of its citizens, by reason of political influence, or wealth, or fluency of speech, have attained prominence for a brief time, and then have been forgotten. Among those whose distinction is deserved, and not short-lived, is Mr. Halcyon Skinner. He came to Yonkers in 1865, an unassuming stranger, neither wealthy nor college bred, in dress plain, in manners quiet, in disposition retiring, a man of more thought than words, and those who met the unpretentious stranger did not know that his labors here would prove such an important factor as they have become, in promoting the growth and prosperity of the town and making it famous at home and abroad as a center of one of the largest carpet industries in the world, and that his great ability as an inventor would materially increase the wealth of the country. Mr. Alexander Smith, his friend and employer, appreciated his talent

* See Chapter XV for a complete history of this factory.

and on more than one occasion, notably when Messrs. A. T. Stewart & Company endeavored to secure his services, he made such arrangements with him that Mr. Skinner remained with him. The annals of Yonkers would be incomplete without a record of Mr. Skinner's contributions of original thought to its development. His father, Joseph Skinner, of New England, was an inventor and natural mechanic whose tastes turned him away from farming, to which he had been bred, and influenced him to engage in mechanical pursuits. Halcyon Skinner's early education was obtained in a log cabin district school in Ohio, and subsequently when the family moved to Massachusetts he attended school at Stockbridge during several winters, working in summer for the neighboring farmers, or for his father in the shop. His father's success in devising and constructing machines for rapidly and efficiently forming the various parts of violins, led him to the construction of a large machine for cutting veneers, and one of his father's large machines for veneer cutting was in use for some years in Mr. Copcutt's mill at West Farms, N. Y. In 1838 the family moved to West Farms, where the father became foreman for Mr. Copcutt, and the son worked with him in the mill. When the mill was destroyed by fire in 1845, Halcyon Skinner found work as a carpenter. He was then twenty-one years old. In 1849, when about twenty-five years of age, Mr. Alexander Smith, who was owner of a small carpet factory at West Farms, and who knew something about his me- chanical skill, had a conversation with him about a new method of dyeing yarns, in which he and an assistant were interested. The carpet factory was not then in operation, but Mr. Smith and Mr. John G. McNair were engaged in devising and con- structing some apparatus for parti-coloring yarns for ingrain carpets. Mr. Smith desired Mr. Skinner to aid them. The ob- ject was to so dye different parts of a skein of yarn that when woven into the fabric each color would appear in its proper place in the design. If this could be accomplished, the striped ap-

HALCYON SKINNER.

pearance, which was a great objection in ingrain carpets, would be avoided. The process required reels of a particular form and a special reeling machine, also an apparatus for immersing parts of the skein in the dye liquor accurately to a measured depth. Mr. Skinner overcame the difficulty with which the experimenters had met, and devised a reeling machine and dipping apparatus which proved to be efficient. A factory was built for manufacturing the new style of carpet on a large scale and Mr. Skinner became the general mechanic of the factory. When his connection with the Alexander Smith & Sons Carpet Company terminated in November, 1889, he had rendered Mr. Smith and his business successors a service of forty years. Only those familiar with the history of carpet manufacture in the United States and abroad, can begin to realize what Mr. Skinner accomplished. The carpet industry as he left it widely differed from what it was when he became connected with it.

In 1855, when Mr. Smith spoke to him about the possibility of constructing a loom for weaving

Axminster carpet, that fabric was woven by a slow and costly process of hand weaving. It seems that no attempt had ever been made to weave it in any other way. Mr. Skinner, at that time, knew little or nothing about power looms of any kind, and had not even seen a power loom in operation for many years. His tools were few, as were the conveniences with which he had to work. The invention of the Axminster loom was the beginning of a new period in the art of carpet weaving, because it first made possible the production of this high grade fabric by automatic machinery. One operative with the new loom could easily produce as many yards per day as seven or eight could produce by the best previously known methods. The weaving of tapestry ingrain by power was also considered to be impossible, until Mr. Skinner devised machinery by which the work was efficiently done. When looms for weaving tapestry Brussels were brought to Yonkers from England and proved defective, Mr. Skinner designed a loom so superior that eventually the number of yards of carpet produced by it was double the number manufactured by the imported loom in the same time. The English looms were sold for half what they cost to make room for the improved ones. When the English yarn-printing machines accompanying the looms were found unsatisfactory, Mr. Skinner designed a new machine as much superior to the old one as the new loom was to the imported loom. The printing machines from England were broken up.

In 1874 he received an offer from A. T. Stewart & Company of a much larger salary than he was receiving from the Smith Company to enter their service and take supervision of the mechanical department of the various factories which they controlled. After careful consideration he decided to remain in Yonkers, and made an engagement with Mr. Smith for a term of years. Immediately after the engagement Mr. Smith broached to him the subject of getting up a power loom for weaving Moquette carpets. Mr. Skinner gave his attention to the matter and made some experiments, but as much of his time was taken up with planning buildings and other matters, it was several years before much progress was made. In 1877 a patent was obtained and half a dozen looms were built. Two of these were sent to England and France, where several concerns were licensed to build and operate looms under the patents which had been obtained in those countries, and he spent a number of months there attending to the construction and starting of them. In 1879 forty looms were built and put in operation by the Smith Company. From that time the manufacture of Moquette carpets increased as experience and skill were acquired in operating the looms, and various improvements in details were made, until one operator attending two looms can weave from twenty-five to thirty times as much in a given time as could be woven by one working by the best methods known previous to the invention of the Moquette power loom. These and other very important inventions did not engross all Mr. Skinner's attention. Much of his time was occupied in oversight of the general mechanical work of the large factory, and in planning and superintending the construction of the new buildings which the expanding business required. Having reserved the right to use in looms for weaving body Brussels carpets the improvements which he had made in tapestry looms, Mr. Skinner, in 1881, designed for the Bigelow Carpet Company, of Clinton, Mass., a loom for weaving that class of goods. He prepared working drawings, and a loom was built at the works of the company, which proved so successful that all the looms put in operation after that time were constructed after his plans in preference to those previously designed by Mr. E. B. Bigelow, the original inventor of the power looms for weaving body Brussels carpets. Mr. Skinner's rights in the subjoined list of patents were assigned to Mr. Alexander Smith, or to the Alexander Smith & Sons Carpet Company:

1, Axminster loom; 2, Improvements on Axminster loom; 3, Improvements on Ingrain loom; 4, Improved Tapestry loom; 5, Moquette loom; 6, Improvements on Moquette loom; 7, Moquette fabric (4 shot); 8, Moquette fabric (3 shot and 2 shot); 9, Improved Chenille Carpet loom; 10, Chenille (or "fur") loom.

When Mr. Skinner began working for Mr. Alexander Smith, in 1849, the establishment consisted of one small wooden building containing nineteen hand-looms for weaving ingrain carpet. The looms were not then in operation, but when in full work would turn out about one hundred and seventy-five yards per day, making about a wagon load to be sent to New York each week. The looms were all in use in the spring of 1850, when the new method of dyeing had proved a success. When Mr. Skinner left in 1889, after a service of forty years, there was a series of large brick buildings, with floor room to the extent of about twenty-three acres, all of which had been planned by Mr. Skinner and erected under his supervision. These buildings contained at that date nearly eight hundred power looms, the more important and valuable of which Mr. Skinner had invented and designed, and the remainder of which he had so greatly improved that the production of each one of them equalled that of two of those used previous to his improvements. About thirty-five hundred operatives were employed in the various departments, and the actual production of all kinds reached 9,217,000 yards per year. In 1892, three years later, the production had increased to 40,000 yards per day, of which 15,000 yards were Moquette, amounting to 4,500,000 yards per year of that kind of carpet. In 1895 the number of looms of all kinds had reached 930.

To show more fully the importance and value of the invention of the Moquette loom, it may be said that the production above mentioned (15,000 yards per day) would yield to the owners of the patents a royalty of twenty cents per yard, amounting to $900,000 for the year, besides a still larger amount in profits to the manufacturer. In addition to this, the Hartford Carpet Company in this country, and several companies in England and France, were paying large amounts in royalties. The most important result of the inventions of the Moquette loom and auxiliary machinery for preparing the materials is the reduction in the price of this very desirable style of carpet from three or three and a half dollars per yard to considerably less than one dollar, thus bringing it within the reach of all who care to have a carpet of any kind. This difference in price, taking the quantity produced by the Smith Company alone (say 15,000 yards per day) represents a saving to the consumer of nearly $12,000,000 a year. The quantity produced by other companies would greatly increase this amount. Notwithstanding the small cost of manufacturing this fabric, which was never produced in this country before the invention of the loom, the daily wages of the operatives are more than double those of the workers under former methods. These statements help to realize what Mr. Skinner has done for Yonkers, and for the country. Since leaving the Smith Carpet Company, he has been engaged a considerable part of his time in designing and constructing a new Moquette loom which has shown a capacity for greatly increased production, and greater economy of material. Having no interest in the royalties or profits derived from his former patents, he is at the present time, at the age of seventy-two years, with the co-operation of a few friends, making preparations for manufacturing carpets in the mill near Nepperhan Avenue, and at the east end of the Glen.

Mr. Halcyon Skinner's two sons are both inventors. In 1879 Charles E. Skinner, who had worked with his father in constructing and putting in operation the Axminster loom, and afterwards on the Moquette loom, studied out some devices by which he thought Moquette goods could be woven in a way different from that in which the original loom operated. Not being a practical weaver, he associated with himself Mr. Eugene Tymeson, who had started many of the Moquette looms at the Smith works, and was an expert at that work. An experimental loom was built which gave good results, and a patent was obtained. Arrangements were made by which the patent, with several others afterwards obtained, were transferred to the Smith Moquette Loom Company, for the consideration of $100,000 in stock. Unfortunately for him *the company did not prove a success* and the stock proved to be of no value, the property being transferred to the Alexander Smith & Sons Carpet Company. His improvements were not put in operation as a whole, but some of them were applied to the original Moquette loom with the result of a considerable increase in production.

About 1881 Mr. Halcyon Skinner's second son, Albert L. Skinner, who had been working for several years in the machine shop connected with the Smith Works, a considerable part of the time on looms, thought he could do something in the way of inventing a Moquette loom. His ideas were quite novel and gave promise of good results if properly carried out. He made drawings of some devices, embodying his ideas, and obtained a patent for the same. He made arrangements with the Bigelow Carpet Company, of Clinton, Mass., and built a loom which was put in operation at their works. It proved very successful, and a large number of the looms were built, and have been profitably operated by the Company ever since.

Another Yonkers inventor, Rudolf Eickemeyer, was born October 18, 1831, in the village of Altenbamberg, in Rhenish Bavaria, his father being an officer of the forestry department of the kingdom of Bavaria. His grandfather, who, at the time of his death, was chief of the forestry department of the province, had been in early life a colonel of engineers in the French Army, and his great-grandfather had been an engineer in the service of the Archbishop of Mainz, and professor of mathematics in the University of Mainz during its existence. His family came originally from Duderstadt in Hanover, and his great-grandfather was the first Eickemeyer in Mainz, where he resided as early as 1753, and where his grand-uncle, Rudolf, was born, a well-known hydraulic and mechanical engineer, whose writings show him to have been well-informed in all branches of engineering science, and possessed of considerable inventive skill in suggestions to improve fire-arms and vessels with defensive armor. All the Eickemeyers were born draughtsmen, and he began to make pictures long before he could write, and the same trait was dominant in his children, and in theirs. Mr. Eickemeyer had a love for mechanical pursuits from his earliest recollections, and as a boy was always busy making wagons and building miniature mills on a small stream which was near his home. When thirteen years of age he was sent to the Real School at Kaiserslautern, and later on to Darmstadt. All mathematical and scientific studies were easy to him, but languages and grammatical studies were the bane of his existence, and although English was one of the languages taught, when he landed in New York on the 22d of November, 1850, he could not speak a dozen English words.

In 1849 the rebellion came to a head in Germany, and he, with a number of schoolmates, joined the rebel army, under August Willich (who became a brigadier-general in our late Civil War), and the well-known veteran of the Union Army, Franz Sigel. After the close of the rebellion, life in Germany was made so unpleasant for the young revolutionist by the Government, that he determined to emigrate. Mr. Eickemeyer, with his schoolmate, fellow-rebel and lifelong friend, George Osterheld, therefore came to this country. They made their way to Buffalo, N. Y., and not finding any employment in the shops, started on foot for Dunkirk, where work could be had on the New York and Erie Railroad. They remained there until spring, returning then to Buffalo, where they found employment in the Steam Engine Works, which was then one of the largest machine-shops in the west. Here they remained until the fall of 1853 when they returned to New York. During the winter of 1853 and the summer of 1854, Mr. Eickemeyer was employed as draughtsman in an office in New York, and his first patented invention was the result of this employment. He had a great deal of shading to do in drawing, so invented an instrument enabling him to draw parallel lines equally distant. This was patented, and later on he started a shop and manufactured them. Mr. Eickemeyer started in business with Mr. Osterheld on September 10, 1854, with the expectation of doing general machine work and repairs in the different factories.

Yonkers was the leading centre of the wool hat industry, and being continuously employed in these factories, he soon found opportunities to suggest improvements in the machinery employed. His first attempt was to fold the edges of the leather bands which were used as substitutes for the ribbons of the so-called "Ledger" hat then in the fashion. The demand for these bands were so great, that it was impossible for the hat manufacturers to obtain them at any price. The little machine he invented would fold and emboss fifty of these bands while a boy or girl could fold one. It was a great success, and simple as it was, it formed the foundation of the leather folding-machines now in use to-day in every hat factory. His next venture was a sewing-machine to sew the sweat-linings into hats. This was patented in 1859, and sewed the sweats with an overhand stitch substantially the same as is now used in all buttonhole machines. He manufactured and sold some hundreds of these machines which remained in use until superseded by others which he introduced in 1863. In the meantime he had been experimenting to find a substitute for the laborious method of stretching and blocking hats then used. This problem was solved when he invented the ribbon and recessed stretching cone, and jointly with his partner, George Osterheld, built the wool hat blocking machine. These inventions revolutionized this part of the manufacture of hats all over the world. Later on he substituted an automatic machine for those in general use in this country. About the time when blocking-machines came into use, pouncing-machines also made their appearance, and he introduced a number of improved machines. For fur hats of a certain style, the pouncing-machine was found to be unsuited, and it was necessary to find a substitute to prepare the hat-body, which is I a conical form, by what the trade called shaving. The long hair which is always present in the fur has to be removed, but not cut off, as the term shaving would imply. The hair is drawn out of the body with a sharp knife held at a certain angle. Mr. Eickemeyer was obliged to learn to shave a hat by hand, and after he had mastered the trade, designed a machine which surpassed all expectations. Other branches of hatting also received his attention, and improvements have been introduced, some to a greater, some to a less extent. During all these years his partner, George Osterheld, attended to the business affairs, and he was left free to devote his time to inventing and improving machinery, and while he made hatting the main object of his investigations, he tried his hand in other lines.

The Clipper Mower and Reaper Company had an establishment in this city, which gave him an opportunity to test another device, a differential gear to produce the reciprocating motion of the cutter bar. The first machine built in 1870 proved the correctness of the device and some hundreds were built during the next few years. In 1876 the Otis Brothers exhibited it at the Centennial Exposition in Philadelphia, and after a field trial the machine proved itself the lightest draught mower of its class. Thousands of machines of this type known as the "Champion" have since been manufactured and are used all over the world. When Mr. Bell astonished the world with his telephone, and Mr. Edison startled it with the phonograph, he began some experiments in electricity, not at first with a view towards doing anything in this line, but simply as a recreation and to understand the principles upon which these instruments acted, all of his knowledge of electricity dating back to the time when he attended school, and was more ancient history than science. To come up to the present he had to begin at the beginning and make sure of his ground, and his bent to improve kept him busy. He finally invented what is considered the most practical form of dynamo machine made, and has proven its excellency in its use as a generator and as a motor, and in the latter capacity, among other things, it has proved a great success in running elevators, Messrs. Otis Brothers having adopted it for use with their hoisting machinery in preference to other motors in the market. The introduction of his machinery had the usual effect. Infringers appropriated it and he had to apply to the courts for redress. He found that a record of the time when his inventions and experiments were made would be valuable, and in July, 1866, he began to keep a written record of his work, which record now fills about twelve volumes of about four hundred pages each. Mr. Eickemeyer was married to Miss Mary T. Tarbell, of Dover, Me., on July 21, 1856. He had been one of the Commissioners of the Water Board since the works were started, and at the time of his death was serving his fifth term of five years, and his tenth year as President of the Board, having been re-appointed every time unanimously by a Democratic Board of Aldermen although he was a Republican. Nearly twenty-two years ago he was elected a member of the Board of Education of one of the school districts and was a member of that Board and of the Board of Education of the Consolidated schools, with the exception of two years, until his death. From 1858 to 1865 he was a member of our Volunteer Fire Department, and from 1860 to 1867 a member of the National Guard, and during Lee's invasion of Pennsylvania, in 1863, he served some thirty days in Fort McHenry. He was a director of the First National Bank of this city from 1878 to 1895. In matters affecting the improvement of the city, Mr. Eickemeyer gave an ardent and intelligent support and his private charities were many, his generous nature finding its greatest pleasure in helping his fellowman. He died at Washington, D. C., after a brief illness, on January 23, 1895.

In the fifties, the citizens of Yonkers were shocked by the tidings that the Hudson River Steamboat, Henry Clay, had been beached at Riverdale, and a large number of her passengers were lying on the shore, dead. An old citizen of Yonkers, Mr. A. R. Van Houten, said, in 1896: "The Henry Clay burned in 1857. At that time I was on the Yonkers dock, just south of the site of the present public dock, building the first Yonkers steamboat house. We knew that the Clay and the Armenia were accustomed to race. Very inflammable material was sometimes thrown into the furnaces in addition to the ordinary fuel to increase the heat of the boilers. On the day of the fire the Clay was ahead. It was off the dock where I was working, when the Armenia was off the present Glenwood shore. I saw smoke issuing from the Clay as the boat sped past Yonkers and I suspected that it was on fire. I watched it, and when I saw it turn toward the Riverdale dock I knew that my suspicions were well-founded. Immediately I started to run to Riverdale and was the first citizen of the village to reach the shore where the steamer lay. Mr. Edwin Forrest, the actor, who lived near, was there, and soon others came. It was an awful sight. The steamer struck the shore and ran up so far that the bow lay across the western railroad track. The passengers were either pitched into the river by the sudden stopping of the boat as it struck the river bank, or they jumped overboard. The bodies were laid along the shore. Eighty or more were drowned or burned. All the bodies were not recovered on the day of the fire. They washed ashore at irregular intervals. This necessitated holding inquests through a period of about two weeks. The coroner was Mr. William H. Lawrence. The inquests were held in the Yonkers Railroad Station. The captain of the boat and other officers escaped from the burning steamer. The Armenia stopped in order to render assistance, if possible. Many of the bodies were buried in a plot in St. John's Cemetery." Mr. George B. Pentz, who is to-day a resident of Yonkers, and who several years ago was the city judge, was one of the passengers on the Henry Clay when it burned. Judge Pentz said in 1896, "The year the Henry Clay burned I was living in New York City. On July 28th of that year, I went to Poughkeepsie to attend to some professional business. Having finished my business I went to the boat landing to take the first south bound steamer. At that time the Henry Clay and the Armenia were running between Albany and New York. The Clay reached Poughkeepsie first. When it left the dock there the Armenia had not yet arrived. After making our last landing that day we were carrying about two hundred and forty or two hundred and fifty people. When off Mt. St. Vincent the boat was somewhat west of the centre of the river.

"I was on the deck. If the boats were racing I was unaware of it. When we saw smoke issuing from below and heard the cry of fire, we immediately began to remove settees and other light and inflammable material. Then we threw water down upon the flames below. The hissing steam as the water was poured down, and the flames shooting up, made us realize our danger. We went aft to assist the passengers to the promenade deck. The gang-way was jammed. We succeeded in clearing a passage, and passing some passengers up to the deck. People were climbing over the guards and clinging to the braces. Many who did this were drowned before the boat reached the shore, for one would pull another off. As we were coming down against the wind the dense smoke rolled aft. Screams and cries were heart-rending. Women seemed stupefied, men were wild.

"The main deck was burning on both sides, preventing escape forward. Flames were issuing from both hatches. The promenade deck was not yet burnt. The port side of the boat was somewhat burnt. When the wind had made the port side untenable, the passengers came to the starboard side. I saw the crowd coming and got up on the promenade deck. We told the people to go forward of the fire. Just as we struck the beach the fire belched up on the promenade deck. When the steamer struck, I was thrown from the main brace and jumped overboard. I found myself in water up to my armpits. A number leaped into the river and got ashore safe.

"After reaching shore we tore the boards from the railroad fence in order to shelter our faces as we approached the intense heat. Throwing off hats, coats and shoes we waded and swam toward the people between us and the flames. We endeavored to push boards toward them and some were thus rescued. A passenger train north bound and another south bound came to a stop and the passengers assisted in the work of rescue. A gentleman living near brought down blankets and other necessary articles. Some people clinging to the braces were drowned, having been pulled off, probably by those clinging to them. Among the passengers who perished were Mr. Stephen Allen, ex-Mayor of New York, Mr. Downing, landscape gardener from Newburgh, and Mr. Crisp, a Brooklyn lawyer. Within a couple of hours from the time we saw the smoke, the whole steamer was a blackened hulk lying with exposed machinery, on the shore.

"In those days, trains ran to Chambers Street. I took the down train and reached Christopher Street. There I alighted and went home without hat, coat or shoes. I can never forget the horror of that July day. The whole scene appeared to me in the night, as I endeavored to sleep. In my dreams I saw it again. That was the most lurid night of my life."

A time like that tries men. It is narrated that as the flames faced the passengers, and they remembered that "it is appointed unto all men once to die and after that the judgment," a wife said to her husband, "John, I am ready to die; how is it with you?"

A monument marks the plot in St. John's Cemetery where many of the dead are buried, but the rains and snows and frosts of decades of years, have so worn the marble column, that it is impossible to decipher a part of the inscription. The monument stands a short distance north of the walk, leading eastward from the entrance of the sloping stone steps of gateway.* Between 1842 and 1855, much of what is now the eastern bank, of was improved city of Yonkers, of rocks and by the removal beautifying of trees, and the Terraces and residences. peared, and, for lovely lawns ap-been admired by years, they have thousands from uncounted up and down all lands, passing yachts, steam-water-craft. the river in boats and other and business New dwellings erected in the places were parts of the town village. Other proved. While were also im-Otis, Alexander Messrs. Waring, Eickemeyer and Smith, Skinner, inventors and other Yonkers were developing business men were bringing industries which prominence, the Yonkers into heavy loss in the town suffered a honored citizen, death of its Warburton Judge William first lawyer, so Scrugham, the who resided in far as is known, was born in Yonkers. He March, 1820, New York in cated at White and was edu-Columbia Col- Plains, and at lege Grammar

JARVIS A. WARING.

School. He studied law with Samuel E. Lyon at White Plains. In the latter part of 1843 he removed to Yonkers, which was then a hamlet. In 1846 he was elected Supervisor of the town, and held the office many consecutive years. In 1847 he was chosen Chairman of the Board of Supervisors. He was elected to the office of District-Attorney, and held it several years (1847–56). In 1849 he was appointed lieutenant-colonel in the Seventeenth Regiment of the State militia. On February 23, 1859, he was married to Miss Mary Kellinger, of Yonkers. In the same year he was elected a Justice of the Supreme Court of New York, and he was incumbent in that office at the time of his death, August 9, 1867. At a term of the Court of Appeals of the State of New York, held at the Capitol in Albany on September 24, 1867, the Hon. Henry E. Davies, Chief Judge, presiding, and seven other Judges being

*The steamer, Isaac Newton, burned in the sixties, a few miles south of the mouth of the Nepperhan. It was on fire off Mount St. Vincent. The injured were brought to a Yonkers dock and to the railroad station.

present, Mr. Samuel E. Lyon presented the Resolutions of the Bar of New York, in honor of Judge Scrugham's memory. Mr. Lyon knew him well and remembered that Mr. Scrugham had lost his parents when he was young, and although deprived of a father's and mother's care, had made an honorable record. He held the Judge in high esteem. Among other sentences of Mr. Lyon's were these: "In private life, Judge Scrugham's intercourse with his friends was delightful. He had a fine sense of humor which surrounded him as with an atmosphere. Yet, withal, his wit never sent a shaft that rankled, and he shrank quite as much from inflicting as from receiving a wound. He honored old age, and loved children. His advent into any circle of his intimates, brought a charm for the old, and a joy for the young, and his death has left a vacant place which will never be filled in the world." Judge Emott also addressed the Court. Among his words of appreciation of his associate, who had been summoned from life, were these: "He took the place of a Judge who was eminent for learning and ability, in age and experience as well as in acquirement, the superior of us all, and whose removal we felt as a loss. Judge Scrugham was inevitably compared with his predecessor, and thus he had to meet, at the outset of his career, not only from the Bar, but from his associates on the Bench, criticism, which was exacting and severe, and perhaps not too friendly. But whatever feelings of regret or reserve he encountered, he speedily disarmed them all. He was so diligent in his duties, so frank in his intercourse, so modest in his bearing, so patient of review and contradiction of his opinion, whether expressed at the trial, or formed upon appeal, so just and honest of purpose, that we soon came to learn his value and esteem him for what he was, a patient, faithful and capable magistrate in such a court."

The Chief Justice also spoke of his ability and learning as a jurist. He said: "We all bear witness to the care, fidelity, intelligence and anxiety to arrive at the truth, which he brought to the investigation of cases to be decided by him. His mind was fair and open, and clear and acute, and he saw the very point of the case quickly and accurately, and expressed it with remarkable neatness and precision." The Chief Justice was impressed by the sudden taking off of one so comparatively young, for Judge Scrugham, at the time of his nomination to the bench, was in his thirty-eighth year, and the youngest man ever elected up to that time to the Supreme Court Bench. He was a little over forty-seven when he died. Life for him was "full of untasted joys." The Chief Justice closed his remarks with the words, "What shadows we are, and what shadows we pursue."

The Resolutions of the New York Bar and the record of the proceedings of the Court of Appeals were engrossed and forwarded to the family of Judge Scrugham. Members in Yonkers, of that profession which is, "ancient as magistracy, noble as virtue, necessary as justice," may always speak with grateful pride of the first Yonkers lawyer. He knew "the science of proof, which is logic." He loved the "gladsome light" of the courts of justice. He never stained the robes of his honorable profession. His kindly voice is silent. His influence abides.

In 1864 *The Yonkers Herald* (established 1852), was purchased by the Yonkers Democratic Publishing Association, and for a short time was edited by Messrs. E. K. Olmstead, and J. G. P. Holden, who came to Yonkers from Poughkeepsie in 1864; he soon became the sole editor. On June 4, 1864, the name of the paper was changed to *The Gazette*. On March 4, 1865, Mr. Henry B. Dawson, of Morrisania, the historian, became editor, Mr. Holden being business manager and associate editor. Mr. Dawson remained editor until March 31, 1866. The "Gazette Series" of historical papers was published during Dawson's editorship. On May 6, 1866, Mr. Holden became editor. On May 15th of that year, the title was lengthened to *The Yonkers Gazette*. Since May, 1864, the paper has been enlarged at least four times. In politics it is Democratic.

In 1863 Messrs. Everett Clapp, Justus Lawrence, G. Hilton Scribner and others, bought *The Examiner* and *The Clarion*, which had been established about 1861, and established *The Yonkers Statesman*. Mr. Martin Van Buren Denslow was the editor, and then Mr. Matthew F. Rowe. Messrs. Lawrence and Rowe became proprietors of the *Statesman* in 1864. Mr. Rowe became sole proprietor in 1869. In 1872 Mr. John W. Oliver, a prominent New York job printer and an editor, who had come to Yonkers in 1866, began to edit the *Statesman*, and is the editor at the present time (1896). It will be remembered that Mr. Thomas Towndrow, with Mr. Thomas Smith, had established *The Yonkers Herald* about three years before the village was incorporated, and that Mr. Towndrow remained in Yonkers only a short time. Mr. Smith conducted the *Herald* until 1864, when he sold it. He remained in the village as a printer. In May, 1866, he established *The Yonkers Herald, Jr.*, and later, for a time, he again published a paper called *The Yonkers Herald*. On a subsequent page of this chapter is a reference to a daily paper which he established. He was widely known and influential among politicians.

His son is now editor of *The New Rochelle Press*. Probably no files of *The Yonkers Herald, Jr.*, or *The Yonkers Weekly Herald* or *The Yonkers Daily Herald*, published by Mr. Smith, are preserved. A few copies may be in existence. Several years' files of *The Yonkers Herald* (from 1852, the year it was established, to the end of May, 1860), are missing. Files from June 2, 1860, to June 4, 1864, when it became *The Gazette* are preserved in the public library. Several years' files of *The Examiner* (from May 23, 1856, when it was established, to the end of June, 1860), are also missing. From May 3, 1860, to November 26, 1863, when the paper merged into *The Yonkers Statesman*, the files are preserved. The files of *The Clarion* (which began to be published January, 1862, and which was merged the next year into *The Statesman*), are not preserved in the public library, nor are any files there of a Yonkers daily paper published during the incorporated village period. If missing files of these village papers are stored away in any of the private residences in the city they should be deposited in the library, to complete the broken files there. Fortunately the papers in the library, which were preserved by Mr. James P. Sanders, one of the oldest lawyers in Yonkers, cover the years of the Civil War and mirror those exciting times more clearly than can the necessarily condensed pages of a history.

THE HUDSON AS SEEN FROM THE RESIDENCE OF GEORGE RAYNER, ESQ., SHONNARD TERRACE.

Beginning with June 2, 1860, the earliest paper on the public library files, and reading to June 4, 1864, (the date the *Herald* became *The Gazette*) the reader finds records of improvements steadily in progress, but slower in the earlier than in the later years. The paragraphs reveal the deep interest of public-spirited citizens in their schools and churches, and in their village, town, county, state and national governments. Political campaigns receive much attention. The names of the supervisors who legislated for the town, and of the trustees who had the care of the incorporated village are recorded. New streets were opened, sidewalks were flagged, provision was made for police protection, and protection against fire. The paragraphs of the papers in the fifties report the coming to the village of famous lecturers, for the lecture platform was popular in those days. Among the lecturers were George William Curtis, who made his first appearance in the village of Yonkers as a lecturer before an American audience, Henry Ward Beecher, Parke Godwin, Prof. O. Doremus, the Rev. Dr. John Lord, Prof. Stephen Alexander, of Princeton, and the Rev. Henry Giles. They belonged to the first year's course. The lecture courses were enjoyed until the winter of 1859-60. Among the lecturers of the four remaining winters, were the village pastors, the Rev. A. A. Livermore, D.D., the Rev. Victor M. Hulbert, the Rev. J. B.

Hagany (two lectures), and the Rev. Henry D. Miller. Other lecturers were the Rev. W. A. Bartlett, (2) the Rev. George W. Bethune, D.D., Park Benjamin, J. B. Brown, the Rev. Henry Ward Beecher, W. H. Burleigh, the Rev. Henry W. Bellows, D.D., George W. Curtis (3), the Rev. E. H. Chapin, D.D., (3) Prof. J. W. Fowler, the Rev. Roswell D. Hitchcock, D.D., (2) Oliver Wendell Holmes, M.D., (2) the Rev. Thomas Starr King (2), Herman Melville, Wendell Phillips, J. C. Richmond, George Sumner (2), Prof. B. Silliman, Jr., John G. Saxe, Hon. John Thompson, the Rev. Joseph P. Thompson, D.D., F. H. Underwood, George Vanderhoef, the Rev. A. A. Willets, D.D., the Rev. A. Woodbury and E. H. Whipple. William M. Thackeray lectured in Yonkers in 1855, and tickets were sold in New York City. Before the village was incorporated, Edwin Forrest gave in the Yonkers Lyceum the only public reading he ever gave in his life. Another course of lectures was advertised in the interest of the Westminster Presbyterian Church. That was in the winter of 1859–60. The lecturers were the Rev. Theodore L. Cuyler, D.D., the Rev. Samuel D. Burchard, D.D., William W. Howe, the Rev. W. H. Milburn, the Rev. Henry M. Scudder, D.D., the Rev. Abraham B. Carter, D.D. (rector of St. John's), the Rev. Rollin A. Sawyer (pastor of the church), the Rev. Samuel H. Cox, D. D., the Rev. William A. Bartlett, D.D., the Rev. Walter F. Clark, D.D., and the Rev. William Adams, D.D. This course was to raise funds for the newly organized church. In that winter, therefore, two courses of lectures were enjoyed in the village. The fact that for five winters (from 1855 to 1860), these lectures were sustained, indicates at once the culture of the villagers, and the spirit of those days, when lectures and debates were popular.

During the years of the Civil War (1861–1865) much space in the small papers of the village was devoted to reports of enlistments of Yonkers men and to news from the quarters of the military organizations temporarily stationed in the village, before going to the front. The papers published letters from the Yonkers soldiers and from some of the soldiers, who, while quartered in the town, had made the acquaintances of the villagers. Among the meetings in those days was that of the society organized to aid the sick and wounded soldiers, for the Sanitary Commission was a prominent organization in the war period and had auxiliaries in small villages and large towns throughout the length and breadth of the loyal States.

A few New York firms advertised in the village papers, but most of the advertisements were of those doing business in Yonkers. The earliest papers on file in the public library (those of 1860), contain names of business men, most of whom have finished their life work, but a few of whom are yet often seen on the city avenues.

[It will be remembered that Alpheus Pierson was the country store-keeper in the hamlet of Yonkers in the early part of the century, and that Aaron Vark, his clerk, succeeded him. Vark was store-keeper, magistrate (justice of the peace), postmaster, and often gave medical as well as legal advice. One of his clerks was John Bashford; another clerk was Levi P. Rose. A reference to some of the store-keepers and other business men between Vark's time and the date of the incorporation of the city helps to an understanding of the growth of the Yonkers dry-goods business and other kinds of business. In 1896, in response to a letter inquiring about the old-time stores of Yonkers, Mr. Bailey Hobbs, an esteemed citizen, wrote: "Before I came to the town, Alpheus Guion kept a country store in the hamlet, but I do not know where. When I came (January 2, 1840), Aaron Vark had a store on what is now the corner of South Broadway and Main Street. Levi P. Rose was his clerk. T. C. Farrington had a store on the east side of the Post-road, a short distance north of the Square and south of the bridge. Duncan McFarland had a bakery north of the tavern, which stood where the Getty House now stands. There was no Palisade Avenue then. John Bashford kept a hotel and store down on Nepperhan Street. At one time he was postmaster. There was no Dock Street then. Levi P. Rose went from Vark's store to go in with Mr. Bashford; but he afterwards bought out Mr. Vark, and kept at the old stand. Samuel W. Chambers opened a store for meats and groceries on Nepperhan Street, and afterwards came up to the site of the present drug store (east corner of North Broadway and the Square). In the forties the village was rural, indeed. Sometimes big hogs would roam through the Square. Cattle also roamed at large."

Mr. A. B. Hoyt's father purchased of Mr. P. F. Peek a lot and building (now Nos. 5 and 7) on the west side of the Post-road. A short time after, the building was rebuilt and enlarged by Mr. A. B. Hoyt. It was then occupied as a dry-goods store by Hoyt Brothers. That was about 1857 or 1858. Thomas O. Farrington kept the store on the opposite side of the street. Hoyt Brothers sold out to Mr. M. W. Rooney, who had opened a dry-goods store where Peck's hat store is now (No. 17 North Broadway). Mr. A. B. Hoyt was appointed chaplain in the army, and, after selling out in 1863, he left Yonkers for the seat of war. Vail & Elting had a dry-goods store, at first just north of Farrington's store. After Hoyt Brothers sold out to Rooney, Vail & Elting built a new building (east side of North Broadway, Nos. 16 and 18). Jarvis A. Waring had a grocery store on the northwest corner of North Broadway and Main Street, after Main Street was opened (1856). George Gaylor had a stove and tinware store where Radcliff's market now stands (No. 3 North Broadway). Where the Getty House is now stood a two-story wooden building kept as a hotel, formerly, by Colonel Williams. The hotel was kept in 1840 by a Mr. Green. The stable stood where the First National Bank now stands, and sheds filled the space between the house and the stable.

About 1852 Mr. Farrington kept a country store in a yellow building where the Radford Building now stands. Mr. Rose kept a feed store at the southwest corner of Mill (Main) Street and the Square. He also kept the mill. The advertisements in the earliest papers (1860), on file in the public library, enable one to realize how steadily changes occur in business circles. Names, then familiar, no longer appear on the Yonkers signs, unless sons have succeeded their fathers. A list of the advertisements in the village papers of 1860, as compared with those in the city papers of 1896, seems to be names of the business men of another town. A generation has moved off the stage of activity, and another has succeeded. Among the advertisements of thirty-six years ago (1860) are: Isaiah Anderson & Bro., saddlery (at the old stand of Joseph Demarest), next door to the bank; Abraham Suydam, house carpenter and builder, opposite Manor Hall; John Moffatt, flour, feed, etc., Dock Street, opposite the post-office; Walter H. Paddock (late Paddock & Terry), groceries, corner of Broadway and Ashburton Avenue; Bailey Hobbs, draper and tailor; Sawyer's dry-goods store, North Broadway, next door above the Baptist Church; Chadeayne & Brother, hardware and house-furnishing, Radford Building; William P. Drummond, tailor, Dock Street, next door to Ackerman & Deyo, grocers; Thomas Cahill, real estate broker; John Isaac, groceries, Dock Street;

The news of the town, as recorded in the village papers, help to mirror the life of the people. Among the paragraphs in the *Herald* and the *Examiner* are the following, which necessarily are unclassified annals:

"1860. The blasting away of a portion of the west side of rocky Locust Hill, to make room for Underhill's row of one-story frame business places (east side of North Broadway); skating on Baldwin's pond, north of present Elm Street; building a bridge over the Nepperhan pond to connect Warburton Avenue and Riverdale Avenue; exhibition of the Yonkers Horticultural Society (Frederick S. Cozzens, Esq., President) in Devoe's building on Dock Street. (For names and officers of this society, see printed pamphlet in rooms of Historical and Library Association); annual meeting of the Library Association—trustees elected: J. B. Colgate, Justus Lawrence, I. H. Knox, William Bell, J. P. Disbrow, R. P. Getty, George Leeds, E. C. Moore, and J. M. Mason; pitching tents for camp-meeting in Staats Fowler's woods (east of Saw Mill River Road, and about a mile north of Yonkers Cemetery); meeting of the Republicans in Humbolt Hall for the organization of a club of 'Wide Awakes,' to parade with torches at political meetings, to be held to advocate the election of Lincoln; the Prince of Wales on his way up the river to West Point in cutter Harriet Lane, is saluted when off Yonkers by a royal salute † fired from Otis Machine Shop (located in bedstead factory), and in acknowledgment, the guns of the cutter are fired and her colors dipped; Garibaldi's fund concert, given in Farrington Hall by Quartette Club in aid of that hero's efforts to liberate Italy; Vail & Elting's new store erected on North Broadway (Nos. 16 and 18), 'an ornament to the whole village'; Hutchinson family gives a concert in Lyceum; meeting of Yonkers Temperance Society; organization of a Yonkers fire insurance company; reports of an up-river parade in which Yonkers Hook and Ladder No. 1, and Neptune Engine Company No. 3, were in line as guests; Hatters' Guard, a hundred muskets strong, board steamer Broadway for excursion to Stryker's Bay; town of Yonkers gives Lincoln and Hamlin 666 votes, and Breckenridge and Lane 662 votes; the *Herald* terms it "an abolition victory"; the victory celebrated by Republicans in procession, escorted by 'Wide Awakes' from Dobb's Ferry and Yonkers; the war cloud grows larger; day of fasting and humiliation appointed.

"1861. The train bearing Lincoln to New York, comes almost to a stand at Yonkers, and about fifteen hundred people who had assembled to catch a glimpse of the President-elect, receive, from the platform, Lincoln's graceful acknowledgement of their salutations; the *Examiner* protests against Sunday liquor-selling; Tom Thumb at Getty Lyceum; Reformed Dutch Excursion to Randall's Island by steamer Sylvan Grove; Mr. M. F. Rowe, editor ‡ of *The Examiner;* Hudson River Railroad Company erect a turn-table at Yonkers station; announcement of the Yonkers Literary Institute (Rev. William H. Gilder, A.M., Principal), which holds its sessions in the hall over Hoyt Brothers' store; lectures in the village; Yonkers Literary Association meeting; news that the Star of the West had been attacked excites the people; the firing on Fort Sumter; the call for 75,000 troops; meeting of citizens of Yonkers to receive volunteers; presentation of a flag to the Starr Academy (stars and stripes were then flying in every hamlet,

E. Y. Morris, grocery and tea store, Farrington Building, Getty Square; S. S. Peck, hatter, Getty House; Charles W. Starr (successor to Samuel D. Rockwell), watchmaker and jeweller; H. W. Bashford, real estate and insurance; Frazier & Curran, blue-stone yard; Leeds Brothers, plaster ornament manufacturing; Stephen C. Chadeayne, boots and shoes; John Wheeler, undertaker and Broadway livery stable; John Grevert & Co., blue-stone yard; T. S. Finin (successor to B. A. Starr), draper and tailor; George Studer, ready-made clothing; Farrington & Buckhart, flour, grain, feed, etc.; Augustus Gaul, cabinet-maker; T. and T. W. Hill, house painters; John C. Boyd, paint store; B. F. Bunker, paint store; William Shaw, house painting; William Wade's clothing warehouse; T. O. Farrington, fire insurance; Metropolitan Market: C. B. Lawrence, meats; J. H. Page, oysters and clams; L. D. Orser, butter, eggs and vegetables. M. Foley, stone mason; E. Hasse, oyster and billiard saloon; William H. Anderson, coach and light wagon manufactory; Jacob Steen (successor to Bute & Steen), lumber, coal, etc.; Francis Getler, fancy articles, toys, etc.; A. R. Van Houten, builder; Wm. P. Mott, builder and house mover; Ackert & Quick, builders and joiners; J. Benson, plumber, tin and sheet-iron worker; Peter E. Radcliff, market (formerly occupied by James Schryver); A. J. Molenoar, Broadway Market; Sickley & Thompson, house, sign and ornamental painters; Conway Pilson, house and sign painting; William Shaw, house and sign painting; Jacob Read, A. P. Speedling, John Nairn, coal, lumber and lime; John Milne, greenhouse conservatories; Chamberlain & Sons, Yonkers and New York Express; William H. Post, Broadway book store; R. J. Toplis, drug store; R. W. Nisbitt, mineral water factory; Thomas Southers, market on Saw Mill River Road; Dr. George W. Perry, dental surgeon; John Davis Hatch, architect and superintendent; L. M. Clark, sash and blind-maker; J. Cable, marble works; J. Logel, liquors; Nicholas Rost's lager bier saloon; Condit's restaurant and billiard saloon; James B. Farrington, flour and feed; James P. Sanders, attorney and counsellor-at-law; E. B. Knox (successor to Noah B. Hoyt) flour, feed, etc.; S. J. Darby, confectionery and restaurant; Thomas O. Farrington's Hall; Riker & Son's Express; Coger, practical plumber; David Cotton, piano tuner; Nicholas Robert, landscape gardener; Jules Lachune, landscape gardener; Auguste Lachaume, landscape gardener; Henry Bussard, gardener and florist; Vail & Elting's new dry-goods store; school for young ladies in Dr. H. L. Gates' former residence, southeast of St. John's Church; Madame Migy's boarding and day-school for boys; Prescott Seminary, boarding and day-school for young ladies, Beuna Vista Avenue, Eliza S. Shaw, Principal; Yonkers Collegiate Institute and Gymnasium, M. N. Wisewell, Principal; Ben Franklin line of sloops, Joseph Peene and H. L. Garrison; the clipper steamer Metamora, Newburgh to New York, Captain R. T. Blanch; steamer Broadway, afternoon boat for Sing Sing; Daniel Drew, day boat for Albany; steamer Aurora, morning boat for Lakes Mahopac and Mohegan, *via* Peekskill; Smith's line steamer, J. P. Smith, for Haverstraw; day boat Armenia for Albany; afternoon boat Edwin for Nyack.

One of the advertisements in one of the village papers recalls a well-known pleasure garden of those early days: "For sale, 'Fairy Grove,' situated on School Street, extending back toward Spring Street two hundred feet, embracing about one acre. Upon it are situated buildings for a boarding-house, hotel, refreshment saloon, and accommodation for pic-nic parties. Apply on the premises. King Griffin." This was the grove to which target companies coming by boat from New York made their way].

† The cannon with which the salute was fired, and which the "Wide Awakes" took with them to Dobb's Ferry and elsewhere, is now on the grounds of ex-Mayor Norton P. Otis.

‡ Mr. Francis N. Bangs, the lawyer, wrote much for *The Examiner*.

village and city in loyal States); forebodings of war; observance of a day of humiliation and prayer; Yonkers Iron Works (Taylor & Pilson, proprietors) advertise improved cannon of every size and style, from twenty weight up to six hundred weight, and cast after the most approved West Point pattern; street lamps lighted;* meeting of public-school teachers' association of Assembly District No. 1; launching of a sloop of about twenty tons burden (built by John Ackerman), from the Glenwood sloop-yard; proposed changing name Guion Street to Nepperhan Avenue; dramatic readings; Mozart Regiment, which had for a time been quartered in Yonkers, marches on July 4th to the dock, to embark at six in the evening, on the steamer Red Jacket; chief of Yonkers police appointed at a salary of $200 a year; concert in the Sans Souci Summer Garden; the building of the Starr Arms Manufactory; donation party to the pastor of the First M. E. Church, the people urged to be present with "a liberal show of life's necessaries and Uncle Abraham's shinplasters" (U. S. currency).

"1862. First number of *The Clarion* (a new paper to be published simultaneously at Yonkers and White Plains) issued by Messrs. J. Burns and Alonzo Bell; a newsdealer fined for selling papers on the Lord's Day;† lectures in the village; village taxes $6,800 (rate, a trifle over twenty-five cents and eight mills on one hundred dollars); Benjamin Mason succeeds Thomas O'Reilly as principal of the Military Academy, west side of Broadway, corner of Hudson Street; young men of Starr Academy parade through the village streets; establishment of a tobacco factory in Devoe's building by the great tobacconist, C. H. Lilienthal, Esq., who at first employs, in Yonkers, three hundred men; the *Yonkers Herald* calls the Republicans, 'piebald and black-striped Abolitionists'; Gottschalk, the composer and pianist, gives an entertainment at Getty Hall, performing choice original compositions; concert in Farrington Hall by a church choir for the benefit of sick and wounded soldiers; *soiree* of Yonkers Harmonic Society at

RESIDENCE OF W. A. BELL, M.D., 104 WARBURTON AVENUE.

the residence of Anson Baldwin; County Agricultural Fair in Yonkers; the *Herald* registers many columns of names of Yonkers voters, (see *Herald* of 1862 and 1863); Hon. William Radford represents the district in Congress.

"1863. Starr Arms Factory Band discourses music in the village; "Copperheads" are unpopular among the Republicans; the *Examiner* describes them as descendants of the cowboys of the Revolution; the *Herald* responds that the army *contractors* should be regarded as descendants of the cowboys who were *abstractors*; post-office at South Yonkers receives for its name, 'Mosholu'; attention of village authorities called to violation of the cattle ordinance, by those who permit their cows to run at large in the upper section of the village, particularly in Warburton Avenue; Father Reed & Company's Old Folks' Concert; Rooney succeeds Hoyt Brothers in dry-goods business on North Broadway (store now Nos.

---

* Street gas lamps were lighted first in Yonkers, April, 1861, when fifty-two lamps were erected, of which twenty-eight were on the east side of Warburton Avenue. This was a decided improvement over the time when the citizens who had occasion to walk at night, on the plank walk on Warburton Avenue, groped their way through the darkness. In 1870, the number of street lamps was one hundred and fifty-five. These were lighted with three feet burners from one hour after sunset till midnight, when there was no moon, at two dollars per year for each lamp. Then the experiment of lighting with naphtha was made for one year. This was unsatisfactory, and in 1871 the gas was reinstated, with the number of lamps increased to three hundred and sixty-one. These were lighted for every night, and all night the year round for twenty-five dollars a year, each.

† A day in which all unnecessary work is forbidden by Divine command.

5 and 7); excitement over the draft; names of Yonkers drafted men published; Masonic election of officers; lecture to the Fenian Brotherhood in Humboldt Hall; meeting of Agricultural and Horticultural Society of Westchester County in the village (for names of officers, regulations, prizes offered for best horses, neat cattle, short horns, Devons, Ayrshires, Alderneys, oxen, fat cattle, sheep, swine, butter, cheese, field crops, garden vegetables, fruits, domestic wines and cider, flowers, agricultural implements, mechanics' work, domestic and household manufacture, bread and honey, names of judges, etc., see printed pamphlet in rooms of Historical Association).

"1864. Holder's piano factory in Spring Street, Yonkers; Mr. and Mrs. J. Freeman Silke's select school in Hudson Street; tidings from the front where Yonkers soldiers were defending the flag."

"ELGEBIA," THE RESIDENCE OF L. G. BLOOMINGDALE, NORTH BROADWAY.

These are among the annals in the *Herald* and the *Examiner* (public-school files) of a part of 1860, all of 1861, 1862, 1863 and a part of 1864.

A few numbers of the *Herald*, published in 1864, just previous to becoming the *Gazette*, and a few numbers of the *Examiner*, published just previous to its becoming (with the *Clarion*) the *Statesman*, are preserved, the *Herald* on the *Gazette* files, the *Examiner* on the *Statesman* files. The *Statesman* hoped "to examine affairs carefully and proclaim them as with a clarion note." Beginning with the files of May, 1864, and reading the papers published in the incorporated village period, the reader finds reports from battlefields, paragraphs relating to village trustee meetings, openings of streets, school and church meetings, regattas in which the Palisade, Vesper and other crews participated, organization of societies, etc., etc. Among the paragraphs are the following:

"1864. The draft commences at Tarrytown; the *Herald's* extra containing names of drafted men 'goes off like hot cakes'; Library Association Rooms located in Getty House; exposure in Yonkers and elsewhere of the frauds of the Davenport Brothers (spiritualists); death of Sergeant Benjamin C. Nodine, of the Sixth Artillery; a Yonkers newsman begins to deliver New York papers in the village at an early hour; 'the wheel of fate' again set in motion in Tarrytown; names of drafted men published (Yonkers quota over three hundred men); reference to Barnum's Museum; New York as a popular place of amusement; Democratic meeting in front of Warner's store, Mosholu; construction of five miles of street railway. One terminus of the road was at the foot of Main Street. The course was through Main Street to Getty Square. Thence one branch was through North Broadway to the north line of the village. The course of the other branch was through South Broadway to Mosholu. The fare was ten cents. The road was not profitable to its owners, and when, in 1866 or 1867, the whole of Broadway northward and southward was widened and regraded, and it was found necessary to take up the rails of the road, they were not relaid.

"1865. Autograph letter from President Lincoln bearing signatures of Cabinet officers, and gratefully acknowledging efforts of Yonkers citizens to relieve sick and wounded soldiers, received and framed for preservation; death of Elon Comstock, Esq., a citizen of Yonkers, some time editor of the *New York Weekly Argus*; illumination of the village upon receipt of tidings of the capture of Richmond, and great victory over Lee's army; flags thrown to the breeze; cannon fired; fireworks displayed; the village with other parts of the land plunged into gloom by tidings of the death of Lincoln; the train bearing Lincoln's remains, and also the body of his little boy, passes Yonkers. Amid tolling of bells a large number of sorrowing citizens made their way to the station to witness the passing of the funeral train. Far up and down the track was lined with spectators. A memorial arch had been erected during the day just south of the station (the village papers contained descriptions of the arch); flowers from York, Penn., were lying on Lincoln's casket. At Poughkeepsie, the ladies brought fresh flowers to strew on the casket; Henry B. Dawson, the historian, assumes editorship of the *Gazette* May 6, 1865, Mr. J. G. P. Holden is associate editor and manager; the *Gazette* historical series appears; two of the blackest contrabands the villagers 'ever laid eyes on' arrive in Yonkers, brought north by an officer of the Sixth Artillery; the Sixth Artillery arrive in New York in July; Smith Carpet Factory begins operations in the village; population of the town, 12,814; specie comes again into use; Yonkers Home Missionary Society appoints Mr. John McCoy village missionary; Reformed Dutch Church calls Professor David Cole, of Rutgers College, to be its pastor; Rutgers College Faculty passes resolutions * complimentary to Professor Cole on the occasion of his resignation.

"1866. Building which was erected by Mr. Thomas O. Farrington about 1857, on north side of Square, and in which was Farrington Hall, burned in 1866; *Gazette* refers to the fire as the burning of the Radford building (owned by the Hon. William Radford); loss, $60,000; insurance, $20,400; the Rev. Dr. David Cole, D.D., installed pastor of the Reformed Church, January, 1866. (He is still the pastor, 1896.) In 1866, Hon. William Radford was Member of Congress; Orrin A. Bills, Member of Assembly; James C. Bell, President of the village; Dr. J. H. Pooley, Health Officer; new steamer (Christinah) built at Nyack, for Smith line; Palisade boat club reorganized; Thomas Smith, Justice of the Peace and Police Justice; closing exercises (25th term) of Professor N. W. Starr's Institute; newly detailed policemen arrive from the Metropolitan force; the *Gazette* asks "who took Drummond's† horse?" the Reformed Dutch Church Sunday-school excursion by steamer Sunnyside; sidewalks flagged; Colonel Oliver C. Denslow, an old citizen, died at his residence, the Denslow House; (he was a prominent Mason, and at one time prevented the surrender of the charter, by putting it in his pocket); King Griffin died, aged 78; Radford Hall erected, 'the largest and most convenient place of entertainment in Yonkers'; Mr. John W. Oliver‡ comes to Yonkers, and is soon active in Yonkers life; Thomas W. Ludlow earns the gratitude

---

* The resolutions appear in the *Gazette* of December 30, 1865.

†Many events never find their way into history. The above recorded question of the *Gazette* was suggested by an incident in the experience of the newly arrived police, who were strangers to the Yonkers people. Mr. Drummond, the practical joker of the village saw two of his friends, who were well-known village lawyers, untie his horse, and drive off for a pleasure ride, without his permission. He waited until they had gone, then went to the police headquarters and reported that his horse and wagon had been taken; the mounted officers set out in pursuit, and arrested the village lawyers (who were strangers to them) at Kingsbridge. No explanations availed. The return ride was not a pleasure trip. The lawyers were detained in the police sitting-room, until well-known citizens came in and introduced them to the police, who had not, up to that hour, the great pleasure of their acquaintance. When the lawyers met their friend Drummond, they made a few remarkable remarks, which they had previously neglected to mention. Drummond enjoyed their pleasure trip more than they did themselves.

"MIDDLEBROOK," THE RESIDENCE OF J. B. BLOOMINGDALE, NORTH BROADWAY.

‡ He had been active and prominent in New York City, as job printer, editor of *The Organ*, founder of the Sons of Temperance and member of the Methodist Church.

of the youth by opening a skating-park on his grounds (Fern Brook ran through his property); Ashburton Avenue (old country road to Eastchester) opened and widened to east line of village (see map); Assembly Hall No. 6 opened; William H. Post's book store on Getty Square, a well-known place of business.

"1867. First Mission Sunday-school under auspices of Westminster Church, is an influence for good; H. A. Underwood is Superintendent, and Mr. and Mrs. Ebenezer Curtice are two steadfast friends of the school; pleasures of the Ivanhoe Boat Club; People's Savings Bank begins business; Freedmen's Union Society gives an entertainment; the West Side and Yonkers Railroad Company is authorized to construct forthwith an experimental railway along Greenwich Street, New York, for a distance of half a mile from its southerly extremity, near Battery Place. It is proposed to operate it with an endless chain. This was the beginning of the present Elevated Railway system; Mr. R. P. Getty was one of its principal projectors; the Yonkers Library Association, after a long and useful life, disbanded. Its books were sold for $1,500, which was not sufficient to meet its debts (being poor, it made many rich in knowledge by its lectures and literature); adoption of a constitution by the Sabbath-school Teachers' Association*; President, Dr. J. H. Pooley; Vice-President, J. T. Travis; Secretary, William Gray; Executive Committee, Walter Underhill, John W. Oliver, R. W. Bogart, Ebenezer Curtice; Thomas Fearon (the swift rower) builds at his boat-house a beautiful yacht and handsome rowboats; Yonkers Cornet Band organized; entertainment by Yonkers Musical Society; the Palisade Boat Club (a young club) at Hoboken with other clubs of the Hudson Amateur Rowing Association; Yonkers Bible Society, an auxiliary of the Westchester County Bible Society (an auxiliary of the American Bible Society), canvasses the town to circulate the Word of God; annual meeting of the Yonkers Freedman's Society, which had sent seven or more teachers into the South; first annual excursion of Yonkers division of the Sons of Temperance (to Myer's Grove, Staten Island); people residing on Palisades opposite Yonkers, build a small, but beautiful M. E. Church at Alpine; organization of Nepperhan Lodge, No. 322, I. O. of G. T.; Mr. Thomas W. Ludlow offers for sale in building lots, forty acres of his property, and opens Ludlow Street through the tract; Clipper Mowing and Reaping Machine Company propose to enlarge their business; the hat factories of Waring and of Baldwin & Flagg running day and night; silk factories of Skinner & Co., William McFarlane, Myers & Copcutt and of Corning & Mensing, all running full time; German-American School held its sessions (Peter Keiper, Principal); drawing-room cars on Hudson River Railroad; Yonkers Home Missionary Society holds Sunday afternoon services at house of Mr. Solomon Corsa, Oliver Avenue, near corner of Walnut Street, A. N. Wittmeyer, a student from Union Theological Seminary, New York, officiates; Mr. M. V. Denslow (son of the late Colonel Denslow of Yonkers) formerly one of the editors of *The Chicago Tribune*, accepts a position on the editorial staff of *The New York Tribune;* Yonkers Cricket Club plays match games; Musical Society meets; anniversary meeting of the Yonkers Home Missionary Society in First Presbyterian Church, the Rev. Drs. Seward, Cole, Crawford and the Rev. Messrs. Mudge, Behrends and Wittmeyer occupied the pulpit platform; Mr. McCoy makes his report and the members of the Society are informed that a house of worship should be built on Nodine Hill, Yonkers; Freedman's Union publish a report; the *Yonkers Daily Herald* (Thomas Smith, editor and proprietor) appears Monday, October 21st; Messrs. F. W. Beers & Co., of New York, propose to publish an atlas of the village of Yonkers; Nepperhan Club engages Horace Greeley to speak on Abraham Lincoln, Dr. Isaac Hayes to narrate some of his experiences in the Arctic regions, and the Rev. E. H. Chapin to lecture on 'Building and Being'; the Rev. Mr. and Mrs. Heron leave Yonkers to labor as missionaries† of the Gospel in India.

"1868. Second annual meeting of the Yonkers Medical Association: President, Dr. Jenkins; Vice-President, Dr. Upham; Treasurer, Dr. Pike; Librarian, Dr. Marmon, of Kingsbridge; Secretary, Dr. Pooley, Jr. Other members: Doctors Arnold, Reinfelder, King and Henry, of Yonkers; Deey, of Kingsbridge, and Pooley, Sr., of Dobb's Ferry. The number afterwards increased by addition of Drs. Varian, of Kingsbridge; Jackson, of Carmansville; Pooley (Thos. R.), of New York; Freeland, of Hastings; Packard, of Fordham, and Rodenstein, of Manhattanville; Dr. Gates was an honorary member; Yonkers Hospital Association organized: President, Justus Lawrence; Vice-President, J. B. Trevor; Secretary, R. W. Bogart; Treasurer, Isaac H. Knox; Board of Trustees consisted of Messrs. Justus Lawrence, Dr. Foster Jenkins, G. Hilton Scribner, Isaac H. Knox, W. T. Coleman, John T. Waring, G. B. Skinner, R. W. Bogart, Dr. Drake, J. B. Trevor, Henry Bowers, and S. H. Thayer; first anniversary of the Sunday-school Association in First Presbyterian Church, on a Saturday afternoon, at which time twelve hundred or fifteen hundred children were assembled; population of Yonkers, 12,756 (2,194 voters, 1,245 natives, 949 naturalized, 366 persons over twenty-one years of age, unable to either read or write); laying of the corner-stone of Warburton Avenue Baptist Church; Yonkers and Alpine Ferry Company incorporated; *Yonkers Daily Herald* still published in 1868; five-mile course on the river surveyed for Palisade and Vesper Boat Clubs; completion of Yonkers Savings Bank; the Rev. A. J. F. Behrends administers the ordinance of Baptism to fifteen candidates in the Hudson, at Glenwood, in the presence of several hundred spectators; decoration of soldiers' graves; Alexander Smith proposed to erect on Palisade Avenue, a large building as a carpet factory, it will be six stories high; large raft in tow of the steamer,

---

*This Association became a power for good. Its debates were vigorous and aroused interest in the best things.

†Ten or twelve years before Miss Seymour left Yonkers to become a missionary in Africa, and several years after Yonkers became a city, Miss Eva Muson went from Yonkers as a missionary to Japan. Miss Ada Daughaday, an accomplished Newburgh, N. Y., lady, well-known as a teacher in Yonkers, went as a missionary to Japan.

Charles E. Mather, passes Yonkers (it was a quarter of a mile long, one hundred feet wide, and valued at $20,000); the Elevated Railway steam-engines will be stationary—one at every half-mile, cars will be drawn by an endless rope; work of preparing Manor Hall for a village hall commenced; new galleries to be placed in First Presbyterian Church; newspapers comment on elegant carriages and teams, with servants in livery, at railroad station, to meet Yonkers ladies and gentlemen arriving on incoming trains, and on the fine residences of Messrs. Ethan Flagg, Union Adams, William Allen Butler (who removed to Yonkers in 1865), and others; 'Lyndon,' the author of 'Margaret,' that delightful and popular romance, referred to as a Yonkers lady; Yonkers Free Reading Room, opened in Radford Building (addresses by William Allen Butler, R. E. Prime, John W. Oliver and Dr. J. H. Pooley); need of a new passenger station.

"1869. Warburton Avenue Baptist Church completed and dedicated. (It was a gift to the congregation by Messrs. John B. Trevor and James B. Colgate, and the entire cost of grounds, building and furniture was nearly $200,000, ten thousand of which for furniture, and surplus, if any, for organ, was contributed by the church and society); Spring Hill Grove, between Glenwood and Hastings, leased for a pleasure grove; Dudley's Grove, near that point, also a well-known pleasure resort for excursions. For many years after the city was incorporated, numbers of pleasure excursions from New York and elsewhere, came to groves at the foot of the Palisades, opposite Yonkers; two divisions of Sons of Temperance (Nos. 64 and 250) in the village; names of soldiers buried in Yonkers Cemetery published in *Gazette*, June 5, 1869, among them General Howard Carrol; citizens begin to propose incorporation of Yonkers as a city; Ivanhoe Boat Club at Glenwood; great fire near Hudson River (just north of Nepperhan River, lumber yard of Parsons, and other property, covering two or three acres in ruins); Protection No. 1, Lady Washington No. 2, Neptune No. 3, Hudson Hose Co. No. 1, Hope Hook and Ladder Co., No. 1, vie with each other to arrest the flames; telegram sent to New York for aid, which comes, but too late to render service; Lady Washington Engine Co. No. 1, from Morrisania, arrives, and does good work; death of Colonel E. Y. Morris (his obituary is in *Gazette* of September 4, 1869); Dr. Carlton Gates, son of Dr. Amos W. Gates, dies; Edge Hill Chapel at Spuyten Duyvil dedicated; citizens discuss question of storing water to extinguish fires; Oloff Park, adjoining Jerome Park on the north, laid out; Frederick S. Cozzens dies, and is buried in Yonkers Cemetery. (He was the author of 'Sparrowgrass Papers.')

"1870. Articles on Frederick S. Cozzens in *Gazette*, January 1, 1870 and May 14, 1870; Edward Underhill, Sr., dies; Hon. William Radford dies; Ferdinand Gervaund, the Yonkers hermit, interviewed, and gives reasons why he lived as a recluse. He spoke several languages with fluency. For report of interview, see *Gazette*, 1870. (This hermit and 'the button man' from up the river, were two well-known persons to the villagers'); proposed improvement of Main Street. 'In its present (1870) state, it is a Slough of Despond, and a muddy disgrace, only equalled by the dilapidated appearance of the railroad station'; the old station is called 'the rat pit'; trustees rent the Grove House, east side of Woodworth Avenue, and a little north of Locust Street, for a hospital; Hebrews in Yonkers lease and fit up for a synagogue, the entire fourth story of Anderson's building, Getty Square, the Rev. M. Bernstein is engaged to minister to them; Elm Street graded; population of the village, 12,693, of town, 18,318; agitation of the question, 'Shall Main Street be widened and a new passenger station be built?' laying of the corner-stone of public hall and reading-room of Mosholu Division No. 208, S. of T., on Broadway, opposite the residence of Hon. Augustus Van Cortlandt; Mrs. M. W. Rooney's dry-goods store, a well-known place of business in 1870.

JEREMIAH BURNS.

"1871. Proposed annexation to New York considered at meeting of citizens; the measure defeated; new Vanderbilt Railroad station at Forty-second Street, New York; semi-annual meeting of Young Men's Lyceum; news items relating to Spring Street (Baptist) Sunday-school; Young People's Christian Association of Westminster Church a power for good; passenger station built near foot of Locust Street; organization of Father Mathew United Total Abstinence Benevolent Society; enlarging and remodeling of St. John's Church; laying corner-stone of St. Joseph's school; G. Hilton Scribner, a Yonkers citizen, elected Secretary of New York State; work on New York and Boston Railroad reported to be progressing; firemen's parade; Y. M. C. A. hold their first meeting in their new rooms over the Yonkers Savings Bank in October; curling club pleasures; Christmas festivals, etc.

"1872. Commissioners on widening and straightening Main Street report; John McClure Club, the offspring of the Fenian Brotherhood, is among Yonkers societies; Yonkers Employment Society at work in the village; *The Yonkers Weekly Herald*, Thomas and Henry T. Smith, editors and proprietors, appears

May 4th, 1872; *The Daily Herald* is to be enlarged; Mr. John W. Oliver succeeds Mr. Ebenezer Curtice as local editor of *The Statesman*; corner-stone of Free Church of St. Mary (now known as Christ Protestant Episcopal Church), laid in April; Dayspring Chapel dedicated in April; *The Herald* building is the first to be moved back to the new line of Main Street; proposed charter of City of Yonkers published."

The above recorded annals present an outline of many of the events of the incorporated village period (1855–1872).

While the Yonkers people were reading these news items of local interest, they were also reading what the village, the New York City, and other papers reported as Westchester County, New York State, National and Foreign news. They were discussing events transpiring in the State during the administrations of six Governors, viz.: Clark, King, Morgan, Seymour, Fenton and Hoffman, and what transpired in the nation during the administrations of five Presidents, viz.: Pierce, Buchanan, Lincoln, Johnson and Grant. Among foreign events which interested them were those in England under Queen Victoria, in France, under Napoleon, in Germany, under William IV., and in other nations under their respective rulers.

The murder of Dr. Burdell in New York, the foundering of the steamer Central America, the panic of 1857, the great religious revival of 1857, the skill of Paul Morphy (the American chess champion), the burning of the steamer Austria, the petroleum excitement in Pennsylvania, the hanging of John Brown, the treaty with Japan, the arrival of the Great Eastern in New York harbor, the tour of the Prince of Wales through the United States, the capture of Fort Sumter, land and naval battles in the south and southwest, the orations of the Rev. Henry Ward Beecher in England, laying of the Atlantic cable, completion of the Pacific Railroad, the burning of Chicago, the war between Prussia and Austria, and the beginning of the Franco-Prussian War.

The sad and tearful faces of the people as they contemplated the lurid and crashing war clouds, dropping their iron hail, were brightened when the Russian serfs and American bondmen were emancipated, and when, over the dear fatherland, from which the scowling storms had fled, floated against the rainbow-spanned sky, the old banner, battle-torn, blood-washed, sun-tipped, and not one bright star missing from its glorious constellation.

CHAPTER XI.

YONKERS DURING THE REBELLION. 1861–1865.

" Mine eyes have seen the glory of the coming of the Lord,
He is trampling out the vintage where the grapes of wrath are stored,
He hath loosed the fateful lightnings of His terrible, swift sword,
His truth is marching on.

" I have seen Him in the watch-fires of a hundred circling camps,
They have builded Him an altar in the evening dews and damps,
I can read His righteous sentence by the dim and flaring lamps,
His day is marching on.

. . . .

" In the beauty of the lilies, Christ was born across the sea,
With a glory in His bosom that transfigures you and me,
As He died to make men holy, let us die to make men free,
While God is marching on."

THE village papers, *The Yonkers Herald* and *The Yonkers Examiner*, reflect the spirit of the people during the exciting years of the Civil War. Like storm-signals, they presaged the coming of the war tempest before it burst upon the land and dropped its iron hail. Their readers hear the muttering thunders, and behold the ominous lightnings, before the lurid clouds break.

January 4, 1861, President Buchanan appointed a fast-day. But fasting did not remove slavery, and slavery was the wrong which was threatening the life of the nation. All, however, did not hold that slavery was an evil. *The Yonkers Herald*, in an editorial, penned just before the war, argued that slavery is not in itself wrong. One of the village papers reported that the American Tract Society refused to publish a tract against the sin of slavery. The officers evidently did not think it expedient, at that time, to denounce the great sin. When Lincoln and Hamlin were nominated, the fire-eaters of the South threatened to break the Union into pieces. *The Yonkers Herald* prophesied that the Union would be severed, and that two sister-confederacies would divide its territory, but the great West refused to consent to another power controlling the mouth of the Mississippi. *The Yonkers Examiner* made known its views by announcing that a mysterious paper had been found in the village. It contained an account of a plot to lead Yonkers to secession. The Corporation fathers were to resolve themselves into a sovereign Congress, with power to levy war, repudiate all debts, import all wines, liquors, etc., and do such other acts as a free and sovereign nation might do. The national standard was to be an ink-bottle, reversed, emblematic of the dark clouds, from which the new kingdom, like the blazing sun, was expected to issue. A prominent citizen of the happy little village was to be crowned king; his palace was to be erected on Hog Hill, which, on penalty of death, was henceforth to be called Boar Hill, in commemoration of those loyal times when George III. held the colonies under his thumb. The tyrannical acts of the Government at Albany, and of the Board of Supervisors of Westchester County, were rehearsed, and it was declared that Yonkers proposed to fall back upon the ancient right of secession. If Federal, State or county power should dare to invade Yonkers soil, blood would be spilled in torrents.

"Therefore, be it known to the world that Yonkers has, by her own free will, cast off all allegiance to the Union, to the State, and to the county, and resumes by her own act, the original sovereignty once possessed by her, when Hendrick Hudson gazed upon her beautiful shores. In confirmation of this declaration of independence, we do hereby affix our signatures, that posterity may know by whom Yonkers was delivered from the oppression of the tyrant." To the threats of the people of the Saw Mill River valley that "they will cut their way to the seaboard with sword in hand," the reply is "let them try it; the mouth of the river can never be controlled by a foreign nation. Yonkers owns it, and Yonkers will spill the last drop of blood to treasure it and maintain it."

The *Examiner* says, "This is but the natural fruits of this secession movement. With New York as a kingdom, Yonkers as an empire, and Tuckahoe a republic, perhaps the ambition of men will be satisfied. We are assured that Yonkers is to be made a free port to all goods, excepting those from New Jersey, which are to be taxed double their value for the purpose of revenue. The mouth of the Nepperhan is to be opened to the free navigation of all vessels sailing under friendly colors. Chicken Island is to be strongly fortified for home protection. A toll is to be laid on every passenger carried by railroad through our borders and speedy measures taken to appoint commissioners to treat with foreign powers, etc. Several forts are to be thrown up without delay, at the mouth of the Nepperhan, so as to command its waters and the harbor of Yonkers."

After an exciting political campaign in which "WideAwakes," with their torches, paraded, Lincoln and Hamlin were elected. At four o'clock on the morning of April 12, 1861, the first gun was fired at Fort Sumter. Intense excitement prevailed. On April 15th, Lincoln's call for 75,000 troops was made. Governor Edwin D. Morgan, commander-in-chief of the New York militia called for 25,000. A call signed by 254 Yonkers citizens and dated April 16th,

JOHN C. SHOTTS.

summoned the people to meet in Farrington Hall on the evening of April 18th. Volunteers were called for. A large number responded. They were assured that their families would be provided for, but the next morning they expressed their apprehensions as to this. Thereupon Mr. John T. Waring gave his personal promise that the support should not be wanting. He and Mr. Ethan Flagg, on investigation, ascertained that sixty-five of the enlisted men had families in varied circumstances. A fixed amount was agreed upon for each family. Subsequently the town reimbursed Mr. Waring. At a meeting in the Mosholu school-house, $414 was subscribed to provide for the families of those who enlisted from the southern district of Yonkers. The names of the subscribers are in the *Examiner* of that period.

Tuesday, April 25th, was a memorable day in the history of the village. Early in the morning groups assembled here and there. "Don't fall with a bullet in your back," say one, as he pats his friend on the back. "Come home a hero," says another. "Stand by that flag with your life," says a third, and thus the fire of words was kept up until about eleven o'clock, when the company formed in line and under the escort of a large number of citizens, including Engine Companies Nos. 1 and 2, with their machines handsomely trimmed and decorated with the national flag, marched to the station. The Yonkers band enlivened the march with excellent music. The smaller church bells chimed. The more deliberate strokes of the heavier bells gave an impression of solemnity to the occasion. At the station it seemed that thousands were assembled to see the boys off to the war. There were mothers bidding farewell—perhaps forever—to their loved ones, sisters taking leave of their brothers, and friends speaking their heartfelt adieus with those whom they hoped might again return to their homes and friends. The German Glee Club sang some patriotic songs, the band chimed in to the echo of the voice, while the thundering notes of the cannon gave emphasis to the expression of feeling. At last the train rounds the curve and sweeps toward the station. Short and fervent are the farewells spoken, "Good-by, my boy; do your duty"; "Shoot Jeff Davis"; "Let 'em have a taste of Yankee pluck"; "Remember Baltimore"; "I'll be after you in a week"; "Stick to your captain" and hundreds of expressions seemed to blend in one loud shout of farewell as the loaded cars left the station, amid the hurrahs of the crowd. Captain Smith stood on the rear platform and kept bowing until lost sight of in the distance. Thus ended the farewell to Company One. Another company was announced to start in a few days.

UNION SOLDIER IN UNIFORM.

The *Examiner* recorded as officers of the first company:

CHARLES H. SMITH, Captain.
GARDNER S. HAWES, Lieutenant.
ROMEYN BOGARDUS, Ensign.
GEORGE REYNOLDS, Orderly Sergeant.
JOHN C. COATES, Second Sergeant.

THOMAS HILL, Third Sergeant.
GEORGE ANDREWS, Fourth Sergeant.
EDWIN CUMBERBEACH, First Corporal.
C. WIGO FITCH, Second Corporal.
ALFRED BOWLER, Third Corporal.

W. J. TOWNSEND, Fourth Corporal.

A handsome sword was presented Captain Smith by Mr. A. R. Larned, of Yonkers. The company received their uniforms in New York. A beautiful flag was raised over St. Paul's church, and a flag was raised over the school-house, at the corner of the Saw Mill River and Tuckahoe Roads. There were speeches, songs, and cheers. One of the school-boys who helped collect the money to buy the flag, and also helped raise the flag was George R. Hendrickson, who enlisted the next year, being at the time of his enlistment thirteen years and ten months old.

September 26, 1861, was observed as a day of fasting, humiliation and prayer, in response to the proclamation of the President. Devout citizens realized that the dependence of the Republic was on the God of their fathers and their God.

Several military organizations were stationed for a time in the village during the war. The Fortieth Mozart Regiment was quartered in Devoe's building on Dock Street. Some of them had seen active service in the Mexican and other wars. The reveille, troop, retreat and tattoo, were each sounded at the proper time, and other duties of the camp adopted. Mounting and relieving guard, grand-rounds, and other formalities were all faithfully executed, with as much strictness as if on the tented field. At first there were ten companies. Subsequently three companies came from Massachusetts. The regiment numbered 800. They drilled daily on the upper and the lower greens. At one time a beautiful flag was raised over the gas works. A company of the Mozart guards, passing up Warburton Avenue, halted and gave three tremendous cheers for the stars and stripes. They were returned with a will. Some refreshments were served, and after a good time all around, the company departed. The low groggeries of the village were a temptation to some of the Mozart men, and the village officials were called upon to shut up those, which were unlicensed. The Yonkers ladies presented the Seventeenth Regiment with 700 havelocks. That regiment was known as the Westchester Chasseurs. The Mozart Regiment removed from the Devoe building and encamped on the hill at the then extreme upper end of Palisade Avenue, where their white tents were pitched to the number of two hundred. The village papers contained letters from members of this regiment, after they had reached the seat of war. A company of German soldiers were also at the barracks on Dock Street, and soldiers attached to a regiment of mounted rifles were there. A company of Yonkers men enlisted in the Anthony Wayne Guard, 135th Regiment, New York State Volunteers. That regiment was in Yonkers for a time. During a part of the war period, the tent of a recruiting officer was pitched near the little green plot in Getty Square.

Lieutenant E. Y. Morris advertised in *The Examiner* for recruits: $2 on enlistment, $25 government bounty, $13 one month's pay in advance, $50 on mustering into service. The colonel of the regiment was Wm. H. Morris, the lieutenant-colonel was Ralph E. Prime. The captain of Company F of Yonkers was Edward Y. Morris, to whom a sword was presented by Lady Washington Engine Company, of which he had been a member. When the 135th departed from Yonkers, they embarked from the bedstead factory dock. The quota of the 135th was more than full. Forty or fifty Yonkers men were expected to go in the 172d. The 172d was not formed, and the men were transferred to the Sixth New York Artillery. Company F was composed of Yonkers and Peekskill men. All the officers were from Yonkers, except the first lieutenant, third sergeant and sixth corporal. *The Examiner* published the following roll of the names of the Yonkers members of the company. Barrett, Hancock and Gilleo were from Peekskill:

MATT. H. ELLIS.

EDWARD Y. MORRIS, Captain.
SAMUEL BARRETT, First Lieutenant.
HENRY A. CHADEAYNE, Second Lieutenant.
THOMAS R. PRICE, First Sergeant.
PATRICK KELLY, Second Sergeant.
GEORGE HANCOCK, Third Sergeant.
ABEL WATERS, Fourth Sergeant.
SAMUEL R. KNIFFEN, Fifth Sergeant.

JOHN J. BRADY, First Corporal.
JAMES T. EARLE, Second Corporal.
THOMAS TUTTLE, Third Corporal.
JAMES E. BEASLEY, Fourth Corporal.
BENJAMIN PRICE, Fifth Corporal.
JACOB GILLEO, Sixth Corporal.
JUDSON ABBOTT, Seventh Corporal.
EDGAR C. NODINE, Eighth Corporal.

ARCHER, NATHANIEL.
BARNES, FREDERICK E.
BURKE, JAMES.
BRAGG, WILLIAM.
BOYLE, JAMES.
BENNETT, MICHAEL.

CASEY, DANIEL.
COLLIN, PATRICK.
CARROLL, JAMES.
COUGHLIN, JOHN.
CONLIN, ANTHONY.
CAIN, JOSEPH.

DARLINGTON, JOHN.
DONAHUE, MICHAEL.
FAGAN, MICHAEL.
FOLEY, JOHN.
GILBERT, JAS. D.
GORMAN, PATRICK.

GOODWIN, FRANCIS.	LINDSAY, WILLIAM.	REIN, GEORGE.
HENRY, JOHN.	LAPHAM, SOLON.	SMITH, THOS. A.
HAINES, JACOB L.	LAUNY, THOMAS.	SHERWOOD, JAMES E.
HART, JAMES.	MCMAHON, JOHN.	STOCKHOLM, FRED E.
HURST, HUGH.	MCGANN, PHILIP.	THOMPSON, WILLIAM.
HAMILTON, WM.	NORRIS, MICHAEL.	VOLZ, GEORGE.
HALLETT, DEMETRIUS B.	O'DONNELL, JOHN.	VAN WART, L. S.
KELLY, TIMOTHY.	O'ROURKE, MICHAEL.	VANDERVLANT, CORN.
KEANILY, JEREMIAH.	PILSON, JAMES.	WELSH, RICHMOND.
KAILY, WILLIAM.	POPE, WILLIAM.	WELSH, JAMES.
LAFFERTY, JAMES.	REIFF, JACOB.	WATSON, WILLIAM.
LANE, THOMAS.	RYAN, THOMAS.	WHITLOCK, AARON.
LOUNSBURY, THOS. N.	REED, JAMES.	

This roll differs somewhat from that published in the volume "Yonkers in the Rebellion," and reproduced on a subsequent page of this chapter.

Charles E. Lawrence, Frederick A. Cowdrey, Ray Howland, George Garrison, Oscar Archer, Archibald E. Miller, Frederick Howlett and William Myers, were in the Eighth Regiment.

About thirty Yonkers men enlisted in the Fifth Regiment, Colonel Duryea's Zouaves. In Company F were George A. Mitchell, James W. Brown, George Hitchcock, James Sheridan, James H. Franklin, John G. Peene, Samuel Parkinson, Charles Fortescue, Charles Allen, Frank Morgan, George Post, Ed. Simmonds, William Stapleton, Henry Wicker, David Wells, Casper Ryer, William Sweeney, James Cochran, Robert Pollock, Cornelius Schermerhorn, Benjamin Sullivan, James Murphy, John Fenner, David Upton, David Crawford, Orville Dudley. William T. Partridge was Captain of Company I; R. E. Prime was Captain of Company C; Charles W. Chamberlain belonged to Company C; George W. Chamberlain was a member of Company E, William Samlar of Company D and James Duff.

The following item appeared in *The Examiner*: "The recent engagements have proved fatal to some of our Yonkers boys. We regret to record in addition to that of Captain Partridge, the death on the battlefield of Charles M. Allen, A. Berrian and C. Ryer, and of severe wounds received by George Mitchell, James Brown and William Sweeney, all of Duryea's Zouaves. Garrett G. Major of the Seventeenth Regiment, formerly an employee in this office was severely wounded by a cannon ball, just as he stepped on board one of the gunboats at West Point. The ball was discharged by the rebels. As

EDWARD J. MITCHELL.

the boats were a good deal below the elevation of the artillery, and the ball was nearly spent, it was not fatal. It struck him on the shoulder and his wound is quite serious."

The following enrolled as Company F, Fifth Regiment, New York State Advance Guards, but when mustered in, the name was dropped and they became a part of Company F, Fifth Regiment, Colonel Duryea's Zouaves.

B. A. SULLIVAN,	WILLIAM SWEENEY,	GEORGE POST,
C. RYER,	STEPHEN BOGARDUS,	WILLIAM SIMS,
GEORGE A. MITCHELL,	HENRY WICKER,	SAMUEL PARKINSON,
JAMES MURPHY,	H. WESTLAKE,	FRANKLIN MORGAN,
JAMES SHERIDAN.	JOHN G. PEENE,	GEORGE HITCHCOCK,
DAVID CRAWFORD,	O. DUDLEY,	JAMES AUSTIN.
JAMES W. BROWN,	C. FORTESCUE,	

The members of the Yonkers Cornet Band also volunteered their services to the country and enlisted in the Seventeenth Regiment, New York Volunteers.

A former pastor of the Methodist Episcopal Church in Yonkers, the Rev. Peletiah Ward, who had been assigned to Ellenville, Ulster County, resigned his charge; in ten days recruited one hundred and thirty men, and led them into Colonel Pratt's command at Kingston. Afterwards, a beautiful sash, sword, belt, pistol and holster, and forty dollars in cash were presented him. The Rev. L. H. King made the presentation address. Captain Ward became the chaplain of his regiment. At the second battle of Bull Run, two of the color bearers of the regiment were shot and instantly killed. As the second one fell, the Rev. Mr. Ward sprang forward, and seizing the flag, waved it and urged the regiment forward. In so doing he received five wounds, which in a few hours resulted in death. He was a man of commanding presence, genial and earnest.

The following paragraph appeared in one of the village papers of 1862: "The Seventy-sixth Regiment, N. Y. S. V., Colonel Green and two artillery companies passed through Yonkers on the Hudson River Railroad for the seat of war. They numbered 1,300 men, and occupied nineteen passenger and six baggage cars, making the largest passenger train that ever passed over the road."

When the report came that the Government proposed to enlist colored men, the editor of the Yonkers Herald raged like an insane man. In 1863, paper money ("shinplaster currency") was in use. William H. Howe, Esq., of Yonkers, received a commission as lieutenant of cavalry of one of the Kansas regiments. In 1863, Messrs. W. C. Meade and Daniel Lyon, Yonkers lawyers, enlisted. Mr. Anson B. Hoyt, a Yonkers merchant, enlisted as a chaplain. A meeting was called in August, 1862, "to take measures to fill the quota of the town, and encourage volunteer enlistment by additional bounties." A number of citizens subscribed to the volunteer bounty fund. As early as 1862, a draft began to be talked about. At one time militia companies were ordered to Yonkers to guard the barracks. It was understood that they were called more for the purpose of looking after the drafted men than the volunteers then in quarters, but the draft did not take place at that time. Yonkers offered $300. In addition to this, the county, State and national bounties amounted to $1,164 for each veteran, of which he received $525 in cash before leaving the State. New recruits were offered $989, of which each received $450 in cash down. About the time the draft was to take place, September, 1863, it was rumored that two gunboats and a body of Federal troops had gone up to Tarrytown. Two hundred and twelve Yonkers men were drawn there, from which one hundred and six were required to fill the quota.

Contributions were made in Yonkers for the sick and wounded soldiers on David's Island. In November, 1862, Yonkers furnished a Thanksgiving dinner to three hundred men on David's Island. During the holidays of 1863, Yonkers subscribed money to send turkeys to the Sixth New York Artillery,

AUGUSTUS KIPP.

that they might have a Christmas dinner. In 1864 a Thanksgiving dinner was provided for the soldiers and sailors. Thousands of turkeys were sent south.

The Ladies' Union Aid Society was in operation from the commencement of the war. It was organized a few days after the bombardment of Fort Sumter. In the winter of 1864, a Sanitary Fair was held. The names of the officers and those who had charge of the various tables and booths are recorded in the volume, "Yonkers in the Rebellion." An interesting feature of the fair was the following letter from President Lincoln and his Cabinet, sent in response to a request from Mrs. Benjamin Rockwell to Mr. Seward:

"WASHINGTON, January 14, 1864.

"The President of the United States and the Heads of the Departments, tender their best wishes to the ladies and managers of the fair to be held at Yonkers for the benefit of the sick and wounded soldiers.
"A. LINCOLN,
"WILLIAM H. SEWARD,
"S. P. CHASE,
"EDWIN M. STANTON,
"GIDEON WELLS."

The letter bore the signature of each official, and was formally sealed. It was sold to three hundred contributors for twenty-five cents each, and presented to the village. The original letter, and a list of the purchasers, in their own handwriting, are framed, and occupy prominent places in the city clerk's office. Several churches contributed to swell the amount the fair aimed to raise. At that time the population of the town was something over 16,000, and the fair netted over one dollar for every man, woman and child within its borders. A festival was given in 1865, the proceeds of which were $1,455.05. The Aid Society forwarded boxes to the Sanitary Commission.

CONFEDERATE BATTLE-FLAG.

George Radford, of Yonkers, who was one of the first to respond to the President's call, enlisted in a New Jersey regiment. He died of wounds, and was buried from the Dutch Reformed Church in Yonkers. Mr. Cyrus Cleveland, while in Norfolk, obtained a "Secesh" flag, and brought it to Yonkers. It was exhibited in Starr's jewelry store. During the war the Starr Arms Company manufactured fire-arms in Yonkers. Mr. William S. Tompkins, the father of Mr. Abraham S. Tompkins (alderman, 1896) manufactured drums in Yonkers. He was at one time a leader of the New York Band. His drums were made for Massachusetts, Connecticut, Illinois and other regiments. They were of superior quality, and very valuable. They cannot be bought now for less than $500 each.

Company F, Fifth Regiment, N. Y. S. V. (Duryea's Zouaves), hailing from Yonkers, received a fine reception on their return from the war. Company A, Seventeenth Regiment, also had a cordial welcome when they came back. The bronzed veterans realized that their services were appreciated. The history of the career of this company is recorded in the *Yonkers Herald* of May 30, 1863. A gold watch was presented by the company to Captain T. V. Foley, who had distinguished himself in the service.

The colonel of the 135th New York Volunteer Infantry, William H. Morris, was the son of Mr. George P. Morris, the author of "Woodman, Spare that Tree." He graduated at West Point, and during the Civil War rendered heroic service. He was elected colonel of the 135th New York Volunteer Infantry, which subsequently became the Sixth New York Volunteer Artillery. He was subsequently promoted to brigadier-general U. S. Volunteers. He was made brevet major-general U. S. Volunteers for "gallant and meritorious services in the battle of the Wilderness."

Colonel Howard J. Kitching, his lieutenant-colonel, became commander of the Sixth Artillery. The regiment had been drilled and instructed and disciplined by Morris, until it was one of the best volunteer regiments in the service. The regiment honored Colonel Kitching, who was worthy of their confidence. A brief biography of his short but useful life is recorded in "Yonkers in the Rebellion."

" Sweet in manner, fair in favor,
Mild in temper, fierce in fight;
Warrior, gentler, nobler, braver,
Never shall behold the light."

CONFEDERATE FLAG OF 1861.

Ralph E. Prime enlisted as a private in the Fifth New York Volunteers, was promoted for gallantry in the field, and was subsequently ordered to the Sixth New York Artillery as lieutenant-colonel.

He found the soldiers in the Sixth strongly attached to Lieutenant-Colonel Kitching, and resigned in his favor. He was nominated by President Lincoln on March 5, 1863, for brigadier-general.

The *Yonkers Daily Statesman* of March, 1896, published a communication recording an event which occurred in Yonkers during the Rebellion.

BREVET MAJOR GENERAL
WM. HOPKINS MORRIS.

"LINCOLN, DANA, RADFORD.—*To the Editor of The Statesman:* I read, with a good deal of interest, the article under the above heading which appeared in *The Statesman*, a few days since. The history of one of the votes cast for the abolition of slavery on the occasion referred to has never yet been written, and, as most of the persons who figured in the matter are dead, no harm can come to any one by giving the following statement.

"In 1862, William Radford was elected to Congress from this district, and was re-elected in 1864. In the early part of January, 1865, I received a note from Mr. Radford, inviting me to call at his house on the Sunday afternoon following, at two o'clock. I went at the time mentioned, and found there about twenty or more leading men of his party from Rockland, Putnam and Westchester Counties, which then formed the Congressional District.

"After awhile, Mr. Radford stated that he had invited the gentlemen present for consultation; that a very important vote was to be taken, that week, on the slavery question, and as he desired to vote understandingly, and in accordance with the views of his constituents, he wished to hear and have expression of the views of those present.

"In accordance with the request of Mr. Radford, I had taken a seat at his desk, and kept a record of the views of the respective gentlemen as they gave them, but took no other part in the meeting.

"The matter was freely discussed, with a large majority in favor of Mr. Radford voting against the proposed measure. About six o'clock the meeting broke up, in not a very harmonious manner—the debate being very warmly contested, and some strong language being used at times.

"As I started to leave the house Mr. Radford stopped me. and requested me to remain after the others had gone, which I did, and I went back to his library, where I found two others. After all the party were gone, Mr. Radford said to me:

"'Now, you have heard what has been said, and know the men; tell me what I shall do. Shall I vote with my party against the measure, or not? Tell me what you would do, under the circumstances.'

"I told him that, if I were in his place, and had a vote, I should certainly vote in the affirmative. He asked for my reasons, and I gave them freely. The vote was taken January 31, 1865, standing 119 in favor and 56 against. Out of all the Democrats in the House—I believe 79 in all—15 voted in favor, and eight did not vote. The four Democrats from the State of New York who voted for the measure were John Ganson of Buffalo, Homer Nelson of Poughkeepsie, Anson Herrick of New York City, and William Radford of Yonkers. If they had voted no, slavery would not have been abolished at that session. All honor to these men! Now for the result politically to them. Not one of these four men were re-elected.

"In connection with this vote of Mr. Radford, a very pleasant incident occurred, and one which I shall never forget. Some little time after the vote on the slavery question was decided, I had occasion to visit Washington, and was invited by Mr. Radford to call on President Lincoln. I gladly accepted and went with him to the White House, was admitted, and introduced to the President by Mr. Radford, who closed his introduction with these words:

"'This is the person who is responsible for that vote.'

"The President answered, while shaking me by the hand: 'If you never did a good deed before, you did it then.'

"When I left he invited me to call again, which I did on some few occasions afterwards, and was always cordially received.

"Of the closing scene I am reminded by a small card, now lying before me, inscribed as follows: On one side, 'East, admit the bearer to the Executive Mansion, on Wednesday, the 19th of April, 1865'; and on the other side, 'Used by me, at the funeral ceremonies at the White House, on the death of President Lincoln, April 19, 1865.'

J. P. SANDERS."

When news of the fall of Richmond reached Yonkers, there was great rejoicing. "Old Glory" was thrown to the breeze, cannons were fired, and a meeting was held at the Getty House, at which speeches were made by Messrs. Getty, Logan, Romer, Pike, M.D., and others.

The town was plunged into gloom when the sad tidings came of the shooting of Lincoln. The uttermost joy was followed suddenly by the uttermost sorrow—"noon and midnight, without a space between."

> " Oh, the inky drop of poison,
>   In our bitter draught of grief;
> Oh, the sorrow of a nation,
>   Mourning for its murdered chief;
> Strongest arms were closely folded,
>   Most impassioned lips at rest;
> Scarcely seemed a heaving motion,
>   In the nation's wounded breast.
> Oh, the land he loved will miss him,
>   Miss him in its hour of need.
> Mourns the nation for the nation,
>   While its teardrops inward bleed."

The following muster rolls and historical paragraphs, with one or two brief exceptions, are transcribed from "Yonkers in the Rebellion":

Company A, Seventeenth Regiment, New York Volunteers. On the fifteenth day of April, 1861, Fort Sumter capitulated, and on the sixteenth day of the same month, the President's call for troops reached Albany. A large and patriotic meeting was held at Farrington Hall, Yonkers, on the evening of April 17th, at which volunteers were called for. In response to this call, over one hundred young men were enrolled to serve in defence of the flag and to preserve the Union. Of this number several joined the Fifth New York Volunteers, while the remainder, about ninety, organized into a company which was known as Company A, Seventeenth New York Volunteers, and which was mustered into the United States service on the 20th of May, 1861, to serve two years, unless sooner discharged.

This company, which was the first to leave Yonkers for the seat of war, and was composed exclusively of Yonkers men, captured, at Hanover Court House, the first cannon taken by the Army of the Potomac. The company was mustered out of the United States service at the expiration of its term of enlistment, June 2, 1863. The majority of those mustered out re-enlisted and returned to the war. We append items, culled from various records, relating to this company.

The following is the record taken from the official archives of the War Department, and from the State card attached to the flags of the Seventeenth Regiment, New York Volunteers, at Albany, N. Y.:

"First.—National Flag, silk, embroidered with number of Regiment. Much worn. Spear-head gone. Presented to the Regiment by eight lady friends of Col. H. S. Lansing.

"Second.—Regimental Banner, white silk, painted on one side with arms of the State of New York, and Seventeenth Regiment New York Volunteers. On the other side, an eagle, shield, and number of Regiment. Staff, with plate inscribed: 'Presented to the Westchester Chasseurs by the ladies of Westchester County, May, 1861.'

"Third.—Regimental Banner, blue silk, painted with arms of the city of New York and inscribed: 'Seventeenth Regiment, N. Y. V. Presented by the City of New York.' Original staff gone."

The Seventeenth Regiment, sometimes known as the Westchester Chasseurs, was organized in the city of New York in the spring of 1861. It was composed of four companies from Westchester County, one from Rockland, two from New York City, one from Wayne, one from Wyoming, and one from Chenango. It left for the seat of war June, 1861, and participated in the siege of Yorktown, and battles of Hanover Court House, where it captured the first cannon taken from the enemy by the Army of the Potomac, Groveton (known as the second battle of Bull Run), where it lost thirteen officers and 250 men, killed and wounded, Antietam, Fredericksburg, and Chancellorsville.

It was mustered out in the spring of 1863 after two years' service, was immediately reorganized for three years' service, and took the field in September, being the first of the thirty-nine old regiments to report for duty.

"Honors of the Empire State in the War of the Rebellion," by Thomas S. Townsend, compiler of "The Library of National Records," on page 292, says:

"Seventeenth Regiment Westchester Chasseurs. The Regiment was commanded by Colonel H. S. Lansing, with Thomas F. Morris as Lieutenant-Colonel. When Lieutenant-Colonel Morris resigned in 1862, Nelson B. Bartram became his successor. The Seventeenth and a Massachusetts Regiment constituted the entire infantry force under General Stoneman on the Peninsula, when he made that hasty, timely and terrible march.

"At Hanover Court House, the Seventeenth took one of the enemy's guns. General Butterfield spoke of the splendid advance of the Brigade, led by the Seventeenth and Forty-fourth New York, at the battle of Groveton. At the battle of Bull Run, no less than four color-bearers lost their lives in defence of the flag; it was saved and rigged to a new staff; was returned to the Common Council of New York as a proof of the valor of the Regiment. The Regiment lost over 200 men at Bull Run out of 550 who went into the battle."

MUSTER-IN ROLL.

Officers.

CHARLES H. SMITH, Captain.
GEORGE REYNOLDS, Lieutenant, discharged on account of disability January 30, 1862.
ROMEYN BOGARDUS, Ensign, resigned August 8, 1861.
MARTIN SKULLY, First Sergeant, wounded August 30, 1862, at the battle of Bull Run, made Second Lieutenant.
JOHN C. COATES, Sergeant.
EDWIN JAMES, Sergeant.
BENJAMIN C. NODINE, Sergeant, wounded August 30, 1862.
EDWIN CUMBERBEACH, Corporal, made Sergeant.
JOHN NOLAN, Corporal.
ALFRED BOWLER, Corporal, made Sergeant.
WILLIAM J. TOWNSEND, Corporal.
JACOB A. GLAZIER, Musician.
RICHARD COOK, Musician, wounded August 30, 1862.

Privates.

AINSWORTH, JOHN, discharged on account of disability August 29, 1861.
AINSWORTH, JOSEPH, discharged on account of disability January 3, 1863.
AMSBY, MARION.
ARCHER, THOMAS O., discharged on account of disability September 20, 1861.
AVERY, WILLIAM.
BARCLAY, JOHN.
BELL, GEORGE.
BRAGG, WILLIAM.
BRAZIL, JAMES, died March 24, 1862.
BROMLEY, JAMES.
BROOKS, GEORGE.
BROWN, CHARLES A.
BURNS, JEREMIAH.
CAIN, MICHAEL, wounded August 30, 1862.
CARLL, JAMES, made Corporal.
CARROLL, WILLIAM, wounded.
CAVANAGH, THOMAS, discharged on account of disability November 11, 1861.
CAWLEY, THOMAS, wounded August 30, 1862; died September 29, 1862.
COLWELL, ATKINS.
CONNELL, WILLIAM, made Corporal; wounded August 30, 1862.
CONNELLY, THOMAS, killed August 30, 1862.
DELANY, DANIEL, killed August 30, 1862.
DONAHUE, JOHN, wounded August 30, 1862.
FISHER, PHILIP.
FLOOD, PETER, wounded August 30, 1862.
FOLKER, WILLIAM, wounded August 30, 1862.
FOSTER, JAMES W.
FOSTER, WILLIAM W., made Corporal; captured August 30, 1862.
GARVIN, FRANK, wounded August 30, 1862.
GLASIER, NEWCOMB B.
HAMPSON, ELI.
HAMPSON, SAMUEL.
HORTON, THERON R., wounded August 30, 1862.
KNOWLES, WILLIAM.
KOHLER, JOHN, wounded August 30, 1862.

Lawrence, Thomas O., wounded August 30, 1862.
Leary, John S.
Leek, Joseph.
Lesnon, Daniel.
Lobdell, Walter C.
Logue, Bernard.
Major, Garrett G., wounded June 30, 1862, and August 30, 1862.
Malloy, Thomas.
Marian, John.
McCabe, Dennis.
McCaul, Thomas.
McNamara, John.
Mills, Thomas.
Murphy, Cornelius, captured August 30, 1862.
Nodine, Edward.
Nodine, Peter, wounded August 30, 1862.
O'Keefe, Patrick, transferred July 1, 1862, to Company E.
O'Rourke, John, transferred July 16, 1862, to Company E.
O'Sullivan, Daniel, transferred July 16, 1862, to Company E.
Plunkett, John.
Rice, Joseph, transferred January 10, 1862, to Company D.
Satzger, Charles C., made Corporal.
Shotts, John C.
Simmonds, Edward.
Tansey, Matthew.
Terry, Thomas F.
Walter, William.
Watson, John, died July 20, 1863.
Welsh, Morris F., made Corporal; killed August 30, 1862.
Whiting, John B., made Corporal; captured August 30, 1862.

The following joined the Company after muster:

Andrews, Joseph.
Arbuckle, William.
Austin, James.
Beardsley, E. H., First Lieutenant.
Beckett, Thomas, Captain, wounded August 30, 1862.
Bell, George, No. 2.
Blauvelt, Isaac D., killed August 30, 1862.
Bowes, Benjamin, discharged on account of disability January 9, 1862.
Brady, Charles.
Bretenshaw, Joshua, wounded.
Brown, Joseph, transferred to Company G, One Hundred and Forty-Sixth Regiment, New York Infantry Volunteers.
Carny, Michael.
Clark, Abner H.
Clark, Peter, wounded August 30, 1862, aged 32.
Clark, Peter, wounded August 30, 1862, aged 20.
Coffey, Michael.
Cook, W. H., discharged on account of disability, May 30, 1862.
Costello, John.
Craft, Isaac, wounded December 16, 1862.
Cullin, Paul, died September 2, 1861.
Doran, John.
Fenner, Henry D., wounded August 30, 1862.
Ferguson, Thomas.
Fitch, C. Wigo, Com. Sergeant.
Foley, T. Vincent, Captain, twice wounded August 30, 1862.
Fox, James, Second Lieutenant.
Gallagher, Martin.
Hardy, John R.
Harrison, Bernard, wounded August 30, 1862.
Hill, Thomas, Sergeant.
Hughes, Patrick.
Irving, Arthur.
Ives, William, killed August 30, 1862.
Kemp, Joseph, wounded August 30, 1862.
Killeon, Daniel, made Sergeant.
McNamara, John, No. 2, made Corporal.
Mills, John, made Corporal.
Mitchell, Peter, captured at Manassas August 30, 1862.
Mitchell, Thomas, transferred to the Twelfth Regiment New York Volunteers, May 14, 1862. Died August 20, 1878.
Moffatt, Andrew, wounded August 30, 1862.

Murphy, William, transferred to Company G, One Hundred and Forty-Sixth Regiment New York Infantry Volunteers, June 25, 1863.
Neil, Walter B.
Nodine, Frederick A., Sergeant, transferred to Company G, One Hundred and Forty-Sixth Regiment New York Infantry Volunteers, June 2, 1863.
O'Mara, John, Sergeant.
Seddin, William, Musician.
Shaw, William.
Sleight, C. T.
Smith, Irving D., Second Lieutenant, transferred to Company F, Seventeenth Regiment New York Volunteers, January 1, 1863.
Stansfield, Thomas.
Taylor, De Witt.
Thompson, George W., transferred to One Hundred and Forty-Sixth Regiment New York Infantry Volunteers, March 8, 1863.
Van Orden, Alfred, transferred to Company G, One Hundred and Fortieth Regiment New York Infantry Volunteers, June 26, 1863.

Sixth New York Volunteer Artillery. In the summer of the year 1862, when the numerous reverses to the Union arms had caused a profound anxiety among the people of the North as to the outcome of the great conflict, in obedience to a call from the President of the United States for three hundred thousand volunteers for three years, the Hon. E. D. Morgan, Governor of the State of New York, appointed a Union Defence Committee for the Eighth Senatorial District of the State, then consisting of the counties of Westchester, Rockland and Putnam—the names of Lewis G. Morris, of Fordham, Chauncey M. Depew, of Peekskill, Gouverneur Morris, of Morrisania, William H. Robertson, of Katonah, Saxton Smith, of Putnam, and Edward F. Shonnard, of Yonkers, being among those so chosen.

This Committee was charged with the duty of obtaining reinforcements for the Union Army. It began its work by promptly effecting the organization in that district of an infantry regiment of ten full companies of more than one hundred men each, enlisted to serve for three years, which was designated by the authorities of the State of New York as the 135th New York Volunteer Infantry, and was named by the Committee, The Anthony Wayne Guard.

Those who thus associated themselves together in defence of the Union were prompted by the same true spirit of patriotism which animated their forefathers in the War of Independence. At that period in the war no large bounties had been offered to stimulate enlistment, and these men, who so promptly responded to the call of the President, fairly represented the best bone and sinew and many of the most substantial families of the three counties.

The following are the names of the original line officers and of the places where they organized their companies:

Company A, Peekskill: Captain A. A. Crookston, Lieutenants George W. Smith and Richard M. Gilleo.

Company B, White Plains: Captain E. W. Anderson, Lieutenants Thomas W. Dick and Horton R. Pratt.

Company C, West Farms: Captain B. B. Valentine, Lieutenants James Smith and George C. Kibbe.

Company D, Somers: Captain Edward Jones, Lieutenants W. S. Scribner and Platt Benedict.

Company E, Port Chester: Captain C. H. Palmer, Lieutenants W. T. Morse and Fordham Morris (son of Lewis G. Morris of the Committee).

Company F, Yonkers: Captain Edmund Y. Morris, Lieutenants Samuel Bassett and Henry A. Chadeayne.

Company G, Carmel: Captain Webster Smith, Lieutenants Stephen Baker and Charles F. Hazen.

Company H, Morrisania: Captain H. B. Hall (wounded), Lieutenants David Harmel (mortally wounded) and Gouverneur Morris, Jr. (son of Gouverneur Morris of the Committee).

Company I, Sing Sing: Captain Clark Peck, Lieutenants Charles C. Hyatt and J. H. Ashton.

Company K, Nyack: Captain Wilson Defendorf, Lieutenants John Davidson and Frederic Shonnard, of Yonkers (son of Edward F. Shonnard of the Committee).

THE YONKERS COMPANY. The following named non-commissioned officers and men, all of Yonkers, were mustered into the United States service in Company F, on September 2, 1862.

Officers.

THOMAS R. PRICE, First Sergeant.
PATRICK KELLY, Second Sergeant.
ABEL WATERS, Fourth Sergeant.
SAMUEL R. KNIFFEN, Fifth Sergeant.
JOHN J. BRADY, First Corporal.

JAMES T. EARLE, Second Corporal.
JAMES E. BEASLEY, Third Corporal, killed.
BENJAMIN PRICE, Fourth Corporal.
JUDSON ABBOTT, Fifth Corporal.
EDGAR C. NODINE, Sixth Corporal.

Privates.

ARCHER, NATHANIEL, killed.
BARNES, FREDERICK E., died in hospital.
BENNETT, MICHAEL.
BOYLE, JAMES.
BRAGG, WILLIAM, killed.
BROWN, JAMES.
BURKE, JAMES.
CAIN, JOSEPH, wounded.
CASEY, DANIEL.
CARROLL, JAMES.
COLLIN, PATRICK.
CONLIN, ANTHONY.
COUGHLIN, JOHN.
DONAHUE, MICHAEL.
FOLEY, JOHN.
FORMAN, SCHUYLER B.
GILBERT, JAMES D.
GOODWIN, FRANCIS.
GORMAN, PATRICK.
HALLETT, DEMETRIUS.
HAMILTON, WILLIAM, taken prisoner, died of wounds.
HARRIS, JACOB L.
HENRY, JOHN.
HUNT, JAMES.
KILEY, WILLIAM, killed.
KEANILY, JEREMIAH.
KELLY, TIMOTHY.
LANE, THOMAS, died of wounds.
LAPHAM, SOLON, wounded.
LAUNY, THOMAS.
LINDSAY, WILLIAM.
LOUNSBURY, PAUL.
McGANN, PHILIP, killed.
McMAHON, JOHN,
MORRIS, JOHN T.
NORRIS, MICHAEL.
O'DONNELL, JOHN.
O'ROURKE, MICHAEL, wounded.
PILSON, JAMES.
POPE, WILLIAM, dead.
REED, JAMES.
REIFF, JACOB.
REIN, GEORGE, wounded and died in prison.
RYAN, THOMAS.
SHERWOOD, JAMES E., died in prison of wounds.
SHERWOOD, RICHARD H.
SMITH, THOMAS A.
THOMPSON, WILLIAM, killed.
VAIL, WILLIAM.
VANDERVLANT, CORNELIUS.
VAN WART, STEPHEN.
VOLZ, GEORGE.
WATSON, WILLIAM.
WELSH, JAMES.
WELSH, RICHARD.
WHITLOCK, AARON, dead.

It is not now possible to give an accurate statement of the names of the killed, wounded, and missing, or even of all those who were members of this Company during these three years' service. Almost to the time of the muster no permanent field officers were chosen, but, pending their appointment, Lewis G. Morris, of the Committee, acted as the provisional colonel.

The experiences of actual war having demonstrated the necessity for having either thoroughly educated or veteran soldiers as field officers of volunteer regiments, the colonelcy was offered to Thomas Arden, of Cold Spring, a graduate of West Point. Upon his declination, the position was tendered to, and accepted by, Captain William Hopkins Morris, also a graduate of West Point, and an officer then in active service in the Army of the Potomac, as chief of staff to Major-General John J. Peck.

Captain Ralph E. Prime, then of White Plains, now of Yonkers, a gallant officer of the Fifth New York Volunteers, who had been wounded in one of the battles on the Peninsula under McClellan, was appointed its lieutenant-colonel. Captain Prime being unable to immediately secure his transfer from the War Department, J. Howard Kitching, of Dobb's Ferry, a brilliant young officer in the Second New York Light Artillery, who had also been wounded on the Peninsula, was made the acting lieutenant-colonel, until Captain Prime could obtain his transfer.

Captain Prime soon after resigned the position, and J. Howard Kitching became the actual lieutenant-colonel, and a few months later, after the promotion of Colonel Morris to the rank of brigadier-general, he became the colonel of the regiment, and, either as its colonel or the commander of the brigade of which it formed a part, he led it in all of the battles in which it was engaged up to and including Cedar Creek, where he received a wound which proved fatal.

J. H. Robinson, of New York City, was chosen the major, but resigned after a few weeks' service. Charles H. Leonard, of Rockland, was appointed adjutant, Frederick Tompkins, also of Rockland, the quartermaster, and Jared G. Wood, M.D., of Brewsters, surgeon.

The regiment was first assembled in Yonkers on or about August 29, 1862, in the old building on the river bank south of the railroad station, then known as the Bedstead Factory, but now as part of the Plough Works. The first dress-parade took place in the open fields then existing south of the old Pistol Factory, now known as the Carpet and Hat Works of the John T. Waring Company. The regiment was not then fully uniformed, and was without arms or other equipments, except that it had received a full stand of National and State colors, which was then for the first time unfurled.

Captain William H. Morris was on that occasion, presented to the regiment as its colonel by Lewis G. Morris in a brief address, which eloquently expressed the Committee's appreciation of the great responsibility resting upon it in the choice of the field officers, and the great care taken in the selections which had been made. He then gracefully touched upon the salient features of the brilliant career of Captain Morris, and closed by warmly commending him to the confidence of the regiment.

Colonel Morris made a soldierly reply, expressing his pride and pleasure in being permitted to command a regiment composed of his life-long neighbors and friends, closing with the announcement that the mustering officers would arrive on September 2d, and that after the formalities of the muster into the service of the United States, the regiment was expected to proceed immediately to the seat of war—an announcement that was received with cheers.

After the ceremonies of the muster by Captain W. S. Edgerton, United States Army, in the presence of Chauncey M. Depew and Lewis G. Morris, of the Union Defence Committee, the command was embarked upon a barge, taken to Perth Amboy, and thence by rail by way of Philadelphia to Baltimore, where it was ordered to report to Major-General Wool. It was a period of intense excitement, because of the misfortunes to the Union arms and the then approaching invasion of the North by the Rebel army. Philadelphia itself had been shocked by the close approach to its suburbs of a band of Rebel rough-riders, who had safely ridden around the city of Baltimore, flanking our forces stationed there, and had made vigorous attempts to destroy the railroad bridges between Baltimore and Philadelphia.

JAMES B. ODELL.

Few such scenes were ever witnessed in any northern city during the war as those participated in by this regiment and the other bodies of troops marching through the city at that exciting period. The streets through which they passed from the New York to the Baltimore depots were crowded with people of all ages and conditions, all in a state of frantic excitement, vying one with another in eager effort to swell the grand proportions of the welcoming ovation.

At Baltimore the regiment was assigned by Major-General Wool to a camp of instruction, where, under Colonel Morris's masterly handling, ably assisted by Lieutenant-Colonel Kitching and the other officers, it made such rapid progress in its military duties that General Wool made public mention of "its soldierly bearing and its proficiency in drill and discipline," and upon his recommendation the War Department raised it to the artillery service, and designated it the Sixth New York Volunteer Artillery. A third battalion and two additional company organizations were added, viz.:

Company L, Cold Spring: Captain A. B. TRUESDELL, Lieutenants GEORGE D. SPENCER and WILLIAM G. FERRIS.

Company M, Elmira: Captain MIAL R. PIERCE, Lieutenants JAMES T. PRICE and C. B. ROBINSON. This company did not, however, join the regiment until early in the spring of 1864.

The regiment, although wearing the red trimmings of the artillery service and having the peculiar organization of that branch, nevertheless during its whole three years of arduous service with the Eighth

Corps, with the Army of the Potomac, with the Army of the James, and with Sheridan's Army of the Shenandoah, continued to serve as Infantry.

On and after December 26, 1862, the regiment was sent to Harper's Ferry, in detachments, upon the receipt by Major-General Schenck, who had in the meantime succeeded General Wool in the command of the Eighth Army Corps, of the following dispatch:

"WAR DEPARTMENT, WASHINGTON,
December 26, 1862.
"MAJOR-GENERAL SCHENCK,
Baltimore, Md.:
"You must defend Harper's Ferry with your command. If necessary, concentrate your forces there. Almost everything available about Washington has been sent to General Burnside. Keep me advised of the enemy's movements.
"H. W. HALLECK,
"*General-in-Chief.*"

After six months or more of very varied service in the Shenandoah Valley with other troops, guarding the Baltimore and Ohio Railroad, performing skirmishing, scouting, and general outpost duties, the regiment formally joined the Army of the Potomac during the Gettysburgh campaign, becoming part of French's Third Corps, which was held in the neighborhood of Frederick City as a reserve to protect Washington, by the orders of the War Department.

The regiment, first with General Morris's Brigade of the Third Division, Third Army Corps, then with the reserve artillery, and afterwards with Ayres's Division of the Fifth Corps, participated in all the campaigns of the Army of the Potomac, from Gettysburg, in July, 1863, to August 13, 1864, in the siege of Petersburg, including the Bristoe Station, the Mine Run, and the great Grant campaigns, and has probably the unique record of having served in battle with every corps of the Army of the Potomac, with Sheridan's Army in the Shenandoah, and with the Army of the James. The following is a list of its more important engagements with the enemy:

THE SOLDIERS' MONUMENT AND ENCLOSURE.

"WITH THE ARMY OF THE POTOMAC.—Wapping Heights, July 23, 1863. The Grant campaign—Wilderness, May 5, 6 and 7, 1864; Spottsylvania, May 8, 9, 10, 11 and 12, 1864. Lieutenant-Colonel W. F. Fox, in his work entitled 'Regimental Losses in the Civil War,' states that the regiment was one of thirty-four regiments at the same time engaged which suffered the heaviest losses of any in the Army of the Potomac on those days. Harris Farm, Spottsylvania, May 19, 1864. In recognition of the services of the troops engaged on this occasion, the following order was issued:

"HEADQUARTERS ARMY OF THE POTOMAC,
"May 20, 1864, 8 A.M.
"The Major-General Commanding desires to express his satisfaction with the good conduct of Tyler's Division and Kitching's Brigade [this Brigade consisted of two regiments, the Sixth and the Fifteenth New York Artillery, both acting as Infantry] of Heavy Artillery, in the affair of yesterday evening. The gallant manner in which those commands, the greater portion being for the first time under fire, met and checked the persistent attacks of a Corps of the enemy led by one of its ablest Generals, justifies the Commanding General in the special commendation of troops who henceforth will be relied upon, as were the tried veterans of the Second and Fifth Corps, at the same time engaged.
"By command of MAJOR-GENERAL MEADE,
"S. S. WILLIAMS."

"Battles at the Ford of the North Anna River, May 23, 24, 25, 26 and 27. In these battles the Sixth Artillery lost more in killed and wounded than any other regiment in the Army of the Potomac at the same time engaged. (*Vide* 'Regimental Losses in the Civil War.') Bethesda Church, May 30."

The New York *Herald* of June 1 said, in reference to one of these battles: "A despatch from the Army of the Potomac, dated on Tuesday night, says that the day before the Fifth Corps, advancing from the Hawe's Store toward Bethesda Church, drove the enemy about two miles. At sunset, while the men were engaged in digging rifle-pits, Rhodes's and Early's Divisions made an attack on Warren's right flank, causing him to fall back from his first line. The enemy then advanced and charged the second line. Kitching's Brigade of Heavy Artillery was posted there, and opened a heavy fire in conjunction with batteries on both flanks, which nearly demolished the Rebel column of attack. The enemy fell back in terrible disorder, and left their dead and wounded on the field."

"Mechanicsville Pike, June 1; Mechanicsville Pike (second position), June 2; battle of Cold Harbor, June 3; Chickahominy, near Long Bridge, June 13; assault on Petersburg, June 18; more or less continuously engaged during June 19, 20, 21, 22, 23, 24 and 25, 1864; siege of Petersburg, June 23 to August 13, 1864, including the Mine Explosion on July 30, 1864."

"WITH GENERAL SHERIDAN'S ARMY IN THE SHENANDOAH VALLEY.—Battle of Cedar Creek, near Winchester, October 14, 1864. J. Howard Kitching, the beloved Colonel of the Regiment, here received a wound which caused his death; Major Jones and Lieutenant Raspberry were killed; and the command of the regiment devolved upon Major George C. Kibbe, a gallant and efficient officer."

THE TOP STONE.
STATUE OF THE COLOR-BEARER.

"WITH THE ARMY OF THE JAMES.—Defences of Bermuda Hundred; sharp engagement, January 22, 1865; repelled assault, January 24; repelled assault on picket-line, February 13, 1865."

Lieutenant-Colonel George C. Kibbe, who had ably and gallantly commanded the regiment since Colonel J. Howard Kitching was wounded, was commissioned colonel March 17, 1865. The last time the regiment was under fire was in a brief engagement at Bermuda Hundred, April 2, 1865.

The original members of the 135th Regiment New York Volunteer Infantry were mustered out of the United States service June 27, 1865. The remainder, with a battalion of the Tenth New York Artillery, became the consolidated Sixth New York Artillery, of which Lieutenant-Colonel Stephen Baker, of the Sixth Artillery, was chosen colonel, on account of brave and meritorious services, and was mustered out July 13, 1865, after having done general provost-marshal duty about Petersburg subsequent to the surrender of Lee.

The following letter was received from Colonel Wm. F. Fox, author of the famous work entitled "Regimental Losses in the Civil War," acknowledging a mistake in his treatment of the record of the Sixth New York Artillery, by which the regiment was omitted from the list of his selected "Three Hundred Fighting Regiments," a position to which it was entitled by "the trail of blood."

AUGUST 1, 1891.

"MAJOR FREDERIC SHONNARD,
"Yonkers, N. Y.:

"*Dear Sir:* In reply I would say that there is no question but that your old regiment, the Sixth Artillery, was a fighting regiment in every sense of the word and I am fully aware of its heroic record. Another edition of the work is to be published soon, in which the omission will be rectified. . . .
"Yours fraternally,
"WILLIAM F. FOX."

The following extract from the report of Brigadier-General Henry J. Hunt, chief of artillery, Army of the Potomac, dated October 31, 1864, in which the regiment is honorably mentioned, will be of interest:

"The Reserve Artillery, May 4, 1864, under the command of Colonel H. S. Burton, Fifth United States Artillery, consisted of two regiments of Foot Artillery—the Sixth New York, Colonel J. Howard Kitching; the Fifteenth New York, Colonel L. Schirmer—twelve batteries of field artillery, twenty-six Napoleons, eighteen 3-inch, twelve 10-pounder, and six 20-pounder Parrotts, and eight 24-pounder Coehorn mortars. The troops of the reserve were organized into three brigades. The first, under the command of Colonel J. Howard Kitching, Sixth New York Artillery, consisted of the Sixth and Fifteenth New York Regiments, six battalions of Foot Artillery armed as Infantry, eighty-four officers, and 2,901 men. This brigade formed the escort and furnished the guards for the reserve and the park attached to it, and was at all times disposable as a reserve and to reinforce the corps in battle. In this way it did valuable service, taking its full share of the marching and fighting of the army in addition to its special duties.

"That afternoon (the 7th), the Reserve Artillery marched to Piney Branch Church, which place it reached on the morning of the 8th, when Kitching's Brigade of Foot Artillery was ordered to report to Major-General Hancock, at Todd's Tavern. General Hancock ordered it back to the reserve the same

ON THE EAST SIDE.
THE INFANTRY STATUE.

night, and again called for it the next morning. From this time this brigade was marched to and fro from one corps to another, being either always in action or on the march, until it was finally, on the breaking up of the reserve, attached to the Fifth Corps, Major-General Warren."

The survivors of this brave regiment, the members of which so signally distinguished themselves by their patriotic promptness in leaving their homes to risk their lives in defence of the Government, and in their conduct on many hard-fought battlefields of the war, again made manifest their sterling qualities as men, and their patriotism as citizens, by their orderly return to the avocations of peace.

On September 2, 1890, the twenty-fifth anniversary of the muster-in to the United States service, the first reunion of the regiment was held in Turn Hall, Yonkers. Over three hundred survivors attended, clasped hands for the first time in a quarter of a century, made speeches, sang songs, laughed, cried, cheered, and embraced each other around the supper-table, after having organized themselves into a society entitled The Fraternity of the Survivors of the Sixth New York Volunteer Artillery, and elected the following officers:

FREDERIC SHONNARD, President, late Major U. S. V.
GEORGE C. KIBBE, First Vice-President, late Colonel U. S. V.
STEPHEN BAKER, Second Vice-President, late Colonel U. S. V.
HENRY B. HALL, Third Vice-President, late Captain and Brevet Major U. S. V.
WILLIAM H. MORRIS, Fourth Vice-President, late Brigadier-General and Brevet Major-General U. S. V.
J. B. EAKINS, Treasurer, late Sergeant U. S. V.
JOHN SMITH, JR., Secretary, late Lieutenant U. S. V.
JOHN FORSYTH, Resident Secretary, late Sergeant U. S. V.
SAMUEL BASSETT, Corresponding Secretary, late Captain U. S. V.

THE THIRTY-DAYS' MEN. On the 8th day of July, 1863, the thirty-days' men, enlisted by John Davis Hatch, were mustered into the service of the United States, at Yonkers, and did valiant service at Fort McHenry, Baltimore, Maryland. Their full official designation was Company H, Seventeenth Regiment, National Guard, State New York. The following names are copied from the muster-in roll:

Officers.

JOHN DAVIS HATCH, Captain.
JAMES STEWART, Second Lieutenant.
EDWARD P. ROBBINS, First Sergeant.
STEPHEN R. STRUTHERS, Second Sergeant.
JOHN MCCLAIN, Third Sergeant.
WALTER H. PADDOCK, Fourth Sergeant.
ROBERT A. GETTY, First Corporal.
CONWAY PILSON, Second Corporal.
JOSIAH RICH, JR., Third Corporal.
WILLIAM MACFARLANE, Fourth Corporal.
JOHN CAHILL, Musician.
JAMES KENNEDY, Musician.

Privates.

ADAMS, CHARLES H.
ARCHER, SAMUEL.
ARCHER, WILLIAM S.
BAIRD, EDWARD P.
BAIRD, WILLIAM C.
BASHFORD, JAMES, JR.
BEALE, WILLIAM R.
BELKNAP, ETHELBERT.
BELL, ALONZO.
BLAUVELT, DANIEL, JR.
BROWN, JAMES H. B.
BROWN, HAVILAND S.
CAMPBELL, JOHN C.
CAMPBELL, JOHN C., JR.
CHAMBERLAIN, GEORGE.
CHAMBERLAIN, ISAAC E.
COEN, THOMAS F.

COEN, JOHN J.
EICKEMEYER, RUDOLF.
FISHER, PHILIP W.
FRISBIE, GEORGE H.
GARRISON, GEORGE O.
HAIGHT, HENRY.
HALEY, THOMAS H.
JENLEY, JOHN W.
MORRISON, DAVID M.
MURPHY, JOHN.
ODELL, JAMES B.
OTIS, CHARLES R.
PORTER, WILLIAM B.
POST, JAMES V.
PROSEUS, JOSEPH L.
RADCLIFF, ABRAM S.

REDDING, JOHN F.
RICE, BENJAMIN.
SAWYER, BENJAMIN F., JR.
SAWYER, HENRY C.
SILKE, FREEMAN J.
SMITH, SAMUEL L.
THAYER, STEPHEN H., JR.
THOMSON, WILLIAM.
TINDALL, RICHARD B.
TYLER, EDWARD H.
VON STORCH, HENRY F.
WARD, JAMES.
WARING, OSCAR.
WILCOX, RICHARD E.
WILSEA, JAMES P.
WOODWORTH, JAMES G.

CAPTAIN PADDEN'S COMPANY. On the 4th of June, 1864, the thirty-days' men enlisted by John W. Padden, were mustered into the service of the United States, at Yonkers, and marched the same day over historic ground on Valentine's Hill, to the village of Mount Vernon, where they found transportation to Mamaroneck, at which place they joined their regiment. Their full official designation was Company B, Fifteenth Regiment, Sixth Brigade, National Guard, State New York Volunteers. On Sunday morning, June 5, 1864, the Fifteenth Regiment sailed on a Government transport to Fort Richmond, New York Harbor, returning home July 6th, the same year. The following names are copied from the muster-in roll:

Officers.

JOHN W. PADDEN, Captain.
A. J. WILLARD, First Lieutenant.
CLEMENT T. DURGIN, Second Lieutenant.
GEORGE W. BROWN, First Sergeant.
CHARLES A. CHAPIN, Second Sergeant.
ROBERT B. CANTRELL, Third Sergeant.
JAMES EDIE, Fourth Sergeant.
WILLIAM R. HINDALS, Fifth Sergeant.

JAMES KEELER, First Corporal.
ALFRED M. BOWLER, Second Corporal.
RICHARD EDIE, Third Corporal.
JAMES GAFFNEY, Fourth Corporal.
GEORGE C. POST, Fifth Corporal.
MARK SPENCER, Sixth Corporal.
JOSEPH A. GEORGE, Seventh Corporal.
ALBERT JOHNSON, Eighth Corporal.

Privates.

ARCHER, CHARLES E.
BAKER, JAMES M.
BRADY, MICHAEL.
BROWN, CALEB V.
CAHILL, JOHN.
CARY, PATRICK.
CASHAN, JAMES.
CHAMBERLAIN, CHARLES W.
CHAMPNEY, EDWARD.
COEN, JOHN.
COON, JOHN W.
CRANE, JOHN.
CROWTHER, TIMOTHY.
DALY, MICHAEL.
DALY, THOMAS F.
DALY, THOMAS J.
DANKS, ELI L.
DONOHUE, CHARLES.
DOOLEY, JOHN.
DOOLUCKTY, JOHN.
DOUGHERTY, JOHN.
ELLOR, JOSEPH.
FISHER, CHARLES R.

FISHER, PHILIP.
FISHER, WILLIAM H.
FRANCIS, KELLOGG.
GARRY, MICHAEL.
GORMAN, JOHN.
GRAHAM, JOHN.
GREITZ, FREDERICK.
GRUNSBRALL, HENRY.
GUION, WILLIAM M.
HALLIHAN, JOHN.
HAMPSON, THOMAS.
JOHNSON, CHARLES L.
JORDAN, THOMAS.
KENNEDY, JAMES.
KERNAN, JAMES.
LAWRENCE, CHARLES.
LAWRENCE, THOMAS C.
LIMBERT, BENJAMIN.
MARSHALL, JOHN.
MCCREADY, THOMAS.
MILLER, FRANKLYN.
MILLS, JOSEPH.

MITCHELL, BENJAMIN.
MOODY, ROBERT.
MORGAN, HENRY D.
MYERS, HENRY S.
PARKINSON, GEORGE N.
PETHIC, CHARLES.
POST, CHARLES J.
POST, SAMUEL.
REGAN, MICHAEL.
RYAN, THOMAS.
SCHNEIDER, FREDERICK.
SIMMONDS, GEORGE.
SIMMONS, WILLIAM.
SMITH, WILLIAM.
STEPHENS, GEORGE.
STEVENS, EDWARD.
TANSEY, ROGER.
TRACY, PATRICK.
VAN TASSELL, S. C.
WILSEA, JAMES P.
WING, MICHAEL.
WOODRUFF, FREDERICK H.

THE HOME GUARDS. During the draft riots in New York, in July, 1863, the lawless spirit reached Yonkers. A company of roughs from below approached Kingsbridge, with the intention, it was rumored, of capturing the Starr Arms Company's stock, in the building now occupied by the John T. Waring Manufacturing Company. Another rumor was that the Croton Aqueduct was to be tapped. There were indications of trouble among the quarrymen at Tuckahoe, and avowed sympathy for the rioters in New York, who were in open rebellion against the laws, destroying private property and assaulting, and even murdering, inoffensive people. The militia organization had gone to the front to meet an emergency, while large numbers of the heads of families were in the army battling to save the Union. It is not strange that, under such circumstances, a general feeling of uneasiness was experienced.

A meeting was held in the store of Acker, Edgar & Co., which resulted in the organization of the Home Guards, to preserve the peace and protect persons and property. Dr. Henry M. Baird gives the following account of the Guards and their work:

"Judge Atkins is correct in his impression that I acted with the Home Guards in the summer of 1863. I fear my services were of no great account, and, indeed, the services of the entire Guards did not amount to much more than to give a little courage to a somewhat despondent community. It was during the time of the 'draft riots' in New York, which had cut off all communication by rail with the metropolis. There were distinct rumors of a probable invasion of Yonkers by men from the marble-quarries near Tuckahoe who were expected to come in quest of pillage, taking advantage of the absence of our Company, then posted on Federal Hill, Baltimore. My brothers, Edward and William, were with the Company.

"To meet the emergency a goodly number of us met and drilled, using Farrington Hall, situated where Radford Building now is, as our headquarters. I remember that as a rule we were on duty upon alternate nights.

"One night a party of us, armed, patrolled the district near the Railroad Depot, where there were several engines brought up from New York, to get them out of harm's way. Another night half a dozen of us, under command of Judge Atkins, slept in the unfinished stable on the present property of Mr. William Allen Butler, at Palisade Avenue and High Street, and repeatedly, during the night, sent out parties of two or more to visit Hog Hill, and see that all was quiet there.

"Another night, Mr. William C. Waring, Sr., and I spent in the tower of the First Presbyterian Church, taking turns in watching for the signal we might receive to ring the great bell as an alarm to call out all good citizens. The watchword had been given us in all secrecy, and it was arranged that, should the messenger from headquarters be unable to reach us, we should accept the word shouted to us from the opposite side of the street as a sufficient warrant for action."

The Home Guards were sworn as special constables. They were divided into four companies, and numbered over three hundred and fifty men. Everett Clapp, then President of the village, was active in organizing the force, and supplied them with carbines from the Starr Arms Company. Lyman Cobb, Jr., acted as Secretary, Thomas F. Morris was Commander, and Gardner P. Haws was Adjutant.

Company A: Captain WILLIAM MONTGOMERY, Lieutenants FREDERICK C. OAKLEY and T. A. ATKINS.
Company B: Captain EDGAR LOGAN, Lieutenants J. W. PADDON and H. A. BROWNELL.
Company C: Captain HENRY A. CHADEAYNE, Lieutenants WIGO FITCH and B. F. BUNKER.
Company D: Captain SYLVANUS MAYO, Lieutenants A. J. WILLARD and T. HILL.

ON THE WEST SIDE.
THE NAVAL STATUE.

A general order, issued by President Clapp, designated that Company A should meet weekly at the armory in Farrington Hall, for drill, on Monday evening at eight o'clock, Company B on Wednesday evening, Company C on Thursday evening, and Company D on Saturday evening.

At a meeting of the force held July 22, 1863, the object was declared to be: When called upon by the village authorities to protect property and preserve the peace; to execute all lawful orders issued by the village authorities; to protect and uphold all well-disposed persons who may be threatened with coercion or spoliation by reason of their refusing to join riotous assemblages.

On the arrival of the carbines at the armory, President Clapp put them in charge of Lyman Cobb, Jr., gave him the password, and ordered him to watch over them until relieved, which would be in the course of an hour or so. In the excitement of the time the promised relief was forgotten. On visiting the armory next morning, President Clapp found Mr. Cobb still on guard. "You here yet!" was the exclamation. "I have obeyed orders," replied Mr. Cobb. "Well," said the President, "you are a good soldier." Explanations followed, and the circumstances caused much merriment.

In addition to the Home Guards, a large force of employees was organized to protect the Starr Arms Company's property, and that force was well equipped with cannon, guns, pistols, etc., for effective service in case of attack. It seems altogether probable that these precautions prevented trouble that might have resulted in the loss of life and property.

"It may be said," remarked one of the Guards, "that the entire body was an awkward squad, and the drills afforded much amusement. The corporations of some were of aldermanic proportions, yet it was insisted that they should line front and rear. Many could not keep step —and when commanded to step off with the left foot, they would start off with the right. To see the Guards go through the manual of arms was truly a comical sight. Still the Home Guards served a very useful purpose."

BENJAMIN F. SAWYER, JR.

Frederick S. Cozzens declared that it was the duty of the Guards to defend the village at all hazards, and not to leave it except in case of invasion by the enemy—and then, to get out on the double-quick.

It is related that two of the Guards, out on patrol duty on North Broadway one night, saw a man with a bundle enter a barn under what they considered suspicious circumstances. On capturing him he proved to be a German, who declared, and no doubt truthfully, that his only object in entering the barn was to seek shelter for the night. However, the prisoner was taken to headquarters and locked up. Next morning he was taken before the "Court Martial." A Judge-Advocate was on hand to prosecute, and the Court mercifully assigned counsel to defend the prisoner's "liberty and life." He was searched, and two matches were found in one of his pockets.

"There!" shouted the Judge-Advocate, with startling emphasis. "What more do you want? Do not those matches afford conclusive evidence that this person intended to fire the barn and blow up Yonkers?"

The prisoner's counsel was earnest and eloquent in the defense of his trembling client—but all to no purpose. The Court found him guilty, and sentenced him to be shot.

"Mein Got!" exclaimed the frightened German. "I lef' New York to keep from bein' murdered—and I fin' you vos verse up here dan dey vos down dere!" His life was spared.

We have been unable to find the rosters of the Home Guards, but it is believed that the following gentlemen were among those who united with their fellow-citizens to protect Yonkers at a critical period:

HENRY F. VON STORCH.

ACKERMAN, JAMES.
ACKERMAN, WILLIAM G.
ACKERT, NELSON.
ANDERSON, WILLIAM H.
ARCHIBALD, WILLIAM.

ATKINS, T. ASTLEY.
BAIRD, HENRY M.
BALDWIN, ANSON.

BARNES, REUBEN.
BARRY, SAMUEL S.
BASHFORD, JAMES.

BELKNAP, CHARLES.
BILLS, ORRIN A.
BREWER, REV. DARIUS R.
BROWN, HENRY.
BURNS, JEREMIAH.
CHADEAYNE, CHARLES L.
CLAPP, EVERETT.

DEVOE, HENRY F.
DEYO, PHILIP A.
DINSMORE, SAMUEL.
DINSMORE, LUTHER.
DORAN, WALTER A.
DOTY, WILLIAM H.
DOUGLASS, ROBERT J.

FARRINGTON, THOMAS O.
FLAGG, ETHAN.
FOOTE, WILLIAM C.
FRANCIS, GEORGE W.
FRANCIS, KELLOGG.
GARRISON, HYATT L.
GETTY, ROBERT P.
GETTY, S. EMMETT.
HAWKINS, JOSEPH W.
HAWS, GARDNER.
HOBBS, JOHN.
JENKINS, DR. J. FOSTER.
KEELER, ALBERT.
KNOX, ISAAC H.
LAWRENCE, JUSTUS.
LAWRENCE, WILLIAM H.
MAJOR, WILLIAM.
MASON, JOHN M.
MERCER, CHARLES T.
MONTGOMERY, WILLIAM.
MOTT, WILLIAM R.
NEVILLE, ROBERT.
OLMSTED, JOHN.
OTIS, E. G.
PAGAN, JOHN.
PEENE, JOSEPH.
PERRY, SAFFORD G.
PILSON, CONWAY.
QUICK, S. FRANCIS.
RADCLIFF, PETER E.
READ, JACOB.
ROBBINS, JEREMIAH.
SANDERS, JAMES P.
SCRIVEN, JAMES.
SHIPMAN, RALPH.
SHONNARD, EDWARD F.
SKINNER, GEORGE B.
SPEEDLING, ALONZO.
STARR, BENJAMIN A.
STARR, CHARLES.
STEWART, DAVID.
STEWART, GEORGE.
STOUT, THEODORE B.
UNDERHILL, EDWARD.
UPHAM, DR. GEORGE B.
VAIL, JONATHAN.
VALENTINE, JAMES M.
VON STORCH, HENRY F.
WARING, WILLIAM C.
WARING, CHARLES E.
WARING, JARVIS.
WARING, JOHN T.
WELLS, LEMUEL.
WOODWORTH, W. W.
YOUMANS, JAMES.

ON THE NORTH SIDE.
THE ARTILLERY STATUE.

CLARK, S. M.
CLEVELAND, CYRUS.
COFFEY, JOHN J.
COLEMAN, WILLIAM T.
CONDON, L. R.
CURRAN, HUGH.
CUTHELL, THOMAS H.

DRUMMOND, WILLIAM P.
EAST, JOHN A.
EDGAR, WILLIAM B.
ELTING, E. J.
EMBREE, JOHN.
EMBREE, ROBERT.

AT THE CLOSE OF THE WAR. From the acceptance of the Village Charter to the close of the Rebellion —ten years, six years of peace, four years of war—was an eventful decade for the little hamlet strung along the banks of the Nepperhan. In these years healthful progress was made, and foundations securely laid whereon have been built the superstructures of the present day.

Many questions there were to be settled, and willing hearts and hands to settle them. The form of government temporarily settled, there quickly arose the potent question as to who should fill the offices, who administer the law. Great strifes there were in those eventful days. There were burning questions as to the roads, the police, the schools, and taxes, and after the war opened there were added the mighty questions of the draft, the substitute, and the bounty. Fierce were the debates in the Getty Lyceum over the town-bonding for bounties to substitutes. Scarcely less fierce were the contests for town supervisor in those sad days of the war, so important were his duties.

Amid the clamor of popular strife, and despite the convulsions of the nation, this little village grew rapidly. Restless and impatient, it still knocked at Mr. Shonnard's gate on the north and Mr. Ludlow's on the south. It was bursting its bonds.

At the close of the war the place had assumed an appearance not unlike that of the present day. At the north end of the village many handsome places had been laid out and built upon. Along the Hudson most of the valuable sites had been taken up and improved. The Flats and the Hill had assumed the appearance which remains to the present day. Along the Nepperhan, once so pure, the mill and factory had come to stay, and make odorous the stream with their filth, and color it with their dyes.

A few streets, or parts of streets, had been opened, and the old roads slightly improved. A better class of buildings was fast taking the place of those small frame structures which always mark a new settlement.

Added to these changes, a new race of men had arrived within our borders, and was fast driving out of power the men of the famous village election contest of ten years before. These newcomers brought with them more progressive ideas and much available capital. Along with these, and chiefly owing to the great demand for labor, came a rougher lot, some very good, some utterly bad, the mass chiefly indifferent.

At this date the ancient town of Yonkers had not been dismembered, and still reached from the Spuyten Duyvil Creek, on the south, to the Greenburgh town line, on the north; while the Bronx chiefly formed its eastern boundary, and the Hudson its western. Around the foundry at Spuyten Duyvil, and again at Riverdale, the population clustered, but north and east of the village

ON THE SOUTH SIDE.
THE CAVALRY STATUE.

line the township was yet in farm-land. Along the Nepperhan, the Bronx, the Sprain and Grassy Sprain, and Tibbet's Brook, were farms and farmers pure and simple, even at this late date. Here and there, upon the old Post-road, north and south of the village line, were the more pretentious villas of the wealthier classes.

The town roads had not increased much in numbers of late years, and they were not models of road-making by any means, being kept up after the ancient method of scooping up dirt from the sides of the road to dump it on the middle. Within the village lines the ways were better kept, but the practice of macadamizing them was not then in vogue. It is but a short time back to mud roads, both in village and township, poor as the improved highways of Yonkers are considered now.

Yonkers to all outward appearance was not affected by the war. For all that the people personally knew of it, it might as well have been in Asia, so remote were its effects. But statistics show that it had a solid share in putting down the Rebellion. It is said that forty men of Yonkers enlisted in the Mozart Regiment, and 135 in the Sixth New York Heavy Artillery; but this is far short of the total of Yonkers enlistment, for one authority says that Yonkers enlisted 254 men in army and navy. We find reported seventeen deaths among our soldiers, of whom eight are reported as buried at Yonkers. All of these figures are far short of the terrible reality. Many of the ordinary items of information are likewise statistically cramped, but they are the best that are to be obtained.

The census of 1865 gives the town a population of over 12,000, and the village nearly 9,000. In the year 1800 the census gave Yonkers 1,176 inhabitants.

A Gazetteer says that "Yonkers, pronounced Yonk'-erz, had 33 stone houses, 194 brick, and 1,328 frame houses," in 1865, and that "a considerable amount of manufactures is carried on at Yonkers and on the Spuyten Duyvil Creek." "It contains 9 churches, several private seminaries, a bank and 3 newspaper offices." This is not exact, but it is near enough for a general Gazetteer. If we add a bank, several churches, a number of mills, a considerable number of both people and houses, and say that Yonkers furnished about 1,000 men for the war, we shall probably come nearer the truth. As to the sinews of war, we paid one quarter of the whole County Special Income Tax, and in all other war contributions were not behind other towns.

We find in the census reports of that year—at the close of the war—such notes as these: "At least nine-tenths of those who reported answers speak cheerfully of the change which the war has brought upon the social condition of the people and the future prospects of the country." Two providential seasons of extraordinary abundance are noted as tending "to restore prosperity and happiness." An increase of expenditure among the people is also noted, and a marked improvement in the condition of the poor. Speaking concerning the soldiers, the historian of that year notes that "much the greater portion quietly returned to the avocations of civil life with an industry in no degree impaired by their recent life in the field." All of which applied to the town of Yonkers at that date.

The year 1865 opened amid much uncertainty and many misgivings as to the future. The people of the town and village of Yonkers were thoroughly tired of the war, as, indeed, were the inhabitants of all the towns of the county. Every one hoped and prayed for peace. On every side now was evidence of this feeling. In February there happened an event which brought the subject anew and sadly to our hearthstones.

The Government had ordered a heavy draft of men. The new quota of Yonkers was 106 of her sons. At Tarrytown the terrible wheel was set turning with 1,528 Yonkers names therein—212 names were drawn. At so late a date, after so many sacrifices on their part, the good people of Yonkers felt the weight of this call, and additional prayers went heavenward that the cruel war might soon be over.

As the weeks wore on into months, and the prospects of peace increased, a more joyous sense prevailed. With other towns Yonkers rejoiced at the downfall of the Confederacy.

A Yonkers journal, of April 8, 1865, said concerning the victory that, "On receipt of the news of the fall of Richmond, at Yonkers, on Monday afternoon last, there was a general rejoicing among the people, which found vent in various ways." In the evening groups of people gathered on the corners or about Getty Square to talk over the events of the war. Cannon thundered forth a joyous salute, and sundry impromptu exhibitions of fire-works were made. The village fathers held a meeting the same evening, and resolved:

"That this Board recommend that the citizens of this village join in celebrating the fall of Richmond, by an illumination of their dwellings, on Thursday evening of this week."

It is chronicled of that eventful Thursday evening, that "Yonkers shone forth amid a perfect blaze of light. The scene from the river was one of enchanting beauty. Music, roar of cannon, and display of fire-works" lent greater interest to the festivities.

The "news of the surrender of Lee's army was received with a great demonstration, with steam-whistles, cannon and church bells. It was a glad day for everybody." The chronicler quaintly adds: "And greatly enjoyed by all."

"The announcement of the assassination of President Lincoln came suddenly upon the people of the village, and produced the most intense feeling of sorrow." Flags were put at half-mast all over the town, for everybody owned a flag or two in those days. Appropriate mention was made in all the churches on the following Sunday. Upon the day of the funeral the village stores were closed, and funeral services were held in several of the churches. "In brief," says a chronicler of that date, "Yonkers, by every means within her power, evinced the depth and sincerity of the sorrow of her people."

On the evening of the 20th of April, a vast mass-meeting was held at Farrington Hall, at which Judge Scrugham presided. The night before the village trustees had met and passed appropriate resolutions.

At the south of the railway station a memorial arch was thrown over the railroad, and under this the funeral train passed northward, while every elevated point along the track was occupied by our saddened citizens, who stood with uncovered heads and tearful eyes as the funeral train moved slowly by.

Among the town items of that eventful year the searcher finds that the street-cars stopped running on North Broadway, "to the no small inconvenience of their many patrons." We may add that the horse-car road of that day was soon thereafter totally eliminated and forgotten. To show how rural we were in those days, the following piece of village news will be not altogether uninteresting:

"The park fronting the Getty House has been fitted up in good style, and now presents quite an attractive appearance. Along the west side of it a strong rail has been erected for the convenience of those who wish to hitch their horses thereto."

It is also related that an officer of the Sixth Artillery brought to Yonkers two of the blackest contrabands Yonkers people had ever laid eyes upon. They were slave boys of Major Robinson, and were respectively of the age of ten and twelve years. It is said that one found a home with Frederick Newman, the village upholsterer, and that the other was taken care of by Thomas Radford, of South Broadway, the brother of Hon. William Radford, who, as our representative in Congress, was one of the immortal seven who voted for Emancipation in opposition to their party.

It is not a pleasant thing to record, but it is nevertheless true, that but little public homage was paid to the heroes of the war when they returned to their homes in Yonkers. A local reporter noticed this, and recorded, for future generations to read, that "in every place but Yonkers, to our shame be it said, the soldiers of the Sixth Artillery are handsomely received and entertained." It is certainly an unpleasant record, for the Sixth Artillery was peculiarly a Yonkers organization.

That the veterans held together for a while is evidenced by the fact that upon Thanksgiving Day of that year the Yonkers soldiers organized a target company, commanded by Colonel E. Y. Morris, and had for once a harmless shooting-party.

But for all the public neglect, each veteran was a hero among his many friends. Some returned minus a leg or arm, but many more in shattered health, and within a very short period after their return quite a number had passed silently away to their long rest from strife and turmoil.

But to pass on to other subjects. For many years now the clink of coin had not been heard in the town. Paper had been exclusively used as current money. When, therefore, we read the following item in a local paper, we are made more fully acquainted with the war phase of the currency:

"While in a car of the Yonkers and New York Railroad, a few days ago, we saw a passenger hand the conductor a fifty cent silver piece. We also learn that several silver half and quarter dollars were taken at the Fenian picnic."

Times were not any too easy that year, and the rate of taxation seemed high to all. "Everything, in short, is taxed, except the air we breathe, and that will probably be taxed by the cholera, next spring."

In that year the Hudson River Railroad still ran to Thirtieth Street, and there were but ten trains each way daily which stopped at Yonkers. It is hard to believe, but it is stated, that there were but two mails daily from Yonkers to New York, and only one mail north. Delays were frequent and often tedious, both as to passengers and mails.

The soldier who returned to his home after four years in the field was apt to find urgent necessity for going to work at once to earn a living for himself and family. No easy task just then, with the labor-market glutted, and prices of living high. When the war broke out he could buy a pound of first-class butter for twenty-three cents; now the same quality was sixty cents. Did he buy cotton cloth, then it did not exceed fourteen cents; now he must pay thirty-three cents. Flour, that in 1860 was $8 a barrel, now sold for $20. Wheat was now $1.30 per bushel, and corn fifty-seven cents. When he went away tea cost fifty cents a pound; when he got home it had risen to three times that price. Pork at twelve cents of old, now, alas! worth thirty cents per pound. Beans were six cents and rice five cents a pound; now he found the former at double their old price, and the cost of the latter nearly trebled. Had he worked as a day-laborer or farm-hand, then he earned a dollar a day; now he was worth only half a dollar more, while all he needed was doubled, trebled, and oftentimes quadrupled. But the brave man only worked the harder, and fought out the bread-and-butter question as he had those questions at stake in the war. In time he had conquered and solved both.

And so another period had passed. Many questions had solved themselves, and many more had been settled by our brave and determined citizens. The day was fast approaching when Yonkers was to lay aside its youthful appearance, to drop its village and rural attire, and assume the airs of a city.

Many of the leading men and women of the town and village who were alive and active in public life and charities at the outbreak of the war, had been called away at a time when their voices and assistance were sadly needed. Much of the work of reconstruction fell upon the younger men of that day, and upon the new men who were moving into the growing village. Such helpful men as Ethan Flagg, Judge William W. Scrugham, James C. Bell, Robert P. Getty, Justus Lawrence, Thomas C. Cornell, and Anson Baldwin were still with us, and coached and applauded the youngsters who had their shoulders to the wheel.

OLD CITIZENS OF YONKERS.

1. Frederick A. Back.
2. Joseph Peene, Sr.
3. Gabriel P. Reevs, M.D.
4. James P. Sanders.
5. Bailey Hobbs.
6. Allen Taylor.
7. James Slade.
8. Ralph E. Prime.
9. R. B. Tompkins.
10. Lewis H. Wiggins.
11. John B. Prote.
12. Sidney S. Peck.

CHAPTER XII.

THE CITY OF YONKERS. 1872–1896.

"In splendor throned, with beauty crowned,
    Fair Queen on classic river's shore,
The lessons of thy Past abound,
    Thy storied Past and blessings pour
In present years from Plenty's horn,
    While beckoning glory brightly glows,
Thy future annals to adorn."

IN April, 1872, a local paper published the following paragraph: "The bill incorporating the City of Yonkers passed the Assembly, and will doubtless pass the Senate. Then good-by to our overgrown village, and a right hearty welcome to the City of Yonkers—the Queen City of the Hudson." The first official information of the signing of the bill was telegraphed from the Executive Chamber at the "Capitol City," June 1st, by the Governor's private secretary, and was received in Yonkers at 1.30 P.M.:

"ALBANY, June 1, 1872.
"TO RALPH E. PRIME:
"Governor Hoffman signed the Yonkers City Charter to-day.
"D. WILLERS, JR."

The southern part of the town was not included within the boundaries of the new city, but was set off,* on December 16, 1872, as the town of Kingsbridge. On January 1, 1874, Kingsbridge was annexed to New York City.

Yonkers (county town and city) is bounded † on the north by the town of Greenburgh, on the east by the middle of the Bronx River, on the south by the City of New York, and on the west by the Hudson River. Its breadth across its north line is a little more than four miles. Its length along its Bronx River line is six and a half miles. Its breadth along its New York City line is a little more than three miles, and its length along its Hudson River line is four and one-third miles. The area of the city is seventeen and one-half square miles. At the time of the incorporation of Yonkers, Manor Hall became the City Hall. The distance of the Yonkers City Hall from the New York City Hall is about seventeen miles, and from the north boundary of New York City is about two miles. At first the number of wards in Yonkers was four; by the charter of 1895 the number is seven.

---

* The town of Kingsbridge was set off by act of the County Supervisors, December 16, 1872. This action was confirmed by the State Legislature, February 28, 1873.

† In the original charter, the boundaries of the City of Yonkers are described as follows: "Bounded westerly by the westerly line of the county of Westchester, northerly by the town of Greenburgh, easterly by the easterly line of the town of Yonkers, and southerly by a line drawn from the westerly line of the said county to the easterly line of the town of Yonkers, in manner following, to wit: Commencing at a point formed by the intersection of the westerly line of the said county with a line of extension westerly of the northerly line of the land belonging to the Sisters of Charity, known as Mount St. Vincent de Paul; thence easterly along said northerly line of the land of said Sisters of Charity to Riverdale Avenue; thence still easterly and in a straight line crossing said Riverdale Avenue and South Broadway to the northwest corner of the land of G. F. Codington; thence still easterly in a straight line to the northwest corner of land known as the Van Cortlandt Estate, near Highland Avenue; thence easterly along the northern boundary line of land known as the Van Cortlandt Estate to the northeasterly corner thereof; thence running easterly in a straight line to the Bronx River to a point in the easterly line of the town of Yonkers, distant northerly twenty-one hundred feet from the northerly boundary line of Woodlawn Cemetery, measured in a course bearing north twenty degrees east (present magnetic bearing) therefrom." The original charter of 1872 has been amended several times and revised, but the boundary lines of the city have not been changed.

At the first municipal election Mr. Robert P. Getty was the Republican candidate for Mayor and Mr. James C. Courter the Democratic candidate. The total vote was 2,344, being 596 more than the highest ever polled in the village. James C. Courter was elected by a majority of eight. He was a young man well known in Yonkers from his boyhood, having been brought up on the farm of his grandfather, Caleb Smith, who was for many years supervisor of Yonkers. His education was for the most part in the Yonkers district and private schools. One of his schoolmates was Mr. John G. Peene, the present Mayor (1896). In 1871, Mr. Courter was elected supervisor, but before his term expired he was honored with the office of Mayor. In his reminiscences of that period he says, "The village merged quietly into the city. The machinery of municipal government ran smoothly. Mr. William H. Doty who had been clerk of the village, and who was conversant with public affairs, became the city clerk. Mr. Ethan

MAYORS OF YONKERS.

1. James C. Courter, (1872-74).
2. Joseph Masten, (1874-76, 1878-80).
3. Wm. Augustus Gibson, (1876-78).
4. Norton P. Otis, (1880-82).
5. Samuel Swift, M.D., (1882-84).
6. Wm. G. Stahlnecker, (1884-86).
7. J. Harvey Bell, (1886-88, 1888-90).
8. James Millward, (1890-92).
9. James H. Weller, (1892-94).
10. John G. Peene, (1894–).

Flagg, who had been a village trustee, became President of the Board of Aldermen, which was composed of substantial citizens. Mr. Flagg was very careful, indeed, I almost considered him punctilious, for I remember that the water bonds were not lithographed, and in compliance with his wishes I signed every one of them, sometimes writing far into the night." Ex-Mayor Courter, whose home is (in 1896) on the Tuckahoe road, a short distance east of the pumping station of the Yonkers water works, recalls other interesting incidents in the annals of the infant city, of which he was the first Mayor, but want of space prevents their record on these pages.

At the time Yonkers became a city, the population of the town, including Kingsbridge, was probably about 20,000. When Kingsbridge was set off, the population of Yonkers was considerably decreased, but in 1880, the city, as now bounded, had about 19,000. In 1896, it has about 40,000. By contrasting the Yonkers of 1872 with the Yonkers of 1896, its wonderful progress, within less than a quarter of a century, is perceived. When the city was incorporated, it had no asphalt avenues and streets, no water works, to supply water for domestic use, for power and for extinguishing fires, no system of sewers,* no fire-bell, no electric fire alarm and no electric lights. There were no steam cars† running to Getty Square, no street-cars (the first horse-car track had been torn up in 1866 or 1867, when Broadway was widened and regraded). Many of the present beautiful streets and avenues were not opened, all the buildings on the narrow, crooked and unpaved street between the Hudson River Railroad and Getty Square had not been moved back to make way for the newly straightened and widened Main Street. The Hudson River Railroad station‡ for passengers, which had been built at the foot of Main Street was in time abandoned and a new station for passengers built near the foot of Locust Street, a site which Yonkers citizens considered inconvenient. There was no bridge spanning the railroad at the foot of Main Street. The highway crossing was a dangerous surface crossing south of the present bridge. The public dock and several of the large private docks of the present day had not been built. Many handsome residences which now ornament the city, were not then erected and their present beautiful grounds, with their winding foot paths and carriage drives were then pasture fields. Many immense brick buildings, in which are now heard the clatter and hum of carpet, hat and other machinery had no existence. St. John's Riverside Hospital was the plain brick building on the east side of Wood-worth Avenue (two or three hundred feet north of Locust Street). The present St. Joseph's and St. John's Hospitals were not erected. There were only fifteen houses of worship, including two at Tuckahoe, and one at Woodhill. St. John's parish house and St. Andrew's Church were not built. The corner-stone of the present Christ Church was laid the year the city was incorporated, but the building, when finished, was smaller than the church as it appears to-day. The parish house was not built, nor was the church organized. St. Andrew's Church Society was not in existence. The First Methodist Church was a plain frame building, standing on the site of the present handsome stone church. The German Methodist Church on Waverly Street and the African Methodist Church on New Main Street were not built. The First Reformed congregation were worshipping

JAMES C. COURTER.

---

* Much of the sewerage was drained into the Nepperhan, and the stream, with its several mill-ponds, became so foul and so seriously menaced the health of the citizens, that by request of some, who realized the danger, the State Board of Health, after inspection by its representatives, condemned the ponds, and eventually the dams were torn down by the city officials' orders.

† When the steam cars began to run on the New York and Northern (now New York and Putnam) Railroad through the Tippitt's brook and Nepperhan valleys, passengers were transferred from Getty Square to the South Yonkers (now Dunwoodie) station by uncomfortable stages. Before the trolley cars ran to Mount Vernon, a line of lumbering stages carried passengers and the United States mail to and fro.

‡ There were at one time two drawbridges near the mouth of the Nepperhan. One was the railroad bridge and the other the highway (wooden) bridge. Sloops came up to the end of Nepperhan Street, and some farther up the stream. The Hudson River Railroad Company was willing to build a new passenger station at the foot of Main Street, provided the city officials would permanently close the railroad drawbridge. This was eventually done and the present passenger station built.

in an old-fashioned brick building, which stood on the site of the present noble house of worship; the Park Hill Reformed Church was not organized. The present St. Joseph's (R. C.) Church on Ashburton Avenue, St. Patrick's (R. C.) Church on Riverdale Avenue, the Monastery on Shonnard Place, the immense Roman Catholic Seminary building on Valentine Hill, the Greek Catholic Church on Ash Street, the Slavonian-Hungarian (R. C.) Church on Walnut Street were not built. The St. Mary's (R. C.) congregation were worshipping in the plain brick church (now an entertainment hall) on St. Mary's Street. Their splendid stone church on South Broadway was not erected. The Westminster Presbyterian congregation were worshipping in a small brick church on the west side of Warburton Avenue, southwest of, and near the site of their present fine stone church. The Dayspring Presbyterian Church was not organized. The Sabbath-school, established a few weeks before the city was incorporated, was holding its sessions in a small frame chapel, southwest corner of Oliver Avenue and Walnut Street. (The chapel was dedicated April 28, 1872, and was enlarged in 1875.) Immanuel Chapel was not in existence, nor was the Lutheran Church on Hudson Street. The Nepperhan Avenue Baptist house of worship was about half its present size. The material of which it is constructed had been removed from the Mount Olivet Baptist Church, which stood on the site of the present Temperance Hall, west side of North Broadway, near Wells Avenue. The Nepperhan Sunday-school was holding its sessions, but the church was not organized, neither were the Messiah Baptist Church, the Woodhill Methodist, nor the German Methodist.

The fine High School building and several other fine public school edifices were not built. Several of the present excellent private schools of the city had not been established. The First National Bank Building, Music Hall, W. C. T. U. Hall, the Women's Institute, Teutonia Hall, Odd Fellows' Hall, the building now rented for Y. M. C. A. Hall, the present Palisade Boat Club House, Yonkers Yacht Club House, the Lawn Tennis Club House, the Park Hill Club House, the Curling Rink, several houses for fire apparatus, the Armory, the Viewville Reading Room, the Home for Aged and Infirm Hebrews, the Leake and Watts Orphan House, and other well-known buildings of to-day, were not yet erected when the city was incorporated. Mail was not collected and distributed by carriers. The Good Government Club and the Board of Trade were not established, nor were a number of fraternities which now enroll hundreds of members. The directory of that day was a small book, as compared with the directory of 1896.

Rocks and trees, hillside fields, woodland and swamps appeared in some parts of the place where now are graded streets and blocks of buildings. A comparison of, for example, Nodine Hill, Park Hill, Lowerre, Ludlow, Glenwood, Shonnard and Hudson Terrace, North Broadway, the extension of Palisade Avenue and other sections with the same localities, as they appear to-day, helps to a realization of the progress Yonkers had made since it became a city. In 1872 there were probably not more than sixty or eighty dwelling-houses on Nodine Hill, east of Walnut Street. On Elm Street, between Linden and Walnut, there were probably not more than four or five houses. Elm Street was not graded, nor were its walks flagged. There were no gas lights on Elm Street, east of Nepperhan Avenue. Oliver, Webster and Washington (the present Elm Street east of Walnut) Avenues were not graded. Garfield Avenue was not opened. At the upper end of Oliver and Webster Avenues, near the crown of the hill were huge rocks, over which it was difficult to drive. Walnut Street did not extend north beyond Yonkers Avenue. No streets extending southward from Washington Avenue (now Elm Street east of Walnut) were opened. The tract between Elm and Poplar, Walnut and Linden was in large part a swamp.

On Park Hill,* now such a lovely section of the city, were woods where squirrels chattered, fields where cattle pastured and ponds where Yonkers boys fished. Lowerre, where now appear graded streets, electric lights and comfortable cottages, was a swamp; many parts of the beautiful section known as Ludlow's was pasture land. Shonnard Terrace and Hudson Terrace and the section near High Street and north were open fields. Now palatial residences, fine lawns and well lighted streets greet the eye, and evidence the rapid and substantial growth of Yonkers since its incorporation as a city.

Clusters of houses, recently built at Woodlawn (a hamlet that sprang up there about 1889), Dunwoodie, Valentine Hill and elsewhere, indicate that within a few years, the hitherto rural districts are soon to take on the characteristics of town life. A number of parks, beside Park Hill, have appeared on the map within a few years and are making rapid improvements. Among them are Armour Villa, Mohegan, Bryn Mawr, Sherwood Hill, Nepera, Victoria, Lincoln, Yonkers and Caryl. Great improvements are projected on Valentine Hill by a new land company. Magnificent views are afforded from that locality.

* The name was first Parkhill, the middle name of Mr. Robert P. Getty, who owned property there.

LAWYERS OF YONKERS.

1. William Warburton Scrugham.
2. John F. Brennan.
3. F. X. Donohue.
4. James M. Hunt.
5. Arthur J. Burns.
6. Cyrus A. Peake.
7. Stephen H. Thayer.
8. Wm. C. Kellogg.
9. Joseph F. Daly.
10. Wm. H. Riley.
11. John C. Harrigan.
12. Thomas F. Curran.
13. Adrian M. Potter.
14. Gabriel Reevs.

When the United States coast survey was at work on Long Island Sound, one of their conspicuous landmarks was a bright piece of tin attached to a pole erected on Valentine Hill. A wealthy New York syndicate has for several years had a surveyor (Mr. John R. Ayer) locating plots, streets and avenues in the Tippett's Brook valley, east of Nodine and Park Hills, where they own a thousand acres of land, more or less. Probably beautiful residences, resembling those on Park Hill, will in time be erected there.

The older citizens, who have witnessed the steady march of improvement in the city, best realize what thought and time and money they represent. Those who dwell in towns which have had little or no growth, have not been confronted with the problems which the public-spirited residents of Yonkers have been solving during recent decades. The minds of many have been broadened, and their knowledge mightily increased by the attention they have given, during a series of years, to public affairs. They have become experienced officials by planning to meet the requirements and supply the increasing needs of a rapidly growing city. They have compared various systems devised for supplying cities with water, various methods of constructing streets and sewers, various systems of lighting towns, of giving fire-alarms, of police protection, and various systems of education. In a city of hundreds of thousands of inhabitants, often the solution of questions, relating to the public welfare, are considered by the few to whom, as officials, the matters are almost entirely left; but in Yonkers the citizens generally have been interested; and while the place has been rapidly growing from a village to a city of 40,000 inhabitants, the people in their homes, in places of business, in public debates, in political meetings, and through the columns of newspapers, have participated in discussions of proposed improvements. It has fallen to them to consider such questions as: Shall the drawbridge at the mouth of the Nepperhan be closed? Shall water for extinguishing fires, and for domestic supply, and for factory and other power be stored in subterranean reservoirs, filled from under-ground or in surface reservoirs, constructed to receive the water of available water-sheds? Shall the Nepperhan be converted into a trunk sewer; or shall a system of sewers be constructed, with the trunk in Main Street and lateral branches where needed? Shall franchises be granted gas, street railroad, telephone, and electric light companies, and if granted, upon what terms? What shall be the grade of these streets and those avenues? Shall pavement be of blocks of wood or of stone, or shall asphalt pavement be laid, and what contracts shall be made with paving companies? How shall assessments be laid? What districts shall they embrace? Upon what terms shall money be borrowed to pay for needed improvements, and when shall bonds mature? What systems of education shall be adopted? Shall there be a Consolidated Board of Education? How shall the criminal class, including law-breaking liquor dealers, be dealt with? How shall the destitute poor be relieved? What shall be done with the indolent and shiftless classes? Where shall the new City Hall be located? Where shall parks be laid out? Shall Yonkers be annexed to New York? These and other questions have, one after another, been discussed, and many of them have been decided.

Reference has already been made to the election of the first Mayor. At the first city election, held under the first city charter on June 18, 1872, Edward P. Baird,* Esq., who had been the police justice of the incorporated village (the successor of T. Astley Atkins, Esq.,) was elected City Judge, and Judge of the City Court in Yonkers. In 1876 he was re-elected City Judge. The names of his successors are recorded at the end of this chapter. The City Court of Yonkers is a court of record presided over by the City Judge of Yonkers. Its jurisdiction has been increased since the city was incorporated. It has had, since 1893, jurisdiction, where the amount claimed does not exceed $2,000, and where the defendant resides in the city of Yonkers, or a town adjoining. The City Judge also has criminal jurisdiction,

J. IRVING BURNS.

* In 1883 Judge Baird removed to Minneapolis, Minn., where he practiced law, until he died (October 26, 1885). He was buried in St. John's Cemetery, Yonkers.

and power to hold courts of special sessions in the city, and to try all complaints for misdemeanors committed in the city. In all criminal complaints, such as assault in the second degree, grand larceny, burglary and the like, the City Judge has power to hold the person accused to await the action of the grand jury.

Under the act of 1870, on the incorporation of Yonkers in 1872 as a city, three excise commissioners were appointed by Mayor Courter. Their names and the names of their successors are recorded among those of other city officials in the latter part of this chapter. The powers of the commissioners, whom the Mayor appointed April 21, 1873, and the common council confirmed, and who continued in office till 1876, were suspended by the act of 1874, which as to the County of Westchester alone, revived the old system of county excise commissioners, but the act of 1874 was soon repealed, and from that time the excise commissioners for Yonkers have been appointed under the city charter, and the act of 1870, for the city alone. The number of licenses granted in 1872, was 159; the number granted in 1895, was 199.* The history of the fire department previous to the incorporation of the city is recorded in Chapters IX. and X. On September 18, 1876, Assistant Engineer E. Alexander Houston was elected chief. The names of his successors are recorded in the latter part of this chapter. He and George A. Mitchell, then treasurer of the department, resolved to collect the money due from foreign insurance companies. Up to that date, little or none had been received. By persistent efforts, they obtained over three hundred and fifty dollars the first year. Previous to 1876, fire alarms had been given by the ringing of church bells. Chief Houston set about the procuring of a fire alarm bell. The securing of the bell was celebrated by a fine torch-light procession of the fire department on July 3, 1877. The fire bell tower was at first located north of and adjoining Manor Hall. It was subsequently erected on the west side of Nepperhan Terrace. When its iron tongue at midnight awakens the people, they are reminded that the city watchmen have been on their rounds, guarding person and property while they have been sleeping, and, perchance, some of them, listening in their homes to the fire bell, recall the poet's lines,

THEODORE H. SILKMAN.

> " Hear the loud alarum bells—
> Brazen bells!
> What a tale of terror now their turbulency tells!
> In the startled ear of night
> How they scream out their affright!"

*It requires only two brief sentences to make this record, but it would require volumes to record the woes, the destruction of happy homes, bodies, minds and souls, resulting from the licenses the city has given to sell as beverages, alcoholic drinks, which science pronounces irritant poisons. Only the revelations of the judgment day will unfold the awful record.

BUSINESS MEN OF YONKERS.

1. Alexander O. Kirkwood.
2. Thomas McVicar.
3. Arnett O. Lawrence.
4. Clarence H. Pearsall.
5. William H. Lake.
6. Felix Murray.
7. Frank Knapper.
8. Nelson A. Ball.

At such an hour the devout citizen remembers the words, "Except the Lord keep the city, the watchman waketh but in vain." In order to make certain of more prompt alarm, in case of fire, an electric system was introduced, which has been improved upon from year to year.

At first the Board of Aldermen supervised the department. By the charter of 1881, it was provided that a Board of Fire Commissioners should be appointed by the Mayor and confirmed by the Common Council. In the revised charter of 1895, the Common Council was authorized to determine fire limits, within which no building of wood shall be constructed, to regulate plans for the construction and repairing of buildings, to require fire-escapes to be provided in mills, factories and other designated buildings, etc., and the Fire Commissioners were authorized to keep idle and suspicious persons away from fires, to procure fire-engines and other fire apparatus, to have control of apparatus and engine-houses, to organize fire, hose, and hook and ladder companies, to appoint and dismiss firemen, and to make rules and regulations for the government of the fire department. The Fire Commissioners are also directed by the charter to examine, at reasonable intervals, all dwellings, yards and buildings of every description, in order to discover whether any of them are in a dangerous condition. The Fire Commissioners are also empowered, with the consent of the Common Council, to make provision for the payment of the officers and members of the fire department if they deem it proper. This has not yet been done. The names of the Board of Fire Commissioners are recorded at the end of this chapter.

Previous to the incorporation of the city (June 1, 1872), Protection Engine Co. No. 1, Lady Washington Engine Co. No. 2, Hope Hook and Ladder Co. No. 1, and Hudson Hose Co. No. 1 were organized. Since Yonkers became a city a number of new fire companies have been organized, and a number of apparatus houses built. The following are the companies of 1896:

Protection Engine Co. No. 1, Engine Place.
Mountaineer Engine Co. No. 2, Oliver Avenue.
Hope Hook and Ladder Co. No. 1, Palisade Avenue.
Columbia Hook and Ladder Co. No. 2, Vineyard Avenue.
Hudson Hose Co. No. 1, Nepperhan Terrace.
Lady Washington Hose Co. No. 2, Palisade Avenue.
City Hose Co. No. 3, Riverdale Avenue.
Palisade Hose Co. No. 4, Vineyard Avenue.
Irving Hose Co. No. 5, North Broadway.
Houston Hose Co. No. 6, Orchard Street.
Shannondale Hose Company, No. 7, near Woodlawn.
Avalanche Hose Co. No. 8, Armour Villa Park.
Lowerre Hose Co. No. 9, near Lowerre Station.

CALEB F. UNDERHILL.

There is in Yonkers, an association of firemen, known as the Veteran Firemen's Benevolent Association. It was organized in May, 1887. A record of its growth is in another chapter.

During a part of the period in which Yonkers has had a corporate life as a city, the fire department has been apprehensive of the dangers of a great conflagration, by reason of the one-story and other frame buildings, which years ago were built here and there. In 1893 a great fire swept away a row of such structures from the east side of Warburton Avenue, between Dock and Main Streets. Substantial and handsome brick buildings have since been erected where the old one-story tinder-boxes stood. A large fire in 1896 swept away another row of inferior frame buildings from the west side of North Broadway, between Getty Square and Dock Street.

The early history of the endeavors of Yonkers officials to guard the health of the people is recorded in Chapter XI. When the city was incorporated the charter contained provisions for a Board of Health. It was to be composed of the following, *ex-officio:* The Mayor, as president; the President of the Common Council, the President of the Board of Police Commissioners, the President of the Board of Water Commissioners, the Supervisor, the Health Officer, and the City Clerk as clerk of the Board. The charter of 1895 provides that the Mayor shall nominate by and with the consent of the Common Council five commissioners of public health, who shall constitute

CHARLES A. MILES, M.D.

the Board of Health. The Health Officer, by provision of the same charter, is appointed by the Board of Health. The Board of Health is empowered to appoint officers to supervise plumbing and drainage of buildings. The Health Officer, by provision of previous charters, was appointed by the Mayor, subject to the approval of the Common Council. On July 1, 1872, Horace B. Pike, M.D., was appointed Health Officer. On April 12, 1873, the old village rules for the protection of public health were adopted. In November, 1873, the Health Officer began furnishing the newspapers with some statistics of his office, among them the number of deaths occurring in the city. Nearly two years afterward the registry of vital statistics began to be kept. In 1875 Dr. Pike estimated, from his records, that there were thirteen deaths among each one thousand residents. Books for registering births, marriages and deaths were opened in the office of the clerk of Yonkers in 1876.

Dr. Galusha B. Balsh succeeded Dr. Pike as Health Officer. He was appointed in the spring of 1876. He had been, during the Civil War, an assistant surgeon of the Ninety-eighth New York Infantry, had rendered service in the general hospital at Yorktown, Va., had charge of the steamer State of Maine, which was used in transporting sick and wounded soldiers to Baltimore, had been assistant surgeon of the Second Veteran Cavalry, New York Volunteers, and during the Red River campaign had been surgeon of his regiment—the Ninety-eighth New York Infantry. For many years after the war he practiced medicine in Yonkers, and is to-day one of the well-known physicians of the city. When he was Health Officer, Yonkers ranked high as to its health record. In a comparison of sixty-eight cities, drawn in 1800, or the National Board of Health, Yonkers was found to be surpassed in the fewness of deaths only by the city of Vallejo, California. The condition, however, of the Nepperhan, at that time, and of its ponds, gave him and other thoughtful citizens much apprehension.

Dr. Valentine Browne succeeded Dr. Balsh, and held the office about seventeen years (from May 15, 1878, to May 21, 1895). At the time of his appointment there were not more than a score of houses in the city having proper sanitary connection with a public sewer, and only a few streets had sewers to connect house drainage with. The old-fashioned vaults and cesspools were everywhere to be seen. There were not less than fifteen ponds in the town, some of them useless, and all of them disease breeding quagmires, detrimental to the public health. The garbage of the city was either fed to pigs, or allowed to become a nuisance for want of proper care and destruction. There was no hospital for the reception and care of persons suffering from contagious diseases, and there was no regular system employed for the protection of school children from contagious diseases, etc. When the doctor's long service as Health Officer came to an end on May 21, 1895, almost every street in Yonkers had a sewer, and every house along the lines of these sewers was connected with them in a thorough sanitary manner, unsurpassed by any city in the United States, or elsewhere. The drainage system for houses is first-class in every respect, and vaults and cesspools in the closely built parts of the city have disappeared. All the filthy ponds have been completely abolished and with them the most dangerous nuisances in Yonkers. The opposition on the part of some to the tearing down of the old dams is still fresh in the memory of every resident of the city. The garbage of Yonkers was reduced to ashes in the crematory erected for that purpose about 1893. A well appointed and commodious hospital was established for the reception of, and care of, persons suffering from contagious

THOMAS C. CORNELL.

diseases. In short, Yonkers was in a thorough sanitary condition, and all that is required now to place the city in the front rank of desirable and healthy cities are public parks and bathing-houses. These, the Board of Health, during eight years of Dr. Browne's term as Health Officer, endeavored to influence the Common Council to provide for the city, but they were unsuccessful.

The next Health Officer was Dr. Garrett N. Banker, who still holds the office in 1896. The names of members of the Board of Health are recorded at the close of this chapter.

The history of the police department previous to the incorporation of the city is in Chapter X.

The history of the detail from the metropolitan police force arriving in Yonkers, and of the subsequent organization of the Yonkers police force is recorded in Chapter X. On August 19, 1873, Roundsman George W. Osborn was detailed as acting sergeant. On July 15, 1874, he was appointed sergeant, in place of James M. King, who had gone to the New York force. Patrolman Frederick H.

Woodruff, on August 18, 1873, was appointed roundsman to the place of Roundsman Osborn, promoted. Patrolman James P. Embree was appointed roundsman on August 19, 1874, and detailed to act at the Bronxville Station. On November 21, 1874, Patrolman Henry J. Quinn was appointed roundsman. Sergeant Charles W. Austin died December 17, 1881. On December 22, 1881, Roundsman James McLaughlin was promoted sergeant. Henry J. Quinn, roundsman, was promoted to roundsman at headquarters. The same day Richard E. Wilcox, patrolman, was detailed as acting roundsman. Captain John Mangin still commands the force. Since December, 1881, the sergeants have been George W. Osborn, James McLaughlin, Henry J. Quinn and Frederick H. Woodruff. The roundsmen since that date have been Henry J. Quinn and Frederick Woodruff. After they became sergeants, two years ago, no roundsmen were appointed. The acting roundsmen have been William M. Lawrence, stationed at the Bronxville sub-station, Richard E. Wilcox, Peter McGowan and William H. Lent. J. Foster Jenkins, M.D., who was the surgeon of police, died October 9, 1883. Samuel Swift, M.D., acting surgeon, was appointed surgeon September 17, 1884. His successor was Albert C. Benedict, M.D., the present surgeon. The force now consists of one captain, four sergeants, one surgeon, thirty-five patrolmen, two doormen and one hostler—forty-four in all. In June, 1872, when Yonkers became a city, the method of forming the police board was changed from the previous method. It was provided that its members should be appointed by the Common Council. They are appointed and confirmed by the Mayor, Council. The names of those who have served as police commissioners, are recorded in the latter part of this chapter. In July, 1874, as Kings-bridge had been annexed to New York, the Kings-bridge sub-station passed under the control of the New York police. The Bronxville sub-station was then the only one connected with the Yonkers headquarters. Joseph E. Johnstone was detailed to duty at that station. No other sub-station has since been added.

JAMES H. WELLER.

The Central Office, on Dock Street, has telegraphic communication with the New York City Central Office, the Bronxville sub-station, all the banks and with the residences of many private citizens. The connection between headquarters and New York was effected June 20, 1867. The line to the Bronxville sub-station was completed February 24, 1874. On April 10, 1874, the first signal box was put in working order. There are at the present time thirty-six boxes. Each bank has a key with which it can call the sergeant at headquarters. By this arrangement a bank can have a policeman on hand in a few minutes if necessary. All the bank safes are connected with police headquarters, so that the slightest tampering with their doors will signal the officer at headquarters.

The department has what was originally termed a "Widows and Orphans Fund," but it is now called the "Police Pension Fund," the object of which is to render assistance to the families of officers who may be injured or killed while in the discharge of their duty. This fund is made up of annual two per cent. assessments on their salaries voluntarily borne by the men, of the proceeds of unclaimed goods, of special fees for sealing weights and measures, of the yield of an entertainment, of donations by a number of citizens, of fines, of interest on deposit in the savings banks, and of loans on bond and mortgage. The fund on March 1, 1896, amounted to $29,822.61.

The total receipts for the maintenance of the force for the year ending March 1, 1896, were $56,860.03. The disbursements were as follows:

Pay Rolls,	$51,227.76
Police Pension Fund,	326.73
Police Telegraph,	1,053.15
Fuel and Light,	551.77
Stationery,	255.12
Contingent Expenses,	939.18
Stables, etc.,	2,016.35
Repairs and Supplies,	489.97
	$56,860.03

The headquarters of the force are in the three-story brick building (formerly known as Melah's Hotel), where they have been from the beginning. A green light is suspended over the entrance door. A sergeant is always at the inrailed desk there, day and night. Various telegraphic instruments, signal bells, telephones, etc., are near his chair. Within the black walnut cases, with glass doors, on the west wall, are a collection of photographs known as "The Rogues' Gallery." Another collection, over the desk in the captain's office, is composed of photographs of Yonkers rogues, for the city has its own criminals, who are known to the police, and who if found on the streets late at night are sent home. On the west side of the captain's office is a case containing pistols, knives, metal knuckles, burglars' tools, masks, etc., etc., taken from prisoners. They are numbered, and each one suggests a sad story of depravity and crime and wretchedness for "the way of the transgressor is hard."

No. 12, for instance, is a wicked-looking, self-acting revolver of French design, to which the following interesting history of the breaking up of the notorious Highland brigands is attached:

On July 29, 1875, this revolver was taken from a daring and expert burglar named George Poxley, alias Chris Pinto, who was arrested near Williamsbridge by the pursuing police. Shortly after midnight of the 27th of July, 1875, the residence of Thomas Ludlow was burglariously

HENRY B. ARCHER.

entered and robbed of some valuables. Mr. Ludlow saw them in his room, and, when they had left, notified his coachman who at once informed police headquarters, and the reserve was sent out immediately.

"Ex-Patrolman Stephenson soon after met three suspicious-looking men on the Hudson River Railroad track, south of Vark Street. They pretended to submit to arrest, but when they found the officer off his guard opened a fusillade with their pistols, firing point blank at him. He being unarmed, they succeeded in effecting their escape, and this escape aroused the captain's ire. He at once called out all the men who were at home, and sent men, horses and wagons to cover all means of exit from the city, and exhausted the energy of the force in his efforts to arrest the thieves. While driving along the line of the Bronx River, Sergeant McLaughlin and ex-Patrolman Pat. Whelan saw a man acting in a suspicious manner, and, on arresting and searching him, found the revolver above-mentioned. In a hand-bag carried by the prisoner, and captured by Officer Stephenson, were some peculiar pin-head cartridges which fitted the pistol. A pair of stockings, damp and stained with grass, that he wore over his shoes to deaden the noise while committing burglary, were also found on his person.

"When confronted by the captain, he said he had no home, no friends or acquaintances, and absolutely failed to identify himself in any way. He was about thirty-two years of age, five feet seven inches in height, strongly built, with dark complexion and beard, and looked the daring man he was subsequently proved to be. After several days of sparring with the captain, who failed to draw from him any admission that would serve as a clew, he was committed to await the action of the Grand Jury.

He appeared elated at having foiled the captain's efforts to locate him, but he was by no means through with that sleuth-hound, for it was arranged to have a trusty man locked in Poxley's cell at the county jail, who, on leaving, asked if he could bear any message for Poxley to his friends.

"The scheme worked, for, after some hesitation, Poxley gave his fellow prisoner a pair of sleeve buttons and directed him to go to a certain dive near the corner of Houston and Wooster Streets, New York, and enquire for a friend of his. Here the amateur detective was coldly received and told no such person was known there, but the production of the sleeve buttons acted as the open sesame and he was ushered into a rear room and introduced to the gang, who were anxious to hear from their comrade in misfortune. He learned that Poxley's companions in the Ludlow robbery were Wm. J. Conroy, of Cold Spring, and an expert known as the Kid. Conroy had secreted himself on a canal boat at Lawrence's dock, and the Kid had escaped on a passing freight train. They all formed a part of a notorious band of burglars and outlaws known as the Highland Brigands of whom a man named Geo. Ellis was leader.

"The amateur detective further learned that William J. Conroy was arrested for a masked burglary in Utica. Captain Mangin, under whose direction the amateur was working, had him arrange with

POLICE OFFICIALS OF YONKERS.

1. CAPTAIN JOHN MANGIN.
2. SERGEANT GEORGE W. OSBORN.
3. SERGEANT HENRY J. QUINN.
4. SERGEANT JAMES MCLAUGHLIN.
5. SERGEANT FREDERICK H. WOODRUFF.

Ellis to commit a robbery. Ellis was met by arrangement about 2 A.M., at the headquarters of the gang, and as they parted at the corner of Houston and Wooster Streets, Captain Mangin and a sergeant jumped on them. and overpowering Ellis brought him to Yonkers, and from here conveyed him to Utica. Ellis was the man whom Supt. Jordan had arrested for the famous Nathan murder in New York City. He was recognized as the head of the New York crooks.

"He told the captain he had spent a couple of days at the Getty house reconnoitring for a favorable prospect to make a haul, and had reported to the gang the folly of an attempt, as he was overhauled by men in citizens' clothes while making his observations. He declared he had no sympathy for Poxley as he had disobeyed orders. Ellis was a polished, gentlemanly individual, who dressed well and possessed a decidedly clerical appearance. While Captain Mangin was taking him handcuffed to Utica, passing through the Highlands, he feigned sickness and jumped from the train, which was travelling at the rate of forty miles an hour. The captain had the train stopped and on going back found him with his head jammed through a picket fence. He was delivered up to the authorities at Utica without further adventure.

"The captain further discovered that the notorious Tom Scott was under arrest in Charleston on suspicion, and he was brought back and delivered at Utica. The results from the arrest of Poxley therefore were as follows: Ellis himself was committed for eighteen years; Tom Scott for eighteen years; Welsh and Bucky Malone were sent up for a term of years; and Poxley was tried for the Ludlow burglary and was sentenced to State Prison for fifteen years.

"Conroy, who had been arrested by Sergeant McLaughlin and Patrolman Redding and brought to Yonkers, at the request of the authorities in Utica. on account of his services in convicting the perpetrators of the Germond Mack burglary was not prosecuted. However, he was arrested a few months later for attempting to blow a house up at Kingston, received a life sentence and died in prison. And thus, by the clever arrest of Sergeant McLaughlin and ex-Patrolman Whelan and the skilful strategy of Captain Mangin, one of the worst gangs that ever infested New York was broken up and most of its members consigned to State's Prison."

BOARD OF WATER COMMISSIONERS OF YONKERS.

1. WILLIAM H. DOTY.
2. MICHAEL WALSH.
3. JOHN EYLER.
4. JACOB READ.
5. JOHN J. TIERNEY.

6. JOSEPH LOCKWOOD, Superintendent.

No thoughtful reader can become conversant with the history of the departments of the city, to which reference has already been made, and to other departments, without being grateful to public-spirited citizens, who have devoted so much of their valuable time to promote public welfare. Many of those who held office, labored without compensation. The splendid system of water works is a monument to many to whose foresight and solid judgment the city owes much. President Eickemeyer alluded to this at the laying of the corner-stone of the High-Service Tower, Nodine Hall (November 13, 1891). On that occasion he made an address in which were these sentences:

"When a disastrous fire on Dock Street, on August 9, 1869, which destroyed a whole square, had proved that water works had to be erected to protect the city, the Board of Trustees of the then village appointed a committee of citizens to act with the Trustees. This Citizens' Committee consisted of nineteen members, and I think, as their action, in co-operation with the Trustees, laid, as it were, the cornerstone of the whole works, it is well to recall their names at the laying of the corner-stone of a structure which will, in time to come, be a very important element in our admirable system of water supply.

"The names of those composing the Citizens' Committee are as follows: Thomas W. Ludlow, Dennis McGrath, Patrick White, Jacob Read, F. A. Back, John T. Waring, Timothy Ryan, G. B. Upham, Samuel Leggett, Cyrus Cleveland, Joseph Masten, Robert P. Getty, Rudolf Eickemeyer, Isaac H. Knox, George B. Skinner, Abijah Curtis, Charles R. Dusenberry, George Stewart, and Professor W. H. C. Bartlett, who was called in by the Committee as an honorary member." The report of the Committee was presented to the Common Council, December, 1872.

The Water Board was organized on March 24, 1873. Mr. M. K. Couzens, civil engineer, and W. W. Grant, also a civil engineer, recommended measures which they considered wise. In March, 1874, Mr. W. W. Wilson was appointed Chief Engineer, at a salary of $4,000 per annum. General George S. Green became Consulting Engineer, at a salary of $2,000 per annum, and Mr. John M. Mason, Counsel. The services of Dr. Newberry (Geologist-in-Chief of the State of Ohio, and Professor in the School of Mines in Columbia College) were procured, to make an examination of the geological structure of the Nepperhan Valley and of the Hudson Valley in the immediate vicinity of Yonkers, in order to ascertain the probability of obtaining a sufficient supply of water for the city from that source.

Mr. Wilson made an elaborate and carefully considered report of his investigations. The report was published by the Board of Water Commissioners. It records Mr. Wilson's comparisons of the Pocantico water-shed (6,500 acres drained), the Bronx water-shed (5,000 acres drained), the Nepperhan water-shed above Riggs dam (10,000 acres drained), and the Sprain brooks. His opinion was that the water of the Sprain and Grassy Sprain would not be so apt to be made impure by their valleys becoming populated, as would the other streams. He included in his report tables showing the amount of waterfall, and number of gallons of water used daily in London, Paris, Montreal, and in many American cities.

ELM STREET WATER TOWER.

He also added that if in time the need should arise of more water than the water-shed of the Sprain brooks affords, recourse could be had to the Bronx, but he demonstrated that the Sprain and Grassy Sprain would suffice for many years.

A sub-committee of the Board visited different cities, in order to inspect different systems. They examined the reservoir system in Syracuse, Buffalo and Detroit, the sandpipe system in Chicago, and the system of pumping directly into the mains, as it existed in Buffalo, Dunkirk, Kalamazoo, Lockport, Peoria and Columbus. The fear was expressed by some citizens that the Sprain brooks would not supply wholesome and pure water. The services of Professor C. F. Chandler, Ph.D., M.D., an expert pre-eminent in his profession, had been secured. An analysis which he made, based on personal examination of the Sprain waters, caused him to form a favorable opinion of the waters. Many citizens were yet apprehensive. The Board to "make assurance doubly sure," engaged Colonel J. W. Adams, another expert, to examine their proposed plans. He also approved of them. The Consulting Engineer and others, who had given careful thought to the enterprise, were not swayed by the opposition of those who doubted the purity of the waters. Their confidence in the opinion of Professor Chandler was unshaken.

The reservoir on Lake Avenue was built in 1873, and supply pipes were laid through the principal streets. On January 1, 1874, water was turned on and those present saw a stream thrown over the Getty House flagstaff. It was thrown from hose attached to a near hydrant. The Lake Avenue reservoir (297 feet above tide water) was at first used to store water for extinguishing fires which might break out in the thickly populated part of the city.

In 1874, no general plan for supplying the city with water for domestic purposes had been adopted. The capacity of the Lake Avenue reservoir was about 3,500,000 gallons, only about one day and a half supply for the city in 1896. After it was completed, the Grassy Sprain storage reservoir was constructed. The pumping station on the Tuckahoe road was erected in 1876. The capacity of the storage reservoir is about 400,000,000 gallons. The waters of the Sprain and Grassy Sprain were joined by means of a canal and the building of a dam on the Sprain, at the height of five feet at the place of diversion—the depression of the dividing ridge between the valleys. Subsequently the high service tower on Lake Avenue was built, and some years later the high service tower on Elm Street (Nodine Hill). Each tower is 450 feet above the Hudson River. The Lake Avenue tower, to the top of the battlements, is one hundred feet above ground. From the water table to the balcony of the Elm Street tower is 129 feet, and from the water table to the peak of the roof is 150 feet. Both towers can be ascended by interior winding stairways and from both, magnificent views from the Hudson to the Sound can be had. The overflows of the two high service towers are on a level with each other, and they are supplied from one high service pumping station, which takes water out of the Lake Avenue distributing reservoir. The two high service systems are connected by pipes which lead from the northern hill down to the Nepperhan, near the bridge southwest of Oakland Cemetery, across the Nepperhan, thence up Walnut Street to

LAKE AVENUE WATER TOWER.

the Nodine Hill system. The high service supplies elevations to a height two hundred and eighty feet and up to four hundred and forty feet above tide, the low service supplies elevations between tide water and two hundred and eighty feet above.

After the Lake Avenue and Grassy Sprain reservoirs and the two high service towers were finished, the next work was the construction of the Fort Field reservoir (capacity about 60,000,000 gallons). That is now completed and the next work will probably be the construction of a dam to hold back the great quantity of the waters of the Sprain and Grassy Sprain which now go to waste over the present dam in seasons of plentiful rains.

For some time the city has sold water to New York (for the Twenty-fourth Ward). When Yonkers needed an additional supply during the drought of 1895, it bought water of New York (taking it from the Croton Aqueduct) and from New Rochelle (by a pipe connecting with the New Rochelle system). The Yonkers water works may also, if necessary, take water from the Pocantico system.

BOARD OF EXCISE COMMISSIONERS.

1. Joseph Miller.   2. Joseph M. Tompkins.   3. John Warneck.

4. Gabriel Reevs, Counsel.   5. Harold C. Housel, Clerk.

There are now in the city $56\tfrac{7}{10}$ miles of water mains, 610 hydrants (all double nozzle), and 3,756 taps and connections. The number of meters is 3,706, and nine indicators are in use. The average daily consumption has been about 3,230,000 gallons. Every purchaser in Yonkers, in factories as well as in private residences, receives city water measured by a water meter. The consumption in some buildings is enormous. The Sugar House, for example, consumes 250,000 to 350,000 gallons per day. Citizens who desire information about the water works and matters relating to the department, find, in Manor Hall, Mr. Joseph A. Lockwood, a graduate of Union College, who is the superintendent, and the bookkeepers, Messrs. A. W. Kingsbury and Hall B. Sims. Mr. Lockwood's report for the year ending December 1, 1895, is a document of great interest to citizens who appreciate the work done by the department. It shows the cost of the works to date, and the amount expended under each account during the year:

REPORT OF MR. JOSEPH A. LOCKWOOD, SUPERINTENDENT, DECEMBER 1, 1895, TO BOARD OF WATER COMMISSIONERS.

ACCOUNTS.	PRIOR TO DEC. 1, 1894.	EXPENDED DEC. 1, 1894, TO DEC. 1, 1895.	TOTAL DEC. 1, 1895.
Lake Avenue Reservoir Land,	$27,457.77		$27,457.77
Grassy Sprain Reservoir and Canal Land,	84,041.04		84,041.04
Low Service Pumping Station, including the land for pipe line,	14,406.11		14,406.11
Engineer's Residence Land,	1,500.00		1,500.00
H. S. Tower, Lake Avenue Land,	6,532.88		6,532.88
H. S. Tower, Elm Street Land,	3,147.80	45.00	3,192.80
Fort Field Reservoir Land,	25,984.46		25,984.46
For Diversion of Water,	34,961.08		34,961.08
Lake Avenue Reservoir Construction,	39,339.33		39,339.33
Pipes and Castings,	334,306.36	14,616.38	348,922.74
Stop-cocks and Gates,	19,488.19	653.07	20,141.26
Trenching and Pipe-laying,	195,614.23	15,305.42	210,919.65
Hydrants,	21,282.91	1,470.51	22,753.42
Grassy Sprain Reservoir Construction,	73,831.04		73,831.04
Sprain Dam and Canal Construction,	10,401.58		10,401.58
Engine House, Low Service,	33,014.09	56.52	33,070.61
Engine House, High Service,	5,890.12		5,890.12
Engine House Aqueduct,		302.84	302.84
Engineer's Residence,	3,639.99		3,639.99
Fireman's Houses,	5,524.75		5,524.75
High Service Tower, Lake Avenue Construction,	19,440.93		19,440.93
High Service Tower, Elm Street Construction,	20,113.09		20,113.09
High Service Stand Pipe, Elm Street Construction,	9,152.56		9,152.56
Shop and Store Room,	1,547.40		1,547.40
Boat House,	440.00		440.00
Engines, Nos. 1 and 2 Boilers L. S.,	17,941.90		17,941.90
Engines, Nos. 2 and 1 Boilers L. S.,	32,168.01		32,168.01
Engines, Nos. 1 and 1 Boiler H. S.,	4,367.50		4,367.50
Engines, Nos. 2 and 1 Boiler H. S.,	6,778.91		6,778.91
Engine and Boiler Aqueduct,		1,768.87	1,768.87
Boilers, Low Service,	1,425.29	2,259.38	3,684.67
Fort Field Reservoir Construction,	159,797.80	73,992.69	233,790.49
Saw Mill River Valley Tests,		4.77	4.77
Engineering,	50,981.01	4,892.85	55,873.86
Counsel Fees, Advertising and Printing, Treasurer's Fees, and other Miscellaneous Expenses,	32,926.68	576.84	33,503.52
	$1,297,444.81	$115,945.14	$1,413,389.95

The Twenty-third Annual Report of the Board of the Water Commissioners of the City of Yonkers was presented December 1, 1895. It contains a report to the Board of Mr. William Henry Baldwin Engineer, which sets forth the following facts:

"The Fort Field distribution reservoir which was under contract with Messrs. Dougherty & Berrigan is finished. The work was commenced in April, 1893. It was completed, and the final certificate given November 27, 1895. Some idea of the magnitude of the work may be derived from a reference to some of the material and labor set forth in the final estimate:

"83,000 cubic yards of earth excavation; 52,000 cubic yards of earth embankment; 57,000 cubic yards of masonry; 11,500 cubic yards of concrete; 8,890 square yards of paving, besides the gate-house and the pipes and valves. The time required to do the work was thirty-two months. The capacity is 60,441,449 gallons. The reservoir is in two compartments, separated by a masonry wall. . . . The bottom of the reservoir is covered with a layer of concrete, consisting of one part hydraulic cement, three parts sand and six parts broken stone. The gate-house is built of stone, selected from the excavations, lined with brick, and all laid in Portland cement. The water from the low service pumping-station, 6,000 feet distant, is brought into the gate-house by a twenty-four inch force main, discharging into a forty-eight inch cast-iron vertical stand pipe, and conducted thence by two thirty-inch pipes passing at an angle of 45° through the core wall, the embankment and pavement, and discharging through screen chambers into the easterly and westerly compartments of the reservoir respectively. The supply to the city is taken through the screen chambers by means of thirty-inch pipes, also passing through the embankment and core walls, and also through the gate-house into the public streets, and thence to the city. All of the gates and valves for controlling the flow of water, both into and out of the reservoir, are situated in the gate-house, and are accessible at all times, as no water is admitted into the gate-house itself, but is passed through it by means of the pipes and valves.

"In addition to the inlet pipes above described, there is another twenty-four inch pipe leading from the forty-eight inch stand pipe along the dividing wall, built into the masonry, and terminating in an elbow, about the middle of the wall, supplied with a movable appliance so arranged as to discharge the water over a weir, into either the easterly or westerly compartment at will. The object is to aerate the water as it comes from the pumps. The entire work is drained by an eight-inch cast-iron mud pipe passing under the concrete bottom of the gate itself. This drain pipe is operated by valves situated in the gate-house.

"The arrangement of gates and valves is such that water can be admitted or discharged independently from either the easterly or westerly compartments of this reservoir at will, or can be turned from the force main directly into the outlet pipe, thence to the city, without entering the reservoir at all.

"The entire property purchased for this reservoir consists of about fifteen and four-tenths acres, of which nearly two acres from the easterly side have been appropriated for a building site, and a dwelling-house will be erected thereon for the use of the keeper. The dwelling will be constructed of stone taken from the premises, and will conform in general appearance to the surroundings.

"The water surface, when the two compartments of the reservoir are full, will contain nine and three-tenths acres, and the area inclosed within the limits of the slope amounts to nine and seven-tenths acres. The exterior slopes of all embankments have been covered with soil, the grounds not occupied by the reservoir have been regulated and graded and paved,

SAMUEL L. COOPER.

gutters have been so placed as to lead all surface water away and discharge it outside the premises. The street front along the Palmer Road and also the exterior property lines have been inclosed with stone walls so that the entire property presents a neat and substantial appearance.

"As to the general supply of water for the requirements of the city, the recent period of dry weather, extending over several years, has directed attention to the matter of securing an additional supply. The attention of the engineer has been carefully given to it, and examination has been made of the records of the amount of water furnished by the rain-fall, together with the amount used for the requirements of the city, and also the amount of water which has run to waste over the dam at the Grassy Sprain reservoir, with a view of determining whether an additional supply of water could be derived from this water-shed. This investigation, when compared with the records made for a period of twenty-five years by the Croton Aqueduct Department brings to light the fact that the rain-fall during the past six years has been unusually small, but, notwithstanding this fact, the amount of water which has gone to waste over the dam during this period of six years has been somewhat more than the entire consumption of the city during that time. The capacity of the Grassy Sprain reservoir is about 400,000,000 gallons, while the amount of water which went to waste over the dam between December 1, 1894, and April 5, 1895, was 900,000,000 gallons, or about double the capacity of the reservoir. These facts show beyond a question of doubt that if the reservoir had been of sufficient size to hold back a reasonable portion of the water which went to waste in the spring-time and save it for use later in the season, there would have been no such scarcity of water as we have been experiencing during the past summer. The question has often been raised whether there is water enough in the stream to fill such a reservoir if it was built. Considering the question in the light of the above statement that enough water has gone to waste over the dam in the driest season on record, to have filled our present reservoir nearly twice over, there seems to be no doubt whatever that such additional storage reservoir as you have contemplated in the proposed enlargement of the Grassy Sprain reservoir, could be most easily filled and made available for use. Your engineer, therefore, most earnestly recommends that you take immediate action to build the proposed enlargement of the Grassy Sprain reservoir, which you have had in contemplation several years."

JOHN G. PEENE.

The site in the old days was a quarry and swamp, and no less than eight hundred cords of wood were cut from the land on which the basins now rest. The gate-house is a solid and substantial looking structure and there is a stone sill over twelve feet in length taken from the property. The enormous carriage blocks are also of home manufacture. The three tablets above the door of the gate-house bear the following inscriptions:

BOARD OF WATER COMMISSIONERS.
RUDOLF EICKEMEYER, President.
JACOB READ, Treasurer.
JOHN J. TIERNEY.
MICHAEL WALSH.
JOHN EYLERS.

YONKERS WATER WORKS.
FORTFIELD RESERVOIR.

WILLIAM H. BALDWIN, Engineer.
EDWIN A. QUICK & SON, Architects.
JOS. A. LOCKWOOD, Superintendent.
DOUGHERTY & BERRIGAN, Contractors.

YONKERS DEPARTMENT OF PUBLIC WORKS. Previous to 1893, street construction work was under the direction of the City Surveyor, and all maintenance and repairs were in the hands of the Street Commissioner. The Yonkers Department of Public Works was created by Act of Legislature, 1893. The Department is charged with the care, maintenance and preservation of the city highways, docks, water courses and bridges.

Mr. Samuel Lispenard Cooper, a graduate of New York University (scientific department) was appointed the first Commissioner of Public Works and still occupies the office. He had been with the Department of Public Works, New York City, from 1879 to 1889, and with the New York City Finance Department as Supervising Engineer from 1889 to 1893.

When Mr. Cooper entered upon the duties of his office there were no paved streets in Yonkers. Since that time there have been laid nearly two miles of granite block pavement and over six miles of asphalt pavement. Twenty-three miles of roadways* have been macadamized, about half of which were not previously macadamized. About eight miles of sewers have been constructed, making a total of about thirty-one miles of sewers in Yonkers on February 1, 1896. The city now owns its own street cleaning equipments, including street sweeper, carts, horses, etc. All the paved streets of the city are cleaned daily. The department has expended (since its creation by act of the Legislature), on street improvements and sewers, about $1,000,000.

The names of the Commissioners of Charities of Yonkers are recorded at the end of this chapter. During the year ending February 29, 1896, the amount expended by the Commissioner for the relief of the poor was about $3,000. The city sends destitute Roman Catholic children to the Home of the Sisters of the Third Order of St. Francis, Peekskill, N. Y. Some are sent to the Roman Catholic Protectory at Westchester. Destitute Protestant

FIRE COMMISSIONERS OF YONKERS.

1. JOHN ROWLAND.   3. ROBERT KELLOCK.
2. JOHN FOERST.   4. ROBERT STEWART.

1. CHARLES STAHL, Chief Engineer.
2. THOMAS F. MULCAHEY, 1st Assistant.   3. JAMES KEARNS, JR., 2d Assistant.

* The drives through and around Yonkers, are among the most beautiful in the United States. To the north, with splendid river views all the way, is the road to Hastings, Dobb's Ferry, Irvington, Sunnyside, Tarrytown and Sleepy Hollow. New York merchants, artists, bankers, retired millionaires and others have their palatial residences along that drive. To the east Valentine Hill, Mount Vernon, New Rochelle, Glen Island and other points, some of them of especial interest (as are those along the northward drive) to the lover of history, song and romance. To the south is Woodlawn, one of the most beautiful cemeteries in the world. Its marbles and mausoleums of great artistic beauty, have been erected at vast cost. The jewelled hand of affection has lavished silver and gold to build enduring memorials of the dear and unforgotten dead. To the southward are Van Cortlandt's Park (a part of which is the New York parade ground, where mock battles occur), Central Park, and Riverside Park, made sacred by the dust of General U. S. Grant. There he sleeps well,

"While the great stars burn, the moons increase,
And the great ages onward roll."

1. JOHN G. PEENE, Mayor.   12. JOHN PAGAN, JR., City Clerk.

ALDERMEN OF YONKERS.

2. LESLIE SUTHERLAND.
3. MICHAEL FITZGERALD.
4. HENRY GAUL.
5. ABRAHAM H. TOMPKINS.
6. JOHN J. BRODERICK.
7. GEORGE H. KALER.
8. MICHAEL MOONEY.
9. EDGAR U. REYNOLDS.
10. E. ALEXANDER HOUSTON.
11. JOHN H. SCHLOBOHM.

children are sent to the Protestant Temporary Home at White Plains; Destitute adults are sent to the Westchester County Alms House at East View, on the New York and Putnam Railroad.

The history of the schools of Yonkers, prior to the incorporation of the city, is recorded in Chapter X. and preceding chapters. When the city was incorporated, there were six school districts in the town, and each was independent of the others. The schools remained separate until May 27, 1881, when they were consolidated. The history of the important movement leading to consolidation is recorded in Chapter XIII. Previous to consolidation, the people of each district were notified of the date of the annual school meeting. The meetings were held in the respective school-houses. Reports were made by the trustees, who informed those attending the meetings what the expenses of the previous year were, and the estimated expenses of the ensuing year. Appropriations were asked to meet those expenses. The amount the people voted to appropriate was raised by separate tax for the public schools. Before the meetings adjourned trustees were elected. This method, which is adapted to

ALDERMEN OF YONKERS.

1. CHARLES E. SKINNER.
2. HYATT GARRISON.
3. ARTHUR W. NUGENT.
4. JOHN SOUTHWICK.
6. PATRICK CURRAN.

5. CHARLES F. HULBERT, Assistant City Clerk.

country districts and small towns, proves cumbersome in large cities. The bill by which the schools were consolidated, provided for the appointment by the Mayor, independent of confirmation by the Common Council, of fifteen citizens as a Yonkers Board of Education, to have the management of the schools of the city. The bill went into operation in 1881, when the Hon. Norton P. Otis was Mayor of Yonkers. The gentlemen whom he appointed held their first meeting July 12, 1881, and divided themselves into five classes, consisting of three members in each class—three to serve one year, three two years, three three years, three four years, and three five years. By the provisions of the act, the Board is authorized to appoint a Superintendent of public schools to act as clerk of the Board, and have oversight of the schools. The Superintendent is not to be chosen from among the members of the Board. The names of citizens who were members of the Board of Education of No. 6, and of those who were members of the Board of Education of No. 2, previous to the consolidation of the schools, are recorded in the latter part of this chapter, where there is also a record of the names of those who have served the city as members of the consolidated Board of Education. The history of the movement leading to consolidation, and of the schools since that important act of the Legislature, is recorded in Chapter XIII., "The Yonkers Schools."

The Board of Civil Service Examiners was organized November 1, 1884. It was at first composed of three citizens appointed by the Mayor. They employed a secretary, not a member of the Board. On July 31, 1894, the Municipal Civil Service rules were amended. The new rules provide for the appointment of four members, one of whom shall act as secretary. The secretary receives a small compensation. The other members serve without salary. It is the duty of the examiners to ascertain the qualifications of those seeking, or named for, positions in the departments and offices of the municipal government, to which the regulations of the Board apply. A printed pamphlet, containing the regulations, can be had on application to the secretary. The names of the examiners are recorded in the latter part of this chapter.

WILLIAM P. CONSTABLE.

The Yonkers Gazette (weekly), *The Yonkers Statesman* (weekly and daily), *The Yonkers Herald* (daily), *The Plaindealer* (weekly, published for a brief time), *The Yonkers Free Press* (weekly, published for a short time), *The Yonkers Home Journal* (weekly, German and English edition, published for a short time), *The Catholic News* (weekly, R. C. newspaper), and other papers (several were small sheets published by Protestant churches), brought to their readers during this period (1872–1896), local and other news. The files of two or three of these papers cover the twenty-four years since Yonkers was incorporated, and impress one who reads them with the multitudinous and varied interests of a rapidly growing city. He finds reports of births, marriages, deaths, school and church and society events, political campaigns (local, state and national), meetings of fraternities and associations, strikes (that of the Smith Carpet Company employees was February 20, 1885), crimes, tragedies, continued improvements of private and public property, erection of residences and of public buildings, including churches, the mounting of new church bells ("preachers reading great sermons with their iron tongues"), the opening of new streets and avenues, and the improving of old streets, the coming of new residents, publication of larger directories, organization of new fraternities, fire companies and bands, society news, the steady growth of long established industries and the establishment of new industries, military, fire and political parades, fairs, lectures, concerts, entertainments, theatrical plays in Music Hall* and elsewhere, efforts of churches and of law and order societies to restrain the deadly liquor traffic, public meetings in the interest of sufferers at home and abroad, the construction of the new Croton Aqueduct, which extends about five

---

* Reference has been made in a previous chapter to several halls, among them "The Long Room," on the first floor of an unoccupied dwelling-house, which stood on the southwest corner of the present Main Street and South Broadway. It was used for public assemblies in the Thirties and Forties, and was afterward moved into Riverdale Avenue, near Washington Street. The first building erected in Yonkers in order to provide the public with a hall, was built in 1845 by Mr. Ethan Flagg, at the corner of the present New Main Street and Palisade Avenue. It was on the second floor and would seat about two hundred and fifty persons. It was called Flagg's Hall. When the Getty Lyceum (in the Getty House) was completed in 1852, it became a popular public hall. The Farrington building, which was erected about 1857, on the north side of the Square, contained a hall known as Farrington Hall. This was burned in 1866. The Radford building, erected on its site, contained a hall, known as Radford Hall. There was, some years ago, a small hall in a building on the west side of Main Street, and not far from Getty Square. It was called Humboldt Hall. The Yonkers Savings Bank has on the second floor the Yonkers Lyceum Hall. The first hall of the Teutonia Society stood and still stands on Main Street at the corner of Brook Street. Turn Verein Hall is on Chicken Island. Washburn Hall, now Warburton, was erected in 1876, by Benjamin S. Washburn & Son. The third story was devoted to a large hall (42 x 85) exclusive of the stage. It would seat, with its gallery, eight hundred and sixty persons. It was opened June 1, 1876. It is now converted into offices. The Warburton Hall Association, incorporated in 1881, by Messrs. William Allen Butler, Warren B. Smith, Walter W. Law, James Stewart and George Stewart, purchased the building and subsequently constructed Music Hall, which was opened April 14, 1884. The Casino Skating Rink, a very large building as to the area it covered, was opened December, 1884. It is said that the galleries would seat a thousand people and that as many as eight hundred skaters were on the floor at one time; The Rink stood at the corner of Riverdale Avenue and Hudson Street. It burned down in April, 1886. Garfield Hall, northeast corner of Main Street and Market Place; Hawthorn Hall, in large brick building, northeast corner of Main Street and Buena Vista Avenue; Teutonia Hall on Buena Vista Avenue; Odd Fellows Hall on North Broadway; Wiggin's Hall, 24 North Broadway; Temperance Hall, North Broadway; The Woman's Institute Hall, Palisade Avenue; St. Mary's Hall, St. Mary's Street; Y. M. C. A. Hall, Main Street, and Montgomery Hall are among the public halls of the city.

miles through Yonkers (work on it was commenced in 1885, only a small part of the structure is above ground), trains beginning to run to Getty Square (1888), Sunday-school, fraternity and social excursions up the river to Iona Island and elsewhere, and down the river, bound for a sail over New York Bay, or up Long Island Sound, New York excursion steamers' announcement of regular trips from Yonkers to Long Branch and other watering places, the establishment of a branch Custom-House at the Yonkers port, trials of skill on land and river, shooting at the Morsemere Range (opposite the residence of G. Livingston Morse, North Broadway), coasting on streets where police permitted it, skating and rowing at Van Cortlandt Park and elsewhere, the running of the tally-ho through Yonkers, the arrival of prominent guests at private residences or at the hotels,* the establishment of a steam ferry to Alpine Dock and to the pleasure groves at the foot of the Palisades, the coming to Yonkers of such well-known evangelists as Mrs. Van Cott, and Messrs. Hammond, Pentecost, Moody, Wells, Greenwood, Smith (Gipsy) and B. Fay Mills, the growth of banking, the slight earthquake

VALENTINE BROWNE, M.D.

shocks of 1874 and 1896, the sale of city lots (in 1873, the average price at auction sale of city lots on the Herriot Property, between Broadway and the Hudson River, was about $1,025), the bi-Centennial celebration of October 18, 1882, when Manor Hall was "aglow with more than light of other days," when seven thousand or more were assembled near the venerable structure, and when there was a fine parade, a salute of twenty guns fired at sunrise from the U. S. Steamer Kearsarge, an oration delivered by the Rev. David Cole, D.D., and fire-works and a search-light display in the evening, etc., (for full record of this important occasion see Scharf's "Westchester County," and the Yonkers newspapers of the time), the great blizzard of March, 1888, which was the heaviest snow-storm ever known in the section, and which stopped trains and suspended traffic, the introduction of mail delivery by uniformed mail carriers, the unveiling of the soldiers' and sailors' monument† on September 17, 1891, when there was another great parade and, on Manor Hall grounds, formal dedicatory exercises, which consisted of a concert by the West Point Band, an opening address by Mr. Charles E. Gorton, President of the Soldiers' and Sailors' Monu-

CHARLES F. BROWN.

* The public houses of former days were Hunt's Tavern (on the site of the Getty House) and the Indian Queen's Inn, or The Nappeckamack House, built on the same site, by Jacob Stout, between 1796 and 1802. Bashford's Tavern, at the sloop wharf, in the Forties, Broadway House, No. 5 North Broadway (the sheds of which extended northward to the Saw Mill River Bridge, North Broadway). Among those of the present day are the Getty House which was built in 1852, the Mansion House (now known as the Arlington Inn), built about 1835, by Dr. DeWitt C. Kellinger at the south corner of South Broadway and Guion Street, and The Dunwellyn, Nos. 35, 37 and 39 Racine Avenue. In 1896, Mr. C. M. Johnson leased the Wynnstay flats, Warburton Avenue, and established a hotel there The Citizens' National Bank, having purchased the southern part of the Getty House, erected on its site a banking house.

† One of the most ardent advocates of the erecting of the monument was Mr. Abram H. Tompkins, subsequently Alderman Tompkins, a soldier of the Union, who, as early as 1873, placed in conspicuous places, boxes to receive contributions toward a monument fund. The remarks on Decoration Day, May 30, 1888, at Music Hall, by Mr. William Allen Butler, and the names of the Committee whom he, as chairman of the memorial meeting, appointed, with power to solicit subscriptions and erect a monument, and also the names of citizens who contributed, are recorded in the memorial volume which the Soldiers' and Sailors' Monument Association published. The influence of Mr. John W. Oliver, editor of *The Daily Statesman*, in forwarding the project, was potent.

ment Association, a prayer by the Rev. Alexander B. Carver, an oration by the Hon. Orlando B. Potter, the singing of "America" by a chorus, the reciting, by the Rev. Thomas McLaughlin, of a poem entitled "The Men who Saved the Union" (written by Mr. S. R. Whitney, of Yonkers), the unveiling of the monument by Miss Susie Leeds Heermance, daughter of Colonel William L. Heermance, the dedicatory address by President Gorton, the firing of a salute by the U. S. war-steamer Boston, (the signal for the salute having been given by the commander of the vessel who was seated on the platform near Manor Hall, at the side of the presiding officer, and having been transmitted to the steamer Boston by signal flags waved from the roof of Manor Hall), the recitation by Miss Eleanor Georgen, of a poem written by Mrs. Jennie L. Lyall, of Yonkers, and entitled, "Honor Our Loyal Men," the singing of "The Star Spangled Banner," with band accompaniment, the closing prayer by the Rev. Dr. John Reid, "taps" by the bugle, played by Mr. William J. Bright, three volleys fired in perfect unison by the Fourth Separate Company, of Yonkers, and the subsequent publication of a full report of the movement to build the monument and its successful culmination, with complete reports of the oration, addresses, poems, prayers, etc., in a handsomely illustrated volume, entitled "Yonkers in the Rebellion," which was edited by Thomas Astley Atkins and John Wise Oliver.*

POLICE COMMISSIONERS OF YONKERS.

1. Theodore H. Silkman.
2. William Moller.
3. J. Foster Jenkins.
4. Henry R. Hicks.

These were among the many local events reported by the press during the period under review. The citizens in conversations, and in the columns of the city papers have from time to time discussed projected improvements (some of which are not yet made), among them, opening of public parks, erection of public bathing-houses, more thorough numbering of houses, methods of educating careless citizens to keep from the streets in front of their dwellings that which gives them an untidy appearance, the need of a public library building (the public library is now in the High School building), and of a museum and art gallery, the extension of the trolley lines up the Hudson, out to White Plains, (the county-seat), over to Glen Island and southward to New York. Citizens have also

---

*The various public meetings, under the auspices of the Grand Army of the Republic, have been of great interest to the citizens. In the early years Decoration Day meetings were held in the cemetery, where addresses were made and other features introduced. Through the influence of Mr. John C. Shotts, afterward Department Commander of New York State, exercises were held annually in Music Hall. Singing by school children, instrumental music, recitations, quartettes, solos, saluting the flag and other parts of the programmes deeply interested the large audiences. The successive orators of those occasions were: 1888, Comrade General Thomas Ewing and Rev. Dr. George E. Strobridge, D.D.; 1889, Comrade Rev. A. J. Palmer, D.D.; 1890, General James R. O'Beirne; 1891, Rev. Edwin A. Schell, Ph. D.; 1892, Rev. Alexander Carver (now Dr. Carver); 1893, Rev. Charles Elmer Allison; 1894, Rev. S. Parkes Cadman; 1895, Hon. Wallace Bruce; 1896, Comrade Cyrus A. Peake.

In 1894, at the suggestion of Comrade William H. Fisher, Department Commander Shotts, moved, at a G. A. R. meeting, that Superintendent Gorton be requested to assist in arranging for a morning open air public meeting on Memorial Day near the soldiers' monument. The meeting of 1894 was greatly enjoyed. The various bodies of school children marched to their assigned places and by their singing delighted the concourse of citizens. Addresses were made and instrumental music was discoursed. The meetings of 1895 and 1896 were equally successful.

considered the pressing need of more rapid transit to the metropolis, the erection of a United States Government building, the need of a large and elegant hotel, the proposed establishment of a zoological garden at Van Cortlandt Park, which would require, if the suggested plan is adopted, one hundred acres, for the collection of animals would be the finest in the whole country. Should this garden be located south of Yonkers, and should the Palisades, on the west, be set apart, as is proposed, for a National Park and Parade Ground, to cost over $4,000,000, and should other projected improvements be completed, Yonkers, already highly favored above other towns, will afford another illustration of the truth, that some cities resemble those men, of whom it is written, "For unto every one that hath, shall be given, and he shall have abundance."

While the residents of the city during this period were considering events of local interest, they were also reading in their own papers, and in the great New York dailies and other papers and periodicals, reports of events transpiring in New York State during the administrations of nine Governors (Hoffman, Dix, Tilden, Robinson, Cornell, Cleveland, Hill, Flower and Morton). The press also brought reports of events transpiring in the country at large, during the administrations of six Presidents (Grant, Hayes, Garfield, Arthur, Cleveland, Harrison, and Cleveland—second term), and the news of the period (1872-1896) from foreign countries. Among the latest events were the war between China and Japan, the persecutions of the Armenians by the bloody Turks, Röntgen's discovery of a method of photographing interior substances more dense than their environment, and the Venezuela boundary dispute, which made excitable citizens apprehensive of a war between Great Britain and the United States. One of the most sensible suggestions which, in the early part of 1896, found place in the press of the country, including that of Yonkers, was the appointment of a Board of Arbitration to decide all disputes arising between the two nations. That would hasten the coming of the day,

"When the war-drum throbs no
  longer,
And the battle-flags are furl'd
In the Parliament of man,
The Federation of the world."

ROLL OF CITY AND TOWN OFFICIALS AND GENERAL STATISTICS.

ELECTIVE OFFICERS AND APPOINTIVE OFFICERS.

The elective officers of the city are a Mayor, a City Judge, four Justices of the Peace, a Supervisor for each of the seven wards, and two Aldermen for each ward.

The appointive officers of the city are a City Clerk, a City Attorney, a Receiver of Taxes, a Commissioner of Public Works, three Assessors, five Commissioners of Public Health, a City Treasurer, a Commissioner of Charities, an Inspector of Buildings, four Fire Commissioners, one or more Pound-keepers, and five Constables—all of whom are nominated, and, with the consent of the Common Council, appointed by the Mayor. A City Auditor is appointed by the Mayor. The Mayor

EDWIN L. THOMAS.

also designated the Civil Service Examiners. The names of these and other officers are recorded on the following pages:

CITY OFFICERS. 1872-3, Mayor, Jas. C. Courter; President of the Common Council, Ethan Flagg; Aldermen: First Ward, Eli L. Seger, John Brennan; Second Ward, Albert Keeler, William Macfarlane; Third Ward, Ethan Flagg, H. L. Garrison; Fourth Ward, Henry R. Hicks, Zeb. H. Brower; City Clerk, W. H. Doty; City Attorney, Matt. H. Ellis. 1873-4, Mayor, Jas. C. Courter; President of the Common Council, William Macfarlane; Aldermen: First Ward, Eli L. Seger, John Brennan; Second Ward, Albert Keeler, William Macfarlane; Third Ward, H. L. Garrison, James Stewart; Fourth Ward, Henry R. Hicks, Michael Mooney; City Clerk, W. H. Doty; City Attorney, Matt. H. Ellis. 1874-5, Mayor, Joseph Masten; President of the Common Council, William Macfarlane; Aldermen: First Ward, Eli L. Seger, Abram S. Radcliff; Second Ward, William Macfarlane, Charles T. Mercer; Third Ward, James Stewart, John S. White; Fourth Ward, Henry R. Hicks, Michael Mooney; City Clerk, W. H. Doty; City Attorney, Matt. H. Ellis. 1875-6, Mayor, Joseph Masten; President of the Common Council, Charles T. Mercer; Aldermen: First Ward, Abram S. Radcliff, Joseph W. Riley; Second Ward, Charles T. Mercer, William H. Copcutt; Third Ward, John S. White, Robert Neville; Fourth Ward, Henry R. Hicks, Michael Mooney; City Clerk, W. H. Doty; City Attorney, R. E. Prime. 1876-7, Mayor, Wm. A. Gibson; President of the Common Council, G. L. Morse; Aldermen: First Ward, Joseph W. Riley, Joseph M. Murphy; Second Ward, Wm. H. Copcutt, James W. Mitchell; Third Ward, Robert Neville, G. L. Morse; Fourth Ward, Henry R. Hicks, Michael Mooney; City Clerk, W. H. Doty; City Attorney, R. E. Prime. 1877-8, Mayor, Wm. A. Gibson; President of the Common Council, G. L. Morse; Aldermen: First Ward, Joseph W. Riley, Joseph M. Murphy; Second Ward, James W. Mitchell, Joseph M. Tompkins; Third Ward, G. L. Morse, Fred. Shonnard; Fourth Ward, Henry R. Hicks, I. V. Underhill; City Clerk, W. H. Doty; City Attorney, Theo. Fitch. 1878-9, Mayor, Joseph Masten; President of the Common Council, Henry R. Hicks; Aldermen: First Ward, Thomas Egan, Bernard Cullen; Second Ward, Jos. M. Tompkins, Edward Underhill; Third Ward, Isaac D. Cole, G. W. Valentine; Fourth Ward, Henry R. Hicks, I. V. Underhill; City Clerk, W. H. Doty; City Attorney, Theo. Fitch. 1879-80, Mayor, Joseph Masten; President of the Common Council, Edward Underhill; Aldermen: First Ward, Thomas Egan, Bernard Cullen; Second Ward, Edward Underhill, Jonathan Vail; Third Ward, Isaac D. Cole, John Pagan; Fourth Ward, Henry R. Hicks, I. V. Underhill; City Clerk, W. H. Doty; City Attorney, Theo. Fitch. 1880-1, Mayor, Norton P. Otis; President of the Common Council, Edward Underhill; Aldermen: First Ward, Thomas Egan, Edward J. Mitchell; Second Ward, Edward Underhill, Jonathan Vail; Third Ward, John Pagan, Wm. P. Ketcham; Fourth Ward, Henry R. Hicks, I. V. Underhill; City Clerk, W. H. Doty; City Attorney, Theo. Fitch. 1881-2, Mayor, Norton P. Otis; President of the Common Council, Henry R. Hicks; Aldermen: First Ward, Thomas Egan, Edward J. Mitchell; Second Ward, Edward Underhill, Jonathan Vail; Third Ward, Wm. P. Ketcham, John F. Thompson; Fourth Ward, Henry R. Hicks, Jas. F. D. Crane; City Clerk, W. H. Doty; City Attorney, Theo. Fitch. 1882-3,

WELLER & WELSH, 5 AND 7 NORTH BROADWAY.

Mayor, Samuel Swift; President of the Common Council, Leander Hodges; Aldermen: First Ward, Thomas Egan, Edward J. Mitchell; Second Ward, Jonathan Vail, Leander Hodges; Third Ward, John F. Thomson, Fisher A. Baker; Fourth Ward, Henry R. Hicks, Jas. F. D. Crane; City Clerk, W. H. Doty; City Attorney, Theo. Fitch. 1883-4, Mayor, Samuel Swift; President of the Common Council, Edward J. Mitchell; Aldermen: First Ward, Edward J. Mitchell, Thomas Egan; Second Ward, Leander Hodges, Charles T. Mercer; Third Ward, Fisher A. Baker, J. Irving Burns; Fourth Ward, Henry R. Hicks, Michael Mooney; City Clerk, W. H. Doty; City Attorney, Jos. F. Daly. 1884-5, Mayor, W. G. Stahlnecker; President of the Common Council, Michael Mooney; Aldermen: First Ward, Edward J. Mitchell, Thomas Egan; Second Ward, Charles T. Mercer, Thomas L. Mottram; Third Ward, J. Irving Burns, Michael F. Murray; Fourth Ward, Michael Mooney, I. V. Underhill; City Clerk, W. H. Doty; City Attorney, Jos. F. Daly. 1885-6, Mayor, W. G. Stahlnecker; President of the Common Council, none appointed; Aldermen: First Ward, Edward J. Mitchell, George H. Lowerre; Second Ward, Thomas L. Mottram, Wm. Greenhalgh; Third Ward, Michael F. Murray, Edwin A. Quick; Fourth Ward, Michael Mooney, I. V. Underhill; City Clerk, W. H. Doty; City Attorney, Jos. F. Daly. 1886-7, Mayor, J. Harvey Bell; President of the Common Council, George H. Lowerre; Aldermen: First Ward, George H. Lowerre, Wm. H. Casey; Second Ward, Wm. Greenhalgh, John Schlobohm; Third Ward, Edwin A. Quick, Maurice H. Downing; Fourth Ward, Michael Mooney, I. V. Underhill; City Clerk, W. H. Doty; City Attorney, Jos. F. Daly. 1887-8, Mayor, J. Harvey Bell; President of the Common Council, Michael Mooney; Aldermen: First Ward, Wm. H. Casey, Thos. J. Lally; Second Ward, John Schlobohm, Edward Underhill; Third Ward, Maurice H. Downing, John J. Broderick; Fourth Ward, Michael Mooney, I. V. Underhill; City Clerk, W. H. Doty; City Attorney, Jos. F. Daly. 1888-9, Mayor, J. Harvey Bell; President of the Common Council, E. Underhill; Aldermen: First Ward, Thos. J. Lally, James P. Gorman; Second Ward, John Schlobohm, Edward Underhill; Third Ward, John J. Broderick, Chas. H. Butler; Fourth Ward, Michael Mooney, John A. Kane; City Clerk,

DRY GOODS ESTABLISHMENT OF CHARLES R. CULVER,
5 AND 7 MAIN STREET.

W. H. Doty; City Attorney, Jos. F. Daly. 1889-90, Mayor, J. Harvey Bell; President of the Common Council, John Schlobohm; Aldermen: First Ward, Jas. P. Gorman, Thos. J. Lally; Second Ward, John Schlobohm, Marvin R. Oakley; Third Ward, Charles H. Butler, John J. Broderick; Fourth Ward, Wm. Austin, John A. Kane; City Clerk, W. H. Doty; City Attorney, Jos. F. Daly. 1890-1, Mayor, James Millward; President of the Common Council, Thos. J. Lally; Aldermen: First Ward, Thos. J. Lally, Finton Phelan; Second Ward, Marvin R. Oakley, John Schlobohm; Third Ward, John J. Broderick, Edwin A. Quick; Fourth Ward, Wm. Austin, John A. Kane; City Clerk, W. H. Doty; City Attorney, Jos. F. Daly. 1891-2, Mayor, James Millward; President of the Common Council, John A. Kane; Aldermen: First Ward, Thos. J. Lally, Finton Phelan; Second Ward, Marvin R. Oakley, John Schlobohm; Third

Ward, John J. Broderick, Edwin A. Quick; Fourth Ward, John A. Kane, David H. Taxter; City Clerk, J. Pagan, Jr.; City Attorney, Jos. F. Daly. 1892-3, Mayor, Jas. H. Weller; President of the Common Council, John Schlobohm; Aldermen: First Ward, John F. Brady, Thomas J. Lally; Second Ward, Marvin R. Oakley, A. H. Tompkins; Third Ward, John J. Broderick, Thomas E. Booth; Fourth Ward, John A. Kane, David H. Taxter; Fifth Ward, John Schlobohm, George U. Stewart; City Clerk, J. Pagan, Jr.; City Attorney, Jas. M. Hunt. 1893-4, Mayor, Jas. H. Weller; President of the Common Council, Thos. J. Lally; Aldermen: First Ward, John F. Brady, Thomas J. Lally; Second Ward, A. H. Tompkins, Henry Gaul; Third Ward, John J. Broderick; Thomas E. Booth; Fourth Ward, John A. Kane, Joseph H. Beall; Fifth Ward, John Schlobohm, James P. Dunn; City Clerk, J. Pagan, Jr.; City Attorney, Jas. M. Hunt. 1894-5, Mayor, John G. Peene; President of the Common Council, J. J. Broderick; Aldermen: First Ward, Thomas J. Lally, Leslie Sutherland; Second Ward, A. H. Tompkins, Henry Gaul; Third Ward, John J. Broderick, George H. Kaler; Fourth Ward, Joseph H. Beall, Michael Mooney; Fifth Ward, John Schlobohm, James P. Dunn; City Clerk, J. Pagan, Jr.; City Attorney, Jas. M. Hunt. 1895-6, Mayor, John G. Peene; President of the Common Council, John Schlobohm; Aldermen: First Ward, Leslie Sutherland, Michael Fitzgerald; Second Ward, A. H. Tompkins, Henry Gaul; Third Ward, John J. Broderick, George H. Kaler; Fourth Ward, Michael Mooney, Edgar U. Reynolds; Fifth Ward, John Schlobohm, E. Alex. Houston; City Clerk, J. Pagan, Jr.; City Attorney, Jas. M. Hunt. 1896-7, Mayor, John G. Peene; President of the Common Council, Leslie Sutherland; Aldermen: First Ward, John H. Southwick, Charles E. Skinner; Second Ward, John H. Schlobohm, E. Alex. Houston; Third Ward, George H. Kaler, Hyatt L. Garrison; Fourth Ward, Leslie Sutherland, Michael Fitzgerald; Fifth Ward, Henry Gaul, Abraham H. Tompkins; Sixth Ward, John J. Broderick, Patrick J. Curran; Seventh Ward, Michael Mooney, Edgar U. Reynolds; City Clerk, John Pagan, Jr.; City Attorney, James M. Hunt.

Alderman Arthur W. Nugent was elected at the annual election, held November, 1895, to succeed Alderman John H. Schlobohm, whose term of office expired April 15, 1896. Charles F. Hulbert, Assistant City Clerk; Joseph O'Brien, Page to the Common Council.

CITY JUDGES. 1872-76, Edward P. Baird; 1876-80, Edward P. Baird; 1880-84, Matt. H. Ellis; 1884-88, George B. Pentz; 1888-92, Stephen H. Thayer; 1892-96, Francis X. Donoghue; 1896-1900, William C. Kellogg.

JUDICIAL. 1894-95, City Judge, F. X. Donoghue; Clerk of City Court, Frederick C. Williams; City Marshal, James J. Quinn; Official Stenographer, James D. Ivers; Deputy Court Clerk, Henry J. Rowan; Justices of the Peace, William Riley, W. W. Scrugham, Adrian M. Potter, Henry A. Ritchie. 1895-96, City Judge, William C. Kellogg; Clerk of City Court, Harry W. Ritchie; City Marshal, Thomas E. Lee; Official Stenographer, Gustave Desgrey, Jr.; Deputy Court Clerk, Henry J. Rowan.

SUPERVISORS OF YONKERS. The town of Yonkers was set apart March 7, 1788. The Supervisors have been: 1788, David Hunt; 1789, James Archer; 1790-94, William Hadley; 1795-96, John Robert; 1797-1800, Garret Dyckman; 1801, William Hadley; 1802-24, Isaac Vermilyea; 1825-41, Caleb Smith; 1842-44, Prince W. Paddock; 1845-49, William W. Scrugham; 1850-53, James L. Valentine; 1854-55, William G. Ackerman; 1856-57, William W. Scrugham; 1858-59, Augustus Van Cortlandt; 1860, Ethan

WILLIAM PALMER EAST, 50 WARBURTON AVENUE.

Flagg; 1861–62, James L. Valentine; 1863, Ethan Flagg; 1864–66, Isaac H. Knox; 1867–68, Ethan Flagg; 1869, Edward DeWitt; 1870–71, Ethan Flagg; 1872–73, Charles R. Dusenberry; 1874, John Henry Williams; 1875–77, Jacob Read; 1878–81, James V. Lawrence; 1882–92, Jacob Read; 1893, First Ward, A. J. Prime; Second Ward, Henrie A. Percival; Third Ward, Patrick A. Conniff; Fourth Ward, Jeremiah J. Clancy; Fifth Ward, William H. McPherson; 1894, First Ward, Michael Fitzgerald; Second Ward, Henrie A. Percival; Third Ward, Elijah M. Yerks; Fourth Ward, Charles R. Dusenberry; Fifth Ward, Isaiah Frazier; 1895, First Ward, Michael Fitzgerald; Second Ward, Isaiah Frazier; Third Ward, Elijah M. Yerks; Fourth Ward, John J. Burns; Fifth Ward, Henrie A. Percival; Sixth Ward, Patrick Whalen; Seventh Ward, Charles R. Dusenberry.

RECEIVERS OF TAXES. 1872–1896. 1872, Kellogg Francis; 1877, Henry B. Archer.

STREET COMMISSIONERS. After the days of roadmasters, and when Yonkers had become a city, street commissioners were appointed. Among those who rendered service in this office were: Captain Joseph Peene, R. P. Getty, Edward M. McElmeel, Charles T. Mercer.

COMMISSIONER OF PUBLIC WORKS. 1893, Samuel Lispenard Cooper; Chief Engineer, E. Ludlow Gould; Assistants, Joseph Sweeny, Jere. S. Clark, Thomas H. See; Book-keeper, E. J. Renahan.

ASSESSORS. The citizens whose names follow, have rendered service as assessors. The charter of 1895, reduced the number of assessors from five to three and provided for the appointment of a clerk of the Board. Mr. William H. Fisher was appointed clerk, June 12, 1895. Hyatt L. Garrison, Frederick A. Back, Caleb F. Underhill, James O'Brien, Frederick W. Rau, P. H. Reardon, Edward Underhill, Michael F. Mitchell, Marvin R. Oakley.

PROTE STORAGE WAREHOUSE, MILL STREET.

HEALTH OFFICERS. 1872, Dr. Horace B. Pike; 1876, Dr. Galusha B. Balsh; 1878, Dr. Valentine Browne; 1895, Dr. Garrett N. Banker.

BOARD OF HEALTH. Dr. Garrett N. Banker (Health Officer), Francis P. Treanor (Health Officer), term expired May 1, 1896; Dr. W. H. Sherman, term expires May 1, 1897; Dr. R. R. Trotter, term expires May 1, 1898; Dr. E. M. Hermance, term expires May 1, 1899; George B. Wray, term expires May 1, 1900; James Handrahan, Secretary, no term.

BOARD OF PLUMBING INSPECTION. The Board of Examiners and Supervisors of Plumbing and Drainage was organized on August 11, 1892. The members were: Dr. Valentine Browne, President; Commissioners, William Henry Baldwin, Robert Harper, Patrick H. Linehan, John A. Lamont.

The members of the present Board are Dr. Garrett N. Banker, President; Commissioners, Samuel L. Cooper, Robert Harper, Patrick H. Linehan, John A. Lamont. The Clerk is James Handrahan.

INSPECTORS OF BUILDINGS. 1872–1896. Anthony Imhoff, appointed June 24, 1889; Augustus Kipp, appointed July 19, 1892.

Within districts defined by the Common Council, no building of wood can be constructed, except with such materials, and in such manner, as shall be approved by the Common Council. Plans of proposed buildings, within said districts, are submitted to the Council or to the Inspector of Buildings for examination.

TREASURERS OF THE CITY OF YONKERS. 1872–1896. George W. Cobb, Bailey Hobbs, Robert P. Getty, John G. P. Holden, Robert P. Getty.

COMMISSIONERS OF CHARITIES. B. A. Starr, April 11, 1873; Michael Galvin, June 21, 1875; Frank Cafferty, October 11, 1877; Michael Galvin, May 13, 1879; George Rayner, February 16, 1880; William P. Constable, July 19, 1892.

CHIEF ENGINEERS OF FIRE DEPARTMENT. 1862, Daniel Blauvelt; 1863–64, Eli L. Seger; 1865–66, Anthony B. Archer; 1867–68, Samuel L. Smith; 1869, Lawrence Page; 1870, John H. Mathews; 1871–72, Lawrence F. Page; 1872–73–74, John Coons; 1874–75–76, Henry L. Myers; 1876–77–78–79–80, E. Alex. Houston; 1880–81–82–84, John Lacy; 1884, John S. Brown; 1886, William Allison; 1888–92, James McVicar; 1892, James Mulcahey; 1894, Charles Stahl. In the Summer of 1896, the city began to pay some of its firemen.

The present Secretary of the Fire Department is Michael A. Kiely.

PROTECTION ENGINE CO. NO. 1. This company was organized June 11, 1853. It has had for its Foremen: August, 1853, to August, 1860, George L. Condit; August, 1860, to August, 1862, Thomas Cogan; August, 1862, to August, 1864, John Houston; August, 1864, to August, 1865, John O'Mara;

WASHINGTON MARKET, W. H. INGHAM, PROPRIETOR, 20 AND 22 NORTH BROADWAY.

August, 1865, to August, 1868, John Crowley; August, 1868, to August, 1869, Thomas Curran; August, 1869, to February, 1870, John O'Mara; February, 1870, to February, 1870, John Smith; August, 1870, to October, 1870, Ralph Bush; October, 1870, to August, 1873, E. J. Mitchell; August, 1873, to August, 1874, Michael Carroll; August, 1874, to August, 1875, John Lacey; August, 1875, to August, 1877, John Brady; August, 1877, to August, 1878, Thomas Mitchell; August, 1878, to August, 1879, E. W. Costello; August, 1879, to August, 1880, J. Merwin; August, 1881, to August, 1882, Patrick Kelly; August, 1882, to August, 1883, Thomas Mitchell; August, 1883, to October, 1883, Thomas Meaney; October, 1883, to August, 1885, Patrick Smith; August, 1885, to August, 1886, P. J. Mitchell; August, 1886, to August, 1887, John Landy; August, 1887, to August, 1888, John T. Lally; August, 1888, to August, 1889, George Graner; August, 1889, to August, 1890, J. J. Bergen; August, 1890, to August, 1892, J. J. Larkin; August, 1892, to August, 1894, Thos. Mulcahey; August, 1894, to August, 1895, J. J. Hogan. The present officers of Protection Engine Co. No. 1, of the City of Yonkers, are as follows: J. J. Hogan, Foreman; Wm. McKenzie, Assistant Foreman; Wm. E. Veideman, Recording Secretary; M. F. Lally, Treasurer; J. J. Larkin and J. J. Hartney, Representatives.

HOPE HOOK AND LADDER CO. NO. 1 was organized August 15, 1853. Those whose names are recorded in the subjoined list have been the Foremen: August 15, 1853, S. W. Chambers; September, 1855, R. L. Bucklin; September, 1856, R. F. Rich; September, 1857, B. A. Starr; September, 1858, David Stewart; September, 1859, Thomas F. Morris; September, 1862, W. B. Edgar; September, 1863, H. F. Brevoort; September, 1864, C. W. Starr; July, 1866, S. L. Smith; November, 1867, W. F. Lawrence; September, 1869, E. A. Rollins; September, 1870, F. H. Woodruff; May, 1871, W. A. Doren; September, 1872, H. S. Wiggens; September, 1873, M. D. Getty; April, 1874, W. A. Doren; December, 1875, J. B. Archibald; September, 1876, W. H. Guernsey; September, 1878, I. S. Lawrence; September, 1879, J. H. Matthews; September, 1880, G. H. Huestis; September, 1881, W. Archibald, Jr.; September, 1883, W. H. Guernsey; September, 1884, A. Taylor; September, 1885, R. L. Stewart; September, 1886, W. M. Hatfield; September, 1888, Robert Kellock; September, 1890, J. George Narr; September, 1891, J. George Narr; September, 1892, Thomas E. Hampson; September, 1893, D. H. Bricker; September, 1894, J. H. Blair; September, 1895, A. M. Keene.

F. J. TOMPKINS, WHOLESALE GROCER, 80 WOODWORTH AVENUE.

LADY WASHINGTON HOSE CO. NO. 2. This company was organized as Lady Washington Engine Co. No. 2, March 2, 1854, and became a hose company March 7, 1876. The names of the Foremen are as follows: 1854-58, Alfred Van Orden; 1859, A. B. Lawrence; 1860-63, Anthony B. Archer; 1864-66, John S. Brown; 1866-69-71-74-76, George A. Mitchell; 1870, William E. Stelwagon; 1872-73, James W. Mitchell; 1877-80, Robert Fawcett; 1881-86, Dennis Lynt; 1882-85, James McVicar; 1887-90-96, John Griffin; 1891, Matthew Eckes; 1892-93, Ferdinand Garnjost; 1894, Benjamin Johnson; 1895, Wiley Tompkins; 1896, John Griffin.

HUDSON HOSE COMPANY NO. 1 was organized January 8, 1868. It has had for its Foremen: January 8, 1868, Ralph I. Bush; January 5, 1869, Lawrence Page; January 4, 1870-75, William R. Wilkison; January 6, 1875, Henry W. Van Wart; January 4, 1876, William R. Wilkison; January 2, 1877-79, John S. Brown; January 7, 1879, William T. White; January 6, 1880, John S. Brown; January 4, 1881, Fred. G. Hill; January 3, 1882, William E. Flandreau; January 2, 1883, James C. Smith; January 8, 1884, Robert Brown; January 6, 1885, Henry Van Wart; January 5, 1886, Charles Stahl; January 2, 1887, Horace Halanbeck; January 3, 1888, William A. Miller; January 8, 1889, Horace Halanbeck; January 7,

1890, Charles Stahl; January 6, 1891, Emmet Nevin; January 5, 1892, Thomas O'Brien; January 3, 1893, John Althoehn; January 2, 1894, Henry A. Landsberg; January 8, 1895, John H. Scholding; January 7, 1896, William A. Miller.

PALISADE HOSE CO. NO. 4. This company was organized January, 1876. It has had for its Foremen: 1876, Edward Whealen; 1877–78, Thomas Coyle; 1879–80, James Mulcahey; 1881, Daniel McGuinness; 1881–83, Jere. Harrigan; 1884, Thomas Tobin; 1885, Richard Fitzgerald; 1886, William Macauley; 1887–88, Dennis Gleason; 1889, Thomas F. Greely; 1890–92, James Mulcahey; 1892–93, Michael McGrath; 1894–95, John Dorney; 1895–96, Thomas Torpey; 1896, John McGuinness.

CITY HOSE CO. NO. 3. This company was organized April, 1876. It has had for its Foremen: 1875–76, Charles Malloy; 1876–81, James Moachler; 1881–82, James Brown; 1882–86, Frederick Kearns; 1886–87, Michael Hays; 1887–89, Edward J. Fitzgerald; 1889–91, Thomas F. Kelly; 1891–92, Jere. P. Lyons; 1892–93, William H. Costello; 1893–94, Richard Atkins; 1894–95, Wright J. Kemp; 1895–96, William H. Costello.

MOUNTAINEER ENGINE CO. NO. 2. This company was organized April, 1876. It has had for its Foremen: 1876–77, Simon Dietzel; 1878, Edward Smith; 1878, Emanuel Fields; 1879, Thomas Moffat; 1880, Simon Dietzel; 1881–82, James F. Smith; 1882–84, George Fischer; 1885, Edward Smith; 1886–87, William E. Townson; 1888–89, William Hallam; 1889–91, William Minnerly; 1892, Edward Cole; 1892, Eugene Hayes; 1893, William Minnerly; 1894–95, John Berrian; 1896, John D. Nodine.

THE PRUYN FURNITURE AND CARPET CO., 107 NEW MAIN STREET.

IRVING HOSE CO. NO. 5. This company was organized May, 1879. It has had numerous Foremen. Among those of recent years, R. W. Anderson, elected in September, 1893, and John Warneck, elected September 6, 1894, who still holds the position.

HOUSTON HOSE CO., NO. 6. This company was organized February 1, 1884. Its Foremen have been: Thomas Coyle, one term; Joseph Keely, two terms; John Shannon, one term; Michael Kane, one term; Abram Laragh, one term; John J. Murray, three terms; James Hart, one term; Michael Moran, one term.

COLUMBIA HOOK AND LADDER CO. NO. 2 was organized February 17, 1887. The company has had six Foremen. 1877–88, Eugene V. Sweeney; 1889–90, Joseph McCarty; 1891, John J. Carroll; 1892–94, James J. Keans; 1895, John A. Boyd; 1896, James J. Sullivan.

AVALANCHE HOSE CO. NO. 7. This company was organized October 17, 1893. It has had for its Foremen: 1893–94, W. Miller, Sr.; 1894–95, E. Barton; 1895–96, E. Barton.

LOWERRE HOSE CO. NO. 9. This company was organized July 26, 1894. It has had for its Foremen: July 26, 1894, R. F. Sharn; September 1, 1895, J. B. Sullivan; April 7, 1896, William L. Mildrum.

SHANNONDALE HOSE CO. NO. 8. This company was organized April 6, 1894. It has had for its Foremen: April 6, 1894, Wm. A. Smith; April 6, 1895, W. V. B. Marquette; April 6, 1896, F. Elliott.

The first Board of Fire Commissioners met for organization October 27, 1881. 1881, John Pentreath, President; George A. Mitchell, Clerk; John O. Campbell, Joseph Peene. 1882, John Pentreath, President; George A. Mitchell, Clerk; John O. Campbell, Joseph Peene—resigned about May 8, 1882, E. Alexander Houston, appointed May 11, 1882. 1883, John Pentreath, President; John O. Campbell, E. Alexander Houston, George A. Mitchell, Clerk. 1884, John O. Campbell, President; John Pentreath, E. Alexander Houston, George A. Mitchell, Clerk. 1885, John Pentreath, President; E. Alexander Houston, reappointed July 13, 1885, John O. Campbell, George A. Mitchell, Clerk. 1886, Lawrence Kelley, appointed January 4, 1886, John Pentreath, President; E. Alexander Houston, George A. Mitchell, Clerk, reappointed October 18, 1886. 1887, E. A. Houston, President; John Pentreath, Lawrence Kelley, George A. Mitchell, Clerk. 1888, E. A. Houston, President; John Pentreath, George A. Mitchell, Lawrence Kelley—resigned about July or August, 1888, James W. Shaughnessy, appointed August 15, 1888. 1889, John Pentreath, James W. Shaughnessy, President; George A. Mitchell, Clerk; James Millward, appointed February 1, 1889. 1890, James W. Shaughnessy, President; John Pentreath, George A. Mitchell, James Millward, resigned about March 9, 1890; W. H. Stewart, appointed about May 9, 1890, died in office November, 1890. 1891, James W. Shaughnessy, President; George A. Mitchell, Clerk; John Pentreath, G. H. Peck, appointed January 27, 1891. 1892, James W. Shaughnessy, resigned January, 1892; Thomas J. Shaughnessy, President, appointed January 13, 1892; John Pentreath—term expired; Robert Kellock, appointed August 5, 1892; G. H. Peck—term expired; John Rowland, appointed October 3, 1892; George A. Mitchell, Clerk—term expired; John Foerst, appointed October 22, 1892; November 14, 1892, J. George Narr (not a commissioner), appointed Clerk by the Board. 1893, R. Kellock, President; John Rowland, Thomas J. Shaughnessy, John Foerst. 1894, R. Kellock, President; John Rowland, Thomas J. Shaughnessy, resigned about April 2, 1894; R. L. Stewart, appointed about May 18, 1894; John Foerst, reappointed October 22, 1894. 1895, John Rowland, President; R. Kellock, John Foerst, Robert L. Stewart. George A. Mitchell served as Clerk of the Board from October 25, 1881, to October 11, 1892. George Narr served as Clerk of the Board from November 14, 1892, to date.

Pound-keeper, Joseph Canepi. Constables: First Ward, John T. McGrath; Second Ward, John L. O'Brien; Third Ward, James J. Quinn; Fourth Ward, M. J. Mooney. Inspector of Engines and Steam Boilers, James Persise. Examiners of Engineers, Halcyon Skinner and W. Garrabrandt.

CITY AUDITOR, Charles F. Brown, appointed June 11, 1895.

EXCISE COMMISSIONERS, 1872–1895. Appointed by Mayor Courter: 1872–73, President, Peter U. Fowler; Clerk, Samuel B. Jones; Patrick Brown; 1873–76, President, Peter U. Fowler; Clerk, Samuel B. Jones; John Wallace. Appointed by Mayor Gibson: 1876–79, President, John S. White; Clerk, Samuel B. Jones; John Wheeler. Appointed by Mayor Masten: 1879–82, President, Henry Stengle; Clerk, Samuel B. Jones; Treasurer, Joseph O'Brien. Appointed by Mayor Swift: 1882–85, President, Henry Stengle; Clerk, Samuel B. Jones; Treasurer, Joseph O'Brien. Appointed by Mayor Stahlnecker: 1885–88, President, Henry Stengle; Clerk, Samuel B. Jones; Treasurer, Joseph O'Brien. This last Board held over, after their terms had expired, until April, 1892, when Mayor Weller made appointments of two new members; Samuel B. Jones continued in office, under former appointment. Appointed by Mayor Weller: 1892–95, President, John Ewald; Clerk, Samuel B. Jones (continued in office under former appointment); Treasurer, Frederick J. Kearns. John Ewald resigned in the spring of 1893, and Theodore J. Bayer was appointed. Appointed by Mayor Peene: 1895–98, President, Joseph Miller; Clerk, John Warneck; Treasurer, Joseph M. Tompkins.

MAHONY & FLOOD, HATTERS AND GENTS' FURNISHING GOODS, 28 NORTH BROADWAY.

COUNSEL FOR THE BOARD OF EXCISE. Prior to May, 1879, James P. Sanders; from May, 1879, Arthur J. Burns; in the spring of 1892, Gabriel Reevs, who is Counsel at the present time. Harold C. Housel is the Clerk. By act of the Legislature, 1896, all Boards of Excise in the State were abolished after April 30th.

BOARD OF WATER COMMISSIONERS ORGANIZED MARCH 18, 1873. 1873-95, Rudolf Eickemeyer; 1873-81, Robt. P. Getty; 1873, David Hawley; 1873, Stephen Banker; 1873-85, Isaac H. Knox; 1873-83, Patrick White; 1873-74, Chas. H. Hamilton; 1874-96, Jacob Read; 1875-84, Ethan Flagg; 1881-90, John Wallace; 1883-88, John G. Peene; 1884-96, Michael Walsh; 1888-93, John C. Shotts; 1891-96, John Eylers; 1893-96, John J. Tierney; 1895-96, Wm. H. Doty. Commissioners, 1896. Wm. H. Doty, President; Jacob Read, Treasurer; Mich'l Walsh, John C. Shotts, John J. Tierney; Jos. A. Lockwood, Clerk and Superintendent; Wm. H. Baldwin, Engineer. Messrs. Banker, Knox, Flagg, Eickemeyer and Doty have been Presidents of the Board. Messrs. Getty and Read, Treasurers. Mr. Hawley was Clerk, March to August, 1873; Mr. Doty from 1873-84; Mr. Jos. A. Lockwood, Clerk from 1884 to date. Mr. W. W. Wilson was Engineer until 1887, and Superintendent, 1876-87; Mr. Lockwood, Superintendent, 1887 to date; Wm. H. Baldwin, Engineer, 1887 to date.

POLICE COMMISSIONERS. 1873-1896. Charles R. Dusenberry, May 14, 1873; George W. Cobb, May 14, 1873; Joseph Peene, May 14, 1873; Dennis McGrath, May 14, 1873; Joseph Masten, May 1, 1876; William L. Hermance, May 1, 1877; Peter U. Fowler, May 1, 1878; E. J. Elting, August 13, 1882; Arthur J. Burns, June 8, 1885; Walter Paddock, May 1, 1887; Leslie M. Saunders, December 10, 1888; Francis P. Treanor, June 25, 1889; Theo. H. Silkman, June 22, 1891; Henry R. Hicks, September 12, 1892; William F. Moller, October 9, 1893; J. Foster Jenkins, November, 1893; Hall B. Waring, March 23, 1896. The Board has had for its counsel, James P. Sanders, Theodore Fitch, Matthew H. Ellis, Joseph F. Daly.

BOARD OF POLICE. William F. Moller, President, term expires May, 1897; J. Foster Jenkins, term expires May, 1899; Henry R. Hicks, term expired May, 1896; Theodore H. Silkman, term expires May, 1898; Dr. A. C. Benedict, Surgeon, no term; John Mangin, Captain, no term; George Osborne, Sergeant, Jas. McLaughlin, Sergeant, four roundsmen, one hostler, two doorkeepers, thirty-five patrolmen, one laborer, hold office during good behavior.

COMMISSIONERS OF DEEDS. J. Foster Jenkins, term expires April 17, 1897; Lyman Cobb, Jr., term expires April 17, 1897; Charles E. Back, term expires April 25, 1897; George H. Warren, term expires April 25, 1897; Patrick Whelan, term expires April 25, 1897; E. A. Oliver, term expires April 25, 1897; Robert B. Light, term expires April 17, 1897; H. C. Donnelly, term expires April 17, 1897; John T. McGrath, term expires April 27, 1897; A. J. Prime, term expired October 27, 1895; John C. Small, term expires April 17, 1897; C. F. Hulbert, term expires December 5, 1896; James J. Handrahan, term expired November 15, 1895; Herman Ehrenspeck, term expired December 1, 1895; Gabriel Reevs, term expires October 11, 1896; Thomas W. Ivers, term expires May 31, 1897; Charles F. Brown, term expires May 19, 1897; William T. McCready, term expires May 19, 1897; Abbie K. Miller, term expires May 19, 1897; Thos. L. Mottram, term expired October 13, 1895.

CORONERS. 1874, Byron Flood, the first Coroner elected in the city, died soon after taking his office; Hugh Hughes was appointed for the unexpired term on July 24, 1875. 1875, Hugh Hughes, elected for three years; no other elected from Yonkers until 1882. 1882, E. J. Mitchell, elected for three years. 1885, E. J. Mitchell, re-elected for three years. 1890, E. J. Mitchell, appointed by the Governor to serve out the unexpired term, caused by the death of Dr. Charles I. Nordquist. 1890, E. J. Mitchell, elected for three years. 1893, C. A. Miles, elected for three years.

BOARDS OF EDUCATION, No. 2 AND No. 6, 1862-1881. The following gentlemen were members of the Board of Education of No. 2 between 1858, the date of its organization as a Union Free School, and 1881, when it passed under the control of the City Board: William N. Seymour, James H. Monckton, John Hobbs, Josiah Rich, Thomas Smith, J. Henry Williams, John M. Mason, George B. Upham, M.D., Jacob Read, James W. Mitchell, Augustus W. Doren, Thomas O. Farrington, Rev. Victor M. Hulbert, Hiram K. Miller, Robert P. Getty, Rev. David Cole, William Radford, William Iles, Rudolf Eickemeyer, William Macfarlane, Edward Simmons, Duncan Smith, George Stewart, Frederick A. Back, John P. Ritter, James V. Lawrence, Halcyon Skinner, John O. Campbell and Rufus Dutton. The Presidents of the Board during the period were John Henry Williams, David Cole, Rudolf Eickemeyer and Duncan Smith.

The following gentlemen were members of the Board of Education of No. 6, between its first opening in 1862 and 1881, when it passed under control of the City Board: John M. Mason, George B. Upham, M.D., Isaac H. Knox, Everett Clapp, Britton Richardson, Stephen H. Thayer, Sr., J. Foster Jenkins, M.D., Abijah Curtis, George B. Pentz, Edward P. Baird, John W. Oliver, William F. Cochran, James P. Sanders, Ezekiel Y. Bell, Edward O. Carpenter, James Stewart, Daniel T. Macfarlan, Frederick C. Oakley, William S. Carr, Matthew H. Ellis, Thomas C. Cornell, Edwin R. Keyes, John H. Keeler, Valentine Browne, M.D., Samuel Swift, M.D., Fayette P. Brown and Dennis Murphy. The Presidents of the Board during the period were in the order named—Justus Lawrence, Dr. George B. Upham, John M. Mason, Edward P. Baird, Isaac H. Knox, James P. Sanders, Matthew H. Ellis and Dr. Samuel Swift.

BOARD OF EDUCATION. 1881–1896. 1881–2, Duncan Smith, President; Matt. H. Ellis, Vice-President. 1882–6, Duncan Smith, President; Frederic Shonnard, Vice-President. 1886–90, Frederic Shonnard, President; G. Livingston Morse, Vice-President. 1890–3, Frederic Shonnard, President; Rudolf Eickemeyer, Vice-President (deceased). Ex-Trustees: Hon. Matt. H. Ellis, William F. Cochran, Thomas B. Caulfield, Duncan Smith, Esq., Rufus Dutton, Peter Mitchell (deceased), Frederick C. Oakley, William H. Thrall, Frederick A. Back, Charles Lockwood, Michael Mooney, John Thurton, Edward M. Le Moyne (deceased), G. Livingston Morse (deceased), Oliver P. Buel, Merwin N. Jones, Francis T. Holder, General Thomas Ewing, David Hawley, Esq., Christian F. Tietjen, Francis O'Neill, Charles Reed, Anthony Imhoff, Samuel Swift, M.D., Alex. Saunders, W. W. Scrugham, Edgar M. Hermance, M.D., James G. Beemer, Jacob Read, Hon. J. Irving Burns.

OFFICERS FOR 1895–6. William F. Nisbet, President; William B. Edgar, Vice-President; Charles E. Gorton, Superintendent and Clerk.

STANDING COMMITTEES. *Teachers and Instruction:* Charles R. Otis, James V. Lawrence, Andrew S. Brownell. *Purchases:* William B. Edgar, Richard L. Condon, Rudolf Eickemeyer. *Buildings:* Ethelbert Belknap, Justus H. Fiedler, James S. Fitch. *Rules:* John H. Hubbell, John F. Brennan, William B. Edgar. *Audit:* R. Oliver Phillips, M.D., Ethelbert Belknap, John Kendrick Bangs. *Evening Schools:* Justus H. Fiedler, James S. Fitch, John F. Brennan. *Libraries:* John F. Brennan, Rudolf Eickemeyer, John Kendrick Bangs. *Census:* Richard L. Condon, Andrew S. Brownell, R. Oliver Phillips, M.D. *New Sites:* James S. Fitch, Charles R. Otis, Charles H. Fancher. *Architecture:* James V. Lawrence, Ethelbert Belknap, Charles R. Otis. *Construction:* Charles H. Fancher, Richard L. Condon, Justus H. Fiedler. *Industrial Education:* John Kendrick Bangs, John H. Hubbell, James V. Lawrence. *Truancy:* Rudolf Eickemeyer, R. Oliver Phillips, M.D., John H. Hubbell. *Finance:* Andrew S. Brownell, William B. Edgar, Charles H. Fancher.

CIVIL SERVICE EXAMINERS. 1884–96: Edward M. LeMoyne, Arthur J. Burns, John G. Peene, Montgomery R. Hooper, James V. Lawrence, Edwin L. Thomas, Charles A. Back, Horace H. Thayer, Charles E. Skinner, William H. Fisher, Robert H. Neville, Stephen T. Bell, Edward K. Martin.

Messrs. LeMoyne, Hooper and Thomas have been Presidents of the Board. Mr. E. L. Thomas has occupied that position since January 4, 1888. Mr. E. Alexander Houston was employed as Secretary up to January 31, 1894. Messrs. Skinner, Fisher and Neville have served about one year each since January 31, 1894.

TOWN CLERKS. The minutes of town meetings from 1788 (when the town was set apart) to 1820, have not been found. The old tavern, which stood where the Getty House stands, was probably the place where the meetings were usually held. Years ago, some of the old citizens were accustomed to talk about going, sometimes, from the Hudson River side of the town to Mile Square to vote, but whether town-meetings were ever held there, the author is unable to ascertain.

Minutes beginning with 1820 are preserved, but they were not carefully written. Some dates were not recorded. The following names constitute the roll of Town Clerks from 1820 to the date of the organization of the city:

1820–4, Caleb Smith; 1825–34, John Williams; 1835–45, John Bashford; 1846, George B. Rockwell; 1847–9, James L. Valentine; 1850, George B. Rockwell; 1851, Henry V. Bashford; 1852–3, Samuel W. Chambers; 1854–6, Anson B. Hoyt; 1857–8, William H. Post; 1859–60, Lyman Cobb, Jr.; 1861, Charles W. Starr; 1862, Abraham R. Van Houten; 1863–5, Charles W. Starr; 1866, John G. P. Holden; 1867, Edmund T. Morris; 1868, John J. Pendergrast; 1869, Henry V. Clark; 1870–1, James W. Mitchell.

CITY CLERKS. 1872–91, William H. Doty; 1891–6, John Pagan, Jr.

POSTMASTERS OF YONKERS. January 1, 1797, Alpheus Pierson; October 20, 1809, Aaron Vark; August 11, 1841, Thomas O. Farrington; August 14, 1843, John Bashford; May 31, 1848, Esther A.

Bashford; May 28, 1860, George L. Andrews; April 8, 1861, William H. Post; September 2, 1865, Levi P. Rose; April 16, 1869, Matthew F. Rowe; March 23, 1881, William Macfarlane; March 3, 1883, Merwin N. Jones; October 25, 1886, Edwin R. Keyes; November 30, 1886, Lillian C. Keyes; June 23, 1890, John Pentreath; August 29, 1894, John G. P. Holden.

During the term of Mr. M. N. Jones, mail delivery by carriers was introduced. In 1896, there were sixteen carriers.

South Yonkers, Westchester County, established July 27, 1854; James B. Warner, postmaster. John Warner was appointed postmaster December 18, 1855. The name of the post-office was changed to Mosholu April 7, 1860, and John Warner continued as postmaster. Mosholu was changed to Riverdale March 7, 1864, and Joseph S. Alger appointed postmaster March 7, 1864. Mary Alger was appointed postmaster January 25, 1875, at which date the office was put in New York County and discontinued March 17, 1875.

Nepera Park post-office was established about 1892. Mr. F. G. Boutelle had the honor to open it and has been the postmaster ever since.

In 1852 the assessed valuation of the town (then including what has since been annexed to the City of New York) was as follows:

Real Estate,	$2,567,095
Personal Property,	374,485
	$2,941,580
Of this valuation the since annexed portion represented about,	650,000
Leaving for the territory now occupied by the city of Yonkers,	$2,291,580

In 1882 the assessed valuation of the city of Yonkers was as follows:

Real Estate,	$17,350,146
Personal Property,	334,375
	$17,684,521

In 1895 the assessed valuation of the city of Yonkers was as follows:

Real Estate,	$28,649,800
Personal Property,	330,141
	$28,979,941
The amount of Tax levied in 1852 was,	$ 9,216.13
The amount of Tax levied in 1882 was,	336,217.34
The amount of Tax levied in 1895 was,	650,000.00

In 1884, according to the Assessors' books, there were in the city as follows: In the First Ward, 685 dwelling-houses, 5 churches, 2 public school-buildings, 1 parish school-building, 1 boarding school-building and factory power, valued at $62,500. In the Second Ward, 1,076 dwelling-houses, 4 churches, 1 public school-building and factory property, valued at $479,259. In the Third Ward, 1,008 dwelling-houses, 6 churches, 1 public school-building, 2 public halls and factory property valued at $277,000. In the Fourth Ward, 155 dwelling-houses, 2 churches, 1 chapel and 3 public school-buildings.

YEAR.	TAXABLE PERSONS.	PROPERTY VALUATION.	YEAR.	TAXABLE PERSONS.	PROPERTY VALUATION.
1790	—	—	1850	448	$1,275,809
1800	175	—	1855	1,629	4,290,672
1810	204	—	1860	1,511	5,173,863
1815	217	—	1865	3,170	4,558,189
1820	210	—	1870	4,890	6,506,164
1825	249	—	1875	5,117	20,906,904
1830	264	—	1880	5,920	17,167,178
1835	250	—	1885	—	18,659,486
1840	269	—	1890	—	22,574,226
1845	286	—	1895	—	28,622,800

BONDED DEBT OF THE CITY. The following is a statement of the bonded debt of the city of Yonkers as it stood on March 16, 1896:

Consolidation Bonds,	$ 220,000 00
Water Bonds,	1,300,000 00
Fire Department Bonds,	30,000 00
Bridge Bonds,	5,500 00
Public Building and Dock Bonds,	28,000 00
Public Building Bonds,	100,000 00
Public Bath Bonds,	20,000 00
School Bonds,	214,500 00
Assessment Bonds,	352,000 00
Redemption Bonds,	84,000 00
Tax Relief Bonds,	145,000 00
Street Paving Bonds,	290,000 00
Street Repair Bonds,	15,000 00
Street Improvement Bonds,	50,000 00
Crematory Bonds,	9,500 00
Deficiency Bonds,	40,000 00
Railway Paving Bonds,	55,764 43
Street Pavement Bonds,	100,000 00
	$3,059,264 43

By Credit—
Water Board Sinking Fund,	$182,755 90	
Tax Relief Bonds,	145,000 00	
		$327,755 90
		$2,731,508 53

Since March 16th, bonds to the amount of $131,000 have been sold—$81,000 by the Board of Education, and $50,000 by the Board of Water Commissioners.

POPULATION. The records of the census of "the Yonkers" furnishes a proof of the rapid growth of the place during recent years. In order to facilitate comparisons the record from the earliest period to the present year, 1896, is here made. Previous to 1788, when Yonkers was erected into a township, the names "the Yonkers" and "Yonkers" sometimes designated a smaller, and sometimes a larger area; therefore it is impossible to be certain as to the number of inhabitants within Yonkers as now bounded, previous to the formation of the town. In Smith's Directory (1858–59) the population of Yonkers is recorded as aggregating 129 in 1674. Bolton records the population as 249 in 1704. Colonel Caleb Heathcote wrote in 1704 to the Secretary of the Gospel Propagation Society, "We have in this county six small towns, viz.: Westchester, Eastchester, New Rochelle, Mamaroneck, Rye and Bedford, besides a place called Lower Yonkers, containing about twenty families, and another, the Manor of Philipsburgh, about forty families." Bolton records the population of Yonkers as 250 in 1708, and 260 in 1712, while the directory of 1758–59 reports it as 608.

The Colonial Government of New York enumerated the people of the colony in 1698, and thereafter at irregular intervals, until 1771. The United States enumerated the people in 1790. Since that date the General Government has taken decennial censuses, and as the State of New York has also enumerated its inhabitants at stated intervals, the records of the population in 1790 and following years, as reported by the National and State Governments, respectively, enable those interested to observe the increase.

YEAR.	POPULATION.	YEAR.	POPULATION.	YEAR.	POPULATION.
1790	1,125	1835	1,879	1870	18,318
1800	1,176	1840	2,968	1875	17,232
1810	1,365	1845	2,517	1880	18,892
1815	954	1850	4,160	1885	
1820	1,586	1855	7,554	1890	32,033
1825	1,621	1860	11,848	1895 (estimated)	40,000
1830	1,761	1865	12,769		

In 1890 the United States Government took the eleventh census. In that year (1890) there were in the United States 124 cities, having 25,000 or more inhabitants; of these 124 cities Yonkers was the 93d city as to population. (In 1840, it was the 61st; in 1850, the 73d; in 1860, the 68th; in 1870, the 91st; in 1880, the 99th.) Yonkers, during 1880 and 1890, grew more rapidly than most of the eastern and southern cities, and also more rapidly than some western cities. Between 1880 and 1890 only eight southern cities increased more rapidly than Yonkers. The eight were, Chattanooga, San Antonio, Dallas, Los Angeles, Memphis, Atlanta, Nashville and Birmingham. Twenty-five western cities and five eastern cities increased more rapidly than Yonkers. The four cities which outdistanced all others were Duluth, which increased during that decade (1880-90) between 3,000 and 4,000 per cent., Tacoma over 3,000 per cent., Seattle over 1,000 per cent. and Kansas City over 1,000 per cent.—but that is phenomenal growth.

Of the 124 cities in the United States in 1890, only forty during the preceding ten years had increased more rapidly than Yonkers. Yonkers grew more rapidly than eighty-three of the 124.

The following table records the per cent. of increase in Yonkers during a period of fifty-six years:

1840,	1850,	1860,	1870,	1880,	1890,	1896.
2,968,	4,160,	11,848,	18,318,	18,892,	32,033,	40,000.
Per cent. increase,	40.16,	136.77,	54.60,	3.13,	69.56,	24.87.

The growth of Yonkers and of other cities was retarded between 1860 and 1870 by the civil war. As Kingsbridge township is not included in the enumeration of 1880, the growth of Yonkers seems small, but it was large. The subjoined statistics indicate the comparative increase of a few cities, between 1880 and 1890:

Minneapolis, 251.35 per cent.; Chicago, 118.58 per cent.; Binghamton, 102.14 per cent.; Brockton, 100.57 per cent.; Trenton, 92.10 per cent.; Long Island City, 78.10 per cent.; Syracuse, 70.19 per cent.; YONKERS, 69.56 per cent.; Elmira, 50.40 per cent.; Rochester, 49.38 per cent.; Brooklyn, 42.30 per cent.; Jersey City, 35.02 per cent.; Newark, 33.20 per cent.; Utica, 29.76 per cent.; St. Louis, 28.89 per cent.; New York, 25.62 per cent.; Philadelphia, 23.58 per cent.; Auburn, 17.94 per cent.; Charleston, 9.95 per cent.; Troy, 7.42 per cent.; Albany, 4.59 per cent.

A comparison of three sister cities, Mount Vernon, Newburgh and Poughkeepsie, with Yonkers, is interesting to thoughtful citizens. In the census of 1890, Mount Vernon is recorded as having 10,830, Newburgh, 23,087, and Poughkeepsie, 22,206. Mount Vernon increased 136.15 per cent.; Newburgh, 27.89 per cent.; and Poughkeepsie, 9.89 per cent.

Another comparison is of interest to the citizen of thoughtful habit. It relates to the percentage of foreign born population in American cities. In twenty-five of twenty-eight great cities in the United States, the native population born of native parents is outnumbered by the native of foreign parents, together with the foreign born and colored. A few cities are designated on this page for comparison with Yonkers. In 1890 San Francisco had a larger percentage of foreign born and colored citizens than any other great city. It was 42.41 per cent.; New York was second with 42.23 per cent.; Louisville, third, with about 42 per cent. After Louisville came Detroit, St. Paul and Washington, each over 40 per cent. colored and foreign born.

Among the cities of New York State smaller than New York City, Long Island City had in 1890 the largest percentage of foreign born population. It was 36.67. Buffalo was second with 35.00 percentage; Yonkers third, 34.14 percentage. Then followed Brooklyn with 32.46; Rochester with 29.71; Troy with 28.32; Utica with 26.74, and Syracuse with 25.35.

"Of the 21,098 nativeborn population in Yonkers in 1890: 43 were born in Maine; 41 in New Hampshire; 60 in Vermont; 316 in Massachusetts; 50 in Rhode Island; 358 in Connecticut; 18,084 in New York; 977 in New Jersey; 331 in Pennsylvania; 9 in Delaware; 78 in Maryland; 20 in District of Columbia; 196 in Virginia; 13 in West Virginia; 40 in North Carolina; 27 in South Carolina; 35 in Georgia; 15 in Florida; 82 in Ohio; 10 in Indiana; 43 in Illinois; 18 in Michigan; 17 in Wisconsin; 5 in Minnesota; 8 in Iowa; 17 in Missouri; 1 was born in North Dakota; 3 were born in Kansas; 14 in Kentucky; 5 in Tennessee; 5 in Alabama; 1 was born in Mississippi; 9 were born in Louisiana; 3 in Texas; 2 in Arkansas; 2 in Colorado; 4 in Washington; 15 in California; 140 in United States (State not specified); 1 was born abroad (an American citizen).

"Of the 9,121 native white population of Yonkers (in 1890) of native parentage: 33 in Maine; 37 in New Hampshire; 38 in Vermont; 202 in Massachusetts; 29 in Rhode Island; 197 in Connecticut; 7,675 in New York; 430 in New Jersey; 159 in Pennsylvania; 4 in Delaware; 36 in Maryland; 7 in District of

Columbia; 35 in Virginia; 1 was born in West Virginia; 3 were born in North Carolina; 7 in South Carolina; 16 in Georgia; 12 in Florida; 54 in Ohio; 6 in Indiana; 23 in Illinois; 10 in Michigan; 11 in Wisconsin; 2 in Minnesota; 2 in Iowa; 12 in Missouri; 1 was born in North Dakota; 3 were born in Kansas; 12 in Kentucky; 2 in Tennessee; 1 was born in Alabama; 4 were born in Louisiana; 1 was born in Texas; 2 were born in Colorado; 7 in California; 46 in United States (State not specified); 1 was born abroad (an American citizen).

"Of the 11,485 native white population of Yonkers of foreign parentage: 10 were born in Maine; 4 in New Hampshire; 22 in Vermont; 112 in Massachusetts; 21 in Rhode Island; 153 in Connecticut; 10,235 in New York; 524 in New Jersey; 166 in Pennsylvania; 2 in Delaware; 10 in Maryland; 7 in District of Columbia; 10 in Virginia; 2 in North Carolina; 5 in South Carolina; 6 in Georgia; 2 in Florida; 27 in Ohio; 4 in Indiana; 20 in Illinois; 6 in Michigan; 6 in Wisconsin; 3 in Minnesota; 6 in Iowa; 5 in Missouri; 1 was born in Kentucky; 2 were born in Tennessee; 4 in Alabama; 2 in Louisiana; 2 in Texas; 2 in Arkansas; 8 in California; 94 in the United States (State not specified)."

1890. Yonkers native born population,	21,098
Yonkers foreign born population,	10,935
	32,033
Yonkers, First Ward native born,	5,344
Yonkers, First Ward foreign born,	3,078
Yonkers, Second Ward native born	8,381
Yonkers, Second Ward foreign born	3,970
Yonkers, Third Ward native born,	6,579
Yonkers, Third Ward foreign born,	3,567
Yonkers, Fourth Ward native born,	794
Yonkers, Fourth Ward foreign born,	320

34.14 per cent. nativeborn; 65.86 per cent. foreignborn.
69.74 per cent. of the Yonkers people in 1890 were of foreign parentage.

In Westchester County, 1890 { native born population, 108,380
foreign born population, 38,392

In 1890 there were in Yonkers 15,259 males and 16,774 females. By way of comparison with a far western city, the proportion in Seattle is here recorded. In that city, in 1890, there were 26,782 males and 16,055 females. In Yonkers, in 1890, were 10,105 native born males, 10,993 native born females, 5,154 foreign born males, 5,781 foreign born females, 9,880 native white males, 10,726 native white females, 4,380 native white males (native parentage), 4,741 native white females (native parentage), 5,500 native white males (foreign parentage), 5,985 native white females (foreign parentage), 5,120 foreign males, 5,774 foreign females, 259 colored males, 274 colored females. (This includes persons of negro descent, Chinese, Japanese and civilized Indians, but probably none of the last named are in Yonkers.)

According to the same census the number of dwellings in Yonkers, in 1890, was 3,746, the number of families, 6,086; persons to a dwelling, 8.55; persons to a family, 5.26. By way of comparison, several other cities are here referred to. In New York City the number of persons to a dwelling was, in 1890, 18.52; the number of persons to a family, 4.84. In Chicago the number of persons to a dwelling was 8.60, number of persons to a family 4.99. In Philadelphia the number of persons to a dwelling was 5.60, the number of persons to a family, 5.10. In Albany the number of persons to a dwelling was 7.22, the number of persons to a family, 4.65.

POPULATION OF WESTCHESTER COUNTY. 1790, 24,003; 1800, 27,373; 1810, 30,272; 1820, 32,638; 1830, 36,456; 1840, 48,686; 1850, 58,263; 1860, 99,497; 1870, 131,348; 1880, 108,988; 1890, 146,722.

BOARD OF EDUCATION OF YONKERS.

1. William F. Nisbet.
2. Richard L. Condon.
3. Andrew S. Brownell.
4. John F. Brennan.
5. R. Oliver Phillips, M.D.
6. Charles R. Otis.
7. Charles H. Fancher.
8. Frederic Shonnard.
9. William B. Edgar.
10. James S. Fitch.
11. Ethelbert Belknap.
12. Rudolf Eickemeyer.
13. John H. Hubbell.
14. Justus H. Fiedler.
15. James V. Lawrence.

CHAPTER XIII.

YONKERS SCHOOLS.

YONKERS is justly proud of its schools. They have an enviable reputation throughout the whole State. Citizens of other cities visit them to observe how they are conducted. Their beneficent influence is refining and uplifting. It has been observed that "no city of the size of Yonkers, without a college or professional school in it, has a larger proportion of scholars, and of minds trained and active in arts and sciences." With the youth under the best educational influences and with many cultured and learned adults, the city is indeed highly favored.

> " The cannon roars on alien shores,
>   And bolts of battle fly,
> But here no din of culverin
>   Disturbs the placid sky,
> Calm learning thrills these listening hills
>   With sounds that sanctify."

In 1713 a school was established in Yonkers by the Gospel Propagation Society. A record of it is in Chapter VI., where there are also other references to other schools of the colonists. The map of 1785, designates the location of two country school-houses. Allusion is made to them in Chapter VIII. About ten years after the Revolution, New York State inaugurated a movement to establish a system of popular education. Reference to that movement, and to the first school monies Yonkers received will be found in Chapter IX. In the same chapter are records of old time country schools in Yonkers, two of which were attended by David Horton, now in his ninety-seventh year. The history of the building of school-houses in the hamlet and village is recorded in Chapters IX., and X., including a description of the old district school-house, which stood until a few years since, at the corner of the Saw Mill Valley and Tuckahoe roads. In the latter part of Chapter XII., will be found the names of citizens, who served No. 2 and No. 6 as trustees, and of those who have been members of the Consolidated Board of Education.

The consolidation of the Board of Education was a movement of vast moment to the city. There were six independent districts, and even before the incorporation of the city, some discerning citizens realized that the independent district system was too cumbersome for a town as large as Yonkers. The history of the steps toward consolidation is substantially as follows:

Mr. Isaac H. Knox, who had been interested in the public schools, was President of the then village of Yonkers. Mr. John M. Mason was counsel for the Board of Water Commissioners and occupied an office in Manor Hall, across the hallway from the present Common Council chamber. It was evident that the time had arrived for the incorporation of the city. The framing of a charter was projected by gentlemen, who came together in Mr. Mason's office, in the evening after the close of the meeting of the Board of Trustees of the village of Yonkers. They were a self-appointed committee of citizens planning for the welfare of their town. Messrs. Isaac H. Knox, President of the village; John M. Mason, Robert P. Getty, afterwards President of the village; J. G. P. Holden, Clerk of the village; John W. Oliver, S. H. Thayer, Sr., and Ralph E. Prime were the citizens who met. It is the impression of at least one of these gentlemen that Mr. M. F. Rowe and possibly Mr. William Augustus Gibson also attended the meetings.

After much consultation, the preparation of a charter was referred to Mr. Ralph E. Prime, it being understood that he would embody the suggestions which had been approved. As Mr. John M. Mason was the best informed on the subject of schools, the preparation of the portion of the charter relating to consolidate schools was assigned to him. He drafted the provision, and it was inserted in the proposed charter as Title 11 of the bill introduced in the Senate, January 25, 1870, known as Senate bill No. 75. The bill failed of passage, but the work of Mr. Mason had been done, and was the foundation for all that was afterward done in the line of consolidating the schools.

In 1872, the city was incorporated, the schools remaining independent each of the other. From January to September, 1873, the subject of consolidation was considered by the Boards of Education of No. 2 and No. 6, and resolutions were passed to submit the proposition to a vote of the districts, but nothing was done. Mr. Mason was the champion of the movement in No. 6, and, it is understood, that Mr. Rudolf Eickemeyer was urging it in No. 2.

In February, 1878, Mr. John M. Mason died. Within one month after his death, efforts were renewed to secure a consolidated Board of Education. A bill embodying Mr. John M. Mason's work, was prepared by Mr. Matt. H. Ellis, and introduced in the Assembly, March 20, 1878. The Legislature adjourned without passing the bill. In 1880 it had become still more evident that deliberation and judgment could no longer be attained at the annual school meetings. Messrs. Prime and Eickemeyer had a conversation upon the subject. Mr. Prime invited to his residence a number of gentlemen to confer. Those present, as now recalled, were Messrs. Rudolf Eickemeyer, Norton P. Otis, Rufus Dutton, Duncan Smith, Halcyon Skinner, Matthew H. Ellis, John W. Oliver, E. A. Nichols, Jonathan Vail, Fayette P. Brown, John G. Campbell, George Stewart and Ralph E. Prime. Mr. Ellis remained but a short time. He had recently been elected City Judge, and questioned the wisdom and right of his participating in the preparation of any matter, which might be the subject of division in the city.

YONKERS HIGH SCHOOL AND PUBLIC LIBRARY.

Several meetings followed, each held at Mr. Prime's residence, and each attended by substantially the same citizens, although all may not have been present at every meeting. As near as can be recalled, the first meeting was held in January, 1881. It is the present impression that a sub-committee, consisting of Messrs. Eickemeyer, Oliver and Prime, were appointed to draft a bill to be submitted to the Legislature. The committee, in the preparation of the bill, had before them the work of Mr. Mason in 1869, and of Mr. Ellis in 1878. The sub-committee requested Mr. Prime to draft the bill. He submitted his work to them and, after some changes, subsequently the draft was submitted to the gentlemen who had been invited to meet at Mr. Prime's house. The proposed bill was then discussed, further changed, and finally approved.

Meanwhile in No. 6 and in No. 2, public meetings were held to consider the proposed consolidation. No. 2 voted for, and No. 6 voted against. The bill having been introduced in the Legislature, a meeting for conference was held at Manor Hall. On that occasion Dr. Swift advocated the election of trustees, or if they were to be appointed by the Mayor, he held it should be with the advice and consent of the Common Council. The bill was reported favorably, and committed to the Committee of the

Whole. It was then referred to a sub-committee, who reported amendments by which, among other features, the entire scope and plan of the bill as to the appointment of trustees was changed. It passed the Assembly in its altered shape. In Yonkers a private conference was held at which Messrs. Edwin R. Keyes and Ralph E. Prime strenuously opposed suggested amendments by which a minority party should have seven members in the Board of fifteen trustees.

The opposition which the bill met in its passage, and the attempt to modify it before it passed, aroused its friends, and a committee of citizens went to Albany to urge its passage just as it was originally drafted, and approved by the gentlemen who had framed it. According to the recollection of a prominent resident, that committee, or delegation, consisted of Messrs. Rudolf Eickemeyer, John W. Oliver, Rufus Dutton, Ethelbert Belknap, William B. Edgar, Joseph L. Proseus and James S. Fitch. These gentlemen took with them copies of the bill, as originally prepared and submitted. Through the influence of Senator William H. Robertson and Assemblyman James W. Husted, the delegation secured a hearing before leaders in both Houses. The result was, that, by agreement, at a meeting in General Husted's private apartment, Mr. Oliver restored the pending bill to its original form, and in that form it became a law without the alteration of a word.

Mr. Norton P. Otis having become Mayor, appointed the fifteen members of the Consolidated Board of Education, of whom eight were Republicans and seven Democrats. Since that date Mayors Swift, Stahlnecker, Bell, Millward, Weller and Peene have appointed members of the Board of Education.

On July 12, 1881, Mr. John Adams Nichols became Superintendent of Public Schools. On June 13, 1882, Mr. Andrew J. Rickoff was appointed. On October 9, 1883, Mr. Charles E. Gorton was appointed. Mr. John H. Claxton, the Secretary of the Board, was appointed in 1887. The rolls of the Yonkers public schools sometimes carry the names of four thousand scholars. A large corps of teachers are employed. No. 1 has two teachers; No. 2 has twenty; No. 3 has ten; No. 4 has four; No. 5 building is not occupied; No. 6 has seventeen; No. 7 has fourteen; No. 8 has two; No. 9 has three; No. 10 has thirteen; No. 11 building is not yet finished. The High School has nine teachers. The Grammar Department of the High School has six. The salaries of the Principals range from $1,000 to $2,200. The salaries of the teachers range from $450 to $1,500.

Principals of Public Schools.

High School: 1882–1883, Charles E. Gorton; 1883–92, Edward R. Shaw; 1892–95, Herbert H. Gadsby; 1895– , Thomas O. Baker.

School No. 1: 1882–83, Oliver Chambers; 1883–85, Annie M. Howes; 1885– , Phoebe E. Palmer.

School No. 2: 1882–84, Mary F. Hyde; 1884– , Caroline J. Dresser.

School No. 3: 1884–88, Ray A. Campbell; 1888–89, Belle J. Harris; 1889–93, Helen M. Blanchard; 1893– , Belle S. Bruce.

School No. 4: 1882–84, William H. Oakley; 1884–85, Jessie T. Bross; 1885– , Etta S. Gracey.

School No. 5: 1882–83, Edith H. Patrick; 1883–84, Ray A. Campbell; 1884–85, Phoebe E. Palmer; 1885, Eliza L. Merrill; 1886, Helen L. Witbeck; 1886–89, Milton C. Palmer; 1889–90, Katharine Hasbrouck; 1890–93, Kate F. Quinn.

School No. 6: 1882–90, Mary E. Spencer; 1890– , Amelia M. Walker.

School No. 7: 1888– , Mary E. Hughes.

School No. 8: 1893– , Kate F. Quinn.

School No. 9: 1895– , Nora R. Baldwin.

School No. 10: 1895– , Lucy A. Earle.

Special Teachers: Musical—William C. Hoff. Drawing—Emma Hentz Nye and Isabelle Imrie. Domestic Science—Georgia M. Gookin. Physical Culture—Sarah M. Wilson. Drill Master—Col. H. S. Farley. Substitute—Emma M. Brennan.

Officers of the Alumni Association, Yonkers High School, 1895–96:

	CLASS OF
President, Miss Margaret R. Brendlinger,	'91
First Vice-President, Miss Lilian B. Clark,	'91
Second Vice-President, Mr. John P. Radcliff, Jr.,	'89
Secretary, Mr. R. V. Howes,	'85
Treasurer, Mr. Frank O. Freethy,	'91
Historian, Miss Carolyn A. Van Tassel,	'84

EXECUTIVE COMMITTEE:

Miss M. R. Brendlinger. Mr. J. P. Radcliff, Jr. Mr. F. O. Freethy.
Miss L. B. Clark. Mr. R. V. Howes, Miss C. A. Van Tassel.
Miss Florence Z. Youmans, '95.

EVENING SCHOOL PRINCIPALS.

SCHOOL NO. 2. 1882–83, Charles E. Gorton; 1883–85, James S. Fitch; 1885–89, F. X. Donoghue; 1889–1892, Herbert H. Gadsby; 1893–96, John A. Byrne.

SCHOOL NO. 6. 1882–86, Oliver Chambers; 1886–95, Wm. C. Kellogg; 1895–96, Tracy E. Clark.

HIGH SCHOOL DRAWING CLASS. 1885–87, A. D. Petersen; 1894–96, C. C. Chipman.

On March 12, 1895, the Common Council appropriated $81,000 for enlarging the school-buildings. The favorable sale of the bonds realized for the Board of Education $91,959.30. They propose to expend more than $26,000 in enlarging No. 10, over $20,000 in enlarging No. 3, and over $35,000 in enlarging No. 2.

ST. MARY'S PARISH SCHOOLS. The early history of St. Mary's parish schools is recorded in Chapter X. In November, 1876, the boy's school was discontinued. It sessions were resumed in September, 1877. When the Rev. Charles R. Corley came to Yonkers he immediately fostered the parish schools. Having reopened the boys' school in September, Brother Elwaren became Principal. He had three assistants and about two hundred and fifteen children. Sister Martina had charge of the girls' department when Father Corley came. About three hundred scholars were enrolled. Sister Maria Magdalena, in September, 1878, took charge. She had several Sisters as assistants. Sister M. Arsenia subsequently had charge. After September, 1882, the boys' school was in charge of Brother Denis, with three Brothers as assistants.

In 1878, the schools enrolled 327 girls and 255 boys: total, 582. In 1884, there were 400 girls and 340 boys: total, 740. In 1885 the building which the Rev. Mr. Lynch had erected in 1860 was greatly enlarged at a cost of about $20,000. On Sabbath, July 5, 1885, the corner-stone of this building was blessed.

Brother Denis was succeeded by Brother Edward, who remained Principal of the boys' school about three years. He was succeeded by Brother Leo, and he by Brother Paphlylinus, who is in charge now. He is assisted by four Brothers. The number of pupils in the Brothers' school is about 210.

Sister Arsenia was succeeded by Sister Monica, who remained about three years. Her successor was Sister Loyola, who is the present Principal. She has been connected with the school about nineteen years. The corps of teachers consists of Sister Loyola, ten Sisters, assistants and four lay teachers. There are about 517 girls and 280 small boys enrolled. The schools have a musical director, a teacher of drawing, and a teacher of elocution.

ST. JOSEPH'S PARISH SCHOOL. In 1872 the present building designed for a school-house and used temporarily as a church, was opened with about three hundred pupils. At the end of June, 1879, the school was discontinued. In 1881 it was reopened under the charge of the Sisters of Charity, for whose use Father Lings purchased the house and lot north of and adjoining the school, and fitted it up at a cost of about $7,000. Sister M. Stephen was placed in charge. In the autumn of 1882, the school numbered 203 boys and 281 girls: total, 484. In June, 1883, the number was 530. Sister Stephen's assistants were Sisters M. Esperanza, Rosa Lima, M. Joseph Berchmans, Marie Angelé and Marie Clotilda. The school now has about 366 boys and 429 girls: total, 795.

ST. JOSEPH'S SEMINARY. The corner-stone of St. Joseph's Seminary was laid in May, 1891. Over 100,000 people were present, according to press reports. The vast structure has cost, with the grounds, over $700,000. It stands in a park of sixty acres which was purchased of the Valentine estate by the Archbishop, March 6, 1890. The building has rooms for the Archbishop and the Rector of the Seminary, apartments for the students, large lecture rooms and class rooms, recreation halls, lavatories, gymnasiums, professors' quarters, large library, chapel, aula maxima, etc. The large one-story buildings, extending east and west, contain the prayer hall and the refectory. A separate building contains the kitchen, quarters for the domestics, and a serving room. The Seminary was formerly located at Troy, N. Y. It is supposed that there will be in the new Seminary building about 250 undergraduates and clergymen. The east wing will be occupied for the philosophical course and the west wing by the theologians.

The following have been appointed members of the Faculty of the new St. Joseph's Seminary on Valentine Hill: Rev. Edward R. Dyer, S.S., President; Rev. Richard K. Wakeham, S.S., Treasurer and Procurator; Rev. Joseph F. Driscoll, S.S., Professor of Dogma; Rev. Joseph Brunean, S. S. Professor of Scripture; Rev. William Temple, Professor of Logic. All of these are members of the Sulpician Order, with the exception of Father Temple, who is a secular priest, but was educated by the Sulpicians.

The following priests, who were members of the Faculty of the old Seminary at Troy, have been retained: Rev. William Livingston, Professor of English, Church History and Rubrics; Rev. Remy Lafort, Professor of Moral Philosophy and Canon Law; and Rev. James Fitzsimmons, Professor of Metaphysics and Philology.

THE MONASTERY PAROCHIAL SCHOOL. The history of the Monastery of the Sacred Heart is recorded in another chapter. The Monastery has a parochial school. It is situated on Convent Avenue, southwest of the Monastery, and is in charge of three Sisters of St. Agnes.

SPENCERIAN BUSINESS COLLEGE. This institution was established in Yonkers, August 3, 1892. Professor B. H. Spencer, of the Kingston, N. Y., Business College, was proprietor and principal. There were three departments: business, shorthand and penmanship. Morris Read had charge of the business department. Mr. John Wemple was resident principal and instructor in the phonographic department. On November 1, 1894, the school was removed to the Warburton Building. On January 1, 1895, it was purchased by Charles B. Hall. In 1895, it enrolled over ninety pupils. Mr. Hall gives his personal attention to the business and penmanship departments. George H. Baxter, formerly official reporter of the New York State Senate, is at the head of the phonographic department. The graduates of the school have good positions in New York, Yonkers, Mount Vernon and elsewhere.

THE YONKERS COLLEGE OF MUSIC. Most excellent work in the domain of musical education is being done by The Yonkers College of Music. The institution was organized in November, 1892. The Director, Mr. Frank Steadman, and his staff of teachers had been working faithfully for two years prior to that time, and their efforts had been so eminently successful, that it was deemed advisable to

THE YONKERS COLLEGE OF MUSIC—PEOPLE'S SAVINGS BANK BUILDING.

reorganize their modest institution and follow the plans and methods of more pretentious institutions of the kind. Mr. Steadman, who is well-known as a successful manager of children's entertainments, first studied, under Eduard Mollenhauer, afterwards under Henry Lambert and Dr. Austin Pearce, of the New York College of Music, and is a popular musician of the day. He devotes his entire time to the College, and those who have had the pleasure of attending many of the concerts and entertainments with which he has been identified can have no doubt of his ability. The rapid and steady growth of the College during its existence has been cause for much congratulation to the management and their friends. The high standard of scholarship established at the outset, has been maintained throughout, while numerous reforms and additional advantages, introduced from time to time, have constantly increased the reputation of the school. The staff of teachers are as follows: Director, Frank Steadman; Piano Department, under the direction of Alfred Andrews, Anton Reiff and Miss Georgiana Moore; Organ, Alfred Andrews; Violin, Frank Steadman and assistants; Violincello, Herm. Brinkman; Vocal, Dr. Carl E. Dufft; Sight Reading, Alfred Andrews; Cornet and Wind Instruments, William Styles, of Sixty-ninth Regiment Band. Harmony and Composition, A. Andrews; Mandolin, W. Graham Lawson; Banjo and Guitar, S. A. Sweet; Zither, James D. Ives; Elocution and Dramatic Art, Livingston Russell.

BUTLER'S BUSINESS COLLEGE. This institution was established in the spring of 1892, by Charles G. Egert, of Ogdensburgh, N. Y., and was known as Egert's School of Stenography. On August 1, 1892, the school was purchased by W. W. Butler, of Potsdam, N. Y., and moved into larger and more convenient quarters. Mr. Butler added the department of business training, after which the institution took the name "Butler's Business College." Owing to the increased patronage it secured its present commodious and elegant quarters in the Grant Building in 1896. The course of study includes book-keeping, penmanship, and all that pertains to a business education. Shorthand and typewriting are also taught. Its graduates hold good positions in New York and elsewhere. Since the establishment of the school in 1892, two of its graduates have been appointed Court Reporters.

In previous chapters there is record of a number of private schools which were established in Yonkers in early years. The academy, of which the Rev. Montgomery R. Hooper, A.M., became the Principal in 1867, was a well-known private school in the days of the incorporated village and in the early years of the city. "The Yale School for Boys" was another well-known Yonkers school. It was established in 1877 by Theodore F. Leighton, A.B. Davison's Institute was established in Yonkers by the Rev. Isaac S. Davison in 1881. Other schools in Yonkers, after the incorporation of the city, were: Mrs. K. T. Holbrook's "School for Young Ladies and Children," Mrs. John Moffat's "Home School for Misses and Children," Miss Crocker's and Miss Herzog's "Day School for Young Ladies and Girls," Miss Anna M. Palmer's "Kindergarten," Miss S. N. MacAdam's "Classes in English and French," Miss Halstead's "College Preparatory School," Mrs. Kellogg's "Select School for Children," Miss A. E. Tompkins' "School for Children" (Froebel Kindergarten), the "Yonkers Military School," of which Mr. Ezra B. Fanchard was the Principal; Miss Mary I. Bliss' "School for Young Ladies," the Misses Corsa's "Parkhill School for Children." All these schools, except two, have either removed to other places or have closed.

The private schools in the city, in 1896, are: the Halstead College Preparatory School, Miss Mary Sicard Jenkins, Principal; the Kingsley School, Miss Helena N. Lowden, Principal; English, German and French Day School, Miss Emma Herzog, Principal, and the Kindergarten School, under the direction of the Misses Blauvelt.

BUTLER'S BUSINESS COLLEGE. GRANT BUILDING, 20 WARBURTON AVENUE.

CHAPTER XIV.

YONKERS CHURCHES.

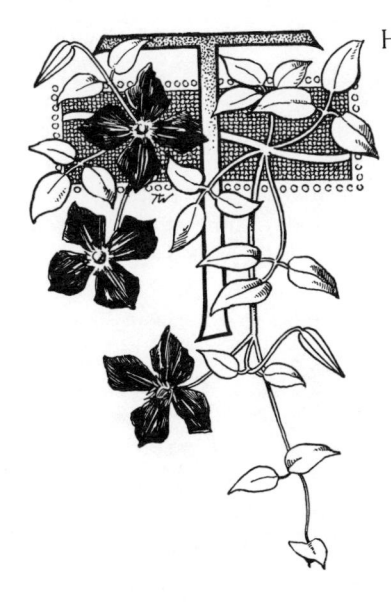

THE original purpose of the Dutch who first came to Manhattan Island was not to colonize, but to trade. The pioneer Pilgrims went to New England to build homes and churches. They were influenced by religious motives. But the Hollanders in New Amsterdam did not ignore religion. How could they, coming as they did from a noble Christian country? Very soon after the arrival of the first company of emigrants a house of worship was built. The first church organized on Manhattan Island was of the Dutch Reformed denomination. The Congregational Church was the first to be established in Westchester County. The New England Congregationalists early made their home in Westchester. The French Protestants, who were the second denomination to erect a church in Westchester County, built their house of worship at New Rochelle. Their primitive church edifices were very quaint as to appearance. The Dutch Reformed denomination built their first house of worship in Westchester County on the banks of the Pocantico, in what is now known as Tarrytown. The third denomination to enter the county was the Church of England. The first church erected at Yonkers was built by members of that denomination.

A number of years before the white man made his home in the woods of "Colen-Donck," or "De Jonkheer's Landt," the villagers on Manhattan Island worshipped in a rude loft above the horse mill. Before a clergyman arrived, their religious teachers were two lay-readers, called "Krankenbezoeckers," or "Visitors of the Sick." The first clergyman who came was the Rev. Jonas Michaelius. He arrived in 1628, and during that year a Reformed Dutch Church was organized. Dominie Michaelius preached in the Dutch language, and occasionally in French. That was during the administration of Director-General Minuit. The next clergyman on Manhattan Island was the Rev. Everardus Bogardus. He came in 1633, with Director-General Van Twiller. Before the end of that year a church, described as "a barn-like structure" was built on Broad Street. In 1642 a stone church was built within the enclosure of the fort on Manhattan Island, and the "barn-like structure" was sold in 1656.

The church in the fort enclosure was, for years, an important centre for the pioneer settlers of New Amsterdam and surrounding places. In 1683, when the village on Manhattan Island contained less than four thousand inhabitants, the stone church was used every Sunday by the representatives of the three leading denominations, and services were held in as many different languages—the Dutch in the morning, the French at noon, and the English in the afternoon. There is no reason to doubt that occasionally inhabitants from "De Jonkheers" were in the congregations which assembled in that church.

When the Congregationalists established themselves at Westchester they also must have sometimes welcomed their neighbors who lived in "Colen-Donck." Westchester was settled by Jonas Bronck in 1639-40. The settlers who came after him were Puritans, who had left New England to escape persecution. They settled in 1642 at what was subsequently known as Throckmorton, also as Throgg's Neck. Mr. John Throckmorton, and a number of English families (probably thirty-five) constituted that company. The Dutch called the place *Vreedlandt*, or the "free land," because the persecuted Puritans found religious freedom there. In 1650 another company of New Englanders settled upon or near the present site of Westchester. They gave that name to the place, but the Dutch called it *Oost-dorp* (East

Town) from its situation east of the Manhattans. The Dutch Commissioners who visited there in December, 1656, reported that "After dinner Cornelius Van Ruyven went to the house where they held their Sunday meeting to see their mode of worship, as they had as yet no preacher. There he found a gathering of about fifteen men and ten or twelve women. Mr. Baly said the prayer, after which Robert Bassett read, from a printed book, a sermon composed by an English clergyman in England. After the reading Mr. Baly gave out another prayer, and sang a psalm, and they all separated." Ecclesiastical business, at this time, was conducted by the town assembled in town meeting, therefore, most of the Church history of the period is registered in the town records. Many historical facts relating to the early churches are recorded in Chapter VI. In 1665, Richard Nicolls, the first English Governor of New York and a loyal adherent of the Duke of York convened delegates from Westchester and other sections at Hempstead, Long Island. The code of laws promulgated at that meeting was called the "Duke's Laws." The code contained no more important provisions than the following:

"WHEREAS, The public worship of God is much discredited for the want of painful and able ministers to instruct the people in true religion, and for want of convenient places capable to receive any assembly of people in a decent manner for celebrating God's holy ordinances;

"*Ordered,* That a church shall be built in the most convenient place in each parish capable to receive and accommodate two hundred persons. To prevent scandalous and ignorant pretenders to the ministry from intruding themselves as teachers, no minister shall be admitted to officiate within the Government, but such as shall produce testimonials to the Governor, that he received ordination either from some Protestant bishop or minister within some part of his Majesty's dominions, or the dominions of any foreign prince of the reformed religion; upon which testimonials the Governor shall induct the said minister into the parish that shall make presentation of him."

The "Duke's Laws" were in force in the province until 1683, when the First Provincial Assembly convened. The Rev. Ezekiel Fogge was in Westchester during those early years. He was probably the first independent clergyman there. His name appears in 1674. A house of worship stood there in the seventeenth century. The meeting-house in Westchester in 1695 must have been erected years before, as in that year it had fallen into decay.

At a town meeting held in Westchester in 1684, the following was passed:

"*Resolved,* That the Justices and Vestrymen of Westchester, Eastchester and Yonkers do accept of Mr. Warham Mather as our minister for one whole year, and that he shall have sixty pounds in country produce, at money price, for his salary, and that he shall be paid every quarter."

In 1693, the colonial Legislature divided the county into the two parishes of Westchester and Rye. The former parish included Westchester, Eastchester, Yonkers and the Manor of Pelham. The latter included Rye, Mamaroneck and Bedford. A church, known as St. Peter's, was located at Westchester. Warham Mather, probably a theological student at the time, conducted services in 1695 as a reader in Westchester parish, to which Yonkers belonged. In 1701, the missionary society known as the "Venerable Society for the Propagation of the Gospel in Foreign Parts," was incorporated in England. Its principal object was to send devout and zealous clergymen as missionaries to the colonies.

How necessary it was to have the Gospel preached is shown by a letter of Colonel Heathcote. He wrote: "When I first arrived in the province (1692), I found it (Westchester) the most rude and heathenish country I ever saw in my whole life, which called themselves Christians, there being not so much as the least marks or footsteps of religion of any sort, Sundays being the only time set apart by them for all manner of vain sports and lewd diversions, and they were grown to such a degree of rudeness that it was intolerable; and having then the command of the militia, I sent an order to all the captains requiring them to call their men under arms, and to acquaint them that in case they would not in every town agree among themselves to appoint readers, and pass the Sabbath in the best manner they could till such times as they could be better provided, that they should every Sunday call their companies under arms, and spend the day in exercise; whereupon it was unanimously agreed on throughout the country to make choice of readers, which they accordingly did, and continued in those methods some time."

The legislation of the Court of Sessions for Westchester County confirms what Colonel Heathcote wrote. In 1693, in view of "greate disorders and prophainness upon the Sabbath days . . . the public worship of God being neglected for want of able ministers to instruct the people. . . . And whereas several places within the County are not in a capacity to maintain a minister, whereby great debaucheries and prophainness are committed on the Lord's day, and the parents and masters of families doe not traine up youths and servants in the feare of God and observing His holy commandments," the Court provides that "within every towne, precinct, and patent within the County, due observance of the Lord's day shall be kept, and for want of an able minister, the inhabitants shall employ a reader to read out of good books two Sermonds every Lord's day (one in the forenoon and one in the afternoon)," and if any person behaved unseemly in the time of public worship, the Justice of the Peace shall commit him to the stocks "one houre" or impose a fine of "tenn shillings."

It was also provided that "noe person should sitt tippling in a publick ordenary on the Lord's day, and no person shall travill on the Lord's day without permission, nor should any person presume to go a-fishing, shooting or hunting of horses on the Lord's day."

All the inhabitants of the county were not indifferent to their religious duties and privileges. The French Huguenots, who built their little frame church at New Rochelle in 1692, were a devout people. When they had no pastor, and when the sacrament was administered four times a year in New York, they walked to the church there in order to obey their Lord's command respecting the ordinance. They remembered that He had said, "Do this in remembrance of Me." Tradition relates that they often set out for New York on Communion Sundays, at a very early hour, reached the old French Church, in Pine Street, in time for the service and returned to their homes on the afternoon or evening of the same day. That necessitated a journey of twenty miles to the church and twenty miles back. The people of Yonkers must have heard the sermons of one or more of the clergymen to whom reference has been made in the foregoing paragraphs. The Huguenot ministers in the seventeenth and eighteenth centuries were the Rev. David De Bourepas, D.D., (1689) the Rev. Daniel Boudet, A.M., (1695) the Rev. Pierre Stouppe, A.M., (1724) the Rev. Michael Houdin, A.M., (1761) and the Rev. Theodolius Bartow (1790). The Rev. Mr. Boudet could preach both in English and French, and at one time it was proposed to call him to Westchester, but the call was not issued.

The inscription on the tablet of the old Dutch Church at Sleepy Hollow records 1699 as the date of the erection of that church, but some circumstances seem to indicate an earlier date. For instance, the dates on the coffins in the crypt beneath the floor, are as early as 1650 and 1660. Reference to the old Sleepy Hollow church is in Chapter VI.

The Rev. John Bartow, A.M., a graduate of Christ College, Cambridge, and one of the first missionaries of the Society, was settled at Westchester as rector of the parish church in 1702. His parish included Yonkers. He wrote in 1702, "I have been at great expense, but I do not grudge it in the service of that God, who, I trust, will bless me in my endeavors. We have a small house built here (Westchester) for public worship, of boards, but there is neither desk, pulpit, nor bell in it. I have neither church Bible nor common prayer-book, which I hope the Society will send me." A report (1704) informs the clergy convened in New York, that "at Yonkers there is a small congregation of Dutch, who have only a reader, and therefore, some of them who understand English, repair to the church at Westchester." In 1708 the Rev. Mr. Bartow wrote to the Society that he occasionally preached at Yonkers, where the population was less than 250 souls. If his congregation resembled his neighboring congregations, representatives of several races must have been present, for in 1710 he reported, "Our Church at Westchester increased, that at Eastchester is constant. We have, sometimes, negroes and Indians come to our assembly and behave themselves orderly." In 1713 a charity school was formed at Yonkers by the Venerable Society. Their abstracts say, "To a schoolmaster at Yonkers, in the province of New York, where there is a large congregation of Dutch and English, for instructing the younger sort of both nations in the catechism and liturgy, £5 per annum, upon producing a certificate of his teaching thirty children in that summer." The Rev. Mr. Bartow wrote in 1717, "Yonkers has no church, but we assemble for divine worship in an house of Joseph Debts, deceased, and sometimes in a barn, when empty, but the people begin to be in a disposition to build a church." In 1719 "Mr. Jones was allowed fifty shillings for teaching children to read at Mile Square." In 1724 Mr. Bartow informed the Bishop of London "that he officiates on Sundays in the four towns under his care, according to their several quotas, in the payment of the £50 per annum, and that he preaches three times a year at Yonkers," etc. Mr. Bartow died in Westchester in 1725, and his remains were interred under the Communion table of the old parish church of St. Peter's.

In 1727, the Rev. Thomas Standard, A.M., M.D., another missionary from England, began his work in the parish of Westchester, which included Yonkers. The church edifice in Yonkers, now known as St. John's, was erected in Dr. Standard's time. It was built in 1752–53, but was not called St. John's until 1792. The Rev. Samuel Johnson, D.D., the first president of King's (now Columbia)

College, wrote from New York in 1759 to the Archbishop of Canterbury: "The next thing is to give your Grace an account of those places where missions are wanted. And here I beg leave first to mention a great part of the province, I mean all the tract on the east side of the Hudson River from Westchester upwards, quite as far as we have any settlements, abounding with people, but almost destitute of ministers of any denomination, except two Dutch and two German, and many people have almost lost all sense of Christianity. Indeed, in the large county of Westchester, there is only good Mr. Wetmore and two dissenting teachers, that are capable of duty. Northward of that is Colonel Philipse's Manor, in which are people enough for a large congregation, without any minister at all. The Colonel has himself built a neat small church, and set off a tract for a glebe, which will be considerable in time, and he and his tenants are very desirous of a minister, but will need the Society's assistance."

The church which Colonel Philipse built, was erected in compliance with the terms of the will of the second Philipse, who took possession of his manor about 1719, and who forwarded the missionary work of the parish of Westchester, carried on between the Hudson and the Bronx. He died in 1751. His will was dated June 6, 1751. By that instrument he devised, in trust to his heirs, a farm with residence and outbuildings for the use of ministers, who might be called to labor here in the service of the Church of England. He directed that his executors should expend £400 from the rentals of his manor, in erecting on the farm a church building for the use of the people.

The third lord known as Colonel Philipse, set apart the farm devised for the use of the ministers, but instead of building the church on the farm, he erected it near the Hudson. The combustible part of that building burned in 1791. When it was restored the next year, without change in its original outward form, it was consecrated by Right Rev. Samuel Provost, D.D., the first bishop of New York State. On that day, August 1, 1792, it first received the name St. John's. The steeple was rebuilt in 1804. Reference to this is made in Chapter IX. Transepts were added in 1849, and at the same time other improvements were made. In 1870 the old building was nearly all taken down and the present church erected. The old south wall, erected in 1752, was retained.

From what has been written, is is evident that previous to regular public religious services in Colen-Donck, the inhabitants probably worshipped in New Amsterdam, and occasionally at Vreedlandt, or Oostdorp, or New Rochelle, or the Upper Mills (Sleepy Hollow), or it may be at Fordham, where the Collegiate Dutch Reformed congregation of New York, organized a society in 1696, the Rev. John Montaigue being minister. The old Dutch meeting-house was erected there in 1706. The two parishes of Westchester and Rye having been formed in 1693, Yonkers became associated with St. Peter's, the parent-church of Westchester, and was supplied with preaching.

Before the erection of the church at Yonkers, in 1752-53, the Rev. Warham Mather and two rectors of St. Peter's, the Rev. John Bartow, A.M., and the Rev. Thomas Standard, A.M., M.D., ministered to the people. From the time the church was erected to the date when the parish was set off (1787) four clergymen labored in Yonkers. One of them was the Rev. John Milner, A.M., third rector of St. Peter's. He was a graduate of Princeton, who went to England for ordination, and was rector of Westchester parish in 1760. He resigned in 1765. His successor was the Rev. Henry Munroe, A.M., a graduate of St. Andrew's, and a chaplain in one of his Majesty's Highland Regiments. He came to Yonkers in 1765 as a missionary. He was not a rector of St. Peter's, but was set apart by the Venerable Society as a special missionary for the precinct of Yonkers. In Chapter VI. is the record of one of his reports to the Society. It is dated Philipsburgh, February 1, 1766. He resigned his license as a missionary in 1764, and his charge of the precinct in 1768, and became rector of St. Peter's, Albany. The next clergyman in Yonkers was the Rev. Luke Babcock, A.M., a graduate of Yale, ordained by the Bishop of London. He began his work as a missionary in Yonkers in 1771, having been set apart by the Venerable Society, to this precinct. He was one of the three hundred and twelve protestors at White Plains. In one of his letters to the Society, dated Philipsburgh, March 22, 1776, he speaks of the "fever excited in men's minds by the late battle of Lexington, then the affairs of Bunker Hill next came, and the Continental Fast, which may be considered as a trial by ordeal of the ministers of the Church of England in America. Most of the clergy in this country (I am sorry to say it) opened their churches on that day. I do not pretend to justify or condemn their conduct; it would certainly have been in opposition to my conscience had I done the same. . . . My refusal to bow down before an altar the Congress had raised, made it necessary to confine myself to my own parish till the packets were discontinued, and I have been threatened with mutilation and death if I go into New England. . . . I have not failed to admonish the people, and in my case plainly, repeatedly and publicly for the year past, that the rebellion will lead its abettors to confusion in this world, and everlasting distraction in the next."

In 1877, the Provincial Congress at Fishkill determined to put a stop to his efforts to influence public opinion. "He was seized by the insurgents, his papers were examined, and because he answered affirmatively to the question, whether he considered himself bound by his oath of allegiance to the king he was deemed an enemy to the liberties of America, and ordered in custody. After four months' confinement his health gave way, and he was then dismissed with a written order to remove within the lines of the king's army. He was in a raging fever and delirious when he reached home, where he died in the thirty-ninth year of his age." His remains were buried in the old family vault of the Van Cortlandts. As a clergyman he was exemplary in his life, and assiduous in his pastoral duty. Mr. Andrew Fowler, a lay reader, says, "Mr. Babcock bore the character of a good preacher, a warm friend, an affectionate husband, an indulgent parent. I became well acquainted with his family, after his death, and was the first person that read prayers and sermons in the church at Yonkers, after the Revolutionary War, A.D. 1784. I prepared the way for the settlement of a clergyman, by collecting a congregation." A fine portrait of the Rev. Mr. Babcock is extant.

The next minister was the Rev. George Panton, A.M., a missionary in Yonkers during a portion of the war period. "During Mr. Panton's ministry the country was very much disturbed by the ravages

ST. JOHN'S PROTESTANT EPISCOPAL CHURCH, CHAPEL, PARISH HOUSE, AND RECTORY.

of the American Revolution, and this parish particularly, being alternately occupied by the British and American forces, felt the sad effects of the war. Some of the congregation were openly attached to the British cause, some as decidedly in favor of the measures of Congress, and others, vibrating in their minds, and undecided what course to pursue in the melancholy struggle." Mr. Panton withdrew in 1782, and no clergyman was called and settled for seven years. Ministers of different denominations were permitted to occupy the pulpit during "this melancholy scene of disorder and distress." The Methodists took advantage of the dissensions then existing, and made proselytes, but subsequently most of them returned to the Protestant Episcopal Church. In 1787 the Yonkers precinct of the parish of Westchester was erected into an independent parish. It was first represented in the convention by Augustus Van Cortlandt and Israel Honeywell as delegates. The property of Frederick Philipse had been confiscated. By act of 1786 and a subsequent act (1792), the State granted to and vested in the corporation of the Episcopal Church of Yonkers, the glebe and other property.

The names of clergymen, which follow, are those of the rectors of the Episcopal Church, which in 1792, was first called St. John's. The Rev. Elias Cooper, A.M., began to labor in Yonkers in 1788, was ordained priest in 1790, remained in the rectorship twenty-seven years, dying in it in 1816.

While he was rector the parish gradually recovered from the ravages of the Revolution. It is written that he was "exemplary in his private deportment, charitable and kind to the poor, liberal to the church, and a steady friend of its ministers. He gained the esteem and affection of all who knew him, and particularly of those who took a lively interest in the prosperity of the church." St. John's contains a wall tablet to his memory. During his pastorate he organized and taught a school. In Chapter IX. is a picture of his school-house and of the rectory and glebe on the Saw Mill River Road, as they appeared in 1809. It was during his rectorship that the tower and roof of the church were destroyed by fire and restored the following year, 1792, and the church consecrated. In 1795 Communion silver was presented by the Van Cortlandt family. In 1798, the chapel at Tuckahoe was erected. The steeple of St. John's, Yonkers, was rebuilt in 1804.

The next rector was the Rev. Wm. Powell, A.M. He became rector in 1816, and resigned in 1819. Mr. Joseph Howland purchased a church bell for St. John's while Rev. Mr. Powell was rector. Reference is made to this in Chapter IX. The Rev. John Grigg, A.M., came in 1820 and resigned in 1823. The Rev. John West, A.M., took charge in 1823, and resigned in 1828. He was succeeded by the Rev. Alexander Hamilton Crosby, A.M., who became rector in 1828, and remained eleven years, dying in the rectorship in 1839. A wall tablet to his memory was erected in the church. The Rev. Smith Pyne, A.M., was chosen rector in 1839 and resigned in 1840. His successor was the Rev. Henry L. Storrs, A.M., who was educated at Hamilton College, Clinton, N. Y., and Union College, Schenectady, N. Y. During his rectorship, the chapel known as St. John's at Tuckahoe was consecrated. The new rectory within the church grounds in Yonkers was also built and transepts were added to the church. The. Rev. Mr. Storrs became rector in 1841, and served eleven years, dying in the rectorship in 1852. His remains were interred in the parochial cemetery.

The Rev. Abraham Beach Carter, A.M., became rector in 1852. He was afterward honored with the title, Doctor of Divinity. He resigned in 1868. His successor was the Rev. Thomas A. Jaggar, D.D., who came in 1869, and resigned in 1870. He was afterward Bishop of the Protestant Episcopal Church for the Southern Diocese of Ohio. In 1870, the Rev. William S. Langford, D.D., became rector. He resigned in 1875, and subsequently became General Secretary of Domestic and Foreign Missions of the Protestant Episcopal Church in America. He was succeeded by the Rev. Addison B. Atkins, D.D., who became rector in 1875, and resigned in 1879. During that year the Rev. James Houghton, A.M., became rector. He resigned in 1887. His successor is the Rev. Alexander B. Carver, D.D., who was elected to the rectorship in 1887, and is the rector at the present time.

The Sunday-school * of the church was founded under the rectorship of the Rev. John West, A.M., October 17, 1823. The interior of the church was remodeled in 1841. In 1845, the old parsonage and glebe was sold for $0,500, excepting the land used as St. John's Cemetery and a new parsonage built near the church. In 1849, the organ was built and put in the gallery, and transepts and chancel were added. In 1853, the chapel at Tuckahoe was set apart as a parish. In 1860, the second chapel of wood was built in the churchyard. In 1870, St. John's Riverside Hospital was organized. In 1872, the present church was erected. The entire south wall of the old building, which was erected in 1752, is retained, with its venerable door and windows, also the south transept and part of the east wall, with two of the windows of the old chancel, the old weather vane and bell. The Cobb memorial font in St. John's Church, erected in memory of Miss Minnie Putnam Cobb, daughter of the Rev. and Mrs. Lyman Cobb, is very artistic. The chancel windows erected in memory of Mrs. Jane Baldwin Smith are beautiful. The memorial pulpit was presented by Mrs. William F. Cochran. On an artistic brass panel in front is the inscription:

I.H.S.
As Though God Did Beseech You Through Us.
Easter, A.D., 1888. A Memorial of
Elizabeth Paddock.
"Christ's faithful soldier and servant unto her life's end."

In 1896, a memorial window to Dr. and Mrs. E. G. Ludlow was placed in the church. These and other interior furnishings, and the large pipe organ increase the beauty of the church. The fine parish house and manse are the gift of Mr. and Mrs. William F. Cochran, who also generously paid the $50,000

---

* The volume "Church and Sunday-school Work in Yonkers" by Miss Agnes E. Kirkwood, records a detailed history of this and other Sunday-schools.

CLERGYMEN OF YONKERS.

1. Albert M. Feeser, Holy Trinity Catholic.
2. George R. Cutting, Westminster Presbyterian.
3. Anthony Molloy, St. Peter's Catholic.
4. James T. Bixby, First Unitarian Congregational.
5. Charles R. Corley, St. Mary's Catholic.
6. James E. Freeman, St. Andrew's Memorial Protestant Episcopal.
7. William P. Bruce, Park Hill Reformed.
8. Alexander B. Carver, St. John's Protestant Episcopal.
9. Frederick M. Davenport, First Methodist Episcopal.
10. Thomas H. Baragwanath, Central Methodist Episcopal.
11. Ephriam S. Widdemer, Christ Episcopal.
12. P. Albert Locher, Church of the Sacred Heart.
13. George P. Krebs, German Methodist Episcopal.
14. John Alison, Immanuel Presbyterian.
15. William B. Bowen, S. African Methodist Episcopal Zion.
16. Albert A. Lings, St. Joseph's Catholic.
17. Alvah S. Hobart, Warburton Avenue Baptist.
18. Enos J. Bosworth, Nepperhan Avenue Baptist.
19. A. H. Holthusen, St. John's German Evangelical Lutheran.

debt of the church. The church in 1896 enrolled about six hundred members, and the Sunday-school about seven hundred. The Rev. Ellis Lyon is the assistant rector. The details of the Sunday-school history are recorded in "Church and Sunday-school Work in Yonkers," by Miss Agnes E. Kirkwood.

CHRONOLOGICAL TABLE.

1753. Episcopal Church erected in Yonkers.
1787. Yonkers became an independent parish.
1797. First Methodist Episcopal Church of Yonkers (at Tuckahoe).
1798. St. John's Protestant Episcopal Church (at Tuckahoe) built, but Tuckahoe not an independent parish until the year 1853.
1828. Methodist Episcopal Church on North Broadway.
1843. Reformed Church on South Broadway.
1848. St. Mary's Roman Catholic Church on South Broadway.
1849. Warburton Avenue Baptist Church, formerly Mount Olivet Baptist.
1852. First Presbyterian Church on North Broadway.
1858. Westminster Presbyterian Church on Warburton Avenue.
1858. St. Paul's Protestant Episcopal Church on North Broadway.
1858. Unitarian Congregational Church on North Broadway.
1870. Central Methodist Episcopal Church on Hudson Street.
1871. African Methodist Episcopal Zion Church on Main Street.
1871. St. Joseph's Roman Catholic Church on Ashburton Avenue.
1872. Christ Protestant Episcopal Church on Nepperhan Avenue.
1873. St. John's German Evangelical Lutheran Church on Hudson Street.
1874. Messiah Baptist Church (colored) on Ashburton Place.

DAVID COLE, D.D., FIRST REFORMED CHURCH.

1879. Dayspring Presbyterian Church, corner of Elm and Walnut Streets.
1880. German Methodist Episcopal Church on Waverly Street.
1891. Nepperhan Avenue Baptist Church.
1891. Church of the Sacred Heart on Shonnard Place.
1892. Park Hill Reformed Church on Ludlow Street.
1892. St. Nicholas United Greek Catholic Church on Ash Street.
1892. Woodhill Methodist Episcopal Church on Saw Mill River Road.
1894. St. Peter's Roman Catholic Church on Riverdale Avenue.
1894. Slavonian-Hungarian Holy Trinity Roman Catholic Church on Walnut Street.
1894. St. Andrew's Memorial Protestant Episcopal Church on Livingston Avenue.
1868. Armour Villa Park Methodist Episcopal Chapel.
1885. Immanuel Chapel on Nepperhan Avenue.
1888. Hebrew Synagogue on New Main Street.
1889. Salvation Army, Dock Street.
1868. Mile Square Sunday School.
1894. Grace Gospel Mission on Palisade Avenue.

FIRST METHODIST EPISCOPAL CHURCH OF YONKERS (AT TUCKAHOE). The early history of this church is recorded in Chapters VI., VIII., IX. and X. The parsonage was built under the pastorate of the Rev. Nathaniel Mead in 1858. The present church is marble. The corner-stone was laid by Bishop Edmund S. Janes in September, 1866. The church was dedicated February 20, 1867. From that date the preachers have been Rev. Gideon Draper, D.D., Rev. S. M. Vernon, Rev. John W. Ackerly, Rev. Oscar Haviland, Rev. Benjamin N. Lewis, Rev. George W. Terbush, Rev. John W. Selleck, Rev. Francis Bottome, D.D., Rev. David McCartney, Rev. Edmund L. Hoffecker, Rev. James Y. Bates. The number of members in 1896 was 134.

In May, 1889, a fine pipe organ was erected in the church. The Sunday-school was established about the year 1797. It now enrolls 118 scholars.

FIRST REFORMED CHURCH.

ST. JOHN'S PROTESTANT EPISCOPAL CHURCH (AT TUCKAHOE). When the Rev. Elias Cooper was rector (1789 to 1816) of the Episcopal Church in Yonkers, he established a branch work at Tuckahoe. A chapel was erected there in 1798. It is still standing and has the characteristics of the old-time architecture. Its quaint steeple, its shingled sides, and its surroundings, divert thoughts from the present and recall past decades. It was consecrated in 1847. In 1853 the parish was erected. In 1867 a chancel was added to the building, to which a vestry room had been added in 1847. Rectors or supplies, 1853-58, Rev. Charles Jones; 1859-60, Rev. Augustus St. Clair; 1860-61, Rev. David Doremus; 1861-65, no incumbent; 1865-80, Rev. Angus M. Ives; 1881-84, Rev. Samuel B. Moore; 1889-92, Rev. John W. Trimble; 1892, Rev. John W. Buckmaster. The church in 1896 had 100 communicants. The Sunday-school, which was organized about 1798, enrolled fifty children in 1896.

METHODIST EPISCOPAL CHURCH ON NORTH BROADWAY. This is known as the First M. E. Church of Yonkers, but the Methodist Church at Tuckahoe was organized first. The early history of the church is recorded in Chapters IX. and X. In 1828 a deed of land on which the present house of worship stands was given to Messrs. Thompson, Oakley, Shonnard, Griffin and Oakley, in trust for the Methodist Episcopal Church. The church was dedicated in the following autumn. In 1839 a plot of ground was deeded to Christ Methodist Episcopal Church—the original corporate name—for a parsonage lot. The successive pastors have been as follows: 1828, Rev. E. Hibbard; 1829–30, Rev. R. Seaman; 1831–32, Rev. E. Hibbard; 1833–34, Rev. E. Smith; 1835, Rev. T. Evans; 1836–37, Rev. E. Oldron and J. D. Bangs; 1838, Rev. J. Davies; 1839, Rev. H. Hatfield; 1840, Rev. Thomas Burch; 1841, Rev. D. I. Wright; 1842–43, Rev. John A. Selleck; 1844–45, Rev. J. C. Green; 1846–47, Rev. C. C. Keyes; 1848–49, Rev. Salmon C. Perry; 1850–51, Rev. Paul R. Brown; 1852, Rev. P. L. Hoyt; 1853, Rev. P. L. Sanford; 1854, Rev. George Brown; 1855–56, Rev. J. B. Hagany; 1857–58, Rev. P. Ward; 1859–60, Rev. L. H. King, D.D.; 1861–62, Rev. Edwin R. Keyes; 1863–65, Rev. Joseph B. Wakeley; 1866, Rev. L. H. King, D.D.; 1866–69, Rev. Morris D'C. Crawford, D.D.; 1870–71, Rev. Frank Bottome, D.D.; 1872–74, Rev. R. M. Stratton, D.D.; 1875–77, Rev. F. Hamlin; 1878–79, Rev. L. H. King, D.D.; 1880–82, Rev. Delos Lull; 1883 to 1886, Rev. William E. Ketcham, D.D.; 1886, Rev. Abraham J. Palmer, D.D.; 1887–90, Rev. George E. Strobridge, D.D.,; 1890, Rev. Edwin A. Schell, Ph.D.; 1893, Rev. Fred M. Daven-port. The Rev. William E. Ketcham, D.D., who was pastor from 1883–86, discerned the need of a new church, and by patient and persistent labor secured subscriptions to the amount of about $28,000. These subscriptions, with the plans of the proposed building, he passed over to his successor. The corner-stone was laid October 19, 1886. The church was dedicated September 9, 1888. Among those whose names were mentioned with gratitude was the Rev. William E. Ketcham, D.D., who had secured the large subscription list during his pastorate. Mr. John E. Andrus and Mr. John C. Havemeyer gave generously on the day of dedication. The gift of the former was one-third of the entire cost of the buildings, which, exclusive of ground, was $60,000. The present membership of the church is five hundred. The Sunday-school was established in 1826, in the country school-house where the first services of the church were held. It has continued its beneficent work down to the present day. The organization and growth of the Chinese department constitute an interesting chapter in the history of the Sunday-school. Messrs. Bloomer & Co., in 1879, opened a shirt manufactory and laundry in the building now owned by the Yonkers Railroad Company, at the western terminus of Main Street. They brought among their employees a number of Chinamen. The Westminster Sunday-school made a partially successful effort to bring the Chinese into that school, but eventually they became members of the First Methodist Sunday-school. Theodore Sewell, Miss Carrie W. Rehorn, Mrs. Catherine B. Sing and other teachers patiently instructed them, beseeching them to abandon their idols and accept Christ as their Saviour. The text-books in use are Chinese primers and Testaments from the American Tract Society. The Chinese department in 1890, enrolled twenty-two pupils. In 1896 it enrolled thirty. The whole school enrolls three hundred members.

WARBURTON AVENUE BAPTIST CHURCH.

FIRST REFORMED CHURCH. Until 1867 this church was known as "The Protestant Reformed Dutch Church." Its early history is recorded in Chapter IX. It originated in a mission movement started in 1841. Its first services were held in the "Long Room." The church was organized April 23, 1843. Its first pastor was the Rev. Victor Moreau Hulbert (subsequently Dr.). The first church edifice was dedicated August 27, 1845. The building was afterward enlarged. The second pastor was the Rev. Isaac S. Demaud, who was installed October 8, 1848. The third pastor was the Rev. Dwight M. Seward (afterward Dr.), who was installed February 12, 1851. The fourth pastor was the Rev. Mr. Hulbert, who was recalled. His second installation was November 9, 1852. The present pastor is the Rev. David Cole, D.D. He succeeded Mr. Hulbert, and was installed January 10, 1866. His long service as a Yonkers pastor has greatly endeared him to his own people and the city at large. In 1891 a large and fine oil portrait of the Rev. Dr. Cole was presented to him by the citizens of Yonkers. The tablet affixed to the frame bears the inscription, "Presented to the Rev. David Cole, D.D., by his fellow citizens of Yonkers-on-the-Hudson—a token of their personal esteem, and of their grateful appreciation of the large services he has rendered Church and State, as a public-spirited citizen, an accurate scholar, and a faithful minister of the Gospel."

On November 9, 1852, a new chapel erected on Ludlow Street by the First Reformed Church, was dedicated to the service of God. It is now the house of worship of the Park Hill Reformed Church.

In 1894, the old house of worship of the Reformed Church was taken down. The corner-stone of the new church was laid on November 14, 1894. The church was first used for Sabbath services on January 12, 1896. It is an ornament to the city. Its cost was over $40,000. The furniture, including the organ, cost about $10,000. The organ, including the water-meter, cost about $5,675. The present membership of the church is 425. The Sunday-school was organized probably in the year 1842. One of its early Superintendents was Mr. Charles W. Baird, afterward the Rev. Dr. Charles W. Baird, the author of "History of the Huguenot Emigration to America." Dr. Baird was for many years the pastor of the Presbyterian Church at Rye, N. Y. Another Superintendent was George Stewart, who was a devoted Christian and earnest teacher. His class erected, in the new church, a window to his memory. The present membership of the Sunday-school is 257.

ST. MARY'S (R.C.) CHURCH. The early history of this church is recorded in Chapters IX. and X. It originated in mission work begun in 1847. A brick church was erected on what is now St. Mary Street in 1848. It is now in use as a public hall. Rev. John Ryan, S.J., had charge of the mission work, and the

ST. MARY'S CATHOLIC CHURCH.

brick church was built while he was in Yonkers. His successor was Rev. Hippolyte Bienvenue, S.J., and he by Rev. Louis Jouin, S.J. The first resident pastor was the Rev. Thomas S. Preston, afterward the Right Rev. Monsignor Preston—a prelate of the Papal household. He was temporarily succeeded by

ST. JOSEPH'S SEMINARY, VALENTINE HILL.

Rev. John McMahon. In 1854, Rev. Eugene Maguire was placed in charge. His successor was Rev. Edward Lynch, who had in 1859 for an assistant priest, Rev. S. A. Mullady. The assistants who succeeded Rev. S. A. Mullady were Father Biretta, an Italian Franciscan, Rev. Patrick Brady, Rev. T. Byrne and Rev. William H. Oram. Father Lynch died while in charge of St. Mary's parish, May 5, 1865. His successor was Rev. Charles T. Slevin. His assistant priest, Rev. Albert A. Lings, was succeeded by Rev. Bernard Goodwin and Rev. J. Byron. While Father Slevin was in Europe, Rev. Edward McKenna occupied his place. Father Byron, the assistant, was succeeded by Rev. Eugene McKenna, and he, by Rev. J. W. Hays. Rev. Andrew O'Reilley was assistant pastor a number of years.

Rev. Charles R. Corley was sent in June, 1877, to supply the place of Father Slevin, who was sick. He still remains in charge of the parish. Rev. Andrew O'Reilley was his assistant. In 1884, Rev. James F. McLaughlin also became an assistant.

WARBURTON AVENUE BAPTIST CHURCH. The early history of this church is recorded in Chapters IX. and X. The first prayer-meeting of Baptists in Yonkers was held March 5, 1847, in the house of Mr. Peter F. Peek. The Rev. John Dow- ling, D.D., was the first Baptist clergy- man who preached in Yonkers. He de- livered a sermon in Mr. Peek's parlors in 1847. Seven persons on May 14, 1849, en- rolled themselves as members of a Bap- tist church in Yon- kers. The Rev. Henry D. Miller, afterward Dr. Miller, was the first pastor. The corner-stone of a church building was laid October 24, 1850. The church was finished and dedicated in 1852. It stood on the lot now occupied by the W. C. T. U. Hall. It was built of brick. Its dimensions were 52 x 63. Its tower was sixty feet high. Its main audience room accommodated three hundred or four hundred, and its basement about two hundred.

TREVOR MEMORIAL PARSONAGE, WARBURTON AVENUE BAPTIST CHURCH.

The pastors of the Warburton Avenue Church have been as follows: 1849-57, Rev. Henry D. Miller; 1858-60, Rev. J. R. Scott; 1861-65, Rev. J. C. C. Clarke; 1865-73, Rev. A. J. F. Behrends;

1874–75; Rev. William T. Burns; 1876–81, Rev. Henry M. Sanders; 1883–86, Rev. Edward P. Farnham; 1887–88, Rev. H. B. Grose, (acting pastor); 1888– , Rev. Alvah S. Hobart, D.D.

During the pastorate of the Rev. A. J. F. Behrends, the noble church edifice on Warburton Avenue, corner of Ashburton Avenue, was built by the Messrs. John B. Trevor and James B. Colgate and presented to the congregation. A special history prepared and published by a committee appointed by the church, June 30, 1869, gives an account of the origin, erection and dedication of the building. The corner-stone was laid April 11, 1868. The church was dedicated June 20, 1869. The entire cost of the ground, building, appointments, etc., was nearly $200,000, all of which with the exception of $10,000 raised by the church and society were contributed by Messrs. Trevor and Colgate, who always gave generously to Baptist churches and institutions. Rochester University with its Trevor Hall and Madison University were recipients of the gifts of Mr. Trevor. Mr. Colgate munificently endowed Madison University and its name was changed to Colgate University.

The Warburton Baptist Church now enrolls 596 members. It supports three mission schools, one at 132 Ravine Avenue, another at 222 Riverdale Avenue, and a third at 10 Florence Street. The Sunday-

FIRST PRESBYTERIAN CHURCH AND MANSE.

school was organized in 1849. It enrolls 225 members. In the Glenwood school are 100 members, in the Riverdale Avenue school 110 members, and in the Florence Street school, 80 members.

FIRST PRESBYTERIAN CHURCH. The early history of this church is recorded in Chapters IX. and X. In 1852, Rev. Dwight M. Seward, then pastor of the Reformed Church with forty-six of the members, separated from the church. On May 10, 1852, they were received by the Third Presbytery of New York and organized into the First Presbyterian Church of Yonkers. The church edifice was dedicated May, 1854. The Rev. Dwight M. Seward (long since Dr. Seward) was succeeded by the Rev. T. Ralston Smith, D.D., who was installed March 1, 1871. During his pastorate the Dayspring Sunday-school, from which has grown the Dayspring Presbyterian Church, was established. The third pastor of the First Presbyterian Church was the Rev. John Reid (subsequently Dr. Reid). He was installed November 6, 1879. During his pastorate Immanuel Chapel was built. His resignation took effect October 31, 1895. The present membership of the First Presbyterian Church is 502. The Sunday-school was organized in 1852. The First Church Sunday-school and the Immanuel Chapel Sunday-school enroll 406 names.

WESTMINSTER PRESBYTERIAN CHURCH. This church is the outgrowth of a movement which began in 1855. A historical pamphlet, by the Rev. Lewis W. Mudge and the Rev. John Dixon, record in full the history of the church to May 20, 1880. On September 16, 1855, "The School Street Mission Sunday-school" opened with ten scholars and five teachers. It was held in the district school-house. Mr. Ebenezer Curtice was the Superintendent. In May, 1856, Mr. Rollin A. Sawyer, a student in Union Theological Seminary, became a missionary in connection with the school. The school was removed to Getty Lyceum in 1857. Preaching services were held there. The first service was on April 26, 1857. About eighty were present. In 1857 the name of the school was changed to "The First Mission Sunday-school of Yonkers." On February 3, 1858, the church was organized with eighteen members. Rev. Mr. Sawyer (long since Dr. Sawyer) was installed February 17, 1858. The first church edifice was erected probably the next year. The Rev. Samuel Thompson Carter was installed November 13, 1862. The Rev. Lewis W. Mudge (now Dr. Mudge) was installed August 1, 1867. The Rev. John Dixon (now Dr. Dixon) was installed October 11, 1877. During his pastorate the present stone church was erected. The corner-stone was laid May 20, 1880. The church was dedicated October 23, 1882. The Rev. Charles P. Fagnani was installed in the spring of 1885. The interior of the church was destroyed by fire April 30, 1886, but was soon restored. The Rev. Edward C. Moore, who came to the church as a stated supply, October, 1886, was installed pastor June 30, 1887. Rev. Zebulon B. Graves was stated supply from October 6, 1889, to January 19, 1890. The Rev. George R. Cutting was installed November 6, 1890.

WESTMINSTER PRESBYTERIAN CHURCH.

The present membership of the Westminster Presbyterian Church is 593. The Sabbath-school enrolls 546, and has a Home Department which enrolls 160. In March, 1895, the church began to publish a local paper called *Tidings*.

ST. PAUL'S PROTESTANT EPISCOPAL CHURCH. In 1858 the Young Men's Missionary Association of St. John's parish prepared a room in Mechanic (now New Main) Street for holding mission services. The Rev. Darius R. Brewer was invited to take charge of the mission. On December 15, 1858, a new parish was incorporated. St. Paul's Church edifice was opened for worship April 8, 1860. The Rev. Mr. Brewer was invested with the office of rector, April 22, 1860. The Rev. Uriah T. Tracy succeeded Mr. Brewer October 4, 1866. On December 9, 1869, Rev. S. G. Fuller was elected rector. The next pastor was the Rev. David F. Banks, who was assisted one year by the Rev. Arthur Sloan. The Rev. C. Maurice Wines succeeded Rev. Mr. Banks. The Rev. William H. Mills, D.D., became rector February 1, 1880. While he was rector the Yonkers "Nursery and Home" was founded by Mrs. J. H. Clark. The St. Paul's Sunday-school was organized in 1858. The first session was held in Humboldt Hall. Mr. Henry Austice was the Superintendent. It now enrolls 125 scholars. The church has a membership of 360.

The successor of the Rev. Dr. Mills was the Rev. G. Ernest Magill, who became rector in September, 1893, and resigned December 30, 1895. His successor is the Rev. W. M. Gilbert, who came in 1896.

UNITARIAN CONGREGATIONAL CHURCH. The first Unitarian sermon preached in Yonkers was delivered by Rev. Samuel S. Osgood, D.D. When the Rev. A. A. Livermore, D.D., editor of the *New York Christian Inquirer* came to Yonkers to reside he preached in the houses of some of the Unitarians. The Society was organized in 1858. In the certificate of incorporation the church is named the First Unitarian Congregational Society of Yonkers, N. Y. The present church building was erected in 1858. The first pastor of the church was Rev. Dr. Livermore. Rev. Israel F. Williams became pastor in June, 1864; Rev. Joseph May in July, 1865; Rev. Rushton D. Burr in June, 1868; Rev. George L. Stowell in December, 1880; Rev. John Heddaeus in 1884, and Rev. James T. Bixby, Ph.D., in 1887.

The church, in 1896, enrolls 85 members. The church does not make baptism and partaking of the Communion a *sine qua non* for church membership. The Sunday-school was established in 1856. It enrolls thirty-seven names.

CENTRAL METHODIST EPISCOPAL CHURCH. On September 23, 1870, a few Methodists decided that they would organize a new Methodist Episcopal Church. The Rev. George W. Lord became pastor in 1870. The church on Hudson Street was dedicated in July, 1873. The second pastor was Rev.

UNITARIAN CONGREGATIONAL CHURCH.

Frederick S. Barnum. He succeeded Mr. Lord in 1872. Rev. A. H. Ferguson became pastor in 1874, Rev. Ezra Tinker in 1877, Rev. Alexander McLean in 1878, Rev. P. R. Hawkhurst in 1881, Rev. Lucius H. King, D.D., in 1884, Rev. Charles W. Millard in 1885, Rev. W. McKendree Darwood, D.D., in 1888, Rev. S. Parkes Cadman in 1893, Rev. John J. Reed, D.D., in 1895. When Rev. S. Parkes Cadman was called to New York, in consideration of his release by the Central M. E. officials, J. Milton Cornell, Esq., in the name of Mr. Cadman's New York friends, placed in the hands of the trustees of the Central M. E. Church a check for $5,000. The Rev. Dr. Reed, with characteristic ability and zeal, planned for the celebration of the twenty-fifth anniversary of the church, and the "Silver Wedding-day," as it was termed, was a joyous occasion. All the ex-pastors living were present. There was an afternoon reception, after which about 200 gathered around the tables in the parlor and enjoyed the banquet and toasts. In the evening ex-Pastor Cadman spoke, and an effort was made to materially reduce the church debt. The church in 1895 enrolled 497 members. The Sunday-school was organized October 20, 1870. It now enrolls between 300 and 400 members. In April, 1896, the Rev. T. H. Baragwanath, Ph.D., became pastor of the church.

AFRICAN METHODIST EPISCOPAL ZION CHURCH. The Rev. Jacob Thomas, of New York, organized this church in May, 1870. The number of members was at first ten. They rented Townsend Hall, No. 50 North Broadway. The first pastor was Rev. Isaac Jenkins. He was succeeded by Rev. Adam Jackson. Rev. George E. Jackson became pastor in 1875, Rev. T. Davis in 1877, and in the same year, Rev.

J. C. Dodge. His successor was Rev. E. J. Miller. The next pastor was Rev. William Dorsey. Rev. J. A. Evans was his successor. Rev. George E. Jackson was recalled in 1883. The corner-stone of the church was laid October 15, 1884. The church was dedicated April 12, 1885. Rev. Charles H. Teneyck became pastor in 1886. In 1891, Rev. T. E. G. Thompson became pastor. Rev. H. M. Cephas succeeded him in 1892. Rev. George S. Adams came in 1893, and the Rev. Wm. B. Bowens was appointed pastor in 1896. There were ten scholars at the first session. The school in 1896 enrolled eighty members. The church now enrolls 125 members. The Sunday-school was organized July 12, 1874, in Townsend Hall, by Gabriel P. Reevs, M.D., an elder in the Reformed Church.

St. Joseph's (R. C.) Church. In May, 1871, St. Joseph's parish was set off from St. Mary's. Rev. Albert A. Lings, an assistant at St. Mary's, was made the first pastor. Rev. Father Shadler was his assistant for about three years. In November, 1876, Rev. Anthony Molloy became assistant. When Father Lings was in Europe in 1881, Father Molloy became acting pastor, with the Rev. Michael Montgomery as assistant. Subsequently, Rev. Fathers Henry Xavier and John F. Coffey became assistants. The corner-stone of the first church was laid in September, 1871. The corner-stone of the present church was laid by Archbishop Corrigan, May 16, 1886. The church was dedicated January 29, 1888. In 1877-78, a new parochial residence was erected. Its site is east of, and adjoining the church plot. St. Joseph's parish schools were established in September, 1872. About three hundred pupils were enrolled. The school was discontinued in June, 1879, and reopened in September, 1881, under the charge of the Sisters of Charity. It now enrolls about three hundred and sixty-six boys and four hundred and twenty-nine girls, according to the last report to the Archbishop of New York. The pastor estimates that his parish numbers about four thousand souls. Rev. Henry F. Xavier is, at present, his only assistant. In 1895, Father Lings became the Very Rev. Dean Lings. His ecclesiastical district includes Westchester, Dutchess and Putnam counties.

Christ Protestant Episcopal Church. In 1867 Miss Caroline Jones gave $1,000 to establish a mission church or school in Yonkers. By her will she increased this fund. Rev. Lyman Cobb, Jr., one of her executors, selected six gentlemen to join with him in organizing a Free Church. In 1872 the fund had grown to about $6,000. The lot at the corner of Nepperhan Avenue and Elm Street was purchased for $4,000, a mortgage was given for that amount, and the $6,000 was used to erect a church. The first service in the church was in July, 1872. The first to officiate was Rev. Lyman Cobb, Jr. Then various clergymen in Yonkers and Riverdale and Hastings officiated. Rev. S. S. Lewis officiated two years. Rev. William Hyde officiated one year. Next came Rev. R. H. Barnes, who was succeeded by Rev. Samuel B. Moore, and he by Rev. Charles Ferris. Mr. Robert S. Carlin, a student in the General Theological Seminary of New York City, officiated for a time. On July 1, 1885, the Rev. August Ulmann (now Dr. Ulmann), who had been the assistant rector of St. John's, became rector of Christ Church. Wardens and vestrymen had been elected Easter Monday. The parish house was built while the Rev. A. Ulmann was rector. Rev. Ephriam S. Widdemer, the present rector, preached his first sermon in Christ Church on October 6, 1890. During his pastorate the church edifice has been enlarged and greatly improved. The church now enrolls 188 members. The Sunday-school was organized July 14, 1872, and took the name of the church which at that time was St. Mary's, but which was subsequently changed. The school now enrolls 234 members.

CENTRAL METHODIST EPISCOPAL CHURCH.

St. John's German Evangelical Lutheran Church. The history of religious work among the Germans is recorded in the pamphlet containing the history of the Westminster Presbyterian Church, which was interested in that work. The Rev. J. H. Sommer became pastor of St. John's German Evangelical Lutheran Church in 1870. The Rev. Leo Koenig succeeded him December 1, 1872. His successor was the Rev. Armindus Volquarts, who became pastor in December, 1877, and remained until November, 1878. He was succeeded by the Rev. Frederick W. Foehlinger. In the fall of 1892, Rev. M. T. Holls entered upon the pastorate. He remained until October, 1894. Rev. A. H. Holthusen, the present pastor, was called to the church on December 16, 1894. In 1896 the church enrolled 30 voting members and 140 communicants.

The Sunday-school was organized September 11, 1869. In 1896 it enrolled 105 scholars. Mr. William Beutler has been Superintendent over twenty-five years.

Messiah Baptist Church (Colored). This church is the outgrowth of a prayer-meeting established in 1872 by Mrs. Henry Peel, Mrs. Grace Purdy and Henry E. Duers. In 1874 a mission was established. The first sermon was preached in Townsend Hall. The mission was first called "Immanuel." In July, 1876, the name was changed to "Messiah." Thomas Peel, Henry Evans, Joseph Maltby, James White, Charles Mann, Richard Bailey, Henry Travis, during 1874-75, held prayer-meetings at the home of Mrs. Peel. The church was organized in the spring or summer of 1874. It was officially recognized as an organized church in 1879. Rev. R. D. Wynn was the stated supply. Mr. James B. Colgate purchased for the society the building formerly known as "Leighton Academy." It was remodelled for a church. The cost of the property and improvements was $15,000. The church was dedicated June 3, 1888. The pastors of the church have been Rev. R. D. Wynn, Rev. Joseph Francis, Rev. William S. Bass, Rev. Joseph Miller, Rev. Joseph Bailey, Rev. Abraham B. Brown, Rev. Alexander M. Conway, Rev. Edward W. Roberts. The church in 1896 enrolled 125 members, and the Sunday-school 50 scholars.

Dayspring Presbyterian Church. Between 1855 and 1860, cottage prayer-meetings were held on Nodine Hill. In 1857, open air services were held. In 1864, Mr. John McCoy was engaged in religious work in Yonkers, and was cordially welcomed when he called on the East Side residents. When the Yonkers Home Missionary Society was organized in 1865, Mr. McCoy continued his religious work under its auspices. Mr. A. W. Wittmeyer was also at work under the auspices of that Society. He was then a Union Theological Seminary student. For many years the Westminster Presbyterian Church sustained cottage prayer-meetings on the hill. In 1871, the First Presbyterian Church Home Missionary Association was organized. The Dayspring Chapel was built by that Association in 1872. For a brief time in 1873, Rev. A. J. Titsworth, a student in the Union Theological Seminary, was at work under the auspices of the First Church Association. Rev. Charles E. Allison, another Union Theological student, began his work in Yonkers in April, 1873. He continued the work in Dayspring Chapel, and on April 21, 1879, the Dayspring Presbyterian Church was organized. A part of a new church building was completed and dedicated on November 13, 1893.

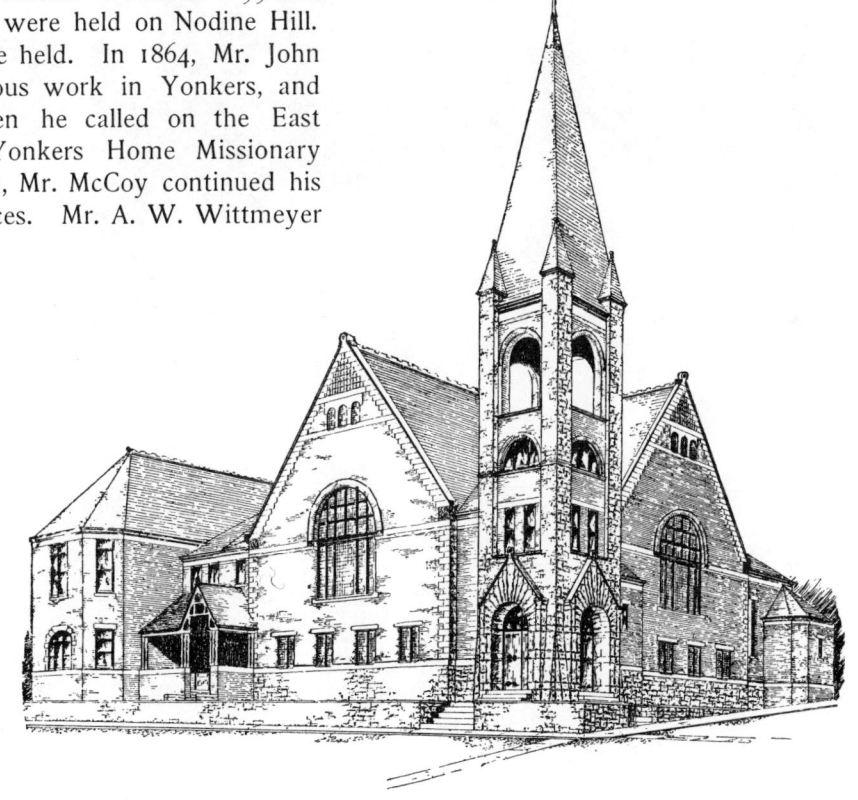

DAYSPRING PRESBYTERIAN CHURCH. (IN COURSE OF CONSTRUCTION.)

The membership of the church in 1896 is 422. The elders are Wm. Smith, John H. Cutbill, Thomas F. Hope and Ezra S. Lefurgy. The Dayspring Sunday-school was organized May 26, 1872, with 43 members. Its first Superintendent was Mr. Charles Lockwood, through whose efforts the school flourished. It was largely through his persevering labor that the school was organized. It now enrolls 377 members. The Superintendent is Mr. William Smith.

GERMAN METHODIST EPISCOPAL CHURCH. In 1880, a mission among the Germans was established by the German Methodists. The Rev. John J. Mesmer preached a sermon in September, to three auditors, Mr. and Mrs. Henry H. Kroenke and Mrs. Augusta Krah. Mr. Kroenke was a zealous friend of the mission. The first services were held in the hall occupied by the W. C. T. U. It stood on the site of the present Getty Square railroad station. Humboldt Hall was the next place of meeting. The ministers of the church have been, 1880–81, Rev. John J. Mesmer: 1881–82, Rev. Ernest Hartmann; 1882–83, Rev. Charles Brockmeier; 1883–86, Rev. Henry Miller; 1886, Rev. Geo. H. Gieger; 1889, Rev. Charles Brockmeier; 1890–92, Rev. Emil Peglow; 1892–94, Rev. John G. Lutz, Sr.; 1894, Rev. Geo. P. Krebs. In 1895, the church enrolled 52 members. In 1880, the Sunday-school with which the mission of the Germans began numbered five teachers and four scholars. In 1895, it enrolled 138.

NEPPERHAN AVENUE BAPTIST CHURCH. This church is the outgrowth of Sunday-school work which was begun in 1863. The Rev. Edward F. Bright, D.D., and his daughter, were the leaders in the movement. The meeting to organize the school was held in the second story of the morocco factory near the corner of Nepperhan Avenue and New Main Street. Almost all who were at the meeting were members of the Mount Olivet Baptist Church. The next Sabbath the teaching began. After a few sessions in the morocco factory the school was removed to a building on Spring Street, now New Main Street. The building is now known as Teutonia Hall. This hall was enlarged in a short time to make room for the Sunday-school scholars. Captain Holmes, a former sea captain, was employed as missionary. Mr. Bromley took up the work when Captain Holmes died. The school held its sessions in the Spring Street building many years.

NEPPERHAN AVENUE BAPTIST CHURCH.

After the Warburton Avenue Church was built, the Mount Olivet Church Building, which stood where the Temperance Hall now stands, was taken down and the material removed to Nepperhan Avenue, where the structure was rebuilt. Some years ago the building was enlarged and thus its capacity was nearly doubled.

The Nepperhan Avenue Baptist Church was organized June 16, 1891. The Rev. H. M. Warren began his pastorate October 18, 1891, ending it August 12, 1894. The Rev. Enos J. Bosworth entered upon his pastorate November 4, 1894. The church membership in 1896 is 325. The Sunday-school, previous to the organization of the church, had at one time about sixty-seven teachers and about 500 scholars in attendance. The roll carried 700 members. As a church-school it enrolls in 1896, about 555 members.

PARK HILL REFORMED CHURCH. The Park Hill Reformed Church is the outgrowth of a religious work begun by the First Reformed Church. In 1884, a chapel was erected on Ludlow Street, principally through the liberality of George Stewart, a member of the Consistory of the First Reformed Church. The chapel was dedicated November 9, 1884. The sermon was preached by the Rev. Dr. David Cole, pastor of the Reformed Church. Services were conducted in the chapel by Rev. Dr. Cole and other city pastors. In 1890, Mr. Robert R. White, a student in Union Theological Seminary, took charge of the work. He remained about one year. His successor was Mr. William Armitage Beardslee, a graduate of the Theological Seminary at New Brunswick. The Park Hill Reformed Church was organized in 1892. Rev. Mr. Beardslee was ordained Jan. 1st, and the same day installed pastor of the Park Hill Reformed Church. He remained about two years, when ill-health necessitated his relinquishing the pastorate. Rev. W. P. Bruce was called as his successor, and was installed April 4, 1895. The present membership of the church is ninety-three. The Sunday-school enrolls 140 members.

ST. NICHOLAS UNITED GREEK CATHOLIC CHURCH. The Greek Catholic Church, commonly called Uniates, represents a body numerous in Austria, Hungary, and other eastern countries in Europe. They are in communion with the Church of Rome, holding, contrary to the other Greek churches of the East, to the procession of the Holy Spirit from the Son as well as from the Father, in accordance with the belief of the Latin Church, but maintaining otherwise their ancient discipline, allowing the lower clergy to marry, administering the communion in both kinds (bread and wine) to the laity, adhering to the old calendar, and using in Greek countries the Greek language in their ritual, in Africa and Asia, the Syric, in Roumania, the Roman, in Hungary and Poland and Russia, the old Slav language. No living language is used in the ritual. It is estimated that there are about 200,000 Greek Catholics in the United States, not including those who may have settled west of St. Louis. In 1895, there were about twenty-four church edifices. In 1895, there were estimated to be 10,000 Greek Catholics in New York State, and three church edifices; the first of which was built in Brooklyn, the second in Yonkers, and the third in Buffalo.

The Yonkers Greek Catholics desired a church of their own order, and were encouraged by Rev. Alex. Dzubay, who was then living in Pennsylvania. The church was organized in 1892. Rev. Eugene Szetala was their first pastor. He came from Hungary and remained in Yonkers about three years, his pastorate beginning in 1892. The Rev. Alex. Jaczkovite was the second pastor. He came in January, 1895, from Streator, Ill. He was originally from Hungary. He speaks both Hungarian and Slav. On account of ill-health, he returned to his own country in October, 1895. The Rev. Basilius Volosin, took charge as pastor in September, 1895. He also came from abroad.

The corner-stone of the church on Ash Street was laid September 26, 1892. The church was dedicated December 18, 1892, the day of St. Nicholas, the patron saint. The membership at first was about six hundred, including baptized children. In 1895, it was about eight hundred or a thousand.

PARK HILL REFORMED CHURCH.

The church is in the diocese of New York. Archbishop Corrigan was present at the second dedicatory service in 1894, when the building was entirely completed.

The cross on the spire has three arms, one end of the lower arm leaning toward one end of the middle arm. The upper arm signifies the tablet on which was the superscription on the Saviour's cross. The central arm signifies the original arm on which the Saviour hung. The lower arm has two, probably three significations. First, it represents the foot rest which was sometimes fastened to the cross; second, forming as it does with the perpendicular beam, a St. Andrew's cross, it represents that cross. St. Andrew was the patron saint of the Slavs. The lower arm of the cross signifies the cross on which the penitent thief hung. In faith he leaned toward the Saviour for comfort and help. In Hungary, the Greek Catholics construct the cross with all the cross-beams horizontal, but in the United States, Poland, Bulgaria, Crotia and other Slav countries are represented, and the cross is constructed according to their views. In some American Greek churches all the cross-bars are horizontal.

The Scriptures are read from the pulpit in Old Slavish. The preaching is in Ruthenian (not Russian, but resembling it). In 1895, the pastors began to preach in the Hungarian language. Probably hereafter there will be preaching in that language once or twice a month. In 1895, three services were held every Sunday. The first called "Matutin," and significant of the resurrection of Christ, the second holy mass, and the third vespers. Sometimes at tvespers there was preaching and sometimes catechetical service, the latter in place of a Sunday-school, but the attendance was principally of adults, and the pastor gave instructions without asking questions. The children attended generally at holy mass.

On the corner-stone of the church is the inscription, "G. C. S. H., 1892," which signifies Greek Catholic Slavish Hungarian, St. Nicholas Church, 1892. The tablet on the church bears the inscription, "Philip O'Reily, Otoza Nas Pohrebnik Ot Svateho Mikoluja Czirkvi." "Nas" means our. "Pohrebnik" means undertaker. "Ot Svateho Otoza" means of saint or holy father. "Mikoluja Czirkvi" means Nicholas Church.

WOODHILL METHODIST EPISCOPAL CHURCH. In 1858, Cornelius W. Thomas, an influential member of the Baptist Church in Hastings established a Sunday-school in the old district school-house on the corner of the Saw Mill River and Tuckahoe roads. Ten teachers were associated with him in the school. Mr. Thomas was the Superintendent about three years. Wallace Pulver succeeded him and held the position two years. Soon after Mr. Pulver's resignation the school was closed. It was reopened in the spring of 1864 by Henry B. Odell, in his house, about one mile beyond the school-house. The scholars assembled in his dining-room. At that time the Rev. Thomas R. G. Peck was the pastor of the Reformed Church at Hastings. He began to hold religious services at Woodhill, and continued his work there for a number of years, sometimes inviting Yonkers clergymen and laymen to conduct the services. The growing Sunday-school had been transferred to one of Mr. Odell's outbuildings which he used as a laundry and kitchen. The Sunday evening congregation worshipped in that building, but it was too small to accommodate all who came. Mr. Odell gave one-quarter of an acre of ground as a site for a house of worship. In order to secure a building-fund the residents of the neighborhood held two fairs, the net proceeds of which were about $1,300. The proceeds of entertainments and of another fair aggregated $1,000. Among those through whose efforts the fairs were held and the entertainments given were Mr. and Mrs. Henry Odell, Mr. and Mrs. Jacob Odell, Mr. and Mrs. Abram Odell, Miss Fannie Dudley, Mr. and Mrs. James Varian, Walter Pulver and Mr. and Mrs. Abram Baxter. The chapel which was erected cost about $3,000. It was opened in 1868, and was known as Woodhill Union Chapel. The services were usually conducted by the Rev. Mr. Peck. Various other ministers led the meetings. Laymen also rendered service as leaders. The attendance on Sunday evenings averaged one hundred and fifty.

THE MOST HOLY TRINITY ROMAN CATHOLIC SLAVONIAN-HUNGARIAN CHURCH.

Woodhill Union Chapel became an organized church May 12, 1892. The M. E. denomination assumed charge of it. The first trustees of the Woodhill Methodist Episcopal Church were: Messrs. Joseph Chamberlain, Furman Lawrence, John E. Andrus, James L. Austin, Abram Austin and Joseph M. Bruce.

The first pastor of the church was the Rev. Robert D. Castle, now deceased. In 1893 he was succeeded by the Rev. William W. Alexander. The present pastor is the Rev. A. E. Barnett. The Sunday-school, which was established in the old district school-house, at first enrolled only twelve or fifteen scholars, but in a few months had an average attendance of over eighty scholars. In the chapel it enrolled one year 125 scholars. Woodhill Sunday-school has had for its Superintendents, Cornelius W. Thomas (the founder), 1858; Wallace Pulver, 1862; Henry B. Odell, 1864; Wallace Pulver, acting Superintendent; Oliver Chambers, 1875; G. Livingston Morse, 1877; William Allen Butler, Jr., 1881; H. C. Fuller, 1883; J. W. Nobles, M. D., 1887; Abram Austin, ——; Joseph Chamberlain, —— the present Superintendent.

St. Peter's (R. C.) Church. This church is called St. Peter's because the Rev. Anthony Molloy, who was appointed to found the new parish, received his appointment on the 29th of June, 1894, the feast of Saints Peter and Paul. Father Molloy had labored in Yonkers eleven years as an assistant of Father Lings, of St. Joseph's Church. He was appointed pastor of a church in Dutchess County, but his Yonkers friends petitioned the Archbishop to permit him to remain in Yonkers and establish a new parish. St. Mary's new church was in contemplation, and the establishment of the new parish was deferred. It was founded on July 13, 1894. The pastor, aided by several business men of the parish, selected as the site of the proposed new church the northeast corner of Riverdale Avenue and Ludlow Street. It is nearly 200 feet square and contains sixteen city lots. The amount paid for it was $20,000. The energetic pastor then erected a tent in which he held services. Plans for a church were drawn by Mr. L. J. O'Connor, and the building was erected at a cost of about $14,000. This amount does not include the cost of heating apparatus, furniture, etc. The corner-stone was laid September 23, 1894, by Archbishop Corrigan. Right Rev. J. M. Farley, V. G., sang the mass, assisted by Rev. A. A. Lings, Deacon; Rev. John McNamee, Sub-deacon. Very Rev. Joseph F. Mooney, V.G., preached the sermon; Rev. J. N. Connolly, Secretary to the Archbishop, was Master of Ceremonies. Eighteen or twenty priests were present. Several societies also were present in full regalia. The flags and banners were numerous. The tent could not accommodate a third of the vast concourse of people.

The Sunday-school organization dates from the founding of the parish. At the beginning it enrolled about sixty children.

The Most Holy Trinity Roman Catholic Slavonian-Hungarian Church. There are twenty Roman Catholic Slavonian-Hungarian churches in the United States. Twenty-eight churches in the United States use their language and their ritual. There are two Roman Catholic Slavonian-Hungarian churches in New York City, one of which was established in 1891, and the other in 1894. The Yonkers Hungarians desired to have public worship and Rev. Father John Pollakovics exerted his influence to establish a church. He came from Hungary and was pastor in Yonkers from July 26, 1894, to January 8, 1895. Rev. Nicolas Reinhart was pastor from February 1, 1895, to June 22, 1895. He was born in New York of German parents. Rev. Francis Denes became pastor June 22, 1895. He was born in Hungary, studied eight years in the King's Gymnasium in Eperis and pursued his theological course of four years in the Seminary at Kassa, where he was priest of the diocese.

The corner-stone of the church on Walnut Street was laid November 9, 1894. The church was dedicated June 6, 1894. The services are in Slavonian, rarely in Hungarian. An English service is held once a month on Sunday mornings. At the beginning about 1,700 belonged to the church. In 1895, the number was 3,000. These figures do not include children under nine years of age. The Sunday-school was not yet established in the autumn of 1895, but in September of that year the pastor said, "We expect to open a Sunday-school in November of this year, and will probably enroll 300 scholars."

The services are held each Sunday morning. Mass at 8 o'clock, at which the attendance is from 200 to 300 worshippers, most of them Irish. A second mass is at 10.30, attended by from 300 to 400, most of whom are Hungarians, but some Irish. The third service is a vesper service at 3 o'clock with an attendance of from 200 to 300.

In 1895 an English service was established. It is held once a month, at 8 o'clock Sunday morning. Rev. Father Albert Feeser preaches at that service. He is a political exile, having been banished from the Republic of Ecuador.

St. Andrew's Memorial Protestant Episcopal Church. In the spring of 1894 a little wooden chapel was erected by Mrs. William F. Cochran at the corner of Livingston Avenue and Morris Street, and placed under the care of St. John's Church. The opening service was held on Sunday, May 20th, of that year. At the first it was designed to accommodate the children in that section of the city with a Sunday-school, and possibly to conduct afternoon service on Sunday. Immediately the venture met with success, the school, which had previously been conducted in a residence by Mrs. K. M. Kellinger and Mrs. George Kerr was transferred to the little chapel and made the nucleus of the new school. So great was the demand of the people of that section for a church service in the morning that, in October, the Rev. James E. Freeman, then assistant rector of St. John's, was assigned by the mother parish to the work of organizing a Board of Trustees to conduct the affairs of the chapel and to the permanent establishment of regular services morning and afternoon. No sooner had this been undertaken than it was apparent that larger accommodations must be secured to hold intact the congregation that affiliated themselves with the movement. Thus it was that in April, 1895 (the following year), Mrs. Cochran, gratified with the results which her little chapel had achieved, proposed the erection of a stone building to be known as St. Andrew's Memorial Church. The corner-stone was laid on June 4, 1895, and the first service held in the new edifice Sunday, October 6th, of the same year. The church was consecrated by Bishop Potter on All Saints' Day, November 1, 1895. It is a memorial to Susannah

ST. ANDREW'S MEMORIAL PROTESTANT EPISCOPAL CHURCH AND RECTORY.

Bailey Baldwin, and her daughters, Susan Baldwin Waring and Jane Baldwin Smith. It is a Gothic structure, built of native granite, with brick trimmings, and has a seating capacity of 400. The interior is richly adorned with memorial gifts presented by members of the congregation. A rectory has recently been completed, built by the congregation, and designed to correspond with the church.

The Rev. James E. Freeman, rector of St. Andrew's Memorial Church, was born in New York City, July 24, 1866. He came to Yonkers as a business man in May, 1890, and after identifying himself with St. John's parish became Superintendent of the Sunday-school of that church. He was associated with the rector, Dr. Carver, in various institutions connected with St. John's, and was President of its Brotherhood at the time the Hollywood Inn was inaugurated. For twelve years he was connected with the Auditing Department of the N. Y. C. & H. R. R. R. Co., and while serving in that capacity took up the study of theology. Being advised by Bishop Potter and his rector, to prosecute a course of study looking to admission into the ministry of the Episcopal Church, he prepared himself, while still in the railroad, and was ordained deacon, May 20, 1894. Immediately after his ordination, he was called as assistant to the rector of St. John's Church, and occupied that pulpit during the absence of the rector in Europe in the summer of 1894. At this time a small chapel had been built by Mrs. Wm. F. Cochran in South Yonkers, and Mr. Freeman was assigned to that post. Since that time, St. Andrew's parish, with its beautiful group of buildings has come into existence. On April 28, 1895, in St. John's Church, Mr. Freeman was advanced to the priesthood and was elected to the rectorate of the new parish of St. Andrew's. He is also conspicuously identified with the Hollywood Inn, as Chairman of its Board of Directors.

THE MONASTERY OF THE SACRED HEART. This monastery is conducted by the Capuchin Fathers. The Capuchins are one branch of the great Franciscan Order, instituted by St. Francis of Assisi in the first decade of the thirteenth century. As a distinct branch, the Capuchins first made their appearance in Italy in 1528. Having received the approbation of Pope Clement (VII.), the new Order spread rapidly throughout the countries of Europe. In the middle of the seventeenth century we find them also laboring on the coast of Maine and Nova Scotia in this country, where they built the first Catholic chapels among the fishing villages of the French colonies. The first priest to officiate in the colony of New Amsterdam (now New York) was likewise a Capuchin.

At present the Capuchin Fathers have two Provinces in the United States, that of St. Joseph and that of St. Augustine. The Province of St. Joseph, to which this monastery belongs, was founded by two secular priests, the Rev. Gregory Haas and the Rev. John Anthony Frey. Coming from Switzerland, their native country, they established themselves at Mt. Calvary, Wisconsin, where they laid the corner-stone of their first convent in the spring of 1857. In 1882 the custody of St. Joseph was raised to the rank of a Province and Fr. Bonaventure Frey elected its first Provincial.

Fr. Bonaventure, the founder of the Monastery of the Sacred Heart, had already in 1866, erected the convent and church of "Our Lady of Sorrows," in Pitt Street, New York; in 1870 he took charge of St. John's Roman Catholic Church in West 30th Street, and in 1886 he established another house of the Order in 112th Street, New York, for the spiritual wants of "Our Lady of Angels'" parish. Five years later, ground was broken on Shonnard Place, Yonkers, for another establishment of the Order. The building erected on these grounds is now well-known as the Capuchin Monastery of the Sacred Heart. Located on one of the highest points in Yonkers, this monastery commands a most picturesque view of the surrounding country, exhibiting the blue hills of Westchester County in the east, and the rocky range of the Palisades to the west.

THE MONASTERY OF THE SACRED HEART.

The present edifice, the corner-stone of which was laid by the Right Rev. Bishop Seidenbush, on Sunday, June 21, 1891, was solemnly dedicated on Sunday, November 15th, of the same year by the Most Rev. Mich. Aug. Corrigan, Archbishop of New York. When completed, the monastery will consist of four wings around a quadrangular court about 100 feet square. The two wings now erected are of gray stone, quarried on the grounds, with brick trimmings and slate roofs. The temporary chapel in the east wing seats 500 people. Later on a more imposing structure, after the early Romanesque basilica style, will be built on Convent Avenue, and form the westerly side of the quadrangle.

The first pastor of the monastery church, Father Bonaventure, with Fr. Casimir and Fr. Peter as assistants, was succeeded in the autumn of 1894 by Fr. Luke as pastor, and Fr. Albert as assistant. At present Fr. Albert, assisted by Fr. Anthony, attends to the spiritual wants of the parish and conducts the divine services at the monastery chapel.

The monastery parochial school is situated on Convent Avenue, southwest of the monastery, and is in charge of three Sisters of St. Agnes.

IMMANUEL CHAPEL. This chapel is a branch of the First Presbyterian Church. It had its origin under the influence of the "Ladies' Missionary Association of the First Presbyterian Church." Mrs. G.

B. Balch and other ladies established a mothers' meeting in No. 6 Moquette Row. On January 6, 1885, a Sunday-school was opened in this house with three teachers and twelve scholars. The teachers were Miss Mary Randolph, Miss F. D. Baird and Miss J. W. Flagg. Wells Olmsted was chosen Superintendent. In February two more Sunday-school teachers, Miss Mary Ewing and Miss Julia F. Baird engaged in the work. The Missionary Association of the First Presbyterian Church assumed the charge of the mission, which was at first known as the "Moquette Mission," and afterward (in 1886) the "Immanuel Mission." The chapel was erected in 1887, and dedicated March 13th of that year.

From time to time theological students from New York conducted Sunday evening services in Moquette Row and in the chapel. The Rev. John S. Penman was placed in charge of the work in May, 1887. The Rev. J. Hendrick de Vries succeeded him in 1888. His successor was the Rev. Frank A. Wales. The present minister in charge is the Rev. John Alison, a recent graduate of the theological seminary. He came about the first Sabbath in July, 1895. The Sunday-school now enrolls about two hundred and twenty-five members.

METHODIST EPISCOPAL CHAPEL. This house of worship is located at Armour Villa Park. It was built in 1868, for religious services and for Sunday-school work, by the late Stephen Barker. It is owned by the Tuckahoe M. E. Church.

HEBREW SYNAGOGUE. Data for a complete history of the religious services of the Hebrews in Yonkers is not at hand. The following item from a Yonkers newspaper published in the village in 1870, seems to indicate that as early as that year public services were held. The paper reports that "the Hebrews of Yonkers have leased and fitted up for a synagogue the entire fourth story of Anderson's Building on Getty Square, and the Rev. M. Bernstein has been engaged to minister to them."

In 1872 there was no synagogue in Yonkers. The Hebrews were few in number. Each year they held services on at least three days. The Hebrew New Year begins in September or October. At the beginning of each year they observed two days. They also in each year held service on the Day of Atonement. Different halls were occupied. In one year, probably 1875, their public worship was in the house of Hermann Lyons, on Yonkers Avenue.

In January, 1887, the Messrs. Adolph Klein and Aaron Abrahamovitz advocated the organization of a congregation, and during about three years the services were in the Grand Army Hall, corner of Palisade Avenue and New Main Street. They were held on every seventh day and on the Hebrew holidays. Then Teutonia Hall, corner of New Main and Brook Streets, was converted into a synagogue and services began there. The Hebrew Benevolent Society bought the hall about 1890. Daily morning and evening services are held. On each Saturday there is a morning service, also an afternoon study of the Psalms and of ethics, followed by prayer and an evening service after sunset. In the morning, the cantor and congregation offer together a prayer in Hebrew. Then the cantor reads from the scroll, kept in the sacred ark. A sermon in German by the rabbi follows the reading. The cantor and congregation offer another prayer. When the rabbi officiates he wears over his shoulder a talith, and on his head a blue black cap, with silk lining. Some of the congregation wear taliths, which are white, with several blue stripes along the edges, and long white tassels on the four corners. The men and women sit apart, the heads of the men as well as those of the women being covered. When prayers are offered, the congregation stands and faces the east.

At first a member of the congregation was called upon to officiate. Mr. Saul Wolf conducted many services. He was assisted by Mr. Morris Mittler, who came from Miskolces, Hungary. The next to officiate was Rabbi Moses S. Wolf, late minister of the congregation in Albany, N. Y. He came to Yonkers in March, 1896. The present cantor is Mr. Copper.

In April, 1896, a Sunday-school was organized. A day school for teaching religion was opened in 1895. After a time it was closed, but was reopened. It was known as Talmud Tora. Daily sessions

IMMANUEL CHAPEL—PRESBYTERIAN.

were held in a room in the synagogue. The school was under the auspices of the Hebrew Benevolent Society. Forty or fifty scholars were in attendance. Two or three teachers gave instruction. One of the instructors was the Rev. Isaac Stemple. Hebrew literature (the Old Testament) and German literature were taught. About ten adults were engaged in the study of the Talmud and other literature. The school is closed at the present time.

SALVATION ARMY. The Salvation Army came to Yonkers in September, 1889. At first there were only two members, the captain and lieutenant. There are fifty-one now on the muster roll. The following named officers have had command in Yonkers: Captains Skidmore and McLallan; Staff Captains, Howell and Watkins; Captains Mimms, Lindsay, Brewer, Snyder, Harrison, Ensign Crawford, and Captain McDowell. Three members of the Army in Yonkers, viz., D. Main, Bessie Main, and Captain Lewis, have left the city to be captains in the "field." A training-school was established in the city in October, 1894. Forty-four cadets have received instruction. In 1896, the barracks of the Army were injured by the burning of an adjoining building. This has terminated the sessions of the school.

THE MILE SQUARE SUNDAY-SCHOOL. Miss Caroline Jones, daughter of William Jones, warden in St. John's Church, Yonkers, opened in 1836-37, a Sunday-school in the old district school-house in Mile Square. She was assisted by Mrs. Tremaine. The Rev. Alexander H. Crosby, the rector of St. John's Church and the Rev. Henry L. Storrs, his successor, frequently visited the school. About 1854, it became a union school and was known as "The Mile Square Union Sunday-school."

The "Mile Square Christian Association," which was organized through the efforts of Mr. John Thurton, co-operated with the Sunday-school in holding a large fair near the school-house. About $800, the profits of the fair, became the nucleus of a building-fund. The Rev. Dr. David Cole, pastor of the Reformed Church in Yonkers, began volunteer preaching services in the spring of 1875. With the assistance of the Rev. Mancius H. Hutton of the Reformed Church, Mount Vernon, an evening service was held every month. When the Rev. Mr. Hutton was unable to continue this extra service, the Rev. Dr. Cole, assisted by some members of his church, conducted the services. Sometimes the building which would accommodate about seventy-five persons, was full. Many of the worshippers publicly professed their faith in Christ as a personal Saviour.

In 1885, the interest in the school began to decrease, some of the teachers and scholars having removed. Within a year or two the Rev. George R. Cutting, pastor of the Westminster Church, Yonkers, assisted by some of his church members has prosecuted religious work in Mile Square, but at the present time no services are held there.

GRACE GOSPEL MISSION. This Mission is a life-saving station. Its doors are open every day and far into every night. Those who have it in charge believe in the power of the Gospel. They hold public services every evening in the year. The services are attended by many homeless men whom the mission lodges and to whom they furnish meals. Those who wish a night's lodging or meals must earn their shelter and food by sawing and splitting wood in the wood-yard of the Mission. The revenue from the sale of this wood partly supports the Mission, but it is mainly dependent upon contributions.

It was organized May 6, 1894, by Charles S. Ferguson. The building at the southeast corner of Palisade Avenue and Elm Street was rented, and is still occupied. On September 1, 1894, Thomas F. Hope became the Superintendent and William E. Duff became Manager, Secretary and Treasurer. The Advisory Board in 1896 had seven members, viz.: Dr. F. A. Cook, Rev. D. T. Macfarlan, F. B. Mee, Charles Carpenter, Dougall MacDougall, George Wixson and William Walsh. The Rev. W. W. Alexander was a member of the Board in 1895. The Secretary's annual report for the year ending August 31, 1895, records that the number lodged from September 1, 1894, to August 1, 1895, was 8,030, an average of 22 each night. The number of meals furnished was 9,855. Employment was found for 143 persons. The number inquiring the way of life was 730, and those who conducted the services hoped that nearly 300 had become Christians. The attendance at the meetings aggregated 12,045, an average of 33 each night.

Yonkers has a society of Theosophists, also one of Spiritualists. Chapter XV. contains a reference to them. The Spiritualist Society was formed in 1894. On September 6, 1895, it became an auxiliary of the National Spiritualists Association, Washington, D.C. Its State charter was issued in April, 1896. The officers for 1895 were: Alfred Andrews, President; Mrs. Mary H. Mosher, Vice-President; Titus Merrit, Secretary; A. Andrews, Treasurer; A. F. Buchanan, William Clapperton, Mrs. F. H. Connolly, Trustees. The society had the same officers in 1896, with one exception. In the place of Mrs. F. H. Connolly, Mrs. Mary E. Embree was a trustee.

PROMINENT FREE MASONS OF YONKERS.

1. Leopold J. Schlesinger.   4. Stephen T. Bell.   7. Isaac G. Downing.
2. Henry M. Anderson.   5. Abraham C. Mott.   9. Elijah M. Yerks.
3. John G. Hatfield.   6. Charles Hepenstal.

8. Raffaelle Cobb.

CHAPTER XV.

YONKERS SOCIETIES.

YONKERS abounds in organizations of various kinds. The City Directory carries the names of scores of orders, clubs, associations, etc. Some are benevolent associations, others literary, others military, and still others social organizations.

The oldest order in Yonkers is that of the Free Masons. In 1896, they have two blue lodges, a chapter, a commandery, and an adjunct to the two lodges, called the Board of Masonic Relief.

RISING STAR LODGE, NO. 450, F. AND A.M. This lodge was organized in 1826. Reference is made to its organization in Chapter IX. On September 7, 1826, the warrant was issued, in which are written the names Amos W. Gates, who was Worshipful Master; Robert Dingee, who was Senior Warden; and Oliver C. Denslow, who was Junior Warden. In 1831 the charter was surrendered. There was at that time popular opposition to Masonry. In 1851 the lodge was reorganized. Its former number was 393. When reorganized the number was changed to 142. The Grand Lodges of the State of New York were reunited in 1858, and the different lodges were renumbered. This lodge then was changed to 450. Prominent citizens were among the first members: Amos W. Gates, M.D., Oliver C. Denslow (it was he who, when it was proposed to surrender the charter, put it in his pocket, and thus prevented the surrender. He died in 1866); M. N. Wisewell, William W. Scrugham, Edward Underhill, Frederic S. Cozzens, John M. Mason, James Jenkinson, Robert F. Rich, J. Foster Jenkins, M.D., and Robert J. Douglass were enrolled among the members in those early days. The member longest connected with the lodge is Mr. A. C. Mott.

The Worshipful Masters of Rising Star Lodge have been: Amos W. Gates, Johnson Ferguson, Fred. A. Lewis, William McCabe, Thomas S. Finin, Oliver C. Denslow, Moses N. Wisewell, Charles W. Cooper, Robert J. Douglass, Lyman Cobb, Jr., Eli L. Seger, Haynes L. Warren, Theodore Terrell, Thomas R. Murphy, Eugene Tymeson, John E. Murphy, Charles E. Skinner, John Smith, George I. Moshier, James E. Irvine, Stephen T. Bell.

The present officers of the lodge are: Master, Stephen T. Bell; S. W., Wm. A. Bate; J. W., Leander Read; Treasurer, Henry M. Anderson; Secretary, Abram C. Mott; Marshal, John R. Murphy; Chaplain, Rev. F. M. Davenport; Organist, J. W. Goodale; S. D., Eugene Tymeson; J. D., James Thomas; Tiler, Wm. H. Fisher; and M. of C., Messrs. Geo. A. Cable and E. M. Yerks. One of the members of this lodge, James Jenkinson, was Grand Master of one of the Grand Lodges of the State, and Oliver C. Denslow was at one time Grand Senior Warden of the State. The present membership of the lodge is 164.

TERRACE CITY CHAPTER NO. 177, R. A. M. (formerly known as Nepperhan Chapter No. 177), was organized August 13, 1863. Ex-Companion J. Foster Jenkins was its first High Priest and the following Companions its charter members: J. Foster Jenkins, Lyman Cobb, Jr., Eli L. Seger, Robert F. Rich, Robert J. Douglass and Edward Underhill. It received its warrant February 30, 1864. It had six members at the date of organization. Its present membership is fifty-four. The name of the chapter was changed by consent of the Grand Chapter to Terrace City Chapter on February 3, 1892. Its High Priests since its organization have been: 1863, J. Foster Jenkins; 1864–65, Lyman Cobb, Jr.; 1866, J. Foster Jenkins; 1867–68, Eli L. Seger; 1869–71, Wm. H. Doty; 1872, Eli L. Seger; 1873–75, George W. White; 1876, Haynes L. Warren; 1877, Oliver Chambers; 1878, Lyman Cobb, Jr.; 1879–80, Ralph E. Prime; 1881, Eli L. Seger; 1882, Edwin A. Quick; 1883, Charles Reed; 1884–88, Ralph E. Prime;

1889-91, Edwin A. Quick; 1892-93, Joseph M. Tompkins; 1894, Moses D. Getty; 1895, Joseph M. Tompkins. Its present officers are: High Priest, Isaac H. Venn; King, Stephen T. Bell; Scribe, Alfred Emery; Treasurer, John G. Hatfield; Secretary, Henry Stengel; Captain of Host, E. Alanson Crandall; Principal Sojourner, Lyman Cobb, Jr.; Royal Arch Captain, Elijah Yerks; Master of the Third Vail, George A. Cable; Master of the Second Vail, John I. Dawkins; Master of the First Vail, Wm. H. Wolfe; Tiler, John Dagg; Trustees, Edwin A. Quick, Samuel L. Berrian, Robert Harper.

YONKERS COMMANDERY, NO. 47, KNIGHTS TEMPLAR. This commandery was organized April 10, 1869. Lyman Cobb, Jr., was the first Eminent Commander, Eli L. Seger, Generalissimo, and W. H. Doty, Captain General. It had nine members when organized. It now enrolls twenty-six. Its present officers are: Eminent Commander, Lyman Cobb, Jr.; Generalissimo, E. Alex. Houston; Captain General, J. Porter Freeman; Prelate, George B. Wray; Treasurer, Joseph M. Tompkins; Recorder, Abram C. Mott; Senior Warden, James S. Fitch; Junior Warden, William H. Doty; Standard Bearer, W. B. Edgar; Sword Bearer, R. H. Mellifont; Warden, Ethelbert H. Belknap; Sentinel, Ambrose Atwell.

NEPPERHAN LODGE, NO. 736, F. AND A. M. This lodge was organized in 1873. At that time it enrolled about sixteen members. It now enrolls ninety-three. Rt. Wor. Bro. M. D. Getty, one of its members, was at one time D.D. Grand Master of the 9th Masonic District. Rt. Wor. Bro. Ralph E. Prime has held the same position.

List of the Masters of Nepperhan Lodge, No. 736, from date of its institution, 5873: Elected 5873, Eli L. Seger; 5874, Eli L. Seger; 5875, Wm. A. Gibson; 5876, Ralph E. Prime; 5877, Ralph E. Prime; 5878, Ralph E. Prime; 5879, Ralph E. Prime; 5880, Ralph E. Prime; 5881, Ralph E. Prime; 5882, Ralph E. Prime; 5883, Wm. W. Wilson; 5884, Charles Reed; 5885, Moses D. Getty; 5886, Moses D. Getty; 5887, Ralph E. Prime; 5888, Ralph E. Prime; 5889, Ralph E. Prime; 5890, Ralph E. Prime; 5891, Ralph E. Prime; 5892, Moses D. Getty; 5893, Ralph E. Prime; 5894, George B. Wray; 5895, Robert L. Calkins.

The present officers are: Wor. Master, Charles Hepenstal; Senior Warden, Eastburn W. Taylor; Junior Warden, Philip Fitz; Treasurer, G. Wm. Curran, and Secretary, Charles Bartelo.

NEPPERHAN COUNCIL, NO. 70, ROYAL AND SELECT MASONS. This council was organized in 1878. Messrs. Ralph E. Prime, Thrice Illustrious Master; Lyman Cobb, Jr., Right Illustrious Deputy Master, and William A. Gibson, Illustrious Principal Conductor of the Work were enrolled in the warrant. The council was removed to Mt. Vernon in 1891. It had nine members when organized. It enrolls fifty-seven now. The past Masters have been: R. E. Prime, Lyman Cobb, Jr., J. H. Murphy, M. D. Getty, G. D. Pond, James H. Jenkins, R. B. Disbrow, Thos. R. Hodge, Franklin T. Davis. Mr. M. D. Getty is now District Deputy Grand Master of the 9th District.

YONKERS BOARD OF MASONIC RELIEF. This board was formed by two Yonkers Masonic lodges in December, 1878. Its first members were Thomas R. Murphy, Theodore Terrell and Eugene Tymeson from Rising Star Lodge, and R. E. Prime, Joseph Lockwood and W. W. Wilson from Nepperhan Lodge. Mr. Abram C. Mott has served as Secretary and Treasurer. The present board consists of Stephen T. Bell, William A. Bate and Leander Read of Rising Star Lodge, and Charles Hepenstal, Philip Fitz and E. W. Taylor of Nepperhan Lodge.

NEPPERHAN LODGE, NO. 181, I. O. O. F. This lodge was organized September 30, 1845. The charter members were Samuel W. Chambers, James Borland, Dr. Horatio S. Gates, Ezra B. Keeler, Alfred H. Hyatt, William Mann, James Hughes, Peter Garrison, Wm. Henry Garrison, Wm. P. Revere and Matthias Warner. Among the subsequent members of the lodge were the following well-known citizens: Samuel W. Chambers, John Moffat, Wm. P. Mott, Ezra B. Keeler, Samuel G. Lawrence, Charles F. Belknap, Searing Howell, John Hawks, Albert Cole, Wm. P. Drummond, John B. Crisfield, Geo. H. Archer, Peter Garrison, Joseph Seely, William Archibald, Wm. H. Lawrence, Samuel Goodman, Richard Francis, Henry W. Bashford, Hyatt L. Garrison, Isaiah Anderson, Frederick R. Bostwick, Jacob Read, George Fisher, Joseph Peene, John Stephens, Matthias Warner, Sr., and Matthias Warner, Jr. The lodge increased in membership until June, 1852. At that time it enrolled eighty-nine. Then it began to decrease. On February 26, 1855, the charter was surrendered. There was no other lodge of the order established in Yonkers until 1870, when Yonkers Lodge, No. 232, was organized.

YONKERS LODGE, NO. 232, I. O. O. F. On May 12, 1870, Yonkers Lodge, No. 232, was instituted. The charter members were Robert B. Light, E. L. Loschenkohl, John N. Kuhn, Henry Symons, John G. C. Macfarlane, Wm. Skidgell. The charter was presented by James P. Sanders, Past Grand Sire, then a member of Cortlandt Lodge, No. 6, of Peekskill, from which he withdrew to become a member of the new lodge which he had fostered. The present membership is 206. The number of week's benefits paid is 1086; number of members relieved, 155; number of brothers of other lodges relieved, 25; widowed families relieved, 9, brothers buried, 20; wives of brothers buried, 23. The amount paid for the relief of brothers, $5,407.36; of widows, $175.00; of orphans, $235.90; for watching with sick, $136.65; burial of brothers, $1,675; burial of wives of brothers, $940. The office of Noble Grand of the lodge has been filled by Robert B. Light, J. C. G. Macfarlane, W. H. Guernsey, Isaac D. Cole, Roger Sullivan, Dr. J. H. Pooley, Thomas P. Doren, D. P. Tasheira, John D. Fowler, James D. McIntyre, J. E. Butler, W. E. Duff, Geo. W. Read, Robert H. Lankester, August Ulrich, George A. Daly, Thomas E. Lee, Jacob Rose, John Bright, Charles Cordery, George W. Nodine, Howard T. Schultz, Theo. J. Bayer, Geo. R. Goss, Robert Hamilton, Samuel Chadburn, Eugene Sherwood, T. Irving Forsyth, Geo. F. Cunningham, Geo. A. Mitchell, D. A. Brown, Richard V. Green, Fred H. Tumber, Henry N. Toole, Geo. W. Sigman, Orlando Nichols, Harry Williams, Edward M. Hill, Robt. P. Nugent, Chas. L. Phinney, Wm. Hartnett, and Aug. Kleine.

The present officers are: Noble Grand, Wm. Hetherington; Vice-Grand, George F. Speedling;

PROMINENT ODD FELLOWS OF YONKERS.

Isaac C. Nodine.   Robert B. Light.
S. William Conklin.   James P. Sanders.   James D. McIntyre.

Recording Secretary, Clarence A. Pearsall; Permanent Secretary, George W. Read; Treasurer, Jacob Rose. Of the membership of this lodge, James P. Sanders was Grand Patriarch of New York State in 1850–51, Grand Master of the State in 1858–59, and Grand Sire of the whole order in 1866–68. James D. McIntyre was Grand Patriarch in 1893–94, and is now the Assistant Grand Secretary. The following members have been honored in their selection as District Deputy Grand Master of all or a portion of Westchester County at various times: Jas. D. McIntyre, John Bright and Theodore J. Bayer.

In 1890, the lodge bought three lots on North Broadway for $4,500. The excavations increased the cost to $5,990.99. The erection of a three-story brick building on a part of the property cost $15,921, making the total cost $21,911.99. The lodge occupied the building July 23, 1891.

SHAFFNER ENCAMPMENT OF PATRIARCHS, NO. 100, I. O. O. F. This encampment was instituted January 29, 1883. The original name was Terrace City Encampment. It was subsequently changed to Shaffner, in honor of Talafiero P. Shaffner, of Kentucky, a well-known and prominent member of the order. The charter members were: J. Edwin Butler, Meyer Loewenthal, Theo. J. Bayer, Roger Sullivan, John Bright, Isaac D. Cole, Robert Fawcett, James Griffin, Richard M. Johnston, Wm. W. Kinnier, John McQuade, Thomas E. Lee, Solon Lapham, George C. Reid, Thomas A. Rhodes, Jacob Rose, August Ulrich, D. P. Tasheira, Robert B. Light, Christian A. Kleine.

Chief Patriarchs: Theo. J. Bayer, Roger Sullivan, Richard M. Johnston, John Bright, William Tompkins, Thomas A. Rhodes, Howard T. Schultz, Quitman F. Shaffer, Chas. P. Ward, George R. Goss, Jacob Rose, Wm. E. Duff, T. Irving Forsyth, S. Wm. Conklin, Eugene Sherwood, George F. Cunningham, Edward M. Hill, Wm. H. Smalley, D. P. Tasheira, James D. McIntyre, George H. Tillotson, Wm. J. McLester, Arthur W. Nugent, Orlando Nichols, and Wm. J. Slagle.

The receipts of the encampment to December 31, 1895, have been $3,372.40; the disbursements, $2,185.18; for sick benefits (114 weeks, twenty members relieved), $271; for burial, three members, $45; widows and orphans, $1,500. Other donations, $35. Present membership is fifty-six, composed of members of the lodges in Yonkers, Tarrytown, North Tarrytown and Dobb's Ferry.

The present officers are: Chief Patriarch, Henry P. Eckert; High Priest, Henry C. Derby; Senior Warden, Wm. J. Lord; Junior Warden, Martin Smith; Recording Scribe, S. T. Given; Financial Scribe, Q. F. Shaffer; Treasurer, D. P. Tasheira; Guide, James D. McIntyre. The membership, December 31, 1895, was fifty-five. The following members of this encampment have held the position of District Deputy Grand Patriarch of this county: Theodore J. Bayer, John Bright, Howard T. Schultz and S. William Conklin. James D. McIntyre was Grand Patriarch of the State in 1893–94.

CANTON YONKERS, NO. 22, PATRIARCHS MILITANT, I. O. O. F. This is a semi-military order of Odd Fellowship. The uniform or regalia gives the members a striking appearance. The motto of the Canton is *pax aut bellum*. It was instituted in Yonkers on December 15, 1886, and was known as Canton Sanders. The first Captain was J. D. McIntyre. Subsequently he was appointed on the staff of the General commanding the Division of the Atlantic. The office was subsequently held by John Bright, Howard T. Schultz, S. William Conklin and Wm. E. Duff. The present Commandant-elect is Jas. D. McIntyre. The membership is about twenty-five. The name was changed from Canton Sanders to Canton Yonkers at the request of Jas. P. Sanders, owing to legislation prohibiting the use of names of living persons for Cantons.

PALISADE LODGE, NO. 571, I. O. O. F. This lodge received its charter August 21, 1890. The first officers were: Noble Grand, S. W. Conklin; Vice-Grand, Wm. Tompkins; Secretary, G. H. Tillotson; Treasurer, Joseph Miller; Permanent Secretary, Wm. A. Bate; Warden, A. M. Beckwith; Conductor, Henry W. Palmer; Outside Guardian, Geo. S. Boyle; Inside Guardian, William J. Lord; Right Supporter of the Noble Grand, D. Henry Kipp; Left Supporter of the Noble Grand, Jno. W. Arbuckle; Right Supporter of the Vice-Grand, J. B. D. Wandell; Left Supporter of the Vice-Grand, E. Thompson; Right Scene Supporter, Pierre Paulding; Left Scene Supporter, Wm. E. Borland; Chaplain, Thaddeus Billings.

These officers and the following were charter members: J. W. Pagan, Charles Schultz, D. C. Dubois, John W. Buckmaster, G. Wallis Smith. The present officers are: Noble Grand, William A. Bate; Vice-Grand, Stanton D. Warner; Secretary, Herbert G. Golding; Treasurer, Charles H. Wilson; Permanent Secretary, Guy R. Stephens; Warden, Harry Schenck; Conductor, William Borland; Outside Guardian, Samuel Bradley; Inside Guardian, Fred C. Wilson; Right Supporter of the Noble Grand, Henry Palmer; Left Supporter of the Noble Grand, Seymour H. Reynolds; Right Supporter of the Vice-Grand, William Grieves; Left Supporter of the Vice-Grand, D. H. Kipp; Chaplain, John W. Arbuckle. The membership is 150.

HERO LODGE, GRAND UNITED ORDER OF ODD FELLOWS. This lodge was instituted in Yonkers in 1872. At first eighteen members were enrolled. Officers: Noble Grand, Samuel Johnson; Vice-Grand, F. J. Moultrie; Noble Father, R. C. Praco; Secretary, A. Feeby; Treasurer, J. Lawson. Present officers: N. G., J. W. Lancaster; V. G., R. Glasso; N. F., J. Header; W. C., Rev. E. Roberts; W. F., R. Singleton; Secretary, S. Giddings.

There is also in Yonkers a branch of the order known as the Queen of the North, No. 330, of the Household of Ruth. It was set apart August 15, 1884. Officers: G. Mason, L. Williams, A. Taylor, K. Taylor, R. Bailey, R. Singleton, M. Thomas.

MONTGOMERY CLUB (CLAN-NA-GAEL), A. This club is composed of Irish and Irish-Americans banded together for social and literary purposes. It was organized about 1871, as the John McClure Club. It does not interfere in religion or politics. It meets every Friday evening in the Grant Building, No. 20 Warburton Avenue. It enrolls between 200 and 300 members. The present officers are: President, Henry V. Doyle; Vice-President, P. F. Higgins.

ANCIENT ORDER OF HIBERNIANS, DIVISION NO. 2. This is a fraternal, benevolent, and patriotic society. It was organized August 15, 1872. Membership at date of organization, thirty-six. Present membership, 118. Presidents since organization: 1872, Patrick Curran; 1873, Thomas Curran; 1874, Patrick Whalen; 1875–76, Thomas Eagan; 1877–78, M. H. Downing; 1879, Patrick Kelly; 1880–82, Daniel Manning; 1883, James P. Dunn; 1884, Patrick Smith; 1885, James Landy; 1886–87, Dennis Gleason; 1889, Patrick Smith; 1890–91, James Mulchey; 1892–96, Michael A. Kiely.

ANCIENT ORDER OF HIBERNIANS, DIVISION NO. 1. This division was organized in Yonkers in 1884 with fifteen members. It now enrolls eighty-five. Its Presidents have been: J. Matthew Reilley, Patrick Clark, William H. McDonough, William F. Cauley. Its Vice-Presidents have been: Andrew Delahanty, William H. McGrath, James V. Healey, Peter J. Brady, Patrick Rohen, Matthew Reilley. Its Recording Secretaries have been: Walter O'Connor, Charles Foster, John McManus, Patrick J. Farrell, John D. Grady. Its Financial Secretaries have been: William F. Cauley, Patrick J. Donahue, William McDonough, Matthew Reilley. Its Treasurers have been: Patrick Clark, T. J. Linehan, Andrew Delahanty.

HOLSATIA LODGE, No. 297, D. O. H. (Deutscher Orden Harngari.) This lodge was instituted November 9, 1872. It received its charter from the Grand Lodge of the United States. Only German speaking men of good moral character are admitted to membership. Sixteen were initiated at the first meeting. Since then 308 have been admitted. The present membership is 106. The first officers were: President, John Knockel; Vice-President, John Schlobohm; Recording Secretary, Max Schmoger; Treasurer, William Knockel; Financial Secretary, E. Jenryensen; Conductor, Christian Toaspern; Warden, W. F. Stettman.

The object of the lodge is the relief of members in case of sickness. In twenty-three years $31,000 have been paid for that purpose. The admission fee is $10. Meetings are held every Thursday evening in the Grant Building, Warburton Avenue. The following have been Presidents: John Schlobohm, John Knockel, Moritz Spreer, Jos. Schall, Will Furma, Jacob Bauer, Charles Muller, Julius Weltzien, Theodore Heinrichs, John W. Bauer, John Foerst, Alexander Piltz, August Nitsch, August Koch, Emil Riegelman, Louis Bochma, Henry Maretzky, Fr. Grossman, Otto Struensee, Erwin Schimpfke, Albert Rose, Louis Wolf, Charles Staib, W. F. Kott, Charles Huchele, Chris. Nielson, Fred Bock, Fred Ebeling, William F. Schlobohm, George Baumeister, Fred Gugel, Chas. Wiese.

The present officers are: President, George Baumeister; Vice-President, George Werner, Corresponding Secretary, Chris. Schlobohm; Financial Secretary, John Rolfs; Treasurer, August Nitsch; Conductor, William Wiseman; Warden, Charles Rentschler; I. G., Henry Kuss; O. G., William Gredo. One of the members, John Schlobohm, has also held the position of President of the National Grand Lodge during the terms of 1892 and 1894. The lodge at present has a relief fund of $8,000.

YONKERS LODGE, No. 1872, KNIGHTS OF HONOR. This lodge was established in Yonkers, November 13, 1879. There were forty charter members. Thirty-six are now enrolled. Its Dictators from date of organization have been: First, C. S. Webster; second, —— Meleney; third, John Doremus; fourth, George L. Odell; fifth, Wm. H. Fisher; sixth, Geo. Fox; seventh, Jerome Barnes; eighth, Wm. Simmonds; ninth, O. C. Eddy; tenth, Moses H. Lester; eleventh, Henry Golding. Present Dictator, Charles P. Bynon.

The following have served as Treasurers: First, A. R. Lutkins; second, J. D. McIntyre; third, I. W. Bynon; fourth, George Jackson; fifth, Chas. P. Bynon; sixth, Ambrose Hill. Present Treasurer, K. Henry Cadds. Its Financial Reporters have been: Chas. P. Bynon, Cornelius Calahan, John Doremus. Present Financial Reporter, I. W. Bynon. When a member dies his family receives $2,000.

Since organization the society has paid for death benefits in Yonkers, $10,000. The Knights of Honor have paid out through the Supreme Treasurer, since organization to date, December 14, 1895, $52,826,761.79. Total membership, 121,085.

COLUMBIA LODGE, No. 122, O. S. ST. G. This lodge was instituted June 27, 1883, with thirty members. It now has seventy-two. Its first chief officers were: Worthy Past President, John Rowland; W. P., Edward Underhill; W. V. P., Daniel Siers; Secretary, Geo. Rayner, Jr.; Assistant Secretary, Thomas Fletcher; Treasurer, Thomas Tyler; Messenger, Jubal Armerod; Trustees, Samuel

Hayward, William Simmonds, Joseph Andrews. The present officers are: President, James Barratt; Vice-President, John Robertshaw; Secretary, John B. Smith; Assistant Secretary, Edgar F. Howorth; Worthy Treasurer, Thomas Tyler; Worthy Messenger, Thomas Sharp; W. Assistant Messenger, Chas. Linegar; W. Inside Sentinel, Thomas Gower; W. Outside Sentinel, Henry Willis; Chaplain, George Peene; Past President, John W. Howorth; District Deputy, Joseph Greenhalgh; Trustees, Fielding Gower, John Pegg and Wm. H. Poole. The lodge has paid for sick benefits, $2,500; for funeral benefits, $1,600.

COLUMBIA LODGE, NO. 122, O. S. ST. G.

Roll of Presidents: Edward Underhill, Joseph Greenhalgh, Charles Atkins, George Walsh, George W. Peene, William H. Poole, Samuel Hayward, Richard Wilkinson, Thomas Arthur, W. P. Constable, John B. Smith, George Peene, James Bennett, Thomas Gower, George W. Peene, Geo. L. Campion, Samuel Hunt, John W. Howorth.

ROSE STANDISH LODGE, NO. 15, INDEPENDENT ORDER DAUGHTERS OF ST. GEORGE, was organized December 14, 1892, with thirty-five members.

MAIDEN CITY L. O. LODGE, NO. 63, was organized November 10, 1884. Officers: W. Master, Samuel Mills; D. Master, William Beatty; Secretary, William J. Bell; Treasurer, Daniel Walker; Chaplain, Harry Bell; Tiler, John Hogg. Mr. William Bruce, of 159 Oliver Avenue, presented the lodge several years ago with a set of jewels. On July 12, 1890, the Lodge paraded in New York. W. J. Bell was Marshal. Two flags were presented to the lodge on July 8, 1892. The Rev. George Y. Lemmon, of Troy, N. Y., made the address. Officers were publicly installed March 13, 1893. The meeting of the New York State Grand Loyal Orange Lodge was held in Yonkers May 2, 1893. Men were present from the English ships lying in New York harbor. A sermon to the lodge was preached by the Rev. George R. Cutting in the Westminster Presbyterian Church, July 9, 1893, by the Rev. Charles E. Allison in the Dayspring Presbyterian Church, July 8, 1894, and by the Rev. Enos J. Bosworth in the Nepperhan Avenue Baptist Church on July 7, 1895.

NEPERA TRIBE, NO. 186, I. O. R. M. The Nepera Tribe of the Improved Order of Red Men was established in Yonkers June 11, 1891. When established it had forty-seven members. It enrolled, in 1895, 130 members. Its first officers were: Sachem, Ferdinand Garnjost; Senior Sagamore, F. C. Randall; Junior Sagamore, George Frazier; Chief of Records, Malcom S. Keyes; Keeper of Wampum, John Pendlebury; Prophet, Jere. S. Clark. Since the tribe was organized, John J. Sloane has served two terms as presiding officer; Ferdinand Garnjost has served one term; F. C. Randall, one term; James A. Taggart, one term; Allen Gower, one term; William Hemingway, one term; Calvin D. Gale, one term.

Jere. S. Clark has been Deputy of Westchester County. The twenty-eighth annual Great Council was held in Tammany Hall, August 13 to August 16, 1895, at which John J. Sloane, James A. Taggart and Allen Gower represented the Nepera Tribe. On August 14, 1895, John J. Sloane was the Great Representative to the Great Council of the United States to represent New York for a term of two years, commencing September 10, 1895.

COURT PALISADE, NO. 192, F. OF A., (formerly No. 8049, A. O. F. of A.), was instituted in this city on October 27, 1891, at Montgomery Hall. Twenty members were initiated that evening. Its presiding officers have been: John H. Watson, John J. Doolity, Joseph H. Whalen, M. J. Walsh and William Duge. Its present officers are: Chief Ranger, John J. Sloane; Sub-chief Ranger, Edward P. Phillips; Treasurer, James T. Lennore; Financial Secretary, William A. Coyle; Recording Secretary, Manus Rodgers; Senior Woodward, Joseph Webb; Junior Woodward, George Simpson; Senior Beadle, Patrick A. O'Donnell; Junior Beadle, Frank M. Baldwin; Trustees, John J. Doolity, James Kelly and Dominick F. Callahan; Deputy Grand Chief Ranger, M. J. Walsh, with jurisdiction over other courts in Westchester County. The present membership is 156. Representatives in the Grand Court of the State of New York are M. J. Walsh and William Duge. Mr. Walsh is also a representative of the Grand Court of the State of New York in the Supreme Court of the order in the United States.

At the last session of the Supreme Court, held in Cleveland, Ohio, in September, the name of the order was changed to the Foresters of America. This action necessitated a change of numbers of the various courts of the order, and Court Palisade is now designated "Court Palisade, No. 192, F. of A."

COURT CITY OF YONKERS, NO. 193, F. OF A., was organized on November 9, 1891, with twenty-eight charter members. On the first regular meeting the following officers were elected: Chief Ranger, Denis Hunihan; Sub-chief Ranger, James Coyle; Treasurer, Peter M. Anderson; Financial Secretary, Edward Brees; Recording Secretary, Edmond E. Brady; Senior Woodward, John Fitzgerald; Junior Woodward, Ambrose Brady; Senior Beadle, John Brophy; Junior Beadle, Wm. Breen; Physician, Dr. N. A. Warren;

Trustees, Dr. N. A. Warren, Joseph Tausig and Wm. E. Hemingway. In 1894, Denis Hunihan was elected Trustee of the Grand Court of the State of New York. Ed. Mallon and Denis Hunihan have served terms as Deputy Grand Chief Ranger for this district. The present membership is 148.

ANCIENT ORDER OF UNITED WORKMEN. The Yonkers branch was established September 18, 1892, and is known as Yonkers Lodge No. 371. It at first enrolled eighteen members. It now enrolls twenty-five. Its presiding officers have been, First Master Workman, D. A. Doren; Second Master Workman, William Wallace; Third Master Workman, J. T. Burrow; Fourth Master Workman, James Lewis. The State Representative, D. A. Doren. Its present officers are: Master Workman, James Lewis; Foreman, James W. Johnson; Overseer, Daniel Devlin; Guide, John T. McGrath; Financier, D. A. Doren; Receiver, Thomas Hadden; Recorder, J. T. Burrow; State Representative, D. A. Doren. The order is a fraternal beneficiary society, which was organized in Meadville, Pa., in 1868, with thirteen members. In 1895 it had a membership of 350,000, and had paid to 1895, death benefits amounting to $66,000,000. All beneficiary certificates are written to the amount of $2,000.

KNIGHTS OF COLUMBUS. A Yonkers Council of the Knights of Columbus, a Catholic benevolent order, was organized in May, 1896, with thirty-seven charter members, who were given the first three degrees. State Deputy John J. Delaney and District Deputy John F. Ward performed the ceremonies.

The following officers were elected: Grand Knight, Judge F. X. Donoghue; Deputy Grand Knight, J. F. McKenna; Treasurer, John A. Byrne; Financial Secretary, Adolph A. Schaefer; Recording Secretary, Edward J. Renahan; Chancellor, Thomas J. Mallon; Warden, Michael J. Walsh; Inside Guard, Charles V. Canavan; Outside Guard, John J. Shannon; Chaplain, Rev. Charles R. Corley; Advocate, Adrian M. Potter; Lecturer, Thomas F. Curran; Trustees, Henry F. Booth, William F. Dee, Andrew B. Barr, Michael J. Walsh and James J. Ford.

After the meeting a collation was served by Steward Campbell, at the City Club. Among those present were Grand Knight Charles A. Webber, of Brooklyn; Rev. Father Cunnion, Judge James A. O'Gorman, Judge Leonard J. Geigerich and Hon. P. H. Flynn, of New York City.

KITCHING POST, NO. 60, GRAND ARMY OF THE REPUBLIC. In 1866 an association of veteran soldiers of the Civil War was formed in the then village of Yonkers. Being crippled by partisan sympathies, it was dissolved. The same company of men, with few exceptions, applied for a charter as a Grand Army Post. Messrs. E. Y. Morris, S. C. Van Tassel, James Stewart, P. Kelly, G. W. Farnham, A. H. Tompkins, E. C. Nodine, James Carter, George R. Hendrickson, William Riley and Daniel S. Munn were granted a charter January 7, 1868. The first officers were: Commander, E. Y. Morris; Senior Vice-Commander, James Stewart; Junior Vice-Commander, George W. Farnham; Adjutant, S. C. Van Tassel; Quartermaster, Abram H. Tompkins.

E. Y. Morris was Commander two years; D. S. Munn two years; John Knester one year; William Riley two years; James Cadis one year; Oscar Barker one year; Henry Osterheld two years; John C. Shotts nine years; Frank A. Curran one year; James V. Lawrence one year; S. C. Van Tassel one year; G. B. Balch, M.D., one year; James Sheridan two years; Augustus Kipp two years. The present membership is 179.

Mr. John C. Shotts has been Department Commander, State of New York; Henry Osterheld has been Senior Vice Department Commander, State of New York; Edward J. Mitchell has been Assistant Quartermaster-General, State of New York. He is Marshal of the Westchester County Association of G. A. R., and Grand Marshal of the Memorial Committee of Yonkers.

The present officers are: Commander, George R. Hendrickson; Senior Vice-Commander, Abram H. Tompkins; Junior Vice-Commander, John H. Reine; Adjutant (twelve years), Edward J. Mitchell; Quartermaster (four years), William H. Fisher; Surgeon (three years), Albert Sieveris; Chaplain, Joseph Andrews; Officer of the Day, James Sheridan; Officer of the Guard, Andrew J. Joslyn; Sergeant-Major (four years), Jere. S. Clark; Quartermaster-Sergeant (four years), George Eimer.

There are 669 posts in New York State. Post 60 (Yonkers) honored itself by choosing for its name Kitching Post, in honor of the beloved General J. Howard Kitching, of whom is a brief record in another chapter.

JOHN C. FREMONT POST, No. 590, G. A. R., was organized May 28, 1886, at first enrolling fifteen members. It now enrolls sixty-seven. At one time its roll carried eighty-two names. Its Commanders have been: Frederic Shonnard, Galusha B. Balch and Thomas Birdsall. Geo. H. Frisbie was Aide on the Staff of Department Commander Shotts with rank of Colonel, Wesley Randall was Aide on the Staff of the Department Commander Atkinson with rank of Colonel, Matt. H. Ellis was Judge Advocate-General on the Staff of the National Commander General Lowler.

The present officers are: Commander, Frederic Shonnard; Senior Vice-Commander, Galusha B. Balch, M.D.; Junior Vice-Commander, Fisher A. Baker; Adjutant, Augustus W. Nicol; Quartermaster, Matt. H. Ellis.

JOHN C. SHOTTS CAMP No. 2, S. V. U. S. A. DIVISION OF NEW YORK. This Society of the Sons of Veterans was organized May 23, 1895, by Messrs. William H. Lent and Frank E. Ellis, with valuable aid from John C. Shotts, Past Department Commander of the G. A. R., New York State. It enrolled at first twenty-nine members. The first officers were: Captain, John W. Pentreath; First Lieutenant, James D. Stewart; Second Lieutenant, John Keeler, Jr.; Chaplain, Rev. F. M. Davenport; First Sergeant, Frank E. Ellis; Quartermaster, George Stewart; Camp Council, William H. Lent, John Andrews, Henry Gaul. Thirty-two members are now enrolled. The present officers are: Captain, John W. Pentreath; First Lieutenant, Joseph Andrews, Jr.; Second Lieutenant, A. James Bowler; Chaplain, J. Harvey Brown; First Sergeant, Frank E. Ellis; Quartermaster, Martin C. Wallace; Camp Council, William H. Lent, John Andrews, Henry Gaul.

The objects of the society are: "To keep green the memories of our fathers, and their sacrifices for the maintenance of the Union. To aid the members of the Grand Army of the Republic in caring for their helpless and disabled veterans; to extend aid and protection to their widows and orphans, to perpetuate the memory and history of their heroic deeds, and the proper observance of Memorial Day. To aid and assist worthy and needy members of our order, to inculcate patriotism and love of our country, not only among our membership, but among all the people of our land, and to spread and sustain the doctrine of equal rights, universal liberty, and justice to all."

Its principles are: "A firm belief and trust in Almighty God, and a realization that under His beneficent guidance the free institutions of our land, consecrated by the services and blood of our fathers, have been preserved, and the integrity and life of the Nation maintained. True allegiance to the Government of the United States of America, based upon a respect for, and devotion and fidelity to, its constitution and laws, manifested by the discountenancing of anything that may tend to weaken loyalty, incite to insurrection, treason or rebellion, or in any manner impair the efficiency and permanency of our National Union."

FOURTH SEPARATE COMPANY, N. G. S. N. Y. During the Civil War, Yonkers and vicinity furnished the Seventeenth Regiment with Company H and Company B. In 1870 a new Third Regiment, N.G.S.N.Y. was formed. Company H of this regiment was from Yonkers. In 1874, the Third Regiment was abandoned. Company H was retained in service, and became Company D of the Sixteenth Battalion. When that battalion was mustered out of service at the end of 1881, Company D was retained in service as the "Fourth Separate Company." It was formally organized as such, January 1, 1882. It occupied for a time an armory on Chicken Island. In 1886 an armory was built for it at the corner of Waverly and Maple Streets. The land cost $4,500, the building $20,000. Subsequent improvements have cost about $3,000 or $4,000. The Captains of the company, from its

ARMORY OF THE FOURTH SEPARATE COMPANY.

beginning under the designation of Company H of the Third Regiment in 1870, have been William Macfarlane, Matt. H. Ellis, Isaac D. Cole, Isaiah Frazier, Raffaelle Cobb, John I. Pruyn. The present officers are: Captain, John I. Pruyn; First Lieutenant, William H. McVicar; Second Lieutenant, William B. Thompson; First Lieutenant and Assistant Surgeon, E. E. Colton, M.D. On several occasions the company has reported under military orders at towns or cities, where riots and strikes necessitated the presence of a military force.

FOURTH SEPARATE COMPANY, VETERAN ASSOCIATION. The Veteran National Guardsmen were organized December 2, 1885. Captain, E. Alexander Houston; First Lieutenant, James P. Stewart; Second Lieutenant, William F. Burgess, who served three years. Augustus Kipp and A. R. Van Houten subsequently served as Captains, each one year. In 1890 the name of the organization was changed to the "Fourth Separate Company, Veteran Association," E. Alex. Houston was elected President, and has continued to hold that office until the present time. There are about sixty members.

EXEMPT FIREMEN'S BENEVOLENT ASSOCIATION. This association was organized May, 1887, with forty members. Its first officers were: President, Henry S. Myers; First Vice-President, John S. Brown; Second Vice-President, John W. Coon; Recording Secretary, George

OFFICERS OF THE FOURTH SEPARATE CO., N. G. S. N. Y.

1. CAPTAIN JOHN I. PRUYN.
2. LIEUTENANT W. H. MCVICAR.
3. SURGEON ELLSWORTH E. COLTON.
4. 2D LIEUT. WILLIAM B. THOMPSON.

Shuler; Financial Secretary, James W. Mitchell; Treasurer, Jacob Read; Chairman of the Board of Directors, John C. Shotts. The society now enrolls 160 members.

All the fire companies are represented in its membership, except the Shannondale, Avalanche, and Lowerre Hose, which have not as yet been organized long enough to have members qualified for membership. The Exempt Association requires as a qualification for membership, active membership for five years. The association has purchased on Buena Vista Avenue, a lot which the last Legislature exempted from taxes. They propose to build on this site. Recently they held a fair, which extended through a week, the proceeds of which will enable them to build in the near future. They have a funeral relief fund for the benefit of members. The present officers are: President, Edward L. Peene; First Vice-President, Thomas S. Walsh; Second Vice-President, Thomas McCaul; Recording Secretary, Wm. H. Devoe; Financial Secretary, Wm. E. Stelwagon; Treasurer, Wm. H. Greenhalgh; Chairman of the Board of Directors, Robert B. Light.

YONKERS TURN VEREIN. This society was established in Yonkers, August, 1875. It organized with thirteen members. Its objects are the physical and mental cultivation of children of German birth and descent. The first President was R. Kersting. The first Secretary was A. Lange. The following named have since served as Presidents: Rudolph Kenting, John Eylers, Henry Merer, Julius Herrmann, John Bauer, August Nitsch, Meyer Loewenthal, Charles Egloffstein, John Ewald. The Secretaries of the society

NON-COMMISSIONED OFFICERS AND HOSPITAL CORPS OF FOURTH SEPARATE CO., N. G. S. N. Y.

No. 1. First Sergeant CHARLES F. NUGENT, Enlisted September 6, 1884, Warranted Corporal, January 4, 1887, Warranted Sergeant, October 16, 1888, Warranted First Sergeant, November 8, 1890.
No. 2. Quartermaster Sergeant GEORGE H. TILLOTSON, Enlisted February 3, 1882, Warranted Quartermaster Sergeant, October 2, 1885.
No. 3. Sergeant JOHN W. ARBUCKLE, Enlisted November 11, 1884, Warranted Corporal, June 1, 1888, Warranted Sergeant, September 4, 1889.
No. 4. Sergeant GEORGE S. MALLINSON, Enlisted January 8, 1884, Warranted Corporal, May 4, 1888, Warranted Sergeant, December 17, 1890.
No. 5. Sergeant ALBERT K. SHIPMAN, Enlisted October 19, 1886, Warranted Corporal, March 12, 1889, Warranted Sergeant, September 19, 1889.
No. 6. Sergeant ARTHUR W. NUGENT, Enlisted July 7, 1885, Warranted Corporal, December 24, 1889, Warranted Sergeant, January 20, 1894.
No. 7. Corporal HORTON W. MALLINSON, Enlisted November 7, 1887, Warranted Corporal, June 26, 1890.
No. 8. Corporal JAMES C. FULTON, Enlisted January 3, 1890, Warranted Corporal, June 8, 1893.
No. 9. Corporal ARTHUR LAND, Enlisted December 6, 1887, Warranted Corporal, June 7, 1893.
No. 10. Corporal JOHN O'NIEL, Enlisted November 22 1889, Warranted Corporal, June 7, 1893.
No. 11. Corporal JOHN MARTIN, Enlisted January 4, 1890, Warranted Corporal, January 18, 1894.
No. 12. Corporal CHARLES E. MALLINSON, Enlisted September 29, 1886, Detailed to Third Brigade Signal Corp, August 5, 1890, Warranted Corporal, January 20, 1894.
No. 13. Corporal WILLIAM HALLEY, Enlisted March 3, 1892, Warranted Corporal, June 23, 1894.
No. 14. Corporal FREDERICK WHITE, Enlisted February 10, 1891, Warranted Corporal, January 6, 1896.
No. 15. Corporal ALBERT N. GARTHWAITE, Enlisted December 28, 1891, Warranted Corporal, January 6, 1896.
No. 16. THOMAS M. FRAZIER, Enlisted November 7, 1884, Detailed for Ambulance Duty, June, 1888, Honorably Discharged, December 31, 1891, Re-enlisted August 15, 1892, Detailed on Hospital Duty, August 18, 1892.

have been Otto Struensee, William Schwanehauser, John Bauer, Henry Merer, Julius Herrmann, John Ewald, Louis Wolf, Charles Gettike, Otto Jager, Charles Lippe, Charles Linke; 125 members are now enrolled. The society meets in Turn Hall, Ann Street. The value of their property is about $1,500. The present officers are: President, John Eylers; Vice-President, Philip Hoffman; Treasurer, Frank Goertelmeyer; Financial Secretary, Conrad Klitzsch; Recording Secretary, Charles Linke; Corresponding Secretary, John W. Bauer; First Turn Wart, Julius Schwartz; Second Turn Wart, Otto Walter; Zeng Wart,

PARK HILL COUNTRY CLUB HOUSE.

Franz Vangerow; Librarian, William Rubin; Trustees: Jaques Jung, William Gernhardt, Henry Wolf.

PARK HILL COUNTRY CLUB. This club was incorporated in the State of New York September 6, 1892. At the time it was organized it enrolled thirty members. Its roll in 1895 carried the names of 130. The first officers of the club were: President, Mr. Andrew S. Brownell; Vice-President, Mr. Joseph C. Earnshaw; Secretary, Mr. E. V. B. Getty; Treasurer, Mr. George S. Ord. The present officers are:

President, Mr. Andrew S. Brownell; Vice-President, Mr. George A. Flagg; Secretary, Mr. Edward E. Vidaud; Treasurer, Mr. Thomas C. Smith. The objects of the club are the recreation of its members and social pleasures. It has musicals, amateur theatricals, readings, lectures, receptions, dances, etc. It has a handsome club-house, built for its especial accommodation, which it leases. The house cost over $6,000, and has a commodious reception hall, bowling alleys, bathrooms, etc. An artistically printed booklet, published by the club, contains a picture of the club-house and lake, and also contains the charter, by-laws and names of officers and members, rules, regulations, etc.

YONKERS BICYCLE CLUB. This club was organized November 19, 1879, with the following named six members: Elliot Mason, George Le Boutillier, Frank Van Vleck, S. B. Hawley, Dr. F. S. Grant, E. Dwight, Jr. President, Dr. F. S. Grant; Secretary, E. Dwight, Jr.; Captain, S. B. Hawley. Since the date of organization the following have been Presidents: Dr. S. F. Grant, Horace Moody, C. E. Nichols, H. O. Talmadge, Mario Lorini, Edwin A. Oliver, Dr. R. A. Fones, John R. Feakins, Charles P. Ward, G. William Curran, Charles F. May. Secretaries: E. Dwight, Jr., Elliot Mason, E. C. Thorne, A. R. Taylor, G. William Curran, C. T. Kuchler, Herbert Golding. Captains: S. B. Hawley, A. Le Due, Mario Lorini, W. B. Ewing, W. H. Ulrich, J. H. Clapp, C. B. Lockwood, W. H. Garratt, C. D. Burnham, Theodore Cox, Graeme Stephens. Treasurer, John Murphy.

THE FORTNIGHTLY CLUB was organized on March 2, 1888. Its object is the study of anthropology. It at first enrolled thirty members. Hon. G. Hilton Scribner has been the President of the club since its organization. The present officers are: President, Hon. G. Hilton Scribner; Vice-Presidents, Fisher A. Baker, Mrs. Justus Lawrence, Mrs. John C. Havemeyer and Charles P. G. Scott; Secretary, Edward P. Shaw; Corresponding Secretary, Mrs. James R. Brevoort. The papers read before the club, by Yonkers writers, are of a high order and have been sought by scientific journals. The club has from time to time been addressed by speakers from out of town, among them: Miss Agnes Crane, Prof. Thomas Frederick Crane, Prof. W. H. Brewer, Prof. Benj. E. Smith, Prof. F. Ward Putnam, Mr. William W. Ellsworth, Prof. Albert S. Bickmore, Dr. Edward C. Mann, Dr. Ameen F. Haddad, Mr. R. L. Garner, Baron de Revier, Dr. Titus Munson Coan.

LAWN TENNIS CLUB (incorporated 1893). This club was organized in 1888. The club-house was built in 1893. The limit of membership is 250, which is the number the club now enrolls.

Previous Directors, 1888-89: President, Rufus King; Vice-President, Mrs. Perit C. Myers; Treasurer, Susie Leeds Heermance; Secretary, Landreth H. King; Wells Olmsted, Victor Elting, Miss Otis. 1889-90: President, Rufus King; Vice-President, Mrs. Perit C. Myers; Treasurer, Susie Leeds Heermance; Secretary, Samuel B. Hawley (Resigned, Landreth H. King elected May 20, 1889); Wells Olmsted, Victor Elting, Miss Otis. 1890-91: President, Landreth H. King; Vice-President, Mrs. Perit C. Myers; Treasurer, Susie Leeds Heermance; Secretary, Theodor S. Oxholm; Wells Olmsted, Victor Elting, Mrs. Willard H. Brownson. 1891-92: President, Hampton D. Ewing; Vice-President, Mrs. W. H. Brownson (Resigned, Mrs. John Reid elected October 10, 1891); Treasurer, Susie Leeds Heermance; Secretary, Henry Martyn Baird, Jr.; William L. Heermance, Wells Olmsted, Theodor S. Oxholm, Miss Waring, Miss Elting. 1892-93: President, Hampton D. Ewing; Vice-President, William L. Heermance; Treasurer, Susie Leeds Heermance; Secretary, Henry Martyn Baird, Jr.; J. Foster Jenkins, Schuyler Alwyn Bogart, Theodor S. Oxholm, Alexander B. Halliday, Mrs. John Reid. 1893-94: President, Hampton D. Ewing; Vice-President, Wm. L. Heermance; Treasurer, Wells Olmsted; Secretary, W. E. Hodgman; W. D. Baldwin, Janet Waring, S. A. Bogart, Mrs. John Reid, H. Holbrook, Jr., H. W. Beecher, J. Foster Jenkins, A. B. Halliday, Susie L. Heermance. 1894-95: President, John K. Bangs; Vice-President, S. A. Bogart; Treasurer, F. B. Allen; Secretary, W. E. Hodgman; Mrs. John Reid, H. Holbrook, Jr., H. W. Beecher, J. Foster Jenkins, A. B. Halliday, Susie L. Heermance, Janet Waring, W. D. Baldwin, H. D. Ewing. 1895-96: President, John K. Bangs; Vice-President, Mrs. John Reid; Treasurer, Francis B. Allen; Secretary, Walter E. Hodgman; J. Foster Jenkins, Alex. B. Halliday, Susie Leeds Heermance, Janet Waring, W. D. Baldwin, H. D. Ewing, Mrs. Arthur White, Wm. R. Innis, James .W Bowden.

THE YONKERS CLERICAL ASSOCIATION was organized February 16, 1891. The officers are a President, Secretary and Treasurer .They have been elected as follows: 1891, President, Rev. A. B. Carver, D.D.; Secretary and Treasurer, Rev. J. Hendrick de Vries; 1892, President, Rev. Charles E. Allison; Secretary and Treasurer, Rev. H. M. Warren; 1893, President, Rev. George R. Cutting; Secretary and Treasurer, Rev. W. Armitage Beardslee; 1894-95, President, Rev. Alvah S. Hobart, D.D.; Secretary and Treasurer,

Rev. Lyman Cobb, Jr.; 1896, President, Rev. David Cole, D.D.; Secretary and Treasurer, Rev. Lyman Cobb, Jr. The following have been members who are not pastors: The Revs. Thos. Armitage, D.D., Wm. E. Ketcham, D.D., James M. Bruce, August Ulmann, W. W. Rand, H. W. Parker, Henry M. Baird, D.D., Jos. H. Bertholf, Lyman Cobb, Jr.

YONKERS CHAPTER, SONS OF THE AMERICAN REVOLUTION. The charter of this chapter was granted prior to December, 1895, and the members organized on December 9, 1895. The jurisdiction of the chapter extends all over Westchester County. The original officers were: President, General Thomas Ewing; Vice-President for Yonkers, Theodore Gilman; Vice-President for Mount Vernon, T. A. M. Ives; Vice-President for Greenburgh, Champion M. Judson; Vice-President for Cortlandt, Cornelius Amory Pugsley; Vice-President for Mamaroneck, John Rogers Hagaman, Jr.; Secretary, David McN.K. Stauffet; Treasurer, Wm. Warburton Scrugham; Chaplain, Rev. A. S. Hobart, D.D.; Registrar, Ralph E. Prime; Manager, W. N. Gilbert Clark.

The chapter now enrolls twenty-five members. The present officers are, President, David McN.K. Stauffet; Secretary, Ralph Earl Prime, Jr.; Vice-President for Pelham, Howard Scribner. The original officers were all re-elected. General Thomas Ewing died in 1896.

KEKESKICK CHAPTER, DAUGHTERS OF THE REVOLUTION. This chapter was organized in June, 1895, by Mrs. Ellen Hardin Walworth, an honorary Vice-President General of the society, with the permission of the State Regent, Miss Forsyth, of Kingston. The officers for the first year are: Regent, Miss Katherine Prime; Secretary, Miss Susie Heermance; Registrar, Mrs. Perit Myers; Treasurer, Miss Janet Flagg; Historian, Miss Fannie A. Jackson; Manager, Mrs. Mary Scrugham. There were thirteen charter members. A reception was held in Manor Hall on February 22, 1896. The societies represented among the guests were "The Sons of the American Revolution," "The Sons of the Revolution," "Military Order of the Loyal Legion," "Colonial Wars," "War of 1812," "G. A. R.," "Mayflower," "Colonial Dames," "Yonkers Historical Society." The speakers were Hon. G. Hilton Scribner, who made the address of welcome; Mr. Morris P. Ferris, who represented the society, "War of 1812"; Mr. Waldo G. Morse, member of the society, the "Colonial Wars"; Mr. Blakemore, of the "Loyal Legion"; Mr. Reynolds, of the "Sons of American Revolution"; Dr. Judson, "Sons of the American Revolution"; Rev. Dr. A. B. Carver, of the "Sons of the Revolution"; Mr. A. O. Kirkwood, of the "G.A.R.," and Rev. Charles E. Allison, of the "Yonkers Historical Society."

YONKERS LODGE, NO. 265, K. OF P. This lodge was organized October 27, 1887. It received its charter August 2, 1888. It enrolled twenty-nine charter members. Its first officers were: Chancellor Commander, George Brown; Vice-Chancellor, Joseph Miller; Prelate, William Dubois; Keeper of Records and Seal, Henry Dayton; Master of Exchequer, James McGregor; Master of Finance, Thomas Mallon; Master-at-Arms, George Taylor. The lodge now enrolls 158 members. The present officers are: Chancellor Commander, Thomas Cook; Vice-Chancellor, Edwin L. Dutcher; Prelate, Robert Hamilton; Master of Work, William G. Long; Master of Exchequer, George S. Powell; Master of Finance, Iretus Beasley; Keeper of Records and Seal, Harry H. Forsyth; Master-at-Arms, Jerome Sleight. The lodge pays benefits to its sick members. It has weekly meetings, and is in a flourishing condition.

YONKERS COUNCIL, ROYAL ARCANUM, NO. 1346. This fraternity was instituted March 9, 1891. Its first officers were: Regent, John J. Littebrandt; Vice-Regent, George P. Bedford; Orator, Thomas Hampson; Secretary, Ernest L. Muller; Collector, Henry M. Anderson; Treasurer, W. D. Barry; Chaplain, J. W. Cole; Guide, John H. Hauser; Warden, George R. Rushforth; Sentry, E. W. Buckhout.

The council enrolls at the present time 143 members. Its present officers are: Regent, Thomas E. Hampson; Vice-Regent, Sidney Welch; Orator, Dr. N. A. Warren; Past Regent, Charles Hepenstal; Secretary, George B. Terrell; Collector, Ernest Longbotham; Treasurer, Harry R. Marsden; Chaplain, A. N. Williams; Guide, George W. Hepenstal; Warden, Thomas Tynen; Sentry, Edgar H. Fisher.

YONKERS REBEKAH LODGE, NO. 93, I. O. O. F. This lodge was organized August 20, 1885. It enrolled nineteen charter members. Among the first officers were: Noble Grand, George W. Nodine; Vice-Grand, Mrs. Nicoline Sievers; Recording Secretary, Miss Ella R. Harber; Treasurer, Mrs. Sarah Skidgel. The lodge now enrolls sixty-eight members. The officers at the present time are: Noble Grand, Mrs. Hattie Lake; Vice-Grand, Mrs. Daisy Penterson; Recording Secretary, Miss Emma P.

Speedling; Financial Secretary, Mrs. Ella R. Harber Montross; Treasurer, Miss Lillian I. Rose; Warden, Mrs. Lena Imholt; Conductress, Miss Emma Kunzmuller; Outer Guardian, Mrs. Barbara Kunzmuller; Inner Guardian, Mrs. M. Gower; R. S. N. G., Mrs. Elizabeth Tompkins; L. S. N. G., Miss Mary Mellor; L. S. V. G., Mrs. Minnie Lowell; R. S. V. G., Mrs. E. Shaffer; R. A. S., Miss Mary Ayers; L. A. S., Mrs. Charles Lynch; Chaplain, Mrs. Lizzie Rose; Organist, Mrs. Rachel Power; Degree Master, George W. Speedling; Trustees, Mrs. Mary Fawcet, Mrs. Barbara Kunzmuller, Mr. Addison Lake.

YONKERS COUNCIL, NO. 33, O. U. A. M. This council was instituted December 19, 1889. Its first officers were: Senior Ex-Councillor, Frederick G. Howlett; Junior Ex-Councillor, Jacob Skerrett; Councillor, Henry Brundage; Vice-Councillor, John Getty; Recording Secretary, Byron Cole; Financial Secretary, George Bedder; Treasurer, John E. Naphey; Inductor, William H. Post; Examiner, Alva Miller; Inside Protector, George Odell; Outside Protector, Robert J. Charlton; Trustees, Alexander Sutherland, Frederick Howlett, Judson Miller.

The council has enrolled 120 members. In the spring of 1896 its officers were: Senior Ex-Councillor, Joseph Phillips; Junior Ex-Councillor, John Phillips; Councillor, Alonzo Kelly; Vice-Councillor, George Conklin; Recording Secretary, John E. Naphey; Financial Secretary, Judson Miller; Treasurer, Henry Wilsea; Inductor, Winslow Brown; Examiner, John Wilcox; Trustees, Robert J. Charlton, John Phillips, John E. Naphey. The order of United American Mechanics has an auxiliary order called the Daughters of Liberty.

LADY HARRISON COUNCIL, NO. 12, D. OF L., was instituted April 13, 1893. The first officers were: Councillor, Judson Miller; Associate Councillor, Catharine Tompkins; Vice-Councillor, Charles Brower; Associate Vice-Councillor, Daisy Miller; Recording Secretary, Wilbur F. Grey; Associate Recording Secretary, Gertie Miller; Financial Secretary, Catharine Walters; Treasurer, Josephine Naphey; Guide, Lulu Lusk; Outside Gnard, Henry Wilsea; Inside Guard, Ida Borland; Junior Ex-Councillor, John E. Naphey; Associate Junior Councillor, Celia Hedger; Trustees, Catharine Tompkins, Ida Borland and Alva Miller. The present officers are: Councillor, Mary Brown; Associate Councillor, Minnie Noble; Vice-Councillor, Lucille Humphrey; Associate Vice-Councillor, Eliza Charlton; Recording Secretary, John E. Naphey; Associate Recording Secretary, Georgia Walters; Financial Secretary, Adelia Doty; Treasurer, Henry Wilsea; Guide, Lena Dean; Inside Guard, Mary Decker; Outside Guard, Robert J. Charlton; Trustees, Mary Decker, Lottie Peene, Lucille Humphrey.

ALGONQUIN TRIBE, NO. 288, I. O. R. M. This tribe was organized September 12, 1894. The first officers were: Prophet, David Devlin; Sachem, Emil Garnjost; Senior Sagamore, —— Valentine; Junior Sagamore, John E. Logue; Chief of Records, George B. Edwards; Collector of Wampum, James W. Gunby; Keeper of Wampum, John F. Hanselmann. Fifty-five charter members were enrolled. The membership rolls now carry sixty-eight names. The present officers are: Prophet, Joseph Braddon; Sachem, Sidney E. Dobson; Senior Sagamore, John E. Logue; Junior Sagamore, John J. Crimmins; Chief of Records, Michael J. Doris; Collector of Wampum, F. Dalton; Keeper of Wampum, Louis King.

The council fire is kindled on the second and fourth Wednesdays in each moon. Visiting brothers are always heartily welcome to sit around the council board.

ST. ANDREW'S GOLF CLUB. This club was organized November 18, 1888, with four members. John Reid was President and John B. Upham, Honorary Secretary and Treasurer. It now enrolls 250 members. Its limit is 300. Its present officers are: President, John Reid; Vice-President, William D. Baldwin; Honorary Secretary, William R. Innis; Treasurer, Walter E. Hodgman; Captain, L. B. Stoddard. Board of Governors, Harry Holbrook, Dr. Henry Moffatt, A. L. Livermore, J. B. Upham, H. O. Talmadge.

First links were on grounds of H. O. Talmadge, Lake Avenue, Yonkers, and the club-house was an apple-tree. In 1892 moved to new links (six holes) at the end of Palisade Avenue. In April, 1894, moved to present location at Gray Oaks station on New York and Putnam Railroad, now called St. Andrew's. The Furman Lawrence farm (located on New York and Putnam Railroad, at Mount Hope station), has been purchased where new links will be laid out and a club-house built at a cost of $30,000. The lease of present links expires in the spring of 1897, when the club will move to its new home. The new property of club will be worth $100,000, within a year or two.

YONKERS BOWLING CLUB. This club was organized September, 1888, with twelve members. It now enrolls forty-five, which is its limited number. The first officers were: President, John Ewald; Secretary, George W. Peene; Treasurer, Fred Goss; Captain, Robert Kellock. The present officers are: President, Philip Fitz; Vice-President, Nelson A. Ball; Secretary, William Graham; Treasurer, Daniel H. Bricker; Captain, A. O. Lawrence; Lieutenant, William B. Brewes.

The club has played with the following New York Clubs—Spartan, Orchard, Golden Rod, West End, Morningside. It has also played with the Tarrytown Lyceum, White Plains, Star and several Mount Vernon clubs, viz., Mount Vernon, Bronx, Lenox, Germania, City Club. It entered twice in the American National Tournament against twenty-one clubs, which bowled games in New York. They occupy the Yonkers Bowling Association Rooms, No. 70 North Broadway.

GOOD GOVERNMENT CLUB. This club was organized in January, 1894. President, Norton P. Otis; Vice-President, William L. Heermance; Secretary, Ralph E. Prime, Jr.; Treasurer, Louis Simpson. These officers served until January, 1896, when the following became the officers of the club: President, S. T. Hubbard, Jr.; Vice-President, L. J. Schlisinger; Secretary, Ralph E. Prime, Jr.; Treasurer, Louis Simpson. The roll carries 160 names.

YOUNG MEN'S REPUBLICAN CLUB. This club was organized June 18, 1894. Its first officers were: President, Theodore Cox; First Vice-President, Richard Edie, Jr.; Second Vice-President, J. E. Howes; Third Vice-President, H. M. Baird, Jr.; Secretary, R. V. Howes; Treasurer, H. W. Bertholf. It enrolled at first sixty members. It now enrolls 254. The second President was Dr. H. W. Bertholf. The Vice-Presidents succeeding Mr. Edie were J. E. Howes and H. M. Baird, Jr. The Secretaries were W. D. Youmans, Charles Ash, Horace Allen, Charles Hunt and George J. Frazier. The Treasurers have been W. D. Youmans and George Christian. The Executive Committee consists of all the officers and one representative from each ward. First Ward, John Sells; second, Charles Ash; third, Edward Forsyth; fourth, E. Yerks; fifth, A. M. King; sixth, Ferd. Garnjost; seventh, E. G. Brown. The following are also officers: Captain, A. K. Shipman; Lieutenant, A. M. Garthway; Sergeant-at-Arms, George Rigby.

PALISADE BOAT CLUB. Previous to 1867, a boat club known as "Excelsior" was organized in Yonkers. Another early club was the "Ivanhoe." The Palisade Base Ball Club in 1866, furnished a company of men to row against the "Excelsiors," and the Palisade Boat Club was organized that year on October 16th. It was incorporated March 2, 1868. It moved from a small boat-house to a larger club-house above Peene's dock. Subsequently it moved to a still finer club-house at Glenwood. Lengthy reports of regattas under its auspices have appeared from time to time in the Yonkers papers. It affords its members facilities for bowling, pool and lawn tennis. There is also a café in the club-house. On January 13, 1896, the assets of the club were $33,453.99, the liabilities, $20,249.26, surplus, $13,204.73.

Officers of the Palisade Boat Club since its organization were, Presidents: 1866–67, Henry Amelung; 1868, John G. P. Holden; 1869, Henry Amelung; 1870–72, E. Adolphus Rollins; 1873–76, Matthew F. Rowe; 1877, William H. Guernsey; 1878–80, William H. King; 1881–83, Horace H. Thayer; 1884, Henry T. Keyser; 1885–87, Robert G. Jackson; 1888, Harrison B. Starr; 1888–89, Lewis N. Morris; 1890–93, Edwin M. Jackson; 1894–95, Charles Philip Easton; 1896, William Y. Frazee. Captains: 1872, Charles H. Martin; 1873–74, Henry M. Underhill; 1875, Horace H. Thayer; 1876, Charles H. Harriot; 1877, Henry T. Keyser; 1878–80, Robert G. Jackson; 1881–82, Charles M. Nicholson; 1882–83, John C. Hays; 1884, Charles H. Harriot; 1884–85, Edward Martin, Jr.; 1886–87, Lewis N. Morris; 1888–89, William W. Scrugham; 1890–91, Edward Martin, Jr.; 1891, Benjamin G. Westcott; 1892–95, Edward Martin, Jr.; 1896, George B. Skinner. Lieutenants: 1872–73, Robert G. Jackson; 1874, William H. Stewart; 1875, Charles H. Harriot; 1876, Henry T. Keyser; 1877, Harrison B. Starr; 1878–80, Andrew Moffat; 1881, Edward Gibson; 1882–83, J. Irving Smith; 1884, Edward Martin, Jr.; 1885, George S. Pentz; 1886, Merritt H. Smith; 1887, Edward R. DeWolfe; 1888, Richmond E. Slade; 1889, Edwin R. Holden; 1890–91, Gabriel Reevs; 1891, Philip P. Getty; 1892–93, Eldridge W. Jones; 1894, John H. Keeler, Jr.; 1895, Thomas Rayner; 1896, Arthur S. Thomson.

PALISADE BOAT CLUB FLAG.

VESPER ROWING ASSOCIATION. This association was organized August 12, 1867. Messrs. Thomas Franklin, R. C. Elliott, Benjamin Mason, William Macfarlane, James T. Howland, Thomas Fearon,

William Hull and George Watt were the original members. It was very prominent for a period, by reason of its successive victories. One crew was especially famous. Thomas Fearon, Bow; Owen Van Winkle, No. 2; William Macfarlane, No. 3; John H. Keeler, Stroke, were the members of that crew. One member of the club was Bob. Cook, of Yale College. The association disbanded some years ago.

VESPER YACHTING ASSOCIATION. This association was organized in the summer of 1881, by Captain Hyatt L. Garrison, Thomas Fearon, James Shaughnessy, Thomas O. Shaughnessy, Augustus Bailey, John Watt and Abram C. Gould. The first Commodore was Thomas Fearon. The association, now disbanded, afforded its members, for a time, much pleasure.

YONKERS YACHT CLUB. This club was organized in 1878. Its first officers were: Commodore, A. J. Prime; Vice-Commodore, Charles T. Mercer; Secretary, Thomas L. Mottram; Treasurer, W. H. Devoe; Trustees. Sylvanus Cokalete, J. W. Garrison and A. W. Serrell. A cruise, at the opening of each season, and a "clam-bake" on May 30th, a regatta in May, another regatta in September, and a cruise in August, were the annual programmes. The membership is seventy-eight at the present time. The officers are: Commodore, W. B. Fink; Vice-Commodore, A. McLaughlin; Fleet Captain. F. C. Williams; Measurer, J. J. Murphy; Recording Secretary, J. B. Pitchford; Financial Secretary, C. Williams; Treasurer, H. P. Allen; Trustees, W. B. Fink, A. A. McLaughlin, H. C. Allen, A. K. Shipman, G. Warren, W. D. Smith and G. Bolwell; Steward, C. Lamkul.

YONKERS YACHT CLUB FLAG.

CORINTHIAN YACHT CLUB. This club was organized January 17, 1889, by twenty-five gentlemen who contributed $100 each for the purchase of property, and the building of a club-house. The club-house was opened May 30, 1889. The cost of the land and house was about $9,000. The total value of the club's property now approximates $11,000. The principal officers for 1896, are: Commodore Alanson J. Prime; Vice-Commodore, Charles E. Valentine; Fleet Captain, Louis Quanchi; Corresponding Secretary, Frank- lin A. Rigby; Financial Secretary, Henry J. Ritchie; Treasurer, J. Howard Clapp. The Trustees are: Halcyon Skinner, James B. Odell, Newton P. Quick, A. T. Rose, T. D. Canfield, Willett H. Clark. A his- tory of the club, written by Mr. J. Joseph Lawrence, appeared in the Regatta Programme of the New York Yacht Racing Association for 1895. Commodore Prime of Yonkers has been President and Admiral of that Association since its organization. It is composed of the following clubs: Audubon, Bayonne, Columbia, Greenville, Hudson River, Jersey City, Kill Von Kull, Newark, New York Athletic Club, Newark Bay Boat Club, New Jersey Athletic Club, New Jersey, Oceanic, Ossining, Pavonia, Shrewsbury, Staten Island Athletic, Tappan Zee, Tower Ridge, Yonkers Corinthian.

THE YONKERS CANOE CLUB. This club was organized February 17, 1886. The Commodores have been John G. Reevs, F. K. Shears, Gabriel Reevs, Everett Masten, Charles C. Rossire, H. Lansing Quick, Jerome W. Simpson, William R. Haviland, D. B. Goodsell, Paul B. Rossire. The club was incorporated in September, 1888. Since that date it has numbered among its officers, besides the Commodores, Captains and Lieutenants. Its first quarters were the old Vesper Boat House. In December, 1888, the club took the entire house, which has since been known as the Yonkers Canoe Club-House. Plans for a new club-house are drawn. In the spring of 1890 the club had the war canoe Ko-ko-ko-ho built. It is thirty-five feet long. The New York Canoe Club International Challenge Cup has been twice held by this club. H. Lansing Quick won it in September, 1890, and T. S. Oxholm won it in June, 1892.

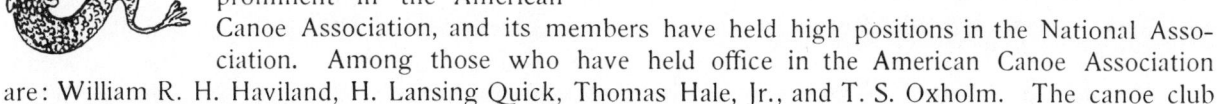

The club is one of the most prominent in the American Canoe Association, and its members have held high positions in the National Association. Among those who have held office in the American Canoe Association are: William R. H. Haviland, H. Lansing Quick, Thomas Hale, Jr., and T. S. Oxholm. The canoe club flag carries the letters Y. C. C. The club emblem is the dolphin.

VOLUNTEER LIFE-SAVING CORPS. The Volunteer Life-Saving Corps of New York State is incorporated at all points of the inland waters of the State, where no United States government provision or appropriation is made therefor, and for the purpose of more fully organizing auxiliary corps, or boat-crews, and to assist them in procuring boats and life-saving equipments, and for the presentation of such rewards and medals for heroic rescuers as shall encourage them to redoubled energy and watchfulness in behalf of the unfortunate. A Volunteer Life- Saving Corps was organized in Yon- kers by W. H. Blakemore. It is aided by the State. There are forty men and twenty boats. The headquarters of the corps are at the Yonkers Yacht Club-House. The men patrol the river front, and from July 30th, up to date saved six lives. The corps is supplied with metallic life-buoys, and rubber life-preservers, with life- lines, also with flags, pennants and burgees and boat-signs of the "Vol- unteer Life-Savers." Private Thomas J. Rollison rescued two men in Aug- ust, 1895, for which he received a bronze medal. The officers are: Captain, William H. Blakemore; First Lieutenants, Messrs. Halley, Frazier and O'Leery; Second Lieu- tenants, Messrs. Williams and Warren; Third Lieutenants, Messrs. Montross and Lonergan.

BADGE OF LIFE-SAVING CORPS.

YONKERS CURLING CLUB. The club was organized in November, 1864, and known as the Yonkers Curling Club. The organizers were Wm. B. Edgar, W. H. Smith, Alex. Clark, H. F. Baldwin, John Moffat, John McLain, Wm. Macfarlane, Wm. H. Doty, E. Underhill and James Stewart. The first officers were: President, Wm. B. Edgar; Secretary, Wm. H. Doty; Treasurer, Wm. Macfarlane. It now has a membership of thirty. The present officers are: President, Thomas Wigley; Vice-President, Alex. Cochrane; Secretary, Robt. Kellock; Treasurer, G. W. Peene.

The rink was built in 1889, by the Yonkers Curling Association, (which was a stock company composed of the members of the club and their friends,) and cost, with the ground, about $13,000. The building is used for curling and skating in the cold weather, but is now rented to H. W. Pagan for a bicycle hall. The club has been a most successful one in curling and is recognized as the strongest club in this vicinity, having won more medals and other trophies than any other. Officers, 1896: President, Thomas Wigley; Vice-President, Alex. Cochrane; Secretary, Robert Kellock; Treasurer, George W. Peene; Representative to Grand National C. C., James Kellock; Representative to Royal Caledonian C. C., Edwin L. Thomas; Committee of Management, George Colquhoun, Robert Kellock, James Johnson.

YONKERS CORINTHIAN YACHT CLUB FLAG.

NEPERA HAYMAKERS' ASSOCIATION, 186½, was instituted December 17, 1891. Good standing in a Tribe of Red Men is a requisite to membership in this association, as only Red Men are eligible. It is a branch or degree of that order. Its first officers were: Chief Haymaker, Ferdinand Garnjost; Assistant Haymaker, George J. Frazier; Collector of Straws, George L. Moir; Keeper of Bundles, Caleb U. Fowler; Past Chief Haymaker, Daniel Devlin; Overseer, James A. Taggart; Stewards, Dr. J. C. Bennett,

J. J. Christian, H. H. Hurst. The present officers are: Past Chief Haymakers, Thomas Moir and Daniel Devlin; Collector of Straws, Michael J. Doris: Keeper of Bundles, Joseph Braddon; Assistant Chief Haymaker, Albert W. Best; Overseer, Philip Trask.

LEO ASSOCIATION. This association was organized June 10, 1886. Its object is to promote the moral, intellectual and social interests of Catholic young men. At first it enrolled thirteen members. At the present time it enrolls eighty-three active members. Its officers are: President, John J. McEnroe; Vice-President, Joseph F. O'Brien; Financial Secretary, William Le Bailly; Recording Secretary, James G. Renahan; Treasurer, William F. Rowan; Librarian, Dennis A. Cooper. These officers, together with Messrs. A. F. Mahony, M. J. Walsh and Jos. M. O'Brien, constitute the Board of Trustees.

LINCOLN LEGION. The Lincoln Legion is a political and social organization, the declared object of which is the furtherance of the interests of the Republican party, and the promoting of honesty in municipal politics. It was organized December 17, 1872. At first eight members were enrolled. The first officers were, President, C. H. Austin; Secretary, W. M. Floyd; Treasurer, D. H. Bricker; Sergeant-at-Arms, L. M. Tillotson. The club now enrolls about 270 members. Only those on whom the Membership Committee report favorably, are accepted; otherwise the number of members would be very much larger. Some of the most prominent men in the city and county are members. Its present officers are: President, W. M. Floyd; Vice-President, W. L. Goddard; Secretary, J. C. Flenchans; Treasurer, D. H. Bricker; Sergeant-at-Arms, George Hayden.

IROQUOIS CLUB. A band of young Democratic citizens of Yonkers, in the spring of 1892, organized for political action. They were known as the Iroquois Club, and declared that their purpose was to co-operate with citizens who desired to elect worthy men to office. The organization was incorporated under the Political and Social Club Laws on December 27, 1894. The incorporators were Messrs. F. C. Williams, James Brouder, F. W. Egloffstein, William M. Kinsella, John T. McGrath, Charles A. Boyd, James M. Claxton and Edward Lester. Most of the members are clerks, mechanics and laborers. The club is supported by small initiation fees and monthly dues.

In 1896, the officers were: President, Julius Rosenthal; Vice-President, Henry Stengel; Corresponding Secretary, James M. Claxton; Recording Secretary, A. W. Nugent; Financial Secretary, James McMinn; Treasurer, Theodore R. Heinrichs; Trustees, Fielding Gower, M. Fitzgerald and Benjamin M. Medina.

THE HALF-HOUR READING CLUB. This club was organized in March, 1889. At that time it enrolled twenty members. Its first officers were: President, Mrs. W. H. Doty; Secretary, Mrs. Benjamin Silliman; Treasurer, Mrs. Peter Elting. Stated meetings are held on the first Wednesdays of June, October, December and February. The annual meeting is on the first Wednesday in April. No course of reading is pursued. Each member chooses her own authors, and at the meetings gives the list of works read since the previous meeting. The members have the privilege of asking about any book mentioned, and are thus able to avoid reading inferior works. This plan also brings valuable books to the notice of the members who otherwise might not hear of them.

All members are required to read at least one half-hour daily, or four hours during the week. Only three novels are to be read in the interval between meetings. No original papers are prepared, but after the business meeting, at the informal discussion of a book selected by a committee at the previous meeting, many original ideas are expressed, as might be expected from a club of twenty-five cultured ladies. The club has been in existence seven years with the same President and Treasurer. Mrs. Norton P. Otis succeeded Mrs. Silliman as Secretary, and each served three years. Mrs. J. L. Porteous was elected Secretary at the last business meeting. The present officers are: President, Mrs. W. H. Doty; Secretary, Mrs. J. L. Porteous; Treasurer, Mrs. Peter Elting.

ROBERT BURNS CLUB. This club was organized December 17, 1890, and was chartered May 6, 1891. Its first officers were: President, James Fullerton; Vice-President, Robert Adam; Treasurer, John Herd; Recording Secretary, John C. Johnston; Corresponding Secretary, Thomas Hadden. Its officers in 1896 are: President, George Colquhoun; Vice-President, John Doherty; Treasurer, David Paton; Recording Secretary, James D. Thompson; Librarian, James Brown; Sergeant-at-Arms, Daniel Watson; Trustees, George Colquhoun, Kenneth McKay, Alexander Cochrane, George Young and David Paton. The club enrolls thirty members at the present time. Judge W. C. Kellogg and the Rev. S. Parkes Cadman are honorary members.

The objects of the club are: First. The preservation of the ancient literature, music and costume, and the encouragement and practice of the ancient games of Scotland. Second. The establishment of a library and the employment of lecturers before the association. Third. Mutual aid and benefit to the members.

SERVIC CLUB, 363, L. L. A. On May 16, 1889, several young people of Yonkers, in order to increase the pleasure and the profit of their social life, organized a society which was named the Servic Club. Edward S. Hine was elected President and Miss Nannie F. Feeter, Secretary. Soon afterwards the scope of the society was broadened by the introduction of debates, and before a year had elapsed it had become a debating society. Early in 1891 it was reorganized, its membership being composed of only young men. Within a brief time it became an auxiliary of the then recently formed Lyceum League of America. Its meetings were at first held in private houses. In February, 1895, through the courtesy of the Board of Education the club was permitted to meet in one of the rooms in the High School. Its membership includes young men in business as well as those who are students. In April, 1896, it enrolled twenty members. The officers in January, 1896, were: President, Edward S. Hine; Vice-President, William Waller; Recording Secretary, Harold P. Van Ness; Corresponding Secretary, Theodore E. Terrell; Treasurer, R. J. Reese; Sergeant-at-Arms, Sidney A. Beckwith.

KITCHING RELIEF CORPS, No. 229, W. R. C. This corps was organized March 5, 1896, with forty-two charter members. On the same date an election was held and officers were installed. The officers are: President, Ida Shotts Pentreath; Senior Vice-President, Mary F. Paulding; Junior Vice-President, Mamie McCaul; Secretary, Mamie Mitchell; Treasurer, Lizzie O'Mara; Chaplain, Minnie Jackson; Conductor, Lillie Yerks; Assistant Conductor, Mary McCauley; Guard, Katie Hooley; Assistant Guard, Annie Carrol.

CITY CLUB. This club was organized and incorporated November 30, 1885. The incorporators were: Edward Underhill, Henry B. Archer, Edwin M. Jackson, Robert H. Howard and Theodore H. Silkman. At first the club enrolled eighteen members. It now enrolls ninety-six resident members and sixty who are non-resident. Its Presidents have been: Messrs. William R. Beers, Ethelbert Belknap, George H. Purser, Robert H. Howard, Theodore H. Silkman and James V. Lawrence. Mr. Edwin M. Jackson was the Treasurer of the club from its organization until December, 1894. The present officers are: President, John C. Shotts; Vice-President, Edwin M. Jackson; Secretary, F. X. Donoghue; Treasurer, Edward Underhill. The Board of Managers is composed of these officers, together with Messrs. William B. Edgar, Henry Osterheld, Theodore H. Silkman, Joseph Miller, James V. Lawrence and John Mulligan. In the spring of 1893, the club purchased the plot and the building No. 47 South Broadway. The property of the club represents an investment of about $25,000.

INSTRUMENTAL BANDS. Yonkers has had a number of instrumental bands. In the village days the Yonkers Band was a well-known organization. Several bands have been organized since the incorporation of the city. The Yonkers Band, Harvey, leader; the Young Men's Catholic Association Band, the Orchestra and Military Band, John W. Murray, leader; the Citizens Military Band, Robt. Thorpe, leader; the Leake and Watts Cornet Band; Schofield's Military Band, Wm. Schofield, leader; the Yonkers Fife and Drum Corps; the Fourth Ward Invincible Flute and Drum Corps, have discoursed stirring music on many occasions. Choral Unions and other associations organized for the study of vocal music, have given musicals, which were greatly enjoyed.

CLAN MACGREGOR, 106, O. S. C. This clan was established in Yonkers on March 10, 1892, with eighteen charter members. The first officers were: Chief, James Brownlie; Tanist, W. S. Barbour; Secretary, Daniel Macindoe; Financial Secretary, James Graham; Treasurer, Willliam Watt. The present membership is twenty-six. The officers in 1896 are: Chief, William Watt; Tanist, John Forbes; Secretary, James Brownlie; Financial Secretary, John Thompson, Jr.; Treasurer, William Brown. The clan held its first meeting in Hawthorn Hall on March 10, 1892. Its present meeting place is Holsatia Hall. It has a fund for sick members, also a fund for the beneficiaries of deceased members. The regalia of a clansman is the Tartan of his clan name, *viz.*, a plaid and buckle, a Scotch bonnet and eagle feather.

THE YONKERS HOMING CLUB. This club was organized April 1, 1896. The officers were: President, Richard Lawson; Secretary and Treasurer, George Eickemeyer. The object of the club is "to promote the homing pigeon fancy, and to fly pigeons from twenty-five to one hundred miles, for honors." The competitors time their swift feathered racers, recording the number of yards covered in a minute, and the number of miles in an hour.

CARPENTERS' UNION, No. 273. The present officers of this society are: President, Champion Thomson; Vice-President, Robert Enright; Recording Secretary, Harry Batchelor; Financial Secretary, Edgar Hulse; Treasurer, George Parry; Conductor, Charles Carlson. The Union was organized in 1887.

CARPENTERS' UNION, NO. 726. The present officers of this society are: President, R. P. Nugent; Vice-President, H. Palmateer; Financial Secretary, Andrew Edwards; Recording Secretary, S. W. Sackett; Conductor, John Hitzelberger.

MASONS' AND PLASTERERS' UNION, NO. 22. The present officers of this large society are: President, Robert Griffin; Vice-President, Edward Connors; Treasurer, James Duffy; Recording Secretary, Thomas Bracken; Financial Secretary, Thomas Burke.

PLUMBERS AND GASFITTERS' UNION, NO. 152. The present officers of this society are: President, Harry F. Fee; Vice-President, James L. Smith; Recording Secretary, James Thomson; Financial Secretary, James Campbell; Treasurer, Charles Dunston.

IRON MOLDERS' UNION, NO. 173. The present officers of this union are: President, James Cuddy; Vice-President, Michael Burns; Recording Secretary, A. Woods; Financial Secretary, Patrick Stafford.

HORSE SHOERS' UNION, NO. 55, M. H. S. N. P. A. This Yonkers union is a branch of the Master Horse Shoers' National Protective Association, a society which exerts an influence in the direction of organization, education and legislation. It maintains that through organization each workman profits by the experience and assistance of all. It aims to educate farriers by making it the duty of each local union to arrange a course of lectures on the anatomy and physiology of the horse's foot and leg in order that horse shoeing may be done scientifically. The arranging of such a course of instruction is compulsory. Influence in the direction of legislation is exerted by each State association. Each endeavors to secure the passage of laws making necessary an apprenticeship of at least three years, to be followed by an examination in anatomy, physiology, scientific horse shoeing, and also requiring the applicant to register at the office of the Clerk of the County. The New York State Association secured the passage of such a bill, but it affects only cities of 50,000 inhabitants or more. The association proposes to secure an amendment in order that the law may affect country as well as city.

The Yonkers Union was organized March 6, 1896. It had six members at first, but its membership has since doubled. The officers are: President, Daniel Devlin; Vice-President, Thomas O'Brien; Recording Secretary, M. J. Flanagan; Treasurer, Thomas Wilkie; Sergeant-at-Arms, Peter Ryan.

THE YONKERS ATHLETIC ASSOCIATION. This association was organized November 1, 1896. Its first officers were: President, John F. Hart; First Vice-President, Edward Sutherland; Second Vice-President, John X. Hackett; Financial Secretary, Frank Madden; Recording Secretary, Thomas See; Treasurer, George W. Cottam; Captain, James J. Gahagan; Lieutenant, John F. Curran. The association enrolls ninety members. It meets in the Chelsea Building.

THE YONKERS TEUTONIA. This German singing and literary society was at first named "Yonkers Liederkrantz." It dates from 1854 or 1855. Among those through whose influence the society was established were: Frederick Hempel, Robert Krapkowski, Albert Ludke and Philip Berenger. They engaged William F. Muller, a well-known teacher of music to give them instructions in music. Eight were enrolled at the beginning. The society was subsequently known as "Mannerchor and Liederkrantz." Yonkers Teutonia is the name by which it is now known. Under this name it was incorporated November 23, 1867.

Its meetings were held at first on Hudson Street at Philip Happel's house, then on North Broadway at Nicholas Rost's house, and then in a school-house which stood on the west side of the Square, where the banks now stand. Afterwards the society again held its sessions in dwelling-houses. Then it purchased the property which was thereafter long known as Teutonia Hall (corner of New Main and Brook Streets). The building has one story and a basement. It contained a stage for amateur theatricals, a dining-room, a bar-room and reading-room. The society generally gave theatricals as often as twice during each winter. In 1885 or 1886, it enrolled about 150 members. The membership included both sexes. In 1892 a new hall was built by the society. It stands on the west side of Buena Vista Avenue, near the western terminus of Hudson Street. The plot cost $5,000. The building cost between $25,000 and $26,000. It contains a large assembly hall, dining-room, etc. In 1896, the roll of members carried 206 names. The officers in 1896 were: President, John Schlobohm; Vice-President, Fred Gugel; Pro. Secretary, Aug. Koch; Financial Secretary, Fritz Cassens; Corresponding Secretary, Max Hettler; Treasurer, Joseph Geitzenauer; Trustees, Otto Fuhrmann, Fred Wangenstein and John Schaefer; Resigneur, Max Josher.

THE MONDAY CLUB. This club is now in its tenth season. It meets each week. Its object is the study of general literature. "The wide range of study can be seen from its programme for the past winter embracing such names as Cuvier, Victor Cousin, Auguste Compte, Guizot, Hugo, Dumas and

Heine of the French writers. Danish and Italian writers were also studied, and papers read on American historical topics, American journalism, English literature, Christian architecture and on the works of Franklin, Hamilton, Irving, Cooper, Moore, De Quincey, Lamb, Scott and Keble."

THE ART CLUB. This is not a society of artists, but an association of lovers of art, who meet to discuss the fine arts. Their discussions are educational and their meetings are as pleasant as they are profitable.

THE CRITICISM CLASS. This class has been conducted by Professor Lioneoh, and has promoted social pleasure while profiting its members. They have enjoyed " opportunities to hear in a less formal way than the lecture platform, public speakers and writers who read from unpublished works or short sketches. These readings are followed by criticism usually friendly and appreciative."

THE ROUND TABLE. This is a literary society, and is in "the seventh year of prosperity." The members meet once every two weeks for the study of English literature. A programme for the year is printed. It assigns two works for each meeting. The discussion is opened by a member selected in advance.

THE YONKERS BRANCH BIBLE ASSOCIATION. This association, an auxiliary to the Westchester County Bible Society, was formed in November, 1857. Its object was to supply all Yonkers residents who had no Bibles, with copies of the sacred volume, and also to send contributions to the American Bible Society. Sometimes the association vigorously prosecuted its work. At other times it did little or nothing. One of its most ardent early friends was Richard Wynkoop. William N. Seymour, Henry Bowers, John W. W. Oliver, John H. Brown and other well-known citizens have been Presidents of the association. Richard Wynkoop, John W. Skinner, Rev. Charles E. Allison and Walter Thomas have, as Secretaries, rendered the society service. For a period of years, Samuel D. Rockwell was the Treasurer, and Gabriel Reevs, M.D., was the Depositary.

THE YONKERS SPIRITUALIST SOCIETY. This organization has a charter from the State society, and also one from the "National Spiritualists Association," of which it is an auxiliary. Its President is Alfred Andrews, an organist and instructor in music, and for years a resident of Yonkers. At the end of the chapter on Yonkers churches is a paragraph relating to the society.

THE YONKERS SOCIETY FOR UNIVERSITY EXTENSION. The extension system was organized October 31, 1891. The committee meeting was held at the Y. M. C. A. rooms in Yonkers, December 12, 1891, and officers and a Board of Managers were elected. Meetings were held in St. John's Church parish house, 1892-93, and in the Woman's Institute from 1893 to the present time. The first officers were: President, Professor A. V. Williams Jackson; Vice-President, Frederic Shonnard; Second Vice-President, Norton P. Otis; Secretary and Treasurer, Theodore Gilman. The officers in 1896 were: President, Professor A. V. Williams Jackson; First Vice-President, Norton P. Otis; Second Vice-President, John Kendrick Bangs; Secretary, J. Harvey Bell; Treasurer, F. W. Eschmann. The Board of Managers consists of over fifty members. Several courses of lectures have been delivered, among them: English Literature, Prof. H. H. Boyesen, of Columbia College; Astronomy, Prof. J. K. Rees, of Columbia College; French Revolution, Prof. A. Cohn, of Columbia College; English Drama, Prof. T. R. Price, of Columbia College, Prof. G. E. Woodberry, of Columbia College, Prof. A. V. W. Jackson, of Columbia College; German Literature, Prof. H. H. Boyesen, of Columbia College; Electricity, Prof. W. Hallock, of Columbia College, Prof. F. B. Crocker, of Columbia College, M. I. Pupin, of Columbia College, W. L. Robb, of Trinity College, Hartford, Mr. Carthy, of New York; Geology, W. B. Scott, of Princeton College; Architecture (five lectures), A. D. F. Hamlin, of Columbia College; Zoology and Geology, W. B. Scott, of Princeton College. Twenty-five students have been awarded the certificates of the Board of Regents at Albany.

The movement in Yonkers in the autumn of 1891, grew out of a vote of the Directors of the Young Men's Christian Association, on a motion by Theodore Gilman, the President of that association. Mr. Gilman then secured the services of Professor James, of Philadelphia, who came to Yonkers in November, and delivered a lecture in the Y. M. C. A. rooms, on the subject of University Extension. This meeting was presided over by William Allen Butler. The final meeting for the election of officers and a Board of Managers was held on December 12, 1891, at the house of the Hon. G. Hilton Scribner, and was addressed by Mr. R. W. Thomas, the representative of the Board of Regents at Albany.

Officers and Managers for year 1894-95: President, A. V. Williams Jackson; First Vice-President, Frederic Shonnard; Second Vice-President, Norton P. Otis; Secretary, J. Harvey Bell; Treasurer, George

P. Butler. Managers: Fisher A. Baker, Mrs. Fisher A. Baker, W. Delavan Baldwin, Mrs. W. Delavan Baldwin, William H. Baldwin, John K. Bangs, Mrs. John K. Bangs, J. Harvey Bell, James R. Brevoort, Mrs. James R. Brevoort, A. S. Brownell, William Allen Butler, George P. Butler, Miss Mary M. Butler, Thomas C. Cornell, Mrs. Thomas C. Cornell, J. J. R. Croes, Mrs. W. W. Ellsworth, P. J. Elting, F. W. R. Eschmann, Mrs. F. W. R. Eschmann, Theodore Gilman, Mrs. Theodore Gilman, Miss Frances Gilman, Nathan Guilford, Samuel B. Hawley, Harry Holbrook, Mrs. Harry Holbrook, Franklin Haynes, Frederick William Holls, A. V. Williams Jackson, Mrs. Justus Lawrence, Dr. E. M. Morrell, Mrs. E. M. Morrell, Waldo G. Morse, Mrs. Waldo G. Morse, Norton P. Otis, Mrs. Norton P. Otis, Frederic Shonnard, Mrs. Frederic Shonnard, George E. Stevens, Mrs. George E. Stevens, Mrs. Alexander Smith, Duncan Smith, Mrs. Duncan Smith, F. C. Train, Charles Vezin, John T. Waring, Mrs. John T. Waring, W. M. Williams, George B. Wray.

Several of the students have passed creditable examinations. One attendant at the lectures, Mr. Henry C. Donnelly, who had for many years been interested in astronomy, becoming still more deeply interested by what he heard and read, built an observatory near his home on Nodine Hill, and erected within it a fine telescope.

THE YONKERS HISTORICAL AND LIBRARY ASSOCIATION. Frequently Galusha B. Balch, M.D., and William E. Ketcham, D.D., conversed about Yonkers historical matters. They were agreed that an organization in the city would doubtless result in much added interest in local history and the preservation of valuable material for the future historian and genealogist. With one accord they proceeded to formulate a paper to be signed by those who would favor such a proposal. The paper read as follows: "We, the undersigned, are of the opinion that an organization should be formed in this city for the preservation of historical, genealogical and biographical records, and for the study of local history." The fourteen citizens to whom it was shown promptly signed it, and the following call was sent in a neat circular to many of our citizens. The names on the printed call sent out were signers of the first paper:

"YONKERS, N. Y., November 2, 1891.

"*Dear Sir:*—We, the undersigned, are of the opinion that an organization should be formed in this city for the preservation of historical, genealogical and biographical records and for the study of local history and kindred subjects.

"With this object in view, we would respectfully request that you will meet with the undersigned and others, at the residence of Mr. Rufus King, 222 North Broadway, on Tuesday evening, November 10th, at 8 o'clock, for the purpose of considering the formation of such an organization.

"HENRY M. BAIRD,	WILLIAM E. KETCHAM,
"DAVID COLE,	EDWARD D. HARRIS,
"RUFUS KING,	JOHN W. OLIVER,
"ROBERT P. GETTY,	JOHN C. HAVEMEYER,
"FREDERIC SHONNARD,	WILLIAM C. RUSSELL,
"RALPH E. PRIME,	DAVID HAWLEY,
"GALUSHA B. BALCH,	T. ASTLEY ATKINS."

The informal meeting at Mr. Rufus King's residence was presided over by David Cole, D.D., and Prof. Edward R. Shaw was appointed Temporary Secretary.

The next notice explains itself:

"YONKERS, December 1, 1891.

"*Dear Sir:*—Pursuant to the adjournment of the informal meeting on Tuesday, November 10th, at the house of Mr. Rufus King, for the purpose of forming a Yonkers Historical and Library Association, we invite you to attend a second meeting to be held in the High School Building, on South Broadway, on Tuesday evening, December 8th, at 8 o'clock. The committee appointed to prepare a constitution and by-laws will be ready to make their report and steps may be taken to perfect the proposed organization.

"DAVID COLE, *Temporary Chairman*.
"EDWARD R. SHAW, *Temporary Secretary*."

The report of the Special Committee on Constitution at the above-named meeting was presented by Dr. Galusha B. Balch, and after sundry modifications the by-laws were adopted, there being no formal constitution other than the principles and rules embraced in the by-laws.

The first election was held January 19, 1892, in the Board of Education Rooms and the following officers were chosen: President, Professor Henry M. Baird, D.D., LL.D.; First Vice-President, David Cole, D.D.; Second Vice-President, T. Astley Atkins; Corresponding Secretary, Thomas C. Cornell; Secretary, Charles Philip Easton; Treasurer, Lyman Cobb, Jr.

The same officers were re-elected for 1893. In 1894, David Cole, D.D., was chosen President, T. Astley Atkins, First Vice-President; W. L. Heermance, Second Vice-President.

In 1895, the following officers were elected: President, Colonel William L. Heermance; First Vice-President, T. Astley Atkins; Second Vice-President, Edward D. Harris; Corresponding Secretary, William E. Ketcham, D.D.; Secretary, Charles Philip Easton; Treasurer, Lyman Cobb, Jr.

In 1896, the following officers were elected: President, Rev. Charles E. Allison; First Vice-President, Charles E. Gorton, Esq.; Second Vice-President, Edward D. Harris; Corresponding Secretary, Rev. William E. Ketcham, D.D.; Recording Secretary, Charles Philip Easton; Treasurer, Rev. Lyman Cobb, Jr.; Librarian, Galusha B. Balch, M.D.

"CERTIFICATE OF INCORPORATION OF THE YONKERS HISTORICAL AND LIBRARY ASSOCIATION.

"STATE OF NEW YORK,
"COUNTY OF WESTCHESTER.

"We, the undersigned citizens of the United States and of the State of New York, of full age, desiring to associate ourselves for historical and literary purposes, and for the purpose of maintaining a library under Chapter 319 of the Laws of 1848, entitled 'An Act for the Incorporation of Benevolent, Charitable, Scientific and Missionary Societies,' and the amendments thereto, do hereby certify as follows:

"1. The name or title by which this society shall be known in law is: 'The Yonkers Historical and Library Association.'

"2. The particular business and objects of such societ yare: The collection and preservation of historical, genealogical and biographical records, and of historical relics; the study of local history and kindred subjects, and the maintaining of a library.

"3. The number of trustees or directors to manage the society is seven.

"4. The names of the Trustees, Directors or Managers for the first year are as follows, *viz.*: Henry M. Baird, David Cole, T. Astley Atkins, Thomas C. Cornell, Charles P. Easton, Lyman Cobb, Jr., and Galusha B. Balch.

"Dated Yonkers, January 26, 1892." "HENRY M. BAIRD.

David Cole, T. Astley Atkins, Thomas C. Cornell, Charles Philip Easton, Lyman Cobb, Jr., Galusha B. Balch, S. H. Thayer, Charles Elmer Allison, William E. Ketcham, Robert P. Getty, E. Alexander Houston, John Reid, Andrew Deyo, Edward Doubleday Harris, William M. Dick, Robert J. Dick, Raffaelle Cobb, William H. Doty, James T. Bixby, William R. Mott, William F. Nisbet, Joseph H. Palmer, A. V. Williams Jackson, Theodore Gilman, Harry Holbrook, J. G. P. Holden, Rufus King, William Warburton Scrugham, William C. Russel, J. Hendrick de Vries, C. H. Montague, J. W. Oliver, W. A. Drinkwater, S. Emmet Getty, Alexander B. Carver, Samuel L. Cooper, H. W. Bashford, Philip Verplanck, Charles R. Corley, Edward R. Shaw, Ethelbert Belknap, James Lawson, Thomas Hale, Robert N. Flagg, W. L. Heermance, Frederic Shonnard, Alfred Jones.

The Certificate of Incorporation having been properly acknowledged, was filed and recorded in the office of Secretary of State at Albany, February 15, 1892.

The association issues interesting bulletins, of which Messrs. William E. Ketcham, Edward D. Harris and Rufus King are the Publishing Committee. The second bulletin contained a full report of the proceedings of the public meeting, called to protest against building new municipal buildings on Manor Hall grounds.

The association has listened to a number of interesting papers. The list of 'the papers is here recorded, also the names of their respective authors and when and where the papers were read:

March 17, 1892. Judge T. Astley Atkins, of Yonkers, N. Y., in High School Building, on "The Indian Wars between the Dutch and the Indians down to 1655."

May 19, 1892. Thomas C. Cornell, Esq., in High School Building, on "Some Reminiscences of the old Manor House and Grounds and Its Surroundings."

October 20, 1892. Robert P. Getty, Esq., in High School Building, on "Chronicles of Yonkers."

December 15, 1892. David Cole, D.D., in High School Building, on "Yonkers—Backlook and Forelook."

March 16, 1893. Judge T. Astley Atkins, in High School Building, on "The Battle at Philipse's Bridge."

May 9, 1893. Edward D. Harris, Esq., in High School Building, on "Genealogical Studies."

December 12, 1893. J. C. L. Hamilton, Esq., in High School Building, on "Sketches from the Manor of Philipsburgh."

March 13, 1894. S. Emmet Getty, Esq., in High School Building, on "Yonkers in the Forties."

May 9, 1894. M. D. Raymond, Esq., of Tarrytown, in High School Building, on "Philipse Manor during the Revolution."

October 9, 1894. Justice J. O. Dykman, in Common Council Chamber, on "Last Twelve Days of Andre."

February 28, 1895. Henry M. Baird, D.D., LL. D., in Common Council Chamber, on "The Recovery of Religious Liberty by the Huguenots."

March 22, 1895. Rev. S. Parkes Cadman, in Hall of Woman's Institute, on "The Pilgrim in England and America."

May 20, 1895. Judge T. Astley Atkins, on "Yonkers Half a Century Ago."

October 29, 1895. Rev. John Reid, D.D., on "Washington Irving."

———   Perre V. B. Hoes, on "Reminiscences of Martin Van Buren."

The rooms of the Yonkers Historical and Library Association are in the Woman's Institute, where it has a collection of lectures, pamphlets, reports and books from nearly every State in the Union.

THE JENKINS MEDICAL ASSOCIATION. This association was organized December 21, 1866, at the house of Dr. Arnold. Doctors Arnold, Jenkins, Reinfelder, Dery and Pooley, Jr., were present. The society was first known as "The Yonkers Medical Association." Its first officers were: President, Dr. Arnold; Vice-President, Dr. Jenkins; Secretary and Treasurer, Dr. Pooley, Jr. On page 196 is a brief reference to an early meeting of the society. It received the name, "The Jenkins Medical Association," September 21, 1883. This name perpetuates the memory of John Foster Jenkins, A.M., M.D., a Yonkers physician of great skill and reputation. (A brief biography of Dr. Jenkins is on page 580, Vol. I. Scharf's "History of Westchester County.") The society now enrolls twenty-four members. Its membership is limited to twenty-five. The death of Dr. Samuel Swift in the summer of 1896, leaves the one vacancy. Yonkers and Mount Vernon are represented in the association. The majority of the members are Yonkers physicians. The society meets on the second Thursday of each month (except June, July and August), at the residence of one of the members. In June the members generally enjoy an outing. In the old papers of the association it is written that it was organized "for medical improvement and promotion of social relations among all its members." The present officers are: President, Dr. Garrett N. Banker, of Yonkers; Vice-President, Dr. S. Oscar Myers, of Mount Vernon; Secretary and Treasurer, Dr. J. L. Porteous, of Yonkers.

YONKERS BRANCH THEOSOPHICAL SOCIETY. The published objects of this society are:

I. To form the nucleus of a Universal Brotherhood of Humanity, without distinction of race, creed, sex, caste, or color.

II. To promote the study of Aryan and other Eastern literatures, and sciences, and demonstrate the importance of that study.

III. To investigate unexplained laws of Nature and the psychical powers latent in man.

Officers: President, H. C. Donnelly; Vice-President, Mrs. Beatrice Towers; Secretary, Miss Elizabeth Towers; Treasurer, Miss Louise J. Kirkwood; Librarian, Miss Maggie Towers.

YOUNG MEN'S CHRISTIAN ASSOCIATION. In December, 1880, the Rev. John Dixon (now Dr. Dixon) and Mr. Ralph E. Prime called a meeting of pastors and others to consider the organization of a Y.M.C.A. in Yonkers. In 1881, Mr. John C. Havemeyer, a member of the State Committee, brought the proposition again to the attention of a few Christian men. The association was organized. Its Presidents have been, John C. Havemeyer, G. Livingston Morse, Lyman Cobb, Jr., Rev. Henry Baird, D.D., LL.D., John T. Sproull, W. W. Ellsworth, Theodore Gilman, George D. Mackay, H. Beattie Brown, M.D., and H. A. Bates. Its General Secretaries have been, Frank R. Wardle, Myron H. Scudder, Asa B. Bixby, A. F. Barrett, Clifton H. Mix, M. D. Brown, Walter F. Haskett. The association at first occupied rooms near the corner of Palisade and Main Streets. Thence it removed to No. 89 North Broadway. In October, 1894, it removed to No. 14 Main Street.

YOUNG MEN'S CHRISTIAN ASSOCIATION BADGE.

YOUNG MEN'S CATHOLIC ASSOCIATION. This association, composed of members of St. Joseph's Church was organized in September, 1871. It occupied at first a room in Public School, No. 6. When the church moved into its new building, a room was fitted up in it for the association.

TERRACE CITY COUNCIL, NO. 433, C. B. L. This council is a branch of the Catholic Benevolent Legion. It was organized January 14, 1894. At first it enrolled fourteen names. Its first officers were: President, J. F. Daley; Vice-President, P. J. Flannery; Treasurer, W. F. Harrigan; Secretary, Ralph E. McGreagle; Collector, John Hennessy. The council now enrolls fifty-four names. It insures its members and " pays death benefits according to the amounts insured." The present officers are: President, Henry J. Miller; Vice-President, John Day; Chancellor, Frank Duffy; Orator, John McCarthy; Treasurer, John E. Crowley; Collector, Patrick H. Linehan; Secretary, John L. Welsh; Marshal, Peter Boyle; Guard, Matthew E. Donnell.

SOCIETY OF ST. VINCENT DE PAUL. This is a benevolent society, and an adjunct of St. Joseph's (R. C.) Church. It was organized February 18, 1877, and chartered in 1882.

THE ALUMNI ASSOCIATION OF YONKERS HIGH SCHOOL, HIGH SCHOOL BUILDING. Executive Committee and Officers for 1894–95: President, Richard Edie, Jr.; First Vice-President, Margaret R. Brendlinger; Second Vice-President, Analusia Barnard; Secretary, Robert V. Howes; Treasurer, Horace P. Allen; Historian, Mary C. Stilwell; John P. Radcliff, Jr. Ex-Officers for 1891–92: President, George V. Fowler; First Vice-President, George P. Holden; Second Vice-President, Jennie C. Marran; Secretary John Avery; Treasurer, James E. Howes; Historian, Lile M. Andrews. 1892–93: President, John Avery; First Vice-President, Richard Edie, Jr.; Second Vice-President, Margaret R. Brendlinger; Secretary, John Martin; Treasurer, James E. Howes; Historian, Sarah F. Mott. 1893–94: President, John Avery; First Vice-President, Margaret R. Brendlinger; Second Vice-President, John C. Harrigan; Secretary, Behrends Messer; Treasurer, Emma Menzer; Historian, Henry H. Banks.

ST. JOHN'S DAY NURSERY. The need of a day nursery in Yonkers having been perceived for some time, the Rev. Dr. Alexander Carver, Rector of St. John's Church, on February 17, 1896, called together the ladies of his parish and organized the charity known as "St. John's Day Nursery." Mrs. John Reid was elected President; Mrs. Kate Kellinger, First Vice-President; Mrs. Theodore H. Silkman, Second Vice-President; Mrs. William M. Williams, Secretary; Mrs. George H. Warren, Treasurer. The Board of Managers included these officers, also, the Rev. Dr. Carver and Messrs. George R. Bunker, John Clark, Mrs. Mary Chapman, Mrs. Thomas Ewing, Jr., Mrs. J. W. Feeter, Mrs. Isaac Milbank, Mrs. Edward S. Perot, Mrs. Edward Underhill, Mrs. Harry Holbrook, Mrs. Grace W. Roberts, Mrs. Albert E. Lawrence, Mrs. M. A. Knight, Mrs. A. Middleton Rose, Mrs. William W. Scrugham, and Mrs. Clark. Mrs. Chapman has since resigned.

The house, No. 144 Warburton Avenue, was rented for the nursery, and on April 15, 1896, was opened for the reception of children of any race and creed. The nursery is supported by voluntary contributions. A small charge of ten cents a day is made for the care of a child. The charity up to this time has proved a success.

YOUNG WOMEN'S CHRISTIAN ASSOCIATION. A meeting to establish a Young Women's Christian Association in Yonkers was held in April, 1891, in the First Methodist Church. Miss Georgia Hicks, since deceased, was chosen President. Previous to that date meetings of young people in various churches had been addressed by Franklin A. Soper, M.D., and Temperance Hall had been rented for a brief period. In May, 1891, the young women began to meet for their religious work in No. 2 Main Street (Getty Square). On June 11th of that year the Y. W. C. A. was organized at that place. The first officers were: President, Mrs. T. M. Lyall; Vice-President, Miss Georgia A. Hicks; Recording Secretary, Miss Minnie Hogel; Treasurer, Miss Anna T. Bate.

The society provided books, games and newspapers. Prayer-meetings were held every week. Membership, Boarding and Comfort Committees were appointed. Miss Anna T. Bate became the General Secretary in May, 1892. She was succeeded by Miss Mary Bartlett in February, 1893. In the autumn of that year a Board of Managers was elected. It consisted of Mrs. Allen Taylor, Mrs. Nathan S. King, Mrs. Joseph Steele, Mrs. Walter Thomas, Mrs. E. Alexander Houston and Mrs. William Okell. In 1893 Miss Mary L. Mellefont became the General Secretary, and a year later she was succeeded by Miss Louise Fuller, who served for a brief time. Her successor was Miss Mariette S. Bailey. The first anniversary of the association was held in June, 1892, in the chapel of St. John's Church.

The association has a Bible-reading Club, and classes which meet on Sunday afternoons for Bible study. It has employment and boarding-house agencies and committees to visit the sick. Class instruction has been given in dressmaking, plain sewing, fancy-work, elocution, vocal music, reading, penmanship and arithmetic. The number of books in the library is slowly increasing. In November, 1894, the association removed to the more cheerful and convenient rooms (No. 32 South Broadway) which it had rented. The work of the society was resumed there January 1, 1895. In February, 1895, the Yonkers society became an auxiliary of the State Association. In the same year it was incorporated, and a Board of Trustees was elected. It consisted of Messrs. Charles R. Otis, Isaac W. Maclay, James C. Beemer, Lyman Cobb, Jr., and Allen Taylor. Lyman Cobb, Jr., was elected President and Treasurer of the Board and Allen Taylor, Secretary.

The present officers of the association are: President, Mrs. T. M. Lyall; First Vice-President, Mrs. E. R. Holden; Second Vice-President, Mrs. F. Davis; Secretary and Treasurer, Miss Anna Bate; Assistant Secretary, Miss S. E. Edwards.

THE HOLLYWOOD INN. On January 23, 1893, free reading and smoking-rooms were opened at No. 18 Main Street, for the purpose of furnishing men a substitute for the saloon. At this time the work was carried on under the direction of a committee of men appointed by the St. John's Chapter of the Brotherhood of St. Andrew, an organization of the Protestant Episcopal Church.

This committee was made up as follows: Chairman, James E. Freeman; Secretary, Edwin A. Smith; Treasurer, Theo. I. Underhill; George B. Wray, Burton D. Bagley and Charles E. Back. The work was established on purely secular lines and supported most liberally by all the denominations of Yonkers. During the first two years the attendance averaged 12,000 per annum. So great was the interest manifested by workingmen in the work that it was determined to secure larger quarters and increase the accommodations. In the fall of 1895, two large floors were secured at No. 3 North Broadway, one floor being arranged with club-rooms and reading-rooms for men and boys, and the other floor devoted exclusively to games.

At this time pool tables were introduced, and a cigar counter, with facilities for serving hot coffee, beef-tea, etc., etc. Immediately the attendance began to increase, and instead of 1,000 per month, it averaged over 1,000 per week. The place became the rendezvous for different trade and social organizations, and the attendance in the reading-rooms kept pace with that in the game-rooms.

Mr. W. F. Cochran, who had, from its inception, been a liberal contributor towards the work, at this time became impressed with the great value of such an institution and the importance of so increasing its accommodations and facilities as to make it a permanent and complete workingmen's club. To this end he addressed the following letter to its President:

"YONKERS, March 16, 1896.

"JAMES E. FREEMAN,
"President of Hollywood Inn, of Yonkers, N. Y.
"MY DEAR SIR:
"Having watched with much interest (especially during the past winter) the establishment and development of the work carried on by the organization known as the 'Hollywood Inn,' I have been and am more and more impressed with its importance, and the great benefit it may become to this community.

"The house now occupied being entirely inadequate to its present requirements, much less to its future extension, it becomes a serious question how best to provide more suitable quarters, such as will enable its managers to add new features which will be educational and social as well as useful mentally, morally and physically.

"Believing this work, when thoroughly organized and established, will be self-supporting, as has been elsewhere demonstrated; and with a conviction of the boon it will prove to the class of men and boys it will reach, and for whose benefit it was conceived and is being conducted, I am led to offer you under certain conditions (hereinafter named) such accommodations as this work requires, and believe the problem of success or failure will be decided during the next three years.

"I now make the following proposition to yourself and Board of Managers, which if accepted, it will soon be ascertained how far the citizens of Yonkers are willing to contribute to the support of an institution which apparently appeals so favorably to the public spirit of this and other communities.

"If you will secure for the next three years annual subscriptions of $3,000, thus insuring the running expenses of the institution, exclusive of rent (which I will contribute), I will erect for the use of the Hollywood Inn a commodious building (on a central site) which will be not only an ornament to our city but a building complete in all its appointments for the fullest and best development of this important work.

"Should the next three years prove its success, in which I have the greatest confidence, satisfactory arrangements will be made such as are deemed best for its permanent home.

"With such a building and suitable managers, many new features may be added, which in turn will place the Hollywood Inn of Yonkers among the great institutions of the land—and who shall say how

HOLLYWOOD INN.

far-reaching its influence for good may be felt? Sincerely trusting you may succeed in meeting the only condition necessary to secure this new home, and which condition is to secure the work until it becomes established,

I remain sincerely yours,

"WM. F. COCHRAN."

In accordance with this letter the Board of Trustees addressed a letter to the public asking them to enable the board to meet the only condition imposed by Mr. Cochran. A very generous response met this appeal, and the ground for the new Inn was broken on Tuesday, the 7th day of July, 1896. The building is the finest and most complete workingmen's club in this country. No cost was spared to build and equip it in the most modern and improved manner. The building occupies the site on the southwest corner of South Broadway and Hudson Street, is forty feet wide, 100 feet deep, having six full stories.

The floors are arranged as follows: In the basement, kitchen, lavatory, baths, bowling alleys and billiard-room. On the first floor, office of the institution, free reading-room and smoking-room; free circulating library of 5,000 volumes, for the exclusive use of workingmen and their families; a lunch room and a large room devoted to the purposes of a workingmen's club. On the second floor, a gymnasium, with shower and needle baths, locker rooms and two large club-rooms. On the third floor, a hall with gallery, seating 500 persons, and class-rooms and dressing-rooms. On the fourth floor, the Board of Directors' room and class-rooms. On the fifth floor, a boys' club, comprising a gymnasium, with baths and lockers, reading-rooms and game-rooms. Janitor's apartments are also on this floor.

The building is fitted with every modern appliance for the comfort and convenience of the men, the reading-rooms being supplied with all the best papers and magazines, and the books in the library selected with a view to furnishing the men with technical works on mechanics and the arts, as well as those on history, fiction, biography, etc., etc.

The workingmen's club is the principal feature of this work. They have their own organization and act in conjunction with the Board of Directors. There is also a co-operative labor bureau and a savings institution. The Board of Directors is as follows: William F. Cochran, James E. Freeman, Edwin A. Smith, Harold Brown, Burton D. Bagley, Geo. B. Wray, Chas. S. Diehl, Chas. E. Gorton, Geo. R. Bunker, S. T. Hubbard, Geo. McNeir, Robert N. Flagg, M.D., Samuel L. Cooper, Wilbur Larremore, Frank P. Treanor, Eugene C. Clark, Alexander Laird, Leslie Sutherland, D. A. Waterman.

THE WOMAN'S CHRISTIAN TEMPERANCE UNION. This society was organized February, 1878. For five years it leased the Grand Army Hall, then on the site of the present Getty Square Railroad station. Mrs. M. M. Smith, a most estimable lady, was President. It began with a coffee-room, which soon developed into a restaurant, where sometimes more than 100 would take their noonday meal. A reading-room was opened. Often from 100 to 175 boys assembled to enjoy games, books, papers and singing. Sabbath afternoon services were sustained. A Band of Hope was organized, and increased until it enrolled over 1,000 members, who had pledged themselves to abstain from alcohol, tobacco and profanity. Mr. Henry H. Kroenke, the janitor, organized a German Sunday-school which held its sessions in the hall. Out of this school the German Methodist Church grew.

When the Railroad Company purchased the hall, the W. C. T. U. was without a home. It hired Humboldt Hall for their Band of Hope meetings, and held business and devotional meetings in church lecture-rooms. The coffee-room was discontinued for about two years. Messrs. Colgate and Trevor generously gave a twenty years lease of their property on the west side of North Broadway, south of Wells Avenue, formerly the site of the Baptist Church, with the promise of a lease of ninety-nine years when the society had paid $10,000 on the building they proposed to erect.

The corner-stone of the W. C. T. U., hall was laid in the spring of 1884. In December a restaurant was opened and has been conducted ever since by the society. Regular business and devotional meetings of the Union are held, also regular meetings of the Loyal Temperance Legion, formerly called Band of Hope. The Band of Hope and Loyal Temperance Legion, since organization, have enrolled in Yonkers 2,815 members.

In addition to the work above described, the other work of the W. C. T. U. is prison and jail visitations, distribution of temperance literature, missionary activity, sales of articles made by the poor, securing situations for those out of work, and superintending the business which the building imposes, for its twenty-two rooms are generally hired by those who appreciate a tidy and pleasant home free from the temptations and discomforts which are so frequently experienced in cheap lodging houses.

The society could accomplish still more, were it relieved of its remaining debt of about $2,000, the balance on the building, which cost $13,000. The two Presidents, the late Mrs. M. H. Smith and Miss Helen A. Rollins, both faithful and persevering workers, have accomplished much for the welfare of the city. They and Mrs. G. B. Balch, Mrs. C. P. Bynon, and Miss G. A. Hicks, Mrs. Raffaelle Cobb, Mrs. Martha A. Dedrick and others, have prosecuted this important work, for which a great number rise up and call them blessed.

The Young Women's Christian Union flourished for a brief time. The members then united with the W. C. T. U.

THE WOMAN'S INSTITUTE. This noble institution is the outgrowth of a small library which was instituted May 1, 1880. As the years increase the citizens of Yonkers more and more realize how large is the debt of gratitude they owe Miss Mary Marshall Butler, the daughter of Mr. William Allen Butler, for the gentle but potent influence whereby ennobling aspirations and brightness have come into so many lives within the city of her home. When, in the spring of 1880, she and other young ladies, her like-minded and earnest colleagues, opened a free library in two small rented rooms in a plain building (No. 49 Palisade Avenue, nearly opposite the carpet factory), they did not anticipate the future dimensions of their unpretentious work. Building better than they knew, they have come to gratefully realize by happy experience the truth of the promise, that a sure reward awaits him who gives a cup of cold water only in a disciple's name.

The library which they opened was small, and almost all of its five hundred volumes were from the book-shelves of friends who had become interested in the work. It was supported by voluntary contributions. During the first summer the library was open for one hour each Saturday afternoon. In the autumn of the same year Miss Mary B. Daniels was engaged as Librarian, and the rooms were open one hour and a half on Monday, Wednesday and Saturday of each week; 600 applied for books the first year; the circulation was 3,000.

When the work had thus expanded and more room was needed, Mr. Samuel Shethar gave the use of a plain brick dwelling-house (No. 48 Palisade Avenue) for a term of years. Some improvements were made, carpets laid, and furniture brought in, and on September 1st the library was transferred to its new quarters. The young ladies who, as a committee, had had the work in charge, realized the need of organization, and they formed themselves into a society under the name "Yonkers Free Circulating Library for Self-supporting Women." Miss Mary M. Butler was President and Treasurer, and Miss Mary B. Daniels, Secretary. The Executive Committee was composed of Miss Butler, Mrs. Walter Graves and the Misses Baird and Uhl.

A free reading-room was opened on appointed evenings; a parlor and class-room were made inviting by taste and by deft fingers. Evening-classes in penmanship, choral music and needlework were formed. Self-supporting women over sixteen years of age were eligible to membership. Membership fees were small. Within five or six years, dating from the opening of the library in 1880, the association had about seventy-five members, and the number of volumes on its shelves had increased by donation and purchase from 500 to 1200.

As the proportions of the work enlarged and the thoughtful managers had time to reflect upon its needs and its possibilities, they became convinced that in order to assure the permanence of the institution and to give it facilities for doing its increasing work, it should be provided with a substantial building. A plot on Palisade Avenue was bought for $1,700, and the present handsome building erected.

Among those who contributed the largest amounts for the building fund were, Warren B. Smith, Mr. and Mrs. William Allen Butler, Walter W. Law, Mrs. John B. Trevor, John Sloane, William D. Sloane, Miss Mary B. Schieffelin, Henry J. Hardenbergh, A. D. Juilliard and the Waring Hat Manufacturing Company. The building and furniture cost about $31,000. The entire property is valued at about $50,000.

"The Institute Building is a substantial brick structure, fifty feet in width and sixty-five feet in depth, designed by Henry J. Hardenbergh, architect, and built by Joseph Perry, mason, and S. Francis Quick, carpenter, on the lots extending from the southerly side of Palisade Avenue, 100 feet to Engine Place. It is constructed and furnished throughout with the best material, is heated by steam, and is lighted by electricity and gas.

"The first floor contains, besides a store that is rented, as a source of income, ample accommodation for the 'Woman's Exchange,' a library and reading-room, social parlor and offices.

"The second floor is mainly occupied by the 'Institute Hall,' (extending the entire depth of the building,) which has been used for lectures, entertainments, calisthenic exercises, etc.

"On the third floor are class-rooms for the various branches of instruction, including dressmaking, needlework, millinery, plain sewing, kitchen-garden, also a large and thoroughly equipped cooking-class room, where by arrangement with the Board of Education, instruction has been given to about 130 girls in the public school in addition to the Institute pupils.

"The basement is fitted up with lavatories and baths, a laundry, janitor's kitchen and sitting-room."

The opening exercises and reception were on April 3, 1893. Several addresses were made on that occasion. The address of Mr. William Allen Butler was published. The following extracts from the address will suffice to indicate the purposes of those who founded the Institute and who, from the beginning, have nourished it. Among other sentences to which Mr. Butler gave utterance were these:

"It is not necessary to dwell on the details of the work which is to go on within these walls. It is in one respect, multiform and many-sided, but in its main purpose it is direct and single. Its aim may be expressed in two words—Christian helpfulness. It is woman's work for woman. It is of the practical, sensible, serviceable type, which is at last beginning to take on shape and substance in our latter-day movements for the benefit of human kind. . . . First and foremost is its relation to the self-supporting working-women. It is meant to draw them to this place as a central point of happy and useful activities, as a circle within which they can avail freely of whatever lightens toil, stimulates capacity and elevates the mental and moral nature. From the basement story to the top floor this building stands for these good and high ends. . . .

"Tried by its fruits, the work stands the test. It has set a bright spot in many experiences otherwise too often overclouded with anxieties and cares. Unravel and tear out from the warp and web of the lives of our working-women the bright threads interwoven by these kindly ministries, shot through and through by the magic shuttle of sympathy, and the golden pattern will be lost, and only the sombre background left. . . . Let it be understood that this work is distinctly Christian, and not restrictively Christian. . . . The Christian churches and ministers of Yonkers have, in The Woman's Institute, an ally and a support whose value they can hardly over-estimate.

"What is done within these walls has in it the element of spirituality and the highest Christian grace, working upon well established lines which have stood the test of experience and have, we think, the seal of the Divine favor. . . .

"The Institute has come to stay in the centre and current of our local activities and interests. All it asks is that cordial co-operation by our citizens which will keep it in touch with the whole life of our city, social, civic and religious."

Since occupying its new building the salutary influence of the Institute has increased.

"By its connection with the University of the State of New York, to which it was admitted June 5, 1894, its educational possibilities are greatly increased, and its library brought under the State aid act, through which it has already received $200 for the purchase and binding of books and periodicals; by its associate membership with the State Committee of the International Board of Women's and Young Women's Christian Association, and The Association of Working Girls' Societies, it keeps in active, sympathetic touch and intimate acquaintance with the work of these organizations, and has the benefit of their conferences, to which its delegates are admitted; through its connection with Pratt and Drexel Institutes and the Teachers' College, by the employment of teachers from these institutions, it receives much stimulus and many practical suggestions; through the University Extension Society it has received the benefit of excellent lecture courses; and last but not least is the great advantage it derives from the helpful and cordial co-operation of the Board of Education of the city of Yonkers.

"The approximate estimate that more than 1200 individuals have been registered in one or more departments of The Institute, and that the building has been visited for one or another purpose by an average of 3,000 per month, testifies to the constant activity of the work of the past year."

The Woman's Institute Club has demonstrated its usefulness. The library probably has 3,000 volumes. The Employment Bureau has rendered inestimable service. The Civic League has promoted an interest in and study of civic affairs, and has endeavored to co-operate with the other societies and with the city authorities "to promote a higher public spirit and better social order," and by becoming a Stamp Station of the Penny Provident Fund, the Institute is helping children as well as adults to form habits of thrift and economy.

The plot on which the Institute stands was bought subject to a mortgage of $10,000. At the beginning of 1896 that had been reduced to $8,500. In the autumn of 1896, Mrs. William F. Cochran, whose name is a synonym for generosity and kindness, gave the Institute $5,000.

Trustees: President, Miss Mary Marshall Butler; First Vice-President and Treasurer, Miss Harriet Allen Butler; Second Vice-President, Mrs. John Reid; Mrs. Wm. H. Doty, Miss Mary S. F. Randolph, Miss Susie Leeds Heermance, Mrs. J. Lindsay Porteous; Advisory Board, Mr. William Allen Butler, Mr. Walter W. Law. Mrs. Perit Coit Myers, Miss Cornelia B. Lawson, Miss Sarah Williams and Miss Joanna Williams, former trustees, rendered long service.

Miss Florence J. Parsons, General Secretary and Superintendent, has done much to promote the usefulness of the Institute. After a long and faithful service as Librarian, Miss Mary B. Daniels resigned, and Miss Grace Hanford succeeded to the office. She is the present incumbent.

HOME FOR THE AGED AND INFIRM, DISTRICT NO. 1, I. O. B. B. This institution was founded by the First District of the Independent Order of B'nai B'rith ("Sons of the Covenant"), a Jewish secret and beneficial order. Each inmate of the home is a member of the "Order," and was for a number of years a contributor to its fund. The amount of contribution was one dollar a year. The grounds and buildings cost $122,000. There is a synagogue in the second story. The building was dedicated June, 1882.

ST. JOHN'S RIVERSIDE HOSPITAL. During 1869, the Rev. Dr. Thomas A. Jagger, now Bishop of Southern Ohio, was the honored and beloved rector of St. John's Episcopal Church, of Yonkers. Some of the poor of his parish were sick. The attention of his people were called to their condition and their need. "St. John's Parish Sick Committee" was organized. The members of this committee were "fifteen noble, capable women, with warm hearts, earnest, and steadfast of purpose." "St. John's Invalid Home," was opened about November 1, 1869. The "Home" was a small house at the southwest corner of Warburton and Ashburton Avenues. Those injured in railroad accidents, and other patients were brought to the home, and it soon proved to be too small. The "Grove House" (east side of Woodworth Avenue and a short distance north of Locust Street), was rented by the founders of the home. A charter for the institution was secured. The name written in the charter is St. John's Riverside Hospital.* The charter is dated May 27, 1870. Soon after this date, St. John's received the proceeds of the sale of the property of the "Yonkers Hospital Association." By act of the Legislature, passed March 15, 1866, the Town Board was authorized to tax the town to raise money for a hospital or pest-house. The money thus raised was used to purchase land in Mile Square, known as the Mott property. The "Yonkers Hospital Association" was formed soon after the levy of the town tax. The Legislature by act dated May 30, 1868, directed the Town Board to convey the Mott property to the "Yonkers Hospital Association," which subsequently sold the property and gave the cash and transferred the mortgage to St. John's Hospital, which retained the mortgage but used the money to pay for the "Grove House."

The St. John's Riverside Hospital, on Woodworth Avenue, was for a long time the only hospital in Yonkers. It proved to be an indispensable institution. Its chaplain, the Rev. Lyman Cobb, Jr., while faithful to the bank of which he was an official, rendered unfailing service to the hospital.

The building on Woodworth Avenue, after some years, proved to be too small and not well adapted for a hospital. Then Mr. Wm. F. Cochran and his wife, Mrs. Eva S. Cochran, generously gave to the society the present large and elegant buildings and grounds on Ashburton Avenue. On June 28, 1894, the deed of the new hospital buildings and grounds was delivered by Mr. Cochran on behalf of himself and Mrs. Cochran to the Board of Managers of the hospital. The record of the dedicatory services is in the hospital annual report of 1894. In closing his address on that occasion Mr. Cochran said:

"And now you will allow me to add that no word can be spoken here to-day that can in any way add to the pleasure we experience in contributing this gift to the cause of humanity.

"'The reward is in the doing.' And while we are spared to go in and out among you, the pleasure that will daily come to us in the consciousness of sickness and suffering relieved will be second only to the precious thought, that when we are called hence, this Christ-work will continue, and that we have been permitted to contribute towards this result, and to lay the corner-stone, as it were, of a lovely charity that will go down 'the ages'—a blessing to the sick, wounded and sorrowful of God's children. And now, gentlemen, for the service of man, and in the name of Christ, my wife and myself present to you the deed of this property. In accepting it you assume a great responsibility. The work will not go on alone, but will need sympathetic care, watchfulness and attention. It requires charity, love and forbearance in its management; perfect peace and harmony must prevail in all its departments; and I assure you that only accepted in the loving spirit in which it is given can it continue to grow and strengthen as it should. May God add His blessing."

* In the History of the Westminster Church, Yonkers, is a record of Dr. J. H. Pooley's influence as an advocate of the building of a hospital. This record seems to question the accuracy of some parts of the generally accepted history of the hospital.

MEDICAL STAFF OF ST. JOHN'S HOSPITAL, YONKERS.

1. William H. Sherman.
2. David John.
3. Emil Schopen.
4. H. Beattie Brown.
5. William S. Coons.
6. E. N. Brandt.
7. Samuel E. Getty.
8. E. M. Morrell.

ST. JOHN'S RIVERSIDE HOSPITAL, ASHBURTON AVENUE, YONKERS.

The officers of St. John's Riverside Hospital for 1895, were: President, William F. Cochran; Vice-President, Norton P. Otis; Secretary, Horace H. Thayer; Treasurer, Lyman Cobb, Jr. Board of Managers: William F. Cochran, Norton P. Otis, Lyman Cobb, Jr., S. Emmet Getty, James Lawson, Horace H. Thayer, Ethelbert Belknap, John O. Campbell, Edward Underhill, J. H. Hubbell, Philip Verplanck, Andrew Deyo, P. J. Elting, Charles E. Gorton, John K. Lasher, William B. Edgar, James Stewart, Jr., William H. Doty, William F. Corwin, Theodore H. Silkman, George R. Bunker, Harold Brown, J. Harvey Bell, F. W. R. Eschmann; Superintendent, Mrs. Mary D. Burnham.

Medical Staff, 1895: Consulting Surgeon, Lewis A. Stimson, M.D., New York City; Consulting Physician, E. G. Janeway, M.D., New York City; Consulting Gynecologist, G. M. Edebohls, M.D., New York City; Consulting Laryngologist, William K. Simpson, M.D., New York City; Consulting Orthopedic Surgeon, T. Halsted Myers, M.D., New York City; Attending Surgeons, William H. Sherman, M.D., Emil Schopen, M.D.; Attending Physicians, David John, M.D., H. Beattie Brown, M.D., E. N. Brandt, M.D.; Dispensary Physicians, William S. Coons, M.D., E. M. Morrell, M.D., S. E. Getty, Jr., M.D.; House Physicians, Clarence W. Buckmaster, M.D., J. DuBois Vanderlyn, M.D.; Bacteriologist, William D. Horne, M.D.; Chairman of Medical Staff, William H. Sherman, M.D.; Secretary of Medical Staff, H. Beattie Brown, M.D.

ST. JOSEPH'S HOSPITAL. St. Joseph's Hospital was built by "The Sisters of Charity of St. Vincent de Paul." Mr. William Schickel, of New York, was the architect. The cornerstone was laid September 24, 1888. The hospital was opened for patients March 19, 1890. The cost of the building, not including furniture, was about $150,000. It is capacious enough to receive sixty-five patients, not including those for whom there is provision in the infant ward.

The chapel, wards and various rooms were furnished by different patrons. Mr. Michael Walsh and Mrs. N. Benziger contributed to purchase the chapel furniture. Among those who furnished private rooms, or gave contributions to furnish the wards were, Mrs. T. C. Connell, Mrs. F. O'Neill, Mrs. ———— Jaffray, Mrs. J. W. Reilly and M. Dee, of Yonkers. The Children of Mary, of St. Mary's Church, Yonkers, also gave contributions for furniture. Among out-of-town patrons who contributed, were the ward pupils of Mount St. Vincent Academy, the firm of Lord & Taylor, and the O'Neill's of New York. In 1896, the Children of Mary, of St. Mary's Church, furnished the ward for infants. Recently the operating-room was refitted at considerable expense. The work was most thoroughly done in a manner that is now deemed essential in aseptic surgery.

ST. JOSEPH'S HOSPITAL, SOUTH BROADWAY, YONKERS.

When the hospital was opened its dispensary was also opened. It is estimated that at the end of the current year, the number of cases treated at the dispensary will have aggregated 5,000. In 1896, a training-school for nurses was opened at St. Joseph's Hospital.

Medical Board, 1896: Consulting Surgeon and President of Medical Board, Peter A. Callan, M.D.; Consulting Surgeon, Joseph D. Bryant, M.D.; Consulting Gynecologists, J. Duncan Emmet, M.D., H. F. Hanks, M.D.; Dermatologist, George H. Fox, M.D.; Neurologist, Landon Carter Gray, M.D.; Consulting Surgeons and Physicians, A. C. Benedict, M.D., E. J. Harrington, M.D., V. Browne, M.D., S. Swift, M.D., E. M. Hermance, M.D.; Visiting Surgeons and Physicians, P. H. Pyne, M.D., N. A. Warren, M.D., H. Moffat, M.D., G. N. Banker, M.D., E. E. Colton, M.D., C. A. Miles, M.D., J. T. Gibson, M.D., J. L. Porteous, M.D.; Pathologist and Curator, Ellsworth E. Colton, M.D.; House Physician and Surgeon, Frederic Van Vliet, M.D.; Assistant, Richard Stinson, M.D.

MEDICAL STAFF OF ST. JOSEPH'S HOSPITAL, YONKERS.

1. P. H. Pyne.
2. Edgar M. Hermance.
3. Samuel Swift.
4. Nathan A. Warren.
5. J. Lindsay Porteous.
6. Henry Moffat.
7. Peter A. Callan.
8. Valentine Browne.
9. Garret N. Banker.
10. Charles A. Miles.
11. Ellsworth E. Colton.
12. Albert C. Benedict.
13. Edwin I. Harrington.
14. James T. Gibson.

The House Physicians and Surgeons from the opening of the hospital until the present time were, Drs. Murphy, Burns, McKay, Littlewood, Mooney and Van Vliet. The present assistant is Richard Stinson, M.D. Two physicians connected with the corps of physicians of St. Joseph's Hospital have died—Dr. Wallace in 1895, and Dr. Swift in 1896. Two of the members of the Advisory Board also have died. The annual report of the hospital for 1895, contains memorial paragraphs. The reference to the deceased physician is as follows:

"It is with deep sorrow and regret that the Medical Board of St. Joseph's Hospital records the death of one of its most valued members—Dr. William B. Wallace, Consulting Gynecologist of the Hospital from its opening until his death, June 7, 1895.

"Dr. Wallace was a physician of sound and practical knowledge, and a gentleman endeared to his colleagues. Of spotless character, genial, tender of heart, and generous, we trust the Great Physician of mankind has given him the eternal reward of peace and rest for his well-spent, self-sacrificing life."

The following appreciative sentences record the esteem in which Mr. Cornell was held:

"St. Joseph's Hospital lost a faithful patron and a generous friend in the death of Mr. Thomas C. Cornell, a member of the Advisory Board. When St. Aloysius' Academy was destroyed by fire, and the Sisters of Charity determined to supply its place by the present structure, no one in the city of Yonkers rendered more willing and effective service than this gentleman. He was ever ready with his purse and advice in giving them assistance. During the fair held on the completion of the building, for the purpose of securing funds to pay the indebtedness, night after night was he present, encouraging the ladies in their philanthropic efforts, and freely bestowing his means for sweet charity's sake."

Mr. Francis O'Neill is referred to as "a kind and generous friend of the hospital," whose death was a loss to the institution. He was a member of the Advisory Board. Sister Aloysius and Sister Lucina have had the charge of the hospital. The latter is in charge at the present time.

HOMŒOPATHIC HOME AND MATERNITY. The society which founded this institution was organized on January 16, 1894, through the influence of Mrs. W. W. Law, who was at that time elected President, and who has remained the President up to this date. The Vice-Presidents were Mrs. (General) Thomas Ewing and Mrs. (Dr.) John Reid. In 1895, Mrs. Reid resigned and Mrs. William A. Butler was elected in her stead. Mrs. Fred D. Blake has been Secretary and Treasurer since the date of organization. The original Board of Managers were: Mrs. H. J. Andrus, Mrs. William Allen Butler, Mrs. F. D. Blake, Mrs. J. Hall Dow, Mrs. (General) Thomas Ewing, Mrs. Walter W. Law, Mrs. Isaac Milbank, Mrs. (Dr.) John Reid, Mrs. Alexander Smith, Mrs. William H. Thorne. In 1895, there were added Mrs. M. H. Brownson, Mrs. (Dr.) R. O. Phillips, Mrs. (Dr.) R. R. Trotter, Mrs. C. W. Flagg, Mrs. S. B. Northrup, Mrs. E. R. Coles. In 1896, Mrs. S. B. Northrup and Mrs. J. Hall Dow resigned. The latter, by reason of her efficient work while on the active list, was made an honorary member.

The home was at first in two rooms on Nepperhan Avenue. After the first year a small house on Woodworth Avenue (No. 246), was rented. The society was incorporated in 1896, and during the same year, through the generosity of Mrs. W. W. Law, purchased a house, No. 127 Ashburton Avenue.

Staff of physicians: President, Dr. R. O. Phillips; Secretary, Dr. R. N. Flagg; Dr. R. R. Trotter, Dr. R. P. Fay, Dr. H. Keith. New York City members of the staff are: Consulting Surgeon, Dr. F. E. Doughty; Surgeon, Dr. E. G. Tuttle; Oculist, Dr. C. H. Heefrich.

THE LEAKE AND WATTS ORPHAN HOUSE. This institution (incorporated in 1831) was founded by the liberality of John G. Leake and John Watts. It was located at Bloomingdale, New York City. The corner-stone of the present house was laid February 22, 1889. The children were brought from New York to their new home October 27, 1891.

Children between three and twelve years old are received in the home, and are kept until they arrive at fifteen years of age. The boys are taught in the class-rooms, and are also taught on the farm, in the shoe shop, carpenter shop, tailoring department and mechanic-room. The girls learn sewing and other useful industries.

Mr. George R. Brown is the popular and efficient Superintendent.

YONKERS SOCIETY FOR THE PREVENTION OF CRUELTY TO CHILDREN. This society was incorporated December 14, 1881. The following were the incorporators: Galusha B. Balch, M.D., S. H. Thayer, Jr., W. H. Wray, Richard W. Bogart, John O. Campbell, Henry Kronke, Edward P. Baird, J. W. Skinner, George Stewart, Cyrus Cleveland and Thomas B. Caulfield.

Galusha B. Balch, M.D., has been the President of the society from its organization. The Secretaries have been Stephen H. Thayer, Jr., Rev. J. Hendrik de Vries, Henry W. Bertholf, D.D.S., and Mrs. Edward R. Shaw. The counsel have been: Hon. Edward P. Baird, William C. Kellogg, Esq., Hon. Matthew H. Ellis, and Hon. Stephen H. Thayer. Most of the court cases have been looked after in court by the President. Since the organization of the society there have been 960 complaints, involving over 2,000 children.

SOCIETY FOR THE PREVENTION OF CRUELTY TO ANIMALS. The American Society for the Prevention of Cruelty to Animals, has an officer stationed in Yonkers. Mr. Ferdinand Garnjost, a citizen of Yonkers, rendered the society service as an officer for fourteen or fifteen years without compensation. A subscription paper circulated in Yonkers was generously signed, and Mr. Garnjost was appointed under pay, January 7, 1896. The officers, uniform is the same as that of the city police, except the helmet, which is of a lighter color.

CHARITY ORGANIZATION SOCIETY. This society was organized in May, 1883. The present officers are: President, Norton P. Otis; Secretary, George Rayner, Jr.; Executive Committee, William F. Cochran, Fisher A. Baker, A. C. Benedict, M.D., Lyman Cobb, Jr.; G. Hilton Scribner, W. W. Scrugham, and the Commissioner of Charities, *ex-officio*. This corps of officers, with but few changes, have served the society from its organization. Thomas C. Cornell was Treasurer almost from the date of organization until his death, December 29, 1894. No successor has as yet been chosen. James S. Fitch was Secretary to May, 1887. W. C. Kellogg was Secretary to March, 1890. From that date to the present time George Rayner, Jr., has been Secretary. The society is a private organization, maintained by voluntary contributions. It is in correspondence with other Charity Organization Societies, when occasion requires. Its object is the discouragement of mendicancy and indiscriminate alms-giving, and the elevation and improvement of the condition of the poor.

The various churches have their young people's associations. In the Protestant churches are such societies as Y. P. S. C. E., Epworth League, Baptist Young People's Association, Social Christian Workers, King's Daughters, etc. In the Roman Catholic churches also are societies of young people.

Yonkers has a Home for Aged Women, and also has several societies or associations which have not been recorded in this chapter because there was at hand no data from which to write even the date of their organization. Among the unrecorded organizations are the Yonkers Symphony Society, the Hatter's Union, the Polish Society, and the Swedish Society, Sons of the North. There also are in the city one or more labor organizations and one or more Building and Loan Associations* which are unmentioned on these pages.

A number of Yonkers social, literary and athletic associations flourished for a time, and then disbanded. In a former chapter, reference is made to the Library Association, an influential society of the village period. Another popular society was the Yonkers Lyceum. It was organized in 1868, and incorporated in 1872. The Osceola Club, organized in 1874, long since disbanded. The Viewville Literary Association flourished for a number of years. Mr. Charles Lockwood built a reading-room on Nodine Hill for the association. Subsequently he gave the property to the Dayspring Presbyterian Church. Two vigorous societies of the past were Athena and Knickerbocker. Their members encouraged debates and literary entertainments. Among the organizations, which flourished for a period were the Yonkers Rifle Association, of which Matthew H. Ellis was Captain in 1875, and the Veteran Base Ball Club, composed of business and professional men, who gave one day in each year to an old-fashioned game of ball. The Good Templars and Sons of Temperance maintained their orders in Yonkers a number of years. The Yonkers Club, which was organized in 1880, had its headquarters a short distance south of the First Presbyterian church. Subsequently it purchased a plot opposite St. Paul's church and erected a fine club-house. When the club disbanded, the house was sold. In the days of the old Lyceum, another organization of young men devoted itself to athletic sports, but, after a while, interest in it decreased. About 1878, the Glenwood Athletic Association was organized, but in a few years it was disbanded. The Mile Square Athletic Association was organized in 1878. It had a life of about four years. About 1879, the Yonkers Athletic Association was organized. It was disbanded about 1882. Five years ago, more or less, still another Athletic Association was formed. It also is now numbered among disbanded associations.

* The number of new buildings (public and private) now in course of construction in "the Yonkers" speaks volumes for the bright future of the city. *The Yonkers Weekly Gazette* of September 5, 1896, contains an article which records the new buildings now in process of construction. The writer of that interesting article claims that the entire building budget for Yonkers for one year will be fully $1,200,000. He names the buildings and specifies the estimated cost of each.

CHAPTER XVI.

YONKERS INDUSTRIES.

WHEN Henry Hudson was in the valley of "The Great River of the Mountains," he bought furs of the "wild men." Previous to that year (1609) the merchants of Holland had resident agents in Russia purchasing furs. When the crew of the Half Moon gave the Hollanders information about the newly-discovered country which abounded in fur-bearing animals, and about the willingness of the Indians to sell beaver, wild-cat, otter, mink, and other skins for trinkets, fur merchants became much interested. In 1610, they fitted up a vessel and dispatched it to the parts from which the Half Moon had come. Unless the fight, which the Indians of the lower Hudson had had the year previous with the crew of the Half Moon, prevented friendly intercourse, it is not improbable that the Hollanders, who came in 1610, bought furs of the red men of Nepperhaem. Either in that year, or soon afterwards, fur trading began. That was the first business in which white men engaged within the boundaries of the territory now known as Yonkers. The next was that of purchasing lands.

In 1626, Director Minuit bought Manhattan Island for the West India Company. He and his officers estimated that the area of the island was 11,000 Dutch morgens, more than 22,000 acres. They paid the Indians sixty guilders ($24) for it. Its present estimated value is over $2,000,000,000. The red men were delighted with the glittering beads and baubles and brightly-colored cloths. About the same year Minuit purchased lands in Westchester County. In 1646 Van Der Donck received his grant, and, although the children of the forest had previously sold their land to Minuit, Van Der Donck paid them for it to obtain a quit-claim. They were unfamiliar with the pale face's idea of ownership, and considered territory, which they had previously sold, as still their own if they retained or regained possession of it. "They understood the right of occupation and use, and nothing more."

The business next in chronological order to fur trading and purchasing real estate was that of sawing logs and grinding grain. When the pioneer settlers began to build their log-houses they needed a saw mill, and as soon as they began to till the ground and raise grain they needed a grist mill. There was a horse mill on Manhattan Island in the time of Governor Minuit. Wind-mills were erected there while he was Governor. The increasing products of the soil necessitated the erection of mills. The wind-mills were used especially for sawing logs. In a paper, written to Holland, Van Der Donck says that previous to 1649 he had built a saw mill on "De Zaag Kill" (the Saw Creek). When the first grist mill was built is not known.

These pioneer industries were followed in due time by others, which were established when there was need for them. On the map of 1813 a "merchant mill" and a saw mill are designated as located west of the Post-road, a fulling mill on or near Chicken Island, and Guion's mills, at the east of the Glen. One writer says that at that time there were five mill buildings on the Nepperhan for grinding grain and plaster and for sawing and fulling. Several industries, which had their beginning in Yonkers, probably within the first twenty-five or thirty years of the nineteenth century, long ago disappeared, and the fact of their having been in the town is retained in the memory of only the oldest inhabitants. For example: There is at Tuckahoe an old stone building, the corner-stone of which is marked 1814. When the Hodgman Rubber Company bought it in 1852, it was used as a cotton factory. For what industry it was built, and when the cotton factory was established there, the author is unable to record.

Among the Yonkers industries of the past were the manufacturing of soldiers' belts, conducted by Robert Dingee in the Glen; the business of the buckskin factory, adjoining and north of the Guion Mill, conducted by Allen Peacock and others; the manufacturing of bone buttons by Abner Sanford, over the grist mill in the Glen; the manufacturing of paper book covers in the mill in the Glen, and the business of the logwood factory, which was conducted in the Glen by a Mr. Griffen. It was probably several years previous to 1850 that he purchased the water power at that point and erected a logwood factory. Logwood and other colored woods were brought up from New York and ground. The acids for dyeing in various colors were extracted. Logwood grinding in the Glen was also at one time conducted, it is said, by Messrs. Russell, Styles & Hibbard. A foundry is said to have been established in Yonkers years ago, and the village papers refer to Holder's piano factory in Spring Street in 1864.

In early years pickle factories were located in Yonkers.* The farmers, however, shipped most of their pickles to New York. Among the Yonkers industries of more recent establishment, not mentioned in the subjoined chronological list, are boat-building, bottling of beverages, carpet-cleaning by steam, manufacturing of awnings, furniture, carriages, baking-powder, coal-bags, concretes, candies, barrels, corks, dynamite, hammer-handles, harness, hat-blocks, ice, monuments, cornices, mouldings, neckwear, patterns, pavement, picture frames, porous plasters, sash-doors, blinds, scrolls, etc.

These and other industries are conducted by citizens whose names are recorded in the Directory of 1895 and 1896. In 1883, Mr. Edward Underhill established the business of storing furniture, general merchandise, etc. He built his storage warehouses, No. 11-17 Ann Street, in 1894. A number of stores (dry-goods, grocery, hardware, book, boot and shoe, carpet and oil-cloth, clothing, confectionery, crockery and glassware, drug, flour and feed, seed, fruit, liquor, toy and jewelry) are the successors of houses established years ago, or have recently been opened in the city. Limited space will not permit more extended reference to them.

CHRONOLOGICAL LIST OF INDUSTRIES.

INDUSTRIES.	ESTABLISHED.	INDUSTRIES.	ESTABLISHED.
Fur Trading with the Indians,	1610	Carpets (Fern Brook Co.),	1881
Purchasing Land,	1626	Medicine Factory,	1881
Saw Mill,	previous to 1649	Paper and Wooden Box Factory,	1881
Grist Mill,	—	Sanitary Plumbing (Washburn & Moore),	1882
Glue Factory,	previous to 1824	Sugar Machinery,	1883
Hat Body Manufacturing,	1828	District Telegraph,	1884
Veneer Mill,	1845	Gear Cutting, etc., (American Co.),	1885
Carpet Factory (Messrs. H. & M.),	about 1846	India Rubber and Gutta Percha Insulation,	1886
Morocco Factory,	1850–69	Electric Lights,	1886
Rubber Manufactory,	1852	Steam Laundry,	1888
Elevator Works,	1854	Wire Picket Fence Factory,	1891
Hat Manufacturing Machinery,	1854	National Sugar Refinery,	1892
Illuminating Gas Manufactory,	1854	Bag Manufactory,	1892
The Silk Works,	1855	Carpet Factory (Yonkers Co.),	1892
Special Machinery,	1857	Electric Motors and Dynamos (Otis Electric Co.),	1893
Brewery,	1858	Hat Bands and Ribbons,	1893
Sugar Refinery (Howell's),	1862	Crown Smyrna Rug Co.,	1894
Arms and Mowing Machines,	1862–63	Nickel, Silver and Gold plating,	1895
Carpet Factory (Alexander Smith),	1865	Elevator and Mill (Deyo),	1895
Soda Water Factory (D. H. Smith),	1866	Postal Telegraph Cable,	1895
Cigar Factory,	1871	Steam Heating (Barr, Reynolds & Co.),	1895
Gas, Light, Fuel and Power,	1875–84	Boat Building (Fearon),	
Wool Extract,	1876	American Laundry,	
Plow Factory,	1878	Carpet Factory (Skinner),	
Telephone Exchange (Westchester Co.),	1880		

* On Sunday afternoon, November 17, 1895, the old saleratus factory of Charles Harriman, at Spring Hill Grove, burned. It had been built some years ago on the ruins of the old pickle factory. It was three stories high, about 50 feet by 100 feet in dimensions. It was in use as a barn and stable when it caught fire.

REPORT OF 1894, SUBMITTED JANUARY 28, 1895, OF NEW YORK STATE FACTORY INSPECTORS, TO THE LEGISLATURE OF THE STATE OF NEW YORK.

NAME OF FIRM.	Goods manufactured.	Males.	Males under 18.	Males under 16.	Females.	Females under 21.	Females under 16.	Number children who cannot read or write English.	Hours of labor of minors.
American Laundry Co.	Laundry work.	3			10	6			55
City Steam Laundry.	Laundry work.	10	2		15	8			60
Dean Plaster Co.	Porous plasters.	10	2	1	6	3	1		59
Eickemeyer & Osterheld Manufacturing Co.	Electrical machinery.	80	6	2					59
Empire Hat Works.	Fur hats.	220	10	6	80	35			58½
Fern Brook Carpet Co.	Ingrain carpets and fleece linings.	81	5	1	135	40	2		60
Flagg, Howard W.	Wool and fur hats.	90	4		40	10	2		59½
Friedman & Wolf.	Cigars.	3			5	1			54
India Rubber and Gutta Percha Insulation Co.	Rubber covered wire.	50			4	2			58½
Maltine Manufacturing Co., The.	Malt extracts.	14			16	8			58
National Sugar Refining Co.	Sugars and syrups.	300							66
New York Pharmacal Association.	Lactopeptine.	12			13	8			58
Otis Bros. & Co.	Elevators.	350	3						59
Otis Electric Co	Electric motors.	60							59
Pass Bros.	Hat bands and ribbons.	27	2		15	5			55
Paton & Hayward.	Paper and wooden boxes.	6			10	8			58
Pentreath, John.	Foundry.	16							60
Rose Leather Co.	Leather.	48							59½
Rowland, J., & Sons.	Fur hats.	67	3		30	10			58
Sanders, D., Sons.	Steam and gasfitters' tools.	52	2						59
Shaughnessy, James W.	Silk ribbon.	16	1		12	4	1		56½
Skinner, Geo. B.	Thrown silk.	11			12	2			60
Skinner & Connolly.	General machinery.	12							59
Smith, Alex., & Sons' Carpet Co.	Tapestry carpets.	180	20	9	509	150	8		60
Smith, Alex., & Sons' Carpet Co.	Printing carpet yarn.	166	35	20	110	20			60
Smith, Alex., & Sons' Carpet Co.	Worsted yarn.	98	20	7	258	100	22		60
Smith, Alex., & Sons' Carpet Co.	Moquette carpets.	267	35	21	364	130	9		60
Thomson, John.	Paper boxes.	6			24	12	2		60
Waring Hat Manufacturing Co.	Fur hats.	700	80	42	300	100	29		60
Washburn, W. F., Brass and Iron Works, The.	Plumbers' tools.	40	3						59
Wolf, Jacob.	Cigars.	4							54
Yonkers Carpet Manufacturing Co.	Carpets.	50	4	1	75	20			60

SAW MILLS. The exact location of the saw mill which Van der Donck built in the woods of Nepperhaem about 250 years ago (1646?) is unknown. Perhaps it stood on the north bank of "De Zaag Kill" (English, The Saw Creek), south of the site, where, probably, less than forty years later (1682?), Frederick Philipse built the southern part of Manor Hall. About the year 1700, Jacobus Van Cortlandt constructed a mill-pond, now called Van Cortlandt Lake, in Yonkers, by damming up Tippett's brook. He also built a saw mill there probably at that time. In 1804, there was a mill on the north bank of the Nepperhan, southwest of Manor Hall. At the same time a small saw mill stood north of the site of the present *Yonkers Statesman* Building, No. 13 Main Street, and another mill which was under the direction of John Guion, was located at the east end of the "Glen." It is said that at one time, there was a dam across the Nepperhan, about west, or a little northwest, of the present stone steps, leading up into St. John's Cemetery, and that a saw mill stood near the dam. About 1813, there was a marble-sawing mill near Kingsbridge. On the map of 1813, a place on the west side of the Post-road, not far from the Nepperhan Bridge, is designated as the site of a saw mill. Guion's mills still stood in 1813, in the "Glen." On the map of 1843, the location of a saw mill is indicated as on the south bank of the Nepperhan, probably north of the site of the present *Yonkers Statesman* Building. On the map of 1847, a point on the north bank of the Nepperhan, southwest of Manor Hall, is designated as the site of Copcutt's mahogany saw mill. On the same map are designated the locations of the pine saw mill of Messrs. O. S. and P. W. Paddock, and the saw mill of Mr. L. P. Rose; the former near what is now the corner of Warburton Avenue and Main Street, and the latter north of the site of the present *Statesman* Building.

GRIST MILLS. When pioneer settlers began to multiply in "De Jonkheer's Landt," a grist mill became indispensable, but the date of the building of the first one is not recorded. It was probably located on the north bank of the Nepperhan, southwest of the site of Manor Hall. Previous to 1700,

Frederick Philipse had built a grist mill on that site. It is probable that the grist mill at Van Cortlandt's was built in 1700, or soon after. About the year 1800, Alexander Macomb erected a four-story grist mill east of Kingsbridge. Its power was supplied by the alternate flow and ebb of the tide, against its under-shot wheel. It 1804, there was a grist mill north of the site of the present *Statesman* Building. In the early part of the century, Gilbert and John Guion had a grist mill at the east end of the "Glen." The foundations of the mill were stone, one side forming a portion of the dam. The mill was a frame structure. It burned in 1844. The Messrs. Guion removed from Yonkers about 1825. Gilbert went to Fordham, and subsequently to Greenburgh. After the Guions removed, the grist mill was operated by Abner Sanford.

On the map of 1813, a point on the north bank of the Nepperhan, southwest of Manor Hall, is designated as the site of a "merchant mill." On the map of 1843, the same place is designated as the location of a "flour mill." On the map of 1847, the site of L. P. Rose's grist mill is designated as the southeast bank of the Nepperhan, about 250 feet west of the Post-road. A flour mill was built in 1851, or 1852, on the site of the Hutchinson & Mitchell Carpet Factory (see map of 1847). The mill was known as the Yonkers Flour Mill. Business was conducted there by F. S. Miles. His successors were Miles & Peek, Peek & Wolf, Peter F. Peek, and Cornelius W. Peek, who was operating the mill as late as the Eighties.

GLUE FACTORY. Northwest of the grist mill in the Glen, and across what was called Guion's lane was a glue factory in the first quarter of the nineteenth century. It was established previous to the year 1824. It is said that Robert Dingee, who established the business there, had previously conducted the same business on Chicken Island.

A few years ago, a glue factory which stood on the south side of Yonkers Avenue, a few rods east of the railroad crossing, burned. It had been conducted many years by the Messrs. Weiderhold.

THE HAT INDUSTRY. In 1828, William C. Waring and Hezekiah Nichols began to manufacture, in Yonkers, bodies for wool hats. Mr. Waring had previously been in charge of the carding-room of a cloth mill in Putnam County. There he had learned to card wool. When he came to Yonkers, he and Mr. Nichols began their manufacturing business in an old-fashioned grist mill at the east end of the Glen at what has been known for years as the sixth fall. In 1834, Messrs. William C. Waring and Obed, and Prince W. Paddock formed a partnership. The firm was Paddock & Waring. Soon after they established their business, John T. Waring, then a youth of about fourteen years of age, came to Yonkers from Southeast, his native town. He entered into their employ and began to learn the business. In 1837 or 1838, Anson Baldwin was a partner in the business, and the firm name was William C. Waring & Co. At first they manufactured hat bodies, and subsequently wool hats. In 1844 the factory was burned. Their business was then removed to the fifth fall, north of the present Elm Street. The privilege was

WILLIAM C. WARING.

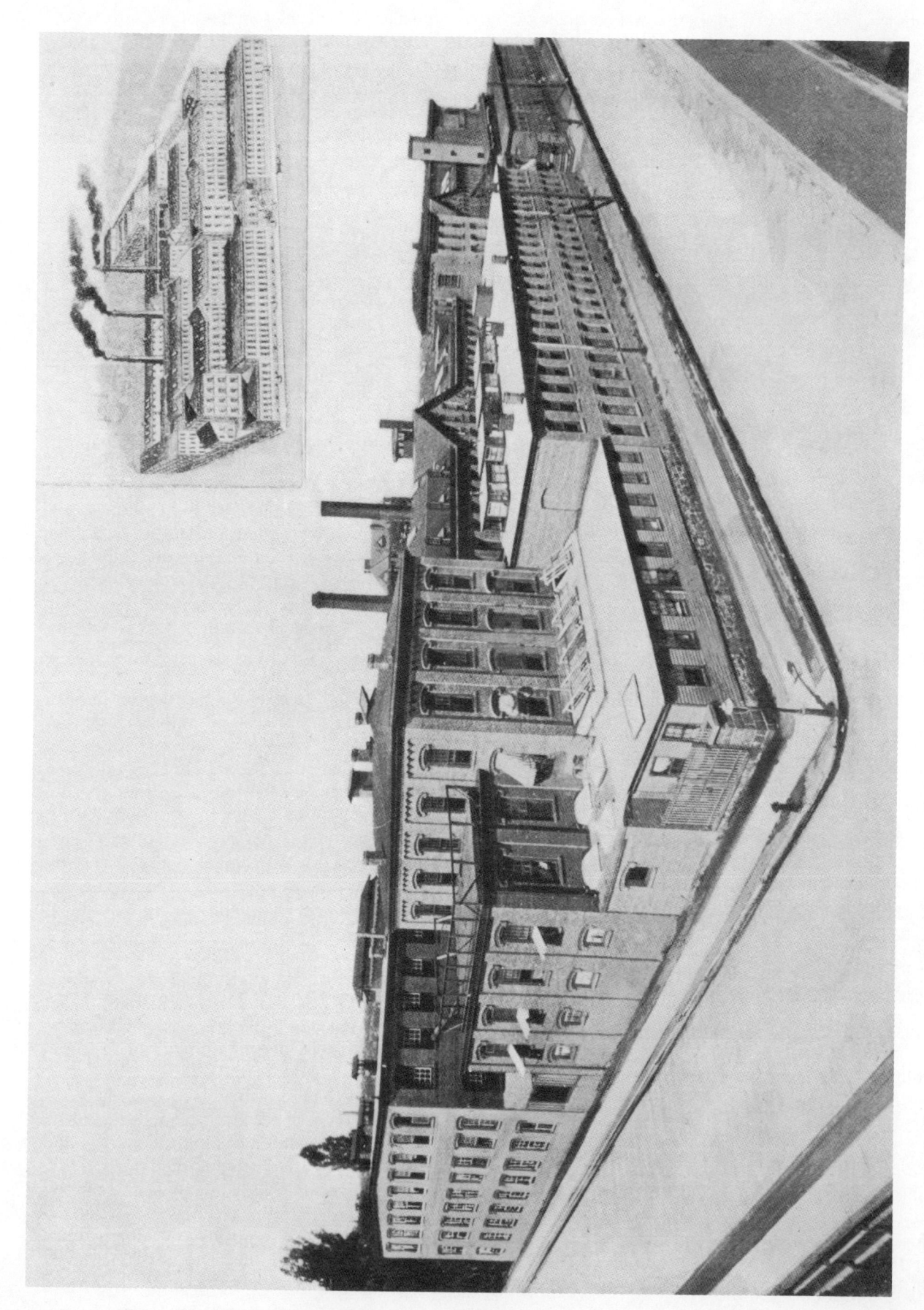

THE WARING HAT MANUFACTURING COMPANY, YONKERS.

purchased of Lemuel W. Wells, and a frame building was erected. Subsequently, the firm of Waring & Co. dissolved partnership. From 1844 to 1849, John T. Waring was associated with his brother. In 1849, he established a business for himself, locating his factory in an old building on Chicken Island, and afterward on the north side of Elm Street. When Waring & Co. dissolved partnership, William C. Waring built another factory farther north. Yonkers then had three hat factories. Subsequently, Mr. Baldwin and William C. Waring were again associated in business. In 1862, Hall F. Baldwin and Ethan Flagg bought out William C. Waring. They conducted business fifteen years. Their factory was known as the "Union Hat Factory." After 1877, which was the year in which Mr. Flagg withdrew, Hall F. Baldwin conducted the business. It closed in 1833. John T. Waring was sole proprietor of the business which he established in 1849. It steadily increased. About 1858 or 1859, his brother, Edward Waring, was associated with him, and the firm was John T. Waring & Co. In 1857, he had bought of William C. Waring & Co., their factory on what is now Elm Street. It was enlarged and business conducted in it for five years. In 1862, the large factory on the south side of Elm Street was erected, and several years afterward, William C. Waring became a member of the firm of John T. Waring & Co. Fourteen years of prosperity were enjoyed in the Elm Street factory. At one time 800 men were employed and between 9,000 and 10,000 hats were manufactured daily. Forty-five hundred dollars was the capital with which John T. Waring began business in 1862. In 1876, capital, property, machinery, etc., of the John T. Waring Hat Company aggregated almost a million. In 1868, he had bought thirty-three acres of land on an eminence overlooking the Hudson, and had there erected a stately residence known as Greystone. Land, building and improvements are said to have cost him nearly $500,000. Reverses struck him in 1876 and swept away his fortune. The Hon. Samuel J. Tilden purchased the Greystone property for $150,000. The factory business was for a time conducted by William C. Waring as agent, and subsequently by Charles H. Coffin, who also was the agent.

The firm of William C. Waring, Belknap & Co., was organized in 1877. Under their direction the business of the "Eagle Hat Factory" was conducted in the Elm Street buildings, one of which is five stories high and as to dimensions 225 x 50. It has two extensions, one of which (200 x 40) is three stories high and contained the engine and boiler and other rooms. The other extension was occupied by the blocking department and dye shops. The steam engines had a capacity of nearly 500 horse-power. The two acres which constitute the premises on which the buildings stand front on Elm Street. The firm at one time manufactured as many as 12,000 hats a day. In 1882, the establishment passed into other hands and has since been occupied by various industries.

John T. Waring was not daunted by his reverses. His genius for business and his characteristic perseverance soon enabled him to acquire another fortune. Removing from Yonkers he made his home in Boston. He formed a partnership with his eldest son, Arthur Baldwin Waring, whose efficient aid he enjoyed in days of reverses and of returning prosperity. The firm was known as The Waring Hat Manufacturing Company. A contract was made with the State of Massachusetts to employ its convict labor. The contract having been fulfilled, the Warings returned to Yonkers about 1878, and purchased a large brick building on Vark Street. It was built during the Civil War for the manufacture of arms, and was originally known as the "Starr Arms Works." It was subsequently occupied by other companies, the last of which was the New York Plow Company. This building was renovated and stocked with the best machinery. In 1878 or 1879, the Waring Hat Manufacturing Company began business in the Vark Street building. Soon after they began to manufacture tapestry velvet carpets, but within about five years their hat business had developed to such proportions that all their room was needed for that industry and they sold out the tapestry machinery. The Vark Street property has at the present time (1896) nearly double the capacity it had in 1878. Some of the processes of hat manufacturing in this factory are Mr. John T. Waring's own inventions. The machine used for sizing hats was invented by him and yields a large income.

In 1895 the Waring Hat Manufacturing Company, purchased the machinery and fixtures of the H. W. Flagg factory, and began that year to manufacture in that building ladies' wool hats. The company is probably, as to the number of hats it manufactures, the largest hat factory in the world. A factory in Belgium employs perhaps more operatives, but its work is slower. The Waring Hat Manufacturing Company employed about 300 hands when they began to do business in Vark Street. In 1895 they employed about 1,700 hands, including 200 in the factory formerly occupied by H. W. Flagg. They manufacture in the Vark Street buildings about 900 dozen fur hats a day, and in the other factory about 250 dozen wool hats for ladies, an average of between 1,100 and 1,200 dozen hats daily. Having so many employees, their pay roll aggregates about $17,000 a week. They purchase most of the rabbit and coney skins in Australia, and the factory requires as its daily supply about 35,000 of these imported skins. The felt is made from them. Some of the skins come from France and New Zealand. The factory covers a plot of ground embraced in two entire city blocks. Most of the buildings are three, and four-story structures. The power which drives the machinery are two powerful Corliss engines—one is 450, and the other 250 horse power. Steam is generated by eight great boilers of 100 horse power each. In 1896 the company began to manufacture leathers for its hat trimmings. Their leather works were established on Chicken Island.

All of the departments are under the direction of expert Superintendents. The President of the company is John T. Waring. The Treasurer and General Director is Arthur B. Waring. Joseph Miller is Superintendent and Le Grand W. Ketchum has charge of the books.

THE H. W. FLAGG HAT FACTORY. In 1876, Ethan Flagg finished a brick building at the corner of James and John Streets. It is four stories high, and 50 x 80 feet. It was occupied at first by Messrs. Howard W. and Wilbur W. Flagg. The former purchased his partner's interest about the first part of the year 1877, and conducted the business until the spring of 1895. He occupied the main building, the engine-house, dye-house and drying-rooms. From about 1890 or 1891, he also occupied the building adjoining on the north which, as to dimensions, is 45 x 100 feet, and three stories in height. William Macfarlane formerly occupied that building as a silk factory. At one time Mr. Flagg employed about 180 operatives, and paid wages amounting annually to from $65,000 to $70,000. The factory had facilities for manufacturing from 350 to 400 dozen hats every ten hours. Mr. Flagg's business closed about April, 1895. The Waring Hat Manufacturing Company purchased the machinery and fixtures, and continued the manufacturing of hats in the building Mr. Flagg had occupied.

THE YONKERS HAT MANUFACTURING COMPANY was incorporated March 22, 1883, with the following officers: President, Eugene V. Connett; Treasurer, Ethelbert Belknap; Secretary, William R. Mott. Other members of the company were William H. Belknap, James Stewart and George W. Beach. The company leased from Samuel Shethar, three buildings on John Street. In May, 1887, Mr. Connett withdrew from the company, and William H. Belknap was elected President, the other officers retaining their former positions. In the spring of 1893, the factory was in operation day and night, employing 400 hands and manufacturing over 400 dozen hats every twenty-four hours. On the morning of May 18, 1893, the principal part of the plant was burned, causing a loss in stock and machinery of $97,000, on which there was an insurance of $53,500. The company then rented a part of the main factory on Elm Street, formerly occupied by John T. Waring & Co. Soon after the fire, Peekskill (N. Y.) Improvement Company made overtures, with the purpose of influencing them to remove their business to Peekskill. Arrangements were finally made, a factory built, and the plant moved to that village, where manufacturing was begun in February, 1894, under the name "Yonkers Hat Manufacturing Company," which was retained until January, 1895, when it was changed to "The Peekskill Hat Manufacturing Company." Other changes in the company have since been made.

THE EMPIRE HAT WORKS were established in 1887, by Messrs. E. V. Connett, Clarence Rutan and William Read. They manufacture fur, felt, and soft hats. After a time Mr. Rutan retired. The firm in 1895, was composed of Messrs. E. V. Connett, William Read, E. V. Connett, Jr., and Ernest R. Connett. The factory from the beginning has been under the management of Mr. John O. Campbell and has increased its output from 100 to 200 dozen hats per day. It has about doubled its production since its establishment. About 400 were employed in 1895. The building, which is on the south side of Dock Street, has been enlarged and the business is flourishing. On December 31, 1895, the co-partnership of Messrs. Connett, Read & Co., was dissolved, and two firms were constituted—Messrs. E. V. Connett & Co., and Messrs William Read & Co., the latter owning, operating and controlling the entire product of the large factory on Dock Street, known as the Empire Hat Works, and the factory on John Street, known as the Simmond's Hat Manufactory. They also secured the product of one of the leading Orange (N. J.) factories, and will do a business similar to that of the old firm. The New York office of Messrs. Connett, Read & Co., was Nos. 17 and 18 Waverly Place. Messrs. William Read & Co., have their office there.

The late John Rowland and his sons established a hat factory in the Shethar Building in the year 1891. John Rowland, Sr., died August 25, 1891. The business is now conducted under the title John Rowland & Sons. The co-partners are Ralph W., and John Rowland. At first about eighty hands were employed. At the present time the full capacity is about 125.

JOHN COPCUTT.

VENEER MILL. In 1835, Mr. John Copcutt, who then lived in New York City, had his veneer mill at West Farms. When it burned, he removed his business of veneer sawing to Yonkers. It was in the year 1845, he built his mill on the Nepperhan, on the foundations of a pre-occupying grist mill, southwest of Manor Hall. He sawed mahogany, rosewood, bird's-eye maple and other fine woods into veneer for cabinet work, using both upright and buzz-saws. The mahogany and other fine timber was sent up from his New York yard. Alfred Anderson had charge of the mill. The logs were brought to Yonkers by the Ben Franklin line, and carted to the mill. The veneer was carted back to be shipped to the city. Mr. Copcutt's mill pond covered what is now Warburton Avenue, between Dock and Main Streets, the site of the present *Yonkers Herald* Building and adjoining structures on the east of the present street. His mill burned about 1875. He then abandoned the business of veneer sawing in Yonkers, and had his sawing done in New York. When the Yonkers mill was rebuilt, the "Eagle" Pencil Company rented it for their factory.

Mr. Copcutt had a thorough knowledge of fine woods. He knew where to purchase the best mahogany, rosewood and satinwood. He knew the quality of the timber of St. Domingo, Cuba, Honduras, Mexico, Porto Rico, Rio Janeiro and other lands. He knew the timber which supplies the prettiest wood pictures, and which has the richest color and grain. The cutting of rosewood veneers into ribbons to veneer picture frames was an interesting process. Mr. Copcutt would often laughingly invite his friends to the Yonkers mill to "see a block of ribbon unrolled." The wood was run off just as quickly as though it were ribbon. Mr. Copcutt was a long-time resident of Yonkers, in which he owned much real estate, and saw the place develop from a village to a city. He died in 1895.

CARPET FACTORY. Messrs. Hutchinson & Mitchell had a carpet factory north of the site of the present *Statesman* Building. It was established probably about 1846. Their looms were hand looms, and their business was conducted on a small scale. Their factory was burned about 1851 or 1852.

MOROCCO FACTORY. About 1850, the business of pulling wool and of manufacturing morocco and sheep-skins from hides was established at the corner of Nepperhan Avenue and New Main Street by Mr. Robert Grant. Mr. James Kitteringham, in 1869, occupied the place for the manufacture of morocco. He remained there about three years. Subsequently he became a member of the firm of Messrs. Rose, McAlpine & Co., which began business at the corner of Nepperhan Avenue and Main Street. He remained with the firm only a short time. In 1882 the firm erected a factory on the south side of Elm Street, near the bridge. Messrs. G. L. Rose, G. L. McAlpine and W. W. McAlpine constituted the firm. The Elm Street works were known as the Nepperhan Leather Works. They had previously manufactured fancy leathers. In the Elm Street building they made morocco of every description. At one time they employed between 150 and 200 hands. The works are not now in operation.

RUBBER MANUFACTORY (Hodgman Rubber Co.) This business was established in New York City in 1838, by Daniel Hodgman, who removed his works to Tuckahoe (town of Yonkers), in 1852. The original building at Tuckahoe, in which he commenced business, is of stone. The date, 1814, is inscribed on the corner stone. It was used as a cotton factory when Mr. Hodgman bought it.

ELISHA G. OTIS.

Daniel Hodgman died in 1874. The business has since been conducted by his sons and grandsons. It was incorporated in 1885, with Geo. F. Hodgman, President, and Charles A. Hodgman, Secretary. The present officers are: President and Treasurer, George F. Hodgman; Vice-President, Charles A. Hodgman, and Secretary, George B. Hodgman. The company employ over 500 hands, men and women. They manufacture rubber mackintoshes, sporting goods, horse clothing and all kinds of druggists' sundries, also a high grade of bicycle tires. Their main office is 459 and 461 Broadway, corner Grand Street, New York. They have a branch factory at Mount Vernon, N. Y., and branch stores at 21 West 23d Street, New York, and in Boston, Mass.

THE OTIS BROTHERS & CO., ELEVATOR WORKS. The company are the foremost builders of passenger and freight elevators in the world. It would not be possible to give a history of the great industry without mentioning the founder.

Elisha Graves Otis, who was the youngest of the six children of Stephen Otis, and was born August 13, 1811, was the inventor of the modern elevator, which has done so much for modern city life and development. Young Otis lived on his father's farm at Halifax, Vt., until the age of nineteen, when he left for Troy, N. Y. In the latter city he resided five years and was engaged in various building operations. On June 2, 1834, he was married to Susan A. Houghton of Halifax. She was the mother of his two sons, Charles R., and Norton P. Otis. She died February 25, 1842. In 1838, Mr. Otis returned to Vermont and engaged for a time in the manufacture of wagons and carriages. He continued in this occupation until 1845. His second wife was Mrs. Betsey A. Boyd, whom he married in August, 1846. A little later he removed to Albany and assumed the charge and direction of the construction of machinery in a large manufacturing establishment. Four years later he withdrew from this employment in order to establish works of his own, but was compelled eventually to give up this undertaking. We next find him holding the position of mechanical superintendent of a furniture manufactory at Hudson City, N. J. In 1852, this establishment was removed to Yonkers. Mr. Otis had charge, as organizer and mechanical superintendent, of what was called the bedstead factory (foot of Vark Street, subsequently occupied by the New York Plow Company), and also superintended the erection of a part of the buildings at Yonkers. It was during this later work that the idea of the elevator occurred to him. The story of his invention has been told as follows: During the building and equipment of this factory it became necessary to construct an elevator for use on the premises during the erection of which Mr. Otis developed some original devices. The most important was one for preventing the fall of the platform in case of the breaking of the lifting rope. The machine attracted the attention of some New York manufacturers, and soon after he secured several orders for elevators to go to that city. This was the beginning of the elevator business. So successful was Mr. Otis in the manufacture and the constant improvement of his new machine that he was obliged to withdraw from the Bedstead Manufacturing Company and confine himself entirely to the construction of elevators. He exhibited his new elevator at the Crystal Palace, New York, in 1851, where he attracted considerable attention by running the elevator car to a considerable height while standing upon it and then cutting the rope. The car did not fall, and by thus demonstrating his own confidence in the usefulness of the invention, orders for machines rapidly increased. Before the year of his death (1861), he had built up quite an extensive business and the Otis elevator had become well-known. In addition to his original invention, he constantly made improvements in the construction of the elevator, and was also the inventor of many important mechanical devices. In personal character Mr. Otis was a man of great worth and integrity. He was a member of the First Methodist Episcopal Church of this city and was also a strong anti-slavery and temperance man.

From 1854 to 1858 from five to fifteen men were employed, and the foreman was Charles R. Otis,

CHARLES R. OTIS.

his eldest son. About 1859 or 1860, Mr. Elisha G. Otis designed, constructed and patented an independent engine capable of high speed, to raise or lower the platform or car. This hoisting-engine marked the beginning of the system of steam elevators. In 1860 and 1861, Charles R. Otis invented and patented many important improvements. After the death of Mr. Elisha G. Otis in 1861, the Otis Brothers—Charles R. and Norton P.—formed a partnership for the continuance of the business. The beginning of the Civil War stimulated trade in war materials, and elevators came into demand for various business houses. Attention to business was required, and both brothers gave close attention to the developing industry. Charles R. Otis worked throughout the day, and sometimes during the entire night. Both sons made many inventions and improvements. Norton P. Otis spent much of his time visiting towns and cities throughout the country introducing the elevator. In 1864, Mr. J. M. Alvord had become a partner and the company was known as Otis Brothers & Co. In 1867, Mr. Alvord sold his interest to the Otis Brothers, after which a stock company was formed. Charles R. Otis was President, Norton P. Otis, Treasurer, and N. H. Stockwell, Secretary. Mr. Stockwell resigned the same year, and J. L. Hubbard became Secretary. The manufactory at the corners of Woodworth, Wells and Ravine Avenues, has been occupied since 1868. In 1872, business had increased to such an extent that during that year it amounted to $393,000. After the company was incorporated, the business continued to increase rapidly, until in 1882, when it was established on a basis of over $600,000 and rapidly increasing. In June, 1882, the brothers retired, selling their interest to a syndicate of capitalists. Later on the control returned to them again, and Charles R. was made President, which position he held until 1890, when he retired, and since then, his brother, Norton P. Otis, has been the President of the company.

Employment is given in this city to about 500 men, and there is a constructing force of about 150 constantly engaged in setting up elevators throughout the country. They have recently perfected an electric elevator. The company has adopted, and made part of its system an electric motor invented by the late Rudolf Eickemeyer of this city. Its valuable features are that it starts and stops with the car, thus economizing power, and it is under perfect control of the operator. The Otis elevators in use in New York City carry daily over 400,000 passengers. These elevators are also used in the Eiffel Tower at Paris, Washington Monument, D. C., the Manufactures and Liberal Arts Building (during the World's Fair in Chicago), Niagara Falls Tower, and the great trestle used by the Hudson County Railroad at Weehawken, N. J. They are also in use in every city of America, every large city in Europe and in South America and Australia, and quite a number in Egypt and China. The Otis Elevating Railroad in the Catskills, which carries passengers up an incline 7,000 feet in length in ten minutes, saving a journey by stage of four hours' duration, and the Prospect Mountain Inclined Railway at Lake George were built by this company. The officers of the company at the present time are: President, Norton P. Otis; Vice-President and Secretary, Abraham G. Mills; Treasurer and General Manager, Wm. Delavan Baldwin.

NORTON P. OTIS.

OTIS BROTHERS & CO.'S ELEVATOR WORKS—OTIS ELECTRIC CO.

OTIS ELECTRIC COMPANY. The Otis Electric Company began business in July, 1893. Norton P. Otis is the President, W. D. Baldwin, Vice-President and Treasurer, and W. E. Hodgman, Secretary. The company is incorporated. They manufacture electric motors and dynamos of a type invented and patented by the late Rudolf Eickemeyer, and they employ about 100 men. Their main building, four stories, brick, is 121 x 58 feet. The annex 46 x 27 feet. The four-story brick building was built in 1893.

HAT MACHINERY. The manufacture of hat machinery has been one of the foremost industries of Yonkers. The business was established by Mr. George Osterheld in 1854. In 1881, the manufacture of mowing machines was begun, this branch being in charge of Messrs. R. Dutton & Co., the hat machine firm being shareholders. Messrs. George Osterheld and Rudolf Eickemeyer constituted the first firm. In 1880, Mr. Osterheld's brother, Henry, came into the firm as his successor. The building in which the business is conducted is large, and is furnished with abundant power. Many hands are employed, most of them being skillful mechanics. All kinds of tools, machines and appliances used in manufacturing felt and wool hats are here made. The business aggregates many thousands of dollars a year. Reference to the many important inventions of Mr. Rudolf Eickemeyer is made in Chapter X.

ILLUMINATING GAS. The Yonkers Gas Light Company was organized in 1854, largely through the influence of Colonel William W. Scrugham. Reference to the early history of the Gas Works is in Chapter X. Works capable of supplying a daily consumption of 10,000 feet were erected, and gas was first delivered in 1854. In 1855, the sales were 1,000,000 feet; in 1860, 4,200,000; in 1870, 11,259,-000; in 1875, 21,144,000. After 1875, the competition of gas companies began to be sharp. In 1860, the illuminating power of the gas was twelve candles. Ten years later it was eighteen candles; in 1880, it was twenty-five candles.

In 1861, the price was $3.50. During the war, when labor and coal were expensive it was $4. In 1865, it had reached $5.75, for the cost of coal was then great. After 1865, the

WM. DELAVAN BALDWIN.

price of gas decreased to $5; in 1866, to $4.50 in 1870, to $4 in 1874, to $3 in 1875, to $2 in 1876, to $1.60 in 1895, and to $1.35 in 1896.

In 1861, fifty-two street gas-lamps were lighted, twenty-eight of them on the east side of Warburton Avenue. In 1870, there were 155 street gas-lamps; in 1871, there were 360; in 1895, there were 1,200 lamps in Yonkers costing $19 per lamp per year, with four feet burners, lighted 4,000 hours per year. In addition there were 781 lamps in the Twenty-Fourth Ward of New York City, supplied by this company.

The Presidents of the company have been James Scrymser, Robert P. Getty, Thomas C. Cornell, and William Warburton Scrugham, son of the first Secretary and Treasurer. The Secretaries of the company have been W. W. Scrugham, J. M. Gardiner, Cyrus Cleveland, J. D. McIntyre. The Treasurers have been W. W. Scrugham, H. W. Bashford, T. C. Cornell, W. W. Scrugham. Superintendents, Isaac

Battin, William Beal, James Slade. The names of those who have been members of the Board of Directors are as follows; those marked with a star were members of of the board in 1895:

	FIRST ELECTED.		FIRST ELECTED.
Sylvester S. Batten,	1854	Thomas W. Ludlow,	1863
Timothy C. Dwight,	1854	Samuel D. Babcock,*	1864
Robert P. Getty,*	1854	James M. Gardiner,	1865
Thomas C. Cornell,	1854	John Olmstead,	1872
Robert Grant,	1854	Stephen H. Condict,	1874
James Scrymser,	1854	Henry Anstice,	1877
Josiah Rich,	1854	Alexander Smith,	1877
Francis S. Mills,	1854	Edward C. Moore,	1877
William Warburton Scrugham,	1854	Warren B. Smith,*	1879
Henry W. Bashford,	1855	James Bruce,*	1880
Ethan Flagg,	1857	James Slade,*	1884
Aaron Peek,	1858	William Warburton Scrugham,*	1889
John Chadwick,	1859	John Kendrick Bangs,*	1894
Stephen H. Plum,	1860	Alfred Jones,*	1895
George Peters,	1862	Harold Brown,*	1895

SEWING SILK. The manufacture of sewing-silk and machine-twist was established in Yonkers in 1855, by George B. Skinner, who had been previously engaged in the same business at Mansfield, Conn. He occupied the stone building on Elm Street, which was erected in 1853 or 1854 for a cotton factory. Subsequently William Iles became a partner under the firm name of George B. Skinner & Co. This was the firm until 1884. They made machine-twist a specialty and at one time employed about 150 hands. The Nepperhan supplied their water-power. In 1887, Mr. Skinner removed the works to the brick building built on Elm Street, by John T. Waring. George B. Skinner, Sr., died in 1881. The business has since been conducted by his son George B. Skinner, as a silk-throwing mill, receiving silk in the raw state and preparing it for weaving purposes. About fifty hands were employed in 1895.

Mr. George B. Skinner is of the well-known New England family of Skinners, silk-throwsters. "He was one of the pioneer silk-throwsters and the most widely known of the family. All the family have been either silk-throwsters or silk-weavers for generations. He started a mill at Northampton, Mass., in 1850. William Skinner, the uncle of the present George B. Skinner, has a silk factory at Holyoke, Mass.

"The Yonkers factory is the only one of its kind in this vicinity. It has an equipment of about 15,000 spindles, and employs, when in full operation, about fifty operatives. George B. Skinner personally conducts the business. He is a practical man, having early mastered the technique of silk-throwsting.

"The operations employed in silk-throwsting are unique and delicate, requiring nice expert handling of the silk and the machinery. The spinning is generally done by women, they seeming to be more skillful and having a greater nicety of touch than men. On an average this mill spins 200 pounds of silk daily. The operation consists in spinning the fine strands of the raw silk into threads or cords of any required size or weight, for the use of silk-weavers.

"After these threads or cords are spun, they are again run into skeins and dyed any color desired. This business was established in 1853, by George B. Skinner, the elder. It has always contributed to the industrial reputation of Yonkers, as its products are used by silk-weavers all over the country. It also has made a reputation for the quality, durability and general excellence of the product. The factory is pleasantly situated on Elm Street near Palisade Avenue. The power employed is steam."

In 1859, another firm established the business of manufacturing machine-twist and sewing-silk. They occupied the basement of the Skinner factory. Messrs. William Macfarlane and William Westney constituted the firm, but within a few months, the latter withdrew and the business was conducted by Mr. Macfarlane. He removed his business twice, first about 1862 or 1863, to a frame building on Chicken Island, and in 1865 to a building on James Street. In 1885, the business was still conducted in that building, occupying two floors (45x100). After the death of Mr. William Macfarlane (1883), his sons, W. W. and Albert E., conducted the business, retaining the father's name. When Albert E. died, the surviving brother continued the business. In 1885, he employed about sixty hands, and a product of the factory was material for warp and filling for silk goods.

Messrs. Wm. H. Copcutt and Wm. A. Myers, in 1866, began to manufacture spool silk, machine-twist and embroideries. Their industry was conducted in Copcutt's mill, a brick building at the east end of the Glen. In 1872, Mr. Myers withdrew and Mr. John Copcutt became a member of the firm, which was known as William H. Copcutt & Co. The William H. Copcutt Manufacturing Company was incorporated in 1883, with a capital of $150,000. At one time about 300 hands were employed. When the Copcutt Manufacturing Company had dissolved, other business men continued to conduct the silk industry in Yonkers. F. A. Straus, manufacturer of thrown-silk, occupied, for a time, the Copcutt Building.

MACHINERY (D. Saunders' Sons). David Saunders, a Scotchman, settled in Yonkers in 1853, having previously lived in New York, from 1850. In 1857, he began business in a shop in a part of Miles & Peek's flour mill. In 1860, he moved into a building below the dam. It was owned by John Copcutt, and was subsequently used as a pencil-factory. In 1868, fire destroyed Mr. Saunders' property. He then built his factory on Atherton Street, occupying it in 1870. Beginning the business of ordinary jobbing, he afterward manufactured lathes and drilling machines as a specialty. In 1868, his drawings for tools, stock of patterns, etc., were destroyed by fire. He then turned his attention to the manufacture of gas and steam fitters' tools. At the beginning the firm consisted of David Saunders and his sons, William, Alexander, Leslie and Andrew. In 1865, William died, and then another son, Ervin, became a member of the firm. David, the father, died in 1873, and Andrew in 1885. The latter was an inventor. The firm own several patents. The main building (65x50) is of brick, and three stories high. There are also a boiler and engine-house and several adjoining shops. The firm has made no changes in its membership since 1885. They built, in 1894, a brick shop and store-house in the rear of the old shop. It faces the Hudson River. It is three stories in height. The wing of the main building is 55x40 feet. In 1892, the firm employed 120 men. Their specialty is machinery and hand tools for cutting and threading iron, steel, brass and copper pipe and fittings.

HENRY OSTERHELD.

They are continually improving their machinery. They ship to Europe, Africa, South America, Australia, Japan, Canada, and the home market.

GENERAL MACHINERY. Messrs. Charles E. Skinner and Frank H. Connolly began the business of manufacturing general machinery in Yonkers, in November, 1888. They located at No. 3 Nepperhan Street. At first they employed three men. In 1895, they employed twenty-five. They make a specialty of general weaving machinery, and their business is principally local, but they fill some orders which come from outside the State. Other machinists are William Garrabrant, John D. Hargraves, Thomas Morris, Walter R. Perrett and Noble Walsh.

BREWERY. The brewery was established by Edward Underhill, Sr. The first barrel of ale was brewed March 1, 1858. Henry & Co. succeeded the founder of the business. Edward Underhill, Jr., William Jackson and Robert Edgar were partners, under the firm name, E. Underhill & Co. H. W.

NATIONAL SUGAR REFINERY.

Underhill was a partner for a while. Then the business was conducted by Edward Underhill, under the name E. Underhill's Son. For several years the firm was Underhill & Jackson. At the present time it is Jackson & Co.

SUGAR REFINERY (Howell's). In 1862, Edward Underhill established a molasses house on the river shore south of the railroad station, to extract brown sugar from molasses, which was sold direct to the grocers. In 1888, the demand ceasing, it was sold to the sugar refiners and made into white sugar.

In 1863, Mr. Underhill and Mr. Wm. C. Waring were associated in this industry, the firm name being Underhill & Waring. In 1864, Mr. Edward W. Cole became a partner in place of Mr. Underhill, who withdrew. Mr. A. W. Doren was admitted in 1864. Mr. Waring retired in 1865. Then Mr. Jacob Read became a partner and the firm was Messrs. Cole, Doren & Read. Mr. Cole withdrew in 1866. Mr. Doren died in 1868. His interest was purchased by Mr. Read, who remained until 1875. The industry then passed into the hands of Messrs. Benjamin Howell & Co. Mr. Read was the Superintendent until 1888. Subsequently, by another change, the business came to be known as Howell's Sugar Refinery.

NATIONAL SUGAR REFINERY. The National Sugar Refining Company was organized in September, 1892. Nathaniel Tooker is the President, George R. Bunker, Manager, Albert Bunker, Secretary and Treasurer. The company began building its refinery in Yonkers in 1892, and began business in December, 1893. It imports raw sugars, cleanses and discolors them, producing white sugar. It also produces syrups. The refinery has a capacity of 2,500 barrels of refined sugar per day. Previous to the late rebellion in Cuba, which cut off supplies from that Island, raw sugar was imported from that country. Now it comes from the other West India Islands, and from Java, Egypt, the Island of Mauritius of the African coast, Porto Rico, Barbadoes and elsewhere. Beet sugars come from Europe. The company do all their own stevedoring work. The number of their employees averages from 300 to 400. In 1894, they secured the passage of a bill by Congress, constituting Yonkers a district of the Port of New York.

JAMES V. LAWRENCE.

FIRE-ARMS AND MOWING MACHINES. In 1862 or 1863, a large brick building was erected on Vark Street as a factory for the manufacturing of fire-arms. The Starr Arms Company was organized. Mr. Everett Clapp was its President. When the Civil War ended, and the demand for fire-arms ceased, the building was unoccupied until 1867. Then the Clipper Mowing Machine Company occupied it. They did business until 1874 or 1875.

THE SIMMONDS HAT MANUFACTURING COMPANY was organized June 15, 1894. The officers were: President, William Simmonds; Treasurer, George Simmonds; Secretary, Harry Forsyth. The present officers are: President, William Simmonds; Secretary and Treasurer, William Read.

The factory is located on John Street. About 250 hands are employed.

ALEXANDER SMITH AND THE FOUNDING OF THE GREAT CARPET MILLS.* As the threads are woven and interwoven in the fabrics manufactured at the great Alexander Smith & Sons' Carpet Mills, so the threads of the history of its founder are woven and interwoven in the history of this enormous industry. Since its inauguration in this city, it has not only been making carpets; it has also been making Yonkers.

Employing as it does to-day about 4,000 operatives, it serves to maintain and support almost one-third of our entire population. Certainly the founder of such an enterprise is worthy of the enduring affection and honor of all the citizens of the Terrace City.

Alexander Smith was born near Trenton, N. J., October 14, 1818. His father, Nathaniel Smith, was a farmer, and his early years were spent "close to nature's heart," where he gained a rugged constitution, and acquired that energy and perseverance which characterized all his efforts in after-life.

When he was sixteen years of age, his father moved to West Farms, N. Y., where he opened a small country store, and here the boy had his first experience in mercantile pursuits. For nine years he worked with his father, becoming during that time Postmaster and Colonel of the local militia. In 1845, having watched with the interest of an inventive mind the small carpet factory at West Farms, owned by James W. Mitchell, then employing twenty-five hand-looms, he purchased the property and turned all his energy and interest to the development of this infant industry. At the first the enterprise did not prove a success, and after operating the factory for several years, he closed its doors and went to Schenectady, where he remained for six months as Superintendent of a similar institution. Returning to West Farms he reopened his factory, experimenting with looms for the manufacture of tapestry ingrain carpets, for which he secured patents. These carpets were the principal product of the mill for a number of years. He carried on business in a modest way until the breaking out of the Rebellion in '61. It is interesting to note here the development of the Axminster loom, which was ultimately to give the firm a world-wide reputation. Its unforeseen, undreamed-of beginning, was due to the meeting, during the winter of 1849-50, of Halcyon Skinner and Mr. Smith. Mr. Skinner had become known

ALEXANDER SMITH.

to Mr. Smith as a skillful artisan, and the carpet manufacturer applied to the young carpenter for aid in designing and making the machinery. In 1856, Mr. Skinner obtained a patent conjointly with Mr. Smith, and an experimental loom was constructed. Changes and improvements were made at frequent intervals, and in 1860, a quite complete and satisfactory loom was in operation. From this time on, constant improvements were effected, until in 1871, Mr. Smith conceived the idea of inventing a power loom for weaving moquette carpets, thus producing a fabric equal to Axminster, and costing considerably less. With the aid of Mr. Skinner this was accomplished, and the large moquette mill on Nepperhan Avenue stands to memorialize this successful venture.

The following, taken from an old journal, will indicate the early development and promise of the factory at West Farms: "One could scarcely expect to find in the village of West Farms, an incipient rival in carpet-making, to the imperial French carpet factory of the Savonnerie, or of the Gobelins. It is

* The author is indebted to others for the preparation of the history of this industry.

nevertheless true. Mr. Alexander Smith, of that place, exhibits a power loom for weaving tufted pile carpeting similar to that now produced by hand, and called Axminster or Wilton. This factory makes twenty-five yards of carpet a day, or two yards an hour." In striking contrast to these figures, is the present output of nearly 42,000 yards per day, or 12,000,000 yards per annum. But the experience at West Farms was not one of unbroken prosperity; indeed, had it not been for the indomitable perseverance and pluck of the young manufacturer through these early years of misfortune, the enterprise must have failed. At the breaking out of the War, he sustained large losses in the South, causing temporary financial embarrassment, from which he quickly recovered.

In 1862, at a time when everything seemed to presage success, a fire destroyed his entire plant, the only thing saved being the American flag that was preserved to wave over one of the largest of America's industries. He immediately rebuilt and again set himself to the task of perfecting the loom for tufted carpets, the model of which had been completely destroyed by the fire. Only two years elapsed before another conflagration swept away his second factory, destroying the loom now almost perfect, over which years of labor had been spent. He said of these first twelve years of his experience, so full of trial and adversity, of anxiety and patient effort, that they were spent in bringing this second invention to the state which he could rely on for future success. "Tried by fire," he stood the test, and out of the trial came the strong, firm, undaunted man, who could fashion and plan an enterprise which was to be the grandest of its kind on the western hemisphere. "Wise men ne'er sit and wail their losses." Alexander Smith was one of those sagacious men who are "better made by ill." It was this last fire of '64 that resulted in his moving his interests from West Farms to Yonkers. "Ill blows the wind that profits nobody." Thus it is that, as a result of the twin disasters at the place where he had first ventured his fortunes, he determined to transfer the operations of his business interests to Yonkers. In 1864, he purchased the property which comprises part of that formerly occupied by the Waring Hat Factory. This was the beginning

WARREN B. SMITH.

of an enterprise which was destined to bring more of the laboring classes to this community, and to maintain more than any other work established here, has accomplished. Nearly thirty-two years have elapsed since its inception.

Below will be found a sketch showing the development of the different mills, together with statistics relating to their production and proportions. We return again to the career of Mr. Smith. He was married when quite young to Miss Jane Baldwin, daughter of Major Ebenezer Baldwin, who was a well-known resident of Yonkers. He had two children who are still residents of Yonkers. Warren B. Smith, who succeeded his father as President of the carpet company, and Eva S., now the wife of Mr. William F. Cochran. He married a second time a Miss Thomas of Baltimore, Md. Mr. Smith was the first President of St. John's Hospital, and was also a member of the Board of Education.

With the great cares which his large business interests laid upon him, he was ever sensible of, and responsive to the call which his duty as a citizen involved. He took an active, personal interest in matters pertaining to the city's welfare. He was a staunch Republican, and was a candidate for mayor of the city in 1874, but was defeated by his Democratic opponent, Joseph Masten, by a small majority.

In 1878, he was nominated by his party for congressman from his district, and after a vigorous personal campaign, was elected by a very large majority. It was the crowning recognition of his talents and ability tendered by those who had known him most intimately for years, but it was the crowning which was bestowed at the goal of a life successful beyond measure, filled to the full with activity, honored and beloved by all who had the good fortune to know him, for he died on the eve of his election November 5, 1878, at the age of sixty. The suddenness of his death at a time when he was apparently about to enter upon a new and larger field of usefulness caused the most widespread disappointment and sorrow.

The loss of no citizen of Yonkers has been more deeply and sincerely mourned than that of Alexander Smith. On the day of his funeral, by unanimous agreement, all the stores were closed and the flags all over the city hanging at half-mast, betokened the passing away of one of Yonkers' most distinguished citizens.

A few days after his death, a memorial service was held at Washburn (now Music) Hall, when addresses were delivered expressive of the love and sympathy of the people. No words could more fittingly conclude the sketch of Mr. Smith's life, than those uttered by William Allen Butler on that occasion. He said: "When we stand by the bier, or near the bier of such a man as we mourn to-night, we reassure ourselves, we take courage, we reassert the supremacy of conscience in the sphere of the human relations, and we take satisfaction and solace in the memory of the good and benevolent actions which belonged to such

WILLIAM F. COCHRAN.

a life, which death *cannot* destroy, and which smell sweet, and blossom in the dust."

THE ALEXANDER SMITH & SONS' CARPET CO.'S MILLS OF TO-DAY. The carpets manufactured by the Alexander Smith & Sons' Carpet Co. are divided into two classes, *viz.:* Tapestry Brussels and tapestry velvets, and moquette or Axminster, the two latter being practically the same weave and embracing the grades known as Savonnerie, neplus ultra and nonpareil—the variation in closeness of texture and the quality of the woolen yarns used, being the essential differences.

The tapestry goods require for their production the joint efforts of three distinct mills, which are known by the names of the Worsted Spinning Mill, Printing Mill or "Drum" room, and the Setting, Weaving and Finishing Departments, commonly known in Yonkers as the Tapestry Mill.

The worsted mill is located on the Saw Mill River Road, close to the Oakland Cemetery's main entrance, on the east side of the Nepperhan River. This plant consists of one main structure of brick, three stories and basement, 500 x 53 feet; a two-story picker room 74 x 50, and two separate systems for

TAPESTRY WEAVING MILLS.

MOQUETTE MILLS.

ALEXANDER SMITH & SONS' CARPET CO., YONKERS.

PRINT MILLS.

WORSTED MILLS.

ALEXANDER SMITH A SONS' CARPET CO., YONKERS.

wool washing and drying contained in buildings of one and two stories, 130 x 80 and 120 x 100, exclusive of boiler and engine-rooms.

This mill is devoted entirely to the production of worsted yarns for carpet purposes, and has a daily product of 14,000 pounds of what is known in the trade, as 11s. and 12s. yarn. The wool used is entirely derived from foreign shores, and is known as carpet combing, is long in staple and is coarser than anything produced in the United States. Donskois from Russia, Scotch fleece, Chinas and Cordovas from South America are the main descriptions used.

The principal machinery in use at this mill is described as follows: fifty-two sets two-cylinder cards, twenty-three Noble combs, 120 spinning frames, sixty-five twisting frames, and all the necessary subsidiary machinery, comprising pickers, washers, dryers, etc., necessary to operate the above; there are four boilers and two engines, with a joint capacity of 1,000 horse-power; the Superintendent in charge is Wm. H. Wolfe, and the number of hands employed is 613.

FRANK T. HOLDER.

The next mill to be considered is the print mill, which takes the worsted yarn and applies the colors to it. This mill is situated opposite the worsted mill, on the western bank of the Nepperhan River. It is a two-story brick building 516 x 110 feet. It contains eighty-five pairs of drums or cylinders, on which the yarn is printed, after being thoroughly scoured and bleached. After being steamed and dried the yarn is then ready for the final processes, and is sent to the tapestry setting and weaving mill. One engine and four boilers are in use at this mill, and there are employed 607 hands. Wm. Webb is in general charge of the printing, and Wm. McKim of the color mixing department.

The tapestry weaving mill comes next, and is the plant around which clusters whatever of sentiment or romance there may be associated with so material a matter as carpet making, as this was the nucleus from which has sprung the

HAROLD BROWN.

present immense works. It is situated on the corner of Palisade Avenue and Elm Street.

The original "wooden" building is still intact, and was bought by Alexander Smith, after leaving West Farms in 1865; he afterwards added fifty feet to the structure; the product of the mill at that time could be removed daily by a single horse wagon, while now about 500 rolls of

EUGENE C. CLARK.

carpeting are daily forwarded to New York from this mill alone. There are still in the employ of the company three or four hands who started in with Alexander Smith the first year he came to Yonkers; the old building is 201x31, three-stories and basement, and it is still in active use for the dressing of warps, carpenter shop, etc.; it is looked upon with somewhat of a feeling akin to reverence, but it is inevitable that some day it will have to give place to a more modern structure.

Immediately on the north side of this building stands the main office and counting-room building, in which are also established a corps of carpet designers.

The main or "weaving" mill is a five-story and basement brick building 428x52 feet. This was built in three sections at different dates; and before its erection its site was occupied by a row of old wooden tenements, coeval with the old mill, in which the employees used to live, long before the era of city water, gas, and electric cars.

In this building are contained eighty-three tapestry setting frames, 455 tapestry and velvet looms, and the necessary finishing machinery. The rumble that these busy looms make, when all at work, is something not easily forgotten. The yards produced average 26,000 daily.

Adjoining the main building is the machine shop. This is a two-story brick building, and employs from eighty to 100 mechanics. Here are built moquette and tapestry looms, printing drums, reels and dyeing machines. The shop has been for fifteen years under the management of Hiram F. Lord.

There are two engines and four boilers in use at this plant, and prior to the destruction by the Health Board of the old dam in 1892, a water-wheel of about fifty horse-power was in operation. The total number of hands employed at this mill is 1,240.

The above paragraphs briefly describe the general characteristics of the worsted, print and tapestry mills. Perhaps a few facts about the consumption of raw materials incidental to the production of this grade of carpets may not be uninteresting.

There are used weekly at the worsted mill 120,000 pounds of combing wool in the "greasy" or raw state, to produce 84,000 pounds of yarn. At the print mill a car of flour is consumed every week to make paste to carry the colors for printing the yarn; 20,000 pounds of soap and 3,000 pounds of sulphur are used weekly to scour and bleach the yarn. At the tapestry weaving mill 84,000 pounds printed worsted yarns, 30,000 pounds of cotton yarn, 100,000 pounds of jute yarn, 45,000 pounds of linen yarn, and 30,000 pounds of starch are used weekly in producing the 156,000 yards of carpet which leave the mill for New York.

We come now to a brief outline of the vast plant which is assembled under the title of the Moquette Mill. The main building is of brick, four-stories and basement, 584x53 feet. This contains 455 moquette, Axminster and Savonnerie looms, sixty-three setting frames, 102 threading machines, and all the necessary finishing machinery, etc., called for by the above looms. The average daily product of this mill is 18,000 yards of the various grades. This mill is the most modern, in construction and equipment, of the company's plant, and embraces all the labor-saving devices that human ingenuity can suggest; the progress of the raw material through its various stages is so arranged as to be steadily onward.

The spinning department is of large dimensions; the building is a two-story brick construction, 319x151, and, together with the picker room adjoining (a two-story building, 274x85), contains 107 sets, two cylinder cards and eighty-six spinning mules or jacks, with the usual picking, washing and drying machinery required for so large a spinning plant. The product of this department is 31,000 pounds daily, using up about 36,000 pounds of raw wool.

Adjoining the picker room is a two-story brick storehouse, 255x100; this is filled with a stock of raw wool, jute and cotton yarns, etc., sufficient to keep the mill going for weeks.

We now come to the dye-house portion of the moquette plant; there are three one-story buildings devoted to dyeing, 172x60, 120x50 and 100x50 respectively; these contain sixty-two power dyeing machines, forty-three of which are made and patented by the company. The daily capacity of this department is an average of 25,000 pounds of dyed yarn. In the same building is located a power yarn washing and drying system. The main dye-house is built entirely of steel and brick, and is considered unique in construction.

One of the chief improvements made at this mill within the past year is the erection of a steel drying tower, 27 x 126 feet in height. This is devoted to drying carpets after they have been sized; and the height of the structure, which is painted a dark red, makes it a prominent landmark in the Saw Mill River Valley.

There are ten boilers and three compound engines in operation at this plant, with a gross capacity of about 1,500 horse-power.

There is quite a large machine-shop adjoining the main engine-rooms, in which are employed mechanics who look after repairs directly connected with the machinery pertaining to this plant.

This mill has the largest number of employees on its pay-roll; the latest count gives 1,640 hands. Reuben Borland is the present Superintendent of the moquette mill.

A unique feature of the mill is the yarn conveyor, which takes the dyed yarn from the store-house directly to the top floor of the main building by means of an endless chain and carrier.

There are used at this mill weekly 60,000 pounds jute yarn, 25,000 pounds cotton yarn, and 31,000 pounds woolen yarn.

The following are a few facts in connection with the mills, as a whole: there are ninety tons of bituminous coal consumed daily, and by an ingenious device attached to the boiler-grates the smoke is consumed; the employees are paid weekly on every Friday: the raw and finished goods handled daily weigh 200 tons; the entire buildings owned by the company have been protected from fire by automatic sprinkling devices; and, in addition, there are four fire pumps of great capacity, in case the city water should fail. The total hands employed number 4,100.

Some idea of the extent of these works may be gathered from the fact, that there are twenty-five acres of floor space in the mills as a whole.

Among the names of those who have been prominent in the service of the company, some of whom are dead, should be mentioned: Halcyon Skinner, John T. Bell, F. T. Holder, John A. Dowe, Thomas Wigley, Wm. McKim, Hiram F. Lord, George Borland, Eugene Tymeson, John Crowther, John H. Coyne, Wm. H. Wolfe, George Moshier, E. C. Clark, Harold Brown, Richard Edie, Jr., William Heatherington, Walter Thomas, Henry Parton, David Paton, Henry J. Laragh, George Stengel, John Crawford. The company give their employees a Saturday half-day holiday, every summer during the months of June, July and August, and allow them their full wages for the time lost.

A large number of the adult male employees own their own homes, and, as the mills have run almost steadily through the past twenty years, the hands are kept more uniformly employed than are those of competing concerns; the last serious stoppage was in the panic year, 1893, when the mills were closed five months, and this resulted in great depression and suffering in the City of Yonkers.

The moquette fabrics made by the company, have been exported quite freely during the past four years, through the general selling agents, Messrs. W. & J. Sloane, of New York City, who have opened an office and established a permanent representative in London; in connection with the recent coronation services of the Czar of Russia, it should be mentioned that 2,500 yards of the company's goods were laid in the palace at Moscow, and this has recently been followed up by orders for several patterns for the private rooms of the Empress of Russia.

Special biographical references will be made elsewhere in this volume, to men who have been prominent in the development of the company.

Upon the death of Alexander Smith, Warren B. Smith, his only son, was elected President (and resigned the office of Treasurer), in January, 1879, which office he held until January 1, 1894, when he resigned. Mr. Smith is a practical carpet man in every respect, as he applied himself to acquiring his knowledge by going into many of the mill departments and working as any other employe might. The present magnitude and success of the works are largely due to his energy and push. Mr. Smith is also largely interested in real estate in Yonkers. During the past three years, he has devoted much time to travelling; his home is still in Yonkers, and his residence is beautifully located at "Hillcrest" where Mrs. Alexander Smith also makes her home.

William F. Cochran, who married Mr. Alex. Smith's daughter, Eva S., held the offices of Treasurer, and Secretary until January 1, 1894, when he also resigned. A special article in this history refers to Mr. Cochran's career.

The present management consists of Mr. F. T. Holder, who became President of the company in January, 1894. He was born in Clinton, Mass., August 18, 1833. He came to the Smiths from the Bigelow Mills in that place in 1870 and since that time has served as Superintendent until his election to the Presidency. He is a man of very large experience, having a practical knowledge of every department, and of every process employed in the manufacture of carpets. He is a self-made man, having begun life in a humble way as watchman in a mill. By close application and industry, he has not only mastered each department of the mills—he has become head master of the entire enterprise—an example of what may be accomplished by brains and energy.

Mr. Harold Brown was born in Toronto, Canada, but resided in England until 1879. He is a young man who came to the Smiths in 1881, and has gradually worked his way up to his present position of Secretary and Treasurer. For many years he was at the head of the office force, and by his ability in that capacity he has earned his present position. Mr. Eugene C. Clark, a Yonkers boy always, became General Superintendent at the time Mr. Holder was advanced to the Presidency. He was formerly Superintendent of the moquette plant. It is a large army that Mr. Clark commands, but it is organized and disciplined with as much care and precision as any military body. The whole system in all its multiplied departments, is as perfect as the machinery that works day by day under the skillful guidance of the thousands of trained hands.

SODA-WATER FACTORY (Mr. David H. Smith). Mr. Smith began his business in Yonkers about 1866, first at the corner of Main Street and Warburton Avenue, then in his new building on Engine Place. He conducts a large manufacturing business; 1,000 bottles are filled daily. If necessary 1,500 can be filled each day. Druggists are supplied, fountains are charged, and bottled soda and other beverages sold. His wagons run to adjoining towns. He has now been in the business about thirty years. Occasionally other dealers have competed, but Mr. Smith has continued to increase his business.

CIGAR FACTORY. A number of tobacconists in Yonkers manufacture cigars. The late W. Lowenthal, long time proprietor of the Terrace City Cigar Store, established his business in the city as early as 1871. The largest business at present is that of M. Friedman, formerly Friedman & Wolf. It was established in Yonkers, January 1, 1886. and conducted at No. 40 Palisade Avenue. Nine men and five girls are employed. The sale is throughout a district extending ten miles around Yonkers.

WESTCHESTER GAS LIGHT COMPANY. "The Peoples Gas Co." received in 1870, from the village of Yonkers, the right to manufacture illuminating gas and to lay distributing pipes. After building a gas holder on Nepperhan Avenue, north of Ashburton, the company sold out in 1872, to "The City Gas Company." This company did nothing. Their property was purchased by the Westchester Gas Light Company, which was incorporated in 1875. This company laid some gas pipes and sold gas for several years.

"The Yonkers Fuel Gas Company" (incorporated in 1879), leased the Westchester Gas Company's property and built additional works for itself on Nepperhan Street. It proposed to deliver a non-illuminating gas for fuel, known as the "Strong Process," but received little encouragement from the citizens. A receiver had charge of the affairs of the Westchester Gas Light Company and the Yonkers Fuel Gas Company in 1883.

"The Yonkers Fuel, Light & Power Company" (incorporated in 1884), leased the works of the two companies from the receiver and began to manufacture gas. The mortgagors of the leased property foreclosed, and the property was advertised for sale.

The company was then purchased by new parties and reorganized under new management. The present officers are: President, Samuel T. Bodine; Secretary and Treasurer, Edward C. Lee.

WOOL EXTRACT. In 1876, Mr. John K. Fleming established in Yonkers the business of extracting wool from rags. He began on Nepperhan Street. In 1877, he removed to Chicken Island. In 1881, the building he had leased of Edward Underhill burned, inflicting a loss of $4,000. Then a factory was built on Bridge Street, near Ludlow Station. Twelve or fifteen hands were employed. A similar establishment was located at Little Falls. The wool extract factories at Yonkers and Little Falls were the only two in the State. After doing business for a time in the Bridge Street factory, the machinery was removed, and the building left vacant. In 1893, it burned and has not been rebuilt, nor has the business been resumed in Yonkers.

THE NEW YORK PLOW COMPANY. As early as 1826, Messrs. Minor and Horton began to manufacture plows at Peekskill, N. Y. The Peekskill Plow Company began to conduct the business in 1863. Subsequently the Peekskill Plow Company and the New York Plow Company, then recently established at Newark, N. J., were consolidated and the business of the new company was established in Yonkers. That was in 1878. They first occupied the Vark Street factory, which had been used by the Clipper Mowing Machine Company. They employed at that time about 200 hands. In 1882, they removed to the foot of Vark Street. At one period they manufactured about 100,000 plows a year, besides other farm utensils. The President was James B. Brown; Secretary, J. W. Douglas; Superintendent, John Pentreath. Among the utensils they manufactured were, cultivators, harrows, ensilage and fodder cutters. They shipped their goods to home markets and to foreign countries.

THE WESTCHESTER TELEPHONE COMPANY. On January 6, 1880, a telephone exchange was established in Yonkers, under the management of the Western Union Telegraph Company. It then had forty-five subscribers: The Metropolitan Telegraph and Telephone Company, of New York City, on July 1, 1880, purchased the property of the Western Union Telegraph Company. About October, 1881, it became the property of the Westchester Company. Mr. George L. Philips became General Manager in place of Mr. L. B. Harris, the Business Manager. Beginning in December, 1881, General C. H. Barney was the General Superintendent. The office of these managers was in New York. Miss A. H. Adgate had general oversight of the local exchange. Mr. W. R. Cabot, in January, 1882, became Assistant General Manager, and his office was in Yonkers. Mr. R. E. Alexander, another Assistant Manager, was appointed Superintendent in 1883. Miss Adgate, who was the first Manager of the Yonkers Exchange, and who served from its opening until April 30, 1884, resigned. The duties of her position were discharged by the Assistant Manager. The stock of the company is held by parties not residing in Yonkers. Mr. Dexter A. Smith was President, and Mr. H. L. Storke, Vice-President and General Manager, and Mr. C. F. Cutler, Secretary and Treasurer. The company's district extends from City Hall, New York, thirty-three and one-third miles north, including Nyack. In 1891 Mr. C. F.

FACTORY OF THE ARLINGTON CHEMICAL CO.,
THE NEW YORK PHARMACAL ASSOCIATION,
THE PALISADE MANUFACTURING CO.

Cutler became President, and Mr. F. W. Sabold, the General Manager, at which time the office of the General Manager was moved to Yonkers. This arrangement continued until June, 1896, when the ownership of the company passed to the New York Telephone Company. Exchanges are at Yonkers, Nyack, Sing Sing, Tarrytown, Dobb's Ferry, White Plains, Mount Vernon, Port Chester, New Rochelle, Westchester, and are connected with smaller towns. The Yonkers Exchange has 450 subscribers, and about 700 miles of wire are in use. The work of operating and maintaining is done by twenty employees.

The territory of the former Westchester Telephone Company now forms the Westchester Division of the New York Telephone Company. The executive offices of the new company are in New York City. The Division headquarters are at 45 Warburton Avenue, Yonkers. F. W. Sabold is Superintendent of the Westchester Division.

MEDICINE MANUFACTORY. The New York Pharmacal Association is an incorporated company of gentlemen of this city engaged in the manufacture and preparation of the medicinal compound called "Lactopeptine," which, with its various combinations of standard products, is used and prescribed by the medicinal profession throughout the world. They, in conjunction with the Arlington Chemical Company, who manufacture beef peptonoids, liquid peptonoids and combinations, also phospho-caffein compound, occupy the present factory, commonly called "The Medicine Factory," situated on Palisade Avenue, near Elm Street.

The Palisade Manufacturing Company, also an occupant in conjunction with the two aforesaid companies, manufacture borolyptol, kola cardinette and velvet skin soap and velvet skin powder.

The New York Pharmacal Association moved from New York to Yonkers in 1885, occupying a small factory, which was destroyed by fire the following year, and from thence into their present commodious and extensive quarters.

The Arlington Chemical Company was organized in 1890, and the Palisade Manufacturing Company in 1894.

The various companies employ much valuable and integrant machinery, an average of seventy-five hands and fifty travellers. All these companies advertise extensively, but to the medical profession only, and their preparations are standard and staple with physicians throughout the United States and all parts of the world. The officers of the companies are: J. E. Andrus, H. J. Andrus and F. W. R. Eschmann.

THE FERNBROOK CARPET COMPANY. This company began business in 1881, near the Ludlow passenger station of the Hudson River Railroad. Previous to that it had been engaged in another project and was known as the Hamilton Wooloid Company. The President of the Wooloid Company was Mr. Charles R. Flint. The Secretary and Treasurer was Mr. Gideon Hamilton. The latter gentleman was the inventor of the chemical process to which hair was subjected, giving it a crimp and spring which resembles wool, and subduing its wiry and glossy appearance. This product was called "wooloid." In 1882, the company began to manufacture ingrain carpet, "wooloid" being used in combination with wool and camel's hair. In 1883, the company was reorganized. Mr. Hamilton was not a member of the new company. The officers were: President, Charles R. Flint; Vice-President and Treasurer, William M. Ivins; Secretary and Superintendent, H. T. Bragg. The company was incorporated in 1885, with a capital of $150,000, taking over the machinery of the Fernbrook Mills, spinners of yarns. The officers of the company have been: Presidents, 1885-87, Walter W. Law; 1888-89, William M. Ivins; 1890-96, Walter W. Law. Treasurers, 1885-87, William M. Ivins; 1887-96, George C. Wetmore, Jr. The number of employees is about 300. The company manufactures ingrain carpets and knit fleece linings.

S. FRANCIS QUICK.

Mr. Law was for years a resident of Yonkers, and contributed generously to strengthen its Sunday-schools and churches. He now resides at Briar Cliff Farm, his splendid country-seat, east of the village of Sing Sing.

YONKERS CARPET MANUFACTURING COMPANY. This company was established in 1892. John H. Coyne was the President, Warren B. Smith, Vice-President, and Francis T. Holder, Treasurer. Their business was conducted in the Shethar Building, south side of Elm Street. It continued a little over two years, at one time employing about 100 hands. Velvet carpets were manufactured. The mill was started in 1892, when the McKinley tariff bill was in force, and the carpet business very prosperous. In the early summer of 1893, the Wilson bill, providing for radical changes in the tariff, among them large reduction in tariff rates, and admission of wool and other raw material free, was formulated. There was great depression in the carpet industry and the outlook was dark. The carpet companies of Yonkers closed indefinitely, and remained closed for more than six months. Business was resumed in the early part of 1894, but not with full force. When the Wilson bill passed, there was a great shrinkage in prices. The Yonkers Carpet Company prudently decided to discontinue business. It paid its obligations, settled its affairs, and closed its factory in the spring of 1895.

PAPER BOXES. John Thompson began to manufacture paper boxes in Yonkers in April, 1881. The business was conducted at first in the Shipman Building, Palisade Avenue, near foot of Locust Hill Avenue. It was removed, in 1885, to the Waring Hat Manufacturing Building, corner of Riverdale Avenue and Vark Street. When the business was established, about fifty dozen boxes were manufactured a day, and about ten hands were employed. In 1895, about fifty hands were employed, and the average number of boxes manufactured was 225 dozen a day. Messrs. Paton & Hayward are also box manufacturers. They are located at Nos. 31 and 39 Buena Vista Avenue. They conduct a wholesale business.

SANITARY PLUMBING (The Washburn & Moore Manufacturing Company). This company began business in 1882, at the corner of Dock and River Streets. It controlled useful fixtures, which Mr. Moore, who was a practical plumber, invented and patented. Among the past patrons of the company were, Professor J. Ogden Doremus, William H. Vanderbilt and Samuel J. Tilden; the Mutual Life Insurance Company of New York and the Chicago Board of Trade. The factory is still located at the corner of Dock and River Streets. The company is now known as The W. F. Washburn Brass Company.

SUGAR MACHINERY. In 1883, Messrs. S. S. Hepworth & Co., who since 1875 had been doing business in New York, established in Yonkers the manufacture of machinery for sugar-plantations and refineries. It was thought to be the only firm in the United States, engaged in manufacturing this machinery. The firm also made engines, tools for machinists, and lathes. Their grounds (300 x 135) are near the Glenwood passenger station. The capacity of the works was equal to the employment of 300 hands. After their business terminated, the building remained for a time unoccupied, and then was occupied by the India Rubber and Gutta-Percha Insulating Company.

THE YONKERS DISTRICT TELEGRAPH COMPANY. This company was incorporated in 1884. The first Board of Directors were Dr. Samuel Swift, Theodore Fitch, Stephen D. Field, George W. Blanchard, George H. Warren, E. L. Moyne and S. E. Simmonds. The first officers were: President, Dr. Samuel Swift; Secretary and General Manager, George W. Blanchard; Treasurer, George H. Warren. The first Manager was Miss A. H. Adgate. An assistant manager, a sergeant, and seven messenger boys were the force.

THE AMERICAN GEAR COMPANY. This company was formed in 1885. It was incorporated with a capital stock of $100,000. Mr. Benjamin W. Cole was the first President, Mr. Henry Y. Chubb the Vice-President and Treasurer, and Mr. William Heckert, the Superintendent. The factory was located near the Glenwood station and its office was in New York. The company cut gears geometrically correct to any regular or fractional pitch, comforming to either the English or metric measurements. Their system was new and exclusively their own. Bevel gearing was not cut accurately and economically before this company, with its improved machinery and system undertook the work. The company manufactured steam, gas and electric motors, universal milling machines, engineers' ruling and routing machines, wire book stitching and calendar eyeleting machines, rosette and jewellers' lathes, fancy color printing presses and ticket label presses. The class of work the company did, required skilled mechanics, and in order to secure the requisite skill, the company combined with its manufacturing industry, a school for teaching mechanical drawing, physical science, etc. It was thought that those who availed themselves of the lectures and other instructions would be valued employees wherever skilled mechanics are in demand.

INDIA RUBBER AND GUTTA PERCHA INSULATION. This company was organized in 1896. It began to do business in Yonkers in 1890. The first members were William S. Wells, James A. Burden, E. Frank Coe, William E. Leach, and John H. Evans. The company was incorporated March 17, 1889. At various times changes took place in the membership. In 1895 the members were: William M. Habirshaw, John Habirshaw, H. E. Wheeler, James O. Bloss, and Otto G. Mayer. The first President was James A. Burden. James Stewart was the first Secretary and Treasurer. William M. Habirshaw became President in 1892. James O. Bloss became Secretary and Treasurer in 1891. In 1894 John Habirshaw became Secretary and Treasurer. The Company began to do business in New York City in 1886. They removed to Glenwood, Yonkers, May 19, 1890. Their New York office is No. 15 Cortlandt Street. The average number of employees is 125.

The company manufactures electrical cables for transmission of power, and arc lighting requiring high potential, for low potential work for electric railroads and house lighting. Also telephone cables, underground and aerial, and underwater cables, armored, for all kinds of electrical service.

The manufacture of this company was, in 1895, adopted for the transmission of high-pressure currents for the electrical work at Niagara Falls, after competitive tests of all other makes.

There has been no attempt on the part of the Manager of these works to use materials otherwise than such as have been known for the past twenty years and proved eminently suitable for the service. It is for this reason, together with the superior style of the machinery used, that the goods have gained their reputation.

Most of the machinery employed in the works was designed by the General Manager (W. M. Habirshaw), and is not in use elsewhere. The sales office is No. 15 Cortlandt Street, New York.

ELECTRIC LIGHT COMPANY. Previous to 1883 the gas company for a very brief time had a few arc lights in Yonkers. In 1885 the Common Council granted to two companies franchises to engage in the electric light business in the city. The Yonkers Light and Power Company (afterward the Thomson-Houston Company) put their wires on the telephone poles. The Yonkers Schuyler Electric Light Company erected poles. Early in 1886 both companies began business. There were several electric lights in the streets, but neither company at that time had a contract for street lighting. They lighted business places. Subsequently the Schuyler Company made a contract with the Common Council for lighting the streets in the central part of the city. After a time the two competing companies were consolidated under the name Yonkers Electric Light Company. Until the summer of 1896 they occupied two stations, one of which was a part of the stone building north of the Elm Street bridge. In 1896 they leased all of that building in order to enlarge and improve their plant.

JOHN CLARK.

CITY STEAM LAUNDRY. The City Steam Laundry was established in the spring of 1888, by George E. Kernochan of Middletown, N. Y. The business was sold in June, 1890, to P. N. Jacobus, of Newton, N. J. It was first conducted in a part of the Shethar Factory Building on Elm Street (formerly John T. Waring & Co., Hat Factory). In February, 1892, it absorbed the business of the Utopian Steam Laundry conducted by S. A. Peene, and the firm name was changed to Jacobus and Peene. The increase of business soon made it necessary to secure larger quarters and the business was removed in 1892, to the ground floor of the Shethar building. The firm thus secured a floor space of about 5,000 square feet. Subsequently much improved machinery was added and the number of employees increased from time to time. In 1895, the number of employees was about sixty. The several delivery wagons cover the territory between the Bronx River on the east and the Hudson on the west, and from Tremont, New York City, north to Tarrytown. The principal business of the laundry is family work, but during the busy season considerable stock work is done for manufacturers of shirts and of ladies' waists.

FENCE MANUFACTORY. In January, 1891, C. E. Parker established the business of manufacturing fences for farms, gardens and city lots, wired picket fence being a specialty. He also manufactures iron fences. The wire fence is manufactured by machinery. His factory is located at the corner of Nepperhan Avenue and King Street. He is the sole manager of the business.

The iron fence works of George R. Merritt are at No. 40 Nepperhan Street, and the iron works of Thomas Morris at No. 58 Nepperhan Street.

BAG MANUFACTORY. The Van O'Linda Manufacturing Company was incorporated in 1892, with Thomas F. Torrey, President; J. D. Van O'Linda, Secretary and Treasurer; H. P. Van O'Linda, General Manager. They began the manufacture of coal bags in Yonkers in the same year under a patent issued to Messrs. H. P. and J. D. Van O'Linda. The Singer Sewing Machine Company manufactures special machines for the Van O'Linda Company. A machine called the Union bag machine is also in use in the factory which is located on Fernbrook Street. The company also manufacture bags for passing ashes in steamships, and bags of other klnds. They ship their bags throughout the United States and Canada. Over 600 retail dealers are using them. The largest dealers in domestic coal in the world have adopted this system of delivering coal. The company supply the American line of steamers and the Red Star line with bags for passing ashes. All the stockholders of the Van O'Linda Manufacturing Company are wholesale coal dealers.

ELEVATOR AND MILL (Andrew Deyo). This grain business was established years ago in Yonkers by Ackerman & Deyo, both of whom are now deceased. The Deyo Elevator and Mill was built on the Deyo Dock, by Andrew Deyo in 1895, and is the only elevator on the Hudson River outside of New York City. The building is 175 feet long, and the tower is 117 feet from the ground. From the tower, the Harbor of New York and the Statue of Liberty can be seen. To the north, Tarrytown, Peekskill and Sing Sing are in sight. The tower is one of the most commanding in the city. The storage capacity of the elevator is about 500,000 bushels, and the elevator capacity about 6,000 bushels an hour. A car of grain containing about 1,000 bushels can be unloaded in about twelve minutes by the steam shovels. A canal boat containing 15,000 bushels can be unloaded in about two hours and a half. There are two mills in the building for grinding corn, oats, etc. There is also a storage building for hay, flour, salt, etc., 120 x 40 feet, on the property not far from the elevator. Mr. Andrew Veitch is the efficient Superintendent of the elevator and mill. The main offices are located at the corner of Wells and Warburton Avenues, and are handsomely fitted up for the business.

CROWN SMYRNA RUG COMPANY. In November, 1894, Thompson & Co. began the manufacture of rugs with hand-looms. They occupied a part of the Washburn Building, corner of Dock and River Streets. In November, 1895, A. B. Buchanan, a member of the firm of A. F. Buchanan & Sons, New York, oil-cloth manufacturers, became a member of the company which was incorporated in that month. They then introduced power-looms. The President is John Thompson, Jr., the Secretary and Treasurer is Andrew Buchanan. The stone building at the east end of the Glen was occupied in November, 1895. In March, 1896, twenty-four hands were employed. The salesrooms of the company are at No. 50 Leonard Street, New York City.

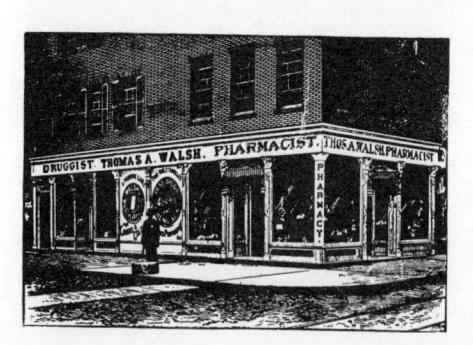

NICKEL, SILVER, AND GOLD PLATING (The Waldor Manufacturing Company). This business was established in Yonkers in 1895, by Messrs. John J. Walsh, son of the Water Commissioner, and D. A. Doran. The name Waldor is composed of the first three letters of each partner's name. Theirs is the pioneer electric plating business in the city, where there is much demand for

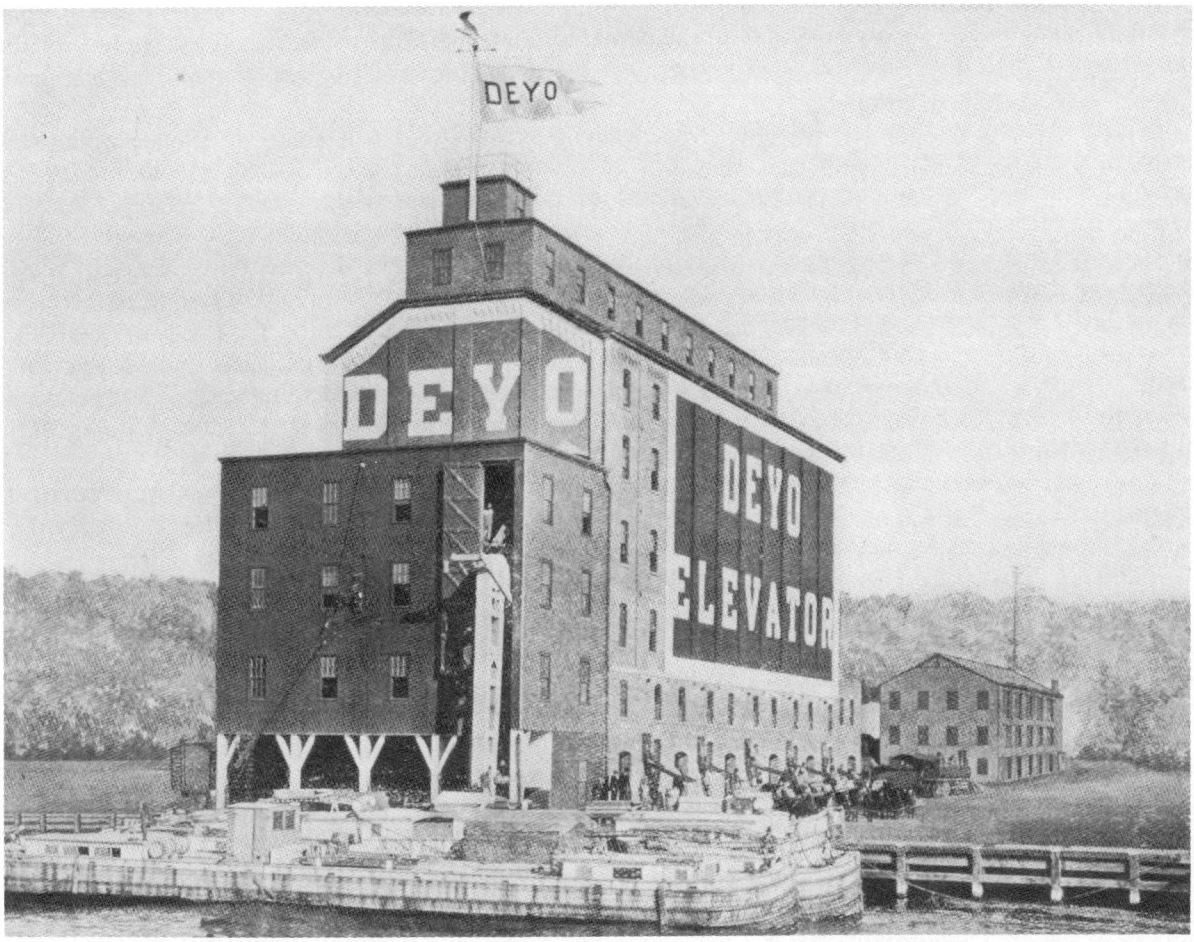
DEYO
DEYO
DEYO
ELEVATOR

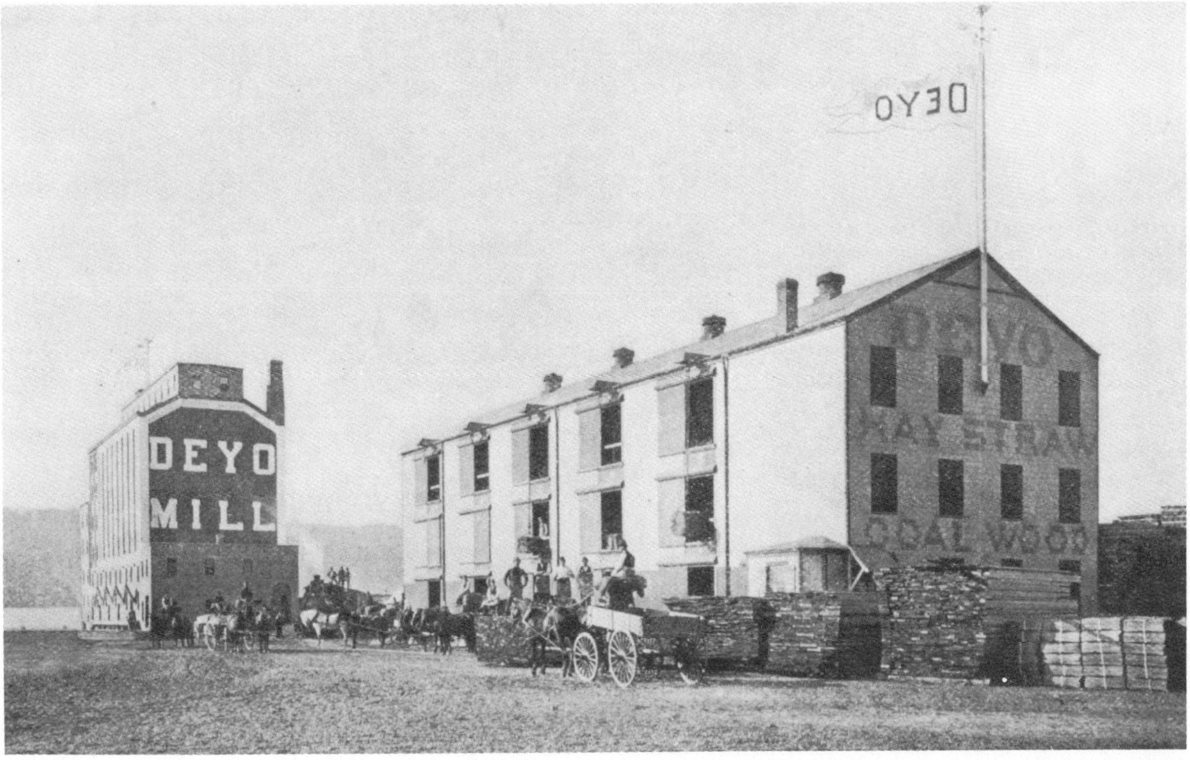
DEYO
MILL
DEYO
HAY STRAW
COAL WOOD

metal finishing. The factory is located at the corner of Dock and River Streets. They restore missing parts, repair and plate surgical instruments, art ornaments, carriage, stove, harness, bicycle parts, musical instruments, tableware, etc.

HAT BANDS AND RIBBONS. Messrs. Pass Brothers established the business of manufacturing hat-bands in Yonkers at the beginning of 1893, and of ribbons in 1894. Messrs. Gustave and Adolph Pass constitute the firm. They conduct their business on the fifth floor of the Shethar Building (formerly Waring Hat Factory), Elm Street, and employed, in 1895, about thirty men and twenty-five girls. Their specialty is hat-bands and their goods are high grade novelties demanded by the trade, on short notice. They have a factory in Rhemish, Prussia, employing about 300 looms. They import eighty per cent. and manufacture in America about twenty per cent. of the goods, which their New York house (Pass & Co., 37 West 4th Street) sells on commission. They get their raw material abroad. Silk comes from Italy, Japan and China. Cotton which is used for filling the hat-bands, comes from England. Their patronage is mostly in New York City, Danbury, Conn., South Norwalk, Conn., Utica, N. Y., Orange Valley, N. J., and Brooklyn, N. Y. Their machinery is of American manufacture.

Mr. Jas. W. Shaughnessy began to manufacture silk ribbons in Yonkers, in May, 1894, locating on Nepperhan Avenue, at Garden Street. He employed, in 1895, about thirty or forty hands when orders were plentiful, and sometimes manufactured from 3,000 to 4,000 yards of ribbon a day.

POSTAL TELEGRAPH CABLE COMPANY. This company, which operates in connection with the Commercial Cable, or Mackay-Bennett Cable Company, and which is a competitor of the Western Union Company, established an office in Yonkers, on July 5, 1895. It maintains a District Messenger Service in Yonkers. The manager is Mr. W. H. Flandreau.

STEAM-HEATING (Barr, Reynolds & Co.). This company, which also has a shop in Rochester, established its business in Yonkers in 1895. They have furnished prominent private residences, and are now fitting up with hot water circulation St. Joseph's Seminary on Valentine Hall. This is the largest building in the State to be heated by hot water, and there are only two or three larger in the country.

The industries to which reference is made in this chapter are with few exceptions those of manufactories. Many paragraphs might be devoted to a record of the kinds of business common to all cities if space permitted. S. Francis Quick and other carpenters and builders, John Clark and other dealers in ice, and many other Yonkers business men have had much to do in increasing the business of the city. Masons and plasterers, house-painters, cabinet makers, plumbers and others are conducting a large business, but reference cannot be made to them all.

CHAPTER XVII.

YONKERS BANKS.

BEFORE a bank was established in their town, the people of Yonkers transacted their banking business in New York. They could reach the city by wagon or sloop, but under the most favorable conditions, a journey of seventeen miles to town, and then, after business was transacted, a return journey of seventeen miles, consumed the best part of the day. As population increased, along with other improvements came banks.

On April 13, 1854, the YONKERS SAVINGS-BANK was incorporated. Two months afterward (June 13th), the new bank began business. The Board of Trustees numbered forty-one. Under the act of 1875 (conforming all savings institutions to a uniformity of powers, rights and liabilities, and fixing their modes of doing business, rates of dividends, etc.), the number of trustees was reduced to twenty-five.

The trustees, who constituted the body corporate and politic by the name of the "Yonkers Savings Bank," were Ethan Flagg, Robert P. Getty, J. Henry Williams, William Radford, Thomas O. Farrington, Horatio G. Prall, John T. Waring, Edward W. Candee, Henry W. Bashford, Lemuel W. Wells, Samuel D. Rockwell, William L. Atwater, William N. Seymour, Bailey Hobbs, Duncan Macfarlane, Charles Archer, Henry F. Devoe, George Gilroy, Amos W. Gates, James C. Bell, James L. Valentine, Joseph S. Hawkins, William G. Ackerman, John Olmsted, Robert Grant, William W. Scrugham, Jonathan Odell, Benjamin Brown, Fielding S. Gant, Joseph H. Jennings, George H. Bell, Frederick A. Coe, Samuel S. Barry, John Stilwell, James Scrymser, Josiah Rich, Edward F. Shonnard, Henry A. Underwood, Lawrence Post, Jr., Jacob Read and Cornelius M. Odell.

The trustees in 1896, are: Robert P. Getty, J. Henry Williams, Jacob Read, S. Francis Quick, J. A. Lockwood, William H. Thorne, H. J. Andrus, W. H. Paddock, Leander Read, Robert L. Stewart, James H. Weller, R. Eickemeyer, Jr., John Eylers, Albert L. Skinner, F. W. R. Eschmann, J. O. Campbell.

The first President of the bank was Ethan Flagg. He held the office for more than thirty years. It became vacant at his death, October 11, 1884. Robert P. Getty was elected his successor, and has remained President until the present time, 1896. The first Cashier (not known as cashier, but as clerk), was Egbert Howland. He served from 1854 to 1859. His successor was Samuel D. Rockwell, who served from 1859 to 1867. During part of this period, Mr. Rockwell was also the Treasurer. He resigned both offices in 1867. Then Lyman Cobb, Jr., who had been an assistant clerk, was elected Clerk, and Isaac H. Knox was chosen Treasurer. It was in 1873, that the title clerk was changed to that of cashier. Mr. Cobb is the Cashier at the present time. Mr. Knox resigned the treasurership in 1874. J. Henry Williams was elected to the office, and holds it to this day.

Raffaelle Cobb was employed by his father in 1867, as Assistant Clerk. In 1874, he was appointed Clerk, by the Trustees, and is still serving the bank in that capacity. F. Eugene Cobb, also rendered service as Clerk during a period of about five years.

Before their present fine banking house was erected, the Yonkers Savings Bank Corporation occupied first the Bank of Yonkers' premises. (The Bank of Yonkers of that day is the First National Bank of to-day.) Then the Savings-Bank transacted its business in the store on the west side of the street. Subsequently it rented and occupied rooms in the Getty House, on the corner of New Main Street. The present banking-house, which is one of the substantial buildings on South Broadway, east of St. John's Church, has a front of brown stone. It contains three stories and a basement. Its ground dimensions are 40 x 70. It is provided with a Lillie safety vault, trustees' rooms, etc., and has a police telegraph attachment to its safe, and a call, which will bring an officer within a minute or two.

The trustees of the Yonkers Savings-Bank in 1896 are: Robert P. Getty, J. Henry Williams, Jacob Read, S. Francis Quick, Joseph A. Lockwood, Wm. H. Thorne, Hamlin J. Andrus, Walter H. Paddock, Leander Read, Robert L. Stewart, Hon. James H. Weller, Rudolf Eickemeyer, John Eylers, Albert L. Skinner, F. W. R. Eschmann, John O. Campbell. Mr. George W. Read became book-keeper, December 1, 1890.

The amount credited to depositors for the first six months in 1854 was: from June 13, 1854, to January 1, 1855, $9,327.46; for year June 13, 1854, to June 13, 1855, $8,887.27. On the first day of January, 1873, the amount deposited had reached $943,638.61. On the first day of January, 1896, the amount deposited was $2,550,267.99.

The present officers of the Yonkers Savings-Bank are: President, Robert P. Getty; Vice-Presidents, Jacob Read and S. Francis Quick; Treasurer, J. Henry Williams; Secretary, Jos. A. Lockwood; Assistant Secretary, Leander Read; Finance Committee, Jacob Read, J. Henry Williams, Jos. A. Lockwood; Cashier, Lyman Cobb, Jr.

There were forty-one charter members in 1854, only seven now living, and but three members of the Board—Robert P. Getty, J. Henry Williams and Jacob Read.

The amount of interest credited to depositors since organization is $1,548,345.33; the item for the first six months was $124.16, the last six months, $45,832.17.

The total amount of deposits received since 1854,	$14,800,894.84
The total amount of interests credited since 1854,	1,548,345.33
	$16,349,240.17

The statement of July 1, 1896, gives the resources as $2,796,337.11; liabilities due depositors, $2,587,071.17, leaving a surplus of $209,265.94. In January, 1883, the bank had a little experience which is a part of its history, and of that of the city. It is thus related by the Rev. Dr. Cole in his "History of Yonkers": "At the beginning of the afternoon of Thursday, the 25th, a rumor was somehow started that the bank was in trouble. How it originated has never been learned. Various statements were made at the time. One was that a woman having called at the bank to draw money just before two o'clock, and finding it not yet open, had immediately afterward remarked on the street, or in a store, that she had been to the bank for money, but that *the bank had closed its doors and she could not get it*. However the rumor was started, the effect was electric. A run on the bank began during the afternoon hours and continued for the next two days dying out gradually with the closing hours of Saturday. The officers,

LYMAN COBB, JR.

had securities in their hands at the time, on which they could have realized $800,000, if it had been necessary.

They continued courteously to meet every demand upon them during all their regular hours, and when they closed successively at twelve and at five, remained with applicants yet in the bank till half-past one and half-past six, till the last applicant had his money. They paid out, in all, $74,000, every dollar of which, as it went out, only strengthened the bank more and more, while those who were the victims of the excitement suffered the loss of their interest due, and a few of them were even so unfortunate as to dissipate, within a few hours, all their principal besides. It is said that nearly all the accounts were redeposited in the bank within the next six months, and that most of them were returned in the identical bills and silver which had been paid out.

THE FIRST NATIONAL BANK OF YONKERS, N. Y., was originally chartered under the name of "The Bank of Yonkers." It was organized in 1854, and began business on August 10th in that year. The directors adopted as an adornment for their bank bills the portrait of the eldest daughter of Mr. John Bashford, who kept the popular inn and stage house down at the sloop wharf. The name of the lady was Miss Joanna C. Bashford, afterwards Mrs. William Hindhaugh. Her portrait remained on the bills until 1865, when the institution became a national bank. One of the old notes is preserved at the bank.

YONKERS SAVINGS BANK.

The original directors were Amos W. Gates, Ethan Flagg, Robert P. Getty, Henry F. Devoe, Lemuel W. Wells, William H. Arthur, William G. Ackerman, Fielding S. Gant, William C. Waring, James L. Valentine, John Olmsted, John Stilwell, Henry W. Bashford. The directors since elected, in the order of their election have been Abraham Hatfield, John T. Waring, Thomas C. Cornell, James C. Bell, Joseph S. Hawkins, William W. Scrugham, Jeremiah Robins, John W. Mills, Edward Underhill, Isaac H. Knox, Cornelius M. Odell, John H. Morris, Jonathan Odell, George B. Skinner, Henry Bowers, Alexander Smith, William L. Cogswell, James Faulkner, James Stewart, William A. Dibble, James W. Drake, Charles Clark, William H. Doty, Warren B. Smith, Rudolf Eickemeyer, Augustus Marsh, William D. Olmsted, Samuel P. Holmes, William F. Cochran, William P. Ketcham, William W. Scrugham, William B. Edgar, Wells Olmsted, W. Delavan Baldwin, Frank T. Holder, Wallis Smith, Harold Brown, R. Eickemeyer, Jr.

John Olmsted was the honored President of the bank from its organization until his decease, which occurred May 30, 1890. He was succeeded by the present incumbent, William H. Doty, on July 1, 1890. Mr. Doty had served as Vice-President from March 11, 1887. W. Delavan Baldwin was elected Vice-President on January 12, 1894, and still occupies the position. The first cashier was Egbert Howland, who resigned May 1, 1875, on account of impaired health. He died January 12, 1878. His business ability was great, and all who were conversant with the affairs of the bank realized how invaluable his services were. William D. Olmsted (Assistant Cashier from September 15, 1871), succeeded him as Cashier. On September 10, 1878, Mr. Olmsted resigned his position and was succeeded

MISS JOANNA C. BASHFORD.

by Wallis Smith, who still occupies the office. James T. Howland entered the bank as clerk when it opened. For many years he was the bank's teller. He resigned in 1895. John H. Keeler was appointed book-keeper April 1, 1868, and resigned February 1, 1873. Wallis Smith succeeded Mr. Keeler and occupied the position until he became cashier. Willard M. Baldwin, who now holds the position of teller, has been in the employ of the bank since 1887. The other teller is James E. Howes, who entered the bank as an employee in 1886. The other employees are Frank O. Freethy, Truman S. Kellogg, Edward L. Schultz, C. W. T. Eylers and Harry C. Miller.

The first place in which the bank transacted business was a small room in the Getty House. Nearly two years after its opening, rooms at the south end of the Getty House were leased. In March, 1863, a safety vault was erected in these rooms and an additional apartment in the rear. These premises were subsequently occupied by the Citizens' National Bank.

The bank erected a substantial banking house on the east side of Getty Square, in 1871–73. The land on which the building stands was purchased of the Anderson estate. Lewis Lillie, formerly of Troy, N. Y., built the vaults, and placed them in position, as soon as the building was enclosed. On April 30, 1873, after business hours, the treasure and books of the bank were removed to the new vaults, and business was begun in the new building the next day. The structure has been thus described:

"Fronting Getty Square, on the east side, with its imposing front of gray stone, wide entrance, and broad, high window, letting in a flood of light, which penetrates to every nook and corner of the interior, it is easily one of the most modern, as well as one of the most pretentious and finest of the commercial buildings in Yonkers.

"Within is a spacious chamber, with a high ceiling, handsomely decorated, in a neutral color, which adds dignity to a perfectly equipped and furnished bank counting-room. The perspective of the interior resembles that of the Independence National Bank of Philadelphia, a bank which, times without number, has been held up as a model institution, in its

FIRST NATIONAL BANK OF YONKERS.

interior construction, for other banks to copy. There is no bank in this country which has a finer counting-room than the First National Bank of Yonkers. This can be said unreservedly and without exaggeration. The fittings are all of rich mahogany. The reception room for customers of the bank and the 'coupon rooms,' where depositors of bonds and stocks in the great $20,000 safety vault, can be snugly ensconced from sight while examining their valuables or cutting off coupons, are 'admirable and up to date.' In all its appurtenances this bank is 'up to date.' Its conveniences are such as one finds in the most modern institutions of its kind, only in the large cities. Taking into consideration these facts and the bank's honorable career and management, there is small wonder that it numbers among its clients several millionaires. Many of the boxes in the safety vault are rented, some of them to people who are multi-millionaires. This circumstance would certainly be a source of great elation to the majority of bank officials, and many would not hesitate to make a public use of such a flattering advertisement, but the officers and directors of the First National Bank of Yonkers have always been as conservative in dealings with their customers as in the conduct of their banking business, and thus they have won the confidence and have received trusts from men whose names are household words, synonymous for millions, throughout the world."

When the institution was a State bank its circulation was $90,000, which was assumed by the new bank—the First National Bank of Yonkers, N. Y. Some of the notes representing the former circulation have never been presented for redemption.

When the institution began business in the small room in the Getty House, at its opening, thirteen deposits were received. They aggregated $11,926. Its first dividend was paid on April 10, 1855, to 133 shareholders. The stock of the bank has always been above par.

THE REPORT OF THE CONDITION OF THE BANK AT THE CLOSE OF BUSINESS, JULY 14, 1896:

RESOURCES.

Loans and discounts,	$809,484.98
Overdrafts, secured and unsecured,	3,666.39
U. S. Bonds to secure circulation,	75,000.00
U. S. Bonds on hand,	5,000.00
Premiums on U. S. Bonds,	8,400.00
Stock, securities, etc.,	21,773.87
Banking-house, furniture and fixtures,	75,000.00
Other real estate and mortgages owned,	81,899.75
Due from National Banks (not reserve agents),	162,552.23
Due from State Banks and bankers,	118,438.64
Due from approved reserve agents,	175,010.06
Checks and other cash items,	7,765.28
Notes of other National Banks,	17,710.00
Fractional paper currency, nickels and cents,	1,251.25
Lawful money reserve in bank, viz.:	
Specie, $51,745.30	
Legal-tender notes, 42,730.00	94,475.30
Redemption fund with U. S. Treasurer (5 per cent. of circulation),	3,375.00
Total,	$1,660,802.75

THE PEOPLE'S SAVINGS BANK.

LIABILITIES.

Capital stock paid in,	$150,000.00
Surplus fund,	65,000.00
Undivided profits, less expenses and taxes paid,	3,489.49
National Bank notes outstanding,	67,500.00
Due to other National Banks,	359,537.46
Due to State Banks and bankers,	53,437.70
Dividends unpaid,	1,555.75
Individual deposits subject to check,	906,389.09
Demand certificates of deposit,	27,798.90
Certified checks,	26,094.36
Total,	$1,660,802.75

THE PEOPLE'S SAVINGS BANK of the town of Yonkers was incorporated April 5, 1866. It began business April 27, 1867. The original Trustees were Robert J. Douglass, Andrew Archibald, Orrin A. Bills, Jonathan Vail, William Radford, William B. Edgar, George B. Skinner, James P. Sanders, William Macfarlane, George E. Coddington, John Phillips, Thomas F. Morris, Eli L. Seger, Nelson Ackert, Levi P. Rose, Henry F. Brevoort, Peter U. Fowler, M. W. Rooney, Clinton M. Davis, George B. Pentz and James W. Mitchell.

The Trustees since elected have been John Wheeler, Philip A. Deyo, Isaac G. Johnson, Lawrence R. Condon, Rudolf Eickemeyer, Joseph Masten, William A. Gibson, George Stewart, Peter E. Radcliff, John G. P. Holden, James C. Courter, William H. Copcutt, J. G. Herriott, Peter J. Elting, Norton P. Otis, Rufus Dutton, Charles Reed, Charles H. Emerson, James E. Bloomer, C. M. Moseman, Frank E. Wheeler, Halcyon Skinner, Robert Neville, John Embree, A. T. Kear, Abram C. Mott, Charles T. Mercer, John Wallace, Charles E. Gorton, George H. Selleck, A. P. Hazard, Robert H. Neville, Richard L. Condon, Frank O. Hartshorn, Charles R. Culver, Albert C. Benedict, Ethelbert B. Embree, Alexander Saunders, Gustav Schlueter, George Vanderlyn, Charles R. Otis, Stephen T. Bell and George W. Cobb. The first President of the bank was William Radford. His successors have been Thomas F. Morris, George B. Pentz, Joseph Masten, Charles Reed, Rufus Dutton and Charles E. Gorton. The Secretaries have been James P. Sanders, J. G. P. Holden, Abram C. Mott and F. E. Wheeler. George W. Cobb is the only Treasurer the bank has had. Frank E. Wheeler is the Secretary, and William H. Shultz, Clerk.

CHARLES E. WARING.

The business of the institution began in the Radford building. It is now conducted in the bank's fine building (adjoining First National Bank), in Getty Square. The fifty-ninth semi-annual statement, July 1, 1896, give the resources as $1,582,494.21; liabilities due depositors $1,506,580.85, leaving a surplus of $75,913.36.

THE CITIZENS' NATIONAL BANK of the City of Yonkers was incorporated December 5, 1872. Its stockholders met on January 31, 1873, to elect officers. The bank began business the next day. The first directors elected were Charles H. Hamilton, Peter U. Fowler, Jonathan Vail, William H. Copcutt, Joseph Peene, Henry R. Hicks, William Macfarlane, James Ackerman, Lyman Cobb, Jr., William G. Ackerman, Charles R. Dusenberry and John Wheeler. Those elected since are as follows: Charles E. Waring, Levi W. Flagg, William S. Carr, Ezekiel J. Elting, William Fred. Lawrence, Philip A. Deyo, Peter J. Elting, John H. Keeler, Joseph Masten, Isaac M. Dyckman, Andrew Deyo, Jacob Levevre, Jos. A. Lockwood, H. J. Andrus, Frederick Von Storch and Stephen Barker. In 1895 the number of directors was reduced from thirteen to nine.

In 1896 the following named are Directors: President, Charles E. Waring; Vice-President, Peter J. Elting; Cashier, John H. Keeler; Henry R. Hicks, Charles R. Dusenberry, E. J. Elting, Andrew Deyo, Jos. A. Lockwood, H. J. Andrus.

Charles H. Hamilton served the bank as President from February 1, 1873, to November 10, 1873. On that date Jonathan Vail was elected President, and to his able and untiring service the success of the institution is in a large measure due. Peter U. Fowler was elected President September 24, 1886, and on the same day Peter J. Elting was elected Vice-President.

CITIZENS' NATIONAL BANK.

On October 1, 1886, Mr. Elting entered the bank as an active officer, in which capacity he still continues. John H. Keeler was the first Cashier and has served continuously to the present day. Henry M. Anderson is the only teller the bank has had. The other employees are: George W. Peene, William H. Radcliff, Horace P. Allen, James W. Shaughnessy, Fred. C. Cummings, Harry P. Bissell and George J. Lancaster.

The bank was organized with a capital of $100,000. The total net profits since organization have been $263,093.59, of which $100,000 is the present surplus. The stockholders have received in dividends $151,500.

The institution began business in the Yonkers Bank Building. On May 1, 1873, it moved into the rooms vacated by the First National Bank. Its architects, Messrs. E. A. Quick & Son, of Yonkers, in 1896, prepared plans for one of the most imposing banking houses in the city. This building is now in course of construction. It will be four stories in height. The banking room (25 x 105 feet) will be fire-proof. It will be lighted by a glass dome. The floors will be mosaic, and the wainscot, marble. A new Herring's burglar-proof vault will assure the best protection for safe deposit boxes and the funds of the bank.

THE REPORT OF THE CONDITION OF THE BANK AT THE CLOSE OF BUSINESS, JULY 14, 1896:

RESOURCES.

Loans and discounts,	$479,238.64
Overdrafts, secured and unsecured,	736.44
U. S. Bonds to secure circulation,	80,000.00
U. S. Bonds on hand,	20,000.00
Premiums on U. S. Bonds,	7,037.50
Stock, securities, etc.,	140,827.46
Banking-House, furniture and fixtures,	35,424.43
Due from National Banks (not reserve agents),	1,110.14
Due from State Banks and bankers,	5,094.82
Due from approved reserve agents,	308,304.20
Checks and other cash items,	3,389.00
Notes of other National Banks,	693.00
Fractional paper currency, nickels and cents,	714.04

Lawful money reserve in bank, *viz.*:

Specie,	$30,507.50	
Legal-tender notes,	18,193.00	
		48,700.50
Redemption fund with U. S. Treasurer (5 per cent. of circulation),		3,600.00
Due from U. S. Treasurer other than 5 per cent. redemption fund,		1,200.00
Total,		$1,136,070.17

LIABILITIES.

Capital stock paid in,	$100,000.00
Surplus fund,	100,000.00
Undivided profits, less expenses and taxes paid,	18,420.68
National Bank notes outstanding,	70,800.00
Due to other National Banks,	11,111.17
Due to State Banks and bankers,	7,774.16
Individual deposits subject to check,	808,430.38
Certified checks,	19,415.63
Cashier's checks outstanding,	118.15
Total,	$1,136,070.17

CHAPTER XVIII.

YONKERS BOARD OF TRADE.

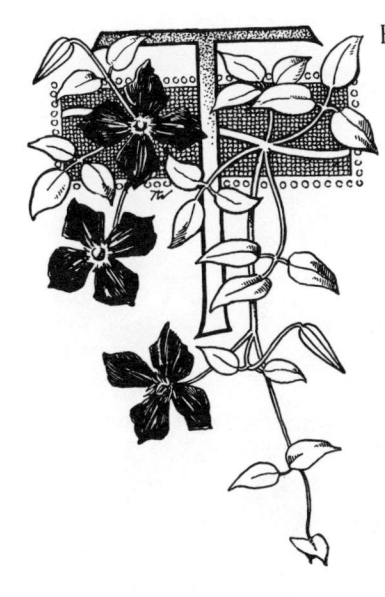

THE Yonkers Board of Trade was organized June 30, 1893. Its objects are to acquire and disseminate useful information of the trades, manufactures and general interests of the city of Yonkers, to encourage intercourse between business men, to co-operate with similar organizations in other cities, and generally, to aid in the promotion and development of the commercial, industrial and other interests of the community. It has committees on membership, trades, needs, public works, transportation and communication, taxes and assessments, public health, legislation, advertising and printing. The names of its trustees, of its executive and other committees, and of its members, are recorded in the printed publications of the board.

In 1893, William F. Cochran was elected its first President; Frederic Shonnard, first Vice-President; James V. Lawrence, second Vice-President; William H. Doty, Treasurer; Philip Verplanck, Secretary. On September 19, 1893, Philip Verplanck resigned as Secretary, and George Rayner was elected in his stead. On January 31, 1894, E. K. Martin was elected second Vice-President in place of James V. Lawrence. On January 15, 1895, E. K. Martin was elected President. Frederic Shonnard, first Vice-President; James V. Lawrence, second Vice-President; William H. Doty, Treasurer, and George Rayner, Secretary. From time to time, important matters relating to the welfare of the city are presented to the Board for consideration. At the meeting of November 19, 1895, Joseph S. Wood, Chairman of the Committee on Water Supply of the Board of Trade of Mount Vernon, was present by invitation, and was heard on the question of a suburban water supply.

He said that the people of Yonkers and Mount Vernon looked forward with bright anticipations o the future growth of their cities. There is reason to believe that if the city of Yonkers will provide facilities and accommodations it will have a much larger population. The Yonkers watershed extends over five miles square, and the limit of production is 1,500,000,000 gallons. This will hardly furnish enough for fifty per cent. increase of population. The watershed is too small for the city. The daily consumption is seventy gallons per capita of population. The use of water is increasing owing to the introduction of baths, water-closets, elevators, etc. In some cities the per capita daily consumption is 100 gallons, and it will soon be so here.

Mount Vernon has a watershed four and one-half miles square, Yonkers five, White Plains two, Mamaroneck seven, Larchmont two and one-half, and New Rochelle three and one-half. Yonkers has, therefore, the smallest watershed in proportion to population of any of these places. How are we to get more water? There is no available water supply in Westchester County that Yonkers or Mount Vernon can get, for what there is has already been appropriated.

Mr. Wood proposed a Metropolitan Water District, similar to that of Boston, whereby the State builds and owns the water works, the cities lay the pipes, and pay to the State for the water used. There is a State Board of Water Commissioners, and no city can pre-empt any water supply without the consent of the State Board,

Mr. Wood said that now is the time for action, and he asked the people of Yonkers to join with those of Mount Vernon in an application to the Legislature for the passage of an act similar to that of

Massachusetts. In union there is strength, and we should act together. He thought that water could be got from the Croton Aqueduct by authority of the Legislature, and that no city would be allowed to monopolize a water supply to the detriment of any other city that may need it.

Mr. McAdoo moved that a committee of three be appointed to act with the Mount Vernon people in relation to a suburban water supply. The motion was carried, and the President appointed William H. Doty, Samuel L. Cooper and W. H. McAdoo.

A vote of thanks was tendered to Mr. Wood, and the meeting adjourned.

At the meeting on January 21, 1896, J. J. R. Croes, Consulting Engineer of the Bronx River sewer, was present, and, on invitation of William H. Baldwin, he was invited to address the meeting. He said, substantially:

About three and a half miles from the east of the Hudson River there is a valley as large as New York City and the annexed district; this valley has only one outlet, and that is in the East River or the Sound. It is practicable and desirable to construct a sewer that will receive sewage only, letting surface water find its way into the Bronx by other means.

A similar system has been in operation in Boston for some years, and it is being extended. It is proposed to take an easement of a strip of land along both sides of the Bronx River, sufficient in breadth to include the channel of the stream, with its crooks and bends, and for land on which to construct the sewer. The total drainage area of the Bronx and Hutchinson Valleys is seventy-five square miles, of which fifteen are in New York City. The area of the city of Yonkers in the drainage is ten miles, and its proportion of the expense would be about twenty per cent. of the total. The chief cost of the proposed sewer will be in the works necessary at its discharge into the Sound. A reservoir will be built to let the sewage out at ebb tide.

The method of payment is easy, running over a number of years. The first ten years the payment is light, the second ten years it would be heavier, and so on with the third and fourth. The assessment is to be apportioned by the Board of Supervisors among the several towns, and the towns will assess on the property benefited, or in any other way they deem best.

EDWIN K. MARTIN.

A proposition has been made for Yonkers to oppose the construction of this sewer, and to drain the Bronx River and Tibbett's Brook Valleys through a tunnel into the Hudson River at the southern part of the city, but this would cost as much as the Yonkers assessment on the Bronx River Sewer, and would make the neighborhood of the outlet of the sewer an undesirable place for residence.

As to the statement that the proposed Bronx River Sewer will take sewage only, it is to be a trunk sewer, and lateral sewers will have to be constructed to connect with it. Where necessary, these lateral sewers will be made to take surface water.

A GROUP OF CHARTER MEMBERS OF THE
YONKERS BOARD OF TRADE.

1. Gen. Thomas Ewing.
2. Peter U. Fowler.
3. Walter H. Paddock.
4. C. E. V. Leliva.
5. John Bellows.
6. Chester W. Newman.
7. Philip Verplanck.
8. Wm. H. Richardson.
9. P. J. Flannery.
10. James Stewart.
11. Andrew Archibald.
12. John B. Copcutt.

The total cost of the Bronx River Sewer is estimated to be $3,716,310, and the share of Yonkers will be about eight per cent. New York county will pay a good proportion. The two counties will issue the bonds. The Commission has not yet finished its report to the Legislature, and there are matters relating to the mode of payment not entirely settled. The report will contain the draft of a bill. One thing is to be considered: The people of the west side of Yonkers have their system of sewers, and they had the Hudson River for an outlet, which cost them nothing. The people on the east side have no Hudson River, but must pay for an outlet, and the people on the west side should help them by placing a portion of the expense on the whole city.

At the annual meeting held on January 21, 1896, President Edwin K. Martin read his annual report, which was approved and ordered published. It is as follows:

"The Yonkers Board of Trade enters upon its third year. There are no brilliant results behind it. Boards of Trade in long settled communities and through periods of depression such as we have passed are affected by their environment very much like individuals. At the same time, it would be unfair to say that we have not accomplished something.

"On March 9, 1895, our Committee on Transportation introduced a bill into the Legislature, for the operation of through trains from Yonkers to Rector Street over the New York and Putnam and Manhattan Railways. This bill passed the House and the Senate Committee, but failed in the latter body because of the lateness of the session. The same bill has again been sent to Albany and is now pending in the present Legislature.

"In April, 1895, the same committee had the 8.40 A.M. train on the New York and Putnam Railroad restored, it having been discontinued for some time. On the 16th of the same month the Chairman of the same committee appeared before the joint committee of the Assembly and Senate in behalf of a reduction of telephone rates in cities of the size of Yonkers from $100 per year to $36 per year.

GEORGE RAYNER.

This bill also failed to pass, and will again be introduced to the present session.

"May 21, the Board of Trade amended its constitution, reducing the initiation fee. This change was made for the purpose of bringing the body in touch with a larger class of people, and giving it greater popular support. It resulted in the Board adding twenty-five members to its rolls at once, and this hearty response to its more liberal policy may be said to be only the beginning of a more prosperous future.

"In June, 1895, the Board secured for Yonkers improved postal facilities. There had, hitherto, been no outgoing mails south after 8 o'clock P.M. on week days, and 8 A.M. on Sundays, a condition of affairs which probably did not exist in any city of similar size in the country. Application to the First Assistant Postmaster-General for relief secured to Yonkers an outgoing mail as late as 10 P.M. week days and 5 P.M. Sundays.

"During the same month, the Board adopted a resolution offering to co-operate with the City Attorney to obtain the money bequeathed by the late Samuel J. Tilden for a public library in Yonkers.

"On the 17th of September, a resolution and report were adopted favoring a system of public parks for Yonkers, and at nearly every meeting since, the Board of Trade has urged upon the Mayor and Aldermen the great necessity of supplying this deficiency before the available lands in suitable localities become too high-priced.

"It is with great pleasure that we notice that at least one breathing spot near the heart of the city, on its highest grounds, has been secured, to which the poorer classes who surround that section may escape when the fierce heat of the summer takes possession of the lower levels. It is probably the only spot in Yonkers from which the magnificent and commanding views of the Palisades and Hudson could be obtained which is to be had at any such sum of money or near it. And before it is too late the public is entitled to at least one of these beautiful heights, which it can call its own. This is only the beginning. Other parks will follow, and ought to, along the river front to the north, and in the heart of the city. But in Nodine Hill Park the Board of Aldermen, in some degree, make amends for what Yonkers lost when it failed to secure Park Hill.

"Nodine Hill can, with a small outlay, be made equally beautiful with Park Hill, and quite as attractive. The Yonkers Electric Railroad has agreed to lay its tracks to the new park the moment it is laid out, and this will put its beautiful views and fresh air at the disposal of the entire city. We understand a lake of three or four acres will be constructed for skating, and many other sources of public amusement and entertainment will be speedily introduced. For this excellent beginning the Board of Trade can take to itself no small share of commendation because of its persistent efforts in behalf of public parks.

"In October of the same year, a committee of the Board called upon H. Walter Webb, Third Vice-President of the New York Central and Hudson River Railroad, presenting a petition signed by more than 1,000 citizens of Yonkers, asking that a new station be erected at the foot of Main Street, and also requesting better sanitary arrangements in the present station until a new one could be had. In response to this visit the sanitary arrangements were at once begun, and are now nearly completed; and of the three new stations to be built on this end of the road, in the near future, Yonkers was promised full consideration.

"Besides these results obtained and sought to be obtained by the Board of Trade, there has been secured the earlier delivery of mail matter to the citizens of Yonkers, so that business men going to New York City might obtain their home letters before leaving in the morning. This, however, has only been partially successful, and is in process of further development. It also secured better electric railway service on Park Avenue and elsewhere, by calling attention to the violation of its contracts by the electric railway company.

"It has requested the proper city authorities to create a supervision of the milk supply, which is greatly needed, and asks that a milk inspector be appointed.

"It has at the present time a committee obtaining information regarding the collection and disposal of garbage in other cities, some of which places the committee, in the discharge of its duties, will shortly visit.

"Besides these matters, the discussion before the Board, of needed public improvements, future water supply, the Bronx and other sewer facilities, assessment and taxation, have lent an interest to its meetings during the past year which we believe has not been surpassed by any voluntary organization in the city of Yonkers.

"It has been said that Cavalry are the eyes of the army. In a similar sense, a keen, alert Board of Health is the eyes of a city. It is on the lookout for what may be said to escape the ordinary observer— the ambushed dangers that threaten our civil life and comfort. There is no more efficient and needful organization among us to-day than the Board of Health. Its splendid work in improving the sanitary rules of the city demands the highest commendation, but it needs the moral support of all classes to reach its greatest efficiency, and needs greater appropriations than the city fathers have been willing to accord hitherto. The Board of Trade has always stood by it and extended its cordial support to these ends.

"As to the Fire Department of Yonkers, it is safe to say that no city of America of the same size and area clings to the old volunteer system with like tenacity. Yonkers, besides being the laughing-stock of the underwriters, pays a heavy penalty for its antiquated methods, in increased insurance premiums. This the Board of Trade has frequently called attention to. Let there be a partly-paid department at least, if the city cannot afford the whole modern idea at one time.

"Yonkers needs a hotel. It will never be a modern town, not to speak of a city until it can properly entertain the stranger within its gates. The seashores and the mountains, Florida and California, the whole United States in fact, are filled with hotels whose very positions insure their failure before they are built. Millions of dollars have been sunk in the erection of splendid caravansaries in absurd places where people could not go more than half the year, or even a few months, if they wanted. And yet capital seems afraid to risk the construction of a modest hotel in Yonkers alongside of 2,000,000 people, and in the midst of 40,000 of our own citizens. And this in the face of the fact that from Poughkeepsie to Spuyten Duyvil on the east bank of the Hudson there is not a first-class spot where a person can get a night's lodgings with the accompaniments of modern hotel life. The Board of Trade has often called the public attention to this situation, and hopes at an early day to take up the question more vigorously. On the whole, our past year has been a profitable one, and 1896 must not fall behind it."

This report indicates some of the lines along which this influential body is working. At one of its last meetings, it planned to encourage the planting and protection of shade trees.

For a long time, the Board of Trade realized that if an opportunity were afforded the citizens of Yonkers to meet and discuss questions of mutual interest, social fellowship would be promoted. To foster this spirit, the Board resolved to have an annual banquet to which all classes should be invited, and where they might fraternize. The first of the proposed annual banquets was on the evening of February 17, 1896, and was spoken of as " one of the most enjoyable of Yonkers social occasions."

The Board, during its brief life as an organization, has been foremost in directing attention to the splendid location of Yonkers, as a city for home building, and to its admirable situation as a manufacturing centre; also to its healthfulness and superior educational advantages.

In its second year, the Board expended more than four thousand dollars for advertising the advantages of Yonkers, in the newspapers of New York and other cities throughout the country. Most, if not all the reforms introduced into the municipal government, originated in the Board of Trade, or were advanced by its influence. It has called together progressive and energetic citizens, united them with a common purpose to further the best interests of the city, and to oppose ill-considered movements. It has not sought to criticise or foster a fault-finding spirit, but to secure for Yonkers all the latest and best municipal improvements. In endeavoring to accomplish this, the Board has attained an encouraging degree of success, and it is yet only at the beginning of its important mission in the city.

CHAPTER XIX.

YONKERS NEWSPAPERS.

HUMAN sources of shaping influences are the parent, the pulpit, the preceptor, the platform and the press. Until in the early fifties, Yonkers had no local press to record and report its news, and to help shape its life. In 1850, the population of the town, including Kingsbridge, was only 4,160. In 1852, Thomas Towndrow, a representative of the New York press in Westchester County, came to Yonkers to collect news items. Thomas C. Cornell suggested to him the establishment of a newspaper in Yonkers. Within a few days, Mr. Towndrow came to the village, accompanied by his associate and printer, Thomas Smith. *The Yonkers Herald* was the name they gave to the paper which they established. Mr. Towndrow remained only a brief time. Mr. Smith continued for years the editor and proprietor of the paper. The Yonkers Democratic Publishing Association bought the *Herald* in 1864, and, for a short time, it was edited by Messrs. E. K. Olmstead and J. G. P. Holden. Mr. Olmstead soon withdrew, and Mr. Holden became the responsible editor. On June 4, 1864, the name was changed. The paper on that date became *The Gazette*. On March 4, 1865, Henry B. Dawson of Morrisania, the historian, became editor, Mr. Holden being associate editor and manager. The "Gazette Series" of historical papers was published about that time. On May 6, 1866, Mr. Holden became the sole editor, and on May 15, 1866, the name of the paper was changed to *The Yonkers Gazette*. In that year, Mr. Holden obtained a controlling interest in the stock, and within a brief time purchased the balance. The paper has been enlarged four times.

On January 20, 1896, *The Yonkers Gazette* was sold to the Yonkers Gazette Company (incorporated). J. G. P. Holden became President; Peter U. Fowler, Vice-President; Edwin R. Holden, Secretary and Treasurer. J. G. P. Holden continued to be the editor. E. R. Holden was associate editor and manager. On March 30, 1896, the first number of *The Evening Gazette* (a daily) was issued. A linotype had been purchased, and was first in use in the office about this time. The advertising manager of the paper was C. H. Du Bois, and the reporters were Frank Ellis, John H. Bangs and George W. Lewis. *The Gazette* was a Democratic organ, but, without regard to politics, advocated the various improvements which have been made in the city. As an original paragrapher, Mr. J. G. P. Holden's *nom de plume* was "Nonpareil Quadrat X. P. D." As a writer he was also known by the name "Ralph Redwood." His work was not exclusively that of an editor. As a city official, a bank officer, and in other capacities, he has for many years been identified with public affairs. He is now the city postmaster; and with characteristic public spirit has endeavored to secure the erection in Yonkers of a United States Government building for a post office. On July 29, 1896, J. G. P. Holden retired as President of the Yonkers Gazette Company, and severed his connection with the paper. Henry Osterheld became President, and I. Sumner Burnstine, Secretary. Edwin R. Holden remained Treasurer. At this time both the daily and weekly *Gazette* became Republican in politics. Edwin R. Holden is the managing editor, Frank H. Cole the business manager, and C. D. Cook, manager of the circulation department. C. H. Du Bois and H. Carlos Fordham are writers on the *Gazette* staff.

In 1856, Thomas C. Cornell, whose political views differed from those which Thomas Smith was publishing in *The Yonkers Herald*, united with other citizens in the establishment of a Whig journal. Jeremiah H. Stedwell, of the then recently formed law firm, Messrs. Stedwell & Mann, was interested in the enterprise. He influenced his friend Matthew F. Rowe, who was at that time publishing a paper at Peekskill, to remove to Yonkers. A weekly paper, known as *The Examiner*, was issued in Yonkers by

Mr. Rowe on February 23, 1856. In 1862, *The Clarion*, another weekly, was established by J. Burns and Alonzo Bell. In 1863, Everett Clapp, Justus Lawrence and G. Hilton Scribner purchased *The Examiner* and *The Clarion*. The two papers were united under the name, *The Yonkers Statesman*, with Mr. Rowe as the editor. Messrs. Lawrence and Rowe owned the paper in October, 1864. Mr. Rowe became sole proprietor in 1869. In 1872, Mr. John W. Oliver was engaged as the editor, and occupies the position at the present time (1896).

Mr. Oliver passed his early years in Baltimore, Md., where he served an apprenticeship of eight years to learn the printing business. Early in May, 1835, he left Baltimore on foot, and reached New York City on the 15th of the same month, a stranger, with only six cents in his pocket. In less than one hour he was at work, within a month he was made foreman of the office, and within two years he had a printing office of his own. He applied some steam machinery to job printing, and revolutionized the trade.

In 1840, he assisted in organizing the Washingtonian movement in New York, and soon after published *The New York Organ*, a temperance paper, which obtained a large circulation, and exerted a wide influence. He and his brother Isaac, under the firm name, Oliver & Brother, conducted an extensive printing and publishing business at the southwest corner of Fulton and Nassau Streets, in what was then known as the *Sun* Building. In 1842, the two brothers organized the Order of the Sons of Temperance. Their printing business increased to such proportions that they sold their publishing business, purchased the lot, No. 32 Beekman Street, erected upon it a five-story white marble building, with cellar, sub-cellar and vault, and furnished it with all the appliances for steam printing.

Some time afterward Mr. Oliver sold his interest in the printing business to his brother, intending to retire, but he was soon convinced that an inactive life was not suitable for him. He fitted up a new printing office and again began business. On October 1, 1866, he removed to Yonkers, having purchased the property on Warburton Avenue, which has since been his home. In 1872, he disposed of his New York business, having a second time decided to retire, but by nine o'clock on the morning after he was released, he had made an arrangement with Mr. Rowe to edit *The Yonkers Statesman*. He put new life into the paper, attacking with characteristic vigor what he considered wrong and supporting what he deemed to be right.

In the spring of 1881, the "practical" politicians

JOHN G. P. HOLDEN.

EDWIN R. HOLDEN.

exerted their influence to have him removed from the editorial chair. He again decided to retire and pass his remaining days on his little farm in Smyrna, Del. A number of leading citizens, desirous of retaining his services as an editor in Yonkers, promised him support should a new paper be established. That resulted in the organization of the Yonkers Publishing Company, with a capital of $10,000, and the purchase of *The Statesman.* Thus within a month from the time of his dismissal, he returned to the establishment as publisher, editor and business manager.

In 1883, in accordance with his advice, the daily *Statesman* was issued. Many friends considered this an unwise venture. They held that Yonkers would not support a daily paper. The result has demonstrated their error. The daily was a pronounced success from the beginning. Its earnings have been sufficient to pay for the fine building occupied for its business, besides paying satisfactory dividends to the stockholders. "All this may be attributed to hard work and good management." In 1884, Mr. Oliver purchased a controlling interest in the Company. The weekly *Statesman* is still continued.

For thirty years, Mr. Oliver has been an active citizen of Yonkers. He served as a Trustee of the village, and also as a Trustee of Union Free School No. 6. He recalls, with great satisfaction, the part he was able to take in inaugurating the sewer system, the establishment of the daily *Statesman*, the consolidation of the public schools, and the erection of the Soldiers' and

JOHN W. OLIVER.

Sailors' Monument. While the *Statesman* is radically Republican, Mr. Oliver has supported Democratic candidates for local offices when, in his judgment, the public interest would be promoted by their election. On April 30, 1895, a number of representative citizens surprised him in his home, on the occasion of his attaining his eightieth birthday, and presented to him a silver pitcher and salver. William Allen Butler made the presentation address. The reply showed that the venerable journalist was deeply affected by the unexpected token of the esteem of his fellow-citizens. Mr. Oliver has been a communicant of the Methodist Episcopal Church, since the autumn of 1842.

His son, Edwin A. Oliver, is assistant editor of *The Statesman,* and is in charge of the business office. He is a graduate of Union Free School No. 6. He excels as a witty and pungent paragrapher, being widely quoted by the press in this country and in Europe. J. Joseph Lawrence, the city editor, is the son of a deceased soldier of the Union. He graduated at Union Free School No. 2. His sound judgment, fine literary taste and his knowledge of music and of the art of printing, admirably fit him for the responsible position he occupies. A number of reporters have been on the *Statesman's* reportorial staff. In the village period, Ebenezer Curtice reported for the paper. James Norwell has long served the *Statesman* as a reporter. He is widely known and popular.

John C. Turner, now of *The Paterson (N. J.) Guardian,* J. Perry Worden, now of Columbia College, were for some time *Statesman* reporters. Elmer J. Craft is a present day collector of news items for the *Statesman*

In May, 1866, Thomas Smith began the publication of *The Yonkers Herald, Jr.*, and later, for a long time he published *The Yonkers Herald*. He began to publish *The Yonkers Daily Herald* on October 21, 1867. It was a small sheet, and was published for several years. Mr. Smith died August, 1874. His son continued to publish the *Herald* after his father's death, but finally he removed from Yonkers and the paper did not make its appearance again for a number of years. The succession of editors and proprietors were Thomas Smith, E. C. Bruce and Charles Schneider. The paper was re-established in 1891 by Frederic Shonnard, with Frank Warner as editor for one week. His successor was Clifford Smythe, who edited the paper for some time. During his absence of thirteen weeks, Joseph Fox was the editor. The paper came under the control of the Yonkers Daily Herald Publishing Company in 1894, and was first published as a morning daily. Alfred Fox became its editor in that year. The city editor of this daily paper is Joseph Fox. In August, 1894, *The Yonkers Herald* removed to its present substantial and commodious building, No. 10 Warburton Avenue. The structure was built for it and is adapted to all the requirements of a modern newspaper office. Excise and Public Bath questions, Manor Hall grounds retention, and other public questions, have received the *Herald's* notice, both reportorial and editorial. Its circulation and the patronage of its advertising columns have increased.

EDWIN A. OLIVER.

Alfred Fox, the editor, was born in Heeley, England, June 20, 1868. He came to America in September, 1884, and acquired a knowledge of business in the newspaper advertising offices of G. P. Rowell & Co., Dun & Co., and Frank E. Randall, President of the Empire Coal Company. While in New York, he wrote for several papers. Some of his newspaper work attracted the notice of those who subsequently became directors of *The Yonkers Herald*, and he was chosen editor. His genial disposition, and his interest in the public welfare, have made him popular in Yonkers. Joseph Fox, the father of the editor of the *Herald*, is a thoughtful observer of city affairs, and his views are often expressed in the columns of the paper. Frank E. Xavier is a member of the reportorial staff.

Thomas L. Mottram established *The Plaindealer* in 1881. William G. Shrive established *The Free Press* in 1882. E. C. Bruce began the publication of *The Yonkers Democrat* in 1882. M. H. Clark afterwards published the same paper as *The Democrat News*. *The Yonkers Home Journal*, a German paper, with a small English edition had a limited circulation.

Home Journal and News. This publication developed from *St. Joseph's News*, an eight-page semi-monthly, 11 x 15, devoted to the interests of St. Joseph's Church. *The St. Joseph's News*, afterward *The Catholic News*, was issued September 12, 1891. *The Catholic News* appeared in May, 1893, published at its own office, 28 South Broadway. Articles of incorporation were filed with the County Clerk, March, 1893, made out in the name of The Yonkers

J. JOSEPH LAWRENCE.

Catholic News Company, and signed by the Rev. Henry F. Xavier, Peter A. Callan, M. D., J. McClure, Fred. S. Taylor and Daniel C. Nolan as directors.

The editors of the publication have been the Rev. Henry F. Xavier and Peter A. Callan, M.D. There was a break in the continuity of the appearance of the paper when its title was changed to *The Catholic News*, owing to the delay of the printing material dealer in furnishing the plant necessary for the issue of the paper from its own office. When the office was in proper working order, the date of issue was changed from the second and fourth Saturdays to every Saturday, and the size increased to twelve pages.

The first change of name (from *Saint Joseph's News* to *The Catholic News*) was necessary on account of its growth from a local paper to one of much wider circulation and interest. The second change (from *The Catholic News* to *The Home Journal and News*) was made in December, 1894, when it was found that the Yonkers paper was often confounded with one of the same name published in New York City. As the latter was first established, its right to the title was conceded by the Yonkers Catholic News Company. In January, 1894, the company acquired an interest in *The Yonkers Herald*, and the plant of *The Catholic News* was moved to the office of the former, No. 63 Main Street. Here it remained until its own building, No 10 Warburton Avenue, was completed, to which it moved in August, 1894. The Christmas (1894) issue consisted of sixteen pages and four-page cover. From that time *The Home Journal and News* has never been less than sixteen pages, 11½ x 15½.

THE STATESMAN BUILDING.

The Westminster Presbyterian Church publishes a church paper called *Tidings*. The Warburton Avenue Baptist Church, for a brief period, published a church paper known as *The Gleaner*, but recently the bright little sheet was discontinued.

New York City papers are represented in Yonkers by several reporters. Frank E. Ellis is the resident reporter of *The New York Tribune*. I. Melville Sheldon, a resident of the village of Sing Sing, reports Yonkers news for *The New York Times*. Representatives of other New York papers are also in Yonkers, when occasion requires.

THE WESTCHESTER PRESS CLUB. A number of Yonkers newspaper men met, on Saturday evening, May 2, 1896, and organized a press club. It was named "The Westchester Press Club," for it is the hope of its charter members that newspaper men in and about the county will become members of it. Frank E. Xavier was chosen President; Frank E. Ellis, Secretary and Treasurer. A committee was appointed to draw up a constitution. The headquarters of the club are in the Holland Building, No. 51 Warburton Avenue, Yonkers, N. Y.

ALFRED FOX.

CHAPTER XX.

LAND AND RIVER TRANSPORTATION.

THE first highways through the forests were the Indian trails. Before a road was built, the pioneers must have driven their oxen and rude carts across the cleared fields, winding around the stumps and big stones, and then through the woods to the river. The Albany Post-road was opened to the Saw Kill about 1669. In course of time it was extended from point to point northward, and finally the Albany stages began to run.

Waterways are Nature's highways. The Hudson and the Spuyten Duyvil Creek afforded access to Yonkers. It may be that with canoes and other light boats, the Indians and pioneer settlers navigated the Bronx also, for its waters, before the forests were laid low, must have flowed in large volume. For a mile or more above its mouth, the Nepperhan ran with too swift a current for even canoe navigation, unless the frail boats were very skillfully guided and controlled, but northward, it ran slow, and with comparatively deeper current, under the ancient forest trees. There the aborigines and the pale face must have launched their boats.

The colonists navigated the Hudson and other waters with the periauger, a boat with two masts, flat bottom, and lee boards. Sloops were in constant use, "their leisurely movements quite suiting the quiet tourists of those days." The boat Yoncker, with her furniture, apparel and appurtenances, was willed by Frederick Philipse (will dated December, 1702), to Frederick Philipse, his grandson. This boat may have been built the latter part of the seventeenth century. It is the only eighteenth century Yonkers boat known to the author. The records of boats coming to Yonkers in the seventeenth and eighteenth centuries, are in Chapters V. and VI., of this volume, but the names of no boats are preserved.

In Chapter IX. are recorded the reminiscences of the venerable David Horton, now ninety-six years old. He says that the first sloop he can remember was the Belvidere, and that he was a small boy when it ran. Another sloop he remembers was known as the Emeline. Both of these were on the river in the first quarter of the nineteenth century. The captain of the Emeline was Isaac Ruton, who at one time kept the tavern in Yonkers. Shares in the sloop Emeline were held by the store-keepers and farmers. Messrs. Oliver Read and Benjamin Archer, about this time, were running the sloop Belvidere between Yonkers and New York.

When Captain Ruton gained a controlling interest in the Emeline and advanced the rates of freight, the displeased freighters built a sloop for themselves about 1825, and called it the Independence. It is said that the owners of this sloop were the most prominent men in Yonkers. Among them were: Captain Benjamin Fowler, Isaac V. Fowler, Samuel Lyon, John M. Lyon, William M. Dyckman, John Dyckman, John Bashford, Judge Aaron Vark, Oliver Read, Benjamin Brown, James H. Blackwell, Garret Ackerman, Elijah Valentine, Joseph Odell, Oliver C. Denslow, David Horton, Thaddeus Rockwell, Anthony Archer, Obed Paddock, William Kerr, Prince W. Paddock, James Haynes, Abram Lent, William P. Jones, Benjamin Haynes, Valentine Odell, Samson Dyckman, Garret Garrison (father of Captain John Garrison), Hezekiah Nichols, William D. Smith, Caleb Smith, Benjamin Lent and Captain John Garrison. The sloop was commanded by the last-named shareholder, who was born at Kingsbridge in 1783.

After a service of about six years the Independence was sold, and another sloop known as the Ben Franklin was put on. This sloop of fifty-seven tons burden was built for the company, and was launched July 4, 1831. Every year from March 1st to about August 15th or thereabouts, the Ben Franklin made one trip each week except during the brief time the farmers were sending their pickles to market. Then she made two or three trips each week, landing at the foot of Murray Street in the city. At Yonkers the sloop was brought to the wharf (see map of 1847), about 100 yards up the Nepperhan.

In 1839, the other owners sold out to Captain John Garrison. One of the active young men on the boat was Joseph Peene, who was born in England and brought up to a seafaring life. Having come to America as a sailor on a passenger vessel in 1834, he was pleased with the country, and in 1835, came to make it his home. In 1839, he found employment on the Ben Franklin. He married, before 1851, Miss Caroline A. Garrison, the Captain's daughter, and when his father-in-law retired from business he became captain of the boat. He and his brother-in-law, Hyatt L. Garrison, who had been with him on the Ben Franklin in 1851, bought the sloop, Elias Hicks (thirty-eight tons). Mr. Garrison commanded that. In 1852, the Hicks and Franklin constituted one line of boats, the latter commanded by Captain Peene and the former by Captain Garrison. Captain Peene left the line in 1855, and with a small tug-boat which he purchased towed vessels around New York harbor. In 1857, he bought the Martin Hynes and in the same year Captain John Garrison sold to him and Captain H. L. Garrison the Ben Franklin, and one-half interest in the Martin Hynes was sold to Captain H. L. Garrison.

Then the two captains (Peene and Garrison, H. L.) were equal owners of boat property. It was in that year (1857) that the line of boats known so long as the Ben Franklin line was started. Three vessels, the Franklin, the Hynes, and the Hicks, then constituted the line. The J. H. Gautier was added in 1862. It was afterward nicknamed the Lizzie.

In 1864 Captain Garrison sold his interest to Captain Peene, who in subsequent years added the propeller John H. Hammitt and the three barges, William Lawrence, Aunt Mary, and Aunt Kate. He also purchased the wharf which he had previously rented. It is the wharf Mr. Wells built in 1831, but is now much more substantial and much larger.

Messrs. John G., Joseph, Jr., and George, sons of Captain Joseph Peene, took charge of the Ben Franklin line in 1873. The "Peene Brothers" have added to the line a lighter known as the City of Yonkers and a steamer which they named Caroline A. Peene, in honor of their mother. They have also added the barge Hudson River and the tugboat Frank A. Sears. The Caroline A. Peene for a number of years made daily trips to New York, carrying passengers and freight. The other boats also make daily trips, carrying freight. In 1831 the Ben Franklin carried about 1,200 tons a week. Now the line carries freight for the factories, markets, stores, and mills of a city of 40,000. It has many transfer trucks.

In 1895, a new boat, the Ben Franklin, was built. It carries passengers and freight and takes the place of the C. A. Peene as a regular boat. The Joseph Peene, Sr., is a tugboat.

In August, 1894, the company became a stock company, and is known as The Ben Franklin Transportation Company. The President is John G. Peene; the Treasurer, Joseph Peene, Jr.; and the Secretary, George Peene.

YONKERS FERRY. Old citizens remember David Sims and his sons, who, with blue rowboats, ferried people across the river between forty and fifty years ago. A ferry company, of which John Wheeler was a prominent member, placed the Kitty Strang on the river as a ferryboat. The Strang burned at the gas-house dock, and the company bought the Armsmere. They ran that boat for a while, but the business was unprofitable. Then another company put on a small propeller. Abram C. Gould, who had rowboats to let, purchased the ferry franchise, and put on, as a ferryboat, the propeller Tornado. He ran that for two years, and in 1885 built the steamer Alpine, which he ran eight years. In 1893 another company, known as the Yonkers and Alpine Ferry Company, was organized, and the steamer Uncas was put on. The Palisade Ferry Company, organized February 22, 1894, purchased the Uncas, and, after running it some time, placed on the river, in 1896, the boat Young

THE ELEVATOR AT PARK HILL STATION.

America. The officers of the company are: President, James V. Lawrence; Vice-President, A. J. Prime; Secretary and Treasurer, M. J. Hays; Manager, W. H. Greenhalgh. One of the former companies was known as the Terrace City and Palisade Ferry Company.

A small steamboat called the Daisy was run in the nineties by David Murray, whose ferry tickets were lettered "Yonkers and Palisade Ferry Company." In 1896 he is building a ferryboat to take the place of the Daisy. The new boat is also called the Daisy. There has been a public road from the river to the top of the Palisades a great many years. The ferryboats have carried horses and wagons, but only a small number. Most of their patrons are foot-passengers, who cross the river for pleasure.

The record of the running of the first steamboats on the Hudson is in a previous chapter. In former chapters are also records of the opening of streets and avenues.

The first railroad in Yonkers was the New York and Harlem. It began to run its trains in the early Forties. The Hudson River Railroad trains began to run in 1849. The New York City and Northern, called the New York and Putnam after it was purchased by the New York Central and Hudson River Railroad, was opened for business in the spring of 1881. The Getty Square branch was completed in 1887.

The passenger stations in Yonkers in 1896 are: Yonkers, Ludlow, and Glenwood; on the New York

STEAMER ALBANY, OF THE HUDSON RIVER DAY LINE.

Central and Hudson River Railroad: Getty Square, Park Hill, Lowerre, Caryl, Lincoln, Dunwoodie, Bryn Mawr Park, Nepperhan, St. Andrew's (formerly Grey Oaks), and Nepera Park.

A horse railroad was constructed in the Sixties. Its brief history is recorded in Chapter X.

YONKERS RAILROAD COMPANY. The Yonkers Railroad Company was one of the several competing applicants for a franchise to lay horse railroad tracks in Yonkers. The franchise was granted this company by the City Government, February, 1886. Daniel N. Stanton was the President. The principal negotiator was Oliver Stahlnecker. The company began laying the rails within that year. The track extended from the foot of Main Street to New Main Street, thence through New Main Street, South Broadway and Ludlow Street to the Ludlow Station. About May, 1888, the company had completed all the track they ever laid. They had laid their track in Riverdale Avenue to the southern boundary of the city, in Nepperhan Avenue to the Moquette Mill, and in Warburton Avenue. In October, 1891, Charles H. Montague was elected President of the company with a view of equipping the road in order to operate it by electricity. At that time Oliver Stahlnecker was acting receiver, and the affairs of the road were in a very bad shape. It was so crippled that electric cars were not run until the following May. During the receivership of Mr. Stahlnecker, in order to raise a small amount of money, all the rails between Main Street and Ludlow Station were torn up and sold at a low price, consequently no electric cars have ever been run on that line.

The first electric car ran in Riverdale Avenue, May 1, 1892. Two weeks later electric cars were running over the Nepperhan Avenue line, and, in the latter part of June, on Warburton Avenue. The Mount Vernon line was built during the first half of 1893, and the cars were running regularly before the end of June, in that year. The business during two years and three months, under electrical equipment, was very satisfactory as to volume, but the road was handicapped because there was no money to provide complete equipments, and the business was not profitable, mainly because of the enormous repair bills, the number of cars being so few that it was necessary to keep them all running all the time. The repairs were very expensive by reason of the old horse-car tracks still remaining. There were no funds with which to replace them with proper rails for electric cars.

In August, 1894, a very wealthy house in Wall Street purchased the entire capital stock and bonds of the road. Since that time they have expended a vast amount of money in new equipments, replacing the old tracks with substantial rails, and also building what is known as the Park Avenue line. They have projected other lines, and have ample means with which to complete them, and it is to be hoped that, in the near future, they will be rewarded by dividends, for, from the day the franchise was granted

STEAMER "NEW YORK" OF THE HUDSON RIVER DAY LINE.

until the present time, a period of over fourteen years, the road has reaped no profits. The investment at the present represents an enormous outlay. Reckoning old rails, worthless cars, dead horses, worthless tracks, paving, repairing, relaying the old tracks with new rails, laying new tracks, improvements and new equipments in the power house, the money expended must aggregate not less than $750,000.

In 1896, the Yonkers, the Tarrytown, and the North and South Electric Railway Companies were consolidated. The three railroads began to be operated as one. Consents were obtained to extend the Warburton Avenue line as far as Main and Constant Streets, Hastings, and efforts were made for an extension of the right-of-way to Tarrytown. The company also proposed to give Yonkers people transportation to New York for ten cents.

THE YONKERS DISTRICT OF THE PORT OF NEW YORK was constituted by act of Congress in 1894. The bill was signed by President Cleveland May 8, 1894. The Port of New York has six districts, North River, East River, Brooklyn, Jersey Shore, Staten Island and Yonkers. Mr. John N. Williams, who had been an Inspector of Customs in New York since 1880, was detailed to the Yonkers district May 9, 1894. The district is favored in having an officer so courteous and capable. He has no official relations to vessels from American ports. He reports the arrival and departure of vessels from foreign countries. They enter the Yonkers district of the Port of New York from various lands, some floating the English flag, some the Spanish, or Dutch or Norwegian. They hail from various harbors. The inspector's books record vessels in the Yonkers district of the Port of New York from Havana, Java, St. Jago, St. Domingo, Demerara, Porto Rico, Danzig, Port Prince, Cienfuegos, Neufarwasser, Manzarillo, Trinidad, Sagua, San Juan, Guantanamo, Antigua, Surinan and elsewhere. Most of the vessels come from Cuba, and the majority them are schooners with bags of sugar. Those freighted with lumber are from St. Johns, N. B. Comparatively few steamers are among the vessels arriving in this district. Some barques and brigs enter Yonkers waters. The larger sailing vessels will sometimes have a cargo of as many as 6,000 bags of sugar. The United States law allows a vessel a specified number of days to discharge her cargo, after that a charge of $4 per day is made. The United States officer stationed at Yonkers has charge of foreign sail vessels. When a foreign steamer bound for Yonkers leaves New York two customs house officers are in charge.

Mr. G. E. Bedell is the United States weigher in the Yonkers district; T. O. Ostrander is his assistant.

The following article appeared in *The Evening Gazette* in 1896:

"The district of Yonkers, of the Port of New York, since the National Sugar Refining Company's works have been located here, has grown remarkably into maritime importance. This is evidenced by the fact that since the establishment of the district in May, 1894, 129 vessels have been cleared from foreign ports. Their cargoes are generally sugar, but some are laden with lumber and lath. Cane sugar is produced in the South American countries and West India Islands, while the beet sugar comes from Germany. The ships bearing these staples come from those countries, and there are often interesting things to be seen on their decks, while they are unloading their cargoes at the foot of Main Street.

"A ship to enter Yonkers must first be registered in New York and get a permit from there to the Customs Inspector here, to unload her cargo.

"The sailors, after long and sometimes stormy voyages, often requiring months, go ashore in New York, and the vessel arrives in Yonkers in charge of the captain and a few deck hands. It requires about ten days to unload the cargo, and as each bag of sugar is taken off a Customs officer jabs a sharp instrument into it and procures a sample. The gruff old captain and sometimes a few of his shipmates remain aboard the ship, and their dress and peculiar seafaring appearance attract general attention as they stroll the streets of Yonkers.

"The largest vessel which ever discharged here was the Waverly, a British steamship, which came in from Java, in November, 1895, loaded with sugar. Her capacity was 2,022 tons, and more than two weeks were required in unloading her."

The river affords Yonkers citizens much pleasure. They enjoyed the fine excursions up the Hudson, down the Bay and through Long Island Sound, on the large passenger excursion steamboats. Some citizens own steam and sail yachts. Reference to the yacht companies is made in another chapter.

HUDSON RIVER DAY LINE STEAMERS. This line during the summer stops at Yonkers every day except Sunday, from May to the middle of October, and is patronized largely by the citizens as an attractive route to the Catskill Mountains, Saratoga and the Adirondacks, and other points to the north and west. Excursionists favor the line, as between the north bound and departure of the south bound steamer, it gives parties three hours to stroll over historical West Point, and at Newburg, one and three-quarters of an hour to inspect Washington's Headquarters and other points of interest. At Poughkeepsie direct connections are made with Sound bound steamers.

"The Albany and the New York, the steamers of this line, are two of the most elegant steamers in the world. They are large and commodious; there is an abundance of comfortable seats, and a good restaurant is located on the main deck. When the boat leaves the dock, you leave the bustle and hum behind you, and enter, as it were, upon a new existence. Now you can stop hurrying for a time, at least, and at your leisure can take in the marvellous beauties of the river as they unfold before your eyes. To float upon the bosom of the majestic Hudson, to gaze upon the mighty hills that fringe its banks, to view those quaint but familiar collections of river craft being towed along, scarcely seeming to move; all these and a myriad of other experiences, are familiar to those who have had the good sense or the good fortune to make the trip between Yonkers and Albany by the day boat. From the time the boat pushes majestically out into the river till it touches the dock at the end of the route, a succession of magnificent panoramas is spread before the tourist. Too much cannot be said regarding the arrangements which have been made for the comfort and pleasure of those who adopt this method of travel." A correspondent of the Boston *Courier* writes: "The journey up the famous Hudson is undoubtedly the most interesting and picturesque inland voyage in the United States. It has been described and re-described, however, until the task of investing an account of its varied and beautiful scenery with any flavor of novelty has become utterly hopeless. But its attractions, though stale in narrative, are perennially charming to the actual sense, and the point of view afforded by the palatial steamers New York and Albany, of the Day Line, is an ideal one. These magnificent boats are unique in one feature, which will be appreciated by tourists: being designed for day service and tourist purposes only, they carry no freight whatever, save personal baggage of passengers. Thus the lower forward decks and other desirable points of view, customarily monopolized by unappreciative packages of merchandise, are open to passengers, and the fittings and accommodations of the craft throughout are enabled to be of a more light and elegant order, and are upon a more uniformly sumptuous plan than is usually possible. Veritable pleasure boats, every suggestion of toil is banished from their decks, and the holiday atmosphere engendered by external circumstances and a happy purpose is thus subtly maintained."

The general offices of the company are at the Desbrosses Street pier, New York City.

CHAPTER XXI.

YONKERS CITIZENS.

PROBABLY no estimate has ever been made of the number of people who have lived within the boundaries of Yonkers, since the first pioneer entered the forests of Keskeskick and Nepperhaem to build his rude dwelling where red Indians and wild animals would be his nearest neighbors. Scores of the thousands who dwelt in Yonkers during different periods of the past three centuries lived quiet lives, served their day and generation, and fell asleep. To-day they are hardly more missed than the autumn leaves, which, during the last three hundred years, fluttered to the ground from the forest trees, or the flowers which bloomed and died. It is not, however, to be inferred, because the lives of these plain people were unknown, that their influence has ceased. The singer dies, but his song lives. Some of them might have become more widely known, had they made self-advancement and prominence the chief end of their lives. Had they devoted to the acquisition of wealth, or of position, or of learning, the same energy, thought and time that they gave to the uplifting of those who were crushed under life's burdens, or to the instructing and counselling of those who sorely needed their fraternal words, they would have achieved more of what the world calls success. But fame is no test of merit. Human opinions of men are largely based upon imperfect knowledge. Only He, who knows inherited tendencies, environment, motive, and all other facts, can pronounce a just judgment. What reversals of human decisions will be made at the judgment throne. Happy the man who has this testimony, that he pleases God.

"Unblemished let me live, or die unknown,
Oh, grant me honest fame, or grant me none."

The landscape is not all rugged mountains, bold hills and rolling river; sweet valleys, at first undiscovered, lie among the hills, and banks of flowers with delicate hue, lovely form and fragrant breath. History is not altogether the record of discovery, settlement, war, politics and feverish competition for "the yellow dust which men call gold." How many happy homes have graced and blessed Yonkers during three centuries. What devoted husbands and fathers have thrown about their families protection like a shield. How rich in counsel and sweet with tenderness were the lives of beloved wives and mothers. With what beauty and loveliness the graces of gentle sisters unfolded, and how symmetrically brothers developed from handsome youth to strong and useful manhood. How winsome were the ways, and unconscious the graces of sweet little children. Must the scribe make no record of these hallowed homes? Do they not also belong to history? Smiling valleys, fragrant gardens, we salute you, reluctantly turning our thoughts to the busy outside world to record its deeds, but a glance at your beauty and loveliness reminds us that most of the best that has been said and done must remain unwritten, except in the book of the recording angel.

The services of some citizens to school, church and state were so large that they deserve recorded commendation. Some became prominent by reason of wealth, or learning, or office. In the Colonial and Revolutionary periods, the pioneers and patriots were conspicuous. Van Der Donck, Archer, Betts, Tippett, Berrian, Heddy, French, Jones, Wescott, Delaval, Lewis, Verveelen, the ferryman at Spuyten Duyvil, Hadden and Frederick Philipse were among the early well-known settlers

During the Philipse period, which covered over a century, the lords of the Manor and their families were pre-eminently prominent. The steward of the Manor was also a man of importance. The Van Cortlandts were an influential family. The Church of England missionaries and the Methodist circuit-riders were well-known. Obviously, the doctor and the school-master were important personages, but no reference of any physician is preserved, except that in Chapter VIII., and while the map of 1785 designates the location of school-houses, there is no record of the names of any who taught within their plain walls. Who the tenants of the third Frederick Philipse were, may be inferred from the list of the names of the buyers of his confiscated lands.

The honored names of the Revolutionary period are those of the patriots who served on the local committees, or who belonged to the Philipsburgh and Lower Yonkers military companies. The names of those committeemen and of the Revolutionary officers are recorded in Chapter VII. Some families were honorably prominent during the Revolution, among them the Odells and the Van Cortlandts. We find the Odells, Pines, Oakleys, Dyckmans, and Posts among the Westchester guides of the Revolution, but whether they were of Yonkers the author is unable to record.

In 1785 and 1786, Yonkers, as now bounded, came into the possession of about seventy or eighty persons. Their names are recorded in Chapter VIII. The names of clergymen, who ministered in the locality at that time, are also on record. A study of those early families is interesting. The Garrisons, Kniffens, Lefurgys, Merrils, and Nodines were in Yonkers more than a century ago. Among the Huguenot names are Devoe, Forshee, Lefurgy, Nodine, and Vermilyea. Besly, Flandreau and Guion are also Huguenot names.

Since the town of Yonkers was erected (1788), a number of prominent citizens have held office. Their names are recorded in the latter part of Chapter XII., where are the lists of postmasters, supervisors, town clerks and other officials. Among well-known citizens in the first half of the nineteenth century were not only descendants of old-time residents, but also many men who subsequently moved into the place—among them Pierson, Vark, Farrington, the Wells family, Major Ebenezer Baldwin, Ethan Flagg, and others who were influential. A prominent land-purchaser of that period at Kingsbridge was Alexander Macomb. Clergymen, lawyers, physicians, teachers and business men, removed to the town, and became identified with it. Their names are recorded in Chapter IX.

After Yonkers was incorporated as a village, the number of influential citizens so increased that it would be very difficult to designate them all. The names of many who established large industries, rendered able professional services, edited papers, wrote books, gave instruction in the schools, assisted in providing the developing city with police protection, fire department, water-works, sewers, etc., are recorded in previous chapters, but the names of many citizens of influence have necessarily been omitted.

The following lists contain the names of physicians, lawyers, resident clergymen (not Yonkers pastors), artists, actors, and humorists.

The record of no other doctors of medicine, practicing in Yonkers in Colonial and Revolutionary times, than those to whom this volume makes reference, has been found by the author. The first physician in Yonkers of whom there is record was the Rev. Thomas Standard, A.M., M.D. He came in 1727, not as a physician, but as a missionary, perhaps as a medical missionary. He came to preach the Gospel, but doubtless often ministered to the sick. In Chapter VIII. reference is made to early physicians, who lived in adjoining places, and rode into Yonkers. Tradition speaks of a doctor of medicine in Philipsburgh (Yonkers) during the Revolution. He was known as "the little doctor." There was also in early times a Dr. ——— Forbes.

PHYSICIANS. Rev. Thomas Standard, A.M., M.D. (missionary, 1727–60); "The Little Doctor" of 1776; ——— Forbes, John Ingersoll, Amos W. Gates, Horatio S. Gates, Timothy R. Hibbard, Levi W. Flagg, George B. Upham, Edmund S. F. Arnold, Maximilian J. Reinfelder, J. Foster Jenkins, J. Henry Pooley, Gabriel P. Reevs, Alfred Robinson, Galusha B. Balch, Horace B. Pike, James Harkness, Isaac N. Swasey, ——— King, ——— Henry, ——— Lozier, ——— Marmon, of Kingsbridge; ——— Deey, of Kingsbridge; ——— Varian, of Kingsbridge; Valentine Browne, A. C. Benedict, N. A. Warren, E. M. Hermance, R. J. Southworth, Samuel Swift, E. I. Harrington, Stephen Hasbrouck, Edwin F. Clark, Paluel De Marmon, P. Hooper, C. Lafayette Loomis, C. D. Marsh, J. S. McLaury, R. Stone, William P. Upham, R. Oliver Phillips, Henry Moffatt, R. R. Trotter, C. A. Miles, W. A. Bell, P. H. Pyne, J. L. Porteous, R. N. Flagg, J. C. Bennett, E. C. Howe, H. Beattie Brown, Ellsworth Colton, W. S. Coons, S. E. Getty, E. Schopen, David John, J. T. Gibson, Frank T. Hopkins, Garrett N. Banker, J. H. Seabury,

William H. Sherman, Alfred Dana, Russell P. Fay, Najib K. Jamal, J. W. Smith, T. H. White, M. Wolf, H. J. Keith, N. S. King, P. A. Callan, Franklin Soper, C. W. Buckmaster, G. W. Bowden, ——— Mooney, Everts M. Morrell, ——— Henderson, ——— Small, F. L. Strong, Stephen Leo, J. H. Carver, Carl H. Kroeber, Bernard Mulligan, George P. Holden, Robert J. Denniston, J. D. Van Derlyn, Frank B. Littlewood, Elizabeth S. Brown, Miriam B. Kennedy.

LAWYERS. William W. Scrugham, William Dean, David Lyon, William Crighton Meade, Reuben W. Van Pelt, Ralph E. Prime, Jeremiah H. Stedwell, ——— Mason, William Romer, James P. Sanders, John M. Mason, Edward P. Baird, H. H. Taylor, Matt. H. Ellis, George B. Pentz, James S. Fitch, Joseph F. Daly, William Riley, Edwin R. Keyes, Allen Taylor, John W. Alexander, John F. Brennan, E. G. Buchanan, Arthur J. Burns, John C. Donohue, John C. Donohue, Jr., Francis X. Donoghue, John H. Ferguson, Charles E. Gorton, John C. Small, William C. Kellogg, Malcolm S. Keyes, Cyrus A. Peake, Alanson J. Prime, Ralph Earl Prime, Jr., Stephen H. Thayer, Jr., Gabriel Reevs, W. W. Bliven, I. J. Beaudrias, John C. Harrigan, William J. McCready, Edwin C. Mott, Adrian M. Potter, Edward Baldwin, Frank Whitney, Henry A. Robinson, John G. Ritter, J. F. Horan, John H. Hubbell, William H. Sweny, Edgar Logan, Edgar Logan, Jr., John T. Geary, James M. Hunt, William Allen Butler, Jr., Fisher A. Baker, George W. Poucher, Benjamin S. Stilwell, Joseph Hover, F. M. Holls, Salter S. Clark, Thomas Ewing, Jr., Frederick C. Train, David Tomlinson, Theodore Tomlinson, Waldo G. Morse, Hampton D. Ewing, Edward Hartley, Alexander Halliday, E. Masten, William G. McAdoo, Thomas Hillhouse, Jacob W. Feeder, S. V. Essick, C. P. Easton, William Cowper Prime, Ernest V. V. Getty, Henry M. Baird, Jr., R. P. Getty, Jr.

Many members of the New York City Bar reside in Yonkers and among them are some whose names appear in the foregoing list. Among other New York lawyers who have had, or have their homes in Yonkers are:

Frederick A. Coe, Martin Van Buren Denslow, G. Hilton Scribner, Francis N. Bangs, Stephen H. Thayer, Sr., Samuel J. Tilden, David Hawley, Thomas Ewing, William Allen Butler, Duncan Smith, James B. Silkman, James Ferguson, T. Astley Atkins, E. Y. Bell, Charles W. Seymour, J. Irving Burns, Oliver P. Buel, Theodore Fitch, Hedding S. Fitch, Francis B. Chedsey, Francis S. Winslow, Samuel Hawley.

The names of those who have been pastors of Yonkers churches are recorded in the general history, or in the chapter on churches. A number of clergymen, not pastors of Yonkers churches, have been citizens of the city. The names of some of them are honorably known abroad as well as in the United States. Among the resident clergymen of the past and present are those recorded on the following roll:

The Revs. Robert Baird, D.D., Henry M. Baird, D.D., LL.D., Robert McCartee, D.D., Robert Kirkwood, Reuben Hubbard, Timothy R. Hibbard, Montgomery R. Hooper, Isaac S. Davison, Livingston Willard, Abram C. Baldwin, William S. Moore, E. A. Hill, James M. Bruce, W. W. Whipple, Edward F. Bright, D.D., William W. Rand, D.D., John G. Shrive, J. S. Shipman, Wendall Prime, D.D., Andrew Longacre, D.D., Thomas Armitage, D.D., J. Henry Bertholf, Alexander Alison, D.D., George B. Waldron, ——— Parker, D.D., J. B. Brown, Isaac Stemple (Hebrew Rabbi), Moses S. Wolf (Hebrew Rabbi), Gustav Gottheil.

ARTISTS. James R. Brevoort, N.A., landscape painter; Benoni Irwin, A.N.A., portrait painter; Alfred Jones, N.A., painter and engraver; Frederick E. Bartlett, landscape painter; Arthur Parton, N.A., landscape painter; Henry Parton, N.A., painter and designer; Virgil Tojetti, figure painter; George Stengel, designer and painter; Edward Lind Morse, portrait painter; Bayard H. Tyler, portrait painter; Walter Blackburn, designer; George Reevs, portrait painter; Frank Airey, landscape painter. Several Yonkers ladies have attained great skill as artists. Several years ago a number of citizens who were much interested in photography, organized a

JAMES RENWICK BREVOORT, N.A.

Camera Club. Their exhibitions were greatly enjoyed. Among the members of the club were Messrs. Rudolf Eickemeyer, Jr., F. W. R. Eschmann, Robert Reevs, John W. Alexander, George Stengel and Walter Blackburn. Mr. Eickemeyer was awarded many medals. Several came from abroad. He is now a photographer in New York City and his artistic work has deserved and received much attention.

AUTHORS. A number of authors have been enrolled among the residents of Yonkers, several of whom are known abroad as well as throughout the length and breadth of their own land.

The town received its name from the lawyer and author, Adriaen Van Der Donck, who was known as "De Jonkheer." He was a graduate of the University of Leyden, and the probable author of "Vertoogh van Niew Nederlandt." He was also the author of "Description of New Netherlands." These two volumes are the sources from which all subsequent writers have derived their information about the early history of New York City.

The Baird family is one of the most prominent of the literary families of Yonkers. The Rev. Robert Baird, D.D., was an author and philanthropist. He spent the close of his industrious life in Yonkers where he died March 15, 1863. From 1835 to 1843, he was much of his time in Europe striving to revive the Protestant faith in the south of the continent, and to promote the cause of temperance in the north.

His son, Professor Henry M. Baird, D.D., LL.D., Ph.D., is the Professor of Greek in New York University, and the Dean of the Faculty. He is the author of a number of important works. Some reviewers have ranked his great histories of the Huguenots with the histories of Prescott and Motley.

Another son, the Rev. Charles W. Baird, D.D., who spent some of his youthful years in Yonkers and was subsequently the American Chaplain in Rome, Italy, and for many years the revered and beloved pastor of the Presbyterian Church at Rye, N. Y., was also an author of prominence. His "History of the Huguenot Emigration to America" ranks high among historical works.

Frederic S. Cozzens, author of the "Sparrowgrass Papers," and contributor to the *Knickerbocker* and *Putnam's Magazine*, was for some time a Yonkers resident.

William Allen Butler, the poet-lawyer, is an influential citizen of Yonkers. His father was the eminent lawyer, Benjamin F. Butler, a member of the cabinets of Jackson and Van Buren. William Allen Butler is a prominent lawyer, and, as a writer, is widely known as the author of "Nothing to Wear," many editions of which have been published in England. The poem was also translated into both German and French. A number of other prose and poetical productions of Mr. Butler's pen form a part of American literature.

Henry B. Dawson, who was for a brief time editor of *The Gazette*, was the author of a number of historical works, which reveal a painstaking and exhausting research, only comprehended by historical writers. A long list of the titles of his numerous works is recorded in Vol. I., Scharf's "Westchester County."

The Rev. David Cole, D.D., senior pastor in Yonkers, was called to the pastorate of the Reformed Church from Rutgers College, where he was the Professor of Greek language and literature. He is the author of a number of works, educational, religious, genealogical and historical. His love of the classics is proverbial among his acquaintances. His knowledge of Hebrew and Greek and Latin, supplemented by his attainments as a theologian, have given him high rank as an able and sound expositor of the inspired Scriptures.

The Rev. William W. Rand, D.D., one of the Secretaries of the American Tract Society, has long resided in Yonkers, and is an experienced writer.

Professor William H. C. Bartlett, who for more than fifty years was identified with the United States Military Academy at West Point, first as a cadet, and subsequently as Professor of Natural and Experimental Philosophy, was a long-time resident of Yonkers. Jefferson Davis, Robert E. Lee, U. S. Grant and others were under his instruction. His books and other writings testify to his scholarship and industry. His "Analytical Mechanics," has reached its ninth edition. As an eminent teacher and scientist, he had no sympathy with Anti-Theism. At the time he retired from his professorship at West Point, he was elected actuary of the Mutual Life Insurance Company of New York. The elaborate tables which he constructed to facilitate their office work can be best appreciated by the able officials of life insurance companies.

Lyman Cobb, Sr., who resided in Yonkers during the last years of his busy life, was well-known as an author of School-books. They were very popular. Millions of copies were sold.

Joseph Howard Palmer (who lived in Yonkers many years, and who rendered long service as a School Commissioner in Westchester County), during about twenty years was First Tutor of

Mathematics in the College of the City of New York. He was the author of a Treatise on Book-keeping, and of text-books on Algebra and Bookkeeping. His books had a large circulation.

The Rev. Robert Kirkwood,* who resided in Yonkers from 1851 to 1866, the year or his death, was the author of several religious works, and a frequent contributor to leading religious papers.

Judge T. Astley Atkins has contributed to the press a series of historical papers, relating to the history of Yonkers. Reference to the value of these papers is made in the Preface of this history. The authors of "Yonkers in the Rebellion," were T. Astley Atkins and John Wise Oliver. Thomas C. Cornell is the author of the volume "The Beginnings of the Roman Catholic Church in Yonkers." He also wrote a genealogical work relating to the Cornell family. His papers treating of local history are valuable.

G. Hilton Scribner, ex-Secretary of New York State, although engrossed with the cares of an active political and business life, has loved litera- ture. He established the "Bancroft Society" of New York and "The Society of Pundits." His mon- ograph entitled "Where Did Life Begin?" has attract- ed the attention of the scientific public. Dr. Dio Lewis, in- ventor of a new system of gymnas- tics, founder of the *Dio Lewis Monthly*, and a lecturer, resided in Yonkers during the closing years of his life. His death occurred in 1886. J. Henry Pooley, M.D., was a frequent writer of pamphlets and articles on profes- sional subjects. He was a brilliant orator, as well as a skillful surgeon, and for years was a prominent citizen of Yonkers. Hon. Samuel J. Tilden, the eminent lawyer and states- man, and at one time candidate for the Presidency of the United States, who spent the closing years of his life in Yonkers, residing at his palatial home, "Greystone," was an able author. His writings and speech- es were edited by John Bigelow. John Kendrick Bangs is a popular writer, whose pages reflect the genial humor of their author. Anson D. F. Ran- dolph, the publisher, who for a time re- sided in Yonkers, was the author of several poems which indicate fine literary taste. The Rev. James T. Bixby, Ph.D., is the author of "Similarities of Physical and Relig- ious Knowledge," and of other literary works.

RESIDENT CLERGYMEN OF YONKERS.

1. Henry M. Baird.
2. William W. Rand.
3. William E. Ketcham.
4. James M. Bruce.

The Rev. William E. Ketcham, D.D., a resident of Yonkers, and the Superintendent of St. Christo- pher's Home at Dobb's Ferry, N. Y., is the editor of "The Preacher's Magazine," and a regular contributor to religious papers and periodicals.

Galusha B. Balch, M.D., is the author of "Genealogy of the Balch Family in America," a work which has involved a wide correspondence and much labor.

---

* Several of the members of the Rev. Robert Kirkwood's family have been industrious workers with their pens. His daughter, Miss Louise J. Kirkwood is the author of "Sewing Illustrated," which is one of her series of works on industrial training of children. It has reached its thirteenth thousand. She is also the originator and General Secretary of the order of the Thread and Needle, to which *St. Nicholas Magazine* devotes one page each month. Miss Anna Watson Kirkwood, eldest daughter of the Rev. Robert Kirkwood, is the author of several booklets, and an acceptable contributor to leading periodicals. The volume "Church and Sunday-school Work in Yonkers," of which another daughter, Miss Agnes Emily Kirkwood, is the author, is well-known in the city. Robert Ogilvie Kirkwood, eldest son of Alexander O. Kirkwood, and grandson of the Rev. Robert Kirkwood, is a student at Princeton University, where he has high honors, and, in 1896, was one of the members of the editorial staff of *The Nassau Literary Magazine*.

Rufus King, of Yonkers, is a writer of genealogies. He is a well-known member of the New York Historical and Genealogical Society.

The Rev. A. J. F. Behrends, D.D., the Rev. Henry M. Sanders, D.D., and the Rev. S. Parkes Cadman, former pastors in Yonkers, are writers whose contributions to the press are read with great interest.

John C. Havemeyer frequently contributed to the press. His latest paper, "The Relations of the United States of America"—an open letter to President Cleveland—was reprinted from the *New York Times* and circulated as a booklet. Mrs. John C. Havemeyer, daughter of the Hon. John M. Francis, wields a facile pen in her sketches of travel.

Miss Mary Crosby, the sister of the late Howard Crosby, D.D., LL.D., compiled "Memorial Papers." It is a handsome volume, containing extracts from the prose and poetical productions of the great scholar and divine, and of newspaper articles referring to his useful life.

Frederic Shonnard is the regimental historian of the Sixth Artillery Association. He is the author of many interesting historical papers. His sentences are compact, clear and instructive.

The Rev. Dr. Wendall Prime, editor of *The New York Observer*, is an interesting writer. His volume entitled "Fifteenth Century Bibles," is a study of the oldest of printed books, and only those which are included in the class called *Incunabula*. Another New York editor residing in Yonkers, is the Rev. Edward Bright, D.D. The columns of *The Examiner* furnish proof of his ability.

The Rev. Thomas Armitage, D.D., who spent the closing years of his useful life in Yonkers, was for many years a prominent clergyman in New York City. He was a lecturer and well-known author. Among writers who were Yonkers citizens, was Professor William C. Russell, formerly teacher of political economy, and at one time acting President of Cornell University. A resident at the present writing is Dr. Norman Wilde of the Columbia College Faculty. His department is Philosophy. Another Columbia College Professor residing in Yonkers is A. V. Williams Jackson, a writer and lecturer well-known by citizens of Yonkers and neighboring towns as an instructor in the University Extension Course.

Salter S. Clark, an alumnus of Yale University (the son of the late honored publisher, Lucius E. Clark, who for years resided in Yonkers), is the author of "Commercial Law, a Text-book for High Schools."

The Rev. Charles E. Allison is the author of "A Historical Sketch of Hamilton College, Clinton, N. Y."

"The Terrace City," as Yonkers is sometimes called, has enrolled several writers of fiction. Some years ago a Yonkers lady wrote the story entitled "Margaret." It was referred to as "that delightful and popular romance." The author's *nom de plume* was "Lyndon." Mrs. E. D. E. N. Southworth, widely known as a voluminous writer, resided in Yonkers many years. She is the author of sixty or more published novels. Mrs. Mary E. Moffat has written a number of entertaining stories. The Rev. Delos Lull wrote "Father Solon, or the Helper Helped," a production which received the prize offered by *The Yonkers Statesman*. Gilson Willets has contributed many short stories to the press.

The volume, "Yonkers in the Rebellion," contains a graceful poem from the pen of Mrs. Jennie L. Lyall, also a stirring poem of which S. R. Whitney is the author.

Some years ago *The Yonkers Statesman* offered a prize for the best original short story and the best original poem contributed to its columns. Several productions ranked so nearly equal that it was difficult to make the award. The prize for the best story was awarded to Mrs. S. L. Cooper. The Committee of Award were Charles E. Gorton, Superintendent of Public Schools, A. V. W. Jackson, Professor of Literature in Columbia College, and Charles E. Allison, Pastor of Dayspring Presbyterian Church, Yonkers. The prize for the best poem was awarded to Ernest L. Bogart. The Committee of Award were Dr. Henry M. Baird, Professor of Greek in New York University, and Messrs. Gorton and Allison.

Several actors and humorists have resided in Yonkers. Years ago Edwin Forrest and R. J. De Cordova were citizens of the town. The home of Clara Morris (Mrs. F. C. Harriot), is in Yonkers, and a prominent humorous writer of the city is John K. Bangs, one of the editors of *Harper's Monthly*.

At least four Yonkers residents lived long enough to become centenarians. Mrs. Hannah Stillwagon died in 1886, aged 103 years. Captain Isaac Denike, who was an old sloop-master, reached the age of 101 years, one month and one day. He had seen Washington, and when he was asked about the personal appearance of the renowned General, exclaimed with enthusiasm, "One man among a multitude!" Captain Denike died in 1880. Thomas Marran, Sr., lived to be 100 years and one month old. He died in 1885. John Farrell was a resident of Yonkers over fifty years. He was reported to be 107 years old. It is said that he fought under Wellington in the battle of Waterloo. He died in Yonkers in 1896.

The biographical sketches which follow, are of citizens whose lives and work constitute no small part of the history of Yonkers. The compilation of so many biographies required much time and labor. The author did not write nor edit them. The patient work was done by others, to whom it was intrusted.

HENRY M. ANDERSON was born in Yonkers, July 13, 1858, and was educated at Public School No. 2. On May 30, 1880, he married Miss Mattie E. Brown. He is teller in the Citizens' National Bank; is a member and the Treasurer of Rising Star Lodge, F. and A. M., and has been the Treasurer of Yonkers Fire Department since 1884.

WILLIAM ARCHIBALD was born at Montrose, Scotland, in 1811. In 1837, he came to America, and in 1841, located at Yonkers, where he resided until his death, which occurred in 1892. When a young man he learned the trade of a blacksmith, which he afterwards successfully followed until he retired from active work in 1867.

In 1835 he married Miss Jane Barrowman, who survived him nearly two years. Seven children were born to them, three sons and four daughters. Mr. Archibald was a member of the Reformed Church of Yonkers from the time of its organization.

ANDREW ARCHIBALD was born at Fordham, N. Y., in December, 1839. After receiving an education in private schools, he engaged in mercantile pursuits. He has resided in Yonkers for the past fifty-five years, where he is still actively engaged in business as a merchant. In April, 1864, he married Miss Mary H. Lyon, and three sons have been born to them. Mr. Archibald is a prominent member of Westminster Church.

HENRY B. ARCHER was born in New York City, September 14, 1833. He attended the public schools until he had completed his education, after which he learned the trade of a carpenter. He has been a resident of Yonkers forty-five years; is a member of the City Club of Yonkers, and also a prominent Mason and attends St. John's Episcopal Church. A Republican in politics, he has held important positions in the post-office and United States revenue departments, and is now filling the position of Receiver of Taxes for the City of Yonkers. On September 16, 1857, Mr. Archer married Miss Mary M. Post. He has had two children, Clara W. and Francis M., both of whom are living.

FREDERICK AUGUSTUS BACK was born in New York City, October 28, 1816, and has resided in Yonkers since 1821. He received his education in the public schools of this city. After leaving school, he learned the trade of a wheelwright. He has always adhered to Democratic principles in politics, and has held several public positions, among which have been those of Village Trustee and City Assessor. He was also a member of the Board of Education for a number of years. He attends St. John's Episcopal Church. On April 15, 1846, Mr. Back married Miss Rebecca J. Brown (deceased December 15, 1893), to whom three sons and one daughter were born.

WILLIAM DELAVAN BALDWIN, a prominent member of the well-known Otis Elevator Company, is a native of Auburn, Cayuga County, N. Y., in which place he was born September 5, 1856. He is the son of Lovewell H. Baldwin, and a descendant of John Baldwin, of Dedham, Mass. The Baldwins came to this country at an early date, and first settled in Vermont, being among the original ancestry of the famous "Green Mountain Boys" of a later date. Mr. Baldwin's mother was Sarah J. Munson, daughter of Aaron Bennett, of New Brunswick, N. J.

Mr. Baldwin received such education as was to be had in the public schools of his native place, his school life continuing until the age of fifteen, when he left school to engage in the business of life, entering the extensive establishment of D. M. Osborne & Co., as an aid and learner. Here the young aspirant for mercantile honors made rapid progress, his energy and ability, with his earnest devotion to the interests of his employers, winning him commendation and advancement until, before he had reached his majority, he held a position of trust and responsibility in the establishment. There could be no higher testimony to his native business ability and the confidence placed in him by his employers than the fact that, at the age of twenty-one, they sent him to Europe to take charge of the European branch of their business. He continued in this responsible position for five years, performing his duties satisfactorily to all concerned, and gaining a wide experience in business management, which was destined to be of much advantage to him in later years. At the end of that period, being desirous of returning to his native land and becoming himself one of the controlling agents in a business concern, he resigned his position with the Osborne Company and crossed the ocean to New York, where he entered the elevator-building firm of Otis Brothers & Co., as a stockholder, and was voted in Treasurer of the company.

Mr. Baldwin is at present one of the largest stockholders in this flourishing firm, of the character and extent of whose business sufficient details have been given in other sketches of the Otis Brothers.

GROUP OF YONKERS CITIZENS.

1. Benjamin S. Washburn.
2. Joseph Peene, Jr.
3. George Peene.
4. Charles E. Gorton.
5. Daniel A. Doran.
6. Charles H. Frazier.
7. William H. Fisher.

He still retains his position as Treasurer of this company, and is, besides, its General Manager. In order that he might be nearer to the factories and spend more time there, he removed in 1887, from his former residence at Montclair, N. J., to Yonkers, N. Y., where the works of the Otis Elevator Company are situated. His success in business life is due to his indomitable will and perseverance, which are distinguishing traits in his character. Personally he is courteous and affable in his intercourse with business men and friends, while no man bears a higher reputation than he for integrity and just dealing. In consequence, while he may be designated a thorough business man in every just and proper sense of the word, his courtesy of manner and high sense of honor in all his dealings have won him hosts of friends and gained him the esteem of all with whom he comes into contact.

Aside from his connection with the Otis Brothers Company, Mr. Baldwin has entered into other business relations. He has been made Vice-President of the First National Bank of Yonkers, and holds the position of director in several financial and other concerns. Politically he is a member of the Republican party, but has never been a seeker for political honors, and in 1892 declined the nomination offered him by the Republican party of his district for member of Congress. He was married in 1881 to Miss Helen R. Sullivan, daughter of Nahum Sullivan, of New York, and has had four sons and three daughters, of whom six—Martin, Delavan, Helen, Louise, Runyon and Roland—are living; one, Elsie, died in infancy. Mr. Baldwin is a member of the Union League, the Lawyers', the Engineers', and other clubs of New York City.

Nelson A. Ball was born in New York City, October 1, 1871, and was educated in the public schools of this city. He has been a resident of this city for twenty years, and is a dealer in hats and gents' furnishing goods. He is a member of the Masonic Lodge, Yonkers Hope Hook and Ladder Fire Truck, and is Republican in politics. In 1895 he married Miss Rachel Jane Bennett.

Garret N. Banker, M.D., was born in Schenectady, N. Y., on April 30, 1860, and received his education in the public schools and Classical Institute of that city, graduating from Bellevue Medical College, of New York City. He has been a practicing physician in this city for six years. He is a member of the New York Academy of Medicine, the Westchester County Medical Society, and is President of Jenkins Medical Association. He is a Republican in politics, and at present is Health Officer of this city and Attending Surgeon of St. Joseph's Hospital.

Isidore J. B. Beaudrias was born in New York City, March 15, 1868. He obtained his rudimentary education in the public schools, after which he attended the College of the City of New York and Columbia Law School. He has resided at Yonkers for twelve years, where he has been engaged in the legal profession. Mr. Beaudrias is a Democrat, and fills the position of Justice of the Peace and Acting Judge of the City of Yonkers. He is a member of the Democratic Club of New York, Knights of Pythias, and Yonkers Turn Verein. He is unmarried.

William A. Bell was born in Bloomingburgh, Orange County, N. Y., in 1853, and is a graduate of Columbia College, New York City. For ten years he has been a resident of this city. He is a physician, having a large and lucrative practice, and a member of the First Methodist Episcopal Church. He has always been an active Republican, but has never held any political office. On June 15, 1886, he was married to Miss Gertrude Aldrich, and they have two daughters, both of whom are living.

ISIDORE J. B. BEAUDRIAS.

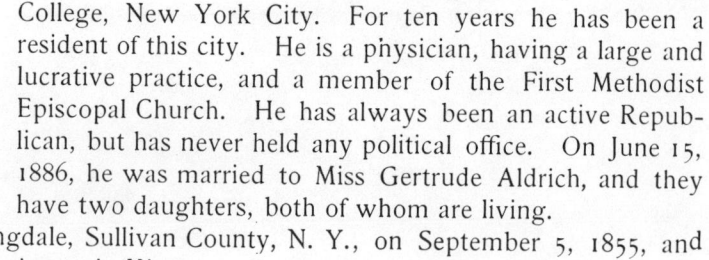

Stephen F. Bell was born at Bloomingdale, Sullivan County, N. Y., on September 5, 1855, and received his education at the Wyoming Seminary, in Kingston, Penn. For nine years he has been a resident of this city, and is a member of the firm of Bell & Cable, Liverymen. He is a member of the Methodist Episcopal Church, Master of Rising Star Lodge, No. 450, F. and A. M., a Republican in politics, and a member of the Civil Service Commission of this city. On June 19, 1884, he married Miss Lilian Millspaugh.

John Bellows became a resident of Yonkers in 1878, and since that time has been engaged in the real estate and fire insurance business, as a member of the firm of Bellows & Warren. He has taken a great interest in the success of the Board of Trade from the time it was first organized, and has been an active worker, serving on various committees and on its Board of Trustees; he is now Second Vice-President.

ETHELBERT BELKNAP was born in Yonkers, March 8, 1843, and was educated in the schools of this city. He is a hat manufacturer. Mr. Belknap is a member of the Knights Templars, a Republican in politics, and was appointed School Trustee, by Mayor Otis, at the time of the consolidation of the school districts, and reappointed by Mayor Millward; he is now a member of the Board of Education. He is one of the Board of Managers of St. John's Riverside Hospital and Chairman of the Executive Committee, also Vice-President of the Yonkers Building and Loan Association. He served seven years in the Seventeenth Regiment, National Guard of the State of New York, and for a number of years was Second Lieutenant. On April 26, 1864, he married Miss Lydia E. Frazee, daughter of the well-known American sculptor, John Frazee.

BLOOMINGDALE. Few of the residents of Yonkers take a greater interest in our city than Mr. Lyman G. Bloomingdale, whose residence, known as "Elgebia," ornaments North Broadway. During the summer months he finds great delight in leaving the details of Bloomingdale Brothers' dry goods establishment, and going over his "farm" as he calls it. Mr. Bloomingdale, although a member of many clubs, societies and associations, is of very domestic tastes, and spends most of his leisure at his home. Adjoining "Elgebia" is "Middlebrook," the summer home of Mr. Joseph B. Bloomingdale, who has spent part of each year since 1890 here. Mr. J. B. Bloomingdale is an enthusiastic "gentleman farmer," and now that he has retired from the firm of Bloomingdale Brothers, he will probably devote more of his time to the elaboration of "Middlebrook."

JOHN F. BRENNAN was born in New York City, December 3, 1853. He attended school in that city and came to Yonkers when a boy of fourteen, completing his elementary training in the public and parochial schools of this city; the same was supplemented by a course at Manhattan College from which he graduated with honors, then entering Columbia College, New York City, graduated, and was then admitted to the bar at Poughkeepsie, in 1877.

Mr. Brennan has always taken an active interest in everything pertaining to the welfare of this city. In 1893, he was appointed a member of the Board of Education by Mayor Weller, and was reappointed in 1895 by Mayor Peene. When the Yonkers Public Library was formed he was chosen President and still holds that office. His legal career has been most successful and he has been connected with many important cases both civil and criminal. In the winter of 1886 and 1887, when former District Attorney Nelson H. Baker was prevented by illness from executing the duties of his office, Mr. Brennan was selected to take charge of the Court work, where he acquitted himself so well and showed such capabilities for the duties of the position as to be highly complimented by the Court of Sessions, presided over by Judge Mills. Mr. Brennan was appointed by the Supreme Court in 1891 as one of the three examiners for the counties of Kings, Rockland, Queens, Richmond, Orange, Putnam, Dutchess and Westchester for the examination of applicants for admission to the bar, and to this position he was reappointed in 1893. He is a member of the Board of Trade, Yonkers Historical Society and numerous social organizations. The Yonkers Railroad Co. was organized in 1886 by him and he was one of the first Directors and has been their counsel since it was formed. In 1889 he married Miss Margaret H. Tiernan, of Dobbs Ferry. A view of his residence will be found on page 173.

HENRY F. BREVOORT was born in New York City, in 1840. He was the son of Elias and Mary Brevoort, who at the time of his birth lived in the old homestead on Fourth Avenue, near Grace Church, New York City. He was educated in the schools of New York and resided in this city for many years, engaging in the coal and wood business. Mr. Brevoort's father was a large stockholder in the Third Avenue Railway of New York City, and it was from him he inherited his fortune. Mr. Brevoort was a widely-known and highly-honored citizen of this city. He died December 20, 1895, leaving a widow and brother—James R. Brevoort, the eminent artist—to mourn his loss, and many friends to whom his sudden death was a great blow. Brusque and

HENRY F. BREVOORT.

abrupt in speech, "Harry" Brevoort, as he was familiarly called, was one of the kindest-hearted men in the world. The poor of Yonkers will long remember him; for he never refused their deserving wants. He was shrewd in business, well posted, able, popular, and a writer of no mean order, being quick to grasp a situation, always seeing the comical side, and having a happy way of putting his ideas on paper, to the pleasure always, and often to the profit, of the reader.

JAMES RENWICK BREVOORT, N. A., was born in Westchester County, July 20, 1832, and is a lineal descendant of Jan Heinrich van Brevoort, who emigrated from Holland and settled in New Amsterdam (now New York) about 1643. He received most of his art education in New York, in the studio of the late Thomas S. Cummings, then Vice-President of the National Academy of Design. In 1873, he went to Europe, where he remained about seven years, visiting nearly all the schools and art centres of Europe, studying the ancient and modern works of art in the galleries of the Old World. Most of the time while in Europe, his residence was in Florence, Italy, where he had his studio and pursued his profession, painting many works of Italian scenery, particularly of the Italian lakes. During his residence in Florence, he received the honor of being made a member of the Royal Academy of Urbino, the birthplace of Raphael. Some of his most important works have been pictures of English heaths and moorlands— such as "A Windy Day on the Border of a Heath," "A Day of Wind and Rain on a Moor," "The Night Wind Swept the Moorland Lea," etc., etc.

The artist's taste has inclined him to paint more of the solemn and weird aspects of nature, to which the heaths and moors of England most readily lend themselves. More recently he has devoted himself to water-colors of American and foreign scenes. His works are well-known, and can be found in various private collections. He was made an Academician of the National Academy of Design in New York in 1863. In 1870, he was appointed Professor of Scientific Perspective at the Academy of Design, upon which subject he gave courses of lectures with demonstrations during three years.

Before devoting himself to the study of landscape painting, he was employed in the office of his cousin, Mr. James Renwick, the well-known architect, during four years, and was Mr. Renwick's assistant in preparing the plans for St. Patrick's Cathedral in New York, the workhouse on Blackwell's Island, and many other public and private buildings. He came to Yonkers in 1880, and in 1890 built his present residence. He was married in 1873 to Miss Marie Louise Bascom, and has three children, two daughters and one son.

JOHN BRODERICK was born at Yonkers, February 22, 1858. He has resided here all his life, and is engaged in the hotel business. He is a Democrat in politics, and in 1877 was elected a member of the Board of Aldermen, and has served continuously ever since. On July 7, 1883, he married Miss Elizabeth Brennan, to whom three children have been born. For the past fifteen years he has been a member of the Volunteer Fire Department.

CHARLES FRANKLIN BROWN was born at Salona, Penn., and received his rudimentary education at the Whitehall Soldiers' Orphans' School. He afterwards took a thorough course at the Central State Normal School at Lockhaven, Penn., and completed a business education at Eastman's Business College at Poughkeepsie, N. Y. Thirteen years ago he located at Yonkers, where he has since resided, being engaged in the profession of an expert accountant. He is a member of the Corinthian Boat Club and the Methodist Episcopal Church of Yonkers, and of United States Lodge, No. 207, F. and A. M., of New York City. On May 11, 1892, he married Miss Effie E. Rote. Mayor Peene appointed Mr. Brown the first City Auditor of the City of Yonkers on June 11, 1895.

H. BEATTIE BROWN, M.D., was born in New York City, November 23, 1862, and has been a resident of Yonkers for thirty-two years. He is a graduate of the College of Physicians and Surgeons (Columbia University), New York City. Dr. Brown is a member of the Palisade Lodge, I. O. O. F., Lincoln Legion, Westchester County Medical Society, and an Elder in the Westminster Presbyterian Church. In politics he is a Republican. He is Consultant Physician to the Westchester County Hospital, Attending Physician to St. John's Riverside Hospital, Secretary of its Medical Board, and Examiner for several lodges and benevolent associations. On June 25, 1896, in Westminster Presbyterian Church, he was married to Miss Frances R. Smith by the Rev. James A. McWilliams, of Sing Sing, N. Y., Rev. George R. Cutting, pastor of the church, assisting in the ceremony.

ANDREW SIMMONS BROWNELL was born at Little Compton, R. I., March 7, 1850, and was educated in the public schools of New Bedford, Mass. He is engaged in the real estate business, and is a member of Park Hill Country Club, St. Andrew's Golf Club, Insurance Club of New York, and Joseph Warren Lodge, F. and A. M., Boston. He is a Republican, and is now a member of the Board of Education. On

February 9, 1888, he married Miss Matilda Geddes Gwyn. He was the pioneer of Park Hill, and in 1890 built and occupied the first house in that part of the City of Yonkers.

VALENTINE BROWNE, M.D., was born in Ireland, where he received his rudimentary education at Newmarket schools, which he attended until he was fourteen years of age, at which time his parents came to America and located in New York. He then entered the University of the City of New York. After completing his studies he decided to study medicine. For the past nineteen years he has been a resident of Yonkers, engaged in his chosen profession. He is a member of the Catholic Club of New York, the Catholic Benevolent Legion Medical Societies, and of St. Joseph's Catholic Church. He has filled the position of School Trustee, was a member of the Board of Health for seventeen years, and President of that body. On November 29, 1865, he married Miss Fannie B. O'Reilly. Eleven children have been born to them, five only of whom are living.

ARTHUR J. BURNS was born at Yonkers, January 11, 1857. He attended St. Mary's School in his native place until he had completed his education. After leaving school he decided to adopt the legal profession. In 1878, he was admitted to the bar, and during the same year he became a member of the law firm of R. E. & A. J. Prime, under the firm name of R. E. & A. J. Prime & Burns. In 1895 the firm was dissolved. In politics, Mr. Burns is a Democrat. He was Counsel to the Board of Excise for Yonkers, from 1879 to 1890. He was one of the first Civil Service Commissioners for Yonkers, and one of the first Police Commissioners of that city, having served from 1885 to 1889. Mr. Burns has been twice married. His first wife was Miss Johanna M. Crowley, who died in 1881; his present wife, whom he married in 1888, was Miss Mary J. Reed. He has two children, a son and a daughter. He is a member of the Church of the Immaculate Conception.

JEREMIAH BURNS was born in Effingham, N. H., November 23, 1817. Naturally studious, he inclined strongly to the profession of law when choosing his life-work. Prevented, however, in carrying out his desires in that direction, he early turned his attention to the study of machinery and manufacturing interests, for that purpose locating in the town of Saco, Me. During his residence there he married Miss Aphia Dennett of Biddeford, Me., and after a few years removed to New York State, and very soon decided to make Yonkers his home. Here he established a manufacturing business, with offices in New York City. Having high ideals of the duties of a citizen, he interested himself in the welfare of Yonkers, and immediately identified himself with all public questions, municipal, political and educational, which tended to the advancement and future prosperity of the growing town. He was a citizen in the truest sense of the term, seeking no office, finding his highest enjoyment in the support of good men and his greatest reward in their triumph. His political principles were well defined and easily understood, he being an ardent Republican, adhering to the party because he believed it the party of liberty, right and justice; he labored devotedly in its cause, and for the advancement of its principles, both with voice and pen. He founded and edited the *Yonkers Clarion*, a weekly newspaper loyally supporting the National Government during the late war, and giving the current news, opinions and events of the day. He was chosen with others to represent his native state during the war on the committee of New England States organized to assist in caring for the welfare of the soldiers.

Mr. Burns removed to New York City in the early part of 1864, but still retained property and a personal interest in Yonkers. He died in New York City, April 25, 1874. The following extract is taken from an article issued soon after his death in *The Republic*, a magazine published in Washington, D. C.: "Although a private citizen, without aspirations for public honors, Mr. Burns was widely known throughout the State of New York and the country for his sterling traits of character, and for the zeal displayed in the cause of freedom and education. The marked traits of his character were his wonderful energy and indomitable will. His principles were as firmly fixed as the granite rock of his native hills, and he was ever ready to sacrifice wealth and popularity in the defence of a just cause, or in an aggressive movement on a wrong one. He was fearless and outspoken against error, having the moral courage to give free expression to his thoughts at all times."

JAMES IRVING BURNS was born in Biddeford, Me., and was educated at Wisewell's Military Academy, Yonkers; Colgate University, Hamilton; and at Union College, Schenectady, N. Y., graduating from the latter with the degree of A.B. He also graduated from the Columbian Law School, Washington, D. C., with the degree of LL.B., and subsequently received the honorary degree of A.M. from Colgate University. His profession was the law. While a resident of New York City, he was an active, public-spirited citizen, and an officer in many public and private institutions. On September 29, 1868, he married Miss Mary C. Russell, of Hamilton, N. Y. They have two children, a son and a daughter.

Having cast his first vote with the Republican party, Mr. Burns became prominently and patriotically identified with it, serving as a member of the Republican Central Committee. Soon after moving to Yonkers, he was elected Alderman for the city, afterward declining a re-election. He was appointed and served as school trustee. He was elected to the State Legislature as a member of Assembly in 1887, 1888, 1890 and 1895, and in the fall of 1895, was nominated and elected State Senator for the term of three years under the new Constitution, receiving the largest plurality of any candidate upon the ticket. As a legislator he has taken high rank and made a most commendable record. He was a champion of the "Greater New York," and supported and voted for it. His party has constantly rewarded his service and loyalty by electing him Chairman of the Republican Central Committee for several consecutive years, and sending him as a delegate to State and other conventions. He is a prominent member of the City Club, Palisade Boat Club, and Yonkers Board of Trade.

CHARLES L. CHADEAYNE was born in New Castle, Westchester County, N. Y., May 12, 1838. His ancestors were among the earliest Huguenots to settle in America. Embracing such opportunities for education as were afforded by the district school system, he completed the same at the Charlotteville Seminary, in Schoharie County, N. Y. At the age of twenty, he came to Yonkers and engaged in the hardware and house-furnishing business, at No. 8 North Broadway, succeeding the firm of W. H. Sleight & Co. Connected with the business was an extensive mechanical department, which was placed under the supervision of the late John S. White. The business was conducted successfully for several years under the firm name of Chadeayne & Bro. (Henry A. Chadeayne), and subsequently as Chadeayne & Garrison (Hyatt L. Garrison), until 1866, when it was purchased by Lemuel Wells.

In 1867, Mr. Chadeayne accepted the agency of the Mutual Life Insurance Co. of New York, for Westchester County, where, having an extensive acquaintance, and being favorably known, he succeeded in building up a large business. In 1884, however, desiring to enter upon a larger field of work, he became connected with the metropolitan department of the company in New York City. He is widely known in insurance circles, and is a frequent contributor to various insurance journals and publications.

He is a member of the Yonkers Historical Society, and has been a diligent collector of historical relics and curios, including many very rare and valuable autographs, in which he manifests a justifiable pride. His married life dates from August 8, 1860, when he married Miss Charlotte Bliven, of Yonkers. Their family consists of two sons and two daughters. During Mr. Chadeayne's thirty-eight years' residence in our beautiful city, he has witnessed most of its phenomenal growth in population, manufacturing interests, material wealth and local improvements.

JOHN CLARK, like A. T. Stewart and many others whose records for business ability and enterprise are the standards set for the youth of America to emulate, was born in Ireland. His birth took place in 1835, and he spent the first nine years of his life in his native land. He then came to America and settled on a farm on Long Island, but fate had decreed that he was not to make his mark as a farmer. At the age of eighteen he went to New York City and engaged in the ice business with the firm of E. Barmore & Co., who at one time were the greatest ice dealers in America, and were the first to go out of New York City for their supply of ice, the ponds within the city limits furnishing all that was needed, until Barmore obtained the privilege of cutting ice from the famous Rockland Lake, and sent the first sloop load to the foot of Hubert Street, North River, then known as the old "Red Fort Dock," in 1855. Two years after Mr. Clark engaged with the Barmore Company, the business was reorganized, and was known as the "Knickerbocker Ice Co.," with Mr. Barmore as President. Mr. Clark was connected with that concern until 1860, five years after the reorganization.

In 1860 Mr. Clark left the Knickerbocker Company and engaged in business on his own account in New York City, under the name of the "Rockland Lake Ice Company, Independent." In fourteen years, by vigorous exercise of his business ability, he had created such a formidable rival to his old employers, that for self-protection they were compelled to buy the plant at his own figures—one-quarter of a million dollars—with the agreement that he was not to engage in the ice business in the City of New York or Brooklyn for five years. In order to pass this period, Mr. Clark with his family went on an extensive European tour. When he returned, in the spring of 1875, taking up his residence in this city, he purchased the ice business and good will of Charles C. Richardson, who was the principal dealer in ice at that time in that locality. Under Mr. Clark, the business was reorganized, and was, and still is, known as the Yonkers City Ice Co. It employs a large number of men and horses in the conduct of its business.

In 1879, at the expiration of the five years' agreement with the Knickerbocker Company, Mr. Clark again engaged extensively in the ice business in New York and Brooklyn, organizing the

A GROUP OF YONKERS CITIZENS.

1. J. Warren Goodale.
2. John Embree.
3. Charles L. Chadeayne.
4. William J. Bright.
5. Alden C. Tompkins.
6. Peter H. Havey.
7. Wm. Palmer East.
8. Charles P. Ward.
9. Wilbur B. Ketcham.

Ridgewood Ice Company, with himself as President, and soon made it the second largest ice business in the United States, the Knickerbocker being its only superior. He then built a number of ice-houses on the Upper Hudson, and became the largest individual owner on the river. He was known in the trade as the "Ice King of the Hudson." When his experience taught him that there was likely to be a failure in the crop of river ice, his agents would go through the lake regions and make contracts for the cutting and storing of ice enough to supply his customers.

Mr. Clark's motto seems to have been "Whatever you do, do it well." He made a study of his business, and is the best posted man on all the details of the trade in this part of the country. He understands the ice business thoroughly, from the time this product is first cut and stored, down to the minutest detail of the retail or wholesale part of the business. History repeats itself. His old rival, the Knickerbocker Company, finding its field to be gradually narrowing by the inroads made by the new company, soon began to make overtures which resulted eventually in the consolidation of the two great concerns, thus forming the largest ice company in the world, with John Clark as one of the chief managers, supplying New York, Brooklyn and adjoining cities.

Rev. Lyman Cobb, Jr., was born at Dryden, N. Y., September 18, 1826. He was educated at a New York collegiate school and the University of the City of New York. He has resided at Yonkers for forty-five years, and for twenty-nine years has been cashier of the Yonkers Savings Bank. He is a Republican, and for seven years was Village Clerk of Yonkers, Town Clerk one year and a Justice of the Peace for thirteen years. On November 4, 1845, he married Miss Cornelia S. Drake. Of the nine children born to them (four male and five female), three sons only are living. Mr. Cobb is a member of St. John's Episcopal Church at Yonkers, also of a number of societies and organizations, prominent among which are:

Masonic: Past Master, Nepperhan Lodge, F. A. M.; Past High Priest, Terrace City Chapter, R. A. M.; Past Illustrious Master, Nepperhan Counsel, R. & S. M.; Past Commander, Yonkers Commandry, K. T.; New York Lodge of Perfection, 14°; New York Council, Princess of Jerusalem, 16°; New York Order of Rose Croix 18°; New York Consistory 32°, Life Member; Masonic Veterans; Order of A. H. H.; Grand Chapter, R. A. M.; Grand Council, R. & S. M.; Grand Commandry, K. T. St. John's Riverside Hospital, Treasurer and Director; Yonkers Society for the Prevention of Cruelty to Children, Treasurer and Director; Yonkers Historical and Library Association, Treasurer and Counsel; Yonkers Clerical Association, Treasurer and Secretary; Westchester Historical Society; New York Prison Association; St. Andrew's Brotherhood; Clergymen's Mutual Insurance League, Director; Protestant Episcopal Society for the Increase of the Ministry, Life Member; Young Men's Christian Association, President; Young Women's Christian Association, President; Oneida Historical Society, Corresponding Member; Buffalo Historical Society, Corresponding Member; Curate St. John's Church, Yonkers; Archdeaconry of Westchester County.

Raffaelle Cobb was born in New York City, January 3, 1850. Almost immediately after his birth his parents removed to Yonkers, where he has resided ever since. Mr. Cobb is Clerk of the Yonkers Savings Bank, having held that position for twenty-nine years. He is a member of Christ's Episcopal Church and is one of the directors and a member of the Y. M. C. A., of Yonkers. On October 29, 1873, he married Miss Martha C. East. Four children have been born to the marriage, two sons and two daughters. The sons are now deceased. Mr. Cobb enlisted as a musician of the Fourth Separate Company, N.G.S.N.Y., in 1870, and was honorably discharged in 1887, after having filled all the official positions from private to captain.

William Francis Cochran. The name and the personality of William F. Cochran are associated with so many of Yonkers philanthropic enterprises that to write of him is to write of the history of some of her most beneficent and useful institutions, for, in a very large measure, to him they owe their present splendid homes and facilities for perpetuating and carrying on their work.

Always ready to lend his support, personal and financial, to any good cause, he has won the honor and affection of all classes, regardless of creed or party. His father, Alexander Gifford Cochran, was born in the city of New York of a good old Scotch family in 1803. He was a man of sterling worth, who brought up his children in the simple, religious way so characteristic of the sturdy Scots. He began his commercial career as a clerk in the old dry-goods house of Doremus, Suydam & Nixon, but in 1830 started his own firm, and soon became known as one of the leading dry-goods merchants of New York. Edward S. Jaffray, one of the most prominent merchants of those days, said of Alexander Cochran that: "he was the ablest and most promising young merchant in that city." After attaining great success in

New York City, his ambition led him to New Orleans, where he soon became widely known. A man of fine presence, most genial in disposition, kindly of heart and liberal to a fault, he gave to his children a heritage greater than wealth could bestow—the heritage of a life lived honestly and nobly before God and men. He died in 1875, honored and beloved of all. He left one daughter, the wife of the Hon. Stephen Sanford, of Amsterdam, N. Y., and one son, William F.

Mr. Cochran's mother, Sarah Phillips, was born at Florida, Montgomery County, N. Y., in 1805, of old Revolutionary stock. She was the youngest of a family of twelve children, all of whom lived to maturity. The Rev. William West Phillips, D.D., for years pastor of the First Presbyterian Church of New York, was her brother. Mr. Cochran's father and mother were devoted members of the Presbyterian Church. The latter died at Amsterdam, the home of her son, in 1893.

DUNCRAGGAN, RESIDENCE OF WILLIAM F. COCHRAN.

William F. Cochran was born in the city of New York, in October, 1835. He was early taught that life was real and earnest, and that industry, integrity, honesty and economy, were the foundation stones upon which commercial success was built, and that regard for the welfare and happiness of others, was a cardinal principle, without which, all life's attainments lacked the true and permanent elements of success. In 1844, his parents removed to Florida, Montgomery County, N. Y., and later they settled in Amsterdam on the Mohawk River, where the early years of his life were spent. He received the educational advantages of a first-class academy, and his academic career as a student was prophetic of the success he should afterwards attain in the social and commercial world. His conception of the uses of wealth as a means to dispense happiness and comfort, and to give to the less favored, advantages and privileges otherwise beyond their reach, it was the ambition of his youth to accomplish, and his whole later life has been eminently successful in the achievement of this noble purpose.

In 1849, he returned to New York to commence his business career, where he entered the service of Swift, Waldron & Co., in Front Street, and afterward Kent, Lowber & Co., both well-known houses. In 1857, he took up his residence in Albany, N. Y., and for several years conducted a business in that city, with unusual success. While there he became interested in the manufacture of Canadian lumber being associated in this business with his brother-in-law, Samuel H. Cook, of Balston Spa, N. Y.

After a close application to business for ten years, he made a tour of Europe in 1867, and on his return devoted all his energies to his lumber interests. In 1869, he married Miss Eva Smith, the only daughter of Alexander Smith, of Yonkers, with whom he soon after became associated in business.

In April, 1869, the firm of Alexander Smith & Sons was formed, and later, in 1873, the company was organized, being composed of Alexander Smith & Sons and the well-known house of W. & J. Sloane of New York. The Alexander Smith & Sons Carpet Company is now one of the largest, if not the largest carpet manufacturing company in the world.

Mr. Cochran was the Secretary and Treasurer of this company, and was devoted to the development of its large interests for almost a quarter of a century; he retired from active participation in its management in 1894. Since then he has given the greater part of his time to the various beneficent institutions with which his name is so closely associated. "Duncraggan," his charming summer home on the banks of the Hudson, is justly celebrated as one of the most beautiful properties on America's Rhine. At this house, where he resides most of the year, and also at his city home in New York, hospitality and hearty cordiality " welcome the coming, and speed the parting guest." He has six children, three sons and three daughters.

Mr. Cochran is a man simple in his tastes, most temperate in his habits, ready always to bestow upon others what he denies himself. In politics he has ever been a strong Republican, taking an active personal interest in the municipal affairs of Yonkers. In 1895 he was his party's choice for the nomination of Congressman, but declined the honor, preferring to devote himself to the enterprises in which he is enlisted here. Mr. Cochran has been a Vestryman of St. John's Protestant Episcopal Church for nineteen years, and during that time he and his wife relieved the church of a large debt, and built the rectory, parish buildings and drinking fountain (which latter is supplied with ice water all through the hot season), at the corner of South Broadway and Hudson Streets.

In many of the good works, indeed in almost all which have been recipients of his benefactions, his good wife has been a partner in his philanthropy. Always exceedingly modest and retiring, ever ready to help, but in the most unostentatious way, Mr. and Mrs. William F. Cochran have done more for the city of Yonkers than any other residents. Their work is not confined to the church of which they are members, but all denominations have received their generous and unstinted support. The beautiful and superbly equipped St. John's Hospital buildings on Ashburton Avenue, opened in 1894, were erected by them, of which institution Mr. Cochran has been President for seventeen years. He has been a member of the Board of Education, first President of the Board of Trade, and Director of the First National Bank. At present he is identified with several large corporations in New York, being a Director of the Western Union Telegraph Company and of the Continental Trust Company.

The Hollywood Inn, at South Broadway and Hudson Street, the largest and best-equipped workingmen's club in this country, was the personal gift of Mr. Cochran, of which also he is the President. To this work, so extensive, so broad, he gives much of his time, ever anticipating and providing for the wants of the thousands who participate in its benefits. Of this man it may be truly said, he lives to make others happy, to dispense the wealth which he regards as committed to his trust, simply and solely as a steward, for the benefit and happiness of others. Yonkers has many enduring monuments which will long commemorate the thoughtfulness, and the generosity, and the nobility, of William F. Cochran.

FREDERICK AUGUSTUS COE was born at New Hartford, N. Y., October 22, 1816, and graduated from Yale College in 1837. Mr. Coe was a lawyer and resided in this city for about twenty years. In 1841 he married Anna Eliza, daughter of Minott Mitchell, of White Plains, N. Y. He was a Republican, and at one time Corporation Counsel of the village of Yonkers, and at the time of his death, January 9, 1870, a member of the Union League Club, of New York City.

ELLSWORTH E. COLTON, M.D., was born at Collinsville, Conn., July 28, 1860. He was educated in the public-schools of his native place, after which he began the study of medicine. Nine years ago he removed to Yonkers, where he has since practiced his chosen profession. He is assistant surgeon to the Fourth Regiment, N. G. S. N. Y., and visiting physician to St. Joseph's Hospital.

WILLIAM P. CONSTABLE was born in London, England, August 24, 1853. For the past thirty-one years he has resided at Yonkers, where he is at present engaged in the printing business. Mr. Constable learned his trade in *The Gazette* office, under J. G. P. Holden. He is a member of the Veterans' National Guards, Westminster Presbyterian Church, is a Republican, and Commissioner of Charities, a position he has held for three years. He served for nine years in the Sixteenth Battalion, Fourth Separate Company, N. G. S. N. Y., also for five years in Irving Hose Company of the Yonkers Fire Department, and for three years of that period was Chairman of the Company. On November 22, 1888, he married Miss S. Jennie Jackson, to whom two children have been born.

RICHARD L. CONDON has been a resident of Yonkers all his life, and was educated at Manhattan College. He is engaged in the coal business, and is a member of the Board of Trade and the Board of Education.

S. WILLIAM CONKLIN, D.D.G.P., was born in New York City on March 19, 1847, and was educated in the public schools of New York. He was married to Kittie Winchell, of Oswego, N. Y., on November 24, 1870. Mr. Conklin is one of the firm of Lawrence & Conklin, proprietors of the Yonkers Planing and Moulding Mills, and has been a resident of this city for fourteen years. He is a member of Otsego Lodge, No. 138, F. and A. M., Palisade Lodge, No. 571, and Shaffner Encampment, No. 100, I. O. O. F. In politics he is a Republican.

WILLIAM S. COONS, M.D., was born at Hudson, Columbia County, N. Y., on October 3, 1864, and received his education at Claverack Institute, Mount Pleasant Military Academy, graduating from the University of New York City. He is a physician and surgeon and has been a resident of this city for five years. On December 3, 1891, he married Miss Carrie Tompkins. He is a member of the Central Methodist Episcopal Church, Knights of Pythias, Westchester County Medical Society, Examiner of the United States Industrial Insurance Company, and Visiting Physician to St. John's Hospital. Independent in politics.

SAMUEL LISPENARD COOPER was born at New York City, January 16, 1858. He is a graduate of the University of the City of New York. For the past eleven years he has been a resident of Yonkers, where he has followed his profession—that of a civil engineer. In politics he is a Democrat, and is at present Commissioner of Public Works for the city of Yonkers. He is a Trustee of Hollywood Inn, a member of the City Club, Palisade Boat Club of Yonkers, the American Society of Civil Engineers, and the Methodist Church. For ten years he was connected as engineer with the New York Water Supply, of which five years were in connection with the new aqueduct and reservoir work, and five years as resident engineer of the old Croton Aqueduct. He also spent three years as examining engineer in the New York Finance Department. On January 6, 1885, Mr. Cooper married Miss Elizabeth Underhill, daughter of the Rev. Dr. George H. Goodsell, of the Methodist Episcopal Church. Three children have been the fruits of the union, one of whom is dead.

JOHN COPCUTT, one of the oldest residents of Yonkers, was born at Oxfordshire, England, in 1805. When twelve years of age his parents removed to New York City, where he was educated in the schools of that place. He followed the vocation of his father, and soon became the largest dealer in and importer of mahogany. He was noted for his extraordinary gift in judging mahogany, and often was laughingly told that "he could see right through a log." In 1824, he made his first visit to this city, accompanied by his father, to make arrangements to have mahogany sawed at the Yonkers mills, coming by sloop from New York. In 1845, Mr. Copcutt purchased a tract of land which included the lower, or first, water power where the Nepperhan River empties into the Hudson, and built upon it a number of mills and stores. In 1854, he made another extensive purchase of woodland and also built his fine stone residence on Nepperhan Avenue. Soon after this he acquired more property and water-power, erecting in the vicinity of his home several substantial factories, besides many small cottages which were rented to the hands employed in the various mills. Having now made Yonkers his permanent home, he watched the growth of the town, taking a great interest in its welfare. Mr. Copcutt delighted in travel and was a great reader. His memory was most remarkable and his reminiscences, extending from his earliest childhood, were most interesting. Mr. Copcutt ascribed his health and activity to the fact that he had always been in active employment. He was a strong free trader and, although at one time largely engaged in silk manufacturing himself, always advocated his views with vigor. In politics he took little active part, but at one time served as village trustee but disliked and declined further office holding. In commercial circles Mr. Copcutt's integrity and financial standing were of the highest; he passed through several financial crises, but always paid his obligations in full. In religion he was a strong Calvinist, and never severed his relations from them in England, and until the time of his death contributed largely to their support. A Church of England magazine said at the time of Mr. Copcutt's demise: "We deeply regret to record the death of the oldest and one of the most appreciative of our transatlantic subscribers. Another of the fathers of the old school has been taken, and the Church of God on earth is the poorer." An English Baptist magazine said: "He was a remarkable man in committing his temporal concerns to God. He was kind to the Lord's poor, who, we fear, will greatly miss him." Mr. Copcutt's death occurred on February 15, 1895, when he succumbed to an attack of acute pneumonia. He was well and strong for his age, being exceedingly active and attending to his business affairs both in this city and New York. In 1833, he was married to Miss Rebecca Medwin Boddington, daughter of Richard Boddington, of Manchester, England. Of the twelve children born to Mr. and Mrs. Copcutt, six survive him—Mrs. A. E. C. Hyde, of this city; Mrs. C. A. Leale and W. H. Copcutt, of New York City; Mrs. James A. Wilcox, of Bloomington, Ills.; John B. Copcutt and Miss Anna C. Copcutt, of this city.

JOHN BODDINGTON COPCUTT was born at Yonkers, August 27, 1855, where he has always resided. He received his education in the private school of Rev. M. R. Hooper of his native place, but afterwards took a thorough course at a business college in New York, after which he engaged in mercantile pursuits. Until recently he was a member of the firm of J. Copcutt, Son & Co., hard-wood merchants and importers, of New York. He is a prominent member of the Yonkers Board of Trade, the South Yonkers Improvement Company, Park Hill Country Club, and is a vestryman of St. Andrew's Memorial Episcopal Church. On October 10, 1888, he married Miss May N. Hill, to whom one child (now deceased), was born.

THOMAS CLAPP CORNELL was born in Flushing, L. I., on January 7, 1819, at which place his parents resided and were engaged in conducting a boarding-school for young ladies. His father, Silas, son of Benjamin Cornell, was born at the old family homestead in Scarsdale, Westchester County, in 1789. His mother, Sarah, daughter of Adam Mott, was born in North Hempstead, Queens County, in 1791, in the old Mott homestead, overlooking Long Island Sound, which had then been in the family more than a century and is still in the possession of the descendants of its founder. The Cornell and Mott families, thus united, had been for many generations among the stanchest Quaker yeomanry of the two counties. At the tender age of four years young Cornell removed with his parents to the neighborhood of Rochester, where they resided on a farm, and the lad enjoyed the meagre opportunity of attending a country district-school during the winter months. This was the only school he ever attended, and the aggregate of his schooling was less than three years, closing before his twelfth year. At the age of fifteen he was doing a man's labor on the farm and continuing his studies in the evening; often before daylight he was at work at his Latin or Greek grammar, or mathematics. His father became the local surveyor of the vicinity, and in 1836 removed to Rochester, adopting the pursuit of surveyor and civil engineer with young Thomas as his assistant.

Upon reaching his majority in 1840, Mr. Cornell accepted employment in the engineering department of the State of New York on the Erie Canal enlargement, and was entrusted with important duties on the combined locks of Lockport. Upon the close of this work he was, in 1844–46, employed by the Canadian Government on the Lachine Canal, near Montreal, and in the office of the Provincial Board of Public Works. Going to Europe in 1846, he spent eighteen months in England, Scotland, France, Switzerland, Germany and Italy, seeking in each country to associate wholly with the natives, that he might thus perfect himself in the local languages. Returning in 1847, he readily found employment as civil engineer on the Hudson River Railroad, then building, having charge of the work between Spuyten Duyvil and Dobb's Ferry, locating in this city, then a mere hamlet. For many years Mr. Cornell was the sole civil engineer in Yonkers and thus directed nearly all of the local improvements. He was also the architect of most of the buildings erected in Yonkers' early development. He was the founder and, for more than forty years, the chief manager of the Yonkers Gas Works, and for the same period director of the Bank of Yonkers and the Yonkers Savings Bank. He was also the founder and early patron of *The Yonkers Gazette* and *The Yonkers Statesman*. He was a Whig, and subsequently Republican in politics, but always refused public office, except that of School Trustee, in which capacity he rendered long and arduous service.

During the course of his European sojourn, Mr. Cornell was induced to abandon the religion of his ancestors, and in 1847, at Lyons, France, he was received into the Roman Catholic Church, of which he was thereafter a zealous and devoted member. He rendered ardent service in founding in Yonkers St. Mary's Church in 1848, and its parish schools in 1859, and St. Joseph's Church in 1871. In the last years of his life he was influential in founding the new church of St. Peter's parish. He promoted the establishment of the Sisters of Charity at Mount St. Vincent in 1859, and continued an active interest in the development of their great institution of learning to the close of his life. He was very prominent in founding the beautiful Hospital of St. Joseph, and was both trustee and treasurer until his death. In 1882 he published a history of the Roman Catholic Church in Yonkers. Mr. Cornell's chief recreation was found in historical studies and genealogical research. He was an active and enthusiastic member of the Westchester Historical Society and the Yonkers Historical and Library Association. He devoted much time and labor to clearing up and elucidating the genealogy of the Cornell and Mott families, and published several contributions regarding them for private circulation. His later work in reference to his mother's family, issued in 1890, was an elaborate and extremely creditable production. In personal appearance Mr. Cornell was about five feet nine, but quite spare in flesh. Although never robust in health, his temperate habits and orderly mode of life enabled him to accomplish much. He was of a peculiarly cheerful and friendly disposition, and in all respects a good neighbor and worthy citizen. On May 2, 1850, he was married to Miss Jane E. Bashford, of Yonkers, who survives him. His only child, a daughter, died in infancy. Mr. Cornell was for nine years a member of the New York Genealogical and Biographical Society, and for six years an active member of the Board of Trustees. He departed this life at his home in Yonkers, December 29, 1894.

JAMES C. COURTER was born at Yonkers, February 26, 1842, where he has resided all his life, with the exception of ten years spent in New York City. He received a careful education in private schools of his native place. On December 27, 1869, he married Elizabeth McClosky. One child (now deceased) was born to them. During the greater part of his life Mr. Courter has been devoted to agricultural pursuits. Politically, he is a Democrat, and has held the position of Mayor of Yonkers, Supervisor and Sheriff of Westchester County. He is a member of the City Club of Yonkers.

CHARLES R. CULVER was born at Poughkeepsie, N. Y., August 6, 1855, and has resided at Yonkers for twenty-six years, where he has been engaged in the dry-goods business since 1879. He is a prominent member of the Presbyterian Church and is prominently identified with various interests in Yonkers.

PATRICK J. CURRAN was born in Ireland in 1851, and received his education in the schools of Ireland and this country. He has been a resident of this city for thirty-three years, for fifteen years was engaged in the silk manufacture, and at one time was foreman of McFarlan's Silk Factory of this city. At present Mr. Curran is engaged in the hotel business. In 1889, he was married to Miss Mary McGrath and they have five children. He is a member of the Fire Department, Hibernian Club and St. Joseph's Church, and in politics a Democrat.

THOMAS F. CURRAN was born at Yonkers in November, 1873. He was educated at parochial and public schools. After completing his education, he, in 1892, entered the office of John F. Brennan, to study law. In September, 1894, he was admitted to the bar, being the youngest man in his class. He is a member of St. Joseph's Catholic Church, St. Joseph's Church Order, Yonkers Corinthian Yacht Club and Yonkers Athletic Club. Politically, he is a Democrat.

JOSEPH F. DALY was born on September 13, 1855, in the city of New York. He received his preliminary education in the common schools of that city, and in his fifteenth year passed his examination for entrance to the College of the City of New York, but, on account of the illness of his father, he was unable to enter. He commenced his legal studies in the office of Hatch & Beneville, and remained with that firm until he was admitted to the bar. In the meantime he completed the course of studies prescribed in the New York Evening High School and in Cooper Union, and on graduating from these schools he entered the University of the City of New York, where, in the year 1877, he received the degree, LL.B., and, on the recommendation of the Faculty of that institution, was admitted to the bar in May of the same year. In 1878, he moved to Yonkers, where he opened an office for the general practice of his profession. In 1882 he was elected Justice of the Peace, and during his entire term of office he was the acting City Judge of the city. In 1883 he received the appointment of City Attorney, which office he held until the spring of 1892. In 1890 he was appointed, by the General Term of the Supreme Court, one of the examiners for the admission of members of the bar for the Second Judicial District, composed of the Counties of Kings, Queens, Richmond, Suffolk, Putnam, and Westchester. During the years he has practiced in Yonkers, both in his private practice and as Attorney for the city and its various departments, he has been engaged in very important litigation, and has been the author of many measures affecting the municipal government. In 1894, upon the recommendation of his political opponents, he was appointed a member of a commission to revise the Charter of the city. He is at present counsel to the Board of Water Commissioners.

JOHN J. DEVITT was born in this city September 22, 1855, and was educated in St. Mary's School and in the public schools of this city and Packard's Business College of New York. He engaged in mercantile pursuits, and at present carries on a large wholesale grocer and commission business in this city and New York. He has always been a Democrat, but never desired any official position. He is a

JOHN J. DEVITT.

Trustee of St. Mary's Church, where, on December 28, 1880, he was married to Miss Mary E. Shaughnessy, by her uncle, the Rev. James H. McGean, pastor of St. Peter's Church, New York, assisted by the Rev. Charles R. Corley, pastor of St. Mary's Church. The children of this marriage have been five, of whom one, Chauncey B., has died, having lived a little over six years, but in that short life displayed such a manly, cheerful character that he endeared himself to all who knew him. The other children are Edmund Booth, John Jay, Sarah M., and Mary Florence. Mr. Devitt is exceedingly popular in business circles, having a large acquaintance and a successful business career.

Francis X. Donoghue was born at Yonkers, March 20, 1856, and was educated in the Christian Brothers' Parochial School and St. Francis Xavier's, graduating June, 1875. He studied law in the office of Thomas Bracken, New York City, and was admitted to practice as an attorney in Brooklyn in February, 1878, and as a Counsellor, September, 1878. He was elected Justice of the Peace in March, 1881; appointed Acting City Judge by Mayor Swift January 1, 1882, and held this appointment until April, 1889. On January 1, 1883, he was appointed by Judge Matt. H. Ellis as Clerk of the City Court of Yonkers, and served till November 1, 1886, when he resigned, being re-elected Justice of the Peace in March, 1885. On April 11, 1889, he was appointed by Surrogate Coffin, Clerk of the Surrogate's Court of Westchester County, and held this office until April 14, 1892, when he was elected City Judge of Yonkers for four years, from April 15, 1892. He is Secretary of the City Club and a member of the Corinthian Yacht Club and Turn Verein.

Daniel A. Doran was born in August, 1860, was educated in public schools, and is a graduate of Cooper Union, N. Y. He has been a resident of Yonkers for thirteen years, being there engaged in the painting and decorating business. He is the State representative of the Ancient Order of United Workmen, member of the Red Men, and Director of the Mercantile Building and Loan Association of N. Y., and of the Atlantic Saving and Loan Association of Syracuse. On June 6, 1886, he was married to Miss Margaret C. McConville, of Spring Valley, N. Y. Mr. Doran is also Secretary and Treasurer of the Waldor Manufacturing Company, and for the past seven years has been largely interested in real estate, owning several desirable pieces of property.

William H. Doty was born at Hyde Park, N. Y., and was educated at Poughkeepsie. For the past thirty-five years, Mr. Doty has resided at Yonkers, and for some years has held the position of President of the First National Bank of Yonkers. He attends the Presbyterian Church, is a member of the F. and A. M., and the Society of Mayflower Descendants and Treasurer of the Board of Trade and the Yonkers Building Association. Politically, he is a Republican, and was for twenty years City Clerk of Yonkers. He is now President of the Board of Water Commissioners. On July 26, 1882, he married Miss Elizabeth C. MacCorkindale, who was born at Campbelltown, Scotland. They have three children, all boys.

Isaac G. Downing was born in December, 1850, at White Plains, N. Y., and was educated at the common schools. He has been a resident of Yonkers for thirty-two years, has been connected with the Post Office Department for over twenty years, and is now holding the position of Assistant Postmaster. He has made himself invaluable, and has served in this position through the different administrations. He is a member of the Nepperhan Lodge, F. and A. M., Yonkers Council, Royal Arcanum and National Provident Union. On December 7, 1892, he was married to Miss Ida A. Vincent, to whom one child, a girl, has been born.

William Bell Edgar was born at Sunnybrae, Annandale, Dumfriesshire, Scotland and educated in the schools of that town. He has been a resident of this city for forty-one years, and is President of the corporation of Acker, Edgar & Co. He is a member of the First Presbyterian Church, Board of Education, Board of Trade and the City Club. Mr. Edgar is a Republican in politics, but never held any official position. On December 6, 1862, he married Miss Mary Bryden, of Clinton, Oneida County, N. Y.

Matt. H. Ellis was born February 25, 1836, at Humphreysville (now called Seymore), New Haven County, Conn. His mother, Charlotte Clinton, was of Puritan descent. His father was born in Wales, and for many years preached as a Methodist minister in Connecticut, western Massachusetts and eastern New York. At the age of seventeen the subject of our sketch shipped as a sailor before the mast and visited many foreign countries, including South America, Australia and the East Indies. Returning after an absence of nearly three years, he entered Hudson River Institute (now known as Claverack College), and graduated therefrom in 1856, the money he earned as a sailor being used to help pay the expense of his education. He subsequently studied law with Wm. Eno, a leading lawyer for many years at Pine Plains, Dutchess County, N. Y., and later married his daughter, Mary Eno. He was admitted to the bar in 1859, and opened a law office in New York City.

After the Civil War broke out and in the dark hours of the summer of 1862, Col. Ellis pitched his recruiting tent in Union Square, New York City, near the Washington Equestrian Statue, and recruited over 200 men. He enrolled as a private, was subsequently commissioned by the Governor as Captain of Company K, 175th New York Volunteers, and served until February 1, 1865. Just before this he was associated with the New York Zouaves, organized for the purpose of competing with Ellsworth's noted Zouaves, of Chicago. The New York Company became famous for perfection in drill. Of this organization he was Secretary, and General Hawkins, afterward Colonel of Hawkins Zouaves, was President. Col. Ellis commanded his company in the battles in which his regiment was engaged in Louisiana, which included the Red River expedition, and at the siege of Port Hudson, he was specially mentioned for gallant conduct for the assault on the citadel, June 14, 1863, and for which he received a commission as Brevet Major. After the capture of Port Hudson he was detailed on general court martial service at New Orleans, where he served as Judge Advocate in the trial of important cases. He was subsequently ordered to Washington as a member of the celebrated general court martial and military commission, of which Gen. Abner Doubleday was President, and acted in conjunction with Gen. Foster, as Judge Advocate of that court. The court tried many important cases, some of them of historical interest. He was also sent to Canada on an important and delicate mission by the Secretary of War.

In 1866, Col. Ellis made his residence in Yonkers, and soon became a prominent member of the Westchester County bar. He became interested in the public affairs of Yonkers and closely identified himself with its interests and growth. He commanded a company of National Guards in the Sixteenth Battalion, which company is now known as the Fourth Separate Company, one of the most efficient and best drilled companies in the state. From this company he was promoted to the rank of Colonel and Assistant-Adjutant General on the staff of Major-General James W. Husted, who commanded the Fifth Division National Guards, of New York, comprising a uniformed force of about 3,000 men.

He was for nearly six years Corporation Counsel of Yonkers, and subsequently four years City Judge, and introduced many new ideas and reform methods in the management of the court. He was prominently identified with drafting the first City Charter, and was counsel for the village and subsequently the city during its transition period, and drafted many legislative enactments, which became necessary by reason of the change in the form of government. He was also several years a member, and for a time, President of the Board of Education of School No. 6, and while acting as such, was prominent in advocating a consolidation of all the school districts under one head.

In February, 1878, he drafted a proposed bill making radical changes in the whole system, notably the appointment of trustees by the Mayor instead of election. His bill met with considerable opposition, but the Colonel was persistent, and sent a petition to the Common Council asking for a hearing, which was granted, and a Committee of the Whole of that body listened to lengthy discussions of the subject from the Colonel and prominent citizens. It was, however, voted down by the council; but the seed was sown, and finally in May, 1881, Col. Ellis' bill, in its essential features, was taken up and passed. The new methods introduced under the new regime have given these schools a national reputation.

Col. Ellis has been identified with the Grand Army of the Republic since 1868, and is a member of Fremont Post, No. 590. He is also a member of the New York Commandery of the Military Order of the Loyal Legion, and has been active for many years in the Yonkers Grand Army Memorial Committee, of which he was one of the organizers. He was one of the original charter members and active workers in organizing the Westchester County Association of the Grand Army of the Republic, which has been an effective power in New York State. He was chief aid on Department Commander John C. Shott's staff in 1874, and upon the election of Commander-in-Chief Lawler was appointed Judge Advocate General of the Grand Army of the Republic for the United States. He is now Vice-President of the Bunnell & Eno Investment Company.

GEN. THOMAS EWING, son of Senator Ewing, of Ohio, was born at Lancaster, Ohio, August 7, 1829, and after graduating from Brown University and the Cincinnati Law School, served President Taylor as private secretary. In 1856 he settled in Kansas, and in 1860 was elected Chief Justice of the Supreme Court of Kansas; in 1862 he recruited and was appointed Colonel of the Eleventh Kansas Infantry. At the close of the war he resigned from the army and resumed the practice of law. He was a representative from Ohio from 1877 to 1881, and in 1879 was the Democratic candidate for Governor of Ohio. He then came to New York City, and practiced law with Milton I. Southard. In 1856 he married Miss Ellen Cox, daughter of the Rev. William Cox, of Piqua, Ohio. General Ewing's sister was the wife of the late General William Tecumseh Sherman. General Ewing died on January 2, 1896, leaving a wife and five children.

JOHN EYLERS was born in Germany, January 5, 1843. He has resided at Yonkers for the past twenty-six years, where he has been engaged in the grocery business. In politics he is a Democrat, and is a member of the Board of Water Commissioners. He is President of the Turn Verein, a member of the Teutonic Society and of Puritan Lodge, No. 338, F. and A. M., of New York. In 1883 he married Mrs. Julia Martina, who has borne him four children.

CHARLES H. FANCHER was born in Warwick, Orange County, N. Y., and was educated in the district schools of that place. He is engaged in the banking business, and has been a resident of Yonkers for about six years, being at present a member of the Board of Education. He is a Republican in politics but has never held any official position.

JUSTUS H. FIEDLER was born in Germany on November 30, 1853, and was educated in the public schools of New York City. He has resided in Yonkers for twenty-one years and is engaged in the dry-goods business, and is a member of various German organizations of this city. Politically, he is a Democrat, and at present is a member of the Board of Education, and Past Master of Putnam Lodge, No. 338, F. and A. M., also 32°, A. A. S. R. Mason. On December 11, 1878, he was married to Miss Delia A. Lester.

WILLIAM H. FISHER was born at West Farms, N. Y., August 19, 1846, and was educated in District School No. 2. He has been a resident of this city for forty-nine years, and was Superintendent in Baldwin & Flagg's, and Howard W. Flagg's hat factories for twenty-five years. He is a member of St. John's Episcopal Church, and served on the Vestry in 1885–1886, a Comrade of Kitching Post No. 60, Grand Army of the Republic, a member of Rising Star Lodge, No. 450, F. and A. M., Past Dictator of Yonkers Lodge No. 1872, Knights of Honor, an honorary member of Hope Hook and Ladder Co., No. 1, and a member of the Westchester County Association Grand Army of the Republic. He is a Republican in politics and in 1892 was appointed Civil Service Commissioner by Mayor Weller, resigning in May, 1895, to accept the position of Clerk of the Board of Assessors. On May 19, 1870, he was married to Elizabeth Reed Raymond, of Danbury, Conn. Mr. Fisher served during the Civil War in Company B., Fifteenth Regiment, New York State National Guard, enlisting June 4, 1864, at the age of seventeen years and being assigned to garrison duty at Fort Richmond, New York Harbor. He was honorably discharged July 6, 1864.

JAMES SEELY FITCH, son of the Rev. Silas Fitch, was born December 2, 1847, in the town of Coeymans, Albany County, N. Y., was educated at Delaware Academy at Delhi, N. Y., and was graduated from Columbia College Law School in 1875. He was Principal of the Hudson Academy, at Hudson, N. Y., during the year 1868. In 1869, he made Yonkers his residence, and was engaged as a teacher in the public schools, for six years. Mr. Fitch is a real estate broker, and makes a specialty of real estate law. He is a member of St. John's Episcopal Church, Nepperhan Lodge, Terrace City Chapter, Yonkers Commandery, the Board of Trade and the Board of Education. He is a Republican, and has taken an active interest in political matters during his residence in Yonkers. In 1876, he was married to Miss Martha P. Munson, at Dedham, Mass. Their children are Edith Munson (deceased), Edward Arthur and Florence Mary.

MICHAEL FITZGERALD was born in Ireland, September 29, 1848, and received his education in the night schools of this city. He came to Yonkers in 1867 and learned the moulding trade in the Clipper Mowing & Reaper Company shops. Mr. Fitzgerald has made one trip to California by way of the Isthmus of Panama through the Golden Gate, returning to Yonkers in 1879, and is now engaged in the foundry business. He is a member of St. Mary's Church, a Democrat in politics, and at the spring election for supervisor in 1894 was the only Democrat elected. In May, 1895, he was elected Alderman of the First Ward, which position he still holds. On May 10, 1880, he married Miss Mary Ann O'Connor, who died at Ware, Mass., on August 1, 1894. After twenty years' residence in the United States he made a trip to his native home.

EDWARD ALBRO FORSYTH.

PATRICK J. FLANNERY was born in Ireland, and came to America when he was a boy eight years of age. After completing an education in the public schools, he attended Eastman's Business College in Poughkeepsie. He has resided in Yonkers for the past fifteen years, and has been engaged in the business of a mason and builder. He is a member of the Catholic Church, City Club and Good Government Club. Politically he is a Democrat. On January 12, 1886, he married Miss Elizabeth A. McCue, to whom five children have been born. Mr. Flannery served seven years in the N. G. S. N. Y.

EDWARD J. FLOOD was born at Yonkers and educated in the schools of this city. In 1892 he entered into partnership with Mr. Mahony, under the firm name of Mahony & Flood. He is a member of St. Mary's Catholic Church and the Knights of Pythias.

JOHN H. FOERST was born at Preetz, Holstein, Germany, January 16, 1855, and was educated at the public schools. Sixteen years ago he located at Yonkers, where he has since that time been engaged in the provision business. On January 12, 1886, he married Miss Agnes J. Fruch. Mr. Foerst is a member of the A. O. of F. and A. M., A. O. O. F., and the German Order of Harugari. He is a Democrat, and a member of the Board of Fire Commissioners.

EDWARD ALBRO FORSYTH was born in Yonkers and was educated in the public schools of this city, graduating from the high school class of 1882. He is a member of the Young Men's Republican Club, and at present is the Supervisor from the Third Ward. He is an architect, and recently the plans prepared by him of the new police station, to be situated at the corner of Wells and Woodworth Avenues, were considered the best submitted, and accepted by the Board of Aldermen. The first prize was awarded to him.

PETER U. FOWLER was born in Yonkers on March 5, 1835, and educated in the schools of this city. For the past thirty years he has been engaged in the grocery business, and is a member of the firm of Thompson & Fowler. He is a Democrat in politics, but has never held any official position. On April 28, 1858, he was married to Miss Sarah A. Codington, to whom three children have been born.

CHARLES H. FRAZIER was born in this city September 3, 1867, and received his education here. For a number of years he has been one of the leading photographers of Yonkers. He is a Republican in politics, but never held any official position. On November 23, 1892, he married Miss Sarah Riele, of Morristown, N. Y., and they have two children.

MUNICIPAL BUILDING IN COURSE OF ERECTION. E. A. FORSYTH, ARCHITECT.

HYATT L. GARRISON was born July 13, 1826, on the farm situated on Odell Avenue, now known as the Flagg Farm, and was educated at the public and district schools of the town of Yonkers. At the age of twenty-one he went as clerk to the grocery store of J. O. Fowler and in 1848, commenced business with his brother on the sloop Mary Kimball, running the sloop as a transient boat, and in 1849 with his brother-in-law Captain Joseph Peene, who was then running the Ben Franklin, which carried the farmers' produce to New York and brought back goods for stores and factories. In 1850, he and Captain Joseph Peene purchased the sloop Eliza Hicks, running it as a transient and freight boat, and in 1851, he formed a partnership with Captain Peene, running the two sloops alternately to New York. In 1851, Captain Peene purchased the sloop Martin Hynes and the same year, together with Captain Peene, Mr. Garrison purchased the Ben Franklin of his father and also bought half interest in the Martin Hynes, running the three sloops under the name of the Ben Franklin Line. This partnership lasted until 1867, when, on account of poor health, Mr. Garrison sold his interest to Captain Peene. In 1868 he became engaged in the flour and feed business with Robert Neville, and in 1870 engaged in the hardware business with Charles L. Chadeayne; in 1872 he entered into the grocery business with S. S. Baldwin, and continued in that line for two years. In 1872 he was elected a trustee of the village of Yonkers. On its incorporation as a city, for two years he served as Alderman, and after retiring from this position in 1874 was appointed Assessor, which office he held for seven years, afterwards engaging in the real estate and fire insurance business, in which he still continues. In 1895 he was again elected as Alderman from the Third Ward. In 1852 he married Miss Sophia A. French, to whom four children were born, three of whom are living.

HENRY GAUL was born at New York City, but has resided at Yonkers for thirty-two years. He was educated at the public schools, and is at present a prosperous merchant. He represents the Second Ward of Yonkers in the Board of Aldermen, having been recently elected to his second term. On November 22, 1882, he married Miss Ellen G. Simmonds. Four children have been born to them. Mr. Gaul is a member of Rising Star Lodge, F. and A. M., and Christ Church of Yonkers.

ROBERT PARKHILL GETTY, who was a member of the first Board of Police Commissioners, and who has been so long identified with the business interests of Yonkers, was born near Londonderry, Ireland, May 1, 1811. His ancestors are said to have lived near Dundee, Scotland, and his grandfather, Robert, was one of the Scotch Covenanters. His father, Samuel, married Mary Parkhill. Their children were Nancy, wife of Richard McCotter; Eliza, wife of Robert Ralston; Mary, wife of Hugh Downs; Jane, Robert P. (the subject of this sketch); Matilda, wife of Thompson Morrison; Eleanor and Samuel. The father of this family was a merchant, and traded in West India goods; was a prominent man in his native place, and an elder in the church for twenty-nine years. Owing to severe reverses he was compelled to retire from business, and, with his family, emigrated to America in 1824.

Robert Parkhill Getty was intended by his father for the ministry, a plan which was defeated by his financial misfortunes. When he, with his father, came to this country, he was thirteen years old, and first obtained employment in the grocery store of James Cleland, in New York. Here he remained till 1828, when he went into business with Sylvanus Schermerhorn, with whom he was afterwards a partner. He set up a grocery and liquor store on his own account, but was induced to give it up by the advice of friends, who were opposed to the liquor traffic. He served a regular apprenticeship at the cooper's trade, and was thoroughly acquainted with the provision-packing business and the inspection laws of the State. His opportunities for attending school ended in 1823, and about this time he became acquainted with Prof. Parker (an ex-professor of Harvard), who took so great an interest in his welfare that he offered to instruct him evenings gratuitously, an act of kindness which was terminated after one meeting by the sudden death of the venerable professor. In 1835 he commenced business with Jeremiah Robins, in which he was successful. His first speculation, which was in city lots in Buffalo, was disastrous. Soon after he was chosen Superintendent of the Association of Inspectors of Beef and Pork, an association which enjoyed peculiar facilities for making money, and when this came to an end, he went into business with Martin Waters, and then with Drake B. Palmer. In 1844 he was appointed Inspector by Governor Bouck, and reappointed by Governor Wright. In 1861 he received the appointment of United States Government Inspector, and during his continuance in office 850,000 packages went through his hands, which represented a value of $29,000,000. He was the first to send American bacon to England, and his brand commanded ever after a premium in the market. He was also largely interested in building in the City of New York. He erected a warehouse in Greenwich Street from No. 115 to No. 123, and leased the same to United States Government as a bonded warehouse, for a sum of $45,000 per year, for three years. In 1849 he came to Yonkers, where he built his present residence. He built the "Getty House," now the principal hotel in Yonkers, in 1851, and also erected the buildings on the southwest corner of Main Street and Broadway; these were sold to John T. Waring in 1868. Very few men have held more local offices than Mr. Getty. In 1848 he was Alderman in New York, and, in 1847 and 1848, a member of the Board of Education. He was for many years one of the Trustees of the village of Yonkers, and was President in 1859 and 1860, and also in 1871 and 1872. A few of the many positions he has held may be mentioned: Director of the Hudson River Railroad, Director of the Bank of North America, of the Yonkers Bank, Merchants' Insurance Company, Corn Exchange, President of the Cumberland Coal and Iron Company, Vice-President of Produce Exchange, Director of West Side Elevated Railroad, First President of the Yonkers Gas Light Co., and has been Director since its organization, and has been Vice-President and President of the Yonkers Savings Bank since its establishment. He filled many offices of a fiduciary character, and in every one his business capacity and integrity have been conspicuous. In politics, Mr. Getty was early among the opponents of slavery, and he was a member of the first Republican Convention. Mr. Getty married Rebecca, daughter of Douw Van Buren, of Schodack Landing. Their children are Samuel E., Harriet G., widow of William A. McDonald; Douw V. B. (deceased), Rebecca M., Robert A., Moses D., William F. H., John, Mary M. (deceased), Eleanor C. (deceased), and Emma.

Mr. Getty is the present City Treasurer of Yonkers, and has held the office for thirteen years. Throughout his entire life he has been distinguished for the utmost promptness in all business matters, and in every position of trust has been thoroughly faithful to his charge.

SAMUEL E. GETTY, M.D., was born in Yonkers on February 11, 1866, received his education at University Medical College, and served eighteen months as interne at Bellevue Hospital, of New York City, after which he located in Yonkers, practicing his profession of medicine. He is Attending Surgeon to St. John's Hospital.

JAMES WARREN GOODALE was born in New Suffolk, L. I., in 1852, and his childhood and youth were spent in Patchogue. He received a thorough elementary education and came to Westchester County in 1870, as an employee of George E. Jayne, shoe merchant at Yonkers and Sing Sing. After a year in the latter city he came to this city, and with Mr. Mesick, purchased Mr. Jayne's Yonkers store, located on North Broadway. In a short time he purchased Mr. Mesick's interest. From North Broadway he moved to his present location at 40 Warburton Avenue, where his trade has largely increased. Though still a young man he has the oldest established shoe-store in the city, having for twenty-three years devoted himself with untiring fidelity to the same with much success. Mr. Goodale is a man of culture, refinement and diversified tastes and accomplishments. He is a musician, also evinces a fondness for boating and other wholesome out-of-door sports. He has been a member of the Central Methodist Episcopal Church, Yonkers, since 1872, and has held official relations as Steward, Trustee and Treasurer since that time. He has served as Organist for twelve years, and in other ways has assisted in building up and maintaining the Church. He is a member and the Organist of Rising Star Lodge, 450, F. and A. M., and has paid special attention to the benevolent work of the order. On October 26, 1880, he was married to Miss Mary C. Williams by the Rev. John Dixon, at that time pastor of the Westminster Presbyterian Church. They have had five children, of whom two only are living, Herbert and Edna. Mr. Goodale is interested in everything tending to the best interests of the city and of mankind at large, being liberal, generous and broad-minded. He has been enabled by industry, economy, courtesy and careful business methods to build up a good trade and accumulate considerable property. He has numerous friends, who rejoice in his high standing and in his well-earned and well-deserved success.

CHARLES EUGENE GORTON was born at North Brookfield, N. Y., December 15, 1845, and was educated at Whitestown Seminary and Michigan University. He is a member of the Bar of the State of New York, and is Superintendent of Schools, having held this position since 1884. He is also President of the People's Savings Bank, Vice-President of the Yonkers Historical Society, Secretary and Treasurer of Yonkers Public Library, Trustee of Hollywood Inn, Trustee of First Presbyterian Church, Trustee of St. John's Riverside Hospital, and a member of the City Club. On December 23, 1875, he married Miss Margaret Malcolm McNab.

JOHN C. HARRIGAN was born at Yonkers, June 22, 1869, and was educated in the schools of this city, and graduated from Columbia College Law School. He is a Democrat, and in 1894 was elected to the Assembly, afterward declining a renomination. Although one of the younger lawyers of this city, he has a large and lucrative practice. On October 1, 1894, he was married to Miss Rose M. Cain, to whom one daughter has been born.

John G. Hatfield was born in Sing Sing, N. Y., and was educated at Tarrytown. He is a baker and confectioner, and has been a resident of this city for thirty-six years. He is a member of the Rising Star Lodge, No. 450, F. and A. M., Ferry City Chapter 177, and Treasurer of Yorke Commandery, No. 55, Mecca Temple. On June 5, 1870, he was married to Miss Mary A. Reeves. He is a Republican, but has never held any official position.

Charles Hepenstal was born December 10, 1855, in Norfolk, Va., and was educated in the schools and commercial colleges of New York. He has been a resident of this city for nineteen years, and is Secretary to Vice-President Hayden of the New York Central and Hudson River Railroad. He is the Past Regent of Yonkers Council, No. 1346, Royal Arcanum, and at present Master of Nepperhan Lodge, No. 736, F. and A. M. In 1876 he was Clerk to the Judiciary Committee of the Assembly of New York State. On June 5, 1878, he was married to Ella Palmer, to whom six children have been born.

Edgar M. Hermance, M.D., was born in New York City, and is the son of Rev. J. P. Hermance, D.D., who for many years has been a prominent Methodist Episcopal clergyman. He is a graduate of Wesleyan University and of the College of Physicians and Surgeons, New York. For eighteen years he has practiced medicine in this city. He is a member of the First Presbyterian Church, Yonkers Public Library Board, N. Y. State Medical Association, New York Academy of Medicine, Westchester County Medical Society, Jenkins Medical Society, Board of Trade, Good Government Club, and is Consulting Physician to St. Joseph's Hospital. In politics he is a Republican, from 1883 to 1888, served as a member of the Board of Education, and is now President of the Board of Health.

Henry R. Hicks was born in New York City, December 14, 1834. He obtained his rudimentary education in the public-schools, after which he graduated from the Grammar School of Columbia College. For the past thirty-two years he has been a resident of Yonkers. He is a prominent Republican, and has filled the positions of Alderman, School Trustee and Police Commissioner; the latter position he received in 1892, for a period of four years. On May 23, 1863, he married Miss Isabell Weed, to whom two children have been born. Mr. Hicks filled the position of Chief Clerk in the Engineering Department of the U. S. Navy, from 1861 to 1874. He is a member of the Masonic order and the Methodist Church.

Bailey Hobbs was born at Princeton, Mass., where he received an education in the common schools. He learned the trade of a tailor. In 1840 he located at Yonkers, and has been a resident of that city ever since. Early in life he espoused the Whig party, in which he remained until the birth of the Republican party. For many years he held the position of village and town trustee in Yonkers, and continued to serve in that capacity until it became a city, in 1872. On October 17, 1842, he married Miss Sarah B. Hasire. He is a member of St. John's Church, of Yonkers.

John G. P. Holden was born at Poughkeepsie, Dutchess County, N. Y., August 22, 1834, being the eldest son of Thomas and Sarah Parker Holden. After a good common school education, he was graduated at the Quintilian Seminary of Rev. Eliphaz Fay. From school life he at once entered upon a thorough preparation for that vocation in life which he has since so highly honored, taking a position as "devil" in the office of *The Poughkeepsie Telegraph*, September 2, 1850, and, through six years of faithful application, working his way step by step to a mastery not only of the practical requirements of newspaper work, but to editorial fitness as well.

During this time he also served two years as Assistant Postmaster of Poughkeepsie (under the administration of Franklin Pierce), and in the summer of 1858 went to New York City for a brief season of work on *The Journal of Commerce*. Returning to Poughkeepsie in November of the same year, he connected himself with *The Daily Press* as local editor and cashier, and in April, 1859, bought a fourth interest in the same, his associate publishers being A. S. Pease and J. W. Spaight. From this time until the spring of 1863 Mr. Holden continued (barring a short service as reporter and proof-reader on *The New York Sun*) his association with *The Poughkeepsie Press*, but in May of that year formed a copartnership with J. H. Hager for the establishment of *The Daily Poughkeepsian*.

With this venture his interests were allied until the close of 1863, and in the following spring, having disposed of his interest in *The Poughkeepsian*, he responded to a telegram from Elon Comstock, Esq., at that time one of the proprietors of *The New York World*, requesting his coming to Yonkers to take charge of *The Yonkers Herald* as business manager and local editor. With this paper—the name of which was shortly after changed to *The Yonkers Gazette*—Mr. Holden has been connected up to the present time.

Mr. Holden's public spiritedness has been manifested throughout his career. He was one of the organizing members of the Palisade Boat Club, eleven years Secretary and now Vice-President of the People's Savings Bank, a charter member of Nepperhan Lodge, No. 736, F. and A. M., and during its life a member of the Board of Directors of the Free Reading Room, and an active member of the committee which raised the money and erected a Soldiers' and Sailors' Monument upon the Manor Hall grounds. He was one of the organizers of the Democratic Editorial Association of the State of New York, and has been its Treasurer since its organization. For twenty-nine years he has been a member of the New York Press Association, having served one year as Secretary and one year as President, and for more than a dozen years as a member of its Executive Committee. He has been chosen four times as delegate for this association to the annual convention of the National Editorial Association.

On August 29, 1894, he was appointed Postmaster, of Yonkers, by President Cleveland, and took possession of the office on October 1, 1894, this being a recess appointment. He was reappointed December 11, 1895, and confirmed by the Senate for a term of four years. His administration of the affairs of the Yonkers post-office has been excellent, and before he had been Postmaster six months he had succeeded, with the assistance of Post-office Inspectors Morris and Jacobs, in capturing a thief who had been committing depredations upon the Yonkers mails for eight or ten years.

Although he has never been an office-seeker, the Democratic party has made repeated recognition of his valuable services, he being in turn chosen Town Clerk and City Treasurer, having been appointed to the last office by Mayor William G. Stahlnecker, and duly confirmed and installed March 11, 1885, and reappointed by Mayor Bell, May 24, 1886. In November, 1864, he was married to Miss Maria E. Le Count, of Brooklyn, N. Y., who, with the three children born to them—Edwin R., George P. and Mary—shares with him the comforts of their charming home.

HAROLD C. HOUSEL was born at Lewisburgh, Penn., February 25, 1864. He received a public-school education, after which he learned the trade of a machinist. In politics he is a Republican, and at present is Clerk to the Excise Board. He is a member of Palisade Lodge, No. 571, I. O. O. F. On September 11, 1889, he married Miss Rosalia S. Miller, and has one son.

E. ALEX. HOUSTON was born in the city of New York. He studied medicine at the New York University, and on leaving college entered the drug business. He came to Yonkers about thirty-two years ago, and, with the exception of four years while holding responsible positions in the United States Treasury and in the Merchants' National Bank in Wall Street, New York, has been engaged in the drug business in this city ever since. He was four years Chief of the Fire Department and seven years Fire Commissioner, also nine years Secretary of the Civil Service Commission.

He has an honorable discharge after serving over five years as First Lieutenant in the National Guard of this State, and has been for nine years President of the Veteran Association of the Fourth Separate Company, N. G. S. N. Y. He is President of the Yonkers Druggists' Association, and was for four years President of the Westchester County Pharmaceutical Association. For many years he has been a contributor to the press, and is well-known in literary circles. He was elected Alderman from the Fifth Ward, March 26, 1895.

CHARLES F. HULBERT was born at Brooklyn, N. Y., April 26, 1836. He attended the private and public-schools of his native place, after which he entered the Grammar School of the University of the City of New York. After completing his education, he entered the profession of an accountant, in which he has since been engaged. He is a member of the City Club and Palisade Boat Club of Yonkers. In politics he is a Republican, and now fills the position of Deputy City Clerk of Yonkers. He also held a position with the Citizens' National Bank of Yonkers.

JAMES M. HUNT was born at East Clarence, N. Y., April 6, 1858. He was educated at Brockport Normal School and the University of Rochester. In September, 1883, he located at Yonkers to engage in his profession, that of a lawyer. He is a Republican and has filled the position of City Attorney, of Yonkers, since April, 1892. He is a member of the Warburton Avenue Baptist Church. On June 5, 1883, he married Miss Normie L. Fanning. Three children have been the fruit of the marriage, all of whom are deceased.

JOHN HENRY HUBBELL was born in Algonac, St. Clair County, Mich., January 19, 1837. In 1839 his parents removed to Jackson, Mich., then a wilderness, containing only about 100 inhabitants. His early educational advantages were necessarily limited, he receiving, however, the benefit of an academical course preparatory to entering college, but, unfortunately, ill-health compelled him to forego completing his studies. Preferring a commercial life, at the age of fifteen he entered the store of

Wiley R. Reynolds, in Jackson, and his rapid acquirement of commercial methods and his aptitude for business was such that in 1855, at the age of eighteen, he commenced a successful business career on his own account. The scope of his business becoming circumscribed, a larger field of operations became necessary, and he removed to Memphis, Tenn., in 1859, where he succeeded in building up a very extended and remunerative business, which was entirely broken up and ruined by the War of the Rebellion. Then followed the additional misfortune of loss of health, his life being despaired of.

During 1862, he returned North, where he improved so rapidly that he was enabled the following year, in connection with capitalists, to devote his energies to the development of the oil wells of Meade County, Ky., which he discovered. In 1866, he embarked in business in St. Louis, bnt remained there a comparatively short time. His experience had suggested to him that he might supply a need that had long been wanted by the lawyers and business men of the country, and in 1870 he commenced the annual publication of "Hubbell's Legal Directory of the United States and Canada," which was designed to be a compendium of the commercial laws of the various States of the Union and Canada, and to contain a list of able and trustworthy attorneys throughout the land. This work now (1896) is in the twenty-seventh year of its publication and has become invaluable in the office of every prominent lawyer in the country. Mr. Hubbell has been admitted to practice as an attorney at law. He removed to New York City in 1870, which has been his place of business since that time. He removed to Yonkers in 1881, where he has since resided. He has been twice appointed a member of the Board of Education, is a member of the Board of Trade, Good Government Club, Trustee of St. John's Hospital, a member of St. John's Protestant Episcopal Church, of which he was Vestryman for several years, and is now President of the Horwood Land and Improvement Company, of Horwood, Fla., where he is largely interested. Mr. Hubbell married Mrs. Martha A. Leman (*née* Baggott), of Dayton, O., June 11, 1871.

J. FOSTER JENKINS was born at Yonkers, July 29, 1861. He was educated at St. Paul's School, of Concord, N. H., and at Columbia College, New York. He has resided at Yonkers all his life and is now engaged in the real estate and insurance business. He is a member of Psi Upsilon Club of New York, St. Andrew's Golf Club and Lawn Tennis Club of Yonkers. He is Junior Warden of St. Paul's Church. On October 25, 1883, he married Miss Alice M. Withers. Mr. Jenkins is a member of the Board of Police Commissioners and a Democrat in politics.

DAVID JOHN, member of the College of Surgeons, England, and Licentiate of College of Physicians, London, for nine years has been a physician and surgeon in this city. He was born at Shanghai, China, in 1858, of British parents, and educated in the schools and colleges of England. He is Attending Surgeon to St. John's Hospital. In 1892, he married Miss Mary Elizabeth Wallace and they have one child.

GEORGE H. KALER was born at Cold Spring, Long Island, N. Y., September 20, 1854, but for the past eighteen years has been a resident of Yonkers, and is now manager for the Chicago Wholesale Beef Company. He attends the Methodist Church and is a member of the Palisade Boat Club of Yonkers. In politics he is a Republican, and in April, 1894, was elected Alderman for the city of Yonkers, being re-elected January 1, 1896. On February 13, 1877, he married Miss Carrie Denike Shotts, of New York City.

JAMES J. KEARNS, JR., was born at Yonkers, February 9, 1868, and was educated at St. Joseph's Parochial and Public School No. 6. He is engaged in the business of a general contractor. He is a member of the Sons of Veterans, Exempt Firemen's Association and the Second District of Sixth Ward Republican Club of Yonkers. On October 15, 1889, he married Miss Mary A. Harrington. He was for eight years a member of Columbia Hook and Ladder Company, and for several years of that period he served as foreman.

ROBERT KELLOCK was born in New York City, May 17, 1858, and was educated in the schools of New York and Yonkers. He has been a resident of Yonkers for twenty-four years, and is engaged in the stone and flagging business. He is a member of Nepperhan Lodge, F. and A. M.; Republican in politics, is now one of the Fire Commissioners, and at one time was President of the Board. On September 11, 1881, he married Miss Jeanette McVicar, to whom four children have been born.

WILLIAM CHANNING KELLOGG was born at Norwich, Vt., July 11, 1850. He was educated at Tilton Seminary, in New Hampshire, Phillips' Exeter Academy of Exeter, N. H., and Wesleyan University of Middletown, Conn. In 1881 he removed to Yonkers, where he has since resided, following his profession, that of a lawyer. He is a member of the City Club, Palisade Lodge, I. O. O. F., Nepperhan Lodge, F. and A. M., Dutch Reformed Church, the Alpha Delta Phi and Phi Beta Kappa Societies. He is a

Republican in politics, and at present fills the position of City Judge of Yonkers, to which he was elected November 5, 1895. On October 3, 1877, he married Miss Emma J. Lewis, of Norwich, Conn., to whom two children have been born, Ruth and Lewis.

AUGUSTUS KIPP was born at Rhinebeck, Dutchess County, N. Y., October 31, 1839, and was educated in the district schools. He has been a resident of this city for thirty years, and is a member of the Warburton Avenue Baptist Church, and a member of Council 33, O. U. A. M. Mr. Kipp is a Republican in politics, and in 1892 was appointed by Mayor Weller as Inspector of Buildings, and still holds that office. In 1864 he was married to Miss Emily C. Olivet, and they have two sons and three daughters. In 1861 he enlisted in the war for the Union, and served for two years in Company D, Thirty-second Regiment, N. Y. S. V., and was discharged as First Sergeant. He also enlisted in N. G. S. of N. Y. in 1874, and was discharged as Sergeant, September 16, 1881. He has also been prominent in G. A. R. circles, and at present is Commander of Kitching Post No. 60.

ALEXANDER OGILVIE KIRKWOOD was born near Auburn, Cayuga County, N. Y., February 20, 1839, and was educated in the public schools of Peekskill, N. Y., Elizabeth, N. J., and at Prof. Washington Hasbrouck's Academy, Yonkers. He has been a public-spirited and useful resident of this city for forty-six years, and is a carpenter and builder. Mr. Kirkwood is the inventor and patentee of the "I X L Reservoir Washstand." He is at present Instructor in Manual Training at Leake and Watts Orphan House. He has been identified with the First Reformed Church, and is now a Ruling Elder of the Westminster Presbyterian Church. He was formerly a Republican in politics, and for a number of years was a member of the Central Committee of that party, but is now a member of the Prohibition party. In 1884 he was nominated by this party as Assemblyman from the First District of Westchester County. He served in the War of the Rebellion in 1862 and 1863 in General Banks' Expedition in Louisiana, in Company A, Forty-seventh Regiment, Massachusetts Infantry Volunteers, and was honorably discharged. In 1896 he was elected Commander of John C. Fremont Post, G. A. R. He was married to Miss Helen M. Blauvelt, of Harrington, Bergen County, September 25, 1867. Their children are Robert Ogilvie, now a student in Princeton University; Allan Stewart, a student in the College of Physicians and Surgeons, New York; Helen Blauvelt, Jennie Olivia, recent graduates of the Oswego Normal College, and the Teachers' College, New York; Grace Louise (deceased), and Rose Effie, pupil in Yonkers High School.

FRANK KNAPPER was born in Germany, on February 22, 1853, and was educated in the schools of that country. He has been a resident of Yonkers for nine years, and is a florist and seedsman. He is a Director of the Mercantile Bank, and a member of the Presbyterian Church. In 1877 he was married to Regina Schnellbach, to whom three children have been born.

WILLIAM HENRY LAKE was born in Brooklyn, N. Y., and was educated at the public schools, graduating from the Brooklyn High School and Chautauqua College. He was for seven years with the First National Bank as bookkeeper, and is now Secretary of the Mercantile Co-operative Bank. He is an extensive dealer in real estate, and through his efforts many homes have been built in Yonkers, and many brought to reside in our city. Mr. Lake is a member of the Baptist Church and the Palisade Boat Club, and is Republican in politics. On October 23, 1890, he married Miss Laura Spofford Wiltsie.

ARNETT ODELL LAWRENCE was born in Yonkers, November 3, 1850, and was educated in the public schools of Yonkers and Bryant & Stratton's Commercial College, New York City. He is a member of the firm of Lawrence & Conklin, proprietors of the Yonkers Planing and Moulding Mills. He is a member of St. John's Episcopal Church, Palisade Boat Club, and a Master Mason. He is a Democrat in politics, but has never held any official position. On December 7, 1887, he was married to Nellie Royce Carr, to whom two sons have been born.

JAMES V. LAWRENCE was born February 6, 1843, in Yonkers, and was educated in the common schools of this city and the Columbian University of Washington, D. C. He is engaged in the lumber business, and is a member of Corinthian Yacht Club, Turn Verein, Nepperhan Lodge, F. and A. M., John C. Fremont Post G. A. R., New York Commandery, Loyal Legion, and is President of the City Club. He is a Democrat, and at one time was Supervisor of the town and city of Yonkers, also Civil Service Commissioner, and is now serving as School Trustee. In May, 1864, he married Charlotte E. Southworth.

WILLIAM H. LAWRENCE was born in Yonkers, February 28, 1813, and received his education in the schools of this city. He was a member of St. John's Episcopal Church, and also a member of the Order of Freemasons. He served for many years as Major in the State militia. In politics he was a Democrat, and held many political positions. He was one of the Coroners of the county for a number of years, and at one time served as Deputy Sheriff of the county. He was also Collector of Taxes for the town of Yonkers for a long time, having been year after year elected to that position. In 1835 he married Miss Maria V. Back, to whom eleven children were born. Mr. Lawrence died January 13, 1879.

WILLIAM FREDERICK LAWRENCE was born at Yonkers, N. Y., January 12, 1841, where he has resided all his life. He received a common school education in the public schools of his native place. He is a member of the Masonic Order, a Trustee of the Citizens' Bank of Yonkers, and has been a Vestryman of St. John's Episcopal Church for the past six years. He is actively engaged in the lumber and building material business. His wife was Miss Mary J. Weddle, of Rochester, N. Y. Four children have been born to them—two sons and two daughters.

CARL EDWARD WILHELM PHILIP VON LELIVA was born in Germany and studied military science, literature, civil engineering, fine arts, architecture, philosophy and natural history in the Cadet Schools, Academies of Art and Universities of Germany. For a number of years he has resided in this city practicing civil engineering, etc. He is a member of several Social and Literary Clubs, of the G. A. R., and the Loyal Legion of the United States of America. His distinguished career as a Line and Staff Officer in the German and American armies ended with the close of our Civil War of 1865.

ROBERT B. LIGHT was born at Fishkill village, Dutchess County, N. Y., March 4, 1841, and was educated in the public schools of Fishkill and Poughkeepsie. For twenty-nine years he has been a resident of this city and at the present time is gate-keeper at Smith & Sons' Carpet Factory. He is a member of Yonkers Lodge No. 232, I. O. O. F., and Exempt Firemen's Association and also a member of Kitching Post No. 60, G. A. R. He is a Republican, and at the present time is Commissioner of Deeds. On January 4, 1870, he married Miss Henrietta Weber, and they have two children.

WILLIAM F. LAWRENCE.

JOS. A. LOCKWOOD was born on November 5, 1847, at Pound Ridge, N. Y., and received his education in public and private schools and at Union College from which he graduated in 1867, receiving the degree of "C. E." He has been a resident of this city for twenty-seven years, is a member of Nepperhan Lodge, F. and A. M., and the Presbyterian Church. For many years he has held the position of Superintendent and Clerk of the Yonkers Water Works. On February 18, 1880, he married Miss Emma L. Clark, and they have three children, one daughter and two sons.

GEORGE DEVEREUX MACKAY was born at Brooklyn, N. Y., in 1854, and was educated at the Polytechnic School in that city. He continued to reside in Brooklyn until 1888, at which time he removed to Yonkers, where he has lived ever since with the exception of three years. He is a member of the banking firm of Vermilye & Co., of New York. On February 5, 1880, Mr. Mackay married Miss Anna Robinson Barnes, of Brooklyn. Eight children have been born to them, two of whom are now deceased.

DANIEL J. MAHONY was born in New York, March 22, 1857, and received his education in the public and Catholic schools. He has been in business in Yonkers for many years, dealing in gents' furnishing and hats. He is independent in politics, and a member of the Montgomery Club, Corinthian Club, Irving Hose Co., and St. Mary's Catholic Church.

JOHN MANGIN was born in the County Tipperary, Ireland, January 10, 1828, and was educated in the schools of that County. In 1857 he came to Yonkers as ticket agent for the New York Central Railroad. In 1860 he resigned this position, and entered the Police Department of New York as patrolman; in due course he was promoted to Roundsman and Sergeant. In 1866, he, with Sergeant James M. Flandrau, and twelve men, was transferred to Yonkers under Captain Alonzo S. Wilson. In 1871 the old Metropolitan Police District force was abolished, and the Municipal substituted. On April 10, 1871, Mr. Mangin was made Captain, and has filled that office up to the present time. He is a member of the Catholic Church, and independent in politics. In 1848 he married Mary Pardy, of his native County, who died in 1892. Nine children were born to this union, four of whom are now living. One of his sons, Thomas H., has been a member of the New York police force for twenty-five years, and is now a Sergeant. One son, Michael J., has charge of the parks in the annexed districts. Mr. Mangin, through his untiring efforts, has brought the police force of this city to a high standard of efficiency.

EDWIN KÖENIGMACHER MARTIN was born in Lancaster County, Penn., in 1844. He fitted for college at Phillips Academy, Andover, Mass., which was then under the direction of the famous New England instructor, Dr. Samuel Taylor, called the Arnold of America. It was while here that the war broke out, and the burial of the Massachusetts dead, killed in the streets of Baltimore and sent to their homes in Lawrence, a few miles distant from Phillips Academy, so fired young Martin's patriotism that he determined to enlist in the ranks of the nation's defenders. Returning to his native county, he entered the Seventy-ninth Pennsylvania, which was then recruiting for the front, and, except the last six months of his army career, when he was attached to Gen. Sherman's headquarters, Mr. Martin remained with his regiment through its perilous services of nearly four years under Thomas, Sherman and Grant, in the southwest. This regiment participated in twenty-three battles and engagements. Many of them, like Perryville, Stone River, Chickamauga, Atlanta, Lookout Mountain, Missionary Ridge, the March to the Sea, involved some of the severest campaigning of the war. After the war drums had ceased, Mr. Martin returned to his college studies. He completed his Andover course, and went for a short time to Princeton, but finally graduated at Amherst College. After graduation he attended Columbia Law School in New York City. Subsequently, owing to the ill-health of his father, who had large lumber and coal interests in Pennsylvania, Mr. Martin entered upon an extensive business career for a number of years in his native state. Finally, in 1876, he was enabled to carry out his long cherished plans of practicing law, which he did successfully for fifteen years in his native state, where he stood high in his profession and built up a large and lucrative practice.

About 1890, Mr. Martin, having previously become interested in real estate in San Francisco, New York and elsewhere in connection with his present associates, discontinued his law practice and removed to Yonkers for the purpose of giving his personal attention and supervision to the growing demands of his New York business. He took position at once in the community in which he made his new home, and where he has now resided for nearly six years. Two years age he was elected President of the Yonkers Board of Trade, and again re-elected for the present year. Mr. Martin is now President of the American Real Estate Company, which owns Park Hill, one of New York's most beautiful suburbs, and a great addition to the beauty and picturesqueness of Yonkers itself. He has spared neither enthusiasm, energy nor capital in carrying forward the bold financial scheme which converted in a few years this raw piece of Yonkers background into some of the loveliest home sites in America.

On June 2, 1881, Mr. Martin married Miss Carrie A. Varick, the daughter of Dr. Theodore R. Varick, a prominent physician and surgeon, of Jersey City, N. J. He has two daughters, Adèle Woolsey, born November 11, 1885, and Anna Romeyn Varick, born April 4, 1890. One son, Theodore Romeyn Varick, born April 23, 1888, died October 23d, of the same year.

In politics Mr. Martin was always an ardent Republican, and while in Pennsylvania an active worker, having presided over the State Convention of his party and helped to shape its platforms and policies. He never held any office, and at the present time prefers to remain a peaceful voter in the ranks. He is still, however, the controlling owner of the *Lancaster Morning News*, a daily newspaper which exercises a wide influence in the Republican ranks of southeastern Pennsylvania, to the columns of which he not infrequently contributes. Mr. Martin has made many warm friends in his new surroundings, and Yonkers people recognize in him one of its builders, and a man thoroughly alive to the widening opportunities which the Queen City of the Hudson is opening up to men of energy and capital. "Overcliff," on Park Hill, where Mr. Martin resides, is one of the handsome country homes of the Hudson River Valley.

JOHN MITCHELL MASON was born in New York City, November 8, 1821, and was educated at Columbia College. He came to this city in 1853. Mr. Mason was a Freemason, and a member of the Bar Association, a Republican, and for ten years was Collector of Internal Revenue. He was also President of the Board of Education, No. 6, for fifteen years. On May 6, 1845, he married Miss Louise Carlisle, who died; and on December 26, 1872, he married Miss Sarah Osborne. Mr. Mason died February 7, 1878, and is now remembered as a much-honored citizen of this city.

CHARLES ADNA MILES, M.D., was born at Waverly, Penn., July 15, 1852. He received a careful education in private and academic schools, after which he attended Madison University, from whence he was graduated. After completing his studies, he decided to adopt the medical profession. He entered Jefferson Medical College of Philadelphia, and was graduated therefrom in 1876. For the past fourteen years he has resided in, and practiced his profession at, Yonkers. He is a member of the City Club, Palisade Boat Club, I. O. O. F., Red Men, and St. John's Church of Yonkers. Politically, he is a Republican, and is at present Coroner of Westchester County, a position to which he was elected in 1893 by over 1,200 majority. On December 27, 1876, he married Miss Angeline Dutcher, of New Haven, Conn. Two children have been born to them, Edith E. and Charles E. Dr. Miles comes of old Revolutionary stock on both sides; his great-grandfathers fought in the War of the Revolution, while his grandfathers fought in the War of 1812.

JOSEPH MILLER was born in Germany, and came to America with his parents when a child. He was educated in the public schools, has resided in Yonkers since 1881, and is a hatter by trade. He is a Republican in politics, and is a President of the Excise Board of Yonkers. He served for two years in the War of the Rebellion in the First and Thirty-seventh New Jersey Volunteers. He belongs to the Order of Odd Fellows, Knights of Pythias, and the G. A. R. On October 20, 1868, he married Miss Rose Harris, of Newark, N. J. Six children have been born to them, four of whom are living.

EDWARD J. MITCHELL was born in Rutland, Vt., on July 10, 1849, and when a year old, his father, Thomas Mitchell, removed to Carbondale, Penn., where he resided until October 1, 1855, when he removed to Yonkers. In 1856 he removed to Tarrytown, but returned in the same year. Colonel Mitchell attended the public school in Carbondale, and St. Mary's Parochial School, Yonkers, up to June, 1859, when he was employed in a grocery store, and soon after in the Eagle Hat Factory. In 1861 his father enlisted in Company A, Seventeenth New York Volunteers, and Mr. Mitchell, being the oldest of seven children, was obliged to stay at home. His father returned in 1863, and his mother died in January, 1864. Three different times he desired to enlist, but his father prevented this action, until finally, on May 10, 1864, he went over to Camp Freelinghuysen in Newark, N. J., and was enrolled as a private in Company E, Thirty-seventh New Jersey Volunteers. On May 25th the regiment was mustered into the United States service at Trenton, N. J., and was at once sent to the front, and in a few days landed at Point of Rocks on Bermuda Hundreds, and was assigned to the Third Brigade, Third Division, Tenth Army Corps, in the Army of the James, under General B. F. Butler. In July, when the Eighteenth Army Corps were sent back from Petersburg, the Tenth Army Corps took their place, and the Thirty-seventh was in the front line of breastworks, and participated in all the movements of the time.

After his term of service had expired he returned home; but in May, 1866, the Fenian excitement broke loose, and he went to New York City and enlisted in the Irish Army for seven years. He was sent to Malone, N. Y., where some thousand men were in camp, who were under orders to march at a minute's notice. In June General Sweeney was arrested at St. Albans, and all the men at Malone were discharged and sent to their homes. On August 18, 1866, he engaged with Otis Brothers, of this city, as a machinist apprentice, and, having served his time, he continued in their employ until May, 1874, when he resigned his position. On November 2, 1869, he joined Protection Fire Engine Company No. 1, and was immediately elected Secretary, serving as such until August 3, 1871, when he was elected Foreman, and served two years. In October, 1874, he was elected First Assistant Engineer of the Department, and served the full term of two years. For fourteen years he was Representative from this Company, and for ten years Secretary and one year Treasurer of the Board of Representatives. After twenty years' service as an active fireman, he resigned. On October 31, 1872, he was married in St. Mary's Church to

Miss Mary McGovern by Rev. Joseph Byron; she died February 22, 1887, leaving one daughter, Mary E. Mitchell. On February 17, 1892, he was again married in St. Mary's Church, by Rev. C. R. Corley, to Miss Emma J. Bentler. Three children have been born to her, of whom Virginia, first born, died July 28, 1893, aged eight months; Christina and Edward B., died August 20, 1895, aged five months. In March, 1880, Mr. Mitchell was elected Alderman for the First Ward, and was re-elected in 1882 and 1884, serving in all six years. In 1883 he was elected President of the Board. During his term as Alderman he was an able worker, and served as a member of the Street Committee for six years, four years of which he was Chairman. He presented the resolutions which, after two years' effort, secured from the Legislature the grant of land at the foot of Main Street, on which the Public Dock is located, and was Chairman of the Committee of the Whole who planned and built the dock. This is now the only plot of land in front of Yonkers which the city owns without cost to it. He also presented resolutions, and had carried the appropriation of the ten thousand dollars which was expended in building new houses for the Fire Department. He was always on the alert, looking out for the interests of his constituents, and retired April 15, 1886, with their good wishes.

On October 4, 1880, he was mustered in as a comrade of Kitching Post No. 60, G. A. R., and in 1883, he became Adjutant of the Post, a position which he still holds. He was a delegate from his Post to the State Encampment in 1886-87-90-94-96, and was Aide-de-camp on the staff of Department Commander N. M. Curtis in 1888, and Department Commander James S. Graham in 1896, and on the National staff of W. G. Veazy in 1891, and John Palmer in 1892. In 1893 he was elected a delegate to the National Encampment at Indianapolis, Ind., and in 1896 to the National Encampment at St. Paul, Minn., and on March 1, 1894, Department Commander John C. Shotts appointed him Quartermaster General of the State of New York, which office he successfully filled until his term expired, May 15, 1895. On May 4, 1894, Governor Roswell P. Flower appointed him as one of the State Board of Managers for the Home of the Aged Dependent Veterans and their wives, Veterans' Mothers, Widows and Army Nurses, which appointment was confirmed by the State Senate on January 23, 1895, for a period of six years. Upon the organization of the Board he was elected Secretary, a position which he holds at present. Mr. Mitchell was one of the organizers of the Westchester County Association of the G. A. R., and is Marshal of that body, which is composed of Past Commanders and Delegates from the posts of this county. In November, 1882, he was elected as one of the Coroners of Westchester County, was re-elected in 1885, and served until January 1, 1889. On March 13, 1890, he was appointed by Governor David B. Hill to fill the vacancy caused by the death of Mr. Charles J. Nordquist and in the Democratic Convention held in October, he was unanimously nominated for the position, being elected in November to serve until January 1, 1894.

Colonel Mitchell is Treasurer of the Yonkers Bowling Association, Treasurer of the A. B. C. Bowling Club, a member of the Montgomery Club, City Club, and the Exempt Firemen's Association. He was elected a delegate to the Democratic State Convention of 1884-87-89-94-96, and has served as County, Congressional, Senatorial and Assembly delegates many times. He is now serving his second year as Grand Marshal of the Memorial Committee of the G. A. R., of this city. In 1895, he was Grand Marshal of the Fourth of July parade, refused a re-election in 1896, and was elected Vice-President of the Fourth of July Celebration Committee. He was chairman of the Committee from Kitching Post which presented flags to St. John's and St. Joseph's Hospitals on July 4, 1896.

Henry Moffat, M.D., was born at Princeton, N. J., December 20, 1855, and received his education at Princeton College, where he graduated in 1875, afterward studying medicine in the College of Physicians and Surgeons, of New York City, and graduated therefrom in 1881. He is Attending Surgeon to St. Joseph's Hospital, and is a member of Academy of Medicine, of New York City, Jenkins Medical Society, Westchester County Medical Society, the University Club of New York, St. Andrew's Society of New York; and the Presbyterian Church of this city. On October 14, 1885, he married Miss Edith Bogart, and they have one son.

Michael Mooney was born in County Galway, Ireland, September 29, 1831. He received an education in a private school. He has resided at Yonkers for the past forty-five years, and has been engaged at farming nearly all his life. In October, 1856, he married Miss Elizabeth O'Neill, to whom seven children have been born, five of whom are living. He is a member of St. Joseph's Catholic Church. In 1873, Mr. Mooney was elected Alderman and served four years. He served for six years as trustee of School No. 5; and in 1881, when the public-schools of Yonkers were consolidated, he was appointed, by Mayor Otis, a member of the first Board of Education. In 1883, he was re-elected Alderman and served three consecutive terms. He was again elected to the office in 1894, and is still a member of that body.

ABRAHAM C. MOTT was born in New York City, February 8, 1835, and removed to Yonkers in 1844, was educated in the private school of Miss Struthers and Public School No. 2 of this city. After leaving school he engaged with Mr. Samuel W. Chambers, who at that time had a grocery store on Nepperhan Street, where he was employed for a number of years. Leaving this position, he engaged with Mr. Levi P. Rose as clerk in his store at the corner of Mill Street (now Main) and Broadway, and continued in his employ until Mr. Rose discontinued his business in Yonkers. He then engaged with his father as a carpenter and continued with him until 1865, when he was appointed Assistant Postmaster under William H. Post, serving under successive Postmasters until 1882. At present he is employed in the purchasing agent's department of the N. Y. C. and H. R. R. R. Co. He is Secretary of the Rising Star Lodge, F. and A. M., and Recorder of Yonkers Commandery No. 47, K. T.

FRANCIS J. MOULTRIE was born at Charleston, S. C., August 22, 1842. He was educated privately. Since 1870 he has been a resident of Yonkers, where he has been engaged in the catering and confectionery business. He is a member of the A. M. E. Church, the G. U. O. Odd Fellows, and Hero Lodge No. 1520. Politically he is a Republican. On July 6, 1870, he married Miss Fanny Allston, to whom two girls have been born, both of whom are now deceased.

THOMAS F. MULCAHEY was born at Waterford, Ireland, on March 21, 1868, and received his education in the public schools. He has been a resident of this city for twenty-two years, and is engaged as a leather worker. He is a member of Protection Engine Company No. 1. In August, 1887, he joined the Fire Department, and in 1891 was elected Foreman of Protection Engine Company, and again re-elected in 1892. In 1894 he was elected First Assistant Engineer of the Department, which position he still holds.

FRANK J. MOULTRIE.

FELIX MURRAY was born in County Down, Ireland, in February, 1852. He obtained an education in the National School of his native country. For seventeen years he has been a resident of Yonkers, where he has been engaged in the grocery business. He is a Republican, and a member of St. Mary's Catholic Church of Yonkers. In 1881 he married Miss Ellen Hessler, to whom six children have been born.

WILLIAM GIBB MCADOO, JR., was born in Marietta, Ga., October 31, 1863, and was educated at the University of Tennessee, the State Military School, at Knoxville, Tenn. He is a lawyer. He is a member of the New York Athletic Club, Reform Club, Board of Trade, of Yonkers, and St. Paul's Episcopal Church. At one time he was Deputy Clerk of the United States Circuit Court, having charge of the Southern Division at Chattanooga, Tenn., for a number of years, and was Alternate Delegate for the Third Congressional District of Tennessee to the Democratic National Convention at Chicago, in 1884, when Mr. Cleveland was first nominated for President. On November 18. 1885, he was married to Miss Sarah Houston Fleming, to whom four children have been born.

JAMES MCLAUGHLIN was born in Ireland, August 16, 1844. He came to America with his parents and settled at Norwalk, Conn., where he attended the public schools. He joined the New York police force in April, 1865. For the past thirty years he has been a resident of Yonkers, and a member of the police force. He is at present attached to the Police Department of Yonkers, in the capacity of Sergeant. On January 16, 1870, he married Miss Catharine Goodwin, to whom twelve children have been born, seven of whom are living. Mr. McLaughlin is a member of the I. O. R. M. and the Catholic Church, and he is an adherent of the Democratic party.

WILLIAM H. MCVICAR was born in New York City, November 24, 1850. He has resided at Yonkers for the past twenty-five years and is engaged in manufacturing metal cornices and skylights. He is a member of the I. O. O. F., Red Men, Yonkers Bicycle Club and several other organizations. Politically, he is a Republican. On November 23, 1886, he married Miss Louisa A. Heliker.

THOMAS MCVICAR was born in Paterson, N. J., May 31, 1855, and was educated in the public schools of Yonkers. In April, 1877, he was married to Miss Eva Lynt. He is engaged in the business of tin, slate and tile roofing, and general metal works, and is a member of Yonkers Lodge, 232, I. O. O. F., Royal Arcanum, Yonkers Counsel, No. 1346, and the Dayspring Presbyterian Church. He is a Republican in politics.

CHESTER W. NEWMAN was born in Brewsters, N. Y., September 10, 1866, and attended the public schools of Yonkers, where he has resided for twenty-one years. He is prominently engaged in the real estate and fire insurance business, and is a member of the Park Hill Country Club, the Palisade Boat Club, the Corinthian Yacht Club and of the Board of Trade of this city. On June 11, 1896, he married Miss Mary Boyd Cark, eldest daughter of James S. Cark.

WILLIAM FULTON NISBET was born February 4, 1835, at Geneva, Ontario County, N. Y. He is the only son of Rev. William Nisbet, a Presbyterian minister (graduated from Washington College, Penn., in 1816), who was settled over a congregation at Geneva, and who died there about the time the son was born. It was on account of this bereavement that in 1836 his widow removed to Yonkers, having been invited to make her home with her sister, the wife of Dr. Amos W. Gates, bringing her two children. Here the boy grew up, attending private and public schools, ending his school life at the Grammar School of the New York University. The first fifteen years of his life having been spent in the home of the very busy village doctor, it was thought to turn his ambition toward the study of medicine, but his intimate acquaintance with its exactions and a decided prejudice against the profession were too strong to be overcome by the wishes of relatives.

Having a *penchant* for agricultural life, which had been fostered by his repeated visits to his native place, where the fine, thrifty farms, the great variety of fruit, the peaceful life and contentment of farmers, forming one of the most intelligent, honest and moral communities to be found, perhaps, in this or any other land, had opened up to his young mind a life congenial it seemed to him, inasmuch as he would be largely in the open air and free from the excitements and worries of a business career. He was allowed to have his own way, and the spring of 1851 found him installed upon the farm of Benjamin Lent, near Tuckahoe. The care of cows, the planting and cultivating, the cutting of grass and making hay were in the order of events, and he was not discouraged by hard work. It was a misfortune that this fine old farmer had a ten-acre lot of cucumbers, which had to be picked over every day from the middle of August until first frost. This was the straw that broke the camel's back, and young Nisbet's love of farming oozed out, so to speak, at his finger ends, and with the first blessed frost and an aching back he retired from the field in October.

The following spring found him acting as assistant bookkeeper and boy of all work in the wholesale grocery house of Wagstaff & Vedder, Cortlandt Street, New York, where he worked early and late for seven months, without remuneration—this was his apprenticeship to business. This house, like all grocery houses of that date, dealt in wines and liquors, and the lad's good mother felt that in that line of business there was always temptation. This it was which largely influenced him in accepting an offer from D. D. Badger & Co., of New York, the most prominent firm employed in the manufacture of architectural iron work and machinery. In 1856 Mr. Nisbet was taken into this company as a partner, and the same year the firm was dissolved, and a corporation known as the Architectural Iron Works was organized. Mr. Nisbet became its Secretary, and the business grew to large proportions, having established a branch in West Philadelphia. It was this firm of D. D. Badger & Co. which built the first iron front building in the United States or the world, *viz.*: the Gilsey Building, still standing on the southwest corner of Broadway and Cortlandt Street.

In 1857 Mr. Nisbet was sent out to Brazil and Buenos Ayres in South America, and succeeded in introducing iron buildings in Rio de Janeiro. The business of the Company ranged over the whole continent of North and South America and the West Indies. During the rebellion the Company manufactured for the Government the fifteen-inch shot and shell, at that time the largest projectiles in use. Mr. Nisbet was at this time a member of the First Regiment, State Militia, a cavalry regiment, and held a commission as its Adjutant for a number of years. On severing his connections with the iron business, he made an extensive trip through Europe and the East, returning *via* the Indies, China and Japan to California, and crossed the continent in the winter of 1869, before the Union and Central Pacific Railroad was finished. After his return he entered upon the business of railroads, and was for a number of years President of the St. Joseph and St. Louis Railroad, which was finally purchased by, and became a part of, the Atchison System. Of late years he has been engaged in the real estate business, and interested in the sale and manufacture of glue. Mr. Nisbet married, in 1872, Mary Anna Browning, of New York, and they have two sons. In 1877, after an absence of twenty-five years, he returned to Yonkers, and has since made it his residence, occupying the old Gates homestead, which is now the property of himself and sister. Mr. Nisbet is independent in politics, attends the First Presbyterian Church, has been for eight years a Trustee of the Board of Education, and is at present serving a second term as the President of the Board.

Mr. Nisbet's family is of Scotch and Scotch Irish descent, his ancestry coming to the Colony of Pennsylvania in the early part of the last century and settling (after various troubles with the Indians) at Great Cove on the southern border, close to Hagerstown, Md. A number of the family fought in the War of Independence, and later on both sides in the great rebellion. On his mother's side his descent is English and Dutch, from Captain Gerrard Smith and Catherine Sebring, married in 1737 in New York. These were his great-grandfather and mother. Mr. Nisbet still owns the ground in the lower part of New York owned and lived upon by his grandfather in 1786. It can be easily understood that there are few men living in Yonkers to-day who can recollect it as it was fifty years ago, and Mr. Nisbet is one of the few who can remember it, with its 1,200 inhabitants, its two churches, its one small public school, its unimpaired Manor house, with its broad glebe stretching away to the river and to a long distance north. The pew holders at St. John's Church had their portable foot-warmers and their cuspidors, for in those days the laymen, and perchance the parsons, used tobacco. It was then the bellows hung in every kitchen and fire-place ere the tinder box had been supplanted by *loco-foco* matches. Shad, fresh from the Hudson, were $6 per hundred, and salmagundi was an appetizing dish upon many a table. Halcyon days of youth! Such are the memories of one of the most entrancing hamlets on the Hudson, its clean and pebbly shores and its well-tried banks affording the most delightful walks, incomparably beautiful, fresh and quiet.

ISAAC COOLEY NODINE was born in New York City, on November 6, 1830, and was educated in the common schools of Boston, Mass. He has resided in Yonkers for forty-six years, and for the past thirty years has been Custodian of the Yonkers Savings Bank. He is a member of Yonkers Lodge, No. 232, I. O. O. F. He is a Republican in politics, and for fourteen years served as Post-office Clerk. In January, 1854, he married Miss Caroline A. Craft. He is one of the original founders of the Fire Department in this city, and, with William Cutbell, is the only surviving member.

ARTHUR W. NUGENT was born at Yonkers, September 11, 1863. By profession he is an electrician. He is a member of St. Paul's Episcopal Church, Yonkers Lodge, No. 232, I. O. O. F., Shaffner Encampment, No. 100, I. O. O. F., and Fourth Separate Company, S. N. Y. Veterans' National Guard. On March 21, 1888, he married Miss Frances A. Ewing, and three children have blessed their union. Mr. Nugent is a Democrat, and in 1895 he was elected a member of the Board of Aldermen.

JAMES B. ODELL was born in Brooklyn, N. Y., on February 5, 1837, and was educated in the public schools. He has been a resident of this city for forty-two years, and is a member of the Rising Star Lodge, F. and A. M., and of the First Methodist Episcopal Church of this city. He is a Republican in politics. His first marriage occurred on November 5, 1859, to Mary A. Hodges, who died on May 19, 1864. On October 18, 1871, he was married to Martha A. Barnes, who died June 18, 1894. Mr. Odell enlisted in the United States Army in July, 1863, and was honorably discharged in August, 1863.

FRANCIS O'NEILL, who lived for many years as one of the foremost and most respected citizens of Yonkers, was born in the north of Ireland on February 22, 1840. While yet a youth of some sixteen years, he came to this country and entered the employ of Robert Irwin & Co., who kept one of the largest boot and shoe establishments in New York City. Growing up with the trade, Mr. O'Neill soon deemed himself capable of starting out in business for himself, and opened a store at 282 Bowery. Here he laid the corner-stone of the famous house of Francis O'Neill, now so widely known throughout the country. Some thirty years ago, Mr. O'Neill moved to the corner of Twenty-eighth Street and Broadway, and since then the store has been the centre of the several boot and shoe concerns he had interested himself in.

As Trustee of St. Patrick's Cathedral, Mr. O'Neill enjoyed until his death the esteem and personal friendship of Archbishop Corrigan, and was consulted in matters concerning the establishment of the new seminary at Dunwoodie and the Catholic Church of Yonkers. He was also a Trustee of St. Mary's Church of this city, and one of the charter members of the Catholic Club of New York City. He served several terms as a member of the Yonkers Board of Education, and was Chairman of the Committee on Census.

His country seat, "Lismore," on Hawthorne Avenue, directly opposite that of his late father-in-law, Mr. C. E. Fitzpatrick, was occupied by him during the summer months, as he was accustomed to take up his residence in New York City during the winter. Mr. O'Neill died February 4, 1895. Mrs. O'Neill and a large family survive him, and a son, Francis O'Neill, is carrying on the business.

HENRY OSTERHELD, of the Eickemeyer & Osterheld Manufacturing Company, was born in a small village in Rhine-Bavaria, on December 10, 1838, and attended school in that place until thirteen years of age, when his parents sent him to Kaiserslantern, where better educational advantages could be found. He entered the Latin preparatory school and after remaining there for two years was admitted to the Real school in the same town where he graduated. The time had now arrived for Mr. Osterheld to choose a profession. His father, who was a forester, as his ancestors had been for many generations, was naturally anxious that he should choose the same profession, the more so as he was the youngest of three sons, and his older brothers had followed other professions. In compliance with his father's wishes he entered the College of Forestry in Ashaffenburg, Bavaria, graduating from this college when twenty years old.

FRANCIS O'NEILL.

Not being favorably impressed with existing conditions in Germany, and foreseeing a long and tedious time of waiting, before he might receive a position, he finally obtained the consent of his parents and came to the United States in the spring of 1859. Coming to a country where forestry is even now in its infancy, and was not even thought of as a profession, he was obliged to look for employment in another direction. He came to Yonkers and obtained work in the machine factory of Osterheld & Eickemeyer, his brother George at that time being a member of the firm, and remained in their employ until April, 1861.

In the fall of 1860, Mr. Osterheld was one of the Elisha Otis Guards of Wideawakes, and in April, 1861, joined the Fifth N. Y. S. M., when Lincoln called the first 75,000 men for three months. After the second Bull Run in August, 1862, he re-enlisted, joining Company F. of the Sixty-eighth N. Y. S. Volunteers, as private. He gradually advanced to the rank of Sergeant, and as such, fought in the battle of Chancellorsville, in May, 1863. In July of the same year, during the battle of Gettysburg, he was made Lieutenant of Company K, of the same regiment. After the battle of Gettysburg the Sixty-eighth regiment was transferred to Tennessee, where they assisted in a series of encounters to raise the siege of Chattanooga and establish a basis of supplies, taking part later in the battle of Chattanooga and Missionary Ridge. In January, 1864, the regiment went on veteran's furlough to New York, and after recruiting, returned to Chattanooga. After returning to the seat of war with his regiment, Mr. Osterheld was appointed on Gen. Rosecrans' staff, in the capacity of Assistant Inspector of railroad defences in the Department of the Cumberland, Major James R. Willet being Chief Inspector. This department was then transferred to Gen. George F. Thomas' command, and Mr. Osterheld was sent to Nashville, Tenn., as Assistant Chief Inspector and took charge of the Topographical Engineers' Department. It was during this time, December, 1864, that the Battle of Nashville was fought and Gen. Hood defeated and driven back. It being very important that a pontoon bridge should be built across the Duck River, which at this time of the year is always very high and rapid, Mr. Osterheld was intrusted with the building of this bridge, which took thirty-six hours. During this time the rain and snow were so severe that the men had to be relieved every four hours, he, however, remaining at his post until the bridge was finished.

Later on he was transferred to the Chief Engineer's office as Assistant Chief Engineer, Major-Gen. Seth B. Tower being the Chief Engineer of the Military Division of Tennessee. In this capacity he remained until the close of the war, when in May, 1866, he was mustered out of service and returned to Yonkers. He again entered the employ of Osterheld & Eickemeyer as bookkeeper, and remained with the firm until 1870, when he accepted a position in the New York Customs House, first as Storekeeper, then as Liquidating Clerk, and finally as United States Gauger, which office he resigned in March, 1880, in order to join Mr. Eickemeyer as partner in place of his brother George, who had been dead two years. Mr. Osterheld married Miss Katherine Eickemeyer, youngest sister of Mr. R. Eickemeyer, Sr., in February, 1864. They have five children, three daughters and two sons. Both sons are graduates of Columbia College, the oldest son having graduated from the School of Mines and the youngest from the School of Physicians and Surgeons.

Mr. Osterheld at one time was active in G. A. R. circles, being Commander of Kitching Post for a number of years, and in 1879 was elected as Senior Vice Department Commander of the State of New York, with the rank of Brigadier General. He had a prominent part in the celebration of the Bi-centennial of October 18, 1882, being Marshal of the Sixth, or business division of the grand parade. Mr. Osterheld is an ardent Republican, and very much interested in whatever appertains to the growth and welfare of our city:

GEORGE W. OSBORN was born at Newcastle, Westchester County, N. Y. He was appointed a patrolman of the Metropolitan Police, New York City, in 1865, and transferred to Yonkers in August, 1866, made Roundsman, April 29, 1871, and Sergeant, August 18, 1873. In politics Mr. Osborn is a Republican.

CHARLES ROLLIN OTIS, the elder of the two sons of Elisha G. Otis, was born in Troy, N. Y., April 29, 1835. During his youth he attended school at Halifax, Vt., and at Albany, N. Y. From early boyhood he manifested a great fondness for mechanics of every kind. At the age of thirteen he entered his father's factory and learned his trade. At fifteen he was greatly interested in steam engines and received the position of engineer in the Hudson Manufactory, of which his father was Superintendent. He was very ambitious to become an engineer on one of the great ocean liners. He was a young man of determined purpose and doubtless but for the removal of his father about this time to this city he would have accomplished it. He accompanied and assisted his father in his early operations in this city. He was quick to see the possibilities of the elevator (a sketch of the Otis Bros. & Co., Elevator Works is given in the Chapter on "Yonkers Industries") that his father had invented and urged him to devote himself exclusively to the making and introducing, etc., throughout the world.

Mr. Otis manifested the same integrity, business ability and genius of invention as his father. He is closely connected with various large business interests, also real estate improvements of this city. He is a member of the Westminster Church, and for years was Superintendent of the Sunday-school, and an elder of the church. He was Chairman of the Committee at the time of the building of the Westminster Presbyterian Church. He was married August 28, 1861, to Carrie F. Boyd. They have had no children but have reared and educated several orphans.

Mr. Otis was appointed a member of the Board of Education in 1886, and has served continuously since then. He has been a member of the Committee on Teachers and Instruction all that time, and is now its Chairman, and is also a member of other important committees. A very considerable part of his time is devoted to visiting and inspecting the schools. He is a steadfast friend of the teachers and children and believes that the public schools should be lifted to the highest standard; to that end he devotes all his efforts. He has been a great traveller, having visited Europe several times. His published letters during his visits abroad are of very great interest. Mr. Otis is an extensive reader, and owner of a valuable special library, including both a classical collection and a wide range of scientific subjects.

NORTON PRENTISS OTIS was born in Halifax, Vt., March 18, 1840. His father was Elisha G. Otis, and his mother Susan A. Houghton. The father died in 1861, and the mother February 25, 1842. Mr. Otis received his early training and education at the public schools in Halifax, Vt., Albany, N. Y., and Hudson City, N. J., at which place his father resided at different times, and on the removal of the family to Yonkers, he completed his studies at District School No. 2, of this city. At eighteen years of age he entered his father's elevator business, then in its infancy. Upon the incorporation of Otis Brothers & Co. in 1867, he became Treasurer, and for the succeeding ten years traveled for the concern throughout the United States and Canada, introducing passenger and freight elevators.

In 1877 he married Miss Lizzie A. Fahs, of York, Pa., a most estimable and accomplished lady. They have seven children—Charles Edwin, Sidney, Arthur Houghton, Norton Prentiss, Katherine Lois, Ruth Adelaide, and James Russell Lowell.

He has always been actively interested in the religious, social and political life of Yonkers, and has filled with honor many offices of distinction in these several departments, and is identified with several of the philanthropic institutions of the city. For years he has been the Vice-President of St. John's Riverside Hospital, and President of the Charity Organization Society. All that concerns the welfare of Yonkers concerns Mr. Otis, and he has always been ready to serve the city of which he is an honored resident.

Politically he is a Republican, and has always sustained the party and its principles. In the spring of 1880 he was nominated for Mayor, and elected by a large majority. During his administration many important and valuable changes were made in the various departments of the city. The Fire Department was reorganized, the system of Public School management was changed and greatly advanced in efficiency (Mr. Otis appointing the first School Board under the Consolidated system), the Water Works were largely augmented by the introduction of new and improved machinery; and with all these improvements, brought about under his practical business administration, when he retired from office the city's debt had been decreased more than $75,000. In the fall of 1883 he was elected to the State Assembly in a district overwhelmingly Democratic. While in the State Legislature he was the author of many important measures, among which were those relating to the reduction of exorbitant rates of fare on State railroads, giving towns the power to regulate or refuse admission to excursion parties, making physicians only eligible to the office of Coroner, etc. The latter bill, however, failed to pass at that time on account of constitutional objections. Since then the Constitution has been amended, and the essential elements of that bill are now the law of the State. In local politics, Mr. Otis is a recognized leader of opinion among the best elements of society. One of the most prominent citizens of Yonkers said of him recently: "Mr. Otis is one of the most sagacious and honorable men that we have to-day in our city. Whatever office he is elected to, he dignifies and discharges its duties with the utmost skill, reflecting credit upon himself, and adding materially to the prosperity and comfort of the community he serves; discountenancing everything that savors of political trickery and corruption, he is pre-eminently qualified to serve his country in any capacity." This just criticism of the man is fully confirmed by his past record both in official and private life.

In 1890, upon the retirement of his brother from business, he was elected President of Otis Brothers & Co., which position he still holds. (A sketch of this Company's Elevator Works is given under the chapter, "Yonkers' Industries.") But Mr. Otis is not only a factor in the political and religious life of the

RESIDENCE OF NORTON P. OTIS. HUDSON TERRACE.

community; he is also a highly respected and valued member of its society. He is a close student, and keeps in touch with the best thought of the day. A Christian gentleman, a cultured member of society, a wise and successful business man—he stands as a representative citizen, honored and respected by the whole community.

PRINCE WILLIAM PADDOCK was born at Southeast, Putnam County, N. Y., and educated in the schools of that place. For many years he was largely engaged in the lumber business, buying large tracts of land in Canada and northwest New York, having the timber cut and brought through the canal to Albany, and then in rafts to Yonkers, where he had extensive steam saw-mills to manufacture the lumber. He was a Democrat and at one time held the position of Supervisor, and was also a member of the Legislature for some time. Mr. Paddock was connected with the Episcopal Church and at one time was a Vestryman of St. John's Episcopal Church of this city. In 1829 he was married to Elizabeth Briggs, to whom four sons and one daughter were born, of whom one son, Walter H. Paddock, and one daughter, Mrs. S. E. Getty, are living. Mr. Paddock died in this city, November 2, 1853.

WALTER HALSEY PADDOCK was born at Yonkers, November 29, 1830. He has resided in his native city all his life, with the exception of about fifteen years, which he spent in New York. Mr. Paddock received a careful education in the schools of Yonkers and later, at Irving Institute of Tarrytown, N. Y. He is not now engaged in business, having several years ago retired. He is a member of St. John's Episcopal Church, Yonkers Board of Trade and is a Trustee of the Yonkers Savings Bank. He is a Republican, and for four years was President of the Yonkers Board of Police Commissioners, and for the same period a member of the Board of Health. On December 7, 1859, he married Miss Ann Maria Waring. Two children were born to them, both of whom are now deceased.

JOHN PAGAN, JR., was born in Yonkers, April 21, 1860, and educated at the public schools. For nine years he was Assistant City Clerk; and he has held the position of City Clerk of Yonkers, since 1890. Politically, he is a Republican, and is a member of the City Club, of Yonkers. On December 9, 1882, Mr. Pagan married Miss Ida Hoag. Two children have been born to them.

CLARENCE A. PEARSALL was born in Alpine, Bergen County, N. J., March 29, 1872, and educated in the public schools of Alpine and Yonkers. He has been a resident of this city for twelve years, and is engaged in the coal and wood business. He is a member of the Y. C. Y. C., I. O. O. F., Red Men, American Mechanics, Board of Trade, and the First M. E. Church. Mr. Pearsall is a Republican, but has never held any official position.

CYRUS AUGUSTUS PEAKE was born in Hamden, Delaware County, N. Y., January 25, 1847. At the age of seventeen years he enlisted in the Union Army and served until the close of the war, receiving an honorable discharge at Hilton Head, S. C., July 4, 1865. In the fall of 1865 he entered the Delaware Academy, at Delhi, N. Y., and afterwards Union College, Schenectady, graduating in the classical course, in 1870, ranking fourth in a class of forty-five. During the commencement week in 1870, he was elected a member of the Phi Beta Kappa Society, membership in which is conditional upon a high rank in scholarship. At the graduating exercises on commencement day, he was awarded the First Blatchford Oratorical Prize, founded by the Hon. Richard M. Blatchford, LL.D., of New York City, consisting of a gold medal of the value of $40 to be given to the member of the graduating class who should, at commencement, deliver the best oration, "regard being had alike to its elevated and classical character and to its graceful and effective delivery." After graduating, Mr. Peake became Principal of the New York Central Academy, at McGrawville, where he remained three years. He then became Principal of the Port Byron Free School and Academy, and after one year resigned that position and came to Yonkers and entered upon the practice of his profession, having been admitted to the Bar at the General Term at Rochester, in April, 1878. In 1879, he was elected Justice of the Peace, and in 1880, was appointed Acting City Judge by Mayor Otis, and served in this capacity for two years. In 1890, he was again elected Justice of the Peace, and was re-appointed Acting City Judge by Mayor Millward.

In 1874 he married Miss Harriet E. Greenman, and has one child, Howard De Ver. Mr. Peake is a staunch Republican, being a firm believer in the policy of Protection to American industries, is a member of the G. A. R., and a charter member of the Yonkers Corinthian Yacht Club.

SIDNEY STARR PECK was born at Danbury, Conn., October 21, 1829, and was educated in the schools of Newtown, Conn. He has been a resident of this city for forty-seven years, and for twenty-five years of that time engaged in the retail hat and fur business. On November 27, 1850, he was married to Mary Jane Wildman, who died November 23, 1853, leaving one child, Charles S., who was born September 22, 1853. On April 20, 1859, his second marriage occurred to Miss Anna Hopkins, daughter of Samuel

Hopkins, of Greenburg, and they had two children, Gideon H. and Milton W. Mr. Peck on coming to Yonkers was employed in Waring & Baldwin's hat factory, then situated on Elm Street, just east of the present gate of the Alex. Smith Carpet Works, and for five years was Superintendent of this factory. Afterwards he succeeded David Wells, who conducted a retail hat store on Dock Street, in a store now occupied by George W. Bruce. From there he moved to the Getty House corner, and afterwards to Wheeler's Row, on North Broadway. His son Charles resides in Danbury, Conn., where he conducts a hat machine factory; he served two years as Alderman and one term as Mayor of the City of Danbury. Gideon H. Peck and Milton W. Peck are engaged in the hat business in this city.

JOHN G. PEENE, the present Mayor of Yonkers, is the eldest son of Captain Joseph Peene, and was born in this city on February 23, 1843. He attended the schools of this city, but at an early age sought employment. In April, 1861, he enlisted with Samuel Parkinson and Cornelius Schemerhorn (who are still living, and they were the first three men who enlisted from this city) in Company F, Fifth New York Volunteer Infantry, known as the Duryea Zouaves, serving for two years, when he was honorably discharged. The company during this period fought in many of the principal battles of the war, and was in the battle of Big Bethel, which was the first engagement of the war fought in the line of battle. After his return from the war in 1863, he connected himself with the Ben Franklin Line owned by his father. In 1873 he was appointed, by Governor John A. Dix, Harbor Master of the Port of New York, a most lucrative position, but after serving for three months he resigned. It has often been remarked that he was the only one appointed to this position that relinquished the same of his own accord.

In 1874, he with his brothers, Joseph Jr., and George, formed the partnership known as Peene Brothers, and bought out their father's interest in the transportation business. In 1893 the business was formed into a corporation and Mr. Peene became the President, which position he holds at present. An extended history of the Ben Franklin Transportation Company will be found in another Chapter of this volume; it is an exceedingly large and prosperous business and all of the owners exert a commanding business influence in the affairs of the city. In 1883, Mr. Peene was elected one of the Water Commissioners by the Board of Aldermen and served for five years. In the spring of 1893, he was nominated for Mayor of Yonkers by the Republican party and defeated John Kendrick Bangs, his Democratic opponent, carrying the city by a majority of 205. On account of the new charter of the City of Yonkers going into effect in November, he was nominated and elected Mayor for a term of two years, from December 1, 1895. This time his opponent on the Democratic ticket was John Eylers, whom he defeated by a majority of 320. Mr. Peene has endeavored to make his administration a business one, and many improvements have been made since he has been Mayor. Our streets have been asphalted and paved, public baths have gone into effect and parks have been introduced. The want of the city for a Municipal building has been solved, and one is now in course of erection, which will cost from $60,000 to $70,000.

In political circles the subject of this sketch has, all his life, associated himself with the Republican party, to whose principles he has strictly adhered. He has served as representative to various County and State Conventions and was a Representative to the National Convention held in St. Louis in July, 1896. Mr. Peene is of an open handed jovial disposition, and has always maintained his position as a representative citizen. His first marriage occurred on November 24, 1864, to Miss Jeanette A. Starr, and his second marriage took place August 1, 1883, to Miss Ava L. Holder. Three of his children are living, Joseph, George and Edna May.

JOSEPH PEENE, JR., was born in Yonkers, July 26, 1845. He received his education in the public and private schools of this city; afterward engaging in the transportation business. He is a member of the New York Athletic Club, Fleetwood Driving Park Club, Suburban Riding and Driving Club, and is a Democrat in politics, but has never held any official position. On November 25, 1875, he married Miss Elenore Jane Brewer and they have had seven children, six of whom are now living. Mr. Peene was the chief supervisor in building all the steam plant of the Ben Franklin Line in which he takes a great interest.

GEORGE PEENE was born in Yonkers, May 14, 1848, and was educated in the public and private schools of the city. He is connected with the Ben Franklin Transportation Company, and a member of the City Club, a Republican in politics, but has never held any official position. On February 7, 1872, he was married to Miss Jennie E. Wood, to whom four children have been born.

RICHARD OLIVER PHILLIPS was born at West Hurley, Ulster County, N. Y., September 11, 1848, and educated at Andes Collegiate Institute, Fairfield Seminary, and New York Homeopathic Medical College. He has been a resident of this city for nineteen years, and is a prominent physician. He is a Republican in politics, a member of Warburton Baptist Church, and a School Trustee. On November 23, 1881, he was married to Miss Anna Preston, of Oneida County, N. Y. They have two sons, Richard Oliver, Jr., and John Preston.

JAMES LINDSAY PORTEOUS, M.D., was born at Riccarton Manse, Ayrshire, Scotland, and was educated by private tutors, and at Ayr Academy, Royal Edinburgh High School, University of St. Andrews and Edinburgh, and the Royal College of Surgeons, Edinburgh. At one time he was Resident Surgeon at Edinburgh Royal Infirmary, and assistant to Dr. Pat. Heron Watson, Professor of Surgery. For two years he was Visiting Physician at the Liverpool Southern Dispensary, and for several years one of the surgeons attached to the British Emigration Service. He is a member of the Royal College of Physicians of Edinburgh, a Fellow of the Royal College of Surgeons, Edinburgh, and a Fellow of the Academy of Medicine of New York City. For some time he was Consultant and Gynæcologist to St. John's Riverside Hospital, and is at present one of the Physicians to St. Joseph's Hospital. Dr. Porteous was also at one time Vice-President of the Westchester Medical Association, and is now Secretary of the Jenkins Medical Association. In 1875 he married Miss Louise C. Mason, daughter of the late John M. Mason, Counsellor-at-law in New York and Yonkers.

WILLIAM H. POST was born at Yonkers, October 14, 1833. He received his education at the public schools, was a carpenter by profession, and was a resident of this place for forty-three years. He was the first Village Clerk of Yonkers, and in 1861 was appointed Postmaster by President Lincoln. He married Miss Sarah M. Sherwood, to whom three children were born, two daughters and one son. Mr. Post was massacred by the Indians at White River Agency, Col., on September 29, 1879.

ADRIAN M. POTTER was born in New York City. He attended the public schools at Hastings, and the State Normal School at Albany, N. Y. He has resided at Yonkers for eight years, where he has studied and followed the profession of a lawyer, he having been admitted to the bar in 1891 at Brooklyn, N. Y. He is a member of the New Manhattan Athletic Club of New York City, and the Corinthian Yacht Club of Yonkers. He is a Democrat, and at present holds the office of Justice of the Peace.

JOHN B. PROTE was born at Albany, N. Y., December 26, 1819, and was educated in the schools of New York City. He is a member of the Blue Lodge (Masonic), a Royal Arch, Knights Templar, and is a Republican in politics. On July 11, 1841, he married Miss Martha A. Nichols and has one son, John R., who is associated with his father in business. Mr. Prote was a member of the old Volunteer Fire Department, and in 1835, he joined the Volunteer Live Oak Engine Company, No. 44, of New York, serving until June, 1854, when he removed to Hastings, N. Y., where he was engaged in the manufacture of lime, for three years, and in the grocery business until coming to this city, in 1867, when he again started in the grocery business, continuing until 1893. He is now agent for the storage warehouse. See illustrations on page 257.

JOHN ISAAC PRUYN was born at Kinderhook, N. Y., December 30, 1854, and was educated at the Kinderhook Academy. In 1869 he located at Yonkers, where he is engaged in the furniture and carpet business. He established his present business in 1892. He is a Republican, and a member and Captain of the Fourth Separate Company, N. G. S. N. Y., and the Reformed Church. On May 19, 1875, he married Miss Mary, daughter of John C. Scott, of Freehold, N. J. Four children have born to them. Mr. Pruyn's military record is as follows: He entered Company D, Sixteenth Battalion, N. G. S. N. Y., as a private, June 6, 1874; was promoted Corporal, March 11, 1876; Sergeant, February 7. 1877; First Sergeant, February 12, 1880, and Sergeant-Major, March 23, 1880. He was honorably discharged, December 10, 1881. He re-enlisted in the Fourth Separate Company, January 2, 1882, was made First Sergeant, March 2, 1882; Second Lieutenant, February 1, 1884; First Lieutenant, August 5, 1885, and Captain, November 26, 1887.

P. H. PYNE, A.M., M.D., was born at Stockbridge, Mass., January 12, 1861, and was educated at the private schools of Huntington, Mass., receiving his collegiate course at Allegheny and Manhattan Colleges. In 1883 he graduated from Bellevue Hospital Medical College, and in 1886 received the Honorary degree of Master of Arts from Manhattan College. Dr. Pyne is a member of the City Club, of Yonkers, ex-President of the Jenkins Medical Society, and a member of the Westchester County Medical Society, also Visiting Physician to St. Joseph's Hospital and to the Royal Seminary of New York, and a Fellow of the New York Academy of Medicine. On April 29, 1885, he married Miss Katheryn R. Fitz Gerald.

S. FRANCIS QUICK was born in Rhinebeck, Dutchess County, N. Y., April 7, 1830. He descended from Hollander and English stock, who settled in Dutchess County, N. Y., at an early date, and his grandfather, Gerardus Quick, was living there during the Revolution. His father, Peter G. Quick, married, first, Rebecca, daughter of Daniel Eckert, and second, Lydia C., daughter of Sebastian Crapser. Their children were S. Francis, Charles W., Peter R., Edwin A., Catharine, wife of William Scoles, Annie, Cornelia, and Mary, wife of Elmore Rickert. In 1854 Mr. Quick married Susan Adams. Their children are: Newton, who married Lucy Bryant, and has two children (one son, Frederick, and a daughter, Mabel), Lucy, wife of Frank E. Wheeler, who have two children (a daughter, Florence, and a son, Francis), Ella, and Arthur. At an early age he learned the carpenter's trade from Henry Latson, a mechanic of rare skill, in his native town. In 1850, when his apprenticeship was completed, a kind and helpful neighbor loaned him $20 to purchase tools, and with these and a capital of $3 (two of these, out of good-heartedness, he loaned to a needy fellow-workman), he came to Yonkers, and with that cash capital of one dollar began his labors. His energy, purpose and honesty were his added equipments, and the real secret that won his fame and fortune. He began as a journeyman with Sylvanus Ferris, with whom he tarried about three years, and then became partner with Nelson Ackert, they having bought out their employer. For twenty years this partnership remained, and with growing success. In 1869 a fire destroyed their buildings, and involved a loss to the young men of $22,000. Such was the confidence reposed in them, that several gentlemen of ample means, among them Martin Bates and William Menzes of New York, promptly and voluntarily offered to supply the funds to start them again in business. With shops rebuilt, they soon began anew a career of prosperous business activity. Yonkers and the adjoining villages grew rapidly, and their business kept pace, and became very extensive. Among the buildings erected by them may be mentioned the Baptist, Unitarian, and St. Paul's Episcopal churches of Yonkers, and Christ Church at Riverdale; the large buildings of the Catholic Institutions of Mount St. Vincent, the foundry and machine shops at Spuyten Duyvil.

In 1876, Mr. Ackert died and Mr. Quick who had already purchased Mr. Ackert's share of the business, has ever since conducted it in his own name. Two-thirds of the factories of this city he has built. The names of a few of the numerous residents for whom he has built private residences, the finest in the city, are of historic interest, and are as follows: William Allen Butler, John B. Trevor, James B. Colgate, G. P. Morosini, Abija Curtis, Percy R. Pyne, H. S. Spaulding, William E. Dodge, S. D. Babcock John E. Andrus, R. C. Vilas, David Hawley and John C. Havemeyer. He also built the high school building, St. John's Rectory and Chapel, St. John's Hospital and numerous other notable structures. His buildings where his shops are located cover many lots and are amply furnished with machinery of modern improvements, and he employs over 100 men. He is a member of the First Methodist Episcopal Church of this city and has held the office of Trustee for thirty-five years with great fidelity. He was an ardent advocate of a new church, which movement was inaugurated by Dr. William E. Ketcham, his pastor in 1885, and was the first to subscribe for its accomplishment. His unwearied toil for the erection of that beautiful edifice attests his love for the church of his choice. He is a staunch Republican in politics but has declined all political honors frequently proffered him. He was for several years a Trustee of the Yonkers Savings Bank and is now honored by being its Vice-President. He is also President of the Yonkers Publishing Company.

EDWIN A. QUICK was born at Rhinebeck, N. Y., where he received an academic education. For several years he was engaged in building operations in New York City, but located at Yonkers twenty years ago, where he has since resided and has been engaged in the profession of an architect. He is a prominent member of the following clubs and societies: City Club, Palisade Boat Club, and Terrace City Chapter of Yonkers; York Lodge, No. 197, and Adelphi Council, No. 7, of New York City; Mokanna Grotto, No. 1, of Hamilton, N. Y., and Supreme Council, M. O. V. P., of the World. Mr. Quick served as a member of the Aldermanic Board, representing the Third Ward of Yonkers in 1885, 1886, 1890, and 1891. On March 25, 1863, he married Miss Martha Stapleton. Three children have been born to them. Elmer E., H. Lansing and Louise B.

EDWIN A. QUICK.

HENRY JOSEPH QUINN was born in County Clare, Ireland, in 1844. He received a common school education, after which he learned a trade in a rolling mill. In April, 1871, he was appointed a Patrolman on the Yonkers Police Force, and in 1874, he was promoted Roundsman. Later on he was promoted Sergeant, a position he now fills. He was the first Patrolman to be appointed when Yonkers became a city. In November, 1879, he married Miss Mary McMahon, to whom one child has been born. Mr. Quinn is a Democrat and a member of St. Mary's Catholic Church. He is the recipient of a set of resolutions engrossed and framed, presented to him by the Board of Police for bravery and efficiency.

PETER E. RADCLIFF was born in Rhinebeck, N. Y., April 2, 1815, and was for many years a leading business man of Yonkers engaged in the market business at 15 North Broadway, which business he successfully carried on until 1870, when his son John succeeded him. He was a member of the First Reformed Church, serving as Elder at the time of his death in August, 1876.

ABRAM S. RADCLIFF, his eldest son, was born at Rhinebeck, N. Y., September 18, 1836, and was foreman in his father's market for several years. In 1867 he purchased the Broadway Market at 29 North Broadway, and in 1885, removed to No. 3 North Broadway where the business is still conducted. He is a member of the Central Methodist Episcopal Church and has been one of the Trustees for the past twenty years, is a member of Rising Star Lodge, F. and A. M., Yonkers Lodge, I. O. O. F., and John C. Fremont Post, G. A. R. He served the city as Alderman for two years, 1875-76.

P. EDWARD RADCLIFF was born December 12, 1860, in Yonkers and received his education in Public School No. 2 of this city. After leaving school he associated with his father in business, in 1890 entering into partnership with his father under the firm name of A. S. Radcliff & Son. He is a member of the Reformed Church and at present holds the office of deacon. In July, 1891, he married Miss Anna Snell, of Palatine Bridge, Principal of School No. 3 of this city at the time of her marriage.

1. PETER E. RADCLIFF.   2. ABRAM S. RADCLIFF.   3. P. EDWARD RADCLIFF.

GEORGE RAYNER, the Secretary of the Yonkers Board of Trade, is of English and Scotch parents. His father, Daniel Rayner, was a native of Sandwich, one of the well-known Cinque Ports, of Kent, England, created by William the Conqueror, many centuries ago. His grandfather was proprietor of a large hostelry at that port for many years, and his ancestors are believed to have settled there about the time of the invasion of England by William the Conqueror. Mr. Rayner's father, upon attaining his majority, entered the service of his Government, and was assigned to duty in the Internal Revenue Department in Scotland, where he met and married Janet Wilson, of Paisley, near Glasgow. There were seven sons and two daughters of this union, George, the third son, being born in the city of Aberdeen, on the northeast coast of Scotland, June 7, 1838. After several promotions his father was assigned to duty in England, and the school-days of George were mainly passed in Cumberland, in the north of England, where at Whitehaven he graduated from Thwaite's Commercial College, and acted as secretary to his father, who, after an honorable service of over thirty years, retired from active duty and settled in the city of Chester, England, where he quietly passed his declining years, and had the pleasure of making acquaintance with several Yonkers citizens *en route* through that ancient and historical city. He died in 1891, in his eighty-seventh year, and is interred in Chester Cemetery, by the side of his beloved wife, who preceded him fifteen years earlier.

Mr. Rayner married Miss Sarah Ainley, of Hyde, Cheshire, England, and in 1860 came to this country, and paid a visit to Yonkers, and a few years later they permanently settled here, where, for about thirty years, Mr. Rayner has followed his profession of Civil Engineer, Surveyor and Architect, being now ably assisted by his sons, George, Jr., and Thomas. After Yonkers was encorporated as a city he received the first appointment of City Surveyor, and in 1880, was made Commissioner of Charities and filled that office for twelve years. From his residence on Shonnard Terrace a very commanding view is had of the Hudson River, the Palisades, and of the open Tappan Zee Bay in the distance. A view of this forms one of the many illustrations in this History.

JACOB READ was born at Southeast, Putnam County, N. Y., on September 30, 1818. His father, Rooney Read, was a soldier in the War of 1812, and his grandfather, Jacob Read, was a soldier in the Revolution. Mr. Read came to Yonkers at the age of eleven, and is one of the oldest and best known citizens. His early reminiscences of this city will be found on page 150. He has held many positions of trust; for fifteen years was Supervisor, and at present is a member of the Board of Water Commissioners, acting as Treasurer. He is a member of the Odd Fellows' and Masons' Orders. On November 23, 1845, he married Miss Catherine L. Mann, who died on December 26, 1891. Five of his children are living— George, Leander and David H., all residents of Yonkers; Mrs. Amanda Gibson, of White Plains, and Helen L., wife of Wilbur B. Ketcham, of this city.

GABRIEL P. REEVS was born January 21, 1820, at Minisink, N. Y. He received his rudimentary education at the Academy of West Town, N. Y., after which he entered the University of the City of New York, graduating therefrom in 1845, with the degree of M.D. After practicing medicine for twelve years at Goshen, N. Y., he removed to Yonkers about thirty years ago. He is now retired from the active practice of his profession. He is a member of the First Presbyterian Church of Yonkers, and has held the office of Ruling Elder for many years. On May 15, 1849, he married Miss Mary M. McCartee (now deceased), to whom seven children were born. On July 13, 1887, he married Miss Julia Reemsey, who died in 1888. On his father's side, Dr. Reeves is descended from the Reeves family, who were among the first settlers of Southold, L. I. On his mother's side he is descended from Matthias Corwin, the first of the Corwin family in America, also of Southold.

GABRIEL REEVS was born at Yonkers, September 28, 1859, and received his rudimentary education at the Rev. Montgomery Hooper's Academy. He afterwards entered Columbia College Law School, and was graduated therefrom with honors in 1882. Mr. Reeves has resided at Yonkers all his life, and is now actively engaged in his legal profession. He is a member and officer of the Palisade Boat Club of Yonkers, is a Republican, and was Acting Judge of Yonkers in 1892 and 1893. In 1892 he was Counsel to the Board of Excise, and was reappointed to the same position in 1895. He is single, and a Protestant.

EDGAR UNDERHILL REYNOLDS was born at Yonkers, was educated at the public schools, and has been a resident of this place for forty-two years. For many years he has followed dairy farming. He is a Republican, and a member of the Board of Aldermen. On June 5, 1879, he married Miss Mary E. Lyon, of Bedford Station, N. Y., to whom two children have been born, Ethel and William. Mr. Reynolds is a member of the Methodist Church.

WILLIAM H. RICHARDSON was born in Washington, N. C., July 30, 1859. In 1878 he located at Yonkers, where he has, since that time, been engaged in the real estate business. He is a member of the Yonkers Board of Trade. Politically, he has always been a Republican. On April 25, 1877, he married Miss Laura G. Youmans.

WILLIAM H. RILEY was born May 18, 1840, in this city, and was educated in the public schools and by private tutors. In 1861 he enlisted in the Civil War and lost his left arm at the battle of Antietam, September 17, 1862, while a private in Company G, Fifty-first Regiment, N. Y. Volunteers, which was also known as "Sheppard Rifles." On his return from the war he was appointed Constable of the town of Eastchester, Tuckahoe District, and Collector of school taxes for the same district. In 1867 he commenced the study of law with R. E. Prime, Esq., and was admitted to the Bar in December, 1868. In March, 1895, he was elected as Justice of the Peace, of this city, to fill a vacancy of nine months, and at the end of that time was re-elected for a full term. In January, 1895, he was appointed Acting City

Judge, of Yonkers, by Mayor J. G. Peene. Mr. Riley is a Republican, and a member of John C. Fremont Post, 590, Department of New York G. A. R., and various other societies of this city. In April, 1869, he married Miss Mary J. Smullen. Mr. Riley's great-grandfather, on his mother's side, Joshua Devoe, was a soldier in the Continental Army under Gen. Sullivan, and his grandfather on the same side, Isaac Devoe, was a soldier in the American Army in the War of 1812.

JOHN ROWLAND was born at Yonkers, July 24, 1861. He was educated at Eickemeyer School, and has resided in his native place for twenty-eight years. He is a prominent hat manufacturer. Politically, he is a Republican, and is President of the Board of Fire Commissioners, of Yonkers. On February 24, 1886, he married Miss Eva Osterheld, who died August 19, 1891, leaving one child.

JAMES P. SANDERS, the oldest lawyer in the city, was born in the Second Ward, of the city of New York. In 1836 he went to Danbury, Conn., where, in 1837, he entered the office of S. H. Hicock, Esq., to study law, where he remained until 1840, when he was entitled to practice; in 1846, he removed to Peekskill, N. Y. In 1856 he opened an office in the town of Westchester; in the fall of 1859 he removed his office to Yonkers. At that time, the only lawyers in practice in Yonkers were W. W. Scrugham, R. W. Van Pelt and I. Stedwell, all of whom have been dead for many years. In 1865, 1866 and 1867, he was counsel for the village of Yonkers. In 1874, 1875 and 1876, he was President of the Board of Education of School District No. 6. During the Rebellion, in connection with Daniel Drew, John G. Holbrook and N. H. Odell, Esq., he was appointed by the Governor of the State, to look after the interests of the drafted men of this Congressional District, and spent much time in the performance of those duties. He has the reputation of being an outspoken man, standing up for what he considers right, and opposed to what he considers wrong. He has always had a good and lucrative practice as a lawyer.

BENJAMIN FRANKLIN SAWYER, JR., was born in the city of Portland, Me., November 27, 1834. His ancestors came from England. After enjoying the advantages of education as afforded by the local schools, he was sent to Boston, Mass., where he completed his education in a creditable manner. In 1860 he became identified with the business interests of Yonkers. From a business point of view Mr. Sawyer was pre-eminently a self-made man. Being possessed of keen natural powers of discernment, he quickly noted the advantages of Yonkers as a location for business, and established the dry-goods store so long and favorably known as "The Bee-Hive," at No. 5 South Broadway, which, by his persistent industry and perseverance, from its modest beginning has proved eminently successful. Thus for nineteen consecutive years he continued here in business. He was materially assisted by his wife, who, with commendable ability and tact, has continued the management of the store with the same marked success since the death of her husband, which occurred September 16, 1879. Mrs. Sawyer was formerly Miss Ellen Von Storch, of Scranton, Penn. She is a sister of the late Henry Ferdinand Von Storch, elsewhere mentioned in this work. Mr. Sawyer is remembered as being one of the most able and popular business men of our city. During the War of the Rebellion he enlisted in Company H., Seventeenth Regiment, National Guard State of New York, and served with the thirty-days' men under Captain John Davis Hatch at Fort McHenry, Baltimore, Md.

ASLAN SAHAGIAN was born at Diarbekir, Armenia, June 2, 1836. He received a collegiate education at Constantinople, Turkey. In 1863 he came to America, and for the past twenty-eight years has been a resident of Yonkers, where he is engaged in the furniture and carpet business. Mr. Sahagian is a self-made man, and has accumulated a large real estate and other property. He is a member of the Board of Trade, and a Republican.

ASLAN SAHAGIAN.

LEOPOLD J. SCHLESINGER was born in Germany, June 18, 1856, and was educated in Charlotteville Institute and Oak Grove Academy, University of Virginia, and New York College of Pharmacy. He has been a resident of this city for fifteen years, and is a druggist. He is a member of the Board of Trade, Irving Hose Company, Good Government Club, Nepperhan Lodge, F. and A. M., Palisade Boat Club, and the

Unitarian Church, and is a Democrat. In July, 1883, he was married to Alice H. Rickett. Their three children are: Harold L., Mildred D., and Malcolm L.

JOHN H. SCHLOBOHM was born in Germany, November 1, 1843. He has been a resident of Yonkers for the past twenty-nine years, most of that time being spent in the hotel business. He is a prominent Republican, and has served ten years as a member of the Aldermanic and Health Boards, and was three times President of the Board of Aldermen. He is also a member of the Lutheran Church, the F. and A. M., the Turn Verein, and the Yonkers Teutonia.

EMIL SCHOPEN, M.D., was born at Dirmstein (Kingdom of Bavaria), Germany, on July 27, 1856. He received his medical education at the Universities of Leipsic (Germany), Paris (France), Geneva and Berne (Switzerland), where he graduated in 1884. After practicing in Europe for several years, he came to this country, locating in Long Island City, where he remained for two years. Dr. Schopen has now been practicing medicine and surgery in Yonkers for seven years, and is Attending Surgeon at St. John's Riverside Hospital. On August 15, 1888, he was married to Miss Henrietta Osterheld, daughter of Henry Osterheld, of this city, who died on August 27, 1894, and on August 25, 1896, he married Miss Celia Ahrens, of New York City.

WILLIAM WARBURTON SCRUGHAM was born in Yonkers, February 18, 1860, and was educated at Rev. Montgomery R. Hooper's Academy, and Columbia College of New York, receiving the degree of A.B. in 1880 with high honors, and the degree of LL.B. in 1882. He studied law in the office of Wm. C. Beecher, Esq., in New York City, and was connected with that office until 1887, when he opened an office in Yonkers. In 1888 he formed a copartnership with Mr. Gabriel Reeves. He is President and Treasurer of the Yonkers Gas Light Company, Director of the First National Bank, Director and Attorney for the Yonkers Building and Loan Association, Vice-President of the Palisade Boat Club, member of Columbia College Alumni Association, the New York City and the Westchester County Bar Associations, the City Club of Yonkers, and the Society of the Sons of the American Revolution. He was, from 1886 to 1892, Vestryman of St. John's Episcopal Church. He is a Democrat, and a member of the Board of Trade of this city. In 1888 and 1890 he was Acting City Judge of Yonkers, and was again appointed in 1893-94. On October 26, 1891, he was married to Miss Margaret B. Otis.

WILLIAM H. SHERMAN, M.D., was born in New York City, July 14, 1859, and is a graduate of Yale College (1880), and Columbia University (Medical Department) 1884. He has been a resident of this city for ten years, and is a

WILLIAM G. SHRIVE.

member of City Club, University Club, New York City, Westchester County Medical Society, New York Academy of Medicine, and St. John's Church. He is a Republican, and at present is one of the Health Commissioners. On June 13, 1893, he married Miss Bessie Snow, of Boston, daughter of Henry C. Snow, and they have one child.

WILLIAM GLENN SHRIVE was born in Equinunc, Pa., September 20, 1862, and received his education at Siglar's Newburgh Institute. He has resided in this city for sixteen years, and is a dealer in bicycles and athletic outfits. He is a member of the Warburton Avenue Baptist Church, Lady Washington Hose Company No. 2 of Yonkers, Palisade Boat Club, and a Veteran of the Twenty-second Regiment, New York. He is independent in politics. On October 18, 1892, he married Miss Nettie J. V. Worth, to whom one daughter has been born. Mr. Shrive came to Yonkers in 1880, and started in the printing business. In 1882 he started the *Yonkers Free Press*, and in 1884 sold his business to M. H. Clark, and entered the employ of the Bank of the State of New York, where he remained until his present business engaged his energies. Mr. and Mrs. Shrive's antecedents were among the first settlers of Putnam County, Mrs. Shrive being the descendant of Stephen Hopkins, signer of the Declaration of Independence. Mr. Shrive's grandmother was first cousin to General Grant's father, and her husband, John Warren, was for twenty-five years pastor of Carmel Baptist Church. The history of Putnam County speaks of Mr. Shrive's great-grandfather, a Revolutionary soldier, escaping from the British prison ship at New York by swimming to the shore. Until a few years ago, a log house at Patterson, N. Y., was still standing which he built in 1770. Mr. Shrive's uncles, Levi and Hiram Warren, respectively, were Surgeon and Assistant Surgeon of the Twenty-fourth Connecticut Volunteers.

JOHN C. SHOTTS, Commander of the Department of New York in 1894, was born August 11, 1844, in West Farms (now the Twenty-third Ward, of the City of New York). He enlisted at Yonkers, April 16, 1861, for two years, and was sworn into the United States service May 22d following, as a member of Company A, Seventeenth New York Volunteers, known as the Westchester Chasseurs. He was discharged June 2, 1863, in New York, having carried a musket in the ranks through the term for which he volunteered. He was at the siege of Yorktown, and engaged in the battles of Mechanicsville, Hanover Court House, Cold Harbor, Whitehouse Junction, Second Bull Run, Antietam, Sheperdstown, Fredericksburgh, Richard's Ford, Chancellorsville and United States Ford. At the battle of Hanover Court House the Seventeenth New York and Eighty-third Pennsylvania captured two guns belonging to Latham's celebrated New Orleans battery, which were the first guns taken in battle by the Army of the Potomac. The charge of the Seventeenth New York was very handsomely made, their superior drill being manifest in the solid front which they presented in moving forward. Comrade Shotts' company (A), being on the skirmish line, was one of the first to reach and take possession of the gun in behalf of the company and regiment. Wherever placed he proved himself to be of the stuff which makes good soldiers, and which saved the Union.

After his discharge Comrade Shotts went into the market business, and since 1883, has been engaged in the wholesale commission business, operating at present three refrigerator houses, one each at Yonkers, Tarrytown and Mount Vernon. He has served one five-year term as Water Commissioner of the city of Yonkers, and has recently been appointed for another five years.

Comrade Shotts is a member of Kitching Post, No. 60, having been mustered in 1879. He was elected Commander of the Post in 1880, and in 1886 was re-elected and served eight consecutive terms. He has for several years been the Chairman of the Yonkers Memorial Committee; in 1893 was a member of the Department Council of Administration, and on February 22, 1894, was elected Department Commander and held office till May 16, 1895. The fidelity with which he attended to his duties is suggested by the fact that in their discharge he journeyed over 22,000 miles and received the fraternal grasp from 20,000 comrades. His sympathy with the private soldier led him to much active endeavor in the halls of legislation, which was not without result. On March 1, 1868, he was married to Miss Ida Kuster, who died September 5, 1877, and on April 28, 1881, he married Miss Sarah M. Smith.

THEODORE HANNIBAL SILKMAN was born at New York City, March 25, 1858. He received a careful academic education under the tutelage of the Rev. M. R. Hooper, of Yonkers, N. Y. He afterwards took a thorough course in law and adopted the legal profession. He is at present Surrogate of Westchester County, having been elected November 6, 1894. Mr. Silkman is a prominent member of the Palisade Boat and City Clubs of Yonkers; a member of the Union League Club, the New York Athletic and New York Riding Clubs of New York City, and President of the City Club. He is a Vestryman of St. John's Episcopal Church of Yonkers, and a Manager of St. John's Riverside Hospital. Politically, Mr. Silkman is a staunch Republican. He has been honored with a number of responsible official positions by his party, prominent among which are the offices of United States Commissioner for the City of Yonkers, Police Commissioner (for four years, at present President of the Board), and Surrogate of Westchester County (he having defeated his opponent, Owen T. Coffin, an extremely popular man, by 3,900 majority). On October 4, 1882, Mr. Silkman married Miss Mary Virginia, daughter of Frederick C. Oakley, Esq. Three children have been born to them—two sons and a daughter, all of whom are living.

CHARLES E. SKINNER was born at West Farms, N. Y., July 24, 1850. He is an engineer and machinist by trade, and is a member of the firm of Skinner & Connally, of Yonkers. He is a Republican, and was for five years a member of the Civil Service Commission for Yonkers, for two years of that period being Secretary of that body. He also served two years as Alderman from the First Ward of Yonkers. He is Past Master of Rising Star Lodge, No. 450, F. and A. M. On January 29, 1884, he married Miss Adaline G. Ackerman, to whom four children have been born.

JAMES SLADE was born at Bath, England, December 22, 1836. He received his rudimentary education in the schools of his native place. While he was a boy his parents came to the United States, nearly forty years ago, and settled at Yonkers, where the subject of this sketch has since resided. Mr. Slade is the Superintendent of the Yonkers Gas Light Company and also a member of the Board of Directors of that corporation. He is a prominent member of St. Paul's Episcopal Church, and in politics, a Republican. He married Miss Mary Nolan, of Yonkers, the union having been blessed with four children, *viz.:* Richmond E. a graduate of Columbia College; Clifford L., Secretary of the Yonkers Electric Light Company; Foster S. and Harry C., who are now students at Cornell University and Harvard College, respectively.

JOHN H. SOUTHWICK was born in New York City, April 12, 1867, where he attended the public schools and the College of the City of New York. He has resided at Yonkers for thirteen years, where he has held the position of Auditor. He is a member of the Protestant Church and of Nepperhan Lodge, F. and A. M. In November, 1895, he was elected Alderman for one year from the First Ward of Yonkers.

CHARLES STAHL was born at Yonkers, January 16, 1860, where he has resided all his life, and where he received his education at the public schools. On May 5, 1882, he married Miss Catherine Byrnes, to whom five children have been born. Mr. Stahl was elected a member of Hudson Hose Company No. 1, August 5, 1884, and held the office until January 7, 1890. September 15, 1890, he was elected Assistant Engineer, resigning from the Company September 23, 1890. September 19, 1892, he was again elected Assistant Engineer, and September 17, 1894, Chief Engineer.

JAMES STEWART was born in Stirling, Scotland, November 13, 1825, and has been a resident of Yonkers for about fifty-one years. He is a builder, having built many of the largest and finest residences and public buildings in this city. He also laid the first water-mains of Yonkers, which extended twenty-one miles. Mr. Stewart is a member and elder of the First Reformed Church, Rising Star Lodge, F. and A. M., Board of Trade, State Militia, Fire Department, Volunteer, and has been a Director of the First National Bank since its organization. He is a Republican in politics, Trustee of the old village, and served as Alderman for two years. He married May E. Porter on May 21, 1851.

ROBERT L. STEWART was born at Yonkers, November 5, 1859. He was a pupil at old Public School No. 6. He has resided at Yonkers, where he has been engaged at his trade, that of a builder. He is a member of the Royal Arcanum and Masonic Lodges, Curling and Quoit Clubs and the First Reformed Church. Politically, he is a Republican, and is a member of the Board of Fire Commissioners. In December, 1881, he married Miss Alice M. James, of Rochester, N. Y. Three children have been born to them, two of whom are deceased.

LESLIE SUTHERLAND was born at New Glasgow, Nova Scotia, April 21, 1866. In 1868 his parents removed to Yonkers, where he received his rudimentary education at the public schools. He afterward attended the School of Science and Art at Cooper Institute, New York City. In 1894 he was elected a member of the Common Council, of Yonkers, from the First Ward, and served two years. In 1895 he was elected to the same body for two years, from the Fourth Ward. In 1896 he was elected President of the Common Council. He is also Clerk of the Surrogate Court of Westchester County, and is a member of Nepperhan Lodge, No. 736, F. and A. M., the Corinthian Yacht Club, and one of the incorporators of the Hollywood Inn.

SAMUEL SWIFT was born in Brooklyn, on August 5, 1849. His father was Samuel Swift, who at that time was a prosperous business man of New York City. His mother was Mary Phelps, a daughter of Samuel Phelps, of West Hampton, Mass. Until 1858, Dr. Swift was a resident of Brooklyn, when he entered Williston Seminary, in Massachusetts. In 1865 he entered Yale College and graduated three years later, receiving the degree of Ph.B. In the fall of 1869 he entered the Medical Department of Cambridge University, but remained there only one year. He then entered the Medical Department of Columbia College, and also studied privately under Dr. T. M. Markoe. He graduated in 1872, and was the valedictorian of his class. Dr. Swift came to this city in 1873, and entered into a partnership with Dr. J. Foster Jenkins, which was terminated by the death of the latter, in 1882. Dr. Swift was a Democrat, and in 1882, was chosen Mayor of the city and served two years. He was also at one time President of the Board of Education. Some years ago Dr. Swift retired from active practice, but resumed the same shortly before his death. At the time of his death, July 29, 1896, he was Medical Inspector for the Yonkers Board of Health.

ALLEN TAYLOR was born in Bangor, N. Y., July, 1832, and received his education at Franklin Academy and Union College. After graduating, he went to Kentucky, and taught school at Munfordsville and Greensburg. In 1861 he studied law in Malone, in the office of Hon. A. B. Parmlee, and was admitted to practice law at Canton, N. Y. In October, 1869, he came to Yonkers, and taught as Vice-Principal of School No. 2. In June, 1872, he married Miss Frank Durant, of Bethel, Conn., who died in 1875, leaving a daughter, who still lives with her father. In 1883 he married Miss Ella McMillan, daughter of Hon. Andrew McMillan, of Utica, N. Y. Mr. Taylor is the grandson of James Taylor, a Revolutionary soldier, who fought under General Montgomery at Quebec, and when that officer was killed, and the army disbanded, suffered greatly in his journey back to Vermont. It is related that for two days they had nothing to eat, when, fortunately, on the third day a squirrel was shot, which was divided between him and his two companions.

STEPHEN HOWARD THAYER, SR., was born at Boston, Mass., January 10, 1811. He was educated at Amherst College. He resided in Yonkers for twenty years, up to the time of his decease, which occurred January 16, 1890. He was by profession a lawyer, was a member of the First Presbyterian Church, was for some years a Village and School Trustee of Yonkers, and a Republican in politics. He was twice married, his first wife being Miss Harriet S. Holden, his second, Miss Elizabeth R. Cox. Mr. Thayer has had seven children.

STEPHEN HOWARD THAYER was born at New York City, May 24, 1842. He was educated at the Polytechnic School, Brooklyn, and Columbia College and Law School, New York. After completing his education, he applied himself to the practice of law, a profession he has been engaged at ever since. He is a member of St. John's Church, Yonkers, the G. A. R., is a Trustee of Oakland Cemetery, is Counsel for the Yonkers Savings Bank, and is also a member of the Palisade Boat Club, and Yonkers Corinthian Yacht Club. He is a Republican in politics, and filled the position of City Judge of Yonkers from 1888 to 1892, prior to which time he served as Justice of the Peace. On April 18, 1870, Mr. Thayer married Miss Anna F. Thurber. Eight children have been born to them, four sons and four daughters, two of them being now deceased.

WILLIAM BRYAN THOMPSON was born at Barbadoes, West Indies, and educated in private schools. He has been a resident of Yonkers for twenty-one years, and is a member of the Odd Fellows, Fire Department, and National Guard. He is a Republican, and now serves the City as Deputy Tax Receiver. In 1878 he enlisted in Company D, Sixteenth Battalion N. G. S. N. Y., and was honorably discharged on January 10, 1884. In 1887 he re-enlisted, and was elected Corporal on November 17, 1887, First Sergeant on April 30, 1883, and Second Lieutenant on September 12, 1890.

EDWIN L. THOMAS was born at Caergwrle, North Wales, on April 6, 1843, and was educated in Willow Academy, Oswestry, England. He has been a resident of this city for twenty-eight years, and is a lumber merchant both in the retail and wholesale trade, being well and favorably known throughout the lumber districts of this country, as a sagacious business man. His lumber yards are on Wells Avenue and Atherton Street. Mr. Thomas is ex-President of the Grand National Curling Club of America, a member of the Board of Trade, and various Yonkers Clubs and Societies. For ten years he has been President of the Civil Service Board of this city, where he has served with honor. On August 6, 1873, he was married to Margaret, eldest daughter of the well-known late Hugh Curran. His residence is on Yonkers Avenue, where he has a most attractive home.

JOHN J. TIERNEY was born in New York City, in 1850, and received his education in the schools of Yonkers. He is a member of St. Joseph's Church, the Catholic Club and Hibernian Society, a Democrat in politics and at present is one of the Water Commissioners. In August, 1884, he married Miss Mary E. Burns, and they have four children living.

ABRAHAM H. TOMPKINS was born at New York City, January 2, 1844. For a time he attended the public schools, after which he enlisted in the army during the War of the Rebellion. He has resided in Yonkers for the past forty years, where he has been engaged in business. He is a member of the Fourth Separate Company Veterans Kitching Post, No. 60, G. A. R., and is a member of the National Staff as

Aide-de-camp. In politics he is a Republican, and has served two terms as a member of the Board of Aldermen. On April 7, 1867, he married Miss Eliza L. Murkey, to whom three children have been born. Mr. Tompkins was the organizer of Kitching Post and served as its first quartermaster. He was the youngest drum-major in the War of the Rebellion. It was through his efforts that the first drinking fountain in Yonkers was erected.

FREDERICK J. TOMPKINS was born at Harrison, N. Y., April 26, 1868. He was educated at private and public schools, after which he engaged in mercantile pursuits. He is a Republican and has been a resident of Yonkers for twenty-six years. On May 12, 1891, he married Miss Zula Smith. Mr. Tompkins is a member of St. John's Episcopal Church.

JOSEPH M. TOMPKINS was born at Newtown, L. I., February 4, 1825, and was educated at the district-school, Newtown. He has resided at Yonkers for twenty-five years, where he was for many years engaged in the manufacturing of carriages. He is a Republican, and has served as Alderman from the Second Ward of Yonkers, for two years. He also served for two years as a member of the Excise Board. On November 3, 1852, he married Miss Elizabeth F. Boyer, to whom three children were born, all of whom are now deceased. Mr. Tompkins is a member of the F. and A. M., and the Dutch Reformed Church.

ROBERT B. TOMPKINS was born at Salt Point, Dutchess County, N. Y., and was educated at the public and collegiate schools of Poughkeepsie. He has been a resident of Yonkers for thirty-one years, and is engaged in the wood and coal business. He is a Republican in politics, and a member of the First Reformed Church of this city. On January 31, 1863, he was married to Miss Annie M. Winters, to whom three children have been born.

CALEB FOWLER UNDERHILL, eldest son of Thomas Bonnett Underhill, was born July 30, 1821, in this city. He was educated in School No. 5, is a member of the Asbury Methodist Episcopal Church, and has held the office of Trustee for thirty years. He is a Republican, and was appointed Assessor in 1858, and again by Mayor Masten, and holds that office up to the present time. He was also a Trustee in School No. 5. On November 11, 1846, he married Emily Sherwood, of New Rochelle. Wilbur Sherwood Underhill, his only son, was born July 5, 1852, and was graduated from School No. 6. In January, 1876, he married Jane Odell Dusenberry. He is a communicant of St. John's Episcopal Church, Tuckahoe, where he has been Vestryman (clerk), and Organist for over twenty years. He is a Superintendent of the Hodgman Rubber Co.'s Works, at Tuckahoe, N. Y.

REUBEN WHALEN VAN PELT was born in Lamington, Somerset County, N. J., on November 7, 1825. After graduating from the University of New York, he studied law and was admitted to the Bar in New York in 1846, at the age of twenty-one years. He was one of the early Trustees of the village of Yonkers, and a Trustee of School No. 1, when that building was first erected. From 1880 to 1883 he was President of the Westchester Gas Light Company. He was also President of the Yonkers Fuel Gas Company, and in the early history of the Reformed Church was its Organist. In 1848 he married Miss Emily S. Chandler, who, with one child, survives him. Mr. Van Pelt was one of the most active and persistent men in all matters of business, never giving himself time for recreation, and it is thought his business reverses did much to hasten the sad ending of an eventful life. He died in 1885.

WILLIAM H. VEITCH was born in New York City, February 9, 1839, and received his education in the schools of that city. He has been a resident of Yonkers for twenty-seven years and is an undertaker. Mr. Veitch is a member of Nepperhan Lodge No. 737, F. and A. M., Terrace City Chapter No. 177, R. A., G. A. R. Post No. 60, and is a Republican in politics, but has never held any official position. On September 29, 1864, he married Miss Mary Eliza Codington, to whom five children have been born.

WILLIAM H. VEITCH.

Two are living, Nellie and his son Norman, who is associated with his father in business.

PHILIP VERPLANCK was born in New York City, in 1825. His father's residence was at Verplanck's Point near Peekskill on the Hudson River, where for eight generations the family have had their home. His earlier education was at the Poughkeepsie collegiate schools until, in 1842, he entered the law office of Mr. Richard L. Riker, of New York City. After two years of study he visited the West India Islands, St. Thomas and St. Croix, to settle some legal claims of the family, and in the course of these matters spent nearly a year visiting all the islands. Returning to New York, he entered the English importing house of Messrs. Sands, Fuller & Co., 59 Pine Street, as a salesman, where he remained for five years. At length the California gold fever broke out and he went to San Francisco *via* Cape Horn, and was one of the first to ascend the Sacramento River in a ship and proceeded to explore the gold placers at Coloma. A very short experience of such exposure was sufficient to undermine his health, and in search of relief he made a voyage to the Sandwich Islands and engaged in trading between those islands and San Francisco.

In 1851, he formed a partnership in San Francisco under the firm name of Verplanck & McMullin, and later as Verplanck, Wellman & Co., passing fourteen years of business life, sharing all the vicissitudes of those early times on the Pacific coast. Fortune favored him in business, but the seeds of disease sown in the mining exposure obliged him to retire from business cares in San Francisco. In hopes of recruiting he passed a year in travel, visiting Europe, Syria and the Holy Land. Returning to New York, he again entered in active business life as a member of the firm of John Verplanck & Co., 89 Wall Street, and so remained until 1883, finishing an active business life within a few blocks of the place where he began it over forty years before. The remaining years have been spent mostly in Yonkers in building and improving real estate and attending to the interests of members of the family who sought him for advice. He has always been deeply interested in the venerable parish church of St. John's, was for many years a Vestryman and Warden, and is now one of the working staff of the St. John's Hospital. He is a member of the Board of Trade, Historical Society, the Holland Society and other societies. Mr. Verplanck has recently erected an apartment house at 12 and 14 School Street, which is considered superior to any ever before erected in this city.

"THE ORIENTAL" APARTMENT HOUSE, 12 AND 14 SCHOOL STREET. PHILIP VERPLANCK, OWNER.

HENRY FERDINAND VON STORCH was descended from prominent German ancestry, who came to America in 1793, and settled in Pennsylvania. He was born in Providence, Luzern County, Pa. (now the City of Scranton), March 27, 1841, and received his education in the schools of that place. In 1861 he came to Yonkers, and engaged in the jewelry business at No. 3 South Broadway, succeeding Charles W. Starr, which business he conducted until his death, which occurred September 14, 1888. Mr. Von Storch attended St. John's Episcopal Church, to which he was a liberal contributor. In politics he was an ardent Republican. His hearty good nature and jovial disposition drew to him hosts of warm friends, and his genial face and presence were always heartily welcomed in social gatherings, of which he was usually the chosen centre, particularly among the business men of our city, where he was so long and favorably known.

Mr. Von Storch was united in marriage to Zelia S. Hobbs, January 11, 1865. Aside from his business and property interests in Yonkers, he held valuable productive mining interests in one of the richest coal deposits in Pennsylvania. Mr. Von Storch was a member of Company H, Seventeenth Regiment, National Guard State of New York, under Captain John Davis Hatch, and was mustered into the service with the thirty-days' men from Yonkers on July 8, 1863. The Company performed valiant service at Fort McHenry, Baltimore, Md.

MICHAEL WALSH was born in Ireland in 1839. He has resided at Yonkers for forty-six years, where he has been engaged in business as a builder. He is a Democrat in politics, and a member of the Board of Water Commissioners. He is a member and a Trustee of St. Joseph's Catholic Church of Yonkers. In November, 1857, he married Miss Margaret Farrell, of Yonkers. Their marriage has been blessed with fifteen children, eight of whom are living.

JOHN WARNECK was born at New Haven, Conn., March 17, 1858. After receiving a common school education, he learned the trade of a butcher. For the past five years he has resided in Yonkers. He attends the Methodist Church, and politically, is independent. He is a member of the Knights of Pythias, Red Men, and is also a member of the Board of Excise Commissioners. He has been a member of Irving Hose Company, No. 5, for the past three years, and has not missed a fire during that time.

CHARLES E. WARING was born January 15, 1826, at the town of Southeast, Putnam County, N. Y. He received a common school education, after which he entered mercantile pursuits. For the past fifty-three years he has been a resident of Yonkers, being engaged in mercantile and manufacturing pursuits. From 1856 to 1870 he was a member of the firm of John T. Waring & Co., and of the Waring Hat Manufactory Company. He is a member of St. John's Episcopal Church of Yonkers, and is a Republican in politics, but has never sought any political honors. On November 7, 1849, Mr. Waring married Miss Julia Weed, to whom four sons have been born, three of whom are living. For a term of years he was a special partner in the firm of Shethar & Nicoll, a hat commission house, doing business at 548 Broadway, New York. Mr. Waring has been President of the Citizens' National Bank, of Yonkers, since January 1, 1888, which position he still holds.

JARVIS A. WARING was born at Southeast, Putnam County, N. Y., and was, for thirty-five years, a resident of Yonkers, where for many years he was engaged in mercantile business. He was a member of the Reformed Church of Yonkers. On December 29, 1834, he married Miss Nancy Odell Boyce, to whom eight children—seven daughters and one son—were born. He died at Yonkers, October 12, 1872.

WILLIAM C. WARING was born at Southeast, Putnam County, N. Y., September 11, 1808, and was educated in the public schools of that town. He was a resident of this city for fifty-two years and was the first to introduce the manufacture of felt hats in this city. For several years he was Senior Warden of St. John's Episcopal Church, and afterward held the same office in St. Paul's Episcopal Church. He was a Republican, and at one time a trustee of the village of Yonkers. His first marriage took place on December 31, 1832, to Miss Susan E. Baldwin, and his second marriage December, 1857, to Miss Sarah E. Foster. In 1883 he removed to Montclair, Fla., where he died February 15, 1886, and was there buried.

BENJAMIN SECOR WASHBURN was born at Mount Pleasant, N. Y., August 20, 1817, and was educated in the public schools. He has been a resident of this city for thirty-four years, and is engaged in the hardware and house-furnishing business. He built Washburn Hall, now known as Warburton Hall. Mr. Washburn is a member of the First Methodist Episcopal Church, and has been one of its Trustees for thirty-four years. He is a Republican in politics, but never held any official position. On October 4, 1844, he married Miss Harriet Palmer, to whom three children have been born.

JAMES H. WELLER was born at Montgomery, Orange County, N. Y., October 10, 1835. He was the eldest of three brothers, the other two being Alanson Y., of the firm of Schoonmaker & Weller, Newburgh, N. Y., and Joseph H., of the firm of Tefft, Weller & Co., of New York City. They all became successful dry-goods merchants.

The subject of this sketch, when but seventeen years of age, became an apprentice with the old dry-goods firm of Scott & Clark, New York City, with whom he remained for eight years, after which he engaged with Demarest & Middleton (leather and findings), of New York City. While with this firm, he became associated with Thomas R. Miller, with whom he embarked in the leather and shoe findings business, under the firm name of Weller & Miller, at 16 Spruce Street, New York City. After a pleasant and successful business career of fifteen years, the firm was dissolved in 1877, by mutual consent. After living in retirement one year, Mr. Weller established the present extensive dry-goods, carpet and furniture house of Weller & Welsh at Yonkers, and it is now the leading establishment of its kind in the city.

On May 21, 1867, Mr. Weller married Miss Adelaide W., daughter of the late Thomas Radford, of Yonkers. Eight children were born to them, five of whom are now living. In the spring of 1892, Mr. Weller received the Republican nomination for Mayor of Yonkers. After a hotly contested election (there being four candidates in the field), he was elected by a plurality of 226. During his term of office he made earnest and honest attempts to reduce the evils of the liquor traffic by the appointment of an Excise Board that would materially reduce the number of drinking places. In his efforts he was opposed by the Aldermen, yet he succeeded in improving the character of the Excise Board, increasing the amount of the license fees, and in holding the demoralizing traffic in check. The most important benefit conferred upon the city under Mayor Weller's administration was the suppression of the threatening nuisances along the Nepperhan River. These nuisances had been indicted by the Grand Jury, and most emphatically condemned by the Yonkers and State Boards of Health; but they continued to offend the senses and imperil human life. At length, firmly supported by the Board of Health, Mayor Weller signed an order for the removal of the dams, and they were summarily removed. The stream, once so offensive, now ripples through the city, sparkling and bright—an ornament rather than a nuisance.

During his administration, also, many entirely new and important improvements were accomplished, among them being the introduction of granite block and sheet asphalt paving for the important thoroughfares of the city, the widening of the arch of the old Croton Aqueduct over Nepperhan Avenue, and the establishing of a hospital for contagious diseases, and a crematory for the burning of garbage and dead animals. Many new streets were also laid out and extended, electric sub-ways put down, sewers constructed, and water and fire systems enlarged. On his retiring from office, he left a public record which, for progressive action and benefit conferred on the city, has been unsurpassed by any of his predecessors.

WILLIAM WELSH, of the firm of Weller & Welsh, was born at New Germantown, N. J., November 20, 1838. When eighteen years of age he left his father's farm and went to New York City, where he engaged as clerk in the retail dry-goods business. When the War of the Rebellion broke out, he volunteered his services, and in May, 1861, joined the Ninth N. Y. S. M., afterwards known as the Eighty-third N. Y. S. V., and went to the front. After serving eighteen months in that regiment as private and non-commissioned officer, he was transferred, by reason of promotion as Second Lieutenant, to Company D, Sixty-eighth N. Y. S. V., and was mustered out with the regiment December, 1864, as Captain, having served in the army three years and seven months, during which time he was in fifteen engagements with his regiment. Among the most notable battles were those of Cedar Mountain, Chantilly, South Mountain, Antietam, Fredericksburg, Chancellorsville, and Gettysburg. After the war he returned to New York City, and re-entered the retail dry-goods business. In 1878 the firm of Weller & Welsh was formed. Mr. Welsh moved to Yonkers, where his partner, Mr. Weller, lived, and the firm started in the dry-goods business on the same spot where their new building now stands.

JOHN WHEELER was born at Fordham, N. Y., March 27, 1819. He had been a resident of Yonkers for forty-three years. He acquired a competence mostly through his investments in real estate, which were many and profitable. He built what is known as the Wheeler Block on North Broadway. He was a man of vigorous constitution, temperate habits, a wise counselor and a warm friend. Many prominent business men of Yonkers owe, in no small degree, their success to his active, practical interest and monetary assistance in their affairs during the days of their early struggles. And as a large-hearted, sympathetic and liberal dispenser of good things to the needy poor he was particularly active, although always in such an unostentatious way as to never let his left hand know what his right hand did in this direction. So modest was he in this respect that most of his charities were dispensed through a personal friend, who alone knows their extent, and the blessings that followed them.

JOHN WHEELER.

Mr. Wheeler was a Democrat of the old school. Although frequently besought, he almost invariably declined public office, the one exception being when he served as a Trustee, in 1861-62, of the then village of Yonkers. March 22, 1867, the date of the organization of the People's Savings Bank of Yonkers, ne was elected one of its Trustees, where he served up to the time of his death, being from May 14, 1867, a member of its Finance Committee, and for most of the time Chairman of said Committee. He served his time as a member of the old Volunteer Fire Department of New York City, and was afterward a member of Lady Washington Engine Company of Yonkers. Mr. Wheeler died at his residence, this city, December 31, 1892, in his seventy-fourth year.

LEWIS H. WIGGINS was born in Greenport, L. I. When he was ten years of age his family removed to Leroy, N. Y., where he resided until 1855, when he came to this city. In 1861 he removed to Peekskill and there started in business, returning to Yonkers in 1864, and in 1865 again starting in business, dealing in hardware, stoves, house furnishing goods, etc. He is a member of the First Reformed Church. On November 6, 1862, he was married to Mary L. Archibald, and they have one son, William A., who is associated with his father in business.

FREDERICK H. WOODRUFF was born at Bristol, England, in 1844. In the year 1848, his parents with their family, consisting of eight children, came to this country. Six of these are now residents of this city. Mr. Woodruff has resided in Yonkers for over forty years. He received his education in the private schools, after which he learned the trade of hatter. On April 27, 1871, he joined the Yonkers Police Department as Patrolman; on August 18, 1873, he was promoted to Roundsman, and on May 10, 1894, made Sergeant, a position he still retains. Prior to becoming a policeman, Mr. Woodruff was for seven years an active fireman in the Fire Department of Yonkers, and was Foreman of Hope Hook and Ladder Company. He is a member of the Veteran Fireman's Association, is a staunch Republican and attends the Methodist Church. In 1869, he married Miss Mary A., daughter of the late well-known D. McGrath of this city. Mr. Woodruff has filled a number of responsible positions. He is a Veteran of the late war, and served in the Fifteenth Regiment New York Infantry, during the Rebellion, being honorably discharged at the expiration of service.

ELIJAH M. YERKS was born in New York City, November 1, 1864, and was educated at the public schools of this city. He is a member of the firm of Yerks & Co., manufacturers and dealers in doors, sashes, mouldings, etc. He is a member of the First Methodist Episcopal Church and for a number of years was the Superintendent of the Sunday-school, also a member of Palisade Lodge No. 571, I. O. O. F., Rising Star No. 450, F. and A. M., Terrace City Chapter No. 177, R. A. M., Young Men's Republican Club, Yonkers Historical and Library Association, and the Board of Supervisors of Westchester County.

CHAPTER XXII.

YONKERS CEMETERIES.

THE locations of the Indian burial grounds (called by the Algonquins *Tawasenthas*, "places of many dead"), within the boundaries of the present Yonkers, are designated in Chapter II. of this volume. In the pioneer days, the settlers and their descendants of the earlier generations buried their dead in family burial grounds, within the boundaries of their respective farms. Families of prominence used gravestones. When stones for marking graves came into general use, granites and marbles were not selected, but stones less enduring.

The plow has obliterated the traces of most of the farm and neighborhood burial places. Some traces of what was probably the burial place of the earliest generations of the Betts and Tippetts family are yet discernible west of the railroad track, and north of the old mills and the pond at Van Cortlandt. Over many a plot in Yonkers the citizen of to-day walks, unconscious that he is treading where

"Each in his narrow cell, forever laid,
The rude forefathers of the hamlet sleep."

On Vault Hill, northeast of the Van Cortlandt Mansion, is the vault where the Van Cortlandts laid their dead. Frederick Philipse, who died in 1702, lies buried in the Sleepy Hollow churchyard. It is said that the Philipses buried their negroes on what was then a high bank, east of the present Hudson River Railroad Station. Near the foot of the present Locust Street was a cove into which sometimes the bodies of drowned persons were washed by the tide. These, and other bodies, were buried at that point. One of the oldest burial grounds in Yonkers was near the corner of the Saw Mill Valley and Tuckahoe roads. Some years ago, in order to make way for projected improvements, the bones and the quaint old headstones were removed to the northeast corner of the St. John's Cemetery.

There are two old cemeteries at Tuckahoe—one in the Methodist and the other in the Episcopal churchyards. The oldest stone in the Methodist yard is inscribed with the date 1800. The people of the country around Tuckahoe bury their dead in that burial yard. It is nearly full of graves. The Sherwoods and many other prominent families have brought their dead to it. The Episcopal Church burial ground also contains many graves. The founders of the church and many other families have laid their dead there.

St. John's Church, South Broadway, received, by bequest of Frederick Philipse, lands on the Saw Mill River Road. A small portion of those lands became a burial ground in the eighteenth century. Bolton says that the first interment in St. John's, the oldest public cemetery in Yonkers, was in 1783. It is recorded that a few years ago there was in this cemetery a tombstone upon which had been inscribed the date 1791. The inscription was then legible, and may be to-day. St. Mary's (R. C.) Cemetery was founded in 1855, in the valley of the Sprain; Oakland in 1882, south of and adjoining St. John's; St. Joseph's (R. C.) in 1877, in the Saw Mill River valley.

The names of members of a large proportion of the families to which reference has been made in the pages of this volume are inscribed on the marbles and granites of one or more of these cemeteries. Laborers, farmers, country store-keepers, boatmen, town and village and city officials, merchants, bankers, judges, clergymen, physicians, lawyers, teachers, authors, founders of many of the large industries of the city, rich and poor, learned and unlearned, high-born and low-born, are among the thousands who lie underneath the sod, waiting the sound of the resurrection trumpet, the opening wide of their tomb-doors, and the judgment day. Sweet little children are there, who were committed, dust to dust, earth to earth, ashes to ashes, the while their bereaved mothers and others stood by, "their eyes moist with the rain of grief." And there, too, are young men, who fell in the strength of their years, and lovely maidens, cut off while yet life for them was full of untasted joys.

> "So perish forms, as fair as those,
> Whose cheeks now living blush the rose,
> Their glory turned to dust."

Near their mounds are the graves of those, to whom, while they were in the vigor of mature manhood, death, unannounced, came with "foot of velvet and hand of steel." The aged are there also, from whose trembling hands, after a long pilgrimage, fell the pilgrim's staff.

It has been well observed that men gain immortality, not so much by what others do for them, as by what they do for others. Among the uncounted multitudes who sleep in St. John's, Oakland, St. Mary's and St. Joseph's Cemeteries, are those who rendered this and all coming generations large service by periling their lives for the Republic. Year after year on Decoration Days, their mounds are gratefully marked with the flag they loved, and embroidered with flowers. The interesting volume, entitled "Yonkers in the Rebellion," thus refers to the bivouac of the dead heroes:

"Many of our brave defenders have crossed the great river never to return. Their memories are dear to us, and we thus silently, with dewy eye and bowed head, tenderly commit their names to our children and children's children to remotest generations, for their reverence and esteem. In the cemeteries of our city lie all that is left of our heroes. Loving hearts and willing hands may decorate their graves." None cherish * their memories more than their comrades, who shared their sacrifices, and were exposed to the same perils on land and on sea.

"OUR HEROES' LAST SLEEP."

NAMES OF SOLDIERS BURIED IN ST. JOHN'S, OAKLAND, ST. MARY'S, AND ST. JOSEPH'S CEMETERIES. Joseph Ainsworth, Charles E. Archer, Frederick E. Barnes, James E. Beasley, Benjamin Bowes, Patrick Burns, John Barklay, Nicholas Burns, Michael Bennett, Charles A. Brown, William C. Blackett, Jacob Brill, John Bashford, James Bashford, William J. Bigelow, Colonel Bills (U. S. Army), Elijah Bowler, James Brazier, Sr., James Brazil, Cornelius Broderick, James W. Brown, James Bromley, George Cook, John J. Cunningham, Eugene Cronin, William Cahill, John J. Cahill, Thomas Cahill, William Connell, Patrick Cary, Thomas Cahill, Dennis Clancey, Patrick Connelly, Anthony Conlin, Bartholomew Conlin, Bernard Carroll, Timothy Cronin, William T. Cummings, James Cadis, Henry B. Cleveland, Joseph Cain, William Cannon, James Cannon, Patrick Cronin, Eugene Cronin, Stephen F. Cropsey, William Cope, Howard Carroll, William Cairns, Joseph Costello, Bernard Donahue, John Durney, Thomas J. Dillon, Andrew L. Donnelly, Henry V. De Witt, Charles A. Downes, A. S. Dwight, William H. Danks, William H. Deboise, James F. Duff, Scott Dean, Harold Doyle, William Dromley, Delmar Duff, Patrick Duffy, James B. Everest, Thomas Ewing, Frederick J. Easton, John Foley, John Fitzgerald, Henry B. Ferguson, Charles W. Foster, Matthew Faulds, John Fenton, Frederick Friend (war of 1812), James H. Green, Patrick H. Greely, Thomas Geary, Martin Geary, Charles Grimshaw, Samuel Granger, George J. Greiner, John R. Gilleo, Joseph Glosque, James Granger, John Grevert, Theodore Gaul, John Gracy, —— Guilford, William Hayes, John Haggerty, James Hanlon, Hugh Hurst, Joseph Humbert, Chauncey Hulse, William Hamilton, Eli Hampson, James Hickton, David M. Howell, Thomas Hill, Thomas M. Haslam, John Hamilton, A. A. Hendrick, Thomas Hickey, Francis Holler, Job Hargraves, Isaac S. Hadden, George Humphreys, Henry Holt, John Hallihan, Eli Hampson, Michael Kane, Michael Kane, Timothy Kelly, John Kelly, Edward Keenan, William Kiley, Abram Kniffen, Patrick Kelly, William Knipe, James Keeler, Edwin R. Keyes, Louis Kunzmuller, Bernard Koch, James Kernan, James Kelly, Thomas Kearnes, John Kniffen, Terrence Lynch, Michael Locke, Nathan Lameraux, Michael Larkin, Robert Lee, Jacob Lynt, Charles Lawrence, Frederick Lynt, Samuel H. Lynt, John H. Lawrence, William J. Murphy, Thomas Mitchell, John Moran, John Mernin, James Maher, James Martin, Jacob Mehlman, Patrick H. Mernin, James Mernin,

---

* About 1888, Mr. George R. Hendrickson was appointed by the Memorial Committee, of the G. A. R., of Yonkers, Chairman of a Committee to ascertain the names of soldiers and sailors buried in Yonkers. For a time James Sheridan was associated with him. He was succeeded by Edward Mitchell, who has served as Secretary of the Committee. Mr. Hendrickson and his associates have for eight years patiently sought information from all quarters, until their roll is nearly complete. It records the name, company, regiment, rank and date of death of each soldier and sailor buried in these cemeteries. Fifty-five of the buried soldiers and sailors belonged to Kitching Post, and four to Fremont Post. Generals, Colonels, and other officers, and privates are enrolled. The author acknowledges the kindness of this Committee in placing their books at his disposal.

Bernard Mulvey, William Murray, Garrett G. Majory, Francis Morgan, Frank A. Morgan, James Murphy, Herman Menzer, Edmund Y. Morris, William H. Myers, Arthur Morris, Thomas F. Morris, Abram B. Mead, Timothy Murphy, John McNamara, Thomas McMinn, John McCoy, James McVicar, William McPherson, John McGraw, Henry Morgan, ―――― McLaughlin, Michael Norris, Clark Nodine, Benjamin C. Nodine, Henry Nessler, W. H. Nodine, Charles B. Nebe, George Nolan, George Nodine, Patrick O'Donnell, Cornelius O'Donnell, Thomas O'Donnell, Charles O'Neil, Henry O'Hara, William S. Oakley, James O'Rourke, Thomas L. Pettit, William Pope, John Pentreath, Thomas R. Price, Prince W. Paddock (war of 1812), Wilder D. Percival, Charles H. Pease, Hollis H. Parse, Charles H. Pollock, Robert C. Perry, Christian Past, Robert A. Pollock, James Price, George Paddock, John J. Quigley, Conrad Roth, George S. Rockwell, Gilbert Riordan, William Right, Wilder Ricever, George Robinson, James A. Reynolds, Thomas Reynolds, John Stephens, Philip Shannon, Edward Shannon, Bernard Seerey, William Seerey, Ernest Smith, O. L. Shepherd, George Stephens, Obadiah Sickley, Jacob Stilling, John M. Still, John W. Skinner, James M. Sickly, John Smith, Abram Shultz, Louis Sprenger, Samuel M. Swift, Edward Starr, Samuel L. Smith, Edward Skelly, George Smith, ―――― Schiling, James Sheridan, Owen Turner, Samuel C. Titus, George P. Trask, Roger Tansey, Peter Tracey, Matthew Tansey, Stephen L. Van Wart, William Van Wagener, Alfred Van Norden, W. C. Wilson, John Wallace, Richard Walsh, James Welsh, Philip Wonderlie, Peter Whelan, Christian Wyeker, Philip Wunderle, John Williams, Michael Wing, Charles Willoughby, Christian Wickel, William Wright, Samuel J. Walton, Caleb T. Wolhiser, William Welsh, William Waldeck, Edwin A. Williams, Patrick Whalan, William W. Yerks, George T. Yerks.

DIED IN YONKERS, BURIED ELSEWHERE. Jacob Gilleo, Henry H. Taylor, Evert H. Wandell.

The historian's latitude for moralizing is limited, but as in meditative mood he walks along the winding footpaths and driveways of the cemeteries, where sleep so many thousands of those who once lived in the town and city whose history he has endeavored to record, he remembers that multitudes whose forms are underneath these mounds once faithfully wrought for the highest welfare of Yonkers, but much as they loved their earthly land and city, they desired a better country, that is, a heavenly, wherefore God is not ashamed to be called their God, for He hath prepared for them a city With eye of faith, from which "trickled the tear of penitence," they saw that city, and rejoiced. Their desire for a heavenly country, more intense than all other desires, was the fruit of no mere belief about Christ, which never yet shaped a human heart, but the fruit of a spirit-given, saving faith in Him.

The solid hills upon which fair Yonkers is enthroned shall melt with fervent heat, and the overarching heavens be rolled together as a scroll, but naught shall ever disturb the gem-adorned foundations of their celestial city, whose streets are pure gold. Thither their Master ascended to prepare mansions for them. Stable those foundations and walls shall stand,

"When the stars are old, and the sun is cold,
And the leaves of the judgment book unfold."

A BIBLIOGRAPHY OF YONKERS

The following bibliography has been reprinted from "A Check List of Books, Maps, Pictures & Other Printed Matter relating to the Counties of Westchester and Bronx," by Otto Hufeland, privately printed in 1929.

The boldface letters to the right indicate location of copies. The letter "H" indicates that the item was in the author's private collection, since then incorporated into the Library of the Huguenot Association of New Rochelle, New York. A supplement to this bibliography will be found on pages 463-464.

2232. Allison, C. E. History of Yonkers from the Earliest Time to the Present, by C. E. Allison. **H**
4to, 460 pp., illust. New York, n.d. (1896).

2233. Allison, C. E. In Memoriam Charles Elmer Allison, D.D., Pastor of Dayspring Presbyterian Church, Yonkers, N. Y. Prepared by Rev. James Freeman. **H**
8vo, 31 pp., port. Yonkers, N. Y., n.d. (1908).

2234. Armitage, Rev. Thos. Record of the Services at the Dedication of the Bust and Tablet Erected in the Fifth Avenue Baptist Church of New York in memory of Thomas Armitage, D.D., LL.D., October 15, 1899. **H**
4to, 91 pp., port and plate. New York, n.d.
Lived in Yonkers at time of his death.

2235. Asbury, Rev. Francis—Portrait, Bishop of the Methodist Episcopal Church in the United States. Portrait engraved by B. Tanner from painting by J. Paradise, Philadelphia, 1814. Also reprint from old plate in 1876. **H**
11 in. x 14 in.
Asbury lived for some time at (old) Tuckahoe in Yonkers.

2236. Assessments. The appeal of Jacob Read, Supervisor, from the Equalization of Assessments by the Board of Supervisors of Westchester County for the year 1876. **H**
8vo, 49 pp. Gazette Steam Printing Office, Yonkers, 1877.

2237. Atkins, T. A. Adrien Van Der Donck. An Address before the Westchester County Historical Society, November 22, 1888. **H**
8vo, 20 pp. The Statesman Print, Yonkers, N. Y., 1888.

2238. Atkins, T. A. The Manor of Philipsburg. A Paper read before the New York Historical Society, June 5, 1894. **H**
8vo, 23 pp. Yonkers, 1894.

2239. Atkins, T. A. Indian Wars and the Uprising of 1655—Yonkers Depopulated. A Paper read before the Yonkers Historical and Literary Association, March 18, 1892. **H**
8vo, 14 pp. n.p., n.d. (1892).

2240. Atkins and Oliver. Yonkers in the Rebellion of 1861-1865. Including a History of the Erection of the Monument to Honor the Men of Yonkers who fought to save the Union, by Thomas Astley Atkins and John Wise Oliver. **H**
8vo, 263 pp., illust. Yonkers, 1892.

2241. Atlas. Property Atlas of Yonkers including portion of the 24th Ward of New York City, from surveys by Thos. C. Cornell and Wm. H. Baldwin. **H**
Folio, 30 pp. New York, 1876.

2242. Atlas of the City of Yonkers, New York, from actual Surveys and Records by Roger Pidgeon, Civil Engineer. **H**
Folio, 25 maps. Published by E. Robinson, New York, 1889.
Another edition, 1896.

2243. Atlas of the City of Yonkers, compiled by E. Kiser.
Folio, 25 maps. Philadelphia, 1907.

2244. Baird, Rev. Robt. The Life of the Rev. Robert Baird, D.D., by his son Henry M. Baird. **H**
12mo, 347 pp., port. New York, 1866.
Lived in Yonkers, 1849-1863.

2245. The Bald Eagle Club of Amateur Fishermen.
8vo, 35 pp. Yonkers, 1865.

2246. Bangs, John K. Three Weeks in Politics. **H**
32mo, 83 pp. New York, 1894.
When Bangs was a candidate for mayor of Yonkers.

2247. Bangs, J. K. The Booming of Acre Hill. Also contains "The Mayor's Lamps" and the "Balance of Power." **H**
16mo, 266 pp., illust. New York, 1900.
All Yonkers subjects.

2248. Baptists. Hudson River (Baptist) Association, South. Fourth Anniversary, held in the Meeting House of Mount Olivet Baptist Church, Yonkers, N. Y., June 20 and 21, 1854. **H**
8vo, 35 pp. New York, 1854.
Another in 1861 and perhaps others.

2249. Baptist Church. History of the erection and dedication of the Warburton Avenue Baptist Church. **H**
8vo, 55 pp., plate. New York, 1869.

2250. Baptist Church. History of the Baptist Church of the Redeemer, Yonkers, N. Y., by Warren G. Hulbert. **H**
12mo, 48 pp., illust. n.p. (Yonkers), 1913.

2251. Bartlett, William H. C. Memoir of, 1804-1893, by Edward Holden. **H**
Biographical Memoirs of National Academy of Sciences, 1911, pp. 173-193.
8vo, 21 pp. Washington, D. C., 1911.
Lived in Yonkers.

2252. Bell, E. Y. Is the Elective System a Failure? Argument of E. Y. Bell in Reply to the Address of M. H. Ellis, entitled "Municipal Government" or should the subordinate officers of the City be appointed or elected. Yonkers, March 10, 1875. **H**
8vo, 21 pp. n.p., n.d.

Bellows, Rev. H. W. See Stowell.

2253. Brewer, Rev. D. R. The Rector's offering—Selections from Sermons. **H**
16mo, 79 pp. New York, 1860.
In aid of St. Paul's Free church, Yonkers, N. Y.

2254. Burton, Frederick R. Hiawatha, a Dramatic Cantata. Book of the Words with analytical notes on the music, Portrait of the Composer, names of Performers, etc. Performance, April 28th and 29th, 1898, by the Yonkers Choral Society.
12mo, 48 pp. New York, n.d.
Composer directed the Society.

2255. Burton, Frederick R. The Legend of Sleepy Hollow, Cantata for Mixed Chorus, Soprano and Bass, Soloists and Orchestra. Words and Music by F. R. Burton.
4to, 79 pp. Yonkers, 1900.

2256. **Butler, Harriet Allen.** In Memoriam. Resolutions adopted at a meeting of the Fortnightly Club for the Study of Anthropology, held January 16, 1914, and memorial addresses. **H**
8vo, 30 pp., port. Yonkers, 1914.
Lived in Yonkers from 1865 to 1914.

2257. **Butler, William Allen.** Memorial of, by George C. Holt. Read before the Association of the Bar of the City of New York, March 10, 1903. **H**
8vo, 33 pp., port. n.p., n.d. (N. Y., 1903).
Lived in Yonkers for many years.

2258. **Butler, Wm. A.** A Retrospect of Forty Years, 1825–65. Edited by Harriet A. Butler. **H**
8vo, 442 pp., illust. New York, 1911.
Lived in Yonkers for many years.

2259. **Butler, Mrs. Wm. Allen.** In Memoriam, Mary Russell Butler, November 30, 1828–February 15, 1919. **H**
8vo, 27 pp., port. New York, 1920.

2260. **Campbell, Rev. I.** History of the Church of the Mediator, Kingsbridge, N. Y. **H**
8vo, 92 pp. New York, 1910.

2261. **Catholic Church.** The Beginnings of the Roman Catholic Church in Yonkers, by Thomas C. Cornell.
8vo, 24 pp. Yonkers "Gazette" Press, Yonkers, 1883.

2262. The **Catholic Church** in Yonkers on the Hudson, by Marion Brunowe.
American Catholic Historical Society, Vol 7, pp. 80-93.
8vo, 14 pp. Philadelphia, 1896.

2263. **Charter of the Village.** Passed April 12, 1855. Renacted with amendments, April, 1857. Amended, 1858, 1860, 1865 and 1866. **H**
8vo, 76 pp. New York, 1868.

2264. **Charter of the City of Yonkers.** Passed, June 1, 1872—reenacted with amendments, February 28, 1873. **H**
8vo, 158 pp. New York, 1873.

2265. **Charter of the City of Yonkers.** **H**
8vo, 54 pp. Albany, 1881.

2265a. **Charter of the City of Yonkers.** **N.Y.P.L.**
8vo, 93 pp. Yonkers, 1897.

2266. **City Reports.** 1880–81, 1881–2, 1882–3. **H**
And others earlier and later.

2267. **Clason vs. Shotwell in Error.** Copy of record and assignment of Errors. **H**
8vo, 59 pp. Albany, 1814.
Ejectment from a farm in Yonkers.

2268. **Cochrane, William Francis.** In Memoriam. **H**
8vo, 80 pp., port. n.p., 1902.
Privately printed.

2269. **Cole, Rev. David.** Yonkers—Historical Address, 25th Anniversary of Reformed Church on the Twenty-third of April, 1868. **H**
8vo, 109 pp., 3 maps and plates. New York, 1868.

2270. **Cole, Rev. D.** A Thanksgiving Sermon. Our American Republic.—The Child of Special Providence. Delivered at a Union Meeting in the Reformed Church, November 30, 1876. **H**
8vo, 52 pp. Yonkers, 1876.

2271. **Cole, Rev. D.** Bi-centennial oration. Two hundred Years of Yonkers. **H**
Folio, 2 pp. Yonkers, 1882.
Extra issue of the Yonkers "Statesman," October 18, 1882, also in Yonkers "Gazette," October 28, November 4 and 11, 1882.

2272. **Cole, Rev. David.** Historical Sermon Commemorative of the Fortieth Anniversary of the Reformed Church, April 22nd, 1883. **H**
8vo, 12 pp. Yonkers "Gazette" Print, Yonkers, 1883.

2273. **Cole, Rev. D.** Reformed Church of Yonkers. Public Exercises at the Twenty-fifth Anniversary of Rev. Dr. Cole's Pastorate, December 11, 1890. **H**
8vo, 29 pp., port. n.p., n.d.

2274. **Collins, Rev. Charles Terry.** In Memoriam. **H**
8vo, 50 pp. n.p., n.d. (1884).
Funeral services at Yonkers, December 25, 1883.

2275. **Couzens, M. K.** Index of Grantees of Lands Sold by the Commissioners of Forfeitures of the Southern District of the State of New York, situate in the Manor of Philipsburg, Westchester County, N. Y. **H**
12mo, 54 pp. n.p., 1880.

2276. **(Cozzens, Frederick S.)** The Sparrowgrass Papers: or Living in the Country (Yonkers). **H**
12mo, 328 pp., front. New York, 1856.

2277. **Cummings.** The President's Hymn—Give thanks all ye People, as sung by the Choir of Hope Church, Yonkers, N. Y. Words by Rev. Dr. William A. Muhlenberg. Music by Edward S. Cummings. **H**
Music folio, 6 pp. Printed for the Author, New York, n.d. (1864).

2278. **Dawson, Henry B.** The (Yonkers) "Gazette" Series.
4 vols., 8vo. 26 copies printed. Yonkers, 1866. **H**

Vol. I. Papers concerning the Capture and Detention of Major John André. **H**
8vo, 247 pp. Yonkers, N. Y., 1866.

2279. Vol. II. Papers concerning the Town and Village of Yonkers, Westchester County. A Fragment. **H**
8vo, 45 pp. Yonkers, N. Y., 1866.

2280. Vol. III. Papers concerning the Boundary between the States of New York and New Jersey. Written by Several Hands. **H**
8vo, 293 pp. Yonkers, N. Y., 1866.

2281. Vol. IV. Rambles in Westchester County, New York. A Fragment. **H**
8vo, 43 pp. Yonkers, N. Y., 1866.
All originally appeared in the Yonkers "Gazette" in 1865.

2282. **Directory.** Smith's Yonkers Directory for 1859–60, with an Appendix containing a Brief History of the Town and Village during the past year, together with advertisements of the most reliable tradesmen in the Village. **H**
12mo, 72 pp., map. Yonkers "Herald," Yonkers, 1859.
The second year.

2283. **Directory.** Rigby and Brady's Yonkers City Directory for the Year ending, May 1st, 1882. **N. Y. Hist. Soc.**
8vo. Yonkers, N. Y., 1881.

2284. **Directory.** Boyd's Yonkers City Directory. **N.Y.P.L.**
8vo. New York and Yonkers, v.y.
1885–6 to 1891–2, and perhaps others.

2285. **Directory.** Thompson and Fowler's Directory for the City of Yonkers. **N.Y.P.L.**
8vo. Newburgh and Yonkers, v.y.
1885 to 1888 and perhaps later.

2286. **Directory.** Thompson and Breed's Sixth Annual Directory of Yonkers for the Year, May 1st, 1890 to May 1st, 1891.
8vo. Newburgh, v.y.

2287. **Directory.** Turner's Directory of the City of Yonkers. **N.Y.P.L.**
8vo. Yonkers, v.y.
Vol. 1, 1892-3. Vol. 19, 1910, and perhaps later.

2288. **Directory.** Richmond's Annual Directory. **N.Y.P.L.**
8vo. Yonkers, v.y.
Begins 1900 to 1916 and probably later.

2289. **Donck, Van Der.** Description of the New Netherlands, translated from the original Dutch by Hon. Jeremiah Johnson. **H**
Collections of the New York Historical Society. Second series, Vol. 1.
8vo, map, pp. 125-242. New York, 1841.

2290. **Donck, Adrian Van der.** Vertoogh van Niew Nederlandt Wegens de Ghelegenheydt, Vruchtbarheydt, en Soberen Staet deszelfs. **N.Y.P.L.**
4to, 49 pp. In 's Graven Haage, 1650.
Translated by H. C. Murphy, New York, 1854.
Also by Dr. E. B. O'Callaghan.

2291. **Donck, Vander.** Beschryvinge van Nieuw-Nederlandt. Adrien Vander Donck. **N. Y. Hist. Soc.**
Small 4to, 100 + 4 pp. Aemsteldam, 1656.
Map with picture of New Amsterdam.

See Vander Donck, Adriaen, under Westchester County Historical Society.

2292. **Donck, Adrian Vander.** Address on, before the New York State Bar Association, by Alfred L. Becker.
1904.

2293. **Edsall, Thomas H.** History of the Kings-Bridge, now part of the 24th Ward, New York City.
8vo, 102 pp., map. New York, 1887.
Privately printed.

2294. **Education.** Second School District. By Laws of the Board of Education—together with the General Act Establishing Union Free Schools. **H**
8vo, 20 pp. Yonkers "Herald" Job Printing Office, Yonkers, 1858.

2295. **Education.** District No. 6. Manual of the Board of Education. **H**
8vo, 56 pp. New York, 1866.

2296. **Education.** Second School District—Reports of the Board of Education. **H**
October 9, 1877, Yonkers, 1878.

2297. Same. **H**
October 8, 1878, Yonkers, 1878.

2298. Same. **H**
October 14, 1879, Yonkers, 1880.

2299. Same. **H**
8vo.
October 12, 1880, Yonkers, 1881. and others.

2300. **Education.** District No. 6. Report of the Board of Education to the Annual Meeting of 1878. **H**
8vo, 22 pp. Yonkers, 1878.
And others.

2301. **Education.** Reports of the Board of Education in the City of Yonkers.
1881 to date.

2302. **Fire Department.** Reports.

2303. **Fourth of July.** Some Account of the Celebration of the Fourth of July, 1857, by the Citizens of Yonkers and Glenwood. Arranged by the Author. **H**
12mo, 41 pp., illust. New York, 1857.

2304. **Fox, Alfred.** Washington and other Pieces from the Yonkers "Herald." **H**
Narrow, 8vo, 21 pp. n.p., 1924.
Contains a number of memorial poems on Yonkers men.

2305. **(Getty, R. P.)** Chronicles of Yonkers. (In rhyme.) **H**
8vo, 23 pp. Yonkers, 1864.
A Waif privately printed for the Benefit of the United State's Sanitary Commission.

2306. **Glenn Park.** Map and Description with drawing of the Botanical Garden. **H**
12mo, 6 pp., map. New York, 1854.

2307. **Glenn Park.** Bemerkungen zu dem Entwurf des Botanischen Gartens zu Glenn Park von W. Benque. **H**
12mo, 12 pp. New York, 1854.

2308. **Glenn Park.** Remarks on the Drawing of the Botanical Garden at Glenn Park by W. Benque. **H**
12mo, 10 pp., plate. New York, 1854.

2309. **Glenn, T. A.** The Manor of Philipborough. **H**
8vo, 32 pp. Philadelphia, 1900.
In Some Colonial Mansions, 2nd series, pp. 245-276.

2310. **"Graphic, The Daily."** November 12, 1878. Views in Woodlawn Cemetery. **H**
Folio. New York, 1878.

2311. **"Graphic, The Daily."** Picturesque Views on the Hudson River. I–The City of Yonkers, February 28, 1877. **H**
Folio. New York, 1877.

2312. **Hall, E. H.** Philipse Manor Hall. The site, the Building and its Occupants by Edward Hagaman Hall. **H**
12mo, 255 pp., illust. New York, 1912.

2313. **Hall, Ed. H.** The Manor of Philipsborough. Address written for the New York Branch of the Order of Colonial Lords of Manors in America. **N.Y.P.L.**
8vo, 52 pp., illust. Baltimore, 1920.

2314. **Havemeyer, John C.** The needs of the Church from a Layman's Standpoint. **H**
12mo, 16 pp. n.p., n.d. (1900).
An address delivered at Yonkers, October, 3, 1900.

2315. **Havemeyer, John C.** Life, Letters and Addresses. **H**
12mo, 372 pp. New York, n.d. (1914).
Lived long in Yonkers.

2316. **Hawley, David.** An address upon the Library, made at the Dedication of the Yonkers High School and Library Building, November 8, 1910.
16 mo, 10 pp. Yonkers, 1890.

2317. **(Holden, J. G. P.)** "A Happy New Year." An Offering to the Owls from Nonpareil Quddrat, P. X. D., January 1, 1867. **H**
8vo, 24 pp. Yonkers, 1867.
Printed at the office of the "Gazette" for J. G. P. Holden exclusively for private circulation.

2318. **Holls, Frederick Wm.** In Memoriam. **H**
8vo, 74 pp., port. n.p., 1904.
Privately printed.
Lived and died in Yonkers.

2319. **Hulbert, Rev. V. M.** Farewell Discourse delivered in the Reformed Dutch Church of Yonkers, April 30, 1848. **H**
8vo, 16 pp. New York, 1848.

2320. **Imprint.** Proceedings of the Board of Supervisors of Westchester County for 1855, 1856 and 1858.
3 vols., 8vo. Yonkers Herald, Yonkers, v.y.

2321. **Imprint.** Fremont and McClellan. Their Political and Military Careers Reviewed by Denslow Van Buren **H**

8vo, 32 pp. Printed at the office of the Semi-Weekly "Clarion," Yonkers, N. Y., 1862.
Second edition.

2322. **Imprint.** The Young Gray-head. A Tale of the Ford. **H**

16mo, 16 pp. William H. Post, Yonkers, 1865.
Originally published in the "Knickerbocker Magazine," January, 1848.

2323. **Imprint.** Lawson, James. Giordano—A Tragedy. **H**

8vo, 98 pp. Yonkers, 1867.
Author lived a long time in Yonkers, 50 copies printed.

2324. **Imprint.** Lawson, James. Liddesdale or the Border Chief. A Tragedy. **N.Y.P.L.**

8vo, 101 pp. Yonkers, 1874.
50 copies.

2325. **Imprint.** (Lawson, James.) The Maiden's Oath. A Domestic Drama. **N.Y.P.L.**

8vo, 195-312 pp. Yonkers, N. Y., 1877.

2326. **Indians.** Indian Wars and the Uprising of 1655. A paper read before the Yonkers Historical and Literary Association by Hon. T. Astley Atkins, March 18, 1892. (See Atkins.) **H**

2327. **Inglis, Rev. Charles.** The Christian Soldier's duty briefly delineated. In a sermon preached at Kingsbridge, Sept. 7, 1777, before the American Corps newly raised for His Majesty's service. by Charles Inglis, rector of Trinity Church.

8vo, 30 pp. New York (Hugh Gaine), n.d. (1777).

2328. **Jenkins, Dr. John F.** Catalogue of the Medical Library of. Sold by Bangs & Co., February 12th, and the four following days, 1883. **H**

8vo, 109 pp. New York, 1883.
1800 lots.

2329. **Jenkins, Dr. J. F.** A Memorial Sketch of the Life and Character of the late John Foster Jenkins, A. M., M.D., of Yonkers, by George Jackson Fisher, M.D., of Sing-Sing, N. Y. **H**

8vo, 21 pp., port. Syracuse, 1884.

2330. **Kauffelt, Mrs. Elizabeth (Nodine).** "Tract" on, by Rev. David Cole.

See address by Dr. Cole in 200th Anniversary of the Old Dutch Church at Sleepy Hollow; note page 120.

2331. **Kingsbridge Water Power.** Report on the Water Power at Kingsbridge near the City of New York belonging to the New York Hydraulic Manufacturing and Bridge Company, by James Renwick. **H**

8vo, 12 pp., 3 maps. New York, 1827.

2332. **Kings Bridge Cottage.** A Revolutionary Tale on an incident that occurred a few days previous to the Evacuation of New York by the British. A Drama in two acts. Written by a Gentleman of New York and performed at the Amateur Theatre. **N. Y. Hist. Soc.**

16mo, 23 pp. New York, 1826.

2333. **Kirkland, Agnes E.** Church and Sunday School Work in Yonkers. Its origin and Progress. **H**

8vo, 523 pp., illust. New York, n.d. (1889).

2334. **Kirkwood, Rev. Robert.** Lectures on the Millennium. Delivered in the Reformed Dutch Church, Yonkers, in September and October, 1855. **H**

12mo, 168 pp. New York, 1856.

2335. **Library.** Yonkers Circulating Library Association. Catalogue of the Library with the certificate of incorporation and by-laws. **H**

12mo, 54 pp. New York, 1864.

2336. **Loan Exhibition,** of the Bicentennial Celebration of Manor Hall, Yonkers, N. Y., October 18-28, 1882. (Catalogue.) **H**

8vo, 32 pp., front. n.p., n.d.

2337. **Lull, Rev. De Los.** Father Solon or the Helper Helped. **H**

12mo, 367 pp. New York, n.d. (1881).
Fiction, scene laid in Yonkers.

2338. **Map** of a Part of the Manor of Philipsburgh in the County of Westchester, showing the Grants from the State of New York in the City of Yonkers and the Town of Greenburgh. Traced and reduced from a Fragment of the original map prepared for the Commissioners of Forfeiture—entitled "A Plan of the Manor of Philipsburgh in the County of Westchester State of New York, surveyed agreeable to the directions of I. Stoutenburg and Philip Van Cortlandt unto John Hills, 1785." Drawn and compiled by M. K. Couzens, May 1st, 1880.

52½ in. x 29½ in.
In Yonkers Manor House.

2339. **Map of the Village of Yonkers.** **Yonkers P. L.**

32 in. x 22 in. Joseph H. Jennings, Publisher, New York, 1850.

2340. **Map** of the Village of Yonkers from original surveys, by Thomas C. Cornell, August, 1851. **Yonkers P. L.**

34 in. x 22 in. New York, 1851.
Scale 300 feet to 1 inch.

2341. **Map** of Walnut Hills in the Village of Yonkers. Surveyed and drawn by J. C. Cornell, September, 1852.

22 in. x 34 in.

2342. **Map** of the Village of Yonkers, N. Y., Surveyed and drawn by Thomas C. Cornell, 1857. **N. Y. Hist. Soc.**

2343. **Map** of part of Yonkers, Showing 200 lots to be sold at the Merchant's Exchange, New York on Wednesday, July 25. **H**

16¼ in. x 30¼ in. New York, 1858 or earlier.

2344. **Map** of Land in the Town of Yonkers belonging to the Estate of the late James H. Blackwell, Esq.

200 feet to the inch. Yonkers, 1859.

2345. **Map of the Woodlawn Cemetery.** **H**

21½ in. x 26 in. New York, 1864.
Also a number of later ones.

2346. **Map** of Part of the Village of Yonkers, showing 72 desirable lots to be sold at Auction on Thursday, June 9, 1859. **N.Y.P.L.**

16¼ in. x 30 in. New York, 1859.
Scale 200 feet to 1 inch.

2347. **Map** of Oloff Park, Yonkers near Kingsbridge. **H**

Scale 100 feet to 1 inch.
34 in. x 23 in. Thomas C. Cornell, C. E., Yonkers, 1869.

2348. **Map** of Bronx River Park situated in the Town of Yonkers, Westchester County, N. Y. Surveyed by Augustus Hepp. **H**

25 in. x 40 in. Dobbs Ferry, August, 1869.

2349. **Map of Woodlawn Heights.** B. Rosa, Surveyor. **H**

17½ in. x 36 in. New York, 1873.

2350. **Map** of North Yonkers, Westchester County, N. Y. Cornell, Bradford & Baldwin, Engineers and Surveyor. **Yonkers P. L.**

35 in. x 26½ in. Yonkers, N. Y., December 11, 1873.

2351. **Map** of the City of Yonkers, 1st Ward, compiled by Cornell, Bradford & Baldwin.

28 in. x 26 in. Approved by Common Council, August 18, 1875.

2351a. Map of the City of Yonkers, 2nd Ward, by William H. Baldwin,
25½ x 27½ inches. Adopted by Common Council August 18, 1875.

2352. Map of the City of Yonkers, 3rd Ward. Compiled by Cornell, Bradford & Baldwin.
14 x 33 inches. Adopted by Common Council, August 18, 1875.

2353. Map. Shonnard Park at Yonkers. Estate of E. F. Shonnard, Esq. Designed from a topographical survey by Egbert L. Viele. C. L. Cooke, Civil Engineer. **N.Y.P.L.**
22 in. x 28 in. New York, n.d.

2354. Map. Part of the Original Shonnard Estate between North Broadway and the Hudson River in the City of Yonkers, N. Y. **H**
28½ in. x 28½ in. n.p., n.d. "Copper plate" map of which only two copies are said to have been printed.

2355. Map of property belonging to Sherwood Park Land and Improvement Co., City of Yonkers, N. Y. Surveyed, March, 1890. Purdy and Sand, C. E. & S. **H**
18½ in. x 17 in.

2356. Map of Property at Lowerre Station, Yonkers, New York. To be sold at Auction, October 28, 1890. F. S. Cook, C. E. **H**
15 in. x 25 in.

2357. Map of the Property of the Yonkers Park Association in the Fourth Ward of the City of Yonkers. Surveyed by A. P. Hartmann. **H**
28 in. x 42 in. New York, 1890.

2358. Map of Central Portion of the Town of Yonkers, showing all buildings in . . . 1847. Yonkers "Daily Herald" Historical Extra. **N.Y.P.L.**
22 in. x 16½ in. Yonkers, January 2, 1892.

2359. Memorial (Day) Ceremonies at the Graves of our Soldiers. Saturday, May 30, 1868. Collected by Frank Moore. **H**
8vo, 736 pp. Washington, D. C., 1869.
Yonkers, pp. 586–588.
First G. A. R. Services.

2360. Methodist. Minutes of the New York Methodist Conference of the Methodist Episcopal Church, held in Central M. E. Church, Yonkers, April 6–13, 1881. **H**
8vo, 86 pp. New York, n.d. (1881).

2361. Methodist. Manual of the Central Methodist Episcopal Church, Yonkers, N. Y., 1895. **H**
16mo, 41 pp. n.p., n.d. (Yonkers, 1895).

2362. Yonkers Military Institute. A Boarding School for Boys. Benjamin Mason, Principal. Established, 1854.
8vo, 16 pp. New York, n.d. **N.Y.P.L.**

2363. Mills, Rev. W. H. God's Providence over Nations. A Sermon preached in St. Paul's, Yonkers, fifteenth Sunday after Trinity, September 25, 1881, on the Death of President Garfield. **H**
12mo, 23 pp. New York, 1881.

2364. Montgomery, Gen. Richard. Biographical Notes concerning—together with hitherto unpublished letters. (By L. L. Hunt.) **H**
8vo, 31 pp. n.p. (Poughkeepsie), 1876.
Had a farm in Kingsbridge.

2365. Mount St. Vincent. A Description and Historical Sketch of Mount St. Vincent Academy, New York City, 1847–1884. **H**
4to, 167 pp. New York, 1884.

2366. Mount St. Vincent. College of Mount Saint Vincent. A Famous Convent School, by Marion J. Brunowe. A new edition with supplementary chapters by Anna C. Browne. **H**
12mo, 205 pp., illust. New York, 1917.

2367. Newspapers. Yonkers "Herald" (First).
Began 1852, changed to the "Gazette," June 4, 1865.

2368. Newspaper. "The Westchester News."
Edited by Thomas Towndrow, removed to Yonkers from New Rochelle in 1854, suspended in 1856. See New Rochelle.

2369. Newspaper. "The Examiner."
Began February, 1856, ended 1865. M. F. Rowe, editor, changed to Yonkers "Statesman"?

2370. Newspaper. "Semi-Weekly Clarion."
Began 1861, ended 1863.

2371. Newspaper. "The Gazette."
Changed from Yonkers "Herald," June 4, 1865, became Yonkers "Gazette," May 15, 1866, still issued in 1910. Weekly.

2372. Newspaper. The Yonkers "Statesman."
Began, 1865. Weekly. Became a daily November, 1883, still issued in 1910.

2373. Newspaper. Yonkers "Herald, Jr."
Began May, 1866.

2374. Newspaper. "Real Estate Bulletin."
1869. Semi-monthly.

2375. Newspaper. "Herald."
Daily, 1867 to 1872.
Weekly, 1872 to 1876.

2376. Newspaper. "Westchester Deutsche Zeitung."
1869 to 1878. Weekly.

2377. Newspaper. Yonkers "Reflector."
1870 to 1871. Weekly.

2378. Newspaper. "Scholars Monthly." **H**
Conducted by the Class of '73 of School No. 6, Yonkers. Vol. 1, No. 1, February, 1873.

2379. Newspaper. "New York Republicaner."
1875 to 1876. Weekly.

2380. Newspaper. "The County Record." **H**
For Westchester, Putnam, Dutchess and Orange Counties, Vol. 1, No. 1, Yonkers, N. Y., July, 1879.
(All issued?)
Folio, 4 pp.

2381. Newspaper. "Plaindealer."
1881 to 1885. Weekly.

2382. Newspaper. Yonkers "Free Press."
1882 to 1884. Weekly.

2383. Newspaper. The Yonkers "Democrat."
1883 to 1884. Weekly.

2384. Newspapers. "Democrat-News."
1883 to 1885. Weekly.

2385. Newspaper. "Home Journal."
1883 to 1893. Weekly.

2386. Newspaper. Yonkers "Journal."
1883 to 1902. German. Weekly.

2387. Newspaper. Yonkers "Times."
1884 to 1885. Weekly.

2388. **Newspaper.** Yonkers "Herald" (later).
Weekly, 1884 to 1889.
Daily, 1889, still issued in 1910.

2389. **Newspaper.** Yonkers "Record."
1884. Daily.

2390. **Newspaper.** "New Christianity."
1888 to 1906. Monthly.

2391. **Newspaper.** "Westchester County Courier."
1891 to 1892. Weekly.

2392. **Newspaper.** "Catholic News."
1891 to 1894. Weekly.

2393. **Newspaper.** "Home Journal & News."
1895 to 1907. Weekly.

2394. **Newspaper.** "Plain Man and Westchester Pictorial Observer."
1899 to 1900. Weekly.

2395. **Newspaper.** "Liberator."
1899 to 1902. Monthly.

2396. **Newspaper.** "New York Review."
1905 to 1909. Bi-Monthly.

2397. **Newspaper.** "Progressive Inquirer."
1906, still issued in 1910. Weekly. Interests of the colored people.

2398. **Newspaper.** "Standard."
1907, still issued in 1910. Weekly.

2399. **Newspaper.** Yonkers "News."
1907 to 1908. Weekly.

2400. **Newspaper.** "Daily News."
1908, still issued in 1910.

2401. **Newspaper.** Yonkers "Workman."
1908, still issued in 1910. Weekly.

2402. **Newspaper.** "Observer."
1908, still issued in 1910. Weekly.

2403. **Newspaper.** "Hudson Valley News."
―――― to 1909. Weekly.

2404. **Nursery.** Yonkers Nursery and Home, 4th Annual Report. **N.Y.P.L.**
12mo, 15 pp. Yonkers, N. Y., 1885.
Probably others.

2405. **Oliver, John Wise.** In Memoriam. H
8vo, 74 pp., port. Privately printed, n.p., 1908.

2406. **Oloff Park.** Peremptory sale at Auction of 300 Plots of Land containing more than 1600 lots at Oloff Park, Part of the Van Cortlandt Estate, adjoining Jerome Park near Kings Bridge, on Thursday, 21st October, 1869. H
8vo, 8 pp., 2 maps. New York, 1869.

2407. **Ordinances** of the Village of Yonkers. H
8vo, 55 pp. n.p., n.d. (1868).

2408. **Ordinances** of the City of Yonkers. H
8vo, 56 pp. New York, 1873.

2409. **Otis Brothers & Co.'s** Patent Safety Hoisting Machinery. Illustrated descriptive catalogue and price list. Manufactory, Yonkers, N. Y. H
8vo, 70 pp., illust. New York, 1869.

2410. **Otis, Norton P.** Memorial Address delivered in the House of Representatives, February 26, 1905. H
8vo, 40 pp., port. Washington, D. C., 1905.

2411. **Park Hill.** An Idyl of the Hudson. 100 Photographs.
4to, 2 maps, 115 views, no text or paging. n.p., n.d. H

Philipsburgh. The Manor of Philipsburg. A Paper read before the New York Historical Society, June 5, 1894, by Hon. T. Astley Atkins. (See Atkins.) H

2412. **Philipse, Frederick.** 1663. H

2413. **Van der Donck, Adrian**
Portraits in February, 1927, number, "The International Studio."
4to. New York, 1927.

2414. **Philipse, Mary.** An Historical and Musical Picture in four Scenes. Founded on certain events in the History of the City of Yonkers, between 1760 and 1776, written by W. G. Van Tassel Sutphen, composed by George F. LeJeune.
16mo, 51 pp. New York, 1892. H

Philipse Manor Hall. American Scenic and Historical Preservation Society.
2415. Report for 1908, pp. 161–247. H

2416. Report for 1912, pp. 77–96. H
8vo. Albany, 1908 and 1912.
Also in other reports.

2417. **Philipse Manor House.** Programme of Bi-Centennial Celebration of the Settlement of Yonkers and the Erection of The Philipse Manor House, October, 1882. H
4to, broadside, 4 pp. Yonkers, 1882.

2418. **Philipse Manor House.** Bi-Centennial Celebration of the Building of. 14 full page photographs.
Oblong 8vo. (Yonkers), 1882.

2419. **Philipse Manor House.** Some Colonial Homesteads and their Stories, by Marion Harland, pp. 239–275.
4to. New York, 1897.

2420. **Picture.** The "Phoenix" and the "Rose" engaged by the Enemy's Fire Ships and Galleys on the 16th August, 1776. Engraved from the Original Picture by D. Serres from a Sketch by Sir James Wallace.
Aquatint in colors.
From Des Barres' "Atlantic Neptune."
11 in. x 19½ in. London, April 2, 1778.

2421. The same. Reproduced in Valentine's Manual of the "Corporation of the City of New York," for 1864. H

2422. **Picture.** Deagles' Hotel, Westchester Side of McComb's Dam.
Small copper plate showing hotel and bridge.

2423. **Picture.** Country Seat near Yonkers. H
Lithograph, colored; residence of Thomas Ludlow.
7 in. x 9¼ in. n.p., n.d.

2424. **Picture.** Soldiers Record. 6th Regiment, Company F, N. Y. V. Artillery. H
Mustered into United States Service at Yonkers, September 2, 1862, by Capt. Edgerton.
19 in. x 14½ in. Lithograph. Chicago, Ill., n.d.

2425. **Picture.** Home for Aged and Infirm. Dist. No. 1, I. O. B. B. H
12½ in. x 16 in. New York, n.d.
Independent Order of Bnai Brith.

2426. **Picture.** A View of Phillips Manor and the Rocks on the Hudson or North River in N. America, June 18th, 1784. D. R. fecit. H
Copy of sepia drawing, 100 copies printed.
11½ in. x 15¼ in. n.p. (Yonkers), 1899.

2427. **Picture.** "Round Oak," Yonkers on the Hudson. **H**
10 in. x 13 in. New York, n.d.
Home of William Allen Butler. Artotype by Bierstadt.

2428. **Picture.** "Duncraggan." Residence of William F. Cochran, Yonkers on the Hudson. **H**
10 in. x 13 in. New York, n.d.
Artotype by Bierstadt.

2429. **Picture.** Residence of James B. Colgate, Southwest View. **H**

2430. **Picture.** Residence of James B. Colgate, Southwest View. **H**

2431. **Picture.** Conservatory of James B. Colgate. **H**
10 in. x 13 in. New York, n.d.
Artotypes by Bierstadt.

2432. **Picture.** Glenview, Residence of John B. Trevor, Southeast View. **H**

2433. **Picture.** Glenview, Parlor. **H**

2434. **Picture.** Glenview, View from Southwest. **H**

2435. **Picture.** Looking south from Glenview. **H**
10 in. x 13 in. New York, n.d.
Artotypes by E. Bierstadt.

2436. **Picture.** Yonkers, N. Y. **H**
27½ in. x 20½ in. New York, n.d.
Colored lithograph view by Sarony.

2437. **Police.** Account of the Police Department.
(1877?)

2438. **Pooley, Dr. J. D.** Report of the Surgical cases treated in the St. John's Riverside Hospital during the year 1870 (19 pp.). **H**

The same, 1871 (20 pp.). **H**

The same, 1872 (30 pp.). **H**

The same, 1873 (29 pp.). **H**
8vo. v.y.

2439. **Potter, Orlando B.** Dedication of the Yonkers Soldiers and Sailors Monument. Oration, September 17, 1891. **H**
8vo, 16 pp. Yonkers, 1891.

2440. **Presbyterian.** Manual of the First Presbyterian Church, Yonkers, N. Y.
Various years, 1856 and later.

2441. **Presbyterian Church.** Piety and Morality. Two Sermons preached in the First Presbyterian Church, Yonkers, N. Y., December 9th and 16th, 1877, by the Pastor, T. Ralston Smith. **H**
8vo, 47 pp. n.p., n.d.

2442. **Presbyterian.** Manual of Westminster Presbyterian Church (First). Yonkers, N. Y. **H**
12mo, 23 pp. Yonkers, 1891.
Probably others.

2443. **Presbyterian.** Year books of the First Presbyterian Church of Yonkers, 1897-1902. **N. Y. Hist. Soc.**
4to, 5 vols. and index, illust. Yonkers, v.y.

2444. **Presbyterian.** An Historical Sketch of the First Presbyterian Church of Yonkers, N. Y. From the change of its ecclesiastical relations from the Reformed (Dutch) Church to the Presbyterian Church (by Ralph E. Prime).
8vo, 42 pp. Yonkers, 1902. **N.Y.P.L.**

2445. **Presbyterian.** Jubilee Year Book First Presbyterian Church, Yonkers, N. Y. **Yonkers P. L.**
4to, 206 pp. Yonkers, 1902.

2446. **Presbyterian.** Jubilee of the Presbyterian History of the First Presbyterian Church of Yonkers, N. Y., April 19th and 20th, 1902. **N. Y. Hist. Soc.**
4to, 47 pp. Yonkers, N. Y., 1902.

2447. **Presbyterian.** History of Westminster Presbyterian Church by Lewis W. Mudge and Rev. John Dixon to May 20, 1880.

2448. **Prime.** In memory of Ruth Havens Prime. Born at Yonkers, June 1, 1874. Died at Yonkers, January 10, 1905. **H**
8vo, 31 pp., port. n.p., 1905.

2449. **Prime.** The Descendants of James Prime who was born at Milford, Conn., in 1644. With some names in allied families. Compiled for private use only by Ralph E. Prime. **H**
8vo, 45 pp. Yonkers, N. Y., G. B. Mottram, 1895.
Of "Yonkers" and "General" interest.

2450. **Rapid Transit Commission.** Minutes of the Proceedings of the Board of Commissioners in the City of Yonkers. **H**
8vo, 45 pp. New York, 1880.

2451. **Robinson, Edith.** A Loyal Little Maid.
12mo, 79 pp. Boston, 1897.
Several editions.
Fiction—in Philipse Manor.

2452. **St. John's Church.** A Sermon occasioned by the Death of the Rev. Alexander H. Crosby, A.M., and preached to the people of his charge on Sunday, March 10, 1839, by Robert William Harris, Rector of Grace Church, White Plains. **H**
12mo, 29 pp. New York, 1839.

2453. **St. John's Church.** The Spirit of the Pastor. Sermon by Dr. H. Anthon in Memory of Rev. H. L. Storrs, January 17, 1852. **H**
8vo, 32 pp. Yonkers, n.d. (1852.)

2454. **St. John's Church.** The Kindred Dead. **H**
8vo, 21 pp. Albany, 1852.
Rev. H. L. Storrs, St. John's Church, John Innes Kane, Sing-Sing, his wife Nancy, Yonkers.

2455. **St. John's Church** in 1753 and in 1853. A sermon preached at the reopening of St. John's Church, March 13th, 1853, by Abraham Beach Carter, M.A., Rector. **N. Y. Hist. Soc.**
8vo, 22 pp. New York, 1853.

2456. **St. John's Church.** The Dangers and Defences of the Church. A Sermon preached, January 22, 1854, by Abraham Beach Carter, M.A., Rector. **H**
8vo, 36 pp. New York, 1854.

2457. **St. John's Church.** The Third Annual Pastoral Letter from the Rector to the Congregation of St. John's Church, January, 1856. **N. Y. Hist. Soc.**
8vo. New York, 1856.

2458. **St. John's Church.** The Crisis and its Duties. Sermon preached on the Sunday before the General and State Elections, November 2nd, 1856, by Abraham Beach Carter, D.D. **H**
8vo., 19 pp. New York, 1856.

2459. **St. John's Church.** The Fourth Annual Pastoral Letter from the Rector to the Congregation of St. John's Church, January, 1857. **H**
8vo, 39 pp. New York, 1857.

2460. **St. John's Church.** A Tribute to the Memory of Rev. Reuben Hubbard, February 15, 1859, by **Abraham Beach Carter.** H
8vo, 23 pp., port. New York, 1860.

2461. **St. John's Church.** The Schoolmate's Grave. Sermon in Memory of Drualt Rollin, preached in St. John's Church, May 7, 1865, by Rev. Ab. B. Carter. H
12mo, 24 pp. New York, 1865.

2462. **St. John's Riverside Hospital.** Incorporated, May, 1870. (Reports for various years.) N.Y.P.L.
8vo. v.p., v.y.

2463. **St. Joseph's Seminary.** Souvenir of the Blessing of the Corner-Stone of the New Seminary of St. Joseph, by the Most Reverend Michael Augustine Corrigan, D.D., May 17, 1891. H
8vo, 117 pp., illust. New York, 1891.

2464. **St. Joseph's Seminary.** History of St. Joseph's Seminary of New York. H
8vo, 151 pp., illust. New York, 1896.

2465. **Seward, Rev. D. M.** The Danger of Misinterpreting and Disregarding the Lessons of Calamity. A Discourse suggested by the burning of the steamer "Henry Clay." Delivered in Yonkers, August 8, 1852, by D. M. Seward, Pastor of the Presbyterian Church. H
8vo, 20 pp. New York, 1852.

2466. **Starr Arms Company,** Armory at Yonkers, N. Y. Sole Manufacturers of Starr's Patent Breech Loading Carbines and Rifles. H
8vo, 20 pp., illust. New York, 1864.

2467. **Stephens, Robert Nelson.** A Continental Dragoon. H
12mo, 299 pp., front. Boston, 1898.
A Love Story of Philipse Manor in 1778.

2468. **Supervisors.** Before the State Assessors of the State of New York. In the matter of the Appeal of Jacob Read, Supervisor of the City of Yonkers, from the Equalization of Assessments by the Board of Supervisors of Westchester County for the year 1876. Argument, etc., by Ralph E. Prime and Matt. H. Ellis. H
8vo, 50 pp. Yonkers, 1877.

2469. **Thackeray** in the United States, 1852-3—1855-6.
2 vols., 8vo, illust. New York, 1901.
Visit to Yonkers and Lecture at Getty House, Vol. I, pp. 41-46.

2470. **Tilden, S. J.** Proceedings of the Senate and Assembly of New York on the Death of Samuel J. Tilden. H
8vo, 73 pp., port. Albany, 1887.
A resident of Yonkers.

2471. **Unitarian Church.** The Beloved High Priest. A Sermon in Memory of Rev. Henry W. Bellows, D.D., preached in the Unitarian Church at Yonkers, Sunday, February 5th, 1882, by its Pastor, George L. Stowell. H
12mo, 26 pp. New York, n.d. (1882).

2472. **Valentine Family.** The Valentines in America, 1644-1874. By T. W. Valentine. H
8vo, 248 pp., illust. New York, 1874.
Also a large paper edition.

2473. **Van Cortlandt House.** Historical Sketch of, prepared for the Society of Colonial Dames of the State of New York, by Mrs. C. V. C. Mathews. N.Y.P.L.
8vo, 17 pp., illust. New York, 1903.

2474. **Van Cortlandt Mansion.** Erected, 1748. Now in the custody of the Colonial Dames of the State of New York, prepared by Mrs. Morris Patterson Ferris. H
8vo, 23 pp., map and illust. n.p., 1927.

2475. **Van Cortlandt Park.** The Story of. H
8vo, 25 pp., illust. New York, 1911.

2476. **Van Cortlandt.** Henry Van Cortlandt (formerly Henry White). Case on Appeal, proving his last Will and Testament. H
8vo, 316 pp. New York, 1840.

2477. **Van Cortlandt.** Henry White and his Family. H
Reprinted from the Magazine of American History, December, 1877, by John Austin Stevens.
8vo, 7 pp., port. (New York, 1899.)
Changed his name to Van Cortlandt.

2478. **Wallin, William J.** Plain History of the Management of the City of Yonkers.
12mo.

2479. **Water Commissioners Reports.** Beginning 1873. 1874 (H), 1875 (H), 1879 (H), 1886 (H), 1887 (H), 1892 (H).
Later issues.

2480. **Water Supply.** Report on Water Supply for the Village of Yonkers made to the Board of Trustees, Dec. 20th, 1869. By William H. Grant, C. E. H
8vo, 46 pp. Yonkers, 1870.

2481. **Woodlawn Cemetery.** Annual Report of the Trustees of, for 1867 and later years. H
8vo. v.y.

2482. **Yale School for Boys,** Yonkers, N. Y. Sixth Year, 1882-3. N.Y.P.L.
8vo.
Probably others.

2483. **Yonkers,** the History and Historical Relics of. Circular invitation of Bi-Centennial Committee. H
4to, 4 pp., plate. Yonkers, 1882.

Yonkers Historical and Library Association Bulletin. H

2484. Vol. 1. April, 1895.

2485. Vol. 2. Manor Hall Number, January, 1896. H
Yonkers, 1895-6.

2486. **Yonkers Illustrated.** H
4to, illust., 192 pp. n.p., n.d.
Issued by the Yonkers Board of Trade.

2487. **Yonkers Military Institute.** Yonkers, N. Y. A boarding school for boys. Benjamin Mason, Principal. N.Y.P.L.
8vo, 16 pp. New York, 185?.

2488. **Yonkers.** Next to the Largest City in the United States. N.Y.P.L.
Oblong 8vo, 96 pp., illust. and map. Yonkers, n.d. (after 1920.)

2489. **Yonkers** in the World War, including The Roll of Honor of the Citizens of Yonkers who served in the Military Forces of the United States during the World War. N.Y.P.L.
4to, 139 pp., illust. Norwood, Mass., 1922.

2490. **Old Yonkers,** 1646-1922. A Page of History by Henry Collins Brown. H
32mo, 192 pp., illust. New York, 1922.

2491. **Yonkers.** Abstract of Title to the property of Lemuel Wells afterward the Village of Yonkers.

SUPPLEMENT

The following supplement to Otto Hufeland's Check List was compiled with the cooperation of the Library of the Westchester County Historical Society, Valhalla, New York, and all items are among the library's vast holdings.

S 1 Asbury Centenary Methodist Episcopal Church, Crestwood, Yonkers. Corporate Centennial Anniversary, 1835-1935, Feb. 21, 1935. 38pp. New York, Talmadge Printing Co., 1935.

S 2 --- The 175th Anniversary of the ... Church, Oct. 13-20th, 1946... A Brief History. 76pp. New York, 1946.

S 3 Brown, Henry Collins. Old Yonkers 1646-1922. 192pp. illus. New York, Valentines Manual Press, 1922.

S 4 Bryn Mawr Park Presbyterian Church, Yonkers, N.Y. 75th Anniversary, Dec. 16, 1906 - Dec. 16, 1981. Illus. Yonkers, 1981.

S 5 Central National Bank of Yonkers. Yonkers through Three Centuries. 16pp. illus. Yonkers, 1946.

S 6 Cornell, Thomas Clapp. Some Reminiscences of the Old Philipse Manor House in Yonkers and its Surroundings. 31pp. New York, Yonkers Chapter, Westch. Co. Hist. Soc., 1932.

S 7 Council of Yonkers Civic Association, Inc. Historical Sketch and By-Laws. 45pp. Yonkers, 1930.

S 8 Hall, Edward H. Philipse Manor Hall at Yonkers, N.Y. 2nd edition, with supplementary notes. 264pp. illus. New York, 1925.

S 9 Hansen, Harry. North of Manhattan. Persons and Places of Old Westchester. 181pp. illus. New York, Hastings House, 1950.

S 10 Johnson, Yolanda. Yonkers Through the Years, by Yolanda Johnson & others. Yonkers, Board of Education, 1962. 72pp. illus.

S 11 Lawrence, John J. History of Rising Star Lodge, no. 450, Free and Accepted Masons in the City of Yonkers, 1826-1926. 99pp. illus. Yonkers, Gazette Press, 1927.

S 12 Map. Atlas of Westchester County. By G.W. Bromley & Co., Philadelphia. Vol. 2, sheets no. 1-8, covering the City of Yonkers. Large folio. Philadelphia, 1911.

S 13 Map. Atlas of Westchester County. By G.M. Hopkins & Co., Philadelphia. Vol. 3, sheets no. 1-27, covering the City of Yonkers. Large folio. Philadephia, 1930.

S 14 Philipse Manor Hall, Yonkers. Loan Exhibition of the Bicentennial Celebration of the Manor Hall, Yonkers, Oct. 18-28, 1882. 32pp. illus. Yonkers, J.W. Oliver, 1882.

S 15 --- Records of the Manor of Philipsburgh. Transcribed by Frederick C. Haacker. 29pp., typewritten, illus. New York, 1951. With appendix: Some Records of the Town of Yonkers.

S 16 Russell, Ellen. Yonkers, U.S.A.; the Development together of One Community and the Nation, (written) for the Mayor's Community Relations Committee of Yonkers in Commemoration of the Bicentennial of the United States, 1776-1976. 44pp., mimeographed, Yonkers, (1976).

S 17 St. Andrew's Golf Club, 1888-1938. 146pp. illus. New York, Rogers, Kellogg, Stillson, Inc., 1938.

S 18 St. Andrew's Golf Club, 1888-1963. 146, 117pp. illus. New York, 1963.

S 19 St. John's Evangelical Lutheran Church, Yonkers. Built On the Rock; 1869-1969, a History... published by the Congregation. 90pp. illus. Yonkers, 1970.

S 20 St. Peter's Church, Yonkers, 1894-1969. Quarto. 30pp. illus. S. Hackensack, 1969.

S 21 Temple Emanu-el, Yonkers. In Commemoration of the Consecration and Dedication of the New Temple Sanctuary and Religious School, May 1960. illus. Yonkers, 1960.

S 22 --- Kodesh; the History, Art and Artifacts of Temple Emanu-el, Yonkers. 97pp. illus. Yonkers, 1975.

S 23 The Trouble with Yonkers. A series of 30 articles, contributed by 12 reporters, under the editorship of Tom Pica, appearing in all Gannett Westchester-Rockland Newspapers, 8 consecutive issues, for May 13 through May 20, 1984. A survey and analysis of the city's financial and political problems.

S 24 Walton, Frank L. The Cedar Knolls. The Story of an American Community located in the Famous Tuckahoe Hills of Historic Yonkers close by the Village of Bronxville with which it is closely associated. 68pp. illus. Bronxville, 1960.

S 25 --- Pillars of Yonkers. 348pp. illus. New York, Stratford House, 1951.

S 26 Yonkers, N.Y. List of the Names which appear upon the Tax Lists for the Years 1822, 1823, 1825, 1826, 1827, 1829, 1830. Copied by Harry A. Archibald. 35 leaves, typewritten. New Rochelle, 1938.

S 27 --- Records of the Town of Yonkers, N.Y. Minutes of the Town Meetings, 1820-1852. Transcribed by Fred C. Haacker. 52pp. typewritten. New York, 1955.

S 28 --- One Hundred Years a City. 16 leaves, illus. Yonkers, 1973.

S 29 Yonkers Art Association, 1915-1940. 6 leaves, illus. Yonkers, 1940.

S 30 Yonkers Chamber of Commerce, Inc. Proudly We Present... the Story of Yonkers... in Words and Pictures. 72pp. illus. Encino, Calif., Windsor Publications, 1971.

S 31 Yonkers Daily News, Yonkers. Old Home Week Souvenir; recording Achievements of Yonkers and its Citizens, with some account of its Growth. 64pp. illus. Yonkers, 1909.

S 32 Yonkers Historical Bulletin. Vol. 1 no. 1, Oct. 1953 to current issue. Publ. by the Yonkers Historical Society semi-annually until v. 23, 1976; annually thereafter.

S 33 Yonkers Historical Society. A Map of the City of Yonkers showing Historic Sites. Yonkers, 1972.

S 34 Yonkers Museum of Science and Arts, Yonkers, June 1926 - June 1931; with a Brief History of its Predecessor. 11pp. Yonkers, 1931.

Books about Westchester County

History of Westchester County from its Earliest Settlement to 1900.

By *Frederic Shonnard & W. W. Spooner.*

While drawing on the two previous works on Westchester history, Bolton's and Scharf's, which were essentially collections of town histories, the authors of this work present an overall view of the county's history, to be enjoyed as continuous reading. It is a scholarly and well-documented work, profusely illustrated, and is well suited also for younger readers. Reprinted from the 1900 edition. 638 pages, profusely illustrated.

buckram $29.50

Westchester County during the American Revolution, 1775-1783.

By *Otto Hufeland.* Foreword by *Dixon Ryan Fox.*

There is no county in all the 13 states where the blight of civil war left an impress so deep as in Westchester County, on the northern border of New York City. Its troubles began in the earliest days of the struggle and did not end until the very day that the enemy left these shores. Hufeland's book is a fascinating and well-documented account of important events which affected the patriot cause at large, both in the State and the Nation. Reprinted from the 1926 edition. 500 pages, 4 foldout maps. cloth $19.95

Place Names of Westchester County.

By *Richard M. Lederer, Jr.*

A Dictionary of origins and meanings of all place names in Westchester (except street names). The elaborate entries form in themselves a fascinating history of the county. With a new bibliography of books on Westchester history supplementing the 1929 bibliography by Otto Hufeland. 1976, with a 1980 updating supplement. 190 pages.

cloth $9.75

Check List of Books, Maps, etc., relating to Westchester and Bronx Counties.

By *Otto Hufeland.*

The standard bibliography of historical material about Westchester County, published through 1929. Arranged by townships. Indispensible reference book. 320 pages.

cloth $15.00

Chronicle of a Border Town: History of Rye, 1660-1870, *including Harrison and White Plains till* 1788.

By *Charles W. Baird.*

In 46 chapters the author traces the history of Rye and vicinity from the Indian Purchases through the Reconstruction period. The individual chapters are devoted to such topics as *Town Matters in Olden Times, Mails & Newspapers, Rye in Connecticut, Harrison's Purchase, The Boston Road, White Plains, Physicians & Lawyers, Slavery in Rye, the Revolution*—to mention only a few. A 105-page appendix contains an alphabetical list of Rye families. Truly a major source work for the history of lower Westchester. Reprinted from the 1871 edition. 570 pages, illus., maps. buckram $35.00

Tuckahoe Marble.

By *Louis Torres.*

History of the rise and fall of an industry in Eastchester, the marble quarries along Marblehead Avenue. 1976. Illustrated, 91 pages. paper $6.95

Harbor Hill Books, P.O. Box 407, Harrison, N. Y. 10528

Books about Westchester County

Historic White Plains.

By *John Rosch*. Preface by *Renoda Hoffman*.

A comprehensive history of the City of White Plains, profusely illustrated with the author's photos and drawings. In the preface is told the story of the preservation and removal of the Purdy House. Reprinted from the 1938 edition. 395 pages. cloth $11.95

The School House at Pine Tree Corner, North Salem, 1784-1916.

By *Helen Trager*.

Teaching and administrative practices in a Westchester rural school, with much bibliographical material on North Salem families. Profusely illustrated, with rare photos and maps. 1976. 180 pages. paper $7.95

A Two Years' Journal in New York (1678-1680).

By *Charles Wolley*. Introduction & notes by *Edward Gaylord Bourne*.

A first-hand account of New York Colony a decade and a half after the English takeover from the Dutch. Charles Wolley, an English clergyman, describes the Indians of Southern New York and Long Island, as he found them during his two years' stay, their dress and customs, their hunting habits and their diet. His book was first published in London in 1701. Reprinted from the 1902 edition. 76 pages. cloth $7.50

General Orders of George Washington, issued at Newburgh on the Hudson, 1782-1783.

Compiled & ed. by *Major Edward C. Boynton*.

New edition, with an introduction by *Alan C. Aimone*.

The general orders issued by General Washington while headquartered at Newburgh during the final years of the American Revolution afford an interesting insight into the life and mood of the Continental Army as it spent its last winter in the New Windsor Cantonment. Reprinted from the 1883 edition, with added illustrations and a new introduction. 144 pages. cloth $11.50

The Spy Unmasked, or, Memoirs of Enoch Crosby,

alias Harvey Birch, the Hero of James Fenimore Cooper's The Spy.

By *H. L. Barnum*.

A facsimile edition of the first edition (1828), with a new introduction by *James H. Pickering*, Michigan State University, and an appendix: Enoch Crosby, Secret Agent of the Neutral Ground: His Own Story.—A fascinating tale of the American Revolution in Westchester County, the story of John Jay's peddler-spy who performed invaluable intelligence service for the American side. Crosby is generally regarded as the model for Cooper's spy-character, Harvey Birch. The introduction adds many new facts to our knowledge of the book and its author, H. L. Barnum. 264 pages, illus. cloth $11.50

Valentine's Manuals: A General Index

to the Manuals of the Corporation of the City of New York, 1841-1870.

Compiled by *Otto Hufeland* and *Richard Hoe Lawrence*.

First combined edition of two separate indexes originally published in limited editions in 1900 and 1906. Indispensible guide to the collation of all Valentines. 1981. 192 pages- cloth $15.00

Harbor Hill Books, P.O. Box 407, Harrison, N.Y. 10528